PREFACE

We wrote *A Community of Voices* to introduce you to some of the voices you will meet in college, voices of professors from fourteen different disciplines and from many of their students as well. We believe that while the university has a common language of communication across the disciplines, its teachers and researchers have also established distinctive ways of viewing their worlds and writing about them. Because those views depend upon subject, we invited the experts to explain their work. Each writer has taken a somewhat different approach to the task, but all hold the same common goal—to share knowledge of their subjects.

THE DESIGN OF THE BOOK

During the two years it took to write this book, we came to agree that every chapter should contain three elements. The first is a conversation with the reader about the discipline. Here a biologist or a historian, a philosopher or a chemist tells about his or her subject—how it views the world, how it does its work, perhaps how it is subdivided. Psychologist Lynne A. Bond describes what she observes when she walks into a party. Amid the clutter of her studio, artist Lynda Reeves McIntyre shows how she turns a napkin sketch into a painting. Each chapter author invites the reader to respond to those questions that arise during this conversation by writing informally.

The second part of every chapter shows how to experience that discipline through writing. These "Suggestions for Research" offer alternatives to the traditional term paper. Sociologist Frederick E. Schmidt shows how to do field research by studying campus bulletin boards. Artist McIntyre suggests a study of two war memorials—Picasso's painting *Guernica* and Maya Ying Lin's Vietnam Veterans Memorial in Washington, D.C. Political scientist Kenneth M. Holland explains how to design and conduct a public opinion poll. Ronald Savitt, our business expert, asks the reader to compare two retail competitors — supermarkets, record shops, pizza parlors. Some other options for research include studying a contemporary life, observing people's eating habits, and writing a philosophical dialogue.

The third part of each chapter is a selection of readings that show the concerns of the discipline. Although most of them are written for the general reader, they explore areas of current interest and controversy in each field. By presenting a variety of voices, they provoke the reader to enter the debate. Selections in the literature chapter, for instance, raise questions about race and gender, peace and war, as well as the very nature of literature. The essays in Chapter 6 — Language, Identity, and Power — reflect that chapter's title as they explore the relationships between language and life. Important issues surface in several chapters; the reader receives varied perspectives on nuclear war, gender equality, the endangered environment, and the nature of a democratic society. Each reading is accompanied by a brief introduction and several "Options for Writing" that allow the student to pursue issues raised by the reading.

Writing is an integral part of each chapter because we believe that writing is a powerful way of learning. That belief inspires this entire book, and we discuss this subject in much greater detail in Chapter 1, "Writing Across the Disciplines." The writing we ask of the reader ranges from brief, informal responses, which are meant to be primarily for the writer's own use (the "Writings 1," "2," "3," etc., within each conversation), to longer, more carefully thought-out pieces, which are drafted and revised over several days (the "Options for Writing" that follow each reading), and finally to essays which are based on research and developed, perhaps collaboratively, over a period of several weeks (the "Suggestions for Research" found at the end of each conversation).

Clearly, we don't expect either the student or the instructor to gain mastery of any of these complex disciplines in a few weeks. Every reader, though, will get a taste of some of the concerns of any college or university. We invite you to join this intellectual community.

ACKNOWLEDGMENTS

We and the chapter authors wish to thank the many people who helped us write this book. At the head of the line is our editor, Eben Ludlow, who understood our vision from the very beginning. In addition, we want to thank our loyal and tenacious permissions editors, Josie Wintch and Jennifer Gordon. We are also grateful to our reviewers, many of them well-known proponents of writing across the curriculum, who contributed valuable time and suggestions to our draft manuscript: Chris M. Anson, University of Minnesota; Kristine Hansen, Brigham Young University; David Shimkin, Queensborough Community College; Barbara R.

Sloan, Santa Fe Community College; Margot Soven, La Salle University; Jo-Ann M. Sipple, Robert Morris College; John Ramage, Arizona State University; Christopher J. Thaiss, George Mason University; and Martha A. Townsend, Arizona State University.

Toby Fulwiler

Arthur W. Biddle

CONTENTS

3   THE NATURE OF HISTORY
Henry Steffens

6 LANGUAGE, IDENTITY, AND POWER
Karen Wiley Sandler   **358**

7 THINKING AS A PSYCHOLOGIST
Lynne A. Bond   **428**

8   THE PURSUIT OF POLITICS
Kenneth M. Holland

READINGS: 513

9 THE INSIGHTS OF SOCIOLOGY
Frederick E. Schmidt

10 THE WORLD OF BIOLOGY
Daniel J. Bean   **630**

READINGS   **641**

12 THE WORLD OF BUSINESS
Ronald Savitt   784

CHAPTER AUTHOR BIOGRAPHIES   959

ACKNOWLEDGMENTS   963

A COMMUNITY
OF VOICES

INTRODUCTION

Toby Fulwiler and Arthur W. Biddle

A Community of Voices is an introduction to reading and writing in the university that presents a close look at the ways reading and writing operate within some key disciplines. We believe that in many ways the university is a small community with common languages and modes of thought that cut across disciplinary lines. However, we also know that the teachers and researchers who inhabit this community have established distinctive ways of viewing their worlds and writing about them. Because those views depend on subject, we invited specialists from more than a dozen disciplines to explain their work. Each writer has taken a somewhat different approach to the task, but all hold the same common goal — to share knowledge of their subjects.

HIGHER EDUCATION

Although they may differ greatly in size and mission, colleges, community colleges, and universities are organized in similar ways. A university is essentially a collection of colleges — Arts and Sciences, Business, Education, Agriculture, and so on. The college in which you are enrolled is further divided into departments such as English and Psychology, or perhaps Finance and Accounting. Within these departments individual professors represent distinct areas of specialization such as American literature and Shakespeare (in English) or marketing and advertising (in business). To some extent, the secondary school you're familiar with is probably arranged in the same way, by disciplines and departments. But the differences between high school and college go beyond organization, to mission.

   If we look at the intellectual as well as the social mission of higher education, we may understand better what these many varied fields of study have in common and what makes them different from other levels of schooling. In addition to teaching students *about* biology, art, and political science, the college professors are themselves often discovering and creating new scientific, aesthetic, and political truths to teach at all levels of education. This research mission is much stronger in the large research universities than in liberal arts colleges and community colleges.

UNITY AND DIVERSITY

Although this book seems to be focused on diversity—with its fourteen chapters representing distinctly different areas of study—it is also about unity. We all realize that chemists pursue a truth about the natural world somewhat different from that pursued by biologists or psychologists and radically different from that sought by philosophers and artists. And it should be equally obvious that professors of education research different issues than do professors of business or political science and that the questions that historians ask are different from those that sociologists or literary scholars ask. Although disciplinary labels or your experience may tell you about the *differences* among these fields of study, they tell you little about their *similarities.*

When you read the various chapters in this book, each written by a specialist in a different academic field, we hope you will see both the differences and the similarities among them. Some differences may be greater than you expect, and some may surprise you by being quite small; in either case, the better you understand the nature of these disciplines, the better you will be able to move from one class to another with your feet still on solid ground.

ASKING QUESTIONS

Researchers and teachers in all the disciplines in the academic community ask questions of themselves and the world. By so doing, they hope to understand how humankind and the physical universe work. Historians ask what happened to human beings in the past, geographers wonder about the world as a physical place, and physics specialists question the laws of space. Biologists ask how living organisms function, psychologists ponder individual behavior, sociologists study our group behavior, and so on. In sum, people in all the disciplines ask questions about who we human beings are, what we are made of, how we function, what it is like where we live, who our neighbors are, how we got here (wherever *here* is), how we live, why we behave as we do (and how ought we to), how we live, and what progress we as a species and a planet are making.

College professors ask these questions through their research and, in turn, ask you similar questions in class discussions, on examinations, and in assigned papers. Professors in one department ask questions different from those in other departments. Even within each department, academic specialists raise different questions. One English professor might ask how gender definition is handled by Mark Twain in *The Adventures of Huckleberry Finn*. Another might wonder about the racial stereotypes in the book, and a third might study the accuracy of Twain's use of dialects.

As you read through this book, notice the questions, stated or implied, that each discipline asks. If you understand a discipline's basic questions, you'll better understand its answers.

FINDING ANSWERS

Each discipline asks questions in order to find answers. In fact, attempting to answer questions seems to be the major preoccupation of most professionals in the academic disciplines. Historians and literary scholars dig through archives and libraries; geologists and paleontologists dig, perhaps, in the more literal ground of fields, mountains, glacial till, prehistoric ruins. Each discipline develops peculiar methods and procedures for *finding answers* to its questions. Each also invents a peculiar vocabulary for articulating these methods and procedures. Learning the kinds of questions asked and answers sought and knowing the methods and language of the practitioners is part of your introduction to any of the subjects you'll be studying. And although these particulars may vary from discipline to discipline — and sometimes even within a single discipline — underneath their sometimes formidable terminology, you may find common beliefs and principles.

As you read through the chapters in this book, notice the disciplines that are more likely to find specific answers, and note those which must be content with answers more approximate than quantifiable.

Observation

All disciplines look at things carefully. They observe specimens under microscopes, objects through telescopes, and species in natural settings and under experimental conditions. They examine concepts in writing and drawing graphically and in three dimensions. Readers of poems in English classes observe language as carefully as readers of aquatic life in biology classes observe organic life: Both look closely, ask questions, and make inferences. So, too, does the writer of a history paper in interpreting the Declaration of Independence, and so does the young philosopher weighing closely the arguments for and against the use of nuclear weapons. Each student makes careful observations in order to find evidence to support theories, make predictions, and discover general laws.

Notice in this text the different objects observed by each field of study. Are they always what you'd expect? Consider also the means of observing.

Evidence

All disciplines require evidence to justify belief and substantiate interpretation. Historians know about Shaker communities because the Shakers left written records explaining their beliefs, architecture, and practices. Written records provide the evidence, the demonstration, the proof that convinces. Someday even more powerful microscopes and telescopes and spaceships will provide scientists with more and better evidence. What exactly moved Frost to compose "Mending Wall," however, may remain forever a matter of speculation and conjecture.

Evidence in history, literature, and philosophy often comes from the close study of texts. Evidence in the social sciences may come from documenting behavior of people. Evidence in biology, chemistry, and physics comes from observation and experimentation.

As you read each author's explanation of how his or her discipline works, see if you notice what kinds of evidence each uses to convince us and make us believe.

Objectivity

Most disciplines attempt to train you to see the world as it is, apart from your own personal biases and beliefs. If the object is a fish (biology), try to see it for what it is whether or not you like that particular species. If the object is a student (education), try to understand him or her without being swayed by the preppy or nerdy clothes unless the clothing itself provides further *objective* clues to the individual's identity as a student. If the object of study is clothing as an index to social status (sociology), attend carefully to the pants, shirt, and shoes, but to interpret rather than to pass judgment.

Most disciplines also ask you to observe the world with the clearest, cleanest, least distorted lens available. The idea is to discover what is true for others as well as yourself, and to do this you need to place your personal beliefs, attitudes, prejudices, and emotions in the background as much as you can. Many teachers and scholars believe that complete objectivity is an unattainable ideal. Other researchers will openly admit and identify their biases, while still arguing that their perspective is the most accurate or most useful (though not necessarily the only) way to pursue knowledge.

As you read the different accounts of disciplinary methods, which strike you as most objective, most verifiable, closest to what you would call "truth"? Which strike you the opposite way?

Relativity

In nearly all disciplines the absolute rightness of answers is questionable. Ironically, this is even more true in the late twentieth century, when we have more sheer data than ever before. Though scholars spend a great deal of their time generating answers to questions and developing trustworthy methods for generating these answers, they seldom believe that what they have found is absolutely the last word. Experience has too often proved final answers to be less than final. As you read college texts and listen to lectures, notice the frequency of qualifiers: "it seems clear," "in many cases," "on the other hand," "it is possible," "in all probability," "for example," "however," "perhaps," and "maybe." In other words, in the academic world, even the most well-established views are open to question. When you, too, find answers in the university community, it will be wise to make your claims for certainty with some caution.

As you read the claims each author makes for the territory of his or her discipline, see if you notice any boundaries that seem shifty, any claims that might apply to one discipline as easily as another. Do authors in some disciplines need to qualify their answers more than others?

Interpretation

No matter what you have closely observed—a poem, frog, building, bacterium, or star—seeing it is only a starting point. The next task of disciplinary training is to find out what it means, why it may be important, or what we can learn from it. It's what we call the "so what?" question: Why does Robert Frost choose to write a poem about farmers mending walls in springtime? Why do some frogs climb trees although most do not? Why do the entrances to Shaker buildings have two doors side by side? These are questions of meaning, of interpretation. The more you are trained to read poems, understand animals, or unravel history, the better you will be at interpreting new data, texts, and theories. Sometimes you will be sure your answer is right: For example, you will *know* that Shaker buildings had two doors to keep men and women apart because the sect did not allow mating or marriage. But other times you will be less sure, and some interpretations will convince you more than others. Scientists respond to an observation in a somewhat different way. Why do these cells divide while those do not? What is a black hole? Their questions of why, how, and what if are answered with a maybe statement, a *hypothesis,* an explanation that can be tested.

As you read the different chapters, notice the nature of each author's interpretation: On what evidence do authors base their claims?

SHARING KNOWLEDGE

When scientists, historians, literary scholars, or artists make a discovery or create new work, they make the results public. They usually do this in articles, books, demonstrations, and lectures, or sometimes on film or in galleries and concert halls. In many colleges and universities, the quality and quantity of a professor's writing correlates directly to his or her rank, salary, and status. From this point of view, the mission of higher education includes providing a forum for sharing results through both teaching and publication. When professors communicate with other professors about ideas in marketing, accounting, or finance, for instance, their talk to each other is loaded with jargon, words the rest of us may find hard to follow but that they find useful in making fine distinctions. As you progress in one discipline or another, you learn certain language and concepts particular to chemistry or biology or English, terms necessary for further study in the discipline. As first-year students, however, you will most often need to communicate in the clearest general language at your disposal. This conflict—between using the specialized language of a subject and using an exact but nonspecialized language of the general population—can be resolved only by the writer's consideration of the circumstances. Answers to these questions help you decide how to approach a writing job: Who is my audience? What are the expectations of this audience? Why am I writing this? Who am I as I write this? We discuss these issues in much greater depth in Chapter 1.

Writing to publish is only one kind of writing that academics do. In truth, writing is one of the most frequently used means of discovering, exploring, and creating knowledge. Scientists, social scientists, humanists, and artists all use writing as a tool to help them ask and answer questions, observe more carefully, and try out the validity of an idea. (In the readings of Chapter 1, see especially Stafford, Emig, and Elbow for more information about the exploratory role of writing.)

As you read through the selections in this book, notice the ones that speak to you most directly and for which you need the least background to understand. Can you identify why one is easier than another? Do these give you any ideas about how to construct your own writing?

HOW TO USE THIS BOOK

During the two years it took to write this book, we came to agree that every chapter should contain three elements. The first is a conversation with the reader about the discipline. Here a biologist, historian, philosopher, or chemist tells about his or her subject—its focus, its procedures, and perhaps its subdivisions. Psychologist Lynne Bond, for example, describes what she observes when she walks into a party, and artist Lynda McIntyre shows how she turns a napkin sketch into a painting. Each chapter author invites the reader to respond to questions that arise during this conversation by writing informally.

The second part of every chapter shows how to experience that discipline through writing. These suggestions for research offer alternatives to the traditional term paper. Sociologist Fred Schmidt shows how to do field research by studying campus bulletin boards. Artist McIntyre suggests a study of two war memorials—Picasso's painting *Guernica* and Maya Ying Lin's memorial to Vietnam Veterans in Washington, D.C.

Political scientist Ken Holland explains how to design and conduct a public opinion poll. Ron Savitt, our business expert, asks the reader to compare retail competitors—supermarkets, record shops, and pizza parlors. Some other options for research include studying a contemporary life, observing people's eating habits, and writing a philosophical dialogue.

The third part of each chapter is a selection of readings that show the concerns of the discipline. Although most of these are written for the general reader, they explore areas of current interest and controversy in each field. By presenting a variety of voices, they provoke the reader to enter the debate. Selections in the literature chapter, for instance, raise questions about race and gender, peace and war, and the very nature of literature. The essays in Chapter 6 explore the relationships between language and life. Important issues surface in numerous chapters: The reader gets varied perspectives, for instance, on nuclear war, gender equality, the endangered environment, and the nature of a democratic society. Each reading is accompanied by a brief introduction and several options for writing that allow the student to pursue issues raised by the reading.

Writing is an integral part of each chapter because we believe that writing is a powerful way of learning. That belief inspires this entire book, and we discuss it in much greater detail in Chapter 1. The writing we ask of the reader ranges from brief, informal responses meant primarily for the writer's own use (the writings 1, 2, 3, and so on within each conversation) to longer, more carefully thought-out pieces drafted and revised over several days (the options for writing that follow each reading) and finally to essays based on research and developed, perhaps collaboratively, over a period of several weeks (the suggestions for research found at the end of each chapter introduction).

Clearly, we don't expect either the student or the instructor to gain mastery of any of these complex disciplines in a few weeks. Every reader, though, will get a taste of some of the concerns of any college or university. We invite you to join this intellectual community.

1

WRITING ACROSS THE DISCIPLINES

Toby Fulwiler and Arthur W. Biddle

Although we learn about the world first through our senses, we soon add a secondary means of knowledge and learn through language, by reading and listening to others and by talking and writing ourselves. By the time we reach college, we have combined and elevated these ways of knowing to higher and more systematic levels.

This chapter is about the student—you—as a writer in the college or university community. We explain the role that audience and purpose play in a piece of writing. Your audience—your professor, your parents, your best friend—will to some extent control not only what you write but how you write it. Your purpose might be to communicate to someone or to imagine or learn something. This last function, learning by writing, is especially important in this book. Sometimes you write primarily to yourself in order to discover what you think or feel, to ponder a question, or to solve a problem. In each chapter of *A Community of Voices* you'll be asked to use exploratory, or discovery, writing to respond to questions, to think about where you stand, or to plan future actions.

READINGS

WRITING TO LEARN
William Stafford Writing

Peter Elbow Freewriting

Toby Fulwiler College Journals

LEARNING TO WRITE
Donald Murray Making Meaning Clear: The Logic of Revision

Janet Emig Writing as a Mode of Learning

Marge Piercy Starting Support Groups for Writers

We learn about the world first through our senses, by looking, listening, smelling, tasting, and touching, and soon after through language, by reading, listening, talking, and writing. In the science laboratory, for instance, we extend the knowledge born of experience (the vibrations we call earthquakes) to knowledge tested by experiment (studying models of the earth's crust) into knowledge explained and examined in language (plate tectonics). Likewise, the study of history starts with perceivable events (George Washington crosses the Delaware River), though we learn about it today through language (written historical records) and explain it with theoretical language (the social, political, military, and economic reasons that necessitated George's crossing).

In fact, inquiries into all forms of knowledge — physical, chemical, historical, sociological — are eventually conducted with and through language of one kind or another (visual, mathematical, verbal) in one mode or another (oral, written). It is writing in particular that we wish to focus on here, because without writing we have no colleges, no curricula, no disciplines to study. Writing lets us codify ideas into disciplines and theories in the first place, and it allows us to hold ideas still so that we can examine, critique, and expand them.

THE ROLE OF WRITING

When professors in virtually every discipline assign essays, reports, and research papers, they have come to expect a barrage of questions from anxious students: How long should it be? When is it due? Does spelling count? How many sources do we need? Does it have to by typed? What form do you want? Will we have a chance to redo it? In fact, after being examined, tested, corrected, and measured in writing throughout high school, it is no wonder that some first-year students have actually come to view writing as their enemy. So, in spite of its centrality to all aspects of learning, writing in academic settings often gets a bad rap. We have written this first chapter — in fact, this whole book — to explain the powerful and positive role writing plays in generating and disseminating knowledge in the university community.

Unlike the subjects in most of the other chapters in *Community of Voices*, writing is not really a discipline in and of itself, or at least we don't look at it that way. Instead, we see writing first as the means by which other disciplines make themselves known to us (we read about them) and, second, as a means we can use to explore and understand these disciplines (we write about them). In the rest of this chapter we'd like to explain how writing works and how you can make it work for you.

A WRITER'S AUDIENCE

It makes perfectly good sense to ask your teachers how long a paper should be, when it's due, and what they expect from it. We professors ask these same questions when we write articles for professional journals or chapters for anthologies. We explored these questions with our publisher before we signed a contract to write this book, and the other fifteen authors asked us the same questions before they agreed to write chapters for us. Writers ask these questions and many others because much of the time they are writing *to* other people *for* specific purposes. We all write better when we understand to whom we are writing and why.

Think for a minute about the audiences for whom you write. Sometimes your audience is known and friendly: for example, when you write a note to a classmate across the room; when you write a letter to thank a friend or relative for a birthday present; or even when you write a journal entry to understand or reassure yourself. Sometimes your audience is known but more critical, such as when you write an essay for a teacher who wants to find out what you know about the plate tectonics or the Revolutionary War. Other times the audience is distant and virtually unknown, such as when you write a letter to the editor of a newspaper to protest the new state drinking age; when you send a request to L. L. Bean to exchange a pair of snowshoes; or when you write a letter to a potential employer with whom you hope to secure a job interview.

As you come to know your audience, so you shape your language. That note or letter to a friend is honest, playful, direct, and probably loosely structured, because the friend is concerned mainly with what you say rather than how you say it. Your journal entry is probably the same way, though maybe less playful. But the letter to an aunt thanking her for the earmuffs is a little more careful, because you want her to think her sister's child is well brought up. The essay to your physics or history teacher is as careful as you can make it—that is, in one draft late the night before it's due. But that hasty level of care won't do for the job interview letter—you have two friends proofread this one to make sure it has no mistakes. We're being hypothetical, of course, but you probably see our drift: We all shape our language, whether spoken or written, according to the audience we're addressing and the impression we want to create.

Another way of thinking about your audience is thinking about how you want to be viewed through your writing. In the letters to a friend and to a prospective employer we see different personas, or masks, created by the same person—at times serious, organized, or careful; at other times playful, self-absorbed, or careless. Skillful writers think hard about who will read their writing and adjust it accordingly, presenting themselves in the way they most want their readers to view them.

Remember that in college your most common academic audience is a professor looking to evaluate what you know. Although he or she is known, to some extent, and perhaps friendly, this audience also expects something from you, such as the ability to explain organic systems accurately, to use terminology correctly, to apply concepts appropriately, to document carefully, and to speculate wisely and cautiously. This audience also expects — or at least hopes — that you will organize your writing logically, compose complete sentences, type neatly and carefully, and spell correctly. In other words, because you want this audience to think well of you and give your paper the most possible points, you adopt a persona that is knowledgeable and literate.

WRITING 1.

Throughout this book, we suggest that you pause periodically in your reading and write informally, to yourself, to gain a better understanding of particular issues raised in each chapter and perhaps to discover their relevance to you. There are, or course, no formulas for how this writing-to-learn gets done; neither is there a right or wrong way to do it. If this idea makes sense to you, the simplest method is to write regularly in a small notebook we call a journal. (For more information on using journals in college classes, see the article by Fulwiler in the readings that follow this chapter.) Here is our first suggestion:

Make a list of people to whom you have written during the last month or so. Next to each name, note a distinguishing characteristic of that person. Finally, write a short journal entry explaining what decisions you made or will make when you write to one of these particular people rather than another.

A WRITER'S PURPOSE

The other part of the writer's equation is purpose: *Why* am I writing to whom I'm writing? Purposes, like audiences, vary greatly; for example, we write in order to ask, answer, explain, persuade, wonder, create, describe, declare, and define. Here again, your purpose determines how you organize, how formal your language is, how much space you use, and even how clear, correct, and conventional you are. To simplify our discussion of purpose, let us describe three distinctly different functions that writing may serve in college or elsewhere: writing to communicate, writing to imagine, and writing to learn.

Writing to Communicate

When many of us think about writing, we think first of its role in *communication*. Our discussion of audience implied that language is used to communicate with other people. When that is our main purpose , we want to appear literate and informed. We can call much of this writing *expository,* writing meant to explain something to an audience and to persuade the audience to believe you.

When you write exposition, you try, above all, to be clear and to avoid mistaken, unintended, or incorrect meanings. Clear writing is generally organized according to a recognizable logic such as cause and effect, chronology, or question and answer. Clear writing likewise contains sentences easily understood by the audience for whom it is intended and may or may not include specialized language, or jargon. Finally, clear writing also uses conventional (dictionary-based) grammar, spelling, and punctuation.

When you write to explain, report, and inform, you want to be believed. For that reason exposition usually contains appropriate illustrations, examples, evidence, references, and documentation. In college, for example, your history paper ought to mention specific and correct names, places, and dates to support your assertions. Likewise, your literature paper should include references to specific plot, characters, and settings, each supported by apt quotations. And, of course, that chemistry lab report needs careful documentation (written in an objective voice) of each subsection—procedure, methods, results, and discussion.

A good example of exposition is this chapter or, for that matter, most of this book. It is our intention to explain as clearly as possible the nature of college-level learning in a variety of disciplines. To that end, we define concepts and terminology as lucidly as we can, supporting our ideas with frequent and often personal examples, making sure our transitions lead smoothly and logically from one paragraph to the next, using frequent subheadings to call attention to organizing concepts, and writing all the while in standard English with conventional grammar, punctuation, and spelling.

Writing to Imagine

When you write *imaginatively,* you write to play, entertain, experiment, and create aesthetic or emotional responses in readers. You may write from your own experience, from what you know, but in a reflective and perhaps fictive way. Actually it's hard to define exactly what such writing does, but you know that effect yourself when you read a novel you can't put down or a poem that creates a lump in your throat. Such writing is commonly called *creative* or *poetic* and includes, in addition to poetry and fiction, drama, essays, and song lyrics.

You can't make any rules for how this kind of writing should look, since imaginative writers frequently experiment with form, style, dialogue, and structure. Consider, for example, some brief passages by three famous American writers who wrote in the last half of the nineteenth century. Walt Whitman's imaginative writing, from the poem "Song of Myself," looks like this:

I am of old and young, of the foolish as much as the wise,
Regardless of others, ever regardful of others,
Maternal as well as paternal, a child as well as a man,
Stuff'd with the stuff that is coarse and stuff'd with the stuff that is fine . . .

Mark Twain's imaginative writing, in the opening lines of *The Adventures of Huckleberry Finn*, looks like this:

You don't know about me, without you have read a book by the name of "The Adventures of Tom Sawyer," but that ain't no matter. That book was made by Mr. Mark Twain, and he told the truth, mainly. There was things which he stretched, but mainly he told the truth.

Emily Dickinson's imaginative writing, in a single untitled poem, looks like this:

Much madness is divinest sense
To a discerning eye
Much sense the starkest madness.
'Tis the majority
In this, as all, prevail.
Assent and you are sane;
Demur, you're straightway dangerous
And handled with chain.

Each of these examples shows written language being used in an inventive, imaginative manner, doing something a little unusual, and looking a little different from conventional expository language. Whitman's language is from a fifty-page poem that takes liberties with spelling and never rhymes. Twain's language is from the first page of a novel claiming to be written by a poorly educated fourteen-year-old boy and meant to sound like him talking to us. Dickinson's language is actually a complete poem in eight tightly compressed lines that rhyme, though they may take several readings on our part to make "divinest sense." Although each passage means and communicates something, that meaning may be created indirectly (Twain) or ambiguously (Dickinson) and be subject to much interpretive debate by readers. In other words, simple clarity is not the goal of such literary language: It is *clearly* up to something else, something neither single nor simple.

Imaginative writing is also quite different from communicative writing insofar as belief is concerned. Although some imaginative writers may try to create belief, as, for example, Twain's young narrator does by speaking in the rhythms of colloquial speech, readers understand that it is not meant to be believed in any literal sense. "Fiction," one form of imaginative writing, means a lie or untruth. This writing is serving a function different from that of straight exposition, and readers are aware of it from the start. (The role of imaginative writing is explored more fully in Chapter 2.)

The majority of the disciplines in the university community ask you to write in order to communicate, not to imagine. As such, imaginative writing is sort of a maverick form, which you will study intensely in literature classes but seldom be asked to write yourself. The exceptions are English department courses in creative writing or courses within subjects such as business or history in which you are asked to role-play a character (for example, by imagining you are an escaped slave) and to explain what you see from that perspective. (When you read Chapter 3 you will find Yourcenar's account of medieval history told from an imagined historical perspective.)

Writing to Learn

Sometimes you write primarily to yourself in order to discover what you think or feel, to ponder a question, or to solve a problem. You do not intend for an audience other than yourself to read this language, because it's often tentative and sometimes messy. We call this writing-to-learn or *discovery writing*, though you might also call it personal, expressive, or simply informal writing.

We write to learn about ourselves or to explore our view of the world in diaries, journals, notes, and rough drafts. Sometimes we also do this when we write of our concerns and frustrations to close friends in letters, sharing our thoughts and exploring our own minds at the same time. Discovery writing takes the loose and often fragmentary strands of thought out of our heads and puts them in concrete language that we can look at and perhaps better understand.

There are no rules for the way discovery writing should look, though it commonly resembles your own informal talk, full of stops and starts, fragments, contractions, exclamations, colloquial words, loose structures, and self-references. If you keep a journal or diary or write letters to friends, you have your own best examples. Here is a sample of such discovery writing by Mary, one of our first-year students who is keeping a journal for her writing class:

> I'm sitting in history right now and I can't take any
> more notes. I'm functioning on 2 hours sleep. The paper
> was due today and every draft I did seemed totally wrong,
> full of B.S. As I look around the classroom I see faces
> that look like they haven't slept either--two guys in back
> of me are actually asleep. The grad student, Tim, looks
> extremely bored. He's sitting beside me drinking coffee
> and writing a letter to someone. All this is going on
> while the teacher is lecturing on the defeat of Islam--I
> wonder if he takes in all that I see? That would depress
> me if I was him.

Mary is really writing to herself here, more to kill time or keep awake, than with any specific purpose in mind, looking around the class and talking to herself on paper. We're calling even this casual sample *discovery writing* because the writer set out to write without knowing in advance where she was going. She lets her eyes and her pen guide her thoughts, not the other way around. As her eyes wander around the room, they actually lead her to a small insight: If the teacher sees all the tired and bored faces she does, that must depress him. At the same time, she writes in a simple, comfortable style—with short sentences, dashes, and contractions—that sounds conversational when we read it.

Notice, too, what Mary does not tell us: We don't know the teacher's name, what he looks like, the title of the course, the point of the lecture, the topic or length of the paper, the age or grade level of the writer, the size or shape of the room, the number of students in it, the type or color of the desks, the day of week or time of day, or whether there's milk in Tim's coffee. The writer is writing to herself and takes all those details for granted: They are clear to her, her only audience.

When people write to themselves they omit details that more distant audiences would need for full understanding. For this kind of writing, omissions, informality, and short-cuts make sense. (For more information on writing-to-learn, or discovery writing, read the following articles by William Stafford, Janet Emig, and Peter Elbow. For more examples, see Fulwiler.)

Although the expository and the imaginative forms of writing are more carefully crafted than discovery writing, discovery writing is most important to the writer. It is through exploratory language—in casual conversation or private notes—that we think ideas through, figure things out, and often locate and discover the ideas that surface when we write in the more formal modes. In many ways, discovery writing is the matrix from which the other forms evolve: Before you can share ideas with someone else, they must make sense to you! For this reason we suggest that you keep a written record of your thoughts as you read this or any other text. If you try to explain what you have just read *to yourself*, you will in fact know the material more thoroughly and be better able to explain it to somebody else on a test or in a more formal paper.

WRITING 2.

Write a journal entry about your previous experiences with discovery writing. Describe the kinds of discovery writing (letters, diaries, journals, rough drafts) you most commonly do. How often do you write to discover? On what particular occasions? Explain in your own terms the value you see in this kind of writing.

What is Good Writing?

We have described these several functions of writing to suggest the variety of roles writing plays in people's lives. We also want you to understand that there's no such thing as only one kind of *good* writing—what's good depends on your audience and the reason for writing. Of course it might be a mistake to write a lab report in a poetic style or a history paper as a journal entry unless the teachers ask for such a style. But wouldn't it be equally silly to write a personal letter in the style of a term paper and use footnotes?

About one thing we're clear: Written language can—if you let it— do virtually everything that oral language can. But perhaps the most important function of all writing is making meaning to readers, both distant and close to the writer's self, in the university community and in the rest of your life. If the writing makes meaning successfully, it must be pretty good writing!

WRITING IN THE UNIVERSITY

Subsequent chapters of *A Community of Voices* introduce you to the various disciplines that comprise the university community. At the same time, each chapter introduces you to the many roles language, especially writing, plays within this community. All the chapters were written for students like yourself, near the beginning of their college studies, so none is written in hard-to-understand disciplinary jargon. However, the writers of each chapter have their own approaches to knowledge, to looking at the world, and occasionally you will notice a word, phrase, rhythm, or metaphor that identifies the author as an artist or scientist or psychologist. As you read the various voices in this text, see if you notice any differences in the way the authors from the different disciplines express themselves. What can you observe in the language of each chapter that separates one from another?

In each chapter (including this one) you have found or will find questions to write about and discuss. Believe us, we are not asking you to pick up your pens or hit your keyboards just to keep you busy. All of us who have written chapters and readings for this book are students, scholars, and writers ourselves. We have learned that the act of writing is one of the most profound of human activities, especially for those of us for whom learning is important.

Your Own Writing

So far we have looked at the role writing plays throughout the university community to communicate, imagine, and discover. We would like to conclude by offering some general advice or counsel for the writing of formal papers in the university. As we have emphasized throughout this chapter, the way you write depends on your audience and purpose: To whom you are writing and why. We don't believe there are any formulas that work for everyone, nor, in fact, any that work for any single writer all the time. However, our experience as both writers and writing teachers has convinced us that certain strategies are more helpful than others, so we'd like to share some of those with you.

Discovering. As you have already seen, we suggest that you pause now and then to write about what you are reading. We also suggest that you keep this informal writing together in a bound notebook called a journal. This is a good habit for whatever reading you are doing for whatever course. Every few pages, ask yourself, "Do I understand what I just read?" The best way to find out is to try to write the idea in your own words: You'll soon know whether the reading is making sense or not. (It happens all too often that the first time you try to write out what you understand is on the examination itself, when it may be too late.)

Something else also happens when you write out ideas to yourself: You find out more than you thought you knew. For instance, you will *see* exactly what you know and what you don't. In addition, if you look carefully, you will *see* the questions to ask in order to find the information that's missing. Finally, as you *see* written down what you already know, you may actually visualize new connections, ideas, and possibilities. So, when you need to think more clearly or creatively, don't just stare at the ceiling or shuffle through old notes. Pick up a pencil or turn on your word processor and start writing. You will see your problem more clearly and soon begin to solve it.

When you need to write a formal paper, we suggest that you do a fair amount of discovery writing first, in a journal or notebook, to experiment with different topics or approaches. We usually start with lists of ideas and begin composing sentences or paragraphs only when one item on the discovery list looks promising. In these discovery drafts, we recommend that you write fast. Let the ideas spill out one after the other in whatever order they appear, and let your pencil (or cursor) help you think. We still do most of our discovery writing by hand in notebooks, though we switch to computers when we begin our formal drafts, preferring the greater freedom to rearrange our writing electronically as we try to give more substance and shape to our writing.

WRITING 3.

As you finish reading this chapter, imagine a good formal writing assignment about an issue related to writing, thinking, or learning, one you can share with others in class or with your teacher. It may involve analysis of a personal experience with a teacher, a time you learned something especially well, the way your own language works in everyday life, or a time when language resulted in catastrophic confusion. Use this occasion to make a list of such possible paper topics, some maybe requiring research, others based on personal experience. Write a paragraph each on two of them. You suggest the topic, direction, nature of your thesis, and possible evidence. (Paper length? Due date? It's your assignment!)

Drafting.   When you need to write a paper for a college assignment—some version of expository writing—plan on writing it in several drafts over several days. If you allow for this in advance, before you even sit down to write your paper, you will be ahead of the game from the start. Drafting, as far as we're concerned, is when you actually sit down to write your paper and attempt to work out the main ideas in the order in which they will appear. Sometimes we work from a quickly sketched outline, other times from a rougher list or from a discovery draft started in a journal or notebook.

When we wrote the first drafts of this chapter, we spent much of our time developing our controlling ideas in relation to the book as a whole. At this stage, we spent very little time on getting our evidence and examples in order; we knew we could do that later once we knew what, exactly, our ideas consisted of. We also used numerous subheadings in these early drafts, because they helped point our writing in useful directions while keeping related ideas together. In subsequent drafts, we changed these around freely, but their value early on was in helping us group ideas and in actually allowing us to see the main outline of our paper. In the early stages of our writing, we especially enjoyed the freedom our computers gave us to change and change again (we used the same software program, which allowed us to share drafts easily). We both also enjoyed how professional and profound even our early ideas looked when they appeared in electronic type on a computer monitor, though careful reading often taught us otherwise.

One more hint: When we write with computers, we find it important to print out several drafts on paper (computer jargon calls this hard copy) and to remove ourselves from the computer to read over what we've first written. The hard copy looks different and allows us to see where to start making changes. Be sure you do this *before* the night before the paper is due.

Revising. *A Community of Voices* was written over a two-year period by seventeen authors. Now that it is finished and published, we believe it is pretty well written—clear, concise, lively, and full of good examples. But it was not always so. In fact, the writing of each chapter was laborious, because each university specialist had to shape his or her prose carefully to suit a nonspecialist audience—to be clear, concise, lively, and to find good examples. Each author eventually achieved this effect by writing and rewriting many times, having the rest of us evaluate the new version each time and tell what we liked, what we didn't like, and where we had questions or wanted more information. *None* of the chapters looks today even remotely like it did at first; each is much better because we planned for rewriting from the beginning. In other words, *revision* was the central process by which this book was written.

By the way, we do not suggest that you allow two years to write the paper due this term, but we do suggest that you make revision a habit if you haven't already done so. Revision is the real secret behind good writing, and, of course, it's not really a secret at all.

In the discovery draft you may not care about how your ideas are ordered. In your first serious draft you may not care whether you have supported and documented all your ideas. But in your final draft, you do care about all of these elements, so you revise. For most of us who wrote this book, revision became a way of life as we shared drafts and ideas with one another. (For more information about revising your writing, read the following article by Don Murray.)

We strongly recommend sharing your early drafts with people you trust and listening to their reactions. No matter how carefully we believe we have crafted our paper or chapter, another pair of eyes will see something we missed. When we ask each other to read our drafts, as we regularly do, we usually tell the reader what we want him or her to look at: "Does my conclusion work?" or "I don't like the way it starts — any suggestions?" or "Do you find anything missing?" We tried at all times to be kind to and supportive of each other but also to make specific suggestions so the chapter writer knew what to do next. (For more information on sharing your writing in groups, read Marge Piercy's article, which follows.)

Editing.   The last operation on any piece of writing, including our book, is *editing*, which we consider to be sentence-level work. When we move to this stage in our writing, we are already pretty sure that the ideas in the paper are solid, in good order, and well supported. But we know from experience that one more reading would help get each idea and example stated in the most precise and careful way possible. While editing we commonly look for strong verbs, omit words that don't carry their weight, and tinker with sentence rhythms.

If it's any consolation, most experienced writers, including ourselves, draft, revise, edit, write, revise, and edit over and over to express the ideas just right. Writing is not easy for any of us, but it's among the most important intellectual work we do, so we work hard at it. We wrote this book believing that if you write about the ideas you read, the ideas make more sense and you will have more fun. In the readings that follow this chapter, you will find further thoughts by writing experts about the complex intellectual process called writing. Read carefully, write often, and have a good time!

SUGGESTIONS FOR RESEARCH
Portrait of Myself as a Writer

Journal Writing.
After you have finished this chapter and the various readings that accompany it, think about your own development as a writer. How

did you learn to write? Who do you remember teaching you? What do you remember most? Was this influence positive or negative? What papers do you remember writing? Which did you think were the best? Which were the worst? Do you still have copies of any of these? Did others share your opinion? Write in your journal about some of these questions, and see what your first-response answers look like. Look for material here to amplify with details and develop with examples.

Draft One.

Now, write a more formal draft in which you profile yourself as a writer, tracing the history of how you got to be the kind of writer you are. Where did you start? How far back can you remember? What do you remember? One of our students, Karen, started her paper here:

> As I look back and review my writing habits I discover a
> pattern: name, date, title, one draft, spell check,
> done!! I handed it in and never looked at it again. My
> senior thesis, I sat down at the computer, typed out a
> draft, and as soon as the page numbers reached ten I
> wrote a conclusion, ran it through spell check, and
> handed it in. I never proofread it. I was content it
> didn't have any spelling errors. So, why did I get a "D"
> on it? I couldn't figure it out.

Draft Two.

See if you can locate any samples of your earlier writing, perhaps at home in folders or boxes saved by you or your parents. If you have none from elementary or secondary school, do you have old letters, journals, notes, or diaries? Or, instead, use samples of the writing you have done so far in college, in this or other classes. Look at this earlier writing and see what story it tells. Karen found this example from her high school commencement speech to her class:

> High school has certainly been an enjoyable experience,
> and although the times may not last forever, at least our
> memories will. I would like to thank every member of the
> class of 1989 for playing a significant role in my high
> school experience. Each of you has contributed to making
> the past four years memorable.

Looking back at this writing of just six months ago, Karen comments, "I can't ever remember talking to my friends or classmates like that. Someone should have handed me a shovel after reading that! Obviously, I wanted to impress the parents."

Draft Three.

Next, think about your writing as it is developing now, in college. What differences do you notice from your earlier writing? Have you

changed the language you use, or your style? The subjects about
which you choose to write? Your attitudes? Here is Karen's assessment
of herself as a writer as she concludes her first-semester writing class:

> I finally learned that clarity and careful editing are
> what make quality papers. Filling page requirements and
> perfect spelling just don't have the same effect. After a
> few weeks in English 1, I learned about editing, and I
> put it to use in my papers. My personal experience paper
> once read, "You have worked too hard to get to this point
> to give up now. Think about every Saturday morning prac-
> tice." Now, after my eighth draft, it reads, "You have
> worked too hard to get to this point only to give up now.
> Think of every sweat-dripping, physically grueling,
> suicide-sprinting, drill-conditioning, nine o'clock
> Saturday morning practice."
>
> I have recognized definite changes in my writing. Now
> I pay attention to detail in order to capture the reality
> of a moment. It took me at least eight drafts, but I fi-
> nally did it. I was no longer content with my work, I was
> proud of it! I even took it home to show my parents. I
> also no longer try to force topics. My personal experi-
> ence paper was originally about my friendship with my
> sister's boyfriend. No matter how hard I wanted to and
> how hard I tried to, I just couldn't develop it. So, I
> switched topics. With my analytical essay I did the same.
> The first poem I chose was too simple, so I found a new
> one. In high school I wrote five-paragraph essays from
> one point of view. Today, my personal experience paper
> has three sections from three different points of view,
> and my research paper is a script for a television show.
>
> Where I stand as a writer today is one who obeys rules
> of editing and ignores rules of format. My new writing
> pattern is draft upon draft, edit, proofread, spell
> check, name, and hand it in. Although it appears first,
> what originally was my first step (my name) is now my
> last.

Other Options:

Finally, think about other options or forms this paper might take:
What would it be like written in the third person, as if you were an
archeologist of your earlier self? What would happen if you presented
your search for self as a series of present-tense journal entries, fabricated to appear written at different stages of your life? Or what if you
presented yourself through a series of scenes in a short play, dramatiz-
ing your earlier self along with those who influenced your story?

We think this is a good paper to have fun with as you find out
important things about yourself. Share these papers with classmates
and give each other as much help as you can in achieving both analytical rigor and a lively voice.

READINGS

Writing to Learn

William Stafford
WRITING

William Stafford (b. 1914) is a poet who won the National Book Award in 1962 for his collection of poetry Traveling Through the Dark. *He has taught at Lewis and Clark College, been a poetry consultant to the Library of Congress, and given poetry readings throughout the world. In the reading that follows, Stafford talks about writing as "one of the great free human activities," more important, perhaps, for its effect on the writer than on the audience. As you read, see if you agree with him about the importance of being receptive to new ideas and fleeting impressions* while you write.

A writer is not so much someone who has something to say as he is someone who has found a process that will bring about new things he would not have thought of if he had not started to say them. That is, he does not draw on a reservoir; instead, he engages in an activity that brings to him a whole succession of unforeseen stories, poems, essays, plays, laws, philosophies, religions, or—but wait!

Back in school, from the first when I began to try to write things, I felt this richness. One thing would lead to another; the world would give and give. Now, after twenty years or so of trying, I live by that certain richness, an idea hard to pin, difficult to say, and perhaps offensive to some. For there are strange implications in it.

One implication is the importance of just plain receptivity. When I write, I like to have an interval before me when I am not likely to be interrupted. For me, this means usually the early morning, before others are awake. I get pen and paper, take a glance out the window (often it is dark out there),and wait. It is like fishing. But I do not wait very long, for there is always a nibble—and this is where receptivity comes in. To get started I will accept anything that occurs to me. Something always occurs, of course, to any of us. We can't keep from thinking. Maybe I have to settle for an immediate impression: it's cold, or hot, or dark, or bright, or in between! Or—well, the possibilities are endless. If I put down something, that thing will help the next thing come, and I'm off. If I let the process go on, things will occur to me that were not at all in my mind when I started. These things, odd or trivial as they may be, are somehow connected. And if I let them string out, surprising things will happen.

If I let them string out. . . . Along with initial receptivity, then, there is another readiness: I must be willing to fail. If I am to keep on writing, I cannot bother to insist on high standards. I must get into

22

action and not let anything stop me, or even slow me much. By "standards" I do not mean "correctness" — spelling, punctuation, and so on. These details become mechanical for anyone who writes for a while. I am thinking about what many people would consider "important" standards, such matters as social significance, positive values, consistency, etc. I resolutely disregard these. Something better, greater, is happening! I am following a process that leads so wildly and originally into new territory that no judgment can at the moment be made about values, significance, and so on. I am making something new, something that has not been judged before. Later others — and maybe I myself — will make judgments. Now, I am headlong to discover. Any distraction may harm the creating.

So, receptive, careless of failure, I spin out things on the page. And a wonderful freedom comes. If something occurs to me, it is all right to accept it. It has one justification: it occurs to me. No one else can guide me. I must follow my own weak, wandering, diffident impulses.

A strange bonus happens. At times, without my insisting on it, my writings become coherent; the successive elements that occur to me are clearly related. They lead by themselves to new connections. Sometimes the language, even the syllables that happen along, may start a trend. Sometimes the materials alert me to something waiting in my mind, ready for sustained attention. At such times, I allow myself to be eloquent, or intentional, or for great swoops (treacherous! not to be trusted!) reasonable. But I do not insist on any of that; for I know that back of my activity there will be the coherence of my self, and that indulgence of my impulses will bring recurrent patterns and meanings again.

This attitude toward the process of writing creatively suggests a problem for me, in terms of what others say. They talk about "skills" in writing. Without denying that I do have experience, wide reading, automatic orthodoxies and maneuvers of various kinds, I still must insist that I am often baffled about what "skill" has to do with the precious little area of confusion when I do not know what I am going to say and then I find out what I am going to say. That precious interval I am unable to bridge by skill. What can I witness about it? It remains mysterious, just as all of us must feel puzzled about how we are so inventive as to be able to talk along through complexities with our friends, not needing to plan what we are going to say, but never stalled for long in our confident forward progress. Skill? If so, it is the skill we all have, something we must have learned before the age of three or four.

A writer is one who has become accustomed to trusting that grace, or luck, or — skill.

Yet another attitude I find necessary: most of what I write, like most of what I say in casual conversation, will not amount to much. Even I will realize, and even at the time, that it is not negotiable. It will be like practice. In conversations I allow myself random remarks — in fact, as I recall, that is the way I learned to talk —, so in writing I launch many expendable efforts. A result of this free way of writing is that I am not writing for others, mostly; they will not see the product at all unless the activity eventuates in something that later appears to be worthy. My guide is the self, and its adventuring in the language brings about communication.

This process-rather-than-substance view of writing invites a final, dual reflection:

1. Writers may not be special—sensitive or talented in any usual sense. They are simply engaged in sustained use of a language skill we all have. Their "creations" come about through confident reliance on stray impulses that will, with trust, find occasional patterns that are satisfying.

2. But writing itself is one of the great, free human activities. There is scope for individuality, and elation, and discovery, in writing. For the person who follows with trust and forgiveness what occurs to him, the world remains always ready and deep, an inexhaustible environment, with the combined vividness of an actuality and flexibility of a dream. Working back and forth between experience and thought, writers have more than space and time can offer. They have the whole unexplored realm of human vision.

OPTIONS FOR WRITING

1. William Stafford describes writing as "a process that will bring about new things he would not have thought of if he had not started to say them." Write an essay describing your own experience finding new things as you write, being as specific as possible.

2. Stafford describes writing as "one of the great, free human activities." What do you think he means by this? What are some of the other great free human activities? Write an essay exploring your own interpretation of these activities.

Peter Elbow
FREEWRITING

> *Peter Elbow (b. 1935) teaches writing at the University of Massachu-*
> *setts. He is widely recognized for his studies of voice in writing and*
> *for the books* Writing Without Teachers *(1973) and* Writing with
> Power *(1981). The following reading is Chapter 2 of* Writing With-
> out Teachers *and describes the technique of fast writing, which he*
> *calls* freewriting. *After you have read this piece, freewrite for ten*
> *minutes about anything on your mind, or freewrite to explore your*
> *opinions about the ideas Elbow presents in this article.*

The most effective way I know to improve your writing is to do freewriting exercises regularly. At least three times a week. They are sometimes called "automatic writing," "babbling," or "jabbering" exercises. The idea is simply to write for ten minutes (later on, perhaps fifteen or twenty). Don't stop for anything. Go quickly without rushing. Never stop to look back, to cross something out, to wonder how to spell something, to wonder what word or thought to use, or to think about what you are doing. If you can't think of a word or a spelling, just use a squiggle or else write, "I can't think of it." Just put down something. The easiest thing is just to put down whatever is in your mind. If you get stuck it's fine to write "I can't think what to say, I can't think what to say" as many times as you want; or repeat the last word you wrote over and over again; or anything else. The only requirement is that you *never* stop.

What happens to a freewriting exercise is important. It must be a piece of writing which, even if someone reads it, doesn't send any ripples back to you. It is like writing something and putting it in a bottle in the sea. The teacherless class helps your writing by providing maximum feedback. Freewritings help you by providing no feedback at all. When I assign one, I invite the writer to let me read it. But also tell him to keep it if he prefers. I read it quickly and make no comments at all and I do not speak with him about it. The main thing is that a freewriting must never be evaluated in any way; in fact there must be no discussion or comment at all.

Here is an example of a fairly coherent exercise (sometimes they are very incoherent, which is fine):

> I think I'll write what's on my mind, but the only thing on my mind right now is what to write for ten minutes. I've never done this before and I'm not prepared in any way — the sky is cloudy today, how's that? now I'm afraid I won't be able to think of what to write when I get to the end of the sentence — well, here I am at the end of the sentence — here I am again, again, again, again, at least I'm still writing — Now I ask is there some reason to be happy that I'm still writing — ah yes! Here comes the question again — What am I getting out of this? What point is there in it? It's almost obscene to always ask it but I seem to question everything that way and I was gonna say something else pertaining to that but I got so busy writing down the first part that I forgot what I was leading into. This is kind of fun oh don't stop writing — cars and trucks speeding by somewhere out the window, pens clittering across people's papers. The sky is cloudy — is it symbolic that I should be mentioning it? Huh? I dunno. Maybe I should try colors, blue, red, dirty words — wait a minute — no can't do that, orange, yellow, arm tired, green pink violet magenta lavender red brown black green — now that I can't think of any more colors — just about done — relief? maybe.

Freewriting may seem crazy but actually it makes simple sense. Think of the difference between speaking and writing. Writing has the advantage of permitting more editing. But that's its downfall too. Almost everybody interposes a massive and complicated series of editings between the time words start to be born into consciousness and when they finally come off the end of the pencil or typewriter onto the page. This is partly because schooling makes us obsessed with the "mistakes" we make in writing. Many people are constantly thinking about spelling and grammar as they try to write. I am always thinking about the awkwardness, wordiness, and general mushiness of my natural verbal product as I try to write down words.

But it's not just "mistakes" or "bad writing" we edit as we write. We also edit unacceptable thoughts and feelings, as we do in speaking. In writing there is more time to do it so the editing is heavier: when speaking, there's someone right there waiting for a reply and he'll get bored or think we're crazy if we don't come out with *something*. Most of the time in speaking, we settle for the catch-as-catch-can way in which the words tumble out. In writing, however, there's a chance to try to get them right. But the opportunity to get them right is a terrible burden: you can work for two hours trying to get a paragraph "right" and discover it's not right at all. And then give up.

Editing, *in itself*, is not the problem. Editing is usually necessary if we want to end up with something satisfactory. The problem is that editing goes on *at the same time* as producing. The editor is, as it were, constantly looking over the shoulder of the producer and constantly fiddling with what he's doing while he's in the middle of trying to do it. No wonder the producer gets nervous, jumpy, inhibited, and finally can't be coherent. It's an unnecessary burden to try to think of words and also worry at the same time whether they're the right words.

The main thing about freewriting is that it is *nonediting*. It is an exercise in bringing together the process of producing words and putting them down on the page. Practiced regularly, it undoes the ingrained habit of editing at the same time you are trying to produce. It will make writing less blocked because words will come more easily. You will use up more paper, but chew up fewer pencils.

Next time you write, notice how often you stop yourself from writing down something you were going to write down. Or else cross it out after it's written. "Naturally," you say, "it wasn't any good." But think for a moment about the occasions when you spoke well. Seldom was it because you first got the beginning just right. Usually it was a matter of a halting or even garbled beginning, but you kept going and your speech finally became coherent and even powerful. There is a lesson here for writing: trying to get the beginning just right is a formula for failure—and probably a secret tactic to make yourself give up writing. Make some words, whatever they are, and then grab hold of that line and reel in as hard as you can. Afterwards you can throw away lousy beginnings and make new ones. This is the quickest way to get into good writing.

The habit of compulsive, premature editing doesn't just make writing hard. It also makes writing dead. Your voice is damped out by all the interruptions, changes, and hesitations between the consciousness and the page. In your natural way of producing words there is a sound, a texture, a rhythm—a voice—which is the main source of power in your writing. I don't know how it works, but this voice is the force that will make a reader listen to you, the energy that drives the meanings through his thick skull. Maybe you don't *like* your voice; maybe people have made fun of it. But it's the only voice you've got. It's your only source of power. You better get back into it, no matter what you think of it. If you keep writing in it, it may change into something you like better. But if you abandon it, you'll likely never have a voice and never be heard.

Freewritings are vacuums. Gradually you will begin to carry over into your regular writing some of the voice, force, and connectedness that creep into those vacuums.

OPTIONS FOR WRITING

1. Follow Peter Elbow's advice and freewrite for ten minutes every day for two weeks. At the end of the period, look back on your freewriting and reflect on its value to you. What surprised you about freewriting? What did you like about it? What did you dislike? What would be the value of continuing to freewrite for the rest of the semester?

2. Reflect again about William Stafford's comment that the act of writing helps you find new things to say. What similarities or differences do you find in Elbow's advice? Drawing on both Stafford and Elbow, make a list of *do*s and *don't*s for writers to follow. Add to this list other items based on your own experience, and compare this list with your classmates' lists. Together make a composite list, and copy it for the class.

Toby Fulwiler
COLLEGE JOURNALS

Toby Fulwiler (b.1942) is a professor of English at the University of Vermont. He is the author of College Writing *(1988) and editor of* The Journal Book *(1986). In the following reading he describes the possible uses for journals in a writing class. Judging from your past experience as a student, do you think journal writing would help with your studies in the way he describes?*

9/7 Perhaps this journal will teach me as much about myself as it will about English. You know, I've never kept a journal or such before. I never knew what a pleasure it is to write. It is a type of cleansing almost a washing of the mind . . . a concrete look at the workings of my own head. That is the idea I like most. The journal allows me to watch my thoughts develop yet, at the same time, it allows me a certain degree of hindsight.

[Peter]

In this passage, Peter describes journals well when he calls them places "to watch [his] thoughts develop" and to allow him a "certain degree of hindsight." Journals are collections of thoughts, impressions, musings, meditations, notes, doubts, plans, and intentions caught chronologically on paper. You write them for yourself in your most comfortable language.

In this chapter I want to share some of the journal entries I have photocopied from student journals (with student permission) over the last few years. Many of them came from the classes I teach in composition and American literature, but a fair number were given to me by colleagues in other disciplines, including botany, philosophy, political science, mathematics, and history. These samples suggest what is possible with journal writing. For the most part, they are interesting samples; I have seen many others much less interesting for outsiders to read, although they may have served their authors well.

OBSERVATIONS

In a small looseleaf notebook, Mary describes the ideas she finds in reading the essay "The American Scholar" by Ralph Waldo Emerson:

> 9/25 In the first few paragraphs of this address, Emerson seems discouraged at the way society is run, that there are no "whole men" left. . . .
> . . . He seems to feel that scholars should learn from books, but he says beware that you don't become a "bookworm." Use the books to inspire your own thoughts, *not* to copy the thoughts of others.

Mary is a freshman enrolled in an American literature class, and she is using her journal to "observe" more carefully what she reads by writing about it. Notice, especially, that she copies direct quotations from what she reads, key phrases that she will remember better because she has written them out. These observations become particularly useful to her the next day when these essays are discussed in class; they are also useful later when she studies for her final examinations.

In a spiral notebook, Alice, a biology major, describes what she sees happening in the petri dishes containing fern spores:

> 9/5 Well, first day of checking the spores. From random observation it seems that the Christmas Fern is much less dense than the Braun's Holly Fern.

Alice makes the following notations amidst other data describing what she sees in each of the 20 petri dishes she is monitoring as part of her senior thesis project:

1a nothing
2a an alive creature swimming around a pile of junk
3a looks like one spore has a rhizoid
4a one spore has a large protrusion (rhizoid beginning?)

In a science class, students commonly keep something like a lab or field notebook in which they both collect and speculate about data. This, too, is a kind of journal—a daily record of observations, speculations, questions, and doubts. Whether observing the words in books or the spores in petri dishes, the journal helps you both remember and understand.

DEFINITIONS

Journals are good places to ask yourself first questions about what you are doing with specific assignments, in specific courses, and in your major. In the following entries, we see students in several different disciplines trying to define or explain to themselves what, exactly, their fields of study are really about.

4/24 What makes politics scientific? How is it related to other disciplines? What tools do political scientists depend on most? Is it really a discipline by itself or does it need to be combined with other disciplines (i.e. the social sciences)? This is a hard subject to write about.
[Oscar]

5/2 Sociologists study groups for various reasons. They teach us to recognize how a group functions, how to seek out and influence the leaders, how to direct and control the masses. There are questions of ethics raised. It is taught as a process. The process is all important. . . . Taking apart a jigsaw puzzle, sociologists learn to unravel and identify distinct parts of the process.
[Marc]

3/7 Unlike math, where you must learn how to add and subtract before you can multiply and divide, philosophy is a smattering of different things with no exact and precise starting place. In philosophy we could start anywhere and end up anywhere without ever having gone anywhere, but we would have uncovered many rocks along the way. Ah Hah! This is our task: uncovering rocks along the way.
[Doug]

On one level, it simply helps to put any concept or term into your own words to try to make sense of it in language you understand. Each of the writers here writes his or her own definition and so increases the chances of truly understanding the concept.

In addition, I think we become immersed in our own disciplines and begin to take too much for granted. Sometimes your instructors stop questioning, at least in public, the basic assumptions around which their disciplines are actually built—assumptions that need periodic re-examining if the disciplines are to remain healthy. Journals are good places in which to ask yourself why you are majoring in what.

CONFUSION

Journals are good places to write about what you do not understand, where you are having trouble, and where you are confused. Sometimes writing about that which does not make sense helps it make sense; sometimes just the venting helps. In the following entry, Mary is venting her frustration about reading Emerson's "American Scholar" essay:

> 9/22 Of course, I'm not a scholar, but if I had to sit and listen to a speech like this I wouldn't be able to figure out what the heck he is talking about. Even after reading it for the third time I still can't figure out half of what he's saying.

If this student's name sounds familiar, you might recall that this is the same Mary who wrote thoughtfully about this same Emerson essay in the earlier section "Observations." Mary wrote the latter entry about three days before she slowed down and looked at the essay more carefully! The act of writing out your frustrations actually helps you focus on them and deal with them productively. In Mary's case, the fact that she earmarked the Emerson essay as difficult made her work harder to understand it—which eventually she did.

SPECULATIONS

One of the best uses for a journal is speculating on the meaning of what you are studying and thinking about. Speculating is really just a fancy name for guessing—making attempts at answers that you are not yet sure of. Speculating on exams or papers is dangerous; doing it in journals is natural. In the following entry, one of my literature students speculates on the meaning of a well-known passage in Henry David Thoreau's *Walden*:

> 10/24 What really caught my attention was the specific description of the fight between the black and red ants. In this chapter is Thoreau trying to put his friends (the wild animals) on the same line as those people in the village?

Bill's question, which poses an answer, is a good one. The more he speculates on the meaning of the various passages in *Walden,* or any other book in any other subject, the more ideas he will have to discuss in class and the more material about which to write further papers or exams. The speculation in his journal could lead to further investigation into other places where Thoreau makes similar comparisons. . . .

INSIGHTS

One of the most exciting things that happens while writing in your journal is that you stumble onto important thoughts in the act of writing. You usually cannot *see* this happening, but sometimes you can. When Missy was writing about writing a report for my advanced composition class the semester before she was to graduate, she wrote this passage:

> 3/12 (after class) Look, we botanists don't ask "Does
> that plant exist?" and we don't ask about the aesthetic
> value of a flower. We ask "What is the economic value of
> this plant?" But that is not the primary interest of a
> true botanist.
>   We want to know why it grows there (ecologists), why
> a plant has the structure it does (evolutionist), how it
> does its stuff (physiologist), etc. The discipline of
> botany has excluded lots of other questions and that is
> why I'm having some problems with it. . . . Yikes! I
> think it's all coming together!

Missy does not explain for us exactly what she sees coming together, but then she is not writing for us either. She is using the journal to think through some important issues that concern her now that she's about to become a professional botanist; in fact, she was using a lot of her composition journal to wrestle with matters closer to botany than English. This is exactly what a journal is for: talking with yourself about the issues that concern you most deeply. Sometimes it seems to answer back.

CONNECTIONS

Use your journal to find connections deliberately. Make as many as you can in any direction that works. Connect to your personal life, connect to other courses, connect one part of your course to another. In the following entries Kevin works on connections in a course on macroeconomics:

> 2/16 One of the things about this course seems to be the
> fact that many theories can be proved algebraically. For
> example, the teacher said that a possible exam question

might be to trace through a Keynesian model. In order to
trace it one has to use a lot of algebra, substituting
variables inside certain functions to prove equations
. . . by explaining it this way you get a better grasp of
things . . . economics becomes less ambiguous. Theories
backed up by mathematical, algebraic, or statistical evidence always seem much more concrete.

2/26 It [economics] is beginning to pull together. After
reading the chapters for the second time, I'm beginning to
see a sequence or passage of ideas from chapter to chapter.

Of course, if you read the material twice, review your notes, and keep
a journal, connections are bound to happen. In Kevin's case he is pulling it together, and the journal is probably helpful in this process.

RESPONSES TO READING

A colleague of mine who teaches history of science asks his students
questions about their reading that are to be answered in their journals.
He enjoys it when students write entries such as the following:

#17 What did Darwin find on the Galapagos Islands? Lions &
tigers & bears? Oh no. Turtles & lizards & seals! That's
what he found. Different from species found anywhere else
in the world. Tame and unafraid of humans. Adapted to a
harsh isolated environment. The birds, such as the wood-
pecker thrush, had learned to use tools. No other
species, except man and baboons, I think, had learned to
use tools. Some birds had no more use for flight so their
wings atrophied.

Journals are places in which to have some fun with language — to amuse
both yourself and your instructor (if you like). Randy's entry is fun to
read while still full of good specific information about his reading.

When I teach my literature classes, I tell my students, "Write about
everything you read in here, even if just for 5 minutes. Whenever you
complete a chapter, a poem, an essay, write something, anything, about
it in your journal. Date your entry and try to identify something specific
in what you are reacting to." By making this assignment I am hoping to
make writing about reading a habit. If you write about what you read,
you increase your chances of (1) remembering it, (2) understanding it,
and (3) asking intelligent, specific questions about it. The following are
two entries written by a first-year literature student while reading *Moby
Dick:*

11/30 The thought of running into that squid makes me
sick. Don't these men get scared of these strange creatures? Nobody can be that strong all the time.

12/1 What I thought was funny is that Stubbs calls the ship
they meet the Rosebud and it is giving off a gross odor because of all the sick and dying whales it carries. What's even
more humorous is that the ambergris (yellow substance) is
used in perfume—it comes from the bowels of dying whales!

The more personal Sarah's reaction, the more I believe that she is engaged in the book; the more she discovers that she finds funny or notable, the more likely she could use that entry as a seed from which to
start an analytic essay or research project.

REACTIONS TO CLASS

Journals are not the place for class notes, which are mere copies of your
professor's thoughts, but they are good places in which to evaluate what
took place in class, to record your opinion of the worth of the lecture or
points made by classmates during a discussion. In the following entry,
Caroline, a senior English major, comments on her Shakespeare class:

2/9 In Shakespeare class today I was aware of my fellow
students and wondered what each one of us was thinking—
about the class in general, about the professor, about
each other's comments, about Shakespeare. I could sense
and see that some students were there only in body. Some
of them obviously hadn't read Hamlet, many hadn't even
brought their books to class. I felt they had closed
themselves to literature—What, in contrast, makes me care
about these plays?

Caroline's candid reaction to class will inevitably help her remember
both the form and substance of that particular class meeting better than
if she had not written about it. Repeated entries such as this would be
likely to sharpen her powers of observation and depth of understanding
as well.

SELF-AWARENESS

Writing in journals promotes more awareness about whatever it is you
are writing about, be it history, economics, literature, or the act of writing itself. Use your journal to examine your attitudes toward ideas,
class, or simply the act of writing. After a few weeks of keeping a journal in his first-year writing class, Kurt wrote:

9/28 I am really amazed at myself! I don't ever recall
writing this much in my life—especially in a journal. I
write down a lot of ideas I get, I write in it when a
class is boring (usually chemistry lecture) and I write
in it because I want to. It helps me get things off my
chest that are bothering me.

Kurt's reaction is fairly typical of students who are starting to get serious about some elements of college (not necessarily chemistry) and are finding the journal a useful companion in advancing their thought—sometimes to their own surprise.

CONVERSATIONS

If your teacher asks to collect and read your journal, then you have a good chance to initiate some dialogue in writing about things that concern you both. Journals used this way take on many of the qualities of letters, with correspondents keeping in touch through the writing. As a writing teacher, I have learned a great deal about my own teaching from written conversations with my students.

Remember Alice, the biology major studying the fern spores in the petri dishes? Her professor responded to nearly every one of her observations, briefly, to let her know if she was on the right track. At midpoint in her project, her professor wrote the following:

```
10/15 Here are some questions designed to organize your
thoughts in groups: (1) What interspecific interactions
are promoted? (2) What intraspecific interactions are
promoted? (3) What about the experimental design casts
doubt on your inferences about interactions?
```

I don't understand these questions, and you probably don't either, but in the context of Alice's project journal, they made complete sense. In journals you can carry on virtually private, closed, tutorial-like conversations with your instructor, even if he or she never asked you to keep one. Sharing journal entries is more like sharing letters than any other kind of writing you are likely to do in college.

REFERENCE

Journals are also good places in which to review, revise, and actually reference your thoughts. Because they represent a progressive and cumulative record, you are bound to evolve perspectives on material and ideas that differ from earlier perspectives you wrote down. In addition, as your course progresses and you switch from one topic to the next, your tentative summations of material can prove to be valuable reference points. In fact, I suggest making it a regular habit to summarize your current thought *and* review your previous thought. In the following entry, John writes about the value of his math "workbook," essentially a journal kept for a mathematics class, as a useful personal reference document:

Well, I take back everything bad I ever said about keeping a workbook. . . . What I like most about my workbook
is that it is a source of reference. When I forget a concept I can look it up. I usually know exactly where to
look because my workbook is a very personal thing. My
workbook also shows my growth and progress in linear
algebra . . . all my homework can be found in one place
and in a very neat and efficient order.

John's workbook was an especially careful production, with sections
clearly labeled with different problem-solving strategies. Such a workbook is clearly a hybrid between a class notebook and a journal, a combination that seemed to suit his purpose for studying mathematics.

EVALUATIONS

Your journal may also prove to be a good place in which to reflect on
the value of journals themselves. I no longer believe journals work for
everyone—some people just don't like to be reflective in language—but
as course assignments go, they are fairly painless. Let me conclude with
some of Jim's observations; he started keeping a journal in my first-year
writing class with some reluctance; later he wrote the following on page
192 of his journal:

11/11 As I scan through my journal, I found a lot of
memories. I wrote consistently on my classes and found
grades to be one of my big hang-ups. . . . The entries
which helped me the most were those about myself and my
immediate surroundings. They helped me to realize who I
am. Maybe I should say what I am. I have a little bit of
everyone inside of me. . . .
    I really enjoyed looking back to see what I wrote.
Some entries were stupid. . . . Many times I wrote what I
really felt. A journal wouldn't be worth keeping if I
didn't. Who wants to read about what other's think? Never
once did I feel it a burden to write. If you would have
told us to write in it everyday, I would have told you
where to go. My roommate says I write too much, but I
think I write too little.

I have presented a lot of examples from college student journals in
a variety of grades and disciplines to make the case that journal writing
can be among the most important writing you do in the academic world.
It *is* the language of thought written down. In the next chapter, I will
describe some of the particular strategies that will make journals work
in easily among your other college assignments.

SUGGESTIONS FOR KEEPING JOURNALS

The following suggestions have proved useful to students enrolled in my literature and composition classes. They are, however, only a few possibilities of the many available. For every one suggestion here I can think of a dozen variations that may work equally well. If you have a good method for keeping your own journal, stick with it. If you have not tried a journal successfully before, see if some of these suggestions help.

1. Buy a looseleaf notebook. The special advantage of a looseleaf over a bound notebook is the ease with which you can add, subtract, and rearrange your writing. With a looseleaf notebook, you share portions of your journal with someone else — your teacher or classmates, for example — but keep on writing. If you write a highly personal entry in a school journal, you can simply withhold it when the teacher asks to read your entries and restore it later. I prefer small thin notebooks, about 7 by 10 inches, because they are easily carried in bookbag, knapsack, or briefcase; other teachers prefer 8½ by 11-inch notebooks because standard handouts can by inserted along with one's journal entries.

2. Divide your notebook/journal into sections. In my own journal I have two sections: the first for personal entries about my life, family, friends, goals, dreams and ambitions; the second section is for professional notes about books and articles I have read or am writing myself; during the year, when I am teaching, I will have additional sections for each class. I would recommend a similar approach for students: keep one part of your journal for private thoughts, another for each class you are taking. If a teacher wants to look at your journal entries, you pull out those entries from his or her class, clip them together, and hand them in — leaving the rest of your journal for you to continue writing in.

3. Date each entry. Your journal will become a record of your thoughts extended through time; the dates will document the distance between one idea and the next, and later will help you see the very evolution of your thought. In my journal I also jot down the time of day, place, and sometimes the weather, quick references that ground my writing/my life.

4. Start each entry on a new page. I do this to give me a good length of page to work with, to remind me that the longer I write the better my chances of finding something interesting to say. I also like the white spaces this method leaves in my journal, as I then have room to add later notes or the occasional clippings I staple into my journal.

5. Write in your natural voice with your most comfortable language. In journals, you want to write in the language that is easiest for you to use, that requires the least attention as you write. Otherwise, you may become distracted by form rather than content — and that's a mis-

take. Journals are places to worry ideas into shape; worry your language into shape when you write formal essays.

6. Write with your favorite pen. This is not, of course, a commandment — none of these suggestions is — but I would try to make writing in your journal something special, and writing with a favorite pen often helps that. I actually use an old fountain pen, preferring the nice lines of black ink it lays down to that of ball points and felt tips.

7. Write at the same time and at different times of the day. Writing in the morning finds me rather on task, making plans, lists of things to accomplish during the day, and the like; writing late at night finds me in a more reflective mood, looking inward, writing more emotionally. I find both moods for writing valuable, just different.

8. Write in the same place and in different places. Here too, I like to write in certain places that I know will be quiet and comfortable: on my front porch, back deck, and airplanes. I also find that writing in different places causes some different thoughts: on the beach, at a shopping mall, in a dentist's waiting room.

9. Write regularly. I really do not mean daily. Theoretically, I intend to write daily; realistically, I never do. More likely, I write four or five times a week, but sometimes two or three times the same day. When writing becomes habit, you will find it an easier and more versatile tool for problem solving and self-reflection both.

10. Prepare your journal for public reading. This advice pertains to journals assigned by teachers for specific courses. In such cases where your journal has a definite beginning, middle, and end, I would recommend that, prior to final submission, you put in page numbers, a title for each entry, a table of contents, an introduction, and a conclusion. This act of final ordering is a review for you and a wonderful courtesy to your reader, showing the seriousness with which you have taken the assignment.

We will now leave the relative privacy of journal writing and move on to writing directed at more public audiences. However, I am convinced that all successful writing is grounded first in personal knowledge and understanding. I never leave my own journal very far behind.

OPTIONS FOR WRITING

1. Describe your experiences keeping a journal or diary, commenting on such things as how old you were, whether it was for school, whether it was voluntary, and its usefulness to you at the time. (If you still have this notebook, review it and describe the writer—your earlier self—who kept it.) If you never kept a journal or diary before, what do you think would be the benefit to you?

2. As an experiment, keep a journal for four weeks, following as best you can the guidelines suggested in this chapter. At the end of the period, compile the following data about your own journal: What topics did you most often write about? How many entries did you write? On average, how many times a week did you write? On average, how many words did you write per entry? At what time of day did you most often write? Finally, write an assessment of the four-week experiment, explaining what you learned from it, what you liked, and what you didn't like.

Learning to Write

Donald Murray
MAKING MEANING CLEAR
The Logic of Revision

> *Donald Murray (b. 1924) is a writer, a journalist, and a teacher who has profoundly influenced the teaching of writing from the 1960s to the 1990s. He won a Pulitzer Prize in 1954 for his editorial writing on the* Boston Herald, *taught for 24 years at The University of New Hampshire, and currently writes a column for the* Boston Globe. *His most influential books include* A Writer Teaches Writing, Write to Learn, *and* Learning by Teaching. *As you read the following chapter, think about your own process of writing. Do you plan to revise when you write? Do you have a consistent strategy for doing so? Do Murray's questions give you any new ideas for revision strategies?*

The writer's meaning rarely arrives by room-service, all neatly laid out on the tray. Meaning is usually discovered and clarified as the writer makes hundreds of small decisions, each one igniting a sequence of consideration and reconsideration.

Revision is not just clarifying meaning, it is discovering meaning and clarifying it while it is being discovered. That makes revision a far more complicated process than is usually thought — and a far simpler process at the same time.

It is complicated because the writer can not just go to the rule book. Revision is not a matter of correctness, following the directions in a manual. The writer has to go back again and again and again to consider what the writing means and if the writer can accept, document, and communicate that meaning. In other words, writing is not what the writer does after the thinking is done; writing is thinking.

This also makes revision simpler. There is a logic to the process. The writer needs only a draft, a pen, and a brain. Each editorial act must relate to meaning. That is the primary consideration that rules each editorial decision. Considerations of audience, structure, tone, pace, usage, mechanics, typography are primarily decided on one issue: do they make the meaning clear?

The process of revision—what the reviser does—is fairly simple. The writer cuts, adds, reorders, or starts over. Each of these acts fits into a sequence most of the time. The writer solves the problems of meaning, and those solutions make it possible to solve the problems of order, and those solutions make it possible to solve the problems of voice.

Unfortunately, many teachers—and, I have discovered recently, many newspaper editors—do not understand the logic of revision and, therefore, do not encourage or even allow revision. They pounce on first-draft writing and make corrections.

Since most writers have not discovered their meaning in their first draft, the corrections editors make must come from the editors' own experience, their own research, their own prejudices. They work in ignorance of the writer's intention and take the writing away from the writer.

When editors or teachers kidnap the first draft, they also remove the responsibility for making meaning from the writer. Writing becomes trivialized, unchallenging, unauthoritative, impersonal, unimportant.

Hemingway told us, "Prose is architecture, not interior decoration . . . " Premature correction by a teacher or an editor must focus mainly on the decoration, the cosmetics of writing. Of course, writers must spell correctly, must follow the conventions of language that make meaning clear. But the writer must do it in relation to the writer's meaning through the medium of the writer's own voice. Writing is too important to be corrected by the book; it must be corrected in relation to meaning.

When revision is encouraged, not as a punishment but as a natural process in the exploration of the text to discover meaning, then basic writers become motivated to revise. It is a slow but miraculous process. The basic writers spot a hint of meaning that surprises them. Usually the meaning is in a primitive form at the time it is first shared with a teacher or fellow student. Basic writers are urged on. Soon they do not revise to become correct, they revise to discover their individual meaning, to hear their own voices making those meanings clear and to hear the readers' delight as an unexpected meaning is recognized as true.

The making of meaning through revision is a logical craft. Once a student has made meaning, the process can be repeated. It is not an act of magic any more than magic acts are; it is a matter of turning an engine, kneading dough, sewing a dress, building a shelf. The act of revision allows the writer to take something that was not and make it something that is; it allows the writer to achieve the satisfaction of completion, closure.

Revision can be the most satisfying part of teaching composition if the teacher is willing to let go. The composition teacher must wean the student. The teacher must give the responsibility for the text to the writer, making clear again and again that it is the student, not the teacher, who decides what the writing means.

The best way for teachers to reveal exploration in revision is by writing in public on the blackboard, or by using an overhead projector, allowing the students to see how writing struggles to find what it has to say. The teacher should not consciously write badly; the teacher should write as well as possible. That will produce copy that is quite bad enough to deserve revision.

The teacher who writes in public will expose the fact that writing often does not come clear, in fact, syntax often breaks down just at the point where a new or significant meaning is beginning to break out of its shell. That meaning has an awkward and clumsy time of it, but if the writer listens carefully and nurtures the meaning it may grow into significance. Or it may not. It may have to be put aside. But first it has to be understood before it can be rejected. Teachers who are willing to share evolving writing will find their class willing to share in a workshop where everyone is trying to help the writer discover and identify the evolving meaning.

I have internalized a checklist that follows the logic of revision. It may be helpful to consider this checklist, but each teacher should work to develop a new checklist with each class. Neither my checklist nor anyone else's checklist should be taken as gospel. The checklist should be formulated while the class experiences the process of making meaning clear.

The principles that underlie my checklist are

- *Build on strength.* The writer searches the text for the meaning that is being developed by the writing and looks for what is working to make it work better. Revising is not so much a matter of correction as it is a matter of discovering the strength of the text and extending that strength.
- *Cut what can be cut.* An effective piece of writing has a single dominant meaning, and everything in the text must advance that meaning.
- *Simplicity is best.* This does not mean writing in pidgin English, merely sending a telegram to the reader. It does mean making the writing as simple as it can be for what is being said. The message may be complex, and that may require linguistic or rhetorical complexity, but that complexity should always be the simplest way to communicate the complexity.
- *The writing will tell you how to write.* In revising I do not look to rule books, to models from other writers, to what I have written before, or how I have written it. The answers to the problems of

this piece of writing lie in the evolving text. I have faith that if I read carefully — if I listen to my own developing voice — I will discover what I have to say.

My checklist requires at least three different kinds of reading for focus, form and voice. This does not mean that I read the text three times; it is possible that the readings overlap and I read it only a couple of times. Most times I read it many more times. There is no ideal number of readings. I read it enough times to discover what I have to say.

During each of the readings I keep my eye and my ear on the single dominant meaning that is evolving from the text. A good piece of writing, I believe, says only one thing. Or to put it a different way, the many things that are said in a piece of writing all add up to a single meaning.

Here is my internal checklist articulated:

FOCUS

First, I read the text as fast as possible, trying to keep my pen capped, trying to see it from a distance the way the reader will so I can ask myself the larger questions of content and meaning. I do not do this "first" reading, of course, until I have the meaning of the writing in mind. In other words, I have to have *a* focus before I can work on *the* focus. If, in each stage of the reading, the meaning does not become clearer and clearer, I go back and discover a potential meaning that can be brought into focus. The questions I ask are

- What does the piece of writing mean? If it isn't clear I will take the time to write a sentence that makes the meaning clear, that achieves what Virginia Woolf calls, "the power of combination," that contains the tensions within the piece of writing in a single statement.
- Are all the reader's questions answered? Many times I will brainstorm the questions that the reader will inevitably ask of the text.
- Is new information needed?
- Is the piece built on undocumented assumptions? Sometimes I will actually write down my assumptions to see if they make sense or stand up as a firm foundation for the piece.
- Is the genre appropriate to the meaning? One of my novels started out as a series of articles. By genre I mean fiction, poetry, or the larger categories of non-fiction — personal narrative, familiar essay, argument, exposition.

- Are there any tangents that can be cut loose? I used to have much more trouble getting rid of those wonderful pieces of evidence or examples of writing that really didn't relate to the meaning. The late Hannah Lees taught me how to solve this problem. For years I wrote one paragraph to a page. Then played solitaire with these paragraphs, analyzed and reanalyzed them until they made a single meaning.
- Is there a section that should be a separate piece of writing?
- Is each point supported by convincing evidence? Sometimes I actually role-play a reader. It is always a specific person I know who does not agree with me and who I believe does not like me. I want to confront my enemies and defeat them before the writing is published.
- Is the piece long enough to satisfy the reader? Most writers underwrite, and I am no exception. The tendency is to say it and not to give the reader enough room to discover the meaning.
- Is the piece short enough to keep the reader involved? The piece of writing must develop its own energy, its own momentum. If my mind wanders during this first quick reading, the reader's certainly will.

FORM

Next, I read the text again, a bit more slowly, only uncapping my pen when a marginal note is necessary, trying to look at the text as a sequence of chunks of writing, perhaps chunks of meaning. I am no longer looking at the text as a whole, although I am aware of the territory now, and I am trying to keep myself free of the concern with detail, for a premature involvement with the details of language may keep me from evaluating the questions of form. The questions are

- Is the title on target? Years ago when I could put my own heads on editorials I found that the effort to write a title is worth the trouble. I may draft as many as a hundred titles, for each one is a way of discovering meaning, and I can draft a number of titles in slivers of time. At this stage of the revision process I check to make sure that the title relates to the meaning as the meaning has now evolved.
- Does the lead catch the reader in three seconds—or less? I hear rumors of good pieces of writing that have poor leads or beginnings, but I have not been able to find any from professional writers. The first few lines of a piece of writing establish the tone, the voice, the direction, the pace, the meaning. I check once more to make sure that the lead will entice the reader.

- Does the lead deliver on its contract with the reader? The lead must be honest. It must relate to the meaning that will evolve through the text.
- Does the piece answer the reader's questions at the point the reader will ask them? This is the key to effective organization. Again and again I will ask questions the reader will ask, even if they are the questions I do not want the reader to ask, and then number them in the order the reader will ask them. A good piece of writing does not need transitional phrases. The information arrives when the reader can use it. The reader's questions and their order can be anticipated.
- How can I get out of the way of the reader and show rather than tell? Orwell instructed writers that they should be like a pane of glass through which the reader sees the subject. I do not want the reader to be impressed with my writing, my arrogance is greater than that; I want the reader to receive the evidence in such a direct fashion that it will cause the reader to think the way I want the reader to think. I want to show so effectively that the reader sees my meaning as inevitable.
- Is there an effective variety of documentation? Most of us fall into a pattern using quotations, citations, anecdotes, statistics, personal experience — whatever we feel comfortable using or whatever we think we do well. The documentation, of course, should be what works best for the point being documented.
- Does the pace reinforce the meaning? The reader should be allowed to absorb each point before moving on to the next one. I tend to write and to teach too intensively; I have to remember to give the reader room.
- Does the pace provide the energy to carry the reader forward?
- Are the dimensions appropriate to the meaning? The size of each section should be in proportion to other sections — appropriate to the meaning.
- Does the end echo the lead and fulfill its promise?

VOICE

At last, I read the text slowly, line by line, my pen uncapped. I usually read the text many times within this category, generally working from the larger issues of voice down to paragraphs to sentences to phrases to single words. This is the most satisfying part of revision. There is a single meaning. It will change and develop and become clearer, but there is a focus, there is an order, and there is the chance to work with language, to combine my voice with the voice that is evolving from the draft. The questions I then ask are

- Can the piece be read aloud? Does it sound as if one person is talking to one person? Reading is a private experience, a human contact from one single person to another single person. I think that effective writing should be conversational. Sometimes the conversation is more formal than others, but it should never be stuffy, pretentious, or incapable of being read aloud by the writer.
- Are important pieces of specific information at the ends and beginnings of key sentences, paragraphs, sections, and the entire piece itself? The 2-3-1 principle of emphasis can do as much as anything else to sharpen up prose and make meaning clear: the second most important point of emphasis is at the beginning: the least important piece of emphasis is at the middle, and the greatest point of emphasis is at the end.
- Does each paragraph make one point?
- Does each paragraph carry a full load of meaning to the reader?
- Do the paragraphs vary in length in relation to meaning—the shorter the more important the information?
- Are the paragraphs in order? If the reader's questions are answered when they will be asked, formal transitions will not be needed.
- Does the reader leave each sentence with more information than the reader entered it?
- Are there sentences that announce what will be said or sum up what has been said and, therefore, can be cut?
- Are most sentences subject-verb-object sentences? At least most sentences that carry the essence of meaning should be direct sentences. The interesting work done in sentence-combining has too often confused this issue. Of course sentences should be combined, but the strength and vigor of the language still lies in simple, direct subject-verb-object sentences. These are the sentences, short and to the point, that will communicate.
- Are there clauses that get in the way of meaning? Many sentences have to be reordered so that the meaning comes clear. This usually means that sentences have to be read aloud again and again until the information in the sentence appears at the moment that the reader can use it.
- Are the verbs active and strong enough to drive the meaning forward? The verbs are the engines of meaning, and during revision the writer must give priority to finding verbs that are accurate and provide energy.
- Has the right word been found? Many times we try to use two almost right words in the hope that we will trap the meaning between them. That does not work. Mark Twain said, "The difference between the right word and the almost-right word is the difference between lightning and a lightning-bug." He was right. Revision is the search for the exactly right word.

- Does the meaning depend on verbs and nouns, not adverbs and adjectives? The right word is rarely an adjective or an adverb. Again, the meaning is not caught best in the crush between adjective and noun, or adverb and verb. I always feel a tiny sense of failure when I use an adjective or an adverb. I have failed to find the right noun or the right verb.
- Is there sexist or racist language that should be changed?
- Can the writing be more specific?
- Are there unnecessary lys, ings, thats, and woulds that should be cut? Each writer must develop a list of linguistic interferences with meaning. I find when I do professional ghost-editing that merely cutting the lys, the ings, the thats, the woulds — and yes, the unnecessary verb be — will make an obscure text start to come clear.
- Are there unnecessary forms of the verb "to be"?
- Is every fact checked?
- Is each word spelled correctly?
- Is there anything I can do to make the writing simple? clear? graceful? accurate? fair?

Do I formally ask all of these questions of myself in every piece of writing I do? Of course not. These concerns are internalized, and they overlap. The process is recursive. I discover meaning by language. I work back and forth from meaning to focus to form to voice and from voice to form to focus to meaning.

The process is, however, logical. Everything on the page must reveal meaning. Every word, every space between words, is put on the page or left on the page because it develops the meaning of the piece of writing.

This checklist can not be dumped on the beginning or the remedial writer, but it can be used by the teacher to establish priorities. The student has to learn that writing is a search for meaning, and once a potential meaning is found it may be clarified through the process of revision.

There is a simple guiding logic to revision, and every question of spelling, usage, structure, mechanics, style, content, documentation, voice, pace, development must be answered in terms of meaning.

Think of a workman who moves in close, measuring, marking, sawing, fitting, standing back to examine the job, moving back in close to plane, chisel, mark and fit, standing back again to study the task, moving in close to nail the piece in place, stepping back for another look, moving in close to set the nails, another step back, another look, then in close to hide the nail holes, to sand, stepping back to make sure the sanding is complete, then in close at last to apply the finish.

Actually the workman probably moved in close many more times before finishing the task and certainly stepped back many times to see the job entire. And so does the writer, working between word and meaning.

What the student can discover is that this process is logical; it can be understood. An effective piece of writing is produced by a craft. It is simply a matter of working back and forth between focus, form, and voice until the meaning is discovered and made clear.

OPTIONS FOR WRITING

1. Describe the process by which you make your own writing better: Explain those processes which are similar to or different from the processes Murray describes. If you are in a hurry, how does your process change? Write a letter advising a younger brother, sister, or friend about how to make his or her writing better.

2. Murray provides guidelines for several dimensions of writing, including *focus, form,* and *voice.* Apply Murray's criteria to a paper you are currently working on, explaining (a) which proved most useful, (b) which were least useful, (c) the completeness of his list, (d) whether it applies to all forms of writing, and (e) additions or deletions you might make to it.

Janet Emig
WRITING AS A MODE OF LEARNING

Janet Emig is a professor of English at Rutgers University. She is a major scholar in the field of composition studies, known especially for her pioneering work The Composing Process of Twelfth Graders *(1970). When she published "Writing as a Mode of Learning" in 1977, she called people's attention to the unique value of writing as a tool for learning as well as a tool for communicating. As you read her article, reflect on your own experiences as a writer. Do you agree with her that writing is fundamentally different from speaking? Can you think of examples in your own experience that support or refute her ideas?*

Writing represents a unique mode of learning—not merely valuable, not merely special, but unique. That will be my contention in this paper. The thesis is straightforward. Writing serves learning uniquely because writing as process-and-product possesses a cluster of attributes that correspond uniquely to certain powerful learning strategies.

Although the notion is clearly debatable, it is scarcely a private belief. Some of the most distinguished contemporary psychologists have at least implied such a role for writing as heuristic. Lev Vygotsky, A. R. Luria, and Jerome Bruner, for example, have all pointed out higher cognitive functions, such as analysis and synthesis, seem to develop most fully only with the support system of verbal language—particularly, it seems, of written language.[1] Some of their arguments and evidence will be incorporated here.

Here I have a prior purpose: to describe as tellingly as possible *how* writing uniquely corresponds to certain powerful learning strategies. Making such a case for the uniqueness of writing should logically and theoretically involve establishing many contrasts, distinctions between (1) writing and all other verbal languaging processes—listening, reading, and especially talking; (2) writing and all other forms of composing, such as composing a painting, a symphony, a dance, a film, a building; and (3) composing in words and composing in the two other major graphic symbol systems of mathematical equations and scientific formulae. For the purposes of this paper, the task is simpler, since most students are not permitted by most curricula to discover the values of composing, say, in dance, or even in film; and most students are not sophisticated enough to create, to originate formulations, using the highly abstruse symbol system of equations and formulae. Verbal language represents the most *available* medium for composing; in fact, the significance of sheer availability in its selection as a mode for learning can probably not be overstressed. But the uniqueness of writing among the verbal languaging processes does need to be established and supported if only because so many curricula and courses in English still consist almost exclusively of reading and listening.

WRITING AS A UNIQUE LANGUAGING PROCESS

Traditionally, the four languaging processes of listening, talking, reading, and writing are paired in either of two ways. The more informative seems to be the division many linguists make between first-order and second-order processes, with talking and listening characterized as first-order processes; reading and writing, as second-order. First-order processes are acquired without formal or systematic instruction; the second-order processes of reading and writing tend to be learned initially only with the aid of formal and systematic instruction.

The less useful distinction is that between listening and reading as receptive functions and talking and writing as productive functions. Critics of these terms like Louise Rosenblatt rightfully point out that the connotation of passivity too often accompanies the notion of receptivity when reading, like listening, is a vital, construing act.

---

[1] Lev S. Vygotsky, *Thought and Language*, trans. Eugenia Hanfmann and Gertrude Vakar (Cambridge: The M.I.T. Press, 1962); A. R. Luria and F. Ia. Yudovich, *Speech and the Development of Mental Processes in the Child*, ed. Joan Simon (Baltimore: Penguin, 1971); Jerome S. Bruner, *The Relevance of Education* (New York: W. W. Norton and Co., 1971).

An additional distinction, so simple it may have been previously overlooked, resides in two criteria: the matters of origination and of graphic recording. Writing is originating and creating a unique verbal construct that is graphically recorded. Reading is creating or re-creating *but not* originating a verbal construct that is graphically recorded. Listening is creating or re-creating but not originating a verbal construct that is *not* graphically recorded. Talking is creating *and* originating a verbal construct that is *not* graphically recorded (except for the circuitous routing of a transcribed tape). Note that a distinction is being made between creating and originating, separable processes.

For talking, the nearest languaging process, additional distinctions should probably be made. (What follows is not a denigration of talk as a valuable mode of learning.) A silent classroom or one filled only with the teacher's voice is anathema to learning. For evidence of the cognitive value of talk, one can look to some of the persuasive monographs coming from the London Schools Council project on writing: *From Information to Understanding* by Nancy Martin or *From Talking to Writing* by Peter Medway.[2] We also know that for some of us, talking is a valuable, even necessary, form of pre-writing. In his curriculum, James Moffett makes the value of such talk quite explicit.

But to say that talking is a valuable form of pre-writing is not to say that writing is talk recorded, an inaccuracy appearing in far too many composition texts. Rather, a number of contemporary trans-disciplinary sources suggest that talking and writing may emanate from different organic sources and represent quite different, possibly distinct, language functions. In *Thought and Language*, Vygotsky notes that "written speech is a separate linguistic function, differing from oral speech in both structure and mode of functioning."[3] The sociolinguist Dell Hymes, in a valuable issue of *Daedalus*, "Language as a Human Problem," makes a comparable point: "That speech and writing are not simply interchangeable, and have developed historically in ways at least partly autonomous, is obvious."[4] At the first session of the Buffalo Conference on Researching Composition (4–5 October 1975), the first point of unanimity among the participant-speakers with interests in developmental psychology, media, dreams and aphasia was that talking and writing were markedly different functions.[5] Some of us who work rather steadily with writing research agree. We also believe that there are hazards, conceptu-

---

[2] Nancy Martin, *From Information to Understanding* (London: Schools Council Project Writing Across the Curriculum. 11–13, 1973); Peter Medway, *From Talking to Writing* (London: Schools Council Project Writing Across the Curriculum, 11–13, 1973).

[3] Vygotsky, 98.

[4] Dell Hymes, "On the Origins and Foundations of Inequality Among Speakers," *Daedalus* 102 (Summer, 1973), 69.

[5] Participant-speakers were Loren Barrett, University of Michigan; Gerald O'Grady, SUNY/ Buffalo; Hollis Frampton, SUNY/ Buffalo; and Janet Emig, Rutgers.

ally and pedagogically, in creating too complete an analogy between talking and writing, in blurring the very real differences between the two.

WHAT ARE THESE DIFFERENCES?

1. Writing is learned behavior; talking is natural, even irrepressible, behavior.
2. Writing then is an artificial process; talking is not.
3. Writing is a technological device—not the wheel, but early enough to qualify as primary technology; talking is organic, natural, earlier.
4. Most writing is slower than most talking.
5. Writing is stark, barren, even naked as a medium; talking is rich, luxuriant, inherently redundant.
6. Talk leans on the environment; writing must provide its own context.
7. With writing, the audience is usually absent; with talking, the listener is usually present.
8. Writing usually results in a visible graphic product; talking usually does not.
9. Perhaps because there is a product involved, writing tends to be a more responsible and committed act than talking.
10. It can even be said that throughout history, an aura, an ambience, a mystique has usually encircled the written word; the spoken word has for the most part proved ephemeral and treated mundanely (ignore, please, our recent national history).
11. Because writing is often our representation of the world made visible, embodying both process and product, writing is more readily a form and source of learning than talking.

UNIQUE CORRESPONDENCES BETWEEN LEARNING AND WRITING

What then are some *unique* correspondences between learning and writing? To begin with some definitions: Learning can be defined in many ways, according to one's predilections and training, with all statements about learning of course hypothetical. Definitions range from the chemophysiological ("Learning is changed patterns of protein synthesis in relevant portions of the cortex")[6] to transactive views drawn from both philosophy and psychology (John Dewey, Jean Piaget) that learning is

---

[6] George Steiner, *After Babel: Aspects of Language and Translation* (New York: Oxford University Press, 1975), 287.

the re-organization or confirmation of a cognitive scheme in light of an experience.[7] What the speculations seem to share is consensus about certain features and strategies that characterize successful learning. These include the importance of the classic attributes of re-inforcement and feedback. In most hypotheses, successful learning is also connective and selective. Additionally, it makes use of propositions, hypotheses, and other elegant summarizers. Finally, it is active, engaged, personal — more specifically, self-rhythmed — in nature.

Jerome Bruner, like Jean Piaget, through a comparable set of categories, posits three major ways in which we represent and deal with actuality: (1) enactive — we learn "by doing"; (2) iconic — we learn "by depiction in an image"; and (3) representational or symbolic — we learn "by restatement in words."[8] To overstate the matter, in enactive learning, the hand predominates; in iconic, the eye; and in symbolic, the brain.

What is striking about writing as a process is that, by its very nature, all three ways of dealing with actuality are simultaneously or almost simultaneously deployed. That is, the symbolic transformation of experience through the specific symbol system of verbal language is shaped into an icon (the graphic product) by the enactive hand. If the most efficacious learning occurs when learning is re-inforced, then writing through its inherent re-inforcing cycle involving hand, eye, and brain marks a uniquely powerful multi-representational mode for learning.

Writing is also integrative in perhaps the most basic possible sense: the organic, the functional. Writing involves the fullest possible functioning of the brain, which entails the active participation in the process of both the left and the right hemispheres. Writing is markedly bispheral, although in some popular accounts, writing is inaccurately presented as a chiefly left-hemisphere activity, perhaps because the linear written product is somehow regarded as analogue for the process that created it; and the left hemisphere seems to process material linearly.

The right hemisphere, however, seems to make at least three, perhaps four, major contributions to the writing process — probably, to the creative process generically. First, several researchers, such as Geschwind and Snyder of Harvard and Zaidal of Cal Tech, through markedly different experiments, have very tentatively suggested that the right hemisphere is the sphere, even the *seat*, of emotions.[9] Second — or perhaps as an illustration of the first — Howard Gardner, in his impor-

[7] John Dewey, *Experience and Education* (New York: Macmillan, 1938); Jean Piaget, *Biology and Knowledge: An Essay on the Relations between Organic Regulations and Cognitive Processes* (Chicago: University of Chicago Press, 1971).

[8] Bruner, 7–8.

[9] Boyce Rensberger, "Language Ability Found in Right Side of Brain," *New York Times*, 1 August 1975, 14.

tant study of the brain-damaged, notes that our sense of emotional appropriateness in discourse may reside in the right sphere:

> Emotional appropriateness, in sum—being related not only to *what* is said, but to how it is said and to what is *not* said, as well—is crucially dependent on right hemisphere intactness.[10]

Third, the right hemisphere seems to be the source of intuition, of sudden gestalts, of flashes of images, of abstractions occurring as visual or spatial wholes, as the initiating metaphors in the creative process. A familiar example: William Faulkner noted in his *Paris Review* interview that *The Sound and the Fury* began as the image of a little girl's muddy drawers as she sat in a tree watching her grandmother's funeral.[11]

Also, a unique form of feedback as well as reinforcement, exists with writing, because information from the *process* is immediately and visibly available as that portion of the *product* already written. The importance for learning of a product in a familiar and available medium for immediate, literal (that is, visual) re-scanning and review cannot perhaps be overstated. In his remarkable study of purportedly blind sculptors, Géza Révész found that without sight, persons cannot move beyond a literal transcription of elements into any manner of symbolic transformation—by definition, the central requirement for reformulation and re-interpretation, i.e., revision, that most aptly named process.[12]

As noted in the second paragraph, Vygotsky and Luria, like Bruner, have written importantly about the connections between learning and writing. In his essay "The Psychobiology of Psychology," Bruner lists as one of six axioms regarding learning: "We are connective."[13] Another correspondence then between learning and writing: in *Thought and Language,* Vygotsky notes that writing makes a unique demand in that the writer must engage in "deliberate semantics"—in Vygotsky's elegant phrase, "deliberate structuring of the web of meaning."[14] Such structuring is required because, for Vygotsky, writing centrally represents an expansion of inner speech, that mode whereby we talk to ourselves, which is "maximally compact" and "almost entirely predicative"; written speech is a mode which is "maximally detailed" and which requires explicitly supplied subjects and topics. The medium then of written verbal language requires the establishment of systematic connections and relationships. Clear writing by definition is that writing which signals

[10] Howard Gardner, *The Shattered Mind: The Person After Brain Damage* (New York: Alfred A. Knopf, 1975), 372.

[11] William Faulkner, *Writers at Work: The Paris Review Interviews,* ed. Malcolm Cowley (New York: The Viking Press, 1959), 130.

[12] Géza Révész, *Psychology and Art of the Blind,* trans. H. A. Wolff (London: Longmans-Green. 1950).

[13] Bruner, 126.

[14] Vygotsky, 100.

without ambiguity the nature of conceptual relationships, whether they be coordinate, subordinate, superordinate, causal, or something other.

Successful learning is also engaged, committed, personal learning. Indeed, impersonal learning may be an anomalous concept, like the very notion of objectivism itself. As Michael Polanyi states simply at the beginning of *Personal Knowledge:* "the ideal of strict objectivism is absurd." (How many courses and curricula in English, science, and all else does that one sentence reduce to rubble?) Indeed, the theme of *Personal Knowledge* is that

> into every act of knowing there enters a passionate contribution of the person knowing what is being known, . . . this coefficient is no mere imperfection but a vital component of his knowledge.[15]

In *Zen and the Art of Motorcycle Maintenance,* Robert Pirsig states a comparable theme:

> The Quality which creates the world emerges as *a relationship* between man and his experience. He is a *participant* in the creation of all things.[16]

Finally, the psychologist George Kelly has as the central notion in his subtle and compelling theory of personal constructs man as a scientist steadily and actively engaged in making and re-making his hypotheses about the nature of the universe.[17]

We are acquiring as well some empirical confirmation about the importance of engagement in, as well as self-selection of, a subject for the student learning to write and writing to learn. The recent Sanders and Littlefield study, reported in *Research in the Teaching of English,* is persuasive evidence on this point, as well as being a model for a certain type of research.[18]

As Luria implies in the quotation above, writing is self-rhythmed. One writes best as one learns best, at one's own pace. Or to connect the two processes, writing can sponsor learning because it can match its pace. Support for the importance of self-pacing to learning can be found in Benjamin Bloom's important study "Time and Learning."[19] Evidence for the significance of self-pacing to writing can be found in the reason

---

[15] Michael Polanyi, *Personal Knowledge: Toward a Post-Critical Philosophy* (Chicago: University of Chicago Press, 1958), viii.

[16] Robert Pirsig, *Zen and the Art of Motorcycle Maintenance* (New York: William Morrow and Co., Inc., 1974), 212.

[17] George Kelly, *A Theory of Personality: The Psychology of Personal Constructs* (New York: W. W. Norton and Co., 1963).

[18] Sara E. Sanders and John H. Littlefield, "Perhaps Test Essays Can Reflect Significant Improvement in Freshman Composition: Report on a Successful Attempt," *RTE* 9 (Fall 1975), 145–153.

[19] Benjamin Bloom, "Time and Learning," *American Psychologist* 29 (September 1974), 682–688.

Jean-Paul Sartre gave last summer for not using the tape-recorder when he announced that blindness in his second eye had forced him to give up writing:

> I think there is an enormous difference between speaking and writing. One rereads what one rewrites. But one can read slowly or quickly: in other words, you do not know how long you will have to take deliberating over a sentence. . . . If I listen to a tape recorder, the listening speed is determined by the speed at which the tape turns and not by my own needs. Therefore I will always be either lagging behind or running ahead of the machine.[20]

Writing is connective as a process in a more subtle and perhaps more significant way, as Luria points out in what may be the most powerful paragraph of rationale ever supplied for writing as heuristic:

> Written speech is bound up with the inhibition of immediate synpractical connections. It assumes a much slower, repeated mediating process of analysis and synthesis, which makes it possible not only to develop the required thought, but even to revert to its earlier stages, thus transforming the sequential chain of connections in a simultaneous, self-reviewing structure. Written speech thus represents a new and powerful instrument of thought.[21]

But first to explicate: writing inhibits "immediate synpractical connections." Luria defines *synpraxis* as "concrete-active" situations in which language does not exist independently but as a "fragment" of an ongoing action "outside of which it is incomprehensible."[22] In *Language and Learning*, James Britton defines it succinctly as "speech-cum-action."[23] Writing, unlike talking, restrains dependence upon the actual situation. Writing as a mode is inherently more self-reliant than speaking. Moreover, as Bruner states in explicating Vygotsky, "Writing virtually forces a remoteness of reference on the language user."[24]

Luria notes what has already been noted above: that writing, typically, is a "much slower" process than talking. But then he points out the relation of this slower pace to learning: this slower pace allows for — indeed, encourages — the shuttling among past, present, and future. Writing, in other words, connects the three major tenses of our experience to make meaning. And the two major modes by which these three aspects are united are the processes of analysis and synthesis: analysis,

[20] Jean-Paul Sartre, "Sartre at Seventy: An Interview," with Michel Contat, *New York Review of Books*, 7 August 1975.

[21] Luria, 118.

[22] Luria, 50.

[23] James Britton, *Language and Learning* (Baltimore: Penguin, 1971), 10–11.

[24] Bruner, 47.

TABLE 1.1.

Unique Cluster of Correspondences between Certain Learning Strategies and Certain Attributes of Writing

SELECTED CHARACTERISTICS OF SUCCESSFUL LEARNING STRATEGIES	SELECTED ATTRIBUTES OF WRITING, PROCESS AND PRODUCT
(1) Profits from multi-representational and integrative re-inforcement	(1) Represents process uniquely multi-representational and integrative
(2) Seeks self-provided feedback:	(2) Represents powerful instance of self-provided feedback:
(a) immediate	(a) provides product uniquely available for *immediate* feedback (review and re-evaluation)
(b) long-term	(b) provides record of evolution of thought since writing is epigenetic as process-and-product
(3) Is connective:	(3) Provides connections:
(a) makes generative conceptual groupings, synthetic and analytic	(a) establishes explicit and systematic conceptual groupings through lexical, syntactic, and rhetorical devices
(b) proceeds from propositions, hypotheses, and other elegant summarizers	(b) represents most available means (verbal language) for economic recording of abstract formulations
(4) Is active, engaged, personal— notably, self-rhythmed	(4) Is active, engaged, personal— notably, self-rhythmed

the breaking of entities into their constituent parts; and synthesis, combining or fusing these, often into fresh arrangements or amalgams.

Finally, writing is epigenetic, with the complex evolutionary development of thought steadily and graphically visible and available throughout as a record of the journey, from jottings and notes to full discursive formulations.

For a summary of the correspondences stressed here between certain learning strategies and certain attributes of writing see Table 1.1.

This essay represents a first effort to make a certain kind of case for writing—specifically, to show its unique value for learning. It is at once over-elaborate and under specific. Too much of the formulation is in the off-putting jargon of the learning theorist, when my own predilection would have been to emulate George Kelly and to avoid terms like *reinforcement* and *feedback* since their use implies that I live inside a certain paradigm about learning I don't truly inhabit. Yet I hope that the essay will start a crucial line of inquiry; for unless the losses to learners of not writing are compellingly described and substantiated by experimental and speculative research, writing itself as a central academic process may not long endure.

OPTIONS FOR WRITING

1. Explain in your own words what Janet Emig means when she says that writing is "a unique mode of learning." Explain further how Emig's thesis is similar to or different from other authors' in this chapter.

2. Locate one of the many sources of Emig's ideas, such as Lev Vygotsgy, Jerome Bruner, Robert Pirsig, William Faulkner, or George Kelly, and conduct further research on this person. Prepare a brief report for your classmates in which you elaborate on these ideas.

Marge Piercy
STARTING SUPPORT GROUPS FOR WRITERS

Marge Piercy (b. 1936) is an influential and innovative feminist novelist whose works include Braided Lives, Fly Away Home, *and* Gone to Soldiers. *As a novelist, she knows firsthand the value of encouragement and support. When you read her rules for making writing support groups work, think about your own experience as a writer: Has your writing received the time, respect, and help she calls for? Can you as a student make sure other writers get such help from you?*

Every writer needs support and feedback to go on writing. Established writers can get some of that from their audiences, but until then, we can only get support and feedback from the people around us and from each other. In Chicago many years ago I had a support group, and then again for a while in New York. I still have a number of writers to whom I show manuscripts or my novels in second draft or with whom I exchange poems. This description of how to set up a support group was written initially for the Feminist Writers' Guild of New England, published in our newsletter, and then expanded some for the National Feminist Writers' Guild Handbook, *Words in Our Pockets.*

For publication here I have changed little. I have retained the female pronouns of its original publications; I am always reading "he's" that are presumed to include me, so why not vice versa? If these suggestions are to be applied to mixed groups, I think it even more important to stress the importance of not allowing one, two, or three individuals to dominate a group and especially to dominate reading or criticism. I once taught a workshop composed of eight women and two men. The two men always spoke first to every poem, and set the tone of reaction so that the women who were timid and had different aesthetic criteria tended to keep silent. I finally had to establish a rule that neither of the men could speak until two women had addressed any particular poem. After two weeks I could lift the rule because the women had begun to gain confidence and the men had become conscious of their overmastering behavior. The workshop was more useful to everybody in it once it reflected the opinions of more than two members.

GROUND RULES FOR A SUPPORT GROUP

1. Respect

Everybody should be able to expect the group to listen to her work and accord it respect. We should try to give another writer criticism for succeeding or failing to do what she is trying to do, not for doing something we wouldn't do. We should not expect that other people want to write the way we do or with the style or content of writers we admire. We should respect women who write directly from their own experiences and women who write from their imagination or their research. A support group is no place to win converts to your ideas.

2. Equal Time

This is an ideal but not a rigid one. Everyone in the group should be able to claim equal time for her work. However, if somebody has low or slow output, the group should not put more pressure on her than she wishes. With a poetry group we might go around the room each time and read one poem by each of maybe half the group. In a drama, fiction, or article group, we might do two or three people each meeting until everyone has been heard and then repeat.

3. Everyone Participates

No one has the right to ask support, feedback or criticism if she is not willing to listen carefully and/or read carefully the work of others and give her responses freely. When we feel we don't know how to express what we sense about somebody's writing, we have to risk trying to say what we mean. We have to risk sounding silly or clumsy or wrong. Silence is not fair to the others in the group; being shy is a luxury. We must share our reactions to other's work so that we can give help as well as receive it. Learning to express my feelings and reactions, my evaluation of another woman's work is important to me because from that exercise I will learn observations I can bring back to my own work. Having to say what I feel is good discipline, and support groups are an environment, unlike a class or a formal workshop or writer's conference, where it should be easy for us to expose our reactions to each other, where we have a right to expect support and respect.

Not every writer can afford to be taking writing workshops all the time, nor are they necessarily the best source of feedback. Often what you learn when you "study" writing with somebody is their mannerisms and their prejudices. Some writing workshops tend to produce a product; a large number of the students who pass through them emerge with similar notions about poetry or prose revealed in their work. Sometimes you will do better with a group of peers.

Often what you learn in a workshop or in a support group is the questions to ask yourself when your poem or piece of fiction is not coming along right. What variables should you consider changing? That way you learn how to revise.

4. We Try to Help

The rule of thumb is always to think what to say to help the other become a better writer. Being witty at the expense of another group member or using their work to put out a pet theory about writing is not being helpful. Each group will set its own emotional tone: how blunt or how gentle people feel comfortable with. But everyone in the group must be able to live with that feeling tone. We should not lie to each other, as that does not help. But we should think how to give feedback that is truly useful.

We must try to be open to each other's criticism too. It's useless to be in a group at all if all we want is adulation. If every criticism is met with "But that's the way it was!," "That's just how I felt!," "That's how it came to me," you can't learn and there's no motivation for others to boil their brains trying to help you.

5. Copies

Each person should take the responsibility for making copies of her own work. Xeroxing is so popular, people often forget that carbon paper exists. Any typewriter will make six or seven legible copies if onion skin or carbon copy manifolds are used. If you give copies to your group, you can expect much better feedback. Many people simply can't get more from a poem or story the first time they hear it than a general emotional sense. That's fine for a reading, but defeats the purpose of a support group.

6. Who Talks

As said above, everybody should make a strong attempt to communicate about each piece of writing. It's also our duty to keep any one or two writers who are more articulate or experienced from dominating the group so that their taste has too much influence.

7. Support in Work Habits

Many of the problems writers face are not in our work, but in our lives. People around us give us little or no support for being writers, for writing. We can give each other that support. We may have trouble sitting down to write. We can encourage each other. We can work in the same building or at certain hours. We can share or circulate child care among our group. We can work out patterns of assistance that help individual women work. Some women want to be nagged. They want a phone call at 10:00 saying, "Have you got to work yet?" Some women need to be praised. They want a phone call at 5:00 saying, "How much did you get done? That's wonderful." Some women want to be let alone while working. They need encouragement in taking the phone off the hook and refusing to answer the door. Some of us need places outside our homes in which to write: we can share office space. Sometimes writers get stuck and need help getting unstuck. Sometimes being listened to about personal problems helps. Praise may be needed. Sometimes a writer needs a sounding board for ideas or needs some help or suggestions for solving a problem that has stymied her.

MECHANICS OF STARTING

1. Somebody must take early responsibility. We need a leader for the first meeting or two. After that, we should rotate the chair.
2. Limit the size of your group. The group can be bigger for poetry than for prose. You do not want a group so big it takes two months before you get to read your work. People will drop out if that is so.
3. Make a real commitment to coming. Death, serious illness, and having to be out of town are valid excuses. Going to a movie, a party, not feeling like it, let other people down who want to read that night, who need help, who need encouragement.
4. Always inform the group if you won't be there.
5. Don't set a time for a meeting when people in your group usually are writing. If the group cuts into work time, it will be resented.
6. Things to do at the first meeting if you don't start right in with reading: You might want to discuss, going around the room:
   What writing experiences you have had,
   What you want to write and why,
   What do you want/need from the group,
   What obstacles do you experience in writing,
   What has helped you to define yourself as a writer and
   What has hurt you,
   What do you hope for and/or fear from the group?

7. In fiction or nonfiction groups, an agreement should be made about roughly how many pages somebody is going to read. It doesn't work well for somebody to read for two hours or even

one hour. No matter how interesting it may be (especially to the author), everybody tunes out eventually and starts thinking about their dental appointment, kids, lovers, and how long it will be till they get to read.

8. Save some time in every other meeting at least to go around and get out anything that's needed. Groups can foul up on little bad interactions if there's no way to work out problems or hurt feelings that arise.

THINGS A GROUP CAN DO EVENTUALLY

Our support group can also provide the beginnings of a group who gives readings. It's much easier for a group of lesser known writers to get a reading someplace together than for each woman individually to secure such a reading. You can each coerce enough close friends to come out to hear you to put together a decent-sized audience. Your writing often improves when you have to read it aloud. Once you have got over your initial fear and nervousness, you can hear what works and what doesn't in prose as well as in poetry.

Your support group can also put out a magazine, a journal, an anthology, or a chapbook. You can sell it at readings you do together as well as hustling it around in the usual bookstores.

Finally, your support group gives you an audience, something which an apprentice writer needs more than anything else except time and determination.

OPTIONS FOR WRITING

1. Compare Marge Piercy's advice on writing groups to your own experience in groups of any kind. Based on your own experience, which advice do you think is most crucial for classroom writers? Share your reflection on group work with others in your class, and agree to try writing groups over a period of time, following Piercy's (and your) advice.

2. Marge Piercy suggests that a writing group can "put out a magazine, a journal, an anthology, or a chapbook." Suggest this idea to your classmates (in writing of course), and volunteer to help edit such a production.

2

STUDYING LITERATURE

Carl G. Herndl and Diane Price Herndl

Sir Arthur Conan Doyle's creation, Sherlock Holmes, provides a useful model of the way skillful readers work as they search for possible meaning in the unfolding events of a narrative or a poem. The Herndls give us useful tips on reading like Holmes, but they also describe the limitations of the mystery-solving approach to reading literature. They encourage us to develop our own personal responses to pieces like Paul Simon's "Graceland" and Gwendolyn Brooks' "The White Troops Had Their Orders But the Negroes Looked Like Men."

READINGS

POETIC RESPONSES TO WAR
Walt Whitman   A Sight in Camp in the Daybreak Gray and Dim
Randall Jarrell   The Death of the Ball Turret Gunner
Denise Levertov   The Altars in the Street
A. R. Ammons   The Eternal City

SHOPPING
John Updike   A & P
Allen Ginsberg   A Supermarket in California

WHAT IS UNSAID
Sylvia Plath   Metaphors
Gabriel García Marquez   One of These Days

WORKS OF AND RESPONSES TO A POET: WANDA COLEMAN
Wanda Coleman   Huh
Wanda Coleman   Doing Battle With the Wolf
Wanda Coleman   Drone
Stacy Gevry   The Apt Anger of Wanda Coleman

60

Tony Magistrale   Doing Battle with the Wolf: A Critical Introduction to
   Wanda Coleman's Poetry

A CRITIC AND A WRITER
Terry Eagleton   Introduction: What Is Literature?
Alice Walker   In Search of Our Mothers' Gardens

We've all read or seen the Sherlock Holmes stories in which Holmes solves the mystery with a flair and ease that amazes his companion, Dr. Watson. And all of us at one time or another have sat in an English class feeling like Dr. Watson in comparison to some Holmeslike reader. Holmes reveals the criminal's motives and methods by identifying seemingly meaningless details as the crucial clues that explain the case. The precision and creativity of his analysis and the clarity of his explanation persuade his listeners that his conclusions are true. The flair with which he demonstrates his discoveries, the surprising revelation, and the witty, confident style of his account make his performance entertaining and convincing. But Holmes is always careful to explain how he reached his conclusion; he deals not in inspiration but in detailed observation and analytic method. His discoveries are so "elementary" because of his careful thinking process.

Although the analogy has limitations, as we'll see, Sherlock Holmes is a useful model of the way skillful readers work. Like Holmes, readers search for possible meaning in the unfolding events of a narrative or a poem. Like Holmes, they too must depend both on the small, sometimes marginal details and on a set of general principles, whether the principles are based on a theory of crime or a theory of literature. (Later in this chapter, we will describe some of the different kinds of questions that suggest general principles for a theory of literature to guide your reading.) And, like Holmes, readers do their investigation because it is an exciting challenge.

WHY STUDY LITERATURE?

People read literature because it is entertaining, but there are other reasons to *study* literature. Studying makes reading even more satisfying and leads readers to see a number of possible meanings, so it makes reading a richer, more active experience. It takes more work, but it provides a different kind of pleasure. Studying literature can be even more vital than pleasurable, though.

In our culture, all sorts of things depend on the printed word: the news, laws, the cereal you buy. Knowing how to *read* those words carefully, how to understand what they mean and how they work, gives a person the power to avoid being misled, manipulated, or dominated by them. Being a practiced reader allows you to choose what interpretation of the world you want to accept. Many of the most important issues today are questions of interpretation; the Supreme Court decision about abortion, for example, depends on how the justices interpret the constitution. It depends not only on *what* they think the constitution means but also on *how* they think it governs lawmaking. Does the constitution mean only what it explicitly says, or does its meaning change with the culture around it? Does it provide a protection for privacy, and does that include abortion? All of these questions are really questions of reading. Studying literature is one of the best ways to become a sophisticated reader, not only of the constitution, but also of any written text: government regulations, business contracts, the newspaper, highway billboards, rock and roll lyrics, your cereal box.

Finally, people study literature as a way to understand the world better. We often explain our lives by telling stories, but where do we get these stories? Why did some stories gain importance while others were ignored? Studying literature helps us to see that meaning is something we make, not something that just exists. Studying literature offers some insight into how we make meaning of our experiences, helps us to understand different points of view (those of different races, classes, or genders), and provides a way to understand how different meanings are connected to different histories.

Holmes at Work

So, how *does* Holmes go about the work of reading? In one of the first Sherlock Holmes stories, "The Red-Headed League," Arthur Conan Doyle, the author of the stories, demonstrates the difference between Holmes' superior powers of perception and those which the rest of us have. When Mr. Jabez Wilson comes to Holmes for help, our narrator, Dr. Watson, gives us this description of him:

> Our visitor bore every mark of being an average commonplace British tradesman, obese, pompous, and slow. He wore rather baggy grey shepherd's check trousers, a not overclean black frockcoat, unbuttoned in the front, and a drab waistcoat with a heavy brassy Albert chain, and a square pierced bit of metal dangling down as an ornament. A frayed top hat and a faded brown overcoat with a wrinkled velvet collar lay upon a chair beside him. Altogether, look as I would, there was nothing remarkable about the man save his blazing red head, and the expression of extreme chagrin and discontent upon his features.

Any one of us would consider this a very thorough description indeed and would pride ourselves on our astute powers of observation. But, of course, Sherlock Holmes sees more than Watson does. He comments, "Beyond the obvious facts that he has at some time done manual labour, that he takes snuff, that he is a Freemason, that he has been in China, and that he has done a considerable amount of writing lately, I can deduce nothing else." Mr. Wilson, Dr. Watson, and we readers are astounded by Holmes' observations. Is he a psychic? How does he know these things? But Holmes explains that good detective work is simply a matter of specialized and careful observation. So, when Mr. Wilson admits that he did do manual labor when he was a ship's carpenter and asks how Holmes knew, Holmes explains how he can read so many things from Jabez Wilson's appearance:

> "Your hands, my dear sir. Your right hand is quite a size larger than your left. You have worked with it and the muscles are more developed."
>
> "Well the snuff, then, and the Freemasonry?"
>
> "I won't insult your intelligence by telling you how I read that, especially as, rather against the strict rules of your order, you use an arc and compass breastpin."
>
> "Ah, of course, I forgot that. But the writing?"
>
> "What else can be indicated by that right cuff so very shiney for five inches, and the left one with the smooth patch near the elbow where you rest it upon the desk."
>
> "Well, but China?"
>
> "The fish which you have tattooed immediately above your right wrist could only have been done in China. I have made a small study of tattoo marks, and have even contributed to the literature of the subject. That trick of staining the fishes' scales of a delicate pink is quite peculiar to China. When, in addition, I see a Chinese coin hanging from your watch-chain, the matter becomes even more simple."

Holmes assures us that such observations are within the power of any one of us if we work at it. In fact, in the later Sherlock Holmes stories, Dr. Watson has learned enough of Holmes' methods to tell as much by looking at a person as Holmes can.

WRITING 1.

Think of some occasion in the past when you've felt like Dr. Watson in an English class while the teacher explained an interpretation of a piece of literature. Write a short description of the difference between your interpretation and the teacher's. Can you explain how the teacher might have developed this interpretation, or does the teacher's method still seem mysterious to you?

LOOKING FOR CLUES

To bring us back to thinking about literature, let's look at how we can apply some Holmeslike techniques to reading a novel. In a recent course on contemporary novels, our students read a novel by Don DeLillo called *White Noise*. It is a novel about a college professor and his family who live through an "airborn toxic event" (a chemical spill) and who must cope with our modern technological age. Even though his topic is serious, DeLillo's novel is a funny look at how technology—from radios, TVs, and medicine to giant chemical and computer companies—affects every aspect of our lives and how little control we often have over it. Early in the novel, DeLillo writes this short passage:

> In the morning I walked to the bank. I went to the automated teller machine to check my balance. I inserted my card, entered my secret code, tapped out my request. The figure on the screen roughly corresponded to my independent estimate, feebly arrived at after long searches through documents, tormented arithmetic. Waves of relief and gratitude flowed over me. The system had blessed my life. I felt its support and approval. The system hardware, the mainframe sitting in a locked room in some distant city. What a pleasing interaction. I sensed that something of deep personal value, but not money, not that at all, had been authenticated and confirmed. A deranged person was escorted from the bank by two armed guards. The system was invisible, which made it all the more impressive, all the more disquieting to deal with. But we were in accord, at least for now. The networks, the circuits, the streams, the harmonies.

This passage tells a lot about DeLillo's novel. You can't understand the whole novel from just one paragraph, of course, but if you approach reading a little bit like Sherlock Holmes, you can deduce some important clues from this one small bit of "evidence." But where do you get started?

First Reactions

You might start simply enough by reading the passage out loud to see what it sounds like. What kind of person would think this way? What frame of mind does it put you in as you read it? It seems pretty odd to get so upset and involved with a simple activity like getting money from the automated teller machine we use every day, or every few days if we can afford it. The speaker seems scared and uncertain about confronting the machine. We do not like to hear that there is no money in our accounts or to have the machine eat our cards, but this speaker feels "waves of relief and gratitude" when he finds out that he can get some cash. That is really pretty strange. Later he talks about "a pleasing interaction" with the machine as if it were alive and could do things to him. In the last sentence, in which he begins with the computer networks and ends with "the harmonies," he sounds a little off the deep end. There is clearly something abnormal about the way this speaker relates to the cash machine. If we felt this way every time we got money from the cash machine, people would think we were crazy.

One good place to start making sense of this passage is to look at the words themselves to see if some kind of pattern stands out. Here, after a little looking, we can see a pattern. DeLillo uses terms like gratitude, blessed, deep personal value, confirmed, and accord. These are words we more typically associate with religion, not with our bank machines. What does it mean to use religious words when discussing a transaction with technology? Maybe DeLillo is suggesting that the narrator, Jack, sees technology as his higher power.

WRITING 2.

Read any one of the poems at the end of this chapter out loud, and record your first reactions to it. How does it make you feel? What does it remind you of?

Connecting Clues

The next step is to see if you can connect this clue to DeLillo's meaning with others you've picked up while you were reading the rest of the novel. But how do you get these clues? You have to learn how to look and practice looking. Like Holmes, you have to investigate a little. The best way to do this is to read with a pen or pencil in your hand and to make notes to yourself in the margins of the book. Ask yourself questions in these notes as you go along, or just note things to look back at when you've finished your first reading. Remember that, like Holmes, you may have to return to the scene of the crime to reexamine evidence. These questions may be simple ones, such as "Why use this image?" or "Haven't I seen that idea before?" They may also be directions, such as "Compare this to page 97," or full-fledged critical commentaries such as "He's using religious language here, maybe suggesting a connection between Jack's faith in technology and the faith that we traditionally reserve for God." All of these little notes, ideas, and questions can be useful to you later in formulating your conclusions about the meaning of the story, poem, novel, or play.

USING A READING JOURNAL

Once you have several small ideas, it is often good to see if you can show connections and illustrate the pattern. The ideal place to do this is a reading journal in which you can record your reactions to the literature and try out ideas you might want to develop further. (In his essay in Chapter 1, Toby Fulwiler describes more fully how to use a journal.) For example, Dana Weinstein, a student in that contemporary novels class, wrote this journal entry about the paragraph from *White Noise:*

> The absurdity of his fascination with these machines almost hits the reader in the face. It's funny to hear Jack notice a person being escorted out of the bank by two guards, and refer to *him* as "deranged," because Jack is the one, after all, feeling that a deep personal value has been confirmed by a computer. At least that other person was interacting with other people, not an extension of some main computer somewhere far away.

In this journal entry, Dana has identified that strange feeling as an absurd fascination with machines. And she realizes how funny this passage sounds, especially when Jack thinks the *other* guy is deranged. After all, it is Jack who thinks about interacting with the automated circuits of the machine as if they were alive and all-powerful. Dana has begun to put a name on her reactions and to describe the specific way in which Jack is abnormal.

In that same journal entry, Dana also begins to compare Jack's reaction with our everyday experience and to speculate about what DeLillo was trying to say when he wrote this:

> Automatic teller machines are as common as telephone booths today. Whoever thought we'd be able to have cold cash on our hands any time we wanted it (if our accounts have the resources, of course)? As DeLillo describes Jack's reaction to the ATM, he highlights the postmodern character of the book. Jack says, "The system had blessed my life," as other people would refer to a miraculous event or a religious figure, but Jack places his faith here. His fascination with this technological advance has allowed him to identify with some microchips stored in "a locked room in some distant place."

Dana's journal isn't a fully worked through "reading" of the novel, but it does try to answer questions she might have had about the paragraph ("Wait a minute. What's this deranged guy doing here?"). In a later journal entry, she connects this idea of treating the machine as a religious entity to other things going on in the novel — Jack's own "derangement," his relationship with his wife, even the title of the novel.

WRITING 3.

Reread the poem you read for the previous writing assignment. Can you identify the specific words or images that caused you to react the way you did when you first read the poem? Can you see any patterns that develop an important theme or idea through the poem? Write a journal entry that connects these words or images, these clues, and describes the way they develop a theme in the poem.

Reading Doesn't Have to Be a Mystery

The analogy of Holmes as a model for reading eliminates some of the sense of mystery and sleight of hand from the process of reading. Dana's journal entry doesn't depend on any privileged insight, but rather on her observations of the details of the passage, her attempt to connect this pattern or issue to other similar issues in the novel, and her knowledge of background information like what postmodernism is. She carefully moves out from specific details to generalizations.

In our discussion of reading *White Noise,* we have concentrated on a single passage and tried to demonstrate different ways to move from this one piece to the novel as a whole. That is one way to read, and it is useful to us here because we can't quote a whole story. But not all readers need to identify single passages and make them the center of a reading. Other ways of reading don't use the technique of beginning with one particular passage and comparing it to the whole piece. You may see an overall pattern emerging, like a recurrent image or idea. What if Jack were to go to his ATM many times? You might begin to ask questions about the book's references to history. What does it mean that Jack is a professor of Hitler studies? You might look at the way the novel is organized; this novel has three major sections of varying length, and each has some relation to the others. There are many ways to begin formulating questions about a literary work.

WHAT'S WRONG WITH THE HOLMES ANALOGY?

Sherlock Holmes' method of examining minute details and leaping outward to huge conclusions is a useful example, but it isn't the only way to read or to think about literature. The Holmes analogy, like all analogies, has limitations. Useful as it is at getting rid of the sense of mystery involved in the expert's reading, it implies a number of inaccuracies about literature and reading.

In the detective story, Holmes always solves the crime; he follows the clues and finds the guilty party. His personal fulfillment and our sense of satisfaction come from the fact that the case is closed and that the right person has been apprehended. The case with reading is very nearly the opposite here. There is no single, right meaning hidden behind or beneath the literary text. The case is never really closed because there is not a single meaning the way there is an individual culprit in the detective story.

Readers' Feelings Matter

Another reason that the Holmes analogy is not entirely accurate is the fact that, unlike the fictional Holmes, real readers are often subjective. Our emotional reaction to a piece of literature can be a part of our determination of its meaning. When Holmes is investigating a case, he is purely rational, purely logical; his sentiments have no place in his conclusions. But when we are reading, our feelings are useful in helping us figure out the writer's point of view, the characters' motives, and our personal position on the moral or social issues involved. These feelings are not the end of the critical story, but they do help us to begin formulating our ideas about what we read. For example, as a way of beginning his interpretation of the paragraph from *White Noise,* another student, Ed Turner, wrote the following journal entry:

> The Automated Teller Machine stands on Church Street next to the doors of the Burlington Square Mall. I need money. It's vital. I must buy the new Rush cassette. I turn the corner from Cherry Street onto Church and head directly for the machine. I focus in on the tiny sign at the bottom right. It is black. The letters are white. OPEN. Yes!
>
> My pace quickens as I get nearer. A few more steps. I'm already taking off my gloves. In the corner of my eye I see the fleeting image of a young woman heading for the same machine. Ha! I'll beat her to it.
>
> My card is in hand, the money almost in my grasp. The window at the bottom right suddenly shifts. Orange. White letters. CLOSED. @#***!#@@%$#&&%*%#!

From here, Ed moves on to talk about how *White Noise* represents the importance and danger of our dependence on machines in our day-to-day life. Ed's frustration at the power the bank machine has over his own life helps him see the way DeLillo's novel is a critique of the invisible systems with which we live. He closes this journal entry with these remarks: "I think that this is another of DeLillo's points. . . . We have spent too much time staring at a television or reading the *Enquirer* rather than learning anything useful. Too much background noise. Too much static on our channels. Too much white noise."

Good Readers Don't Always Agree

As the two journal entries we have seen suggest, readers develop unique interpretations, which doesn't necessarily mean that one of them is wrong. Other people reading the paragraph by DeLillo have noticed other things going on there. Someone focusing on the main character, Jack, might look at how this paragraph develops our sense of his personality, his insecurity and need for personal affirmation; someone else might concentrate on the "deranged person" being led from the bank and ask whether the "tormented arithmetic" and the "invisible system" caused the derangement. Someone else might compare the first line of the paragraph, which suggests health and energy, to the last two lines, which seem somewhat ominous and threatening: He is "in accord" only for now, so what will happen when he is not? Will he become the deranged person? Of course, none of these insights is a "reading" of the novel, but all are places to start asking the kinds of questions that will lead to an interpretation.

Literature can have many meanings, depending on who is doing the reading, when he or she is reading, and even where the person is reading. Think of how many times you have heard people talking about something they have just read in an English class, saying "I wish I could get it to make sense." We have all said something like this, but it is actually the reader, not the piece of literature, that makes the sense. Reading is a process of understanding the relations between the literary text and a number of possible frames of reference. Readers have traditionally looked at the text's relations to the author's personal or historical world, its relations to our world, and its relations to the literary and linguistic tradition. With this range of possibilities, it is not unfair to the piece of literature or the author to see numerous meanings; in fact, one could argue that the strength of literature is exactly its ability to mean many things at once. The process of reading cannot be arrested the way the criminal can; reading and interpretation have no end.

The fact that reading is open ended and that there are many possible ways to interpret any work can make reading fun, but the process does have limits. Literature does not simply mean whatever any one reader wants to say it does. Reasonable readers have argued that *Huckleberry Finn* is an attack on slavery, and others have argued that it condones slavery. For your interpretation to be effective, you must be able to persuade other readers that it is possible and that it makes sense.

WRITING 4.

Get a friend to read the poem about which you wrote a journal entry. What was the friend's reaction? How did it differ from yours? Write a short description of how the two readings differ, and try to explain why they are different.

READING IN EVERYDAY LIFE

So far, we have been discussing the kind of reading that goes on in an English class—you read carefully, analyze what you read, and look for ways to create meanings, to make sense. But people also read outside of classrooms; they read many things other than "serious literature" and have many reasons for reading. You may read a newspaper to learn about the world around you, a romance or science fiction to relax or speculate about the future, or an article in *The Rolling Stone* to learn about a new style of rock and roll.

We read every day, sometimes without even knowing it. For example, when you listen to a song, a lot of things happen. You get a kick from the rhythm and rhyme and the clever witty expression; you enjoy the way it says something you feel deeply, the way it reminds you of other lyrics, and the way it helps you identify what you have in common with your friends. What is happening here, even though you probably do not notice it, is that you are enjoying the form or the poetry of the lyric, and you are relating the song's theme to something in your life. When we study literature, we are trying to figure out why it entertains us, why it interests us, what effects it has on us, and how it works.

Reading Rock 'N Roll

Most of the time when the two of us listen to Paul Simon's "Graceland" in the car, we sing along, and it makes us feel good, but we could read it the way we read a poem. If you look on the back of the album cover, the lyrics *look* like a poem. If we were going to study the lyrics in a literature class, we might start looking for formal features — metaphors, similes, repeated images — or we might start looking at the social, historical, or political context in which the song was written. We might ask, "What does Simon mean by 'Graceland'?" since he repeats the word so many times. Because he says he's going to Memphis, Tennessee, we know that he is referring to Elvis Presley's home, which is now a tourist attraction to some and a shrine to others. But is that all he means? You wouldn't talk as he does in the song about being "received" at a tourist attraction. Probably, then, he is playing with the idea of Graceland as heaven (the land of grace). Simon might mean this in a straightforward way (he is, after all, a rock and roll star and Elvis was the "father" of rock), but he might also mean it ironically. Simon might be making fun of people who think of Elvis this way. To a lot of people, the Elvis "cult," with all its impersonators and headlines in the *National Enquirer,* seems pretty silly. So Graceland could represent three things: the history of rock and roll, a heaven where we all belong and can be safe, or a comment on popular American culture.

In the song, Simon says that he is taking a trip with his young daughter along the Mississippi River to Graceland. From here, you might want to ask why Simon talks about pilgrims and poorboys going to Graceland, why he's taking his child from his first marriage, and why at the end he's worried about having to defend all the loves and all the endings in his life. The reading that you would develop from these questions would be very different depending on whether you believe Simon is being straight or ironic in his attitude toward Elvis.

Another line of questioning which you could pursue would begin by looking at the context in which "Graceland" appeared: It was the title song for an album featuring the music of South Africa and the lead for a concert Simon gave to protest apartheid. What do the lyrics have to do with racism? Notice that he says he's traveling down the Mississippi into the birthplace of the Civil War. This, of course, refers to the southern United States, the center of this country's civil rights struggles. Simon cannot explain why he wants to go to Graceland. Could it have something to do with his own part in the struggle with or against racism?

What Counts as Literature

When we are listening to the song, this is not what we are thinking, but this kind of academic reading may explain our reactions to it. We don't usually read rock lyrics this way because they are not usually considered "literature." Nobody prints them in the major anthologies of British, American, or World literature. They do not even get printed in anthologies of contemporary literature. We have a sense of what serious literature is, and people just don't read rock lyrics or Harlequin romances in literature classes.

What people *do* read in literature classes is always changing, though, and in the year 3,000, Paul Simon may be considered a great poet of the twentieth century. This probably will not happen, but we cannot know for sure. Questions of what is and is not literature, and what is and is not great, are asked every day; standards change as history changes. There was a time when American literature did not get taught in college at all because no one believed it was worthwhile. That has certainly changed. As Terry Eagleton argues in one of the readings for this chapter, what counts as literature is a debatable issue. He compares the difficulty of defining literature to the difficulty of defining a weed; the difference may depend less on the thing itself than on the purpose for which you are growing a garden. For everyone, some books stand out as great books, but even among literary scholars there is no clear agreement about what those books are; there is currently a heated debate about what makes a book worth reading and about what should be taught. Is it form? Is it the history represented in that book? Is it the social perspective the book provides? Is it the book's relation to other literary works?

WRITING 5.

Write a journal entry that describes what you think makes a book "literature" and makes it worth reading. Can you connect this to specific books you have read?

READING IN ENGLISH CLASS

As you have probably noticed, the kinds of questions scholars ask to determine what is worth reading are very similar to those we had earlier called the possible frames of reference. These are the types of questions readers use to understand a work and to construct their interpretation.

People who study literature ask themselves a number of different kinds of questions as they read. Not all readers ask all the questions, and one reader does not ask the same questions about all the different things he or she reads. But good readers always have a repertoire of questions that they might ask, questions that can guide them in making sense of what they read. Like Holmes, they have a sense of "the usual suspects" to interrogate.

Although we can't cover all the questions that readers ask themselves, we can offer you five general sets of questions. Readers ask questions about the following:

- the reader's reaction to the literary work
- the text's form and structure
- the historical context

- possible relations between literature and social issues
- the text's place in literary history

We'll examine each of these methods in some detail. These questions form conceptual frameworks that describe the ways in which literature can be meaningful. To illustrate how you might use these questions to read a piece of literature, we will use the poem "The White Troops Had Their Orders But the Negroes Looked Like Men" written in 1945 by the contemporary poet Gwendolyn Brooks as an example.

> They had supposed their formula was fixed.
> They had obeyed instructions to devise
> A type of cold, a type of hooded gaze.
> But when the Negroes came they were perplexed.
> These Negroes looked like men. Besides it taxed   5
> Time and temper to remember those
> Congenital iniquities that cause
> Disfavor of the darkness. Such as boxed
> Their feelings properly, complete to tags —
> A box for dark men and a box for Other —   10
> Would often find the contents had been scrambled.
> Or even switched. Who really gave two figs?
> Neither the earth nor the heaven ever trembled.
> And there was nothing startling in the weather.

Questions of the Reader's Reaction

There are two ways that you can focus on a reaction to a piece of literature. You can focus on your own reaction—did the story or poem make you angry? sad? happy? anxious?—and try to figure out what, exactly, made you feel that way. Or you can focus on what other readers would be likely to feel and examine the techniques the writer uses to cause those feelings. Is the author deliberately trying to make readers cry? How can you tell? Did it work? What would be gained by making the reader cry? This is not a matter of simply saying that literature means something because you feel a certain way when you read, but of figuring out *how* and *why* the literature makes you feel that way and *how* that feeling is connected to the meaning. Sometimes this reaction is just the beginning of other readings; at other times, this perspective can help you develop detailed analyses of how a text works.

The Emotion in Brooks' Poem.   When you read Brooks' poem "The White Troops Had Their Orders," what kinds of feelings does it generate? When we read that the white troops were perplexed because "These Negroes looked like men," we are puzzled at first. Of course they look like men: They are men! The idea of being ordered to look at the world with "cold" and "hooded gaze" and to "box" our "feelings properly" makes us feel as if we are being manipulated and forced to act less than human; we have feelings and don't like being forced to deny them by putting them into boxes. When we get near the end, the speaker asks us "Who really gave two figs?" We are not sure, but we do not like the way the question ignores our feelings and seems to deny the Negro soldiers' humanity. Our general reaction in our first or second reading of the poem is to be angry at the way the orders dehumanize the Negro soldiers and force people to box their feelings. When we become aware of this kind of carefully controlled anger, we realize that this is an angry poem that expresses its outrage subtly in the satirical tone of understatement.

Questions of Form

You can also investigate the form of a piece of literature and ask yourself how that form is related to meaning. Are there repeated words, images, patterns, or structures? Does the writer use words in a particular way? Are there certain kinds of metaphors (using a word to stand for something else) that can reveal what the author is doing? Does the author use a particular kind of structure to aid our understanding of the literature? Does she use rhyme? Does she present events in the story out of the order they would have happened? Does she set up chapters in a novel in a meaningful way? For example, if a writer dealt with a very serious topic in the form of a limerick (a common form of comic poetry), she might be using that form to reveal irony about her subject.

Breaking Forms. If we look at the formal features of this poem by Brooks, it is hard to know where to start. Because this is a poem, we might begin by noticing that, unlike much modern poetry, it rhymes very regularly even if some of the rhymes are a little unusual. The first four lines and the second four lines rhyme in a regular pattern: "Fixed" and "perplexed" in lines one and four and "devise" and "gaze" in lines two and three make one set. "Taxed" and "boxed" in lines five and eight and "those" and "cause" in lines six and seven make a second set. The last six lines rhyme, but in a different pattern: "tags" and "figs" (lines nine and twelve); "Other" and "weather" (lines ten and fourteen); "scrambled" and "trembled" (lines eleven and thirteen). You might also notice that each rhyme unit—lines one through four, five through eight, and nine through fourteen—generally coincides with an idea or theme: the perplexed feeling, the Negroes and the distrust, and the problem of boxing their feelings. This is clearly a pretty tight pattern of rhyme. The poem, then, seems to have something of the "fixed formula" that the first line mentions.

Despite this tight structure, the poem begins to break out of its formula in places. For example, the sentence that runs from line five through the middle of line eight is the theme of that unit, but the new sentence and theme of the last piece overlap line eight. That is, the poem tends to fight against the fixed formula. Given this clue, you might notice that the word "boxed" is the only repeated word; feelings are boxed, men are boxed, and in a formal sense the poem is boxed.

This all suggests that being boxed or fixed is crucial to the poem. Finally, the kind of language the speaker uses seems relatively normal until we get to "congenital iniquities" and "Disfavor of darkness," and at the end we get the almost slang question "Who really gave two figs?" Why does Brooks change her language to draw our attention to these two points in the poem?

Questions of History

All works of literature are part of their own times, and often we need to know something of history in order to understand the literature fully — and sometimes literature helps us to understand the times fully. To read a text historically, you might ask yourself first if there are words used here that meant something different in their own time. But you can also ask bigger questions. What was going on in the world at this time? Is this story a commentary on those historical events? Has the literature been affected by a particular event? You can also ask more specialized historical questions related to particular kinds of history: What were social conditions like when this was written? What would the author's life have been like? What were the political issues of the day, and how are they represented here? Did the author write anything else about that time that can shed light on this piece of literature? This kind of study requires some background research, looking up words and historical events, but it can be well worth the effort. Remember the fish tattoo that Holmes identified? Often the only way he is able to solve a crime is by doing extensive study.

Brooks and World War II.   To use these kinds of historical questions to read Brooks' poem, you may need to do a little research. You might begin, however, by noticing that the poem was published in 1945 and that it is clearly about soldiers at war. This suggests that the poem was written during World War II and that it concerns the relations between black and white troops fighting in the same army. What you will not know without some research is that the Army shipped the bodies of black and white soldiers home in segregated coffins. This was only one case of what was a systematic segregation of black soldiers during the war. As Brooks points out in other poems, black soldiers fought and died but were regularly segregated to lesser positions in the army.

Questions of Sociology

Sociological questions examine literature as an important part of our society, as something that affects how we see other people and how we relate to them. If you want to approach a story, poem, novel, or play from a sociological perspective, you might ask how it represents women, minorities, or people of different classes and examine in detail how that representation is a part of the meaning. Are certain people stereotyped? Why? Does the text make judgments about people? On what basis? Does it make any kind of social commentary? Are workers mistreated?

Does it show abuses of people of color? Does it represent all rich people as good or bad? And how is that commentary related to the meaning?

Racism Then and Now.   Once we have thought about the historical circumstances of Brooks' poem, the related questions of sociological perspective become clear. Gwendolyn Brooks is a black poet writing about the injustice black soldiers experienced during the war. They were fighting and dying for a country in which they were not equal, in which they were not treated as if they were, in fact, really men. This complicates the question "Who really gives two figs?" Some white soldiers did, but those who obeyed the formula and believed in the "congenital iniquities" did not. But the question is also addressed to us, to our contemporary world. The "congenital iniquities" are the inherited inequality and prejudice against racial minorities in our culture. The poem asks us if they still exist. Do we really give two figs?

Questions of Literary Tradition

Every piece of literature is part of a growing body of literary works, and one way to read a book is to examine its relations to other works. Sometimes a book is written as a commentary on or a play against another work. Comic works, for example, often exploit the possible alternatives in familiar stories or plot lines, playing off our knowledge and expectations. You might ask whether the book deliberately uses other literary works as a background. What are those other works, and how does the writer use them? Does she imitate them? Parody them? Rewrite them in terms of her own era and set of problems? This is a question about how a writer uses and changes previous stories.

Brooks and the Sonnet.   In the case of Brooks' poem, questions about its place in the literary tradition are very similar to the questions about its form. "The White Troops" is a sonnet (it has fourteen lines and a specific rhyme structure), one of the oldest poetic forms. Sonnets are often written in sequences, and usually each sonnet in a sequence treats one aspect of a large, important issue. Shakespeare's sonnets were about love, death, and fame. The form here is a Petrarchan sonnet (the lines are arranged in two groups of four and a final group of six). Petrarch's sonnets were Italian love poems, and Brooks is using this form satirically; that is, she takes a form usually used for love poetry to discuss the hatred of prejudice and war. She is breaking the formula of the Petrarchan sonnet as a way of questioning whether we can break the rules of other inherited forms, like racism.

FROM READING TO WRITING

We have not given you a fully worked out reading of "The White Troops," but just the beginning questions. If you were going to write a paper on the poem, you would need to do more research, ask more questions, make connections between the ideas, organize them, and provide an introduction and conclusion. We have simply sketched out five different frames of reference, or sets of questions, that might be a place to start with your journal entries, so that like our students Dana and Ed, you can begin to ask the kinds of questions that will help you build a reading of a literary text.

The kind of reading that goes on in English classes is not essentially different from the everyday reading we all do: It involves many of the same language skills but has a different purpose and takes more practice. It does not depend on some special insight, just on informed and careful observation. You do not have to read like Sherlock Holmes all the time; Holmes works only on the most mysterious, baffling cases and gets bored the rest of the time. But it is nice to know how Holmes does it, to be able to use that skill when it is necessary.

SUGGESTION FOR RESEARCH

After you've read the stories and poems that follow, pick one in which you are especially interested. Use one of the sets of questions we've described, and write an essay about the poem. You'll need to go to the library: to learn how other readers have reacted to the text; to discover something about the formal features the author uses; to find out something about the history, the society, or the politics of the time; or to become acquainted with the "genre," the literary tradition of the piece. Once you have done this research, explain what you think this text means, using this background material. You should end up making an argument for your interpretation of the piece.

READINGS

Poetic Responses to War

Walt Whitman
A SIGHT IN CAMP IN THE DAYBREAK GRAY AND DIM

In the introductory essay, we discussed a war poem by Gwendolyn Brooks that deals with racism and war. The following four poems examine different aspects of war: the deaths of soldiers, the resistance to war, and the devastation war leaves. Like Brooks, Randall Jarrell (1914–1965) writes about World War II, but Walt Whitman (1819–1892) writes about the Civil War, and Denise Levertov (b. 1923) about the Vietnam War. A. R. Ammons (b. 1926) could be writing about any city destroyed by war. All four poems examine the destructive power of war and question how we keep on living and hoping.

As you read, jot down your ideas about the metaphors and images these poets use to frame and describe the experience of war. How does this poetry help to make it more bearable? How do the poems help us to understand it?

A sight in camp in the daybreak gray and dim,
As from my tent I emerge so early sleepless,
As slow I walk in the cool fresh air the path near by the hospital
    tent,
Three forms I see on stretchers lying, brought out there untended
    lying,
Over each the blanket spread, ample brownish woolen blanket,
Gray and heavy blanket, folding, covering all.

Curious I halt and silent stand,
Then with light fingers I from the face of the nearest the first just
    lift the blanket;
Who are you elderly man so gaunt and grim, with well-gray'd hair,
    and flesh all sunken about the eyes?
Who are you my dear comrade?

Then to the second I step—and who are you my child and darling?
Who are you sweet boy with cheeks yet blooming?

Then to the third—a face nor child nor old, very calm, as of beauti-
    ful yellow-white ivory;

Young man I think I know you — I think this face is the face of the
   Christ himself,
Dead and divine and brother of all, and here again he lies.

                                                        1865,1867

Randall Jarrell
THE DEATH OF THE BALL TURRET
GUNNER

From my mother's sleep I fell into the State,
And I hunched in its belly till my wet fur froze.
Six miles from earth, loosed from its dream of life,
I woke to black flak and the nightmare fighters.
When I died they washed me out of the turret with a hose.

Denise Levertov
THE ALTARS IN THE STREET

> *On June 17th, 1966, The New York Times reported that, as part of
> the Buddhist campaign of non-violent resistance, Viet-Namese children
> were building altars in the streets of Saigon and Hue, effectively jam-
> ming traffic.*

Children begin at green dawn nimbly to build
topheavy altars, overweighted with prayers,
thronged each instant more densely

with almost-visible ancestors.
Where tanks have cracked the roadway
the frail altars shake; here a boy

with red stumps for hands steadies a corner,
here one adjusts with his crutch the holy base.
The vast silence of Buddha overtakes

and overrules the oncoming roar
of tragic life that fills alleys and avenues;
it blocks the way of pedicabs, police, convoys.

The hale and maimed together
hurry to construct for the Buddha
a dwelling at each intersection. Each altar

made from whatever stones, sticks, dreams, are at hand,
is a facet of one altar; by noon
the whole city in all its corruption,

all its shed blood the monsoon cannot wash away,
has become a temple,
fragile, insolent, absolute.

A. R. Ammons
THE ETERNAL CITY

After the explosion or cataclysm, that big
display that does its work but then fails
out with destructions, one is left with the

pieces: at first, they don't look very valuable,
but nothing sizable remnant around for
gathering the senses on, one begins to take

an interest, to sort out, to consider closely
what will do and won't, matters having become
not only small but critical: bulbs may have been

uprooted: they should be eaten, if edible, or
got back in the ground: what used to be garages,
even the splinters, should be collected for

fires: some unusually deep holes or cleared
woods may be turned to water supplies or
sudden fields: ruinage is hardly ever a

pretty sight but it must when splendor goes
accept into itself piece by piece all the old
perfect human visions, all the old perfect loves.

OPTIONS FOR WRITING

1. All four of these poems come to terms with the destruction and loss of
war, but they do so in different ways. Make a list of the images and
metaphors each poet uses and then compare the lists to see if any pattern
emerges. Choose two poems, and write a journal entry that discusses how
those patterns of images develop an idea about war.

2. These four poems describe different wars, from very different time
periods. In some sense, wars are always the same — the pain and suffering,
loss and death do not change — but in other ways, they are different and

specific to their own time periods. Write an essay comparing Whitman's and Levertov's poems, discussing how the historical situations of the wars they describe — the Civil War and the Vietnam War — affect how we read them.

3. In the chapter on philosophy, there are two essays on the bombing of Hiroshima during World War II ("Hiroshima: A Soldier's View," by Paul Fussell, and "Hiroshima: An Act of Terrorism," by Michael Walzer). Consider these poems as complementary pieces on the ethics of war and its relation to religion; think of them as philosophical essays. Write an essay or a journal entry about how and why these poems connect war and religion or ethics.

4. Artists respond to war in a variety of media. Look, for example, at the responses by Pablo Picasso and Maya Ying Lin in Chapter 5. Which medium do you find most powerful? Write an essay exploring your reaction to these differing responses.

Shopping

John Updike
A & P

If there is one experience that is common to almost everyone in the United States, it is the weekly visit to a supermarket. The supermarket represents the convenience, abundance, and richness that Americans expect in their lives and is in some ways a symbol of American life. In these two readings, we have two distinctly different views of supermarkets. Novelist and short story writer John Updike (b. 1932) focuses on one check-out clerk's experience in his short story "A & P." In "A Supermarket in California," poet Allen Ginsberg (b. 1926) muses on what Walt Whitman might think of America if he were to visit a modern supermarket.

Make notes, as you read these pieces, about what the supermarket represents for each of these writers. Is it symbolic of America as a whole or of a particular aspect of the country? What is it about the supermarket that draws these writers' attention? Are they using it to make some kind of social comment?

In walks these three girls in nothing but bathing suits. I'm in the third checkout slot, with my back to the door, so I don't see them until they're over by the bread. The one that caught my eye first was the one in the plaid green two-piece. She was a chunky kid, with a good tan and a sweet broad soft-looking can with those two crescents of white just under it, where the sun never seems to hit, at the top of the backs of her legs. I stood there with my hand on a box of HiHo crackers trying to remember if I rang it up or not. I ring it up again and the customer starts giving me hell. She's one of these cash-register-watchers, a witch about fifty with rouge on her cheekbones and no eyebrows, and I know it made her day to trip me up. She'd been watching cash registers for fifty years and probably never seen a mistake before.

By the time I got her feathers smoothed and her goodies into a bag — she gives me a little snort in passing, if she'd been born at the right time they would have burned her over in Salem — by the time I get her on her way the girls had circled around the bread and were coming back, without a pushcart, back my way along the counters, in the aisle between the checkouts and the Special bins. They didn't even have shoes on. There was this chunky one, with the two-piece — it was bright green and the seams on the bra were still sharp and her belly was still pretty pale so I guessed she just got it (the suit) — there was this one, with one of those chubby berry-faces, the lips all bunched together under her nose, this one, and a tall one, with black hair that hadn't quite frizzed right, and one of these sunburns right across under the eyes, and a chin that was too long — you know, the kind of girl other girls think is very "striking" and "attractive" but never quite makes it, as they very well know, which is why they like her so much — and then the third one, that wasn't quite so tall. She was the queen. She kind of led them, the other two peeking around and making their shoulders round. She didn't look around, not this queen, she just walked straight on slowly, on these long white primadonna legs. She came down a little hard on her heels, as if she didn't walk in bare feet that much, putting down her heels and then letting the weight move along to her toes as if she was testing the floor with every step, putting a little deliberate extra action into it. You never know for sure how girls' minds work (do you really think it's a mind in there or just a little buzz like a bee in a glass jar?) but you got the idea she had talked the other two into coming in here with her, and now she was showing them how to do it, walk slow and hold yourself straight.

She had on a kind of dirty-pink — beige maybe, I don't know — bathing suit with a little nubble all over it and, what got me, the straps were down. They were off her shoulders looped loose around the cool tops of her arms, and I guess as a result the suit had slipped a little on her, so all around the top of the cloth there was this shining rim. If it hadn't been there you wouldn't have known there could have been anything whiter than those shoulders. With the straps pushed off, there was nothing between the top of the suit and the top of her head except just *her*, this clean bare plane of the top of her chest down from the shoulder bones like a dented sheet of metal tilted in the light. I mean, it was more than pretty.

She had a sort of oaky hair that the sun and salt had bleached, done up in a bun that was unravelling, and a kind of prim face. Walking into the A & P with your straps down, I suppose it's the only kind of face you *can* have. She held her head so high her neck, coming up out of those white shoulders, looked kind of stretched, but I didn't mind. The longer her neck was, the more of her there was.

She must have felt in the corner of her eye me and over my shoulder Stokesie in the second slot watching, but she didn't tip. Not this queen. She kept her eyes moving across the racks, and stopped, and turned so slow it made my stomach rub the inside of my apron, and buzzed to the other two, who kind of huddled against her for relief, and then they all three of them went up the cat-and-dog-food-breakfast-cereal-macaroni-rice-raisins-seasonings-spreads-spaghetti-soft-drinks-crackers-and-cookies aisle. From the third slot I look straight up this aisle to the meat counter, and I watched them all the way. The fat one with the tan sort of fumbled with the cookies, but on second thought she put the package back. The sheep pushing their carts down the aisle — the girls were walking against the usual traffic (not that we have one-way signs or anything) — were pretty hilarious. You could see them, when Queenie's white shoulders dawned on them, kind of jerk, or hop, or hiccup, but their eyes snapped back to their own baskets and on they pushed. I bet you could set off dynamite in an A & P and the people would by and large keep reaching and checking oatmeal off their lists and muttering "Let me see, there was a third thing, began with A, asparagus, no, ah, yes, applesauce!" or whatever it is they do mutter. But there was no doubt, this jiggled them. A few house-slaves in pin curlers even looked around after pushing their carts past to make sure what they had seen was correct.

You know, it's one thing to have a girl in a bathing suit down on the beach, where what with the glare nobody can look at each other much anyway, and another thing in the cool of the A & P, under the fluorescent lights, against all those stacked packages, with her feet paddling along naked over our checker-board green-and-cream rubber-tile floor.

"Oh Daddy," Stokesie said beside me. "I feel so faint."

"Darling," I said. "Hold me tight." Stokesie's married, with two babies chalked up on his fuselage already, but as far as I can tell that's the only difference. He's twenty-two, and I was nineteen this April.

"Is it done?" he asks, the responsible married man finding his voice. I forgot to say he thinks he's going to be manager some sunny day, maybe in 1990 when it's called the Great Alexandrov and Petrooshki Tea Company or something.

What he meant was, our town is five miles from a beach, with a big summer colony out on the Point, but we're right in the middle of town, and the women generally put on a shirt or shorts or something before they get out of the car into the street. And anyway these are usually women with six children and varicose veins mapping their legs and nobody, including them, could care less. As I say, we're right in the middle of town, and if you stand at our front doors you can see two banks and the Congregational church and the newspaper store and three real-estate offices and about twenty-seven old freeloaders tearing up Central Street because the sewer broke again. It's not as if we're on the Cape; we're north of Boston and there's people in this town haven't seen the ocean for twenty years.

The girls had reached the meat counter and were asking McMahon something. He pointed, they pointed, and they shuffled out of sight behind a pyramid of Diet Delight peaches. All that was left for us to see was old McMahon patting his mouth and looking after them sizing up their joints. Poor kids, I began to feel sorry for them, they couldn't help it.

Now here comes the sad part of the story, at least my family says it's sad, but I don't think it's so sad myself. The store's pretty empty, it being Thursday afternoon, so there was nothing much to do except lean on the register and wait for the girls to show up again. The whole store was like a pinball machine and I didn't know which tunnel they'd come out of. After a while they come around out of the far aisle, around the light bulbs, records at discount of the Caribbean Six or Tony Martin Sings or some such gunk you wonder they waste the wax on, six-packs of candy bars, and plastic toys done up in cellophane that fall apart when a kid looks at them anyway. Around they come, Queenie still leading the way, and holding a little gray jar in her hand. Slots Three through Seven are unmanned and I could see her wondering between Stokes and me, but Stokesie with his usual luck draws an old party in baggy gray pants who stumbles up with four giant cans of pineapple juice (what do these bums *do* with all that pineapple juice? I've often asked myself) so the girls come to me. Queenie puts down the jar and I take it into my fingers icy cold. Kingfish Fancy Herring Snacks in Pure Sour Cream: 49¢. Now her hands are empty, not a ring or a bracelet, bare as God made them, and I wonder where the money's coming from. Still with that prim look she lifts a folded dollar bill out of the hollow at the center of her nubbled pink top. The jar went heavy in my hand. Really, I thought that was so cute.

Then everybody's luck begins to run out. Lengel comes in from haggling with a truck full of cabbages on the lot and is about to scuttle into that door marked MANAGER behind which he hides all day when the girls touch his eye. Lengel's pretty dreary, teaches Sunday school and the rest, but he doesn't miss that much. He comes over and says, "Girls, this isn't the beach."

Queenie blushes, though maybe it's just a brush of sunburn I was noticing for the first time, now that she was so close. "My mother asked me to pick up a jar of herring snacks." Her voice kind of startled me, the way voices do when you see the people first, coming out so flat and dumb yet kind of tony, too, the way it ticked over "pick up" and "snacks." All of a sudden I slid right down her voice into her living room. Her father and the other men were standing around in ice-cream coats and bow ties and the women were in sandals picking up herring snacks on toothpicks off a big glass plate and they were all holding drinks the color of water with olives and sprigs of mint in them. When my parents have somebody over they get lemonade and if it's a real racy affair Schlitz in tall glasses with "They'll Do It Every Time" cartoons stenciled on.

"That's all right," Lengel said. "But this isn't the beach." His repeating this struck me as funny, as if it had just occurred to him, and he had been thinking all these years the A & P was a great big dune and he was the head lifeguard. He didn't like my smiling—as I say he doesn't miss much—but he concentrates on giving the girls that sad Sunday-school-superintendent stare.

Queenie's blush is no sunburn now, and the plump one in plaid, that I liked better from the back—a really sweet can—pipes up, "We weren't doing any shopping. We just came in for the one thing."

"That makes no difference," Lengel tells her, and I could see from the way his eyes went that he hadn't noticed she was wearing a two-piece before. "We want you decently dressed when you come in here."

"We *are* decent," Queenie says suddenly, her lower lip pushing, getting sore now that she remembers her place, a place from which the crowd that runs the A & P must look pretty crummy. Fancy Herring Snacks flashed in her very blue eyes.

"Girls, I don't want to argue with you. After this come in here with your shoulders covered. It's our policy." He turns his back. That's policy for you. Policy is what the kingpins want. What the others want is juvenile delinquency.

All this while, the customers had been showing up with their carts but, you know, sheep, seeing a scene, they had all bunched up on Stokesie, who shook open a paper bag as gently as peeling a peach, not wanting to miss a word. I could feel in the silence everybody getting nervous, most of all Lengel, who asks me, "Sammy, have you rung up their purchase?"

I thought and said "No" but it wasn't about that I was thinking. I go through the punches, 4, 9, GROC, TOT—it's more complicated than you think, and after you do it often enough, it begins to make a little song, that you hear words to, in my case "Hello (*bing*) there, you (*gung*) hap-py *pee*-pul (*splat*)!"—the *splat* being the drawer flying out. I uncrease the bill, tenderly as you may imagine, it just having come from between the two smoothest scoops of vanilla I had ever known there were, and pass a half and a penny into her narrow pink palm, and nestle the herrings in a bag and twist its neck and hand it over, all the time thinking.

The girls, and who'd blame them, are in a hurry to get out, so I say "I quit" to Lengel quick enough for them to hear, hoping they'll stop and watch me, their unsuspected hero. They keep right on going, into the electric eye; the door flies open and they flicker across the lot to their car, Queenie and Plaid and Big Tall Goony-Goony (not that as raw material she was so bad), leaving me with Lengel and a kink in his eyebrow.

"Did you say something, Sammy?"

"I said I quit."

"I thought you did."

"You didn't have to embarrass them."

"It was they who were embarrassing us."

I started to say something that came out "Fiddle-de-do." It's a saying of my grandmother's, and I know she would have been pleased.

"I don't think you know what you're saying," Lengel said.

"I know you don't," I said. "But I do." I pull the bow at the back of my apron and start shrugging it off my shoulders. A couple of customers that had been heading for my slot begin to knock against each other, like scared pigs in a chute.

Lengel sighs and begins to look very patient and old and gray. He's been a friend of my parents for years. "Sammy, you don't want to do this to your Mom and Dad," he tells me. It's true, I don't. But it seems to me that once you begin a gesture it's fatal not to go through with it. I fold the apron, "Sammy" stitched in red on the pocket, and put it on the counter, and drop the bow tie on top of it. The bow tie is theirs, if you've ever wondered. "You'll feel this for the rest of your life," Lengel says, and I know that's true, too, but remembering how he made that pretty girl blush makes me so scrunchy inside I punch the No Sale tab and the machine whirs "pee-pul" and the drawer splats out. One advantage to this scene taking place in summer, I can follow this up with a clean exit, there's no fumbling around getting your coat and galoshes, I just saunter into the electric eye in my white shirt that my mother ironed the night before, and the door heaves itself open, and outside the sunshine is skating around on the asphalt.

I look around for my girls, but they're gone, of course. There wasn't anybody but some young married screaming with her children about some candy they didn't get by the door of a powder-blue Falcon station wagon. Looking back in the big windows, over the bags of peat moss and aluminum lawn furniture stacked on the pavement, I could see Lengel in my place in the slot, checking the sheep through. His face was dark gray and his back stiff, as if he's just had an injection of iron, and my stomach kind of fell as I felt how hard the world was going to be to me hereafter.

Allen Ginsberg
A SUPERMARKET IN CALIFORNIA

What thoughts I have of you tonight, Walt Whitman, for I walked down the sidestreets under the trees with a headache self-conscious looking at the full moon.

In my hungry fatigue, and shopping for images, I went into the neon fruit supermarket, dreaming of your enumerations!

What peaches and what penumbras! Whole families shopping at night! Aisles full of husbands! Wives in the avocados, babies in the tomatoes!—and you, García Lorca, what were you doing down by the watermelons?

I saw you, Walt Whitman, childless, lonely old grubber, poking among the meats in the refrigerator and eyeing the grocery boys.

I heard you asking questions of each: Who killed the pork chops? What price bananas? Are you my Angel?

I wandered in and out of the brilliant stacks of cans following you, and followed in my imagination by the store detective.

We strode down the open corridors together in our solitary fancy tasting artichokes, possessing every frozen delicacy, and never passing the cashier.

Where are we going, Walt Whitman? The doors close in an hour. Which way does your beard point tonight?

(I touch your book and dream of our odyssey in the supermarket and feel absurd.)

Will we walk all night through solitary streets? The trees add shade to shade, lights out in the houses, we'll both be lonely.

Will we stroll dreaming of the lost America of love past blue automobiles in driveways, home to our silent cottage?

Ah, dear father, graybeard, lonely old courage-teacher, what America did you have when Charon quit poling his ferry and you got out on a smoking bank and stood watching the boat disappear on the black waters of Lethe?

Berkeley, 1955

OPTIONS FOR WRITING

1. In "The World of Business" (Chapter 13), we will see how a business person would look at a grocery store. How do Updike's and Ginsberg's views differ? What kinds of things does the businessperson overlook and what does the creative writer overlook? How could the two views gain from each other? Imagine either Ginsberg or Updike as a supermarket owner and write a journal entry about how he might run the store, or write an imaginary conversation between Ginsberg, Updike, and a marketing student.

2. In "A & P," the young women in the swimsuits stop at the meat counter to ask for information; when they leave, we see the butcher "looking after them sizing up their joints." Updike implies that these girls are being looked at as if they were pieces of meat. Are there other instances of this in the story? How are women described in this story? Think through the way Sammy talks about women, and write a journal entry about the role of women in the American society described in "A & P."

3. Both Updike and Ginsberg seem to see the supermarket as in some way symbolic of America and its social problems. Think about how they represent those problems, how they use their symbolism, and write an essay about these literary texts as social criticism.

What is Unsaid

Sylvia Plath
METAPHORS

American writer Sylvia Plath's poem "Metaphors" (1932–1963) is a riddle. Use the form of the poem and the meaning of the metaphors to get its answer. (Hint: Count the number of lines and the number of syllables in each line.) To what is she referring?

I'm a riddle in nine syllables,
An elephant, a ponderous house,
A melon strolling on two tendrils.
O red fruit, ivory, fine timbers!
This loaf's big with its yeasty rising.
Money's new-minted in this fat purse.
I'm a means, a stage, a cow in calf.
I've eaten a bag of green apples,
Boarded the train there's no getting off.

OPTIONS FOR WRITING

1. Analyze the way Plath uses form to express meaning in this little poem.
2. Think through the different metaphors in this poem; are they complimentary or disparaging? How to they make you feel? Are they funny or sad? Write a short essay on how our responses to the imagery helps develop the meaning in this poem.
3. Write your own riddle in poetic form.

Gabriel García Marquez
ONE OF THESE DAYS

Gabriel García Marquez (b. 1928) is a South American writer and the author of the best-selling novels One Hundred Years of Solitude *and* Love in the Time of Cholera. *He won the Nobel prize for literature in 1982. In this odd little story, he takes the common experience of going to the dentist—and our common fear of it—as an occasion for a comment on revenge and small town South American politics.*

In your reading, pay attention to the details of the interaction between dentist and mayor, both to what is said and to what is unsaid. Take note also of the symbolism and imagery in the poem: What could false teeth represent here?

Monday dawned warm and rainless. Aurelio Escovar, a dentist without a degree, and a very early riser, opened his office at six. He took some false teeth, still mounted in their plaster mold, out of the glass case and put on the table a fistful of instruments which he arranged in size order, as if they were on display. He wore a collarless striped shirt, closed at the neck with a golden stud, and pants held up by suspenders. He was erect and skinny, with a look that rarely corresponded to the situation, the way deaf people have of looking.

When he had things arranged on the table, he pulled the drill toward the dental chair and sat down to polish the false teeth. He seemed not to be thinking about what he was doing, but worked steadily, pumping the drill with his feet, even when he didn't need it.

After eight he stopped for a while to look at the sky through the window, and he saw two pensive buzzards who were drying themselves in the sun on the ridgepole of the house next door. He went on working with the idea that before lunch it would rain again. The shrill voice of his eleven-year-old son interrupted his concentration.

"Papá."

"What?"

"The Mayor wants to know if you'll pull his tooth."

"Tell him I'm not here."

He was polishing a gold tooth. He held it at arm's length, and examined it with his eyes half closed. His son shouted again from the little waiting room.

"He says you are, too, because he can hear you."

The dentist kept examining the tooth. Only when he had put it on the table with the finished work did he say:

"So much the better."

He operated the drill again. He took several pieces of a bridge out of a cardboard box where he kept the things he still had to do and began to polish the gold.

"Papá."

"What?"

He still hadn't changed his expression.

"He says if you don't take out his tooth, he'll shoot you."

Without hurrying, with an extremely tranquil movement, he stopped pedaling the drill, pushed it away from the chair, and pulled the lower drawer of the table all the way out. There was a revolver. "O.K.," he said. "Tell him to come and shoot me."

He rolled the chair over opposite the door, his hand resting on the edge of the drawer. The Mayor appeared at the door. He had shaved the left side of his face, but the other side, swollen and in pain, had a five-day-old beard. The dentist saw many nights of desperation in his dull eyes. He closed the drawer with his fingertips and said softly:

"Sit down."

"Good morning," said the Mayor.

"Morning," said the dentist.

While the instruments were boiling, the Mayor leaned his skull on the headrest of the chair and felt better. His breath was icy. It was a poor office: an old wooden chair, the pedal drill, a glass case with ceramic bottles. Opposite the chair was a window with a shoulder-high cloth curtain. When he felt the dentist approach, the Mayor braced his heels and opened his mouth.

Aurelio Escovar turned his head toward the light. After inspecting the infected tooth, he closed the Mayor's jaw with a cautious pressure of his fingers.

"It has to be without anesthesia," he said.

"Why?"

"Because you have an abscess."

The Mayor looked him in the eye. "All right," he said, and tried to smile. The dentist did not return the smile. He brought the basin of sterilized instruments to the worktable and took them out of the water with a pair of cold tweezers, still without hurrying. Then he pushed the spittoon with the tip of his shoe, and went to wash his hands in the washbasin. He did all this without looking at the Mayor. But the Mayor didn't take his eyes off him.

It was a lower wisdom tooth. The dentist spread his feet and grasped the tooth with the hot forceps. The Mayor seized the arms of the chair, braced his feet with all his strength, and felt an icy void in his kidneys, but didn't make a sound. The dentist moved only his wrist. Without rancor, rather with a bitter tenderness, he said:

"Now you'll pay for our twenty dead men."

The Mayor felt the crunch of bones in his jaw, and his eyes filled with tears. But he didn't breathe until he felt the tooth come out. Then he saw it through his tears. It seemed so foreign to his pain that he failed to understand his torture of the five previous nights.

Bent over the spittoon, sweating, panting, he unbuttoned his tunic and reached for the handkerchief in his pants pocket. The dentist gave him a clean cloth.

"Dry your tears," he said.

The Mayor did. He was trembling. While the dentist washed his hands, he saw the crumbling ceiling and a dusty spider web with spider's eggs and dead insects. The dentist returned, drying his hands. "Go to bed," he said, "and gargle with salt water." The Mayor stood up, said goodbye with a casual military salute, and walked toward the door, stretching his legs, without buttoning up his tunic.

"Send the bill," he said.

"To you or the town?"

The Mayor didn't look at him. He closed the door and said through the screen:

"It's the same damn thing."

(1962)

OPTIONS FOR WRITING

1. Much is left unsaid in this story; "twenty dead men" are mentioned, but we learn little about them. How does García Marquez use the unsaid? How does it affect our reading? Write a paragraph about what you suspect is missing and about how its absence affects your reading of the story.

2. Think about the symbolism of the dentist and the teeth. Certainly, García Marquez appeals to our common dread of the dentist and uses our common experience of pain in the dentist's chair to make the story more effective. How else does he use dentistry here? How does his use of dentistry build the meaning of the story? Is that meaning simple, or might it have different interpretations? Explore the possible implications of this symbolism in an essay.

Works of and Responses to a Poet: Wanda Coleman

Wanda Coleman

HUH

Wanda Coleman is a contemporary African-American poet who writes about the physical, emotional, and spiritual condition of African-American women in language and imagery that is sometimes overpowering. The poems that follow are taken from two of her collections, Mad Dog Black Lady *(1979) and* Heavy Daughter Blues *(1987). In these poems, Coleman uses the blunt language of the street and the rhythms and style of the blues tradition to give voice to the anger and suffering she sees around her. In doing so, she creates a harsh and painful beauty.*

In his essay "Doing Battle with the Wolf: A Critical Introduction to Wanda Coleman's Poetry," Tony Magistrale, a professor of contemporary literature at the University of Vermont, points out that Coleman's work has been largely overlooked by literary critics because it is so different from much contemporary poetry. He illustrates here the power of literary history to determine both how and what we read. His article helps us understand the major themes and poetic strategies that run through Coleman's writing — the historical/social problems that motivate her poetry and the forms her poetry takes. He does this by describing the cultural context for Coleman's work and by offering readings of some of her most striking poems.

Stacy Gevry, a student in an American literature class at the University of Vermont, provides a personal reaction to Wanda Coleman's poetry in "The Apt Anger of Wanda Coleman." Ms. Gevry wrote this response after she heard Wanda Coleman read some of her poems aloud; she uses both the experience of that evening and her own experiences of racism in America to help her better understand the poetry.

We have provided these poems and the writings about them to help you see the difference between informal writing and formal literary criticism. Stacy Gevry's response essay and Tony Magistrale's essay are examples of the ways different readers go about making sense of Coleman's poetry. As you read this material, compare your reactions to Coleman with those of Gevry and Magistrale.

whatcha gonna do girl
get married. let me see the ring. it's only glass
but it look like a whole lot of diamond. he only a boy
but he look like a whole lot of man. you only a
child but you look like a whole lot of woman
it's only the world and it's a whole lot of trouble
whatcha gonna do girl when the weddin's thru
and the moon's wine turns to vinegar
whatcha gonna do when you got no one but you
and baby to feed. whatcha gonna do
when the sun go down and the wind move in to stay?

DOING BATTLE WITH THE WOLF

1.
i drip blood
on my way to and from work
i drip blood
down the aisles while shopping at the supermarket
i drip blood
standing in line at the bank
filling my tank at the gas station
visiting my man in prison
buying money orders at the post office
driving the kids to school
walking to bed at night
i drip blood

an occasional transfusion arrives in the mail
or i find plasma in the streets
an occasional vampire flashes my way

but they don't take much
my enemy is the wolf
who eats even the mind

the wolf will come for me sooner or later
i know this
the wolf makes no sexual distinctions
i am the right color
he has a fetish for black meat and
frequently hunts with his mate along side him

he follows my trail of blood

i drip blood for hours
go to the bathroom and apply bandages
i've bled enough
it's my monthly bleeding of poison
getting it out of my system
watching it as it flows from the
open sore of my body into the toilet stool

making a red ring
so pretty
flushing it away—red swirls
a precious painful price i pay

my man cannot protect me
the wolf has devoured most of my friends
i watched them die horribly
saw the
raw hunks of meat skin bone
swallowed
watched as full, the wolf crept away
to sleep

2.
the wolf has a beautiful coat
it is white and shimmers in moonlight/a coat of diamonds
his jaws are power
teeth sharp as guns glisten against his red tongue
down around his feet the fur is dirty with the caked blood of my friends

i smile
i never thought it would come to this

scratching
scratching at my door
scratching to get in

howls howls howls
my children are afraid
i send them to hide in the bedroom

scratch scratch scratch
the door strains
howl howl howl
cries of my children "mama! mama! who is it?"

i am ready
—armed with my spear inherited from my father as he from his mother
(who was a psychic) as she from her father (who was a runaway slave)
    as he
from his mother (who married the tribal witch doctor)—me—african
    warrior
imprisoned inside my barely adequate female form
determined
i open the door
a snarl
he lunges
the spear
against his head
he falls back
to prepare for second siege
i wait
the door will not close
i do not see the wolf
my children scream
i wait
look down
am wounded
drip blood
cannot move
or apply bandages
must wait
wolf howls and the roar of police sirens

DRONE

i am a clerk
i am a medical billing clerk
i sit here all day and type
the same type of things all day long
insurance claim forms
for people who suffer chronic renal failure

fortunately these people i rarely see
these are hard core cases
most of them are poor, black or latin
they are cases most other doctors refuse
they are problem cases
some of them have complications like heroin abuse
some of them are very young
most of them have brief charts
which means they died within a year of beginning treatment
sometimes a patient gets worried about his or her
coverage and calls the office
i refer them to the dialysis unit case worker
a few of the patients do bad things. for instance
some of them might refuse treatment as scheduled
sometimes they get drunk and call up
the nurses or attendants and curse them out
sometimes they try to fight the attendants
because they feel neglected/afraid
sometimes they wait until the last minute
to show up and it is the last minute
most of the patients, good patients,
quietly expire
i retire their charts to the inactive file
a few more claims i won't be typing up anymore
they are quickly replaced by others black, latin or poor
i make out crisp new charts
and the process starts all over again
the cash flows and flows and flows
so that the doctors can feed their race horses
and play tennis and pay the captains of their yachts
and keep up their children's college tuition and
trusts and maintain their luxury cars
for this service i am paid a subsistence salary
i come in here each morning
and bill the government for the people by the people
for these patients
i sit here and type
is what i do and that's very important
day after day/adrift in the river of forms
that flows between my desk and the computer that
prints out the checks
there are few problems here. i am a very good clerk
i sit here all day and type
i am a medical billing clerk
i am a clerk
i clerk

Stacy Gevry
THE APT ANGER OF WANDA COLEMAN

If I had to identify one pervading theme prevalent in Wanda Coleman's poetry it would be anger. I felt her anger at the injustices suffered by blacks, women especially. There were several poems she read which I felt epitomized her anger; "Arrest," "Stella," "They'll Starve You," and "Drone." Although I often classify anger as a potentially destructive force the anger of Wanda Coleman seemed appropriate and apt for her subjects. Of all of Coleman's poems I had the strongest reaction to "Arrest." I felt the hate and power of the white cop contrasting sharply with the silent defenseless black women. Her powerful reading persona conveyed the pure hatred emulating from the cop. Her intense reading made me feel as though I had fallen and had the wind knocked out of me. Her deliberate omission of any female voice gave me an image of the black woman as a silent defenseless sufferer. The woman had no power or even words to combat the hatred of the policeman. The persona and voice that Wanda Coleman adopted to read the cop oozed with the poisonous hatred of racism that I'm sure many people feel towards me. The black woman like many blacks everywhere has no voice, no power, no justice, and no control. The black woman in "Arrest" reminded me of the black mother "Stella" who lost her children because she could not support them. What struck me about the mother was the fact that she did not want charity or a free ride—she wanted a fair chance. Stella wanted to raise her children and support them, but she was held down by the system. The mother had no control or power over the lives of her children or herself because she could not receive an adequate paying job. The injustice of this situation I feel lies in the fact that she will never be given the opportunity she deserves simply because she is black. That particular poem evoked a sense of despair in me. I felt disgust at the social and economic establishments which deliberately work to ensure poverty for the blacks of Coleman's poetry which exist in reality.

The undisguised disgust in the poems "Drone" and "They'll Starve You" seemed apt and well directed when Coleman read her works. I felt her disgust at the social systems and the people which allowed them to exist. In "Drone" Coleman's tone fluctuated between the mundane repetition of the clerks tasks and a syrupy sweet sarcasm when describing the institution and doctors. I read in her sickly sweet reading voice disgust and disdain for the employers of the billing clerk in the poem. The closing lines represented a poignant contrast for me; the image of the patients as money to feed the doctor's racehorses, pay the captains of their yachts, and provide the means for tennis contrasted drastically with the image of the sick drug addicted patients of these doctors. "They'll Starve You" also had vividly contrasting themes. The list of desires and feelings felt by the blacks answered only with racism on the side of whites seemed to symbolize the whole meaning of Wanda Coleman's poetry for me. I felt the wall of prejudice that the blacks encounter from society and it depressed me.

Wanda Coleman's poetry brought to mind my sister, who is black, and created a tangible force which I feel she will someday encounter in one form or another. Because my sister is black prejudice is not a new sensation for me. However, I have conveniently forgotten to what extent racism still exists. I suppose that because I know and love my sister I assume that anyone would look and see the same things I do. What I have forgotten is that many people would look at Joy and never see anything other than her color. The fact that such widespread bigotry and racism still exists seems horrifying and criminal to me. I thank and applaud Wanda Coleman for bringing up the subjects of discrimination and racism for examination using such a powerful and profound style and voice.

Tony Magistrale
DOING BATTLE WITH THE WOLF:
A Critical Introduction
to Wanda Coleman's Poetry

> they tug at me, the children
> persistent at hem of my weary skirt
> we must eat. we must have shelter
> we must
> live. out of my hand/sweat/bread
> scheme. no time to idle in
> green pastures or chase stray dogs
> through daisy laden fields
>
> — "Worker" Imagoes 131

Since 1979, Wanda Coleman has produced three lengthy volumes of poetry — Mad Dog Black Lady, Imagoes, and Heavy Daughter Blues — , all published by a well-known and respected house, Black Sparrow Press. Yet, to date her poems have failed to receive serious critical attention and recognition. Although her books have been reviewed favorably in The Los Angeles Times,[1] she has been completely ignored by American literary scholars. Her work has been neither the subject of a full-length scholarly essay nor included in recent poetry anthologies compiled by editors pursuing an array of new American voices.[2]

I suspect that the most convincing explanation for this neglect has to do with Coleman's status as a writer. First, she is a poet, and her marginalization is in part a measure of the current status of poetry in the Afro-American literary canon. Second, she is a radical feminist who produces poems that are not similar in tone, style, or subject matter to the technically elegant and solipsistic verse that is currently being produced by graduates of advanced writing programs. Since she has never been an "academic poet," making her living outside the world of the university, she has been essentially cut off from the "network" that controls both the dissemination and audience for contemporary poetry.[3] Kate Adams argues in a recent essay that this "professionalizing" of poetry has served to "narrow the range of the American poetic voice":

> Just as an advanced degree seems to be an essential for the corporate climber, so it is becoming for the aspiring poet.
> The workshops, university presses, and literary journals associated with the strongest graduate programs now dominate the production and publication of poetry in this country. That dominance, while perhaps increasing the number of active poets, has narrowed the range of the American poetic voice. . . .
> The poet-professors and the institutions they serve collaborate in the production of American poetry—or at least in that body of work that academe and mainstream intellectual culture recognize and reward.
> . . . [this system] overwhelmingly suggests that the American poet is a white, male, highly educated university employee. (A48)

Neither white nor male nor university-affiliated, Wanda Coleman remains unread by that small minority of Americans who still appreciate the art of poetry. She is, on the other hand, a writer who embraces one of the most vital traditions of black American poetry (a body of literature that has always distinguished itself from the workshop laboratories of academe): Coleman writes about the life and death rhythms of the street.

The subjects of Wanda Coleman's poetry are black oppression, female persecution, and the inequitable class structure of contemporary America. Pared of romantic illusions and academic pretensions, her poems are honest and uncompromising commentaries about those who have been excluded from the American Dream. Her dramatic personae are prostitutes, single mothers, office clerks, victims of sexual assault, and female observers of black urban life—and in animating each of these roles Coleman's poetry demonstrates a clarity of vision and perspective that is at once powerful and convincing. The solitary female voice speaking in these poems is one intimately acquainted with the realities of poverty and oppression. She captures the bitter intensity of urban struggles, lamenting misspent black energy at the same time that she indicts the social forces responsible for so thoroughly restricting the lives of the poor.

In most of Coleman's work, the obstacles that black women confront on a daily basis are physically and psychologically debilitating, and the pain attendant to this condition is reflected through stark language, vivid imagery, and explicit sexual references. She examines her subjects without flinching. The dryness, the absence of pathos, the refusal of all idealism, and the indefatigable examination of black suffering are the great virtues of Coleman's poetry. Her work is charged with passion and outrage on the verge of erupting into some type of violent response. Yet it seldom does. She exerts a tremendous control over her emotions. As in Claude McKay's best verse, anger never interferes with Coleman's eloquence; the best poems never descend into the realm of blind rage.

Just as Coleman's poems reflect the themes of black urban struggle, her poetics capture the distinctive sounds and rhythms of black music, especially jazz and the blues. Coleman makes frequent reference to specific blues musicians, Billie Holiday, in particular, throughout her poetic canon, and several of her poems either deal directly with the relationship between music and language or suggest this relationship within their very titles. "Blue Lady Things," "Trouble on My Doorstep Blues," "Variations on a Blues Motif," "Blues for a Man on Sax," "Jass Man," "Walkin' Papers Blues," "At the Jazz Club He Comes on a Ghost," and "The Saturday Afternoon Blues" are just a few examples that illustrate Coleman's awareness of the connection between the blues tradition and its offspring, black American poetry.

The early anonymous singers of the blues were frequently wanderers who carried their songs from one black community to another. They sang on street corners and in railroad stations. From the time of their origin, however, the blues have always been associated with the poor and the downtrodden — embraced by the brothel and saloon, but rejected by the respectable. Coleman's poetry shows the influence of this tradition not only in her themes but also in the very style of the poems' composition. As in blues melodies, often a word, a phrase, or a complete line will repeat itself several times in an individual poem, serving as an explanation for the condition of her protagonist at the same time that it sustains a rhythmical cadence through the length of the work. The restatement of the phrase "whatcha gonna do" in "Huh," a short poem from *Heavy Daughter Blues*, for example, is a refrain that supplies a disquieting comment upon the romantic expectations of a young girl:

> whatcha gonna do girl
> get married. let me see the ring. it's only glass
> but it look like a whole lot of diamond. he only a boy
> but he look like a whole lot of man. you only a
> child but you look like a whole lot of woman
> it's only the world and it's a whole lot of trouble
> whatcha gonna do girl when the weddin's thru
> and the moon's wine turns to vinegar
> whatcha gonna do when you got no one but you
> and baby to feed. whatcha gonna do
> when the sun go down and the wind move in to stay? (33)

Coleman's language is the speech of urban blacks: rhythmical, dynamic, direct. It is tough and street-smart. Her decision to eschew the standard conventions of punctuation and grammar mirrors the poet's desire to create accessible work that is a challenge to those readers reluctant to associate poetry with the daily language of ghetto life. Moreover, Coleman seeks to produce a "breathless" quality in her poetics: Like the blues tradition itself, most of her poems attempt to record verbatim the dynamics of human conflict and speech, and this rendition is signaled through a random use of punctuation and lines which run together, obscuring clear poetic breaks.

In her discourse on the affiliation between Afro-American poetry and the blues, Sherley Anne Williams argues that "blues songs are almost always literal. . . . much of the verbal strength of the blues resides in the directness with which the songs confront experience" (131). Coleman often relies upon techniques which approximate or parallel blues devices. Arguably, the most obvious nexus is that her poems are composed from the everyday realities of black life and rendered in language that either describes the black world personally or confronts white society and its values directly. As the blues are an oral form meant to be heard rather than read, Coleman seldom writes poems of contemplation; the impulse of action is inherent within her verse. There is, moreover, a persistent element of affirmation in her poetry that manages to defy the range of suffering the poet entertains. As Eileen Southern points out in *The Music of Black Americans*, "By singing about his misery, the blues singer achieves a kind of catharsis and life becomes bearable again" (333). Embodied in the imagery of loneliness and exploitation there is an exaltation of pain; Coleman's songs of black sorrow often become a means for transcendence.

8 P.M. DISPUTE
       featuring pain on drums
         fear on bass
       heartbreak on piano
        jealousy on tenor sax

there isn't space enuff for us to blow
wah wah wah
and he say i don't play love enuff
he wants to know what to do
(whatever's cool)

a door slammed. a glass thrown
my eye blackens

i won't give

summer wind dance in the torn drape jazz

he won't give

winter light dance in the cracked glass blues

harmonic possibilities
discordant hope

what should i do? he asks, applying lots of hot
whatever's cool, i answer

and day comes to a bad jam
my jerks and clowns and muthafuckers
his bitch-i-could-kill-yous

whatever's cool (*Heavy Daughter Blues* 103)

Coleman frequently writes to illuminate the lives of the underclass and the disenfranchised, the invisible men and women who populate America's downtown streets after dark, the asylums and waystations, the inner city hospitals and clinics. Several poems in *Mad Dog Black Lady* are about the "poor, black or latin cases" who must visit the clinics of affluent white physicians seeking medical treatment that merely prolongs their agony. In "Drone," the best of these autobiographical poems, the narrator is a medical billing clerk who is conscious of her own exploitation and that of the patients suffering chronic renal failure. The patients are victimized by their disease, by their poverty and hopelessness, and by a bureaucracy that quantifies their humanity into the "crisp charts" of a medical file:

most of the patients, good patients,
quietly expire
i retire their charts to the inactive file
a few more claims i won't be typing up anymore (91)

Like the patients, the poet finds herself trapped by a "subsistence salary" and by her own workplace alienation. She is, as the title implies, a worker "drone" whose sole purpose is to process sick people:

i sit here and type
is what i do and that's very important
day after day/ adrift in the river of forms
that flows between my desk and the computer that
prints out the checks
there are few problems here. (92)

The poem is a scathing attack on the American medical profession. This clinic is a human factory in which the quiet desperations of debilitated men and women are "referred to the dialysis case worker." As patients "quietly expire," they are replaced by

others black, latin or poor
i make out crisp new charts
and the process starts all over again (91)

Instead of the accumulation of honey, this clinical hive produces money:

"the cash flows and flows and flows." Presiding over this lucrative arrangement are doctors who are nothing more than soulless technocrats. Their interests are purely mercantile; they care only about the smooth maintenance of the system that sustains the health of their bank portfolios. These parasites thrive off the suffering of others, exploiting both the patients and the government that pays their bills in order to

> feed race horses
> and play tennis and pay the captains of their yachts
> and keep up their children's college tuition and
> trusts and maintain their luxury cars (91–92)

Coleman's poetry dramatizes the differences that distinguish the haves from the have nots. She is aware that obtaining power in America is directly related to economic status—and that, in turn, is tied to race and gender. Many of Coleman's poems detail the lives of street prostitutes who are locked into patterns of violence and exploitation, forced out of economic necessity to perform intimate acts that are drained of all emotion. The irony inherent in the poem "Sweet Mama Wanda Tells Fortunes for a Price" is that there is no indication the future promises anything different from the particular night's reality described by the poem's narrator. Indeed, the voice in this poem appears resigned to a mechanical routine that is destined to repeat itself:

> dark stairs
> me walking up them
> the room
> is cold
> i am here to fuck
> then go back
> to the streets
>
> he sighs
> touches
> likes my lips
> my cocoa thighs
> we lay down
> the bed yields
> he comes off calling mama
>
> outside
> i count my cash
> it's been a good night
> the street is cold
> i head east
> i am hungry
> i smile
>
> i know what tomorrow
> is all about (Mad Dog Black Lady 79)

It is interesting that the language of this poem maintains a consistent minimalist tone of dispassionate observation in describing the actions which take place inside the room with her john and back on the streets afterwards. Both the street and the room are "cold" places where the woman finds neither sanctuary nor meaning. The offering of her body is rendered in strictly objective terms; like the bed itself, the narrator "yields" herself in order to "count my cash." Sex is reduced to the purest of business transactions, and in the process the woman surrenders control over her own life. The only occasion in which she is provided the opportunity to render any kind of personal response is when she expresses her "hunger" at the conclusion of the poem, an awareness that is symbolically appropriate given the emptiness she has just defined.

Coleman emphasizes continually the gap—perhaps *chasm* is more accurate—separating the worlds of male and female. Men and women fail to communicate on a variety of levels in her poetry; indeed, men are described as incapable of empathizing with the emotional, economic, and sexual needs of women. Instead of promoting a closer bond between future parents, the pregnancy in "Television Story" merely highlights the inability of men to respond sympathetically to women. The woman in the poem yearns to spend a romantic evening with her lover, but "he wants to go trip with his brothers." Devoted to the health of her fetus, the pregnant mother "wants to stay clean," so she is excluded from his self-indulgent behavior even as "she hates it / when he does acid." Although the man "feels her resentment," he chooses to ignore it; left alone in their home the woman senses that her altered physical appearance has diluted his desire for sexual intimacy. Since he is no longer interested in her sexually, she believes he has no interest in her personally. Influenced by his lack of sensitivity, the woman internalizes his rejection, and is consequently disgusted by the hormonal changes taking place in her body:

> she listens to the door shut
> goes over to the bed and takes off her muumuu
> in the mirror her belly full of child distended round fat
> gobs of dimpled cocoa flesh
> fat climbing upward settling into her face and neck
>
> "he can't stand to look at me," she says aloud
> she puts her muumuu back on (*Imagoes* 104–05)

The women in Coleman's poetry assume the daily pain that men—strangers, lovers, relatives—force upon them. In "Rape," neither the male authorities (policemen and doctors) nor the woman's boyfriend comprehend, much less sympathize with, the humiliation the female victim has experienced. Coleman's poem dramatically validates Susan Brownmiller's thesis in *Against Our Will* that rape codifies the perception of women as property in a patriarchal culture.[4] The boyfriend reacts as though he has been personally insulted in the violation of his girlfriend, and he further misdirects his anger not at the woman's assailants but at the victim herself. Less concerned about her psychological and physical conditions than he is indignant over her failure to prevent the rape, the boyfriend assaults the woman himself. His own contribution to this woman's defilement can be read as a desperate attempt to reclaim his threatened masculinity by re-establishing his dominance in the relationship; as a punishment to his girlfriend for "allowing" her own violation; and, most perverse of all, as a furtive, particularly masculine identification with the earlier burglar/rapists, who also viewed her body merely as chattel, something else to be appropriated and abused:

> the boyfriend
>
> came in. she was feeling shrunken dirty suicide
> she hadn't douched. the wetness still pouring
> out/a sticky riverlet on her inner thighs
> he got indignant. why didn't she call the police
> why didn't she call her mama. why didn't she die
> fighting. she remained silent. he asked her where
> it happened. she showed him the spot. he
> pulled down his pants, forced her back onto the sheets
> i haven't cleaned up, she whined. but he was
> full saddle hard dicking and cumming torrents (*Imagoes* 122–23)

Coleman's poems highlight the specific entrapments and consequent frustration that oppress black women. Although she employs a first-person-singular voice in the majority of her verse, she rarely writes only about a particular individual; her characters come to speak for an entire race or gender. In "Women of My Color," as is frequently the case in Coleman's poetry, the sexual translates into the political. The poem begins and ends in an act of fellatio. The graphic sexual refrain "i follow the curve of his penis / and go down" shocks the reader into attentiveness, while also stating the politics of gender that are in operation throughout the poem. Oral sex is employed as a symbol of domination; the act of "going down" is a physical event and an image of the greater social oppression of females by males: "being on the bottom where pressures / are greatest is least desirable." The isolation and persecution of black women victimized as a consequence of both their sex and race is underscored throughout the poem. Coleman is accentuating that black women's exploitation is not merely racial, but also gender-specific; the woman in this poem does not indicate any awareness of the *color* of the penis she is accommodating. The poem criticizes the dynamics of patriarchal authority, its color notwithstanding:

> there is a peculiar light in which women
> of my race are regarded by black men
> > as saints
> > as mothers

                    as sisters
                    as whores

  but mostly as the enemy

  it's not our fault   we are victims
  who have chosen to struggle and stay alive

  there is a peculiar light in which women
  of my race are regarded by white men
                    as exotic
                    as enemy

  but mostly as whores

  it's enough to make me cry
  but i don't

  following the curve of his penis
  i go down

  will i ever see
  the sun? (*Mad Dog Black Lady* 24)

The range of black male responses in this poem is perhaps broader than what the poet associates with white men, but both races nonetheless reduce the black woman to stereotyped categories that effectively restrict or deny her individuality. Black men, oppressed by the white world and in need of reasserting their own potency, in turn oppress black women. White men, existing in a cultural vacuum, are even further removed from the lives of black women, perceiving them only as "enemy" or "exotic" sexual toys. Both white and black male worlds want her "down," conforming to an emotional and economic "curve" where men are able to assert their power and pleasure at the expense of her identity. Coleman insists that, from either racial perspective, women of color are misinterpreted and victimized; the narrator's only occasion to exert what remains of her human dignity is in her stoic refusal to cry.

Although Coleman is most acutely sensitive to feminist issues in poems such as "Women of My Color," "A Black Woman's Hole," "Television Story," "Rape," and "No Woman's Land," in which she fully appreciates that "love politics" are governed by "a legislature of pricks," she is continually frustrated in her search for a feminist alternative to the oppression described in these poems. In "Women in My Life," for example, Coleman yearns for contact with other women—"my sisters do not write. unrequited letters beg communication"—,but her "anxious welcomes" are received only by a "silent door." The poem suggests not only that her "sisters" are busy living their own lives in distant places, but that they are likewise unwilling to expend the energy necessary to maintain a relationship with another woman. Coleman implies that, without the allure of sex or a masculine presence, the women in her life cannot retain sufficient interest: "would asking love be too much? . . . *the women in my life cut deeper than the men*" (*Mad Dog Black Lady* 40).

In one of the most eloquent poems Coleman has written to date, "Luz," the quest for a deep and lasting female relationship with an Hispanic woman is thwarted by Luz's desire to assimilate into the white world:

> for there was that to which you aspired/the whiteness
> of the white world/a door closed and bolted to me
> you entered, i remained outside

Although the persona shared an interest in her friend's ethnic background—"used to teach me some [Spanish] and introduce me to [her] culture, food, ways"—and an honest sympathy toward the fact that her "poverty went deeper than mine," their mutual status as outsiders living in white America was not basis enough for a commitment to one another:

> oh luz, i had so many things
> to say—so many tight chic referrals to the
> latin-black conflicts over white socio-eco crumbs
>
> i wanted to say them through you

Thus, the opportunity to forge a sympathetic union that might have helped both women to comprehend better their similar social circumstances and perhaps to transcend such limitations is lost. In the spurning of this ethnic union, the persona measures her isolation against the bitter recollection of the potential that has been sacrificed:

> all i do is remember, think of us/our people as we were
> or could have been—apart, the awful silence
> together, the awesome storm (*Mad Dog Black Lady* 29)

At the same time that Coleman recognizes and appears to long for a supportive union with another woman, her poetry reflects the dissatisfaction she has experienced in this pursuit. Her failure to portray a successful feminist relationship does not, however, invalidate a feminist reading of her poetry. Surely the most plausible explanation for many of the barriers that separate individual women in her work is due in no small measure to the influence of a patriarchal culture that continues to shape sexual priorities and preferences. In "Beyond Sisters," for example, the narrator apprehends the love she shares with another woman, but remains reluctant to become involved in a lesbian relationship because of her own sexual orientation: "she spoke words i forbade with/ my sexology and lust for man-flesh" (*Mad Dog Black Lady* 33). Coleman's work thus illustrates both the direct and indirect influence of a societal order that maintains its dominion over women by keeping them alienated from themselves as well as one another. When women discover they can do without men sexually, they defy power. The limits of feminist and lesbian unions in Coleman's poetry is less a criticism of the individual women involved than a comment on the restrictive patriarchal world surrounding these "illicit" relationships.

All of the themes I have traced in Wanda Coleman's poetry—the acute sensitivity to economic exploitation; the gender and racial gaps that separate men and women, black and white; and the vague yearning for the strength inherent in a feminist bond with another woman— coalesce in one of Coleman's most powerful poems to date, "Doing Battle with the Wolf." The wolf in this poem is clearly meant to symbolize the aggressiveness of the white world,[5] and it stalks the narrator, "wounded" by virtue of her color and sex, as she goes about her daily business. Indeed, each of her contacts within a world dominated by white employers and merchants steadily drains her of life fluid:

> i drip blood
> on my way to and from work
> i drip blood
> down the aisles while shopping at the supermarket
> i drip blood
> standing in line at the bank . . .
>
> the wolf will come for me sooner or later
> i know this
> the wolf makes no sexual distinctions
>
> i am the right color
> he has a fetish for black meat and
> frequently hunts with his mate along side him (*Mad Dog Black Lady* 17)

As we have already seen in many of Coleman's other poems, the bond that should exist among women against all forms of exploitation is once again betrayed. The wolf's power is so great that white women, who are in a position to identify with black oppression, choose to join in the "hunt" on the side of white males. Since its inception, the feminist movement in America has been vulnerable to the charge that its emphasis has centered on middle- and upper-class white issues, and that this predominantly white movement has virtually ignored the immense, twofold struggle of black women.[6] Coleman's poem effectively exaggerates such criticism in the suggestion that white men and women find a racist alliance in their mutual quest for "black meat."

"Doing Battle with the Wolf" is pervaded with blood imagery, as the poet repeats the refrain "i drip blood." And just as the narrator finds her blood everywhere—depositing a trail from her workplace in the morning to her bedroom at night—, the wolf is also silently omnipresent. There is no safety or recourse from his attacks, "the wolf has devoured most of my friends / i watched them die horribly," as the beast does not wound enough to kill, but merely to weaken progressively through a daily draining of blood. And when "the wolf / who eats even the mind" is satisfied that his victim is vulnerable enough, he launches a more aggressive assault:

scratch scratch scratch
the door strains

howl howl howl
cries of my children "mama! mama! who is it?"

i am ready
—armed with my spear inherited from my father as he from his mother
    (who was a psychic) as she from her father (who was a runaway slave)
    as he from his mother (who married the tribal witch doctor)—me—
    african warrior imprisoned inside my barely adequate female form
determined
i open the door
a snarl
he lunges
the spear
against his head
he falls back
to prepare for a second siege
i wait
the door will not close
i do not see the wolf
my children scream
i wait
look down
am wounded
drip blood
cannot move
or apply bandages
must wait
wolf howls and the roar of police sirens (18–19)

This exchange gives meaning to the symbolic roles of the wolf and
the woman. As the wolf comes clawing at her door, instilling fear in her
children, the poet is suddenly transformed into a black warrior, "armed
with my spear inherited from my father as he from his mother." The
strength to do battle against the wolf emerges from a familial line that
connects the speaker with her great-grandfather's rebellion against the
institution of slavery, the psychic powers of her grandmother, and the
magic of an African witch doctor. Summoning the courage both inherent
in her maternal instincts and in a heightened sensitivity to her own
black ancestry, the solitary heroine repudiates the passive bleeding that
characterizes the earlier sections of the poem and identifies with the
"african warrior / imprisoned inside my barely adequate female form." It
is her duty to defend her children and to assert herself as a representative for the entire black race. But the reality of the wolf's power proves
too much: Although the narrator strikes the creature once and wounds
him, she is unable to triumph over his superior and invisible strengths.
While she has learned patience and defiance in her battle, she also
knows the wolf will come again, incensed by the scent of her blood. She

knows, too, that "the door will not close," allowing the wolf final access to her and her family. The "roar" of sirens closes the poem, nearly indistinguishable from the "howls" of the beast. These are probably not sirens coming to her rescue, but rather the police of a lupine world — the remainder of the pack — summoned to aid the wolf in subduing his defiant victim.

Coleman's characters struggle against circumstances over which they exert little control. The dual burdens of sexism and racism keep her women confined to subservient lives. For them, happiness and self-determination are far removed, at the pole of some distant horizon. And yet so many of these poems tell a story that is larger than existential despair. These are also portraits of endurance. They do not romanticize the black woman — forging her into the supreme matriarch, or a model of feminist radicalism, or a self-sufficient being who revels in her isolation. Coleman's poems focus rather on women who do what they must to survive in a world that seeks constantly to rob them of their individuality and humanity. They are not superhuman nor do they often triumph over the severe circumstances that encumber their young lives. But they are strong people nonetheless; not one of them settles for a release in suicide, drug addiction, or institutionalization. They are victims of history and economics, but they do not expend their valuable energies in self-lamentation. Like Camus' Sisyphus, Coleman's women have been cursed by the gods; however, they assert whatever remains of their humanity in their stubborn refusal to surrender to forces greater than themselves. As Coleman reminds us in a line from "Women of My Color," that embodies the crux of her poetry, "it's not our fault we are victims / who have chosen to struggle and stay alive" (24).

In the last decade or two, a new generation of scholars has focused attention on the need to re-evaluate and enlarge the literary canon. In a recent article published in the *New York Times Magazine*, James Atlas summarized this impulse succinctly:

> . . . shaped by intellectual trends that originated in the 60's: Marxism, feminism, deconstruction, a skepticism about the primacy of the West . . ., for these scholars, the effort to widen the canon is an effort to define themselves, to validate their own identities. In the 80's, literature is us.(26)

In the laudable effort to widen the scope of our literary corpus, teachers and scholars of American literature must open themselves not only to the full range of varying voices in American fiction — women, blacks, Asians, Hispanics — but also to the individual voices of these communities not yet heard or recognized. Wanda Coleman, like Gwendolyn Brooks before her, has much to tell us about what it is like to be a poor black woman in America. This information is of particular importance to readers who have never thought deeply about this perspective, much less experienced it themselves. At its best, Coleman's poetic spirit enlarges the perimeters of our common humanity; her women characters take us, as Holly Prado notes in her *Los Angeles Times* review of *Mad Dog Black Lady*, "beyond brutality to fierce dignity" (qtd. in "Coleman, Wanda" 66). Indeed, Coleman's heated sensibility remains a sobering challenge to the naïve optimism that characterized the Reagan era. Her voice, and those of others like her, must no longer go unheard.

NOTES

[1] See *The Los Angeles Times* 31 Jan. 1982 and 13 Nov. 1983.

[2] In a random sampling of recent poetry anthologies published since 1979 (the date of Coleman's first book), I discovered that she has been excluded from the following collections: *A Geography of Poets: An Anthology of the New Poetry; Dear Dark Faces; Black Sister: Poetry by Black American Women; New Poetry of the American West; Carriers of the Dream Wheel;* and *Sylvan Song: America Singing.*

[3] According to the entry in *Contemporary Authors*, Coleman's *vita* is an interesting one. She has lived most of her life in the Los Angeles area, working an assortment of occupations besides that of poet, including magazine editor, waitress, medical transcriber and billing clerk, co-host of an interview program for Pacific Radio, proofreader, assistant recruiter for Peace Corps/Vista, staff writer for NBC's daytime soap opera *Days of Our Lives* (for which she won an Emmy in 1976), as well as a scriptwriter for Hollywood.

[4] As Brownmiller details throughout her monumental study, " . . . rape became not only a male prerogative, but man's basic weapon of force against woman, the principal agent of his will and her fear. His forcible entry into her body, despite her physical protestations and struggle, became the vehicle of his victorious conquest over her being, the ultimate test of his superior strength, the triumph of his manhood" (5).

[5] The employment of a wolf to represent white America as seen through the eyes of a black woman is an appropriate and complex personification. Throughout Western mythology, the wolf has been associated with war and rapacious behavior. The animal was, for example, sacred to the gods Apollo and Mars. In the Middle Ages, the wolf was an archetype of evil, connoting fierceness, cunning, greed, and gluttony. Except during the summer, when the young families of cubs are being separately provided for by the parents, wolves assemble in troops or packs and, by their combined efforts, are able to overpower and kill wounded animals of all sizes. As a scavenger, the wolf is known not so much for its ability to kill, but rather for its willingness to exploit the vulnerabilities of other animals. It is curious that, while wolves can be found extending over nearly the whole of Europe and Asia, and North America from Greenland to Mexico, they are not indigenous to Africa (*Encyclopedia Britannica* 697). These details obviously deepen the meaning of the animal's symbolic purpose in Coleman's poem, since all of these vulpine characteristics are embodied in the poet's personification of the white world.

[6] For a more thorough examination of this issue, see Terrelonge, La Rue, and Lewis. Lewis represents the most penetrating examination into the subject, as she supplies a survey of literature in the field as well as her own critique: "The woman's liberation movement has generated a number of theories about female inequality. Because the models usually focus exclusively upon the effects of sexism, they have been of limited applicability to minority women subjected to the constraints of both racism and sexism. In addition, black women have tended both to see racism as a more powerful cause of their subordinate position than sexism and to view the women's liberation movement with considerable distrust" (169).

WORKS CITED

Adams, Kate. "Academe's Dominance of Poetic Culture Narrows the Range of American Poetry." *Chronicle of Higher Education* 18 (May 1988): A48.

Atlas, James. "The Battle of the Books." *New York Times Magazine* (5 June 1988): 24–26, 72–74, 85.

Black Sister: Poetry by Black American Women. Ed. Erlene Stetson. Bloomington: Indiana UP, 1981.

Brownmiller, Susan. *Against Our Will: Men, Women, and Rape.* New York: Bantam, 1975.

Carriers of the Dream Wheel. Ed. Duane Niatum. New York: Harper, 1981.

Coleman, Wanda. *Heavy Daughter Blues.* Santa Barbara: Black Sparrow, 1987.

——— .*Imagoes.* Santa Barbara: Black Sparrow, 1983.

——— .*Mad Dog Black Lady.* Santa Barbara: Black Sparrow, 1979.

"Coleman, Wanda." *Contemporary Authors.* Gale Research 119. Ed. Hal May. Detroit: Gale, 1987: 66.

Dear Dark Faces. Ed. Helen Simcox. Los Angeles: Lotus, 1980.

A Geography of New Poets: An Anthology of New Poetry. Ed. Edward Field. New York: Bantam, 1979.

La Rue, Linda, J. M. "Black Liberation and Woman's Liberation." *Transaction* 8 (1970): 59–64.

Lewis, Diane K. "A Response to Inequality: Black Women, Racism, and Sexism." *The Signs Reader: Women, Gender, and Scholarship.* Ed. Elizabeth Abel and Emily Abel. Chicago: U of Chicago P, 1983. 169–91.

New Poetry of the American West. Ed. Peter Wild and Frank Graziano. Durango: Logbridge-Rhodes, 1982.

Southern, Eileen. *The Music of Black Americans: A History.* New York: Norton, 1971.

Sylvan Song: America Singing. Ed. Sylvia H. Manoltos. Northville: Sylvan, 1982.

Terrelonge, Pauline. "Feminist Consciousness in Black Women." *Women: A Feminist Perspective.* Ed. Joe Freeman. Palo Alto: Mayfield, 1984. 557–67.

Williams, Sherley A. "The Blues Roots of Contemporary Afro-American Poetry." *Chant of Saints: A Gathering of Afro-American Literature, Art, and Scholarship.* Ed. Michael S. Harper and Robert B. Stepto. Urbana: U of Illinois P, 1979. 123–36.

"Wolf." *Encyclopedia Britannica.* 1959 ed.

OPTIONS FOR WRITING

1. Read both Stacy Gevry's journal entry about Coleman's poetry and Magistrale's essay. What kinds of things does Gevry say? What kinds of things does Magistrale say? How do the writers support their claims? Do they both try to persuade their reader, or does the writing have a different purpose? If the writing is persuasive, what makes it so? Write a short essay exploring some of these questions.

2. Did your responses to Wanda Coleman differ from either Gevry's or Magistrale's? In what ways? Write your own response in a form of your choice.

3. If, as Terry Eagleton argues in the next reading, what we read in literature classes depends on a set of judgments that reflect cultural values and power, why is Wanda Coleman so overlooked by literary scholars? What about her poetry goes against our own values or expectations of literature? Write a critical essay that defends either her inclusion in or her exclusion from a literature class.

A Critic and a Writer

Terry Eagleton
INTRODUCTION: WHAT IS LITERATURE?

Terry Eagleton (b. 1943) is an English professor at the University of Pennsylvania whose work represents much of the newer, more radical thinking about literature, literary interpretation, and the relation of literature to culture. Like a number of other writers, he has questioned many of the assumptions that scholars had long taken for granted. In doing so, he has contributed to the current debates about what we read and teach in literature courses—what is called the literary canon—and about where we find the standards of value and meaning we use when we read.

The selection that follows is taken from his influential book Literary Theory: An Introduction. *In this provocative essay, Eagleton has a lot of fun with the seemingly simple, but very important, question of what "literature" is. He describes a number of different ways that scholars have tried to define literature in the past but shows that none is adequate. He argues that as a category, literature cannot be objectively defined according to an unchanging set of qualities or attributes. He concludes that, in the end, what counts as literature always depends on value judgments. While you read this essay, think about where these values come from and who decides on them.*

If there is such a thing as literary theory, then it would seem obvious that there is something called literature which it is the theory of. We can begin, then, by raising the question: what is literature?

There have been various attempts to define literature. You can define it, for example, as 'imaginative' writing in the sense of fiction—writing which is not literally true. But even the briefest reflection on what people commonly include under the heading of literature suggests that this will not do. Seventeenth-century English literature includes Shakespeare, Webster, Marvell and Milton; but it also stretches to the essays of Francis Bacon, the sermons of John Donne, Bunyan's spiritual autobiography and whatever it was that Sir Thomas Browne wrote. It might even at a pinch be taken to encompass Hobbes's *Leviathan* or Clarendon's *History of the Rebellion*. French seventeenth-century literature contains, along with Corneille and Racine, La Rochefoucauld's maxims, Bossuet's

funeral speeches, Boileau's treatise on poetry, Madame de Sévigné's let-
ters to her daughter and the philosophy of Descartes and Pascal.
Nineteenth-century English literature usually includes Lamb (though not
Bentham), Macaulay (but not Marx), Mill (but not Darwin or Herbert
Spencer).

A distinction between 'fact' and 'fiction', then, seems unlikely to get
us very far, not least because the distinction itself is often a questionable
one. It has been argued, for instance, that our own opposition between
'historical' and 'artistic' truth does not apply at all to the early Icelandic
sagas.[1] In the English late sixteenth and early seventeenth centuries, the
word 'novel' seems to have been used about both true and fictional
events, and even news reports were hardly to be considered factual.
Novels and news reports were neither clearly factual nor clearly fictional:
our own sharp discriminations between these categories simply did not
apply.[2] Gibbon no doubt thought that he was writing the historical
truth, and so perhaps did the authors of Genesis, but they are now read
as 'fact' by some and 'fiction' by others; Newman certainly thought his
theological meditations were true but is now for many readers 'literature'. Moreover, if 'literature' includes much 'factual' writing, it also
excludes quite a lot of fiction. *Superman* comic and Mills and Boon novels
are fictional but not generally regarded as literature, and certainly not as
Literature. If literature is 'creative' or 'imaginative' writing, does this
imply that history, philosophy and natural science are uncreative and
unimaginative?

Perhaps one needs a different kind of approach altogether. Perhaps
literature is definable not according to whether it is fictional or 'imaginative', but because it uses language in peculiar ways. On this theory,
literature is a kind of writing which, in the words of the Russian critic
Roman Jakobson, represents an 'organized violence committed on ordinary speech'. Literature transforms and intensifies ordinary language,
deviates systematically from everyday speech. If you approach me at a
bus stop and murmur 'Thou still unravished bride of quietness,' then I
am instantly aware that I am in the presence of the literary. I know this
because the texture, rhythm and resonance of your words are in excess of
their abstractable meaning — or, as the linguists might more technically
put it, there is a disproportion between the signifiers and the signifieds.
Your language draws attention to itself, flaunts its material being, as
statements like 'Don't you know the drivers are on strike?' do not.

This, in effect, was the definition of the 'literary' advanced by the
Russian formalists, who included in their ranks Viktor Shklovsky,
Roman Jakobson, Osip Brik, Yury Tynyanov, Boris Eichenbaum and
Boris Tomashevsky. The Formalists emerged in Russia in the years before the 1917 Bolshevik revolution, and flourished throughout the 1920s,
until they were effectively silenced by Stalinism. A militant, polemical
group of critics, they rejected the quasi-mystical symbolist doctrines
which had influenced literary criticism before them, and in a practical,
scientific spirit shifted attention to the material reality of the literary text

itself. Criticism should dissociate art from mystery and concern itself with how literary texts actually worked: literature was not pseudo-religion or psychology or sociology but a particular organization of language. It had its own specific laws, structures and devices, which were to be studied in themselves rather than reduced to something else. The literary work was neither a vehicle for ideas, a reflection of social reality nor the incarnation of some transcendental truth: it was a material fact, whose functioning could be analysed rather as one could examine a machine. It was made of words, not of objects or feelings, and it was a mistake to see it as the expression of an author's mind. Pushkin's *Eugene Onegin*, Osip Brik once airily remarked, would have been written even if Pushkin had not lived.

Formalism was essentially the application of linguistics to the study of literature; and because the linguistics in question were of a formal kind, concerned with the structures of language rather than with what one might actually say, the Formalists passed over the analysis of literary 'content' (where one might always be tempted into psychology or sociology) for the study of literary form. Far from seeing form as the expression of content, they stood the relationship on its head: content was merely the 'motivation' of form, an occasion or convenience for a particular kind of formal exercise. *Don Quixote* is not 'about' the character of that name: the character is just a device for holding together different kinds of narrative technique. *Animal Farm* for the Formalists would not be an allegory of Stalinism; on the contrary, Stalinism would simply provide a useful opportunity for the construction of an allegory. It was this perverse insistence which won for the Formalists their derogatory name from their antagonists; and though they did not deny that art had a relation to social reality — indeed some of them were closely associated with the Bolsheviks — they provocatively claimed that this relation was not the critic's business.

The Formalists started out by seeing the literary work as a more or less arbitrary assemblage of 'devices', and only later came to see these devices as interrelated elements or 'functions' within a total textual system. 'Devices' included sound, imagery, rhythm, syntax, metre, rhyme, narrative techniques, in fact the whole stock of formal literary elements; and what all of these elements had in common was their 'estranging' or 'defamiliarizing' effect. What was specific to literary language, what distinguished it from other forms of discourse, was that it 'deformed' ordinary language in various ways. Under the pressure of literary devices, ordinary language was intensified, condensed, twisted, telescoped, drawn out, turned on its head. It was language 'made strange'; and because of this estrangement, the everyday world was also suddenly made unfamiliar. In the routines of everyday speech, our perceptions of and responses to reality become stale, blunted, or, as the Formalists would say, 'automatized'. Literature, by forcing us into a dramatic awareness of language, refreshes these habitual responses and renders objects more 'perceptible'. By having to grapple with language in a more strenuous, self-conscious way than usual, the world which that language contains is vividly renewed. The poetry of Gerard Manley Hopkins might provide a particularly graphic example of this. Literary discourse estranges or alienates ordinary speech, but in doing so, paradoxically, brings us into a fuller, more intimate possession of experience. Most of the time we breathe in air without being conscious of it: like language, it is the very medium in which we move. But if the air is suddenly thickened or infected we are forced to attend to our breathing with new vigilance, and the effect of this may be a heightened experience of our bodily life. We read a scribbled note from a friend without paying much attention to its narrative structure; but if a story breaks off and begins again, switches constantly from one narrative level to another and delays its climax to keep us in suspense, we become freshly conscious of how it is constructed at the same time as our engagement with it may be intensified. The story, as the Formalists would argue, uses 'impeding' or 'retarding' devices to hold our attention; and in literary language, these devices are 'laid bare'. It was this which moved Viktor Shklovsky to remark mischievously of Laurence Sterne's *Tristram Shandy*, a novel which impedes its own story-line so much that it hardly gets off the ground, that it was 'the most typical novel in world literature'.

The Formalists, then, saw literary language as a set of deviations from a norm, a kind of linguistic violence: literature is a 'special' kind of language, in contrast to the 'ordinary' language we commonly use. But to spot a deviation implies being able to identify the norm from which it swerves. Though 'ordinary language' is a concept beloved of some Oxford philosophers, the ordinary language of Oxford philosophers has little in common with the ordinary language of Glaswegian dockers. The language both social groups use to write love letters usually differs from the way they talk to the local vicar. The idea that there is a single 'normal' language, a common currency shared equally by all members of society, is an illusion. Any actual language consists of a highly complex range of discourses, differentiated according to class, region, gender, status and so on, which can by no means be neatly unified into a single homogeneous linguistic community. One person's norm may be another's deviation: 'ginnel' for 'alleyway' may be poetic in Brighton but ordinary language in Barnsley. Even the most 'prosaic' text of the fifteenth century may sound 'poetic' to us today because of its archaism. If we were to stumble across an isolated scrap of writing from some long-vanished civilization, we could not tell whether it was 'poetry' or not merely by inspecting it, since we might have no access to that society's 'ordinary' discourses; and even if further research were to reveal that it was 'deviatory', this would still not prove that it was poetry as not all linguistic deviations are poetic. Slang, for example. We would not be able to tell just by looking at it that it was not a piece of 'realist' literature, without much more information about the way it actually functioned as a piece of writing within the society in question.

It is not that the Russian Formalists did not realize all this. They recognized that norms and deviations shifted around from one social or historical context to another—that 'poetry' in this sense depends on where you happen to be standing at the time. The fact that a piece of language was 'estranging' did not guarantee that it was always and everywhere so: it was estranging only against a certain normative linguistic background, and if this altered then the writing might cease to be perceptible as literary. If everyone used phrases like 'unravished bride of quietness' in ordinary pub conversation, this kind of language might cease to be poetic. For the Formalists, in other words, 'literariness' was a function of the *differential* relations between one sort of discourse and another; it was not an eternally given property. They were not out to define 'literature', but 'literariness'—special uses of language, which could be found in 'literary' texts but also in many places outside them. Anyone who believes that 'literature' can be defined by such special uses of language has to face the fact that there is more metaphor in Manchester than there is in Marvell. There is no 'literary' device—metonymy, synecdoche, litotes, chiasmus and so on—which is not quite intensively used in daily discourse.

Nevertheless, the Formalists still presumed that 'making strange' was the essence of the literary. It was just that they relativized this use of language, saw it as a matter of contrast between one type of speech and another. But what if I were to hear someone at the next pub table remark 'This is awfully squiggly handwriting!' Is this 'literary' or 'non-literary' language? As a matter of fact it is 'literary' language, because it comes from Knut Hamsun's novel *Hunger*. But how do I know that it is literary? It doesn't, after all, focus on any particular attention on itself as a verbal performance. One answer to the question of how I know that this is literary is that it comes from Knut Hamsun's novel *Hunger*. It is part of a text which I read as 'fictional', which announces itself as a 'novel', which may be put on university literature syllabuses and so on. The *context* tells me that it is literary; but the language itself has no inherent properties or qualities which might distinguish it from other kinds of discourse, and someone might well say this in a pub without being admired for their literary dexterity. To think of literature as the Formalists do is really to think of all literature as *poetry*. Significantly, when the Formalists came to consider prose writing, they often simply extended to it the kinds of technique they had used with poetry. But literature is usually judged to contain much besides poetry—to include, for example, realist or naturalistic writing which is not linguistically self-conscious or self-exhibiting in any striking way. People sometimes call writing 'fine' precisely because it *doesn't* draw undue attention to itself: they admire its laconic plainness or low-keyed sobriety. And what about jokes, football chants and slogans, newspaper headlines, advertisements, which are often verbally flamboyant but not generally classified as literature?

Another problem with the 'estrangement' case is that there is no kind of writing which cannot, given sufficient ingenuity, be read as estranging. Consider a prosaic, quite unambiguous statement like the one sometimes seen in the London underground system: 'Dogs must be carried on the escalator.' This is not perhaps quite as unambiguous as it seems at first sight: does it mean that you *must* carry a dog on the escalator? Are you likely to be banned from the escalator unless you can find some stray mongrel to clutch in your arms on the way up? Many apparently straightforward notices contain such ambiguities: 'Refuse to be put in this basket,' for instance, or the British road-sign 'Way Out' as read by a Californian. But even leaving such troubling ambiguities aside, it is surely obvious that the underground notice could be read as literature. One could let oneself be arrested by the abrupt, minatory *staccato* of the first ponderous monosyllables; find one's mind drifting, by the time it had reached the rich allusiveness of 'carried', to suggestive resonances of helping lame dogs through life; and perhaps even detect in the very lilt and inflection of the word 'escalator' a miming of the rolling, up-and-down motion of the thing itself. This may well be a fruitless sort of pursuit, but it is not significantly more fruitless than claiming to hear the cut and thrust of the rapiers in some poetic description of a duel, and it at least has the advantage of suggesting that 'literature' may be at least as much a question of what people do to writing as of what writing does to them.

But even if someone were to read the notice in this way, it would still be a matter of reading it as *poetry*, which is only part of what is usually included in literature. Let us therefore consider another way of 'misreading' the sign which might move us a little beyond this. Imagine a late-night drunk doubled over the escalator handrail who reads the notice with laborious attentiveness for several minutes and then mutters to himself 'How true!' What kind of mistake is occurring here? What the drunk is doing, in fact, is taking the sign as some statement of general, even cosmic significance. By applying certain conventions of reading to its words, he prises them loose from their immediate context and generalizes them beyond their pragmatic purpose to something of wider and probably deeper import. This would certainly seem to be one operation involved in what people call literature. When the poet tells us that his love is like a red rose, we know by the very fact that he puts this statement in metre that we are not supposed to ask whether he actually had a lover who for some bizarre reason seemed to him to resemble a rose. He is telling us something about women and love in general. Literature, then, we might say, is 'non-pragmatic' discourse: unlike biology textbooks and notes to the milkman it serves no immediate practical purpose, but is to be taken as referring to a general state of affairs. Sometimes, though not always, it may employ peculiar language as though to make this fact obvious — to signal that what is at stake is a *way of talking* about a woman, rather than any particular real-life woman. This focusing on the way of talking, rather than on the reality of what

is talked about, is sometimes taken to indicate that we mean by literature a kind of *self-referential* language, a language which talks about itself.

There are, however, problems with this way of defining literature
too. For one thing, it would probably have come as a surprise to George
Orwell to hear that his essays were to be read as though the topics he
discussed were less important than the way he discussed them. In much
that is classified as literature, the truth-value and practical relevance of
what is said *is* considered important to the overall effect. But even if
treating discourse 'non-pragmatically' is part of what is meant by 'literature', then it follows from this 'definition' that literature cannot in fact
be 'objectively' defined. It leaves the definition of literature up to how
somebody decides to *read*, not to the nature of what is written. There
are certain kinds of writing — poems, plays, novels — which are fairly obviously intended to be 'non-pragmatic' in this sense, but this does not
guarantee that they will actually be read in this way. I might well read
Gibbon's account of the Roman empire not because I am misguided
enough to believe that it will be reliably informative about ancient Rome
but because I enjoy Gibbon's prose style, or revel in images of human
corruption whatever their historical source. But I might read Robert
Burns's poem because it is not clear to me, as a Japanese horticulturalist,
whether or not the red rose flourished in eighteenth-century Britain.
This, it will be said, is not reading it 'as literature'; but am I reading
Orwell's essays as literature only if I generalize what he says about the
Spanish civil war to some cosmic utterance about human life? It is true
that many of the works studied as literature in academic institutions
were 'constructed' to be read as literature, but it is also true that many
of them were not. A piece of writing may start off life as history or
philosophy and then come to be ranked as literature; or it may start off
as literature and then come to be valued for its archaeological significance. Some texts are born literary, some achieve literariness, and some
have literariness thrust upon them. Breeding in this respect may count
for a good deal more than birth. What matters may not be where you
came from but how people treat you. If they decide that you are literature
then it seems that you are, irrespective of what you thought you were.

In this sense, one can think of literature less as some inherent quality or set of qualities displayed by certain kinds of writing all the way
from *Beowulf* to Virginia Woolf, than as a number of ways in which
people *relate themselves* to writing. It would not be easy to isolate, from
all that has been variously called 'literature', some constant set of inherent features. In fact it would be as impossible as trying to identify the
single distinguishing feature which all games have in common. There is
no 'essence' of literature whatsoever. Any bit of writing may be read
'non-pragmatically', if that is what reading a text as literature means,
just as any writing may be read 'poetically'. If I pore over the railway
timetable not to discover a train connection but to stimulate in myself
general reflections on the speed and complexity of modern existence,
then I might be said to be reading it as literature. John M. Ellis has

argued that the term 'literature' operates rather like the word 'weed': weeds are not particular kinds of plant, but just any kind of plant which for some reason or another a gardener does not want around.[3] Perhaps 'literature' means something like the opposite: any kind of writing which for some reason or another somebody values highly. As the philosophers might say, 'literature' and 'weed' are *functional* rather than *ontological* terms: they tell us about what we do, not about the fixed being of things. They tell us about the role of a text or a thistle in a social context, its relations with and differences from its surroundings, the ways it behaves, the purposes it may be put to and the human practices clustered around it. 'Literature' is in this sense a purely formal, empty sort of definition. Even if we claim that it is a non-pragmatic treatment of language, we have still not arrived at an 'essence' of literature because this is also so of other linguistic practices such as jokes. In any case, it is far from clear that we can discriminate neatly between 'practical' and 'non-practical' ways of relating ourselves to language. Reading a novel for pleasure obviously differs from reading a road sign for information, but how about reading a biology textbook to improve your mind? Is that a 'pragmatic' treatment of language or not? In many societies, 'literature' has served highly practical functions such as religious ones; distinguishing sharply between 'practical' and 'non-practical' may only be possible in a society like ours, where literature has ceased to have much practical function at all. We may be offering as a general definition a sense of the 'literary' which is in fact historically specific.

We have still not discovered the secret, then, of why Lamb, Macaulay and Mill are literature but not, generally speaking, Bentham, Marx and Darwin. Perhaps the simple answer is that the first three are examples of 'fine writing', whereas the last three are not. This answer has the disadvantage of being largely untrue, at least in my judgement, but it has the advantage of suggesting that by and large people term 'literature' writing which they think is *good*. An obvious objection to this is that if it were entirely true there would be no such thing as 'bad literature'. I may consider Lamb and Macaulay overrated, but that does not necessarily mean that I stop regarding them as literature. You may consider Raymond Chandler 'good of his kind', but not exactly literature. On the other hand, if Macaulay were a *really* bad writer — if he had no grasp at all of grammar and seemed interested in nothing but white mice — then people might well not call his work literature at all, even bad literature. Value-judgements would certainly seem to have a lot to do with what is judged literature and what isn't — not necessarily in the sense that writing has to be 'fine' to be literary, but that it has to be *of the kind* that is judged fine: it may be an inferior example of a generally valued mode. Nobody would bother to say that a bus ticket was an example of inferior literature, but someone might well say that the poetry of Ernest Dowson was. The term 'fine writing', or *belles lettres*, is in this sense ambiguous: it denotes a sort of writing which is generally highly regarded, while not necessarily committing you to the opinion that a particular specimen of it is 'good'.

With this reservation, the suggestion that 'literature' is a highly valued kind of writing is an illuminating one. But it has one fairly devastating consequence. It means that we can drop once and for all the illusion that the category 'literature' is 'objective', in the sense of being eternally given and immutable. Anything can be literature, and anything which is regarded as unalterably and unquestionably literature—Shakespeare, for example—can cease to be literature. Any belief that the study of literature is the study of a stable, well-definable entity, as entomology is the study of insects, can be abandoned as a chimera. Some kinds of fiction are literature and some are not; some literature is fictional and some is not; some literature is verbally self-regarding, while some highly-wrought rhetoric is not literature. Literature, in the sense of a set of works of assured and unalterable value, distinguished by certain shared inherent properties, does not exist. When I use the words 'literary' and 'literature' from here on in this book, then, I place them under an invisible crossing-out mark, to indicate that these terms will not really do but that we have no better ones at the moment.

The reason why it follows from the definition of literature as highly valued writing that it is not a stable entity is that value-judgements are notoriously variable. 'Times change, values don't,' announces an advertisement for a daily newspaper, as though we still believed in killing off infirm infants or putting the mentally ill on public show. Just as people may treat a work as philosophy in one century and as literature in the next, or vice versa, so they may change their minds about what writing they consider valuable. They many even change their minds about the grounds they use for judging what is valuable and what is not. This, as I have suggested, does not necessarily mean that they will refuse the title of literature to a work which they have come to deem inferior: they may still call it literature, meaning roughly that it belongs to the *type* of writing which they generally value. But it does mean that the so-called 'literary canon', the unquestioned 'great tradition' of the 'national literature', has to be recognized as a *construct*, fashioned by particular people for particular reasons at a certain time. There is no such thing as a literary work or tradition which is valuable *in itself*, regardless of what anyone might have said or come to say about it. 'Value' is a transitive term: it means whatever is valued by certain people in specific situations, according to particular criteria and in the light of given purposes. It is thus quite possible that, given a deep enough transformation of our history, we may in the future produce a society which was unable to get anything at all out of Shakespeare. His works might simply seem desperately alien, full of styles of thought and feeling which such a society found limited or irrelevant. In such a situation, Shakespeare would be no more valuable than much present-day graffiti. And though many people would consider such a social condition tragically impoverished, it seems to me dogmatic not to entertain the possibility that it might arise rather from a general human enrichment. Karl Marx was troubled by the question of why ancient Greek art retained an 'eternal charm', even though the social conditions which produced it had long passed; but how do we know that it will remain 'eternally' charming, since history has not yet ended? Let us imagine that by dint of some deft archaeological research we discovered a great deal more about what ancient Greek tragedy actually meant to its original audiences, recognized that these concerns were utterly remote from our own, and began to read the plays again in the light of this deepened knowledge. One result might be that we stopped enjoying them. We might come to see that we had enjoyed them previously because we were unwittingly reading them in the light of our own preoccupations; once this became less possible, the drama might cease to speak at all significantly to us.

The fact that we always interpret literary works to some extent in the light of our own concerns — indeed that in one sense of 'our own concerns' we are incapable of doing anything else — might be one reason why certain works of literature seem to retain their value across the centuries. It may be, of course, that we still share many preoccupations with the work itself; but it may also be that people have not actually been valuing the 'same' work at all, even though they may think they have. 'Our' Homer is not identical with the Homer of the Middle Ages, nor 'our' Shakespeare with that of his contemporaries; it is rather that different historical periods have constructed a 'different' Homer and Shakespeare for their own purposes, and found in these texts elements to value or devalue, though not necessarily the same ones. All literary works, in other words, are 'rewritten', if only unconsciously, by the societies which read them; indeed there is no reading of a work which is not also a 're-writing'. No work, and no current evaluation of it, can simply be extended to new groups of people without being changed, perhaps almost unrecognizably, in the process; and this is one reason why what counts as literature is a notably unstable affair.

I do not mean that it is unstable because value-judgements are 'subjective'. According to this view, the world is divided between solid facts 'out there' like Grand Central station, and arbitrary value-judgements 'in here' such as liking bananas or feeling that the tone of a Yeats poem veers from defensive hectoring to grimly resilient resignation. Facts are public and unimpeachable, values are private and gratuitous. There is an obvious difference between recounting a fact, such as 'This cathedral was built in 1612,' and registering a value-judgement, such as 'This cathedral is a magnificent specimen of baroque architecture.' But suppose I made the first kind of statement while showing an overseas visitor around England, and found that it puzzled her considerably. Why, she might ask, do you keep telling me the dates of the foundation of all these buildings? Why this obsession with origins? In the society I live in, she might go on, we keep no record at all of such events: we classify our buildings instead according to whether they face north-west or south-east. What this might do would be to demonstrate part of the unconscious system of value-judgements which underlies my own descriptive statements. Such value-judgements are not necessarily of the same kind as 'This cathedral is a magnificent specimen of baroque architecture,' but they are value-judgements nonetheless, and no factual pronouncement I make can escape them. Statements of fact are after all *statements*, which presumes a number of questionable judgements: that those statements are worth making, perhaps more worth making than certain others, that I am the sort of person entitled to make them and perhaps able to guarantee their truth, that you are the kind of person worth making them to, that something useful is accomplished by making them, and so on. A pub conversation may well transmit information, but what also bulks large in such dialogue is a strong element of what linguists would call the 'phatic', a concern with the act of communication itself. In chatting to you about the weather I am also signalling that I regard conversation with you as valuable, that I consider you a worthwhile person to talk to, that I am not myself anti-social or about to embark on a detailed critique of your personal appearance.

In this sense, there is no possibility of a wholly disinterested statement. Of course stating when a cathedral was built is reckoned to be more disinterested in our own culture than passing an opinion about its architecture, but one could also imagine situations in which the former statement would be more 'value-laden' than the latter. Perhaps 'baroque' and 'magnificent' have come to be more or less synonymous, whereas only a stubborn rump of us cling to the belief that the date when a building was founded is significant, and my statement is taken as a coded way of signalling this partisanship. All of our descriptive statements move within an often invisible network of value-categories, and indeed without such categories we would have nothing to say to each other at all. It is not just as though we have something called factual knowledge which may then be distorted by particular interests and judgements, although this is certainly possible; it is also that without particular interests we would have no knowledge at all, because we would not see the point of bothering to get to know anything. Interests are *constitutive* of our knowledge, not merely prejudices which imperil it. The claim that knowledge should be 'value-free' is itself a value-judgement.

It may well be that a liking for bananas is a merely private matter, though this is in fact questionable. A thorough analysis of my tastes in food would probably reveal how deeply relevant they are to certain formative experiences in early childhood, to my relations with my parents and siblings and to a good many other cultural factors which are quite as social and 'non-subjective' as railway stations. This is even more true of that fundamental structure of beliefs and interests which I am born into as a member of a particular society, such as the belief that I should try to keep in good health, that differences of sexual role are rooted in human biology or that human beings are more important than crocodiles. We may disagree on this or that, but we can only do so because we share certain 'deep' ways of seeing and valuing which are bound up with our social life, and which could not be changed without transforming that life. Nobody will penalize me heavily if I dislike a particular Donne poem, but if I argue that Donne is not literature at all then in certain circumstances I might risk losing my job. I am free to vote Labour or Conservative, but if I try to act on the belief that this choice itself merely masks a deeper prejudice—the prejudice that the meaning of democracy is confined to putting a cross on a ballot paper every few years—then in certain unusual circumstances I might end up in prison.

The largely concealed structure of values which informs and underlies our factual statements is part of what is meant by 'ideology'. By 'ideology' I mean, roughly, the ways in which what we say and believe connects with the power-structure and power-relations of the society we live in. It follows from such a rough definition of ideology that not all of our underlying judgements and categories can usefully be said to be ideological. It is deeply ingrained in us to imagine ourselves moving forwards into the future (at least one other society sees itself as moving backwards into it), but though this way of seeing *may* connect significantly with the power-structure of our society, it need not always and everywhere do so. I do not mean by 'ideology' simply the deeply entrenched, often unconscious beliefs which people hold; I mean more particularly those modes of feeling, valuing, perceiving and believing which have some kind of relation to the maintenance and reproduction of social power. The fact that such beliefs are by no means merely private quirks may be illustrated by a literary example.

In his famous study *Practical Criticism* (1929), the Cambridge critic I. A. Richards sought to demonstrate just how whimsical and subjective literary value-judgements could actually be by giving his undergraduates a set of poems, withholding from them the titles and authors' names, and asking them to evaluate them. The resulting judgements, notoriously, were highly variable: time-honoured poets were marked down and obscure authors celebrated. To my mind, however, much the most interesting aspect of this project, and one apparently quite invisible to Richards himself, is just how tight a consensus of unconscious valuations underlies these particular differences of opinion. Reading Richards' undergraduates' accounts of literary works, one is struck by the habits of perception and interpretation which they spontaneously share—what they expect literature to be, what assumptions they bring to a poem and what fulfilments they anticipate they will derive from it. None of this is really surprising: for all the participants in this experiment were, presumably, young, white, upper- or upper middle-class, privately educated English people of the 1920s, and how they responded to a poem

depended on a good deal more than purely 'literary' factors. Their critical responses were deeply entwined with their broader prejudices and
beliefs. This is not a matter of *blame:* there is no critical response which
is not so entwined, and thus no such thing as a 'pure' literary critical
judgement or interpretation. If anybody is to be blamed it is I. A.
Richards himself, who as a young, white, upper-middle-class male Cambridge don was unable to objectify a context of interests which he himself largely shared, and was thus unable to recognize fully that local,
'subjective' differences of evaluation work within a particular, socially
structured way of perceiving the world.

If it will not do to see literature as an 'objective', descriptive category, neither will it do to say that literature is just what people whimsi-
cally choose to call literature. For there is nothing at all whimsical about
such kinds of value-judgement: they have their roots in deeper structures of belief which are as apparently unshakeable as the Empire State
building. What we have uncovered so far, then, is not only that literature does not exist in the sense that insects do, and that the value-judgements by which it is constituted are historically variable, but that these
value-judgements themselves have a close relation to social ideologies.
They refer in the end not simply to private taste, but to the assumptions
by which certain social groups exercise and maintain power over others.
If this seems a far-fetched assertion, a matter of private prejudice, we
may test it out by an account of the rise of 'literature' in England.

NOTES

[1] See M. I. Steblin-Kamenskij. *The Saga Mind* (Odense, 1973).

[2] See Lennard J. Davis. "A Social History of Fact and Fiction: Authorial Disavowal in
the Early English Novel," in Edward W. Said (ed.), *Literature and Society* (Baltimore and
London, 1980).

[3] *The Theory of Literary Criticism: A Logical Analysis* (Berkeley, 1974), pp. 37–42.

OPTIONS FOR WRITING

1. If you did Writing 5 from earlier in this chapter, go back to your journal
entry and compare your definition of literature with those Eagleton describes. Which of the strategies for defining literature did you follow? Has
Eagleton's essay changed your mind about what counts as literature? Why
or why not? Write a response to your previous journal entry.

2. When Eagleton says that any definition of "literature" depends on value
judgements, he opens the door to a whole range of troubles. What are
some of the problems for thinking about literature that follow from this
definition, and how does Eagleton suggest that we solve them? In a
speculative essay, explore your own answers to these questions.

3. Pick a reading from one of the other chapters in this book, and see if
you can make a case that it should be considered a piece of literature.

Alice Walker
IN SEARCH OF OUR MOTHERS' GARDENS

*Alice Walker (b. 1944) is a prominent and popular contemporary
writer. She is the author of the novels* The Color Purple *and*
Medallion *as well as many short stories and essays. Much of
Walker's work focuses on the lives of African-American women —
their courage and creativity despite the great hardships they have
faced.*

*In this essay, she addresses the question of how black women
have maintained their creativity despite centuries of oppression. What
happened to slave women who were born with artistic gifts? To answer this question, Walker looks to the life of her own mother — a
poor, hard-working woman who was famous for her beautiful flower
gardens. Walker argues that we may just have been looking in the
wrong places for "art" when it was all around us, in quilts, in unwritten stories, and in flower gardens. Walker asks us to think about
what keeps creativity alive, about what we count as artistic expression, and about the courage and resilience of generations of African-
American women.*

I described her own nature and temperament. Told how they
needed a larger life for their expression. . . . I pointed out that
in lieu of proper channels, her emotions had overflowed into
paths that dissipated them. I talked, beautifully I thought,
about an art that would be born, an art that would open the
way for women the likes of her. I asked her to hope, and build
up an inner life against the coming of that day. . . . I sang, with
a strange quiver in my voice, a promise song.

—Jean Toomer, "Avey," Cane

The poet speaking to a prostitute who falls asleep while he's talking —

When the poet Jean Toomer walked through the South in the early
twenties, he discovered a curious thing: black women whose spirituality
was so intense, so deep, so *unconscious*, that they were themselves unaware of the richness they held. They stumbled blindly through their
lives: creatures so abused and mutilated in body, so dimmed and confused by pain, that they considered themselves unworthy even of hope.
In the selfless abstractions their bodies became to the men who used
them, they became more than "sexual objects," more even than mere
women: they became "Saints." Instead of being perceived as whole persons, their bodies became shrines: what was thought to be their minds

became temples suitable for worship. These crazy Saints stared out at
the world, wildly, like lunatics—or quietly, like suicides; and the "God"
that was in their gaze was as mute as a great stone.

Who were these Saints? These crazy, loony, pitiful women?

Some of them, without a doubt, were our mothers and grandmothers.

In the still heat of the post-Reconstruction South, this is how they
seemed to Jean Toomer: exquisite butterflies trapped in an evil honey,
toiling away their lives in an era, a century, that did not acknowledge
them, except as "the *mule* of the world." They dreamed dreams that no
one knew—not even themselves, in any coherent fashion—and saw visions no one could understand. They wandered or sat about the countryside crooning lullabies to ghosts, and drawing the mother of Christ in
charcoal on courthouse walls.

They forced their minds to desert their bodies and their striving
spirits sought to rise, like frail whirlwinds from the hard red clay. And
when those frail whirlwinds fell, in scattered particles, upon the ground,
no one mourned. Instead, men lit candles to celebrate the emptiness
that remained, as people do who enter a beautiful but vacant space to
resurrect a God.

Our mothers and grandmothers, some of them: moving to music
not yet written. And they waited.

They waited for a day when the unknown thing that was in them
would be made known; but guessed, somehow in their darkness, that
on the day of their revelation they would be long dead. Therefore to
Toomer they walked, and even ran, in slow motion. For they were
going nowhere immediate, and the future was not yet within their
grasp. And men took our mothers and grandmothers, "but got no pleasure from it." So complex was their passion and their calm.

To Toomer, they lay vacant and fallow as autumn fields, with harvest time never in sight: and he saw them enter loveless marriages,
without joy; and become prostitutes, without resistance; and become
mothers of children, without fulfillment.

For these grandmothers and mothers of ours were not Saints, but
Artists; driven to a numb and bleeding madness by the springs of
creativity in them for which there was no release. They were Creators,
who lived lives of spiritual waste, because they were so rich in spirituality—which is the basis of Art—that the strain of enduring their unused
and unwanted talent drove them insane. Throwing away this spirituality
was their pathetic attempt to lighten the soul to a weight their work-
worn, sexually abused bodies could bear.

What did it mean for a black woman to be an artist in our grandmothers' time? In our great-grandmothers' day? It is a question with an
answer cruel enough to stop the blood.

Did you have a genius of a great-great-grandmother who died
under some ignorant and depraved white overseer's lash? Or was she

required to bake biscuits for a lazy backwater tramp, when she cried out in her soul to paint watercolors of sunsets, or the rain falling on the green and peaceful pasturelands? Or was her body broken and forced to bear children (who were more often than not sold away from her)— eight, ten, fifteen, twenty children—when her one joy was the thought of modeling heroic figures of rebellion, in stone or clay?

How was the creativity of the black woman kept alive, year after year and century after century, when for most of the years black people have been in America, it was a punishable crime for a black person to read or write? And the freedom to paint, to sculpt, to expand the mind with action did not exist. Consider, if you can bear to imagine it, what might have been the result if singing, too, had been forbidden by law. Listen to the voices of Bessie Smith, Billie Holiday, Nina Simone, Roberta Flack, and Aretha Franklin, among others, and imagine those voices muzzled for life. Then you may begin to comprehend the lives of our "crazy," "Sainted" mothers and grandmothers. The agony of the lives of women who might have been Poets, Novelists, Essayists, and Short-Story Writers (over a period of centuries), who died with their real gifts stifled within them.

And, if this were the end of the story, we would have cause to cry out in my paraphrase of Okot p'Bitek's great poem:

> O, my clanswomen
> Let us all cry together!
> Come,
> Let us mourn the death of our mother,
> The death of a Queen
> The ash that was produced
> By a great fire!
> O, this homestead is utterly dead
> Close the gates
> With *lacari* thorns,
> For our mother
> The creator of the Stool is lost!
> And all the young women
> Have perished in the wilderness!

But this is not the end of the story, for all the young women—our mothers and grandmothers, *ourselves*—have not perished in the wilderness. And if we ask ourselves why, and search for and find the answer, we will know beyond all efforts to erase it from our minds, just exactly who, and of what, we black American women are.

One example, perhaps the most pathetic, most misunderstood one, can provide a backdrop for our mothers' work: Phillis Wheatley, a slave in the 1700s.

Virginia Woolf, in her book *A Room of One's Own*, wrote that in order for a woman to write fiction she must have two things, certainly:

a room of her own (with key and lock) and enough money to support herself.

What then are we to make of Phillis Wheatley, a slave, who owned not even herself? This sickly, frail black girl who required a servant of her own at times—her health was so precarious—and who, had she been white, would have been easily considered the intellectual superior of all the women and most of the men in the society of her day.

Virginia Woolf wrote further, speaking of course not of our Phillis, that "any woman born with a great gift in the sixteenth century [insert "eighteenth century," insert "black woman," insert "born or made a slave"] would certainly have gone crazed, shot herself, or ended her days in some lonely cottage outside the village, half witch, half wizard [insert "Saint"], feared and mocked at. For it needs little skill and psychology to be sure that a highly gifted girl who had tried to use her gift for poetry would have been so thwarted and hindered by contrary instincts [add "chains, guns, the lash, the ownership of one's body by someone else, submission to an alien religion"], that she must have lost her health and sanity to a certainty."

The key words, as they relate to Phillis, are "contrary instincts." For when we read the poetry of Phillis Wheatley—as when we read the novels of Nella Larsen or the oddly false-sounding autobiography of that freest of all black women writers, Zora Hurston—evidence of "contrary instincts" is everywhere. Her loyalties were completely divided, as was, without question, her mind.

But how could this be otherwise? Captured at seven, a slave of wealthy, doting whites who instilled in her the "savagery" of the Africa they "rescued" her from . . . one wonders if she was even able to remember her homeland as she had known it, or as it really was.

Yet, because she did try to use her gift for poetry in a world that made her a slave, she was "so thwarted and hindered by . . . contrary instincts, that she . . . lost her health. . . . " In the last years of her brief life, burdened not only with the need to express her gift but also with a penniless, friendless "freedom" and several small children for whom she was forced to do strenuous work to feed, she lost her health, certainly. Suffering from malnutrition and neglect and who knows what mental agonies, Phillis Wheatley died.

So torn by "contrary instincts" was black, kidnapped, enslaved Phillis that her description of "the Goddess"—as she poetically called the Liberty she did not have—is ironically, cruelly humorous. And, in fact, has held Phillis up to ridicule for more than a century. It is usually read prior to hanging Phillis's memory as that of a fool. She wrote:

> The Goddess comes, she moves divinely fair,
> Olive and laurel binds her *golden* hair.
> Wherever shines this native of the skies,
> Unnumber'd charms and recent graces rise. [My italics]

It is obvious that Phillis, the slave, combed the "Goddess's" hair every morning; prior, perhaps, to bringing in the milk, or fixing her mistress's lunch. She took her imagery from the one thing she saw elevated above all others.

With the benefit of hindsight we ask, "How could she?"

But at last, Phillis, we understand. No more snickering when your stiff, struggling, ambivalent lines are forced on us. We know now that you were not an idiot or a traitor; only a sickly little black girl, snatched from your home and country and made a slave; a woman who still struggled to sing the song that was your gift, although in a land of barbarians who praised you for your bewildered tongue. It is not so much what you sang, as that you kept alive, in so many of our ancestors, *the notion of song.*

Black women are called, in the folklore that so aptly identifies one's status in society, "the *mule* of the world," because we have been handed the burdens that everyone else—*everyone* else—refused to carry. We have also been called "Matriarchs," "Superwomen," and "Mean and Evil Bitches." Not to mention "Castraters" and "Sapphire's Mama." When we have pleaded for understanding, our character has been distorted; when we have asked for simple caring, we have been handed empty inspirational appellations, then stuck in the farthest corner. When we have asked for love, we have been given children. In short, even our plainer gifts, our labors of fidelity and love, have been knocked down our throats. To be an artist and a black woman, even today, lowers our status in many respects, rather than raises it: and yet, artists we will be.

Therefore we must fearlessly pull out of ourselves and look at and identify with our lives the living creativity some of our great-grandmothers were not allowed to know. I stress *some* of them because it is well known that the majority of our great-grandmothers knew, even without "knowing" it, the reality of their spirituality, even if they didn't recognize it beyond what happened in the singing at church—and they never had any intention of giving it up.

How they did it—those millions of black women who were not Phillis Wheatley, or Lucy Terry or Frances Harper or Zora Hurston or Nella Larsen or Bessie Smith; or Elizabeth Catlett, or Katherine Dunham, either—brings me to the title of this essay, "In Search of Our Mothers' Gardens," which is a personal account that is yet shared, in its theme and its meaning, by all of us. I found, while thinking about the far-reaching world of the creative black woman, that often the truest answer to a question that really matters can be found very close.

In the late 1920s my mother ran away from home to marry my father. Marriage, if not running away, was expected of seventeen-year-old girls. By the time she was twenty, she had two children and was pregnant with a third. Five children later, I was born. And this is how I came to know my mother: she seemed a large, soft, loving-eyed woman who was rarely impatient in our home. Her quick, violent temper was on view only a few times a year, when she battled with the white landlord who had the misfortune to suggest to her that her children did not need to go to school.

She made all the clothes we wore, even my brothers' overalls. She made all the towels and sheets we used. She spent the summers canning vegetables and fruits. She spent the winter evenings making quilts enough to cover all our beds.

During the "working" day, she labored beside—not behind—my father in the fields. Her day began before sunup, and did not end until late at night. There was never a moment for her to sit down, undisturbed, to unravel her own private thoughts; never a time free from interruption—by work or the noisy inquiries of her many children. And yet, it is to my mother—and all our mothers who were not famous—that I went in search of the secret of what has fed that muzzled and often mutilated, but vibrant, creative spirit that the black woman has inherited, and that pops out in wild and unlikely places to this day.

But when, you will ask, did my overworked mother have time to know or care about feeding the creative spirit?

The answer is so simple that many of us have spent years discovering it. We have constantly looked high, when we should have looked high—and low.

For example: in the Smithsonian Institution in Washington, D.C., there hangs a quilt unlike any other in the world. In fanciful, inspired, and yet simple and identifiable figures, it portrays the story of the Crucifixion. It is considered rare, beyond price. Though it follows no known pattern of quilt-making, and though it is made of bits and pieces of worthless rags, it is obviously the work of a person of powerful imagination and deep spiritual feeling. Below this quilt I saw a note that says it was made by "an anonymous Black woman in Alabama, a hundred years ago."

If we could locate this "anonymous" black woman from Alabama, she would turn out to be one of our grandmothers—an artist who left her mark in the only materials she could afford, and in the only medium her position in society allowed her to use.

As Virginia Woolf wrote further, in *A Room of One's Own:*

> Yet genius of a sort must have existed among women as it must have existed among the working class. [Change this to "slaves" and "the wives and daughters of sharecroppers."] Now and again an Emily Brontë or a Robert Burns [change this to "a Zora Hurston or a Richard Wright"] blazes out and proves its presence. But certainly it never got itself on to paper. When, however, one reads of a witch being ducked, of a woman possessed by devils [or "Sainthood"], of a wise woman selling herbs [our root work-

ers], or even a very remarkable man who had a mother, then I think we are on the track of a lost novelist, a suppressed poet, of some mute and inglorious Jane Austen. . . . Indeed, I would venture to guess that Anon, who wrote so many poems without signing them, was often a woman. . . .

And so our mothers and grandmothers have, more often than not anonymously, handed on the creative spark, the seed of the flower they themselves never hoped to see: or like a sealed letter they could not plainly read.

And so it is, certainly, with my own mother. Unlike "Ma" Rainey's songs, which retained their creator's name even while blasting forth from Bessie Smith's mouth, no song or poem will bear my mother's name. Yet so many of the stories that I write, that we all write, are my mother's stories. Only recently did I fully realize this: that through years of listening to my mother's stories of her life, I have absorbed not only the stories themselves, but something of the manner in which she spoke, something of the urgency that involves the knowledge that her stories—like her life—must be recorded. It is probably for this reason that so much of what I have written is about characters whose counterparts in real life are so much older than I am.

But the telling of these stories, which came from my mother's lips as naturally as breathing, was not the only way my mother showed herself as an artist. For stories, too, were subject to being distracted, to dying without conclusion. Dinners must be started, and cotton must be gathered before the big rains. The artist that was and is my mother showed itself to me only after many years. This is what I finally noticed:

Like Mem, a character in *The Third Life of Grange Copeland*, my mother adorned with flowers whatever shabby house we were forced to live in. And not just your typical straggly country stand of zinnias, either. She planted ambitious gardens—and still does—with over fifty different varieties of plants that bloom profusely from early March until late November. Before she left home for the fields, she watered her flowers, chopped up the grass, and laid out new beds. When she returned from the fields she might divide clumps of bulbs, dig a cold pit, uproot and replant roses, or prune branches from her taller bushes or trees—until night came and it was too dark to see.

Whatever she planted grew as if by magic, and her fame as a grower of flowers spread over three counties. Because of her creativity with her flowers, even my memories of poverty are seen through a screen of blooms—sunflowers, petunias, roses, dahlias, forsythia, spirea, delphiniums, verbena . . . and on and on.

And I remember people coming to my mother's yard to be given cuttings from her flowers; I hear again the praise showered on her because whatever rocky soil she landed on, she turned into a garden. A garden so brilliant with colors, so original in its design, so magnificent with life and creativity, that to this day people drive by our house in

Georgia—perfect strangers and imperfect strangers—and ask to stand or walk among my mother's art.

I notice that it is only when my mother is working in her flowers that she is radiant, almost to the point of being invisible—except as Creator: hand and eye. She is involved in work her soul must have. Ordering the universe in the image of her personal conception of Beauty.

Her face, as she prepares the Art that is her gift, is a legacy of respect she leaves to me, for all that illuminates and cherishes life. She has handed down respect for the possibilities—and the will to grasp them.

For her, so hindered and intruded upon in so many ways, being an artist has still been a daily part of her life. This ability to hold on, even in very simple ways, is work black women have done for a very long time.

This poem is not enough, but it is something, for the woman who literally covered the holes in our walls with sunflowers:

> They were women then
> My mama's generation
> Husky of voice—Stout of
> Step
> With fists as well as
> Hands
> How they battered down
> Doors
> And ironed
> Starched white
> Shirts
> How they led
> Armies
> Headragged Generals
> Across mined
> Fields
> Booby-trapped
> Kitchens
> To discover books
> Desks
> A place for us
> How they knew what we
> *Must* know
> Without knowing a page
> Of it
> Themselves.

Guided by my heritage of a love of beauty and a respect for strength—in search of my mother's garden, I found my own.

And perhaps in Africa over two hundred years ago, there was just such a mother; perhaps she painted vivid and daring decorations in oranges and yellows and greens on the walls of her hut; perhaps she sang—in a voice like Roberta Flack's—*sweetly* over the compounds of her village; perhaps she wove the most stunning mats or told the most ingenious stories of all the village storytellers. Perhaps she was herself a poet—though only her daughter's name is signed to the poems that we know.

Perhaps Phillis Wheatley's mother was also an artist.

Perhaps in more than Phillis Wheatley's biological life is her mother's signature made clear.

OPTIONS FOR WRITING

1. Using what you know of the history of slavery, invent a brief biography describing the life of a slave woman trying to express her creativity in a world where she was forbidden to write, paint, or sculpt. How would she do it? (You may want to develop this idea by going to the library and doing some research on slave women's lives or on the art of African-American women.)

2. Walker suggests that we learn to see different things as art, to understand quilts and flower gardens as being as much art as poems and paintings. Write an essay expressing whether you believe history and social conditions are important in defining literature and art. In a longer, more complex essay, you could compare her view to Terry Eagleton's notion of redefining literature (in "Introduction: What is Literature?").

3

THE NATURE OF HISTORY

Henry Steffens

History is more than simply what happened in earlier times; it is also our understanding and interpretation of those events. Even now historians are rewriting the stories of our past from changing perspectives. Historian Steffens shows us how we, too, can study a document like the Declaration of Independence and write history. With a little practice at using facts as evidence to support conclusions, we're ready for the challenge of researching the life of a historical figure and writing a sketch of his or her life.

READINGS

REASONS FOR WRITING HISTORY

Barbara W. Tuchman A Distant Mirror: The Period, the Protagonist, the Hazards

Garrett Mattingly The Armada

Oron J. Hale The Great Illusion

Barbara W. Tuchman The Proud Tower, A Portrait of the World Before the War, 1890–1914

THE NATURE AND USES OF HISTORY

R. G. Collingwood The Idea of History

Michael Kammen On Knowing the Past

George F. Kennan American Diplomacy, 1900–1950

ISSUES FOR HISTORIANS

Leon Litwack Patterns of Social and Political Interaction

Marguerite Yourcenar Reflections on the Composition of *The Memoirs of Hadrian*

Marguerite Yourcenar   The Memoirs of Hadrian

Mike Carter   Crewmen Who Dropped A-Bomb Tour Nation Selling
   Mementos

Theo Sommer   Why We Can Be Trusted

Angus Deming   Korea's Heartbreaking Hills: An American Veteran
   Relives a Bloody War

WHY STUDY HISTORY?

> How could you tell how much of it was lies? It *might* be true that the
> average human being was better off now than he had been before the Rev-
> olution. The only evidence to the contrary was the mute protest in your
> own bones, the instinctive feeling that the conditions you lived in were
> intolerable and that at some other time they must have been different. . . .
>   He reached down and scratched his ankle again. Day and night the
> telescreens bruised your ears with statistics proving that people today had
> more food, more clothes, better houses, better recreations — that they lived
> longer, worked shorter hours, were bigger, healthier, stronger, happier,
> more intelligent, better educated, than the people of fifty years ago. Not a
> word of it could ever be proved or disproved. . . . It was like a single equa-
> tion with two unknowns. It might very well be that literally every work in
> the history books, even the things that one accepted without question, was
> pure fantasy. . . .
>   Everything faded into mist. The past was erased, the erasure was for-
> gotten, the lie became truth. . . . (p. 63–64)

George Orwell's novel *1984* depicts a society that has lost the ability to
think historically. People know that they are not especially happy, but
because they have no access to accurate records and information, no one
knows with any accuracy whether things were better in the past or
whether it is possible for things to be any better in the present. "Big
Brother" and the government in power control information. Communications are limited, and there are no accessible records of the past. The
main character in the novel, Winston Smith, knows that unless he can
gain some accurate information about the way things were, he will
never be able to understand the full dimensions of his problems or to
see any pathway out of his current condition.

Winston Smith thinks that he remembers good-quality, delicious
chocolate bars that were inexpensive and easily available many years
ago. They must have been better than the tasteless, crumbly bars that
cost so much now and that are going up in price. Because his memory
is not especially accurate, and because he has not tasted good chocolate
for so long, he cannot be sure if his dissatisfaction is justified or just a
temporary and unjustified discontent. Because there are neither records
nor good chocolate, he cannot be sure. With no history of his past,
Winston Smith cannot be sure about the present.

Novelists like Orwell are free to make up any interesting situation or episode to further their plot and interest their readers. Now let's take an example that really happened. When Joseph Stalin consolidated his power over the Union of Soviet Socialist Republics in the 1930s, he not only controlled communications throughout the USSR, but he began to rewrite the histories of the Revolution of 1917. By 1939 Stalin had eliminated thousands of his political opponents as well as many who took part in the 1917 revolution. With no one to know better, Stalin rewrote his own role in the revolution. Instead of recording the minor role he really played, Stalin claimed he was one of Lenin's most trusted and indispensable comrades. For people growing up in the USSR of the 1930s and 1940s, Stalin became the person that he claimed to be. No one could be sure that his version was incorrect, and without access to any other records or accounts, no other believable alternative could be suggested. People believed Stalin's version because they had no history, no records of the past, no ability to gain a perspective on the account to judge its accuracy or inaccuracy.

If we ignore our historical past, we lose our ability to make informed judgments, like the people deceived by Big Brother and Joe Stalin. We orient ourselves by knowing what has gone before us. History also gives us a sense of what people have done and what people are capable of doing. If we understand the range of human actions in the past, we can envision likely courses of action in the future.

WHAT IS HISTORY?

History is the sum total of human actions in the past. But what interests us about human actions in the past is not just the fact that they occurred, but the hope that we can somehow come to appreciate and understand them and find some meaning in them for our own lives in the present. History may be better defined as a process — a process of investigation, a search in the past. Just as all investigators have some purpose in mind when they begin their investigations and all searchers search for something, we take an interest in the past for reasons that make sense to ourselves in our present lives. The reasons for an interest in the past are as varied as the number of people who study and write history.

Some historians study the Middle Ages because they are interested in religion and want to know about a time when people took their religious beliefs seriously. Others study the Middle Ages because they want to discover the role of women in a society where both religion and military prowess were important. Still others study the Middle Ages to gain an understanding of the beginnings of the Western-style economic structure and commerce. Each historian will view the Middle Ages with a different interest and perspective. The information that they gather to develop their understanding will also be different.

Historians rely as much as possible on written documents and records. Contemporary written records are the bedrock of our information about the past. The historian of religion will turn to church documents, monastic records, ecclesiastical correspondence, religious tracts, and the like to supply information to match his or her special interest. The historian interested in the lives of women will need to search out letters, household records, building designs, descriptions of clothing, paintings and illustrations of contemporary people, and a whole range of possible sources of information that hold less interest to the historian who is searching for an understanding of the governing structure of the Archbishopric of Paris in A.D. 1100. The historian interested in commerce and the economic life of the Middle Ages will search for yet other sources. The interests of historians in their present lives shape the kinds of interests that they seek to fulfill about the past.

WHY ARE THERE DIFFERENT KINDS OF HISTORY?

There are numerous kinds of history because so many people have individual interests that lead them to different sources of information. Each particular source needs special skills to be understood fully. Students of nineteenth century intellectual history, for example, usually look at the published pieces of writing by the nineteenth century people who interest them—perhaps John Stuart Mill, Marie Curie, or Charles Darwin. These pieces are often difficult to understand fully. It takes training to read them well, so it is of special interest to a historian who has developed the necessary skills in reading nineteenth century sources to discuss these sources with another historian who has developed similar skills. That is why there are special sessions of annual meetings of historians devoted solely to topics in nineteenth century intellectual history. It is also why there are special journals devoted entirely to intellectual history, such as the *Journal of the History of Ideas*. Historians interested in intellectual history would subscribe to this rather specialized journal. This does not mean that they neglect all other kinds of history. But, just like everything else in our lives, we all enjoy talking to and being with people who share our interests and who understand what we mean when we speak.

The different kinds of history and the diverse sources of information about our past indicate the vitality and dynamism of history as a discipline. Historians are currently willing to learn about the past by allying themselves with scholars from a broad range of related disciplines. Literary scholars and philosophers are now sources of ideas and techniques to be used by historians when considering texts and documents. Cultural anthropologists are sources of information about different cultural groups and about research techniques to be used to understand human societies. Although archeologists who have studied human societies before there were written records have always supplied valuable information to historians, today they provide even more data with their increasingly sophisticated techniques and equipment. Archeologists have allied themselves with physicists and geologists to provide more accurate systems for dating artifacts and remains. They work with paleobotanists to provide more accurate information on the food people ate and with paleoastronomers to give us a better idea of calendars and timekeeping. In short, the historian now has more information available about the past than ever before.

Historians are now rewriting the histories of all episodes of human actions in the past. This is not because previous histories were wrong; rather, new sources of information have cast new light on well-known episodes. This new information forces us to reconsider and rewrite. In addition, our interests in the present are constantly changing, so our interests in the past produce new kinds of history. For example, during the first part of the twentieth century, few historians were interested in women's roles in historical events. Since the 1970s, however, our societal interests have changed, and many more historians are attempting to understand the historical role of women. In order to pursue this new interest, historians have had to discover how to use different sources of information and to process that information in sophisticated ways. Local birth and death records now provide demographic information as well as clues to local conditions of life for all inhabitants. Household artifacts reveal other clues about home life, and school books and popular literature reveal societal attitudes and beliefs. The list of new sources of information for the historian is endless; there will always be an opportunity to study the past through fresh eyes.

HOW DO WE KNOW THAT HISTORIANS ARE TELLING US THE TRUTH?

Should we worry about whether historians are telling us the truth about the past? Yes and no. We have seen the historian in the role of investigator and searcher. Investigators try to persuade us that the outcome of their investigation is correct, and searchers try to convince us that their discoveries are both interesting and important. So, historians are also out to convince us that their particular stories of the past are better than those that have gone before. We need to make the same kind of decisions about whether to believe a historical account as we need to make whenever we read a newspaper or magazine article or hear a report on the radio or TV. We know that all accounts are presented from an individual's point of view and are dependent on the individual's sources of information, background, socioeconomic status, and so on. It is always up to us to decide the truthfulness of any account. The oil company executive who claimed that "only a million gallons of oil was leaked" and the environmentalist who reported that "a million gallon oil spill was an environmental disaster" were both describing the same event. We already know that reports are neither wholly complete nor permanent for all time. The worry comes in our own ability or inability to make an informed judgment.

Our ability to make judgments about historical accounts depends heavily on two of our own characteristics: our own current interests and our own current knowledge and experience. If we are not interested in political history, for example, we are unlikely to be able to make an informed judgment about the importance of a newly written history of the unification of Germany during the nineteenth century. Because we are not interested, we are also probably uninformed about the complexities of political and diplomatic maneuverings during the last century. Not being interested, and not knowing anything, we are unlikely to be able to assess the truthfulness of one historian's account over that of another's on this subject.

But suppose that we really are interested in a historical topic, such as the role of women in Western society, especially the role of women in the late nineteenth and early twentieth centuries. Then the situation is quite changed. We are dependent, at least at first, on historical accounts for our information about that aspect of our historical past. We now care whether the histories that we read are true. But our concern is not enough. We need to know something about the role of women before we can begin to make evaluative judgments about individual histories. At first, this is a bit of a "which came first, the chicken or the egg?" problem. We first need to obtain some information about our topic. During this first phase of our process of judgment, we need not be overly concerned about our sources. Once we begin to become informed, however, we begin to develop our own sense of the correctness of the author's point of view toward our topic of mutual interest. We also begin to develop a sense of the extent to which a particular author utilized all the sources of information available. We begin to believe one historian over another when we ourselves know more about history. In other words, we need to be historians ourselves if we are to judge historical accounts of situations that interest us in the past.

WRITING 1.

Write an unbiased history of one event that you witnessed during the last week. How easy is it to be unbiased? What decisions do you need to make to ensure objectivity? Compare your history to that of a classmate writing on the same or a similar event.

THINKING LIKE A HISTORIAN

We act like historians every day of our lives. We all remember past events and assess their importance for our present and future. Historians think in precisely the same patterns. A historian who is interested in the American Civil War, for example, is not old enough to have personal memories of the 1860s. That historian's remembrances must be created by his or her own research: reading, studying artifacts, and visiting the sites of important Civil War events. Even though we cannot remember the Civil War years directly, historical research provides us with the necessary information to allow us to imagine what it was like. We are able to recreate a portrait of the Civil War period imaginatively because we have taken the trouble to gather information about those times. We are also able to imagine those times because we assume that people back then behaved very much as we ourselves would have behaved in similar circumstances. Without information, we would have no basis for imagination, and without the assumption that, generally speaking, people in the past were pretty much the same as people in the present, we could not write history. If people who lived during the nineteenth century were fundamentally different from you or me, we could not write their history because we could not imagine their ideas and actions. Of course, people who lived in the past have many obvious and rather superficial differences from us: They may have worn different clothing, eaten different kinds of food, lived at different levels of comfort, had different entertainments, and so on. But we can discover these differences by historical research. We can understand these things, and we can use our understanding of our own lives to imaginatively recreate the lives of our predecessors, taking the known differences in lifestyle into account.

Historians develop a very personal link to the past. L. Pearce Williams, the biographer of the nineteenth-century scientist Michael Faraday, told me, on completing the biography, that he felt that he had lived the past ten years with Faraday and his family, in addition to his own. The Renaissance is as real to the historian of fifteenth-century Italy as is his or her own life in the present—more real in some respects because the historian pays closer attention to it.

Without Writing There Would Be No History

We need accurate information about the past in order to imagine it, and writing leaves the best record. Written documents give us access to the thoughts behind human actions. Artifacts and historical sites are mute: They say nothing to us directly. We must have written sources to determine their meaning and importance. The same is true about human actions. Unless we can know the ideas behind people's actions, we cannot truly understand them. People usually convey ideas with words. However, reading and interpreting written records is no simple task. Finding the significance of documents involves a complex mixture of our own experiences, abilities, and personalities. The first part of a familiar document from our American past, the Declaration of Independence, is a good example of this.

In Congress, July 4, 1776.
A DECLARATION
By the Representatives of the
United States of America,
In General Congress Assembled.

When in the Course of human Events, it becomes necessary for one People to dissolve the Political Bands which have connected them with another, and to assume among the Powers of the Earth, the separate and equal Station to which the Laws of Nature and of Nature's God entitle them, a decent Respect to the Opinions of Mankind requires that they should declare the causes which impel them to the Separation.

We hold these Truths to be self-evident, that all Men are created equal, that they are endowed by their Creator with certain unalienable Rights, that among these are Life, Liberty, and the Pursuit of Happiness—That to secure these Rights, Governments are instituted among Men, deriving their just Powers from the Consent of the Governed, that whenever any Form of Government becomes destructive of these Ends, it is the Right of the People to alter or to abolish it, and to institute new Government, laying its Foundation on such Principles, and organizing its Powers in such Form, as to them shall seem most likely to effect their Safety and Happiness. Prudence, indeed, will dictate that Governments long established should not be changed for light and transient Causes; and accordingly all Experience hath shewn, that Mankind are more disposed to suffer, while evils are sufferable, than to right themselves by abolishing the Forms to which they are accustomed. But when a long Train of Abuses and Usurpations, pursuing invariably the same Object, evinces a Design to reduce them under absolute Despotism, it is their Right, it is their Duty, to throw off such Government, and to provide new Guards for their future Security. Such has been the patient Sufferance of these Colonies; and such is now the Necessity which constrains them to alter their former Systems of Government.

Some Clues from the Document

When a document is available, historians must draw their clues directly from the words of the document. Let's see what we can discover about the writers of the Declaration of Independence.

1. *Point of view*. What made these men so confident that they were right? Listen to the tone of these phrases: "to assume among the Powers of the Earth, the separate and equal Station to which the Laws of Nature and of Nature's God entitle them," "these Truths to be self-evident," "it is the Right of the People to alter or to abolish it, and to institute a new Government," and "it is their Right, it is their Duty, to throw off such Government." Does the basis of the writer's point of view become clear as we read these two paragraphs? (God has entitled them to a station. They are capable of seeing self-evident truths. They have specific rights and a specific duty in their political lives.)

2. *Models of thought*. These self-confident men lived at the end of the

century that saw the successful completion of the scientific revolution. The model of science was a powerful one, both in Europe and in America. See the connection between the model of science and the words in these phrases: "the Laws of Nature and of Nature's God," "unalienable Right, that among these are Life, Liberty, and the Pursuit of Happiness," and "accordingly all Experience hath shewn."

The writers believed that God created the universe—nature as well as the world of men—and endowed this universe with laws. Just as there were laws in the natural world, laws governing motion, or mass, so too were there laws governing the affairs of men. These laws were permanent, unchanging, "unalienable" in all domains. The test of experience was the most trusted test in science. We should also rely on the test of experience in the affairs of men. These assumptions are all operative in the Declaration of Independence.

The writers also had a rather well-defined view of God and God's rule in the affairs of men, as these lines suggest: "the separate and equal Station to which the Laws of Nature and of Nature's God entitle them," and "that all men are created equal, that they are endowed by their Creator with certain unalienable Rights." What image does this create in your mind? Do you see their image of God and God's nature? The words in the document would be very different if the writers had had different beliefs or had lived during a different century.

WRITING 2.

WRITING ABOUT THE DECLARATION OF INDEPENDENCE—How did you respond to this document? This is the kind of question that historians must ask themselves about every document they read. Does this make sense to me? Do I agree with the point of view of the writer? Where do I differ? Do I know what the words are telling me?

In your opinion, after reading our brief selection, did the writers make their case for independence in the Declaration of Independence? Why or why not?

Facts Vs. Evidence

We all respond in a personal way to a document from the past. It is this personal response that turns historical "facts" into "evidence." The distinction between facts and evidence in history is very complex; facts are important, but they are not as useful and interesting as evidence. Facts need to be set into a context. The formation of a context turns facts into evidence. For example, we know that the Declaration of Independence was signed on 4 July 1776. We have the document, and we can see the date and signatures. So what? This question turns a fact into evidence in the following way.

Suppose that we would like to support the ideas that we have just developed that the writers of the Declaration had a model of scientific laws and scientific truth in mind as they wrote. This transforms 4 July 1776 from fact to evidence. The 4 July part is not so important, but the 1776 certainly is. In order to make the transformation from fact to evidence, historians must collect some information about the eighteenth century. We need to develop a point of view toward that century. As historians interested in the eighteenth century, we would know from our research that by that year the progress of science was well advanced in both America and Europe. We would know that by then Ben Franklin and Thomas Jefferson, two of the writers of the Declaration of Independence, were well versed in the works of European natural philosophers (as scientists were called in those days). Now, by using the date 1776 as evidence, we could establish which European natural philosophers Franklin and Jefferson knew. Holding 1776 in mind and doing some further research to find out about important natural philosophers of the eighteenth century, we would quickly discover the importance of the French chemist Lavosier. Lavosier is called the father of modern chemistry, at least by the French. Because a good deal of his important work occurred before 1776, it could have been known to Franklin and Jefferson before they participated in the writing of the Declaration. Doing a bit more research, we would discover that Lavosier corresponded with Franklin many times and that he was well known to Thomas Jefferson, the American ambassador to the French court. The date 1776 allows us to discover the link between Lavosier and Jefferson. It also allows us to reject the possibility of the influence of the work of the English natural philosopher Michael Faraday, for example, for the simple reason that Faraday did his work in the 1830s.

With just the little bit of evidence, 1776, we can begin to construct a more accurate portrait of just what intellectual model the writers of the Declaration of Independence had in mind. To continue, we need to use information that we, as historians interested in the eighteenth century, know from other sources. Suddenly, another fact—"and accordingly all Experience hath shewn"—transforms itself into a bit of evidence. We all know a little bit about chemistry. Chemistry is an inductive science, which means that it starts with specific facts, or pieces of data, and builds toward more general principles. Chemistry depends on experiments to produce these specific pieces of data. It also depends on our sense experience, in that we observe these experiments carefully. Therefore, with the inductive method, chemistry builds on bits of experience to draw more general conclusions. Each bit helps us in the process of drawing a conclusion and supports the conclusion that we draw. So, if we list "a long Train of Abuses and Usurpations," each one, bit by bit, will lead us to the general conclusion that we must "throw off such Government." Each one will also support our general conclusion. Therefore, in the eighteenth century perspective — the perspective of Lavosier, Franklin, and Jefferson — because the conclusion was based on experience and arrived at by proper scientific reasoning, the process of induction, it must be true and unquestionable. We, as historians, now understand more about the context within which the Declaration of Independence was framed. The date 1776 was an important piece of evidence to support our interpretation of the intellectual model that Franklin and Jefferson had in mind as they thought through and wrote the Declaration, a model of reasoning drawn from the natural philosophy of that time.

Historians always turn facts into evidence to support their imaginatively created portraits of the past. Facts are dull until you turn them into accounts of how you think people acted in the past. But the process of turning facts into evidence involves many subjective factors that may shape our use of evidence; some might even say it actually distorts the facts. Historians need to be very self-aware so that they can at least attempt to keep their own prejudices, beliefs, and preferences from shading their portraits of the past too greatly.

Writing About Self-Awareness

Think again about the Declaration of Independence in light of our discussion. Read the two paragraphs again. Then answer the following question.

WRITING 3.

Were the writers of the Declaration of Independence "your kind of people," people with whom you could have had a meaningful conversation, or were they very different from you? How do you know?

SUGGESTIONS FOR RESEARCH

Writing Biography

Write a brief historical biography of someone who holds special interest for you. This historical person can be from any place and from any time! The point is to pick someone you truly want to know more about. Try to discover some of this person's most important ideas and actions. As a historian, you will also want to decide how the person's thoughts and actions were shaped by his or her times. You will also want to decide how great an influence your person had on his or her society during and after his or her lifetime. This is by no means easy to do. But with a bit of research in the library to learn some biographical information, a bit of general reading about the times during which the person lived, and a lot of historical imagination, you will be able to write a brief piece of history of your own.

Prewriting and Reading

1. *Make a list* of at least four people who have always interested you. Let your imagination run over the whole of history: all times and cultures. They can be very recent people, or people who lived many centuries ago.

Think about these people, then pick one. Write a paragraph on why that figure interests you. What attracts you to the person? What would you really like to know? What aspect of his or her life do you think will be most interesting?

Pick another person, perhaps someone very different. (Don't shortchange yourself.) Write another paragraph about his person. Perhaps you might discuss both people with a classmate. Explaining your interests to another person might help you to decide who interests you more.

2. *Pick your historical person.* You will now need to go to the library to find some biographical information. Start in the reference section of the library, with biographical dictionaries and encyclopedias. It is usually helpful to learn a bit about your figure before you begin to look at full biographies located from the card catalogue. Once you have read a bit about your person, you will also need to find some information about the historical period during which the person flourished. (Be alert to how reading begins to change your initial impression of that person.) Take some reading notes.

3. After you have read a good bit about your person, do some writing. Write a short piece describing the person. Describe his or her important actions, ideas, and relationships to other people. Try to choose the really crucial ideas and actions, those that seem to you to characterize your figure best. Try to include as much detailed information as you have collected thus far. (You will have begun to develop your own point of view toward your figure at this point. Because you have a great deal of information available, you will need to decide which aspects of the life of your person you will focus on.)

Write a second short piece about the backgrounds to your person's life. Describe the person's early life experiences and education, the people who influenced the person, and the "climate of the times" as he or she grew to maturity. Try to think about the whole context of your person's life. What factors shaped his or her life? Under what conditions did he or she grow up? Include as much information about the times as you have discovered in your readings.

Write a third short piece about your person as an influence on his or her age. What were his or her most important contributions? Whom did he or she influence most? How did he or she represent or characterize the age? Do you think that your person was important?

Reread your three pieces. You will now have a good sense of how much you know about your person. You will also know what aspects of his or her life you will need to know more about. Go back to your sources to do some further reading and research.

Drafting

Clearly you will have to think about writing. You have just found hundreds, if not thousands, of pages of biographical information about your figure. You will really need to think like a historian to focus on your figure. What is your personal point of view? What did you find most important? What was most important about your person, from your point of view? Your own interpretation and conclusions and your own sense of the times during which your figure lived will enable you to focus your attention so that you can write your own short biographical piece.

Instead of writing a five- or six-page biographical narrative, you have four possible alternatives:
1. Present your figure through letters written and received.
2. Write a brief play revealing some aspect of your figure's life.
3. Write journal or diary entries for your figure.
4. Allow your person to speak about life in his or her own voice.
Abandoning the straight narrative form, the form that you read in order to collect information, will require you to recast your knowledge about your person in your own terms. This will make your piece unique.

READINGS

Reasons for Writing History

Barbara W. Tuchman
A DISTANT MIRROR:
The Period, The Protagonist, The Hazards

> *Barbara Tuchman (1912–1989) told us specifically why she undertook*
> *what was for her a new historical interest in the fourteenth century*
> *in writing her book* A Distant Mirror: *"The genesis of this book was*
> *a desire to find out what were the effects on society of the most lethal*
> *disaster of recorded history — that is to say, of the Black Death of*
> *1348–50, which killed an estimated one third of the population living*
> *between India and Iceland. Given the possibilities of our own time,*
> *the reason for my interest is obvious."*
>
> *Ms. Tuchman, like all historians, was attracted to the past for*
> *reasons in her present. She was an excellent and prolific historian,*
> *writing books on such diverse topics as Europe before World War I,*
> *the American experience in China, and the American Revolution. She*
> *never accepted an academic position after her graduation from college,*
> *but she possessed the primary qualification of being a historian: She*
> *wrote history.*

The genesis of this book was a desire to find out what were the effects
on society of the most lethal disaster of recorded history — that is to say,
of the Black Death of 1348–50, which killed an estimated one third of
the population living between India and Iceland. Given the possibilities
of our own time, the reason for my interest is obvious. The answer
proved elusive because the 14th century suffered so many "strange and
great perils and adversities" (in the words of a contemporary) that its
disorders cannot be traced to any one cause; they were the hoofprints
of more than the four horsemen of St. John's vision, which had now
become seven — plague, war, taxes, brigandage, bad government, insur-
rection, and schism in the Church. All but plague itself arose from conditions that existed prior to the Black Death and continued after the
period of plague was over.

Although my initial question has escaped an answer, the interest of
the period itself — a violent, tormented, bewildered, suffering and disintegrating age, a time, as many thought, of Satan triumphant — was compelling and, as it seemed to me, consoling in a period of similar disarray.
If our last decade or two of collapsing assumptions has been a period of
unusual discomfort, it is reassuring to know that the human species has
lived through worse before.

Curiously, the "phenomenal parallels" have been applied by another historian to earlier years of this century. Comparing the aftermaths of the Black Death and of World War I, James Westfall Thompson found all the same complaints: economic chaos, social unrest, high prices, profiteering, depraved morals, lack of production, industrial indolence, frenetic gaiety, wild expenditure, luxury, debauchery, social and religious hysteria, greed, avarice, maladministration, decay of manners. "History never repeats itself," said Voltaire; "man always does." Thucydides, of course, made that principle the justification of his work.

Simply summarized by the Swiss historian, J. C. L. S. de Sismondi, the 14th century was "a bad time for humanity." Until recently, historians tended to dislike and to skirt the century because it could not be made to fit into a pattern of human progress. After the experiences of the terrible 20th century, we have greater fellow-feeling for a distraught age whose rules were breaking down under the pressure of adverse and violent events. We recognize with a painful twinge the marks of "a period of anguish when there is no sense of an assured future."

The interval of 600 years permits what is significant in human character to stand out. People of the Middle Ages existed under mental, moral, and physical circumstances so different from our own as to constitute almost a foreign civilization. As a result, qualities of conduct that we recognize as familiar amid these alien surroundings are revealed as permanent in human nature. If one insists upon a lesson from history, it lies here, as discovered by the French medievalist Edouard Perroy when he was writing a book on the Hundred Years' War while dodging the Gestapo during World War II. "Certain ways of behavior," he wrote, "certain reactions against fate, throw mutual light upon each other."

The fifty years that followed the Black Death of 1348–50 are the core of what seems to me a coherent historical period extending approximately from 1300 to 1450 plus a few years. To narrow the focus to a manageable area, I have chosen a particular person's life as the vehicle of my narrative. Apart from human interest, this has the advantage of enforced obedience to reality. I am required to follow the circumstances and the sequence of an actual medieval life, lead where they will, and they lead, I think, to a truer version of the period than if I had imposed my own plan.

The person in question is not a king or queen, because everything about such persons is *ipso facto* exceptional, and, besides, they are overused; nor a commoner, because commoners' lives in most cases did not take in the wide range that I wanted; nor a cleric or saint, because they are outside the limits of my comprehension; nor a woman, because any medieval woman whose life was adequately documented would be atypical.

The choice is thus narrowed to a male member of the Second Estate — that is, of the nobility — and has fallen upon Enguerrand de Coucy VII, last of a great dynasty and "the most experienced and skillful of all the knights of France." His life from 1340 to 1397 coincided with the period that concerned me, and, from the death of his mother in the great plague to his own perfectly timed death in the culminating fiasco of the century, seemed designed for my purpose.

Through marriage to the eldest daughter of the King of England, he acquired a double allegiance bridging two countries at war, which enlarged the scope and enriched the interest of his career; he played a role, usually major, in every public drama of his place and time, and he had the good sense to become a patron of the greatest contemporary chronicler, Jean Froissart, with the result that more is known about him than might otherwise have been the case. He has one grievous imperfection — that no authentic portrait of him exists. He has, however, a compensating advantage, for me: that, except for a single brief article published in 1939, nothing has been written about him in English, and no formal, reliable biography in French except for a doctoral thesis of 1890 that exists only in manuscript. I like finding own way.

I must beg the reader to have patience in making Coucy's acquaintance because he can only be known against the background and events of his time which fill the first half dozen chapters. Enguerrand (pronounced with a hard "g") made his first mark on history at the age of eighteen in 1358. . . .

I come now to the hazards of the enterprise. First are uncertain and contradictory data with regard to dates, numbers, and hard facts. Dates may seem dull and pedantic to some, but they are fundamental because they establish sequence — what precedes and what follows — thereby leading toward an understanding of cause and effect. Unfortunately, medieval chronology is extremely hard to pin down. The year was considered to begin at Easter and since this could fall any time between March 22 and April 22, a fixed date of March 25 was generally preferred. The change over to New Style took place in the 16th century but was not everywhere accepted until the 18th, which leaves the year to which events of January, February, and March belong in the 14th century a running enigma — further complicated by use of the regnal year (dating from the reigning King's accession) in official English documents of the 14th century and use of the papal year in certain other cases. Moreover, chroniclers did not date an event by the day of the month but by the religious calendar — speaking, for example, of two days before the Nativity of the Virgin, or the Monday after Epiphany, or St. John the Baptist's Day, or the third Sunday in Lent. The result is to confuse not only the historian but the inhabitants of the 14th century themselves, who rarely if ever agree on the same date for any event.

Numbers are no less basic because they indicate what proportion of the population is involved in a given situation. The chronic exaggeration of medieval numbers — of armies, for example — when accepted as factual, has led in the past to a misunderstanding of medieval war as analogous to modern war, which it was not, in means, method, or purpose. It should be assumed that medieval figures for military forces, battle casualties, plague deaths, revolutionary hordes, processions, or any groups en masse are generally enlarged by several hundred percent. This is because the chroniclers did not use numbers as data but as a device of literary art to amaze or appall the reader. Use of Roman numerals also made for lack of precision and an affinity for round numbers. The figures were uncritically accepted and repeated by generation after generation of historians. Only since the end of the last century have scholars begun to re-examine the documents and find, for instance, the true strength of an expeditionary force from paymaster' records. Yet still they disagree. J. C. Russell puts the pre-plague population of France at 21 million, Ferdinand Lot at 15 or 16 million, and Edouard Perroy at a lowly 10 to 11 million. Size of population affects studies of everything else — taxes, life expectancy, commerce and agriculture, famine or plenty — and here are figures by modern authorities which differ by 100 percent. Chroniclers' figures which seem obviously distorted appear in my text in quotation marks.

Discrepancies of supposed fact were often due to mistakes of oral transmission or later misreading of a manuscript source, as when the Dame de Courcy, subject of an international scandal, was mistaken by an otherwise careful 19th century historian for Coucy's second wife, at a cost, for a while, of devastating confusion to the present author. The Comte d'Auxerre in the Battle of Poitiers was variously rendered by English chroniclers as Aunser, Aussure, Soussiere, Usur, Waucerre, and by the *Grandes Chroniques* of France as Sancerre, a different fellow altogether. Enguerrand was written as Ingelram in England. It is not surprising that I took the name Canolles to be a variant of the notorious brigand captain Arnaut de Cervole, only to find, when the circumstances refused to fit, that it was instead a variant of Knowles or Knollys, an equally notorious English captain. Though minor, this sort of difficulty can be unnerving.

Isabeau of Bavaria, Queen of France, is described by one historian as a tall blonde and by another as a "dark, lively, little woman." The Turkish Sultan Bajazet, reputed by his contemporaries to be bold, enterprising, and avid for war, and surnamed Thunderbolt for the rapidity of his strikes, is described by a modern Hungarian historian as "effeminate, sensual, irresolute and vacillating."

It may be taken as axiomatic that any statement of fact about the Middle Ages may (and probably will) be met by a statement of the opposite or a different version. Women outnumbered men because men were killed off in the wars; men outnumbered women because women died in childbirth. Common people were familiar with the Bible; common people were unfamiliar with the Bible. Nobles were tax exempt; no, they were not tax exempt. French peasants were filthy and foul-smelling and lived on bread and onions; French peasants ate pork, fowl, and game and enjoyed frequent baths in the village bathhouses. The list could be extended indefinitely.

Contradictions, however, are part of life, not merely a matter of conflicting evidence. I would ask the reader to expect contradictions, not uniformity. No aspect of society, no habit, custom, movement, development, is without cross-currents. Starving peasants in hovels live alongside prosperous peasants in featherbeds. Children are neglected and children are loved. Knights talk of honor and turn brigand. Amid depopulation and disaster, extravagance and splendor were never more extreme. No age is tidy or made of whole cloth, and none is a more checkered fabric than the Middle Ages.

One must also remember that the Middle Ages change color depending on who is looking at them. Historians' prejudices and points of view — and thus their selection of material — have changed considerably over a period of 600 years. During the three centuries following the 14th, history was virtually a genealogy of nobility, devoted to tracing dynastic lines and family connections and infused by the idea of the noble as a superior person. These works of enormous antiquarian research teem with information of more than dynastic interest, such as Anselm's item about the Gascon lord who bequeathed a hundred livres for the dowries of poor girls he had deflowered.

The French Revolution marks the great reversal, following which historians saw the common man as hero, the poor as *ipso facto* virtuous, nobles and kings as monsters of iniquity. Simeon Luce, in his history of the Jacquerie, is one of these, slanted in his text, yet unique in his research and invaluable for his documents. The giants of the 19th and early 20th centuries who unearthed and published the sources, annotated and edited the chronicles, collected the literary works, read and excerpted masses of sermons, treatises, letters, and other primary material, provided the ground on which we latecomers walk. Their work is now supplemented and balanced by modern medievalists of the post–Marc Bloch era who have taken a more sociological approach and turned up detailed hard facts about daily life — for example, the number of communion wafers sold in à particular diocese, as an indicator of religious observance.

My book is indebted to all these groups, beginning with the primary chroniclers. I realize it is unfashionable among medievalists today to rely on the chroniclers, but for a sense of the period and its attitudes I find them indispensable. Furthermore, their form is narrative and so is mine.

With all this wealth, empty spaces nevertheless exist where the problem is not contradictory information but no information. To bridge the gap, one must make use of what seems the likely and natural explanation, which accounts for the proliferation of "probably" and "presumably" in my text — annoying but, in the absence of documented certainty, unavoidable.

A greater hazard, built into the very nature of recorded history, is overload of the negative: the disproportionate survival of the bad side — of evil, misery, contention, and harm. In history this is exactly the same as in the daily newspaper. The normal does not make the news. History is made by the documents that survive, and these lean heavily on crisis and calamity, crime and misbehavior, because such things are the subject matter of the documentary process — of lawsuits, treaties, moralists' denunciations, literary satire, papal Bulls. No Pope ever issued a Bull to approve of something. Negative overload can be seen at work in the religious reformer Nicolas de Clamanges, who, in denouncing unfit and worldly prelates in 1401, said that in his anxiety for reform he would not discuss the good clerics because "they do not count beside the perverse men."

Disaster is rarely as pervasive as it seems from recorded accounts. The fact of being on the record makes it appear continuous and ubiquitous whereas it is more likely to have been sporadic both in time and place. Besides, persistence of the normal is usually greater than the effect of disturbance, as we know from our own times. After absorbing the news of today, one expects to face a world consisting entirely of strikes, crimes, power failures, broken water mains, stalled trains, school shutdowns, muggers, drug addicts, neo-Nazis, and rapists. The fact is that one can come home in the evening — on a lucky day — without having encountered more than one or two of these phenomena. This has led me to formulate Tuchman's Law, as follow: "The fact of being reported multiplies the apparent extent of any deplorable development by five- to tenfold" (or any figure the reader would care to supply).

Difficulty of empathy, of genuinely entering into the mental and emotional values of the Middle Ages, is the final obstacle. The main barrier is, I believe, the Christian religion as it then was: the matrix and law of medieval life, omnipresent, indeed compulsory. Its insistent principle that the life of the spirit and of the afterworld was superior to the here and now, to material life on earth, is one that the modern world does not share, no matter how devout some present-day Christians may be. The rupture of this principle and its replacement by belief in the worth of the individual and of an active life not necessarily focused on God is, in fact, what created the modern world and ended the Middle Ages.

What compounds the problem is that medieval society, while professing belief in renunciation of the life of the senses, did not renounce it in practice, and no part of it less so than the Church itself. Many tried, a few succeeded, but the generality of mankind is not made for renunciation. There never was a time when more attention was given to money and possessions than in the 14th century, and its concern with the flesh was the same as at any other time. Economic man and sensual man are not suppressible.

The gap between medieval Christianity's ruling principle and everyday life is the great pitfall of the Middle Ages. It is the problem that runs through Gibbon's history, which he dealt with by a delicately malicious levity, pricking at every turn what seemed to him the hypocrisy of the Christian ideal as opposed to natural human functioning. I do not think, however great my appreciation of the master otherwise, that Gibbon's method meets the problem. Man himself was the formulator of the impossible Christian ideal and tried to uphold it, if not live by it, for more than a millennium. Therefore it must represent a need, something more fundamental than Gibbon's 18th century enlightenment allowed for, or his elegant ironies could dispose of. While I recognize its presence, it requires a more religious bent than mine to identify with it.

Chivalry, the dominant political idea of the ruling class, left as great a gap between ideal and practice as religion. The ideal was a vision of order maintained by the warrior class and formulated in the image of the Round Table, nature's perfect shape. King Arthur's knights adventured for the right against dragons, enchanters, and wicked men, establishing order in a wild world. So their living counterparts were supposed, in theory, to serve as defenders of the Faith, upholders of justice, champions of the oppressed. In practice, they were themselves the oppressors, and by the 14th century the violence and lawlessness of men of the sword had become a major agency of disorder. When the gap between ideal and real becomes too wide, the system breaks down. Legend and story have always reflected this; in the Arthurian romances the Round Table is shattered from within. The sword is returned to the lake; the effort begins anew. Violent, destructive, greedy, fallible as he may be, man retains his vision of order and resumes his search.

OPTIONS FOR WRITING

1. This book enabled Barbara Tuchman to formulate Tuchman's Law: "The fact of being reported multiplies the apparent extent of any deplorable development by five- to tenfold (or any figure the reader would care to supply)." Ms. Tuchman was referring to written historical documents, but her law also applies to news reporting today. Describe an event that you are familiar with that seemed distorted by the media coverage.

2. Voltaire said: "History never repeats itself, man always does." What do you think he means by this? Make a case that something happening today has an accurate historical precedent.

3. Can we really compare human life 600 years ago to our own lives today? Have people changed fundamentally from the Medieval Ages to the twentieth century? Explore these questions in a brief essay.

Garrett Mattingly
THE ARMADA

Garrett Mattingly (1900–1962) was also drawn to the past for reasons in his present life: "The idea of writing a book about the defeat of the Spanish Armada first came to me, as it must have come to others, in June 1940, when the eyes of the world were again turned to the shores of England and their surrounding seas." England was once again under attack, this time by the Germans, not the Spanish. Mattingly, at the time a middle-aged academic, found himself in the war effort, engaged in naval and amphibious operations in the same waters sailed by the Armada. He began the book in 1940 and finished it after his war years. His reasons for writing and his point of view should be clear from this excerpt.

PREFACE

The idea of writing a book about the defeat of the Spanish Armada first came to me, as it must have come to others, in June 1940, when the eyes of the world were again turned to the shores of England and their surrounding seas. If the idea attracted me, in spite of all that had already been written on the subject, it was because it seemed there might be some interest in replacing the narrative of the naval campaign in the broader European context in which it had once been viewed but from which, in the peaceful years before 1914, it had become more and more detached. To minds formed by A. T. Mahan and the theorists of empire, the issue in 1588 seemed to be the command of the ocean seas and the opportunity to exploit the newly discovered routes to Asia and the Americas. To such minds it was rational and right to fight for economic interests, but absurd and rather shocking to fight about the relative validity of conflicting systems of ideas.

The men of 1588 did not think so. To them the clash of the English and Spanish fleets in the Channel was the beginning of Armageddon, of a final struggle to the death between the forces of light and the forces of darkness. Which side was which depended, of course, on where one stood, but all across Europe the lines were drawn, and though most of the nations were technically noncombatants there were no real neutrals. All Europe watched the battle in the Channel with breathless suspense because upon its outcome was felt to hang not just the fates of England and Scotland, France and the Netherlands, but all of Christendom. Ideological wars are revolutionary wars, easily transcending national boundaries, and always, at least in intention, and in the imaginations of the men involved in them, total wars. It was easier in 1940 to appreciate this point of view than it had been in, say, 1890.

In 1940 I contemplated a short book, based on the standard accounts, and mainly devoted to pointing out the various issues which depended, or were felt to depend, on the success of the Spanish attempt to invade England, the first of those efforts by continental military powers to establish a European hegemony which have provided a recurrent pattern in modern history. Before I could get very far with my notion other matters intervened. Before I could get back to it I had acquired some acquaintance — no more than a nodding acquaintance certainly, but more than I would have supposed likely to befall a sedentary, middle-aged historian — with some aspects of naval and amphibious operations, and with some of the waters through which the Armada had sailed.

When I had time to think about the Armada again, although it no longer seemed urgent to finish a book about it right away, the idea of doing one which would present the campaign not just as a naval duel between Spain and England, but as the focus of the first great international crisis in modern history still appealed to me. Since there was no hurry, I decided to start over, working this time from the original sources, in the archives and in print, and visiting or revisiting as many as possible of the places I would want to talk about, not because I had any conviction of the higher purity of such procedures, or even because I expected to make any startling discoveries, but because that is the way I enjoy working. Besides, Professor Michael Lewis's brilliant series of articles in *The Mariner's Mirror*, "Armada Guns" (Vols. XXVIII–XXIX, 1942–1943), had shown me that a fresh eye and a few fresh documents could make evidence long in the public domain yield a fresh and significant interpretation, and my friend Bernard DeVoto's *The Year of Decision* (1943) and *Across the Wide Missouri*, the manuscript of which I began to read not long after I got out of uniform, made me wonder whether it might not be possible, with luck, to re-create for the late sixteenth century a series of connected historical scenes perhaps half as alive as those DeVoto evoked from the history of the Rocky Mountain West.

In the end, I found no startling fresh interpretation, but excavations among the unpublished documents and re-examination of the published ones did yield scraps of new evidence weakening certain accepted views and strengthening others. And the same spade work did turn up, now and then, a communicative and resonant phrase or a concrete visual image to freshen a familiar tale. So, although this account agrees, in the main, with currently accepted scholarship, I hope it may prove to have enough shifts of emphasis and unfamiliar details to keep it from seeming completely trite.

Since this book is addressed not to specialists but to the general reader interested in history, there are no footnotes. But on the chance that some student of the period, turning these pages, might feel a bit of curiosity about the grounds for some judgment or assertion, I have appended a general account of the documents and printed books most relied on, followed by short notes on the chief sources for each chapter, with special reference to the evidence for any views which depart from those generally accepted.

EPILOGUE

New York, New Year's, 1959

Historians agree that the defeat of the Spanish Armada was a decisive battle, in fact one of the Decisive Battles of the World, but there is much less agreement as to what it decided. It certainly did not decide the issue of the war between England and Spain. Though no fleet opposed Drake, and only local defense forces opposed Norris, the English enterprise of Portugal in 1589 ended in disastrous failure, and thereafter the war dragged itself out for nearly fourteen years more, as long, in fact, as Queen Elizabeth lived, and ended in no better than a draw. Some historians say that the defeat of the Armada "marked the decline of the Spanish colonial empire and the rise of the British." It is hard to see why they think so. By 1603, Spain had not lost to the English a single overseas outpost, while the English colonization of Virginia had been postponed for the duration. Nor did the Armada campaign "transfer the command of the sea from Spain to England." English sea power in the Atlantic had usually been superior to the combined strengths of Castile and Portugal, and so it continued to be, but after 1588 the margin of superiority diminished. The defeat of the Armada was not so much the end as the beginning of the Spanish navy. The English could raid the Spanish coast, but they were not able to blockade it. Drake and Hawkins had dreamed of bringing Philip to his knees by cutting off his revenues from the New World, but, in fact, more American treasure reached Spain in the years between 1588 and 1603 than in any other fifteen years in Spanish history. In the War of Elizabeth, nobody commanded the seas.

It is sometimes said that the defeat of the Armada produced the mood of buoyant optimism which characterized the Elizabethan temper, and led to the great explosion of literary genius which marked the last fifteen years of Elizabeth's reign.

> Come the three quarters of the world in arms
> And we shall shock them

from *King John* is usually quoted by way of illustration. Some doubt is cast on the validity of the first part of this assertion, even for those who have no doubts about characterizing with a phrase the whole mood and temper of a people, by the difficulty of demonstrating that "buoyant optimism" was any more prevalent in England in the decade and a half after 1588 than in the decade and a half before. The second part, the assertion of a causal connection between the defeat of the Armada and the flowering of Elizabethan drama, is hard to refute; even harder, except by the method of *post hoc, propter hoc,* to prove. There is no link in England between the Armada campaign and any literary work as clear as one we can find in Spain. According to the accepted story, a maimed veteran of Lepanto, a minor poet, in the confusing weeks before the Armada sailed from Lisbon, got his accounts of collections he was making for the fleet so embroiled that nobody could tell whether he was trying to cheat the crown or not, and in due time he was sent to prison until somebody could straighten out his books. In his enforced leisure, he found time to begin to write *Don Quixote*. Perhaps this proves that defeat may be just as stimulating to genius as victory, a proposition for which history can furnish considerable support. Or perhaps Cervantes and Shakespeare would have written much as they did whether the Armada had sailed or not.

The older historians, Froude and Motley, Ranke and Michelet, who said that the defeat of the Armada decided that the Counter Reformation was not to triumph throughout Europe have a much better case. Perhaps there was nothing that Medina Sidonia could have done to win the naval battle, but Howard could certainly have lost it. Had he done so, perhaps some way could have been found to get Parma's army across to England. Had Parma landed and taken Rochester, as he meant to do, and then marched to London, supported by a victorious Spanish fleet in the Thames, the course of history in England, and on the Continent, might have been altered in any one of a number of ways. Even had Parma failed to conquer England, or to dethrone the queen, just a limited Spanish success might have dealt the cause of Protestantism a serious, possibly even a fatal blow.

It seems more likely, however, that even had the Spaniards snatched a victory at sea, the final picture of Europe, when peace came, would not have been much different. Philip and his militant advisers dreamed of a great crusade which should wipe out heresy and impose on Christendom the king of Spain's Catholic peace. Drake and his fellow Puritans dreamed of spreading the religious revolution throughout Europe until Anti-Christ was hurled from his throne. Both dreams were wide of reality. Neither the Catholic nor the Protestant coalition had the necessary unity, or could dispose of the necessary force. Systems of ideas, though usually self-limiting in their spread, are harder to kill than men, or even than nations. Of all the kinds of war, a crusade, a total war against a system of ideas, is the hardest to win. By its very nature, the war between Spain and England was likely to be indecisive, and, men being what they are, even its object lesson proved to be in vain. Most of Europe had to fight another war, thirty years long, before deciding that crusades were a poor way of settling differences of opinion, and that two or more systems of ideas could live side by side without mortal danger to either.

Nevertheless, the defeat of the Spanish Armada was, in one sense, a decisive event. Less for the combatants than for the onlookers. For the experts on both sides, the outcome at Gravelines was surprising chiefly because the Armada had done as well as it had. But the landsmen, English and Spanish, were less certain which way the scales of victory would incline, and other people were less certain still. France and Germany and Italy had seen the Spanish colossus advance from victory to victory. Providence, God's increasingly obvious design, the wave of the future, seemed to be on the side of Spain, and, as Catholics, French and German and Italian Catholics rejoiced that Spain was clearly the elected champion of God's Church, little as they relished the prospect of Spanish dominance, while Protestants everywhere were correspondingly alarmed and dismayed. When the Spanish Armada challenged the ancient lords of the English Channel on their own grounds, the impending conflict took on the aspect of a judicial duel in which, as was expected in such duels, God would defend the right. The solemnity of the occasion was heightened by the portentous prophecies about the year of the conflict, prophecies so ancient and respectable that even the most enlightened and skeptical could not quite ignore them. So, when the two fleets approached their appointed battleground, all Europe watched.

For the spectators of both parties, the outcome, reinforced, as everyone believed, by an extraordinary tempest, was indeed decisive. The Protestants of France and the Netherlands, Germany and Scandinavia saw with relief that God was, in truth, as they had always supposed, on their side. The Catholics of France and Italy and Germany saw with almost equal relief that Spain was not, after all, God's chosen champion. From that time forward, though Spain's preponderance was to last for more than another generation, the peak of her prestige had passed. France, in particular, after Henry III's coup d'état at Blois, began to come back to her role of balance against the house of Austria, and so to being the chief guarantor of the liberties of Europe as long as those liberties were threatened by the Habsburgs. Without the English victory at Gravelines and its ratification by the news from Ireland, Henry III might never have summoned the courage to throw off the Leaguer yoke, and the subsequent history of Europe might have been incalculably different.

So, in spite of the long, indecisive war which followed, the defeat of the Spanish Armada really was decisive. It decided that religious unity was not to be reimposed by force on the heirs of medieval Christendom, and if, in doing so, it only validated what was already by far the most probable outcome, why, perhaps that is all that any of the battles we call decisive have ever done. Whether or not Parma could have reconquered Holland and Zeeland for Spain as he had reconquered the southern provinces, we shall never know. After 1588 he never had a chance; too much of his slender force had to go to sustaining the League against Henry of Navarre. The pattern of territorial, ultimately "national" states which was to characterize modern Europe was beginning to emerge, and after 1588 each major state was not only to be free, but increasingly to feel free, to develop its own individual potentialities without conforming to any externally imposed system of beliefs. Since the powers of Europe were were not strong enough, and would not be strong enough for centuries, to inflict irreparable harm on one another, the problem of how to combine freedom to differ with safety from utter destruction could be left to the century in which it would arise.

Meanwhile, as the episode of the Armada receded into the past, it influenced history in another way. Its story, magnified and distorted by a golden mist, became a heroic apalogue of the defense of freedom against tyranny, an eternal myth of the victory of the weak over the strong, of the triumph of David over Goliath. It raised men's hearts in dark hours, and led them to say to one another, "What we have done once, we can do again." Insofar as it did this, the legend of the defeat of the Spanish Armada became as important as the actual event— perhaps even more important.

OPTIONS FOR WRITING

1. In what ways does knowing about episodes in the past, when people in our country have overcome difficulties, help us to deal with our problems in the present? Write a letter to the editor of your local paper in which you suggest a solution to a present problem by citing a historical example.

2. What *was* the importance of the Spanish Armada, according to Mattingly? Does this defeat strike you as important? Describe what the world would be like today if Spain had prevailed.

3. Religious belief was one of the strong motivations for launching the Spanish Armada. Does religion still motivate us strongly today? Write a brief essay about a modern event that was shaped by religious belief.

Oron J. Hale
THE GREAT ILLUSION

Oron Hale (1902–1982) looked to the past so that he could better understand his own age: "the assumption underlying this book is that the years from 1900 to 1914 were not simply the sunset of the nineteenth century—or the last act in a Victorian play—but rather a period that clearly belongs to the twentieth century, and one in which our present-day concerns and achievements had their beginning. Wherever the historian of my generation delves in this epoch he encounters his own present." Hale's book is one of 20 volumes in the famous Rise of Modern Europe series. It is quite an honor to be selected to write one of the volumes, so it must be perfectly acceptable for a real historian to take an interest in the past for reasons in the present.

PREFACE

A distinguished French historian, the late Marc Bloch, tells of a student's paper that contained this sly or naïve statement: "It is well known that the eighteenth century begins in 1715 and ends in 1789." One can imagine another student writing: "It is well known that the nineteenth century begins in 1815 and ends in 1914." Such a view indeed is widely held, but the assumption underlying this book is that the years from 1900 to 1914 were not simply the sunset of the nineteenth century—or the last act in a Victorian play—but rather a period that clearly belongs to the twentieth century, and one in which our present-day concerns and achievements had their beginning. Wherever the historian of my generation delves in this epoch he encounters his own present. To be sure the period was one of seedtime rather than of harvest; in science, in art and literature, in technical advances, in economic growth and development, indeed in almost every respect, these were gigantic years in which Europeans gained enormously in knowledge, wisdom, wealth, and power. Discoveries and developments originating in these decades were later to revolutionize the world.

The significance of the epoch is well illustrated by the emergence of a new appreciation of the universe and the world of nature. First among theoretical physicists, then among the philosophers of science, and finally through them to a wider public, the implications of Max Planck's quantum theory and Einstein's relativity turned men's minds away from the Newtonian conception of the universe and the belief that nature functioned like a great machine. Discontinuity, indeterminacy, and the relativity of space, time, and mass developed a competing, and eventually a dominating, image of nature.

Also in the political sphere the period had its revolutionary aspects. The year 1905 witnessed the first Russian revolution, the victory of a modernized Japan over one of the great powers, and a diplomatic revolution in the relations of the principal European states. The Boer war, the Russo-Japanese War, and the public exposure of conditions in the Congo manifestly marked a turning point in the history of Western imperialism. Internally, or domestically, the mystery of economic growth began to replace social injustice as the dominant theme in economic history, and the transition from wealth to welfare, which distinguishes the nineteenth from the twentieth century, became an acknowledged social goal. The fact that the leaders in the various fields of endeavor— Freud, Max Planck, Bergson, Diesel, Max Weber, J. J. Thomson—all experienced life in two centuries was a characteristic feature of these years and constituted as it were a bridge between two worlds which science and technology were rendering ever more dissimilar. The automobile, the airplane, the gene theory, abstract art, and the first wireless signal flashed across the Atlantic were germinal achievements of the first decade of the 1900's.

The posturing of the "decadents" at the turn of the century should not be given undue weight, for the real mood was broadly optimistic and anticipatory. Some pessimists envisioned a "shipwrecked Europe," but most observers were convinced that they lived in an age of peace and progress and that there would be more prosperity to come. The "road to disaster" theme, so often applied to these years, is a highly retrospective construction. No one, including this author, whose youthful years fell before 1914, really anticipated the approaching chaos of our times. I have therefore tried to avoid mistaking the natural optimism of youth and the contrasting sadness of later years for a cosmic transformation.

THE CRITICAL THIRTY-NINE DAYS — 1914

The Great Illusion in an Era of Confidence

Scarcely had the "guns of August" sounded when publicists and historians began to ask: Was this war willed by individuals or was it an inevitable product of historic forces that could not be contained? More than a half-century has elapsed and the *Kriegsschuldfrage* is no nearer resolution than it was in the 1920's when first bruited. The personal responsibility of the diplomats, military leaders, and statesmen is incontestable because only individuals can make decisions and act. And yet the men of 1914 did not act irresponsibly in violation of the powers and terms of their office. Only the French ambassador in St. Petersburg, Maurice Paléologue, has been charged with exceeding the limits of his instructions, pursuing a personal policy, and concealing from his superiors in Paris the critical decisions being taken by the Russian government in the matter of mobilization. Schooled diplomats and experienced statesmen made every move by the book — predictably, unimaginatively, without an original idea that might have broken the chain of decisions which was dragging them all to the brink. It is historically inconceivable that a Metternich, Castlereagh, a Bismarck, or even a Salisbury would have acted so conventionally and with so little wisdom and vision. Furthermore, it is significant that in all the volumes of diplomatic dispatches, notes, and memoranda pertaining to the 1914 crisis, there is not to be found a recorded discussion of the crucial question: What will a civil war mean to Europe, and how will it affect the position of predominance that the European nations enjoy in the world? And it was not too much to expect of statesmanship that this question be raised; but statesmanship was lacking in large quantities in 1914.

The impersonal forces in play require somewhat more detailed consideration. In this connection, it cannot be argued convincingly that the First World War was predestined or prefigured in the arts and sciences, in economic relations, in the area of ideas, or even in the public relations of the peoples of Europe. In other areas — social and political — institutions and policies seemed adequate to accomplish the necessary adjustments and compromises. Europe before 1914 had an inner unity and a common ideology arising from its social institutions, its history, and its religions. The network of contacts and communications was very thick among the educated classes and businessmen, and there was a consciousness of sharing a common European culture. There was also a good deal of imitation and much borrowing from others' experiences.

The number of international congresses, organizations, and commissions founded between 1900 and 1914 is both impressive and significant. All this reinforced the optimism and belief in progress which was dominant in popular thought during these years. Interpreters who must divine a *Zeitgeist* in every era have insisted that the end of the century was "decadent" and the period covered by this study the tag end of a heroic age. This judgment must be repudiated. As has been well said, the *fin de siècle* was really a beginning rather than an end; it was not the twilight of a golden age but the seedbed of our twentieth-century problems and concerns. Confident of the future and proud of the past, Europe welcomed the twentieth century.

This leads us to conclude that if there was a fatal flaw threaded through this era of confidence—and this was the great illusion—it was the humanitarian belief that a general war among Europeans was really unthinkable. But while this popular conviction was spreading among the enlightened, the European governments in their international relationships continued to wear the outmoded garments of the nineteenth century. Never were values associated with the nation state so grossly inflated—and this in a period when interdependence in all vital matters was weaving a girdle around the world. But this new reality was only faintly reflected in the relations of governments. Every country had its contingent of "jump-to-glory" militarists and navalists and second-rate statesmen engrossed in the mechanics of power. In the crisis of 1914 both the men and the mechanism failed. This brings us close to the view prevalent at the time: The war resulted from a series of fateful human decisions—mostly mistaken and erroneous—involving risks that decision makers would have avoided had they been endowed with a larger measure of foresight and prudence. Dawning light, rich in promise for a fair day, never became high noon because of the failures and miscalculations of Europe's political and military leaders.

OPTIONS FOR WRITING

1. The great illusion in the years before the Great War, according to Hale, "was the humanitarian belief that a general war among Europeans was really unthinkable." Explain why this belief is not possible today.

2. Hale claims that World War I resulted from mistaken and erroneous human decisions. "Dawning light, rich in promise for a fair day, never became high noon because of the failures and miscalculations of Europe's political and military leaders." Are today's military and political leaders responsible for modern events or do world circumstances really control what happens? Choose a recent event and make a case for one point of view.

3. Decide the extent to which "the great illusion," the "failures and miscalculations of . . . political and military leaders," or both are shaping a current event. Write a letter to the editor of your local paper in which you try to alert citizens to this problem.

Barbara W. Tuchman
THE PROUD TOWER, A PORTRAIT OF THE WORLD BEFORE THE WAR, 1890 – 1914

This selection should be read in conjunction with the selection by Oron Hale. Barbara Tuchman's point of view toward the same years before World War I is rather different from Hale's: "The Great War of 1914–18 lies like a band of scorched earth dividing that time from ours. In wiping out so many lives which would have been operative on the years that followed, in destroying beliefs, changing ideas, and leaving incurable wounds of disillusion, it created a physical as well as psychological gulf between two epochs. This book is an attempt to discover the quality of the world from which the Great War came." Two historians can view the same historical period very differently.

Yet, despite a difference in point of view, see how Tuchman's vivid description of Lord Salisbury and the British patrician class supports Hale's claim for a "grand illusion."

FOREWORD

The epoch whose final years are the subject of this book did not die of old age or accident but exploded in a terminal crisis which is one of the great facts of history. No mention of that crisis appears in the following pages for the reason that, as it had not yet happened, it was not a part of the experience of the people of this book. I have tried to stay within the terms of what was known at the time.

The Great War of 1914–18 lies like a band of scorched earth dividing that time from ours. In wiping out so many lives which would have been operative on the years that followed, in destroying beliefs, changing ideas, and leaving incurable wounds of disillusion, it created a physical as well as psychological gulf between two epochs. This book is an attempt to discover the quality of the world from which the Great War came.

It is not the book I intended to write when I began. Preconceptions dropped off one by one as I investigated. The period was not a Golden Age or *Belle Epoque* except to a thin crust of the privileged class. It was not a time exclusively of confidence, innocence, comfort, stability, security and peace. All these qualities were certainly present. People *were* more confident of values and standards, more innocent in the sense of retaining more hope of mankind, than they are today, although they were not more peaceful nor, except for the upper few, more comfortable. Our misconception lies in assuming that doubt and fear, ferment, protest, violence and hate were not equally present. We have been mis-led by the people of the time themselves who, in looking back across the gulf of the War, see that earlier half of their lives misted over by a lovely sunset haze of peace and security. It did not seem so golden when they were in the midst of it. Their memories and their nostalgia have conditioned our view of the pre-war era but I can offer the reader a rule based on adequate research: all statements of how lovely it was in that era made by persons contemporary with it will be found to have been made after 1914.

A phenomenon of such extended malignance as the Great War does not come out of a Golden Age. Perhaps this should have been obvious to me when I began but it was not. I did feel, however, that the genesis of the war did not lie in the *Grosse Politik* of what Isvolsky said to Aeh-renthal and Sir Edward Grey to Poincaré; in that tortuous train of Rein-surance treaties, Dual and Triple Alliances, Moroccan crises and Balkan imbroglios which historians have painstakingly followed in their search for origins. It was necessary that these events and exchanges be examined and we who come after are in debt to the examiners; but their work has been done. I am with Sergei Sazonov, Russian Foreign Minis-ter at the time of the outbreak of the War, who after a series of investi-gations exclaimed at last, "Enough of this chronology!" The *Grosse Politik* approach has been used up. Besides, it is misleading because it allows us to rest on the easy illusion that it is "they," the naughty statesmen, who are always responsible for war while "we," the innocent people, are merely led. That impression is a mistake.

The diplomatic origins, so-called, of the Great War are only the fever chart of the patient; they do not tell us what caused the fever. To probe for underlying causes and deeper forces one must operate within the framework of a whole society and try to discover what moved the people in it. I have tried to concentrate on society rather than the state. Power politics and economic rivalries, however important, are not my subject.

The period of this book was above all the culmination of a century of the most accelerated rate of change in man's record. Since the last explosion of a generalized belligerent will in the Napoleonic wars, the industrial and scientific revolutions had transformed the world. Man had entered the Nineteenth Century using only his own and animal power, supplemented by that of wind and water, much as he had entered the Thirteenth, or, for that matter, the First. He entered the Twentieth with his capacities in transportation, communication, production, manufac-ture and weaponry multiplied a thousandfold by the energy of machines. Industrial society gave man new powers and new scope while at the same time building up new pressures in prosperity and poverty, in growth of population and crowding in cities, in antagonisms of classes and groups, in separation from nature and from satisfaction in individ-ual work. Science gave man new welfare and new horizons while it took away belief in God and certainty in a scheme of things he knew. By the time he left the Nineteenth Century he had as much new unease as ease. Although *fin de siècle* usually connotes decadence, in fact society at the turn of the century was not so much decaying as bursting with new tensions and accumulated energies. Stefan Zweig who was thirty-three in 1914 believed that the outbreak of war "had nothing to do with ideas and hardly even with frontiers. I cannot explain it otherwise than by this surplus force, a tragic consequence of the internal dynamism that had accumulated in forty years of peace and now sought violent release."

In attempting to portray what the world before the war was like my process has been admittedly highly selective. I am conscious on finishing this book that it could be written all over again under the same title with entirely other subject matter; and then a third time, still without repeating. There could be chapters on the literature of the period, on its wars — the Sino-Japanese, Spanish-American, Boer, Russo-Japanese, Balkan — on imperialism, on science and technology, on business and trade, on women, on royalty, on medicine, on painting, on as many different subjects as might appeal to the individual historian. There could have been chapters on Leopold II, King of the Belgians, Chekhov, Sargent, The Horse, or U.S. Steel, all of which figured in my original plan. There should have been a chapter on some ordinary everyday shopkeeper or clerk representing the mute inglorious anonymous middle class but I never found him.

I think I owe the reader a word about my process of selection. In the first place I confined myself to the Anglo-American and West European world from which our experience and culture most directly derive, leaving aside the East European which, however important, is a separate tradition. In choice of subjects the criterion I used was that they must be truly representative of the period in question and have exerted their major influence on civilization before 1914, not after. This consideration ruled out the automobile and airplane, Freud and Einstein and the movements they represented. I also ruled out eccentrics, however captivating.

I realize that what follows offers no over-all conclusion but to draw some tidy generalization from the heterogeneity of the age would be invalid. I also know that what follows is far from the whole picture. It is not false modesty which prompts me to say so but simply an acute awareness of what I have not included. The faces and voices of all that I have left out crowd around me as I reach the end.

THE PATRICIANS

The last government in the Western world to possess all the attributes of aristocracy in working condition took office in England in June of 1895. Great Britain was at the zenith of empire when the Conservatives won the general election of that year, and the Cabinet they formed was her superb and resplendent image. Its members represented the greater landowners of the country who had been accustomed to govern for generations. As its superior citizens they felt they owed a duty to the State to guard its interests and manage its affairs. They governed from duty, heritage and habit—and, as they saw it, from right.

The Prime Minister was a Marquess and lineal descendant of the father and son who had been chief ministers to Queen Elizabeth and James I. The Secretary for war was another Marquess who traced his inferior title of Baron back to the year 1181, whose great-grandfather had been Prime Minister under George III and whose grandfather had served in six cabinets under three reigns. The Lord President of the Council was a Duke who owned 186,000 acres in eleven counties, whose ancestors had served in government since the Fourteenth Century, who had himself served thirty-four years in the House of Commons and three times refused to be Prime Minister. The Secretary for India was the son of another Duke whose family seat was received in 1315 by grant from Robert the Bruce and who had four sons serving in Parliament at the same time. The President of the Local Government Board was a preeminent country squire who had a Duke for brother-in-law, a Marquess for son-in-law, an ancestor who had been Lord Mayor of London in the reign of Charles II, and who had himself been a Member of Parliament for twenty-seven years. The Lord Chancellor bore a family name brought to England by a Norman follower of William the Conqueror and maintained thereafter over eight centuries without a title. The Lord Lieutenant for Ireland was an Earl, a grandnephew of the Duke of Wellington and a hereditary trustee of the British Museum. The Cabinet also included a Viscount, three Barons and two Baronets. Of its six commoners, one was a director of the Bank of England, one was a squire whose family had represented the same county in Parliament since the Sixteenth Century, one—who acted as Leader of the House of Commons—was the Prime Minister's nephew and inheritor of a Scottish fortune of £4,000,000, and one, a notable and disturbing cuckoo in the nest, was a Birmingham manufacturer widely regarded as the most successful man in England.

Besides riches, rank, broad acres and ancient lineage, the new Government also possessed, to the regret of the Liberal Opposition and in the words of one of them, "an almost embarrassing wealth of talent and capacity." Secure in authority, resting comfortably on their electoral majority in the House of Commons and on a permanent majority in the House of Lords, of whom four-fifths were Conservatives, they were in a position, admitted the same opponent, "of unassailable strength."

Enriching their ranks were the Whig aristocrats who had seceded from the Liberal party in 1886 rather than accept Mr. Gladstone's insistence on Home Rule for Ireland. They were for the most part great landowners who, like their natural brothers the Tories, regarded union with Ireland as sacrosanct. Led by the Duke of Devonshire, the Marquess of Lansdowne and Mr. Joseph Chamberlain, they had remained independent until 1895, when they joined with the Conservative party, and the two groups emerged as the Unionist party, in recognition of the policy that had brought them together. With the exception of Mr. Chamberlain, this coalition represented that class in whose blood, training and practice over the centuries, landowning and governing had been inseparable. Ever since Saxon chieftains met to advise the King in the first national assembly, the landowners of England had been sending members to Parliament and performing the duties of High Sheriff, Justice of the Peace and Lord Lieutenant of the Militia in their own counties. They had learned the practice of government from the possession of great estates, and they undertook to manage the affairs of the nation as inevitably and unquestionably as beavers build a dam. It was their ordained role and natural task.

But it was threatened. By a rising rumble of protest from below, by the Radicals of the Opposition who talked about taxing unearned increment on land, by Home Rulers who wanted to detach the Irish island from which so much English income came, by Trade Unionists who talked of Labour representation in Parliament and demanded the legal right to strike and otherwise interfere with the free play of economic forces, by Socialists who wanted to nationalize property and Anarchists who wanted to abolish it, by upstart nations and strange challenges from abroad. The rumble was distant, but it spoke with one voice that said Change, and those whose business was government could not help but hear.

Planted firmly across the path of change, operating warily, shrewdly yet with passionate conviction in defence of the existing order, was a peer who was Chancellor of Oxford University for life, had twice held the India Office, twice the Foreign Office and was now Prime Minister for the third time. He was Robert Arthur Talbot Gascoyne-Cecil, Lord Salisbury, ninth Earl and third Marquess of his line.

Lord Salisbury was both the epitome of his class and uncharacteristic of it — except insofar as the freedom to be different was a class characteristic. He was six feet four inches tall, and as a young man had been thin, ungainly, stooping and shortsighted, with hair unusually black for an Englishman. Now sixty-five, his youthful lankiness had turned to bulk, his shoulders had grown massive and more stooped than ever, and his heavy bald head with full curly gray beard rested on them as if weighted down. Melancholy, intensely intellectual, subject to sleepwalking and fits of depression which he called "nerve storms," caustic, tactless, absent-minded, bored by society and fond of solitude, with a penetrating, skeptical, questioning mind, he had been called the Hamlet of English politics. He was above the conventions and refused to live in Downing Street. His devotion was to religion, his interest in science. In his own home he attended private chapel every morning before breakfast, and had fitted up a chemical laboratory where he conducted solitary experiments. He harnessed the river at Hatfield for an electric power plant on his estate and strung up along the old beams of his home one of England's first electric light systems, at which his family threw cushions when the wires sparked and sputtered while they went on talking and arguing, a customary occupation of the Cecils.

Lord Salisbury cared nothing for sport and little for people. His aloofness was enhanced by shortsightedness so intense that he once failed to recognize a member of his own Cabinet, and once, his own butler. At the close of the Boer War he picked up a signed photograph of King Edward and, gazing at it pensively, remarked, "Poor Buller [referring to the Commander-in-Chief at the start of the war], what a mess he made of it." On another occasion he was seen in prolonged military conversation with a minor peer under the impression that he was talking to Field Marshal Lord Roberts.

For the upper-class Englishman's alter ego, most intimate companion and constant preoccupation, his horse, Lord Salisbury had no more regard. Riding was to him purely a means of locomotion to which the horse was "a necessary but extremely inconvenient adjunct." Nor was he addicted to shooting. When Parliament rose he did not go north to slaughter grouse upon the moors or stalk deer in Scottish forests, and when protocol required his attendance upon royalty at Balmoral, he would not go for walks and "positively refused," wrote Queen Victoria's Private Secretary, Sir Henry Ponsonby, "to admire the prospect or the deer." Ponsonby was told to have his room in the dismal castle kept "warm" — a minimum temperature of sixty degrees. Otherwise he retired for his holidays to France, where he owned a villa at Beaulieu on the Riviera and where he could exercise his fluent French and lose himself in *The Count of Monte Cristo,* the only book, he once told Dumas *fils,* which allowed him to forget politics.

His acquaintance with games was confined to tennis, but when elderly he invented his own form of exercise, which consisted in riding a tricycle through St. James's Park in the early mornings or along paths cemented for the purpose in the park of his estate at Hatfield. Wearing for the occasion a kind of sombrero hat and a short sleeveless cloak with a hole in the middle in which he resembled a monk, he would be accompanied by a young coachman to push him up the hills. At the downhill slopes, the young man would be told to "jump on behind," and the Prime Minister, with the coachman's hands on his shoulders, would roll away, cloak flying and pedals whirring.

Hatfield, twenty miles north of London in Hertfordshire, had been the home of the Cecils for nearly three hundred years since James I had given it, in 1607, to his Prime Minister, Robert Cecil, first Earl of Salisbury, in exchange for a house of Cecil's to which the King had taken a fancy. It was the royal residence where Queen Elizabeth had spent her childhood and where, on receiving news of her accession, she held her

first council, to swear in William Cecil, Lord Burghley, as her chief Secretary of State. Its Long Gallery, with intricately carved paneled walls
and gold-leaf ceiling, was 180 feet in length. The Marble Hall, named for
the black and white marble floor, glowed like a jewel case with painted
and gilded ceiling and Brussels tapestries. The red King James Drawing
Room was hung with full-length family portraits by Romney and
Reynolds and Lawrence. The library was lined from floor to gallery and
ceiling with 10,000 volumes bound in leather and vellum. In other rooms
were kept the Casket Letters of Mary Queen of Scots, suits of armor
taken from men of the Spanish Armada, the cradle of the beheaded
King, Charles I, and presentation portraits of James I and George III.
Outside were yew hedges clipped in the form of crenelated battlements,
and the gardens, of which Pepys wrote that he never saw "so good
flowers, nor so great gooseberries as big as nutmegs." Over the entrance
hall hung flags captured at Waterloo and presented to Hatfield by the
Duke of Wellington, who was a constant visitor and devoted admirer of
the Prime Minister's mother, the second Marchioness. In her honor Wellington wore the hunt coat of the Hatfield Hounds when he was on
campaign. The first Marchioness was painted by Sir Joshua Reynolds
and hunted till the day she died at eighty-five, when, half-blind and
strapped to the saddle, she was accompanied by a groom who would
shout, when her horse approached a fence, "Jump, dammit, my Lady,
jump!"

It was this exceptional person who reinvigorated the Cecil blood,
which, after Burghley and his son, had produced no further examples of
superior mentality. Rather, the general mediocrity of succeeding generations had been varied only, according to a later Cecil, by instances of
"quite exceptional stupidity." But the second Marquess proved a vigorous and able man with a strong sense of public duty who served in
several mid-century Tory cabinets. His second son, another Robert Cecil,
was the Prime Minister of 1895. He in turn produced five sons who
were to distinguish themselves. One became a general, one a bishop,
one a minister of state, one M.P. for Oxford, and one, through service
to the government, won a peerage in his own right. "In human beings
as in horses," Lord Birkenhead was moved to comment on the Cecil
record, "there is something to be said for the hereditary principle."

At Oxford in 1850 the contemporaries of young Robert Cecil agreed
that he would end as Prime Minister either because or in spite of his
remorselessly uncompromising opinions. Throughout life he never
bothered to restrain them. His youthful speeches were remarkable for
their virulence and insolence; he was not, said Disraeli, "a man who
measures his phrases." A "salisbury" became a synonym for a political
imprudence. He once compared the Irish in their incapacity for self-government to Hottentots and spoke of an Indian candidate for Parliament
as "that black man." In the opinion of Lord Morley his speeches were
always a pleasure to read because "they were sure to contain one blaz-

ing indiscretion which it is a delight to remember." Whether these were altogether accidental is open to question, for though Lord Salisbury delivered his speeches without notes, they were worked out in his head beforehand and emerged clear and perfect in sentence structure. In that time the art of oratory was considered part of the equipment of a statesman and anyone reading from a written speech would have been regarded as pitiable. When Lord Salisbury spoke, "every sentence," said a fellow member, "seemed as essential, as articulate, as vital to the argument as the members of his body to an athlete."

Appearing in public before an audience about whom he cared nothing, Salisbury was awkward; but in the Upper House, where he addressed his equals, he was perfectly and strikingly at home. He spoke sonorously, with an occasional change of tone to icy mockery or withering sarcasm. When a recently ennobled Whig took the floor to lecture the House of Lords in high-flown and solemn Whig sentiments, Salisbury asked a neighbor who the speaker was and on hearing the whispered identification, replied perfectly audibly, "I thought he was dead." When he listened to others he could become easily bored, revealed by a telltale wagging of his leg which seemed to one observer to be saying, "When will all this be over?" Or sometimes, raising his heels off the floor, he would set up a sustained quivering of his knees and legs which could last for half an hour at a time. At home, when made restless by visitors, it shook the floor and made the furniture rattle, and in the House his colleagues on the front bench complained it made them seasick. If his legs were at rest his long fingers would be in motion, incessantly twisting and turning a paper knife or beating a tattoo on his knee or on the arm of his chair.

He never dined out and rarely entertained beyond one or two political receptions at his town house in Arlington Street and an occasional garden party at Hatfield. He avoided the Carlton, official club of the Conservatives, in favor of the Junior Carlton, where a special luncheon table was set aside for him alone and the library was hung with huge placards inscribed SILENCE. He worked from breakfast to one in the morning, returning to his desk after dinner as if he were beginning a new day. His clothes were drab and often untidy. He wore trousers and waistcoat of a dismal gray under a broadcloth frock coat grown shiny. But though careless in dress, he was particular about the trimming of his beard and carefully directed operations in the barber's chair, indicating "just a little more off here" while "artist and subject gazed fixedly in the mirror to judge the result."

Despite his rough tongue and sarcasms, Salisbury exerted a personal charm upon close colleagues and equals which, as one of them said, "was no small asset in the conduct of affairs." He gave detailed attention to party affairs and even sacrificed his exclusiveness for their sake. Once he astonished everyone by accepting an invitation to the traditional dinner for party supporters given by the Leader of the House of Commons. He asked to be given in advance biographical details about each guest. At the dinner the Prime Minister charmed his neighbor at table, a well-known agriculturist, with his expert knowledge of crop rotation and stock-breeding, chatted amiably afterward with every guest in turn, and before leaving, beckoned to his Private Secretary, saying, "I think I have done them all, but there was someone I have not identified who, you said, made mustard."

Mr. Gladstone, though in political philosophy his bitterest antagonist, acknowledged him "a great gentleman in private society." In private life he was delightful and sympathetic and a complete contrast to his public self. In public acclaim, Salisbury was uninterested, for — since the populace was uninstructed — its opinions, as far as he was concerned, were worthless. He ignored the public and neither possessed nor tried to cultivate the personal touch that makes a political leader a recognizable personality to the man in the street and earns him a nickname like "Pam" or "Dizzy" or the "Grand Old Man." Not in the press, not even in *Punch,* was Lord Salisbury ever called anything but Lord Salisbury. He made no attempt to conceal his dislike for mobs of all kinds, "not excluding the House of Commons." After moving to the Lords, he never returned to the Commons to listen to its debates from the Peers' Gallery or chat with members in the Lobby, and if compelled to allude to them in his own House, would use a tone of airy contempt, to the amusement of visitors from the Commons who came to hear him. But this was merely an outward pose designed to underline his deep inner sense of the patrician. He was not rank-conscious; he was indifferent to honors or any other form of recognition. It was simply that as a Cecil, and a superior one, he was born with a consciousness in his bones and brain cells of ability to rule and saw no reason to make any concessions of this prescriptive right to anyone whatever.

Having entered the House of Commons in the customary manner for peers' sons, from a family-controlled borough in an uncontested election at the age of twenty-three, and, during his fifteen years in the House of Commons, having been returned unopposed five times from the same borough, and having for the last twenty-seven years sat in the House of Lords, he had little personal experience of vote-getting. He regarded himself not as responsible *to* the people but as responsible *for* them. They were in his care. What reverence he felt for anyone was directed not down but up — to the monarchy. He revered Queen Victoria, who was some ten years his senior, both as her subject and, with chivalry toward her womanhood, as a man. For her he softened his brusqueness even if at Balmoral he could not conceal his boredom.

She in turn visited him at Hatfield and had the greatest confidence in him, giving him, as she told Bishop Carpenter, "if not the highest, an equal place with the highest among her ministers," not excepting Disraeli. Salisbury, who was "bad on his legs at any time," was the only man she ever asked to sit down. Unlike in every quality of mind except in their strong sense of rulership, the tiny old Queen and the tall, heavy, aging Prime Minister felt for each other mutual respect and regard.

In unimportant matters of state as in dress, Salisbury was inclined to be casual. Once when two clergymen with similar names were candidates for a vacant bishopric, he appointed the one not recommended by the Archbishop of Canterbury, and this being sorrowfully drawn to his attention, he said, "Oh, I daresay he will do just as well." He reserved high seriousness for serious matters only, and the most serious to him was the maintenance of aristocratic influence and executive power, not for its own sake, but because he believed it to be the only element capable of holding the nation united against the rising forces of democracy which he saw "splitting it into a bundle of unfriendly and distrustful fragments."

Class war and irreligion were to him the greatest evils and for this reason he detested Socialism, less for its menace to property than for its preaching of class war and its basis in materialism, which meant to him a denial of spiritual values. He did not deny the need of social reforms, but believed they could be achieved through the interplay and mutual pressures of existing parties. The Workmen's Compensation act, for one, making employers liable for work-sustained injuries, though denounced by some of his party as interference with private enterprise, was introduced and passed with his support in 1897.

He fought all proposals designed to increase the political power of the masses. When still a younger son, and not expecting to succeed to the title, he had formulated his political philosophy in a series of some thirty articles which were published in the *Quarterly Review* in the early 1860's, when he was in his thirties. Against the growing demand at the time for a new Reform law to extend the suffrage, Lord Robert Cecil, as he then was, had declared it to be the business of the Conservative party to preserve the rights and privileges of the propertied class as the "single bulwark" against the weight of numbers. To extend the suffrage would be, as he saw it, to give the working classes not merely a voice in Parliament but a preponderating one that would give to "mere numbers a power they ought not to have." He deplored the Liberals' adulation of the working class "as if they were different from other Englishmen" when in fact the only difference was that they had less education and property and "in proportion as the property is small the danger of misusing the franchise is great." He believed the workings of democracy to be dangerous to liberty, for under democracy "passion is not the exception but the rule" and it was "perfectly impossible" to commend a farsighted passionless policy to "men whose minds are unused to thought and undisciplined to study." To widen the suffrage among the poor while increasing taxes upon the rich would end, he wrote, in a complete divorce of power from responsibility; "the rich would pay all the taxes and the poor make all the laws."

He did not believe in political equality. There was the multitude, he said, and there were "natural" leaders. "Always wealth, in some countries birth, in all countries intellectual power and culture mark out the man to whom, in a healthy state of feeling, a community looks to undertake its government." These men had the leisure for it and the fortune, "so that the struggles for ambition are not defiled by the taint of sordid greed. . . . They are the aristocracy of a country in the original and best sense of the word . . . The important point is, that the rulers of a country should be taken from among them," and as a class they should retain that "political preponderance to which they have every right that superior fitness can confer."

So sincere and certain was his conviction of that "superior fitness" that in 1867 when the Tory Government espoused the Second Reform Bill, which doubled the electorate and enfranchised workingmen in the towns, Salisbury at thirty-seven flung away Cabinet office within a year of first achieving it rather than be party to what he considered a betrayal and surrender of Conservative principles. His party's reversal, engineered by Disraeli in a neat enterprise both to "dish the Whigs" and to meet political realities, was regarded with abhorrence by Lord Cranborne (as Lord Robert Cecil had then become, his elder brother having died in 1865). Though it might ruin his career he resigned as Secretary for India and in a bitter and serious speech spoke out in the House against the policy of the party's leaders, Lord Derby and Mr. Disraeli. He begged the members not to do for political advantage what would ultimately destroy them as a class. "The wealth, the intelligence, the energy of the community, all that has given you that power which makes you so proud of your nation and which makes the deliberations of this House so important, will be numerically absolutely overmatched." Issues would arise in which the interests of employers and employed would clash and could only be decided by political force, "and in that conflict of political force you are pitting an overwhelming number of employed against a hopeless minority of employers." The outcome would "reduce to political insignificance and extinction the classes which have hitherto contributed so much to the greatness and prosperity of their country."

A year later, on his father's death, he entered the House of Lords as third Marquess of Salisbury. In 1895, after the passage of nearly thirty years, his principles had not shifted an inch. With no belief in change as improvement, nor faith in the future over the present, he dedicated himself with "grim acidity" to preserving the existing order. Believing that "rank, without the power of which it was originally the symbol, was a sham," he was determined, while he lived and governed England, to resist further attack on the power of that class of which rank was still the visible symbol. Watchful of approaching enemies, he stood against the coming age. The pressures of democracy encircled, but had not yet closed in around, the figure whom Lord Curzon described as "that strange, powerful, inscrutable, brilliant, obstructive deadweight at the top."

The average member of the ruling class, undisturbed by Lord Salisbury's too-thoughtful, too-prescient mind, did not worry deeply about the future; the present was so delightful. The Age of Privilege, though assailed at many points and already cracking at some, still seemed, in the closing years of the Nineteenth Century and of Victoria's reign, a permanent condition. To the privileged, life appeared "secure and comfortable. . . . Peace brooded over the land." Undoubtedly Sir William Harcourt's budget of 1894, enacted by the Liberals during the premiership of Lord Rosebery, Mr. Gladstone's rather inappropriate successor sent a tremor through many. It introduced death duties — and what was worse, introduced them on a graduated principle from 1 per cent on estates of £500 to 8 per cent on estates of over a million pounds. And it increased the income tax by a penny to eightpence in the pound. Although to soften the blow and equalize the burden it imposed a tax on beer and spirits so that the working class, who paid no income tax, would contribute to the revenue, this failed to muffle the drumbeat of the death duties. The eighth Duke of Devonshire was moved to predict a time which he "did not think can be deferred beyond the period of my own life" when great estates such as his of Chatsworth would be shut up solely because of "the inexorable necessities of democratic finance."

But a greater, and from the Conservative point of view a happier, event of 1894 compensated for the budget. Mr. Gladstone retired from Parliament and from politics. His last octogenarian effort to force through Home Rule had been defeated in the House of Lords by a wrathful assembly of peers gathered for the purpose in numbers hardly before seen in their lifetime. He had split his party beyond recall, he was eighty-five, the end of a career had come. With the Conservative victory in the following year there was a general feeling, reflected by *The Times*, that Home Rule, that "germ planted by Mr. Gladstone in our political life which has threatened to poison the whole organism," being now disposed of, at least for the present, England could settle down sensibly to peace and business. The "dominant influences" were safely in the saddle.

"Dominant influences" was a phrase, not of the Conservative-minded *Times*, but strangely enough of Mr. Gladstone himself, who was a member of the landed gentry and never forgot it nor ever abandoned the inborn sense that property is responsibility. He owned an estate of 7,000 acres at Hawarden with 2,500 tenants producing an annual rent roll between £10,000 and £12,000. In a letter to his grandson who would inherit it, the Great Radical urged him to regain lands lost through debt by earlier generations and restore Hawarden to its former rank as a "leading influence" in the county, because, as he said, "society cannot afford to dispense with its dominant influences." No duke could have put it better. This was exactly the sentiment of the Conservative landowners, who were his bitterest opponents but with whom, at bottom, he shared a belief both in the "superior fitness" conferred by inherited ownership of land and in the country's need of it. Their credo was the exact opposite of the idea prevailing in the more newly minted United States, that there was a peculiar extra virtue in being lowly born, that only the self-made carried the badge of ability and that men of easy circumstances were more likely than not to be stupid or wicked, if not both. The English, on the contrary, having evolved slowly through generations of government by the possessing class, assumed that prolonged retention by one family of education, comfort and social responsibility was natural nourishment of "superior fitness."

It qualified them for government, considered in England as nowhere else the proper and highest profession of a gentleman. A private secretaryship to a ministerial uncle or other relative could be either a serious apprenticeship for Cabinet office or merely a genial occupation for a gentleman like Sir Schomberg McDonnell, Lord Salisbury's Private Secretary, a brother of the Earl of Antrim. Diplomacy, too, offered a desirable career, often to persons of talent. The Marquess of Dufferin and Ava, when British Ambassador in Paris in 1895, taught himself Persian and noted in his diary for that year that besides reading eleven plays of Aristophanes in Greek, he had learned by heart 24,000 words from a Persian dictionary, "8,000 perfectly, 12,000 pretty well, and 4,000 imperfectly." Military service in one of the elite regiments of Guards or Hussars or Lancers was an equally accepted role for men of wealth and rank, although it tended to attract the weaker minds. The less wealthy went into the Church and the Navy; the bar and journalism provided careers when earning power was a necessity. But Parliament above all was the natural and desirable sphere for the exercise of "superior fitness." A seat in Parliament was the only way to a seat in the Cabinet, where power and influence and a membership in the Privy Council, and on retirement a peerage, were to be won. The Privy Council, made up of 235 leaders in all fields, though formal and ceremonial in function, was the badge of importance in the nation. A peerage was still the magic mantle that set a man apart from his fellows. Cabinet office was highly coveted and the object of intense maneuvering behind the scenes. When governments changed, nothing so absorbed the attention of British society as the complicated minuet of Cabinet-making. Clubs and drawing rooms buzzed, cliques and alliances formed and reformed, and the winners emerged proudly wearing fortune's crown of laurel. The prize required hard work and long hours, though rarely knowledge of the department. A minister's function was not to do the work but to see that it got done, much as he managed his estate. Details such as decimal points, which Lord Randolph Churchill when Chancellor of the Exchequer shrugged aside as "those damned dots," were not his concern.

OPTIONS FOR WRITING

1. Ms. Tuchman questioned an interpretation of war which placed all the blame on military and political leaders. She argued that "it is misleading because it allows us to rest on the easy illusion that it is 'they,' the naughty statesmen, who are always responsible for a war while 'we,' the innocent people, are merely led. That impression is a mistake." Can 'we' — you and I — be held responsible for the decisions of our leaders today? To what extent are 'we' to blame? Argue your point of view in the context of a recent or historical confrontation.

2. Ms. Tuchman provides us with a vivid portrait of members of the British patrician class. Are there still people like that today in our modern world? Describe one.

3. People are often puzzled when two different historians view the same period of history in two different ways. To understand why this happens join with one or more of your classmates in writing a history of yesterday.

The Nature and Uses of History

R. G. Collingwood
THE IDEA OF HISTORY

This is the most difficult piece in these readings, but it is well worth careful and thoughtful reading. Collingwood (1889–1943) found himself in a teaching environment at Oxford in the 1930s that stressed the importance of the sciences and analytical philosophy. Philosophers like Bertrand Russell and G. E. Moore tried to assert the general argument that "if it wasn't logical and analytical, it really wasn't worth doing." Many tried to argue that history is an inductive science — facts piled up to make general statements about our past — and that historians should behave and think just as scientists do. Collingwood knew that historians are not scientists. He gave some systematic thought to the nature of history and concluded, in part, that historians imaginatively recreate the past. History, for him, was much more interesting than science because it is produced by people and because we can imagine their lives and actions.

INTRODUCTION

The Philosophy of History

This book is an essay in the philosophy of history. The name 'philosophy of history' was invented in the eighteenth century by Voltaire, who meant by it no more than critical or scientific history, a type of historical thinking in which the historian made up his mind for himself instead of repeating whatever stories he found in old books. The same name was used by Hegel and other writers at the end of the eighteenth century; but they gave it a different sense and regarded it as meaning simply universal or world history. A third use of the phrase is found in several nineteenth-century positivists for whom the philosophy of history was the discovery of general laws governing the course of the events which it was history's business to recount.

The tasks imposed on the 'philosophy' of history by Voltaire and Hegel could be discharged only by history itself, while the positivists were attempting to make out of history, not a philosophy, but an empirical science, like meteorology. In each of these instances, it was a conception of philosophy which governed the conception of the philosophy of history: for Voltaire, philosophy meant independent and critical thinking; for Hegel, it meant thinking about the world as a whole; for nineteenth-century positivism, it meant the discovery of uniform laws.

My use of the term 'philosophy of history' differs from all of these, and in order to explain what I understand by it I will first say something of my conception of philosophy.

Philosophy is reflective. The philosophizing mind never simply thinks about an object, it always, while thinking about any object, thinks also about its own thought about that object. Philosophy may thus be called thought of the second degree, thought about thought. For example, to discover the distance of the earth from the sun is a task for thought of the first degree, in this case for astronomy; to discover what it is exactly that we are doing when we discover the distance of the earth from the sun is a task for thought of the second degree, in this instance for logic or the theory of science.

This is not to say that philosophy is the science of mind, or psychology. Psychology is thought of the first degree; it treats mind in just the same way in which biology treats life. It does not deal with the relation between thought and its object, it deals directly with thought as something quite separate from its object, something that simply happens in the world, as a special kind of phenomenon, one that can be discussed by itself. Philosophy is never concerned with thought by itself; it is always concerned with its relation to its object, and is therefore concerned with the object just as much as with the thought.

This distinction between philosophy and psychology may be illustrated in the different attitudes adopted by these disciplines to historical thinking, which is a special kind of thinking concerned with a special kind of object, which we will provisionally define as the past. The psychologist may interest himself in historical thinking; he may analyze the peculiar kinds of mental events that go on in historians; he might for example argue that historians are people who build up a fantasy-world, like artists, because they are too neurotic to live effectively in the actual world, but, unlike artists, project this fantasy-world into the past because they connect the origin of their neuroses with past events in their own childhood and always go back and back to the past in a vain attempt to disentangle these neuroses. This analysis might go into further detail, and show how the historian's interest in a commanding figure such as Julius Caesar expresses his childish attitude to his father, and so on. I do not suggest that such analysis is a waste of time. I only describe a typical case of it in order to point out that it concentrates its attention exclusively on the subjective term in the original subject-object relation. It attends to the historian's thought, not to its object the past. The whole psychological analysis of historical thought would be exactly the same if there were no such thing as the past at all, if Julius Caesar were an imaginary character, and if history were not knowledge but pure fancy.

For the philosopher, the fact demanding attention is neither the past by itself, as it is for the historian, nor the historian's thought about it by itself, as it is for the psychologist, but the two things in their mutual relation. Thought in its relation to its object is not mere thought but knowledge; thus, what is for psychology the theory of mere thought, of mental events in abstraction from any object, is for philosophy the theory of knowledge. Where the psychologist asks himself: How do historians think? the philosopher asks himself: How do historians know? How do they come to apprehend the past? Conversely, it is the historian's business, not the philosopher's, to apprehend the past as a thing in itself, to say for example that so many years ago such-and-such events actually happened. The philosopher is concerned with these events not as things in themselves but as things known to the historian, and to ask, not what kind of events they were and when and where they took place, but what it is about them that makes it possible for historians to know them.

Thus the philosopher has to think about the historian's mind, but in doing so he is not duplicating the work of the psychologist, for to him the historian's thought it not a complex of mental phenomena but a system of knowledge. He also thinks about the past, but not in such a way as to duplicate the work of the historian: for the past, to him, is not a series of events but a system of things known. One might put this by saying that the philosopher, insofar as he thinks about the subjective side of history, is an epistemologist, and so far as he thinks about the objective side a metaphysician; but that way of putting it would be dangerous as conveying a suggestion that the epistemological and metaphysical parts of his work can be treated separately, and this would be a mistake. Philosophy cannot separate the study of knowing from the study of what is known. This impossibility follows directly from the idea of philosophy as thought of the second degree.

If this is the general character of philosophical thinking, what do I mean when I qualify the term 'philosophy' by adding, 'of history'? In what sense is there a special philosophy of history different from philosophy in general and from the philosophy of anything else?

It is generally, though somewhat precariously, agreed that there are distinctions within the body of philosophy. Most people distinguish logic or the theory of knowledge from ethics or the theory of action;

although most of those who make the distinction would also agree that knowing is in some sense a kind of action, and that action as it is studied by ethics is (or at least involves) certain kinds of knowing. The thought which the logician studies is a thought which aims at the discovery of truth, and is thus an example of activity directed towards an end, and these are ethical conceptions. The action which the moral philosopher studies is an action based on knowledge or belief as to what is right or wrong, and knowledge or belief is an epistemological conception. Thus logic and ethics are connected and indeed inseparable, although they are distinct. If there is a philosophy of history, it will be no less intimately connected with the other special philosophical sciences than these two are connected with each other.

We have then to ask why the philosophy of history should be a subject of special study, instead of being merged in a general theory of knowledge. Throughout the course of European civilization people have in some degree thought historically; but we seldom reflect on the activities which we perform quite easily. It is only the difficulties which we encounter that force upon us a consciousness of our own efforts to overcome them. Thus the subject-matter of philosophy, as the organized and scientific development of self-consciousness, depends from time to time on the special problems in which, at any given time, men find special difficulties. To look at the topics specially prominent in the philosophy of any given people at any given period of their history is to find an indication of the special problems which they feel to be calling forth the whole energies of their minds. The peripheral or subsidiary topics will reveal the things about which they feel no special difficulty.

Now, our philosophical tradition goes back in a continuous line to sixth-century Greece, and at that time the special problem of thought was the task of laying the foundations of mathematics. Greek philosophy therefore placed mathematics in the center of its picture, and when it discussed the theory of knowledge it understood by it first and foremost the theory of mathematical knowledge.

Since then there have been, down to a century ago, two great constructive ages of European history. In the Middle Ages the central problems of thought were concerned with theology, and the problems of philosophy therefore arose out of reflection on theology and were concerned with the relations of God and man. From the sixteenth to the nineteenth centuries the main effort of thought was concerned with laying the foundations of natural science, and philosophy took as its main theme the relation of the human mind as subject to the natural world of things around it in space as object. All this time, of course, people were also thinking historically, but their historical thought was always of a comparatively simple or even rudimentary kind; it raised no problems which it did not find easy to solve, and was never forced to reflect upon itself. But in the eighteenth century people began thinking critically about history, as they had already learnt to think critically about the external world, because history began to be regarded as a special form of thought, not quite like mathematics or theology or science.

The result of this reflection was that a theory of knowledge proceeding on the assumption that mathematics or theology or science, or all three together, could exhaust the problems of knowledge in general, was no longer satisfactory. Historical thought has an object with peculiarities of its own. The past, consisting of particular events in space and time which are no longer happening, cannot be apprehended by mathematical thinking, because mathematical thinking apprehends objects that have no special location in space and time, and it is just that lack of peculiar spatio-temporal location that makes them knowable. Nor can the past be apprehended by theological thinking, because the object of that kind of thinking is a single infinite object, and historical events are finite and plural. Nor by scientific thinking, because the truths which science discovers are known to be true by being found through observation and experiment exemplified in what we actually perceive, whereas the past has vanished and our ideas about it can never be verified as we verify our scientific hypotheses. Theories of knowledge designed to account for mathematical and theological and scientific knowledge thus do not touch on the special problems of historical knowledge; and if they offer themselves as complete accounts of knowledge they actually imply that historical knowledge is impossible.

This did not matter so long as historical knowledge had not yet obtruded itself on the consciousness of philosophers by encountering special difficulties and devising a special technique to meet them. But when that happened, as it did, roughly speaking, in the nineteenth century, the situation was that current theories of knowledge were directed towards the special problems of science, and inherited a tradition based on the study of mathematics and theology, whereas this new historical technique, growing up on all sides, was unaccounted for. A special inquiry was therefore needed whose task should be the study of this new problem or group of problems, the philosophical problems created by the existence of organized and systematized historical research. This new inquiry might justly claim the title philosophy of history, and it is to this inquiry that this book is a contribution.

Two stages are to be expected as the inquiry proceeds. First, the philosophy of history will have to be worked out, not, indeed, in a watertight compartment, for there are none in philosophy, but in a relatively isolated condition, regarded as a special study of a special problem. The problem requires special treatment just because the traditional philosophies do not deal with it, and it requires to be isolated because it is a general rule that what a philosophy does not assert it denies, so that the traditional philosophies carry with them the implication that historical knowledge is impossible. The philosophy of history has therefore to leave them alone until it can build up an independent demonstration of how history is possible.

The second stage will be to work out the connexions between this new branch of philosophy and the old traditional doctrines. Any addition to the body of philosophical ideas alters to some extent everything that was there already, and the establishment of a new philosophical science necessitates a revision of all the old ones. For example, the establishment of modern natural science, and of the philosophical theory produced by reflection upon it, reacted upon the established logic by producing widespread discontent with the syllogistic logic and substituting for it the new methodologies of Descartes and Bacon; the same thing reacted upon the theological metaphysics which the seventeenth century had inherited from the Middle Ages and produced the new conceptions of God which we find for example in Descartes and Spinoza. Spinoza's God is the God of medieval theology as revised in the light of seventeenth-century science. Thus, by the time of Spinoza, the philosophy of science was no longer a particular branch of philosophical investigation separate from the rest: it had permeated all the rest and produced a complete philosophy all conceived in a scientific spirit. In the present case this will mean a general overhauling of all philosophical questions in the light of the results reached by the philosophy of history in the narrower sense, and this will produce a new philosophy which will be a philosophy of history in the wide sense, i.e., a complete philosophy conceived from an historical point of view.

Of these two stages, we must be content if this book represents the first. What I am attempting here is a philosophical inquiry into the nature of history regarded as a special type or form of knowledge with a special type of object, leaving aside, for the present, the further question how that inquiry will affect other departments of philosophical study.

History's Nature, Object, Method, and Value

What history is, what it is about, how it proceeds, and what it is for, are questions which to some extent different people would answer in different ways. But in spite of differences there is a large measure of agreement between the answers. And this agreement becomes closer if the answers are subjected to scrutiny with a view to discarding those which proceed from unqualified witnesses. History, like theology or natural science, is a special form of thought. If that is so, questions about the nature, object, method, and value of this form of thought must be answered by persons having two qualifications.

First, they must have experience of that form of thought. They must be historians. In a sense we are all historians nowadays. All educated persons have gone through a process of education which has included a certain amount of historical thinking. But this does not qualify them to give an opinion about the nature, object, method, and value of historical thinking. For in the first place, the experience of historical thinking which they have thus acquired is probably very superficial; and the opinions based on it are therefore no better grounded than a man's opinion of the French people based on a single week-end visit to Paris.

In the second place, experience of anything whatever gained through the ordinary educational channels, as well as being superficial, is invariably out of date. Experience of historical thinking, so gained, is modelled on text-books, and text-books always describe not what is now being thought by real live historians, but what was thought by real live historians at some time in the past when the raw material was being created out of which the text-book has been put together. And it is not only the results of historical thought which are out of date by the time they get into the text-book. It is also the principles of historical thought: that is, the ideas as to the nature, object, method, and value of historical thinking. In the third place, and connected with this, there is a peculiar illusion incidental to all knowledge acquired in the way of education: the illusion of finality. When a student is *in statu pupillari* with respect to any subject whatever, he has to believe that things are settled because the text-books and his teachers regard them as settled. When he emerges from that state and goes on studying the subject for himself he finds that nothing is settled. The dogmatism which is an invariable mark of immaturity drops away from him. He looks at so-called facts with a new eye. He says to himself: 'My teacher and text-books told me that such and such was true; but is it true? What reasons had they for thinking it true, and were these reasons adequate?' On the other hand, if he emerges from the status of pupil without continuing to pursue the subject he never rids himself of this dogmatic attitude. And this makes him a person peculiarly unfitted to answer the questions I have mentioned. No one, for example, is likely to answer them worse than an Oxford philosopher who, having read Greats in his youth, was once a student of history and thinks that this youthful experience of historical thinking entitles him to say what history is, what it is about, how it proceeds, and what it is for.

The second qualification for answering these questions is that a man should not only have experience of historical thinking but should also have reflected upon that experience. He must be not only an historian but a philosopher; and in particular his philosophical thought must have included special attention to the problems of historical thought. Now it is possible to be a quite good historian (though not an historian of the highest order) without thus reflecting upon one's own historical thinking. It is even easier to be a quite good teacher of history (though not the very best kind of teacher) without such reflection. At the same time, it is important to remember that experience comes first, and reflection on that experience second. Even the least reflective historian has the first qualification. He possesses the experience on which to reflect; and when he is asked to reflect on it his reflections have a good chance of being to the point. An historian who has never worked much at philosophy will probably answer our four questions in a more intelligent and valuable way than a philosopher who has never worked much at history.

I shall therefore propound answers to my four questions such as I think any present-day historian would accept. Here they will be rough and ready answers, but they will serve for a provisional definition of our subject-matter and they will be defended and elaborated as the argument proceeds.

a. *The definition of history*. Every historian would agree, I think, that history is a kind of research or inquiry. What kind of inquiry it is I do not yet ask. The point is that generically it belongs to what we call the sciences: that is, the forms of thought whereby we ask questions and try to answer them. Science in general, it is important to realize, does not consist in collecting what we already know and arranging it in this or that kind of pattern. It consists in fastening upon something we do not know, and trying to discover it. Playing patience with things we already know may be a useful means towards this end, but it is not the end itself. It is at best only the means. It is scientifically valuable only insofar as the new arrangement gives us the answer to a question we have already decided to ask. That is why all science begins from the knowledge of our own ignorance: not our ignorance of everything, but our ignorance of some definite thing—the origin of parliament, the cause of cancer, the chemical composition of the sun, the way to make a pump work without muscular exertion on the part of a man or a horse or some other docile animal. Science is finding things out: and in that sense history is a science.

b. *The object of history*. One science differs from another in that it finds out things of a different kind. What kind of things does history find out? I answer, *res gestae*: actions of human beings that have been done in the past. Although this answer raises all kinds of further questions many of which are controversial, still, however they may be answered, the answers do not discredit the proposition that history is the science of *res gestae*, the attempt to answer questions about human actions done in the past.

c. *How does history proceed?* History proceeds by the interpretation of evidence: where evidence is a collective name for things which singly are called documents, and a document is a thing existing here and now, of such a kind that the historian, by thinking about it, can get answers to the questions he asks about past events. Here again there are plenty of difficult questions to ask as to what the characteristics of evidence are and how it is interpreted. But there is no need for us to raise them at this stage. However they are answered, historians will agree that historical procedure, or method, consists essentially of interpreting evidence.

d. Lastly, *what is history for?* This is perhaps a harder question than the others; a man who answers it will have to reflect rather more widely than a man who answers the three we have answered already. He must reflect not only on historical thinking but on other things as well, because to say that something is 'for' something implies a distinction between A and B, where A is good for something and B is that for which something is good. But I will suggest an answer, and express the opinion that no historian would reject it, although the further questions to which it gives rise are numerous and difficult.

My answer is that history is 'for' human self-knowledge. It is generally thought to be of importance to man that he should know himself: where knowing himself means knowing not his merely personal peculiarities, the things that distinguish him from other men, but his nature as man. Knowing yourself means knowing, first, what it is to be a man; secondly, knowing what it is to be the kind of man you are; and thirdly, knowing what it is to be the man *you* are and nobody else is. Knowing yourself means knowing what you can do; and since nobody knows what he can do until he tries, the only clue to what man can do is what man has done. The value of history, then, is that it teaches us what man has done and thus what man is.

The Problem of Parts I–IV

The idea of history which I have just briefly summarized belongs to modern times. . . . Historians nowadays think that history should be *(a)* a science, or an answering of questions; *(b)* concerned with human actions in the past; *(c)* pursued by interpretation of evidence; and *(d)* for the sake of human self-knowledge. But this is not the way in which people have always thought of history. For example, a recent author[1] writes of the Sumerians in the third millennium before Christ:

> Historiography is represented by official inscriptions commemorating the building of palaces and of temples. The theocratic style of the scribes attributes everything to the action of the divinity, as can be seen from the following passage, one of many examples.
> "A dispute arises between the kings of Lagash and of Umma about the boundaries of their respective territories. The dispute is submitted to the arbitration of Mesilim, king of Kish, and is settled by the gods, of whom the kings of Kish, Lagash, and Umma are merely the agents or ministers:
> "Upon the truthful word of the god Enlil, king of the territories, the god Ningirsu and the god Shara deliberated. Mesilim, king of Kish, at the behest of his god, Gu-Silim, . . . erected in [this] place a stela. Ush, *isag* of Umma, acted in accordance with his ambitious designs. He removed Mesilim's stela and came to the plain of Lagash. At the righteous word of the god Ningirsu, warrior of the god Enlil, a combat with Umma took place. At the word of the god Enlil, the great divine net laid low the enemies, and funerary *tells* were placed in their stead in the plain."

Monsieur Jean, it will be noticed, says not that Sumerian historiography *was* this kind of thing, but that in Sumerian literature historiography *is represented by* this kind of thing. I take him to mean that this kind of thing is not really history, but is something in certain ways resembling history. My comment on this would be as follows. An inscription like this expresses a form of thought which no modern histo-

---

[1] Monsier Charles F. Jean, in Edward Eyre, *European Civilization* (London, 1935), vol. i, p. 259.

rian would call history, because, in the first place, it lacks the character of science: it is not an attempt to answer a question of whose answer the writer begins by being ignorant; it is merely a record of something the writer knows for a fact; and in the second place the fact recorded is not certain actions on the part of human beings, it is certain actions on the part of gods. No doubt these divine actions resulted in actions done by human beings; but they are conceived in the first instance not as human actions but as divine actions; and to that extent the thought expressed is not historical in respect of its object, and consequently is not historical in respect of its method, for there is no interpretation of evidence, nor in respect of its value, for there is no suggestion that its aim is to further human self-knowledge. The knowledge furthered by such a record is not, or at any rate is not primarily, man's knowledge of man, but man's knowledge of the gods.

From the writer's point of view, therefore, this is not what we call an historical text. The writer was not writing history, he was writing religion. From our point of view it can be used as historical evidence, since a modern historian with his eye fixed on human *res gestae* can interpret it as evidence concerning actions done by Mesilim and Ush and their subjects. But it only acquires its character as historical evidence posthumously, as it were, in virtue of our own historical attitude towards it; in the same way in which prehistoric flints or Roman pottery acquire the posthumous character of historical evidence, not because the men who made them thought of them as historical evidence, but because *we* think of them as historical evidence.

The ancient Sumerians left behind them nothing at all that we should call history. If they had any such thing as an historical consciousness, they have left no record of it. We may say that they must have had such a thing; to us, the historical consciousness is so real and so all-pervasive a feature of life that we cannot see how anyone can have lacked it; but whether we are right so to argue is very doubtful. If we stick to facts as revealed to us by the documents, I think we must say that the historical consciousness of the ancient Sumerians is what scientists call an occult entity, something which the rules of scientific method forbid us to assert on the principle of Occam's Razor that *entia non sunt multiplicanda praeter necessitatem*.

Four thousand years ago, then, our forerunners in civilization did not possess what we call the idea of history. This, so far as we can see, was not because they had the thing itself but had not reflected upon it. It was because they did not possess the thing itself. History did not exist. There existed, instead, something which in certain ways resembled what we call history, but this differed from what we call history in respect of every one of the four characteristics which we have identified in history as it exists to-day.

History as it exists to-day, therefore, has come into existence in the last four thousand years in western Asia and Europe. How did this happen? By what stages has the thing called history come into existence?

OPTIONS FOR WRITING

1. Would you characterize yourself as being more interested in human lives and actions or in events in the physical world? Are you more a "humanist" or a "scientist"? Define yourself one way or the other in a brief character sketch.

2. Collingwood placed difficult requirements upon us if we are to think like historians. It is not good enough to listen to a teacher, read a textbook, and memorize names and dates to become a historian. Questions about the nature of history are much too important for that kind of meager preparation. In a wonderfully irritating sentence he claimed: "No one, for example, is likely to answer them worse than an Oxford philosopher who, having read Greats in his youth, was once a student of history and thinks that this youthful experience of historical thinking entitles him to say what history is, what it is about, how it proceeds, and what it is for." Real live historians deal with the raw material of history, in Collingwood's view.

Choose a recent event, and list the "raw material" you need in order to study the event to enable you to be a real historian of that event. Look carefully at your list and describe your next move as if you were going to make it.

3. Collingwood claimed that "history is 'for' human self-knowledge." Does knowing about human actions in the past help you to know who you are in the present? How else could you know about yourself? How might people trained in another discipline—sociology, psychology, biology—respond to this question? Choose one of these perspectives (see other chapters in this book) and write a response to Collingwood.

Michael Kammen
ON KNOWING THE PAST

Michael Kammen (b. 1936) is a well-published and well-known professor of American history, whose People of Paradox: An Inquiry Concerning the Origins of American Civilization *won the* Pulitzer Prize for history in 1973. In this short piece he tries to assess the place of "real" history in our current lives.

Have we recently reached a critical juncture in our relationship to History? Abundant signs say yes. To judge by rising museum attendance, increasing book sales, successful television programs and historical-preservation activities, nostalgia is surely in the saddle.

Nostalgia would seem to be a mindless, if not headless horseman, however, because newspaper surveys reveal a woeful ignorance of the national past by Americans with above-average educational backgrounds. . . .

This problem exemplifies a more general American ambivalence about the past—an ambivalence that has been visible for three centuries. Americans who are policy-makers and opinion-makers, for example, have had a strangely ambiguous relationship to history.

Let us look at three of the most interesting Americans in our pantheon: Thomas Jefferson, Ralph Waldo Emerson and Henry Ford. Associated with each is a provocative statement about our need to be released from the burdens of an oppressive or meaningless past. Each statement is actually more complex than a one-line excerpt can reveal, but at least the one-liners serve to jog our memories:

> "The earth belongs in usufruct to the living . . . the dead have neither powers nor rights over it."(Jefferson to James Madison, Sept. 6, 1789.)
>   "Our age is retrospective. . . . It writes biographies, histories, and criticism. The foregoing generations beheld God and nature face to face, we, through their eyes. . . . Why should not we have a poetry and philosophy of insight and not of tradition, and a religion by revelation to us, and not the history of theirs?" (Emerson, "Nature," 1836.)
>   "History is more or less bunk." (Ford in a newspaper interview, 1916.)

The problem with taking any of these pithy remarks too seriously is that they are not only misguided as declarations, in my opinion, but they are not even representative of the three men who offered them.

Consider the fact that Jefferson, in his 1781 "Notes on the State of Virginia," the only book he ever wrote and a classic of American thought, pleaded for the necessary centrality of History in the curriculum of secondary-school students. "History, by apprizing them of the past, will enable them to judge of the future; it will avail them of the experience of other times and other nations; it will qualify them as judges of the actions and designs of men."

Consider the fact that Emerson wrote an 1841 essay called "History" in which he declared that "Man is explicable by nothing less than all his history. . . . There is a relation between the hours of our life and the centuries of time."

And consider the fact that emblazoned on an iron sign in front of Greenfield Village and the Henry Ford Museum in Dearborn, Michigan, are these words from a Henry Ford grown wiser than the 1916 curmudgeon: "The farther you look back, the farther you can see ahead."

How are we supposed to make sense of such contradictory utterances?

First, of course, we must recognize that their views were as variable as ours. All lived long lives, witnessed and participated in the making of history, and changed their minds on certain key matters from time to time.

Second, we should appreciate that they distinguished between the desirability of knowing history and the imperative that we not be prisoners of the past.

Third, we must recognize that there is a tension contained within the cliché that we ought to learn from the lessons of the past. Do we learn from the so-called wisdom of the past, or do we profit from the follies of the past? Jefferson made that distinction, and preferred the second alternative.

One reason why Americans may frequently recite the negative statements of Jefferson, Emerson and Ford and prefer to neglect their affirmations of historical study is that we have been—most of us, most of the time—an optimistic and opportunistic people. We want to believe that "it" will all work out for the best.

The problem is that history shows us that "it" doesn't always. History, real history, isn't chock full of happy endings.

Listen to Walter Lippmann back in 1914: "Modern men are afraid of the past. It is a record of human achievement, but its other face is human defeat." How right he was—all the more reason why we must know and understand the past. We have at least as much to learn from our defeats as from our achievements.

Why, then, should we really want to know the past? Here are a few reasons that I find most compelling:

To make us more cognizant of human differences and similarities, over time and through space.

To help us appreciate far more fully than we do the nonrational and irrational elements in our behavior: what James Boswell called, in 1763, "the unaccountable nature of the human mind."

To enhance our awareness of the complexity of historical causation—the unanticipated intertwining of opinion and events—and their consequences for our understanding of that whirlwind we call social change.

To acknowledge more fully and critically than we do the consequences of what is at stake when powerful people interpret history for partisan purposes on the basis of insufficient or inaccurate information about the past.

To avoid the tendency to ascribe equal value to all relationships and events. Worse than no memory at all is the undiscriminating memory that cannot differentiate between important and inconsequential experiences.

It is the historian's vocation to provide society with a discriminating memory.

OPTIONS FOR WRITING

1. Compare these two statements by Michael Kammen and Oron Hale: "History, real history, isn't chock full of happy endings" (Kammen). "[The great illusion] was the humanitarian belief that a general war among Europeans was really unthinkable" (Hale). Describe the advantages of knowing that often people have succeeded in the past and that often they have failed.

2. What relationship do you see between Kammen's claim that history helps us to "enhance our awareness of the complexity of historical causation — the unanticipated intertwining of opinion and events" and our ability to interpret and evaluate TV evening news broadcasts? Evening news broadcasters must say things that are short, concise, and relatively simple. Explain how the need for short, simple statements on TV distorts our understanding of events.

George F. Kennan
AMERICAN DIPLOMACY, 1900–1950

If ever we needed the aid of history as a guide to diplomacy, we need it right now on the 1990s. Events in China, Russia, Eastern Europe, the Middle East, and Africa have all presented new and fundamental challenges to American diplomacy. George Kennan (b. 1904) was the dean of American diplomatic historians. He also served in the Foreign Service of the United States immediately after World War II. It was during his official duties that he came to realize the full importance of historical understanding for the formulation of foreign policy. In this foreword to his six famous lectures at Princeton in 1951, Kennan explains the connection between history and diplomacy.

FOREWORD

After many years of official duty in the Foreign Service of the United States, it fell to me to bear a share of the responsibility for forming the foreign policy of the United States in the difficult years following World War II. The Policy Planning Staff — it was my duty to set up this office and direct it through the first years of its existence — was the first regular office of the Department of State to be charged in our time with looking at problems from the standpoint of the totality of American national interest, as distinct from a single portion of it. People working in this institutional framework soon became conscious of the lack of any general agreement, both within and without our government, on the basic concepts underlying the conduct of the external relations of the United States.

It was this realization of the lack of an adequately stated and widely accepted theoretical foundation to underpin the conduct of our external relations which aroused my curiosity about the concepts by which our statesmen had been guided in recent decades. After all, the novel and grave problems with which we were forced to deal seemed in large measure to be the products of the outcome of these past two world wars. The rhythm of international events is such that the turn of the century seemed a suitable starting point for an examination of American diplomacy and its relation to these two great cycles of violence. One and a half decades elapsed between the conclusion of the war with Spain and the dispatch of the first "Open Door" notes, on the one hand, and the outbreak of World War I, on the other. Measured against what we know of the relationships between cause and effect in the great matters of international life, this is a respectable period of time and one in which the influence of a country as powerful as the United States of that day could, if exerted consistently and with determination, have affected perceptibly the course of world affairs. The same was plainly true of the interval between the two world wars. By 1900 we were generally aware that our power had world-wide significance and that we could be affected by events far afield; from that time on our interests were constantly involved in important ways with such events.

By what concepts were our statesmen animated in their efforts to meet these new problems? What assumptions had they made concerning the basic purposes of this country in the field of foreign policy? What was it they felt they were trying to achieve? And were these concepts, in the light of retrospect, appropriate and effective ones? Did they reflect some deeper understanding of the relationship of American democracy to its world environment—something which we, perhaps, had forgotten but ought to resurrect and place again at the foundation of our conduct? Or had they been inadequate and superficial all along?

It was these questions which drew my curiosity to the record of American's diplomatic activity in this past half-century, a record which has become steadily richer with the continued appearance of private memoirs and papers and the excellent efforts of American scholarship in the study and analysis of this material. As a novice in the field of diplomatic history, I could not hope to contribute to this work of research or even to make a comprehensive examination of all the secondary material which has appeared on these subjects. The lectures included in this volume, therefore, represent only an attempt to apply what might be called a layman's reading of the main published materials—fortified by the curiosity described above—to the questions at hand and to indicate the answers that suggested themselves.

Two somewhat contradictory considerations gave to this inquiry a special edge of interest from my own standpoint. The first of these was the recognition that the formulation of American foreign policy from the time of the Spanish-American War until the end of World War II had absorbed the energies and contributions of a number of outstanding Americans—men of exceptional intelligence and education, deeply respected for their integrity of character and breadth of experience. In certain instances, they were substantially the best we had to offer. If their approaches to the philosophy of external relations were inadequate, then the deficiencies of America's understanding of her own relationship to the rest of the globe, and her interest in shaping this relationship, were deeply rooted in the national consciousness, and any corrections would be difficult indeed.

Coupled with this, one had the inescapable fact that our security, or what we took to be our security, had suffered a tremendous decline over the course of the half-century. A country which in 1900 had no thought that its prosperity and way of life could be in any way threatened by the outside world had arrived by 1950 at a point where it seemed to be able to think of little else but this danger.

What was the explanation for this? To what extent was it the fault of American diplomacy? To the extent that it *was* the fault of American diplomacy, what was wrong—the concepts or the execution? To the extent that it might be the result of things outside the range of our influence, what were these things and what did they portend? Were they still operable, and where would they carry us? There could be no thought of answering these questions exhaustively in six lectures, even had one felt that he had the answers. The lectures in this volume, then, constitute attempts to discuss individual episodes and situations in the light of these questions, in the hope that this impressionistic pattern may communicate better than any attempt at direct presentation my own reactions to the material at hand. Only in the last of them is there any effort at generalization. I am sure they will be vulnerable in matters of detail to the critical judgment of the experienced diplomatic historian. The conclusions they indicate will certainly be widely challenged. If they serve as a stimulus to further thought on these problems and to worthier efforts by wiser and more learned people, their purpose will be served.

The lectures given at the University of Chicago, embracing as they did American diplomacy up to and through World War II, had little direct reference to the problems of Soviet-American relations, which have agitated so deeply the public opinion of our day. For this reason, it may not be easy for everyone to discern the full measure of their relevance to current problems. It was thought appropriate, therefore, to include in this volume two articles on Russian-American relations which can be taken as reflecting the application of the same intellectual approach to problems of the present day.

I acknowledge here my gratitude to the officers of the Charles R. Walgreen Foundation for the Study of American Institutions, which sponsored these six lectures, and to the Editor of *Foreign Affairs*, in which the two articles were originally published.

OPTIONS FOR WRITING

1. "By 1900," Kennan wrote, "we were generally aware that our power had world-wide significance and that we could be affected by events far afield. . . . " This was a major transition in American diplomacy, requiring thought about our position in the world.

Choose *one* recent event and, in a short essay, show how *both* American power and our sense of distant events affecting our own self-interest shaped our behavior during that event.

2. Kennan suggests that diplomats must have a "deeper understanding of the relationship of American democracy to its world environment." Do you agree? Argue your position in a letter to the editor of your campus newspaper.

3. Kennan believed that "a country which in 1900 had no thought that its prosperity and way of life could be in any way threatened by the outside world had arrived by 1950 at a point where it seemed to be able to think of little else but this danger." How might George Kennan revise this essay if he were writing today?

Issues for Historians

Leon Litwack
PATTERNS OF SOCIAL AND POLITICAL INTERACTION

> *Racism is a problem in our lives. The ways in which history is*
> *taught may help or hinder us in our attempts to display the advan-*
> *tages of our knowing about other cultures and other peoples. Specifi-*
> *cally concerned with the teaching of history, Litwack (b. 1929) argues:*
> *"History is not a set of indigestible facts and "great events" arrayed*
> *in chronological order—no sooner memorized than forgotten. Stu-*
> *dents need to be able to* feel *the facts to which they are exposed; they*
> *need to be engaged in the social complexity and diversity of the past.*
> *Teachers face an equally formidable task in helping their students to*
> *overcome racial and ethnic stereotypes and cultural parochialism."*
> *History students and teachers alike need to be sensitive to the issues*
> *of cultural diversity.*

When the Bradley Commission noted "the new prominence of women, minorities, and the common people in the study of history, and their relation to political power and influential elites," it acknowledged the far reaching changes in writing, teaching, and documentation of the American past. Until recently, the American history the typical student learned in high school or college was the history of exceptional people, mostly white, literate men. If women, racial minorities, or common people appeared at all, it was largely as picturesque appendages, not as active shapers of their own history; their experience was not only peripheral but said to be impossible to reclaim, because traditional methods of historical scholarship emphasized the importance of records and documents which the "inarticulate"—working class racial and ethnic communities—have not usually kept.

Historians played a significant role in creating, shaping, and reinforcing racial, gender, and ethnic biases; they succeeded in miseducating several generations of Americans. The history they wrote did have consequences. The ways in which the past is interpreted often have had a profound impact on the present. The traditional view of Reconstruction in American history, for example, as a period of unrelieved debauchery and black rule, helped to explain why blacks were unfit to participate in political life and why the South needed to eliminate them as voters and officeholders; it not only rationalized the South's denial of constitutional rights to black people but northern acquiescence in that denial. And for nearly a century this distorted image of Reconstruction shaped white southern responses to any threat to white supremacy, to any proposal to end segregation and readmit blacks as voters.

To provide a deeper understanding of the cultural and racial diversity of American society, the quality, depth, and resourcefulness of the response of racial minorities, women, and ordinary people to their place in that society, it becomes necessary to reassess the traditional documentation of the past, to appreciate the diverse ways in which the "inarticulate" have related their experiences and communicated their feelings. It has often been in their music, in their folk beliefs and proverbs, in their humor, in their hero traditions, in their language and dialect, in their superstitions, in their art and dances that people have expressed their innermost thoughts and preoccupations, their sorrows, frustrations, and joys, their triumphs and defeats. That scholars and teachers neglected these sources revealed not only a lack of historical imagination but ethnocentric complacency and racial chauvinism. In the conclusion of his work *Deep Blues*, Robert Palmer asked, "How much thought can be hidden in a few short lines of poetry? How much history can be transmitted by pressure on a guitar string?" And he answered, "The thought of generations, the history of every human being who's ever felt the blues come down like showers of rain." In that spirit, teachers need to instill in their students an appreciation of the complexities and varieties of cultural documentation, the enormous possibilities those documents afford us to bring into our historical consciousness people ordinarily left outside the framework of history. The kinds of records found in most documentary readers—state papers, legislative enactments, court decisions, speeches and proclamations—reveal only a fragment of the past and do little to illuminate the character and culture of a people, the range and depth of the human experience.

History is not a set of indigestible facts and "great events" arrayed in chronological order—no sooner memorized than forgotten. Students need to be able to *feel* the facts to which they are exposed; they need to be engaged in the social complexity and diversity of the past. Teachers face an equally formidable task in helping their students to overcome racial and ethnic stereotypes and cultural parochialism. That challenge has seldom taken on such critical proportions as it does today. Racism remains the most debilitating virus in the American system, deeply embedded in our culture and politics (as graphically revealed in the last presidential election), and its consequences spill over into almost every facet of American life. It is nourished by historical and cultural illiteracy.

OPTIONS FOR WRITING

1. Litwack claims that historical documents "state papers, legislative enactments, court decisions, speeches and proclamations — reveal only a fragment of the past and do little to illuminate the character and culture of a people, the range and depth of the human experience." Documents are rather easily available, but it is often difficult to study and understand other sources of information.

Write an essay about a recent experience that helped you to appreciate "the character and culture of a people" somewhat unfamiliar to you. What type of evidence helped you gain this new appreciation?

2. Until very recently, the "inarticulate" members of a culture have been neglected in our history books. Access to these people — racial minorities, women, and ordinary people — must be gained through sources other than written documents. Litwack suggests that alternative sources such as music, folk beliefs and proverbs, humor, language and dialect, dances, and art give us access to knowing about the portion of a population previously neglected by most historians. Do you agree that these alternative sources are better than documents for our understanding of the culturally and racially diverse aspects of a culture? Can we understand them? Make a case one way or another and address your answer to another historian mentioned in this chapter.

3. Litwack gives a harsh criticism of the neglect of alternative historical sources: "That scholars and teachers neglected these sources revealed not only a lack of historical imagination but ethnocentric complacency and racial chauvinism." In a short essay, defend these past historians from Litwack's attack.

Marguerite Yourcenar
REFLECTIONS ON THE COMPOSITION OF
THE MEMOIRS OF HADRIAN

Marguerite Yourcenar (1903–1987) has written a unique and wonderful portrait of the Roman emperor Hadrian. She has imaginatively recreated his life, writing her historical account in the first person. She lets Hadrian speak for himself: "Surely Hadrian could speak more forcibly and more subtly of his life than could I." In these selections from her reflections on her historical writing, she gives us a fine sense of a historian at work.

I left for Taos, in New Mexico, taking with me the blank sheets for a fresh start on the book (the swimmer who plunges into the water with no assurance that he will reach the other shore). Closed inside my compartment as if in a cubicle of some Egyptian tomb, I worked late into the night between New York and Chicago; then all the next day, in the restaurant of a Chicago station where I awaited a train blocked by storms and snow; then again until dawn, alone in the observation car of a Santa Fé limited, surrounded by black spurs of the Colorado mountains, and by the eternal pattern of the stars. Thus were written at a single impulsion the passages on food, love, sleep, and the knowledge of men. I can hardly recall a day spent with more ardor, or more lucid nights.

Portrait of a voice. If I have chosen to write these *Memoirs of Hadrian* in the first person it is in order to dispense with any intermediary, in so far as possible, even were that intermediary myself. Surely Hadrian could speak more forcibly and more subtly of his life than could I.

* * * *

Those who put the historical novel in a category apart are forgetting that what every novelist does is only to interpret, by means of the techniques which his period affords, a certain number of past events; his memories, whether consciously or unconsciously recalled, whether personal or impersonal, are all woven of the same stuff as History itself. The work of Proust is a reconstruction of a lost past quite as much as is *War and Peace.* The historical novel of the 1830's, it is true, tends toward melodrama, and to cloak-and-dagger romance; but not more than does Balzac's magnificent *Duchess of Langeais,* or his startling *Girl with the Golden Eyes,* both of wholly contemporary setting. Flaubert painstakingly rebuilds a Carthaginian palace by charging his description with hundreds of minute details, thus employing essentially the same method as for his picture of Yonville, a village of his own time and of his own Normandy. In our day, when introspection tends to dominate literary forms, the historical novel, or what may for convenience's sake be called by that name, must take the plunge into time recaptured, and must fully establish itself within some inner world.

* * * *

Time itself has nothing to do with the matter. It is always surprising to me that my contemporaries, masters as they consider themselves to be over space, apparently remain unaware that one can contract the distance between centuries at will.

* * * *

We lose track of everything, and of everyone, even ourselves. The facts of my father's life are less known to me than those of the life of Hadrian. My own existence, if I had to write of it, would be reconstructed by me from externals, laboriously, as if it were the life of someone else: I should have to turn to letters, and to the recollections of others, in order to clarify such uncertain memories. What is ever left but crumbled walls, or masses of shade? Here, where Hadrian's life is concerned, try to manage so that the lacunae of our texts coincide with what he himself might have forgotten.

* * * *

Which is not to suggest, as it too often done, that historical truth is never to be attained, in any of its aspects. With this kind of truth, as with all others, the problem is the same: one errs *more* or *less*.

* * * *

The rules of the game: learn everything, read everything, inquire into everything, while at the same time adapting to one's ends the *Spiritual Exercises* of Ignatius of Loyola, or the method of Hindu ascetics, who for years, and to the point of exhaustion, try to visualize ever more exactly the images which they create beneath their closed eyelids. Through hundreds of card notes pursue each incident to the very moment that it occurred; endeavor to restore the mobility and suppleness of life to those visages known to us only in stone. When two texts, or two assertions, or perhaps two ideas, are in contradiction, be ready to reconcile them rather than cancel one by the other; regard them as two different facets, or two successive stages, of the same reality, a reality convincingly human just because it is complex. Strive to read a text of the Second Century with the eyes, soul, and feelings of the Second Century; let it steep in that mother solution which the facts of its own time provide; set aside, if possible, all beliefs and sentiments which have accumulated in successive strata between those persons and us. And nevertheless take advantage (though prudently, and solely by way of preparatory study) of all possibilities for comparison and cross-checking, and of new perspectives slowly developed by the many centuries and events separating us from a given text, a fact, a man; make use of such aids more or less as guide-marks along the road of return toward one particular point in time. Keep one's own shadow out of the picture; leave the mirror clean of the mist of one's own breath; take only what is most essential and durable in us, in the emotions aroused by the senses or in the operations of the mind, as our point of contact with those men who, like us, nibbled olives and drank wine, or gummed their fingers with honey, who fought bitter winds and blinding rain, or in summer sought the plane tree's shade: who took their pleasures, thought their own thoughts, grew old, and died.

Marguerite Yourcenar
THE MEMOIRS OF HADRIAN

In this brief selection from the Memoirs *Hadrian has just succeeded Trajan as Emperor of Rome. Hadrian's aspirations as a ruler im-*

mediately conflict with the political realities of the Roman empire.
This selection raises some interesting questions about the similarities
and differences between history and historical fiction: What are some
differences? What can novelists do that historians cannot? What free-
doms do novelists enjoy in their narratives that historians do not?
What constraints do both novelists and historians have as they write?
How important are "the facts" for both?

Order was restored in my life, but not in the empire. The world which
I had inherited resembled a man in full vigor of maturity who was still
robust (though already revealing, to a physician's eyes, some barely perceptible signs of wear), but who had just passed through the convulsions of a serious illness. Negotiations were resumed, this time openly;
I let it be generally understood that Trajan himself had told me to do so
before he died. With one stroke of the pen I erased all conquests which
might have proved dangerous: not only Mesopotamia, where we could
not have maintained ourselves, but Armenia, which was too far away
and too removed from our sphere, and which I retained only as a vassal
state. Two or three difficulties, which would have made a peace conference drag on for years if the principals concerned had had any advantage in lengthening it out, were smoothed over by the skillful mediation
of the merchant Opramoas, who was in the confidence of the Satraps. I
tried to put into these diplomatic conversations the same ardor that
others reserve for the field of battle; I forced a peace. Osroës, moreover,
desired peace at least as much as I: the Parthians were concerned only
to reopen their trade routes between us and India. A few months after
the great crisis I had the joy of seeing the line of caravans re-form on
the banks of the Orontes; the oases were again the resort of merchants
exchanging news in the glow of their evening fires, each morning re-
packing along with their goods for transportation to lands unknown a
certain number of thoughts, words, and customs genuinely our own,
which little by little would take possession of the globe more securely
than can advancing legions. The circulation of gold and the passage of
ideas (as subtle as that of vital air in the arteries) were beginning again
within the world's great body; earth's pulse began to beat once more.

The fever of rebellion subsided in its turn. In Egypt it had been so
violent that they had been obliged to levy peasant militia at utmost
speed while awaiting reinforcements. Immediately I sent my comrade
Marcius Turbo to re-establish order there, a task which he accomplished
with judicious firmness. But order in the streets was hardly enough for
me; I desired to restore order in the public consciousness, if it were
possible, or rather to make order rule there for the first time. A stay of
a week in Pelusium was given over entirely to adjusting differences between those eternal incompatibles, Greeks and Jews. I saw nothing of
what I should have wished to see: neither the banks of the Nile nor the

Museum of Alexandria, nor the temple statues; I barely found time to devote a night to the temple statues; I barely bound time to devote a night to the agreeable debauches of Canopus. Six interminable days were passed in the steaming vat of a courtroom, protected from the heat without by long slatted blinds which slapped to and fro in the wind. At night enormous mosquitoes swarmed round the lamps. I tried to point out to the Greeks that they were not always the wisest of peoples, and to the Jews that they were by no means the most pure. The satiric songs with which these low-class Hellenes were wont to antagonize their adversaries were scarcely less stupid than the grotesque imprecations from the jewries. These races who had lived side by side for centuries had never had the curiosity to get to know each other, nor the decency to accept each other. The exhausted litigants who did not give way till late into the night would find me on my bench at dawn, still engaged in sorting over the rubbish of false testimony; the stabbed corpses which they offered me as evidence for conviction were frequently those of invalids who had died in their beds and had been stolen from the embalmers. But each hour of calm was a victory gained, though precarious like all victories; each dispute arbitrated served as precedent and pledge for the future. It mattered little to me that the accord obtained was external, imposed from without and perhaps temporary; I knew that good like bad becomes a routine, that the temporary tends to endure, that what is external permeates to the inside, and that the mask, given time, comes to be the face itself. Since hatred, stupidity, and delirium have lasting effects, I saw no reason why good will, clarity of mind and just practice would not have their effects, too. Order on the frontiers was nothing if I could not persuade a Jewish peddler and a Greek grocer to live peaceably side by side.

Peace was my aim, but not at all my idol; even to call it my ideal would displease me as too remote from reality. I had considered going so far in my refusal of conquests as to abandon Dacia, and would have done so had it been prudent to break openly with the policy of my predecessor; but it was better to utilize as wisely as possible those gains acquired before my accession and already recorded by history. The admirable Julius Bassus, first governor of that newly organized province, had died in his labors there, as I myself had almost succumbed in my year on the Sarmatian frontiers, exhausted by the thankless task of endless pacification in a country which had supposedly been subdued. I ordered a funeral triumph for him in Rome, an honor reserved ordinarily only for emperors; this homage to a good servitor sacrificed in obscurity was my last, and indirect, protest against the policy of conquest; nor had I need to denounce it publicly from the time that I was empowered to cut it short. On the other hand, military measures had to be taken in Mauretania, where agents of Lusius Quietus were fomenting revolt; nothing, however, required my immediate presence there. It was the same in Britain, where the Caledonians had taken advantage of withdrawal of troops for the war in Asia to decimate the reduced garrisons left on the frontiers. Julius Severus saw to what was most urgent there while awaiting the time when restoration of order in Roman affairs would permit me to undertake that long voyage. But I greatly desired to take charge myself in the Sarmatian war, which had been left inconclusive, and this time to throw in the number of troops requisite to make an end of barbarian depredations. For I refused, here as everywhere, to subject myself to a system. I accepted war as a means toward peace where negotiations proved useless, in the manner of a physician who decides to cauterize only after having tried simples. Everything is so complicated in human affairs that my rule, even if pacific, would have also its periods of war, just as the life of a great captain has, whether he likes it or not, its interludes of peace.

Before heading north for the final settlement of the Sarmation conflict, I saw Quietus once more. The butcher of Cyrene remained formidable. My first move had been to disband his columns of Numidian scouts, but he still had his place in the Senate, his post in the regular army, and that immense domain of western sands which he could convert at will either into a springboard or a hiding-place. He invited me to a hunt in Mysia, deep in the forests, and skilfully engineered an accident in which with a little less luck or less bodily agility I should certainly have lost my life. It seemed best to appear unsuspecting, to be patient and to wait. Shortly thereafter, in Lower Moesia, at a time when the capitulation of the Sarmatian princes allowed me to think of an early return to Italy, an exchange of dispatches in code with my former guardian warned me that Quietus had come back abruptly to Rome and had just conferred there with Palma. Our enemies were strengthening their positions and realigning their troops. No security was possible so long as we should have these two men against us. I wrote to Attianus to act quickly. The old man struck like lightning. He overstepped his orders and with a single stroke freed me of the last of my avowed foes: on the same day, a few hours apart, Celsus was killed at Baiae, Palma in his villa at Terracina, and Nigrinus at Faventia on the threshold of his summer house. Quietus met his end on the road, on departing from a conference with his fellow conspirators, struck down on the step of the carriage which was bringing him back to the City. A wave of terror broke over Rome. Servianus, my aged brother-in-law, who had seemed resigned to my success but who was avidly anticipating my errors to come, must have felt an impulse of joy more nearly akin to ecstasy than any experience of his whole life. All the sinister rumors which circulated about me found credence anew.

I received this news aboard the ship which was bringing me back to Italy. I was appalled. One is always content to be relieved of one's adversaries, but my guardian had proceeded with the indifference of age for the far-reaching consequences of his act: he had forgotten that I should have to live with the after effects of these murders for more than twenty years. I thought of the proscriptions of Octavius, which had forever stained the memory of Augustus; of the first crimes of Nero, which had been followed by other crimes. I recalled the last years of Domitian, of that merely average man, no worse than another, whom fear had gradually destroyed (his own fear and the fears he caused), dying in his palace like a beast tracked down in the woods. My public life was already getting out of hand: the first line of the inscription bore in letters deeply incised a few words which I could no longer erase. The Senate, that great, weak body, powerful only when persecuted, would never forget that four of its members had been summarily executed by my order; three intriguing scoundrels and a brute would thus live on as martyrs. I notified Attianus at once that he was to meet me at Brundisium to answer for his action.

He was awaiting me near the harbor in one of the rooms of that inn facing toward the East where Virgil died long ago. He came limping to receive me on the threshold, for he was suffering from an attack of gout. The moment that I was alone with him, I burst into upbraiding: a reign which I intended to be moderate, and even exemplary, was beginning with four executions, only one of which was indispensable and for all of which too little precaution had been taken in the way of legal formalities. Such abuse of power would be cause for the more reproach to me whenever I strove thereafter to be clement, scrupulous, and just; it would serve as pretext for proving that my so-called virtues were only a series of masks, and for building about me a trite legend of tyranny which would cling to me perhaps to the end of history. I admitted my fear; I felt no more exempt from cruelty than from any other human fault; I accepted the commonplace that crime breeds crime, and the example of the animal which has once tasted blood. An old friend whose loyalty had seemed wholly assured was already taking liberties, profiting by the weakness which he thought that he saw in me; under the guise of serving me he had arranged to settle a personal score against Nigrinus and Palma. He was compromising my work of pacification, and was preparing for me a grim return to Rome, indeed.

The old man asked leave to sit down, and rested his leg, swathed in flannel, upon a stool. While speaking I arranged the coverlet over his ailing foot. He let me run on, smiling meanwhile like a grammarian who listens to his pupil making his way through a difficult recitation. When I had finished, he asked me calmly what I had planned to do with the enemies of the regime. It could be proved, if need were, that these four men had plotted my death; it was to their interest, in any case, to do so. Every transition from one reign to another involved its operations of mopping up; he had taken this task upon himself in order to leave my hands clean. If public opinion demanded a victim, nothing was simpler than to deprive him of his post of Praetorian prefect. He had envisaged such a measure; he was advising me to take it. And if more were needed to conciliate the Senate, he would approve my going as far as relegation to the provinces, or exile.

Attianus had been the guardian from whom money could be wheedled, the counselor of my difficult days, the faithful agent; but this was the first time that I had ever looked atttentively at that face with its carefully shaven jowls, at those crippled hands tranquilly clasped over the handle of his ebony cane. I knew well enough the different elements of his life as a prosperous citizen: his wife, whom he loved, and whose health was frail; his married daughters and their children, for whom he was modest but tenacious in his ambitions, as he had been for himself; his love of choice dishes; his decided taste for Greek cameos and for young dancing girls. He had given me precedence over all these things: for thirty years his first care had been to protect me, and next to serve me. To me, who had not yet given first place to anything except to ideas or projects, or at the most to a future image of myself, this simple devotion of man to man seemed prodigious and unfathomable. No one is worthy of it, and I am still unable to account for it. I followed his counsel: he lost his post. His faint smile showed me that he expected to be taken at his word. He knew well that no untimely solicitude toward an old friend would ever keep me from adopting the more prudent course; this subtle politician would not have wished me otherwise. Let us not exaggerate the extent of his disgrace: after some months of eclipse, I succeeded in having him admitted to the Senate. It was the greatest honor that I could offer to this man of equestrian rank. He lived to enjoy the easy old age of a wealthy Roman knight, much sought after for his perfect knowledge of families and public affairs; I have often been his guest at his villa in the Alban Hills. Nevertheless, like Alexander on the eve of a battle, I had made a sacrifice to Fear before entering into Rome: I sometimes count Attianus among my human victims.

OPTIONS FOR WRITING

1. Marguerite Yourcenar wrote a good part of these *Memoirs* all at once, on a several day train trip to Santa Fe. Describe a time when you were so ready to write something that you sat down and wrote it in one sitting. What do you think made this burst of writing possible?

2. Do you think that it would be possible for you to know some historical figure better than you know a person in your present life? Describe how you would begin to gain such intimate knowledge.

3. The previous selection by Litwack raised the problem of racial and cultural diversity in the context of writing history. Ms. Yourcenar told us her "rules of the game: learn everything, read everything, inquire into everything. . . . " Do you think her unique portrayal of Hadrian reflects this? Write a short essay explaining your answer.

Mike Carter
CREWMEN WHO DROPPED A-BOMB TOUR NATION SELLING MEMENTOS

*It has been over forty-five years since the crew of the bomber Enola
Gay dropped the atomic bomb on the Japanese city of Hiroshima on 6
August 1945. The war in Europe had ended with the surrender of
Germany on 8 May 1945, so the Allied attention turned to the defeat
of Japan. After three years of war in the Pacific, the stage was set
for the full-scale invasion of Japan.*

*Scientists — Americans and European refugees — had secretly been
developing atomic bombs at Los Alamos, New Mexico, during the
last four years of the war. The bomb dropped by the Enola Gay destroyed the city of Hiroshima, causing the loss of about 78,000 lives.
Three days later a more powerful version of the atomic bomb was
dropped on Nagasaki, with even greater destruction and loss of life.
The Japanese offered peace, and a formal surrender was signed 2
September 1945.*

*American servicemen and servicewomen who fought during
World War II are in their sixties and seventies today. Japanese people
from Hiroshima and Nagasaki who survived the bombs are forty-five
years old and older. Most people alive today have had no direct experience of World War II.*

*Is it appropriate for the crew members of the Enola Gay to tour
the nation? Will they bring a bit of history into your life? Should
they?*

The pilot, navigator and bombardier of the plane that dropped the
atomic bomb on Hiroshima say they have no reservations about making
a buck off their place in history.

In recent months, they've been hopscotching the country, hawking
books, T-shirts, caps and coffee mugs commemorating the Aug. 6, 1945,
bombing that claimed nearly 100,000 Japanese lives and hastened the
end of World War II.

It's simple supply and demand, said 75-year-old retired Brig. Gen.
Paul W. Tibbets Jr., the pilot of the bomber Enola Gay.

Setsuko Thurlow, founder and co-chairwoman of Hiroshima-Naga-
saki Relived, a Toronto-based anti-nuclear group, finds that attitude
appalling. She was 13 when she was buried in the rubble from the
bomb, which killed her sister and niece.

"I think it is commercial exploitation of the hundreds of thousands
of people who were killed," she said. "I do question their sense of mor-

ality. Whatever they did, you would think they would feel at least a part of the collective guilt."

But Tibbets said: "It's never dawned on me that I'm trying to capitalize on anybody's death. My reaction to that is, I tell them that they're wrong."

Last August, Tibbets hooked up with an agent, Clark St. John of Buckeye Aviation Publishing Co., which published his book, "Flight of the Enola Gay."

They began touring shopping malls and air shows, and later persuaded Enola Gay navigator Theodore "Dutch" Van Kirk and bombardier Tom Ferebee to join them.

Tibbets said it quickly became apparent they were an attraction.

"We found out that people came in and they had all kinds of pictures—they wanted pictures autographed," he said. "They were interested in the book, but they had their own mementos. You know, 'Will you autograph this, will you autograph that?''

That prompted St. John and Tibbets to develop their own package of wares, including Enola Gay coffee mugs ($6), T-shirts ($9), sweatshirts ($12.95), videos ($19.95 and $24.95), photographs ($6 and $9) and a copy of the order authorizing use of the atomic bomb ($5).

Big sellers, said St. John, are Tibbets' book ($14.95) and a limited edition color lithograph, selling for $24.95, depicting the bomber climbing away as the mushroom cloud blossomed over Hiroshima.

Autographs and handshakes are free.

"The general does not charge for an autograph," St. John said. "He refuses to get involved in a gimmick like that."

Van Kirk said he joined Tibbets and Ferebee on the road because it gives him an opportunity to refresh the memories of his countrymen, fading 45 years after V-J Day.

"If I'm lending even a little bit of knowledge to some people. . . . I think I'm making a contribution," he said.

OPTIONS FOR WRITING

1. Should we consider living people who played a role in an important historical event famous? Have they earned their fame any more or less than, for example, a modern rock star? Argue your position as persuasively as you can.

2. Michael Kammen argued that we should know about the past so that we can develop a discriminating memory. "[We should] avoid the tendency to ascribe equal value to all relationships and events. Worse than no memory at all is the undiscriminating memory that cannot differentiate between important and inconsequential experiences." The navigator of the Enola Gay, Dutch Van Kirk, gave this reason for joining the tour: "If I'm lending even a little bit of knowledge to some people. . . . I think that I'm making a contribution." Speculate on the nature of the contribution Van Kirk made.

Theo Sommer
WHY WE CAN BE TRUSTED

Germany was first unified after the Franco-Prussian war in 1871. This newly unified German empire soon made its presence felt in all areas of European life. German technology, science, music, literature, drama, and the arts all flourished. At the end of the nineteenth century, Germany belatedly joined the European race for overseas colonial possessions. This German empire also played a major role in the beginning and progress of World War I.

German unification took a very different turn in the years between the wars. The Weimar government, put in place by the Allies after World War I, experienced continuous difficulties. The rise of the Nazi party and the election of Adolf Hitler to the German presidency in 1933 set Germany on its new European course. World War II and the Holocaust soon followed.

Germany was fragmented once again after World War II. But the surprising and rapid events in Europe and the USSR during 1990 have presented the reality of a unified Germany once again.

This account of Germany's recent past was written by Theo Sommers, the editor-in-chief of one of West Germany's major newspapers, Die Zeit. *Sommers is also a columnist for* Newsweek International. *Are you convinced that all Germans will once again say "Deutschland," but this time without the "uber alles"?*

The Random House Dictionary of the English Language defines "Germany" as follows: "a former country in central Europe, having Berlin as its capital, now divided into East Germany and West Germany." The Great Soviet Encyclopedia has almost the same definition: "a state in Europe (capital Berlin) which existed until the end of World War II." Now these definitions will have to be revised.

Not many Germans expected reunification to happen in their lifetime. Like many of my countrymen, I thought that with luck the Berlin wall might come down before the end of the century and that the German Question might be placed on the world agenda by 2030 or 2050. And I expected it to result from a slow process of societal change, not from revolutionary upheaval. But now unity is suddenly upon us: an unexpected gift of history, the fulfillment of an undreamt dream.

The Germans did not make unity happen: it happened to them. It wasn't the upshot of an operative West German policy. Rather it was the outcome of a fortuitous combination of factors: reform in the Soviet Union, upheaval in Eastern Europe, and most of all the impatience and determination of the East Germans. What started as an assertion of the democratic spirit against a dictatorial regime soon turned into a national uprising against division.

Can the Germans live with the new givens? Can the world? I think so, for a number of reasons.

First: in 1990, German unity is not a Bismarckian product of "blood and iron." It is the product of a democratic revolution. While there was deep joy when the wall came down, there was no chauvinist frenzy. In fact, since the heady days and nights of November 1989, exuberance has given way to self-doubt and apprehension. The East Germans worry about the hardships of transition, the West Germans fret about the high cost of unity. The are no fanfares; there is only the subdued roll of drums. We do not goose-step in where angels fear to tread.

Second: in 1990, the Germans are not embittered and embattled. They live in peace with themselves and their neighbors. Their commitment to democracy and free enterprise, to social caring and the rule of law, are beyond doubt.

Third: reunification will be expensive. The East German salvage operation is going to cost anywhere from 470 billion to $1.2 trillion over the next 10 years. There has never been a time when the West Germans could afford that kind of money more easily. But had history sprung the present opportunity of them back in 1974 or 1979, at the height of the first or the second world oil crisis, they might have been hard put to meet the challenge. Today they find themselves in an excellent economic situation. Last year they produced a gross national product of close to $1.3 trillion, invested $63.8 billion abroad, and rang up a trade surplus of $71.2 billion. Their GNP is expected to grow by better than 4 percent in 1990. The burden of unity will be heavy, but they can shoulder it.

As a historian, I know that the past casts a very long shadow. Germany was truly united in one central state for only 75 years during its thousand-year history: 1871 to 1945, from Bismarck to Hitler. It was not our happiest period, nor our neighbors' happiest. And with a population soon to count 78 million people we'll tower over the European landscape. Not only unforgiving or unreasonable contemporaries worry about the critical mass of a united Germany.

But one can overdo the worrying. The new Germany will not be the Big Bad Wolf. And with 31 percent of the combined gross domestic product of the European Economic Community (compared with West Germany's current 26.7 percent), it will be much less of an economic juggernaut than is generally assumed. I don't hesitate to venture three propositions.

For one thing, we shall be more European, not less. The Germans have often been suspected of wanting to bolt the Western stable. Remember the catchwords: *dérive allemande*, eastward drift, lure of neutralism. None of this was ever true. In fact, now that unity comes to pass, it turns out that it works exactly the other way round: German unification has become a driving force for European unification. Thus

Bonn consented to the moving up of the Intergovernmental Conference about European Monetary Union. Likewise, West Germany redoubled its efforts to bring about political union in the European Economic Community. That is the whole point of the recent Kohl-Mitterand initiative. We think it is absolutely indispensable to contain the emerging united Germany within the larger framework of a united Europe—with Western Europe at its core, but Eastern Europe not forever beyond the pale.

Of course, we shall remain loyal to NATO, which we consider the foundation of post-post-war adjustment. At the same time we agree with those who think NATO will have to undergo profound changes— and can afford such changes after having prevailed in the cold war. Specifically, we press for an agonizing reappraisal of prevailing doctrines: forward defense, flexible response, first use of nuclear weapons. We envision NATO as a building block of an overarching European security arrangement including the United States and Canada.

Lastly, we favor affiliation with the newly liberated countries of Eastern Europe in the Council of Europe, the World Bank and the International Monetary Fund. We even see them as full EEC members in the long run. And we are urging a concerted Western effort to help these countries help themselves.

Once again: the West Germans have truly changed. We value freedom and democracy—and so do the East Germans who have quite recently taught us a lesson in democratic fortitude. As we grow together again, we are both determined not to revert to our old ways. We harbor no hegemonic designs. The militarism of yesteryear has given way to robust antimilitarism. Reunification will not tear us from our postwar moorings.

Not only the Germans have forsworn their past—so have the other Europeans. The ground rules of European politics have been profoundly altered. The age of nationalism, of state rivalry, of destructive arms races between neighbors is over. European union is the mighty vision to which the Germans want to harness themselves. We will carry our weight—but not throw it around. We know that we'll have power, economic power above all—but we have no delusions of omnipotence. We say *"Deutschland"* again, but we say so quite diffidently—and we don't add *"über alles."*

OPTIONS FOR WRITING

1. Describe a German influence on your own life today.

2. Can you write a brief portrayal of a typical German? A typical American? Write a letter describing what is wrong with these questions.

3. George Kennan argued that we must be informed by history in order to proceed diplomatically. Do you think that you know enough about German history to reach a personal decision about a new, unified Germany? Are

you glad or apprehensive? Explain why you either need to know more history or know enough to decide about your own feelings.

4. Some Americans call themselves neo-Nazis, claiming to follow the statements and beliefs of Adolf Hitler. Do you consider these American neo-Nazis to be "Americans"? In a short essay, explain your answer carefully.

Angus Deming
KOREA'S HEARTBREAKING HILLS:
An American Veteran Relives a Bloody War

Our "police action" in Korea, beginning in June 1950, resulted in the death of about 33,870 Americans—about one-half as many as died during World War I. An estimated 100,000 Americans were wounded. North and South Korea each suffered about one million killed, wounded, or missing.

When the Soviet-backed and supplied North Korea invaded the American-supported and supplied South Korea, President Harry Truman convinced the Security Council of the United Nations to condemn North Korea as an aggressor and to take military action. He committed American troops to an American-led United Nations force led by General Douglas MacArthur. MacArthur rapidly pushed the North Korean forces north of the thirty-eighth parallel of latitude, which approached the border of North Korea and Manchuria, a province of Communist China. In November 1950, the People's Republic of China attacked with hundreds of thousands of troops and support from Soviet-supplied jet fighter planes. The American-led United Nations forces were thrown back toward South Korea. General MacArthur wanted to take military action against China, but President Truman, aware of the political climate during this Cold War period, feared another world war. MacArthur was relieved of his command.

Indecisive fighting continued. In July 1953 an armistice was signed to stop the major fighting. Negotiations over prisoners of war went on for two years. Finally an armistice was signed in 1953. Political conditions reverted to approximately the state they were in at the start in 1950. But this police action in Korea involved the United States in Asia. The Vietnam war was a result of this involvement during the 1960s.

Angus Deming fought in the Korean conflict as Lieutenant Deming of the U.S. Marine Corps and was awarded the Silver Star in 1951. His return to Korea was prompted by the hope of finding answers to questions. "Now I was hoping to find answers to questions that had haunted me for years: Would I be able to find the hills where my comrades and I fought? What would my emotions be if I

*did? Would being in Korea again, even for a brief visit, change my
feelings about the war?"*

*Lt. Deming summarized, "I believed then that we were right to
hold the line against communist aggression in Korea, and I still
do. . . . Thank God I will never have to do it again." What do you
conclude from this statement? Who will hold the line now?*

While Roh Tae Woo was in the United States last week discussing
Korea's future, I was in Korea—searching for the past. In 1951, I served
in the Korean War as a lieutenant in the U.S. Marine Corps. I had not
been back since. Now I was hoping to find answers to questions that
had haunted me for years: Would I be able to find the hills where my
comrades and I fought? What would my emotions be if I did? Would
being in Korea again, even for a brief visit, change my feelings about the
war?

Seoul did not seem to provide many answers at first. South Korea's
capital is a bustling, sprawling, neon-lit metropolis striving to get ahead
in the world. It does not display its battle scars. People there do not
spend time dwelling on a war that took place before many of them were
born. It took a visit to Seoul's War Museum to recall the violence of the
conflict and the lives lost at such aptly named places as Heartbreak
Ridge, Bloody Ridge and Massacre Valley. Poster-size photographs depict horror and suffering: the frozen corpses of U.S. Marines killed at
the Choson Reservoir, lines of panic-stricken refugees, half-starved war
orphans.

The museum's meticulously compiled books of remembrance list the
names of every one of the 33,870 American servicemen killed in the
Korean War. On consecutive pages, I found two men I had known well,
and whose deaths had always saddened me. One was a classmate from
Officer Training School. Although he was an only son and was enrolled
in graduate school, he had been called up and sent to Korea anyway.
There were no easy deferments in those days. He had been afraid of
going into combat. But he had accepted it, and he won the Silver Star
twice before dying on a Korean hilltop in May 1951. The other name
was that of a 19-year-old corporal in my own platoon. He, too, died in
an assault on a hill. He was about 15 feet away from me when an
enemy grenade landed nearby. At first I had not realized how badly
wounded he was. But when I passed him a while later he looked at me
with unforgettable anguish and said: "I'm dying, Lieutenant." There was
no way to save him. Later I wrote his parents. He, too, was an only
son. I told them he died instantly and felt no pain.

I wanted to find some South Koreans who had fought in the war.
Kim Chong Un, a former ROK (Republic of Korea) Army officer who
now teaches English and American literature at Seoul National University, was the sort of person I was looking for. Kim had been a KATUSA—
a Korean attached to a U.S. Army unit. His outfit had been the Second

Infantry Division, which saw much heavy combat. "It was the most traumatic experience of my entire life," Kim told me. "I still have night-mares, 40 years later." I did not press him for details. I didn't need to. I knew what he meant.

Other South Koreans told me curious things. Na Chong Il, dean of the graduate School at Seoul's Kyung Hee University, spoke of a confer-ence he had organized in May to promote "reconciliation and under-standing" among veterans of the war. The participants included a retired U.S. Air Force general, a former Soviet colonel who claimed to have shot down 14 American planes over North Korea and a former North Korean POW who now manages a golf course in Seoul and has a son studying biology in the United States. "We achieved good reconciliation—we got on well together," says Na Chong Il. "But we were less successful with understanding. After [talking] for three days, the participants couldn't understand why they had fought each other so hard 40 years ago."

That was fine, but what I really wanted to find was hills—if possi-ble, the ones where we actually fought. I started out by car from Seoul and headed toward Inje, a town on the eastern side of the peninsula. Hills of the sort I remembered began just outside Seoul. They looked greener and more heavily wooded than I recalled, but otherwise just as I remembered them: steep, massive and very forbidding. Did we actu-ally struggle up those hills with packs on our backs and heavy weapons on our shoulders and live in holes in the ground, like animals? And then fight and die up there? Good Lord.

HEAVY PRICE

Finally we came to a remote village called Yanggu, surrounded by ridge lines and mountains that seemed even steeper and more desolate. In early June 1951, various rifle companies of the Fifth Marine Regiment, my own included, had clawed and fought their way along these same ridgelines in pursuit of Chinese and North Korean troops that were fall-ing back slowly—but exacting a heavy price all the way. The car wound its way up over a twisting dirt road. We stopped in a pass at the top of the ridge. Thirty nine years earlier, almost to the day, my company assaulted the enemy-held hill looming above the road. It was an all-day struggle. Casualties were heavy.

So here I was at last. Had it been worth it? I had gone quite will-ingly to Korea, back then. It was only a few years after the end of World War II, and patriotism was a value that few questioned. We felt we were doing our duty. More than that, we were Marines. Wasn't that explana-tion enough?

I believed than that we were right to hold the line against commun-ist aggression in Korea, and I still do. Revisionism is not for me. The tactics, at least those followed by the Marines, were sound. Controlling the high ground is one of the basic laws of warfare, and that's why we had to climb all those hills. But it was awful. Thank God I will never have to do it again.

OPTIONS FOR WRITING

1. Describe a time when you returned to a place to relive an experience.

2. How does revisiting a place change your memories about the place and the events that happened to you there?

3. There is a saying, "you never can go home again." Can you? Did you ever try? Share your written responses to these questions with your classmates.

4. Is it easier to learn about and understand some historical event that you had no personal connection with or one in which you had a part? Have you had any experience with a situation like this? Explore your answer in a brief essay.

4

QUESTIONS OF PHILOSOPHY

Derk Pereboom

Will I live on forever after I die? Does the universe have a beginning?
Is life only a dream? If you've ever pondered questions like these, you
understand the beginnings of philosophy. Join philosopher Derk
Pereboom as he explains why we ask these questions and how we can
search for answers. Can you prove that you are not dreaming your
life? What is it that makes your existence meaningful? Pereboom challenges you to try to answer your own question.

READINGS

Gar Alperovitz Hiroshima Remembered: The U.S. Was Wrong

John Connor Hiroshima Remembered: The U.S. Was Right

Jeremy Bentham Of the Principle of Utility

Michael Walzer Supreme Emergency

Jean-Paul Sartre Existentialism Is a Humanism

Thomas Nagel Death

Peter Singer Famine, Affluence, and Morality

Daniel C. Dennett Where Am I?

When I was young, I asked myself the question: Will I live on forever
after I die? Suppose the answer is yes. Then after living for one million
years, I would be alive for another million, and after that a million times
a million, and that wouldn't even amount to the smallest fraction of the
years I would get to live. I would live to *infinity*! The thought of living
forever gave me a feeling of fascination, a feeling that thinking about
many other questions has given me since then.

Figure 4.1   Calvin and Hobbes philosophize. (*Calvin and Hobbes*, Copyright © 1988 Universal Press Syndicate. Reprinted with permission. All rights reserved.)

Does the universe have a beginning? Or has the universe always existed? Did some being create it? God, perhaps? Is there a God, or is religion just a story? Does space have limits? Is life a dream? Is merely good behavior morally praiseworthy, or must my motivations be good as well? What is it to live a happy and fulfilled human life, and how do I achieve it? All of these questions have something in common—they are *philosophical* questions.

QUESTIONS PHILOSOPHERS ASK

Philosophers recognize four main branches of philosophy—metaphysics, epistemology, ethics, and logic—and several more specialized areas.

What Is the World Made of?

Consider the atom. In elementary school we learned that all material objects are made up of atoms. You may not have learned that our atomic theory took more than 2,000 years to develop from the time the ancient Greeks first thought of atoms. The picture of atoms that Democritus thought up in the sixth century B.C. is very different from today's theory. Yet Democritus was asking a question that you might have

Figure 4.2   Calvin considers fatalism. (*Calvin and Hobbes*, Copyright © 1989 Universal Press Syndicate. Reprinted with permission. All rights reserved.)

posed in a reflective moment. What are material things made of? Matter, of course, might have been our answer! But this answer suggests another question: What is matter made of? Democritus said atoms, indivisible chunks of material stuff. But what are these atoms made of? Philosophers say these questions belong in an area called *metaphysics*, the investigation into what there really is in the world and how it all hangs together.

According to legend, the word "metaphysics" comes from an editor of the Greek philosopher Aristotle, who called Aristotle's book on metaphysical issues *ta meta ta physica*, or the one that comes after the *Physics*, another work by Aristotle. There are other questions in metaphysics: Are human beings free, or is all human action determined by natural laws? What makes you the same person now as the infant you were years ago? What is time? What is space? Does the world go back in time to infinity, or was there a time it all began?

A metaphysical question that has concerned people ever since philosophy began is the question of what we human beings are made of. Muscles, nerves, blood and guts, we might reply. This answer says that the human being is a completely material thing. Materialism is perhaps the most widely held position among philosophers and scientists today. But many other philosophers and religious thinkers have argued that the human being is partly immaterial, or spiritual—that human beings have a soul, for instance, which is not made of matter. The Greek philosopher Plato believed this, as did the father of modern philosophy, René Descartes. Still others, like George Berkeley, maintained that we are completely immaterial, that physical bodies are just perceptions in the mind, like dreams or hallucinations. This idea may seem odd to us, but Berkeley argued for it quite brilliantly.

WRITING 1.

In the comic strip in Figure 4.2, Calvin considers the view that because everything that happens is preordained and unalterable, we human beings are not free. He is attracted to this philosophical position because he believes it exempts him from responsibility for his actions because his actions are also preordained and unalterable. What would it be like to believe what Calvin does? Would your views on criminal punishment change? Would your responses to both the good and the bad things people do to you be different? Write your reflections in your journal.

How Do We Know Anything?

Consider the atom again. No one has actually ever seen an atom. Scientists believe that they have a lot of evidence that atoms exist, but no one has ever seen an atom in the way that we see tables and chairs. But, then, do we really *know* that atoms exist? Or is it just a theory? More generally, for us to really know that something exists, shouldn't *somebody* be able to perceive it? Or, maybe, shouldn't somebody have *actually* perceived it?

We've now come to an issue in a second main branch of philosophy, *epistemology*, the study of knowledge. The word comes from the Greek word for knowledge, *episteme*, and from the word for theory, *logos*. Epistemology is theory of knowledge. These are some questions that worry epistemologists: Can I know there is a world outside of my own mind? If I can, how much of it can I know? Can I come to know everything about the physical world? Can I ever know whether God exists?

But how can we know anything with certainty? The view that we cannot know anything, *skepticism*, is a very old epistemological position. Some skeptics have argued that there is no way to distinguish our present experience from dream experience, so we don't know that we're not dreaming. We therefore don't know whether any of the objects we are experiencing are real. Although philosophers have tried to defend skepticism, many more have tried to defeat it.

Another important job for epistemologists is to think about what it is to acquire knowledge. What is to know something rather than merely to have an opinion? You know that $2 + 2 = 4$, but it is only your opinion that the Dodgers will win the World Series within the next ten years. What makes the one belief knowledge and the other only opinion?

WRITING 2.

Chances are that you don't believe you are dreaming right now. But why do you think you know this? Sure, you have dreams that are so wild that they couldn't be real. But couldn't your experiences right now be just one of those ordinary dreams? Write your thoughts about these questions in your journal.

What Is the Nature of the Good?

Near the close of World War II, American scientists developed the atomic bomb, a weapon vastly more powerful than any that had ever been made before. Hoping to end the war against Japan, the Americans dropped an atomic bomb on the Japanese city of Hiroshima on 6 August 1945 and did the same to Nagasaki three days later. Many people were killed, including children and the elderly. People have wondered ever since if it was right to attack these Japanese cities with nuclear weapons.

This is an issue in the area of philosophy called *ethics*, an investigation into what it is to live a good life, how we know what the good is, and why we should care about it. There are many ethical questions: Is what is wrong for me always wrong for you? Is what is right and wrong for a member of a tribe of South African natives the same as what is right and wrong for us? Is a life of nothing but sheer physical ecstacy meaningful?

Ethicists have tried to provide general formulas that determine what's right and wrong in every possible situation. In one influential picture, our sole concern should be to maximize happiness minus unhappiness. This theory is known as *utilitarianism*. Suppose that you must choose between two possible courses of action, such as working or going to college. Utilitarianism says that you must determine all the happiness and unhappiness that will result for everyone if you work and calculate the difference. After doing the same for going to college, you check to see for which of the two the difference is greater, and you must take on that course of action.

One problem with utilitarianism is the idea that it seems to allow individuals to be harmed or killed for the benefit of society. For example, utilitarianism might allow some innocent person to be punished as a scapegoat in order to keep a vengeful mob from rioting and causing more harm. According to a rival view that avoids this problem, morality consists mainly in respecting a system of basic human rights. The eighteenth century philosopher Kant advocated a closely related anti-utilitarian view: To be moral is to treat a person not merely as a means, but always as an end in him- or herself. Kant believed that at the core of being moral is the resolve never to merely use people, but always to treat them as beings with infinite worth. An innocent person therefore cannot be punished, even if it would maximize happiness minus unhappiness for everyone.

Ethicists also discuss many more specific issues. Is it acceptable to punish criminals at all? If so, why? Is it right to favor members of groups that have in the past suffered from discrimination when employees were being hired or students were being admitted to desirable programs? Is it permissible to kill people who are terminally ill, are in great pain, and want to die? Is the right to an abortion a license to murder, or is it a legitimate freedom?

The meaning and purpose of life is one of the oldest and most central ethical concerns. The Greek and Roman Stoics argued that meaning is found through rational control of one's passions and through obedience to the laws of the universe discernible through reason. Their main rivals, the Epicureans, thought that meaning could be achieved through limiting one's desires to the desires that one can reasonably expect to be satisfied. The ancient Pyrrhonists believed that it is the search for knowledge that makes people tense and unhappy and that one can achieve the ideal state, *ataraxia*, or mellowness, only by becoming a skeptic. The nineteenth century philosopher Kierkegaard thought that real fulfillment can be achieved through an infinitely passionate relationship with God. According to Sartre, one of the most important *existentialist* philosophers, life has no meaning independent of one's own choices, and one can create meaning only by freely taking on projects to shape one's life.

WRITING 3.

What makes your life meaningful? Is it just pleasure? Are your family, friends, and education meaningful just because they provide you with pleasure, or is there more to it? Must God exist for life to be meaningful? Respond to these questions in your journal.

What Is It to Reason Correctly?

What kinds of arguments can human beings devise to support their theories and opinions, and what makes these arguments good or bad? These are issues in the fourth main branch of philosophy, *logic*, the study of correct reasoning processes.

Logic is often divided into formal and informal disciplines. Informal logic is the study of standards and criticism of ordinary written or spoken arguments. For instance, in informal logic we try to isolate the various mistakes in reasoning that people tend to make in ordinary circumstances. Mike might reason in this way: "Everything the Bible says is true. I know this because the Bible tells me so." You might criticize Mike for *begging the question*, assuming what he wants to prove.

The formal discipline investigates symbolic idealizations of arguments. For example, the formal logician typically has the variables p and q stand for sentences. As it turns out, any argument of this form is a good argument:

1. If p, then q.
2. p.
3. Therefore, q.

This argument form is called *modus ponens*. There are many other forms of this kind for good arguments, and also for bad arguments. The formal logician studies these various forms. Philosophers have come to recognize that formal logic is very close to mathematics. Hence, during the last twenty years courses in formal logic have moved from philosophy to mathematics departments.

Some Specialized Areas

The more specialized philosophical disciplines often combine elements from two or three of the main branches. *Philosophy of religion* considers questions about God. Does God exist? What kind of being would God be? Can we justify a belief in a God? Is the existence of God compatible with the evil in the universe? Can a relationship with God bring meaning to life?

The political state is the topic of *political philosophy*, a special branch of ethics. Perhaps the central issue in this area is the justification of state authority. What gives the state the right to make laws and to have us obey them? Popular among seventeenth century European rulers was the view called the divine right of kings, according to which the authority of the ruler emanates directly from God. Some rival theorists, such as Thomas Hobbes and John Locke, insisted that the right to rule comes from the consent of the ruled, by means of a contract made with other people in society or with the ruler.

Philosophers have also asked fundamental questions about art and the artistic process. What separates artistic activity from other human pursuits? What makes a work of art good? Is it good if people like it? Or is it good if it accurately expresses the emotions of the artist? Does the excellence of a work of art have to do with its form rather than its content? This area of inquiry is called *aesthetics*.

WHAT MAKES ALL OF THESE ISSUES PHILOSOPHICAL?

By now a different kind of question may have occurred to you: What makes all these various issues *philosophical*? You might suspect that philosophy is just a group of disciplines that don't fit anywhere else. This is partly right, because philosophers try to answer so many different types of questions, but there is also a common characteristic to all areas of philosophy. To see how this is so, let's consider the origins and history of philosophical investigation.

When people started asking philosophical questions about the world, there were no special sciences like physics or psychology. When Thales, in 600 B.C., wondered what everything is made of and suggested that it is water, there was no science in place to evaluate his view. Since then, however, special scientific disciplines have developed around different kinds of questions. In the seventeenth century, for example, the science of physics emerged after an intense philosophical struggle among various camps. Isaac Newton created a general agreement on how to study physics with the publication of his *Principia* in 1687. This work demonstrated the power of his mathematical and experimental method to generate results on which everyone could agree. The

Figure 4.3   Calvin and Hobbes consider existence. (*Calvin and Hobbes*, Copyright ©
1989 Universal Press Syndicate. Reprinted with permission. All rights reserved.)

emergence of this successful methodology for physics allowed it to separate off from philosophy. In general, when a specific area of inquiry
developed its own methodology and successful results, it was able to
leave the mother discipline, philosophy. Many of the contemporary special sciences, such as economics, psychology, and sociology, were able
to leave the philosophical nest in the eighteenth and nineteenth centuries.

Some disciplines still haven't split off from philosophy. One example is *cognitive science*, a fairly new discipline devoted to investigating
how the mind works. Philosophers, neurophysiologists, computer
theorists, and artificial intelligence researchers all work together in this
field. According to one view, the philosophers participate because the
issues about the right method haven't been settled and because no
agreed-on body of results exists. What kinds of questions should be
asked? What will a theory of the mind look like? Do we develop a
theory of the mind by trying to build a machine that can do what humans can, by studying the brain, or by building a machine that replicates brain processes? Should the study of the mind instead be independent of brain and artificial intelligence research? These questions have
not been answered satisfactorily. But philosophers are important because
they possess the special skills to formulate these questions precisely and
to propose interesting answers to them.

The story may seem to imply that if philosophy is successful, then
all of its branches will be special sciences and philosophy itself will go
out of business. In fact, a significant number of philosophers believe that
this will eventually happen. Philosophy, according to these philosophers, will only really succeed when it destroys itself. Such a view
is sometimes linked to a suspicion about the way philosophers pose
questions, suspicions that the kinds of questions philosophers ask cannot be answered because they haven't been formulated in a genuinely
scientific way, and that when these questions are taken as scientific
questions, as they should be, their mysterious philosophical aura van-
ishes (see Figure 4.3).

But most philosophers believe that philosophy will always be with us. They think that some philosophical questions will never have answers everyone can accept. Many philosophers think that this is true for ethical issues, and for many metaphysical and epistemological questions. Philosophy, they believe, will always be in business since it has a special system of reasoning for questions that don't have answers everyone can agree on.

Reading Philosophy

To develop skills in writing philosophy, you must first learn how to read it. Philosophical texts can't be read quickly, and it's not often that you can understand them completely after reading them only once.

There are several reasons for this. First, philosophical thoughts and arguments are usually conceptually complex. To understand what a philosophical author is saying you must think it through for yourself, which takes time. You won't be able to speed-read philosophical texts. A professional philosopher working on a difficult passage may read it over fifteen to twenty times.

Second, philosophy often uses technical terminology as a kind of shorthand. Rather than repeat complex doctrines in detail, philosophers give them names, such as materialism and skepticism. As a beginning student, you may be intimidated by technical terminology, but this is easy to avoid. You can understand a technical term simply by understanding its definition. But keep in mind that change and evolution in technical terminology can make it hard to understand texts in the history of philosophy. Technical terms vary in meaning over time; it's sometimes difficult even for professional scholars to track down the meanings of some of them.

Third, the conciseness of philosophical prose can be daunting. Sometimes you'll have to spend half an hour on a single page before you even begin to understand it because there is so much on that page. To keep from being intimidated here, you need only *keep in mind* the fact that the prose is concise.

Finally, an author's perspective can also keep you from understanding a text easily. All of us think about the world from our own point of view, a perspective molded by our unique background and experience. Understanding another author often demands that you see the subject matter sympathetically from his or her point of view. This requires intellectual effort, and more effort for points of view further removed from your own.

Writing Philosophy

In your own writing, you should make things as easy as possible for your reader. Here are two points to keep in mind: First, always be *clear* in your writing; clarity is one of the cardinal philosophical virtues. Philosophical discussions are often complex, and they shouldn't be made confusing by unclear expression. The philosopher Schopenhauer wrote, "The real philosopher will always look for clearness and distinctness; he will invariably try to resemble not a turbid, impetuous torrent, but rather a Swiss lake which by its calm combines great depth with clearness, the depth revealing itself precisely through its clearness." Second, *develop* all of the important points you make. Do not be content to make an important point in a single sentence; rather, explain it so that the reader knows exactly what you are thinking. Attempting to develop an idea will often deepen your own understanding as well.

One of the oldest forms of philosophical writing is the dialogue, a written report of an actual or fictional conversation. The dialogue is an especially good vehicle for presenting philosophical reasoning that is *critical*, reasoning that challenges other philosophical views. In what specific ways should you go about challenging philosophical theories and the arguments for them? You might criticize a philosophical view by pointing out tensions, or inconsistencies, in it. Consider the following dialogue:

Phyllis. I believe that abortion is murder. The fetus is a human being from conception on, and to destroy it is to kill a human being.
Mike.   What if a woman becomes pregnant by being raped? Would you allow abortion in such a case?
Phyllis. That's different. I would allow for exceptions to the general rule in cases of rape.
Mike.   But if you believe that to abort a fetus is to kill a human being, what makes killing a human right just because that human being came into being as a result of rape? You base your opposition to abortion on the value of the life of the fetus. Is a fetus less valuable because it came into being as a result of rape?

Phyllis believes that abortion is murder but that it is morally permissible in the case of rape. Mike challenges Phyllis's position by pointing out an apparent inconsistency, or tension. If Phyllis wants to base her opposition to abortion on the claim that to abort a fetus is to kill a human being, she must also accept the view that to abort a fetus caused by rape is to kill a human being. The debate doesn't end here, but Mike has challenged Phyllis to be consistent. To become consistent, Phyllis might accept that abortion is wrong even in cases of rape or come to believe that abortion is not murder and not generally wrong.

You may choose to challenge someone's philosophical opinion by means of a parallel illustration. Consider this dialogue:

Madeline. There is no God. By definition, God is good and can do anything. So if there were a God, he would prevent all wars and diseases. But there are lots of wars and diseases. So there is no God.

Paul. But God tests our love for him by putting us through trials and tribulations, like diseases and wars. If we continue to love God through these trials, then he will reward us in the end. It's morally okay for God to behave in this way.

Madeline. If God did that, he would be evil. Imagine a parent who wants to test his child's love for him. The parent purposely does not have the child vaccinated against polio and the child develops the disease. He then tells the child that if she continues to love him in spite of all this, then she will be rewarded with the best college education and a million dollars. Is such a parent morally good? Of course not—he's evil.

In this case, Madeline shows that Paul's belief about what God can legitimately do conflicts with what we believe to be morally acceptable. Perhaps Paul's intuitions about standards for God's behavior are insulated from her general beliefs about morality. Madeline's illustration breaks down the barrier and should make Paul rethink his view.

You may want to challenge a general theory by pointing out a counterexample. Philosophers often want to devise general theories, and they can sometimes be tested by particular examples. An illustration of this is a famous counterexample to the act utilitarian theory of ethics. According to the act utilitarian theory, we should always act so that the greatest amount of happiness (minus unhappiness) results for all affected by the action. So suppose that you must make a choice between two different actions. The first will result in 1,000 units of happiness, but 600 units of unhappiness. The second will produce 700 units of happiness but merely 100 units of unhappiness. Act utilitarianism will tell you to pick the second alternative, because the net difference is 600 units, whereas the net difference for the first alternative is only 400 units. Now consider this exchange between an act utilitarian and his opponent:

Jeremy. One should always act so that the most happiness (after subtracting unhappiness) results for all affected by the action.

Mary. Here is a counterexample to the theory: You are a surgeon. In your hospital there are six patients who live very happy lives, but each has a problem. The first will die unless he receives a new heart, the second will die unless she receives a new kidney, and so on. You do not have the right organs in the refrigerator, but you have a very unhappy person on the operating table. You know that if you turn up the power on the respirator just a bit this patient will die, and you'll be able to save the six other patients with the use of his organs. Suppose in addition that no one will find out that you turned up the power and that no one will blame you for your patient's death. The act utilitarian theory would instruct you to scrap the patient's body for organs, since this would maximize overall happiness. But we know that such an action is wrong. So the act utilitarian theory is mistaken.

This counterexample provides a challenge to the act utilitarian's generalization. The act utilitarian must show that his position can accommodate the counterexample or either revise or abandon his theory.

SUGGESTIONS FOR RESEARCH

Writing a Dialogue

Sometimes philosophical theories apply to real-life situations. This is most often true in the area of ethics. Sometimes you will be required to make very difficult ethical decisions, and you will have to try to justify your course of action philosophically. Such difficult decisions must often be made in time of war.

Let's look closely at the decision to drop the atomic bomb on Hiroshima. Was it wrong for the Americans to do this? Even now there are many people on both sides of the issue. In order to defend either position, we need to consider some basic philosophical positions on ethical questions.

Whenever we are faced with an ethical choice, shouldn't we choose the action that brings about the most happiness? The act utilitarians think that this view lies at the core of ethics. As we have seen, the act version of utilitarianism is the view that one should always act so as to maximize happiness minus unhappiness for all affected by the action.

But although act utilitarianism might seem uncontroversial at first glance, counterexamples show that it has problems. The preceding hospital example is one such counterexample. Perhaps this case doesn't show that act utilitarianism is mistaken, but just that its followers have some explaining to do. Yet many philosophers believe that examples such as this one reveal a fatal flaw in act utilitarian ethical theory.

Some opponents of utilitarianism believe that it is always wrong to harm people in order to maximize happiness for all. In this second view, which we will call *absolutism*, human beings have certain *rights* that can never be violated, even if such violations contribute to maximizing happiness. These human rights include the right to life, the right not to be psychologically or physically tortured, and the right to liberty. Absolutists do allow, however, that one may severely hurt or even kill, if necessary, people who are threatening to violate one's own rights or those of others. In virtue of being such a threat, people forgo the rights they had when they were not a threat. One should note that absolutists never allow us to violate the rights of people who are not threats in order to defend ourselves or others. Suppose, for instance, that we can divert the attention of an assailant by wounding his innocent child. This, according to absolutists, is prohibited.

According to absolutism, then, it is always wrong to perform an action that has the foreseeable consequence that someone's basic rights will be violated, although one may hurt or kill, if necessary, someone who threatens to violate rights. This view may seem obviously correct at first, but important objections have been raised. Consider the following case: Suppose that a great but evil power is developing a device with which it intends to destroy millions of people. We can prevent this evil power from succeeding by bombing the factory where the device is being built. But we know that the evil power has enslaved innocent people to work around the clock as janitors in the factory. Bombing the plant would kill these innocent people, and hence violate their rights, so absolutism says that we cannot bomb the plant.

The standards of absolutism are relaxed somewhat by a third view, the *doctrine of double effect*, which is a theory developed in the twelfth century by the great Catholic philosopher, Thomas Aquinas. This doctrine makes a distinction between foreseen violations of rights that are allowable and those that are not. In the preceding case, suppose that bombing the factory would, by itself, be a good thing. The doctrine of double effect would allow us to bomb it because the bad effect of the action, the deaths of the innocent slaves, is neither (1) a *goal* of our action, nor (2) a *means* whereby we achieve our goal. Our goal is to destroy the plant, not to kill the innocent people, and we do not destroy the plant by means of killing the innocent people. The doctrine of double effect captures these two conditions by saying that the bad effect of the action cannot be *intended* but that it may be allowed as a *side effect* of one's action.

The doctrine of double effect adds one further condition, that the bad consequences of the action that we foresee do not outweigh the good consequences. In short, the doctrine says that we may perform an action that will foreseeably violate rights, as long as no violations of rights are intended and all the bad results of the action do not outweigh the good results.

Some people think that the doctrine of double effect is still too strict. Suppose a terrorist threatens to blow up Europe with a nuclear device unless we kill one innocent person (who, let us suppose, would not be killed by the terrorist). The doctrine says that it is wrong to appease the terrorist because we would be intentionally violating the innocent person's rights. Or suppose that the only way to defeat an evil power that is threatening to destroy civilization is to demoralize its population by bombing its cities. Suppose that some of the inhabitants of the cities are innocent children. In this case, the doctrine tells us that it's wrong to bomb these cities because we would be killing innocent people as a means of achieving our goal.

Review these general views on ethical questions. Ask yourself which view is most reasonable. Construct some cases on your own to illustrate and perhaps support these views.

You are now equipped to write a dialogue. Take careful notes on the following selections by Alperovitz, Connor, and Walzer, and suppose that one could foresee that the bombing of Hiroshima would kill between 100,000 and 200,000 Japanese civilians. Now write a dialogue with two or more participants. You might have one be an act utilitarian and another an absolutist or a proponent of the doctrine of double effect. Perhaps you will have the character who represents your own view defend an ethical theory that differs from those we have discussed. Have the participants take varying positions on whether it was morally permissible for the United States to drop the atomic bomb on Hiroshima. You might want to make one of the participants win the debate, or you might want it to be a stalemate. Have your characters use various cases and counterexamples to advance their views.

READINGS

Gar Alperovitz
HIROSHIMA REMEMBERED:
The U.S. Was Wrong

*In August 1985, forty years after Hiroshima and Nagasaki were
devastated by atomic bombs, the* New York Times *solicited two
comments on the event. Gar Alperovitz (b. 1935) has worked as an
assistant at the U.S. Senate and in the Department of State. He has
written several books, including* Atomic Diplomacy: Hiroshima
and Potsdam. *John Connor (b. 1930), professor of anthropology at
California State University, Sacramento, was at General MacArthur's
headquarters in Tokyo in 1949 and 1950. As you read, summarize
the evidence and reasons these authors give for their respective positions. When doubts about the evidence and reasons come to mind,
think about them and write then down. Why do you think these
authors disagree? Does the evidence used by one author ever contradict that used by the other? Do they provide different evidence?
Or do they draw different conclusions based on the same evidence?*

Though it has not yet received broad public attention, there exists overwhelming historical evidence that President Harry S. Truman knew he
could almost certainly end World War II without using the atomic bomb:
The United States had cracked the Japanese code, and a stream of documents released over the last 40 years show that Mr. Truman had two
other options.

The first option was to clarify America's surrender terms to assure
the Japanese we would not remove their Emperor. The second was simply to await the expected Soviet declaration of war — which, United
States intelligence advised, appeared likely to end the conflict on its
own.

Instead, Hiroshima was bombed Aug. 6, 1945, and Nagasaki on
Aug. 9. The planned date for the Soviet Union's entry into the war
against Japan was Aug. 8.

The big turning point was the Emperor's continuing June–July decision to open surrender negotiations through Moscow. Top American officials — and, most critically, the President — understood the move was
extraordinary: Mr. Truman's secret diaries, lost until 1978, call the key
intercepted message "the telegram from Jap Emperor asking for peace."

Other documents — among them newly discovered secret memoran-
dums from William J. Donovan, director of the Office of Strategic Services — show that Mr. Truman was personally advised of Japanese peace

initiatives through Swiss and Portuguese channels as early as three months before Hiroshima. Moreover, Mr. Truman told several officials he had no objection in principle to Japan's keeping the Emperor, which seemed the only sticking point.

American leaders were sure that if he so chose "the Mikado could stop the war with a royal word" — as one top Presidential aide put it. Having decided to use the bomb, however, Mr. Truman was urged by Secretary of State James F. Byrnes not to give assurances to the Emperor before the weapon had been demonstrated.

Additional official records, including minutes of top-level White House planning meetings, show the President was clearly advised of the importance of a Soviet declaration of war: it would pull the rug out from under Japanese military leaders who were desperately hoping the powerful Red Army would stay neutral.

Gen. George C. Marshall in mid-June told Mr. Truman that "the impact of Russian entry on the already hopeless Japanese may well be the decisive action levering them into capitulation at that time or shortly thereafter if we land."

A month later, the American-British Combined Intelligence Staffs advised their chiefs of the critical importance of a Red Army attack. As the top British general, Sir Hastings Ismay, summarized the conclusions for Prime Minister Winston Churchill: "If and when Russia came into the war against Japan, the Japanese would probably wish to get out on almost any terms short of the dethronement of the Emperor."

Mr. Truman's private diaries also record his understanding of the significance of this option. On July 17, 1945, when Stalin confirmed that the Red Army would march, Mr. Truman privately noted: "Fini Japs when that comes about."

There was plenty of time: The American invasion of Japan was not scheduled until the spring of 1946. Even a preliminary landing on the island Kyushu was still three months in the future.

Gen. Dwight D. Eisenhower, appalled that the bomb would be used in these circumstances, urged Mr. Truman and Secretary of War Henry L. Stimson not to drop it. In his memoirs, he observed that weeks before Hiroshima, Japan had been seeking a way to surrender. "It wasn't necessary," he said in a later interview, "to hit them with that awful thing."

The man who presided over the Joint Chiefs of Staff, Adm. William D. Leahy, was equally shocked: "The use of this barbarous weapon at Hiroshima and Nagasaki was of no material assistance in our war against Japan. The Japanese were already defeated and ready to surrender."

Why, then, was the bomb used?

American leaders rejected the most obvious option — simply waiting for the Red Army attack — out of political, not military, concerns.

As the diary of one official put it, they wanted to end the war before Moscow got "in so much on the kill." Secretary of the Navy

James V. Forrestal's diaries record that Mr. Byrnes "was most anxious to get the Japanese affair over with before the Russians got in."

United States leaders had also begun to think of the atomic bomb as what Secretary Stimson termed the "master card" of diplomacy. President Truman postponed his Potsdam meeting with Stalin until July 17, 1945—one day after the first successful nuclear test—to be sure the atomic bomb would strengthen his hand before confronting the Soviet leader on the shape of a postwar settlement.

To this day, we do not know with absolute certainty Mr. Truman's personal attitudes on several key issues. Yet we do know that his most important adviser, Secretary of State Byrnes, was convinced that dropping the bomb would serve crucial long-range diplomatic purposes.

As one atomic scientist, Leo Szilard, observed: "Mr. Byrnes did not argue that it was necessary to use the bomb against the cities of Japan in order to win the war. Mr. Byrnes' . . . view [was] that our possessing and demonstrating the bomb would make Russia more manageable."

John Connor
HIROSHIMA REMEMBERED:
The U.S. Was Right

Forty years ago this week in Hiroshima: the dreadful flash, the wrist watches fused forever at 8:16 A.M. The question still persists: Should we have dropped the atomic bomb?

History seldom gives decisive answers, but recently declassified documents point to a clear judgment: Yes, it was necessary to drop the bomb. It was needed to end the war. It saved countless American and Japanese lives.

In the early summer of 1945, Japan, under tight control of the militarists, was an implacable, relentless adversary. The Japanese defended territory with a philosophy we had seldom encountered: Soldiers were taught that surrender was worse than death. There was savage resistance to the end in battle after battle.

Of the 5,000-man Japanese force at Tarawa in November 1943, only 17 remained alive when the island was taken. When Kwajalein was invaded in February 1944, Japanese officers slashed at American tanks with samurai swords; their men held grenades against the sides of tanks in an effort to disable them.

On Saipan, less than 1,000 of the 32,000 defending Japanese troops survived. Casualties among the Japanese-ruled civilians on the island numbered 10,000. Parents bashed their babies' brains out on rocky cliff sides, then leaped to their deaths. Others cut each other's throats; children threw grenades at each other. America suffered 17,000 casualties.

Just 660 miles southeast of Tokyo, Iwo Jima's garrison was told to defend the island as if it were Tokyo itself. They did. In the first day of fighting, there were more American casualties than during "D-Day" in Normandy. At Okinawa—only 350 miles south of Kyushu—more than 110,000 Japanese soldiers and 100,000 civilians were killed. Kamikaze attacks cost the Navy alone some 10,000 casualties. The Army and Marines lost more than 50,000 men.

In the early summer of 1945, the invasion of Japan was imminent and everyone in the Pacific was apprehensive. The apprehension was justified, because our intelligence was good: With a system code-named "Magic," it had penetrated Japanese codes even before Pearl Harbor. "Magic" would play a crucial role in the closing days of the war.

Many have maintained that the bomb was unnecessary because in the closing days of the war intercepted Japanese diplomatic messages disclosed a passionate desire for peace. While that is true, it is irrelevant. The Japanese Government remained in the hands of the militarists: *Their* messages indicated a willingness to fight to the death.

Japanese planes, gasoline and ammunition had been hoarded for the coming invasion. More than 5,000 aircraft had been hidden everywhere to be used as suicide weapons, with only enough gas in their tanks for a one-way trip to the invasion beaches. More than two million men were moving into positions to defend the home islands.

The object was to inflict such appalling losses that the Americans would agree to a treaty more favorable than unconditional surrender. The Army Chief of Staff, Gen. George C. Marshall, estimated potential American casualties as high as a million.

The willingness of the Japanese to die was more than empty bravado. Several of my colleagues at Kyushu University told me that as boys of 14 or 15, they were being trained to meet the Americans on the beaches with little more than sharpened bamboo spears. They had no illusions about their chances for survival.

The Potsdam declaration calling for unconditional surrender was beamed to Japan on July 27. On July 30, the Americans were informed that Japan would officially ignore the ultimatum. A week later, the bomb was dropped.

Could we not have warned the Japanese in advance, critics asked, and dropped a demonstration bomb? That alternative was vetoed on the grounds the bomb might not work, or that the plane carrying it might be shot down. Moreover, it is questionable how effective a demonstration bomb might have been. The militarists could have imposed a news blackout as complete as the one imposed after the disastrous battle of Midway and continued on their suicidal course. That is exactly what happened at Hiroshima. Within hours, the Japanese Government sent in a team of scientists to investigate the damage. Their report was immediately suppressed and was not made public until many years after the war.

After midnight on Aug. 10, a protracted debate took place in an air-raid shelter deep inside the Imperial Palace. The military insisted that

Japan should hold out for terms far better than unconditional surrender. The peace faction favored accepting the Potsdam declaration, providing that the Emperor would be retained. The two factions remained at an impasse. At 2 A.M., Prime Minister Kantaro Suzuki asked the Emperor to decide. In a soft, deliberate voice, the Emperor expressed his great longing for peace. The war had ended.

It was impossible, in August 1945, to predict the awesome shadow the bomb would cast on humanity. The decision to drop it seemed both simple and obvious. Without it, the militarists might have prevailed, an invasion ordered. And the loss of both American and Japanese lives would have been awesome.

The atomic bomb accomplished what it had been designed to do. It ended the war.

OPTIONS FOR WRITING

1. List the reasons each author provides for his respective views. Which side makes the stronger case? Write out your reasoning in a short essay.

2. Team up with a classmate, and select an issue with a strong ethical dimension. Each write a short essay defending your position. Share your essays with the class, and discuss which essay makes the most persuasive case.

Jeremy Bentham
OF THE PRINCIPLE OF UTILITY

Jeremy Bentham (1748–1832), an English philosopher, was the founder of utilitarianism. Bentham was very interested in moral reform, especially reform of the judicial system. He believed that the judicial torture of his day was morally abhorrent and used his utilitarian theory of ethics to advocate the elimination of these vicious punishment practices. This reading is an excerpt from his most important work, An Introduction to the Principles of Morals and Legislation, *in which he argues for a utilitarian position on public policy. What does Bentham believe about the nature of the good for human life? Do you think that he is right? Exactly how, according to Bentham, should we decide what to do in any particular situation?*

I. Nature has placed mankind under the governance of two sovereign masters, *pain* and *pleasure*. It is for them alone to point out what we ought to do, as well as to determine what we shall do. On the one hand the standard of right and wrong, on the other the chain of causes and effects, are fastened to their throne. They govern us in all we do, in all we say, in all we think: every effort we can make to throw off our subjection, will serve but to demonstrate and confirm it. In words a man may pretend to abjure their empire: but in reality he will remain subject to it all the while. The *principle of utility*[1] recognises this subjection, and assumes it for the foundation of that system, the object of which is to rear the fabric of felicity by the hands of reason and of law. Systems which attempt to question it, deal in sounds instead of sense, in caprice instead of reason, in darkness instead of light.

But enough of metaphor and declamation: it is not by such means that moral science is to be improved.

II. The principle of utility is the foundation of the present work: it will be proper therefore at the outset to give an explicit and determinate account of what is meant by it. By the principle[2] of utility is meant that principle which approves or disapproves of every action whatsoever, according to the tendency which it appears to have to augment or diminish the happiness of the party whose interest is in question: or, what is the same thing in other words, to promote or to oppose that happiness. I say of every action whatsoever; and therefore not only of every action of a private individual, but of every measure of government.

III. By utility is meant that property in any object, whereby it tends to produce benefit, advantage, pleasure, good, or happiness, (all this in

---

[1] Note by the Author, July 1822.

To this denomination has of late been added, or substituted, the *greatest happiness* or *greatest felicity* principle: this for shortness, instead of saying at length *that principle* which states the greatest happiness of all those whose interest is in question, as being the right and proper, and only right and proper and universally desirable, end of human action: of human action in every situation, and in particular in that of a functionary or set of functionaries exercising the powers of Government. The word *utility* does not so clearly point to the ideas of *pleasure* and *pain* as the words *happiness* and *felicity* do: nor does it lead us to the consideration of the *number*, of the interests affected; to the *number*, as being the circumstance, which contributes, in the largest proportion, to the formation of the standard here in question; the *standard of right and wrong*, by which alone the propriety of human conduct, in every situation, can with propriety be tried. This want of a sufficiently manifest connexion between the ideas of *happiness* and *pleasure* on the one hand, and the idea of *utility* on the other, I have every now and then found operating, and with but too much efficiency, as a bar to the acceptance, that might otherwise have been given, to this principle.

[2] The word principle is derived from the Latin principium: which seems to be compounded of the two words *primus*, first, or chief, and *cipium*, a termination which seems to be derived from *capio*, to take, and in *mancipium*, *municipium*; to which are analogous, *auceps*, *forceps*, and others. It is a term of very vague and very extensive signification: it is applied to any thing which is conceived to serve as a foundation or beginning to any series of operations: in some cases, of physical operations; but of mental operations in the present case.

The principle here in question may be taken for an act of the mind; a sentiment; a sentiment of approbation; a sentiment which, when applied to an action, approves of its utility, as that quality of it by which the measure of approbation or disapprobation bestowed upon it ought to be governed.

the present case comes to the same thing) or (what comes again to the same thing) to prevent the happening of mischief, pain, evil, or unhappiness to the party whose interest is considered: if that party be the community in general, then the happiness of the community: if a particular individual, then the happiness of that individual.

IV. The interest of the community is one of the most general expressions that can occur in the phraseology of morals: no wonder that the meaning of it is often lost. When it has a meaning, it is this. The community is a fictitious *body*, composed of the individual persons who are considered as constituting as it were its *members*. The interest of the community then is, what? — the sum of the interests of the several members who compose it.

V. It is in vain to talk of the interest of the community without understanding what is the interest of the individual.[3] A thing is said to promote the interest, or to be *for* the interest, of an individual, when it tends to add to the sum total of his pleasures: or, what comes to the same thing, to diminish the sum total of his pains.

VI. An action then may be said to be conformable to the principle of utility, or, for shortness sake, to utility, (meaning with respect to the community at large) when the tendency it has to augment the happiness of the community is greater than any it has to diminish it.

VII. A measure of government (which is but a particular kind of action, performed by a particular person or persons) may be said to be conformable to or dictated by the principle of utility, when in like manner the tendency which it has to augment the happiness of the community is greater than any which it has to diminish it.

VIII. When an action, or in particular a measure of government, is supposed by a man to be conformable to the principle of utility, it may be convenient, for the purposes of discourse, to imagine a kind of law or dictate, called a law or dictate of utility: and to speak of the action in question, as being conformable to such law or dictate.

IX. A man may be said to be a partizan of the principle of utility, when the approbation or disapprobation he annexes to any action, or to any measure, is determined by and proportioned to the tendency which he conceives it to have to augment or to diminish the happiness of the community: or in other words, to its conformity or unconformity to the laws or dictates of utility.

X. Of an action that is conformable to the principle of utility one may always say either that it is one that ought to be done, or at least that it is not one that ought not to be done. One may say also, that it is right it should be done; at least that it is not wrong it should be done: that it is a right action; at least that it is not a wrong action. When thus interpreted, the words *ought*, and *right* and *wrong*, and others of that stamp, have a meaning: when otherwise, they have none.

---

[3] Interest is one of those words, which not having any superior *genus*, cannot in the ordinary way be defined.

XI. Has the rectitude of this principle been ever formally contested? It should seem that it had, by those who have not known what they have been meaning. Is it susceptible of any direct proof? it should seem not: for that which is used to prove every thing else, cannot itself be proved: a chain of proofs must have their commencement somewhere. To give such proof is as impossible as it is needless.

XII. Not that there is or ever has been that human creature breathing, however stupid or perverse, who has not on many, perhaps on most occasions of his life, deferred to it. By the natural constitution of the human frame, on most occasions of their lives men in general embrace this principle, without thinking of it: if not for the ordering of their own actions, yet for the trying of their own actions, as well as of those of other men. There have been, at the same time, not many, perhaps, even of the most intelligent, who have been disposed to embrace it purely and without reserve. There are even few who have not taken some occasion or other to quarrel with it, either on account of their not understanding always how to apply it, or on account of some prejudice or other which they were afraid to examine into, or could not bear to part with. For such is the stuff that man is made of: in principle and in practice, in a right track and in a wrong one, the rarest of all human qualities is consistency.

XIII. When a man attempts to combat the principle of utility, it is with reasons drawn, without his being aware of it, from that very principle itself.[4] His arguments, if they prove any thing, prove not that the principle is *wrong*, but that, according to the applications he supposes to be made of it, it is *misapplied*. Is it possible for a man to move the earth? Yes; but he must first find out another earth to stand upon.

[4] 'The principle of utility, (I have heard it said) is a dangerous principle: it is dangerous on certain occasions to consult it.' This is as much as to say, what? that it is not consonant to utility, to consult utility: in short, that it is *not* consulting it, to consult it.

Addition by the Author, July 1822.

Not long after the publication of the Fragment on Government, anno 1776, in which, in the character of an all-comprehensive and all-commanding principle, the principle of *utility* was brought to view, one person by whom observation to the above effect was made was *Alexander Wedderburn*, at that time Attorney or Solicitor General, afterwards successively Chief Justice of the Common Pleas, and Chancellor of England, under the successive titles Lord Loughborough and Earl of Rosslyn. It was made—not indeed in my hearing, but in the hearing of a person by whom it was almost immediately communicated to me. So far from being self-contradictory, it was a shrewd and perfectly true one. By that distinguished functionary, the state of the Government was thoroughly understood: by the obscure individual, at that time not so much as supposed to be so: his disquisitions had not been as yet applied, with any thing like a comprehensive view, to the field of Constitutional Law, nor therefore to those features of the English Government, by which the greatest happiness of the ruling *one* with or without that of a favoured few, are now so plainly seen to be the only ends to which the course of it has at any time been directed. The *principle of utility* was an appellative, at that time employed—employed by me, as it had been by others, to designate that which, in a more perspicuous and instructive manner, may, as above, be designated by the name of the *greatest happiness principle*. 'This principle (said Wedderburn) is a dangerous one.' Saying so, he said that which, to a

XIV. To disprove the propriety of it by arguments is impossible; but, from the causes that have been mentioned, or from some confused or partial view of it, a man may happen to be disposed not to relish it. When this is the case, if he thinks the settling of his opinions on such a subject worth the trouble, let him take the following steps, and at length, perhaps, he may come to reconcile himself to it.

1. Let him settle with himself, whether he would wish to discard this principle altogether; if so, let him consider what it is that all his reasonings (in matters of politics especially) can amount to?

2. If he would, let him settle with himself, whether he would judge and act without any principle, or whether there is any other he would judge and act by?

3. If there be, let him examine and satisfy himself whether the principle he thinks he has found is really any separate intelligible principle; or whether it be not a mere principle in words, a kind of phrase, which at bottom expresses neither more nor less than the mere averment of his own unfounded sentiments; that is, what in another person he might be apt to call caprice?

4. If he is inclined to think that his own approbation or disapprobation, annexed to the idea of an act, without any regard to its consequences, is a sufficient foundation for him to judge and act upon, let him ask himself whether his sentiment is to be a standard of right and wrong, with respect to every other man, or whether every man's sentiment has the same privilege of being a standard to itself?

5. In the first case, let him ask himself whether his principle is not despotical, and hostile to all the rest of human race?

6. In the second case, whether it is not anarchial, and whether at this rate there are not as many different standards of right and wrong as there are men? and whether even to the same man, the same thing, which is right to-day, may not (without the least change in its nature) be wrong to-morrow? and whether the same thing is not right and wrong in the same place at the same time? and in either case, whether

certain extent, is strictly true: a principle, which lays down, as the only *right* and justifiable end of Government, the greatest happiness of the greatest number—how can it be denied to be a dangerous one? dangerous it unquestionably is, to every government which has for its *actual* end or object, the greatest happiness of a certain *one*, with or without the addition of some comparatively small number of others, whom it is matter of pleasure or accommodation to him to admit, each of them, to a share in the concern, on footing of so many junior partners. *Dangerous* it therefore really was, to the interest—the sinister interest—of all those functionaries, himself included, whose interest it was, to maximize delay, vexation, and expense, in judicial and other modes of procedure, for the sake of the profit, extractible out of the expense. In a Government which had for its end in view the greatest happiness of the greatest number, Alexander Wedderburn might have been Attorney General and then Chancellor: but he would not have been Attorney General with £15,000 a year, nor Chancellor, with a peerage with a veto upon all justice, with £25,000 a year, and with 500 sinecures at his disposal, under the name of Ecclesiastical Benefices, besides *et cæteras.*

all argument is not at an end? and whether, when two men have said, 'I like this,' and 'I don't like it,' they can (upon such a principle) have any thing more to say?

7. If he should have said to himself, No: for that the sentiment which he proposes as a standard must be grounded on reflection, let him say on what particulars the reflection is to turn? if on particulars having relation to the utility of the act, then let him say whether this is not deserting his own principle, and borrowing assistance from that very one in opposition to which he sets it up: or if not on those particulars, on what other particulars?

8. If he should be for compounding the matter, and adopting his own principle in part, and the principle of utility in part, let him say how far he will adopt it?

9. When he has settled with himself where he will stop, then let him ask himself how he justifies to himself the adopting it so far? and why he will not adopt it any farther?

10. Admitting any other principle than the principle of utility to be a right principle, a principle that it is right for a man to pursue; admitting (what is not true) that the word *right* can have a meaning without reference to utility, let him say whether there is any such thing as a *motive* that a man can have to pursue the dictates of it: if there is, let him say what that motive is, and how it is to be distinguished from those which enforce the dictates of utility: if not, then lastly let him say what it is this other principle can be good for?

OPTIONS FOR WRITING

1. Bentham believes that pleasure is the good for human life. Is he right about this? Suppose that a substance were developed that would make you experience ecstatic pleasure but would render you incapable of any productive activity. Would your life be a good one if you did nothing but ingest this substance? In a persuasive essay, argue for or against this theory of pleasure.

2. If pleasure is not the only good for human life, what else is? Look at the works of Picasso and Maya Ling Lin in Chapter 5, or Wanda Coleman in Chapter 2, then present alternative justifications for the creation of art.

Michael Walzer
SUPREME EMERGENCY

Michael Walzer (b. 1935) is a professor of social science at the Institute for Advanced Study in Princeton, New Jersey. He has written many books, including Radical Principles, Just and Unjust Wars,

and Spheres of Justice. *In this excerpt from his* Just and Unjust
Wars, *Walzer considers the morality of bombing the German cities in
1940 and compares these actions to dropping the atomic bomb on
Hiroshima. (Note: According to the "sliding scale" conception, one
forfeits one's rights to the extent that one engages in immoral behavior.) State the facts relevant to deciding the morality of dropping
the bomb on Hiroshima, as Walzer reports them. Outline Walzer's
argument for the view that bombing the German cities was justified
but that dropping the bomb on Hiroshima was wrong.*

THE NATURE OF NECESSITY

Everyone's troubles make a crisis. "Emergency" and "crisis" are cant
words, used to prepare our minds for acts of brutality. And yet there
are such things as critical moments in the lives of men and women and
in the history of states. Certainly, war is such a time: every war is an
emergency, every battle a possible turning point. Fear and hysteria are
always latent in combat, often real, and they press us toward fearful
measures and criminal behavior. The war convention is a bar to such
measures, not always effective, but there nevertheless. In principle at
least, as we have seen, it resists the ordinary crises of military life. Churchill's description of Britain's predicament in 1939 as a "supreme
emergency" was a piece of rhetorical heightening designed to overcome
that resistance. But the phrase also contains an argument: that there is
a fear beyond the ordinary fearfulness (and the frantic opportunism) of
war, and a danger to which that fear corresponds, and that this fear and
danger may well require exactly those measures that the war convention
bars. Now, a great deal is at stake here, both for the men and women
driven to adopt such measures and for their victims, so we must attend
carefully to the implicit argument of "supreme emergency."

Though its use is often ideological, the meaning of the phrase is a
matter of common sense. It is defined by two criteria, which correspond
to the two levels on which the concept of necessity works: the first has
to do with the imminence of the danger and the second with its nature.
The two criteria must both be applied. Neither one by itself is sufficient
as an account of extremity or as a defense of the extraordinary measures
extremity is thought to require. Close but not serious, serious but not
close—neither one makes for a supreme emergency. But since people at
war can rarely agree on the seriousness of the dangers they face (or pose
for one another), the idea of closeness is sometimes made to do the job
alone. Then we are offered what might best be called the back-to-the-
wall argument: that when conventional means of resistance are hopeless
or worn out, anything goes (anything that is "necessary" to win). Thus
British Prime Minister Stanley Baldwin, writing in 1932 about the dangers of terror bombing:

Will any form of prohibition of bombing, whether by convention, treaty, agreement, or anything you like, be effective in war? Frankly, I doubt it, and in doubting it, I make no reflection on the good faith of either ourselves or any other country. If a man has a potential weapon and has his back to the wall and is going to be killed, he will use that weapon, whatever it is and whatever undertaking he has given about it.[1]

The first thing that has to be said about this statement is that Baldwin does not mean his domestic analogy to be applied literally. Soldiers and statesmen commonly say that their backs are to the wall whenever military defeat seems imminent, and Baldwin is endorsing this view of extremity. The analogy is from survival at home to victory in the international sphere. Baldwin claims that people will necessarily (inevitably) adopt extreme measures if such measures are necessary (essential) either to escape death or to avoid military defeat. But the argument is wrong at both ends. It is simply not the case that individuals will always strike out at innocent men and women rather than accept risks for themselves. We even say, very often, that it is their duty to accept risks (and perhaps to die); and here as in moral life generally, "ought" implies "can." We make the demand knowing that it is possible for people to live up to it. Can we make the same demand on political leaders, acting not for themselves but for their countrymen? That will depend upon the dangers their countrymen face. What is it that defeat entails? Is it some minor territorial adjustment, a loss of face (for the leaders), the payment of heavy indemnities, political reconstruction of this or that sort, the surrender of national independence, the exile or murder of millions of people? In such cases, one's back is always to the wall, but the dangers one confronts take very different forms, and the different forms make a difference.

If we are to adopt or defend the adoption of extreme measures, the danger must be of an unusual and horrifying kind. Such descriptions, I suppose, are common enough in time of war. One's enemies are often thought to be—at least they are often said to be—unusual and horrifying.[2] Soldiers are encouraged to fight fiercely if they believe that they are fighting for the survival of their country and their families, that freedom, justice, civilization itself are at risk. But this sort of thing is only sometimes plausible to the detached observer, and one suspects that its propagandistic character is also understood by many of the participants. War is not always a struggle over ultimate values, where the victory of one side would be a human disaster for the other. It is necessary to be skeptical about such matters, to cultivate a wary disbelief of wartime rhetoric, and then to search for some touchstone against which arguments about extremity might be judged. We need to make a map of human crises and to mark off the regions of desperation and disaster. These and only these constitute the realm of necessity, truly understood. Once again, I am going to use the experience of World War II in Europe to suggest at least the rough contours of the map. For Nazism lies at the outer limits of exigency, at a point where we are likely to find ourselves united in fear and abhorrence.

That is what I am going to assume, at any rate, on behalf of all those people who believed at the time and still believe a third of a century later that Nazism was an ultimate threat to everything decent in our lives, an ideology and a practice of domination so murderous, so degrading even to those who might survive, that the consequences of its final victory were literally beyond calculation, immeasurably awful. We see it—and I don't use the phrase lightly—as evil objectified in the world, and in a form so potent and apparent that there could never have been anything to do but fight against it. I obviously cannot offer an account of Nazism in these pages. But such an account is hardly necessary. It is enough to point to the historical experience of Nazi rule. Here was a threat to human values so radical that its imminence would surely constitute a supreme emergency; and this example can help us understand why lesser threats might not do so.

In order to get the map right, however, we must imagine a Nazi-like danger somewhat different from the one the Nazis actually posed. When Churchill said that a German victory in World War II "would be fatal, not only to ourselves, but to the independent life of every small country in Europe," he was speaking the exact truth. The danger was a general one. But suppose it had existed for Britain alone. Can a supreme emergency be constituted by a particular threat—by a threat of enslavement or extermination directed against a single nation? Can soldiers and statesmen override the rights of innocent people for the sake of their own political community? I am inclined to answer this question affirmatively, though not without hesitation and worry. What choice do they have? They might sacrifice themselves in order to uphold the moral law, but they cannot sacrifice their countrymen. Faced with some ultimate horror, their options exhausted, they will do what they must to save their own people. That is not to say that their decision is inevitable (I have no way of knowing that), but the sense of obligation and of moral urgency they are likely to feel at such a time is so overwhelming that a different outcome is hard to imagine.

Still, the question is difficult, as its domestic analogue suggests. Despite Baldwin, it is not usually said of individuals in domestic society that they necessarily will or that they morally can strike out at innocent people, even in the supreme emergency of self-defense.[3] They can only attack their attackers. But communities, in emergencies, seem to have different and larger prerogatives. I am not sure that I can account for the difference, without ascribing to communal life a kind of transcendence that I don't believe it to have. Perhaps it is only a matter of arithmetic: individuals cannot kill other individuals to save themselves, but to save a nation we can violate the rights of a determinate but smaller number of people. But then large nations and small ones would have different entitlements in such cases, and I doubt very much that that is true. We might better say that it is possible to live in a world where individuals are sometimes murdered, but a world where entire peoples are enslaved or massacred is literally unbearable. For the survival and freedom of political communities—whose members share a way of life, developed by their ancestors, to be passed on to their children—are the highest values of international society. Nazism challenged these values on a grand scale, but challenges more narrowly conceived, *if they are of the same kind*, have similar moral consequences. They bring us under the rule of necessity (and necessity knows no rules).

I want to stress again, however, that the mere recognition of such a threat is not itself coercive; it neither compels nor permits attacks on the innocent, so long as other means of fighting and winning are available. Danger makes only half the argument; imminence makes the other half. Now let us consider a time when the two halves came together: the terrible two years that followed the defeat of France, from the summer of 1940 to the summer of 1942, when Hitler's armies were everywhere triumphant.

OVERRIDING THE RULES OF WAR

The Decision to Bomb German Cities

There have been few decisions more important than this one in the history of warfare. As a direct result of the adoption of a policy of terror bombing by the leaders of Britain, some 300,000 Germans, most of them civilians, were killed and another 780,000 seriously injured. No doubt, these figures are low when compared to the results of Nazi genocide; but they were, after all, the work of men and women at war with Nazism, who hated everything it stood for and who were not supposed to imitate its effects, even at lagging rates. And the British policy had further consequences: it was the crucial precedent for the fire-bombing of Tokyo and other Japanese cities and then for Harry Truman's decision to drop atomic bombs on Hiroshima and Nagasaki. The civilian death toll from Allied terrorism in World War II must have exceeded half a million men, women, and children. How could the initial choice of this ultimate weapon ever have been defended?

The history is a complex one, and it has already been the subject of several monographic analyses.[4] I can review it only briefly, attending especially to the arguments put forward at the time by Churchill and other British leaders, and always remembering what sort of a time it was. The decision to bomb cities was made late in 1940. A directive issued in June of that year had "specifically laid down that targets had to be identified and aimed at. Indiscriminate bombing was forbidden." In November, after the German raid on Coventry, "Bomber Command was instructed simply to aim at the center of the city." What had once been called indiscriminate bombing (and commonly condemned) was now required, and by early 1942, aiming at military or industrial targets was barred: "the aiming points are to be the built-up areas, *not*, for instance, the dockyards or aircraft factories."[5] The purpose of the raids was explicitly declared to be the destruction of civilian morale. Following the famous minute of Lord Cherwell in 1942, the means to this demoralization were specified: working-class residential areas were the prime targets. Cherwell thought it possible to render a third of the German population homeless by 1943.[6]

Before Cherwell provided his "scientific" rationale for the bombing, a number of decisions had already been offered for the British decision. From the beginning, the attacks were defended as reprisals for the German blitz. This is a very problematic defense, even if we leave aside the difficulties of the doctrine of reprisals (which I have already canvassed). First of all, it appears possible, as one scholar has recently argued, that Churchill deliberately provoked the German attacks on London — by bombing Berlin — in order to relieve pressure on R.A.F. installations, until then the major *Luftwaffe* target.[7] Nor was it Churchill's purpose, once the blitz began, to deter the German attacks or to establish a policy of mutual restraint.

> We ask no favor of the enemy. We seek from them no compunction. On the contrary, if tonight the people of London were asked to cast their votes whether a convention should be entered into to stop the bombing of all cities, the overwhelming majority would cry, "No, we will mete out to the Germans the measure, and more than the measure, that they have meted out to us."[8]

Needless to say, the people of London were not in fact asked to vote on such a convention. Churchill assumed that the bombing of German cities was necessary to their morale and that they wanted to hear (what he told them in a radio broadcast in 1941) that the British air force was making "the German people taste and gulp each month a sharper dose of the miseries they have showered upon mankind."[9] This argument has been accepted by many historians: there was "a popular clamor" for revenge, one of them writes, which Churchill had to satisfy if he was to maintain a fighting spirit among his own people. It is especially interesting to note, then, that a 1941 opinion poll showed that "the most determined demand for [reprisal raids] came from Cumberland, Westmoreland, and the North Riding of Yorkshire, rural areas barely touched by bombing, where some three-quarters of the population wanted them. In central London, conversely, the proportion was only 45 percent."[10] Men and women who had experienced terror bombing were less likely to support Churchill's policy than those who had not — a heartening statistic, and one which suggests that the morale of the British people (or perhaps better, their conventional morality) allowed for political leadership of a different sort than Churchill provided. The news that

Germany was being bombed was certainly glad tidings in Britain; but as late as 1944, according to other opinion surveys, the overwhelming majority of Britishers still believed that the raids were directed solely against military targets. Presumably, that is what they wanted to believe; there was by then quite a bit of evidence to the contrary. But that says something, again, about the character of British morale. (It should also be said that the campaign against terror bombing, run largely by pacifists, attracted very little popular support.)

Reprisal was a bad argument; revenge was a worse one. We must concentrate now on the military justifications for terror bombing, which were presumably paramount in Churchill's mind, whatever he said on the radio. I can discuss these only in a general way. There was a great deal of dispute at the time, some of it technical, some of it moral in character. The calculations of the Cherwell minute, for example, were sharply attacked by a group of scientists whose opposition to terrorism may well have had moral grounds, but whose position, to the best of my knowledge, was never stated in moral terms.[11] Explicit moral disagreement developed most importantly among the professional soldiers involved in the decision-making process. These disagreements are described, in characteristic fashion, by a strategic analyst and historian who has studied the British escalation: "The . . . debate had been beclouded by emotion on one side of the argument, on the part of those who as a matter of moral principle objected to making war on civilians."[12] The focus of these objections seems to have been some version of the doctrine of double effect. (The arguments had, to the mind of the strategic analyst, "a curiously scholastic flavor.") At the height of the blitz, many British officers still felt strongly that their own air attacks should be aimed only at military targets and that positive efforts should be made to minimize civilian casualties. They did not want to imitate Hitler, but to differentiate themselves from him. Even officers who accepted the desirability of killing civilians still sought to maintain their professional honor: such deaths, they insisted, were desirable "only insofar as [they] remained a by-product of the primary intention to hit a military target. . . ."[13] A tendentious argument, no doubt, yet one that would drastically have limited the British offensive against cities. But all such proposals ran up against the operational limits of the bomber technology then available.

Early in the war, it became clear that British bombers could fly effectively only at night, and, given the navigational devices with which they were equipped, that they could reasonably aim at no target smaller than a fairly large city. A study made in 1941 indicated that of those planes that actually succeeded in attacking their target (about two-thirds of the attacking force), only one-third dropped their bombs within five miles of the point aimed at.[14] Once this was known, it would seem dishonest to claim that the intended target was, say, this aircraft factory and that the indiscriminate destruction around it was only an unintended, if foreseeable, consequence of the justified attempt to stop the production of planes. What was really unintended but foreseeable was that the factory itself would probably escape harm. If any sort of strategic bombing offensive was to be maintained, one would have to plan for the destruction that one could and did cause. Lord Cherwell's minute was an effort at such planning. In fact, of course, navigational devices were rapidly improved as the war went on, and the bombing of specific military targets was an important part of Britain's total air offensive, receiving top priority at times (before the June 1944 invasion of France, for example) and cutting into the resources allowed for attacks on cities. Today many experts believe that the war might have ended sooner had there been a greater concentration of air power against targets such as the German oil refineries.[15] But the decision to bomb cities was made at a time when victory was not in sight and the specter of defeat ever present. And it was made when no other decision seemed possible if there was to be any sort of military offensive against Nazi Germany.

Bomber Command was the only offensive weapon available to the British in those frightening years, and I expect there is some truth to the notion that it was used simply because it was there. "It was the only force in the West," writes Arthur Harris, chief of Bomber Command from early 1942 until the end of the war, "which could take offensive action . . . against Germany, our only means of getting at the enemy in a way that would hurt at all."[16] Offensive action could have been postponed until (or in hope of) some more favorable time. That is what the war convention would require, and there was also considerable military pressure for postponement. Harris was hard-pressed to keep his Command together in the face of repeated calls for tactical air support—which would have been coordinated with ground action largely defensive in character, since the German armies were still advancing everywhere. Sometimes, in his memoirs, he sounds like a bureaucrat defending his function and his office, but obviously he was also defending a certain conception of how the war might best be fought. He did not believe that the weapons he commanded should be used because he commanded them. He believed that the tactical use of bombers could not stop Hitler and that the destruction of cities could. Later in the war, he argued that only the destruction of cities could bring the fighting to a quick conclusion. The first of these arguments, at least, deserves a careful examination. It was apparently accepted by the Prime Minister. "The bombers alone," Churchill had said as early as September 1940, "provide the means of victory."[17]

The bombers alone—that poses the issue very starkly, and perhaps wrongly, given the disputes over strategy to which I have already referred. Churchill's statement suggested a certainty to which neither he nor anyone else had any right. But the issue can be put so as to accommodate a degree of skepticism and to permit even the most sophisticated among us to indulge in a common and a morally important fantasy: suppose that I sat in the seat of power and had to decide whether to use Bomber Command (in the only way that it could be used systematically and effectively) against cities. Suppose further that unless the bombers were used in this way, the probability that Germany would eventually be defeated would be radically reduced. It makes no sense at this point to quantify the probabilities; I have no clear notion what they actually were or even how they might be calculated given our present knowledge; nor am I sure how different figures, unless they were very different, would affect the moral argument. But it does seem to me that the more certain a German victory appeared to be in the absence of a bomber offensive, the more justifiable was the decision to launch the offensive. It is not just that such a victory was frightening, but also that it seemed in those years very close; it is not just that it was close, but also that it was so frightening. Here was a supreme emergency, where one might well be required to override the rights of innocent people and shatter the war convention.

Given the view of Nazism that I am assuming, the issue takes this form: should I wager this determinate crime (the killing of innocent people) against that immeasurable evil (a Nazi triumph)? Obviously, if there is some other way of avoiding the evil or even a reasonable chance of another way, I must wager differently or elsewhere. But I can never hope to be sure; a wager is not an experiment. Even if I wager and win, it is still possible that I was wrong, that my crime was unnecessary to victory. But I can argue that I studied the case as closely as I was able, took the best advice I could find, sought out available alternatives. And if all this is true, and my perceptions of evil and imminent danger not hysterical or self-serving, then surely I must wager. There is no option; the risk otherwise is too great. My own action is determinate, of course, only as to its direct consequences, while the rule that bars such acts is founded on a conception of rights that transcends all immediate considerations. It arises out of our common history; it holds the key to our common future. But I dare to say that our history will be nullified and our future condemned unless I accept the burdens of criminality here and now.

This is not an easy argument to make, and yet we must resist every effort to make it easier. Many people undoubtedly found some comfort in the fact that the cities being bombed were German and some of the victims Nazis. In effect, they applied the sliding scale and denied or diminished the rights of German civilians so as to deny or diminish the horror of their deaths. This is a tempting procedure, as we can see most clearly if we consider again the bombing of occupied France. Allied fliers killed many Frenchmen, but they did so while bombing what were (or were thought to be) military targets. They did not deliberately aim at the "built-up areas" of French cities. Suppose such a policy had been proposed. I am sure that we would all find the wager more difficult to undertake and defend if, through some strange combination of circumstances, it required the deliberate slaughter of Frenchmen. For we had special commitments to the French; we were fighting on their behalf (and sometimes the bombers were flown by French pilots). But the status of the civilians in the two cases is no different. The theory that distinguishes combatants from noncombatants does not distinguish Allied from enemy noncombatants, at least not with regard to the question of their murder. I suppose it makes sense to say that there were more people in German than in French cities who were responsible (in some fashion) for the evil of Nazism, and we may well be reluctant to extend to them the full range of civilian rights. But even if that reluctance is justified, there is no way for the bombers to search out the right people. And for all the others, terrorism only reiterates the tyranny that the Nazis had already established. It assimilates ordinary men and women to their government as if the two really made a totality, and it judges them in a totalitarian way. If one is forced to bomb cities, it seems to me, it is best to acknowledge that one has also been forced to kill the innocent.

Once again, however, I want to set radical limits to the notion of necessity even as I have myself been using it. For the truth is that the supreme emergency passed long before the British bombing reached its crescendo. The greater number by far of the German civilians killed by terror bombing were killed without moral (and probably also without military) reason. The decisive point was made by Churchill in July of 1942:

> In the days when we were fighting alone, we answered the question: "How are you going to win the war?" by saying: "We will shatter Germany by bombing." Since then the enormous injuries inflicted on the German Army and manpower by the Russians, and the accession of the manpower and munitions of the United States, have rendered other possibilities open.[18]

Surely, then, it was time to stop the bombing of cities and to aim, tactically and strategically, only at legitimate military targets. But that was not Churchill's view: "All the same, it would be a mistake to cast aside our original thought . . . that the severe, ruthless bombing of Germany on an ever-increasing scale will not only cripple her war effort . . . but will create conditions intolerable to the mass of the German population." So the raids continued, culminating in the spring of 1945—when the war was virtually won—in a savage attack on the city of Dresden in which something like 100,000 people were killed.[19] Only then did Churchill have second thoughts. "It seems to me that the moment has come when the question of bombing German cities simply for the sake of increasing the terror, though under other pretexts, should be reviewed. . . . The destruction of Dresden remains a serious query against the conduct of Allied bombing."[20] Indeed it does, but so does the destruction of Hamburg and Berlin and all the other cities attacked simply for the sake of terror.

The argument used between 1942 and 1945 in defense of terror bombing was utilitarian in character, its emphasis not on victory itself but on the time and price of victory. The city raids, it was claimed by men such as Harris, would end the war sooner than it would otherwise end and, despite the large number of civilian casualties they inflected, at a lower cost in human life. Assuming this claim to be true (I have already indicated that precisely opposite claims are made by some historians and strategists), it is nevertheless not sufficient to justify the bombing. It is not sufficient, I think, even if we do nothing more than calculate utilities. For such calculations need not be concerned only with the preservation of life. There is much else that we might plausibly want to preserve: the quality of our lives, for example, our civilization and morality, our collective abhorrence of murder, even when it seems, as it always does, to serve some purpose. Then the deliberate slaughter of innocent men and women cannot be justified simply because it saves the lives of other men and women. I suppose it is possible to imagine situations where that last assertion might prove problematic, from a utilitarian perspective, where the number of people involved is small, the proportions are right, the events hidden from the public eye, and so on. Philosophers delight in inventing such cases in order to test out our moral doctrines. But their inventions are somehow put out of our minds by the sheer scale of the calculations necessary in World War II. To kill 278,966 civilians (the number is made up) in order to avoid the deaths of an unknown but probably larger number of civilians and soldiers is surely a fantastic, godlike, frightening, and horrendous act.[21]

I have said that such acts can probably be ruled out on utilitarian grounds, but it is also true that utilitarianism as it is commonly understood, indeed, as Sidgwick himself understands it, encourages the bizarre accounting that makes them (morally) possible. We can recognize their horror only when we have acknowledged the personality and value of the men and women we destroy in committing them. It is the acknowledgment of rights that puts a stop to such calculations and forces us to realize that the destruction of the innocent, whatever its purposes, is a kind of blasphemy against our deepest moral commitment. (This is true even in a supreme emergency, when we cannot do anything else.) But I want to look at one more case before concluding my argument—a case where the utilitarian accounting, however bizarre, seemed so radically clear-cut to the decision-makers to leave them, they thought, no choice but to attack the innocent.

THE LIMITS OF CALCULATION

Hiroshima

"They all accepted the 'assignment' and produced The Bomb," Dwight Macdonald wrote in August 1945 of the atomic scientists.

"Why?" It is an important question, but Macdonald poses it badly and then gives the wrong answer. "Because they thought of themselves as specialists, technicians, and not as complete men."[22] In fact, they did not accept the assignment; they sought it out, taking the initiative, urging upon President Roosevelt the critical importance of an American effort to match the work being done in Nazi Germany. And they did this precisely because they were "complete men," many of them European refugees, with an acute sense of what a Nazi victory would mean for their native lands and for all mankind. They were driven by a deep moral anxiety, not (or not most crucially) by any kind of scientific fascination; they were certainly not servile technicians. On the other hand, they were men and women without political power or following, and once their own work was done, they could not control its use. The discovery in November 1944 that German scientists had made little progress ended their own supreme emergency, but it did not end the program they had helped to launch. "If I had known that the Germans would not succeed in constructing the atom bomb," Albert Einstein said, "I would never have lifted a finger."[23] By the time he found that out, however, the scientists had largely finished their work; now indeed technicians were in charge, and the politicians in charge of them. And in the event, the bomb was not used against Germany (or to deter its use by Hitler, which is what men like Einstein had in mind), but against the Japanese, who had never posed such a threat to peace and freedom as the Nazis had.[24]

Still, it was an important feature of the American decision that the President and his advisors believed the Japanese to be fighting an aggressive war and, moreover, to be fighting it unjustly. Thus Truman's address to the American people August 12, 1945:

> We have used [the bomb] against those who attacked us without warning at Pearl Harbor, against those who have starved and beaten and executed American prisoners of war, against those who have abandoned all pretense of obeying international laws of warfare. We have used it to shorten the agony of war. . . .

Here again the sliding scale is being used to open the way for utilitarian calculations. The Japanese have forfeited (some of) their rights, and so they cannot complain about Hiroshima so long as the destruction of the city actually does, or could reasonably be expected to, shorten the agony of war. But had the Japanese exploded an atomic bomb over an American city, killing tens of thousands of civilians and thereby shortening the agony of war, the action would clearly have been a crime, one more for Truman's list. This distinction is only plausible, however, if one renders a judgment not only against the leaders of Japan but also against the ordinary people of Hiroshima and insists at the same time that no similar judgment is possible against the people of San Francisco, say, or Denver. I can find, as I have said before, no way of defending such a procedure. How did the people of Hiroshima forfeit their rights? Perhaps their taxes paid for some of the ships and planes used in the attack on Pearl Harbor; perhaps they sent their sons into the navy and air force with prayers for their success; perhaps they celebrated the actual event, after being told that their country had won a great victory in the face of an imminent American threat. Surely there is nothing here that makes these people liable to direct attack. (It is worth noting, though the fact is not relevant in judging the Hiroshima decision, that the raid on Pearl Harbor was directed entirely against naval and army installations: only a few stray bombs fell on the city of Honolulu.)[25]

But if Truman's argument on August 12 was weak, there was a worse one underlying it. He did not intend to apply the sliding scale with any precision, for he seems to have believed that, given Japanese aggression, the Americans could do anything at all to win (and shorten the agony of war). Along with most of his advisors, he accepted the "war is hell" doctrine; it is a constant allusion in defenses of the Hiroshima decision. Thus Henry Stimson:

> As I look back over the five years of my service as Secretary of War, I see too many stern and heartrending decisions to be willing to pretend that war is anything else but what it is. The face of war is the face of death; death is an inevitable part of every order that a wartime leader gives.[26]

And James Byrnes, Truman's friend and his Secretary of State:

> . . . war remains what General Sherman said it was.[27]

And Arthur Compton, chief scientific advisor to the government:

> When one thinks of the mounted archers of Ghengiz Khan . . . the Thirty Years War . . . the millions of Chinese who died during the Japanese invasion . . . the mass destruction of western Russia . . . one realizes that in whatever manner it is fought, war is precisely what General Sherman called it.[28]

And Truman himself:

> Let us not become so preoccupied with weapons that we lose sight of the fact that war itself is the real villain.[29]

War itself is to blame, but also the men who begin it . . . while those who fight justly merely participate in the hell of war, choicelessly, and there are no moral decisions for which they can be called to account. This is not, or not necessarily, an immoral doctrine, but it is radically one-sided; it evades the tension between *jus ad bellum* and *jus in bello;* it undercuts the need for hard judgments; it relaxes our sense of moral restraint. When he was choosing a target for the first bomb, Truman reports, he asked Stimson which Japanese cities were "devoted exclusively to war production."[30] The question was reflexive; Truman did not want to violate the "laws of war." But it wasn't serious. Which American cities were devoted exclusively to war production? It is possible to ask such questions only when the answer doesn't matter. If war is hell however it is fought, then what difference can it make how we fight it? And if war itself is the villain, then what risks do we run (aside from the strategic risks) when we make decisions? The Japanese, who began the war, can also end it; only they can end it, and all we can do is fight it, enduring what Truman called "the daily tragedy of bitter war." I don't doubt that that was really Truman's view; it was not a matter of convenience but of conviction. but it is a distorted view. It mistakes the actual hellishness of war, which is particular in character and open to precise definition, for the limitless pains of religious mythology. The pains of war are limitless only if we make them so — only if we move, as Truman did, beyond the limits that we and others have established. Sometimes, I think, we have to do that, but not all the time. Now we must ask whether it was necessary to do it in 1945.

The only possible defense of the Hiroshima attack is a utilitarian calculation made without the sliding scale, a calculation made, then, where there was no room for it, a claim to override the rules of war and the rights of Japanese civilians. I want to state this argument as strongly as I can. In 1945, American policy was fixed on the demand for the unconditional surrender of Japan. The Japanese had by that time lost the war, but they were by no means ready to accept this demand. The leaders of their armed forces expected an invasion of the Japanese main islands and were prepared for a last-ditch resistance. They had over two million soldiers available for fighting, and they believed that they could make an invasion so costly that the Americans would agree to a negotiated peace. Truman's military advisors also believed that the costs would be high, though the public record does not show that they ever recommended negotiations. They thought that the war might continue late into 1946 and that there would be as many as a million additional American casualties. Japanese losses would be much higher. The capture of Okinawa in a battle lasting from April to June of 1945 had cost almost 80,000 American casualties, while virtually the entire Japanese garrison of 120,000 men had been killed (only 10,600 prisoners were taken).[31] If the main islands were defended with a similar ferocity, hundreds of thousands, perhaps millions, of Japanese soldiers would die. Meanwhile, the fighting would continue in China and in Manchuria, where a Russian attack was soon due. And the bombing of Japan would also continue, and perhaps intensify, with casualty rates no different from those anticipated from the atomic attack. For the Americans had adopted in Japan the British policy of terrorism: a massive incendiary raid on Tokyo early in March 1945 had set off a firestorm and killed an estimated 100,000 people. Against all this was set, in the minds of American decision-makers, the impact of the atomic bomb — not materially more damaging but psychologically more frightening, and holding out the promise, perhaps, of a quick end to the war. "To avert a vast, indefinite butchery . . . at the cost of a few explosions," wrote Churchill in support of Truman's decision, "seemed, after all our toils and perils, a miracle of deliverance."[32]

"A vast indefinite butchery" involving quite probably the deaths of several million people: surely this is a great evil, and if it was imminent, one could reasonably argue that extreme measures might be warranted to avert it. Secretary of War Stimson thought it was the sort of case I have already described, where one had to wager; there was no option. "No man, in our position and subject to our responsibilities, holding in his hand a weapon of such possibilities for . . . saving those lives, could have failed to use it."[33] This is by no means an incomprehensible or, on the surface at least, an outrageous argument. But it is not the same as the argument I suggested in the case of Britain in 1940. It does not have the form: if we don't do x (bomb cities), they will do y (win the war, establish tyrannical rule, slaughter their opponents). What Stimson argued is very different. Given the actual policy of the U.S. government, it amounts to this: if we don't do x, *we* will do y. The two atomic bombs caused "many casualties," James Byrnes admitted, "but not nearly so many as there would have been had our air force continued to drop incendiary bombs on Japan's cities."[34] Our purpose, then, was not to avert a "butchery" that someone else was threatening, but one that we were threatening, and had already begun to carry out. Now, what great evil, what supreme emergency, justified the incendiary attacks on Japanese cities?

Even if we had been fighting in strict accordance with the war convention, the continuation of the struggle was not something forced upon us. It had to do with our war aims. The military estimate of casualties was based not only on the belief that the Japanese would fight almost to the last man, but also on the assumption that the Americans would accept nothing less than unconditional surrender. The war aims of the American government required either an invasion of the main islands, with enormous losses of American and Japanese soldiers and Japanese civilians trapped in the war zones, or the use of the atomic bomb. Given that choice, one might well reconsider those aims. Even if we assume that unconditional surrender was morally desirable because of the character of Japanese militarism, it might still be morally undesirable because of the human costs it entailed. But I would suggest a stronger argument than this. The Japanese case is sufficiently different from the German so that unconditional surrender should never have been asked. Japan's rulers were engaged in a more ordinary sort of military expansion, and all that was morally required was that they be defeated, not that they be conquered and totally overthrown. Some restraint upon their war-making power might be justified, but their domestic authority was a matter of concern only to the Japanese people. In any case, if killing millions (or many thousands) of men and women was militarily necessary for their conquest and overthrow, then it was morally necessary—in order not to kill those people—to settle for something less. I have made this argument before . . . ; here is a further example of its practical application. If people have a right not to be forced to fight, they also have a right not to be forced to continue fighting beyond the point when the war might justly be concluded. Beyond that point, there can be no supreme emergencies, no arguments about military necessity, no cost-accounting in human lives. To press the war further than that is to re-commit the crime of aggression. In the summer of 1945, the victorious Americans owed the Japanese people an experiment in negotiation. To use the atomic bomb, to kill and terrorize civilians, without even attempting such an experiment, was a double crime.[35]

These, then are the limits of the realm of necessity. Utilitarian calculation can force us to violate the rules of war only when we are face-to-face not merely with defeat but with a defeat likely to bring disaster to a political community. But these calculations have no similar effects when what is at stake is only the speed or the scope of victory. They are relevant only to the conflict between winning and fighting well, not to the internal problems of combat itself. Whenever that conflict is absent, calculation is stopped short by the rules of war and the rights they are designed to protect. Confronted by those rights, we are not to calculate consequences, or figure relative risks, or compute probable casualties, but simply to stop short and turn aside.

NOTES

[1] Quoted in George Quester, *Deterrence Before Hiroshima* (New York, 1966), p. 67.

[2] See J. Glen Gray, *The Warriors: Reflections on Men in Battle* (New York, 1967), ch. 5: "Images of the Enemy."

[3] But the claim that one can never kill an innocent person abstracts from the question of coercion and consent.

[4] See Quester, *Deterrence* and F. M. Sallagar, *The Road to Total War: Escalation of World War II* (Rand Corporation Report, 1969); also the official history by Sir Charles Webster and Noble Frankland, *The Strategic Air Offensive Against Germany* (London, 1961).

[5] Noble Frankland, *Bomber Offensive: The Devaluation of Europe* (New York, 1970), p. 41.

[6] The story of the Cherwell minute is told, most unsympathetically, in C. P. Snow, *Science and Government* (New York, 1962).

[7] Quester, pp. 117–18.

[8] Quoted in Quester, p. 141.

[9] Quoted in Angus Calder, *The People's War: 1939–1945* (New York, 1969), p. 491.

[10] Calder, p. 229; the same poll is cited by Vera Brittain, a courageous opponent of British bombing policy: *Humiliation with Honor* (New York, 1943), p. 91.

[11] " . . . it was not [Cherwell's] ruthlessness that worried us most, it was his calculations." Snow, *Science and Government*, p. 48. Cf. P. M. S. Blackett's post-war critique of the bombing, worked out in narrowly strategic terms: *Fear, War, and the Bomb* (New York, 1949), ch. 2.

[12] Sallagar, p. 127.

[13] Sallagar, p. 128.

[14] Frankland, *Bomber Offensive*, pp. 38–39.

[15] Frankland, *Bomber Offensive*, p. 134.

[16] Sir Arthur Harris, *Bomber Offensive* (London, 1947), p. 74.

[17] Calder, p. 229.

[18] *The Hinge of Fate*, p. 770.

[19] For a detailed account of this attack, see David Irving, *The Destruction of Dresden* (New York, 1963).

[20] Quoted in Quester, p. 156.

[21] George Orwell has suggested an alternative utilitarian rationale for the bombing of German cities. In a column written for the leftist journal *Tribune* in 1944, he argued that the bombing brought the true character of contemporary combat home to all those people who supported the war, even enjoyed it, only because they never felt its effects. It shattered "the immunity of civilians, one of the things that have made war possible," and so it made war less likely in the future. See *The Collected Essays, Journalism and Letters of George Orwell*, ed. Sonia Orwell and Ian Angus, New York, 1968, Vol. 3, pp. 151–152. Orwell assumes that civilians had really been immune in the past, which is false. In any case, I doubt that his argument would lead anyone to begin bombing cities. It is an apology after the fact, and not a convincing one.

[22] *Memoirs of a Revolutionist* (New York, 1957), p. 178.

[23] Robert C. Batchelder, *The Irreversible Decision: 1939–1950* (New York, 1965), p. 38. Batchelder's is the best historical account of the decision to drop the bomb, and the only one that treats the moral issues in a systematic way.

[24] In his novel *The New Men*, C. P. Snow describes the discussions among atomic scientists as to whether or not the bomb should be used. Some of them, his narrator says, answered that question with "an absolute no," feeling that if the weapon were used to kill hundreds of thousands of innocent people, "neither science nor the civilization of which science is bone and fibre, would be free from guilt again." But the more common view was the one I have been defending: "Many, probably the majority, gave a conditional no with much the same feeling behind it; but if there were *no other way* of saving the war against Hitler, they would be prepared to drop the bomb." *The New Men*, New York, 1954, p. 177 (Snow's emphasis).

[25] A. Russell Buchanan, *The United States and World War II* (New York, 1964), I, 75.

[26] "The Decision to Use the Atomic Bomb," *Harpers Magazine* (February 1947), repr. in ed. Paul R. Baker, *The Atomic Bomb: The Great Decision* (New York, 1968), p. 21.

[27] *Speaking Frankly* (New York, 1947), p. 261.

[28] *Atomic Quest* (New York, 1956), p. 247.

[29] *Mr. Citizen* (New York, 1960), p. 267. I owe this group of quotations to Gerald McElroy.

[30] Batchelder, p. 159.

[31] Batchelder, p. 149.

[32] *Triumph and Tragedy* (New York, 1962), p. 639.

[33] "The Decision to Use the Bomb," p. 21.

[34] *Speaking Frankly*, p. 264.

[35] The case would be even worse if the bomb were used for political rather than military reasons (with the Russians rather than the Japanese in mind): on this point, see the careful analysis of Martin J. Sherwin, *A World Destroyed: The Atomic Bomb and the Grand Alliance* (New York, 1975).

OPTIONS FOR WRITING

1. Walzer's argument depends on his view that in the 1940s, the Japanese were not the threat to civilization that the Nazis were. Do you agree or disagree? Is he right in believing that as a result we were wrong in dropping the atomic bomb? Write a critical review of Walzer's argument.

2. Would you make a similar case for the American decision to attack Iraq on January 16, 1991? Explain your answer in a persuasive essay.

Jean-Paul Sartre
EXISTENTIALISM IS A HUMANISM

Jean-Paul Sartre (1905–1980) was a French philosopher, novelist, and playwright who had a profound effect on twentieth century philosophy, literature, theater, and film. He was perhaps the most influential proponent of existentialism, the theory that holds that there is no meaning to life to be found outside of ourselves and that we create meaning by the projects we choose to form our lives. In this reading, Sartre provides a concise statement of this existentialist philosophy. This is a difficult reading, and you may have to read it more than once. Write down questions about the reading for class discussion. Outline the main features of Sartre's existentialist philosophy. What does Sartre mean by the terms "existence" and "essence"? What does Sartre mean when he says that we are condemned to be free?

What is meant by the term *existentialism*?

Most people who use the word would be rather embarrassed if they had to explain it, since, now that the word is all the rage, even the work of a musician or painter is being called existentialist. A gossip columnist in *Clartés* signs himself *The Existentialist*, so that by this time the word has been so stretched and has taken on so broad a meaning, that it no longer means anything at all. It seems that for want of an advance-guard doctrine analogous to surrealism, the kind of people who are eager for scandal and flurry turn to this philosophy which in other respects does not at all serve their purposes in this sphere.

Actually, it is the least scandalous, the most austere of doctrines. It is intended strictly for specialists and philosophers. Yet it can be defined easily. What complicates matters is that there are two kinds of existentialist; first, those who are Christian, among whom I would include Jaspers and Gabriel Marcel, both Catholic; and on the other hand the atheistic existentialists, among whom I class Heidegger, and then the French existentialists and myself. What they have in common is that they think that existence precedes essence, or, if you prefer, that subjectivity must be the starting point.

Just what does that mean? Let us consider some object that is manufactured, for example, a book or a paper-cutter: here is an object which has been made by an artisan whose inspiration came from a concept. He referred to the concept of what a paper-cutter is and likewise to a known method of production, which is part of the concept, something which is, by and large, a routine. Thus, the paper-cutter is at once an object produced in a certain way and, on the other hand, one having a specific use; and one can not postulate a man who produces a paper-cutter but does not know what it is used for. Therefore, let us say that, for the paper-cutter, essence — that is, the ensemble of both the production routines and the properties which enable it to be both produced and defined — precedes existence. Thus, the presence of the paper-cutter or book in front of me is determined. Therefore, we have here a technical view of the world whereby it can be said that production precedes existence.

When we conceive God as the Creator, He is generally thought of as a superior sort of artisan. Whatever doctrine we may be considering, whether one like that of Descartes or that of Leibnitz, we always grant that will more or less follows understanding, or, at the very least, accompanies it, and that when God creates He knows exactly what He is creating. Thus, the concept of man in the mind of God is comparable to the concept of paper-cutter in the mind of the manufacturer, and, following certain techniques and a conception, God produces man, just as the artisan, following a definition and a technique, makes a paper-cutter. Thus, the individual man is the realization of a certain concept in the divine intelligence.

In the eighteenth century, the atheism of the *philosophes* discarded the idea of God, but not so much for the notion that essence precedes existence. To a certain extent, this idea is found everywhere; we find it in Diderot, in Voltaire, and even in Kant. Man has a human nature; this human nature, which is the concept of the human, is found in all men, which means that each man is a particular example of a universal concept, man. In Kant, the result of this universality is that the wild-man, the natural man, as well as the bourgeois, are circumscribed by the same definition and have the same basic qualities. Thus, here too the essence of man precedes the historical existence that we find in nature.

Atheistic existentialism, which I represent, is more coherent. It states that if God does not exist, there is at least one being in whom existence precedes essence, a being who exists before he can be defined by any concept, and that this being is man, or, as Heidegger says, human reality. What is meant here by saying that existence precedes essence? It means that, first of all, man exists, turns up, appears on the scene, and, only afterwards, defines himself. If man, as the existentialist conceives him, is indefinable, it is because at first he is nothing. Only afterward will he be something, and he himself will have made what he will be. Thus, there is no human nature, since there is no God to conceive it. Not only is man what he conceives himself to be, but he is also only what he wills himself to be after this thrust toward existence.

Man is nothing else but what he makes of himself. Such is the first principle of existentialism. It is also what is called subjectivity, the name we are labeled with when charges are brought against us. But what do we mean by this, if not that man has a greater dignity than a stone or table? For we mean that man first exists, that is, that man first of all is the being who hurls himself toward a future and who is conscious of imagining himself as being in the future. Man is at the start a plan which is aware of itself, rather than a patch of moss, a piece of garbage, or a cauliflower; nothing exists prior to this plan; there is nothing in heaven; man will be what he will have planned to be. Not what he will want to be. Because by the word "will" we generally mean a conscious decision, which is subsequent to what we have already made of ourselves. I may want to belong to a political party, write a book, get married; but all this is only a manifestation of an earlier, more spontaneous choice that is called "will." But if existence really does precede essence, man is responsible for what he is. Thus, existentialism's first move is to make every man aware of what he is and to make the full responsibility of his essence rest on him. And when we say that a man is responsible for himself, we do not only mean that he is responsible for his own individuality, but that he is responsible for all men.

The word subjectivism has two meanings, and our opponents play on the two. Subjectivism means, on the one hand, that an individual chooses and makes himself; and, on the other, that it is impossible for man to transcend human subjectivity. The second of these is the essential meaning of existentialism. When we say that man chooses his own self, we mean that every one of us does likewise; but we also mean by that that in making this choice he also chooses all men. In fact, in creating the man that we want to be, there is not a single one of our acts which does not at the same time create an image of man as we think he ought to be. To choose to be this or that is to affirm at the same time the value of what we choose, because we can never choose evil. We always choose the good, and nothing can be good for us without being good for all.

If, on the other hand, existence precedes essence, and if we grant that we exist and fashion our image at one and the same time, the image is valid for everybody and for our whole age. Thus, our responsibility is much greater than we might have supposed, because it involves all mankind. If I am a workingman and choose to join a Christian trade-union rather than be a communist, and if by being a member I want to show that the best thing for man is resignation, that the kingdom of man is not of this world, I am not only involving my own case—I want to be resigned for everyone. As a result, my action has involved all humanity. To take a more individual matter, if I want to marry, to have children; even if this marriage depends solely on my own circumstances or passion or wish, I am involving all humanity in monogamy and not merely myself. Therefore, I am responsible for myself and for everyone else. I am creating a certain image of man of my own choosing. In choosing myself, I choose man.

This helps us understand what the actual content is of such rather grandiloquent words as anguish, forlornness, despair. As you will see, it's all quite simple.

First, what is meant by anguish? The existentialists say at once that man is anguish. What that means is this: the man who involves himself and who realizes that he is not only the person he chooses to be, but also a lawmaker who is, at the same time, choosing all mankind as well as himself, can not help escape the feeling of his total and deep responsibility. Of course, there are many people who are not anxious; but we claim that they are hiding their anxiety, that they are fleeing from it. Certainly, many people believe that when they do something, they themselves are the only ones involved, and when someone says to them, "What if everyone acted that way?" they shrug their shoulders and answer, "Everyone doesn't act that way." But really, one should always ask himself, "What would happen if everybody looked at things that way?" There is no escaping this disturbing thought except by a kind of double-dealing. A man who lies and makes excuses for himself by saying "not everybody does that," is someone with an uneasy conscience, because the act of lying implies that a universal value is conferred upon the lie.

Anguish is evident even when it conceals itself. This is the anguish that Kierkegaard called the anguish of Abraham. You know the story: an angel has ordered Abraham to sacrifice his son; if it really were an angel who has come and said, "You are Abraham, you shall sacrifice your son," everything would be all right. But everyone might first wonder, "Is it really an angel, and am I really Abraham? What proof do I have?"

There was a madwoman who had hallucinations; someone used to speak to her on the telephone and give her orders. Her doctor asked her, "Who is it who talks to you?" She answered, "He says it's God." What proof did she really have that it was God? If an angel comes to me, what proof is there that it's an angel? And if I hear voices, what proof is there that they come from heaven and not from hell, or from the subconscious, or a pathological condition? What proves that they are addressed to me? What proof is there that I have been appointed to impose my choice and my conception of man on humanity? I'll never find any proof or sign to convince me of that. If a voice addresses me, it is always for me to decide that this is the angel's voice; if I consider that such an act is a good one, it is I who will choose to say that it is good rather than bad.

Now, I'm not being singled out as an Abraham, and yet at every moment I'm obliged to perform exemplary acts. For every man, everything happens as if all mankind had its eyes fixed on him and were guiding itself by what he does. And every man ought to say to himself, "Am I really the kind of man who has the right to act in such a way that humanity might guide itself by my actions?" And if he does not say that to himself, he is masking his anguish.

There is no question here of the kind of anguish which would lead to quietism, to inaction. It is a matter of a simple sort of anguish that anybody who has had responsibilities is familiar with. For example, when a military officer takes the responsibility for an attack and sends a certain number of men to death, he chooses to do so, and in the main he alone makes the choice. Doubtless, orders come from above, but they are too broad; he interprets them, and on this interpretation depend the lives of ten or fourteen or twenty men. In making a decision he can not help having a certain anguish. All leaders know this anguish. That doesn't keep them from acting; on the contrary, it is the very condition of their action. For it implies that they envisage a number of possibilities, and when they choose one, they realize that it has value only because it is chosen. We shall see that this kind of anguish, which is the kind that existentialism describes, is explained, in addition, by a direct responsibility to the other men whom it involves. It is not a curtain separating us from action, but is part of action itself.

When we speak of forlornness, a term Heidegger was fond of, we mean only that God does not exist and that we have to face all the consequences of this. The existentialist is strongly opposed to a certain kind of secular ethics which would like to abolish God with the least possible expense. About 1880, some French teachers tried to set up a secular ethics which went something like this: God is a useless and costly hypothesis; we are discarding it; but, meanwhile, in order for there to be an ethics, a society, a civilization, it is essential that certain values be taken seriously, and that they be considered as having an *a priori* existence. It must be obligatory, *a priori*, to be honest, not to lie, not to beat your wife, to have children, etc., etc. So we're going to try a little device which will make it possible to show that values exist all the same, inscribed in a heaven of ideas, though otherwise God does not exist. In other words — and this, I believe, is the tendency of everything called reformism in France — nothing will be changed if God does not exist. We shall find ourselves with the same norms of honesty, progress, and humanism, and we shall have made of God an outdated hypothesis which will peacefully die off by itself.

The existentialist, on the contrary, thinks it very distressing that God does not exist, because all possibility of finding values in a heaven of ideas disappears along with Him; there can no longer be an *a priori* Good, since there is no infinite and perfect consciousness to think it. Nowhere it is written that the Good exists, that we must be honest, that we must not lie; because the fact is we are on a plane where there are only men. Dostoyevsky said, "If God didn't exist, everything would be possible." That is the very starting point of existentialism. Indeed, everything is permissible if God does not exist, and as a result man is forlorn, because neither within him nor without does he find anything to cling to. He can't start making excuses for himself.

If existence really does precede essence, there is no explaining things away by reference to a fixed and given human nature. In other words, there is no determinism, man is free, man is freedom. On the other hand, if God does not exist, we find no values or commands to turn to which legitimize our conduct. So, in the bright realm of values, we have no excuse behind us, nor justification before us. We are alone, with no excuses.

That is the idea I shall try to convey when I say that man is condemned to be free. Condemned, because he did not create himself, yet, in other respects is free; because, once thrown into the world, he is responsible for everything he does. The existentialist does not believe in the power of passion. He will never agree that a sweeping passion is a ravaging torrent which fatally leads a man to certain acts and is therefore an excuse. He thinks that man is responsible for his passion.

The existentialist does not think that man is going to help himself by finding in the world some omen by which to orient himself. Because he thinks that man will interpret the omen to suit himself. Therefore, he thinks that man, with no support and no aid, is condemned every moment to invent man. Ponge, in a very fine article, has said, "Man is the future of man." That's exactly it. But if it is taken to mean that this future is recorded in heaven, that God sees it, then it is false, because it would really no longer be a future. If it is taken to mean that, whatever a man may be, there is a future to be forged, a virgin future before him, then this remark is sound. But then we are forlorn.

To give you an example which will enable you to understand forlornness better, I shall cite the case of one of my students who came to see me under the following circumstances: his father was on bad terms with his mother, and, moreover, was inclined to be a collaborationist; his older brother had been killed in the German offensive of 1940, and the young man, with somewhat immature but generous feelings, wanted to avenge him. His mother lived alone with him, very much upset by the half-treason of her husband and the death of her older son; the boy was her only consolation.

The boy was faced with the choice of going to England and joining the Free French Forces — that is, leaving his mother behind — or remaining with his mother and helping her to carry on. He was fully aware that the woman lived only for him and that his going-off — and perhaps his death — would plunge her into despair. He was also aware that every act that he did for his mother's sake was a sure thing, in the sense that it was helping her to carry on, whereas every effort he made toward going off and fighting was an uncertain move which might run aground and prove completely useless; for example, on his way to England he might, while passing through Spain, be detained indefinitely in a Spanish camp; he might reach England or Algiers and be stuck in an office at a desk job. As a result, he was faced with two very different kinds of action: one, concrete, immediate, but concerning only one individual; the other concerned an incomparably vaster group, a national collectivity, but for that very reason was dubious, and might be interrupted en route. And, at the same time, he was wavering between two kinds of ethics. On the one hand, an ethics of sympathy, of personal devotion; on the other hand, a broader ethics, but one whose efficacy was more dubious. He had to choose between the two.

Who could help him choose? Christian doctrine? No. Christian doctrine says, "Be charitable, love your neighbor, take the more rugged path, etc., etc." But which is the more rugged path? Whom should he love as a brother? The fighting man or his mother? Which does the greater good, the vague act of fighting in a group, or the concrete one of helping a particular human being to go on living? Who can decide *a priori*? Nobody. No book of ethics can tell him. The Kantian ethics says, "Neither treat any person as a means, but as an end." Very well, if I stay with my mother, I'll treat her as an end and not as a means; but by virtue of this very fact, I'm running the risk of treating the people around me who are fighting, as means; and, conversely, if I go to join those who are fighting, I'll be treating them as an end, and, by doing that, I run the risk of treating my mother as a means.

If values are vague, and if they are always too broad for the concrete and specific case that we are considering, the only thing left for us is to trust our instincts. That's what this young man tried to do; and when I saw him, he said, "In the end, feeling is what counts. I ought to choose whichever pushes me in one direction. If I feel that I love my mother enough to sacrifice everything else for her—my desire for vengeance, for action, for adventure—then I'll stay with her. If, on the contrary, I feel that my love for my mother isn't enough, I'll leave."

But how is the value of a feeling determined? What gives his feeling for his mother value? Precisely the fact that he remained with her. I may say that I like so-and-so well enough to sacrifice a certain amount of money for him, but I may say so only if I've done it. I may say "I love my mother well enough to remain with her" if I have remained with her. The only way to determine the value of this affection is, precisely, to perform an act which confirms and defines it. But, since I require this affection to justify my act, I find myself caught in a vicious circle.

On the other hand, Gide has well said that a mock feeling and a true feeling are almost indistinguishable; to decide that I love my mother and will remain with her, or to remain with her by putting on an act, amount somewhat to the same thing. In other words, the feeling is formed by the acts one performs; so, I can not refer to it in order to act upon it. Which means that I can neither seek within myself the true condition which will impel me to act, nor apply to a system of ethics for concepts which will permit me to act. You will say, "At least, he did go to a teacher for advice." But if you seek advice from a priest, for example, you have chosen this priest; you already knew, more or less, just about what advice he was going to give you. In other words, choosing your adviser is involving yourself. The proof of this is that if you are a Christian, you will say, "Consult a priest." But some priests are collaborating, some are just marking time, some are resisting. Which to choose? If the young man chooses a priest who is resisting or collaborating, he has already decided on the kind of advice he's going to get. Therefore, in coming to see me he knew the answer I was going to give him, and I had only one answer to give: "You're free, choose, that is, invent." No general ethics can show you what is to be done; there are no omens in the world. The Catholics will reply, "But there are." Granted—but, in any case, I myself choose the meaning they have.

When I was a prisoner, I knew a rather remarkable young man who was a Jesuit. He had entered the Jesuit order in the following way: he had had a number of very bad breaks; in childhood, his father died, leaving him in poverty, and he was a scholarship student at a religious institution where he was constantly made to feel that he was being kept out of charity; then, he failed to get any of the honors and distinctions that children like; later on, at about eighteen, he bungled a love affair; finally at twenty-two, he failed in military training, a childish enough matter, but it was the last straw.

This young fellow might well have felt that he had botched everything. It was a sign of something, but of what? He might have taken refuge in bitterness or despair. But he very wisely looked upon all this as a sign that he was not made for secular triumphs, and that only the triumphs of religion, holiness, and faith were open to him. He saw the hand of God in all this, and so he entered the order. Who can help seeing that he alone decided what the sign meant?

Some other interpretation might have been drawn from this series of setbacks; for example, that he might have done better to turn carpenter or revolutionist. Therefore, he is fully responsible for the interpretation. Forlornness implies that we ourselves choose our being. Forlornness and anguish go together.

As for despair, the term has a very simple meaning. It means that we shall confine ourselves to reckoning only with what depends upon our will, or on the ensemble of probabilities which make our action possible. When we want something, we always have to reckon with probabilities. I may be counting on the arrival of a friend. The friend is coming by rail or street-car; this supposes that the train will arrive on schedule, or that the street-car will not jump the track. I am left in the realm of possibility; but possibilities are to be reckoned with only to the point where my action comports with the ensemble of these possibilities, and no further. The moment the possibilities I am considering are not rigorously involved by my action, I ought to disengage myself from them, because no God, no scheme, can adapt the world and its possibilities to my will. When Descartes said, "Conquer yourself rather than the world," he meant essentially the same thing.

The Marxists to whom I have spoken reply, "You can rely on the support of others in your action, which obviously has certain limits because you're not going to live forever. That means: rely on both what others are doing elsewhere to help you, in China, in Russia, and what they will do later on, after your death, to carry on the action and lead it to its fulfillment, which will be the revolution. You even *have* to rely upon that, otherwise you're immoral." I reply at once that I will always rely on fellow-fighters insofar as these comrades are involved with me in a common struggle, in the unity of a party or a group in which I can more or less make my weight felt; that is, one whose ranks I am in as a fighter and whose movements I am aware of at every moment. In such a situation, relying on the unity and will of the party is exactly like counting on the fact that the train will arrive on time or that the car won't jump the track. But, given that man is free and that there is no human nature for me to depend on, I can not count on men whom I do not know by relying on human goodness or man's concern for the good of society. I don't know what will become of the Russian revolution; I may make an example of it to the extent that at the present time it is apparent that the proletariat plays a part in Russia that it plays in no other nation. But I can't swear that this will inevitably lead to a triumph of the proletariat. I've got to limit myself to what I see.

Given that men are free and that tomorrow they will freely decide what man will be, I can not be sure that, after my death, fellow-fighters will carry on my work to bring it to its maximum perfection. Tomorrow, after my death, some men may decide to set up Fascism, and the others may be cowardly and muddled enough to let them do it. Fascism will then be the human reality, so much the worse for us.

Actually, things will be as man will have decided they are to be. Does that mean that I should abandon myself to quietism? No. First, I should involve myself; then, act on the old saw, "Nothing ventured, nothing gained." Nor does it mean that I shouldn't belong to a party, but rather that I shall have no illusions and shall do what I can. For example, suppose I ask myself, "Will socialization, as such, ever come about?" I know nothing about it. All I know is that I'm going to do everything in my power to bring it about. Beyond that, I can't count on anything. Quietism is the attitude of people who say, "Let others do what I can't do." The doctrine I am presenting is the very opposite of quietism, since it declares, "There is no reality except in action." Moreover, it goes further, since it adds, "Man is nothing else than his plan; he exists only to the extent that he fulfills himself; he is therefore nothing else than the ensemble of his acts, nothing else than his life."

According to this, we can understand why our doctrine horrifies certain people. Because often the only way they can bear their wretchedness is to think, "Circumstances have been against me. What I've been and done doesn't show my true worth. To be sure, I've had no great love, no great friendship, but that's because I haven't met a man or woman who was worthy. The books I've written haven't been very good because I haven't had the proper leisure. I haven't had children to devote myself to because I didn't find a man with whom I could have spent my life. So there remains within me, unused and quite viable, a host of propensities, inclinations, possibilities, that one wouldn't guess from the mere series of things I've done."

Now, for the existentialist there is really no love other than one which manifests itself in a person's being in love. There is no genius other than one which is expressed in works of art; the genius of Proust is the sum of Proust's works; the genius of Racine is his series of tragedies. Outside of that, there is nothing. Why say that Racine could have written another tragedy, when he didn't write it? A man is involved in life, leaves his impress on it, and outside of that there is nothing. To be sure, this may seem a harsh thought to someone whose life hasn't been a success. But, on the other hand, it prompts people to understand that reality alone is what counts, the dreams, expectations, and hopes warrant no more than to define a man as a disappointed dream, as miscarried hopes, as vain expectations. In other words, to define him negatively and not positively. However, when we say, "You are nothing else than your life," that does not imply that the artist will be judged solely on the basis of his works of art; a thousand other things will contribute toward summing him up. What we mean is that a man is nothing else than a series of undertakings, that he is the sum, the organization, the ensemble of the relationships which make up these undertakings.

OPTIONS FOR WRITING

1. Discuss how you view the meaning and purpose of your own life. What makes your life worth living? Describe some scenarios in which you would find your life meaningless. In which ways are your own views similar to and different from Sartre's existentialism? Write a reflective essay in which you address some of these issues.

2. Sartre believes that belief in God has no role in making human life meaningful. Critically analyze his argument for this view in a short, pointed essay.

Thomas Nagel
DEATH

Thomas Nagel (b. 1937) taught philosophy at Princeton University and is now a professor at New York University. He is the author of several books, including The Possibility of Altruism *and* The View

From Nowhere, *and of a collection of essays,* Mortal Questions, *from which this selection is taken. Here Nagel addresses the issue of death, whether death is a bad thing for the person who dies. Many of us fear death as the worst thing that might happen to us, yet this sentiment has been seriously challenged by philosophers in the past. The ancient Epicureans argued that death cannot be bad for the person who dies because nothing can be bad for someone unless it is unpleasant for that person, and nothing can be unpleasant for a person who does not exist. Besides, we do not fear the time before we were born, when we did not exist, so why should we fear the time after we die, when we also do not exist? Nagel nevertheless does believe that death is bad for the person who dies, and hence attempts to answer these arguments. Why does Nagel believe that death is a bad thing for the person who dies? How does Nagel argue that something (like death) may be bad for a person without being positively unpleasant for him or her? How does Lucretius argue that death is not a bad thing for the person who dies, and how does Nagel answer him?*

If death is the unequivocal and permanent end of our existence, the question arises whether it is a bad thing to die.

There is conspicuous disagreement about the matter: some people think death is dreadful; others have no objection to death *per se,* though they hope their own will be neither premature nor painful. Those in the former category tend to think those in the latter are blind to the obvious, while the latter suppose the former to be prey to some sort of confusion. On the one hand it can be said that life is all we have and the loss of it is the greatest loss we can sustain. On the other hand it may be objected that death deprives this supposed loss of its subject, and that if we realize that death is not an unimaginable condition of the persisting person, but a mere blank, we will see that it can have no value whatever, positive or negative.

Since I want to leave aside the question whether we are, or might be, immortal in some form, I shall simply use the word 'death' and its cognates in this discussion to mean *permanent* death, unsupplemented by any form of conscious survival. I want to ask whether death is in itself an evil; and how great an evil, and of what kind, it might be. The question should be of interest even to those who believe in some form of immortality, for one's attitude toward immortality must depend in part on one's attitude toward death.

If death is an evil at all, it cannot be because of its positive features, but only because of what it deprives us of. I shall try to deal with the difficulties surrounding the natural view that death is an evil because it brings to an end all the goods that life contains. We need not give an account of these goods here, except to observe that some of them, like perception, desire, activity, and thought, are so general as to be constitutive of human life. They are widely regarded as formidable benefits in themselves, despite the fact that they are conditions of misery as well as of happiness, and that a sufficient quantity of more particular evils can perhaps outweigh them. That is what is meant, I think, by the allegation that it is good simply to be alive, even if one is undergoing terrible experiences. The situation is roughly this: There are elements which, if added to one's experience, make life better; there are other elements which, if added to one's experience, make life worse. But what remains when these are set aside is not merely *neutral:* it is emphatically positive. Therefore life is worth living even when the bad elements of experience are plentiful, and the good ones too meager to outweigh the bad ones on their own. The additional positive weight is supplied by experience itself, rather than by any of its contents.

I shall not discuss the value that one person's life or death may have for others, or its objective value, but only the value it has for the person who is its subject. That seems to me the primary case, and the case which presents the greatest difficulties. Let me add only two observations. First, the value of life and its contents does not attach to mere organic survival: almost everyone would be indifferent (other things equal) between immediate death and immediate coma followed by death twenty years later without reawakening. And second, like most goods, this can be multiplied by time: more is better than less. The added quantities need not be temporally continuous (though continuity has its social advantages). People are attracted to the possibility of long-term suspended animation or freezing, followed by the resumption of conscious life, because they can regard it from within simply as a *continuation* of their present life. If techniques are ever perfected, what from outside appeared as a dormant interval of three hundred years could be experienced by the subject as nothing more than a sharp discontinuity in the character of his experiences. I do not deny, of course, that this has its own disadvantages. Family and friends may have died in the meantime; the language may have changed; the comforts of social, geographical, and cultural familiarity would be lacking. Nevertheless these inconveniences would not obliterate the basic advantage of continued, though discontinuous, existence.

If we turn from what is good about life to what is bad about death, the case is completely different. Essentially, though there may be problems about their specification, what we find desirable in life are certain states, conditions, or types of activity. It is *being* alive, *doing* certain things, having certain experiences, that we consider good. But if death is an evil, it is the *loss of life*, rather than the state of being dead, or nonexistent, or unconscious, that is objectionable.[1] This asymmetry is important. If it is good to be alive, that advantage can be attributed to

---

[1] It is sometimes suggested that what we really mind is the process of *dying*. But I should not really object to dying if it were not followed by death.

a person at each point of his life. It is a good of which Bach had more than Schubert, simply because he lived longer. Death, however, is not an evil of which Shakespeare has so far received a larger portion than Proust. If death is a disadvantage, it is not easy to say when a man suffers it.

There are two other indications that we do not object to death merely because it involves long periods of nonexistence. First, as has been mentioned, most of us would not regard the *temporary* suspension of life, even for substantial intervals, as in itself a misfortune. If it ever happens that people can be frozen without reduction of the conscious lifespan, it will be inappropriate to pity those who are temporarily out of circulation. Second, none of us existed before we were born (or conceived), but few regard that as a misfortune. I shall have more to say about this later.

The point that death is not regarded as an unfortunate *state* enables us to refute a curious but very common suggestion about the origin of the fear of death. It is often said that those who object to death have made the mistake of trying to imagine what it is like to *be* dead. It is alleged that the failure to realize that this task is logically impossible (for the banal reason that there is nothing to imagine) leads to the conviction that death is a mysterious and therefore terrifying prospective *state*. But this diagnosis is evidently false, for it is just as impossible to imagine being totally unconscious as to imagine being dead (though it is easy enough to imagine oneself, from the outside, in either of those conditions). Yet people who are averse to death are not usually averse to unconsciousness (so long as it does not entail a substantial cut in the total duration of waking life).

If we are to make sense of the view that to die is bad, it must be on the ground that life is a good and death is the corresponding deprivation or loss, bad not because of any positive features but because of the desirability of what it removes. We must now turn to the serious difficulties which this hypothesis raises, difficulties about loss and privation in general, and about death in particular.

Essentially, there are three types of problem. First, doubt may be raised whether *anything* can be bad for a man without being positively unpleasant to him: specifically, it may be doubted that there are any evils which consist merely in the deprivation or absence of possible goods, and which do not depend on someone's *minding* that deprivation. Second, there are special difficulties, in the case of death, about how the supposed misfortune is to be assigned to a subject at all. There is doubt both as to *who* its subject is, and as to *when* he undergoes it. So long as a person exists, he has not yet died, and once he has died, he no longer exists; so there seems to be no time when death, if it is a misfortune, can be ascribed to its unfortunate subject. The third type of difficulty concerns the asymmetry, mentioned above, between our attitudes to posthumous and prenatal nonexistence. How can the former be bad if the latter is not?

It should be recognized that if these are valid objections to counting death as an evil, they will apply to many other supposed evils as well. The first type of objection is expressed in general form by the common remark that what you don't know can't hurt you. It means that even if a man is betrayed by his friends, ridiculed behind his back, and despised by people who treat him politely to his face, none of it can be counted as a misfortune for him so long as he does not suffer as a result. It means that a man is not injured if his wishes are ignored by the executor of his will, or if, after his death, the belief becomes current that all the literary works on which his fame rests were really written by his brother, who died in Mexico at the age of 28. It seems to me worth asking what assumptions about good and evil lead to these drastic restrictions.

All the questions have something to do with time. There certainly are goods and evils of a simple kind (including some pleasures and pains) which a person possesses at a given time simply in virtue of his condition at that time. But this is not true of all the things we regard as good or bad for a man. Often we need to know his history to tell whether something is a misfortune or not; this applies to ills like deterioration, deprivation, and damage. Sometimes his experimental *state* is relatively unimportant—as in the case of a man who wastes his life in the cheerful pursuit of a method of communicating with asparagus plants. Someone who holds that all goods and evils must be temporally assignable states of the person may of course try to bring difficult cases into line by pointing to the pleasure or pain that more complicated goods and evils cause. Loss, betrayal, deception, and ridicule are on this view bad because people suffer when they learn of them. But it should be asked how our ideas of human value would have to be constituted to accommodate these cases directly instead. One advantage of such an account might be that it would enable us to explain *why* the discovery of these misfortunes caused suffering—in a way that makes it reasonable. For the natural view is that the discovery of betrayal makes us unhappy because it is bad to be betrayed—not that betrayal is bad because its discovery makes us unhappy.

It therefore seems to me worth exploring the position that most good and ill fortune has as its subject a person identified by his history and his possibilities, rather than merely by his categorical state of the moment—and that while this subject can be exactly located in a sequence of places and times, the same is not necessarily true of the goods and ills that befall him.[2]

These ideas can be illustrated by an example of deprivation whose severity approaches that of death. Suppose an intelligent person receives a brain injury that reduces him to the mental condition of a contented infant, and that such desires as remain to him can be satisfied by a

---

[2] It is certainly not true in general of the things that can be said of him. For example, Abraham Lincoln was taller than Louis XIV. But when?

custodian, so that he is free from care. Such a development would be widely regarded as a severe misfortune, not only for his friends and relations, or for society, but also, and primarily, for the person himself. This does not mean that a contented infant is unfortunate. The intelligent adult who has been *reduced* to this condition is the subject of the misfortune. He is the one we pity, though of course he does not mind his condition—there is some doubt, in fact, whether he can be said to exist any longer.

The view that such a man has suffered a misfortune is open to the same objections which have been raised in regard to death. He does not mind his conditions. It is in fact the same condition he was in at the age of three months, except that he is bigger. If we did not pity him then, why pity him now; in any case, who is there to pity? The intelligent adult has disappeared, and for a creature like the one before us, happiness consists in a full stomach and a dry diaper.

If these objections are invalid, it must be because they rest on a mistaken assumption about the temporal relation between the subject of a misfortune and the circumstances which constitute it. If, instead of concentrating exclusively on the oversized baby before us, we consider the person he was, and the person he *could* be now, then his reduction to this state and the cancellation of his natural adult development constitute a perfectly intelligible catastrophe.

This case should convince us that it is arbitrary to restrict the goods and evils that can befall a man to nonrelational properties ascribable to him at particular times. As it stands, that restriction excludes not only such cases of gross degeneration, but also a good deal of what is important about success and failure, and other features of a life that have the character of processes. I believe we can go further, however. There are goods and evils which are irreducibly relational; they are features of the relations between a person, with spatial and temporal boundaries of the usual sort, and circumstances which may not coincide with him either in space or in time. A man's life includes much that does not take place within the boundaries of his body and his mind, and what happens to him can include much that does not take place within the boundaries of his life. These boundaries are commonly crossed by the misfortunes of being deceived, or despised, or betrayed. (If this is correct, there is a simple account of what is wrong with breaking a deathbed promise. It is an injury to the dead man. For certain purposes it is possible to regard time as just another type of distance.) The case of mental degeneration shows us an evil that depends on a contrast between the reality and the possible alternatives. A man is the subject of good and evil as much because he has hopes which may or may not be fulfilled, or possibilities which may or may not be realized, as because of his capacity to suffer and enjoy. If death is an evil, it must be accounted for in these terms, and the impossibility of locating it within life should not trouble us.

When a man dies we are left with his corpse, and while a corpse can suffer the kind of mishap that may occur to an article of furniture, it is not a suitable object for pity. The man, however, is. He has lost his life, and if he had not died, he would have continued to live it, and to possess whatever good there is in living. If we apply to death the account suggested for the case of dementia, we shall say that although the spatial and temporal locations of the individual who suffered the loss are clear enough, the misfortune itself cannot be so easily located. One must be content just to state that his life is over and there will never be any more of it. That *fact*, rather than his past or present condition, constitutes his misfortune, if it is one. Nevertheless if there is a loss, someone must suffer it, and *he* must have existence and specific spatial and temporal location even if the loss itself does not. The fact that Beethoven had no children may have been a cause of regret to him, or a sad thing for the world, but it cannot be described as a misfortune for the children that he never had. All of us, I believe, are fortunate to have been born. But unless good and ill can be assigned to an embryo, or even to an unconnected pair of gametes, it cannot be said that not to be born is a misfortune. (That is a factor to be considered in deciding whether abortion and contraception are akin to murder.)

This approach also provides a solution to the problem of temporal asymmetry, pointed out by Lucretius. He observed that no one finds it disturbing to contemplate the eternity preceding his own birth, and he took this to show that it must be irrational to fear death, since death is simply the mirror image of the prior abyss. That is not true, however, and the difference between the two explains why it is reasonable to regard them differently. It is true that both the time before a man's birth and the time after his death are times when he does not exist. But the time after his death is time of which his death deprives him. It is time in which, had he not died then, he would be alive. Therefore any death entails the loss of *some* life that its victim would have led had he not died at that or any earlier point. We know perfectly well what it would be for him to have had it instead of losing it, and there is no difficulty in identifying the loser.

But we cannot say that the time prior to a man's birth is time in which he would have lived had he been born not then but earlier. For aside from the brief margin permitted by premature labor, he *could* not have been born earlier: anyone born substantially earlier than he was would have been someone else. Therefore the time prior to his birth is not time in which his subsequent birth prevents him from living. His birth, when it occurs, does not entail the loss to him of any life whatever.

The direction of time is crucial in assigning possibilities to people or other individuals. Distinct possible lives of a single person can diverge from a common beginning, but they cannot converge to a common conclusion from diverse beginnings. (The latter would represent not a set of different possible lives of one individual, but a set of distinct possible individuals, whose lives have identical conclusions.) Given an identifiable individual, countless possibilities for his continued existence are imaginable, and we can clearly conceive of what it would be for him to go on existing indefinitely. However inevitable it is that this will not come about; its possibility is still that of the continuation of a good for him, if life is the good we take it to be.[3]

We are left, therefore, with the question whether the nonrealization of this possibility is in every case a misfortune, or whether it depends on what can naturally be hoped for. This seems to me the most serious difficulty with the view that death is always an evil. Even if we can dispose of the objection against admitting misfortune that is not experienced, or cannot be assigned to a definite time in the person's life, we still have to set some limits on how possible a possibility must be for its nonrealization to be a misfortune (or good fortune, should the possibility be a bad one). The death of Keats at 24 is generally regarded as tragic; that of Tolstoy at 82 is not. Although they will both be dead for ever, Keats' death deprived him of many years of life which were allowed to Tolstoy; so in a clear sense Keats' loss was greater (though not in the sense standardly employed in mathematical comparison between infinite quantities). However, this does not prove that Tolstoy's loss was insignificant. Perhaps we record an objection only to evils which are gratuitously added to the inevitable; the fact that it is worse to die at 24 than at 82 does not imply that it is not a terrible thing to die at 82, or even at 806. The question is whether we can regard as a misfortune any limitation, like mortality, that is normal to the species. Blindness or near-blindness is not a misfortune for a mole, nor would it be for a man, if that were the natural condition of the human race.

The trouble is that life familiarizes us with the goods of which death deprives us. We are already able to appreciate them, as a mole is not

---

[3] I confess to being troubled by the above argument, on the ground that it is too sophisticated to explain the simple difference between our attitudes to prenatal and posthumous nonexistence. For this reason I suspect that something essential is omitted from the account of the badness of death by an analysis which treats it as a deprivation of possibilities. My suspicion is supported by the following suggestion of Robert Nozick. We could imagine discovering that people developed from individual spores that had existed indefinitely far in advance of their birth. In this fantasy, birth never occurs naturally more than a hundred years before the permanent end of the spore's existence. But then we discover a way to trigger the premature hatching of these spores, and people are born who have thousands of years of active life before them. Given such a situation, it would be possible to imagine *oneself* having come into existence thousands of years previously. If we put aside the question whether this would really be the same person, even given the identity of the spore, then the consequence appears to be that a person's birth at a given time *could* deprive him of many earlier years of possible life. Now while it would be cause for regret that one had been deprived of all those possible years of life by being born too late, the feeling would differ from that which many people have about death. I conclude that something about the future *prospect* of permanent nothingness is not captured by the analysis in terms of denied possibilities. If so, then Lucretius' argument still awaits an answer. I suspect that it requires a general treatment of the difference between past and future in our attitudes toward our own lives. Our attitudes toward past and future pain are very different, for example. Derek Parfit's unpublished writings on this topic have revealed its difficulty to me.

able to appreciate vision. If we put aside doubts about their status as goods and grant that their quantity is in part a function of their duration, the question remains whether death, no matter when it occurs, can be said to deprive its victim of what is in the relevant sense a possible continuation of life.

The situation is an ambiguous one. Observed from without, human beings obviously have a natural lifespan and cannot live much longer than a hundred years. A man's sense of his own experience, on the other hand, does not embody this idea of a natural limit. His existence defines for him an essentially open-ended possible future, containing the usual mixture of goods and evils that he has found so tolerable in the past. Having been gratuitously introduced to the world by a collection of natural, historical, and social accidents, he finds himself the subject of a *life*, with an undeterminate and not essentially limited future. Viewed in this way, death, no matter how inevitable, is an abrupt cancellation of indefinitely extensive possible goods. Normality seems to have nothing to do with it, for the fact that we will all inevitably die in a few score years cannot by itself imply that it would not be good to live longer. Suppose that we were all inevitably going to die in *agony*—physical agony lasting six months. Would inevitability make *that* prospect any less unpleasant? And why should it be different for a deprivation? If the normal lifespan were a thousand years, death at 80 would be a tragedy. As things are, it may just be a more widespread tragedy. If there is no limit to the amount of life that it would be good to have, then it may be that a bad end is in store for us all.

OPTIONS FOR WRITING

1. Reflect on your own intuitions about fear of death. Is your fear of death really fear of nonexistence, apprehension about the unknown, or something else? Explain your ideas in a short reflective essay.

2. Is Nagel right when he argues that what you will never know may in fact hurt you? Analyze his arguments, and argue for or against his view.

3. Do you think that someone's dying at age 24 is worse than her dying at age 82? Compare your view to Nagel's position on this issue.

Peter Singer
FAMINE, AFFLUENCE, AND MORALITY

Peter Singer (b. 1946) is a professor of philosophy at Monash University in Australia. He is well known for his book Animal Liberation, *which has been very influential in the development of the animal rights movement. In this reading, Singer asks whether we have an obligation to provide for the starving. Many people believe that al-*

though it is a good thing to provide charity for the poor and starving, we do not have to do it—it is not a moral obligation. Singer argues that this view is mistaken. But if it is mistaken, we must radically alter our lifestyles, forgoing many of the luxuries that we have become used to, in order to provide charity. Outline the main points of Singer's argument. State the Sidgwick-Urmson objection to Singer's view and Singer's reply to it. How does Singer respond to the argument that we should allow the Bengal refugees to die because the population in the area will increase and cause more people to die of starvation in the future?

As I write this, in November 1971, people are dying in East Bengal from lack of food, shelter, and medical care. The suffering and death that are occurring there now are not inevitable, not unavoidable in any fatalistic sense of the term. Constant poverty, a cyclone, and a civil war have turned at least nine million people into destitute refugees; nevertheless, it is not beyond the capacity of the richer nations to give enough assistance to reduce any further suffering to very small proportions. The decisions and actions of human beings can prevent this kind of suffering. Unfortunately, human beings have not made the necessary decisions. At the individual level, people have, with very few exceptions, not responded to the situation in any significant way. Generally speaking, people have not given large sums to relief funds; they have not written to their parliamentary representatives demanding increased government assistance; they have not demonstrated in the streets, held symbolic fasts, or done anything else directed toward providing the refugees with the means to satisfy their essential needs. At the government level, no government has given the sort of massive aid that would enable the refugees to survive for more than a few days. Britain, for instance, has given rather more than most countries. It has, to date, given £14,750,000. For comparative purposes, Britain's share of the non-recoverable development costs of the Anglo-French Concorde project is already in excess of £275,000,000, and on present estimates will reach £440,000,000. The implication is that the British government values a supersonic transport more than thirty times as highly as it values the lives of the nine million refugees. Australia is another country which, on a per capita basis, is well up in the "aid to Bengal" table. Australia's aid, however, amounts to less than one-twelfth of the cost of Sydney's new opera house. The total amount given, from all sources, now stands at about £65,000,000. The estimated cost of keeping the refugees alive for one year is £464,000,000. Most of the refugees have now been in the camps for more than six months. The World Bank has said that India needs a minimum of £300,000,000 in assistance from other countries before the end of the year. It seems obvious that assistance on this scale will not be forthcoming. India will be forced to choose between letting the refugees starve or diverting funds from her own development program, which will mean that more of her own people will starve in the future.[1]

These are the essential facts about the present situation in Bengal. So far as it concerns us here, there is nothing unique about this situation except its magnitude. The Bengal emergency is just the latest and most acute of a series of major emergencies in various parts of the world, arising both from natural and from man-made causes. There are also many parts of the world in which people die from malnutrition and lack of food independent of any special emergency. I take Bengal as my example only because it is the present concern, and because the size of the problem has ensured that it has been given adequate publicity. Neither individuals nor governments can claim to be unaware of what is happening there.

What are the moral implications of a situation like this? In what follows, I shall argue that the way people in relatively affluent countries react to a situation like that in Bengal cannot be justified; indeed, the whole way we look at moral issues — our moral conceptual scheme — needs to be altered, and with it, the way of life that has come to be taken for granted in our society.

In arguing for this conclusion I will not, of course, claim to be morally neutral. I shall, however, try to argue for the moral position that I take, so that anyone who accepts certain assumptions, to be made explicit, will, I hope, accept my conclusion.

I begin with the assumption that suffering and death from lack of food, shelter, and medical care are bad. I think most people will agree about this, although one may reach the same view by different routes. I shall not argue for this view. People can hold all sorts of eccentric positions, and perhaps from some of them it would not follow that death by starvation is in itself bad. It is difficult, perhaps impossible, to refute such positions, and so for brevity I will henceforth take this assumption as accepted. Those who disagree need read no further.

My next point is this: if it is in our power to prevent something bad from happening, without thereby sacrificing anything of comparable moral importance, we ought, morally, to do it. By "without sacrificing anything of comparable moral importance" I mean without causing anything else comparably bad to happen, or doing something that is wrong in itself, or failing to promote some moral good, comparable in significance to the bad thing that we can prevent. This principle seems almost as uncontroversial as the last one. It requires us only to prevent what is bad, and not to promote what is good, and it requires this of us only when we can do it without sacrificing anything that is, from the moral

---

[1] There was also a third possibility: that India would go to war to enable the refugees to return to their lands. Since I wrote this paper, India has taken this way out. The situation is no longer that described above, but this does not affect my argument, as the next paragraph indicates.

point of view, comparably important. I could even, as far as the application of my argument to the Bengal emergency is concerned, qualify the point so as to make it: if it is in our power to prevent something very bad from happening, without thereby sacrificing anything morally significant, we ought, morally, to do it. An application of this principle would be as follows: if I am walking past a shallow pond and see a child drowning in it, I ought to wade in and pull the child out. This will mean getting my clothes muddy, but this is insignificant, while the death of the child would presumably be a very bad thing.

The uncontroversial appearance of the principle just stated is deceptive. If it were acted upon, even in its qualified form, our lives, our society, and our world would be fundamentally changed. For the principle takes, firstly, no account of proximity or distance. It makes no moral difference whether the person I can help is a neighbor's child ten yards from me or a Bengali whose name I shall never know, ten thousand miles away. Secondly, the principle makes no distinction between cases in which I am the only person who could possibly do anything and cases in which I am just one among millions in the same position.

I do not think I need to say much in defense of the refusal to take proximity and distance into account. The fact that a person is physically near to us, so that we have personal contact with him, may make it more likely that we *shall* assist him, but this does not show that we *ought* to help him rather than another who happens to be further away. If we accept any principle of impartiality, universalizability, equality, or whatever, we cannot discriminate against someone merely because he is far away from us (or we are far away from him). Admittedly, it is possible that we are in a better position to judge what needs to be done to help a person near to us than one far away, and perhaps also to provide the assistance we judge to be necessary. If this were the case, it would be a reason for helping those near to us first. This may once have been a justification for being more concerned with the poor in one's own town than with famine victims in India. Unfortunately for those who like to keep their moral responsibilities limited, instant communication and swift transportation have changed the situation. From the moral point of view, the development of the world into a "global village" has made an important, though still unrecognized, difference to our moral situation. Expert observers and supervisors, sent out by famine relief organizations or permanently stationed in famine-prone areas, can direct our aid to a refugee in Bengal almost as effectively as we could get it to someone in our own block. There would seem, therefore, to be no possible justification for discriminating on geographical grounds.

There may be a greater need to defend the second implication of my principle—that the fact that there are millions of other people in the same position, in respect to the Bengali refugees, as I am, does not make the situation significantly different from a situation in which I am the only person who can prevent something very bad from occurring.

Again, of course, I admit that there is a psychological difference between the cases; one feels less guilty about doing nothing if one can point to others, similarly placed, who have also done nothing. Yet this can make no real difference to our moral obligations.[2] Should I consider that I am less obliged to pull the drowning child out of the pond if on looking around I see other people, no further away than I am, who have also noticed the child but are doing nothing? One has only to ask this question to see the absurdity of the view that numbers lessen obligation. It is a view that is an ideal excuse for inactivity; unfortunately most of the major evils — poverty, overpopulation, pollution — are problems in which everyone is almost equally involved.

The view that numbers do make a difference can be made plausible if stated in this way: if everyone in circumstances like mine gave £5 to the Bengal Relief Fund, there would be enough to provide food, shelter, and medical care for the refugees; there is no reason why I should give more than anyone else in the same circumstances as I am; therefore I have no obligation to give more than £5. Each premise in this argument is true, and the argument looks sound. It may convince us, unless we notice that it is based on a hypothetical premise, although the conclusion is not stated hypothetically. The argument would be sound if the conclusion were: if everyone in circumstances like mine were to give £5, I would have no obligation to give more than £5. If the conclusion were so stated, however, it would be obvious that the argument has no bearing on a situation in which it is not the case that everyone else gives £5. This, of course, is the actual situation. It is more or less certain that not everyone in circumstances like mine will give £5. So there will not be enough to provide the needed food, shelter, and medical care. Therefore by giving more than £5 I will prevent more suffering than I would if I gave just £5.

It might be thought that this argument has an absurd consequence. Since the situation appears to be that very few people are likely to give substantial amounts, it follows that I and everyone else in similar circumstances ought to give as much as possible, that is, at least up to the point at which by giving more one would begin to cause serious suffering for oneself and one's dependents — perhaps even beyond this point to the point of marginal utility, at which by giving more one would cause oneself and one's dependents as much suffering as one would prevent in Bengal. If everyone does this, however, there will be more

[2] In view of the special sense philosophers often give to the term, I shall say that I use "obligation" simply as the abstract noun derived from "ought," so that "I have an obligation to" means no more, and no less, than "I ought to." The usage is in accordance with the definition of "ought" given by the *Shorter Oxford English Dictionary*: "the general verb to express duty or obligation." I do not think any issue of substance hangs on the way the term is used; sentences in which I use "obligation" could all be rewritten, although somewhat clumsily, as sentences in which a clause containing "ought" replaces the term "obligation."

than can be used for the benefit of the refugees, and some of the sacrifice will have been unnecessary. Thus, if everyone does what he ought to do, the result will not be as good as it would be if everyone did a little less than he ought to do, or if only some do all that they ought to do.

The paradox here arises only if we assume that the actions in question—sending money to the relief funds—are performed more or less simultaneously, and are also unexpected. For if it is to be expected that everyone is going to contribute something, then clearly each is not obliged to give as much as he would have been obliged to had others not been giving too. And if everyone is not acting more or less simultaneously, then those giving later will know how much more is needed, and will have no obligation to give more than is necessary to reach this amount. To say this is not to deny the principle that people in the same circumstances have the same obligations, but to point out that the fact that others have given, or may be expected to give, is a relevant circumstance: those giving after it has become known that many others are giving and those giving before are not in the same circumstances. So the seemingly absurd consequence of the principle I have put forward can occur only if people are in error about the actual circumstances—that is, if they think they are giving when others are not, but in fact they are giving when others are. The result of everyone doing what he really ought to do cannot be worse than the result of everyone doing less than he ought to do, although the result of everyone doing what he reasonably believes he ought to do could be.

If my argument so far has been sound, neither our distance from a preventable evil nor the number of people who, in respect to that evil, are in the same situation as we are, lessens our obligation to mitigate or prevent that evil. I shall therefore take as established the principle I asserted earlier. As I have already said, I need to assert it only in its qualified form: if it is in our power to prevent something very bad from happening, without thereby sacrificing anything else morally significant, we ought, morally, to do it.

The outcome of this argument is that our traditional moral categories are upset. The traditional distinction between duty and charity cannot be drawn, or at least, not in the place we normally draw it. Giving money to the Bengal Relief Fund is regarded as an act of charity in our society. The bodies which collect money are known as "charities." These organizations see themselves in this way—if you send them a check, you will be thanked for your "generosity." Because giving money is regarded as an act of charity, it is not thought that there is anything wrong with not giving. The charitable man may be praised, but the man who is not charitable is not condemned. People do not feel in any way ashamed or guilty about spending money on new clothes or a new car instead of giving it to famine relief. (Indeed, the alternative does not occur to them.) This way of looking at the matter cannot be justified.

When we buy new clothes not to keep ourselves warm but to look "well-dressed" we are not providing for any important need. We would not be sacrificing anything significant if we were to continue to wear our old clothes, and give the money to famine relief. By doing so, we would be preventing another person from starving. It follows from what I have said earlier that we ought to give money away, rather than spend it on clothes which we do not need to keep us warm. To do so is not charitable, or generous. Nor is it the kind of act which philosophers and theologians have called "supererogatory"—an act which it would be good to do, but not wrong not to do. On the contrary, we ought to give the money away, and it is wrong not to do so.

I am not maintaining that there are no acts which are charitable, or that there are no acts which it would be good to do but not wrong not to do. It may be possible to redraw the distinction between duty and charity in some other place. All I am arguing here is that the present way of drawing the distinction, which makes it an act of charity for a man living at the level of affluence which most people in the "developed nations" enjoy to give money to save someone else from starvation, cannot be supported. It is beyond the scope of my argument to consider whether the distinction should be redrawn or abolished altogether. There would be many other possible ways of drawing the distinction— for instance, one might decide that it is good to make other people as happy as possible but not wrong not to do so.

Despite the limited nature of the revision in our moral conceptual scheme which I am proposing, the revision would, given the extent of both affluence and famine in the world today, have radical implications. These implications may lead to further objections, distinct from those I have already considered. I shall discuss two of these.

One objection to the position I have taken might be simply that it is too drastic a revision of our moral scheme. People do not ordinarily judge in the way I have suggested they should. Most people reserve their moral condemnation for those who violate some moral norm, such as the norm against taking another person's property. They do not condemn those who indulge in luxury instead of giving to famine relief. But given that I did not set out to prevent a morally neutral description of the way people make moral judgments, the way people do in fact judge has nothing to do with the validity of my conclusion. My conclusion follows from the principle which I advanced earlier, and unless that principle is rejected, or the arguments shown to be unsound, I think the conclusion must stand, however strange it appears.

It might, nevertheless, be interesting to consider why our society, and most other societies, do judge differently from the way I have suggested they should. In a well-known article, J. O. Urmson suggests that the imperatives of duty, which tell us what we must do, as distinct from what it would be good to do but not wrong not to do, function so as to prohibit behavior that is intolerable if men are to live together in society.[3] This may explain the origin and continued existence of the present division between acts of duty and acts of charity. Moral attitudes are shaped by the needs of society, and no doubt society needs people who will observe the rules that make social existence tolerable. From the point of view of a particular society, it is essential to prevent violations of norms against killing, stealing, and so on. It is quite inessential, however, to help people outside one's own society.

If this is an explanation of our common distinction between duty and supererogation, however, it is not a justification of it. The moral point of view requires us to look beyond the interests of our own society. Previously, as I have already mentioned, this may hardly have been feasible, but it is quite feasible now. From the moral point of view, the prevention of the starvation of millions of people outside our society must be considered at least as pressing as the upholding of property norms within our society.

It has been argued by some writers, among them Sidgwick and Urmson, that we need to have a basic moral code which is not too far beyond the capacities of the ordinary man, for otherwise there will be a general breakdown of compliance with the moral code. Crudely stated, this argument suggests that if we tell people that they ought to refrain from murder and give everything they do not really need to famine relief, they will do neither, whereas if we tell them that they ought to refrain from murder and that it is good to give to famine relief but not wrong not to do so, they will at least refrain from murder. The issue here is: Where should we draw the line between conduct that is required and conduct that is good although not required, so as to get the best possible result? This would seem to be an empirical question, although a very difficult one. One objection to the Sidgwick-Urmson line of argument is that it takes insufficient account of the effect that moral standards can have on the decisions we make. Given a society in which a wealthy man who gives five percent of his income to famine-relief is regarded as most generous, it is not surprising that a proposal that we all ought to give away half our incomes will be thought to be absurdly unrealistic. In a society which held that no man should have more than enough while others have less than they need, such a proposal might seem narrowminded. What it is possible for a man to do and what he is likely to do are both, I think, very greatly influenced by what people around him are doing and expecting him to do. In any case, the possibility that by spreading the idea that we ought to be doing very much more than we are to relieve famine we shall bring about a general breakdown of moral behavior seems remote. If the stakes are an end to wide-

---

[3] J. O. Urmson, "Saints and Heroes," in *Essays in Moral Philosophy*, ed. Abraham I. Melden (Seattle and London, 1958), p. 214. For a related but significantly different view see also Henry Sidgwick, *The Methods of Ethics*, 7th edn. (London, 1907), pp. 220–221, 492–493.

spread starvation, it is worth the risk. Finally, it should be emphasized that these considerations are relevant only to the issue of what we should require from others, and not to what we ourselves ought to do.

The second objection to my attack on the present distinction between duty and charity is one which has from time to time been made against utilitarianism. It follows from some forms of utilitarian theory that we all ought, morally, to be working full time to increase the balance of happiness over misery. The position I have taken here would not lead to this conclusion in all circumstances, for if there were no bad occurrences that we could prevent without sacrificing something of comparable moral importance, my argument would have no application. Given the present conditions in many parts of the world, however, it does follow from my argument that we ought, morally, to be working full time to relieve great suffering of the sort that occurs as a result of famine or other disasters. Of course, mitigating circumstances can be adduced — for instance, that if we wear ourselves out through overwork, we shall be less effective than we would otherwise have been. Nevertheless, when all considerations of this sort have been taken into account, the conclusion remains: we ought to be preventing as much suffering as we can without sacrificing something else of comparable moral importance. This conclusion is one which we may be reluctant to face. I cannot see, though, why it should be regarded as a criticism of the position for which I have argued, rather than a criticism of our ordinary standards of behavior. Since most people are self-interested to some degree, very few of us are likely to do everything that we ought to do. It would, however, hardly be honest to take this as evidence that it is not the case that we ought to do it.

It may still be thought that my conclusions are so wildly out of line with what everyone else thinks and has always thought that there must be something wrong with the argument somewhere. In order to show that my conclusions, while certainly contrary to contemporary Western moral standards, would not have seemed so extraordinary at other times and in other places, I would like to quote a passage from a writer not normally thought of as a way-out radical, Thomas Aquinas.

> Now, according to the natural order instituted by divine providence, material goods are provided for the satisfaction of human needs. Therefore the division and appropriation of property, which proceeds from human law, must not hinder the satisfaction of man's necessity from such goods. Equally, whatever a man has in superabundance is owed, of natural right, to the poor for their sustenance. So Ambrosius says, and it is also to be found in the *Decretum Gratiani*: "The bread which you withhold belongs to the hungry; the clothing you shut away, to the naked; and the money you bury in the earth is the redemption and freedom of the penniless."[4]

---

[4] *Summa Theologica*, II-II, Question 66, Article 7, in *Aquinas, Selected Political Writings*, ed. A. P. d'Entreves, trans. J. G. Dawson (Oxford, 1948), p. 171.

I now want to consider a number of points, more practical than philosophical, which are relevant to the application of the moral conclusion we have reached. These points challenge not the idea that we ought to be doing all we can to prevent starvation, but the idea that giving away a great deal of money is the best means to this end.

It is sometimes said that overseas aid should be a government responsibility, and that therefore one ought not to give to privately run charities. Giving privately, it is said, allows the government and the noncontributing members of society to escape their responsibilities.

This argument seems to assume that the more people there are who give to privately organized famine relief funds, the less likely it is that the government will take over full responsibility for such aid. This assumption is unsupported, and does not strike me as at all plausible. The opposite view—that if no one gives voluntarily, a government will assume that its citizens are uninterested in famine relief and would not wish to be forced into giving aid—seems more plausible. In any case, unless there were a definite probability that by refusing to give one would be helping to bring about massive government assistance, people who do refuse to make voluntary contributions are refusing to prevent a certain amount of suffering without being able to point to any tangible beneficial consequences of their refusal. So the onus of showing how their refusal will bring about government action is on those who refuse to give.

I do not, of course, want to dispute the contention that governments of affluent nations should be giving many times the amount of genuine, no-strings-attached aid that they are giving now. I agree, too, that giving privately is not enough, and that we ought to be campaigning actively for entirely new standards for both public and private contributions to famine relief. Indeed, I would sympathize with someone who thought that campaigning was more important than giving oneself, although I doubt whether preaching what one does not practice would be very effective. Unfortunately, for many people the idea that "it's the government's responsibility" is a reason for not giving which does not appear to entail any political action either.

Another, more serious reason for not giving to famine relief funds is that until there is effective population control, relieving famine merely postpones starvation. If we save the Bengal refugees now, others, perhaps the children of these refugees, will face starvation in a few years' time. In support of this, one may cite the now well-known facts about the population explosion and the relatively limited scope for expanded production.

This point, like the previous one, is an argument against relieving suffering that is happening now, because of a belief about what might happen in the future; it is unlike the previous point in that very good evidence can be adduced in support of this belief about the future. I will not go into the evidence here. I accept that the earth cannot support indefinitely a population rising at the present rate. This certainly poses a problem for anyone who thinks it important to prevent famine. Again, however, one could accept the argument without drawing the conclusion that it absolves one from any obligation to do anything to prevent famine. The conclusion that should be drawn is that the best means of preventing famine, in the long run, is population control. It would then follow from the position reached earlier that one ought to be doing all one can to promote population control (unless one held that all forms of population control were wrong in themselves, or would have significantly bad consequences). Since there are organizations working specifically for population control, one would then support them rather than more orthodox methods of preventing famine.

A third point raised by the conclusion reached earlier relates to the question of just how much we all ought to be giving away. One possibility, which has already been mentioned, is that we ought to give until we reach the level of marginal utility—that is, the level at which, by giving more, I would cause as much suffering to myself or my dependents as I would relieve by my gift. This would mean, of course, that one would reduce oneself to very near the material circumstances of a Bengali refugee. It will be recalled that earlier I put forward both a strong and a moderate version of the principle of preventing bad occurrences. The strong version, which required us to prevent bad things from happening unless in doing so we would be sacrificing something of comparable moral significance, does seem to require reducing ourselves to the level of marginal utility. I should also say that the strong version seems to me to be the correct one. I proposed the more moderate version—that we should prevent bad occurrences unless, to do so, we had to sacrifice something morally significant—only in order to show that even on this surely undeniable principle a great change in our way of life is required. On the more moderate principle, it may not follow that we ought to reduce ourselves to the level of marginal utility, for one might hold that to reduce oneself and one's family to this level is to cause something significantly bad to happen. Whether this is so I shall not discuss, since, as I have said, I can see no good reason for holding the moderate version of the principle rather than the strong version. Even if we accepted the principle only in its moderate form, however, it should be clear that we would have to give away enough to ensure that the consumer society, dependent as it is on people spending on trivia rather than giving to famine relief, would slow down and perhaps disappear entirely. There are several reasons why this would be desirable in itself. The value and necessity of economic growth are now being questioned not only by conservationists, but by economists as well.[5]

---

[5] See, for instance, John Kenneth Galbraith, *The New Industrial State* (Boston, 1967); and E. J. Mishan, *The Costs of Economic Growth* (London, 1967).

There is no doubt, too, that the consumer society has a distorting effect on the goals and purposes of its members. Yet looking at the matter purely from the point of view of overseas aid, there must be a limit to the extent to which we should deliberately slow down our economy; for it might be the case that if we gave away, say, forty percent of our Gross National Product, we would slow down the economy so much that in absolute terms we would be giving less than if we gave twenty-five percent of the much larger GNP that we would have if we limited our contribution to this smaller percentage.

I mention this only as an indication of the sort of a factor that one would have to take into account in working out an ideal. Since Western societies generally consider one percent of the GNP an acceptable level for overseas aid, the matter is entirely academic. Nor does it affect the question of how much an individual should give in a society in which very few are giving substantial amounts.

It is sometimes said, though less often now than it used to be, that philosophers have no special role to play in public affairs, since most public issues depend primarily on an assessment of facts. On questions of fact, it is said, philosophers as such have no special expertise, and so it has been possible to engage in philosophy without committing oneself to any position on major public issues. No doubt there are some issues of social policy and foreign policy about which it can truly be said that a really expert assessment of the facts is required before taking sides or acting, but the issue of famine is surely not one of these. The facts about the existence of suffering are beyond dispute. Nor, I think, is it disputed that we can do something about it, either through orthodox methods of famine relief or through population control or both. This is therefore an issue on which philosophers are competent to take a position. The issue is one which faces everyone who has more money than he needs to support himself and his dependents, or who is in a position to take some sort of political action. These categories must include practically every teacher and student of philosophy in the universities of the Western world. If philosophy is to deal with matters that are relevant to both teachers and students, this is an issue that philosophers should discuss.

Discussion, though, is not enough. What is the point of relating philosophy to public (and personal) affairs if we do not take our conclusions seriously? In this instance, taking our conclusion seriously means acting upon it. The philosopher will not find it any easier than anyone else to alter his attitudes and way of life to the extent that, if I am right, is involved in doing everything that we ought to be doing. At the very least, though, one can make a start. The philosopher who does so will have to sacrifice some of the benefits of the consumer society, but he can find compensation in the satisfaction of a way of life in which theory and practice, if not yet in harmony, are at least coming together.

OPTIONS FOR WRITING

1. Much of the Third World is very poor, and its people would greatly benefit from our financial aid. Suppose that these people would be greatly helped, but not even brought up to our standard of living, if we donated to them all of the money we now spend on arts and culture, beautiful homes, cars, appliances, fine food and drink in restaurants, and vacation travel to far-flung destinations. By the type of argument that Singer advances, would we be obligated to donate this money to the Third World? If so, is this result acceptable to you? Explain your answer in a brief essay.

2. Singer is a utilitarian, and the argument in this essay draws from utilitarian principles. Utilitarians believe that, in principle, we are wrong when we are partial to our own situation over that of strangers. But consider the following case: Suppose that a flood has occurred and you are in a rescue boat. There are two groups of people on housetops—group A with five people, and group B with seven—but because the flood waters are rising, you can save only one group. Suppose that group A contains your three children and that all of the members of group B are total strangers to you. Is it wrong, as the utilitarian would seem to think, to save group A rather than B? You are in the boat with Singer: Reconstruct the dialogue with Singer about which group to save.

Daniel C. Dennett
WHERE AM I?

Daniel Dennett (b. 1942) is a professor of philosophy at Tufts University in Medford, Massachusetts. The primary focus of his writing is the nature of the human mind, and he is one of the primary advocates of materialism, *or* physicalism. *According to physicalism, we humans do not have immaterial souls or nonphysical mental states but are best understood by the natural sciences, such as physics and biology. Dennett has recently argued that knowing evolutionary biology is crucial to understanding human mental life. The main topic of this essay is the issue of personal identity. To what is my identity as a person connected? Is it my immaterial soul? My body as a whole? A certain specific part of my body, the brain? Or is it something more abstract, like states of a mind connected by memories? In this essay, the two positions Dennett considers most closely are the view that identity is connected to the brain and the view that it is connected to the body. Does reading this essay lead you to puzzle about what kind of a thing you are? Does Dennett's essay implicitly contain an argument for some particular view on this issue?*

Now that I've won my suit under the Freedom of Information Act, I am at liberty to reveal for the first time a curious episode in my life that may be of interest not only to those engaged in research in the philosophy of mind, artificial intelligence, and neuroscience but also to the general public.

Several years ago I was approached by Pentagon officials who asked me to volunteer for a highly dangerous and secret mission. In collaboration with NASA and Howard Hughes, the Department of Defense was spending billions to develop a Supersonic Tunneling Underground Device, or STUD. It was supposed to tunnel through the earth's core at great speed and deliver a specially designed atomic warhead "right up the Red's missile silos," as one of the Pentagon brass put it.

The problem was that in an early test they had succeeded in lodging a warhead about a mile deep under Tulsa, Oklahoma, and they wanted me to retrieve it for them. "Why me?" I asked. Well, the mission involved some pioneering applications of current brain research, and they had heard of my interest in brains and of course my Faustian curiosity and great courage and so forth. . . . Well, how could I refuse? The difficulty that brought the Pentagon to my door was that the device I'd been asked to recover was fiercely radioactive, in a new way. According to monitoring instruments, something about the nature of the device and its complex interactions with pockets of material deep in the earth had produced radiation that could cause severe abnormalities in certain tissues of the brain. No way had been found to shield the brain from these deadly rays, which were apparently harmless to other tissues and organs of the body. So it had been decided that the person sent to recover the device should *leave his brain behind*. It would be kept in a safe place where it could execute its normal control functions by elaborate radio links. Would I submit to a surgical procedure that would completely remove my brain, which would then be placed in a life-support system at the Manned Spacecraft Center in Houston? Each input and output pathway, as it was severed, would be restored by a pair of microminiaturized radio transceivers, one attached precisely to the brain, the other to the nerve stumps in the empty cranium. No information would be lost, all the connectivity would be preserved. At first I was a bit reluctant. Would it really work? The Houston brain surgeons encouraged me. "Think of it," they said, "as a mere *stretching* of the nerves. If your brain were just moved over an *inch* in your skull, that would not alter or impair your mind. We're simply going to make the nerves indefinitely elastic by splicing radio links into them."

I was shown around the life-support lab in Houston and saw the sparkling new vat in which my brain would be placed, were I to agree. I met the large and brilliant support team of neurologists, hematologists, biophysicists, and electrical engineers, and after several days of discussions and demonstrations, I agreed to give it a try. I was subjected to an enormous array of blood tests, brain scans, experiments, interviews, and the like. They took down my autobiography at great length, recorded tedious lists of my beliefs, hopes, fears, and tastes. They even listed my favorite stereo recordings and gave me a crash session of psychoanalysis.

The day for surgery arrived at last and of course I was anesthetized and remember nothing of the operation itself. When I came out of anesthesia, I opened my eyes, looked around, and asked the inevitable, the traditional, the lamentably hackneyed postoperative question: "Where am I?" The nurse smiled down at me. "You're in Houston," she said, and I reflected that this still had a good chance of being the truth one way or another. She handed me a mirror. Sure enough, there were the tiny antennae poling up through their titanium ports cemented into my skull.

"I gather the operation was a success," I said. "I want to go see my brain." They led me (I was a bit dizzy and unsteady) down a long corridor and into the life-support lab. A cheer went up from the assembled support team, and I responded with what I hoped was a jaunty salute. Still feeling lightheaded, I was helped over to the life-support vat. I peered through the glass. There, floating in what looked like ginger ale, was undeniably a human brain, though it was almost covered with printed circuit chips, plastic tubules, electrodes, and other paraphernalia. "Is that mine?" I asked. "Hit the output transmitter switch there on the side of the vat and see for yourself," the project director replied. I moved the switch to OFF, and immediately slumped, groggy and nauseated, into the arms of the technicians, one of whom kindly restored the switch to its ON position. While I recovered my equilibrium and composure, I thought to myself: "Well, here I am sitting on a folding chair, staring through a piece of plate glass at my own brain. . . . But wait," I said to myself, "shouldn't I have thought, 'Here I am, suspended in a bubbling fluid, being stared at by my own eyes'?" I tried to think this latter thought. I tried to project it into the tank, offering it hopefully to my brain, but I failed to carry off the exercise with any conviction. I tried again. "Here am *I*, Daniel Dennett, suspended in a bubbling fluid, being stared at by my own eyes," No, it just didn't work. Most puzzling and confusing. Being a philosopher of firm physicalist conviction, I believed unswervingly that the tokening of my thoughts was occurring somewhere in my brain: yet, when I thought "Here I am," where the thought occurred to me was *here*, outside the vat, where I, Dennett, was standing staring at my brain.

I tried and tried to think myself into the vat, but to no avail. I tried to build up to the task by doing mental exercises. I thought to myself, "The sun is shining *over there*," five times in rapid succession, each time mentally ostending a different place: in order, the sunlit corner of the lab, the visible front lawn of the hospital, Houston, Mars, and Jupiter. I found I had little difficulty in getting my "there"'s to hop all over the celestial map with their proper references. I could loft a "there" in an instant through the farthest reaches of space, and then aim the next "there" with pinpoint accuracy at the upper left quadrant of a freckle on my arm. Why was I having such trouble with "here"? "Here in Houston" worked well enough, and so did "here in the lab," and even "here in this part of the lab," but "here in the vat" always seemed merely an unmeant mental mouthing. I tried closing my eyes while thinking it. This seemed to help, but still I couldn't manage to pull it off, except perhaps for a fleeting instant. I couldn't be sure. The discovery that I couldn't be sure was also unsettling. How did I know *where* I meant by "here" when I thought "here"? Could I *think* I meant one place when in fact I meant another? I didn't see how that could be admitted without untying the few bonds of intimacy between a person and his own mental life that had survived the onslaught of the brain scientists and philosophers, the physicalists and behaviorists. Perhaps I was incorrigible about where I *meant* when I said "here." But in my present circumstances it seemed that either I was doomed by sheer force of mental habit to thinking systematically false indexical thoughts, or where a person is (and hence where his thoughts are tokened for purposes of semantic analysis) is not necessarily where his brain, the physical seat of his soul, resides. Nagged by confusion, I attempted to orient myself by falling back on a favorite philosopher's ploy. I began naming things.

"Yorick," I said aloud to my brain, "you are my brain. The rest of my body, seated in this chair, I dub 'Hamlet.'" So here we all are: Yorick's my brain, Hamlet's my body, and I am Dennett. *Now,* where am I? And when I think "where am I?" where's that thought tokened? Is it tokened in my brain, lounging about in the vat, or right here between my ears where it *seems* to be tokened? Or nowhere? Its *temporal* coordinates give me no trouble; must it not have spatial coordinates as well? I began making a list of the alternatives.

1. *Where Hamlet goes, there goes Dennett.* The principle was easily refuted by appeal to the familiar brain-transplant thought experiments so enjoyed by philosophers. If Tom and Dick switch brains, Tom is the fellow with Dick's former body—just ask him; he'll claim to be Tom, and tell you the most intimate details of Tom's autobiography. It was clear enough, then, that my current body and I could part company, but not likely that I could be separated from my brain. The rule of thumb that emerged so plainly from the thought experiments was that in a brain-transplant operation, one wanted to be the *donor,* not the recipient. Better to call such an operation a *body* transplant, in fact. So perhaps the truth was,

2. *Where Yorick goes, there goes Dennett.* This was not at all appealing, however. How could I be in the vat and not about to go anywhere, when I was so obviously outside the vat looking in and beginning to make guilty plans to return to my room for a substantial lunch? This begged the question I realized, but it still seemed to be getting at something important. Casting about for some support for my intuition, I hit upon a legalistic sort of argument that might have appealed to Locke.

Suppose, I argued to myself, I was now to fly to California, rob a bank, and be apprehended. In which state would I be tried: in California, where the robbery took place, or in Texas, where the brains of the outfit were located? Would I be a California felon with an out-of-state brain, or a Texas felon remotely controlling an accomplice of sorts in California? It seemed possible that I might beat such a rap just on the undecidability of that jurisdictional question, though perhaps it would be deemed an interstate, and hence Federal, offense. In any event, suppose I were convicted. Was it likely that California would be satisfied to throw Hamlet into the brig, knowing that Yorick was living the good life and luxuriously taking the waters in Texas? Would Texas incarcerate Yorick, leaving Hamlet free to take the next boat to Rio? This alternative appealed to me. Barring capital punishment or other cruel and unusual punishment, the state would be obliged to maintain the life-support system for Yorick though they might move him from Houston to Leavenworth, and aside from the unpleasantness of the opprobrium, I, for one, would not mind at all and would consider myself a free man under those circumstances. If the state has an interest in forcibly relocating persons in institutions, it would fail to relocate *me* in any institution by locating Yorick there. If this were true, it suggested a third alternative.

3. *Dennett is wherever he thinks he is.* Generalized, the claim was as follows: At any given time a person has a *point of view*, and the location of the point of view (which is determined internally by the content of the point of view) is also the location of the person.

Such a proposition is not without its perplexities, but to me it seemed a step in the right direction. The only trouble was that it seemed to place one in a heads-I-win/tails-you-lose situation of unlikely infallibility as regards location. Hadn't I myself often been wrong about where I was, and at least as often uncertain? Couldn't one get lost? Of course, but getting lost *geographically* is not the only way one might get lost. If one were lost in the woods one could attempt to reassure oneself with the consolation that at least one knew where one was: one was right *here* in the familiar surroundings of one's own body. Perhaps in this case one would not have drawn one's attention to much to be thankful for. Still, there were worse plights imaginable, and I wasn't sure I wasn't in such a plight right now.

Point of view clearly had something to do with personal location, but it was itself an unclear notion. It was obvious that the content of one's point of view was not the same as or determined by the content of one's beliefs or thoughts. For example, what should we say about the point of view of the Cinerama viewer who shrieks and twists in his seat as the roller-coaster footage overcomes his psychic distancing? Has he forgotten that he is safely seated in the theater? Here I was inclined to say that the person is experiencing an illusory shift in point of view. In other cases, my inclination to call such shifts illusory was less strong.

The workers in laboratories and plants who handle dangerous materials by operating feedback-controlled mechanical arms and hands undergo a shift in point of view that is crisper and more pronounced than anything Cinerama can provoke. They can feel the heft and slipperiness of the containers they manipulate with their metal fingers. They know perfectly well where they are and are not fooled into false beliefs by the experience, yet it is as if they were inside the isolation chamber they are peering into. With mental effort, they can manage to shift their point of view back and forth, rather like making a transparent Necker cube or an Escher drawing change orientation before one's eyes. It does seem extravagant to suppose that in performing this bit of mental gymnastics, they are transporting *themselves* back and forth.

Still their example gave me hope. If I was in fact in the vat in spite of my intuitions, I might be able to train myself to adopt that point of view even as a matter of habit. I should dwell on images of myself comfortably floating in my vat, beaming volitions to that familiar body *out there*. I reflected that the ease or difficulty of this task was presumably independent of the truth about the location of one's brain. Had I been practicing before the operation, I might now be finding it second nature. You might now yourself try such a *trompe l'oeil*. Imagine you have written an inflammatory letter which has been published in the *Times*, the result of which is that the government has chosen to impound your brain for a probationary period of three years in its Dangerous Brain Clinic in Bethesda, Maryland. Your body of course is allowed freedom to earn a salary and thus to continue its function of laying up income to be taxed. At this moment, however, your body is seated in an auditorium listening to a peculiar account by Daniel Dennett of his own similar experience. Try it. Think yourself to Bethesda, and then hark back longingly to your body, far away, and yet *seeming* so near. It is only with long-distance restraint (yours? the government's?) that you can control your impulse to get those hands clapping in polite applause before navigating the old body to the rest room and a well-deserved glass of evening sherry in the lounge. The task of imagination is certainly difficult, but if you achieve your goal the results might be consoling.

Anyway, there I was in Houston, lost in thought as one might say, but not for long. My speculations were soon interrupted by the Houston doctors, who wished to test out my new prosthetic nervous system before sending me off on my hazardous mission. As I mentioned before, I was a bit dizzy at first, and not surprisingly, although I soon habituated myself to my new circumstances (which were, after all, well nigh indistinguishable from my old circumstances). My accommodation was not perfect, however, and to this day I continue to be plagued by minor coordination difficulties. The speed of light is fast, but finite, and as my brain and body move farther and farther apart, the delicate interaction of my feedback systems is thrown into disarray by the time lags. Just as one is rendered close to speechless by a delayed or echoic hearing of one's speaking voice so, for instance, I am virtually unable to track a moving object with my eyes whenever my brain and my body are more than a few miles apart. In most matters my impairment is scarcely detectable, though I can no longer hit a slow curve ball with the authority of yore. There are some compensations of course. Though liquor tastes as good as ever, and warms my gullet while corroding my liver, I can drink it in any quantity I please, without becoming the slightest bit inebriated, a curiosity some of my close friends may have noticed (though I occasionally have *feigned* inebriation, so as not to draw attention to my unusual circumstances). For similar reasons, I take aspirin orally for a sprained wrist, but if the pain persists I ask Houston to administer codeine to me *in vitro*. In times of illness the phone bill can be staggering.

But to return to my adventure. At length, both the doctors and I were satisfied that I was ready to undertake my subterranean mission. And so I left my brain in Houston and headed by helicopter for Tulsa. Well, in any case, that's the way it seemed to me. That's how I would put it, just off the top of my head as it were. On the trip I reflected further about my earlier anxieties and decided that my first postoperative speculations had been tinged with panic. The matter was not nearly as strange or metaphysical as I had been supposing. Where was I? In two places, clearly: both inside the vat and outside it. Just as one can stand with one foot in Connecticut and the other in Rhode Island, I was in two places at once. I had become one of those scattered individuals we used to hear so much about. The more I considered this answer, the more obviously true it appeared. But, strange to say, the more true it appeared, the less important the question to which it could be the true answer seemed. A sad, but not unprecedented, fate for a philosophical question to suffer. This answer did not completely satisfy me, of course. There lingered some question to which I should have liked an answer, which was neither "Where are all my various and sundry parts?" nor "What is my current point of view?" Or at least there seemed to be such a question. For it did seem undeniable that in some sense *I* and not merely *most of me* was descending into the earth under Tulsa in search of an atomic warhead.

When I found the warhead, I was certainly glad I had left my brain behind, for the pointer on the specially built Geiger counter I had brought with me was off the dial. I called Houston on my ordinary radio and told the operation control center of my position and my progress. In return, they gave me instructions for dismantling the vehicle, based upon my on-site observations. I had set to work with my cutting torch when all of a sudden a terrible thing happened. I went stone deaf. At first I thought it was only my radio earphones that had broken, but when I tapped on my helmet, I heard nothing. Apparently the auditory transceivers had gone on the fritz. I could no longer hear Houston or my own voice, but I could speak, so I started telling them what had happened. In midsentence, I knew something else had gone wrong. My vocal apparatus had become paralyzed. Then my right hand went limp—another transceiver had gone. I was truly in deep trouble. But worse was to follow. After a few more minutes, I went blind. I cursed my luck, and then I cursed the scientists who had led me into this grave peril. There I was, deaf, dumb, and blind, in a radioactive hole more than a mile under Tulsa. Then the last of my cerebral radio links broke, and suddenly I was faced with a new and even more shocking problem: whereas an instant before I had been buried alive in Oklahoma, now I was disembodied in Houston. My recognition of my new status was not immediate. It took me several very anxious minutes before it dawned on me that my poor body lay several hundred miles away, with heart pulsing and lungs respiring, but otherwise as dead as the body of any heart-transplant donor, its skull packed with useless, broken electronic gear. The shift in perspective I had earlier found well nigh impossible now seemed quite natural. Though I could think myself back into my body in the tunnel under Tulsa, it took some effort to sustain the illusion. For surely it was an illusion to suppose I was still in Oklahoma: I had lost all contact with that body.

It occurred to me then, with one of those rushes of revelation of which we should be suspicious, that I had stumbled upon an impressive demonstration of the immateriality of the soul based upon physicalist principles and premises. For as the last radio signal between Tulsa and Houston died away, had I not changed location from Tulsa to Houston at the speed of light? And had I not accomplished this without any increase in mass? What moved from A to B at such speed was surely myself, or at any rate my soul or mind—the massless center of my being and home of my consciousness. My *point of view* had lagged somewhat behind, but I had already noted the indirect bearing of point of view on personal location. I could not see how a physicalist philosopher could quarrel with this except by taking the dire and counterintuitive route of banishing all talk of persons. Yet the notion of personhood was so well entrenched in everyone's world view, or so it seemed to me, that any denial would be as curiously unconvincing, as systematically disingenuous, as the Cartesian negation, "non sum."

The joy of philosophic discovery thus tided me over some very bad minutes or perhaps hours as the helplessness and hopelessness of my situation became more apparent to me. Waves of panic and even nausea swept over me, made all the more horrible by the absence of their normal body-dependent phenomenology. No adrenaline rush of tingles in the arms, no pounding heart, no premonitory salivation. I did feel a dread sinking feeling in my bowels at one point, and this tricked me momentarily into the false hope that I was undergoing a reversal of the process that landed me in this fix—a gradual undisembodiment. But the isolation and uniqueness of that twinge soon convinced me that it was simply the first of a plague of phantom body hallucinations that I, like any other amputee, would be all too likely to suffer.

My mood then was chaotic. On the one hand, I was fired up with elation of my philosophic discovery and was wracking my brain (one of the few familiar things I could still do), trying to figure out how to communicate my discovery to the journals; while on the other, I was bitter, lonely, and filled with dread and uncertainty. Fortunately, this did not last long, for my technical support team sedated me into a dreamless sleep from which I awoke, hearing with magnificent fidelity the familiar opening strains of my favorite Brahms piano trio. So that was why they had wanted a list of my favorite recordings! It did not take me long to realize that I was hearing music without ears. The output from the stereo stylus was being fed through some fancy rectification circuitry directly into my auditory nerve. I was mainlining Brahms, an unforgettable experience for any stereo buff. At the end of the record it did not surprise me to hear the reassuring voice of the project director speaking into a microphone that was now my prosthetic ear. He confirmed my analysis of what had gone wrong and assured me that steps were being taken to re-embody me. He did not elaborate, and after a few more recordings, I found myself drifting off to sleep. My sleep lasted, I later learned, for the better part of a year, and when I awoke, it was to find myself fully restored to my senses. When I looked into the mirror, though, I was a bit startled to see an unfamiliar face. Bearded and a bit heavier, bearing no doubt a familiar resemblance to my former face, and with the same look of spritely intelligence and resolute character, but definitely a new face. Further self-explorations of an intimate nature left me no doubt that this was a new body, and the project director confirmed my conclusions. He did not volunteer any information on the past history of my new body and I decided (wisely, I think in retrospect) not to pry. As many philosophers unfamiliar with my ordeal have more recently speculated, the acquisition of a new body leaves one's *person* intact. And after a period of adjustment to a new voice, new muscular strengths and weaknesses, and so forth, one's *personality* is by and large also preserved. More dramatic changes in personality have been routinely observed in people who have undergone extensive plastic surgery, to say nothing of sex-change operations, and I think no one contests the survival of the body in such cases. In any event I soon accommodated to my new body, to the point of being unable to recover any of its novelties to my consciousness or even memory. The view in the mirror soon became utterly familiar. That view, by the way, still revealed antennae, and so I was not surprised to learn that my brain had not been moved from its haven in the life-support lab.

I decided that good old Yorick deserved a visit. I and my new body, whom we might as well call Fortinbras, strode into the familiar lab to another round of applause from the technicians, who were of course congratulating themselves, not me. Once more I stood before the vat and contemplated poor Yorick, and on a whim I once again cavalierly flicked off the output transmitter switch. Imagine my surprise when nothing unusual happened. No fainting spell, no nausea, no noticeable change. A technician hurried to restore the switch to ON, but still I felt nothing. I demanded an explanation, which the project director hastened to provide. It seems that before they had even operated on the first occasion, they had constructed a computer duplicate of my brain, reproducing both the complete information-processing structure and the computational speed of my brain in a giant computer program. After the operation, but before they had dared to send me off on my mission to Oklahoma, they had run this computer system and Yorick side by side. The incoming signals from Hamlet were sent simultaneously to Yorick's transceivers and to the computer's array of inputs. And the outputs from Yorick were not only beamed back to Hamlet, my body; they were recorded and checked against the simultaneous output of the computer program, which was called "Hubert" for reasons obscure to me. Over days and even weeks, the outputs were identical and synchronous, which of course did not *prove* that they had succeeded in copying the brain's functional structure, but the empirical support was greatly encouraging.

Hubert's input, and hence activity, had been kept parallel with Yorick's during my disembodied days. And now, to demonstrate this, they had actually thrown the master switch that put Hubert for the first time in on-line control of my body—not Hamlet, of course, but Fortinbras. (Hamlet, I learned, had never been recovered from its underground tomb and could be assumed by this time to have largely returned to the dust. At the head of my grave still lay the magnificent bulk of the abandoned device, with the word STUD emblazoned on its side in large letters—a circumstance which may provide archaeologists of the next century with a curious insight into the burial rites of their ancestors.)

The laboratory technicians now showed me the master switch, which had two positions, labeled B, for Brain (they didn't know my brain's name was Yorick) and H, for Hubert. The switch did indeed point to H, and they explained to me that if I wished, I could switch it back to B. With my heart in my mouth (and my brain in its vat), I did this. Nothing happened. A click, that was all. To test their claim, and with the master switch now set at B, I hit Yorick's output transmitter switch on the vat and sure enough, I began to faint. Once the output switch was turned back on and I had recovered my wits, so to speak, I continued to play with the master switch, flipping it back and forth. I found that with the exception of the transitional click, I could detect no trace of a difference. I could switch in mid-utterance, and the sentence I had begun speaking under the control of Yorick was finished without a pause or hitch of any kind under the control of Hubert. I had a spare brain, a prosthetic device which might some day stand me in very good stead, were some mishap to befall Yorick. Or alternatively, I could keep Yorick as a spare and use Hubert. It didn't seem to make any difference which I chose, for the wear and tear and fatigue on my body did not have any debilitating effect on either brain, whether or not it was actually causing the motions of my body, or merely spilling its output into thin air.

The one truly unsettling aspect of this new development was the prospect, which was not long in dawning on me, of someone detaching the spare — Hubert or Yorick, as the case might be — from Fortinbras and hitching it to yet another body — some Johnny-come-lately Rosencrantz or Guildenstern. Then (if not before) there would be *two* people, that much was clear. One would be me, and the other would be a sort of super-twin brother. If there were two bodies, one under the control of Hubert and the other being controlled by Yorick, then which would the world recognize as the true Dennett? And whatever the rest of the world decided, which one would be *me*? Would I be the Yorick-brained one, in virtue of Yorick's causal priority and former intimate relationship with the original Dennett body, Hamlet? That seemed a bit legalistic, a bit too redolent of the arbitrariness of consanguinity and legal possession, to be convincing at the metaphysical level. For suppose that before the arrival of the second body on the scene, I had been keeping Yorick as the spare for years, and letting Hubert's output drive my body — that is, Fortinbras — all that time. The Hubert-Fortinbras couple would seem then by squatter's rights (to combat one legal intuition with another) to be the true Dennett and the lawful inheritor of everything that was Dennett's. This was an interesting question, certainly, but not nearly so pressing as another question that bothered me. My strongest intuition was that in such an eventuality *I* would survive so long as *either* brain-body couple remained intact, but I had mixed emotions about whether I should want both to survive.

I discussed my worries with the technicians and the project director. The prospect of two Dennetts was abhorrent to me, I explained, largely for social reasons. I didn't want to be my own rival for the affections of my wife, nor did I like the prospect of the two Dennetts sharing my modest professor's salary. Still more vertiginous and distasteful, though, was the idea of knowing *that much* about another person, while he had the very same goods on me. How could we ever face each other? My colleagues in the lab argued that I was ignoring the bright side of the matter. Weren't there many things I wanted to do but, being only one person, had been unable to do? Now one Dennett could stay at home and be the professor and family man, while the other could strike out on a life of travel and adventure — missing the family of course, but happy in the knowledge that the other Dennett was keeping the home fires burning. I could be faithful and adulterous at the same time. I could even cuckold myself — to say nothing of other more lurid possibilities my colleagues were all too ready to force upon my overtaxed imagination. But my ordeal in Oklahoma (or was it Houston?) had made me less adventurous, and I shrank from this opportunity that was being offered (though of course I was never quite sure it was being offered to *me* in the first place).

There was another prospect even more disagreeable: that the spare, Hubert or Yorick as the case might be, would be detached from any input from Fortinbras and just left detached. Then, as in the other case, there would be two Dennetts, or at least two claimants to my name and possessions, one embodied in Fortinbras, and the other sadly, miserably disembodied. Both selfishness and altruism bade me take steps to prevent this from happening. So I asked that measures be taken to ensure that no one could ever tamper with the transceiver connections or the master switch without my (our? no, *my*) knowledge and consent. Since I had no desire to spend my life guarding the equipment in Houston, it was mutually decided that all the electronic connections in the lab would be carefully locked. Both those that controlled the life-support system for Yorick and those that controlled the power supply for Hubert would be guarded with fail-safe devices, and I would take the only master switch, outfitted for radio remote control, with me wherever I went. I carry it strapped around my waist and—wait a moment—here it is. Every few months I reconnoiter the situation by switching channels. I do this only in the presence of friends, of course, for if the other channel were, heaven forbid, either dead or otherwise occupied, there would have to be somebody who had my interests at heart to switch it back, to bring me back from the void. For while I could feel, see, hear, and otherwise sense whatever befell my body, subsequent to such a switch, I'd be unable to control it. By the way, the two positions on the switch are intentionally unmarked, so I never have the faintest idea whether I am switching from Hubert to Yorick or vice versa. (Some of you may think that in this case I really don't know *who* I am, let alone where I am. But such reflections no longer make much of a dent on my essential Dennettness, on my own sense of who I am. If it is true that in one sense I don't know who I am then that's another one of your philosophical truths of underwhelming significance.)

In any case, every time I've flipped the switch so far, nothing has happened. *So let's give it a try. . . .*

"THANK GOD! I THOUGHT YOU'D NEVER FLIP THAT SWITCH! You can't imagine how horrible it's been these last two weeks—but now you know; it's your turn in purgatory. How I've longed for this moment! You see, about two weeks ago—excuse me, ladies and gentlemen, but I've got to explain this to my . . . um, brother, I guess you could say, but he's just told you the facts, so you'll understand—about two weeks ago our two brains drifted just a bit out of synch. I don't know whether *my* brain is now Hubert or Yorick, any more than you do, but in any case, the two brains drifted apart, and of course once the process started, it snowballed, for I was in a slightly different receptive state for the input we both received, a difference that was soon magnified. In no time at all the illusion that I was in control of my body — our body — was completely dissipated. There was nothing I could do — no way to call you. YOU DIDN'T EVEN KNOW I EXISTED! It's been like being carried around in a cage, or better, like being possessed — hearing my own voice say things I didn't mean to say, watching in frustration as my own hands performed deeds I hadn't intended. You'd scratch our itches, but not the way I would have, and you kept me awake, with your tossing and turning. I've been totally exhausted, on the verge of a nervous breakdown, carried around helplessly by your frantic round of activities, sustained only by the knowledge that some day you'd throw the switch.

"Now it's your turn, but at least you'll have the comfort of knowing *I* know you're in there. Like an expectant mother, I'm eating — or at any rate tasting, smelling, seeing — for *two* now, and I'll try to make it easy for you. Don't worry. Just as soon as this colloquium is over, you and I will fly to Houston, and we'll see what can be done to get one of us another body. You can have a female body — your body could be any color you like. But let's think it over. I tell you what — to be fair, if we both want this body, I promise I'll let the project director flip a coin to settle which of us gets to keep it and which then gets to choose a new body. That should guarantee justice, shouldn't it? In any case, I'll take care of you, I promise. These people are my witnesses.

"Ladies and gentlemen, this talk we have just heard is not exactly the talk *I* would have given, but I assure you that everything he said was perfectly true. And now if you'll excuse me, I think I'd — we'd — better sit down."

OPTIONS FOR WRITING

1. Where do you think that Dennett is at each stage of his story? Is your view always the same as the one Dennett seems to be advocating? Does your view have any implications about the nature of personal identity? Explain, in writing, to a skeptical classmate.

2. Suppose that you are a completely physical thing, and that after you die your body decomposes. Suppose that there is a God, who remembers the arrangement of every atom in your body just before death. Fifty years after you die, God creates an exact replica of you in heaven. This replica has all the mental states, including all of the memories, that you had when you died. Would this replica *be* you? Are there reasons to think it would not be? Suppose God created this replica while you were still alive. Would this replica be you?

5

A PERSPECTIVE ON THE ARTS

Lynda Reeves McIntyre

Through words and drawings artist McIntyre shows us the clutter of her studio and the order of her mind. As she takes us from an impromptu napkin sketch to finished work, she explains how an artist perceives and develops visual images. Along the way she reveals the striking parallels between the writing process and the art-making process. In one section McIntyre invites the reader to examine two powerful pieces of art—Picasso's *Guernica* and Maya Ying Lin's Vietnam Veterans Memorial—and to consider their inspiration, creation, and significance. She then challenges us to see and listen—to map a laundromat or sketch an argument or describe in words what a shelf of books sounds like.

READINGS

Eberhard Fisch   A Study of Picasso's *Guernica*

Brent Ashabranner   The Vision of Maya Ying Lin

Ann Truit   Daybook: The Journal of an Artist

Henry Moore   On Sculpture and Primitive Art

Paul Klee   On Modern Art

John Dewey   Art as Experience

My studio is cluttered. Every vertical and horizontal surface wants to be covered. Morning light streams over my left shoulder onto my first cup of pale tea. Walls are covered with pictures: photos of olive groves, Italian hill towns, an elderly friend in China against a clear blue sky; daily photos of Ayer's Rock; postcards of layered terra cotta roofs in

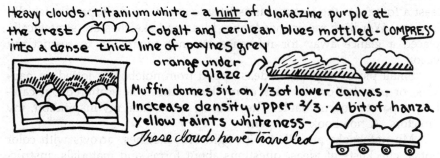

Heavy clouds · titanium white - a _hint_ of dioxazine purple at the crest. Cobalt and cerulean blues mottled - COMPRESS into a dense thick line of paynes grey

orange under glaze

Muffin domes sit on ⅓ of lower canvas - Increase density upper ⅔ · A bit of hanza yellow taints whiteness-
These clouds have traveled

Figure 5.1   Notebook sketches and notes.

Lucca. More postcards of brilliantly colored bath houses and umbrellas by the sea are tacked to stick board and molding. Pieces of faded floral fabrics drape from push pins. Tapering wolf's hair brushes hang from wooden Chinese brush racks. An army of empty baby food jars huddle in the corner of my large, paint-spattered wooden work table.

THE STUDIO AND THE ARTIST

This is my studio, the studio of a working visual artist. All artists have their own work territories, their own inspirations, materials, and languages. When I refer to the arts, I am referring to a broad variety of disciplines including dance, music, theater, writing, and visual arts. Each of these disciplines contains numerous diverse fields of study. A choreographer may work in the field of jazz dance, ballet, or improvisation. The visual artist's primary interest may be architecture, painting, film making, or graphic design. Other professionals study arts as historians, critics, or educators. What is important is the fact that the process of thinking about, making, and responding to the arts is parallel from art form to art form; this process is quite similar to the writing process. Artists write? Of course. In this chapter we will examine how various artists think, and why and how they write. Through assignments we will attempt to "try on" some of the conceptual processes of artists. I will present examples from many art forms but will rely most heavily on my experience as a visual artist and teacher, confident that the parallels in art forms will begin to reveal themselves.

Back to the studio. As I work I glance longingly at my paints. Crinkled metal tubes of cobalt blue with labels long worn off, jars of dioxazine purples, new plastic tubes imprinted with health warnings, and empty clear glass jars with rings of paint sit side by side. Three green plastic tubs sit filled with twisted tubes of paints. A piece of Plexiglas® is nearly invisible under moonscape mountains of cadmium red, ochre, cerulean blue, and green paints: This is my pallet, and a little piece of every recent painting is right here. A cup of hot tea is kept at least a foot from the rinsing jar as I try to avoid my daily paintbrush dip into tea. Wordless music moves me. Ideas and sketches are strategically placed a glance away for reference but not square on to restrict my vision.

Small pieces of paper—ideas ripped from notebooks, jotted on napkins, or penciled on the back of my bank stubs—lie scattered but carefully separated on my table. They are my reminders, my inspiration, my directors. A notebook lies open.

My notebooks are filled with light line sketches, arrows with color notes, checklists of ideas, questions about forms and materials, instructions, and pep talks (see, for example, Figure 5.1). Turquoise green, vicious red . . . circles here and there reinforce these ideas or forms that seem most powerful. Saved notes on napkins, developed while I waited for a tardy friend, are tucked into the artist's sketchbook, with its page after page of line, word, arrow, and gesture in a personal language. The sketches in Figure 5.2 were the foundations for larger acrylic paintings such as the one you'll see later in Figure 5.5.

THE ARTIST'S JOURNAL

These notes and doodles are my first steps. They are the prewriting of my visual text. The creative process of making a painting, composing a

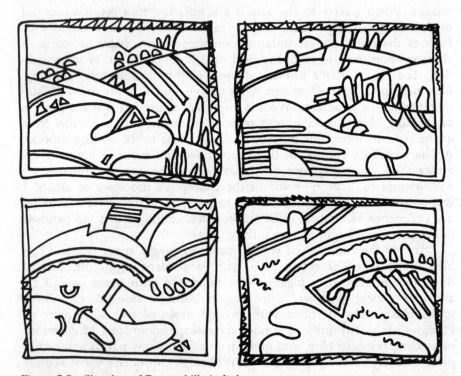

Figure 5.2   Sketches of Tuscan hills in Italy.

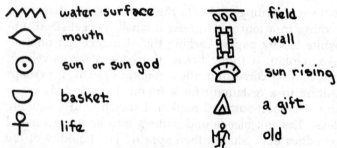

Figure 5.3   Common hieroglyphics.

piece of music, choreographing a dance, or planning a theatrical piece is often sequential and similar to the writing process. Each process involves an inventing or exploring phase much like prewriting. In my work this is the note taking, the journal writing, and the quick sketch gathering of ideas. A dancer might jot down observed movements or ideas about qualities of movement. A musician might observe a hawk and attempt to note its movements and soaring to express in music. The drafting, or manipulating and shaping, stages come next, followed by a refining and revising stage and eventually an editing and evaluating phase. Each artwork is in itself a "text," and though the main medium of communication may be sound or movement or color, the process of exploration and execution in which writing is often an important part runs parallel form to form. The resulting artwork texts can best be read by an audience that has learned to look at, listen to, and understand the language.

WRITING 1.

In ancient Egypt, as in many cultures, the first written communication was accomplished through pictographs, simple visual images symbolic of objects or ideas. Figure 5.3 shows a few common hieroglyphics.

For the next week, create your own visual language, or hieroglyphics, in your journal. See if you can record your observations, thoughts, and ideas in your own symbols. You may choose to vary your color, size of form, medium (ink, charcoal, pencil), or implement (quill, cotton swab, ballpoint pen). You might try combinations or repetitions of symbols. How will you order your page or scroll? Will it be horizontal, vertical, circular? Reread your journal at the end of the week. Do certain similar systems arise? What symbols and means are uniquely your own? Did you change or evolve any symbols? Have you discovered anything from this investigation?

From Journal to Napkin

Each artist has his or her own method of keeping ideas, a unique blending of images, personal hieroglyphics, and words. As we look at the relationship between writing and art, the most direct interactions surface through writing in a journal. I prefer a small, pocket-sized, unlined book with white toothy paper. Lacking this, I quickly jot on anything I can find—a napkin, a traffic ticket, the back of an envelope. Some of my best ideas have come from these napkin drawings, perhaps scribbled while waiting in a restaurant for a friend. I particularly enjoy the feel of the pen on the soft-surfaced napkin. I sketch with a liquidity that seems effortless. The ink bleeds and softens into amusing lines. I observe and follow edges first. Shapes then appear. The liquidity of the line invites me to continue, so even if my friend is very late, the time is engagingly spent. As I draw, I am not thinking, "I am an artist, I am making art," I am simply looking, observing, noting, gathering information, and enjoying myself. I am not judging the drawing but am effortlessly making decisions as I go along about what I want to include, where I would like to put it. I leave out objects, lines, forms that I find uninteresting. I welcome the random placement of objects on the table. The tablecloth and the salt and pepper shakers were not arranged by me. Instead, they are observed and captured by me. Like a writer, I jot down ideas and thoughts that I may later move and manipulate to form a final piece. I try to suspend my heavy-handed judgments. The objects take on a life of their own, and each requires a certain weight of line, a certain attention to character. I relax into the pleasure of observation, the fluidity and tactile quality of drawing, and the quiet decisions of inclusion, placement, and scale (see Figure 5.4).

My friend arrives, and my attention shifts. The salt and pepper shakers no longer hold my attention with their reflective metal caps, faceted glass bodies, and half-filled dusty insides. I push them aside as I lean into a focused conversation. Without thought I use the napkin to cushion my teacup, and it absorbs tan pools in the saucer. If an image or idea has pleased me I might fold the napkin and tuck it into my bag to be surprised by the tea drawing later.

From Napkin to Canvas

These napkin drawings have a vitality and honesty I admire. I am direct in my drawing, less immediately judgmental. The drawings never seem labored or overworked. They are often humorous and have a sense of freedom, spontaneity, and spirit that I value. They join other scraps, notes, and doodles as resources for future work. These napkin sketches and two-inch notebook sketches may be the beginning of eight-foot paintings. Or they may join a thousand other ideas in stacks of paper, notebooks, and boxes awaiting another review, another judgment. Some I will circle, approve, and begin to rework; others I will save again; and still others I will throw out.

The saved notes I refine and rework. This is the beginning of my drafting stage—the sketching out of colors, forms, and ideas to embrace or discard. I write down my "mind decisions" as I map out alternatives

Figure 5.4   A napkin sketch.

and ideas. This process continues to ebb and flow as I execute the painting. I proceed with an ongoing dialogue between the piece in process and my intentions. Each mark changes the piece and creates, perhaps, a new avenue for exploration. I never really know exactly where the final piece will go or how it will look. I usually know only how I want it to feel.

Even as I am working I will be noting on paper directions for my next project, ideas this one has given me. Notes often surround these developing works. Sometimes these notes are technical, regarding color, gesture, and so on; sometimes they are organizational listings of things to do; and sometimes they are simply thoughts or reflections that seem relevant that day. "Should the triangular shape of the shadowed cypress be lilac or a gray green?" This might be considered the parallel of the revision process in writing.

Even the completion of a piece is not its end. I then allow myself time to look at the painting to reflect, to evaluate, and to question. I attempt to enjoy the elements I believe are successful and at the same time to address the areas that are problematic. I also attempt to be generous with myself, to allow the painting to wash over me before I become too judgmental. Does this idea need to be reworked, or has it reached a point of successful completion that would make reworking redundant? Upon completion of a piece or a series, I often need time to simply sit back, absorb, question, and delight in the work.

There is great satisfaction in a hard day of this physical, intellectual, and emotional labor. These little doodles can and do grow with effort and refinement into a variety of often magical paintings. From visual notes to sketches, to preliminary paintings, to the moving of forms and colors, to the refinements and attention to detail, and to the final scanning of the whole piece, this art-making, creative process runs parallel to the writing process with its prewriting, drafting, revision, and editing stages. Although an audience seldom experiences the total process directly, it is a rare work that springs forth whole, complete, perfect, and processless. In most art forms, the success of the final product depends on the successful involvement and use of this creative process. The acrylic painting in Figure 5.5 grew out of a series of sketches of the Tuscan landscape illustrated in Figure 5.2. The watercolor in Figure 5.6 integrated elements from the previously illustrated napkin drawing into its composition.

WRITING 2.

In the following activities I am not looking for correct answers. In fact, there are no correct answers. I am asking you to suspend your judgment and to try on different ways of seeing. Choose one of the following approaches to seeing differently.

Figure 5.5   The completed painting of the Tuscan landscape.

Figure 5.6 A watercolor.

Seeing Lines and Shapes

Look around you. Look at the objects and shapes in your environment. A clock may be a circle, a table a rectangular. Layers of rectangular doors, circular door knobs, vertical lines of wall corners and door frames surround you. Take time and note the shapes, particularly the edges of shapes, not the details. Now draw the shapes and edges that you see. Do not try to "make art." Simply record the shapes that you see. Follow the edge of a form. This drawing of shapes is the beginning of abstracting. The clock, a teacup, a doorknob may all become circles. This is also parallel in some ways to your previous creation of hieroglyphics. The circle may have become the symbol for the sun. If you follow the edges of the forms, you will begin to see the building blocks of visual language. Simply observe—really look—and enjoy the looking; use your pen or pencil as you move your eyes, following the edges of forms. Fill up your page with as much information as you can. The resulting picture will be an abstraction of what you see. How does the process feel? Take some time to reflect on this in your journal. You might choose to extend this exercise by trying different approaches. Try to draw the room from another view. What if you were looking down on the room? What if you were viewing the area as an ant might see it? Experiment. Look and draw. Enjoy the looking, the drawing, the process of taking in and recording information.

Seeing Movement and Interaction

Go to a cafeteria, restaurant, or laundromat—anywhere there are people interacting with each other and with their environment. How are people moving? How fast? Alone? In small groups? As small herds? Are the movements done with their whole bodies or just hands or faces? Do many people use similar movements, or are most of the movements individual? Are there qualities or intensities of energy that you can see in these movements? For example, two lovers talking over coffee might be more intense than a person buying a token at a laundromat or a subway station. How will you show these differences? Once you have found an interesting site, begin to draw or diagram the movements and energy in the situation. You could map the scene from the air or head on. You might include snippets of conversation. How would you draw someone bending? An argument? Someone folding laundry? Experiment. Find your own visual language to communicate the movement, pace, and intensity of the situation. This is your prewriting note taking. Can you now reassemble and compose your information and craft a piece that, to you, captures the energy and movement of the situation?

Seeing the Potential for Sound

Can you see sound or potential sound? Look around you. A venetian blind through its visual rhythm tells you it can be strummed, as can a shelf of books. Book pages could be fanned, metal chair legs sound different from wooden ones when tapped, and trash cans can become drums and reveal different sounds played upside down or sideways. Some objects make sounds during use — a refrigerator, a push-button telephone, a door latch. Look around you again. What objects could make a sound? How would you "play" the room? That's right, play the room. Take time, experiment. Actually attempt to create sounds in and from your environment. How many objects can make sounds? What varieties of sounds can they make? Change rhythm and volume. Involve others if you wish (incorporate more instruments at one time). How could you write this music? Compose and write a piece written for your chosen site. Can this work be played? Try it. Again, you are taking prewriting information and drafting it into workable form. Have you any thoughts about the process? Have you discovered anything from this investigation?

WRITING ABOUT ART

From Idea to Form

Why and how does one write about art? The connections between art and writing are often obscure. This is probably most apparent in the work of a studio artist, like myself, who paints and dances.

As a studio artist and a teacher, I am painfully aware of my own initial resistance to writing. I was of the mind that art works or it doesn't and that the less said or written, the better. As a student I could draw myself through nearly anything, and I coasted through school with minimal writing, called creative writing. I later realized I wanted and needed to communicate with others both visually and verbally. Upon reflection, I also realized that I had been writing all my life — poems, short stories, journals, letters, notes in my calculus books, and so on. I had started my first newspaper, "The Hilton Street Tattler," at age six. At this time I also began to document my paintings by having my next-door neighbor prop them up as I held my breath and shot black and white photos of landscape and horse paintings with my prized maroon Brownie camera. At seven I began to keep sporadic journals.

Today as I drive down a road, I make notes on the color of the sky or the quality of light that I hope to capture and evoke in my next work. Surprisingly, these verbal notes get closer to the heart of what I hope to accomplish than a photograph. Photographs can give me composition, but the notes give me the renewal, the soul, the texture. I also use writing to generate lists for new works or concepts to explore. I brainstorm an idea on paper, expand it, play with changes, and pull it back in. These notes are guidelines for my work, and my artwork is stronger for this process. Over the last twenty-four years I have consistently used journals to solve visual problems both compositionally and verbally.

As artists begin to show work more often, they are frequently asked to write narratives about their work, about its history and purpose. A narrative can also elaborate on ideas and give the viewer a sense of the artist's inspirations, goals. It also can help the viewer locate a particular series of work within the breadth of works and concerns of the artist. The following is an excerpt from a narrative for a painting show of mine, a show that included the Tuscan landscape shown in Figures 5.2 and 5.5.

Dances from the Land

This series of works is based on sketches and impressions of landscapes as viewed from the air. The work comes directly from experiences in natural surroundings and a fascination with light and atmospheric qualities that change momentarily. This fascination, combined with a passion for gesture, for color and its boundaries, has evolved into various series of stained and assembled acrylic paintings. The language of gesture and strokes are based on the energy of the landscape, the layering of cultivated fields, the changes in crop colors, the winding of rivers, the deliberate directional plowing of fields and the movement and density of the atmosphere in relation to the land. Each moment brings changes to even a familiar landscape. These changing patterns and often illusive qualities of emotional experience are the direct inspiration and resources for this series of paintings. I paint, respond, reassemble, paint over, and attempt to capture the feeling, the liquidity, the gesture, and the spirit of the changing land.

—Lynda Reeves McIntyre

In the narrative the artist tells the story, and in the review the art critic responds to the work. The reviewer not only paints a verbal picture of the work for those who might not be able to view the work in person but also attempts to put the work in context, describe artistic elements and techniques, and even make quality judgments about the work. Here is a review that critic Emmie Donadio wrote for *Art in New England*.

Summers end suddenly in Vermont. No sooner do the schools reopen than the heat and humidity evaporate. Despite the chill air and the twilight colors of the season, there are "sunny spells," and one of the sunniest places in Vermont this month is the Frame of Mind Gallery in Burlington, where Lynda McIntyre is showing her summer work.

Three canvases, about three by three and a half feet, comprise this exhibition, all of them completed recently during McIntyre's summer stay at the MacDowell Colony in Peterborough, New Hampshire. Delicious color, eloquent gesture, and luxuriant talent radiate from these drawings. Working with acrylic on paper, the artist lavishes fugitive notations in a gorgeous range of pastels and deeper hues, overlapping and interweaving strokes to achieve a texture as rich and resonant as it is diaphanous.

What one confronts here are drawings painted on paper onto which small squares of still other drawings have been superimposed. The result of these layerings is a loosely-woven counterpoint that runs from harmonies of high density and excitement to ones clearer and more limpid, depending on the color key and mood of the particular drawings juxtaposed.

Color and texture are the key ingredients of these compositions, and McIntyre is in perfect control of both. Despite the apparent spontaneity and ease — the sprezzatura — of her brush stroke, the programs or strategies of the works have been planned with precision: Each drawing has a regular grid of two-by-two-inch insets of the complementary composition, and the impression conveyed by the whole is one of vibrant and luminous energy. Although one is reminded of Sol LeWitt's programmatic recipes for works, or even of Mel Brochner's (with whom McIntyre studied briefly at Yale), the personality of each stroke here demonstrates a far livelier and more idiosyncratic performance than anything executed on command by a committee or a prior conception.

Something of the dancer's discipline shines through these gestures, each one elegantly tuned to the particular occasion, but each still obviously the result of inspired and continuous practice. And if her notations convey McIntyre's love of the elegant gestures of dance, the colors she elects to display yield pleasures that are purely visual. Shades of lavender, chartreuse, vermilion and gold vie with pale blue, green, and salmon, reminding one visitor of an array of tropical flora, and another of the festive hues of a birthday party.

Sensuous and careful, these tasteful works linger vividly in memory, bearing overtones of summer into fall.

Asking Questions About Art

Reviewing artwork requires asking questions. What is the purpose of the piece? Who is the artist? When was it executed? How was it crafted or composed? Does it remind you of something? How does it make you feel? Does it fall into a historical style? Are there elements of line, shape, form, color, texture, repetition, movement? What medium was used? Are there parallels to other art forms? Art, music, dance, and poetry all have rhythm, for instance. The painter Wassily Kandinski refers to the color yellow as a "blare of the trumpet." Probing with a variety of questions generates a great wealth of information about a piece without relying on "I like it" or "I don't like it."

As my students begin to write reviews and criticism, I encourage them to search out and attend art experiences with which they are not familiar. They then analyse and respond to these experiences honestly, first by exploring the work through questions such as those just listed, by journal writing, and by freewriting, and then by pulling that information together into a short, informative, and engaging critical review. This process helps a viewer more thoroughly explore the work of art and attempt to explore the content and context beyond a simple value judgment. Responses may range from analytical to emotional to interpretive. Each response reveals much about both the artwork and the writer.

In each of my beginning drawing and design classes, I ask students to participate in at least six arts experiences and to write a compelling critique of that experience. The following critiques were pulled from a variety of basic art classes. Each approaches writing and art from a different perspective. These essays are not meant to serve as "right" approaches but as examples of using words to explore nonverbal material and experiences.

Kate Schmidt describes to us her personal visual and eavesdropping experience as she encounters an art show. She looks at the environment, the people involved, her own changing focus and attitude. The art pieces in the show became but a small part of the total experience.

Kelly McVeary approaches a visual and written archaeological show analytically. She draws questions from the presented materials and explores cultural connections, analyzing both the materials and her own responses.

As you read these pieces, consider these questions: How did this person approach the work? What questions did she ask? How did she choose to present the work? Do you become an observer or a participant? Did you get a feeling for the art or experience? Did these pieces raise any questions?

The Opening of "Faces in the Parlor"
Kate Schmidt

My artsy and invincible feeling (stemming from my recently acquired "Santa Fe" style outfit) was squelched as I walked back to the main entrance of the Fleming yesterday afternoon. I was humbled by the sudden snow and the flurry of elderly people leaving the museum. Both made me feel very underdressed—what the hell was I going to do with my cowboy hat now? Humbly, with hat crushed under my arm, I entered the opening.

It seemed to be an event celebrating the artwork. A pianist dressed in a traditional outfit of the 1800s played in the middle of the gallery, and chairs were set up to create a feeling of a parlor. As many people gathered around a table with cookies and coffee as did around the paintings themselves.

I observed these paintings only superficially; I felt

rushed through, there were too many people. I will go back and study it more carefully when there are fewer distractions.

The portraits were much like ones my grandparents have of their grandparents, my ancestors, similar, and yet my relatives lived and were painted in Germany.

"There's Okrissa," the old woman next to me exclaimed to her friend. "Now, she used to hang in my living room at home, but then Lorraine and George had her. They asked Lorraine to borrow it."

She turned to me with one hand around her mouth as if she were confiding a secret and said, "she was my relative way back."

Then to her friend, "Matthew's sister." Her friend nodded in understanding.

The person who accompanied me to the show is a Vermonter of many generations. There were several portraits that could have been her distant relatives, last or middle names that were or are family names. I've lived here 19 of my 21 years, but I have occasionally felt on the outside of the very strong sense of community in Vermont. Yesterday was one of those times.

I don't think it was really a celebration of art at the Fleming yesterday; it was a celebration of these long-time Vermonters who donated portraits of relatives. My friend and I were easily the youngest guests present. It was amazing to have gone to see the exhibit yesterday. Eavesdropping on the conversation of others caused me to come to a deeper understanding and appreciation of the exhibit, and the meaning of a portrait beyond just a popular art form of an era past.

I will go back and study value, line, form, motion, and color in the portraits, but for me that is not where the lesson lies. I do not know exactly what I learned. Part of it has something to do with my self-identification--personal, historical, and even geographical. Not one of my German ancestors or any of these aging Vermonters had ever had occasion to wear a cowboy hat.

"WO/MAN"
Kelly McVearny

The exhibit at the Fleming Museum entitled "WO/MAN: The Culture of Gender" is a collection of paintings, sculpture, and household paraphernalia that suggest the relationship between the sexes throughout history. A view of these objects is a shocking experience that illuminates male dominance and female submissiveness. The exhibit's introduction states the theme that underlies the collection's four components of GENDER IMAGES, TEACHING GENDER, GENDER AND WORK, and GENDER PROPS:

GENDER--the cultural expression of biological sexual differences--is a powerful force. It defines who you are and what you can do. Throughout history, women have been subordinate to men. Today this is challenged by a view of women and men as two essential versions of humanity with equal rights.

The GENDER IMAGES section begins the exhibit by depicting male and female status in different societies. A nineteenth century scrimshaw on whale teeth shows Adam and Eve, the earliest male/female relationship.

The artwork is delicate, but subject is of greater significance. Eve, with her head bowed and twisted form, suggests humility and submission; Adam, with outstretched arms and spread, active legs, expresses his confidence and control of his environment.

A black and white Lysistrata is a simple but compelling print. This work titled "Adoration of the Penis" is necessarily repulsive. Here a clothed man stands proudly exposing only enormous, erect genitals as a girl in pigtails buries her face in his testicles. This epitomizes female exploitation, for mutual love is absent and affection and pleasure is one-sided.

From Germany are hand-colored photographs by Paul Albert titled "The Old School" (c. 1900). This small-scale work uses accurate coloring and is a relatively uneventful composition. Important for its subject matter, it depicts men in full uniforms or business attire, in positions of power and control. Shortly after in 1918, a war poster was printed by Sachete and Wilhelms Corporation in the United States. On this lithograph is a young woman--slender and attractive--who is referred to as a "lassie" and is portrayed making her big contribution to WWI: passing out doughnuts to male soldiers, primping and smiling.

Primitive statues, whether from Mexico, China, Zaire, the United States, or Easter Island, portray similar images of males and females. Women were shown with child or lying prostrate and spread eagled. Men, on the other hand, were upright and solitary and seemed confident, not humble.

The TEACHING GENDER section effectively showed how societies' values are unconsciously translated through children's toys. Little girls' encourage domesticity, whereas boys' encourage adventure. In a 1934 book *Happy Hours: Photographs of Happy Children*, verse by Elizabeth Daniel accompanies a B&W picture of a cute girl wearing a party dress and drying dishes:

My mother praises me and says
There's only one thing that she wishes--

That when I'm big I'll be as glad
To help her with the dishes.

This photograph makes good use of space and is an organized composition. However, the verse is disquieting. One might hope a mother would have higher aspirations for her daughter. In fact, it is this attitude and resignation to domesticity that perpetuated the female position of subordination for so long.

An interesting object was the 1939 Revised Handbook for Boys by the Boy Scouts of America. An entire page was devoted to "Respect for Womanhood." Good Scouts were instructed to walk on side of street nearest traffic, offer their seat, and always make way for "her." The entire tone assumes the helplessness and fragility of women, as though they do not have functioning legs and could not dare to be splashed by a drop or two of mud from passing traffic.

Wooden dolls from the Hopi people of Arizona in the twentieth century establish similar roles for the sexes. The Male Kachina is extravagant, colorful, adorned with feathers, and dressed for a great tribal ceremony. In stark contrast, the Kachina Maiden is plain and dully dressed, and her only prop is a bowl--probably for preparing a feast for her family.

Recently, Mattel Toys manufactured in 1987 a "Dr. Barbie" doll. Almost revolutionary in the toy world, it signifies a woman in a traditionally male role that requires intelligence. Still, the transition is not complete, as Dr. Barbie is dressed in a silky white doctor jacket with a hot pink dress underneath, is wearing flashy earrings, and has the makeup caked on for the operating room. Also displayed was an F14 USA jet fighter manufactured in 1988 by Son Ai Toys. Chances are not too many girls received them as presents this past Christmas.

The GENDER PROPS section presented objects related solely to each sex's identity in a given society. From nineteenth century China was a dainty cloth and leather woman's shoe for a bound foot. Approximately four inches long, the delicate floral embroidery adorns an object that crippled many Chinese women for the sake of maintaining a petite appearance. From nineteenth century Japan was a man's sword. It is an awesome piece--statuesque, antique craftsmanship of steel, brass, lacquer, wood, and silk--that commands respect and was certainly never handled by a woman. Displayed next to the sword was a woman's pincushion. This nineteenth century American piece was exclusively feminine, complete with floral embroidery on pink satin. These props from various countries share the view of women as domestic and showpieces, and the view of men as participants in the outside world.

Some displays were not revealing, but merely natural. The man's urinal made in 1988 by the Kohler Company simply acknowledges the fact that men and women are anatomically different. The sexes are different, but in this modern age we are learning that one sex is not superior to another. The artistic value of most pieces in this exhibition was a far cry from spectacular and dynamic. Individually, the works and objects were relatively dull or quaint. Together, they projected a powerful, if not disquieting, social message that forces the viewer to evaluate his/her role in the world. Personally, I left the exhibit determined to help end the subordination of women and be on guard for subtle sex discrepancies and discriminations in my society.

WRITING 3.

Take some time and view or participate in an artwork or performance with which you are not totally familiar. Go to a play. Look at paintings. Listen to unfamiliar music. Go to a poetry reading. Look at the work and how it was created. What do you think the artist was trying to do? How did he or she use color, lighting, scale, rhythm, placement, timing, and so on to do this? What was the context of the piece, the way in which it was presented? What was your response? Did you think anything? Feel anything? Did it remind you of something? How did others respond? What was the total environment like? Would you change this piece if it were yours? Take notes and make drawings while you are involved with the experience. Talk with others. Take time out and freewrite about the experience.

Actually, the best way to do this is to go through the experience twice. First let the artwork simply affect you, and then try to analyze why you were affected. It is also helpful to do this with friends and then all by yourself. When you think you have experienced the artwork thoroughly, pull together your resource material, notes, doodles, eavesdropped lines, and so forth.

Write a short critical essay about this artwork or experience. Who is the artist? What was he or she attempting to do? How did the artist go about this? Was he or she successful? Where does this piece stand historically? Does it have emotional content? Do elements of color, harmony, line, and rhythm appear? How was the total experience crafted? Attempt to engage the readers and bring them through the experience.

Speaking for Art

Another interesting and interpretive approach to writing about art is to take on the role of the piece of art and to "speak for the art." This approach attempts to project the spirit of the piece through words. Form and rhythm can be integrated into critical writing. This approach often comes close to the essence of the visual or performed piece but also leaves a great deal of room for the writer's interpretation. The same beginning questions are asked, but others are added. Does this artwork want to be a poem, a narrative? Should the text be in color?

The following student reviews are expressive in nature as they try to speak for the art. Again, they are included to serve as examples of alternative approaches, not as the correct approaches. In each case, the student attempts to find an appropriate voice for the artwork or problem explored. These pieces review an art show of computer-generated graphics, executed in silkscreen by a young Chinese artist. Wendy Werner gives the piece a poetic voice. Lauri Robinson uses the more technological aspect and speaks for the work. Each written piece reveals a certain aspect or viewpoint of the overall art show. As you read you might compare and contrast these pieces. Do you see any similarities? Do they help you to visualize the work? Where are areas of conflict? Do they provoke any questions?

Hui Chu Ying's Exhibit
at the Colburn Gallery
Wendy Werner

I am Small	I am Large
I am Whole	I am Parts
I am New	I am Old
I am Science	I am Art
I am Technology	I am Tradition
I am Western	I am Eastern
I am Computer Generated	I am Handmade
I am Calculated	I am Random
I am Programmed	I am Inspiration
I am Design	I am Color
I am Tomorrow	I am Yesterday
I am Independent	I am Interdependent
I am Right Side Up	I am Up Side Down
I Pull Opposites Together	I Push Likenesses Apart
I am Balanced	I am Complementary
I am Each of These Things	I am All of These Things

I am Yin, I am Yang

Hui Chu Ying's Exhibit
at the Colburn Gallery
Lauri Robinson

CPU (i8086) Pass
ROM Module Pass
DMA Timer   Pass
DMA Control Pass

```
      Interrupts  Pass
      RT Clock    Pass
      Fixed Disk  Not Present
      Floppy (A:) Ready
Primary Boot-strap . . .
A>/SCRNSAVE
A>B:
B>A:WP
```

```
This is the age of computers. That's what they keep say-
ing. People walk in here looking skeptical at first, then
surprised. How can this be made by a computer, many of
them wonder aloud. I smirk to myself; they are so ignor-
ant. Computers can do anything nowadays. I am a beautiful
example of one of the many artistic uses of a computer.
Of course, I am not actually made by the computer; I am a
silkscreen image of the computer-generated ideas on the
wall to my left. I am of course much more striking than
these images, more versatile as well. Every day my
squares are moved to form a new design. The possibilities
are infinite; well, there is probably a program to figure
out the exact number, but you get the idea. Today I feel
great. My pattern is quite dynamic with majestic colors,
green and gold, which make me feel noble. The gold X
crossing my chest is like some sort of royal sash, and
the gold diamond on the right reminds me of a crown. Yes
today I am royalty; tomorrow who knows.
A>SAVE
B>EXIT
```

WRITING 4.

Again take some time to view or participate in an artwork or performance with which you are not totally familiar. Be inquisitive. Use all
your senses to take in information. Look at elements of rhythm, intensity, harmony, discord. Record your insights and observations in your
journal. Really listen to the work.

Using words, find a voice for the artwork. Would this experience be
a poem? Would it speak in sentences? Would there be color in the
words? Shapes? Ask yourself the same questions as those proposed in
Writing 3, but craft an expressive written work that doesn't necessarily
document the original artwork but attempts to replicate the feeling, effect, or power of the original piece, only this time through your chosen
and crafted verbal/written medium.

Form from Ideas

Art and ideas—art is ideas. The idea, the concept, is the most important element in the making of art. It is the seed from which the

artwork begins to take form. To be successful a strong idea must be partnered with appropriate media, skill, and spirit. Artistic problems — whether visual, musical, physical — find their roots in ideas, but each individual artist solves these sometimes universal problems in very personal ways.

Artists may address similar issues but use different imagery, materials, and scale to attempt to convey their message. The issues of war and conflict, for example, have been successfully and powerfully addressed by many artists. The final artistic pieces, however, have rarely been at all similar. Picasso's *Guernica* — a large, mostly black and white painting that uses human and animal figures with powerful and emotive expressions — portrays a strong statement about war and suffering in general but was painted in response to a specific bombing incident during the Spanish Civil War. It addresses historical and political issues of fascism, mechanism, and war that are at once specific and universal.

Maya Ying Lin's Vietnam Veterans Memorial in Washington, DC is another piece that addresses similar issues. Here the artist has made quite different choices concerning imagery, materials, scale, and placement. Her vision, historical context, and media, provide a differing perspective on a universal issue. The readings at the end of this chapter expand on the historical and artistic contexts of both Picasso's and Maya Ying Lin's pieces.

These two pieces — Picasso's *Guernica* (Figure 5.7) and Maya Ying Lin's Vietnam Veterans Memorial (Figure 5.8) — are artistic functions of differing times, issues, and aesthetics. One was commissioned, the other a competition winner; one executed by a well-known mature artist, the other designed by a young artist while still a student. One was painted on canvas, the other carved in stone. Both artists have attempted to use a language of shapes, lines, color, scale, and media to communicate information to the viewer. The viewer will also bring his or her own experience and interpretations to the piece.

Figure 5.7   *Guernica* by Pablo Picasso, 1937.

Figure 5.8   The Vietnam Veterans Memorial by Maya Ying Lin, 1982.

If you look at a piece of artwork from a historical point of view, you look beyond the specifics of colors and canvas to the artistic history, political climate, personal issues, and other factors that affected the imagery, information, and processes by which the work was made. This enriches the work, but a successful work of art has the power to affect people even if the viewers are not educated about the specifics of the piece. The critical consensus holds that both *Guernica* and the Vietnam Veterans War Memorial are successful.

SUGGESTION FOR RESEARCH

A Look at *Guernica* and the Vietnam Veterans War Memorial

This research and writing assignment will involve you in looking at human and artistic issues as an artist, historian, and critic. There is a lot of information out there on these artworks, and the process of uncovering it can in itself be invigorating.

In small groups, take a look at these two works—*Guernica* and the Vietnam Veterans Memorial. It would be most powerful to view them in person, but since they are in Spain and Washington, DC, respectively, you may have to compare them through photographs or videos. Ask yourself a number of questions. What do you think the artists were attempting to do? What was the historical context of the work? Why did they choose their materials? Why did they make specific site and scale decisions? What qualities do you believe they attempted to portray? Were they successful? What was the initial public response to their pieces? Has that response changed? What is your response? What is the difference between actually experiencing the work and experiencing only the reproductions? Keep notes and sketches while you look at the works. Read about the works, look at photos, visit them if you can, and talk to people who have seen the works or have some connection with them. Take time and freewrite about each. Discuss ideas and opinions within your group.

As a group you can decide on an approach that seems most interesting. For example, each person in the group might approach the writing from a different perspective. What questions would the studio artist need to ask to create this work? How would you attempt to generate ideas regarding appropriate materials, site, scale, and imagery to accomplish the defined task? You might approach the piece from the perspective of an art historian. What larger political and artistic places does the piece hold in a social context? As a critic, you might analyze the elements of the artwork and its overall success at the time of its creation and as time passes. You might choose to try on the problem and propose your own solution using your researched information and rationales. Depending on the size of your group, you may choose to compare the two works of art or to explore one work in depth. You might choose to expand this exercise and compare other war pieces in literature, music, or theatre. It might be interesting to share your final works in written form and in discussions, panels, or debates.

Our Visual and Verbal Worlds

As we look around it becomes clear that our visual and verbal worlds have inextricable and complex connections. Our minds think and see in pictures, but seem to concretize, to generate alternatives and sequences, through writing and words. We take in information visually and through all our senses. We also have the ability to communicate through these modes. It is said that a fine writer paints with words and, similarly, that a strong picture is worth a thousand words. The dance between these exploring and expressive methods of communication is often overlooked, underrated, and thus underused because of habit or the familiar use of one approach. This often happens because of the fear of an unfamiliar or untested approach.

Combining languages has a synergistic effect; that is, the resulting experience is greater than the sum of the individual parts. If you encourage yourself to investigate ideas through the limitless combinations of available languages, you can expand your own verbal, visual, and sensory vocabularies. You can use these many paths to explore unfamiliar territories and perhaps to push the boundaries of the predictable toward the profound. You can bring magic and insight to that which seemed common. This process of exploration, or finding the right voice and getting to the heart of an idea, is the core of creative thought and work. It is an eye-opening, often surprising, and invigorating experience that promises a lively and provocative approach to living.

READINGS

Eberhard Fisch
A STUDY OF PICASSO'S *GUERNICA*

Eberhard Fisch's Guernica by Picasso: A Study of the Picture
and Its Context *is one of several book-length studies of Picasso's
monumental painting. In his book Fisch (b. 1936) analyzes the composition and the pictorial elements of* Guernica. *He also examines
the work in the context of earlier paintings by Peter Paul Rubens,
William Blake, Francisco Goya, Salvador Dalí and others.*

THE SPANISH CIVIL WAR AND THE
BOMBARDMENT OF GUERNICA

In the year 1930, Spain was an economically retarded agrarian state
ruled over by a king, but actually governed by rich landowners, by the
army, and by the church. In 1931, the monarchy was replaced by a
socialist republic, which openly tried to combat the influence of the army
and the church. There were attempts at agrarian reforms as well as an
extensive school reform aimed at abolishing the church's monopoly on
education. Widespread discontent with such measures resulted in a
swing to the right and a nationalist victory in the 1934 elections, which
were followed by a general strike and the rebellion of the miners in the
province of Asturias. The army, commanded by General Franco, suppressed the revolt violently. About two thousand people were killed;
thirty thousand miners were imprisoned. Months of oppression followed.

In February 1936, elections led to the "Popular Front" government,
in which republicans, socialists, communists, and even anarchists formed
a coalition. The still-imprisoned Asturian miners were finally released.
But a wave of about three hundred strikes then followed, crippling
Spanish industry. The immense poverty and the long pent-up rage led
to revolts and outbreaks of looting in which churches and abbeys were
burned down. To restore order, the government felt impelled to restrict
civil liberties, such as the freedom of the press.

On 17 July 1936, a group of generals in Spanish Morocco used the
assassination of a conservative member of parliament as a pretext for
proclaiming the overthrow of the government. When the rightist rebellion also spread to the motherland, the republican government defended
the country with loyal troops and with the massive support of the trade
unions. Within a few days, all of Spain was engulfed in civil war.

The industrial areas and the capital, Madrid, sided with the republicans. The marines and the air force dismissed their officers and did not
take part in the putsch, so that the insurgent generals were unable to
leave North Africa with their troops. To escape from this predicament,
Franco asked Hitler and Mussolini for support, and they at once put

planes, ships, and soldiers at his disposal. The republican government's call for help remained unheeded by France and Great Britain, who, afraid of a new world war, pursued a policy of nonintervention. But the Soviet Union did respond, supplying the Spanish Republic with arms and money. Soviet workers even had to sacrifice one-half percent of their monthly wages to show their solidarity with the Popular Front in Spain. Volunteers from many countries went to Spain to fight for their political ideals. In the autumn of 1936, Franco's nationalists controlled practically half of Spanish territory and besieged Madrid. On 29 September 1936, General Franco was appointed head of state by the military junta. Step by step he established a military dictatorship in the parts of Spain that were occupied by the nationalist troops. Members of the German armed forces, the so-called Condor Legion headed by Lieutenant General Sperrle, cooperated with the junta. The German forces consisted of fighter planes, a bomber squadron, and a squadron of reconnaissance planes, and were assisted by three heavy antiaircraft units, intelligence units, infantry regiments, marines, and four tank divisions. This military operation was at first kept secret in Germany; later the costs were officially placed at 381 million reichsmarks.

On 26 April 1937, the Condor Legion flew a major attack against the undefended Basque town of Guernica and destroyed it completely: this ranks as one of the most blatant acts of unmitigated cruelty in the history of mankind.

On 29 September 1938, Germany, Italy, Great Britain, and France came to an agreement in Munich, which was widely, but erroneously, regarded as an important step toward keeping the peace in Europe. It was this concession that finally shattered the Spanish Republic's hopes of receiving support. On 28 March 1939, Franco's troops were able to march into Madrid practically unopposed. The fierce, three-year struggle for power in Spain had now come to an end. On 1 September 1939, World War II broke out.

PICASSO'S COMMISSION

On 24 May 1937, a world exhibition was opened in Paris. Although not very large, the Spanish pavilion attracted attention on account of its ultra-modern style. The chief architect was José Luis Sert, who had spent some time working in Paris with Le Corbusier. Sert and the poet Juan Larrea were in charge of the Spanish information bureau. At the beginning of 1937, they arranged for Picasso to be given the commission for a large mural, for which the artist was supposed to be receiving the respectable sum of 150,000 francs. To this very day, it is still a moot point whether Picasso remained the legal owner of the painting or not. At all events, the mural was meant to be the chief attraction in the entrance hall, in the center of which there stood a mercury fountain by Alexander Calder.

There were several reasons for Picasso being given the commission. The main ones were:

- In the spring of 1936, a group of young Spanish painters and poets calling themselves "Friends of the New Arts" had organized a big Picasso exhibition which had traveled to various cities in Spain (Barcelona, Madrid, and Bilbao). Picasso himself had not attended it: he had had a friend, the poet Eluard, speak for him at the opening ceremony.
- On 29 November 1936, Picasso had been offered the post of honorary director of the Prado Museum in Madrid, which he did not hesitate to accept.
- In those years, Picasso (according to an estimate of the Spanish Aid Fund) contributed about 400,000 francs in order to ease the poverty in his native country, as well as giving money to compatriots in need.
- Since January 1937, Picasso had been working on eighteen etchings, which he later published under the title *Dream and Lie of Franco*. These etchings, the proceeds of which were also to benefit the country of his birth, were a passionate indictment of Franco.
- Thus, Picasso had definitely taken the side of the Spanish Republic. Of course, Picasso's being awarded the commission was undoubtedly also due to the fact that he was the most famous Spanish painter and that he lived in Paris.

As the flat in the rue de la Boétie was too small for a mural of such monumental dimensions as he had in mind (11 feet 5½ inches × 25 feet 5¾ inches or 350 × 777 centimeters), Picasso rented two stories in a seventeenth-century building, which had seen more splendid days, situated in the rue des Grands-Augustins near the Seine. In the months that followed, he painted still lifes and portraits of his two mistresses, Marie-Thérèse Walter and Dora Maar. However, it would not be quite accurate to say that Picasso did not do any work on the enormous task that was ahead of him. In mid-February he was preoccupied with a picture of an extremely wide oblong format that probably had something to do with the commission. In the Musée Picasso in Paris, there is a series of twelve preliminary drawings Picasso made for his commissioned work with the quite unpolitical theme "Painter and His Model."[1] Their remoteness from the theme of the commissioned work may be surprising, but from other commissions it can be seen that Picasso was not in the habit of approaching his task with such external relationships in mind.

On 28 April 1937, the news of the bomb attack reached France. When Picasso heard about it, he was infuriated; on the other hand, his inspiration was affected to the utmost. On 1 May 1937, he started on the preliminary drawings for *Guernica*. . . .

The mural was probably completed on 4 June[2] and in mid-June erected in the still unfinished Spanish pavilion. Those who had commissioned the painting had obviously been thinking of a more realistic picture, that would make a passionate and unambiguous appeal to the masses, and they were immensely disappointed. At first, the mural was to be removed again. It was only because a decent replacement for the mural was, of course, not to be found and because of Picasso's artistic reputation that *Guernica* was allowed to remain in the Spanish pavilion to the end of the exhibition.

PICASSO'S ARTISTIC AND PRIVATE SITUATION

In 1924, the young poet and friend of Picasso's, André Breton—inspired by Sigmund Freud's psychoanalytical discoveries—published the first surrealist manifesto, a programmatic impulse that had a galvanizing effect on a host of young poets and artists. In 1925, the first surrealist exhibition was held in Paris and showed pictures by Arp, Chirico, Ernst, Klee, Miró, and Picasso. Picasso himself never became a member of the surrealist group because he was too much of an individualist; in those years, however, he gave up his neoclassical style for the time being and vehemently devoted himself to the unexplored land of the unconscious. He painted insectlike, demonic figures. Discovering the human being as an animal, as a monster, and as a technical construction, he began to shift eyes, mouths, breasts, arms, and so forth, in order to create new effects. To the inexperienced layman, such contorted forms may well appear to be a destruction of the human figure and, hence, an insult to man's dignity. For the artist, however, such techniques fulfill quite a different purpose. In modern art especially, real objects must not be confused with their visual representations in a work of art, since the latter only nave meaning within the unique context of the work of art and are governed by its logic alone. Picasso experimented with forms, colors, and meanings in order to reveal what people had never perceived before and to share his novel insights with those who looked at his pictures. Some of these surrealistic paintings can be compared to nightmares, but one must not forget that dreams, too, bear the stamp of reality.

The changes that affected Picasso's artistry were accompanied by changes in his private life. His marriage with Olga Koklowa, a Russian ballet dancer of noble birth, was slowly disintegrating, though in 1921 a son, named Paolo, had been born. Olga's primary interests were attending social functions and similar kinds of amusement, whereas Picasso's life revolved only around his artistic work. His quarrels with Olga became increasingly bitter, especially when, in 1927, Picasso developed a relationship with the young, blond-haired Marie-Thérèse Walter, whom he often visited and painted. In many pictures she is portrayed as a gentle woman, radiant with happiness. In 1935, Olga left Picasso, taking Paolo with her. At first, Picasso apparently intended to get a divorce.

But since Spain did not recognize divorces and Picasso did not want to become a French citizen, the outcome of it was merely an informal separation. Picasso was fifty-four years old at the time.

In 1936, he became acquainted with another woman, Dora Maar (Markowitch), an intelligent young photographer of aristocratic appearance. In contrast to Marie-Thérèse Walter, she had dark hair. Her father was a Yugoslav architect married to a French lady. For several years, the family had lived in Argentina, where Dora Maar had learned to speak Spanish; thus, she was able to talk to Picasso in his mother tongue. The numerous pictures of her reveal that she was an earnest, often melancholy and tearful woman. For many years, she shared the role of being Picasso's mistress with Marie-Thérèse Walter, who had given birth to a daughter in 1935. The baby was christened María de la Concepción, "Maya" for short.

Those years were overshadowed by economic crises and increasingly severe political tensions. In 1933, the National Socialists took over in Germany, and in 1936, the Spanish Civil War broke out, splitting Picasso's native land into two parts and wreaking devastation. The threat of a second world war loomed.

"In the late twenties Picasso became disillusioned with the *beau monde*. He retreated into himself. During the thirties his work was mostly introspective. (*Guernica*, as we shall see later, is a highly introspective work and only the political uses to which it was rightly put have confused people about this.) The imagery of this period is Spanish, mythological, and ritualistic. Its symbols are the bull, the horse, the woman, and the Minotaur."[3]

This statement shows how Picasso, at the beginning of the thirties, gradually withdrew into himself, turning aside from his social activities to retreat into a kind of mental seclusion. He invented a very private artistic world and language, an individual mythology, in which he employed the motifs of the woman, the bull, the horse, and the minotaur as actors. But the assumption that he did not care about the political changes of his time can be refuted by careful study of his work.

From 1925 onward, many of Picasso's pictures depicted women: some of these—many portraying Marie-Thérèse Walter—are full of peace and color; others show women that appear to be wild, grotesque, and demonic. These latter works can often be proved to be connected with his jealous wife, Olga. In those years, the surrealists liked to talk about the praying mantis, an insect which often eats up its male partner during the sexual act. This seems to have exerted a strong influence on Picasso. Picasso was practically spellbound by the juxtaposition of contrasting elements, exemplified for him by the surrealist symbol of the minotaur, a combination of bull and man. In Picasso's work, the minotaur has nothing to do with its model in Greek mythology; here it must be regarded as a varying synthesis of humanity and primitive, uncivilized bestiality.

Picasso's immense artistic body of work on the motifs of woman, the minotaur, and the bullfight is extremely rich in meaning and is worth comparing to his more numerous cubist compositions. In both these spheres, his imagery runs through a multitude of variations. In both types of work, it can be said that the motifs and meanings are of less importance, and the artistic and compositional elements are given priority. The consequence is that the artistic quality is greatly enhanced and the message is given more depth, so that the semantic content of each picture is complex and takes on a certain degree of ambiguity.

GUERNICA — A MONUMENT

Covering more than 292 square feet (roughly 27 square meters), *Guernica* is one of Picasso's largest pictures. The observer usually sees only relatively small reproductions of the picture, which, of course, enormously reduces the effect. The original has gigantic proportions: its larger-than-life figures add to the total impact. That the artistic quality of *Guernica* is of equal stature is beyond dispute. Once the message of the picture has been made comprehensible to a larger public, *Guernica* will be regarded as Picasso's masterpiece, as the culmination of his life's work: he was fifty-five when he painted the picture.

The twentieth century has been shaped by wars. Two world wars and innumerable smaller wars and conflicts, the scope of which is still unpredictable, have completely changed the face of the earth. Like many other painters, Picasso took up the theme of this century — war — and painted a "war picture" that has often been called the most important picture of this century. In point of fact, it is the most important *anti*-war picture in the history of art.

Guernica is a monument in the widest sense of the word. The bombing of the Basque town of Guernica with its seven thousand or so inhabitants would now be almost forgotten if it were not for the picture; the significance of the raid would have paled before the horrors of World War II, which it foreshadowed. Picasso's picture reminds mankind of one of the first acts of modern "total war" waged against a defenseless population.

Earlier war pictures often glorified war and victory. In *Guernica* there is no victory. There is only suffering.

NOTES

[1] Cf. Werner Spies, ed., *Pablo Picasso — Werke aus der Sammlung Marina Picasso* (Munich: Prestel Verlag, 1981), pp. 21–33.

[2] Anthony Blunt, *Picasso's "Guernica"* (London: Oxford University Press, 1969): "The final state can be dated to about 4 June on the basis of two drawings for the soldier's head. The first, dated 3 June, shows the head facing downwards, as it had been in all the earlier stages. The second shows it in its final form, with the mouth gaping towards the sky" (p. 60).

[3] John Berger, *The Success and Failure of Picasso* (Harmondsworth, England: Penguin Books, 1965), p. 102.

OPTIONS FOR WRITING

1. Write a proposal for a monument whose reference is a recent or important conflict or event. Why must it be made? Describe its purpose, its audience, its placement, its materials, and so on.

2. Look at the plate of *Guernica*. See the original or a number of prints, if possible; remember it is a vast mural. Describe your responses to this work.

3. Look at books on Picasso. Look at slides, prints, or actual work, if possible. Fisch refers to a "very private artistic work and language" that Picasso invented. Expand on this idea.

4. "In Guernica there is no victory. There is only suffering." Can you make an argument for this statement?

5. Look at the plate of *Guernica*, and look at the original or various prints, if possible. Using words, try to speak for the work. Try to go beyond description to the essence of the power of the piece. Can you capture and project the imagery, color, rhythm, and emotion of the work?

6. Picasso's life was long and his work varied. Read other articles on or by Picasso. Write him a letter regarding your thoughts and questions.

Brent Ashabranner
THE VISION OF MAYA YING LIN

Brent Ashabranner has written widely on American history and complex social issues. His books include The New Americans: Changing Patterns in U.S. Immigration, To Live in Two Worlds: American Indian Youth Today, *and* Dark Harvest: Migrant Farmworkers in America. *Ashabranner spent a number of years working as an education advisor in developing countries for the Agency for International Development (AID). He was director of Peace Corps programs in Nigeria and India and later was deputy director of the Peace Corps in Washington, DC. Ashabranner lives in Williamsburg, Virginia, where he devotes all of his time to writing.*

The memorial had been authorized by Congress "in honor and recognition of the men and women of the Armed Forces of the United States who served in the Vietnam War." The law, however, said not a word about what the memorial should be or what it should look like. That was left up to the Vietnam Veterans Memorial Fund, but the law did state that the memorial design and plans would have to be approved by the Secretary of the Interior, the Commission of Fine Arts, and the National Capital Planning Commission.

What would the memorial be? What should it look like? Who would design it? Scruggs, Doubek, and Wheeler didn't know, but they were determined that the memorial should help bring closer together a nation still bitterly divided by the Vietnam War. It couldn't be something like the Marine Corps Memorial showing American troops planting a flag on enemy soil at Iwo Jima. It couldn't be a giant dove with an olive branch of peace in its beak. It had to sooth passions, not stir them up. But there was one thing Jan Scruggs insisted on: the memorial, whatever it turned out to be, would have to show the name of every man and woman killed or missing in the war.

The answer, they decided, was to hold a national design competition open to all Americans. The winning design would receive a prize of $20,000, but the real prize would be the winner's knowledge that the memorial would become a part of American history on the Mall in Washington, D.C. Although fund raising was only well started at this point, the choosing of a memorial design could not be delayed if the memorial was to be built by Veterans Day, 1982. H. Ross Perot contributed the $160,000 necessary to hold the competition, and a panel of distinguished architects, landscape architects, sculptors, and design specialists was chosen to decide the winner.

Announcement of the competition in October, 1980, brought an astonishing response. The Vietnam Veterans Memorial Fund received over five thousand inquiries. They came from every state in the nation and from every field of design; as expected, architects and sculptors were particularly interested. Everyone who inquired received a booklet explaining the criteria. Among the most important: the memorial could not make a political statement about the war; it must contain the names of all persons killed or missing in action in the war; it must be in harmony with its location on the Mall.

A total of 2,573 individuals and teams registered for the competition. They were sent photographs of the memorial site, maps of the area around the site and of the entire Mall, and other technical design information. The competitors had three months to prepare their designs, which had to be received by March 31, 1981.

Of the 2,573 registrants, 1,421 submitted designs, a record number for such a design competition. When the designs were spread out for jury selection, they filled a large airplane hangar. The jury's task was to select the design which, in their judgment, was the best in meeting these criteria:

- a design that honored the memory of those Americans who served and died in the Vietnam War.
- a design of high artistic merit.
- a design which would be harmonious with its site, including visual harmony with the Lincoln Memorial and the Washington Monument.
- a design that could take its place in the "historic continuity" of America's national art.

- a design that would be buildable, durable, and not too hard to maintain.

The designs were displayed without any indication of the designer's name so that they could be judged anonymously, on their design merits alone. The jury spent one week reviewing all the designs in the airplane hangar. On May 1 it made its report to the Vietnam Veterans Memorial Fund: the experts declared Entry Number 1,026 the winner. The report called it "the finest and most appropriate" of all submitted and said it was "superbly harmonious" with the site on the Mall. Remarking upon the "simple and forthright" materials needed to build the winning entry, the report concludes:

> This memorial with its wall of names, becomes a place of quiet reflection, and a tribute to those who served their nation in difficult times. All who come here can find it a place of healing. This will be a quiet memorial, one that achieves an excellent relationship with both the Lincoln Memorial or Washington Monument, and relates the visitor to them. It is uniquely horizontal, entering the earth rather than piercing the sky.
>
> This is very much a memorial of our own times, one that could not have been achieved in another time and place. The designer has created an eloquent place where the simple meeting of earth, sky and remembered names contain messages for all who will know this place.

The eight jurors signed their names to the report, a unanimous decision.

When the name of the winner was revealed, the art and architecture worlds were stunned. It was not the name of a nationally famous architect or sculptor, as most people had been sure it would be. The creator of Entry Number 1,026 was a twenty-one-year-old student at Yale University. Her name—unknown as yet in any field of art or architecture—was Maya Ying Lin.

How could this be? How could an undergraduate student win one of the most important design competitions ever held? How could she beat out some of the top names in American art and architecture? Who was Maya Ying Lin?

The answer to that question provided some of the other answers, at least in part. Maya Lin, reporters soon discovered, was a Chinese-American girl who had been born and raised in the small midwestern city of Athens, Ohio. Her father, Henry Huan Lin, was a ceramicist of considerable reputation and dean of fine arts at Ohio University in Athens. Her mother, Julia C. Lin, was a poet and professor of Oriental and English literature. Maya Lin's parents were born to culturally prominent families in China. When the Communists came to power in China in the 1940s, Henry and Julia Lin left the country and in time made their way to the United States.

Maya Lin grew up in an environment of art and literature. She was interested in sculpture and made both small and large sculptural figures, one cast in bronze. She learned silversmithing and made jewelry. She was surrounded by books and read a great deal, especially fantasies such as *The Hobbit* and *Lord of the Rings*.

But she also found time to work at McDonald's. "It was about the only way to make money in the summer," she said.

A covaledictorian at high school graduation, Maya Lin went to Yale without a clear notion of what she wanted to study and eventually decided to major in Yale's undergraduate program in architecture. During her junior year she studied in Europe and found herself increasingly interested in cemetery architecture. "In Europe there's very little space, so graveyards are used as parks," she said. "Cemeteries are cities of the dead in European countries, but they are also living gardens."

In France, Maya Lin was deeply moved by the war memorial to those who died in the Somme offensive in 1916 during World War I. The great arch by architect Sir Edwin Lutyens is considered one of the world's most outstanding war memorials.

Back at Yale for her senior year, Maya Lin enrolled in Professor Andrus Burr's course in funerary (burial) architecture. The Vietnam Veterans Memorial competition had recently been announced, and although the memorial would be a cenotaph—a monument in honor of persons buried someplace else—Professor Burr thought that having his students prepare a design of the memorial would be a worthwhile course assignment.

Surely, no classroom exercise ever had such spectacular results.

After receiving the assignment, Maya Lin and two of her classmates decided to make the day's journey from New Haven, Connecticut, to Washington to look at the site where the memorial would be built. On the day of their visit, Maya Lin remembers, Constitution Gardens was awash with a late November sun; the park was full of light, alive with joggers and people walking beside the lake.

"It was while I was at the site that I designed it," Maya Lin said later in an interview about the memorial with *Washington Post* writer Phil McCombs. "I just sort of visualized it. It just popped into my head. Some people were playing Frisbee. It was a beautiful park. I didn't want to destroy a living park. You use the landscape. You don't fight with it. You absorb the landscape. . . . When I looked at the site I just knew I wanted something horizontal that took you in, that made you feel safe within the park, yet at the same time reminded you of the dead. So I just imagined opening up the earth. . . ."

When Maya Lin returned to Yale, she made a clay model of the vision that had come to her in Constitution Gardens. She showed it to Professor Burr; he liked her conception and encouraged her to enter the memorial competition. She put her design on paper, a task that took six weeks, and mailed it to Washington barely in time to meet the March 31 deadline.

A month and a day later, Maya Lin was attending class. Her roommate slipped into the classroom and handed her a note. Washington was calling and would call back in fifteen minutes. Maya Lin hurried to her room. The call came. She had won the memorial competition.

OPTIONS FOR WRITING

1. Maya Lin was a student in a funerary architecture class when she entered and won the Vietnam Veterans Memorial competition. Are you involved with any courses whose content, issues, or ideas deserve a monument? Write a proposal describing such a monument, its purpose, and your solution.

2. If you have had the opportunity to visit the Vietnam Veterans Memorial, describe the experience. If there is a monument close to your home, visit it and describe the experience. If possible, compare the experiences.

3. What are memorials? What are their purposes? Are they necessary? Discuss these ideas.

4. Maya Lin traveled to Washington to experience the site where the memorial was to be placed. She said it was there that she designed it. Explore your surroundings. Locate a site that interests you. Is it a site for a monument? What kind? What scale or materials? Discuss the appropriateness of your site for a specific monument.

5. Imagine that you are one of the many names on the granite wall of the Vietnam Memorial. Write a letter to Maya Lin regarding your experience of this monument.

Anne Truit
DAYBOOK: THE JOURNAL OF AN ARTIST

Anne Truit was born in Baltimore, Maryland, in 1921. She received her Bachelor of Arts degree from Bryn Mawr College and had her first one-person exhibit at Andre Emnerich Gallery in New York in 1963. Her paintings, sculptures, and drawings have won international praise, and she has had a number of retrospective exhibitions at the Whitney museum in New York and the Corcoran Gallery in Washington, DC. The following journal selections were written in a seven-year period during which Anne Truit was determined to come to terms with the artist in herself. As you read these passages, you might ask yourself some questions. Can a journal help one explore ideas in our time? Do these snippets of thought help to paint a picture of this artist? Do the dilemmas and ideas explored seem relevant at all to your own life? Do you find any repeated themes or questions?

14 July

Three sculptures are finished, small ones: *Parva* I, II, and III. And I have now started a series of drawings I am calling *Stone South*. These are pencil and white paint, very spare: attempts to catch the threshold of consciousness, the point at which the abstract nature of events becomes perceptible. This comes down to the placement of interval: lines meeting and not meeting as close as the force of their lengths will allow; a metaphor for the virtually imperceptible ways in which our lives turn, critical turns of change determined by interval.

I have settled into the most comfortable routine I have ever known in my working life. I wake very early and, after a quiet period, have my breakfast in my room: cereal, fruit, nuts, the remainder of my luncheon Thermos of milk and coffee. Then I write in my notebook in bed. By this time, the sun is well up and the pine trees waft delicious smells into my room. My whole body sings with the knowledge that nothing is expected of me except what I expect of myself. I dress, do my few room chores, walk to the mansion to pick up my lunch box (a sandwich, double fruit, double salad — often a whole head of new lettuce) and Thermos of milk, and walk down the winding road to my Stone South studio.

At noon, I stop working, walk up through the meadow to West House, have a reading lunch at my desk, and nap. By 2:30 or so I am back in the studio. Late in the afternoon, I return to my room, have a hot bath, and dress for dinner. It is heavenly to work until I am tired, knowing that the evening will be effortless. Dinner is a peaceful pleasure. Afterward I usually return to my solitude, happy to have been in good company, happy to leave it. I read, or write letters, have another hot bath in the semidarkness of my room, and sink quietly to sleep.

31 July

A group of resident poets read their work last night in the living room of West House. They read in sequence, a man's voice, a woman's voice, each a poem, sometimes quietly repeated until it had settled into us all.

The pain of poets seems to me unmitigated. They are denied the physical activity of studio work, which in itself makes a supportive context for thought and feeling. In my twenties, when I was writing poetry steadily, I heard words at a high pitch. On the deep, full notes of three-dimensional form, demanding for its realization the physical commitment of my whole body, I floated into spaciousness. Using all my faculties, I could plumb deeper, without sinking forever.

Poetry was drawn out of my life, pulled out into lines. Sculpture is not. The works stand as I stand; they keep me company. I realize this clearly here because I miss them. I brought only table sculptures with me. In making my work, I make what comforts me and is home for me.

I expanded into love with the discipline of sculpture. Although my intellectual reason for abandoning writing for sculpture in 1948 was that I found myself uninterested in the sequence of events in time, I think now that it was this love that tipped the balance. Artists have no choice but to express their lives. They have only, and that not always, a choice of process. This process does not change the essential content of their work in art, which *can* only be their life. But in my own case the fact that I have to use my whole body in making my work seems to disperse my intensity in a way that suits me.

6 August

In skirting the role of the artist, I now begin to think that I have made too wide a curve, that I have deprived myself of a certain strength. Indeed, I am not sure that I can grow as an artist until I can bring myself to accept that I am one. This was not true, I think, before last winter. I was underground until the two retrospective exhibits of my work. Part of my intense discomfort this past year has been that I was pried out of my place there. I was attached to my secret burrow, which now begins to feel a little stale.

And also egotistic, confined, even imprisoning. I begin to see that by clinging to this position I was limiting what I had to handle in the world to what I could rationalize. As long as I stayed within my own definition of myself, I could control what I admitted into that definition. By insisting that I was "just me," I held myself aloof. Let others claim to be artists, I said to myself, holding my life separate and unique, beyond all definition but my own.

The course of events in my life has blasted this fortification, as it had blasted another in Japan. The fact of financial insecurity since my divorce in 1971, and the momentum of my own work and my efforts to be responsible for it, have thrown me into the open.

The open being: I am an artist. Even to write it makes me feel deeply uneasy. I am, I feel, not good enough to be an artist. And this leads me to wonder whether my distaste for the inflated social definition of the artist is not an inverse reflection of secret pride. Have I haughtily rejected the inflation on the outside while entertaining it on the inside? In my passion for learning how to make true for others what I felt to be true for myself (and I cannot remember, except very, very early on, ever not having had this passion), I think I may have fallen into idolatry of those who were able to communicate this way. Artists. So to think myself an artist was self-idolatry.

In a clear wind of the company of artists this summer, I am greatly disarmed. We are artists because we are ourselves.

18 September

I did not see a painting of high quality until I was thirteen. One hot afternoon, my father took my sisters and me to a friend's house to swim. We were led through a wide central hall at the end of which a screen door opened out onto a sunny lawn bordering a broad river. On the left of this door hung a small painting, the head of a girl in brilliant, clear colors. I gazed, transfixed. I remember swiftly calculating whether it would be rude to ask about it. I felt shy to thrust my curiosity forward, but I was blocking the way as I stood in front of it and I finally found it less awkward to ask who had made it. "Renoir," was the answer, "a French painter." Pressed by our small group, I moved on, but I have remembered the radiance of that little painting ever since, along with the dazzling insight that such beauty could be *made*.

Now, when I am called upon to look critically at the work of another artist, I watch for this response—the spontaneous rise of my whole being.

This instantaneous recognition of quality has been very, very rare in my experience with artists I am called upon to gauge, and in these modest circumstances I make it a habit to start by coming to respectful attention. It is such an act of courage to put pencil to paper that I begin by honoring the artist's intention.

Usually the work falls into a range I have to examine with my mind, in the light of what I know about the history of art and about its techniques. If the work is the result of honest effort, I acknowledge its validity but I look for the skill and talent that set apart potentially significant art. I try to discern the range of the artist's gift. When this range coincides with contemporary artistic concerns, the work has cogency in an historical context. This seems to me to be a matter of luck. A perfectly articulated range of sensibility may be just plain irrelevant to the problems confronting artists ambitious to make work of the highest quality in this historical sense. The degree to which an artist addresses these problems usually indicates the degree of his or her ambition. There is a sort of "feel" that marks relevant art. To some extent it can be learned, and here I find that young artists can badly deceive themselves: They can fall into using intelligence the wrong way; they can fail to realize that the purpose of scanning contemporary art is to use its articulations for the purer realization of their own work. As a carpenter might reach out for a newly invented saw, the work of other artists may suggest techniques or even solutions. But the essential struggle is private and bears no relation to anyone else's. It is of necessity a solitary and lonely endeavor to explore one's own sensibility, to discover how it works and to implement honestly its manifestations.

It is ultimately character that underwrites art. The quality of art can only reflect the quality and range of a person's sensitivity, intellect, perception, and experience. If I find an artist homing in on himself or herself, I bring maximum warmth to bear, knowing full well that the process is painful and, lonely as it is, susceptible to encouragement. Companionship helps. And the pleasure of being with younger or less experienced artists can be intense—the delight of watching people grow into themselves, becoming more than they have known that they are.

Sometimes artists use their work for ends that have nothing to do with art, placing it rather in the service of their ambitions for themselves in the world. This forces their higher parts to serve their lower parts in a sad inversion of values. And is, in art perhaps more than in any other profession, self-defeating. Purity of aspiration seems virtually prerequisite to genuine inspiration.

7 January

Of all the Ten Commandments, "Thou shalt not murder" always seemed to me the one I would have to worry least about, until I got old enough to see that there are many different kinds of death, not all of them physical. There are murders as subtle as a turned eye. Dante was inspired to install Satan in ice, cold indifference being so common a form of evil.

10 January

There is an appalling amount of mechanical work in the artist's life: lists of works with dimensions, prices, owners, provenances; lists of exhibitions with dates and places; bibliographical material; lists of supplies bought, storage facilities used. Records pile on records. This tedious, detailed work, which steadily increases if the artist exhibits to any extent, had been something of a surprise to me. It is all very well to be entranced by working in the studio, but that has to be backed up by the common sense and industry required to run a small business. In trying to gauge the capacity of young artists to achieve their ambition, I always look to see whether they seem to have this ability to organize their lives into an order that will not only set their hands free in the studio but also meet the demands their work will make upon them when it leaves the studio. The "enemies of promise," in Cyril Connolly's phrase, are subtle, guileful, and resourceful. Talent is mysterious, but the qualities that guard, foster, and direct it are not unlike those of a good quartermaster.

11 January

An exhibit that is coming along well is cheerful. Yesterday John Gossage and Renato Danese, the co-curators of the Baltimore Museum of Art exhibit, and I strode around the museum as if on our native heath, making decisions together, with the zest of experience. This light-heartedness in no way denies our knowledge that much could go wrong before our concept of the exhibit becomes real.

The point at which decision is brought to bear on process is that at which two opposing forces meet and rebound, leaving an interval in which a third force can act. The trick of acting is to catch this moment. When it all happens well, a happy feeling of swinging from event to event results, a sort of gymnastic pleasure. Yesterday Renato thought an exhibition room should be unified by pigeon gray; John thought the photographs would line up into nonentity in such a flat environment. They turned to me. I suggested a third solution incorporating both insights; we all rose to it and took the wave of decision as one.

It was Gurdjieff who dissected this process for me to examine, and I like to watch it happening. His analysis of process into octaves is also fascinating to me, and very helpful. An undertaking, he says, begins with a surge of energy that carries it a certain distance toward completion. There then occurs a drop in energy, which must be lifted back to an effective level by conscious effort, in my experience by bringing to bear hard purpose. It is here that years of steady application to a specific process can come into play. It is, however, in the final stage, just before completion, that Gurdjieff says pressure mounts almost unendurably to a point at which it is necessary to bring to bear an even more special kind of effort. It is at this point, when idea is on the verge of busting into physicality, that I find myself meeting maximum difficulty. I sometimes have the curious impression that the physical system seems in its very nature to *resist* its invasion by idea. The desert wishes to lie in the curves of its own being: It resists the imposition of the straight line across its natural pattern. Matter itself seems to have some mysterious intransigency.

It is at this critical point that most failures seem to me to occur. The energy required to push the original concept into actualization, to finish it, has quite a different qualitative feel from the effort needed to bring it to this point. It is this strange, higher-keyed energy to which I find I have to pay attention—to court, so to speak, by living in a particular way. Years of training build experience capable of holding a process through the second stage. The opposition of purpose to natural indolence, the friction of this opposition, maintained year after year, seems to create a situation that attracts this mysterious third force, the curious fiery energy required to raise an idea into realization. Whether or not it does so attract remains a mystery.

The Baltimore exhibit is in the second stage of this process. We are bringing our experience to it and are prepared to bear down hard through the final stage. Whether the exhibit will lift into the light in which we conceive it to exist remains in jeopardy.

3 February

When I painted a chair recently, I noticed that I put the paint on indifferently, smoothly but without particular attention. The results were satisfactory but not in any sense beautiful. Does the attention in itself with which paint is applied in art actually change the effect of the paint? Does the kind of consciousness with which we act determine the quality of our actions? It would follow, if this were true, that the higher the degree of consciousness, the higher the quality of the art. I think it likely. Training in art is, then, a demand that students increase the consciousness with which they employ techniques that are, in themselves, ordinary.

9 February

I feel a little brittle and have decided to try to go to Ossabaw Island, off the coast of Georgia, for two weeks in late March. Work thins me out. We, my sculptures and I, are symbiotic while they are in process. My energy nourishes them to completion. And their completion depletes me.

Last night I didn't take off my work clothes until bedtime, hoping to get back into the studio, but was in the end too tired to go. . . .

OPTIONS FOR WRITING

1. Compare two of Truit's journal entries that you find in some way provocative or in conflict. Attempt to expand on ideas Truit has introduced.

2. Truit seems to find it difficult to call herself an artist. Why? Analyze her self-discussions. Can this difficulty be generalized? Is it difficult for you to call yourself an artist in your own field?

3. "Purity of aspiration seems virtually prerequisite to genuine inspiration." Can you make an argument for this statement?

4. September 18: "I did not see a painting of high quality until I was thirteen." Do you remember the first powerful quality work of art you experienced? Describe the experience. Flesh out the details.

5. Ms. Truit speaks of painting a chair indifferently and comments on the results (January 13). Have you had similar experiences? Analyze the importance of attention in its relationship to quality.

Henry Moore
ON SCULPTURE AND PRIMITIVE ART

Henry Moore (1898–1985) was born in Castleford, Yorkshire. His organic stone sculptures are well known and respected worldwide. Much of his work is designed for open-air viewing and is monumental in scale. He did not often write about sculpture, but in the following three pieces he invites us into the visions and purpose of a sculptor; reflects on the processes, issues, and elements of dimensional work; and acquaints us with a perspective on primitive art. Two of these essays were originally lectures.

"The Sculptor's Aims" was first published in Unit One *in 1934, edited by Herbert Read. "Notes on Sculpture" and "Primitive Art" appeared first in* The Listener. *These three pieces are often published together.*

As you read these pieces on sculpture, you might ask yourself some simple questions. What is sculpture, its purpose, its power? Are there parallels between this and other expressive art forms? If you were to express yourself sculpturally, what medium would you choose, and why? What seems to make primitive work powerful? Can you recall a time you were engaged by a sculpture or sculptural form?

THE SCULPTOR'S AIMS

Each sculptor through his past experience, through observation of natural laws, through criticism of his own work and other sculpture, through his character and psychological make-up, and according to his stage of development, finds that certain qualities in sculpture become of fundamental importance to him. For me these qualities are:

Truth to material. Every material has its own individual qualities. It is only when the sculptor works direct, when there is an active relationship with his material, that the material can take its part in the shaping of an idea. Stone, for example, is hard and concentrated and should not be falsified to look like soft flesh — it should not be forced beyond its constructive build to a point of weakness. It should keep its hard tense stoniness.

Full three-dimensional realization. Complete sculptural expression is form in its full spatial reality.

Only to make relief shapes on the surface of the block is to forego the full power of expression of sculpture. When the sculptor understands his material, has a knowledge of its possibilities and its constructive build, it is possible to keep within its limitations and yet turn an inert block into a composition which has a full form existence, with masses of varied size and section conceived in their air-surrounded entirety, stressing and straining, thrusting and opposing each other in spatial relationship — being static, in the sense that the center of gravity lies within the base (and does not seem to be falling over or moving off its base) — and yet having an alert dynamic tension between its parts.

Sculpture fully in the round has no two points of view alike. The desire for form completely realized is connected with asymmetry. For a symmetrical mass being the same from both sides cannot have more than half the number of different points of view possessed by a nonsymmetrical mass.

Asymmetry is connected also with the desire for the organic (which I have) rather than the geometric.

Organic forms, though they may be symmetrical in their main disposition, in their reaction to environment, growth, and gravity, lose their perfect symmetry.

Observation of natural objects. The observation of nature is part of an artist's life, it enlarges his form-knowledge, keeps him fresh and from working only by formula, and feeds inspiration.

The human figure is what interests me most deeply, but I have found principles of form and rhythm from the study of natural objects such as pebbles, rocks, bones, trees, plants, etc.

Pebbles and rocks show nature's way of working stone. Smooth, sea-worn pebbles show the wearing away, rubbed treatment of stone and principles of asymmetry.

Rocks show the hacked, hewn treatment of stone, and have a jagged nervous block rhythm.

Bones have marvelous structural strength and hard tenseness of form, subtle transition of one shape into the next, and great variety in section.

Trees (tree trunks) show principles of growth and strength of joints, with easy passing of one section into the next. They give the ideal for wood sculpture, upward twisting movement.

Shells show nature's hard but hollow form (metal sculpture) and have a wonderful completeness of single shape.

There is in nature a limitless variety of shapes and rhythms (and the telescope and microscope have enlarged the field) from which the sculptor can enlarge his form-knowledge experience.

But beside formal qualities there are qualities of vision and expression:

Vision and expression. My aim in work is to combine as intensely as possible the abstract principles of sculpture along with the realization of my idea.

All art is an abstraction to some degree (in sculpture the material alone forces one away from pure representation and toward abstraction).

Abstract qualities of design are essential to the value of a work, but to me of equal importance is the psychological, human element. If both abstract and human elements are welded together in a work, it must have a fuller, deeper meaning.

Vitality and power of expression. For me a work must first have a vitality of its own. I do not mean a reflection of the vitality of life, of movement, physical action, frisking, dancing figures, and so on, but that a work can have in it a pent-up energy, an intense life of its own, independent of the object it may represent. When a work has this powerful vitality we do not connect the word Beauty with it.

Beauty, in the later Greek or Renaissance sense, is not the aim in my sculpture.

Between beauty of expression and power of expression there is a difference of function The first aims at pleasing the senses, the second has a spiritual vitality which for me is more moving and goes deeper than the senses.

Because a work does not aim at reproducing natural appearances it is not, therefore, an escape from life—but may be a penetration into reality, not a sedative or drug, not just the exercise of good taste, the provision of pleasant shapes and colors in a pleasing combination, not a decoration to life, but an expression of the significance of life, a stimulation to greater effort in living.

NOTES ON SCULPTURE

It is a mistake for a sculptor or a painter to speak or write very often about his job. It releases tension needed for his work. By trying to express his aims with rounded-off logical exactness, he can easily become a theorist whose actual work is only a caged-in exposition of conceptions evolved in terms of logic and words.

But though the non-logical, instinctive, subconscious part of the mind must play its part in his work, he also has a conscious mind which is not inactive. The artist works with a concentration of his whole personality, and the conscious part of it resolves conflicts, organizes memories, and prevents him from trying to walk in two directions at the same time.

It is likely, then, that a sculptor can give, from his own conscious experience, *clues* which will help others in their approach to sculpture, and this article tries to do this, and no more. It is not a general survey of sculpture, or of my own development, but a few notes on some of the problems that have concerned me from time to time.

Appreciation of sculpture depends upon the ability to respond to form in three dimensions. That is perhaps why sculpture has been described as the most difficult of all arts; certainly it is more difficult than the arts which involve appreciation of flat forms, shape in only two dimensions. Many more people are "form-blind" than color-blind. The child learning to see, first distinguishes only two-dimensional shape; it cannot judge distances, depths. Later, for its personal safety and practical needs, it has to develop (partly by means of touch) the ability to judge roughly three-dimensional distances. But having satisfied the requirements of practical necessity, most people go no farther. Though they may attain considerable accuracy in the perception of flat form, they do not make the further intellectual and emotional effort needed to comprehend form in its full spatial existence.

This is what the sculptor must do. He must strive continually to think of, and use, form in its full spatial completeness. He gets the solid shape, as it were, inside his head—he thinks of it, whatever its size, as if he were holding it completely enclosed in the hollow of his hand. He mentally visualizes a complex form *from all round itself*; he knows while he looks at one side what the other side is like; he identifies himself with its center of gravity, its mass, its weight; he realizes its volume, as the space that the shape displaces in the air.

And the sensitive observer of sculpture must also learn to feel shape simply as shape, not as description or reminiscence. He must, for example, perceive an egg as a simple single solid shape, quite apart from its significance as food, or from the literary idea that it will become a bird. And so with solids such as a shell, a nut, a plum, a pear, a tadpole, a mushroom, a mountain peak, a kidney, a carrot, a tree-trunk, a bird, a bud, a lark, a lady-bird, a bulrush, a bone. From these he can go on to appreciate more complex forms or combinations of several forms.

Since the Gothic, European sculpture had become overgrown with moss, weeds — all sorts of surface excrescences which completely concealed shape. It has been Brancusi's special mission to get rid of this overgrowth, and to make us once more shape-conscious. To do this he has had to concentrate on very simple direct shapes, to keep his sculpture, as it were, one-cylindered, to refine and polish a single shape to a degree almost too precious. Brancusi's work, apart from its individual value, has been of historical importance in the development of contemporary sculpture. But it may now be no longer necessary to close down and restrict sculpture to the single (static) form unit. We can now begin to open out. To relate and combine together several forms of varied sizes, sections, and directions into one organic whole.

Although it is the human figure which interests me most deeply, I have always paid great attention to natural forms, such as bones, shells, and pebbles, etc. Sometimes for several years running I have been to the same part of the seashore — but each year a new shape of pebble has caught my eye, which the year before, though it was there in hundreds, I never saw. Out of the millions of pebbles passed in walking along the shore, I choose out to see with excitement only those which fit in with my existing form-interest at the time. A different thing happens if I sit down and examine a handful one by one. I may then extend my form-experience more, by giving my mind time to become conditioned to a new shape.

There are universal shapes to which everybody is subconsciously conditioned and to which they can respond if their conscious control does not shut them off.

Pebbles show nature's way of working stone. Some of the pebbles I pick up have holes right through them.

When first working direct in a hard and brittle material like stone, the lack of experience and great respect for the material, the fear of ill-treating it, too often result in relief surface carving, with no sculptural power.

But with more experience the completed work in stone can be kept within the limitations of its material, that is, not be weakened beyond its natural constructive build, and yet be turned from an inert mass into a composition which has a full form-existence, with masses of varied sizes and sections working together in spatial relationship.

A piece of stone can have a hole through it and not be weakened — if the hole is of a studied size, shape, and direction. On the principle of the arch, it can remain just as strong.

The first hole made through a piece of stone is a revelation.

The hole connects one side to the other, making it immediately more three-dimensional.

A hole can itself have as much shape-meaning as a solid mass.

Sculpture in air is possible, where the stone contains only the hole, which is the intended and considered form.

The mystery of the hole — the mysterious fascination of caves in hill-sides and cliffs.

There is a right physical size for every idea.

Pieces of good stone have stood about my studio for long periods, because though I've had ideas which would fit their proportions and materials perfectly, their size was wrong.

There is a size to scale not to do with its actual physical size, its measurement in feet and inches — but connected with vision.

A carving might be several times over life size and yet be petty and small in feeling — and a small carving only a few inches in height can give the feeling of huge size and monumental grandeur, because the vision behind it is big. Example, Michelangelo's drawings or a Massacio madonna — and the Albert Memorial.

Yet actual physical size has an emotional meaning. We relate every-thing to our own size, and our emotional response to size is controlled by the fact that men on the average are between five and six feet high.

An exact model, to one-tenth scale, of Stonehenge, where the stones would be less than us, would lose all its impressiveness.

Sculpture is more affected by actual size considerations than paint-ing. A painting is isolated by a frame from its surroundings (unless it serves just a decorative purpose) and so retains more easily its own imaginary scale.

If practical considerations allowed me, cost of material, of transport, etc., I should like to work on large carvings more often than I do. The average in-between size does not disconnect an idea enough from pro-saic everyday life. The very small or the very big takes on an added size emotion.

Recently I have been working in the country, where, carving in the open air, I find sculpture more natural than in a London studio, but it needs bigger dimensions. A large piece of stone or wood placed almost anywhere at random in a field, orchard, or garden, immediately looks right and inspiring.

My drawings are done mainly as a help toward making sculpture — as a means of generating ideas for sculpture, tapping oneself for the initial idea; and as a way of sorting out ideas and developing them.

Also, sculpture compared with drawing is a slow means of expression, and I find drawing a useful outlet for ideas which there is not time enough to realize as sculpture. And I use drawing as a method of study and observation of natural forms (drawings from life, drawings of bones, shells, etc.).

And I sometimes draw just for its own enjoyment.

Experience though has taught me that the difference there is between drawing and sculpture should not be forgotten. A sculptural idea which may be satisfactory as a drawing always needs some alteration when translated into sculpture.

At one time, whenever I made drawings for sculpture I tried to give them as much the illusion of real sculpture as I could — that is, I drew by the method of illusion, of light falling on a solid object. But I now find that carrying a drawing so far that it becomes a substitute for the sculpture either weakens the desire to do the sculpture, or is likely to make the sculpture only a dead realization of the drawing.

I now leave a wider latitude in the interpretation of the drawings I make for sculpture, and draw often in line and flat tones without the light and shade illusion of three dimensions; but this does not mean that the vision behind the drawing is only two-dimensional.

The violent quarrel between the abstractionists and the surrealists seems to me quite unnecessary. All good art has contained both abstract and surrealist elements, just as it has contained both classical and romantic elements — order and surprise, intellect and imagination, conscious and unconscious. Both sides of the artist's personality must play their part. And I think the first inception of a painting or a sculpture may begin from either end. As far as my own experience is concerned, I sometimes begin a drawing with no preconceived problem to solve, with only the desire to use pencil on paper, and make lines, tones, and shapes with no conscious aim; but as my mind takes in what is so produced, a point arrives where some idea becomes conscious and crystallizes, and then a control and ordering begin to take place.

Or sometimes I start with a set subject; or to solve, in a block of stone of known dimensions, a sculptural problem I've given myself, and then consciously attempt to build an ordered relationship of forms, which shall express my idea. But if the work is to be more than just a sculptural exercise, unexplainable jumps in the process of thought occur; and the imagination plays its part.

It might seem from what I have said of shape and form that I regard them as ends in themselves. Far from it. I am very much aware that associational, psychological factors play a large part in sculpture. The meaning and significance of form itself probably depends on the countless associations of man's history. For example, rounded forms convey an idea of fruitfulness, maturity, probably because the earth, women's breasts, and most fruits are rounded, and these shapes are important because they have this background in our habits of perception. I think the humanist organic element will always be for me of fundamental importance in sculpture, giving sculpture its vitality. Each particular carving I make takes on in my mind a human, or occasionally animal, character and personality, and this personality controls its design and formal qualities, and makes me satisfied or dissatisfied with the work as it develops.

My own aim and direction seems to be consistent with these beliefs, though it does not depend upon them. My sculpture is becoming less representational, less an outward visual copy, and so what some people would call more abstract; but only because I believe that in this way I can present the human psychological content of my work with the greatest directness and intensity.

PRIMITIVE ART

The term *Primitive Art* is generally used to include the products of a great variety of races and periods in history, many different social and religious systems. In its widest sense it seems to cover most of those cultures which are outside European and the great Oriental civilizations. This is the sense in which I shall use it here, though I do not much like the application of the word "primitive" to art, since, through its associations, it suggests to many people an idea of crudeness and incompetence, ignorant gropings rather than finished achievements. Primitive art means far more than that; it makes a straightforward statement, its primary concern is with the elemental, and its simplicity comes from direct and strong feelings, which is a very different thing from that fashionable simplicity-for-its-own-sake which is emptiness. Like beauty, true simplicity is an unselfconscious virtue; it comes by the way and can never be an end in itself.

The most striking quality common to all primitive art is its intense vitality. It is something made by people with a direct and immediate response to life. Sculpture and painting for them was not an activity of calculation or academism, but a channel for expressing powerful beliefs, hopes, and fears. It is art before it got smothered in trimmings and surface decorations, before inspiration had flagged into technical tricks and intellectual conceits. But apart from its own enduring value, a knowledge of it conditions a fuller and truer appreciation of the later developments of the so-called great periods, and shows art to be a universal continuous activity with no separation between past and present.

All art has its roots in the "primitive," or else it becomes decadent, which explains why the "great" periods, Pericles' Greece and the Renaissance for example, flower and follow quickly on primitive periods, and then slowly fade out. The fundamental sculptural principles of the Archaic Greeks were near enough to Phidias' day to carry through into his carvings a true quality, although his conscious aim was so naturalistic; and the tradition of early Italian art was sufficiently in the blood of Massacio for him to strive for realism and yet retain a primitive grandeur and simplicity. The steadily growing appreciation of primitive art among artists and the public today is therefore a very hopeful and important sign.

Excepting some collections of primitive art in France, Italy, and Spain, my own knowledge of it has come entirely from continual visits to the British Museum during the past twenty years. Now that the Museum has been closed [during World War II], one realizes all the more clearly what one has temporarily lost — the richness and comprehensiveness of its collection of past art, particularly of primitive sculpture, and perhaps by taking a memory-journey through a few of the Museum's galleries I can explain what I believe to be the great significance of primitive periods.

At first my visits were mainly and naturally to the Egyptian galleries, for the monumental impressiveness of Egyptian sculpture was nearest to the familiar Greek and Renaissance ideals one had been born to. After a time, however, the appeal of these galleries lessened; excepting the earlier dynasties. I felt that much of Egyptian sculpture was too stylized and hieratic, with a tendency in its later periods to academic obviousness and a rather stupid love of the colossal.

The galleries running alongside the Egyptian contained the Assyrian reliefs — journalistic commentaries and records of royal lion hunts and battles, but beyond was the Archaic Greek room with its lifesize female figures, seated in easy, still naturalness, grand and full like Handel's music; and then near them, downstairs in the badly lit basement, were the magnificent Etruscan Sarcophagus figures — which, when the Museum reopens, should certainly be better shown.

At the end of the upstairs Egyptian galleries were the Sumerian sculptures, some with a contained bull-like grandeur and held-in energy, very different from the liveliness of much of the early Greek and Etruscan art in the terracotta and vase rooms. In the prehistoric and Stone Age room an iron staircase led to gallery wall-cases where there were originals and casts of Paleolithic sculptures made 20,000 years ago — a lovely tender carving of a girl's head, no bigger than one's thumbnail, and beside it female figures of very human but not copyist realism with a full richness of form, in great contrast with the more symbolic two-dimensional and inventive designs of Neolithic art.

And eventually to the Ethnographical room, which contained an inexhaustible wealth and variety of sculptural achievement (Negro, Oceanic Islands, and North and South America), but overcrowded and jumbled together like junk in a marine store, so that after hundreds of visits I would still find carvings I had not discovered there before. Negro art formed one of the largest sections of the room. Except for the Benin bronzes it was mostly woodcarving. One of the first principles of art so clearly seen in primitive work is truth to material; the artist shows an instinctive understanding of his material, its right use and possibilities. Wood has a stringy fibrous consistency and can be carved into thin forms without breaking, and the Negro sculptor was able to free arms from the body, to have a space between the legs, and to give his figures long necks when he wished. This completer realization of the component parts of the figure gives to Negro carving a more three-dimensional quality than many primitive periods where stone is the main material used. For the Negro, as for other primitive peoples, sex and religion were the two main interacting springs of life. Much Negro carving, like modern Negro spirituals but without their sentimentality, has pathos, a static patience and resignation to unknown mysterious powers; it is religious and, in movement, upward and vertical like the tree it was made from, but in its heavy bent legs is rooted in the earth.

Of works from the Americas, Mexican art was exceptionally well represented in the Museum. Mexican sculpture, as soon as I found it, seemed to me true and right, perhaps because I at once hit on similarities in it with some eleventh-century carvings I had seen as a boy on Yorkshire churches. Its "stoniness," by which I mean its truth to material, its tremendous power without loss of sensitiveness, its astonishing variety and fertility of form-invention, and its approach to a full three-dimensional conception of form, make it unsurpassed in my opinion by any other period of stone sculpture.

The many islands of the Oceanic groups all produced their schools of sculpture with big differences in form-vision. New Guinea carvings, with drawn out spider-like extensions and bird-beak elongations, made a direct contrast with the featureless heads and plain surfaces of the Nukuoro carvings; or the stolid stone figures of the Marquesas Islands against the emasculated ribbed wooden figures of Easter Island. Comparing Oceanic art generally with Negro art, it has a livelier thin flicker, but much of it is more two-dimensional and concerned with pattern making. Yet the carvings of New Ireland have, besides their vicious kind of vitality, a unique spatial sense, a bird-in-a-cage form.

But underlying these individual characteristics, these featural peculiarities in the primitive schools, a common world-language of form is apparent in them all; through the working of instinctive sculptural sensibility, the same shapes and form relationships are used to express similar ideas at widely different places and periods in history, so that the same form-vision may be seen in a Negro and a Viking carving, a Cycladic stone figure and a Nukuoro wooden statuette. And on further familiarity with the British Museum's whole collection it eventually became clear to me that the realistic ideal of physical beauty in art which sprang from fifth-century Greece was only a digression from the main world tradition of sculpture, whilst, for instance, our own equally European Romanesque and Early Gothic are in the main line.

Primitive art is a mine of information for the historian and the anthropologist, but to understand and appreciate it, it is more important to look at it than to learn the history of primitive peoples, their religions and social customs. Some such knowledge may be useful and help us to look more sympathetically, and the interesting titbits of information on the labels attached to the carving in the Museum can serve a useful purpose by giving the mind a needful rest from the concentration of intense looking. But all that is really needed is response to the carvings themselves, which have a constant life of their own, independent of whenever and however they came to be made, and they remain as full of sculptural meaning today to those open and sensitive enough to perceive it as on the day they were finished.

OPTIONS FOR WRITING

1. Walk around campus, visit a local museum. Take time to look at sculpture and sculptural forms around you. Choose two sculptures of differing images and/or materials, and using Moore's suggestions and notes, compare the two pieces as to form, material, image, execution, honesty, and power.

2. You have something to say that is important to you. You are a sculptor and you must write an overview of your upcoming project explaining what you are trying to do, why sculpture is the vehicle, what materials must be used and how they will be handled, and where this piece is to be placed for its important purpose.

3. You are a creative and articulate native from a past "primitive" civilization, and you were somehow able to read Henry Moore's future writing on primitive art. You were deeply affected and have decided to write Moore a letter regarding his essay.

Paul Klee
ON MODERN ART

Paul Klee (1879–1940) was a native of Switzerland. He moved to Munich to study art in 1898 and joined the second BlaueReiter exhibition in 1912. He joined the Bauhaus, an extremely important arts institution, at Weimar. His "Pedagogical Sketchbook" of 1925 was a Bauhaus publication that came directly from his teaching. In "On Modern Art," Klee speaks more of his aesthetic. This lecture accompanied a show of his works in 1924 and was later reassembled through his notes.

While reading these selected lecture materials, take notes and ask yourself questions. What is modern art? (The lecture was given in 1925, remember.) What is the source of artistic expression? What are the elements of design that make up a painting? What does Klee mean by construction becoming composition? Does the metaphor of a tree ring true to you? Is this information relevant today? Tomorrow?

Speaking here in the presence of my work, which should really express itself in its own language, I feel a little anxious as to whether I am justified in doing so and whether I shall be able to find the right approach.

For, while as a painter I feel that I have in my possession the means of moving others in the direction in which I myself am driven, I doubt whether I can give the same sure lead by the use of words alone.

But I comfort myself with the thought that my words do not address themselves to you in isolation, but will complement and bring into focus the impressions, perhaps still a little hazy, which you have already received from my pictures.

If I should, in some measure, succeed in giving this lead, I should be content and should feel that I had found the justification which I had required.

Further, in order to avoid the reproach "Don't talk, painter, paint," I shall confine myself largely to throwing some light on those elements of the creative process which, during the growth of a work of art, take place in the subconscious. To my mind, the real justification for the use of words by a painter would be to shift the emphasis by stimulating a new angle of approach; to relieve the formal element of some of the conscious emphasis which is given and place more stress on content.

I shall try to give you a glimpse of the painter's workshop, and I think we shall eventually arrive at some mutual understanding.

For there is bound to be some common ground between layman and artist where a mutual approach is possible and where the artist no longer appears as a being totally apart.

But, as a being, who like you, has been brought, unasked, into this world of variety, and where, like you, he must find his way for better or for worse.

A being who differs from you only in that he is able to master life by the use of his own specific gifts; a being perhaps happier than the man who has no means of creative expression and no chance of release through the creation of form.

This modest advantage should be readily granted the artist. He has difficulties enough in other respects.

May I use a simile, the simile of the tree? The artist has studied this world of variety and has, we may suppose, unobtrusively found his way in it. His sense of direction has brought order into the passing stream of image and experience. This sense of direction in nature and life, this branching and spreading array, I shall compare with the root of the tree.

From the root the sap flows to the artist, flows through him, flows to his eye.

Thus he stands as the trunk of the tree.

Battered and stirred by the strength of the flow, he molds his vision into his work.

As, in full view of the world, the crown of the tree unfolds and spreads in time and in space, so with his work.

Nobody would affirm that the tree grows its crown in the image of its root. Between above and below can be no mirrored reflection. It is obvious that different functions expanding in different elements must produce vital divergences.

But it is just the artist who at times is denied those departures from nature which his art demands. He has even been charged with incompetence and deliberate distortion.

And yet, standing at his appointed place, the trunk of the tree, he does nothing other than gather and pass on what comes to him from the depths. He neither serves nor rules—he transmits.

His position is humble. And the beauty at the crown is not his own. His is merely a channel.

Before starting to discuss the two realms which I have compared with the crown and the root, I must make a few further reservations.

It is not easy to arrive at a conception of a whole which is constructed from parts belonging to different dimensions. And not only nature, but also art, her transformed image, is such a whole.

It is difficult enough, oneself, to survey this whole, whether nature or art, but still more difficult to help another to such a comprehensive view.

What the so-called spatial arts have long succeeded in expressing, what even the time-bound art of music has gloriously achieved in the harmonies of polyphony, this phenomenon of many simultaneous dimensions which helps drama to its climax, does not, unfortunately, occur in the world of verbal didactic expression.

Contact with the dimensions must, of necessity, take place externally to this form of expression; and subsequently.

And yet, perhaps I shall be able to make myself so completely understood that, as a result, you will be in a better position with any given picture, to experience easily and quickly the phenomenon of simultaneous contact with these many dimensions.

As a humble mediator—not to be identified with the crown of the tree— I may well succeed in imparting to you a power of rich, brilliant vision.

And now to the point—the dimensions of the picture.

I have already spoken of the relationship between the root and the crown, between nature and art, and have explained it by a comparison with the difference between the two elements of earth and air, and with the correspondingly differing functions of below and above.

The creation of a work of art — the growth of the crown of the tree — must of necessity, as a result of entering into the specific dimensions of pictorial art, be accompanied by distortion of the natural form. For, therein is nature reborn.

What, then, are these specific dimensions?

First, there are the more or less limited, formal factors, such as line, tone value, and color.

Of these, line is the most limited, being solely a matter of simple Measure. Its properties are length (long or short), angles (obtuse or acute), length of radius and focal distance. All are quantities subject to measurement.

We now have three formal means at our disposal — Measure, Weight, and Quality, which in spite of fundamental differences, have a definite interrelationship.

Leaving this subject of formal elements I now come to the first construction using the three categories of elements which have just been enumerated.

This is the climax of our conscious creative effort.
This is the essence of our craft.
This is critical.

From this point, given mastery of the medium, the structure can be assured foundations of such strength that it is able to reach out into dimensions far removed from conscious endeavor.

This phase of formation has the same critical importance in the negative sense. It is the point where one can miss the greatest and most important aspects of content and thus fail, although possibly possessing the most exquisite talent. For one may simply lose one's bearings on the formal plane. Speaking from my own experience, it depends on the mood of the artist at the time which of the many elements are brought out of their general order, out of their appointed array, to be raised together to a new order and form an image which is normally called the subject.

This choice of formal elements and the form of their mutual relationship is, within narrow limits, analogous to the idea of motif and theme in musical thought.

With the gradual growth of such an image before the eyes an association of ideas gradually insinuates itself which may tempt one to a material interpretation. For any image of complex structure can, with some effort of imagination, be compared with familiar pictures from nature.

These associative properties of the structure, once exposed and labelled, no longer correspond wholly to the direct will of the artist (at least not to his most intensive will) and just these associative properties have been the source of passionate misunderstandings between artist and layman.

While the artist is still exerting all his efforts to group the formal elements purely and logically so that each in its place is right and none clashes with the other, a layman, watching from behind, pronounces the devastating words "But that isn't a bit like uncle."

The argument is therefore concerned less with the question of the existence of an object, than with its appearance at any given moment—with its nature.

I only hope that the layman who, in a picture, always looks for his favorite subject, will, as far as I am concerned, gradually die out and remain to me nothing but a ghost which cannot help its failings. For a man only knows his own objective passions. And admittedly it gives him great pleasure when, by chance, a familiar face of its own accord emerges from a picture.

The objects in pictures look out at us serene or severe, tense or relaxed, comforting or forbidding, suffering or smiling.

They show us all the contrasts in the psychic-physiognomical field, contrasts which may range from tragedy to comedy.

But it is far from ending there.
The figures, as I have often called these objective images, also have their own distinctive aspects, which result from the way in which the selected groups of elements have been put in motion.

This, firstly, identified the dimensions of the elemental ingredients of the picture with line, tone value, and color. And then the first constructive combination of these ingredients gave us the dimension of figure or, if you prefer it, the dimension of object.

These dimensions are now joined by a further dimension which determines the question of content.

Certain proportions of line, the combination of certain tones from the scale of tone values, certain harmonies of color, carry with them at the time quite distinctive and outstanding modes of expression.

The linear proportions can, for example, refer to angles: movements which are angular and zigzag—as opposed to smooth and horizontal—strike resonances of expression which are similarly contrasting.

In the same way a conception of contrast can be given by two forms of linear construction, the one consisting of a firmly jointed structure and the other of lines loosely scattered.

Contrasting modes of expression in the region of tone value are given by:

> The wide use of all tones from black to white, implying full-bodied strength.
> Or the limited use of the upper light half or the lower dark half of the scale.
> Or medium shades around the grey which imply weakness through too much or too little light.
> Or timid shadows from the middle. These, again, show great contrasts in meaning.

And what tremendous possibilities for the variation of meaning are offered by the combination of colors.

Color as tone value: e.g. red in red, i.e. the entire range from a deficiency to an excess of red, either widely extended, or limited in range. Then the same in yellow (something quite different). The same in blue — what contrasts!

Or colors diametrically opposed — i.e. changes from red to green, from yellow to purple, from blue to orange.

Tremendous fragments of meaning.

Or changes of color in the direction of chords,[1] not touching the grey center, but meeting in a region of warmer or cooler grey.

What subtleties of shading compared with the former contrasts.

Our picture has, as has been described, progressed gradually through dimensions so numerous and of such importance, that it would be unjust to refer to it any longer as a "Construction." From now on we will give it the resounding title of "Composition."

I would like now to examine the dimensions of the object in a new light and so try to show how it is that the artist frequently arrives at what appears to be such an arbitrary "deformation" of natural forms.

First, he does not attach such intense importance to natural form as do so many realist critics, because, for him, these final forms are not the real stuff of the process of natural creation. For he places more value on the powers which do the forming than on the final forms themselves.

He is, perhaps unintentionally, a philosopher, and if he does not, with the optimists, hold this world to be the best of all possible worlds, nor to be so bad that it is unfit to serve as a model, yet he says:

"In its present shape it is not the only possible world."

Thus he surveys with penetrating eye the finished forms which nature places before him.

The deeper he looks, the more readily he can extend his view from the present to the past, the more deeply he is impressed by the one essential image of creation itself, as Genesis, rather than by the image of nature, the finished product.

Then he permits himself the thought that the process of creation can today hardly be complete and he sees the act of world creation stretching from the past to the future. Genesis eternal!

He goes still further!

He says to himself, thinking of life around him: this world at one time looked different and, in the future, will look different again.

Then, flying off to the infinite, he thinks: it is very probable that, on other stars, creation has produced a completely different result.

Such mobility of thought on the process of natural creation is good training for creative work.

It has the power to move the artist fundamentally, and since he is himself mobile, he may be relied upon to maintain freedom of development of his own creative methods.

This being so, the artist must be forgiven if he regards the present state of outward appearances in his own particular world as accidentally fixed in time and space. And as altogether inadequate compared with his penetrating vision and intense depth of feeling.

Does then the artist concern himself with microscopy? History? Paleontology?

Only for purposes of comparison, only in the exercise of his mobility of mind. And not to provide a scientific check on the truth of nature.

Only in the sense of freedom.
In the sense of freedom, which does not lead to fixed phases of development, representing exactly what nature once was, or will be, or could be on another star (as perhaps may one day be proved).

But in the sense of a freedom which merely demands its rights, the right to develop, as great Nature herself develops.

From type to prototype.

Presumptuous is the artist who does not follow his road through to the end. But chosen are those artists who penetrate to the region of that secret place where primeval power nurtures all evolution.

There, where the powerhouse of all time and space — call it brain or heart of creation—activates every function; who is the artist who would not dwell there?

In the womb of nature, at the source of creation, where the secret key to all lies guarded.

But not all can enter. Each should follow where the pulse of his own heart leads.

So, in their time, the Impressionists—our opposites of yesterday—had every right to dwell within the matted undergrowth of everyday vision.

But our pounding heart drives us down, deep down to the source of all.

What springs from this source—whatever it may be called, dream, idea or fantasy—must be taken seriously only if it unites with the proper creative means to form a work of art.

Then those curiosities become realities—realities of art which help to lift life out of its mediocrity.

For not only do they, to some extent, add more spirit to the seen, but they also make secret visions visible.

I said "with the proper creative means." For at this stage is decided whether pictures or something different will be born. At this stage, also, is decided the kind of the pictures.

These unsettled times have brought chaos and confusion (or so it seems, if we are not too near to judge).

But among artists, even among the youngest of them, one urge seems to be gradually gaining ground:
The urge to the culture of these creative means, to their pure cultivation, to their pure use.

The legend of the childishness of my drawing must have originated from those linear compositions of mine in which I tried to combine a concrete image, say that of a man, with the pure representation of the linear element.

Had I wished to present the man "as he is," then I should have had to use such a bewildering confusion of line that pure elementary representation would have been out of the question. The result would have been vagueness beyond recognition.

And anyway, I do not wish to represent the man as he is, but only as he might be.

And thus I could arrive at a happy association between my vision of life [Weltanschauung] and pure artistic craftsmanship.

And so it is over the whole field of use of the formal means: in all things, even in colors, must all trace of vagueness be avoided.

This then is what is called the untrue coloring in modern art.

As you can see from this example of "childishness" I concern myself with work on the partial processes of art. I am also a draughtsman.

I have tried pure drawing, I have tried painting in pure tone values. In color, I have tried all partial methods to which I have been led by my sense of direction in the color circle. As a result, I have worked out methods of painting in colored tone values, in complementary colors, in multicolors and methods of total color painting.

Always combined with the more subconscious dimensions of the picture.

Then I tried all possible syntheses of two methods. Combining and again combining, but, of course, always preserving the culture of the pure element.

Sometimes I dream of a work of really great breadth, ranging through the whole region of element, object, meaning, and style.

This, I fear, will remain a dream, but it is a good thing even now to bear the possibility occasionally in mind.

Nothing can be rushed. It must grow, it should grow of itself, and if the time ever comes for that work—then so much the better!

> We must go on seeking it!
> We have found parts, but not the whole!
> We still lack the ultimate power, for:
> the people are not with us.

But we seek a people. We began over there in the Bauhaus. We began there with a community to which each one of us gave what he had. More we cannot do.

NOTES

[1] [The word used by the author was "segment." This would appear to be a geometrical slip which has been corrected in the translation—Translator's note.]

OPTIONS FOR WRITING

1. Describe the process by which a construction becomes a composition.

2. "That doesn't *look* like anything." Present an argument for the source of validity of modern art.

3. Klee queries whether perhaps creative people are happier because of their ability to release creative expression. Expand on this idea.

4. Look at a number of paintings or reproductions of works by Paul Klee. Compare the actual visual works with the theories and explanations Klee has presented about modern art.

5. Reread this selection by Paul Klee, and write a letter to Mr. Klee regarding your thoughts and questions.

John Dewey
ART AS EXPERIENCE

John Dewey (1859–1952) was born and educated in Burlington, Vermont. A philosopher and educator, Dewey's teachings and writings spanned nearly a century. He was called a democratic philosopher whose concerns addressed concepts of inquiry and freedom. He served at the University of Michigan as the chairman of the department of philosophy and at the University of Chicago as the chairman of the department of philosophy, psychology, and pedagogy. He founded the Laboratory School and the American Association of University Professors and helped found the original teachers' union movement in New York City. He visited and taught widely in Japan and China. His writings include "The School and Society," "Ethics," "Schools of Tomorrow," "Democracy and Education," "Experience and Nature," "Art as Experience," and "Freedom and Culture," among others.
Dewey's works stress experience and inquiry, participation and interdependence, choices and freedom.

This selection from "Art as Experience" examines the ideas of "artistic" and "aesthetic." While reading you might ask yourself a number of questions. What do the terms artistic and aesthetic mean? What is their relationship to each other and to you? What differentiates art from artifacts? What is the role and the attitude of the maker of an art piece? What is the role and the attitude of the viewer? How important is each?

We have no word in the English language that unambiguously includes what is signified by the two words "artistic" and "esthetic." Since "artistic" refers primarily to the act of production and "esthetic" to that of perception and enjoyment, the absence of a term designating the two processes taken together is unfortunate. Sometimes, the effect is to separate the two from each other, to regard art as something superimposed upon esthetic material, or, upon the other side, to an assumption that, since art is a process of creation, perception and enjoyment of it have nothing in common with the creative act. In any case, there is a certain verbal awkwardness in that we are compelled sometimes to use the term "esthetic" to cover the entire field and sometimes to limit it to the receiving perceptual aspect of the whole operation. I refer to these obvious facts as preliminary to an attempt to show how the conception of conscious experience as a perceived relation between doing and undergoing enables us to understand the connection that art as production and perception and appreciation as enjoyment sustain to each other.

Art denotes a process of doing or making. This is as true of fine as of technological art. Art involves molding of clay, chipping of marble, casting of bronze, laying on of pigments, construction of buildings, singing of songs, playing of instruments, enacting rôles on the stage, going through rhythmic movements in the dance. Every art does something with some physical material, the body or something outside the body, with or without the use of intervening tools, and with a view to production of something visible, audible, or tangible. So marked is the active or "doing" phase of art, that the dictionaries usually define it in terms of skilled action, ability in execution. The Oxford Dictionary illustrates by a quotation from John Stuart Mill: "Art is an endeavor after perfection in execution" while Matthew Arnold calls it "pure and flawless workmanship."

The word "esthetic" refers, as we have already noted, to experience as appreciative, perceiving, and enjoying. It denotes the consumer's rather than the producer's standpoint. It is Gusto, taste; and, as with cooking, overt skillful action is on the side of the cook who prepares, while taste is on the side of the consumer, as in gardening there is a distinction between the gardener who plants and tills and the householder who enjoys the finished product.

These very illustrations, however, as well as the relation that exists in having an experience between doing and undergoing, indicate that the distinction between esthetic and artistic cannot be pressed so far as to become a separation. Perfection in execution cannot be measured or defined in terms of execution; it implies those who perceive and enjoy the product that is executed. The cook prepares food for the consumer and the measure of the value of what is prepared is found in consumption. Mere perfection in execution, judged in its own terms in isolation, can probably be attained better by a machine than by human art. By itself, it is at most technique, and there are great artists who are not in the first ranks as technicians (witness Cézanne), just as there are great performers on the piano who are not great esthetically, and as Sargent is not a great painter.

Craftsmanship to be artistic in the final sense must be 'loving'; it must care deeply for the subject matter upon which skill is exercised. A sculptor comes to mind whose busts are marvelously exact. It might be difficult to tell in the presence of a photograph of one of them and of a photograph of the original which was of the person himself. For virtuosity they are remarkable. But one doubts whether the maker of the busts had an experience of his own that he was concerned to have those share who look at his products. To be truly artistic, a work must also be esthetic—that is, framed for enjoyed receptive perception. Constant observation is, of course, necessary for the maker while he is producing. But if his perception is not also esthetic in nature, it is a colorless and cold recognition of what has been done, used as a stimulus to the next step in a process that is essentially mechanical.

In short, art, in its form, unites the very same relation of doing and undergoing, outgoing and incoming energy, that makes an experience to be an experience. Because of elimination of all that does not contribute to mutual organization of the factors of both action and reception into one another, and because of selection of just the aspects and traits that contribute to their interpenetration of each other, the product is a work of esthetic art. Man whittles, carves, sings, dances, gestures, molds, draws and paints. The doing or making is artistic when the perceived result is of such a nature that *its* qualities *as perceived* have controlled the question of production. The act of producing that is directed by intent to produce something that is enjoyed in the immediate experience of perceiving has qualities that a spontaneous or uncontrolled activity does not have. The artist embodies in himself the attitude of the perceiver while he works.

Suppose, for the sake of illustration, that a finely wrought object, one whose texture and proportions are highly pleasing in perception, has been believed to be a product of some primitive people. Then there is discovered evidence that proves it to be an accidental natural product. As an external thing, it is now precisely what it was before. Yet at once it ceases to be a work of art and becomes a natural "curiosity." It now belongs in a museum of natural history, not in a museum of art. And the extraordinary thing is that the difference that is thus made is not one of just intellectual classification. A difference is made in appreciative perception and in a direct way. The esthetic experience — in its limited sense — is thus seen to be inherently connected with the experience of making.

The sensory satisfaction of eye and ear, when esthetic, is so because it does not stand by itself but is linked to the activity of which it is the consequence. Even the pleasures of the palate are different in quality to an epicure than in one who merely "likes" his food as he eats it. The difference is not of mere intensity. The epicure is conscious of much more than the taste of the food. Rather, there enter into the taste, as directly experienced, qualities that depend upon reference to its source and its manner of production in connection with criteria of excellence. As production must absorb into itself qualities of the product as perceived and be regulated by them, so, on the other side, seeing, hearing, tasting, become esthetic when relation to a distinct manner of activity qualifies what is perceived.

There is an element of passion in all esthetic perception. Yet when we are overwhelmed by passion, as in extreme rage, fear, jealousy, the experience is definitely non-esthetic. There is no relationship felt to the qualities of the activity that has generated the passion. Consequently, the material of the experience lacks elements of balance and proportion. For these can be present only when, as in the conduct that has grace or dignity, the act is controlled by an exquisite sense of the relations which the act sustains — its fitness to the occasion and to the situation.

The process of art in production is related to the esthetic in perception organically — as the Lord God in creation surveyed his work and found it good. Until the artist is satisfied in perception with what he is doing, he continues shaping and reshaping. The making comes to an end when its result is experienced as good—and that experience comes not by mere intellectual and outside judgment but in direct perception. An artist, in comparison with his fellows, is one who is not only especially gifted in powers of execution but in unusual sensitivity to the qualities of things. This sensitivity also directs his doings and makings.

As we manipulate, we touch and feel, as we look, we see; as we listen, we hear. The hand moves with etching needle or with brush. The eye attends and reports the consequence of what is done. Because of this intimate connection, subsequent doing is cumulative and not a matter of caprice nor yet of routine. In an emphatic artistic-esthetic experience, the relation is so close that it controls simultaneously both the doing and the perception. Such vital intimacy of connection cannot be had if only hand and eye are engaged. When they do not, both of them, act as organs of the whole being, there is but a mechanical sequence of sense and movement, as in walking that is automatic. Hand and eye, when the experience is esthetic, are but instruments through which the entire live creature, moved and active throughout, operates. Hence the expression is emotional and guided by purpose.

Because of the relation between what is done and what is undergone, there is an immediate sense of things in perception as belonging together or as jarring; as reënforcing or as interfering. The consequences of the act of making as reported in sense show whether what is done carries forward the idea being executed or marks a deviation and break. In as far as the development of an experience is *controlled* through reference to these immediately felt relations of order and fulfillment, that experience becomes dominantly esthetic in nature. The urge to action becomes an urge to that kind of action which will result in an object satisfying in direct perception. The potter shapes his clay to make a bowl useful for holding grain; but he makes it in a way so regulated by the series of perceptions that sum up the serial acts of making, that the bowl is marked by enduring grace and charm. The general situation remains the same in painting a picture or molding a bust. Moreover, at each stage there is anticipation of what is to come. This anticipation is the connecting link between the next doing and its outcome for sense. What is done and what is undergone are thus reciprocally, cumulatively, and continuously instrumental to each other.

The doing may be energetic, and the undergoing may be acute and intense. But unless they are related to each other to form a whole in perception, the thing done is not fully esthetic. The making for example may be a display of technical virtuosity, and the undergoing a gush of sentiment or a revery. If the artist does not perfect a new vision in his process of doing, he acts mechanically and repeats some old model fixed like a blue print in his mind. An incredible amount of observation and of the kind of intelligence that is exercised in perception of qualitative relations characterizes creative work in art. The relations must be noted not only with respect to one another, two by two, but in connection with the whole under construction; they are exercised in imagination as well as in observation. Irrelevancies arise that are tempting distractions; digressions suggest themselves in the guise of enrichments. There are occasions when the grasp of the dominant idea grows faint, and then the artist is moved unconsciously to fill in until his thought grows strong again. The real work of an artist is to build up an experience that is coherent in perception while moving with constant change in its development.

When an author puts on paper ideas that are already clearly conceived and consistently ordered, the real work has been previously done. Or, he may depend upon the greater perceptibility induced by the activity and its sensible report to direct his completion of the work. The mere act of transcription is esthetically irrelevant save as it enters integrally into the formation of an experience moving to completeness. Even the composition conceived in the head and, therefore, physically private, is public in its significant content, since it is conceived with reference to execution in a product that is perceptible and hence belongs to the common world. Otherwise it would be an aberration or a passing dream. The urge to express through painting the perceived qualities of a landscape is continuous with demand for pencil or brush. Without external embodiment, an experience remains incomplete; physiologically and functionally, sense organs are motor organs and are connected, by means of distribution of energies in the human body and not merely anatomically, with other motor organs. It is no linguistic accident that "building," "construction," "work," designate both a process and its finished product. Without the meaning of the verb that of the noun remains blank.

Writer, composer of music, sculptor, or painter can retrace, during the process of production, what they have previously done. When it is not satisfactory in the undergoing or perceptual phase of experience, they can to some degree start afresh. This retracing is not readily accomplished in the case of architecture — which is perhaps one reason why there are so many ugly buildings. Architects are obliged to complete their idea before its translation into a complete object of perception takes place. Inability to build up simultaneously the idea and its objective embodiment imposes a handicap. Nevertheless, they too are obliged to think out their ideas in terms of the medium of embodiment and the object of ultimate perception unless they work mechanically and by rote. Probably the esthetic quality of medieval cathedrals is due in some measure to the fact that their constructions were not so much controlled by plans and specifications made in advance as is now the case. Plans grew as the building grew. But even a Minerva-like product, if it is artistic, presupposes a prior period of gestation in which doings and perceptions projected in imagination interact and mutually modify one another. Every work of art follows the plan of, and pattern of, a complete experience, rendering it more intensely and concentratedly felt.

It is not so easy in the case of the perceiver and appreciator to understand the intimate union of doing and undergoing as it is in the case of the maker. We are given to supposing that the former merely takes in what is there in finished form, instead of realizing that this taking in involves activities that are comparable to those of the creator. But receptivity is not passivity. It, too, is a process consisting of a series of responsive acts that accumulate toward objective fulfillment. Otherwise, there is not perception but recognition. The difference between the two is immense. Recognition is perception arrested before it has a chance to develop freely. In recognition there is a beginning of an act of perception. But this beginning is not allowed to serve the development of a full perception of the thing recognized. It is arrested at the point where it will serve some *other* purpose, as we recognize a man on the street in order to greet or to avoid him, not so as to see him for the sake of seeing what is there.

In recognition we fall back, as upon a stereotype, upon some previously formed scheme. Some detail or arrangement of details serves as cue for bare identification. It suffices in recognition to apply this bare outline as a stencil to the present object. Sometimes in contact with a human being we are struck with traits, perhaps of only physical characteristics, of which we were not previously aware. We realize that we never knew the person before; we had not seen him in any pregnant sense. We now begin to study and to "take in." Perception replaces bare recognition. There is an act of reconstructive doing, and consciousness becomes fresh and alive. *This* act of seeing involves the coöperation of motor elements even though they remain implicit and do not become overt, as well as coöperation of all funded ideas that may serve to complete the new picture that is forming. Recognition is too easy to arouse vivid consciousness. There is not enough resistance between new and old to secure consciousness of the experience that is had. Even a dog that barks and wags his tail joyously on seeing his master return is more fully alive in his reception of his friend than is a human being who is content with mere recognition.

Bare recognition is satisfied when a proper tag or label is attached, "proper" signifying one that serves a purpose outside the act of recognition—as a salesman identifies wares by a sample. It involves no stir of the organism, no inner commotion. But an act of perception proceeds by waves that extend serially throughout the entire organism. There is, therefore, no such thing in perception as seeing or hearing *plus* emotion. The perceived object or scene is emotionally pervaded throughout. When an aroused emotion does not permeate the material that is perceived or thought of, it is either preliminary or pathological.

The esthetic or undergoing phase of experience is receptive. It involves surrender. But adequate yielding of the self is possibly only through a controlled activity that may well be intense. In much of our intercourse with our surroundings we withdraw; sometimes from fear, if only of expending unduly our store of energy; sometimes from preoccupation with other matters, as in the case of recognition. Perception is an act of the going-out of energy in order to receive, not a withholding of energy. To steep ourselves in a subject-matter we have first to plunge into it. When we are only passive to a scene, it overwhelms us and, for lack of answering activity, we do not perceive that which bears us down. We must summon energy and pitch it at a responsive key in order to *take* in.

Every one knows that it requires apprenticeship to see through a microscope or telescope, and to see a landscape as the geologist sees it. The idea that esthetic perception is an affair for odd moments is one reason for the backwardness of the art among us. The eye and the visual apparatus may be intact; the object may be physically there, the cathedral of Notre Dame, or Rembrandt's portrait of Hendrik Stoeffel. In some bald sense the latter may be "seen." They may be looked at, possibly recognized, and have their correct names attached. But for lack of continuous interaction between the total organism and the objects, they are not perceived, certainly not esthetically. A crowd of visitors steered through a picture-gallery by a guide, with attention called here and there to some high point, does not perceive; only by accident is there even interest in seeing a picture for the sake of subject matter vividly realized.

For to perceive, a beholder must *create* his own experience. And his creation must include relations comparable to those which the original producer underwent. They are not the same in any literal sense. But with the perceiver, as with the artist, there must be an ordering of the elements of the whole that is in form, although not in details, the same as the process of organization the creator of the work consciously experienced. Without an act of recreation the object is not perceived as a work of art. The artist selected, simplified, clarified, abridged and condensed according to his interest. The beholder must go through these operations according to his point of view and interest. In both, an act of abstraction, that is of extraction of what is significant, takes place. In both, there is comprehension in its literal signification — that is, a gathering together of details and particulars physically scattered into an experienced whole. There is work done on the part of the percipient as there is on the part of the artist. The one who is too lazy, idle, or indurated in convention to perform this work will not see or hear. His "appreciation" will be a mixture of scraps of learning with conformity to norms of conventional admiration and with a confused, even if genuine, emotional excitation.

The considerations that have been presented imply both the community and the unlikeness, because of specific emphasis, of *an* experience, in its pregnant sense, and esthetic experience. The former has esthetic quality; otherwise its materials would not be rounded out into a single coherent experience. It is not possible to divide in a vital experience the practical, emotional, and intellectual from one another and to set the properties of one over against the characteristics of the others.

The emotional phase binds parts together into a single whole; "intellectual" simply names the fact that the experience has meaning; "practical" indicates that the organism is interacting with events and objects which surround it. The most elaborate philosophic or scientific inquiry and the most ambitious industrial or political enterprise has, when its different ingredients constitute an integral experience, esthetic quality. For then its varied parts are linked to one another, and do not merely succeed one another. And the parts through their experienced linkage move toward a consummation and close, not merely to cessation in time. This consummation, moreover, does not wait in consciousness for the whole undertaking to be finished. It is anticipated throughout and is recurrently savored with special intensity.

Nevertheless, the experiences in question are dominantly intellectual or practical, rather than *distinctively* esthetic, because of the interest and purpose that initiate and control them. In an intellectual experience, the conclusion has value on its own account. It can be extracted as a formula or as a "truth," and can be used in its independent entirety as factor and guide in other inquiries. In a work of art there is no such single self-sufficient deposit. The end, the terminus, is significant not by itself but as the integration of the parts. It has no other existence. A drama or novel is not the final sentence, even if the characters are disposed of as living happily ever after. In a distinctively esthetic experience, characteristics that are subdued in other experiences are dominant; those that are subordinate are controlling—namely, the characteristics in virtue of which the experience is an integrated complete experience on its own account.

In every integral experience there is form because there is dynamic organization. I call the organization dynamic because it takes time to complete it, because it is a growth. There is inception, development, fulfillment. Material is ingested and digested through interaction with that vital organization of the results of prior experience that constitutes the mind of the worker. Incubation goes on until what is conceived is brought forth and is rendered perceptible as part of the common world. An esthetic experience can be crowded into a moment only in the sense that a climax of prior long enduring processes may arrive in an outstanding movement which so sweeps everything else into it that all else is forgotten. That which distinguishes an experience as esthetic is conversion of resistance and tensions, of excitations that in themselves are temptations to diversion, into a movement toward an inclusive and fulfilling close.

Experiencing like breathing is a rhythm of intakings and outgivings. Their succession is punctuated and made a rhythm by the existence of intervals, periods in which one phase is ceasing and the other is inchoate and preparing. William James aptly compared the course of a conscious experience to the alternate flights and perchings of a bird. The flights and perchings are intimately connected with one another; they are not so many unrelated lightings succeeded by a number of equally unrelated hoppings. Each resting place in experience is an undergoing in which is absorbed and taken home the consequences of prior doing, and, unless the doing is that of utter caprice or sheer routine, each doing carries in itself meaning that has been extracted and conserved. As with the advance of an army, all gains from what has been already effected are periodically consolidated, and always with a view to what is to be done next. If we move too rapidly, we get away from the base of supplies—of accrued meanings—and the experience is flustered, thin, and confused. If we dawdle too long after having extracted a net value, experience perishes of inanition.

The *form* of the whole is therefore present in every member. Fulfilling, consummating, are continuous functions, not mere ends, located at one place only. An engraver, painter, or writer is in process of completing at every stage of his work. He must at each point retain and sum up what has gone before as a whole and with reference to a whole to come. Otherwise there is no consistency and no security in his successive acts. The series of doings in the rhythm of experience give variety and movement; they save the work from monotony and useless repetitions. The undergoings are the corresponding elements in the rhythm, and they supply unity; they save the work from the aimlessness of a mere succession of excitations. An object is peculiarly and dominantly esthetic, yielding the enjoyment characteristic of esthetic perception, when the factors that determine anything which can be called *an* experience are lifted high above the threshold of perception and are made manifest for their own sake.

OPTIONS FOR WRITING

1. Dewey speaks of the difference between perception and recognition. Take time to review your own participation in creative work. Compare these two processes.

2. Dewey states that both the making of art and the perceiving of artworks are active and interrelated processes. Do you agree? Present an argument for your point of view.

3. A splendid African mask is donated to a University. Is it art? Is it an artifact? Does it belong in a museum of art or of natural history? How do the processes of creation and perception affect the interpretation of such a piece? How would you evaluate such a piece? What criteria would you use? Present an evaluation of this situation.

4. Compare the concepts of artistic and aesthetic.

5. This selection comes from a book titled *Art as Experience*. Based on your reading and your experience, examine and analyze the phrase, "art as experience."

6

LANGUAGE, IDENTITY, AND POWER

Karen Wiley Sandler

Picture yourself in a place where you don't speak the language, when, say, the airplane you're on begins to make strange noises, or you experience sudden sharp pains in your abdomen. That picture gives you some idea of the importance of language as a connection to other people and to your world. Sandler explains how language can be used not only to connect us to others but also to define our identity, to include or exclude us from groups, even to grant or deny us power. Not all language is verbal—we use our bodies, the space between us, and even time to communicate our messages. Sandler invites you to explore the role that language of all types plays in your life, through a language log, interviews, or close observation of people in social settings.

READINGS

Frank Conroy Think About It: Ways We Know; and Don't

Edward T. Hall Proxemics in a Cross-Cultural Context: Germans, English, and French

John Fire Lame Deer Talking to the Owls and Butterflies

Margaret Atwood The Handmaid's Tale

Ursula K. LeGuin Bryn Mawr Commencement Address

Neil Postman The Medium is the Metaphor

Muriel Rukeyser Myth

Mark Twain That Awful German Language

Lewis Thomas Social Talk

Lewis Thomas The Tucson Zoo

I guess I should have known better back then at my high school graduation. Known better than to have said, "Never! No Way!" This may
seem like a strange way to begin a chapter in a college textbook, but
after you hear my story, maybe you'll agree with me that it's the best
way I can tell you about language and personal power.

In high school I frequently got good grades even in courses that
didn't particularly interest me. But I needed good grades to get into
college, and I *was* interested in that. I even got good grades in French.
In fact, my high school French teacher's parting words to me before
graduation were "I do hope you'll major in French in college." That's
when I replied with great fervor, "Never!"

I hated French. To me, it was just an intellectual exercise, a way to
prove to myself that I could do any academic task that came my way. It
certainly wasn't fun. I used to think about my French homework as a
coding and decoding exercise. You know, you take the words in English, find their French equivalents, plug them in in the right place in
the sentence, and that's it. Fini!

I certainly wasn't going to major in French. I was destined to do
something really interesting.

Well, sometimes interesting things happen in unexpected ways. I
had to take French in college to complete distribution requirements. One
warm spring afternoon, after two terms of studying intermediate French,
I sat in class barely able to stay awake. It was a scene familiar to most
students: a classroom with windows facing the college green where blue
sky, fluffy clouds, dogs, green grass, and frisbee-playing students tease
you to come out and join them. "Can we have class outside today?" has
just fallen on deaf ears—again—and the hour has just started.

Fortunately, I had a great teacher, Mrs. Posgate (even though she
wouldn't let us have class outside). This was my second term with her,
and I loved the stories she told about her years in France, about starving
through the war years, freezing in low-rent Paris flats, and conversing
for hours in cafés about life, love, philosophy, religion, and great art.
She made Paris come alive for me; she made the language sing. But she
couldn't give the language itself life beyond that intellectual code I had
constructed for myself in high school. *La table* = *table*, *parler* = *to speak*,
bon = *good*, and that was that. French was English translated into strange
sounds, no matter how pleasant.

But sometimes the combination of a great teacher and total relaxation helps your mind rearrange information you have known for a while
into a pattern that finally makes sense. At least that's what happened
for me. My teacher was explaining a grammatical point, making the
distinction between two expressions that differ only by the use of the
small preposition following the verb. In French, if you want to talk
about your opinion, you use the expression *penser de*. If you want to say
simply that you have given some thought to something, you must use
a different preposition after the verb: You say *penser à*. The important

decision is choosing which word follows the verb *penser*. Is it *de* for opinion or *à* for a simple thought?

As I wrote this all down in my notebook for the hundredth time—objectively and remotely processing the intellectual code—I began to picture a French person talking, using these expressions. And suddenly I realized that for a French person that choice between *de* and *à* isn't governed by an English translation. It isn't a conscious decision directed by a grammar rule or a dictionary. It's the unconscious way the person thinks because that's the way the person has grown up thinking. Those two expressions mean completely different things, so the structure of the language has come to reflect that difference. The language has followed the meaning, not the other way around, as I had been trying to learn it. I had been looking at things backward, trying to make the meaning follow the language. For the first time, I saw language as a tool, a necessary tool, for thinking and self-expression. People cannot understand themselves, other people, or other cultures until they can use the tool to gain access to the thinking behind it. I had failed to understand the power of language because I had not seen the thinking behind it.

I didn't begin to understand then why language serves as such a helpful tool. All I knew at that moment was the fascination of being inside someone else's head, if only for an instant. That experience, as I began to see the connection between thought and action, changed the way I thought about studying French. You might say that I had glimpsed the human instead of the mechanical side of language.

LANGUAGE AS A COPING MECHANISM

Why do people need language? Imagine a situation in which you cannot use language. What aspects of our everyday life might be missing as a result? For example, imagine that you are traveling on a foreign airline. You speak English, but the predominant language is Japanese. There will be no problem following directions such as "fasten your seat belt" or "no smoking" because there are internationally recognizable pictograms to help communicate those ideas. And you will probably be able to gesture your need for coffee or for a magazine by nodding, pointing, or even by drawing pictures.

But let's complicate the picture a bit. Suppose that you are terrified of flying and that just after takeoff a series of bells and buzzers begin to sound. Now you are really in trouble! You cannot ask if the plane is about to crash, although that is your predominant thought! Do the sounds indicate something you should do (such as fasten your seat belt or press the attendant call button)? Or do they have meaning only for the pilots? What is the meaning, and how life threatening is it? You, the foreign traveler, cannot find out what the sounds mean and so lose the logical connection to your world.

Language, then, provides connections to other people and to the larger world. Language also gives us conscious control over the *things* in our world. If things are important to us, we name them or learn their names. Naming a thing helps us figure out what it is, what it does, and how we can use it. Things for which we do not find names usually have little benefit for us. They remain in a large sense beyond our grasp, as anyone who has ever asked someone to bring the "thingamajig" will attest.

That's part of what I understood on that warm, lazy afternoon in my college French class. I saw that language was a way of connecting me with someone who had grown up in a different culture in another part of the world. I saw the potential for learning about the differences and similarities between someone who grew up speaking French and me. Language offered me the link to thinking like a native speaker of French, and, thus, I could cope — act, interact, define, and discover — in more than my own comfortable world.

WRITING 1.

Pick someone whose major is a foreign language or who teaches it, and spend about 15 minutes with him or her. Ask this person about his or her decision to study a foreign language. When did this decision take place? Why does that person enjoy foreign languages? Can he or she give you some examples of the kind of connection between language and thought I described? For the next class, write about your interview in a journal.

THINKING LIKE A NATIVE

If you've ever traveled abroad or spent a great deal of time with people who speak a language different from your own, you know that thinking like a native speaker isn't easy. The first few days I'm in France, I end the day exhausted, sometimes with a headache. I think the reason for this reaction is quite simple: The unconscious control that I exert over my own environment when I speak English must suddenly become conscious control. It's like learning a new stroke in swimming: You have to pay attention to *every* move — you have to be aware of the interaction of moves that will later become routine. Or you could say it's similar to the way you feel when you are sleeping away from home and wake up in the middle of the first night. It takes concentrated effort to remember where you are and why you are there. At home when you wake up, everything is right where you know it will be. Away, you must figure out where things are, and this takes conscious effort.

For the first few days I live in a foreign culture, things that are natural and unconscious demand thought, attention, and energy. Nothing is familiar. Every language has elements of nonverbal as well as verbal communication. In a foreign setting, nothing can be spontaneous or taken for granted. The simplest things—how to sneeze politely, whether to shake hands, how to answer the telephone, and where to keep my hands while I'm eating—all become self-conscious decisions. After all, no one wants to look like a fool!

So during my first few days abroad, I keep pretty still and watch my step. The focus, the concentration, and the fear of making a significant goof all produce a change in my personality. I'm quieter, much more reserved, and certainly not so quick with a joke or a wisecrack. A friend from France, fluent in both English and French, told me that he has the same experience each time he visits the United States. One time, when we were discussing a serious issue, I insisted on speaking English. He complained that this gave me an advantage. Even though his English is excellent, I knew he was right!

You don't have to travel abroad to know about the concentration, effort, and anxiety associated with speaking a foreign language. Why is it that we all feel so vulnerable, so inept, sometimes so stupid when we are learning a foreign language? Without language we feel somehow alone, voiceless, and powerless. We don't like to lose our control over the way we let people understand who we are. I never like losing (even temporarily) my sense of humor and wit during my first few days in France.

LANGUAGE AND MEANING

So far I've been using my experience in learning and using French to help me talk about verbal language. Language, however, is a much broader concept than that. For example, the most common language used by scientists, engineers, and mathematicians is mathematics. Philosophers have a common language called "symbolic logic." Language can also be composed of sounds (as in music), feelings (as in poetry or religion), visual forms (as in art), or gestures (as in dance or mime).

When you look at language this way, you can see that it crosses all disciplinary lines. What we will consider in this chapter is the broader meaning of language and its impact on your life. Just as you've seen in Chapter 1 how writing touches all aspects of our lives and varies according to our use of it, so language in general encompasses more than a single discipline or activity. Although there is a specific field of study, linguistics, that focuses on the ways languages are formed, developed, and used, the aim of this chapter is to help you understand the general importance of language for all people, whether or not they choose to study a specific aspect of language. And we're not going to consider only the study of a *foreign language*. In this chapter, we will focus on the universal aspects of language in its broadest sense (spoken, written, nonverbal, symbolic) and on the ways language connects us with others. For example, English is the tool that all the writers of this book have in common. It is also the connection between you and everyone else in the English-speaking world.

We have to be careful, however, when we talk about this connection. Many scholars of language point out that there is an essential difference between the name of something and the thing itself. In other words, language and meaning are not always related in a simple and straightforward way. In an example made famous by S. I. Hayakawa, the word "cow" means, on one level, Bessie, the animal in the barn owned by a family; "cow" on another level is a dictionary definition of a four-legged mammal that gives milk; "cow" on another level is part of the farm assets, worth a certain amount of money; and "cow" may also be a metaphoric verb, as in "She was cowed," meaning "intimidated." In other words, cow is one thing to one person in one context, another thing to another person in another context.

There's always a danger of being too literal when words can be used for many different meanings. For instance, Hayakawa talks about "snarl words" and "purr words"; that is, words that are used to indicate one's mood or attitude and not necessarily a fact or a condition. I'm sure many examples spring to mind. If you walk into class late for the third day in a row and your professor stops class to mutter, "I'm so glad you decided to honor us with your presence this morning," you are surely not going to think you are being flattered! As a native speaker of the language, you have learned to distinguish between the words and the real meaning. And you won't miss the snarl in the words!

WRITING 2.

Make a list of as many types of languages as you can think of (use examples). For instance, mathematics is a language; you speak in mathematical language by writing $2+2=4$. What does shaking your head mean in your own body language? See what examples you can come up with that others may overlook.

LANGUAGE AND CONTROL

We have already seen that language can do many things for us. Because it provides the connection between us and the concepts and things that surround us, language can give us ease and comfort, a means of expressing ourselves and of organizing our thoughts, and it can empower us by allowing us to name and define our world. However, language can disable and mislead as readily as it can empower and enlighten. Through our own ignorance or another's maliciousness, language can hinder as much as it can help. The individuals who know how to control language are much better able to control their experience.

An example of what I mean is the function of names. We all know people who insist on being called by their title. Why? "Dr." or "Professor" or "General" adds a different element to the conversation. My friend Freny Daruvala asks most people to call her by her first name from the start. Her last name is difficult to pronounce. Her first name isn't much easier, but it's shorter. While she's teaching people how to say her name, she's putting them at ease with her. Freny's profession is speech therapy, so she takes advantage of a language barrier to break down other kinds of barriers. The opposite would happen if someone like that insisted on using her title and the unpronounceable last name.

Here's another example. Imagine that your family moved from where you now live all the way across the United States to another region. The first day of school your classmates invite you to join them after school for a grinder and a cabinet. You find out later that day that a grinder is a sandwich, which you call a submarine, hero, or hoagie. A cabinet is a milkshake. How soon will you be comfortable among your new friends? When you know their language, and probably not before then.

The same kind of thing happened to me my sophomore year in college. My roommate was from London, and despite our different accents, we understood each other from the start. Then one morning, she woke me before my alarm went off (not a smart thing for her to do!) with a puzzled question. "Should I wear a jumper to class today?" she asked, looking out the window at the beautiful fall morning. I thought grumpily that she needed to learn quickly not to consult me on her choice of wardrobe that early in the morning, and I began to tell her what I thought as kindly as possible, given the hour. After a brief and confusing conversation, I discovered that what she really wanted to know was whether or not she should take a sweater with her to class. The British word for sweater is "jumper." Her question had to do with the new climate and not at all with fashion! We had several conversations of the same sort during the year; she insisted on calling my stereo a "gramophone" despite my best efforts to change her vocabulary. Interestingly enough, it was only at the end of the first month that she noticed she had been mispronouncing my name, a habit I liked so much that all my best friends from college still call me Karen with an "ah" sound instead of the usual American pronunciation (with a short "a" sound).

OUT OF CONTROL

These examples illustrate the way language allows us to fit ourselves in or allows others to keep us out. You probably have memories of excluding or being excluded through language. Children frequently develop a code with a friend so that younger siblings cannot follow the conversation. When I was very young, my parents spelled things out loud to each other so that I could not understand what they were saying. (At Christmas time, for example, you might have heard "T-R-I-C-Y-C-L-E" frequently whispered.) You probably use language your teachers cannot understand at times, and you have probably thought that your professors were speaking a different language when you first heard lectures in a new or difficult course.

Every day we can find examples of the ways language is tied to issues of autonomy and respect. In 1988 at Gallaudet University, a university for deaf students, the Board of Trustees appointed someone as president who could not communicate with the students in sign language. The students and faculty wanted another candidate, one who was deaf. Although the trustees didn't think this was important, the student revolution eventually brought about the change they desired. In a way sign language was the key to the whole situation. The presidential candidate who could speak to the students and faculty was the one they preferred. Why? Because mastery of a group's language gives you access to that group. No one can exclude you to the same extent, and frequently no one will want to exclude you once you speak the same language.

The Gallaudet example illustrates an important focus of this chapter: We are discussing *language*, not necessarily *speech*. Although most languages are spoken languages, we have already talked about several that are not, some that don't even use words the way we know them. For example, computer languages are composed of digital impulses. Music is composed of graduated tones. And there are nonverbal languages as complex and influential as the verbal ones. Each of these languages shares characteristics with the spoken languages we think of most frequently when we talk about language. They are all, for instance, highly organized; they are composed of a system of symbols that are predictable and reconstructible. If we use these symbols in unpredictable ways, we lose meaning. Many of us have had this experience on a very practical level when typing the wrong commands on the computer and getting the response "syntax error." Essentially, when the computer does not recognize meaning, it will tell us to fix up our computer language.

VERBAL AND NONVERBAL LANGUAGES

Because all languages are composed of symbols arranged in a systematic way, these symbols will be recognizable by the native speaker from context, experience, tradition, or structural organization. The trouble occurs when a symbol looks or sounds the same in more than one language, though it may have a completely different meaning or no meaning at all unless it is linked with another symbol. An engineer once told me about a translation he read that referred to a "wet male sheep." He finally figured out that the original reference, in another language, was to a "hydraulic ram."

Sociologists of language argue that 60 percent to 70 percent of human communication is nonverbal. Others go further to assert that if any given message contains contradictions between the verbal and the nonverbal content, the nonverbal will prevail. Think about the implications of this assertion. Can you imagine times when the two types of language might be in conflict? For example, imagine someone close to tears saying, "I don't love you any more." What is the possible message conveyed by the contradictory languages? Or imagine someone saying, "Of course I still love you" in a gruff or distant tone. Which message would you take as real? The words or the tone?

When we are traveling together, my husband and I have learned to pay close attention to nonverbal messages. Because I do not intuitively understand the difference between right and left (I still have to stop and think each time I indicate direction), my husband has become used to hearing me say, "Take a sharp right here," while pointing to the left. He almost always double-checks before taking the turn, and he's become adroit at U-turns on country roads! Similarly, I quickly learned that in France when I am asked if I wish to have seconds, I must shake my head to indicate "no" while saying "merci" (which means "thank you"). If I fail to use the nonverbal clue, I'll get seconds of something I may not wish to eat.

Probably one of the most interesting areas of nonverbal language is body language, an area in which all of us who have grown up in the same culture are native speakers. But it's a different story when we are transplanted into another culture. For example, remember the last time someone stood either too close or too far away while talking to you? If the person stood too close, how did you feel? Annoyed? Threatened? Slightly nervous? Your reaction probably depended on the distance. Likewise, someone standing too far from you may have given you the impression that he or she was aloof, uninterested, maybe even untrustworthy. Personal space, the physical perimeter within which we want to remain sovereign, varies with individuals and cultures. Violating that personal space can be a serious breach of etiquette. Yet the definition of that space is variable, so we run the risk of offending without knowing that we are doing so when we leave our own culture and become a speaker of a foreign body language.

Another aspect of nonverbal language is time. The way we use it, the way we view it, whether we even think of it—all are indications of our cultural language. In some Latin American cultures, it's acceptable and even normal to be thirty or more minutes late to an important business interview. In North American culture, however, we'd probably be in trouble if we did that too often. Still another aspect of nonverbal language is sound. People react to the invasion of their personal sense of sound privacy the same way they react to invasion of their space boundaries. These reactions depend on culture and individual traits. Most of you—and your parents—would probably agree that these reactions are also dependent on age. How many times do your parents complain that music is too loud when you don't notice any extreme noise yourself?

WRITING 3.

Make a list of situations in which you've experienced verbal and nonverbal messages that contradict each other. Does the nonverbal prevail each time? Why or why not?

THE DARK SIDE: SILENCING

It may not be readily apparent, but language can also have oppressive aspects. For example, what if someone is incapable of using language to express his or her ideas? We have all experienced the frustration of forgetting the word we're searching for or the embarrassment of not recognizing someone's meaning. This kind of difficulty happens on a daily basis to foreigners trying to become a part of a new culture. I knew a recent Soviet immigrant who consistently referred to the "fire distinguisher" and used the expression "toes over nose" when she meant "head over heels." When you think about it, each of these strange expressions has its own logic to a nonnative.

Forgetfulness or ignorance can be annoying, temporary obstacles. However, more serious damage can be inflicted by robbing us of the use of language, by silencing us, or by making us speak in ways that violate our personal beliefs or identity. One of the first steps undertaken by any dictator is to limit what people can say both publicly and privately. Most politically powerless people cannot or may not speak or write freely. Stifling our language will ultimately limit our control over our own lives. And when we are denied the use of language to reflect our individuality, we are at quite a disadvantage.

An example of this misuse of language can be found in a sociolinguistic study of the customs of courtroom stenographers. The long-standing public perception of the role of these court stenographers holds that they take a verbatim record of the trial proceedings and that their reports accurately include all speech that occurs during the trial. However, according to the author of the study, some stenographers take liberties when they transcribe the conversations by correcting grammatical errors in the language of the judges, the attorneys, and educated expert witnesses. They do not, however, make any such corrections when they transcribe the language of other witnesses. Citing a handbook published by the National Shorthand Reporters Association, Anne Graffam Walker points out a guideline headed "Judges and Lawyers are Supposed to be Educated Men":

> Another important thing to remember is that all judges and most if not all lawyers are men of education, and they will resent having attributed to them in stenographic reports ungrammatical and carelessly phrased remarks. Witnesses often are illiterate, and as a rule they do not see the reports of their testimony.

Our own culture restricts linguistic freedom in small ways that are not immediately apparent. For instance, articles that refer to a doctor as "he" and a nurse as "she" subtly deprive the female doctors and the male nurses of their credibility. Perhaps you noticed that the writer of the guideline cited above assumed that judges and lawyers are "educated men." A female attorney may feel excluded from the generalization. Indeed, our language may communicate assumptions like this to others who are learning about our culture. This sexist use of language not only cheats us of proper understanding but also begins to control the way we express ourselves, the way we think about ourselves. That is why, for instance, minority groups such as Native Americans and blacks would rather name themselves than accept the names the ruling majority gives them.

WRITING 4.

Keep a log for a week of the language you hear around you that could subtly influence people's attitudes. You may wish to use some of the preceding examples to start with, but try to find your own examples as well. Be sure to listen to different types of language, from your professors' lectures to informal conversation at the lunch table. Do you remember language taught to you by friends or family that expresses a certain attitude? Have you changed some of the expressions that you were taught since you arrived on campus? At the end of the week, pick one entry in your log that you think no one else will select. Can you explain to your classmates why you think this language should be changed?

LANGUAGE AND IDENTITY

Let's look further at the relationship between language and a person's identity. For instance, most people would resist the idea of being called by a number instead of a name. Why? What is the difference between a number and a name? A partial answer relates to identity. A number is just one more part of a long series. It has no history, no story connected with it, no tradition, no possibility of being shortened into a nickname. Yet a number is distinctly individual. I believe that our names gradually grow their own histories along with us, as we mature and accumulate experience and adventures. Our names, like the word "cow" that we talked about earlier, are not limited to one concrete thing; they represent meaning. The number, in our society, does not offer us this possibility. In another context, it might; but for us, the name has many potential meanings and associations that the number just does not possess. Language gives us a name and then helps us grow the name along with our identity.

Language reveals a great deal about us, too. Not just in the obvious ways, such as how much we talk, how well we talk, and what words we select, but in more subtle ways. For instance, do artistic people tend to use images and metaphors more frequently than other people do? Do shy people use shorter sentences and simpler words? When we are excited, we talk faster and at a higher pitch than when we are depressed or sad. At one point in my life, I spent a great deal of my time worrying about what I was going to do with my career. Everything seemed up in the air and incomplete as I tried to find a direction for my life. A good friend pointed out to me one day that I rarely finished any sentence I began in conversation. My language directly mirrored the incomplete state of my life plans at that moment.

Language also gives identity to groups and communities. In French-speaking Quebec Province, the French majority insists that the official language be French instead of the language of the English-speaking minority. Parts of the United States provide bilingual education, voting instructions, and legal assistance for Spanish-speaking Americans. Language in these cases is used as a way of providing economic or political power and access to groups of citizens. Moreover, language provides a sense of belonging (or not belonging), and it is frequently used in this way. For example, Robbins Burling points out in *Man's Many Voices* that the Walbiri tribe in central Australia have a secret language used only among the Walbiri men. Learning the language (which is an extremely sophisticated form of pig latin) determines a youth's readiness to be accepted as an adult. Boys must infer the rules of the secret language by listening carefully to the older men. Only when they have gained a certain adeptness at using this language are they accepted as full-fledged members of the male elite.

Students in college also have to learn new varieties of language. An understanding of how language functions in a different setting helps us feel more comfortable in that setting. Think, for instance, of the lectures you hear in biology or chemistry classes as opposed to those in your sociology or history classes. What are some of the characteristics of those lectures? Which predominate, words or symbols? Do the teachers talk with different tones of voice? How long are their sentences? What do they write on the board or on an overhead? Next think about the small class discussions you participate in. What are the differences between these discussions and the lectures you attend?

And what are the differences between these discussions and your conversations with close friends over dinner? Would you tell the same stories, use the same words, even speak with the same volume of voice? What about the words, the slang, and the tone of voice you would use if you were interviewing for a job you wanted very much? Would they be the same as a late night phone conversation with your best friend? Language shapes your image as seen by others. It gives you access to various groups (as when Walbiri boys become men and when prospective computer scientists learn to use computer languages), and it allows you tremendous flexibility. Knowing how to use language to fit into various contexts gives you a great deal of personal power and choice.

USING THE KEY

Language is the essential key to discovering the link between you and your world and is the key to understanding other cultures and other people's views. Like any key, it fits only certain locks. Different settings require different languages. And like any other tool, language is useful only when the user is skilled at manipulating it and when it is carefully maintained. In the university, you will gain familiarity and skill in the languages of art, poetry, dance, or music; in computer and mathematical languages; and in scientific symbols. And as you become assimilated into the culture of the university, you may see your own verbal and nonverbal languages change. Each chapter in this book introduces elements of the language of a discipline. An understanding of the varying voices in the university offers access to the college community you've just joined, and the study of language will open many doors for you.

Notes.   I wish to acknowledge the assistance of a Gettysburg College freshman composition class taught by Ms. Anne Showalter in the spring semester of 1988.

SUGGESTIONS FOR RESEARCH
Lobbying for Language Change

After your class has discussed Writing 4, go back to your log to review the comments on language that you made in light of the class discussion. Pick one or two examples from your log that seem to be related. You might have noticed several nonverbal examples, for instance, or you may find that your professors' language includes examples that interest you. Once you have a few related examples, try reading your campus newspaper, the local paper, and one national paper or magazine with attention to the same types of language. Keep these examples in your log as well. The purpose of this exercise is twofold: You will be gaining sensitivity to the role language plays in influencing attitudes, and you will be accumulating evidence for the assignment that follows.

As a final preparatory step, use your university library to find a recent article on language and culture (these are two good keywords to use in a computer search) or set up an appointment to interview one of the following people:

1. The Director of African-American Studies or the African-American Center on your campus
2. The Director of Women's Studies or the Women's Center on your campus
3. Your university's Affirmative Action officer
4. Someone recommended by your teacher who is an expert in linguistics, sociology, psychology, or anthropology
5. One of your own professors who has shown sensitivity to language usage in class

Spend about fifteen minutes interviewing this individual. Use the examples you have selected from your log to begin the conversation. You should ask this person for his or her opinion about your examples, for suggestions for further study on these or other related examples, and for an assessment of the effect of such language used in spoken or written form. Speculate with this person about ways to change the effects of this type of language or about ways to use language with positive effects. When you finish the interview, spend about fifteen more minutes writing about what you learned in the conversation.

Write a letter to the University President, the Dean of your college, or to one of the newspapers or magazines you have been reading. Point out what you have discovered about the use of language in the context you have selected, and make a suggestion about the ways that language should be amended. If you believe that a linguistic practice should be eliminated, you will need to provide some evidence about how the language is currently being used and why it should stop. Use your own observations to back up your recommendation.

Observing Social Language

For this project, work in groups of three. Each person should select two different settings in which he or she participates on a regular basis, such as classes, jobs, social settings, or family situations. You will be using these settings to conduct some linguistic research. First you will need to construct a listening/observation log, and then you will record your observations over a fixed period of time.

Divide each page of your log into two sections by drawing a line down the middle of the page. On one side, record your observations of the verbal patterns you hear, and on the other side, record your observations of nonverbal patterns. For instance, if you selected a large lecture class in introductory math or science, your log entry might look like this:

Verbal	Nonverbal
Defines terms	One person speaks at a time
Uses symbols/numbers	Lecture mode predominates
Short sentences	Prof draws on board
Repetition for emphasis	Students sit in groups toward
	rear of classroom
Uses examples	Prof's voice distinct and clear

If you select dinner with your family as another setting, your log will have very different observations.

It's not always easy to get beyond the first obvious observations, but as you persist you will find that you notice more and more verbal and nonverbal clues. After you have kept the log for a week, read and discuss your entries with your group. From the six settings your group has worked with, select the two that offer the most contrast. Arrange for all the group members to attend these two settings at least once. Each group member should keep his or her own log, trying to move beyond the initial observations to find more details or linguistic behaviors.

Your group report will draw on these observations by comparing and contrasting the linguistic activity—both verbal and nonverbal—as if you were a team of anthropologists who travel back from the future to visit your campus. Your team's assignment is to study American college student culture and to draw some conclusions from the linguistic behavior you have observed. You will be making a report on your return. This report will include the following:

1. A brief description of the linguistic activity you observed in each setting
2. A discussion of the differences and similarities in the language observed in these settings
3. A general conclusion about American college student culture drawn from the data observed
4. (Optional) Recommendations for further study or action by your team's government

Feel free to be imaginative in writing this report.

READINGS

Frank Conroy
THINK ABOUT IT:
Ways We Know; and Don't

At the beginning of this chapter, we looked at ways that nonverbal language operates: time, space, gestures. In this essay, Frank Conroy (b. 1936) reflects on ways that he has learned new things during his lifetime, many of which reflect nonverbal and cultural uses of language to communicate. As you read, notice how often Conroy actually describes the physical, or nonverbal, communication in addition to or in place of the verbal communication. Can you find times when these two types of language conflict? If so, which one predominates? How is language (verbal and nonverbal) used to exclude in this piece? How is language related to Conroy's personal identity and power?

When I was sixteen I worked selling hot dogs at a stand in the Fourteenth Street subway station in New York City, one level above the trains and one below the street, where the crowds continually flowed back and forth. I worked with three Puerto Rican men who could not speak English. I had no Spanish, and although we understood each other well with regard to the tasks at hand, sensing and adjusting to each other's body movements in the extremely confined space in which we operated, I felt isolated with no one to talk to. On my break I came out from behind the counter and passed the time with two old black men who ran a shoeshine stand in a dark corner of the corridor. It was a poor location, half hidden by columns, and they didn't have much business. I would sit with my back against the wall while they stood or moved around their ancient elevated stand, talking to each other or to me, but always staring into the distance as they did so.

As the weeks went by I realized that they never looked at anything in their immediate vicinity—not at me or their stand or anybody who might come within ten or fifteen feet. They did not look at approaching customers once they were inside the perimeter. Save for the instant it took to discern the color of the shoes, they did not even look at what they were doing while they worked, but rubbed in polish, brushed, and buffed by feel while looking over their shoulders, into the distance, as if awaiting the arrival of an important person. Of course there wasn't all that much distance in the underground station, but their behavior was so focused and consistent they seemed somehow to transcend the physical. A powerful mood was created, and I came almost to believe that these men could see through walls, through girders, and around corners to whatever hyperspace it was where whoever it was they were waiting and watching for would finally emerge. Their scattered talk was hip, elliptical, and hinted at mysteries beyond my white boy's ken, but it was the staring off, the long, steady staring off, that had me hypnotized. I left for a better job, with handshakes from both of them, without understanding what I had seen.

Perhaps ten years later, after playing jazz with black musicians in various Harlem clubs, hanging out uptown with a few young artists and intellectuals, I began to learn from them something of the extraordinarily varied and complex riffs and rituals embraced by different people to help themselves get through life in the ghetto. Fantasy of all kinds— from playful to dangerous—was in the very air of Harlem. It was the spice of uptown life.

Only then did I understand the two shoeshine men. They were trapped in a demeaning situation in a dark corner in an underground corridor in a filthy subway system. Their continuous staring off was a kind of statement, a kind of dance. Our bodies are here, went the statement, but our souls are receiving nourishment from distant sources only we can see. They were powerful magic dancers, sorcerers almost, and thirty-five years later I can still feel the pressure of their spell.

The light bulb may appear over your head, is what I'm saying, but it may be a while before it actually goes on. Early in my attempts to learn jazz piano, I used to listen to recordings of a fine player named Red Garland, whose music I admired. I couldn't quite figure out what he was doing with his left hand, however; the chords eluded me. I went uptown to an obscure club where he was playing with his trio, caught him on his break, and simply asked him. "Sixths," he said cheerfully. And then he went away.

I didn't know what to make of it. The basic jazz chord is the seventh, which comes in various configurations, but it is what it is. I was a self-taught pianist, pretty shaky on theory and harmony, and when he said sixths I kept trying to fit the information into what I already knew, and it didn't fit. But it stuck in my mind—a tantalizing mystery.

A couple of years later, when I began playing with a bass player, I discovered more or less by accident that if the bass played the root and I played a sixth based on the fifth note of the scale, a very interesting chord involving both instruments emerged. Ordinarily, I suppose I would have skipped over the matter and not paid much attention, but I remembered Garland's remark and so I stopped and spent a week or two working out the voicings, and greatly strengthened my foundations as a player. I had remembered what I hadn't understood, you might say, until my life caught up with the information and the light bulb went on.

I remember another, more complicated example from my sophomore year at a small liberal-arts college outside Philadelphia. I seemed never to be able to get up in time for breakfast in the dining hall. I

would get coffee and a doughnut in the Coop instead—a basement area
with about a dozen small tables where students could get something to
eat at odd hours. Several mornings in a row I noticed a strange man
sitting by himself with a cup of coffee.

He was in his sixties, perhaps, and sat straight in his chair with
very little extraneous movement. I guessed he was some sort of distinguished visitor to the college who had decided to put in some time at
a student hangout. But no one ever sat with him. One morning I
approached his table and asked if I could join him.

"Certainly," he said. "Please do." He had perhaps the clearest eyes
I had ever seen, like blue ice, and to be held in their steady gaze was
not, at first, an entirely comfortable experience. His eyes gave nothing
away about himself while at the same time creating in me the eerie
impression that he was looking directly into my soul. He asked a few
quick questions, as if to put me at my ease, and we fell into conversation. He was William O. Douglas from the Supreme Court, and when
he saw how startled I was he said, "Call me Bill. Now tell me what
you're studying and why you get up so late in the morning." Thus
began a series of talks that stretched over many weeks. The fact that I
was an ignorant sophomore with literary pretentions who knew nothing
about the law didn't seem to bother him. We talked about everything
from Shakespeare to the possibility of life on other planets. One day I
mentioned that I was going to have dinner with Judge Learned Hand. I
explained that Hand was my girlfriend's grandfather. Douglas nodded,
but I could tell he was surprised at the coincidence of my knowing the
chief judge of the most important court in the country save the Supreme
Court itself. After fifteen years on the bench Judge Hand had become a
famous man, both in and out of legal circles—a living legend, to his
own dismay. "Tell him hello and give him my best regards," Douglas
said.

Learned Hand, in his eighties, was a short, barrel-chested man with
a large, square head, huge, thick, bristling eyebrows, and soft brown
eyes. He radiated energy and would sometimes bark out remarks or
questions in the living room as if he were in court. His humor was
sharp, but often leavened with a touch of self-mockery. When something caught his funny bone he would burst out with explosive laughter—the laughter of a man who enjoyed laughing. He had a large
repertoire of dramatic expressions involving the use of his eyebrows—
very useful, he told me conspiratorially, when looking down on things
from behind the bench. (The court stenographer could not record the
movement of his eyebrows.) When I told him I'd been talking to William
O. Douglas, they first shot up in exaggerated surprise, and then lowered
and moved forward in a glower.

"*Justice* William O. Douglas, young man," he admonished. "Justice
Douglas, if you please." About the Supreme Court in general, Hand
insisted on a tone of profound respect. Little did I know that in private

correspondence he had referred to the Court as "The Blessed Saints, Cherubim and Seraphim," "The Jolly Boys," "The Nine Tin Jesuses," "The Nine Blameless Ethiopians," and my particular favorite,"The Nine Blessed Chalices of the Sacred Effluvium."

Hand was badly stooped and had a lot of pain in his lower back. Martinis helped, but his strict Yankee wife approved of only one before dinner. It was my job to make him the second and somehow slip it to him. If the pain was particularly acute he would get out of his chair and lie flat on the rug, still talking, and finish his point without missing a beat. He flattered me by asking for my impression of Justice Douglas, instructed me to convey his warmest regards, and then began talking about the Dennis case, which he described as a particularly tricky and difficult case involving the prosecution of eleven leaders of the Communist party. He had just started in on the First Amendment and free speech when we were called into dinner.

William O. Douglas loved the outdoors with a passion, and we fell into the habit of having coffee in the Coop and then strolling under the tress down toward the duck pond. About the Dennis case, he said something to this effect: "Eleven Communists arrested by the government. Up to no good, said the government; dangerous people, violent overthrow, etc., First Amendment, said the defense, freedom of speech, etc." Douglas stopped walking. "Clear and present danger."

"What?" I asked. He often talked in a telegraphic manner, and one was expected to keep up with him. It was sometimes like listening to a man thinking out loud.

"Clear and present danger," he said. "That was the issue. Did they constitute a clear and present danger? I don't think so. I think everybody took the language pretty far in Dennis." He began walking, striding along quickly. Again, one was expected to keep up with him. "The F.B.I. was all over them. Phones tapped, constant surveillance. How could it be clear and present danger with the F.B.I. watching every move they made? That's a ginkgo," he said suddenly, pointing at a tree. "A beauty. You don't see those every day. Ask Hand about clear and present danger."

I was in fact reluctant to do so. Douglas's argument seemed to me to be crushing—the last word, really—and I didn't want to embarrass Judge Hand. But back in the living room, on the second martini, the old man asked about Douglas. I sort of scratched my nose and recapitulated the conversation by the ginkgo tree.

"What?" Hand shouted. "Speak up, sir, for heaven's sake."

"He said the F.B.I. was watching them all the time so there couldn't be a clear and present danger," I blurted out, blushing as I said it.

A terrible silence filled the room. Hand's eyebrows writhed on his face like two huge caterpillars. He leaned forward in the wing chair, his face settling, finally, into a grim expression. "I am astonished," he said softly, his eyes holding mine, "at Justice Douglas's newfound faith in the Federal Bureau of Investigation." His big, granite head moved even closer to mine, until I could smell the martini. "I had understood him to consider it a politically corrupt, incompetent organization, directed by a power-crazed lunatic." I realized I had been holding my breath throughout all of this, and as I relaxed, I saw the faintest trace of a smile cross Hand's face. Things are sometimes more complicated than they first appear, his smile seemed to say. The old man leaned back. "The proximity of the danger is something to think about. Ask him about that. See what he says."

I chewed the matter over as I returned to campus. Hand had pointed out some of Douglas's language about the F.B.I. from other sources that seemed to bear out his point. I thought about the words "clear and present danger," and the fact that if you looked at them closely they might not be as simple as they had first appeared. What degree of danger? Did the word "present" allude to the proximity of the danger, or just the fact that the danger was there at all—that it wasn't an anticipated danger? Were there other hidden factors these great men were weighing of which I was unaware?

But Douglas was gone, back to Washington. (The writer in me is tempted to create a scene here—to invent one for dramatic purposes—but of course I can't do that.) My brief time as a messenger boy was over, and I felt a certain frustration, as if, with a few more exchanges, the matter of *Dennis v. United States* might have been resolved to my satisfaction. They'd left me high and dry. But, of course, it is precisely because the matter did not resolve that has caused me to think about it, off and on, all these years. "The Constitution," Hand used to say to me flatly, "is a piece of paper. The Bill of Rights is a piece of paper." It was many years before I understood what he meant. Documents alone do not keep democracy alive, nor maintain the state of law. There is no particular safety in them. Living men and women, generation after generation, must continually remake democracy and the law, and that involves an ongoing state of tension between the past and the present which will never completely resolve.

Education doesn't end until life ends, because you never know when you're going to understand something you hadn't understood before. For me, the magic dance of the shoeshine men was the kind of experience in which understanding came with a kind of click, a resolving kind of click. The same with the experience at the piano. What happened with Justice Douglas and Judge Hand was different, and makes the point that understanding does not always mean resolution. Indeed, in our intellectual lives, our creative lives, it is perhaps those problems that will never resolve that rightly claim the lion's share of our energies. The physical body exists in a constant state of tension as it maintains homeostasis, and so too does the active mind embrace the tension of never being certain, never being absolutely sure, never being done, as it engages the world. That is our special fate, our inexpressibly valuable condition.

OPTIONS FOR WRITING

1. Write a letter to an old friend, reminiscing about some important event in your childhood. Select an event that made a significant impression on you, and try to think through with your friend the surroundings, the mood you were in, the event itself, and the lessons you learned from it.

2. Conroy, as a white person, describes his experience with the two black shoeshiners as expressing a difference in culture that he understood only later. In his other encounters, how does he make other differences known to you as the reader, and what role does "language" play in pointing out these differences?

3. Ask a friend with a different major or someone from a different cultural, ethnic, or age group if you can follow him or her around for a morning. Take your journal with you, and note only those events involving language (verbal or nonverbal) that are different from your accustomed way of thinking. (You may have to listen hard and force yourself to notice things you might not normally pay attention to.) After you have made a list, talk over these elements with your friend, and write about your shared reaction to this exercise.

4. In a short essay, write about an experience you have had that later taught you something you didn't know.

5. Write a play or a poem in which one character knows something and the other character is unaware that he or she knows it.

Edward T. Hall
PROXEMICS IN A CROSS-CULTURAL CONTEXT:
Germans, English, and French

Edward Hall's two most popular books, The Silent Language *(1959) and* The Hidden Dimension *(1966), offer a linguist's view of nonverbal language. Edward Hall (b. 1914) helped to bring the attention of Americans to the importance of understanding cultural aspects of language as well as the grammatical and spoken aspects. Nonverbal language is sometimes discussed in terms of kinesics (movement) and proxemics (space and use of distance). In the following excerpt from a longer chapter in* The Hidden Dimension, *Hall outlines significant differences among the English, the Germans, and Americans when it comes to the use and interpretation of space and body language. As you read, think of your attitudes toward your own private space, and try to imagine how you react to the various actions Hall describes. You might also think of other uses of body language that are important in American society and consider how people react when these standard practices are ignored.*

The Germans, the English, the Americans, and the French share significant portions of each other's cultures, but at many points their cultures clash. Consequently, the misunderstandings that arise are all the more serious because sophisticated Americans and Europeans take pride in correctly interpreting each other's behavior. Cultural differences which are out of awareness are, as a consequence, usually chalked up to ineptness, boorishness, or lack of interest on the part of the other person.

THE GERMANS

Whenever people from different countries come into repeated contact they begin to generalize about each other's behavior. The Germans and the German Swiss are no exception. Most of the intellectual and professional people I have talked to from these two countries eventually get around to commenting on American use of time and space. Both the Germans and the German Swiss have made consistent observations about how Americans structure time very tightly and are sticklers for schedules. They also note that Americans don't leave any free time for themselves (a point which has been made by Sebastian de Grazia in *Of Time, Work, and Leisure*).

Since neither the Germans nor the Swiss (particularly the German Swiss) could be regarded as completely casual about time, I have made it a point to question them further about their view of the American approach to time. They will say that Europeans will schedule fewer events in the same time than Americans do and they usually add that Europeans feel less "pressed" for time than Americans. Certainly, Europeans allow more time for virtually everything involving important human relationships. Many of my European subjects observed that in Europe human relationships are important whereas in the United States the schedule is important. Several of my subjects then took the next logical step and connected the handling of time with attitudes toward space, which Americans treat with incredible casualness. According to European standards, Americans use space in a wasteful way and seldom plan adequately for public needs. In fact, it would seem that Americans feel that people have no needs associated with space at all. By overemphasizing the schedule Americans tend to underemphasize individual space needs. I should mention at this point that all Europeans are not this perceptive. Many of them go no further than to say that in the United States they themselves feel pressured by time and they often complain that our cities lack variety. Nevertheless, given these observations made by Europeans one would expect that the Germans would be more upset by violations of spatial mores than the Americans.

Germans and Intrusions

I shall never forget my first experience with German proxemic patterns, which occurred when I was an undergraduate. My manners, my status, and my ego were attacked and crushed by a German in an instance where thirty years' residence in this country and an excellent command of English had not attenuated German definitions of what constitutes an intrusion. In order to understand the various issues that were at stake, it is necessary to refer back to two basic American patterns that are taken for granted in this country and which Americans therefore tend to treat as universal.

First, in the United States there is a commonly accepted, invisible boundary around any two or three people in conversation which separates them from others. Distance alone serves to isolate any such group and to endow it with a protective wall of privacy. Normally, voices are kept low to avoid intruding on others and if voices are heard, people will act as though they had not heard. In this way, privacy is granted whether it is actually present or not. The second pattern is somewhat more subtle and has to do with the exact point at which a person is experienced as actually having crossed a boundary and entered a room. Talking through a screen door while standing outside a house is not considered by most Americans as being inside the house or room in any sense of the word. If one is standing on the threshold holding the door open and talking to someone inside, it is still defined informally and experienced as being *outside*. If one is in an office building and just "pokes his head in the door" of an office he's still outside the office. Just holding on to the doorjamb when one's body is inside the room still means a person has one foot "on base" as it were so he is not quite inside the other fellow's territory. None of these American spatial definitions is valid in northern Germany. In every instance where the American would consider himself *outside* he has already entered the German's territory and by definition would become involved with him. The following experience brought the conflict between these two patterns into focus.

It was a warm spring day of the type one finds only in the high, clean, clear air of Colorado, the kind of day that makes you glad you are alive. I was standing on the doorstep of a converted carriage house talking to a young woman who lived in an apartment upstairs. The first floor had been made into an artist's studio. The arrangement, however, was peculiar because the same entrance served both tenants. The occupants of the apartment used a small entryway and walked along one wall of the studio to reach the stairs to the apartment. You might say that they had an "easement" through the artist's territory. As I stood talking on the doorstep, I glanced to the left and noticed that some fifty to sixty feet away, inside the studio, the Prussian artist and two of his friends were also in conversation. He was facing so that if he glanced to one side he could just see me. I had noted his presence, but not wanting to appear presumptuous or to interrupt his conversation, I unconsciously applied the American rule and assumed that the two activities — my quiet conversation and his conversation — were not involved with each other. As I was soon to learn, this was a mistake, because in less time than it takes to tell, the artist had detached himself from his friends, crossed the intervening space, pushed my friend aside, and with eyes flashing, started shouting at me. By what right had I entered his studio without greeting him? Who had given me permission?

I felt bullied and humiliated, and even after almost thirty years, I can still feel my anger. Later study has given me greater understanding of the German pattern and I have learned that in the German's eyes I really had been intolerably rude. I was already "inside" the building and I intruded when I could *see* inside. For the German, there is no such thing as being inside the room without being inside the zone of intrusion, particularly if one looks at the other party, no matter how far away.

Recently, I obtained an independent check on how Germans feel about visual intrusion while investigating what people look at when they are in intimate, personal, social, and public situations. In the course of my research, I instructed subjects to photograph separately both a man and a woman in each of the above contexts. One of my assistants, who also happened to be German, photographed his subjects out of focus at public distance because, as he said, "You are not really supposed to look at other people at public distances *because it's intruding.*" This may explain the informal custom behind the German laws against photographing strangers in public places without their permission.

The "Private Sphere"

Germans sense their own space as an extension of the ego. One sees a clue to this feeling in the term "Lebensraum," which is impossible to translate because it summarizes so much. Hitler used it as an effective psychological lever to move the Germans to conquest.

In contrast to the Arab, as we shall see later, the German's ego is extraordinarily exposed, and he will go to almost any length to preserve his "private sphere." This was observed during World War II when American soldiers were offered opportunities to observe German prisoners under a variety of circumstances. In one instance in the Midwest, German P.W.s were housed four to a small hut. As soon as materials were available, each prisoner built a partition so that he could have *his own space*. In a less favorable setting in Germany when the *Wehrmacht* was collapsing, it was necessary to use open stockades because German prisoners were arriving faster than they could be accommodated. In this situation each soldier who could find the materials built his own tiny dwelling unit, sometimes no larger than a foxhole. It puzzled the Americans that the Germans did not pool their efforts and their scarce materials to create a larger, more efficient space, particularly in view of the very cold spring nights. Since that time I have observed frequent instances of the use of architectural extensions of this need to screen the ego. German houses with balconies are arranged so that there is visual privacy. Yards tend to be well fenced; but fenced or not, they are sacred.

The American view that space should be shared is particularly troublesome to the German. I cannot document the account of the early days of World War II occupation when Berlin was in ruins but the following situation was reported by an observer and it has the nightmarish quality that is often associated with inadvertent cross-cultural blunders. In Berlin at that time the housing shortage was indescribably acute. To provide relief, occupation authorities in the American zone ordered those Berliners who still had kitchens and baths intact to share them with their neighbors. The order finally had to be rescinded when the already overstressed Germans started killing each other over the shared facilities.

Public and private buildings in Germany often have double doors for soundproofing, as do many hotel rooms. In addition, the door is taken very seriously by Germans. Those Germans who come to America feel that our doors are flimsy and light. The meanings of the open door and the closed door are quite different in the two countries. In offices, Americans keep doors open; Germans keep doors closed. In Germany, the closed door does not mean that the man behind it wants to be alone or undisturbed, or that he is doing something he doesn't want someone else to see. It's simply that Germans think that open doors are sloppy and disorderly. To close the door preserves the integrity of the room and provides a protective boundary between people. Otherwise, they get too involved with each other. One of my German subjects commented, "If our family hadn't had doors, we would have had to change our way of life. Without doors we would have had many, many more fights. . . . When you can't talk, you retreat behind a door. . . . If there hadn't been doors, I would always have been within reach of my mother."

Whenever a German warms up to the subject of American enclosed space, he can be counted on to comment on the noise that is transmitted through walls and doors. To many Germans, our doors epitomize American life. They are thin and cheap; they seldom fit; and they lack the substantial quality of German doors. When they close they don't sound and feel solid. The click of the lock is indistinct, it rattles and indeed it may even be absent.

The open-door policy of American business and the closed-door patterns of German business culture cause clashes in the branches and subsidiaries of American firms in Germany. The point seems to be quite simple, yet failure to grasp it has caused considerable friction and misunderstanding between American and German managers overseas. I was once called in to advise a firm that has operations all over the world. One of the first questions asked was, "How do you get the Germans to keep their doors open?" In this company the open doors were making the Germans feel exposed and gave the whole operation an unusually relaxed and unbusinesslike air. Closed doors, on the other hand, gave the Americans the feeling that there was a conspiratorial air about the place and that they were being left out. The point is that whether the door is open or shut, it is not going to mean the same thing in the two countries.

Order in Space

The orderliness and hierarchical quality of German culture are communicated in their handling of space. Germans want to know where they stand and object strenuously to people crashing queues or people who "get out of line" or who do not obey signs such as "Keep out," "Authorized personnel only," and the like. Some of the German attitudes toward ourselves are traceable to our informal attitudes toward boundaries and to authority in general.

However, German anxiety due to American violations of order is nothing compared to that engendered in Germans by the Poles, who see no harm in a little disorder. To them lines and queues stand for regimentation and blind authority. I once saw a Pole crash a cafeteria line just "to stir up those sheep."

Germans get very technical about intrusion distance, as I mentioned earlier. When I once asked my students to describe the distance at which a third party would intrude on two people who were talking, there were no answers from the Americans. Each student knew that he could tell when he was being intruded on but he couldn't define intrusion or tell how he knew when it had occurred. However, a German and an Italian who had worked in Germany were both members of my class and they answered without any hesitation. Both stated that a third party would intrude on two people if he came within seven feet!

Many Americans feel that Germans are overly rigid in their behavior, unbending and formal. Some of this impression is created by differences in the handling of chairs while seated. The American doesn't seem to mind if people hitch their chairs up to adjust the distance to the situation—those that do mind would not think of saying anything, for to comment on the manners of others would be impolite. In Germany, however, it is a violation of the mores to change the position of your chair. An added deterrent for those who don't know better is the weight of most German furniture. Even the great architect Mies van der Rohe, who often rebelled against German tradition in his buildings, made his handsome chairs so heavy that anyone but a strong man would have difficulty in adjusting his seating position. To a German, light furniture is anathema, not only because it seems flimsy but because people move it and thereby destroy the order of things, including intrusions on the "private sphere." In one instance reported to me, a German newspaper editor who had moved to the United States had his visitor's chair bolted to the floor "at the proper distance" because he couldn't tolerate the American habit of adjusting the chair to the situation.

THE ENGLISH

It has been said that the English and the Americans are two great people separated by one language. The differences for which language gets blamed may not be due so much to words as to communications on other levels beginning with English intonation (which sounds affected to many Americans) and continuing to ego-linked ways of handling time, space, and materials. If there ever were two cultures in which differences of the proxemic details are marked it is in the educated (public school) English and the middle-class Americans. One of the basic reasons for this wide disparity is that in the United States we use space as a way of classifying people and activities, whereas in England it is the social system that determines who you are. In the United States, your address is an important cue to status (this applies not only to one's home but to the business address as well). The Joneses from Brooklyn and Miami are not as "in" as the Joneses from Newport and Palm Beach. Greenwich and Cape Cod are worlds apart from Newark and Miami. Businesses located on Madison and Park avenues have more tone than those on Seventh and Eighth avenues. A corner office is more prestigious than one next to the elevator or at the end of a long hall. The Englishman, however, is born and brought up in a social system. He is still Lord—no matter where you find him, even if it is behind the counter in a fishmonger's stall. In addition to class distinctions, there are differences between the English and ourselves in how space is allotted.

The middle-class American growing up in the United States feels he has a right to have his own room, or at least part of a room. My American subjects, when asked to draw an ideal room or office, invariably drew it for themselves and no one else. When asked to draw their present room or office, they drew only their own part of a shared room and then drew a line down the middle. Both male and female subjects identified the kitchen and the master bedroom as belonging to the mother or the wife, whereas Father's territory was a study or a den, if one was available; otherwise it was "the shop," "the basement," or sometimes only a workbench or the garage. American women who want to be alone can go to the bedroom and close the door. The closed door is the sign meaning "Do not disturb" or "I'm angry." An American is available if his door is open at home or at his office. He is expected not to shut himself off but to maintain himself in a state of constant readiness to answer the demands of others. Closed doors are for conferences, private conversations, and business, work that requires concentration, study, resting, sleeping, dressing, and sex.

The middle- and upper-class Englishman, on the other hand, is brought up in a nursery shared with brothers and sisters. The oldest occupies a room by himself which he vacates when he leaves for boarding school, possibly even at the age of nine or ten. The difference between a room of one's own and early conditioning to shared space,

while seeming inconsequential, has an important effect on the Englishman's attitude toward his own space. He may never have a permanent "room of his own" and seldom expects one or feels he is entitled
to one. Even Members of Parliament have no offices and often conduct
their business on the terrace overlooking the Thames. As a consequence,
the English are puzzled by the American need for a secure place in
which to work, an office. Americans working in England may become
annoyed if they are not provided with what they consider appropriate
enclosed work space. In regard to the need for walls as a screen for the
ego, this places the Americans somewhere between the Germans and
the English.

The contrasting English and American patterns have some remarkable implications, particularly if we assume that man, like other animals,
has a built-in need to shut himself off from others from time to time. An
English student in one of my seminars typified what happens when
hidden patterns clash. He was quite obviously experiencing strain in his
relationships with Americans. Nothing seemed to go right and it was
quite clear from his remarks that we did not know how to behave. An
analysis of his complaints showed that a major source of irritation was
that no American seemed to be able to pick up the subtle clues that
there were times when he didn't want his thoughts intruded on. As he
stated it, "I'm walking around the apartment and it seems that
whenever I want to be alone my roommate starts talking to me. Pretty
soon he's asking 'What's the matter?' and wants to know if I'm angry.
By then I am angry and say something."

It took some time but finally we were able to identify most of the
contrasting features of the American and British problems that were in
conflict in this case. When the American wants to be alone he goes into
a room and shuts the door—he depends on architectural features for
screening. For an American to refuse to talk to someone else present in
the same room, to give them the "silent treatment," is the ultimate form
of rejection and a sure sign of great displeasure. The English, on the
other hand, lacking rooms of their own since childhood, never developed the practice of using space as a refuge from others. They have
in effect internalized a set of barriers, which they erect and which others
are supposed to recognize. Therefore, the more the Englishman shuts
himself off when he is with an American the more likely the American
is to break in to assure himself that all is well. Tension lasts until the
two get to know each other. The important point is that the spatial and
architectural needs of each are not the same at all.

Using the Telephone

English internalized privacy mechanisms and the American privacy
screen result in very different customs regarding the telephone. There is
no wall or door against the telephone. Since it is impossible to tell from
the ring who is on the other end of the line, or how urgent his business

is, people feel compelled to answer the phone. As one would anticipate, the English when they feel the need to be with their thoughts treat the phone as an intrusion by someone who doesn't know any better. Since it is impossible to tell how preoccupied the other party will be they hesitate to use the phone; instead, they write notes. To phone is to be "pushy" and rude. A letter or telegram may be slower, but it is much less disrupting. Phones are for actual business and emergencies.

I used this system myself for several years when I lived in Santa Fe, New Mexico, during the depression. I dispensed with a phone because it cost money. Besides, I cherished the quiet of my tiny mountainside retreat and didn't want to be disturbed. This idiosyncrasy on my part produced a shocked reaction in others. People really didn't know what to do with me. You could see the consternation on their faces when, in answer to the question, "How do I get in touch with you?" I would reply, "Write me a post card. I come to the post office every day."

Having provided most of our middle-class citizens with private rooms and escape from the city to the suburbs, we have then proceeded to penetrate their most private spaces in their home with a most public device, the telephone. Anyone can reach us at any time. We are, in fact, so available that elaborate devices have to be devised so that busy people can function. The greatest skill and tact must be exercised in the message-screening process so that others will not be offended. So far our technology has not kept up with the needs of people to be alone with either their families or their thoughts. The problem stems from the fact that it is impossible to tell from the phone's ring who is calling and how urgent his business is. Some people have unlisted phones but then that makes it hard on friends who come to town who want to get in touch with them. The government solution is to have special phones for important people (traditionally red). The red line bypasses secretaries, coffee breaks, busy signals, and teen-agers, and is connected to White House, State Department, and Pentagon switchboards.

Neighbors

Americans living in England are remarkably consistent in their reactions to the English. Most of them are hurt and puzzled because they were brought up on American neighboring patterns and don't interpret the English ones correctly. In England propinquity means nothing. The fact that you live next door to a family does not entitle you to visit, borrow from, or socialize with them, or your children to play with theirs. Accurate figures on the number of Americans who adjust well to the English are difficult to obtain. The basic attitude of the English toward the Americans is tinged by our ex-colonial status. This attitude is much more in awareness and therefore more likely to be expressed than the unspoken right of the Englishman to maintain his privacy against the world. To the best of my knowledge, those who have tried to relate to the English purely on the basis of propinquity seldom if ever succeed. They may get to know and even like their neighbors, but it won't be because they live next door, because English relationships are patterned not according to space but according to social status.

Whose Room Is the Bedroom?

In upper middle-class English homes, it is the man, not the woman, who has the privacy of the bedroom, presumably as protection from children who haven't yet internalized the English patterns of privacy. The man, not the woman, has a dressing room; the man also has a study which affords privacy. The Englishman is fastidious about his clothes and expects to spend a great deal of time and attention in their purchase. In contrast, English women approach the buying of clothes in a manner reminiscent of the American male.

Talking Loud and Soft

Proper spacing between people is maintained in many ways. Loudness of the voice is one of the mechanisms which also varies from culture to culture. In England and in Europe generally, Americans are continually accused of loud talking, which is a function of two forms of vocal control: (a) loudness, and (b) modulation for direction. Americans increase the volume as a function of distance, using several levels (whisper, normal voice, loud shout, etc.). In many situations, the more gregarious Americans do not care if they can be overheard. In fact, it is part of their openness showing that we have nothing to hide. The English do care, for to get along without private offices and not intrude they have developed skills in beaming the voice toward the person they are talking to, carefully adjusting it so that it just barely overrides the background noise and distance. For the English to be overheard is to intrude on others, a failure in manners and a sign of socially inferior behavior. However, because of the way they modulate their voices the English in an American setting may sound and look conspiratorial to Americans, which can result in their being branded as troublemakers.

Eye Behavior

A study of eye behavior reveals some interesting contrasts between the two cultures. Englishmen in this country have trouble not only when they want to be alone and shut themselves off but also when they want to interact. They never know for sure whether an American is listening. We, on the other hand, are equally unsure as to whether the English have understood us. Many of these ambiguities in communication center on differences in the use of the eyes. The Englishman is taught to pay strict attention, to listen carefully, which he must do if he is polite and there are not protective walls to screen out sound. He doesn't bob his head or grunt to let you know he understands. He blinks his eyes to let you know that he has heard you. Americans, on the other hand, are taught not to stare. We look the other person straight in the eye without wavering only when we want to be particularly certain that we are getting through to him.

The gaze of the American directed toward his conversational partner often wanders from one eye to the other and even leaves the face for long periods. Proper English listening behavior includes immobilization of the eyes at social distance, so that whichever eye one looks at gives the appearance of looking straight at you. In order to accomplish this feat, the Englishman must be eight or more feet away. He is too close when the 12-degree horizontal span of the macula won't permit a steady gaze. At less than eight feet, one *must* look at either one eye or the other.

OPTIONS FOR WRITING

1. Imagine yourself a newly arrived visitor to campus. Write a letter home to explain the body language you observe on campus. For example, how do people regulate the distances between themselves and friends? Between faculty and students? Between students and staff? What other observations can you make that would help someone who has never visited your campus understand the normal body language behavior?

2. How can proxemics help you in your career and in your social life? Write a letter to a friend explaining how proxemics can assist him or her in the search for an important job or social acceptance.

3. Genelle G. Morain, a sociolinguist, observed recently, "Enmeshed in the warp and woof of words, teachers find it hard to believe that the average American speaks for only ten to eleven minutes a day, and that more than 65 percent of the social meaning of a typical two-person exchange is carried by nonverbal cues." Go to your campus snack bar or to the library with a classmate, and observe some conversations between people there. Take notes independently, and then share your observations with each other. How many nonverbal gestures can you find compared to the number of times that people speak?

4. Describe in a humorous essay a misunderstanding or confusion that arose as a result of ignorance of appropriate nonverbal language. If you can't think of an actual experience of your own, draw on the experience of a good friend or family member or make up a story.

John Fire Lame Deer
TALKING TO THE OWLS AND BUTTERFLIES

John Fire Lame Deer (Tahca Ushte) is a Sioux Indian born in South Dakota on the Rosebud Reservation. He is a medicine man who found his vocation through a vision that came to him in the traditional "vision pit," and he shares his vision of the oneness of all life in his outspoken and perceptive book Lame Deer Seeker of Visions: The Life of a Sioux Medicine Man *(published in 1972). As you*

read this short excerpt, keep in mind that John Lame Deer and his
fellow medicine man, Pete Catches, speak without hesitation about the
shortcomings of white American culture and about the cultural defi-
ciencies they observe in that culture. Do you agree with the basic
assumption that all life can teach us? And do you believe that ani-
mals and other natural forms can "speak" to us? How can this as-
sumption affect the way an individual behaves?

An animal doesn't have to be big to be powerful. There's an ant power.
Some ants have no eyes, but they can feel their way. They go out and
bring back those rocks, called *yuwipi*, to put on their anthills. Tiny rocks,
the size of seed beads, shiny, agate-like, little stones as clear as snow.
Sometimes instead of these they bring tiny fossils. It takes two ants to
get one of those rocks. One might be stepped upon and die. The ants
take no chances.

We medicine men go out to look for anthills and get these tiny
rocks. They are sacred. We put 405 of them into our gourds and rattles
which we use in our ceremonies. They represent the 405 trees which
grow in our land. *Taśuśka śaśa* — the red ants — we mash them up and
put them in our medicine. If somebody gets shot we give this to him to
drink. This ant medicine makes the wound heal faster. As to what you
people call fossils, these too are used by us. Deep in the Badlands we
find the bones of *unktegila*, the giant, the water monster, which lived
long before human beings appeared. On a hill there lies the back-
bone of one of them, right along the spine of that mound. I have been
up there, riding the ridge like a horse; that's the only way you can
move on it. It's spooky, like riding the monster. At night there are
spirit lights flitting about on that hill. I find things there which I use
in my doctoring.

Iktomé — the spider — has a power, too, but it is evil. His body is
short, and everything is in one place, the center, with its legs spread
out. It's sitting in its web, waiting for a fly. Iktomé is really a man. He's
a foolish guy, a smart-ass; he wants to trick everybody, wants to tan-
talize people, make them miserable. But he is easy to outwit.

You have to listen to all these creatures, listen with your mind.
They have secrets to tell. Even a kind of cricket, called *ptewoyake*, a
wingless hopper, it used to tell us where to find buffalo. It has nothing
to tell us now.

Butterflies talk to the women. A spirit will get into a beautiful butterfly, fly over to a young squaw, sit on her shoulder. The spirit will talk
through that butterfly to the young squaw and tell her to become a
medicine woman. We still have a couple of these ladies. I helped one,
taught her what she must know, and she is doing a good job on the
reservation. She is honest, so honest that the very poor, the down-and-
out winos, really believe in her. She doesn't take any money from them,
just does her best for the sake of helping them.

I have a nephew, Joe Thunderhawk, who is a healer. He has the coyote power. On his drum is painted the picture of a coyote, showing Joe's vision. This coyote power has been in the Thunderhawk family for a long time. Many years ago Joe's grandfather traveled in the wintertime. The snows were deep and darkness surprised him in a canyon. He had to hole up in there, trying to keep from freezing to death. In the middle of the night something came up to him, settling down by his legs. He saw that it was a coyote. They gave each other warmth, keeping each other alive, until the next morning. When that man got up to travel again, the coyote followed him.

After that, Joe's grandfather would hear the coyote bark at night, near his home. It would bark in two ways — one bark sounding like a dog, the other like a little boy. One barking meant that something good was about to happen, the other foreshadowed misfortune. Joe's grandfather became a medicine man and a prophet. The coyote told him of things to come. When the old man died, his knowledge died with him. He had not been able to pass it on.

One day Joe Thunderhawk passed through that same canyon where his grandfather and the coyote had warmed each other long ago. My nephew was in a wagon. Suddenly he had a feeling that someone was following him. He looked back and there was a coyote, right behind him. It was kind of lame and very thin. It started to bark in two ways — like a dog and like a child.

That night Joe Thunderhawk dreamed about this coyote and understood that he was meant to be a medicine man, that he would carry on his grandfather's work. He is working now in the Indian way, with his own medicines, curing sick people who would have to undergo surgery otherwise. Thus the coyote power has returned to the Thunderhawk family.

As for myself, the birds have something to tell me. The eagle, the owl. In an eagle there is all the wisdom of the world; that's why we have an eagle feather at the top of the pole during a *yuwipi* ceremony. If you are planning to kill an eagle, the minute you think of that he knows it, knows what you are planning. The black-tailed deer has this wisdom, too. That's why its tail is tied farther down at the *yuwipi* pole. This deer, if you shoot at him, you won't hit him. He just stands right there and the bullet comes right back and hits you. It is like somebody saying bad things about you and they come back at him.

In one of my great visions I was talking to the birds, the winged creatures. I was saddened by the death of my mother. She had held my hand and said just one word: "pitiful." I don't think she grieved for herself; she was sorry for me, a poor Indian she would leave in a white man's world. I cried up on that vision hill, cried for help, stretched out my hands toward the sky and then put the blanket over myself — that's all I had, the blanket and the pipe, and a little tobacco for an offering. I didn't know what to expect. I wanted to touch the power, feel it. I had the thought to give myself up, even if it would kill me. So I just gave myself to the winds, to nature, not giving a damn about what could happen to me.

All of a sudden I hear a big bird crying, and then quickly he hit me on the back, touched me with his spread wings. I heard the cry of an eagle, loud above the voices of many other birds. It seemed to say, "We have been waiting for you. We knew you would come. Now you are here. Your trail leads from here. Let our voices guide you. We are your friends, the feathered people, the two-legged, the four-legged, we are your friends, the creatures, little tiny ones, eight legs, twelve legs—all those who crawl on the earth. All the little creatures which fly, all those under water. The powers of each one of us we will share with you and you will have a ghost with you always—another self."

That's me, I thought, no other thing than myself, different, but me all the same, unseen, yet very real. I was frightened. I didn't understand it then. It took me a lifetime to find out.

And again I heard the voice amid the bird sounds, the clicking of beaks, the squeaking and chirping. "You have love for all that has been placed on this earth, not like the love of a mother for her son, or of a son for his mother, but a bigger love which encompasses the whole earth. You are just a human being, afraid, weeping under that blanket, but there is a great space within you to be filled with that love. All of nature can fit in there." I was shivering, pulling the blanket tighter around myself, but the voices repeated themselves over and over again, calling me "Brother, brother, brother." So this is how it is with me. Sometimes I feel like the first being in one of our Indian legends. This was a giant made of earth, water, the moon and the winds. He had timber instead of hair, a whole forest of trees. He had a huge lake in his stomach and a waterfall in his crotch. I feel like this giant. All of nature is in me, and a bit of myself is in all of nature.

PETE CATCHES: "I too feel this way. I live in an age which has passed. I live like fifty years ago, a hundred years ago. I like it that way. I want to live as humbly, as close to the earth as I can. Close to the plants, the weeds, the flowers that I use for medicine. The Great Spirit has seen to it that man can survive in this way, can live as he is meant to live. So I and my wife are dwelling in a little cabin—no electricity, no tap water, no plumbing, no road. This is what we want. This simple log cabin knows peace. That's how we want to be for the rest of our lives. I want to exist apart from the modern world, get out, way out, in the sticks, and live much closer to nature, even, than I am doing now. I don't even want to be called a medicine man, just a healing man, because this is what I am made for. I don't ask for anything. A white doctor has a fee, a priest has a fee. I have no fee. A man goes away from me healed. That is my reward. Sometimes I do not have the power—it makes me sad. When I have the power, then I am happy. Some men think of money, how to get it. That never comes into my mind. We live off nature, my wife and I; we hardly need anything. We will somehow live. The Great Spirit made the flowers, the streams, the pines, the cedars—takes care of them. He lets a breeze go through there, makes them breathe it, waters them, makes them grow. Even the one that is down in the crags, in the rocks. He tends to that, too. He takes care of me, waters me, feeds me, makes me live with the plants and animals as one of them. This is how I wish to remain, an Indian, all the days of my life. This does not mean that I want to shut myself off. Somehow many people find their way to my cabin. I like this. I want to be in communication, reach out to people everywhere, impart a little of our Indian way, the spirit's way, to them.

"At the same time, I want to withdraw further and further away from everything, to live like the ancient ones. On the highway you sometimes see a full-blood Indian thumbing a ride. I never do that. When I walk the road, I expect to walk the whole way. That is deep down in me, a kind of pride. Someday I'll still move my cabin still farther into the hills, maybe do without a cabin altogether, become part of the woods. There the spirit still has something for us to discover—a herb, a sprig, a flower—a very small flower, maybe, and you can spend a long time in its contemplation, thinking about it. Not a rose—yellow, white, artificial, big. I hear they are breeding black roses. That's not natural. These things are against nature. They make us weak. I abhor them.

"So as I get older, I burrow more and more into the hills. The Great Spirit made them for us, for me. I want to blend with them, shrink into them, and finally disappear in them. As my brother Lame Deer has said, all of nature is in us, all of us is in nature. That is as it should be. Tell me, what are you going to call the chapter of your book in which you put the things we have talked about today? I know, you will call it 'Talking to the Owls and the Butterflies.'"

OPTIONS FOR WRITING

1. Recent efforts to teach some animals to speak have included teaching sign language to primates and attempting to communicate with whales and dolphins. Write a story about a human being and an animal who learned to communicate.

2. John Fire Lame Deer claims that "you have to listen to all these creatures, listen with your mind." Write about a time when a creature taught you something, or speculate on how you could have learned something from nature.

3. What aspects of our culture prevent us from communicating with other living creatures?

4. Write a letter to your pet about what you have learned from him or her. Include some suggestions on what you hope your pet has learned (or not learned) from you!

5. Write a poem that captures the sense of a common language so apparent in "Talking to the Owls and Butterflies."

Margaret Atwood
THE HANDMAID'S TALE

*Margaret Atwood, a Canadian novelist, is known for her thoughtful
and provocative novels. She frequently gives attention to issues of
grave concern to women. In* The Handmaid's Tale, *Atwood imagines a future world governed by a tyrannical religious dictatorship, a
world in which women have been forbidden any rights or education.
Women fill one of three roles: Wife (a ceremonial figure, lacking any
sexual relation with the husband), Martha, (a household servant
named in reference to the busily serving Martha in the Bible), and
Handmaid (a female whose duty it is to produce children for the
sterile wife and the usually impotent husband). The husband in the
family is called the Commander; he possesses power of life and death
over the Handmaid, the narrator of this story. In this excerpt, the
Handmaid (who had been an educated, cultured woman before her
enslavement) recounts a strange visit she pays to the Commander at
his request. Knowing that she is in grave danger if she refuses, she
goes to his study late at night, thus risking the danger of being
caught in forbidden territory. As you read, imagine how you would
react to this situation. If you were deprived of the ability to read and
to write; if you were allowed to speak only the most rudimental
words and then only if you were addressed first, what would be your
sense of your own intellectual being? What is the ultimate effect of
forcing someone's speech into a preconceived mold? Does the Handmaid behave like a freely functioning intelligent being, or does she
exhibit behavior that strikes you as bizarre? How can you explain her
behavior?*

The clock in the hall downstairs strikes nine. I press my hands against
the sides of my thighs, breathe in, set out along the hall and softly
down the stairs. Serena Joy may still be at the house where the Birth
took place; that's lucky, he couldn't have foreseen it. On these days the
Wives hang around for hours, helping to open the presents, gossiping,
getting drunk. Something has to be done to dispel their envy. I follow
the downstairs corridor back, past the door that leads into the kitchen,
along to the next door, his. I stand outside it, feeling like a child who's
been summoned, at school, to the principal's office. What have I done
wrong?

My presence here is illegal. It's forbidden for us to be alone with
the Commanders. We are for breeding purposes: we aren't concubines,
geisha girls, courtesans. On the contrary: everything possible has been
done to remove us from that category. There is supposed to be nothing
entertaining about us, no room is to be permitted for the flowering of
secret lusts; no special favors are to be wheedled, by them or us, there

are to be no toeholds for love. We are two-legged wombs, that's all: sacred vessels, ambulatory chalices.

So why does he want to see me, at night, alone?

If I'm caught, it's to Serena's tender mercies I'll be delivered. He isn't supposed to meddle in such household discipline, that's women's business. After that, reclassification. I could become an Unwoman.

But to refuse to see him could be worse. There's no doubt about who holds the real power.

But there must be something he wants, from me. To want is to have a weakness. It's this weakness, whatever it is, that entices me. It's like a small crack in a wall, before now impenetrable. If I press my eye to it, this weakness of his, I may be able to see my way clear.

I want to know what he wants.

I raise my hand, knock, on the door of this forbidden room where I have never been, where women do not go. Not even Serena Joy comes here, and the cleaning is done by Guardians. What secrets, what male totems are kept in here?

I'm told to enter. I open the door, step in.

                    *   *   *

What is on the other side is normal life. I should say: what is on the other side looks like normal life. There is a desk, of course, with a Computalk on it, and a black leather chair behind it. There's a potted plant on the desk, a pen-holder set, papers. There's an oriental rug on the floor, and a fireplace without a fire in it. There's a small sofa, covered in brown plush, a television set, an end table, a couple of chairs.

But all around the walls there are bookcases. They're filled with books. Books and books and books, right out in plain view, no locks, no boxes. No wonder we can't come in here. It's an oasis of the forbidden. I try not to stare.

The Commander is standing in front of the fireless fireplace, back to it, one elbow on the carved wooden overmantel, other hand in his pocket. It's such a studied pose, something of the country squire, some old come-on from a glossy men's mag. He probably decided ahead of time that he'd be standing like that when I came in. When I knocked he probably rushed over to the fireplace and propped himself up. He should have a black patch, over one eye, a cravat with horseshoes on it.

It's all very well for me to think these things, quick as staccato, a jittering of the brain. An inner jeering. But it's panic. The fact is I'm terrified.

I don't say anything.

"Close the door behind you," he says, pleasantly enough. I do it, and turn back.

"Hello," he says.

It's the old form of greeting. I haven't heard it for a long time, for years. Under the circumstances it seems out of place, comical even, a flip backward in time, a stunt. I can think of nothing appropriate to say in return.

I think I will cry.

He must have noticed this, because he looks at me, puzzled, gives a little frown I choose to interpret as concern, though it may merely be irritation. "Here," he says. "You can sit down." He pulls a chair out for me, sets it in front of his desk. Then he goes around behind the desk and sits down, slowly and it seems to me elaborately. What this act tells me is that he hasn't brought me here to touch me in any way, against my will. He smiles. The smile is not sinister or predatory. It's merely a smile, a formal kind of smile, friendly but a little distant, as if I'm a kitten in a window. One he's looking at but doesn't intend to buy.

I sit up straight on the chair, my hands folded on my lap. I feel as if my feet in their flat red shoes aren't quite touching the floor. But of course they are.

"You must find this strange," he says.

I simply look at him. The understatement of the year, was a phrase my mother uses. Used.

I feel like cotton candy: sugar and air. Squeeze me and I'd turn into a small sickly damp wad of weeping pinky-red.

"I guess it is a little strange," he says, as if I've answered.

I think I should have a hat on, tied with a bow under my chin.

"I want . . . " he says.

I try not to lean forward. Yes? Yes, yes? What, then? What does he want? But I won't give it away, this eagerness of mine. It's a bargaining session, things are about to be exchanged. She who does not hesitate is lost. I'm not giving anything away: selling only.

"I would like—" he says. "This will sound silly." And he does look embarrassed, *sheepish* was the word, the way men used to look once. He's old enough to remember how to look that way, and to remember also how appealing women once found it. The young ones don't know those tricks. They've never had to use them.

I'd like you to play a game of Scrabble with me," he says.

I hold myself absolutely rigid. I keep my face unmoving. So that's what's in the forbidden room! Scrabble! I want to laugh, shriek with laughter, fall off my chair. This was once the game of old women, old men, in the summers or in retirement villas, to be played when there was nothing good on television. Or of adolescents, once, long long ago. My mother had a set, kept at the back of the hall cupboard, with the Christmas decorations in their cardboard boxes. Once she tried to interest me in it, when I was thirteen and miserable and at loose ends.

Now of course it's something different. Now it's forbidden, for us. Now it's dangerous. Now it's indecent. Now it's something he can't do with his Wife. Now it's desirable. Now he's compromised himself. It's as if he's offered me drugs.

"All right," I say, as if indifferent. I can in fact hardly speak.

He doesn't say why he wants to play Scrabble with me. I don't ask him. He merely takes a box out from one of the drawers in his desk and opens it up. There are the plasticized wooden counters I remember, the board divided into squares, the little holders for setting the letters in. He dumps the counters out on the top of his desk and begins to turn them over. After a moment I join in.

"You know how to play?" he says.

I nod.

We play two games. *Larynx*, I spell. *Valance. Quince. Zygote.* I hold the glossy counters with their smooth edges, finger the letters. The feeling is voluptuous. This is freedom, an eyeblink of it. *Limp*, I spell. *Gorge.* What a luxury. The counters are like candies, made of peppermint, cool like that. Humbugs, those were called. I would like to put them into my mouth. They would taste also of lime. The letter C. Crisp, slightly acid on the tongue, delicious.

I win the first game, I let him win the second: I still haven't discovered what the terms are, what I will be able to ask for, in exchange.

Finally he tells me it's time for me to go home. Those are the words he uses: *go home.* He means to my room. He asks me if I will be all right, as if the stairway is a dark street. I say yes. We open his study door, just a crack, and listen for noises in the hall.

This is like being on a date. This is like sneaking into the dorm after hours.

This is conspiracy.

OPTIONS FOR WRITING

1. Imagine that in some future world, you have been forbidden to read and write. You have, however, found writing utensils and paper. Although your life is at risk, you begin to keep a journal. What would you write? Invent the first few pages of your journal.

2. Why is the choice of the Scrabble game particularly useful for Atwood to use in this scene? Can you find examples in the text of the sensual quality of her descriptions? Try writing some of your own to continue the description of the Scrabble game.

3. On campus, pay close attention to the language used in class and among your peers. Make a list of the times you find people being silenced or ignored by others in the group. Write a journal entry imagining the feelings of a person being so silenced.

4. Try going to a day's classes without speaking unless you are spoken to. (Tell your teachers ahead of time that this is a linguistic experiment.) At the end of the day, write a letter to a close friend telling how you felt about yourself and your ideas. Did your feelings change from the early part of the day to the later part?

5. Write a poem that you think the Handmaid would write after her Scrabble game.

Ursula K. Le Guin
BRYN MAWR COMMENCEMENT ADDRESS

Ursula Le Guin (b. 1929) is probably best known for her fiction, a blend of fantasy and science fiction. She is also an outspoken feminist and essayist. In this address to the class of 1986 at Bryn Mawr College, a prestigious women's college, she speculates on the connections between language, power, gender, and art. As you read, keep in mind that this was an address given to young women, most of whom had led privileged social and intellectual lives, most of whom had higher than average expectations for their own lives and careers. What is Le Guin warning them about? How does she use her ideas of "father tongue" and "mother tongue" to provoke thought and invite speculation? Would her own language have been different at another college? At your college? Does her own language in this address connect or distance her in relation to the reader/listener?

Thinking about what I should say to you made me think about what we learn in college; and what we unlearn in college; and then how we learn to unlearn what we learned in college and relearn what we unlearned in college, and so on. And I thought how I have learned, more or less well, three languages, all of them English; and how one of these languages is the one I went to college to learn. I thought I was going to study French and Italian, and I did, but what I learned was the language of power—of social power; I shall call it the father tongue.

This is the public discourse, and one dialect of it is speechmaking—by politicians, commencement speakers, or the old man who used to get up early in a village in Central California a couple of hundred years ago and say things very loudly on the order of "People need to be getting up now, there are things we might be doing, the repairs on the sweathouse aren't finished and the tarweed is in seed over on Bald Hill; this is a good time of day for doing things, and there'll be plenty of time for lying around when it gets hot this afternoon." So everybody would get up grumbling slightly, and some of them would go pick tarweed—probably the women. This is the effect, ideally, of the public discourse. It makes something happen, makes somebody—usually somebody else—do something, or at least it gratifies the ego of the speaker. The difference between our politics and that of a native Californian people is clear in the style of the public discourse. The difference wasn't clear to the White invaders, who insisted on calling any Indian who made a speech a "chief," because they couldn't comprehend, they wouldn't admit, an authority without supremacy—a non-dominating authority. But it is such an authority that I possess for the brief—we all hope it is decently brief—time I speak to you. I have no right to speak to you. What I have is the responsibility you have given me to speak to you.

The political tongue speaks aloud—and look how radio and television have brought the language of politics right back where it belongs—but the dialect of the father tongue that you and I learned best in college is a written one. It doesn't speak itself. It only lectures. It began to develop when printing made written language common rather than rare, five hundred years ago or so, and with electronic processing and copying it continues to develop and proliferate so powerfully, so dominatingly, that many believe this dialect—the expository and particularly the scientific discourse—is the *highest* form of language, the true language, of which all other uses of words are primitive vestiges.

And it is indeed an excellent dialect. Newton's *Principia* was written in it in Latin, and Descartes wrote Latin and French in it, establishing some of its basic vocabulary, and Kant wrote German in it, and Marx, Darwin, Freud, Boas, Foucault—all the great scientists and social thinkers wrote it. It is the language of thought that seeks objectivity.

I do not say it is the language of rational thought. Reason is a faculty far larger than mere objective thought. When either the political or the scientific discourse announces itself as the voice of reason, it is playing God, and should be spanked and stood in the corner. The essential gesture of the father tongue is not reasoning but distancing—making a gap, a space, between the subject or self and the object or other. Enormous energy is generated by that rending, that forcing of a gap between Man and World. So the continuous growth of technology and science fuels itself; the Industrial Revolution began with splitting the world-atom, and still by breaking the continuum into unequal parts we keep the imbalance from which our society draws the power that enables it to dominate every other culture, so that everywhere now everybody speaks the same language in laboratories and government buildings and headquarters and offices of business, and those who don't know it or won't speak it are silent, or silenced, or unheard.

You came here to college to learn the language of power—to be empowered. If you want to succeed in business, government, law, engineering, science, education, the media, if you want to succeed, you have to be fluent in the language in which "success" is a meaningful word.

White man speak with forked tongue; White man speak dichotomy. His language expresses the values of the split world, valuing the positive and devaluing the negative in each redivision: subject/object, self/other, mind/body, dominant/submissive, active/passive, Man/Nature, man/woman, and so on. The father tongue is spoken from above. It goes one way. No answer is expected, or heard.

In our Constitution and the works of law, philosophy, social thought, and science, in its everyday uses in the service of justice and clarity, what I call the father tongue is immensely noble and indispensably useful. When it claims a privileged relationship to reality, it becomes dangerous and potentially destructive. It describes with exquisite accuracy the continuing destruction of the planet's ecosystem by its speakers. This word from its vocabulary, "ecosystem," is a word unnecessary except in a discourse that excludes its speakers from the ecosystem in a subject/object dichotomy of terminal irresponsibility.

The language of the fathers, of Man Ascending, Man the Conqueror, Civilized Man, is not your native tongue. It isn't anybody's native tongue. You didn't even hear the father tongue your first few years, except on the radio or TV, and then you didn't listen, and neither did your little brother, because it was some old politician with hairs in his nose yammering. And you and your brother had better things to do. You had another kind of power to learn. You were learning your mother tongue.

Using the father tongue, I can speak of the mother tongue only, inevitably, to distance it — to exclude it. It is the other, inferior. It is primitive: inaccurate, unclear, coarse, limited, trivial, banal. It's repetitive, the same over and over, like the work called women's work; earthbound, housebound. It's vulgar, the vulgar tongue, common, common speech, colloquial, low, ordinary, plebeian, like the work ordinary people do, the lives common people live. The mother tongue, spoken or written, expects an answer. It is conversation, a word the root of which means "turning together." The mother tongue is language not as mere communication but as relation, relationship. It connects. It goes two ways, many ways, an exchange, a network. Its power is not in dividing but in binding, not in distancing but in uniting. It is written, but not by scribes and secretaries for posterity; it flies from the mouth on the breath that is our life and is gone, like the outbreath, utterly gone and yet returning, repeated, the breath the same again always, everywhere, and we all know it by heart. John have you got your umbrella I think it's going to rain. Can you come play with me? If I told you once I told you a hundred times. Things here just aren't the same without Mother, I will now sign your affectionate brother James. Oh what am I going to do? So I said to her I said if he thinks she's going to stand for that but then there's his arthritis poor thing and no work. I love you. I hate you. I hate liver. Joan dear did you feed the sheep, don't just stand around mooning. Tell me what they said, tell me what you did. Oh how my feet do hurt. My heart is breaking. Touch me here, touch me again. Once bit twice shy. You look like what the cat dragged in. What a beautiful night. Good morning, hello, goodbye, have a nice day, thanks. God damn you to hell you lying cheat. Pass the soy sauce please. Oh shit. Is it grandma's own sweet pretty dear? What am I going to tell her? There there don't cry. Go to sleep now, go to sleep. . . . Don't go to sleep!

It is a language always on the verge of silence and often on the verge of song. It is the language stories are told in. It is the language spoken by all children and most women, and so I call it the mother tongue, for we learn it from our mothers and speak it to our kids. I'm trying to use it here in public where it isn't appropriate, not suited to the occasion, but I want to speak it to you because we are women and I can't say what I want to say about women in the language of capital M Man. If I try to be objective I will say, "This is higher and that is lower," I'll make a commencement speech about being successful in the battle of life, I'll lie to you; and I don't want to.

Early this spring I met a musician, the composer Pauline Oliveros, a beautiful woman like a grey rock in a streambed; and to a group of us, women, who were beginning to quarrel over theories in abstract, objective language — and I with my splendid Eastern-women's-college training in the father tongue was in the thick of the fight and going for the kill — to us, Pauline, who is sparing with words, said after clearing her throat, "Offer your experience as your truth." There was a short silence. When we started talking again, we didn't talk objectively, and we didn't fight. We went back to feeling our way into ideas, using the whole intellect not half of it, talking with one another, which involves listening. We tried to offer our experience to one another. Not claiming something: offering something.

How, after all, can one experience deny, negate, disprove, another experience? Even if I've had a lot more of it, *your* experience is your truth. How can one being prove another being wrong? Even if you're a lot younger and smarter than me, *my* being is my truth. I can offer it; you don't have to take it. People can't contradict each other, only words can: words separated from experience for use as weapons, words that make the wound, the split between subject and object, exposing and exploiting the object but disguising and defending the subject.

People crave objectivity because to be subjective is to be embodied, to be a body, vulnerable, violable. Men especially aren't used to that; they're trained not to offer but to attack. It's often easier for women to trust one another, to try to speak our experience in our own language, the language we talk to each other in, the mother tongue; so we empower one another.

But you and I have learned to use the mother tongue only at home or safe among friends, and many men learn not to speak it at all. They're taught that there's no safe place for them. From adolescence on, they talk a kind of degraded version of the father tongue with each other — sports scores, job technicalities, sex technicalities, and TV politics. At home, to women and children talking mother tongue, they respond with a grunt and turn on the ball game. They have let themselves be silenced, and dimly they know it, and so resent speakers of the mother tongue; women babble, gabble all the time. . . . Can't listen to that stuff.

Our schools and colleges, institutions of the patriarchy, generally teach us to listen to people in power, men or women speaking the father tongue; and so they teach us not to listen to the mother tongue, to what the powerless say, poor men, women, children: not to hear that as valid discourse.

I am trying to unlearn these lessons, along with other lessons I was taught by my society, particularly lessons concerning the minds, work, works, and being of women. I am a slow unlearner. But I love my unteachers—the feminist thinkers and writers and talkers and poets and artists and singers and critics and friends, from Wollstonecraft and Woolf through the furies and glories of the seventies and eighties—I celebrate here and now the women who for two centuries have worked for our freedom, the unteachers, the unmasters, the unconquerors, the unwarriors, women who have at risk and at high cost offered their experience as truth. "Let us NOT praise famous women!" Virginia Woolf scribbled in a margin when she was writing *Three Guineas*, and she's right, but still I have to praise these women and thank them for setting me free in my old age to learn my own language.

The third language, my native tongue, which I will never know though I've spent my life learning it: I'll say some words now in this language. First a name, just a person's name, you've heard it before. Sojourner Truth. That name is a language in itself. But Sojourner Truth spoke the unlearned language; about a hundred years ago, talking it in a public place, she said, "I have been forty years a slave and forty years free and would be here forty years more to have equal rights for all." Along at the end of her talk she said, "I wanted to tell you a mite about Woman's Rights, and so I came out and said so. I am sittin' among you to watch; and every once and awhile I will come out and tell you what time of night it is." She said, "Now I will do a little singing. I have not heard any singing since I came here."[1]

Singing is one of the names of the language we never learn, and here for Sojourner Truth is a little singing. It was written by Joy Harjo of the Creek people and is called "The Blanket Around Her."[2]

> maybe it is her birth
> which she holds close to herself
> or her death
> which is just as inseparable
> and the white wind
> that encircles her is a part
> just as
>   the blue sky
> hanging in turquoise from her neck
>
> oh woman
> remember who you are
> woman
> it is the whole earth

So what am I talking about with this "unlearned language"—poetry, literature? Yes, but it can be speeches and science, any use of language when it is spoken, written, read, heard as art, the way dancing is the body moving as art. In Sojourner Truth's words you hear the coming together, the marriage of the public discourse and the private experience, making a power, a beautiful thing, the true discourse of reason. This is a wedding and welding back together of the alienated consciousness that I've been calling the father tongue and the undifferentiated engagement that I've been calling the mother tongue. This is their baby, this baby talk, the language you can spend your life trying to learn.

We learn this tongue first, like the mother tongue, just by hearing it or reading it; and even in our overcrowded, underfunded public high schools they still teach *A Tale of Two Cities* and *Uncle Tom's Cabin*; and in college you can take four solid years of literature, and even creative writing courses. But. It is all taught as if it were a dialect of the father tongue.

Literature takes shape and life in the body, in the womb of the mother tongue: always: and the Fathers of Culture get anxious about paternity. They start talking about legitimacy. They steal the baby. They ensure by every means that the artist, the writer, is male. This involves intellectual abortion by centuries of women artists, infanticide of works by women writers, and a whole medical corps of sterilizing critics working to purify the Canon, to reduce the subject matter and style of literature to something Ernest Hemingway could have understood.

But this is our native tongue, this is our language they're stealing: we can read it and we can write it, and what we bring to it is what it needs, the woman's tongue, that earth and savor, that relatedness, which speaks dark in the mother tongue but clear as sunlight in women's poetry, and in our novels and stories, our letters, our journals, our speeches. If Sojourner Truth, forty years a slave, knew she had the right to speak that speech, how about you? Will you let yourself be silenced? Will you listen to what men tell you, or will you listen to what women are saying? I say the Canon has been spiked, and while the Eliots speak only to the Lowells and the Lowells speak only to God, Denise Levertov comes stepping westward quietly, speaking to us.[3]

> There is no savor
> more sweet, more salt
>
> than to be glad to be
> what, woman,
>
> and who, myself,
> I am, a shadow
>
> that grows longer as the sun
> moves, drawn out
>
> on a thread of wonder:
> If I bear burdens
>
> they begin to be remembered
> as gifts, goods, a basket

of bread that hurts
my shoulders but closes me

in fragrance. I can
eat as I go.

As I've been using the word "truth" in the sense of "trying hard not to lie," so I use the words "literature," "art," in the sense of "living well, living with skill, grace, energy" — like carrying a basket of bread and smelling it and eating as you go. I don't mean only certain special products made by specially gifted people living in specially privileged garrets, studios, and ivory towers — "High" Art; I mean also all the low arts, the ones men don't want. For instance, the art of making order where people live. In our culture this activity is not considered an art, it is not even considered work. "Do you work?" — and she, having stopped mopping the kitchen and picked up the baby to come answer the door, says, "No, I don't work." People who make order where people live are by doing so stigmatized as unfit for "higher" pursuits; so women mostly do it, and among women, poor, uneducated, or old women more often than rich, educated, and young ones. Even so, many people very much want to keep house but can't, because they're poor and haven't got a house to keep, or the time and money it takes, or even the experience of ever having seen a decent house, a clean room, except on TV. Most men are prevented from housework by intense cultural bias; many women actually hire another woman to do it for them because they're scared of getting trapped in it, ending up like the women they hire, or like that woman we all know who's been pushed so far over by cultural bias that she can't stand up, and crawls around the house scrubbing and waxing and spraying germ killer on the kids. But even on her kneebones, where you and I will never join her, even she has been practicing as best she knows how a great, ancient, complex, and necessary art. That our society devalues it is evidence of the barbarity, the aesthetic and ethical bankruptcy, of our society.

As housekeeping is an art, so is cooking and all it involves — it involves, after all, agriculture, hunting, herding. . . . So is the making of clothing and all it involves. . . . And so on; you see how I want to revalue the word "art" so that when I come back as I do now to talking about words it is in the context of the great arts of living, of the woman carrying the basket of bread, bearing gifts, goods. Art not as some ejaculative act of ego but as a way, a skillful and powerful way of being in the world. I come back to words because words are my way of being in the world, but meaning by language as art a matter infinitely larger than the so-called High forms. Here is a poem that tries to translate six words by Hélène Cixous, who wrote *The Laugh of the Medusa*; she said, "Je suis là où ça parle," and I squeezed those six words like a lovely lemon and got out all the juice I could, plus a drop of Oregon vodka.

I'm there where
it's talking
Where that speaks I
am in that talking place
    Where
that says
my being is
  Where
my being there
is speaking
I am
  And so
laughing
in a stone ear

The stone ear that won't listen, won't hear us, and blames us for its being stone. . . . Women can babble and chatter like monkeys in the wilderness, but the farms and orchards and gardens of language, the wheatfields of art—men have claimed these, fenced them off: No Trespassing, it's a man's world, they say. And I say,

oh woman
remember who you are
woman
it is the whole earth

We are told, in words and not in words, we are told by their deafness, by their stone ears, that our experience, the life experience of women, is not valuable to men—therefore not valuable to society, to humanity. We are valued by men only as an element of their experience, as things experienced; anything we may say, anything we may do, is recognized only if said or done in their service.

One thing we incontestably do is have babies. So we have babies as the male priests, lawmakers, and doctors tell us to have them, when and where to have them, how often, and how to have them; so that is all under control. But we are *not to talk about* having babies, because that is not part of the experience of men and so nothing to do with reality, with civilization, and no concern of art. —A rending scream in another room. And Prince Andrey comes in and sees his poor little wife dead bearing his son— Or Levin goes out into his fields and thanks his God for the birth of his son— And we know how Prince Andrey feels and how Levin feels and even how God feels, but we don't know what happened. Something happened, something was done, which we know nothing about. But what was it? Even in novels by women we are only just beginning to find out what it is that happens in the other room— what women do.

Freud famously said, "What we shall never know is what a woman wants." Having paused thoughtfully over the syntax of that sentence, in

which WE are plural but "a woman" apparently has no plural, no individuality—as we might read that a cow must be milked twice a day or
a gerbil is a nice pet—WE might go on then to consider whether WE
know anything about, whether WE have ever noticed, whether WE have
ever asked a woman what she *does*—what women do.

Many anthropologists, some historians, and others have indeed
been asking one another this question for some years now, with pale
and affrighted faces—and they are beginning also to answer it. More
power to them. The social sciences show us that speakers of the father
tongue are capable of understanding and discussing the doings of the
mothers, if they will admit the validity of the mother tongue and listen
to what women say.

But in society as a whole the patriarchal mythology of what "a
woman" does persists almost unexamined, and shapes the lives of
women. "What are you going to do when you get out of school?" "Oh,
well, just like any other woman, I guess I want a home and family"—
and that's fine, but what is this home and family just like other
women's? Dad at work, mom home, two kids eating apple pie? This
family, which our media and now our government declare to be normal
and impose as normative, this nuclear family now accounts for seven
percent of the arrangements women live in in America. Ninety-three
percent of women don't live that way. They don't do that. Many
wouldn't if you gave it to them with bells on. Those who want that,
who believe it's their one true destiny—what's their chance of achieving
it? They're on the road to Heartbreak House.

But the only alternative offered by the patriarchal mythology is that
of the Failed Woman—the old maid, the barren woman, the castrating
bitch, the frigid wife, the lezzie, the libber, the Unfeminine, so beloved
of misogynists both male and female.

Now indeed there are women who want to be female men; their
role model is Margaret Thatcher, and they're ready to dress for success,
carry designer briefcases, kill for promotion, and drink the Right Scotch.
They want to buy into the man's world, whatever the cost. And if that's
true desire, not just compulsion born of fear, O.K.: if you can't lick 'em
join 'em. My problem with that is that I can't see it as a good life even
for men, who invented it and make all the rules. There's power in it,
but not the kind of power I respect, not the kind of power that sets
anybody free. I hate to see an intelligent woman voluntarily double herself up to get under the bottom line. Talk about crawling! And when she
talks, what can she talk but father tongue? If she's the mouthpiece for
the man's world, what has she got to say for herself?

Some women manage it—they may collude, but they don't sell out
as women; and we know that when they speak for those who, in the
man's world, are the others: women, children, the poor. . . .

But it is dangerous to put on Daddy's clothes, though not, perhaps,
as dangerous as it is to sit on Daddy's knees.

There's no way you can offer your experience as your truth if you deny your experience, if you try to be a mythical creature, the dummy woman who sits there on Big Daddy's lap. Whose voice will come out of her prettily hinged jaw? Who is it says yes all the time? Oh yes, yes, I will. Oh I don't know, you decide. Oh I can't do that. Yes hit me, yes rape me, yes save me, oh yes. That is how A Woman talks, the one in What-we-shall-never-know-is-what-A-Woman-wants.

A Woman's place, need I say, is in the home, plus at her volunteer work or at the job where she's glad to get sixty cents for doing what men get paid a dollar for but that's because she's always on pregnancy leave but childcare? No! A Woman is home caring for her children! even if she can't. Trapped in this well-built trap, A Woman blames her mother for luring her into it, while ensuring that her own daughter never gets out; she recoils from the idea of sisterhood and doesn't believe women have friends, because it probably means something unnatural, and anyhow, A Woman is afraid of women. She's a male construct, and she's afraid women will deconstruct her. She's afraid of everything, because she can't change. Thighs forever thin and shining hair and shining teeth and she's my Mom, too, all seven percent of her. And she never grows old.

There are old women—little old ladies, as people always say; little bits, fragments of the great dummy statue goddess A Woman. Nobody hears if old women say yes or no, nobody pays them sixty cents for anything. Old men run things. Old men run the show, press the buttons, make the wars, make the money. In the man's world, the old man's world, the young men run and run and run until they drop, and some of the young women run with them. But old women live in the cracks, between the walls, like roaches, like mice, a rustling sound, a squeaking. Better lock up the cheese, boys. It's terrible, you turn up a corner of civilization and there are all these old women running around on the wrong side—

I say to you, you know, you're going to get old. And you can't hear me. I squeak between the walls. I've walked through the mirror and am on the other side, where things are all backwards. You may look with a good will and a generous heart, but you can't see anything in the mirror but your own face; and I, looking from the dark side and seeing your beautiful young faces, see that's how it should be.

But when you look at yourself in the mirror, I hope you see yourself. Not one of the myths. Not a failed man—a person who can never succeed because success is basically defined as being male—and not a failed goddess, a person desperately trying to hide herself in the dummy Woman, the image of men's desires and fears. I hope you look away from those myths and into your own eyes, and see your own strength. You're going to need it. I hope you don't try to take your strength from me, or from a man. Secondhand experience breaks down a block from the car lot. I hope you'll take and make your own soul; that you'll feel your life for yourself pain by pain and joy by joy; that you'll feed your life, eat, "eat as you go" — you who nourish, be nourished!

If being a cog in the machine or a puppet manipulated by others isn't what you want, you can find out what you want, your needs, desires, truths, powers, by accepting your own experience as a woman, as this woman, this body, this person, your hungry self. On the maps drawn by men there is an immense white area, terra incognita, where most women live. That country is all yours to explore, to inhabit, to describe.

But none of us lives there alone. Being human isn't something people can bring off alone; we need other people in order to be people. We need one another.

If a woman sees other women as Medusa, fears them, turns a stone ear to them, these days, all her hair may begin to stand up on end hissing, *Listen, listen, listen!* Listen to other women, your sisters, your mothers, your grandmothers — if you don't hear them how will you ever understand what your daughter says to you?

And the men who can talk, converse with you, not trying to talk through the dummy Yes-Woman, the men who can accept your experience as valid — when you find such a man love him, honor him! But don't obey him. I don't think we have any right to obedience. I think we have a responsibility to freedom.

And especially to freedom of speech. Obedience is silent. It does not answer. It is contained. Here is a disobedient woman speaking, Wendy Rose of the Hopi and Miwok people, saying in a poem called "The Parts of a Poet,"[4]

> parts of me are pinned
> to earth, parts of me
> undermine song, parts
> of me spread on the water,
> parts of me form a rainbow
> bridge, parts of me follow
> the sandfish, parts of me
> are a woman who judges.

Now this is what I want: I want to hear your judgments. I am sick of the silence of women. I want to hear you speaking all the languages, offering your experience as your truth, as human truth, talking about working, about making, about unmaking, about eating, about cooking, about feeding, about taking in seed and giving out life, about killing, about feeling, about thinking; about what women do; about what men do; about war, about peace; about who presses the button and what buttons get pressed and whether pressing buttons is in the long run a fit occupation for human beings. There's a lot of things I want to hear you talk about.

This is what I don't want: I don't want what men have. I'm glad to let them do their work and talk their talk. But I do not want and will not have them saying or thinking or telling us that theirs is the only fit work or speech for human beings. Let them not take our work, our words, from us. If they can, if they will, let them work with us and talk with us. We can all talk mother tongue, we can all talk father tongue, and together we can try to hear and speak that language which may be our truest way of being in the world, we who speak for a world that has no words but ours.

I know that many men and even women are afraid and angry when women do speak, because in this barbaric society, when women speak truly they speak subversively—they can't help it: if you're underneath, if you're kept down, you break out, you subvert. We are volcanoes. When we women offer our experience as our truth, as human truth, all the maps change. There are new mountains.

That's what I want—to hear you erupting. You young Mount St. Helenses who don't know the power in you—I want to hear you. I want to listen to you talking to each other and to us all: whether you're writing an article or a poem or a letter or teaching a class or talking with friends or reading a novel or making a speech or proposing a law or giving a judgment or singing the baby to sleep or discussing the fate of nations, I want to hear you. Speak with a woman's tongue. Come out and tell us what time of night it is! Don't let us sink back into silence. If we don't tell our truth, who will? Who'll speak for my children, and yours?

So I end with the end of a poem by Linda Hogan of the Chickasaw people, called "The Women Speaking."[5]

> Daughters, the women are speaking.
> They arrive
> over the wise distances
> on perfect feet.
> Daughters, I love you.

NOTES

[1] Sojourner Truth, in Sandra M. Gilbert and Susan Gubar, eds., *The Norton Anthology of Literature by Women* (New York: W. W. Norton & Co., 1985), pp. 255–56.

[2] Joy Harjo, "The Blanket Around Her," in Rayna Green, ed., *That's What She Said: Contemporary Poetry and Fiction by Native American Women* (Bloomington: Indiana University Press, 1984), p. 127.

[3] Denise Levertov, "Stepping Westward," in *Norton Anthology*, p. 1951.

[4] Wendy Rose, "The Parts of a Poet," in *That's What She Said*, p. 204.

[5] Linda Hogan, "The Women Speaking," in ibid., p. 172.

OPTIONS FOR WRITING

1. After reading this passage, write a long entry (10 minutes) in your journal about your first personal response to this address. Share with two classmates, one male and one female, and then write another journal entry reflecting on how your responses differ from (or resemble) each other's.

2. Find an example of the third language Le Guin describes. Select something that means a great deal to you, and speculate in your journal about why this piece meets the specifications Le Guin sets up for unlearned language.

3. Think about the experience of a woman you know well, and write her a letter telling her what you have learned from Le Guin's address that helps you value her experience in a different way.

4. Write a poem or essay that contrasts or illustrates father tongue and mother tongue usage.

5. As a class, design a father tongue dictionary and a mother tongue dictionary. Working in small groups, write a few entries for each dictionary.

Neil Postman
THE MEDIUM IS THE METAPHOR

Neil Postman is a professor of communication at New York University and editor of Et Cetera, *a journal of general semantics. As an educator, he is very concerned with communications theory as it relates to teaching and learning in the United States. In* Amusing Ourselves to Death, *Postman claims that the threat posed to our free society by a dictatorship such as the one portrayed by George Orwell in his* 1984, *is unlikely to catch us without warning. He suggests instead that a more troubling threat is posed by the type of world envisioned by Aldous Huxley in his novel* Brave New World, *a story about a society too sated by amusement and diversion to care about protecting its liberties. As you read his first chapter, you might want to ask yourself about Postman's assumptions about language and the role of metaphor in shaping culture. Do you agree that there is an intimate and powerful connection between a civilization's metaphors and the quality of its culture? What are the predominant metaphors that govern our current public discourse?*

At different times in our history, different cities have been the focal point of a radiating American spirit. In the late eighteenth century, for example, Boston was the center of a political radicalism that ignited a shot heard round the world—a shot that could not have been fired any other place but the suburbs of Boston. At its report, all Americans, including Virginians, became Bostonians at heart. In the mid-nineteenth century, New York became the symbol of the idea of a melting-pot America—or at least a non-English one—as the wretched refuse from all over the world disembarked at Ellis Island and spread over the land their strange languages and even stranger ways. In the early twentieth century, Chicago, the city of big shoulders and heavy winds, came to symbolize the industrial energy and dynamism of America. If there is a statue of a hog butcher somewhere in Chicago, then it stands as a reminder of the time when America was railroads, cattle, steel mills and entrepreneurial adventures. If there is no such statue, there ought to be, just as there is a statue of a Minute Man to recall the Age of Boston, as the Statue of Liberty recalls the Age of New York.

Today, we must look to the city of Las Vegas, Nevada, as a metaphor of our national character and aspiration, its symbol a thirty-foot-high cardboard picture of a slot machine and a chorus girl. For Las Vegas is a city entirely devoted to the idea of entertainment, and as such proclaims the spirit of a culture in which all public discourse increasingly takes the form of entertainment. Our politics, religion, news, athletics, education and commerce have been transformed into congenial adjuncts of show business, largely without protest or even much popular notice. The result is that we are a people on the verge of amusing ourselves to death.

As I write, the President of the United States is a former Hollywood movie actor. One of his principal challengers in 1984 was once a featured player on television's most glamorous show of the 1960's, that is to say, an astronaut. Naturally, a movie has been made about his extraterrestrial adventure. Former nominee George McGovern has hosted the popular television show "Saturday Night Live." So has a candidate of more recent vintage, the Reverend Jesse Jackson.

Meanwhile, former President Richard Nixon, who once claimed he lost an election because he was sabotaged by makeup men, has offered Senator Edward Kennedy advice on how to make a serious run for the presidency: lose twenty pounds. Although the Constitution makes no mention of it, it would appear that fat people are now effectively excluded from running for high political office. Probably bald people as well. Almost certainly those whose looks are not significantly enhanced by the cosmetician's art. Indeed, we may have reached the point where cosmetics has replaced ideology as the field of expertise over which a politician must have competent control.

America's journalists, i.e., television newscasters, have not missed the point. Most spend more time with their hair dryers than with their scripts, with the result that they comprise the most glamorous group of people this side of Las Vegas. Although the Federal Communications Act makes no mention of it, those without camera appeal are excluded from addressing the public about what is called "the news of the day." Those with camera appeal can command salaries exceeding one million dollars a year.

American businessmen discovered, long before the rest of us, that the quality and usefulness of their goods are subordinate to the artifice of their display; that, in fact, half the principles of capitalism as praised by Adam Smith or condemned by Karl Marx are irrelevant. Even the Japanese, who are said to make better cars than the Americans, know that economics is less a science than a performing art, as Toyota's yearly advertising budget confirms.

Not long ago, I saw Billy Graham join in with Shecky Green, Red Buttons, Dionne Warwick, Milton Berle and other theologians in a tribute to George Burns, who was celebrating himself for surviving eighty years in show business. The Reverend Graham exchanged one-liners with Burns about making preparations for Eternity. Although the Bible makes no mention of it, the Reverend Graham assured the audience that God loves those who make people laugh. It was an honest mistake. He merely mistook NBC for God.

Dr. Ruth Westheimer is a psychologist who has a popular radio program and a nightclub act in which she informs her audience about sex in all of its infinite variety and in language once reserved for the bedroom and street corners. She is almost as entertaining as the Reverend Billy Graham, and has been quoted as saying, "I don't start out to be funny. But if it comes out that way, I use it. If they call me an entertainer, I say that's great. When a professor teaches with a sense of humor, people walk away remembering."[1] She did not say what they remember or of what use their remembering is. But she has a point: It's great to be an entertainer. Indeed, in America God favors all those who possess both a talent and a format to amuse, whether they be preachers, athletes, entrepreneurs, politicians, teachers or journalists. In America, the least amusing people are its professional entertainers.

Culture watchers and worriers — those of the type who read books like this one — will know that the examples above are not aberrations but, in fact, clichés. There is no shortage of critics who have observed and recorded the dissolution of public discourse in America and its conversion into the arts of show business. But most of them, I believe, have barely begun to tell the story of the origin and meaning of this descent into a vast triviality. Those who have written vigorously on the matter tell us, for example, that what is happening is the residue of an exhausted capitalism; or, on the contrary, that it is the tasteless fruit of the maturing of capitalism; or that it is the neurotic aftermath of the Age of Freud; or the retribution of our allowing God to perish; or that it all comes from the old stand-bys, greed and ambition.

I have attended carefully to these explanations, and I do not say there is nothing to learn from them. Marxists, Freudians, Lévi-Straussians, even Creation Scientists are not to be taken lightly. And, in any case, I should be very surprised if the story I have to tell is anywhere near the whole truth. We are all, as Huxley says someplace, Great Abbreviators, meaning that none of us has the wit to know the whole truth, the time to tell it if we believed we did, or an audience so gullible as to accept it. But you *will* find an argument here that presumes a clearer grasp of the matter than many that have come before. Its value, such as it is, resides in the directness of its perspective, which has its origins in observations made 2,300 years ago by Plato. It is an argument that fixes its attention on the forms of human conversation, and postulates that how we are obliged to conduct such conversations will have the strongest possible influence on what ideas we can conveniently express. And what ideas are convenient to express inevitably become the important content of a culture.

I use the word "conversation" metaphorically to refer not only to speech but to all techniques and technologies that permit people of a particular culture to exchange messages. In this sense, all culture is a conversation or, more precisely, a corporation of conversations, conducted in a variety of symbolic modes. Our attention here is on how forms of public discourse regulate and even dictate what kind of content can issue from such forms.

To take a simple example of what this means, consider the primitive technology of smoke signals. While I do not know exactly what content was once carried in the smoke signals of American Indians, I can safely guess that it did not include philosophical argument. Puffs of smoke are insufficiently complex to express ideas on the nature of existence, and even if they were not, a Cherokee philosopher would run short of either wood or blankets long before he reached his second axiom. You cannot use smoke to do philosophy. Its form excludes the content.

To take an example closer to home: As I suggested earlier, it is implausible to imagine that anyone like our twenty-seventh President, the multi-chinned, three-hundred-pound William Howard Taft, could be put forward as a presidential candidate in today's world. The shape of a man's body is largely irrelevant to the shape of his ideas when he is addressing a public in writing or on the radio or, for that matter, in smoke signals. But it is quite relevant on television. The grossness of a three-hundred-pound image, even a talking one, would easily overwhelm any logical or spiritual subtleties conveyed by speech. For on television, discourse is conducted largely through visual imagery, which is to say that television gives us a conversation in images, not words. The emergence of the image-manager in the political arena and the concomitant decline of the speech writer attest to the fact that television demands a different kind of content from other media. You cannot do political philosophy on television. Its form works against the content.

To give still another example, one of more complexity: The information, the content, or, if you will, the "stuff" that makes up what is called "the news of the day" did not exist—could not exist—in a world that lacked the media to give it expression. I do not mean that things like fires, wars, murders and love affairs did not, ever and always, happen in places all over the world. I mean that lacking a technology to advertise them, people could not attend to them, could not include them in their daily business. Such information simply could not exist as part of the content of culture. This idea—that there is a content called "the news of the day"—was entirely created by the telegraph (and since amplified by newer media), which made it possible to move decontextualized information over vast spaces at incredible speed. The news of the day is a figment of our technological imagination. It is, quite precisely, a media event. We attend to fragments of events from all over the world because we have multiple media whose forms are well suited to fragmented conversation. Cultures without speed-of-light media—let us say, cultures in which smoke signals are the most efficient space-conquering tool available—do not have news of the day. Without a medium to create its form, the news of the day does not exist.

To say it, then, as plainly as I can, this book is an inquiry into and a lamentation about the most significant American cultural fact of the second half of the twentieth century: the decline of the Age of Typography and the ascendancy of the Age of Television. This change-over has dramatically and irreversibly shifted the content and meaning of public discourse, since two media so vastly different cannot accommodate the same ideas. As the influence of print wanes, the content of politics, religion, education, and anything else that comprises public business must change and be recast in terms that are most suitable to television.

If all of this sounds suspiciously like Marshall McLuhan's aphorism, the medium is the message, I will not disavow the association (although it is fashionable to do so among respectable scholars who, were it not for McLuhan, would today be mute). I met McLuhan thirty years ago when I was a graduate student and he an unknown English professor. I believed then, as I believe now, that he spoke in the tradition of Orwell and Huxley—that is, as a prophesier, and I have remained steadfast to his teaching that the clearest way to see through a culture is to attend to its tools for conversation. I might add that my interest in this point of view was first stirred by a prophet far more formidable than McLuhan, more ancient than Plato. In studying the Bible as a young man, I found intimations of the idea that forms of media favor particular kinds of content and therefore are capable of taking command of a culture. I refer specifically to the Decalogue, the Second Commandment of which prohibits the Israelites from making concrete images of anything. "Thou shalt not make unto thee any graven image, any likeness of any thing that is in heaven above, or that is in the earth beneath, or that is in the water beneath the earth." I wondered then, as so many others have, as to why the God of these people would have included instructions on how they were to symbolize, or not symbolize, their experience. It is a strange injunction to include as part of an ethical system *unless its author assumed a connection between forms of human communication and the quality of a culture.* We may hazard a guess that a people who are being asked to embrace an abstract, universal deity would be rendered unfit to do so by the habit of drawing pictures or making statues or depicting their ideas in any concrete, iconographic forms. The God of the Jews was to exist in the Word and through the Word, an unprecedented conception requiring the highest order of abstract thinking. Iconography thus became blasphemy so that a new kind of God could enter a culture. People like ourselves who are in the process of converting their culture from word-centered to image-centered might profit by reflecting on this Mosaic injunction. But even if I am wrong in these conjectures, it is, I believe, a wise and particularly relevant supposition that the media of communication available to a culture are a dominant influence on the formation of the culture's intellectual and social preoccupations.

Speech, of course, is the primal and indispensable medium. It made us human, keeps us human, and in fact defines what human means. This is not to say that if there were no other means of communication all humans would find it equally convenient to speak about the same things in the same way. We know enough about language to understand that variations in the structures of languages will result in variations in what may be called "world view." How people think about time and space, and about things and processes, will be greatly influenced by the grammatical features of their language. We dare not suppose therefore that all human minds are unanimous in understanding how the world is put together. But how much more divergence there is in world view among different cultures can be imagined when we consider the great number and variety of tools for conversation that go beyond speech. For although culture is a creation of speech, it is re-created anew by every medium of communication — from painting to hieroglyphs to the alphabet to television. Each medium, like language itself, makes possible a unique mode of discourse by providing a new orientation for thought, for expression, for sensibility. Which, of course, is what McLuhan meant in saying the medium is the message. His aphorism, however, is in need of amendment because, as it stands, it may lead one to confuse a message with a metaphor. A message denotes a specific, concrete statement about the world. But the forms of our media, including the symbols through which they permit conversation, do not make such statements. They are rather like metaphors, working by unobtrusive but powerful implication to enforce their special definitions of reality. Whether we are experiencing the world through the lens of speech or the printed word or the television camera, our media-metaphors classify the world for us, sequence it, frame it, enlarge it, reduce it, color it, argue a case for what the world is like. As Ernst Cassirer remarked:

> Physical reality seems to recede in proportion as man's symbolic activity advances. Instead of dealing with the things themselves man is in a sense constantly conversing with himself. He has so enveloped himself in linguistic forms, in artistic images, in mythical symbols or religious rites that he cannot see or know anything except by the interposition of [an] artificial medium.[2]

What is peculiar about such interpositions of media is that their role in directing what we will see or know is so rarely noticed. A person who reads a book or who watches television or who glances at his watch is not usually interested in how his mind is organized and controlled by these events, still less in what idea of the world is suggested by a book, television, or a watch. But there are men and women who have noticed these things, especially in our own times. Lewis Mumford, for example, has been one of our great noticers. He is not the sort of a man who looks at a clock merely to see what time it is. Not that he lacks interest in the content of clocks, which is of concern to everyone from moment to moment, but he is far more interested in how a clock creates the idea of "moment to moment." He attends to the philosophy of clocks, to clocks as metaphor, about which our education has had little to say and clock makers nothing at all. "The clock," Mumford has concluded, "is a piece of power machinery whose 'product' is seconds and minutes." In manufacturing such a product, the clock has the effect of disassociating time from human events and thus nourishes the belief in an independent world of mathematically measurable sequences. Moment to moment, it turns out, is not God's conception, or nature's. It is man conversing with himself about and through a piece of machinery he created.

In Mumford's great book *Technics and Civilization*, he shows how, beginning in the fourteenth century, the clock made us into time-keepers, and then time-savers, and now time-servers. In the process, we have learned irreverence toward the sun and the seasons, for in a world made up of seconds and minutes, the authority of nature is superseded. Indeed, as Mumford points out, with the invention of the clock, Eternity ceased to serve as the measure and focus of human events. And thus, though few would have imagined the connection, the inexorable ticking of the clock may have had more to do with the weakening of God's supremacy than all the treatises produced by the philosophers of the Enlightenment; that is to say, the clock introduced a new form of conversation between man and God, in which God appears to have been the loser. Perhaps Moses should have included another Commandment: Thou shalt not make mechanical representations of time.

That the alphabet introduced a new form of conversation between man and man is by now a commonplace among scholars. To be able to *see* one's utterances rather than only to hear them is no small matter, though our education, once again, has had little to say about this. Nonetheless, it is clear that phonetic writing created a new conception of knowledge, as well as a new sense of intelligence, of audience and of posterity, all of which Plato recognized at an early stage in the development of texts. "No man of intelligence," he wrote in his Seventh Letter, "will venture to express his philosophical views in language, especially not in language that is unchangeable, which is true of that which is set down in written characters." This notwithstanding, he wrote voluminously and understood better than anyone else that the setting down of views in written characters would be the beginning of philosophy, not its end. Philosophy cannot exist without criticism, and writing makes it possible and convenient to subject thought to a continuous and concentrated scrutiny. Writing freezes speech and in so doing gives birth to the grammarian, the logician, the rhetorician, the historian, the scientist—all those who must hold language before them so that they can see what it means, where it errs, and where it is leading.

Plato knew all of this, which means that he knew that writing would bring about a perceptual revolution: a shift from the ear to the eye as an organ of language processing. Indeed, there is a legend that to encourage such a shift Plato insisted that his students study geometry before entering his Academy. If true, it was a sound idea, for as the great literary critic Northrop Frye has remarked, "the written word is far more powerful than simply a reminder: it re-creates the past in the present, and gives us, not the familiar remembered thing, but the glittering intensity of the summoned-up hallucination."[3]

All that Plato surmised about the consequences of writing is now well understood by anthropologists, especially those who have studied cultures in which speech is the only source of complex conversation. Anthropologists know that the written word, as Northrop Frye meant to suggest, is not merely an echo of a speaking voice. It is another kind of voice altogether, a conjurer's trick of the first order. It must certainly have appeared that way to those who invented it, and that is why we should not be surprised that the Egyptian god Thoth, who is alleged to have brought writing to the King Thamus, was also the god of magic. People like ourselves may see nothing wondrous in writing, but our anthropologists know how strange and magical it appears to a purely oral people—a conversation with no one and yet with everyone. What could be stranger than the silence one encounters when addressing a question to a text? What could be more metaphysically puzzling than addressing an unseen audience, as every writer of books must do? And correcting oneself because one knows that an unknown reader will disapprove or misunderstand?

I bring all of this up because what my book is about is how our own tribe is undergoing a vast and trembling shift from the magic of writing to the magic of electronics. What I mean to point out here is that the introduction into a culture of a technique such as writing or a clock is not merely an extension of man's power to bind time but a transformation of his way of thinking—and, of course, of the content of his culture. And that is what I mean to say by calling a medium a metaphor. We are told in school, quite correctly, that a metaphor suggests what a thing is like by comparing it to something else. And by the power of its suggestion, it so fixes a conception in our minds that we cannot imagine the one thing without the other: Light is a wave; language, a tree; God, a wise and venerable man; the mind, a dark cavern illuminated by knowledge. And if these metaphors no longer serve us, we must, in the nature of the matter, find others that will. Light is a particle; language, a river; God (as Bertrand Russell proclaimed), a differential equation; the mind, a garden that yearns to be cultivated.

But our media-metaphors are not so explicit or so vivid as these, and they are far more complex. In understanding their metaphorical function, we must take into account the symbolic forms of their information, the source of their information, the quantity and speed of their information, the context in which their information is experienced. Thus, it takes some digging to get at them, to grasp, for example, that a clock recreates time as an independent, mathematically precise sequence; that writing recreates the mind as a tablet on which experience is written; that the telegraph recreates news as a commodity. And yet, such digging becomes easier if we start from the assumption that in every tool we create, an idea is embedded that goes beyond the function of the thing itself. It has been pointed out, for example, that the invention of eyeglasses in the twelfth century not only made it possible to improve defective vision but suggested the idea that human beings need not accept as final either the endowments of nature or the ravages of time. Eyeglasses refuted the belief that anatomy is destiny by putting forward the idea that our bodies as well our minds are improvable. I do not think it goes too far to say that there is a link between the invention of eyeglasses in the twelfth century and gene-splitting research in the twentieth.

Even such an instrument as the microscope, hardly a tool of everyday use, had embedded within it a quite astonishing idea, not about biology but about psychology. By revealing a world hitherto hidden from view, the microscope suggested a possibility about the structure of the mind.

If things are not what they seem, if microbes lurk, unseen on and under our skin, if the invisible controls the visible, then is it not possible that ids and egos and superegos also lurk somewhere unseen? What else is psychoanalysis but a microscope of the mind? Where do our notions of mind come from if not from metaphors generated by our tools? What does it mean to say that someone has an IQ of 126? There are no numbers in people's heads. Intelligence does not have quantity or magnitude, except as we believe that it does. And why do we believe that it does? Because we have tools that imply that this is what the mind is like. Indeed, our tools for thought suggest to us what our bodies are like, as when someone refers to her "biological clock," or when we talk of our "genetic codes," or when we read someone's face like a book, or when our facial expressions telegraph our intentions.

When Galileo remarked that the language of nature is written in mathematics, he meant it only as a metaphor. Nature itself does not speak. Neither do our minds or our bodies or, more to the point of this book, our bodies politic. Our conversations about nature and about ourselves are conducted in whatever "languages" we find it possible and convenient to employ. We do not see nature or intelligence or human motivation or ideology as "it" is but only as our languages are. And our languages are our media. Our media are our metaphors. Our metaphors create the content of our culture.

NOTES

[1] As quoted in the *Wisconsin State Journal* (August 24, 1983), Section 3, page 1.
[2] Cassirer, p. 43.
[3] Frye, p. 227.

OPTIONS FOR WRITING

1. Toward the end of his chapter, Postman speculates about the changes brought about by the introduction of writing into a culture that had previously depended on speech alone. To test his theory, spend a day depending solely on oral communication. Don't take class notes, don't make "to do" lists, don't write checks. Then, write a letter to a friend describing what you noticed during the course of the day and explaining the usefulness of written language to your life (or explain why you intend to depend more on oral communication from now on).

2. Find a metaphor that is currently in popular use to describe an event, an attitude, or a phenomenon. In a speculative essay, explore a different metaphor for the same thing. Does your view of the item you're describing change? If so, how?

3. Postman says "you cannot use smoke [signals] to do philosophy. Its form excludes the content." Do you agree? Find at least two further examples of intellectual content that cannot be communicated by a particular medium. In a brief essay, compare these two examples with Postman's examples of television and political philosophy and of the media and the news of the day.

4. Make as long a list as you can of the intellectual and aesthetic advantages of written language. Then, using this list, write a story or a poem illustrating one or more of these advantages.

5. Write the next few pages of Postman's book on the role of television in modern American culture. Base your writing on the argument in his essay and on the title of his book.

Muriel Rukeyser
MYTH

Muriel Rukeyser (1913–1980) was a teacher, poet, social activist, and novelist passionately interested in human rights and social justice. An active participant in the civil rights movement, the women's movement, and the anti-Vietnam protests of the 1960s, she wrote and translated until her death in 1980. Her poem "Myth" appeared in The Collected Poems of Muriel Rukeyser, *a collection that won several awards in the year of its publication (1979).*

Mark Twain (the pen name of Samuel Clemens) is known to most Americans as the nineteenth century author of The Adventures of Tom Sawyer *and* Huckleberry Finn. *An essayist and social critic with a trenchant humor, Mark Twain often found himself in the position of pointing out to American society what people should have found most obvious, and he enjoyed the game of playing — sometimes outrageously — with language. In "That Awful German Language," Twain has a great deal of fun with the notion of gender, which many languages assign to nouns regardless of the gender (or lack of it) of the thing being described. He also reminds us of the obvious: how it feels to be transported into a culture whose arbitrary but time-honored rules make little sense to us.*

As you read these two passages together, speculate on the role played by language in the creation of each. What do they have in common? What assumptions are made (or challenged) by the writers? What assumptions do the writers seem to accept without question? How can language be used to clarify, to confuse, or to deceive? How can language be used humorously?

Long afterward, Oedipus, old and blinded, walked the roads. He smelled a familiar smell. It was the Sphinx. Oedipus said, "I want to ask one question. Why didn't I recognize my mother?" "You gave the wrong answer," said the Sphinx. "But that was what made everything possible," said Oedipus. "No," she said. "When I asked, What walks on four legs in the morning, two at noon, and three in the evening, you answered, Man. You didn't say anything about woman." "When you say Man," said Oedipus, "you include women too. Everyone knows that." She said, "That's what you think."

Mark Twain
THAT AWFUL GERMAN LANGUAGE

Every noun has a gender, and there is no sense or system in the distribution; so the gender of each must be learned separately and by heart. There is no other way. To do this, one has to have a memory like a memorandum book. In German, a young lady has no sex, while a turnip has. Think what overwrought reverence that shows for the turnip, and what callous disrespect for the girl. See how it looks in print — I translate this from a conversation in one of the best of the German Sunday-school books:

"Gretchen.   Wilhelm, where is the turnip?
"Wilhelm.   She has gone to the kitchen.
"Gretchen.   Where is the accomplished and beautiful English maiden?
"Wilhelm.   It has gone to the opera."

To continue with the German genders: a tree is male, its buds are female, its leaves are neuter; horses are sexless, dogs are male, cats are female, — Tomcats included, of course; a person's mouth, neck, bosom, elbows, fingers, nails, feet, and body, are of the male sex, and his head is male or neuter according to the word selected to signify it, and *not* according to the sex of the individual who wears it, — for in Germany all the women wear either male heads or sexless ones; a person's nose, lips, shoulders, breast, hands, hips, and toes are of the female sex; and his hair, ears, eyes, chin, legs, knees, heart, and conscience, haven't any sex at all. The inventor of the language probably got what he knew about a conscience from hearsay.

Now, by the above dissection, the reader will see that in Germany a man may *think* he is a man, but when he comes to look into the matter closely, he is bound to have his doubts; he finds that in sober truth he is a most ridiculous mixture; and if he ends by trying to comfort himself with the thought that he can at least depend on a third of this mess as being manly and masculine, the humiliating second thought will quickly remind him that in this respect he is no better off than any woman or cow in the land.

In the German it is true that by some oversight of the inventor of the language, a Woman is a female; but a Wife, (*Weib,*) is not, — which is unfortunate. A wife, here, has no sex; she is neuter; so, according to the grammar, a fish is *he,* his scales are *she,* but a fishwife is neither. To describe a wife as sexless, may be called under-description; that is bad enough, but over-description is surely worse. A German speaks of an Englishman as the *Engländer;* to change the sex, he adds *inn,* and that stands for Englishwoman, — *Engländerinn.* That seems descriptive enough, but still it is not exact enough for a German; so he precedes the word with that article which indicates that the creature to follow is feminine, and writes it down thus: *"die* Engländer*inn,"* — which means "the *she-Englishwoman.*" I consider that that person is over-described.

Well, after the student has learned the sex of a great number of nouns, he is still in a difficulty, because he finds it impossible to persuade his tongue to refer to things as *"he"* and *"she,"* and *"him"* and *"her,"* which it has always been accustomed to refer to as *"it."* When he even frames a German sentence in his mind, with the hims and hers in the right places, and then works up his courage to the utterance-point, it is no use, — the moment he begins to speak his tongue flies the track and all those labored males and females come out as *"its."* And even when he is reading German to himself, he always calls those things *"it;"* whereas he ought to read in this way:

Tale of the Fishwife and It's Sad Fate.[1]

It is a bleak Day. Hear the Rain, how he pours, and the Hail, how he rattles; and see the Snow, how he drifts along, and oh the Mud, how deep he is! Ah the poor Fishwife, it is stuck fast in the Mire; it has dropped its Basket of Fishes; and its Hands have been cut by the Scales as it seized some of the falling Creatures; and one Scale has even got into its Eye, and it cannot get her out. It opens its Mouth to cry for Help; but if any Sound comes out of him, alas he is drowned by the raging of the Storm. And now a Tomcat has got one of the Fishes and she will surely escape with him. No, she bites off a Fin, she holds her in her Mouth — will she swallow her? No, the Fishwife's brave Mother-Dog deserts his Puppies and rescues the Fin, — which he eats, himself, as his Reward. O, horror, the Lightning has struck the Fish-basket; he sets him on Fire; see the Flame, how she licks the doomed Utensil with her red and angry Tongue; now she attacks the helpless Fishwife's Foot, — she burns him up, all but the big Toe, and even *she* is partly consumed; and still she spreads, still she waves her fiery Tongues; she attacks the Fishwife's Leg and destroys *it*; she attacks its Hand and destroys *her*; she attacks its poor worn Garment and destroys *her* also; she attacks its Body and consumes *him*; she wreathes herself about its Heart and *it* is consumed; next about its Breast, and in a Moment *she* is a Cinder; now she reaches its Neck, —*he* goes; now its Chin, —*it* goes; now its Nose, —*she* goes. In another Moment, except Help come, the Fishwife will be no more. Time presses, — is there none to succor and save? Yes! Joy, joy, with flying Feet the she-Englishwoman comes! But alas, the generous she-Female is too late; where now is the fated Fishwife? It has ceased from its Sufferings, it has gone to a better Land; all that is left of it for its loved Ones to lament over, is this poor smouldering Ash-heap. Ah, woful, woful Ash heap! Let us take him up tenderly, reverently, upon the lowly Shovel, and bear him to his long Rest, with the Prayer that when he rises again it will be in a Realm where he will have one good square responsible Sex, and have it all to himself, instead of having a mangy lot of assorted Sexes scattered all over him in Spots.

There, now, the reader can see for himself that this pronoun-business is a very awkward thing for the unaccustomed tongue.

OPTIONS FOR WRITING

1. Do you believe that "man" used generically includes "woman"? Imagine that you are running for President of the United States. How would you defend your position (pro or con) on this issue if you were making a speech to the Women's Legislative Caucus of your political party? (Remember, you need their votes, so you must be convincing!)

2. Think about some aspect of the English language that could appear confusing and perhaps silly to a foreigner trying to learn the English language. Write a short humorous piece similar to Twain's in which you poke fun at this aspect of the language.

---

[1] I capitalize the nouns in the German (and ancient English) fashion. —M. T.

3. Notice that Mark Twain uses the generic male pronoun while laughing at the German use of gendered pronouns. Imagine that Twain and Rukeyser appeared on a talk show together to discuss sexist language. Write their dialogue. Remember that both were astute and clever social critics.

4. Both Rukeyser and Twain make gentle fun of the concept of "everyone knows" as it applies to language and society. Write a story, an essay, or a poem that does the same thing: satirizes something that everyone knows but which may not be so universally understood and supported as it first appears.

5. Write a letter to your teacher explaining why you think these two pieces were chosen for a chapter on language. Defend or attack their inclusion in the readings.

Lewis Thomas
SOCIAL TALK

Lewis Thomas is a respected physician who has written frequently about his profession and his observations of life. An active researcher and now a healthcare administrator, Thomas mixes his acute powers of observation with a dry wit and an imaginative flair in his many essays on all aspects of life, from the Manhattan downtown to anthropological discussions to music, art, and language. The two essays that follow are related by Thomas's interest in language as a genetically predetermined behavior peculiar to humans and by his insistent speculation on human interconnectedness through language. As you read, you might ask yourself how Thomas's definition of language fits with others in this chapter. Can you find similarities between Thomas and Lame Deer as they consider human reactions to animals? Does Thomas identify functions of language that are new to you? Are there some functions he overlooks?

Not all social animals are social with the same degree of commitment. In some species, the members are so tied to each other and interdependent as to seem the loosely conjoined cells of a tissue. The social insects are like this; they move, and live all their lives, in a mass; a beehive is a spherical animal. In other species, less compulsively social, the members make their homes together, pool resources, travel in packs or schools, and share the food, but any single one can survive solitary, detached from the rest. Others are social only in the sense of being more or less congenial, meeting from time to time in committees, using social gatherings as *ad hoc* occasions for feeding and breeding. Some animals simply nod at each other in passing, never reaching even a first-name relationship.

It is not a simple thing to decide where we fit, for at one time or another in our lives we manage to organize in every imaginable social arrangement. We are as interdependent, especially in our cities, as bees or ants, yet we can detach if we wish and go live alone in the woods, in theory anyway. We feed and look after each other, constructing elaborate systems for this, even including vending machines to dispense ice cream in gas stations, but we also have numerous books to tell us how to live off the land. We cluster in family groups, but we tend, unpredictably, to turn on each other and fight as if we were different species. Collectively, we hanker to accumulate all the information in the universe and distribute it around among ourselves as though it were a kind of essential foodstuff, ant-fashion (the faintest trace of real news in science has the action of a pheromone, lifting the hairs of workers in laboratories at the ends of the earth), but each of us also builds a private store of his own secret knowledge and hides it away like untouchable treasure. We have names to label each as self, and we believe without reservation that this system of taxonomy will guarantee the entity, the absolute separateness of each of us, but the mechanism has no discernible function in the center of a crowded city; we are essentially nameless, most of our time.

Nobody wants to think that the rapidly expanding mass of mankind, spreading out over the surface of the earth, blackening the ground, bears any meaningful resemblance to the life of an anthill or a hive. Who would consider for a moment that the more than 3 billion of us are a sort of stupendous animal when we become linked together? We are not mindless, nor is our day-to-day behavior coded out to the last detail by our genomes, nor do we seem to be engaged together, compulsively, in any single, universal, stereotyped task analogous to the construction of a nest. If we were ever to put all our brains together in fact, to make a common mind the way the ants do, it would be an unthinkable thought, way over our heads.

Social animals tend to keep at a particular thing, generally something huge for their size; they work at it ceaselessly under genetic instructions and genetic compulsion, using it to house the species and protect it, assuring permanence.

There are, to be sure, superficial resemblances in some of the things we do together, like building glass and plastic cities on all the land and farming under the sea, or assembling in armies, or landing samples of ourselves on the moon, or sending memoranda into the next galaxy. We do these together without being quite sure why, but we can stop doing one thing and move to another whenever we like. We are not committed or bound by our genes to stick to one activity forever, like the wasps. Today's behavior is no more fixed than when we tumbled out over Europe to build cathedrals in the twelfth century. At that time we were convinced that it would go on forever, that this was the way to live, but it was not; indeed, most of us have already forgotten what it was all about. Anything we do in this transient, secondary social way, compulsively and with all our energies but only for a brief period of our history, cannot be counted as social behavior in the biological sense. If we can turn it on and off, on whims, it isn't likely that our genes are providing the detailed instructions. Constructing Chartres was good for our minds, but we found that our lives went on, and it is no more likely that we will find survival in Rome plows or laser bombs, or rapid mass transport or a Mars lander, or solar power, or even synthetic protein. We do tend to improvise things like this as we go along, but it is clear that we can pick and choose.

For practical purposes, it would probably be best for us not to be biologically social, in the long run. Not that we have a choice, or course, or even a vote. It would not be good news to learn that we are all roped together intellectually, droning away at some featureless, genetically driven collective work, building something so immense that we can never see the outlines. It seems especially hard, even perilous, for this to be the burden of a species with the unique attribute of speech, and argument. Leave this kind of life to the insects and birds, and lesser mammals, and fish.

But there is just that one thing. About human speech.

It begins to look, more and more disturbingly, as if the gift of language is the single human trait that marks us all genetically, setting us apart from all the rest of life. Language is, like nest-building or hive-making, the universal and biologically specific activity of human beings. We engage in it communally, compulsively, and automatically. We cannot be human without it; if we were to be separated from it our minds would die, as surely as bees lost from the hive.

We are born knowing how to use language. The capacity to recognize syntax, to organize and deploy words into intelligible sentences, is innate in the human mind. We are programmed to identify patterns and generate grammar. There are invariant and variable structures in speech that are common to all of us. As chicks are endowed with an innate capacity to read information in the shapes of overhanging shadows, telling hawk from other birds, we can identify the meaning of grammar in a string of words, and we are born this way. According to Chomsky, who has examined it as a biologist looks at live tissue, language "must simply be a biological property of the human mind." The universal attributes of language are genetically set; we do not learn them, or make them up as we go along.

We work at this all our lives, and collectively we give it life, but we do not exert the least control over language, not as individuals or committees or academies or governments. Language, once it comes alive, behaves like an active, motile organism. Parts of it are always being changed, by a ceaseless activity to which all of us are committed; new words are invented and inserted, old ones have their meaning altered or abandoned. New ways of stringing words and sentences together come into fashion and vanish again, but the underlying structure simply grows, enriches itself, expands. Individual languages age away and seem to die, but they leave progeny all over the place. Separate languages can exist side by side for centuries without touching each other, maintaining their integrity with the vigor of incompatible tissues. At other times, two languages may come together, fuse, replicate, and give rise to nests of new tongues.

If language is at the core of our social existence, holding us together, housing us in meaning, it may also be safe to say that art and music are functions of the same universal, genetically determined mechanism. These are not bad things to do together. If we are social creatures because of this, and therefore like ants, I for one (or should I say we for one?) do not mind.

Lewis Thomas
THE TUCSON ZOO

Science gets most of its information by the process of reductionism, exploring the details, then the details of the details, until all the smallest bits of the structure, or the smallest parts of the mechanism, are laid out for counting and scrutiny. Only when this is done can the investigation be extended to encompass the whole organism or the entire system. So we say.

Sometimes it seems that we take a loss, working this way. Much of today's public anxiety about science is the apprehension that we may forever be overlooking the whole by an endless, obsessive preoccupation with the parts. I had a brief, personal experience of this misgiving one afternoon in Tucson, where I had time on my hands and visited the zoo, just outside the city. The designers there have cut a deep pathway between two small artificial ponds, walled by clear glass, so when you stand in the center of the path you can look into the depths of each pool, and at the same time you can regard the surface. In one pool, on the right side of the path, is a family of otters; on the other side, a family of beavers. Within just a few feet from your face, on either side, beavers and otters are at play, underwater and on the surface, swimming toward your face and then away, more filled with life than any creatures I have ever seen before, in all my days. Except for the glass, you could reach across and touch them.

I was transfixed. As I now recall it, there was only one sensation in my head: pure elation mixed with amazement at such perfection. Swept off my feet, I floated from one side to the other, swiveling my brain, staring astounded at the beavers, then at the otters. I could hear shouts across my corpus callosum, from one hemisphere to the other. I remember thinking, with what was left in charge of my consciousness, that I wanted no part of the science of beavers and otters; I wanted never to know how they performed their marvels; I wished for no news about the physiology of their breathing, the coordination of their muscles, their vision, their endocrine systems, their digestive tracts. I hoped never to have to think of them as collections of cells. All I asked for was the full hairy complexity, then in front of my eyes, of whole, intact beavers and otters in motion.

It lasted, I regret to say, for only a few minutes, and then I was back in the late twentieth century, reductionist as ever, wondering about the details by force of habit, but not, this time, the details of otters and beavers. Instead, me. Something worth remembering had happened in my mind, I was certain of that; I would have put it somewhere in the brain stem; maybe this was my limbic system at work. I became a behavioral scientist, an experimental psychologist, an ethologist, and in the instant I lost all the wonder and the sense of being overwhelmed. I was flattened.

But I came away from the zoo with something, a piece of news about myself: I am coded, somehow, for otters and beavers. I exhibit instinctive behavior in their presence, when they are displayed close at hand behind glass, simultaneously below water and at the surface. I have receptors for this display. Beavers and otters possess a "releaser" for me, in the terminology of ethology, and the releasing was my experience. What was released? Behavior. What behavior? Standing, swiveling flabbergasted, feeling exultation and a rush of friendship. I could not, as the result of the transaction, tell you anything more about beavers and otters than you already know. I learned nothing new about them. Only about me, and I suspect also about you, maybe about human beings at large: we are endowed with genes which code out our reaction to beavers and otters, maybe our reaction to each other as well. We are stamped with stereotyped, unalterable patterns of response, ready to be released. And the behavior released in us, by such confrontations, is, essentially, a surprised affection. It is compulsory behavior and we can avoid it only by straining with the full power of our conscious minds, making up conscious excuses all the way. Left to ourselves, mechanistic and autonomic, we hanker for friends.

Everyone says, stay away from ants. They have no lessons for us; they are crazy little instruments, inhuman, incapable of controlling themselves, lacking manners, lacking souls. When they are massed together, all touching, exchanging bits of information held in their jaws like memoranda, they become a single animal. Look out for that. It is a debasement, a loss of individuality, a violation of human nature, an unnatural act.

Sometimes people argue this point of view seriously and with deep thought. Be individuals, solitary and selfish, is the message. Altruism, a jargon word for what used to be called love, is worse than weakness, it is sin, a violation of nature. Be separate. Do not be a social animal. But this is a hard argument to make convincingly when you have to depend on language to make it. You have to print up leaflets or publish books and get them bought and sent around, you have to turn up on television and catch the attention of millions of other human beings all at once, and then you have to say to all of them, all at once, all collected and paying attention: be solitary; do not depend on each other. You can't do this and keep a straight face.

Maybe altruism is our most primitive attribute, out of reach, beyond our control. Or perhaps it is immediately at hand, waiting to be released, disguised now, in our kind of civilization, as affection or friendship or attachment. I don't see why it should be unreasonable for all human beings to have strands of DNA coiled up in chromosomes, coding out instincts for usefulness and helpfulness. Usefulness may turn out to be the hardest test of fitness for survival, more important than aggression, more effective, in the long run, than grabbiness. If this is the sort of information biological science holds for the future, applying to us as well as to ants, then I am all for science.

One thing I'd like to know most of all: when those ants have made the Hill, and are all there, touching and exchanging, and the whole mass begins to behave like a single huge creature, and *thinks*, what on earth is that thought? And while you're at it, I'd like to know a second thing: when it happens, does any single ant know about it? Does his hair stand on end?

OPTIONS FOR WRITING

1. Write a brief essay based on the model of "The Tucson Zoo" in which you recount an experience you have had and relate it to some intellectual interest or theory of your own.

2. Imagine that one of the otters is a budding otter biologist observing Lewis Thomas at the zoo. Write a few pages in the otter's log.

3. Thomas observes that "Language, once it comes alive, behaves like an active, motile organism." Make a list of examples of language's self-generating, self-perpetuating, and independent nature. Share these examples with your classmates, and develop a longer list as a class project.

4. Do you agree that language is essential to thought? Thomas says, "We cannot be human without [language]; if we were to be separated from it our minds would die, as surely as bees lost from the hive." Write a letter to Thomas based on your own observations and the readings in this chapter.

7

THINKING AS A PSYCHOLOGIST

Lynne A. Bond

When people-watcher Lynne Bond goes to a party, she notices her own initial nervousness among strangers as well as the ways other guests act. That sort of curiosity about human behavior often leads psychologists to design experiments to find out what makes people tick. Bond shows how psychologists use the scientific method in their research and encourages readers to conduct some experiments for themselves. In the first of these experiments, readers record their own behavior, then search for its roots. Next they observe public behavior in a classroom and a restaurant and finally prepare written observations and an analysis of the experiment.

READINGS

428

Parties always remind me how strange and amazing people are—predictable, but so hard to predict, if you know what I mean. I guess that's why people-watching is such a great pastime. Of course, what we see people do may be only the tip of the iceberg; there's all that thinking and feeling going on inside that we can't really see—we just surmise. That's what makes the whole puzzle even more baffling. We can never be absolutely sure why people do what they do, feel what they feel, or think what they think. Or can we?

Just what makes people tick? What makes *you* and *me* tick? This is the subject of psychology. And as I said, whenever I go to a party I'm reminded what an odd assortment of characters we all are. Perhaps that's one of the reasons that I'm a psychologist.

OBSERVING

Whether or not I feel geared up to go to a party, there's often that moment (it *can* feel like a lifetime) when I walk in the door and that little voice in the back of my head says "What am I doing here? I hope this isn't a disaster."

You know that dull feeling. I walk into a strange new house and don't know where to throw my coat. (Is this the closet? Oh no, it's the bathroom—face flushes, pulse throbs.) I hear the strained laughter and exaggerated animation of voices from the next room. Why does everyone's voice suddenly get 20 decibels louder when they open their mouths at a party? I take a deep breath—that usually helps—and walk in. The smell of food and drink from one corner eases my body a bit.

At first it seems so dark that I can't see people's faces clearly; it's funny how people seem to feel safer when the lights are dimmed (Or do they? When they're outside the dark can feel dangerous—maybe it depends on who you're with and where). Anyway, I stand still for a moment so my eyes can adjust. Despite the large and relatively empty room, everyone is jammed together into two little huddles, one around the food and drinks and the other in the corner. Wouldn't everyone be much more comfortable if they all took one big step back and got some breathing room? I guess not.

As I stand there alone for five or ten seconds (it feels like an eternity) the room seems to brighten, and I make out some faces. My heart starts racing, and my stomach knots up: I don't recognize anyone. Just take a few deep breaths and try to relax—no big deal, right? Oh, now I recognize Travis and Cheryl, that strange duo who are always walking around arm in arm (what on earth could they see in each other?). Travis always tries to act like a tough guy, but he seems to be putty underneath. Everyone around them is howling. Travis obviously said something that got his crowd roaring. He usually does. Why does everyone always find him such a stitch? He's actually a jerk, and he's always clutching a can of beer as if it's his security blanket.

Why do I come to these things anyway? It always gets better, I reassure myself, or at least usually. I wonder how many parties actually leave me feeling good at the end. I seem to go through phases when I'm into the party scene and then phases when I'm not. Maybe it depends on how well the rest of my social life is going.

I find myself wandering up to the food table and shoveling chips and dip into my mouth. The dip is that lousy stuff that comes right out of a can. Why do people buy this junk when it always tastes like plastic? Better yet, why do I eat it? But somehow the chips and plastic dip make me feel better for the moment, so I continue to scoop food into my mouth.

I realize that I'm easing closer to Travis's group, trying not to make eye contact with him but sort of hoping that the jerk will notice me. He does, and in his bellowing voice he shouts some ridiculous greeting, wraps his arm around me, and regales a story about the two of us getting his car stuck in the mud. It had been a rather ho-hum event on that drizzly day in May when I got stuck, but as he embellishes the tale it sounds like the laugh of a lifetime. The crowd roars again. I find myself relaxing, easing closer to the center of the crowd. The chill of the room gradually subsides, and a small grin creeps across my face.

One tale leads to another—stuck in mud and no shoes on, stuck on a freeway in a friend's new car, out of gas on the town's main drag with a car full of costumed friends on Halloween. Others wander into the party with carefully crafted nonchalance. Some ease up to the periphery of my huddle, but one parades right into the middle of the gang and assumes center stage. The group swells, and the group ethic fades; the team disperses into quieter, relaxed conversations in small groups that splinter off from the huddle. I find myself moving from one cluster to another, enjoying the exchanges and marveling at the incredible cast of characters I'm meeting. All the while I've got to laugh at myself for being such a character: I mean, what's the big deal? Why get so worked up over nothing? It's just another party.

THE PSYCHOLOGICAL ANALYSIS

So what *does* make us tick? I have been living with myself all of my life, but I still can't figure "me" out entirely. How well can *you* explain your own feelings, thoughts, and behaviors? Well, this is what the field of psychology is all about: understanding the bases of the behavior, thoughts, and feelings of humans and other animals and thinking about the different ways we experience our world. Imagine that the world is a huge party and that psychologists are wandering around trying to figure out what everyone is feeling, thinking, and doing and what's shaping these experiences. Of course, they do much more than that. Applied psychologists try to use their understanding of human and animal behavior to reshape social policy, communities, institutions, and organizations to improve individuals' lives.

There's no trick to the field of psychology. Contrary to what the media sometimes suggests, psychologists can't read people's minds or see through to their subconscious in mystical ways. (How many times have I been at a party when someone has turned to a friend during our conversation and said, "Watch what you say. Don't you know that she's a psychologist?") In fact, psychologists ask the same sorts of questions and make the same sorts of speculations that you do as you go through your day-to-day life: "Why do I get so worked up over parties when they usually turn out just fine?" "Gee, my whole body is jittery; I guess I'm more nervous than I thought." "I'll bet that he acts tough on the outside to hide his insecurities on the inside." Let's face it. We are *all* psychologists to some degree, even from the time we are very young.

Psychologists assume that thoughts, feelings, and behaviors do not simply occur in a random way, so we look for rules or laws that describe, explain, or predict actions, emotions, and thoughts from one situation to another. For example, we ask if our ability to see in a dimly lit room improves with the length of time we spend in dimly lit situations. We also question whether there are *patterns* of behaviors, thoughts, and feelings that characterize particular groups of individuals. For example, are teenagers more self-conscious about their social interaction than children and adults? Are women more likely than men to eat when they feel anxious? Is there such a thing as an addictive personality type that is associated with certain mental and physical characteristics? Psychologists try to understand what *motivates* behavior as well; why do people do what they do, think what they think, feel what they feel? Why do I eat that awful dip even though it reminds me of plastic? Do I always behave that way? Am I an obsessive eater? Is there something about that situation, in particular, that leads me to behave in such a way? Have my past experiences with eating or party-going shaped my behavior?

In our quest we also explore how behaviors, feelings, and thoughts are modified and ask about the major influences that shape them. How important are the people or things around us, experiences of the past, anticipations of the future, physical and chemical changes in our bodies, subconscious activity, and the amount of sunlight in our days? The possibilities seem almost endless.

THE SCIENTIFIC METHOD

The major difference between professional and amateur psychologists is that professionals have been trained to use a technique we call the scientific method to pursue these issues carefully and systematically. This method includes the following steps:

1. *Make an observation.* For example, I am feeling really uncomfortable and nervous and am shoveling junk food into my mouth.

2. *Raise questions regarding the observation.* Do I eat when I feel anxious? Do I eat to distract myself? Is eating actually making me feel better?

3. *Formulate a hypothesis, or possible explanation.* Anxious people eat in order to calm themselves.

4. *Test the hypothesis by experimentation.* Make identical refreshments freely available in two classrooms. In one class, but not the other, make a sudden announcement that the class is about to have a surprise quiz (in order to arouse anxiety). Observe how much each student eats during the next five minutes in each class. Also, give the students a brief questionnaire to measure their levels of anxiety at the end of the five-minute period. According to your original hypothesis, students in the high-anxiety class should eat more than those in the low-anxiety class. You can predict that among students in the high-anxiety class, those who eat most will end up the least anxious.

5. *Formulate a scientific theory.* Form your theory if your hypothesis is repeatedly confirmed in this and other experiments. In reality, most hypotheses are only partially confirmed in a given experiment. This leads to a modification of the hypothesis and to experiments to test the revised and refined hunch. For example, in this experiment, you might have found that nearly all of those in the low-anxiety class ate a moderate amount. Meanwhile, one-half the students in the high-anxiety class ate a tremendous amount but one-half ate nothing at all, and after the five-minute period, there was little difference between the anxiety levels of the big and small eaters.

Note that professional psychologists are taught to refrain from simply generalizing from their own experiences to the experiences of others. They learn that careful, varied observations are the key to posing meaningful questions, collecting useful data, and deriving worthwhile conclusions. Ideally, systematic observations lead to careful experimentation that reveals new observations and understanding and hence refined experimentation and understanding; the cycle, then, continues as we engage in the ongoing process of constructing knowledge. Meanwhile, psychologists are becoming increasingly more sensitive to the dangers of creating artificial experimental contexts. The experimental settings that are most carefully controlled by the researcher are often those that are furthest removed from the natural environment and are hence least likely to allow the researcher to study behavior as it actually occurs in our everyday world. Thus, some psychologists debate whether controlled experiments can tell us much about real human or animal behavior. What do you think?

WRITING 1.

Now you set up the next experiment. Continue our investigation of eating and anxiety using the outline for the scientific method. (1) Restate our new observation (that most of the students in the low-anxiety class ate a moderate amount, that one-half of the students in the high-anxiety class ate a lot but one-half ate nothing at all, and that after five minutes there was no difference in anxiety among any of the students. (2) Raise new questions regarding this observation. (3) Formulate a new, improved hypothesis. (4) Propose a test for the hypothesis by experimentation, and describe what results you might expect.

DIFFERENT PSYCHOLOGISTS OBSERVE DIFFERENTLY

There's no denying that thoughts, emotions, and behaviors are extremely complex phenomena. They are so complex, in fact, that the field of psychology itself has evolved into a large number of subfields, including personality, social psychology, environmental psychology, physiological psychology, perception, developmental psychology, learning and motivation, cognition, memory, neuropsychology, psychopharmacology, clinical psychology, counseling psychology, school psychology, and organizational psychology. Each subfield of psychology looks at behavior, thinking, and emotion but does so from slightly different angles — with different-colored glasses, so to speak. Each group asks certain types of questions, emphasizes different sorts of observations, and tries to explain particular kinds of phenomena with different levels of analysis.

Let's consider some of the ways that different types of psychologists think. In fact, we'll find that we were conducting many of those sorts of psychological analyses ourselves.

For a start, what is that little voice in the back of your head that converses with you in these and other situations? Some of us talk to ourselves aloud, though others converse more discretely. But all of us have had conversations with ourselves in one form or another. Do we all have some deeper, inner self that knows us better than we know ourselves? How can we reach that inner voice and hear what it has to say? What's the relationship between this inner self and the self that we observe on the outside? Are the two selves really distinct, or are they the same — just different sides of our complex personalities at different levels of consciousness, or awareness? These are issues that you and the *personality psychologist* might consider. In fact, these are some of the questions that the great Sigmund Freud asked back in the nineteenth century, questions that led psychology to become a household topic of discussion. An interest in personality also leads us to ask at the party why certain people stand on the periphery of a crowd while others stride to the center without hesitation. Think too about Travis clutching his beer can: Is he really so gutsy, or is he terrified?

How are people's feelings, thoughts, and behavior affected by interactions with others? At the beginning of the party I heard strained laughter and the exaggerated animation of voices. I wondered why people speak so much more loudly at parties than in other contexts. And why were people jammed into two little huddles, despite the big and relatively empty room? Why squish together when you don't have to? Then there was the strange duo of Travis and Cheryl. What makes certain people attracted to each other (and how many hours have we all spent trying to figure this out)? Is it true that "birds of a feather flock together," or do "opposites attract"? Can both be right? Neither? Can we predict at all? Certainly much of advertising relies on everyone's assumption (or hope!) that we can identify and then acquire the sorts of things that make people attractive to each other. Social psychologists and probably all humans think about these sorts of things.

But we recognize that not only people affect our thoughts, emotions, and behavior. Our general environments affect us as well, and that's the heart of environmental psychology. When you think about the reasons why dimmed lights are appreciated at parties but not when you're walking down an unfamiliar street, you're acting as an *environmental psychologist*. You're considering general rules about the ways that the environment affects thoughts and behavior. Can we determine what sorts of surroundings will lead people to drink more or less alcohol at a party or in a restaurant? (In fact, people drink more when slow rather than fast music is playing.) What sorts of classroom seating arrangements will encourage students to speak up? Can the dentist's office be designed in a way to make us feel more at ease? In terms of individual differences in response to the environment, do you concentrate best when it's quiet or when there's some background noise? Do you get energized or overwhelmed by a bustling city street? These are all concerns of the environmental psychologist.

The perspective of the *physiological psychologist* prevailed at the party as I made observations about the relationship between my body's functioning and my feelings and behavior — my flushed face and throbbing pulse as I mistook the bathroom for the coat closet, that dull feeling that swept over me when I first walked in the door, my racing heart and knotted stomach when I recognized no one, the slight easing of body tension when I smelled the food and drink, and my muscle relaxation as I became part of the group storytelling and laughter. The body does amazing things in conjunction with our thoughts, feelings, and behavior.

I not only observed my body functions changing but also tried to use my body to alter my thoughts and feelings, to make myself feel more calm and in control. I took a deep breath when I walked into the room, and I tried to make myself breathe slowly and steadily as I stood alone attempting to decipher whether I knew anyone at the party. Similarly, the physiological psychologist is interested in the ways our bodies both affect and are affected by the ways we feel, think, and act.

Psychologists are also curious about the ways we perceive or sense things around us. At the party I noted the smell of the food and drink: How do we recognize these smells? I detected a plastic taste in the dip:

Why does it taste like plastic to me but nectar to another? I noted the changing sounds of the crowd's laughter and conversation, the chill and then warming of the room, and the brightening of the room as I stood there a few moments. How much of the sound change was real, and how much imagined? Did the room temperature actually vary? Why did the lights seem to brighten when no one adjusted them? And I sensed the passage of time, but wondered whether those uncomfortable moments at the beginning of the party were really seconds, minutes, or hours. How do we sense the passage of time, anyway? Do we have some internal clock? How accurate are we? And what affects our accuracy? When do hours seem like minutes and minutes like hours? These questions are all matters of *perception,* one of the oldest fields within the study of psychology.

I even engaged in a bit of *psychological experimental design* at the party. I asked, "How many parties actually leave me feeling good at the end?" And following an observation ("I seem to go through phases when I'm into the party scene and then phases when I'm not"), I formulated a hypothesis: "Whether or not I'm into the party scene depends on how well the rest of my social life is going."

WRITING 2.

In just a few paragraphs, describe an informal experiment you might conduct or a systematic set of observations you might make to examine the truth of the hypothesis that "whether or not you're drawn to the partygoing depends on how well the rest of your social life is going."

ON THE NATURE OF PSYCHOLOGICAL DATA

Being an experimental psychologist can be particularly tough because these psychologists are often trying to examine things that are difficult to define or point to. For example, how do we measure feelings such as fear, pleasure, hunger, love, or anger? We can't actually see them or touch them. How do we observe people's thoughts, quantify their motivation, and evaluate the strength of their preferences? We can't put these intangible things under a microscope or place them in a jar to study; moreover, they seem to be forever changing. For psychologists and many other scientists and social scientists, this is a constant problem — how do we get meaningful and reliable data on which to base our scientific observations, hypotheses, and experimentation?

Self-Reports

Webster's Ninth New Collegiate Dictionary defines data as "factual information (as measurements or statistics) used as a basis for reasoning, discussion, or calculation." What might this factual information be for the psychologist? How might it be gathered? Obviously, the answers to these questions depend in part on the particular issue we're examining. Let's return once again to an observation I made at the party and explore the nature of psychological data in that context.

Feeling anxious, I scooped the chips and plastic-tasting dip into my mouth, and that somehow made me feel better for the moment. What data was I using to surmise that eating lousy dip and chips made me feel better? I was turning to my "gut feelings," or, as psychologists might say, using introspection. Introspection means, literally, to look inside, to examine one's own thoughts and feelings. Sometimes this strategy is referred to as "self-report"; the person is being asked to report on herself or himself. Many folks used to believe that psychology had to be based primarily on data derived from introspection or self-reports—that it provided the only meaningful, accurate, and reliable data. Today we continue to use introspection, but most psychologists believe that it's only one of several important techniques for gathering information.

WRITING 3.

Use introspection to explore the ways in which your feelings of anxiety are related to the way you eat. Think about some recent situations in which you felt anxious. In your journal or notebook, write an informal but detailed description of ways your anxiety affected what and how much you ate. In turn, consider the ways in which eating seems to affect how anxious you feel.

Other-Reports

Introspection is criticized by many. Some people argue that you can't be purely objective about yourself, that you may have something to hide or be unable to admit certain things about yourself. Even if you try to be totally honest, perhaps you lack a broad perspective when you look at yourself alone. And, no doubt, that's true in some situations. It certainly isn't unusual to turn to a friend and ask, for example, "Am I being unreasonable?" or "Am I being defensive?" In our daily lives, we, ourselves, sometimes recognize that it's difficult to be objective about our own feelings and behavior, so we turn to an acquaintance and ask for an opinion. That is, we look for reports from others.

Similarly, psychologists use data from *other-reports*. For example, they ask teachers or parents to report on the feelings and actions of children; they ask family members to evaluate the reactions and behaviors of one another; they ask coworkers to comment on ways in which their colleagues respond to situations. Other-reports may be collected using personal interviews or, alternatively, written questionnaires or tests. In collecting your other-reports, you might guide the respondent in a very structured way, asking specific questions (for example, "Do I seem to eat more when I'm feeling extremely anxious about a test?").

Or you might use semistructured or even open-ended questions, encouraging the respondents to interpret the query in whatever way is most meaningful for them (for example, "How does the amount I eat seem to be affected by how anxious I'm feeling?").

Of course, although other-reports allow us to avoid some of the problems of self-reports, they're likely to have shortcomings of their own. How well can anyone else know what you're actually thinking? Even your closest friends see you only in selective situations—they don't follow you everywhere you go. Doesn't the way in which someone else observes and interprets your behavior depend on that person's own experiences and feelings?

WRITING 4.

Select someone who knows you very well—a friend or family member who spends a great deal of time with you. Interview this person about the ways in which he or she believes that *your* personal eating behavior and level of anxiety relate to each other. In your journal or notebook, take careful notes on what your interviewee says.

Carefully prepare for the interview. First make a list of questions that you plan to pose. Begin by jotting down as many relevant questions as you can imagine. You may want to review the introspective summary you completed in the last writing assignment to get some ideas for questions or probes. Now revise your list of questions: Omit those that are redundant, and identify those that seem most clear and relevant to the question at hand; you may want to combine several of your preliminary questions or break one big question into a couple of smaller ones in order to be more precise and concise. Finally, put the polishing touches on your interview: Reorder and rework your questions so that they are clear and understandable and flow in a logical sequence. You are now ready to interview.

After the interview, compare your results with the introspective data you constructed earlier. In just a few pages, describe the similarities and differences in impressions in the two data sets. In what ways do the self-report and other-report appear to use different sorts of information in arriving at conclusions? In what other ways do these two sets of observations resemble or contrast with each other? Discuss some explanations for the dissimilarities between your self-report and the other-report. What might underlie these different points of view? In what ways do you think that one report is more accurate than the other?

Behavioral Observation

The impressions that we form about the thoughts, feelings, and behaviors of ourselves and others—that is, our self-reports and other-reports—are undoubtedly affected by a variety of things. What we perceive depends partly on what we're attending to. Have you ever sat unknowingly tapping your foot, tearing a styrofoam cup into little pieces, biting your nails, twirling your hair, or sniffling while you were deep in thought about something else? Even if we're paying attention, the way we perceive and then remember an emotion or action may be distorted as a result of our experiences. For example, our observations can be shaped by our stereotypes (conforming to or contrasting with our expectations) and by the stories and opinions we've heard from others. In fact, sometimes we get confused about whether we actually remember a very early childhood experience or just think we recall it because we've seen photographs or heard others talk about it.

Given the limitations of self-report and other-report data, many psychologists rely heavily on *observational* data as well. That is, they gather information by systematically defining and then observing the behavior in which they are interested. This sounds nice and simple, doesn't it? Well, it's not. In fact, we come back to the problem we started with: We're often trying to examine thoughts and feelings that are difficult to observe or even define in precise behavioral terms. How do we define and measure, for example, hunger, love, anger, pleasure, or anxiety?

There's no perfect solution to this problem, but in an effort to be very clear about what they're doing, psychologists present operational definitions of the issues they're examining; that is, they define the issue in terms of the precise operations they will use to measure it. For example, hunger may be defined in one experiment as the number of hours since an animal last ingested any solid substance. Anger may be defined as the number of seconds during which the individual displays an "angry" facial grimace (of course, such a grimace would have to be precisely defined: furrowed eyebrows and chin, down-turned corners of the mouth, baring of teeth, and so on).

Behavioral observation may seem more objective and accurate than self-reports and other-reports, but remember, observers still play an important role in shaping the results of behavioral observations. Observers define the setting in which the behavior will be observed (shall we look at eating at home, at school, or in a fancy restaurant?). The observers define the ways in which the behavior will be measured (shall we quantify eating in terms of total amount of food consumed, the amount of time spent chewing, hand-to-mouth movement?). And most behavior, regardless of where it is observed and how it is defined, is subject to some interpretation, so *observer bias* can easily shape the outcome of the observations.

We've considered a variety of psychological observations including self-reports, other-reports, and behavioral observations. I imagine that none of this was totally new to you, because as we go through our daily lives, all of us rely on these strategies as we try to understand ourselves and others. As we said before, we're *all* psychologists to one degree or another, even from a very early age.

And what do we do with all the observations we make day to day? We integrate them with one another to create our general impressions and understandings of the world around us. Psychologists do precisely the same thing, but perhaps in a more conscious and systematic way. Psychologists are aware that conclusions that result from only one source or type of observation are unlikely to be as valuable or accurate as those that emerge from a combination of sources. Multiple sources of data collected at several times and in varied contexts will probably provide us with meaningful and reliable information. That is the key to constructing knowledge: Build on careful and varied observations.

SUGGESTIONS FOR RESEARCH
Watching People Eat

Working with a friend or classmate, conduct a behavioral observation of the effect of eating behavior on feelings of pleasure. Conduct your study in your school cafeteria or a nearby restaurant.

1.   You and your partner should each independently develop definitions both of eating behavior and of pleasure. Try to make these definitions as meaningful as you can, but don't tell each other what definitions you're using.

2.   Go to your observation spot (the cafeteria or restaurant) together. Select one person whom you will both observe for the same ten-minute period. During this time, each of you should record your observational data using the definitions you have devised independently.

3.   After your first ten-minute observation, agree with your partner on one common set of operational definitions to guide a second ten-minute observational period. Don't worry about which definitions you choose—simply agree to use one person's set. Then select another individual for both of you to observe for the next ten-minute period, again examining the effect of eating behavior on feelings of pleasure.

4.   Write a three- to five-page summary of your two sets of behavioral observations. Begin by describing the operational definitions you used for each observational period. Describe the results you recorded in each period and your interpretations of your findings. Consider the following questions as you summarize results:

  a. Compare the observations that you and your partner made during the first observational period when you were using different operational definitions. How did your definitions affect your results?

  b. Compare the observations that you and your partner made during the second observational period when you were using the same operational definitions. How might you explain differences between the observations that you and your partner made?

  c. Compare the behavioral observations you made in the first and second periods. In what ways were your results and interpretations similar or dissimilar? What might explain some of the differences between your two sets of outcomes?

5. In the final section of your report, consider some of the advantages and limitations of the different observational strategies you've used throughout this chapter as you examined the relationship between eating and emotions. Now, as any good psychologist would do, try to integrate the data you've gathered from these varied sources and contexts. Write a four- to six-page summary of your new understanding of the relationship between eating and emotions. As you write, consider the following questions as well: What are the different strategies that might be used to explore this relationship? What are the difficulties and issues involved in trying to observe or measure this relationship? How consistent does the relationship appear to be from person to person and from situation to situation? What sort of new data do we need to gather in order to understand more thoroughly the ways in which eating relates to emotion?

READINGS

Ellen J. Langer
THE MINDSET OF HEALTH

The relationship between the mind and the body has fascinated people
for centuries. Approaching the study from many angles as psycholo-
gists, philosophers, and physicians, humans have been intrigued with
the ways in which the mind and body relate to, reflect, and influence
each other. Is there a simple distinction to be made between the men-
tal and the physical aspects of the self? Perhaps not. Over the years,
mind and body have been thought of, alternately, as one and the
same, totally independent, and recently as unique but highly interde-
pendent. We now find a renewed interest in the ways in which our
mental and physical activities can support each other.

The first two essays, "The Mindset of Health" by Ellen J.
Langer and "The Healing Brain" by Robert Ornstein and David
Sobel, address one aspect of the mind-body relationship. They argue
that the mind can exert amazing influence over the body, power that
we can harness to improve our health. Although both articles are
written for a lay audience rather than for experts in the field, note
that the authors use somewhat different strategies to present their
arguments. Langer is the chair of the social psychology program at
Harvard University and has won an award from the American Psy-
chological Association for Distinguished Contributors to Psychology
in the Public Interest. Ornstein is a cognitive psychologist and presi-
dent of the Institute for the Study of Human Knowledge. His
coauthor Sobel is an M.D. and director of preventive medicine for
Kaiser-Permanente in northern California. As you go through the
articles, think about the ways that the authors' backgrounds and
training might explain the different approaches they have taken. But
before you begin to read, jot down some of your own ideas about the
ways your mind might be able to affect your body's health.

Consider this scenario: During a routine physical, your doctor notices a
small lump in your breast and orders a biopsy as a cancer-screening
measure. Your immediate reaction is fear, probably intense fear. Yet in
some cases, a tiny breast lump or mole requires only a tiny incision,
comparable to removing a large splinter. Fear in such a situation is
based not on the procedure but on your interpretation of what the doctor is doing. You're not thinking splinters or minor cuts: you're thinking
biopsy, cancer, death.

Our thoughts create the context that determines our feelings. In
thinking about health, and especially in trying to change the conse-

441

quences of an illness or the behavior that leads to it, an awareness of context—or what I have come to call a "mindfulness"—is crucial.

UNDERSTANDING THE POWER OF CONTEXT

"Is there a split between mind and body?" the comedian Woody Allen once asked. "And if so, which is better to have?" With these questions he penetrates to one of our most potent mindsets. From earliest childhood we learn to see mind and body as separate—and to regard the body as without question the more essential of the two. We are taught that "sticks and stones can break my bones, but names can never hurt me." And later, we take our physical problems to one sort of doctor, our mental problems to another. But the mind/body split is not only one of our strongest beliefs, it is a dangerous and premature psychological commitment.

When we think of various influences on our health, we tend to think of many of them as coming from the outside environment. But each outside influence is mediated by context. Our perceptions and interpretations influence the ways in which our bodies respond to information in the world. If we automatically—"mindlessly"—accept preconceived notions of the context of a particular situation, we can jeopardize the body's ability to handle that situation. Sometimes, for the sake of our health, we need to place our perceptions intentionally, that is, mindfully in a different context.

Context can be so powerful that it influences our basic needs. In an experiment on hunger, subjects who chose to fast for a prolonged time for personal reasons tended to be less hungry than those who fasted for external reasons—for money, for example. Freely choosing to perform a task means that one has adopted a certain attitude toward it. In this experiment, those who had made a personal psychological commitment not only were less hungry on a subjective measure, but they also showed a smaller increase in free fatty acid levels, a physiological indicator of hunger. The obvious conclusion: State of mind shapes state of body.

BUILDING IMMUNITY THROUGH EMOTION

A wide body of recent research has been devoted to investigating the influence of attitudes on the immune system, which is thought to be the intermediary between psychological states and physical illness. The emotional context, our interpretation of the events around us, could thus be the first link in a chain leading to serious illness. And since context is something we can control, the clarification of these links between psychology and illness is good news. Diseases that were once thought to be purely physiological and probably incurable may be more amenable to personal control than we once believed.

Even when a disease may appear to progress inexorably, our reactions to it can be mindful or mindless and thus influence its effects. A very common mindset, as mentioned before, is the conviction that cancer means death. Even if a tumor has not yet had any effect on any body function, or how you feel physically, rarely will you think of yourself as healthy after having a malignancy diagnosed. At the same time, there are almost certainly people walking around with undiagnosed cancer who consider themselves healthy, and may remain so. Yet many doctors have noticed that following a diagnosis of cancer, some patients seem to go into a decline that has little to do with the actual course of the disease. They appear, in a sense, to "turn their faces to the wall" and begin to die. But they needn't. By reinterpreting the context, they might avoid the unnecessary failure attributable to fear alone.

HARNESSING THE POWER OF THE MIND

In recent years there has been much new research that now supports the value of a mindful approach in handling a variety of health situations such as:

Pain: Patients have been successfully taught to tolerate rather severe pain by seeing how pain varies depending on context (thinking of bruises incurred during a football game that are easily tolerated, versus the attention we require to nurse a mere paper cut).

This mindful exercise helped the patients get by with fewer pain relievers and sedatives and to leave the hospital earlier than a comparison group of patients. And the results seem to indicate more than a simple, temporary distraction of the mind, because once the stimulus — the source of pain — has been reinterpreted so that the person has a choice of context, one painful, one not, the mind is unlikely to return to the original interpretation. It has, in effect, changed contexts.

Hospitals: Part of the hospital context is its strangeness, a strangeness that has been found to be life-threatening in some cases. In a dramatic investigation, Klaus Jarvinen, lecturer in internal medicine at the University of Helsinki, studied patients who had suffered severe heart attacks and found that they were five times as likely to die suddenly when unfamiliar staff members made the rounds.

Had these patients been able to meet these staff members and helped to see the way they were much like the people the patients already knew and cared for, making the new staff seem less strange, the consequences might have been different.

OUTSMARTING TEMPTATION

We all know people who have quit smoking "cold turkey." Do they succeed because their commitment to stop puts withdrawal symptoms into a new context? For many years I quit smoking from time to time, found it too difficult, and began again, as many people do. But when I stopped the last time, almost ten years ago, I surprisingly felt no withdrawal symptoms. There was no willpower involved. I simply did not have an urge to continue smoking. Where did it go?

Jonathan Margolis, a graduate student at Harvard, and I explored this question in two stages. First we tried to find out if smokers in a nonsmoking context experienced strong cravings for cigarettes. We questioned smokers in three situations that prohibited smoking: in a movie theater, at work, and on a religious holiday (Orthodox Jews are not permitted to smoke on the Sabbath). The results in each setting were very similar. People did not suffer withdrawal symptoms when they were in any of the nonsmoking contexts. But when they returned to a context where smoking was allowed—a smoke break at work, for instance—their cravings resurfaced.

All of these people escaped the urge to smoke in a mindless manner. Could they have achieved the same thing deliberately? Can people control the experience of temptation?

In designing a second experiment to answer this question, we assumed that a mindful person would look at addiction from more than one perspective. For instance, it is clear that there are actually advantages as well as disadvantages to addictions. But this is not the usual point of view of someone trying to break a habit.

People who want to stop smoking usually remind themselves of the health risks, the bad smell, the cost, others' reactions to their smoking—the drawbacks of smoking. But these effects are not the reason they smoke, so trying to quit for those reasons alone often leads to failure. The problem is that all of the *positive* aspects of smoking are still there and still have strong appeal—the relaxation, the concentration, the taste, the sociable quality of smoking.

A more mindful approach would be to look carefully at these pleasures and find other, less harmful, ways of obtaining them. If the needs served by an addiction or habit can be satisfied in different ways, it should be easier to shake.

To test whether this dual perspective was at work when people quit smoking, we picked a group of people who had already quit and complimented each one for their success. We then paid careful attention to their responses to our compliments on their will power.

To understand our strategy, imagine being complimented for being able to spell three-letter words. A compliment doesn't mean much when the task is very easy. If you solve a horrendously difficult problem and then receive a compliment, it is probably most welcome.

We then asked these former smokers what factors they considered when they decided to stop smoking. Those who gave single-minded answers, citing only the negative consequences, were more likely to be the ones who accepted the compliment. Those who saw both sides usually shrugged it off, suggesting that quitting was easier for them. And months later, these people who did not experience a hardship when quitting were more likely to remain successful in staying off cigarettes.

PUTTING ADDICTION OUT OF MIND

Similar evidence of the importance of context in dealing with temptation comes from work on alcoholism and drug addiction, both often seen as intractable problems. For instance, even the degree of intoxication experienced can be changed by altering the drinker's expectations.

In one experiment, psychologists G. Alan Marlatt of the University of Washington and Damaris J. Rohsenow of the V.A. Medical Center in Providence, Rhode Island, divided a group of subjects according to whether they expected to receive an alcoholic drink (vodka and tonic) or a nonalcoholic drink (tonic alone). Despite the presumed physiological effects of alcohol on behavior, expectations were the major influence. What the people expected, tonic or vodka and tonic, determined how aggressively they behaved and how socially anxious and sexually aroused they became. In a similar study, researchers found that groups of men who believed they had been given alcohol, whether or not they had, showed a tendency for reduced heart rate, a condition associated with drinking.

These are just two of the many investigations showing that thoughts may be a more important determinant of the physiological reactions believed to be alcohol-related than the actual chemical properties of alcohol. The antics of high school kids at parties, generation after generation, are probably also influenced by context just as much as they are by the quantity of beer guzzled.

Here is another example. Informal reports from people who work with heroin addicts show that those addicts who are sent to prisons with the reputation of being "clean" (that is, the addicts believe there is absolutely no chance they will be able to get drugs there) did not seem to suffer withdrawal symptoms, while addicts sent to prisons whose reputations included easy access to drugs and who believed they would be able to get their hands on drugs—but didn't—experienced the pain of withdrawal.

FOOLING THE MIND

The deliberate nature of mindfulness is what makes its potential so enormous. And that potential has important precursors in methods we've developed to "fool" ourselves into better health. In the 1960s, experiments with biofeedback made it clear that it was possible to gain intentional control of such "involuntary" functions as heart rate, blood flow and brain activity. Through trial and error, people learned to control the workings of their own bodies and, for example, lower their blood pressure or counteract painful headaches.

Another method for harnessing the healing powers of the mind in a passive way is through the use of placebos, inert substances that in appearance resemble active drugs. Although inert, placebos are known to have powerful effects on health. But who is doing the healing? Why can't we just say to our minds, "Repair this ailing body." Why must we fool our minds in order to enlist our own powers of self-healing?

Placebos, hypnosis, autosuggestion, faith healing, visualization, positive thinking, biofeedback—these are among the ways we have learned to invoke our own powers. Each can be seen as a device for changing mindsets, enabling us to move from an unhealthy to a healthy context. The more we can learn about how to do this mindfully and deliberately, rather than having to rely on elaborate, indirect strategies, the more control we will gain over our own health.

THE MIND'S ACTIVE PLACEBO

Ever since we relied on our mothers to make a bruised knee better with a Band-Aid and a kiss, we have held on to the assumption that someone out there, somewhere, can make us better. If we go to a specialist and are given a Latin name for our problem, and a prescription, this old mindset of that magical someone helping is reconfirmed.

But what if we get the Latin name without the prescription? Imagine going to the doctor for some aches and pains and being told you have Zapalitis and that little can be done for this condition. Before you were told it was Zapalitis, you paid attention to each symptom in a mindful way and did what you could to feel better. But now you have been told that nothing can be done. So you do nothing. Your motivation to do something about the aches, to listen to your body, has been thwarted by a label. With the loss of motivation eventually comes the loss of the skill of caring for ourselves, to whatever degree we otherwise would have been able.

In the past decade or so, a new brand of empowered patient/consumer movement has tried to restore our control over our own health. Many of the alternative therapies sought out by these people have as their most active ingredient the concept of mindfulness.

Whenever we try to heal ourselves and do not abdicate this responsibility completely to doctors, each step is mindful. We welcome new information, whether from our bodies or from books. We look at our illness from more than the single perspective of medicine. We work on changing contexts, whether it is a stressful workplace or a depressing view of the hospital. And finally, when we attempt to stay healthy rather than to be made well, we become involved in the process rather than the outcome.

In applying mindfulness theory to health, I have worked a good deal with elderly people. Success in increasing longevity by making more mental demands on nursing-home residents or by teaching meditation or techniques of flexible, novel thinking gives us strong reason to believe that the same techniques could be used to improve health and shorten illness earlier in life. In a recent experiment we gave arthritis sufferers various interesting word problems to increase their mental activity. Compared to a group given a less stimulating task, the mindful patients not only reported increased comfort and enjoyment, but some of the chemistry of the disease changed as well.

There are two ways in which we have learned to influence our health: exchanging unhealthy mindsets for healthy ones and increasing a generally mindful state. The latter method is more lasting and results in more personal control. Understanding the importance of abandoning the mind/body dualism that has shaped both our thinking and the practice of medicine for so long can make a profound difference in both what we do and how we feel. The real value of fostering the idea of "active placebos" will come when people put them to work for themselves.

Consider how you learned to ride a bike. Someone older held on to the seat as you peddled to keep you from falling until you found your balance. Then, without your knowledge, that strong hand let go and you were riding on you own. You controlled the bicycle without even knowing you had learned how.

The same is true for all of us most of our lives. We control our health, and the course of disease, without really knowing that we do. But just as on the bike, at some point we all discover that we are in control. Now may be the time for many of us to learn how to recognize and use the control we possess over illness through mindfulness.

OPTIONS FOR WRITING

1. Langer has argued that diseases may be more amenable to personal control than we once believed. If we accept this notion, how should we then define the roles and responsibilities of physicians in today's world? What sorts of activities need to be included in physicians' training?

2. Imagine that you are about to have some painful dental work done. Discuss some mental strategies that you might use (no medication allowed!) to minimize the pain while the dentist is working on your mouth.

3. Test Langer's strategy for breaking habits. Focus on a habit that you would like to break. For one week, keep a record of the contexts in which you perform this habit and of your thoughts about both the negative and the positive aspects associated with this habit. Then review your observa-

tions, and propose alternative ways of obtaining the pleasures that your habit provides you. During the next week, try to substitute these alternative behaviors for your habit, maintaining an observational record of your successes and failures and their contexts. Summarize your results, and draw conclusions about the effectiveness of Langer's strategy and the factors that affect its success.

Robert Ornstein and David Sobel
THE HEALING BRAIN

Every day hundreds upon hundreds of people receive the phone call they dreaded ever receiving: A disembodied voice informs them that a loved one has died. The circumstances might be violent and shocking or the death may have been expected for some time, but in any case the survivors suffer greatly while grieving their losses during the months that follow.

Since the mid 1970s, R. W. Bartrop and his colleagues in New South Wales, Australia, have been systematically studying the effects of bereavement, not only the emotional consequences but the effects on physical health as well—specifically, the body's ability to fight off disease. They followed the lives of surviving spouses, charting the transient changes in immune function during mourning, and in one 1977 study they reported that the immune systems of grieving spouses were indeed weakened. Specifically, they had lower activity levels of what are called "T cells"—one of the blood cells that attack foreign invaders.

That study was the first to show, in human beings, a measurable weakening of the body's defense system following severe psychological stress in a real-life setting. It precipitated a number of investigations into the larger question of how mind, brain, body and society are intertwined. At first glance it may seem that changes in one's social world, and in related emotional and mental states, have little to do with disease. But there is mounting evidence that "real," organic diseases are linked to changing beliefs about oneself, to the nature of one's relationships with others and to one's position in the social world. Such links only seem impossible—or at least irrelevant—from the early and simplistic medical view of the body as automaton. Our lungs, hearts and stomachs are hardly independent, autonomous organs. While they certainly have autonomous functions, they are all in communication with and regulated by the brain.

While there is much we still don't know about the relationship of brain, mind, body and society, evidence from many areas of research is beginning to make some of the connections clear. The heart cannot decide that a loved one's death in a train wreck is too much to bear; the liver does not feel the shame of embarrassment; the immune system does not know whether its client is employed or not, divorced or happily married. It is the brain that knows and feels. Indeed a primary function of the brain, perhaps as important as rational thought or language, is health maintenance. The brain has evolved complex "bodyguards," designed to ward off disease, and it may even be that our human tendency toward social connectedness may help keep us well.

There have been many studies since the original Australian investigation. A study at the Mount Sinai School of Medicine confirmed and went beyond those findings. Men who were married to women with terminal breast cancer showed a similar drop in responsiveness of the lymphocytes (another of the blood cells specialized for defense) immediately after their wives' deaths, a drop that continued for two months. But between 4 and 14 months after the death, the husbands' immune functioning had recovered, a change that occurred as their bereavement diminished.

But how can grief and bereavement "get into" the immune system? Is it something the bereaved do differently than others? Changes in nutrition, exercise and general activity do affect the workings of the immune system, but the people in this study had maintained their normal habits. What appears more likely is that the numerous connections between the nervous system and the immune system allow the mind to influence resistance or susceptibility to disease. For example, extensive networks of nerve endings have been found in the thymus gland, an organ that plays an essential role in the maturation of certain cells in the immune system. Similarly, the spleen, bone marrow and lymph nodes are richly supplied with nerves supporting a brain-immune system link.

In addition, the cells of the immune system appear equipped to respond to chemical signals from the central nervous system. Receptors for a variety of chemical messengers — catecholamines, prostaglandins, growth hormone, thyroid hormone, sex hormones, serotonin and endorphins — have been found on the surfaces of lymphocytes. These neuroendocrines, neurotransmitters and neuropeptides may somehow stimulate the differentiation, migration and activity of the lymphocytes.

Given the links between the nervous system and the immune system, the idea that instability in the social world can affect immunity becomes less far-fetched. Research shows that physical and psychological upsets release several powerful neurohormones, including catecholamines, corticosteroids and endorphins. These, in turn, alter immune function. For example, corticosteroids exert such powerful immunosuppressive effects that steroids are widely used as drugs to suppress immunity in allergic conditions like asthema and hay fever and autoimmune disorders like rheumatoid arthritis and to suppress rejection of transplanted organs.

During certain types of stress the brain also releases endorphins, the brain's own morphine-like chemicals, which block pain sensation. Psychologist John Liebeskind and colleagues were able to stimulate the release of endorphins by delivering brief, mild electrical shocks to rats, and psychologist Yehuda Shavit later reported a corresponding decrease in tumor-fighting ability in natural killer cells, yet another fighter in the body's immune response.

To test whether this immune suppression was mediated by the release of endorphins, the researchers injected the rats with an endorphin antagonist—a drug that blocks the effects of endorphins. They found that the activity of the natural killer cells had been restored, supporting the idea that the immune suppression was caused by endorphins. This explanation was reinforced by the additional finding that natural killer cell potency was also suppressed when the animals were actually given a dose of morphine.

Other animal research links stress and the development of disease. The late Vernon Riley and his colleagues performed scores of experiments on a strain of mice that are genetically predisposed to develop breast cancer. In one series of experiments the mice were subjected to what was called "rotational stress"—that is, they were spun on a record turntable at various speeds (ranging from 16 RPM to 78 RPM). They found that the faster the rotation, the larger the growth in tumors.

Other studies suggest that tumors grow more rapidly in animals exposed to uncontrollable stress than in those exposed to stress they could control. Rats were implanted with tumor cells and the next day experienced either no electrical shock, escapable shock or inescapable shock. Fifty-four percent of the first group rejected the tumor; 63 percent of the rats receiving escapable shock and only 27 percent of the rats receiving inescapable shock rejected the tumors.

These findings are supported by changes in immune function. Steven Maier, Mark Laudenslager and coworkers at the University of Colorado studied how exposing animals to controllable or uncontrollable electric shocks affected immunity. One group of rats was taught that they could terminate a mild electric shock by turning a wheel in their cages. Another group of rats received a shock every time the first group did, but nothing they could do would control the shock. Immune function was assessed by the ability of the T-cells to multiply in response to stimulation. The results showed decreased immune function only in the rats receiving the uncontrollable shocks.

Generalizing from rats to humans is always difficult, but scores of studies on humans show that various types of social instability and the lack of resources to regain stability are associated with subsequent illness. For example, psychologist Stanislav Kasl and his colleagues at Yale University followed the development of infectious mononucleosis among West Point cadets in a study published in 1979. All the entering cadets were given blood tests over a four-year period to screen for the presence of antibodies to Epstein-Barr virus, the agent that causes mononucleosis. In addition the investigators reviewed interview data, which included information about the cadets' expectations and family backgrounds.

Each year about one in five of the susceptible cadets were infected, but only about one-quarter of those infected actually developed symptoms of mono. Cadets who had fathers who were described as "overachievers" and who themselves strongly wanted success in a career but were doing poorly academically were most likely to get sick. The combination of high expectation and poor performance was reflected in increased susceptibility to infectious disease.

More recent studies link the onset and course of virus infections with stress-altered immune function. For example, approximately one person in four suffers from recurrent infections of oral herpes simplex. In a recent study, 18 people between 20 and 43 years old with a history of three to four recurrent episodes of oral herpes per year completed a stress questionnaire twice: once within three days of the first appearance of a lesion marking the recurrence of herpes and another time when they had no active lesions.

In the week prior to a recurrence of infection, the group reported increased stressful life events, daily "hassles" and anxiety, indicating that such stressful circumstances are associated with an increased likelihood of recurrent herpes lesions. Later studies suggest that it probably is not the actual stress that brings on the herpes but the person's emotional reaction to the disease. If someone is continually depressed about having herpes, this reaction itself keeps bringing it back.

Psychologist Janice Kiecolt-Glaser, virologist Ronald Glaser and colleagues at Ohio State University College of Medicine have shown that even mild upsets—milder, that is, than the loss of a spouse—can affect the immune system. In this study, medical students reported on the number of their "life change events" in the previous months as well as their loneliness. Both loneliness and the mild life stress were associated with decreased immune cell activity.

During a situation where there are conflicting signals or a sudden unexplained threat or a threat that is beyond the organism's ability to handle easily, the sympathetic nervous system is activated. This increases the level of circulating hormones that suppress immune function.

Most of the research on the relationship of psychological states and immunity has focused on stress-induced immune suppression. But the question of whether positive states of mind enhance immunity is the subject of a growing amount of research. There have been many extravagant claims made for the effects of "positive attitude" and "imagery" on subsequent diseases, but there is little hard evidence that attitude alone can cure serious disease. There is, however, some real evidence that people can voluntarily improve their own immune function and thus prevent disease.

In one study, psychologist Howard Hall of Pennsylvania State University and colleagues gave 20 healthy people ages 22 to 85 blood tests before hypnosis, one hour after and one week later in order to measure the response of the lymphocytes to hypnotic suggestion. When they were hypnotized they were told to visualize their white blood cells as powerful "sharks" swimming through the bloodstream attacking weak, confused germs (this is not too far from the truth about lymphocytes). They were told to practice the visualization. The people did self-hypnosis two times a day for a week, each time telling themselves the shark story.

Not everyone showed changes in immune function; the older people were less likely to. But enough did show improvement to suggest a link between the separate worlds of the "soft" mental images and the "harder" phenomena of lymphocytes. The younger people showed a small but real increase in the responsiveness of their immune systems following the hypnosis and visualization. In addition, those people who were easily hypnotized showed increased numbers of lymphocytes after their hypnotic sessions.

These changes in immune functioning were small, but so was the experimental "treatment" — just two hypnotic sessions and self-hypnosis for a week. But if such a minor series of events can lead to real changes in immune functioning, what might the possibilities be for increasing our ability to control our own immunity?

Kiecolt-Glaser and colleagues have found that relaxation training can also enhance cellular immune function. Forty-five geriatric residents of an independent-living facility were taught progressive relaxation and guided imagery techniques three times a week for one month. Relaxation was presented to these residents as a way to gain some control over their world. By the end of the training period the group showed a significant increase in natural killer cell activity compared to a control group and a group that merely had "social contact" visits from a college student. The relaxation group also showed significant decreases in antibodies to herpes simplex virus, possibly because the herpes virus was being controlled better by the immune system. These relaxation-induced improvements in immune function were accompanied by self-reports of less psychological distress.

A series of interesting and still controversial studies by Boston University psychologist David McClelland and colleagues suggests that the need to exercise power over others is related to differences in immune function and susceptibility to disease. In McClelland's view, some people have a greater need for power — the desire for prestige or influence over others — than they do for affiliation — the desire to form close affectionate relationships. When people who need power are for some reason unable to exercise it, there seem to be changes in their immune function.

McClelland and colleagues have found that college students who were high in power-related life stresses — a major personal achievement, for example, or the threat of physical attack — reported more frequent and more severe illnesses than other individuals. They also showed elevated levels of epinephrine and depressed levels of salivary immunoglobulin A (S-IgA) — considered a factor in resistance to respiratory infections. As expected, lower levels of S-IgA correlated with reports of more frequent illness. McClelland interpreted the findings as indicating that if a strong need for power is inhibited, there is chronic overactivity of the sympathetic nervous system, which suppresses the immune system.

Similar results were obtained in a 1982 study of first-year dental students. Psychologist John Jemmott and colleagues found that students with an inhibited high need for power reported greater incidence of upper respiratory infections following periods of high academic stress than after periods of low stress. However, variations in stress did not appear to correlate significantly with reported illness in students who were below average in their need for power.

Other studies show how feelings, expressed or not, are associated with immune function and disease. In a 1979 study that compared long-term survivors of breast cancer with those who did not survive, psychologist Leonard Derogatis and colleagues at Johns Hopkins University School of Medicine found that long-term survivors expressed much higher levels of anxiety, hostility, alienation and other negative moods and were perceived as having negative attitudes toward their illness.

We take a somewhat controversial approach to interpreting many psychological effects on the immune system, looking not only at the individual's attitudes, moods and thoughts but at his or her relationship to the larger social environment. The well-known increase in mortality rates among bereaved spouses cannot be fully understood as individual reactions alone. There seem to be some mechanisms in animals and in human beings that respond to social needs. When the Sika deer suffer from overcrowding, many of the herd die more quickly, even though they have adequate food. Maybe the same phenomenon occurs in humans; the immune system may cut down resistance to disease when a person is grieving or is no longer part of a viable social unit, as in widowhood. It may be an accident of the close neural connection of the systems, or it may well have resulted from some evolutionary selection pressures. But in any case there are relationships between health and the social world that might well be considered from this simple perspective.

And conversely, a solid and stable connection to a larger social group, or to humanity in general, may have the opposite result: improved resistance because the person is probably more valuable as a member of a group. From our speculative viewpoint this may be one reason why almost all societies have developed conventions emphasizing the same virtues and why there is such an emphasis in most religions upon caring for others, being generous to others and serving them. Perhaps one of the many reasons is that doing so is not only helpful to the entire community but also to the health of the donor.

Consider a final study. When college students were shown a film of Mother Teresa, winner of the Nobel Peace Prize, tending to the sick and dying of Calcutta, their immune functioning (as measured by S-IgA concentrations) immediately increased. So even watching a person engaged in a selfless act of service to others may have important functions for the health of the community. McClelland noted in an interview that this immune effect occurred even in people who said they disliked Mother Teresa: "The results," he suggests, "mean that she was contacting these consciously disapproving people in a part of their brains that they were unaware of and that was still responding to the strength of her tender loving care."

We wouldn't necessarily describe it that way and in fact think that McClelland has gone beyond what the data support; but even so, looking outside of the dominant self-system seems to be important. Even attending to a pet or a plant seems to have health benefits. We don't mean to be absurdly reductionist and imply that all social norms exist for health purposes, but one aim of social and religious communities over the millennia has been to keep their adherents alive and well, to encourage health through specific diets and prohibitions, through cleansing rituals and other means.

Could attention to the larger group, away from our biologically primary but primitive focus upon ourselves, and away from the hostile reactions to others, be something we are also organized to resound to? All this is very speculative, but we may well have to think differently about how closely we are related to others in order to understand ourselves, our organs, even our white blood cells.

OPTIONS FOR WRITING

1. The authors state that "the immune system may cut down resistance to disease when a person is grieving or is no longer part of a viable social unit." What are the implications of this statement for the design of healthcare and social community services? Suggest some specific services or organizations that would promote healthier communities.

2. Compare "The Mindset of Health" and "The Healing Brain." Which article most convincingly argues that the mind can have strong influence over the body? Analyze which components of their respective arguments are most and least effective, and discuss why.

3. "The Mindset of Health" and "The Healing Brain" both discuss the ways in which people can gain greater control over their bodies and their health. Discuss the advantages and possible disadvantages that might be associated with feeling greater control of your health.

Jeffrey Z. Rubin, Frank J. Provenzano, Zella Luria
THE EYE OF THE BEHOLDER:
Parents' Views on Sex of Newborns

Are males and females different? In some ways, of course! Otherwise, we wouldn't be able to tell men from women. But there is little agreement regarding sex differences in behavior and, in particular, in the causes of the behavioral differences that do exist. Are these differences inevitable? Are they purely a result of training? What factors shape the development of girls and boys?

The following article addresses this issue from a psychological viewpoint. It examines the ways parents make assumptions about their boy and girl infants during the baby's first day of life, assumptions that in turn might influence the ways the parents raise their infants. Jeffrey Rubin is a professor of social psychology at Tufts University; Zella Luria is a professor of developmental psychology at the same institution. Frank Provenzano was a graduate student working with Rubin and Luria when the report was completed. As you read the study, notice how it brings together both a social and a developmental psychology orientation. It examines parents' earliest social impressions of their infants, which may affect parents' treatment of the babies and, hence, the children's development.

This article is an example of a research report, *one of the most common forms of writing in psychology. The psychological research report has a specific structure that allows psychologists from around the world to know where and how to obtain specific sorts of essential information from the report. Research reports begin with* abstracts, *brief synopses of the most essential information from the report, followed by an* introduction, *in which the authors summarize research and theory that are relevant to their study and present their hypotheses. Then the* method *section includes details about the subjects of the experiment and the exact procedure that was used to conduct the research project. Ideally, this section provides enough information to permit a reader to replicate the experiment precisely. In the* results *section, the findings of the research are presented. Don't be intimidated by the report of the statistical analyses (the "analysis of variance" and "X^2 analyses"). A good research report, such as this one, describes the findings in clear narrative as well as in statistical terms. The* discussion *section follows, in which the authors comment on their interpretations of their findings and the implications of this work. Finally, the* reference *section lists complete bibliographic information for each citation in the report, enabling readers to locate the original references if they so wish.*

A good research report is precise and clear. As you read the following article, think about its organization and structure. In what ways do they help or hinder your efforts to understand the content of the paper? Are there portions of the report that are more important for certain audiences than for others? Placing yourself in the role of a psychologist, determine whether the report provides you with the sorts of information you would need to replicate the study.

ABSTRACT

Thirty pairs of primiparous parents, fifteen with sons and fifteen with daughters, were interviewed within the first 24 hours postpartum. Although male and female infants did not differ in birth length, weight, or Apgar scores, daughters were significantly more likely than sons to be described as little, beautiful, pretty, and cute, and as resembling their mothers. Fathers made more extreme and stereotyped rating judgments of their newborns than did mothers. Findings suggest that sex-typing and sex-role socialization have already begun at birth.

INTRODUCTION

As Schaffer[10] has observed, the infant at birth is essentially an asocial, largely undifferentiated creature. It appears to be little more than a tiny ball of hair, fingers, toes, cries, gasps, and gurgles. However, while it may seem that "if you've seen one, you've seen them all," babies are *not* all alike—a fact that is of special importance to their parents, who want, and appear to need, to view their newborn child as a creature that is special. Hence, much of early parental interaction with the infant may be focused on a search for distinctive features. Once the fact that the baby is normal has been established, questions such as, "Who does the baby look like?" and "How much does it weigh?" are asked.

Of all the questions parents ask themselves and each other about their infant, one seems to have priority: "Is it a boy or a girl?" The reasons for and consequences of posing this simple question are by no means trivial. The answer, "boy" or "girl," may result in the parents' organizing their perception of the infant with respect to a wide variety of attributes—ranging from its size to its activity, attractiveness, even its future potential. It is the purpose of the present study to examine the kind of verbal picture parents form of the newborn infant, as a function both of their own and their infant's gender.

As Asch[2] observed years ago, in forming our impressions of others, we each tend to develop a *Gestalt*—a global picture of what others are like, which permits us to organize our perceptions of the often discrepant, contradictory aspects of their behavior and manner into a unified whole. The awareness of another's status,[13] the belief that he is "warm" or "cold,"[2, 5] "extroverted" or "introverted,"[6] even the apparently trivial knowledge of another's name[4]—each of these cues predisposes us to develop a stereotypic view of that other, his underlying nature, and how he is likely to behave. How much more profound, then, may be the consequences of a cue as prominent in parents' minds as the gender of their own precious, newborn infant.

The study reported here is addressed to parental perceptions of their infants at the point when these infants first emerge into the world. If it can be demonstrated that parental sex-typing has already begun its course at this earliest of moments in the life of the child, it may be possible to understand better one of the important antecedents of the complex process by which the growing child comes to view itself as boy-ish or girl-ish.

Based on our review of the literature, two forms of parental sextyping may be expected to occur at the time of the infant's birth. First, it appears likely that parents will view and label their newborn child differentially, as a simple function of the infant's gender. Aberle and Naegele[1] and Tasch,[12] using only fathers as subjects, found that they had different expectations for sons and daughters: sons were expected to be aggressive and athletic, daughters were expected to be pretty, sweet, fragile, and delicate. Rebelsky and Hanks[9] found that fathers spent more time talking to their daughters than their sons during the first three months of life. While the sample size was too small for the finding to be significant, they suggest that the role of father-of-daughter may be perceived as requiring greater nurturance. Similarly, Pedersen and Robson[8] reported that the fathers of infant daughters exhibited more behavior labeled (by the authors) as "apprehension over well being" than did the fathers of sons.

A comparable pattern emerges in research using mothers as subjects. Sears, Maccoby and Levin,[11] for example, found that the mothers of kindergartners reported tolerating more aggression from sons than daughters, when it was directed toward parents and peers. In addition, maternal nurturance was seen as more important for the daughter's than the son's development. Taken together, the findings in this body of research lead us to expect parents (regardless of their gender) to view their newborn infants differentially—labeling daughters as weaker, softer, and therefore in greater need of nurturance, than sons.

The second form of parental sextyping we expect to occur at birth is a function both of the infant's gender *and* the parent's own gender. Goodenough[3] interviewed the parents of nursery school children, and found that mothers were less concerned with sex-typing their child's behavior than were fathers. More recently, Meyer and Sobieszek[7] presented adults with videotapes of two seventeen-month-old children (each of whom was sometimes described as a boy and sometimes as a girl), and asked their subjects to describe and interpret the children's behavior. They found that male subjects, as well as those having little contact with small children, were more likely (although not always significantly so) to rate the children in sex-stereotypic fashion—attributing "male qualities" such as independence, aggressiveness, activity, and alertness to the child presented as a boy, and qualities such as cuddliness, passivity, and delicacy to the "girl." We expect, therefore, that sex of infant and sex of parent will interact, such that it is fathers, rather than mothers, who emerge as the greater sex-typers of their newborn.

In order to investigate parental sex-typing of their newborn infants, and in order, more specifically, to test the predictions that sex-typing is a function of the infant's gender, as well as the gender of both infant and parent, parents of newborn boys and girls were studied in the maternity ward of a hospital, within the first 24 hours postpartum, to uncover their perceptions of the characteristics of their newborn infants.

METHOD

Subjects

The subjects consisted of 30 pairs of primiparous parents, fifteen of whom had sons, and fifteen of whom had daughters. The subjects were drawn from the available population of expecting parents at a suburban Boston hospital serving local, predominantly lower-middle-class families. Using a list of primiparous expectant mothers obtained from the hospital, the experimenter made contact with families by mail several months prior to delivery, and requested the subjects' assistance in "a study of social relations among parents and their first child." Approximately one week after the initial contact by mail, the experimenter telephoned each family, in order to answer any questions the prospective parents might have about the study, and to obtain their consent. Of the 43 families reached by phone, eleven refused to take part in the study. In addition, one consenting mother subsequently gave birth to a low birth weight infant (a 74-ounce girl), while another delivered an unusually large son (166 ounces). Because these two infants were at the two ends of the distribution of birth weights, and because they might have biased the data in support of our hypotheses, the responses of their parents were eliminated from the sample.

All subjects participated in the study within the first 24 hours postpartum—the fathers almost immediately after delivery, and the mothers (who were often under sedation at the time of delivery) up to but not later than 24 hours later. The mothers typically had spoken with their husbands at least once during this 24 hour period.

There were no reports of medical problems during any of the pregnancies or deliveries, and all infants in the sample were full-term at time of birth. Deliveries were made under general anesthesia, and the fathers were not allowed in the delivery room. The fathers were not permitted to handle their babies during the first 24 hours, but could view them through display windows in the hospital nursery. The mothers, on the other hand, were allowed to hold and feed their infants. The subjects participated individually in the study. The fathers were met in a small, quiet waiting room used exclusively by the maternity ward, while the mothers were met in their hospital rooms. Every precaution was taken not to upset the parents or interfere with hospital procedure.

Procedure

After introducing himself to the subjects, and after congratulatory amenities, the experimenter (FJP) asked the parents: "Describe your baby as you would to a close friend or relative." The responses were tape-recorded and subsequently coded.

The experimenter then asked the subjects to take a few minutes to complete a short questionnaire. The instructions for completion of the questionnaire were as follows:

> On the following page there are 18 pairs of opposite words. You are asked to rate your baby in relation to these words, placing an "x" or a checkmark in the space that best describes your baby. The more a word describes your baby, the closer your "x" should be to that word.
>
> Example: Imagine you were asked to rate Trees.

Good   :___:___:___:___:___:___:___:___: Bad

Strong   :___:___:___:___:___:___:___:___: Weak

> If you cannot decide or your feelings are mixed, place your "x" in the center space. Remember, the more you think a word is a good description of your baby, the closer you should place your "x" to that word. If there are no questions, please begin. Remember, you are rating your baby. Don't spend too much time thinking about your answers. First impressions are usually the best.

Having been presented with these instructions, the subjects then proceeded to rate their baby on each of the eighteen following, eleven-point, bipolar adjective scales: firm-soft; large featured–fine featured; big-little; relaxed-nervous; cuddly–not cuddly; easy going–fussy; cheerful-cranky; good eater–poor eater; excitable-calm; active-inactive; beautiful-plain; sociable-unsociable; well coordinated–awkward; noisy-quiet; alert-inattentive; strong-weak; friendly-unfriendly; hardy-delicate.

Upon completion of the questionnaire, the subjects were thanked individually, and when both parents of an infant had completed their participation, the underlying purposes of the study were fully explained.

Hospital Data

In order to acquire a more objective picture of the infants whose characteristics were being judged by the subjects, data were obtained

TABLE 7.1 **Mean Ratings on the 18 Adjective Scales, as a Function of Sex of Parent (Mother vs. Father) and Sex of Infant (Son vs. Daughter)***

SCALE	EXPERIMENTAL CONDITION				
(I)–(II)	M-S	M-D	F-S	F-D	$\overline{X}$
Firm–Soft	7.47	7.40	3.60	8.93	6.85
Large featured–Fine featured	7.20	7.53	4.93	9.20	7.22
Big–Little	4.73	8.40	4.13	8.53	6.45
Relaxed–Nervous	3.20	4.07	3.80	4.47	3.88
Cuddly–Not cuddly	1.40	2.20	2.20	1.47	1.82
Easy going–Fussy	3.20	4.13	3.73	4.60	3.92
Cheerful–Cranky	3.93	3.73	4.27	3.60	3.88
Good eater–Poor eater	3.73	3.80	4.60	4.53	4.16
Excitable–Calm	6.20	6.53	5.47	6.40	6.15
Active–Inactive	2.80	2.73	3.33	4.60	3.36
Beautiful–Plain	2.13	2.93	1.87	2.87	2.45
Sociable–Unsociable	4.80	3.80	3.73	4.07	4.10
Well coordinated–Awkward	3.27	2.27	2.07	4.27	2.97
Noisy–Quiet	6.87	7.00	5.67	7.73	6.82
Alert–Inattentive	2.47	2.40	1.47	3.40	2.44
Strong–Weak	3.13	2.20	1.73	4.20	2.82
Friendly–Unfriendly	3.33	3.40	3.67	3.73	3.53
Hardy–Delicate	5.20	4.67	3.27	6.93	5.02

*The larger the mean, the greater the rated presence of the attribute denoted by the second (right-hand) adjective in each pair.

from hospital records concerning each infant's birth weight, birth length, and Apgar scores. Apgar scores are typically assigned at five and ten minutes postpartum, and represent the physician's ratings of the infant's color, muscle tonicity, reflex irritability, and heart and respiratory rates. No significant differences between the male and female infants were found for birth weight, birth length, or Apgar scores at five and ten minutes postpartum.*

RESULTS

In Table 7.1, the subjects' mean ratings of their infant, by condition, for each of the eighteen bipolar adjective scales, are presented. The right-extreme column of Table 7.1 shows means for each scale, which have been averaged across conditions. Infant stimuli, overall, were characterized closer to the scale anchors of soft, fine featured, little, relaxed,

* Birth weight $\overline{X}_{Sons} = 114.43$ ounces, $\overline{X}_{Daughters} = 110.00$, $t\,(28) = 1.04$); Birth length ($\overline{X}_{Sons} = 19.80$ inches, $\overline{X}_{Daughters} = 19.96$, $t\,(28) = 0.52$); 5 minute Apgar score ($\overline{X}_{Sons} = 9.07$, $\overline{X}_{Daughters} = 9.33$, $t\,(28) = 0.69$); and 10 minute Apgar score ($\overline{X}_{Sons} = 10.00$, $\overline{X}_{Daughters} = 10.00$).

cuddly, easy going, cheerful, good eater, calm, active, beautiful, sociable, well coordinated, quiet, alert, strong, friendly, and hardy. Our parent-subjects, in other words, appear to have felt on Day 1 of their babies' lives that their newborn infants represented delightful, competent new additions to the world!

Analysis of variance of the subjects' questionnaire responses (1 and 56 degrees of freedom) yielded a number of interesting findings. There were *no* rating differences on the eighteen scales as a simple function of Sex of Parent: parents appear to agree with one another, on the average. As a function of Sex of Infant, however, several significant effects emerged: Daughters, in contrast to sons, were rated as significantly softer ($F = 10.67$, $p < .005$), finer featured ($F = 9.27$, $p < .005$), littler ($F = 28.83$, $p < .001$), and more inattentive ($F = 4.44$, $p < .05$). In addition, significant interaction effects emerged for seven of the eighteen scales: firm-soft ($F = 11.22$, $p < .005$), large featured-fine featured ($F = 6.78$, $p < .025$), cuddly-not cuddly ($F = 4.18$, $p < .05$), well coordinated-awkward ($F = 12.52$, $p < .001$), alert-inattentive ($F = 5.10$, $p < .05$), strong-weak ($F = 10.67$, $p < .005$), and hardy-delicate ($F = 5.32$, $p < .025$).

The meaning of these interactions becomes clear in Table 7.1, in which it can be seen that six of these significant interactions display a comparable pattern: fathers were more extreme in their ratings of *both* sons and daughters than were mothers. Thus, sons were rated as firmer, larger featured, better coordinated, more alert, stronger, and hardier— and daughters as softer, finer featured, more awkward, more inattentive, weaker, and more delicate—by their fathers than by their mothers. Finally, with respect to the other significant interaction effect (cuddly–not cuddly), a rather different pattern was found. In this case, mothers rated sons as cuddlier than daughters, while fathers rated daughters as cuddlier than sons—a finding we have dubbed the "oedipal" effect.

Responses to the interview question were coded in terms of adjectives used and references to resemblance. Given the open-ended nature of the question, many adjectives were used—healthy, for example, being a high frequency response cutting across sex of babies and parents. Parental responses were pooled, and recurrent adjectives were analyzed by X^2 analysis for sex of child. Sons were described as big more frequently than were daughters (X^2 (1) = 4.26, $p < .05$); daughters were called little more often than were sons (X^2 (1) = 4.28, $p < .05$). The "feminine" cluster—beautiful, pretty, and cute—was used significantly more often to describe daughters than sons (X^2 (1) = 5.40, $p < .05$). Finally, daughters were said to resemble mothers more frequently than were sons (X^2 (1) = 3.87, $p < .05$).

DISCUSSION

The data indicate that parents—especially fathers—differentially label their infants, as a function of the infant's gender. These results are particularly striking in light of the fact that our sample of male and female infants did *not* differ in birth length, weight, or Apgar scores. Thus, the results appear to be a pure case of parental labeling—what a colleague has described as "nature's first projective test" (personal communication, Leon Eisenberg). Given the importance parents attach to the birth of their first child, it is not surprising that such ascriptions are made.

But why should posing the simple question, "Is it a boy or a girl?", be so salient in parents' minds, and have such important consequences? For one thing, an infant's gender represents a truly *distinctive* characteristic. The baby is either a boy or a girl—there are no ifs, ands, or buts about it. A baby may be active sometimes, and quiet at others, for example, but it can always be assigned to one of two distinct classes: boy or girl. Secondly, an infant's gender tends to assume the properties of a *definitive* characteristic. It permits parents to organize their questions and answers about the infant's appearance and behavior into an integrated *Gestalt*. Finally, an infant's gender is often a *normative* characteristic. It is a property that seems to be of special importance not only to the infant's parents, but to relatives, friends, neighbors, and even casual passersby in the street. For each of these reasons, an infant's gender is a property of considerable importance to its parents, and is therefore one that is likely to lead to labeling and the investment of surplus meaning.

The results of the present study are, of course, not unequivocal. Although it was found, as expected, that the sex-typing of infants varied as a function of the infant's gender, as well as the gender of both infant and parent, significant differences did not emerge for all eighteen of the adjective scales employed. Two explanations for this suggest themselves. First, it may simply be that we have overestimated the importance of sex-typing at birth. A second possibility, however, is that sex-typing is more likely to emerge with respect to certain classes of attributes— namely, those which denote physical or constitutional, rather than "internal," dispositional, factors. Of the eight different adjective pairs for which significant main or interaction effects emerged, six (75%) clearly refer to external attributes of the infant. Conversely, of the ten adjective pairs for which no significant differences were found, only three (30%) clearly denote external attributes. This suggests that it is physical and constitutional factors that specially lend themselves to sex-typing at birth, at least in our culture.

Another finding of interest is the lack of significant effects, as a simple function of sex of parent. Although we predicted no such effects, and were therefore not particularly surprised by the emergence of "non-findings," the implication of these results is by no means trivial. If we had omitted the sex of the infant as a factor in the present study, we might have been led to conclude (on the basis of simply varying the sex of the parent) that *no* differences exist in parental descriptions of new-born infants—a patently erroneous conclusion! It is only when the infant's and the parent's gender are considered together, in interaction, that the lack of differences between overall parental mean ratings can be seen to reflect the true differences between the parents. Mothers rate both sexes closer together on the adjective pairs than do fathers (who are the stronger sex-typers), but *both* parents agree on the direction of sex differences.

An issue of considerable concern, in interpreting the findings of the present study appropriately, stems from the fact that fathers were not permitted to handle their babies, while mothers were. The question then becomes: Is it possible that the greater sex-typing by fathers is simply attributable to their lesser exposure to their infants? This, indeed, may have been the case. However it seems worthwhile to consider some of the alternative possibilities. Might not the lesser exposure of fathers to their infants have led not to greater sex-typing, but to a data "wash out" — with no differences emerging in paternal ratings? After all, given no opportunity to handle their babies, and therefore deprived of the opportunity to obtain certain first-hand information about them, the fathers might have been expected to make a series of neutral ratings — hovering around the middle of each adjective scale. The fact that they did not do this suggests that they brought with them a variety of sex stereotypes that they then imposed upon their infant. Moreover, the fact that mothers, who were allowed to hold and feed their babies, made distinctions between males and females that were in keeping with cultural sex-stereotypes (see Table 7.1), suggests that even if fathers had had the opportunity of holding their infants, similar results might have been obtained. We should also not lose sight of the fact that father-mother differences in exposure to infants continue well into later years. Finally, one must question the very importance of the subjects' differential exposure on the grounds that none of the typical "exposure" effects reported in the social psychological literature[14] were observed. In particular, one might have expected mothers to have come to rate their infants more favorably than fathers, simply as a result of greater exposure. Yet such was not the case.

The central implication of the study, then, is that sex-typing and sex-role socialization appear to have already begun their course at the time of the infant's birth, when information about the infant is minimal. The *Gestalt* parents develop, and the labels they ascribe to their newborn infant, may well affect subsequent expectations about the manner in which their infant ought to behave, as well as parental behavior itself. This parental behavior, moreover, when considered in conjunction with the rapid unfolding of the infant's own behavioral repertoire, may well lead to a modification of the very labeling that affected parental behavior in the first place. What began as a one-way street now bears traffic in two directions. In order to understand the full importance and implications of our findings, therefore, research clearly needs to be conducted in which delivery room stereotypes are traced in the family during the first several months after birth, and their impact upon parental behavior is considered. In addition, further research is clearly in order if we are to understand fully the importance of early paternal sex-typing in the socialization of sex-roles.

REFERENCES

1. Aberle, D. and Naegele, K. 1952. Middle-class fathers' occupational role and attitudes toward children. Amer. J. Orthopsychiat. 22(2):366–378.
2. Asch, S. 1946. Forming impressions of personality. J. Abnorm. Soc. Psychol. 41:258–290.
3. Goodenough, E. 1957. Interest in persons as an aspect of sex differences in the early years. Genet. Psychol. Monogr. 55:287–323.
4. Harari, H. and McDavid, J. Name stereotypes and teachers' expectations. J. Educ. Psychol. (in press)
5. Kelley, H. 1950. The warm-cold variable in first impressions of persons. J. Pers. 18:431–439.
6. Luchins, A. 1957. Experimental attempts to minimize the impact of first impressions. In The Order of Presentation in Persuasion, C. Hovland, ed. Yale University Press, New Haven, Conn.
7. Meyer, J. and Sobieszek, B. 1972. Effect of a child's sex on adult interpretations of its behavior. Develpm. Psychol. 6:42–48.
8. Pedersen, F. and Robson, K. 1969. Father participation in infancy. Amer. J. Orthopsychiat. 39(3):466–472.
9. Rebelsky, F. and Hanks, C. 1971. Fathers' verbal interaction with infants in the first three months of life. Child Develpm. 42:63–68.
10. Schaffer, H. 1971. The Growth of Sociability. Penguin Books, Baltimore.
11. Sears, R., Maccoby, E. and Levin, H. 1957. Patterns of Child Rearing. Row, Peterson, Evanston, Ill.
12. Tasch, R. 1952. The role of the father in the family. J. Exper. Ed. 20:319–361.
13. Wilson, P. 1968. The perceptual distortion of height as a function of ascribed academic status. J. Soc. Psychol. 74:97–102.
14. Zajonc, R. 1968. Attitudinal effects of mere exposure. J. Pers. Soc. Psychol. Monogr. Supplement 9:1–27.

OPTIONS FOR WRITING

1. Ideally, reports are structured to fit the needs of their audiences. The research report is designed to provide special clarity for scientists. Rewrite the report as a brief article for a parents' magazine aimed at a lay audience of new parents. Keep the goals, interests, and experience of your new audience in mind as you work.

2. Imagine that you repeated this study today, some 20 years or so after it was originally conducted. In what ways might the results be similar to or different from the original findings, and *why?* As you consider this question, think too about the ways in which your subjects might differ from the subjects in Rubin, Provenzano, and Luria's sample. That might well affect your results!

3. Few people would deny that parents treat their female and male children differently. Go to a public place such as a playground or shopping center, and observe parents' interactions with their male and female children for 30 to 60 minutes, recording your observations in a journal. Then summarize your notes in writing, drawing conclusions about what you observed. Consider the ways in which the characteristics of your subjects (for example, their ages, income, or educational levels) and your procedures (such as the time and place at which you made your observations) affected your results. How might your personal experiences and biases have shaped your conclusions as well?

Carl G. Jung
SIGMUND FREUD

Perhaps the greatest triumvirate in the history of modern psychology included Sigmund Freud, Carl Jung, and Alfred Adler, three individuals who probed into the depths of personality development. They brought new sophistication to the study of factors that motivate behavior, the power of the unconscious, and the significance of dreams. The following essay offers a fascinating glimpse of the evolving relationship between two of these great theorists, Freud and Jung. It is, in fact, a selection from Jung's autobiography, Memories, Dreams, Reflections, *in which Jung traces his growing respect for and then disenchantment with the ideas of Freud.*

In this autobiographical account, Jung provides us with an unusual opportunity to experience the intellectual and emotional struggles of a great theorist as he grapples with the politics of his discipline. What will his colleagues say when Jung admits that he endorses the originally unpopular beliefs of Freud? What are at the roots of Jung's inability to accept Freud's sexual theory in total? Jung reflects on his own professional and intellectual development as he develops an increasingly distinct impression of Freud not only as a theorist but also as a man.

Jung offers the reader an insider's view of the human and political dynamics that shape a scholarly field. His account of Freud also reminds us of the power with which the personal lives of scholars shape both what they study and the conclusions they draw. Jung wonders what it was that drew Freud to regard sexuality as one might view a religion — with unwavering conviction of its omnipresence and power.

You'll find that Jung's criticism of Freud stems from Jung's more general conviction about principles that are essential to good science. In the following selection, Jung writes that "a scientific truth was a hypothesis which might be adequate for the moment but was not to be preserved as an article of faith for all time." This notion fits with the scientific method we discussed earlier. On the other hand, do you believe that scientists can be purely open and noncommittal regarding their hypotheses? Is it realistic or even desirable for them simply to follow their empirical findings without keeping strong ties to their intuitive beliefs and personal experiences?

As you read, think about whether you trust Jung's account of Freud and why. How might Freud have explained Jung's resistance to his sexual theory?

I embarked on the adventure of my intellectual development by becoming a psychiatrist. In all innocence I began observing mental patients, clinically, from the outside, and thereby came upon psychic processes of a striking nature. I noted and classified these things without the slightest understanding of their contents, which were considered to be adequately evaluated when they were dismissed as "pathological." In the course of time my interest focused more and more upon cases in which I experienced something understandable — that is, cases of paranoia, manic-depressive insanity, and psychogenic disturbances. From the start of my psychiatric career the studies of Breuer and Freud, along with the work of Pierre Janet, provided me with a wealth of suggestions and stimuli. Above all, I found that Freud's technique of dream analysis and dream interpretation cast a valuable light upon schizophrenic forms of expression. As early as 1900 I had read Freud's *The Interpretation of Dreams.* I had laid the book aside, at the time, because I did not yet grasp it. At the age of twenty-five I lacked the experience to appreciate Freud's theories. Such experience did not come until later. In 1903 I once more took up *The Interpretation of Dreams* and discovered how it all linked up with my own ideas. What chiefly interested me was the application to dreams of the concept of the repression mechanism, which was derived from the psychology of the neuroses. This was important to me because I had frequently encountered repressions in my experiments with word association; in response to certain stimulus words that patient either had no associative answer or was unduly slow in his reaction time. As was later discovered, such a disturbance occurred each time the stimulus word had touched upon a psychic lesion or conflict. In most cases the patient was unconscious of this. When questioned about the cause of the disturbance, he would often answer in a peculiarly artificial manner. My reading of Freud's *The Interpretation of Dreams* showed me that the repression mechanism was at work here, and that the facts I had observed were consonant with his theory. Thus I was able to corroborate Freud's line of argument.

The situation was different when it came to the content of the repression. Here I could not agree with Freud. He considered the cause of the repression to be a sexual trauma. From my practice, however, I was familiar with numerous cases of neurosis in which the question of sexuality played a subordinate part, other factors standing in the foreground — for example, the problem of social adaptation, of oppression by tragic circumstances of life, prestige considerations, and so on. Later I presented such cases to Freud; but he would not grant that factors other than sexuality could be the cause. That was highly unsatisfactory to me.

At the beginning it was not easy for me to assign Freud the proper place in my life, or to take the right attitude toward him. When I became acquainted with his work I was planning an academic career, and was about to complete a paper that was intended to advance me at the university. But Freud was definitely *persona non grata* in the academic world at the time, and any connection with him would have been damaging in scientific circles. "Important people" at most mentioned him surreptitiously, and at congresses he was discussed only in the corridors, never on the floor. Therefore the discovery that my association experiments were in agreement with Freud's theories was far from pleasant to me.

Once, while I was in my laboratory and reflecting again upon these questions, the devil whispered to me that I would be justified in publishing the results of my experiments and my conclusions without mentioning Freud. After all, I had worked out my experiments long before I understood his work. But then I heard the voice of my second personality: "If you do a thing like that, as if you had no knowledge of Freud, it would be a piece of trickery. You cannot build your life upon a lie." With that, the question was settled. From then on I became an open partisan of Freud's and fought for him.

I first took up the cudgels for Freud at a congress in Munich where a lecturer discussed obsessional neuroses but studiously forbore to mention the name of Freud. In 1906, in connection with this incident, I wrote a paper for the *Münchner Medizinische Wochenschrift* on Freud's theory of the neuroses, which had contributed a great deal to the understanding of obsessional neuroses. In response to this article, two German professors wrote to me, warning that if I remained on Freud's side and continued to defend him, I would be endangering my academic career. I replied: "If what Freud says is the truth, I am with him. I don't give a damn for a career if it has to be based on the premise of restricting research and concealing the truth." And I went on defending Freud and his ideas. But on the basis of my own findings I was still unable to feel that all neuroses were caused by sexual repression or sexual traumata. In certain cases that was so, but not in others. Nevertheless, Freud had opened up a new path of investigation, and the shocked outcries against him at the time seemed to me absurd.

I had not met with much sympathy for the ideas expressed in "The Psychology of Dementia Praecox." In fact, my colleagues laughed at me. But through this book I came to know Freud. He invited me to visit him, and our first meeting took place in Vienna in February 1907. We met at one o'clock in the afternoon and talked virtually without a pause for thirteen hours. Freud was the first man of real importance I had encountered; in my experience up to that time, no one else could compare with him. There was nothing the least trivial in his attitude, I found him extremely intelligent, shrewd, and altogether remarkable. And yet my first impressions of him remained somewhat tangled; I could not make him out.

What he said about his sexual theory impressed me. Nevertheless, his words could not remove my hesitations and doubts. I tried to advance these reservations of mine on several occasions, but each time he would attribute them to my lack of experience. Freud was right; in those days I had not enough experience to support my objections. I could see that his sexual theory was enormously important to him, both personally and philosophically. This impressed me, but I could not decide to what extent this strong emphasis upon sexuality was connected with subjective prejudices of his, and to what extent it rested upon verifiable experiences.

Above all, Freud's attitude toward the spirit seemed to me highly questionable. Wherever, in a person or in a work of art, an expression of spirituality (in the intellectual, not the supernatural sense) came to light, he suspected it, and insinuated that it was repressed sexuality. Anything that could not be directly interpreted as sexuality he referred to as "psychosexuality." I protested that this hypothesis, carried to its logical conclusion, would lead to an annihilating judgment upon culture. Culture would then appear as a mere farce, the morbid consequence of repressed sexuality. "Yes," he assented, "so it is, and that is just a curse of fate against which we are powerless to contend." I was by no means disposed to agree, or to let it go at that, but still I did not feel competent to argue it out with him.

There was something else that seemed to me significant at the first meeting. It had to do with things which I was able to think out and understand only after our friendship was over. There was no mistaking the fact that Freud was emotionally involved in his sexual theory to an extraordinary degree. When he spoke of it, his tone became urgent, almost anxious, and all signs of his normally critical and skeptical manner vanished. A strange, deeply moved expression came over his face, the cause of which I was at a loss to understand. I had a strong intuition that for him sexuality was a sort of *numinosum.* This was confirmed by a conversation which took place some three years later (in 1910), again in Vienna.

I can still recall vividly how Freud said to me, "My dear Jung, promise me never to abandon the sexual theory. That is the most essential thing of all. You see, we must make a dogma of it, an unshakable bulwark." He said that to me with great emotion, in the tone of a father saying, "And promise me this one thing, my dear son: that you will go to church every Sunday." In some astonishment I asked him, "A bulwark—against what?" To which he replied, "Against the black tide of mud"—and here he hesitated for a moment, then added—"of occultism." First of all, it was the words "bulwark" and "dogma" that alarmed me; for a dogma, that is to say, an undisputable confession of faith, is set up only when the aim is to suppress doubts once and for all. But that no longer has anything to do with scientific judgment; only with a personal power drive.

This was the thing that struck at the heart of our friendship. I knew that I would never be able to accept such an attitude. What Freud seemed to mean by "occultism" was virtually everything that philosophy and religion, including the rising contemporary science of parapsychology, had learned about the psyche. To me the sexual theory was just as occult, that is to say, just as unproven an hypothesis, as many other speculative views. As I saw it, a scientific truth was a hypothesis which might be adequate for the moment but was not to be preserved as an article of faith for all time.

Although I did not properly understand it then, I had observed in Freud the eruption of unconscious religious factors. Evidently he wanted my aid in erecting a barrier against these threatening unconscious contents.

The impression this conversation made upon me added to my confusion; until then I had not considered sexuality as a precious and imperiled concept to which one must remain faithful. Sexuality evidently meant more to Freud than to other people. For him it was something to be religiously observed. In the face of such deep convictions one generally becomes shy and reticent. After a few stammering attempts on my part, the conversation soon came to an end.

I was bewildered and embarrassed. I had the feeling that I had caught a glimpse of a new, unknown country from which swarms of new ideas flew to meet me. One thing was clear; Freud, who had always made much of his irreligiosity, had now constructed a dogma; or rather, in the place of a jealous God whom he had lost, he had substituted another compelling image, that of sexuality. It was no less insistent, exacting, domineering, threatening, and morally ambivalent than the original one. Just as the psychically stronger agency is given "divine" or "daemonic" attributes, so the "sexual libido" took over the role of a *deus absconditus*, a hidden or concealed god. The advantage of this transformation for Freud was, apparently, that he was able to regard the new numinous principle as scientifically irreproachable and free from all religious taint. At bottom, however, the numinosity, that is, the psychological qualities of the two rationally incommensurable opposites— Yahweh and sexuality—remained the same. The name alone had changed, and with it, of course, the point of view: the lost god had now to be sought below, not above. But what difference does it make, ultimately, to the stronger agency if it is called now by one name and now by another? If psychology did not exist, but only concrete objects the one would actually have been destroyed and replaced by the other. But in reality, that is to say, in psychological experience, there is not one whit the less of urgency, anxiety, compulsiveness, etc. The problem still remains; how to overcome or escape our anxiety, bad conscience, guilt, compulsion, unconsciousness, and instinctuality. If we cannot do this from the bright, idealistic side, then perhaps we shall have better luck by approaching the problem from the dark, biological side.

Like flames suddenly flaring up, these thoughts darted through my mind. Much later, when I reflected upon Freud's character, they revealed their significance. There was one characteristic of his that preoccupied me above all; his bitterness. It had struck me at our first encounter, but it remained inexplicable to me until I was able to see it in connection with his attitude toward sexuality. Although, for Freud, sexuality was undoubtedly a *numinosum*, his terminology and theory seemed to define it exclusively as a biological function. It was only the emotionality with which he spoke of it that revealed the deeper elements reverberating within him. Basically, he wanted to teach—or so at least it seemed to me—that, regarded from within, sexuality included spirituality and had an intrinsic meaning. But his concretistic terminology was too narrow to express this idea. He gave me the impression that at bottom he was working against his own goal and against himself; and there is, after all, no harsher bitterness than that of a person who is his own worst enemy. In his own words, he felt himself menaced by a "black tide of mud"—he who more than anyone else had tried to let down his buckets into those black depths.

Freud never asked himself why he was compelled to talk continually of sex, why this idea had taken such possession of him. He remained unaware that his "monotony of interpretation" expressed a flight from himself, or from that other side of him which might perhaps be called mystical. So long as he refused to acknowledge that side, he could never be reconciled with himself. He was blind toward the paradox and ambiguity of the contents of the unconscious, and did not know that everything which arises out of the unconscious had a top and a bottom, an inside and an outside. When we speak of the outside—and that is what Freud did—we are considering only half of the whole, with the result that a countereffect arises out of the unconscious.

There was nothing to be done about this one-sidedness of Freud's. Perhaps some inner experience of his own might have opened his eyes; but then his intellect would have reduced any such experience to "mere sexuality" or "psychosexuality." He remained the victim of the one aspect he could recognize, and for that reason I see him as a tragic figure; for he was a great man, and what is more, a man in the grip of his daimon.

OPTIONS FOR WRITING

1. Imagine that Freud and Jung are sitting in your classroom today trying to explain one another's behavior. Write a dialogue you might hear as Freud tries to argue why Jung is resisting his sexual theory and Jung asserts why Freud is holding so steadfastly to his position regarding the power of sexuality.

2. Like students of all ilks, famous thinkers choose their scholarly interests in reaction to their personal histories—experiences they have had, people they have met, actions they have observed. Think about one or two areas of study that interest you. In a page or two, describe and analyze the ways in which your own personal experiences have contributed to those interests in some way.

3. Both Freud and Jung appreciated the tremendous power of the unconscious in motivating people's behavior. This idea is widely accepted today. Think about your own behavior over the past couple of weeks. In a brief essay, discuss some of the unconscious factors that, in retrospect, you believe motivated some of your actions.

Oliver Sacks
THE PRESIDENT'S SPEECH

A common form of presenting psychological data is the case study. *Much of Sigmund Freud's pioneering work grew from these sorts of observations. In contrast to experiments in which various conditions are systematically manipulated, case studies generally involve observations of naturally occurring events. Often these are events that differ from the norm—experiments of nature, so to speak. For example, we might study the case of a dog that was accidentally stranded alone in a cellar for the first months of its life in order to examine the contributions of early social contact to later sociability.*

Case studies help us to understand the effects of circumstances that would be inappropriate and even unethical to manipulate intentionally. Sometimes case studies provide us with insights about events that we might never have imagined would be important to investigate. But case studies of unusual disorders also help us understand normal development and functioning. In fact, they can be extraordinarily revealing of the complex processes that are involved in our typical day-to-day lives—processes that we take for granted.

The following essay by Oliver Sacks provides an intriguing example of this point. It describes the repercussions of global aphasia, which is damage to the central nervous system of the brain that results in the inability to understand words. We find that by examin-

ing the abilities and limitations that accompany this rare syndrome, we learn a great deal about the complex ways in which humans normally process speech. Sacks's essay is best described as a modified clinical case study. Written especially for a lay audience, it is less systematic and detailed than a formal case study, and probably more entertaining!

Before you read, make a list of some of the verbal and nonverbal cues you use to interpret spoken words. Think about situations in which you process verbal communication without access to all possible cues—for example, on the telephone and television, through books and letters. Are there situations in which you'd prefer to have limited cues?

What was going on? A roar of laughter from the aphasia ward, just as the President's speech was coming on, and they had all been so eager to hear the President speaking. . . .

There he was, the old Charmer, the Actor, with his practiced rhetoric, his histrionisms, his emotional appeal—and all the patients were convulsed with laughter. Well, not all: some looked bewildered, some looked outraged, one or two looked apprehensive, but most looked amused. The President was, as always, moving—but he was moving them, apparently, mainly to laughter. What could they be thinking? Were they failing to understand him? Or did they, perhaps, understand him all too well?

It was often said of these patients, who though intelligent had the severest receptive or global aphasia, rendering them incapable of understanding words as such, that they none the less understood most of what was said to them. Their friends, their relatives, the nurses who knew them well, could hardly believe, sometimes, that they *were* aphasic.

This was because, when addressed naturally, they grasped some or most of the meaning. And one does speak 'naturally,' naturally.

Thus, to demonstrate their aphasia, one had to go to extraordinary lengths, as a neurologist, to speak and behave un-naturally, to remove all the extraverbal cues—tone of voice, intonation, suggestive emphasis or inflection, as well as all visual cues (one's expressions, one's gestures, one's entire, largely unconscious, personal repertoire and posture): one had to remove all of this (which might involve total concealment of one's person, and total depersonalization of one's voice, even to using a computerized voice synthesizer) in order to reduce speech to pure words, speech totally devoid of what Frege called 'tone-colour' *(Klangenfarben)* or 'evocation.' With the most sensitive patients, it was only with such a grossly artificial, mechanical speech—somewhat like that of the computers in *Star Trek*—that one could be wholly sure of their aphasia.

Why all this? Because speech—natural speech—does *not* consist of words alone, nor (a Hughlings Jackson thought) 'propositions' alone. It consists of *utterance*—an uttering-forth of one's whole meaning with one's whole being—the understanding of which involves infinitely more

than mere word-recognition. And this was the cue to aphasiacs' understanding, even when they might be wholly uncomprehending of words
as such. For though the words, the verbal constructions, *per se*, might
convey nothing, spoken language is normally suffused with 'tone,' embedded in an expressiveness which transcends the verbal—and it is precisely this expressiveness, so deep, so various, so complex, so subtle,
which is perfectly preserved in aphasia, though understanding of words
be destroyed. Preserved—and often more: preternaturally enhanced. . . .

This too becomes clear—often in the most striking, or comic, or
dramatic way—to all those who work or live closely with aphasiacs:
their families or friends or nurses or doctors. At first, perhaps, we see
nothing much the matter; and then we see that there has been a great
change, almost an inversion, in their understanding of speech. Something has gone, has been devastated, it is true—but something has
come, in its stead, has been immensely enhanced, so that—at least with
emotionally-laden utterance—the meaning may be fully grasped even
when every word is missed. This, in our species *Homo loquens*, seems
almost an inversion of the usual order of things: an inversion, and
perhaps a reversion too, to something more primitive and elemental.
And this perhaps is why Hughlings Jackson compared aphasiacs to dogs
(a comparison that might outrage both!) though when he did this he
was chiefly thinking of their linguistic incompetences, rather than their
remarkable, and almost infallible, sensitivity to 'tone' and feeling. Henry
Head, more sensitive in this regard, speaks of 'feeling-tone' in his (1926)
treatise on aphasia, and stresses how it is preserved, and often enhanced, in aphasiacs.[1]

Thus the feeling I sometimes have—which all of us who work
closely with aphasiacs have—that one cannot lie to an aphasiac. He cannot grasp your words, and so cannot be deceived by them; but what he
grasps he grasps with infallible precision, namely the *expression* that goes
with the words, that total, spontaneous, involuntary expressiveness
which can never be simulated or faked, as words alone can, all too
easily. . . .

We recognize this with dogs, and often use them for this purpose—
to pick up falsehood, or malice, or equivocal intentions, to tell us who
can be trusted, who is integral, who makes sense, when we—so susceptible to words—cannot trust our own instincts.

---

[1] 'Feeling-tone' is a favorite term of Head's, which he uses in regard not only to
aphasia but to the affective quality of sensation, as it may be altered by thalmic or
peripheral disorders. Our impression, indeed, is that Head is continually half-unconscious-
ly drawn toward the exploration of 'feeling-tone'—toward, so to speak, a neurology of
feeling-tone, in contrast or complementarity to a classical neurology of proposition and
process. It is, incidentally, a common term in the U.S.A., at least among blacks in the
South: a common, earthy and indispensable term. 'You see, there's such a thing as a
feeling tone. . . . And if you don't have this, baby, you've had it' (cited by Studs Terkel
as epigraph to his 1967 oral history *Division Street: America*).

And what dogs can do here, aphasiacs do too, and at a human and immeasurably superior level. 'One can lie with the mouth,' Nietzsche writes, 'but with the accompanying grimace one nevertheless tells the truth.' To such a grimace, to any falsity or impropriety in bodily appearance or posture, aphasiacs are preternaturally sensitive. And if they cannot see one—this is especially true of our blind aphasiacs—they have an infallible ear for every vocal nuance, the tone, the rhythm, the cadences, the music, the subtlest modulations, inflections, intonations, which can give—or remove—verisimilitude to or from a man's voice.

In this, then, lies their power of understanding—understanding, without words, what is authentic or inauthentic. Thus it was the grimaces, the histrionisms, the false gestures and, above all, the false tones and cadences of the voice, which rang false for these wordless but immensely sensitive patients. It was to these (for them) most glaring, even grotesque, incongruities and improprieties that my aphasic patients responded, undeceived and undeceivable by words.

This is why they laughed at the President's speech.

If one cannot lie to an aphasiac, in view of his special sensitivity to expression and 'tone,' how is it, we might ask, with patients—if there are such—who *lack* any sense of expression and 'tone,' while preserving, unchanged, their comprehension for words: patients of an exactly opposite kind? We have a number of such patients, also on the aphasia ward, although, technically, they do not have aphasia, but, instead, a form of *agnosia*, in particular a so-called 'tonal' agnosia. For such patients, typically, the expressive qualities of voices disappear—their tone, their timbre, their feeling, their entire character—while words (and grammatical constructions) are perfectly understood. Such tonal agnosias (or 'aprosodias') are associated with disorders of the *right* temporal lobe of the brain, whereas the aphasias go with disorders of the *left* temporal lobe.

Among the patients with tonal agnosia on our aphasia ward who also listened to the president's speech was Emily D., with a glioma in her right temporal lobe. A former English teacher, and poetess of some repute, with an exceptional feeling for language, and strong powers of analysis and expression, Emily D. was able to articulate the opposite situation—how the President's speech sounded to someone with tonal agnosia. Emily D. could no longer tell if a voice was angry, cheerful, sad—whatever. Since voices now lacked expression, she had to look at people's faces, their postures and movements when they talked, and found herself doing so with care, an intensity, she had never shown before. But this, it so happened, was also limited, because she had a malignant glaucoma, and was rapidly losing her sight too.

What she then found she had to do was to pay extreme attention to exactness of words and word use, and to insist that those around her did just the same. She could less and less follow loose speech or slang—speech of an allusive or emotional kind—and more and more required of her interlocutors that they speak *prose*—'proper words in proper places.' Prose, she found, might compensate, in some degree, for lack of perceived tone or feeling.

In this way she was able to preserve, even enhance, the use of 'expressive' speech—in which the meaning was wholly given by the apt choice and reference of words—despite being more and more lost with 'evocative' speech (where meaning is wholly given in the use and sense of tone).

Emily D. also listened, stony-faced, to the President's speech, bringing to it a strange mixture of enhanced and defective perceptions—precisely the opposite mixture to those of our aphasiacs. It did not move her—no speech now moved her—and all that was evocative, genuine or false completely passed her by. Deprived of emotional reaction, was she then (like the rest of us) transported or taken in? By no means. 'He is not cogent,' she said. 'He does not speak good prose. His word-use is improper. Either he is brain-damaged, or he has something to conceal.' Thus the President's speech did not work for Emily D. either, due to her enhanced sense of formal language use, propriety as prose, any more than it worked for our aphasiacs, with their word-deafness but enhanced sense of tone.

Here then was the paradox of the President's speech. We normals— aided, doubtless, by our wish to be fooled, were indeed well and truly fooled (*'Populus vult decipi, ergo decipiatur'*). And so cunningly was deceptive word-use combined with deceptive tone, that only the brain-damaged remained intact, undeceived.

OPTIONS FOR WRITING

1. In a brief essay, compare the power of written and oral verbal communication. Beyond the choice of the words themselves, what other aspects of communications (such as tone or tempo) influence the ways we interpret their meaning? It's probably less obvious how we can alter the meaning of written words without changing the words themselves. Write a two-sentence description of a person you know. Then rewrite it once or twice using essentially the same words but altering their presentation (for example, through punctuation, sequence, or even print) in order to convey different meaning.

2. Describe whether you think you communicate more effectively in speaking or in writing, and why. Consider whether your answer depends on what you're attempting to communicate. What sorts of personal characteristics might lead a person to feel more effective at one sort of communication rather than another?

3. Watch ten minutes of television without the sound. In your journal, record your reactions to this experience, and note how they change over the ten-minute period.

4. Think about a significant event in your own past, and describe it in the form of a case study. Present relevant details of the experience, and draw conclusions about its contributions to your subsequent behavior and experiences.

Elizabeth F. Loftus
EYEWITNESSES:
Essential but Unreliable

In many fields, including psychology, distinctions are made between basic and applied research. Basic research investigates core processes and operations without particular concern for the ways in which these facts can be applied to activities and settings in our everyday lives. Applied research focuses on the latter, the application of knowledge or facts to real-life settings such as classrooms (will the timing of the lunch hour affect student behavior?), roadways (what shape and color of stop sign will be most effective?), and hospitals (would a constant rather than rotating nursing crew provide greater comfort for patients?).

As the following article suggests, the courtroom is full of intriguing questions for the applied psychologist, questions that illustrate the ways in which basic psychological research can be extended into applied research. Memory, perception, attitude formation, and learning are just some of the psychological processes that shape courtroom proceedings.

Our judicial system has long relied on eyewitness testimony as a valuable resource. Have we been relying on the unreliable? In the following essay, author Elizabeth Loftus, a professor of psychology at the University of Washington, scrutinizes whether eyewitnesses can provide accurate details of events they have observed. As you read, try to identify some of the basic psychological processes that are involved in presenting accurate testimony. Ask yourself, as well, what characteristics of the witness, defendant, jury, or general courtroom scene may influence the degree to which testimony is perceived by others as credible. Clearly there are many psychological dimensions of the courtroom that may affect the ways in which a court case evolves.

The ladies and gentlemen of William Bernard Jackson's jury decided that he was guilty of rape. They made a serious mistake, and before it was discovered, Jackson had spent five years in prison. There he suffered numerous indignities and occasional attacks until the police discovered that another man, who looked very much like Jackson, had committed the rapes.

If you had been on the jury, you would probably have voted for conviction too. Two women had positively identified Jackson as the man who had raped them in September and October of 1977. The October victim was asked on the witness stand, "Is there any doubt in your mind as to whether this man you have identified here is the man who had the sexual activity with you on October 3, 1977?" She answered "No doubt." "Could you be mistaken?" the prosecutor asked. "No, I am not mistaken," the victim stated confidently. Jackson and other defense witnesses testified that he was home when the rapes occurred. But the jury didn't believe him or them.

This is just one of the many documented cases of mistaken eyewitness testimony that have had tragic consequences. In 1981, Steve Titus of Seattle was convicted of raping a 17-year-old woman on a secluded road; the following year he was proven to be innocent. Titus was luckier than Jackson; he never went to prison. However, Aaron Lee Owens of Oakland, California, was not as fortunate. He spent nine years in a prison for a double murder that he didn't commit. In these cases, and many others, eyewitnesses testified against the defendants, and jurors believed them.

One reason most of us, as jurors, place so much faith in eyewitness testimony is that we are unaware of how many factors influence its accuracy. To name just a few: what questions witnesses are asked by police and how the questions are phrased; the difficulty people have in distinguishing among people of other races; whether witnesses have seen photos of suspects before viewing the lineup from which they pick out the person they say committed the crime; the size, composition and type (live or photo) of the lineup itself.

I know of seven studies that assess what ordinary citizens believe about eyewitness memory. One common misconception is that police officers make better witnesses than the rest of us. As part of a larger study, my colleagues and I asked 541 registered voters in Dade County, Florida, "Do you think that the memory of law enforcement agents is better than the memory of the average citizen?" Half said yes, 38 percent said no and the rest had no opinion. When A. Daniel Yarmey of the University of Guelph asked judges, lawyers and policemen a similar question, 63 percent of the legal officials and half the police agreed that "The policeman will be superior to the civilian" in identifying robbers."

This faith in police testimony is not supported by research. Several years ago, psychologists A. H. Tinkner and E. Christopher Poulton showed a film depicting a street scene to 24 police officers and 156 civilians. The subjects were asked to watch for particular people in the film and to report instances of crimes, such as petty theft. The researchers found that the officers reported more alleged thefts than the civilians but that when it came to detecting actual crimes, the civilians did just as well.

More recently, British researcher Peter B. Ainsworth showed a 20-minute videotape to police officers and civilians. The tape depicted a number of staged criminal offenses, suspicious circumstances and traffic offenses at an urban street corner. No significant differences were found between the police and civilians in the total number of incidents reported. Apparently neither their initial training nor subsequent experience increases the ability of the police to be accurate witnesses.

Studies by others and myself have uncovered other common misconceptions about eyewitness testimony. They include:

- *Witnesses remember the details of a violent crime better than those of a nonviolent one.* Research shows just the opposite: The added stress that violence creates clouds our perceptions.
- *Witnesses are as likely to underestimate the duration of a crime as to overestimate it.* In fact, witnesses almost invariably think a crime took longer than it did. The more violent and stressful the crime, the more witnesses overestimate its duration.
- *The more confident a witness seems, the more accurate the testimony is likely to be.* Research suggests that there may be little or no relationship between confidence and accuracy, especially when viewing conditions are poor.

The unreliability of confidence as a guide to accuracy has been demonstrated outside of the courtroom too; one example is provided by accounts of an aircraft accident that killed nine people several years ago. According to *Flying* magazine, several people had seen the airplane just before impact, and one of them was certain that "it was heading right toward the ground, straight down." This witness was profoundly wrong, as shown by several photographs taken of the crash site that made it clear that the airplane hit flat and at a low enough angle to skid for almost 1,000 feet.

Despite the inaccuracies of eyewitness testimony, we can't afford to exclude it legally or ignore it as jurors. Sometimes, as in cases of rape, it is the only evidence available, and it is often correct. The question remains, what can we do to give jurors a better understanding of the uses and pitfalls of such testimony? Judges sometimes give the jury a list of instructions on the pitfalls of eyewitness testimony. But this method has not proved satisfactory, probably because, as studies show, jurors either do not listen or do not understand the instructions.

Another solution, when judges permit, is to call a psychologist as an expert witness to explain how the human memory works and describe the experimental findings that apply to the case at hand. How this can affect a case is shown by a murder trial in California two years ago. On April 1, 1981, two young men were walking along Polk Street in San Francisco at about 5:30 in the evening. A car stopped near them and the driver, a man in his 40s, motioned one of the men to get in, which he did. The car drove off. Up to this point, nothing appeared unusual. The area was known as a place where prostitutes hang out; in fact, the young man who got in the car was there hustling for "tricks." Three days later, he was found strangled in a wooded area some 75 miles south of San Francisco.

Five weeks later, the victim's friend was shown a six-person lineup and picked out a 47-year-old I'll call D. The quick selection of D's photograph, along with the strong emotional reaction that accompanied it (the friend became ill when he saw the photo), convinced the police that they had their man. D was tried for murder.

At his trial, the defense lawyer introduced expert testimony by a psychologist on the factors that made accurate perception and memory difficult. For example, in the late afternoon of April 1, the witness had been using marijuana, a substance likely to blur his initial perceptions and his memory of them. Furthermore, just before viewing the lineup, the witness had seen a photograph of D on a desk in the police station, an incident that could have influenced his selection. During the five weeks between April 1 and the time he saw the photographs, the witness had talked about and been questioned repeatedly about the crime, circumstances that often contaminate memory.

In the end, the jury was unable to reach a verdict. It is difficult to assess the impact of any one bit of testimony on a particular verdict. We can only speculate that the psychologist's testimony may have made the jury more cautious about accepting the eyewitness testimony. This idea is supported by recent studies showing that such expert testimony generally increases the deliberation time jurors devote to eyewitness aspects of a case.

Expert testimony on eyewitness reliability is controversial. It has its advocates and enemies in both the legal and psychological professions. For example, several judicial arguments are used routinely to exclude the testimony. One is that it "invades the province of the jury," meaning that it is the jury's job, not an expert's, to decide whether a particular witness was in a position to see, hear and remember what is being claimed in court. Another reason judges sometimes exclude such testimony is that the question of eyewitness reliability is "not beyond the knowledge and experience of a juror" and thus is not a proper subject matter for expert testimony.

In virtually all the cases in which a judge has prohibited the jury from hearing expert testimony, the higher courts have upheld the decision, and in some cases have driven home the point with negative comments about the use of psychologists. In a recent case in California, *People v. Plasencia*, Nick Plasencia Jr. was found guilty of robbery and other crimes in Los Angeles County. He had tried to introduce the testimony of a psychologist on eyewitness reliability, but the judge refused to admit it, saying that "the subject matter about which (the expert) sought to testify was too conjectural and too speculative to support any opinion he would offer." The appellate court upheld Plasencia's conviction and made known its strong feelings about the psychological testimony:

"Since our society has not reached the point where all human conduct is videotaped for later replay, resolution of disputes in our court system depends almost entirely on the testimony of witnesses who re-count their observations of a myriad of events.

"These events include matters in both the criminal and civil areas of the law. The accuracy of a witness's testimony of course depends on factors which are as variable and complex as human nature itself. . . . The cornerstone of our system remains our belief in the wisdom and integrity of the jury system and the ability of 12 jurors to determine the accuracy of witnesses' testimony. The system has served us well. . . .

"It takes no expert to tell us that for various reasons, people can be mistaken about identity, or even the exact details of an observed event. Yet to present these commonly accepted and known facts in the form of an expert opinion, which opinion does nothing more than generally question the validity of one form of traditionally accepted evidence, would exaggerate the significance of that testimony and give a 'scientific aura' to a very unscientific matter.

"The fact remains, in spite of the universally recognized fallibility of human beings, persons do, on many occasions, correctly identify indi-viduals. Evidence that under contrived test conditions, or even in real-life situations, certain persons totally unconnected with this case have been mistaken in their identification of individuals is no more relevant than evidence that in other cases, witnesses totally unconnected with this event have lied.

"It seems beyond question that the identifications in this case were correct. We find no abuse of discretion in the trial court's rejecting the proffered testimony."

Quite the opposite view was expressed by the Arizona Supreme Court in *State v. Chapple*. At the original trial, defendant Dolan Chapple had been convicted of three counts of murder and two drug-trafficking charges, chiefly on the testimony of two witnesses who identified him at the trial. Earlier they had selected him from photographs shown them by the police more than a year after the crime.

Chapple's lawyer tried to introduce expert psychological testimony on the accuracy of such identification. The judge refused to permit it on the grounds that the testimony would pertain only to matters "within the common experience" of jurors. The high court disagreed, maintain-ing that expert testimony would have provided scientific data on such pertinent matters as the accuracy of delayed identification, the effect of stress on perception and the relationship between witness confidence and accuracy. "We cannot assume," the court added, "that the average juror would be aware of the variables concerning identification and memory" about which the expert would have testified. Chapple's con-viction was reversed, and he has been granted a new trial.

Like lawyers and judges, psychologists disagree on whether expert testimony is a good solution to the eyewitness problem. Two of the most outspoken critics are Michael McCloskey and Howard Egeth of The

Johns Hopkins University. These experimental psychologists offer four reasons why they believe that expert testimony on eyewitness reliability is a poor idea. They say that there is no evidence that such testimony is needed; that the data base on which the expert must rely is not sufficiently well-developed; and that conflicting public testimony between experts would tarnish the profession's image. Given this sorry state of affairs, they argue, psychologists may do more harm than good by intruding into judicial proceedings.

Obviously, many psychologists disagree with this assessment and believe that both the law and psychology gain from mutual interaction. In the area of eyewitness testimony, information supplied by psychologists to lawyers has stimulated responses that have suggested a number of important ideas for future research.

For example, psychologists need to learn more about the ideas that the rest of us have about the operation of human perception and memory. When these ideas are wrong, psychologists need to devise ways to educate us so that the judgments we make as jurors will be more fully informed and more fair. Only through this give-and-take, and occasional biting controversy, will progress be made. It is too late to help William Jackson, or Steve Titus, or Aaron Lee Owens, but it is not yet too late for the rest of us.

OPTIONS FOR WRITING

1. Imagine that you are a lawyer preparing a case for trial and that a psychologist offers her services as a consultant. Think about the varied dynamics of a courtroom trial, such as the physical setting, the selection of jurors, and the ways in which the lawyers and clients impress the jurors. Write a short essay describing some of the issues the psychologist might be able to advise you on as you prepare to defend your client, who was accused of robbing a jewelry store.

2. Clearly there is great controversy regarding whether psychologists should provide expert testimony to jurors on eyewitness reliability. There is some concern about the ways in which such testimony will affect jurors' responses to eyewitness reports. But jurors always need to make judgments about the validity and accuracy of witness testimony. Imagine that you are a juror. What sorts of instruction would you want to receive regarding factors that may influence eyewitness testimony? What sorts of factors will influence the degree to which you accept a witness' testimony as accurate and reliable?

3. Recalling the reading and related discussions, describe the advantages and disadvantages of allowing expert testimony of psychologists in the courtroom. After you have explored the various sides of the argument, take a stand regarding whether or under what conditions such expert testimony should be permitted.

Robert J. Sternberg and Janet E. Davidson
THE MIND OF THE PUZZLER

"Water lilies double in area every 24 hours. At the beginning of the summer there is one water lily on a lake. It takes 60 days for the lake to become covered with water lilies. On what day is the lake half covered?"

This insight problem, drawn from the following essay, "The Mind of the Puzzler," is actually part of a research assessment used to examine the ways in which people think. How do people solve problems? What skills and processes are involved in problem-solving activity? These issues form the core of much psychological inquiry. For example, physiological psychologists examine changes in the chemistry and structure of the brain that accompany learning and problem-solving; educational psychologists study strategies that seem to facilitate thinking processes; clinical psychologists investigate why certain people appear to interpret information consistently in unusual and stress-producing ways; developmental psychologists examine the ways in which problem-solving strategies change over course of the life span.

The following essay was written by two cognitive psychologists interested in the skills involved in problem solving and in the relationship of these skills to intelligence. Robert Sternberg, a professor of psychology at Yale University, has received several awards for his outstanding research on human intelligence, thinking, and intellectual development, including the Boyd R. McCandless Young Scientists Award of the American Psychological Association. Sternberg is also well known for his efforts to apply his research findings to help people become more effective problem solvers. The coauthor of this essay, Janet Davidson, was a graduate student in psychology at Yale at the time this paper was written.

Sternberg and Davidson trace the ongoing development of their research hypotheses, methods, and findings related to problem-solving insight and intelligence. Their essay is particularly useful in several ways: (1) It raises important questions about the concept of intelligence and problem solving; (2) It presents a good example of an informal review of research; and (3) It illustrates the ways in which a line of research actually evolves. The results of successive investigations lead to the hypotheses for the next, as we described in our discussion of the scientific method.

As you read this essay, underline each successive hypothesis that is posed. Not the ways in which the hypotheses emerge from the preceding investigations. Consider, as well, the concepts that are being studied: Are problem solving and intelligence the same? Write a brief definition of each before you read the article, and compare your defi-

nitions with those that the authors appear to be using. Before you read any further, return to the water lilies problem at the beginning of this introduction. Think about the different sorts of skills and knowledge you need to use to solve the problem effectively. Do different types of problem solving require different sorts of intelligence?

Before departing from San Francisco on a flight to New York recently, a colleague of ours picked out some reading to test his wits. A professor of some accomplishment, he expected to make short work of the problems in *Games for the Superintelligent, More Games for the Superintelligent,* and *The Mensa Genius Quiz Book.* By the time he crossed the Rocky Mountains, however, he had realized that he was neither a genius nor, as *The Genius Quiz Book* puts it, "a secret superbrain who doesn't even know it." By the time he crossed the Mississippi River, he knew that he wasn't "superintelligent," either.

More often than not, the puzzles stumped him. How could two men play five games of checkers and each win the same number of games without any ties? He couldn't figure it out. How could you plant a total of 10 trees in five rows of four trees each? He drew several diagrams, and none of them worked. But he couldn't put the books down.

Mental puzzles have been a staple of the publishing industry for years. Martin Gardner's mathematical puzzles, from the monthly column he used to write for *Scientific American,* have been collected in 10 different books, with total sales of more than half a million copies. *Solve It, Games for the Superintelligent,* and *More Games for the Superintelligent,* all by James Fixx, have together sold nearly one million copies.

Many of the problems in these books require flashes of insight or "leaps of logic" on the part of the solver, rather than prior knowledge or laborious computation. We wondered just how people approach such puzzles—which are commonly called insight problems—and whether they provide a valid measure of a person's intelligence. To answer these questions, we examined the literature on problem-solving, and then conducted a mini-experiment to measure the relationship between performance on insight problems and scores on standard intelligence tests.

On the basis of our research, we identified three types of intellectual processes that, separately or together, seem to be required in solving most insight problems: the ability to select and "encode" information—that is, to understand what information is relevant to solving the problem, and how it is relevant; the ability to combine different and seemingly unrelated bits of useful information; and the ability to compare the problem under consideration with problems previously encountered. For example, in solving the problem of the checker players, faulty encoding would lead one to assume that the two men were playing each other. Correctly combining the facts that there were no ties and that each player won the same number of games should lead one to conclude that they couldn't be playing each other.

Similarly, to plant 10 trees in five rows of four trees each, one must get away from the idea of making the five rows parallel. People who are accustomed to thinking in geometric terms will usually imagine several other kinds of patterns, until they hit on the correct one [Figure 7.1].

The literature on how people solve insight problems is meager, and includes almost no reports on research relating solution of these problems to intelligence. One of the few studies of this sort was done in 1965 by Norman Maier and Ronald Burke at the University of Michigan. Maier and Burke compared people's scores on a variety of aptitude tests with their skill at solving the "hat-rack problem." The problem calls on them to build a structure, sufficiently stable to support a man's overcoat, using only two long sticks and a C-clamp. The opening of the clamp is wide enough so that the two sticks can be inserted and held together securely when the clamp is tightened. Participants are placed in a small room and are asked to build a hat rack in the center of the room. The solution is shown [in Figure 7.2].

When the researchers compared people's ability to solve the hat-rack problem with their scores on the Scholastic Aptitude Test, the correlations were all trivial. In other words, whatever insight people needed to build the hat rack seemed to be unrelated to their scores on standardized intelligence tests. Burke and Maier concluded that the abilities needed to solve insight problems may be different from those required to solve problems of the kinds found on such tests. Their study is of limited value, however: They used only one problem, and scored the responses only in terms of "right" or "wrong."

We did find in the literature some theoretical basis for the lack of relationship between intelligence and performance on the hat-rack problem. Kjell Raaheim, a psychologist at the University of Bergen, in Norway, wrote in *Problem Solving and Intelligence* that "it is unreasonable to

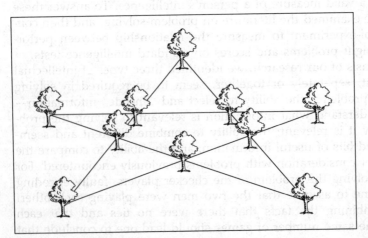

Figure 7.1   Solution to the "tree" puzzle.

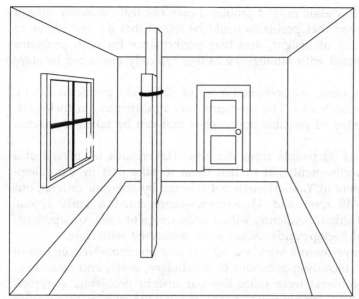

Figure 7.2   Solution to the Maier/Burke "hat-rack" puzzle.

expect intelligence to be an important factor of success in solving tasks which are totally unfamiliar to the individual facing them." According to Raaheim, problems will best measure intelligence if they present a situation that is *intermediate* in its degree of familiarity to a problem-solver. Problems presenting situations that are either too familiar or too unfamiliar will provide poorer measures of a person's intelligence.

In an ingenious set of experiments, Robert Weisberg and Joseph Alba, of Temple University, asked people to solve a set of insight problems. One was the familiar nine-dot problem, in which they were shown a three-by-three array of nine equally spaced dots and asked to connect the nine dots using four straight lines without lifting pencil from paper. The solution requires an approach similar to that used to plant the five rows of trees.

What is unique about Weisberg and Alba's study is that participants were actually given the insight they needed to solve the problem: They were told that it could be solved only by drawing the lines beyond the boundaries formed by the dots. Still, even after they were given the relevant insights, people in this study had considerable difficulty in solving the problem. Weisberg and Alba interpreted the results as suggesting that such problems may not really measure insight, but rather problem-specific prior knowledge. Our interpretation is a bit different. As we see it, subjects not only needed to know that they could draw the lines outside the boundaries; they also had to know how to combine what went outside the dots with what went inside. Performance on these insight problems therefore might not correlate with performance on intelligence-test problems.

Even though classic insight problems may not truly measure insight alone, we believed that problems could be found that do provide fairly accurate measures of insight, and that performance on such problems would be correlated with intelligence as it is typically measured by standardized tests.

To test this view, we compiled a set of 12 insight problems from a number of popular books. The problems vary in difficulty, in trickiness, and in the number of possible approaches that can be taken to reach a solution.

We recruited 30 people from the New Haven area by means of a newspaper advertisement that invited them to take part in a problem-solving experiment at Yale. Though not selected by scientific criteria, our small sample — 19 men and 11 women — represented a fairly typical cross-section of urban residents, with a wide range of ages, occupations, and educational backgrounds. None were connected with Yale.

First, we gave them a standard IQ test (the Henmon-Nelson Test of Mental Ability), including questions of vocabulary, math, and reasoning. None of the problems were quite like our insight problems. A typical reasoning problem, for example, might require the person to solve an analogy such as: CAR is to GASOLINE as HUMAN is to (a.OIL b. ENERGY c.FOOD d.FUEL); or a number series such as: 3, 7, 12, 18, —? (a. 24 b. 25 c. 26 d. 27). The IQ test problems were multiple-choice, whereas the insight problems we used required people to generate their own answers.

The average IQ score of our sample on this test was 112, 12 points above the national average. (Elevated average IQs are typical in such experiments, since those who volunteer for studies on problem-solving are likely to be of above-average intelligence. People with very low IQs may not read newspapers, and probably wouldn't volunteer for experiments on problem-solving even if they do.)

Second, we gave our subjects a deductive-reasoning test on non-sense syllogisms, such as "All trees are fish. All fish are horses. Therefore, all trees are horses. Please indicate whether the conclusion is logically valid or not." (This one is.) Third, in a test of inductive reasoning, we presented our subjects with five sets of letters (for example, NOPQ, DEFL, ABCD, HIJK, UVWX) and asked them to choose the set that was based on a rule different from the rule used as a basis for the other sets.

We included these two specific tests, as well as the more general IQ test, to judge the accuracy of a prediction we had made: If our problems genuinely measured insight, they should be more highly correlated with the inductive test, which requires one to go beyond the information given, than with the deductive test, which merely requires one to analyze the given information and draw the proper conclusion. Normal arithmetic or logic problems, for example, require primarily deductive rather than inductive reasoning skills.

Our subjects found the insight problems fun but sometimes frustrating, since the items varied considerably in difficulty. The easiest item, answered correctly by 73 percent of our sample, was this:

"Next week I am going to have lunch with my friend, visit the new art gallery, go to the Social Security office, and have my teeth checked at the dentist's. My friend cannot meet me on Wednesday; the Social Security office is closed weekends; the art gallery is closed Tuesday, Thursday, and weekends; and the dentist has office hours only on Tuesday, Friday, and Saturday. What day can I do everything I have planned?" Reaching the answer (Friday) is easy because one can simply check off which days don't work.

The hardest item, answered correctly by only 7 percent of our subjects, was:

"A bottle of wine cost $10. The wine was worth $9 more than the bottle. How much was the bottle worth?" People probably had a hard time coming up with the answer (50 cents) because they misunderstood the word 'more.'

The average score on our insight problem test was 4.4 correct out of 12, or roughly 37 percent. The individual scores ranged from a low of one to a high of 10, with no difference between the average scores of the men and the women. The times people spent solving the problems ranged from 11 minutes to 47 minutes, with an average of 28 minutes.

When we examined the relationship between scores on the set of 12 insight problems and scores on the mental-ability tests, we found relatively high correlations between the insight-problem scores and the scores on the tests of IQ (.66 on a scale from zero to one, on which a correlation of zero means no relationship, and a correlation of one means a perfect relationship) and inductive reasoning (.63), and only a moderate correlation with the scores on the test of deductive reasoning (.34). (All of the correlations were statistically significant.) These correlations suggest that performance on insight problems does provide a good index of intelligence, and that such performance may be more closely related to inductive than to deductive reasoning.

We then looked at the relationship between the test scores and time spent on the insight problems, and found that people who spent the most time working on the problems tended to have a higher number of correct solutions, and higher IQ scores. (The correlation between time spent and number of insight problems correctly solved was .62. The correlation between time spent and IQ was .75, which is remarkably high.) Why did smart people take longer on this task? Although we can only speculate, we suspect it is because they became more absorbed in the problems and more motivated to solve them. Our observations suggested that the less bright people either were too quick to choose the seemingly obvious but wrong answers on trick questions, or simply didn't know how to get started on the tougher problems and gave up more quickly.

When we looked at the correlations between the test scores on the insight problems and the scores on the standardized intelligence test, we found that the problems varied considerably in their validity as indicators of IQ. The problem of which day to schedule a lunch date with a friend had almost no correlation with IQ; the problem that proved to be the best predictor of IQ score was the following:

"Water lilies double in area every 24 hours. At the beginning of the summer there is one water lily on a lake. It takes 60 days for the lake to become covered with water lilies. On what day is the lake half covered?" To find the answer, people must realize that since the water lilies double in area every 24 hours, the lake will be half covered on the 59th day in order to be completely covered on the 60th.

What made some items better measures of IQ than others? We discovered two patterns among the "good" and "bad" indicators of IQ that we thought were striking, at least as preliminary hypotheses.

The best indicators of IQ seemed to be those problems that presented both relevant and irrelevant information: The key to success was the ability to distinguish necessary information from unnecessary. For example, people with high IQs tended to realize that "water lilies double in area every 24 hours" was an important clue to solving this problem. People with low IQs frequently ignored this information and tried to solve the problem by dividing the 60 days by two.

Our interpretation of performance on the problems supports the theory that the ability to detect and use clues embedded in the context of what one reads plays an important role in solving verbal problems. When reading a test—whether it is a newspaper, a science book, or a verbal or arithmetic problem—much of the information may be irrelevant to one's needs; often the hard part is figuring out what is relevant, and how it is relevant.

The problems that proved to be poor indicators of IQ were the "trick" problems in which errors were due primarily to misreading the problem situation—fixing on the apparent question rather than on the actual question. Take the following problem: "A farmer has 17 sheep. All but nine break through a hole in the fence and wander away. How many are left?" People making errors generally failed to comprehend exactly what "all but nine" meant; many assumed that the nine had escaped and thus subtracted that number from 17 to get the number of sheep that remained behind.

If, as we have shown, insight problems do provide a good measure of intellectual ability—at least when they require one to make inductive leaps beyond the given data and when they require one to sift out relevant from irrelevant information—we must ask: Just what is insight? The reason that others have not found any common element in the various insights they have studied is that no one model works for all cases. We have identified three basic kinds of cognitive processes or insightful performance, one or more of which may be required to solve a given problem:

Selective Encoding, or processing of information. This kind of insight occurs when one perceives in a problem one or more facts that are not immediately obvious. Earlier, we referred to the importance of being able to sort out relevant from irrelevant information. This skill can provide the solver with a basis for selective encoding.

Consider the following problem: "If you have black socks and brown socks in your drawer, mixed in the ratio of 4 to 5, how many socks will you have to take out to make sure of having a pair the same color?" Subjects who failed to realize that "mixed in the ratio of 4 to 5" was irrelevant information consistently came up with the wrong solution. (The correct answer: three.) In the hat-rack problem, noticing the relevance of the floor and ceiling as elements in the problem is also an example of selective encoding.

Selective Combination. This type of insight takes place when one sees a way of combining unrelated (or at least not obviously related) elements, as one must do in the following problem: "With a seven-minute hourglass and an 11-minute hourglass, what is the simplest way to time the boiling of an egg for 15 minutes?" Our subjects had all of the necessary facts, but they had to figure out how to combine the two timers to measure 15 minutes. In the hat-rack problem, figuring out how to combine the use of the floor, ceiling, C-clamp, and two sticks constitutes a similar insight of selective combination.

Selective Comparison. This kind of insight occurs when one discovers a nonobvious relationship between new and old information. It is here that analogy, metaphor, and models come into play. In the hat-rack problem, for example, one might think of how a pole lamp can be stabilized by wedging it between the floor and ceiling of a room, and how the same principle could be used in the construction of a hat rack.

Consider another type of selective comparison: If someone doesn't know a word on a vocabulary test, he can often figure out its definition by thinking of words he does know that have the same word stems. For example, if he doesn't know the word 'exsect,' he might be able to guess its meaning by thinking of a word that has the same prefix (such as 'extract,' where *ex* means out) and a word that has the same root (such as 'dissect,' where *sect* means cut). This information might help him realize that 'exsect' means 'to cut out.'

We emphasize the critical role of selection in each kind of information-processing. In Selective Encoding, one must choose elements to encode from the often numerous and irrelevant bits of information presented by the problem; the trick is to select the right elements. In Selective Combination, there may be many possible ways for the encoded elements to be combined or otherwise integrated; the trick is to select the right way of combining them. In Selective Comparison, new information must be related to one or more of many possible old pieces of information. There are any number of analogies or relations that might be drawn; the trick is to make the right comparison or comparisons.

Thus, to the extent that there is a communality in the three kinds of insight, it appears to be in the importance of selection to each kind.

We believe that much of the confusion in the past and present literature on problem-solving stems from a failure to recognize the existence of and differences among these three kinds of insight, which together seem to account for the mental processes that have been labeled as insight, and which are involved in everything from solving problems in puzzle books to making major scientific breakthroughs.

Although we have focused on the importance of insight in problem-solving—and also in intelligence—insight alone is not enough to solve problems. Certain other essential ingredients exist, including:

Prior Knowledge. Even apparently simple problems often require a store of prior knowledge for their solution; complex problems can require a vast store of such knowledge. Consider the problem of the seven-minute and 11-minute hourglasses, and how to time a 15-minute egg. If people have used hourglass timers before, and can remember that they can turn them over at any point, the knowledge will certainly help.

Executive Processes. These are the processes used to plan, monitor, and evaluate one's performance in problem-solving. To start with, one must first study the problem carefully, in order to figure out exactly what question is being asked.

Another executive process involves monitoring one's solution process (keeping track of what one has done, is doing, and still needs to do) and then switching strategies if one isn't making progress. Sometimes it helps to try a new approach if an old one doesn't work.

Motivation. Really challenging problems often require a great deal of motivation on the part of the solver. Successful problem-solvers are often those who simply are willing to put in the necessary effort. Indeed, in our mini-study we found that the better problem-solvers were more persevering than the poorer ones.

Style. People approach problems with different cognitive styles. In particular, some tend to be more impulsive and others more reflective. It seems to us—although we have no hard experimental evidence to support our view—that the most successful problem solvers are those who manage to combine both impulsive and reflective styles. We do not believe that most people follow just one style or the other. Rather, at certain points in the problem-solving process, people act on impulse; at other times, they act only after great reflection. The hard part is knowing which style will pay off at which point in solving problems.

Successful problem-solving involves a number of different abilities. For many problems, one kind of insight may provide a key to a quick solution. But we believe that most problems are like the apartment doors one finds in some of our larger cities: They have multiple locks requiring multiple keys. Without combining different kinds of insights, as well as prior knowledge, executive processes, motivation, and style, the problems remain locked doors, waiting for the clever solver to find the right set of keys.

OPTIONS FOR WRITING

1. Sternberg and Davidson defined insight as "leaps in logic." In your journal, brainstorm about the sorts of conditions that would be most likely to foster insights in thinking. Consider the physical, mental, social, and environmental contexts that you think would be most likely to support insightful thinking and those that would likely interfere.

2. Present the water lily insight problem (from the beginning of the introduction to this essay) to two or three friends, one at a time. Ask them to think aloud and to describe the ways in which they go about trying to reason through the problem. Record what each friend says in your journal, then compare the problem-solving approaches described by each in a brief entry.

3. In a short essay, discuss the different ways that intelligence is defined in our society. Describe different notions of the characteristics of an intelligent person. In concluding your essay, present your own position on what characterizes intelligence.

Susan Chollar
CONVERSATIONS WITH THE DOLPHINS

Have you ever watched a family pet, an animal in a zoo, or even a bird soaring in the sky and wondered what was going through its mind? Do animals think the same kinds of thoughts as humans do? Do they feel humanlike emotions? Comparative psychologists, among others, have long asked such questions, comparing the behavior and functioning of different species. They study which sorts of behavioral and psychological patterns are common to various groups of animals and which patterns set certain species apart.

There are a number of reasons for doing this research. Certainly some investigators are simply interested in gaining a more thorough understanding of the different animal species in our world. Other researchers have a particular interest in learning about human functioning and find that a greater understanding of other animals helps to clarify the origins, functions, and evolution of human processes.

Are some characteristics uniquely human? Take a moment to answer this question yourself. Can you identify skills, interests, or behaviors that are found in humans alone? By studying the psychological functioning of other animals, social psychologists, personality psychologists, developmental psychologists, learning and motivation psychologists, and others have been forced to reexamine some of those concepts that they had presumed set humans apart from others.

The next essay, "Conversations with the Dolphins," examines the dolphins' cognitive and, in particular, linguistic skills. You'll find that although much of the reported research was conducted by psychologists, other professionals, including computer specialists and biologists, have been involved as well. In fact, psychologists often work in interdisciplinary teams because the questions that are being asked typically do not fall into neat disciplinary categories.

This essay is not a psychological report, per se. *Rather, it is written by a general science writer for a popular magazine,* Psychology Today. *Examine the opening paragraphs, and note the rich, descriptive, literary quality of the first paragraph, in particular. What is the apparent goal of this opening paragraph? How might it have been written differently had the essay been written for professional psychologists whose expertise is dolphins?*

As you read through Chollar's essay, think about the ways in which the research findings add to your understanding not only of dolphins but also of humans. Does this information challenge the assumptions you've held about what characteristics are uniquely human?

Piercing the turquoise water of two interconnected pools, the hot Hawaiian sun projects dappled images on dolphins at play. Four powerful gray forms knife through the water, first skimming along the bottom, then tracing the pools' circumferences. From time to time 350 pounds of dolphin bursts effortlessly skyward, showering bystanders with cool drops.

Then a female, named Akeakamai, breaks with the game and swims tankside, where she peers over the rim at a group of humans gathering equipment and buckets of freshly thawed fish. Her trainer, Mark Xitco, deeply tanned and looking more like a surfer than a scientist, beckons to Akeakamai and speaks to her in a soft voice while stroking her head.

Then Xitco and Ake, as she is affectionately called, get down to business. He dons a pair of goggles dark enough to prevent Ake from seeing what he is looking at and, in quick succession, forms four hand signals that mean *basket, right, Frisbee* and *fetch*. Ake has been taught the meaning of each sign but has never before been given this particular combination. Unlike performing dolphins, which must be painstakingly taught each new trick, Ake immediately understands that this command tells her to "go to the Frisbee to your right and take it to the basket."

Ignoring a Frisbee floating near the left side of the pool, the dolphin heads to her right and scoops up the Frisbee floating there. She nudges it along the water's surface to a plastic basket floating thirty feet away and flips it in. A shrill whistle informs her that she has done well, and she swims over to Xitco for a plump herring and a word of encouragement.

To those reared on tales of Dr. Doolittle, the spectacle of a human "talking" to a dolphin may not seem surprising. But only a generation ago, the ability to use systems of abstract symbols, such as language, was defined as the exclusive purview of Homo sapiens — a skill that separated us from the beasts. In the past 10 years, however, language researchers have shown that dolphins do have the cognitive skills to understand simple language, including concepts such as direction and basic rules governing the sequence of words. Recently, dolphins have even started to talk back.

In the tank, two paddles are positioned along the edge: a white one, which to Ake symbolizes *yes* and a black one meaning *no*. With an index finger pointing skyward, Xitco calls the dolphin to attention, then forms two hand-signals that inquire, "Is a pipe in the pool?" Ake casts a quick glance around her water world then resolutely swims to the "no" paddle and presses it firmly with her snout.

Akeakamai (whose name, not coincidentally, means "lover of wisdom" in Hawaiian) lives at the Kewalo Basin Marine Mammal Laboratory, part of the University of Hawaii in Honolulu. The lab is also home to three other Atlantic bottle-nosed dolphins. Elele, a fast learner, and her rather recalcitrant male companion, Hiapo, are four-year-olds just getting to know the language-research ropes. Phoenix, a 13-year-old female like Ake, is a seasoned veteran. Both have been in language studies at the lab since 1979.

Psychologist Louis Herman, director of the lab, became interested in dolphin research in the mid-1970s, when studies of language in chimpanzees and other great apes were very much in vogue. He saw an excellent opportunity to parallel this type of research using dolphins, which he calls the "cognitive cousins" of the great apes.

Both types of animals are intelligent and highly social. "Primates and dolphins really depend upon a very complex network of social affiliations and interactions in order to make their living in the world," Herman says. "The glue that holds this network together is communication."

Wary of the difficulties encountered by researchers who had been trying to teach primates to "speak," Herman approached the animal language problem in a different way. He set out to test whether dolphins can comprehend language.

This approach appealed to Herman for several reasons. When an animal "speaks," it is sometimes difficult to determine if it knows what it's talking about. Koko, the gorilla that Penny Patterson trained in American Sign Language, once strung together a series of hand signals to produce the following sentence: "Please milk please me like drink apple bottle." Although it is evident that Koko was trying to convey a desire for something, it is not clear what.

Evaluating comprehension, in contrast, is fairly straightforward. When you ask an animal to carry out a specific task and offer it an edible reward, it is quickly apparent whether or not the animal understands. If Phoenix, for example, is asked to place the Frisbee in the basket but instead places it through the hoop, she will miss out on a tasty herring treat from her trainer.

Comprehension also appealed to Herman because he felt it was the most logical place to begin searching for language competency in animals. Human infants understand language before they begin to produce it, and some research indicates that comprehension may involve less complex mental skills than does language production.

To test dolphin comprehension, Herman designed two artificial languages. Ake mastered a vocabulary of hand signals. Phoenix learned an acoustic language composed of computer-generated, whistle-like sounds that are broadcast into the tank through an underwater speaker. Each gestural or auditory sign stands for either an object such as *Frisbee*, an action such as *fetch*, or a description of position such as *under*.

Phoenix and Ake have each learned approximately 50 "words," but according to Herman, the size of their vocabulary is not as important as the possibilities it presents. Herman and his staff have recombined the words, as one can do with a set of building blocks, to construct more than 1,000 different sentences, each eliciting an unlearned, unrehearsed response.

Teaching the animals to understand individual words or groups of words, however, wasn't enough. Herman wanted to test whether the dolphins could also master word order and syntax. It appears that they can. Phoenix learned a straightforward left-to-right grammar. To her, "Frisbee, in, basket" means place the Frisbee in the basket. Ake, however, was taught an inverse grammar, which requires her to comprehend the entire sequence before acting. The same request to Ake would be stated "basket, Frisbee, in."

Language can also conjure up images of things that aren't there—a skill known as displacement. Traditionally, linguists and other humans did not consider animals capable of using symbols to recall such images, but Herman's studies have shown that dolphins are indeed able to do so. That's what Ake was doing when Xitco asked if a pipe was in her tank. When asked whether a missing object is present, Ake and Phoenix press a paddle which stands for *no*. This suggests that an arbitrary symbol can conjure up an image of the missing object in the dolphin's mind.

Symbolic communication in dolphins is not confined to an observation tank. Out in the ocean, dolphins routinely use at least some of these language skills. Several studies have shown that dolphins use sound signals to identify themselves to other dolphins and to communicate their emotional state.

In the wild, dolphins produce two general categories of sounds: clicks, which they use to probe the world around them, the way a submarine uses sonar; and whistles, which play a central role in dolphin-to-dolphin communication. The function of many dolphin whistles is unknown, but biologist Peter Tyack of Woods Hole Oceanographic Institution in Massachusetts has found that, when dolphins swim together, at least half of the whistles that each produces are signature whistles, which identify the sender to the rest of the group.

At Kewalo Basin, psychologist James Ralston and computer specialist Humphrey Williams have found that the signature whistle can convey more than just a dolphin's identity. There may be messages about the dolphin's emotional state nested within the primary message.

Ralston and Williams compared acoustic pictures, or sonograms, of the dolphins' signature whistles during normal social activities and in stressful situations, such as when they are removed from the tank for routine veterinary procedures. They found that, when the animals are stressed, each dolphin's signature whistle keeps its general configuration but may change in pitch and duration. In other words, although dolphins may not have the words to say "I am worried," or "Danger is at hand," the manner in which they broadcast their signature whistle may convey that information to other members of their group.

Beyond identity or emotional state, there is no evidence that dolphins communicate more complex messages to each other in nature. "Can they talk about things in the past or in the future? Can they talk about things that never existed?" asks veteran dolphin watcher Kenneth Norris, a biologist at the University of California, Santa Cruz. "To date I see no syntactic language in dolphins at sea—no strings of abstract symbols like verbs, nouns and prepositions, which can carry nearly any message."

Even if they don't use symbolic communication systems in nature, Herman's work indicates that dolphins are capable of doing so, and this goes a long way toward knocking humans off the pedestal on which they were placed by linguists such as Noam Chomsky, who argues that teaching animals human language makes as much sense as teaching humans to fly: They don't have the capacity. "Some people think of language like pregnancy—you either have it or you don't," says Herman. "Others look at it as simply a continuum of skills. A linguist reviewing what our dolphins are doing might say that this is a relatively minor accomplishment. I would answer, 'If the dolphins saw us trying to make our way about through the water, would they call it swimming?'"

"People are getting less and less hung up on the notion that language should have evolved en masse in humans," Norris says. "In the animal kingdom, the precursors of language are all over the place."

Herman is now gearing up to find out whether dolphins are capable of producing language—of talking about things other than their identities or their moods. The yes/no paddles are a start, but Herman is now designing a device, similar to one being used in primate language research, that will allow the dolphins to say more. A large board displaying 16 different symbols will be placed on the floor of the dolphin tank. Each symbol will be selected from a vocabulary of as many as 50 symbols for objects, actions and modifiers.

When a dolphin presses one of the symbols, a visual record of that symbol will appear on a TV monitor that is visible to the dolphin through a window in the tank. As the dolphin continues to press "words," the visual record will grow, allowing the dolphin to keep track of what it has "said."

Herman can come up with many pragmatic reasons for teaching dolphins to talk to humans. "We may be able to interrogate them," he says. "We now ask, 'Is there a Frisbee in the tank?' It's not much of a stretch to say, 'Is there a whale out there? A submarine? What's on the bottom?'"

As you listen to Herman describe his work, though, you get the distinct impression that practical applications are not foremost in his mind. "What we're trying to do," he explains, "is to map out the many dimensions of their intellect, so that we can come to an understanding of what it's like cognitively to be a dolphin."

"The way [dolphins] think about the world is different," adds one of Herman's graduate students, Adam Pack. "We may never really know what it's like to be a dolphin, but it may be possible to meet on a common plane."

From Herman's office, you can look across a small courtyard through a window into one of the dolphin tanks. From time to time a dolphin peers back. What do the dolphins think of when they see scientists scurrying about, clipboards under arms, or hear the cacaphonic PA system paging members of the staff? Does Ake miss the murky waters of the Atlantic, where predators constantly lurk just out of sight? Does Phoenix enjoy her meals of smelt and herring?

Someday soon talking with the animals may not just be the stuff of fairy tales. Maybe then they will answer our questions.

OPTIONS FOR WRITING

1. This essay raises questions regarding how we should define language. Is it a continuum of skills or something whole and unique unto itself? Write a one- to two-page essay defining language. One strategy for doing so is to consider the criteria you would use to decide whether a particular animal or individual has language.

2. Researchers must frequently explain why their governments, their institutions, and other organizations should invest money in their research when there are so many other national and international needs such as starving and homeless people and life-threatening diseases. Write an essay of one or two pages in which you support the investment of funds in research on the linguistic abilities of dolphins. Then write a one- to two-page essay that argues against such an investment of money. End with a synopsis of what you personally think is the most reasonable stand on this issue.

8

THE PURSUIT
OF POLITICS

Kenneth M. Holland

> Politics is one subject on which almost everyone has an opinion,
> which is good because as citizens of a democracy, we have a wide
> range of political responsibilities. Many students, for instance, are at-
> tracted by the glamour and excitement of campaigning and working
> for local and national candidates and frequently spend their time
> analyzing and discussing the results of public opinion polls. Kenneth
> Holland explains how to read a poll and then shows us how to design
> and conduct our own public opinion survey.

READINGS

Thomas Jefferson   The Declaration of Independence

PUBLIC OPINION AND MASS SOCIETY

W. H. Auden   The Unknown Citizen

Alexis de Tocqueville   Of the Principal Source of Belief Among
Democratic Nations

James Madison   The Federalist No. 10: To the People of the State of
New York

MAJORITY TYRANNY: AMERICAN DEMOCRACY AND THE AFRICAN-AMERICAN EXPERIENCE

Frederick Douglass   What to the Slave is the Fourth of July? An Address
Delivered in Rochester, New York, on 5 July 1852

Martin Luther King, Jr.   Letter from Birmingham Jail

Abraham Lincoln   The Gettysburg Address, 1863

Edward Banfield, Allan Bloom, and Charles Murray   The Pursuit of Happiness: Then and Now

The Baltimore Sun   Election System Flawed, Poll Shows

Everett Carll Ladd   Abortion—The Partisan Consequences: Trouble for
Both Parties

The scene: a frozen lake in Vermont.

"Here's one," Arthur Thomas shouted across the frozen pond. Brad ran, or rather trotted, dressed as he was in heavy boots, wool pants, parka, and long underwear, to where his father knelt peering down at his discovery and brushing away the powdery snow blanketing the ice. "You can go through this one with no trouble at all. Looks like it was made yesterday. It didn't drop below zero last night, so it's probably only a couple of inches thick," he exclaimed, looking at a circular outline of about four inches in diameter on the ice.

"Hey, this is a great spot—it's not too far from the shanty." Brad's voice came from deep within his fur-lined hood, his much-valued shield from the icy wind blowing unimpeded from the hills to the north across the open pond, which the real estate developers had begun calling a lake, only a few miles from the Canadian border. "Let's hope there are some others nearby." Brad squatted over what had been an open hole the day before, where ice two feet thick had been cut in a few seconds by a power auger. Placing the point of his hand-operated tool over the center of the disk, he turned the crank with one gloved hand and pressed down on the handle with the other. Soon the ice began to yield, but a full minute passed before the drill broke through to the water below. As a kid, Brad had always complained that he and his father didn't have a power auger like most of the other fishers who braved the pond in winter, but as he cranked in the silence of the early morning January sun, somehow that didn't seem to matter anymore.

Later the pair sat inside the wooden shanty, which was dragged on skids out to the center of the pond each December. Arthur filled Brad's plastic cup with piping hot coffee from the large, metallic thermos. "Brad, you know, if you're going to vote in the March primary, you have to register soon. According to the state supreme court, because you're a college student, you can register here in Newport or in Burlington. Did you know my law firm represented one of the plaintiffs in that suit?"

"Yea, you mentioned that last year. To tell you the truth, Dad, I haven't given that too much thought. I've had a few other things on my mind, like enjoying my vacation. Anyway, I don't think most of my friends are registered. Besides, Chuck Feeley said that if you are registered to vote you can be called up for jury duty and might have to miss classes."

"I don't mean to be a pain, but did you register with the Selective Service System on your birthday?"

"I had basketball practice on the fifteenth, but I did drop by the post office after my math exam the next day. I thought about putting it off, but the college paper had a story about two guys who were arrested and put on trial last year for not registering. My sociology prof, Dr. Stokes, says the government is keeping draft registration because it's planning to invade a lot of Third World countries. Now that the Russians are no threat, he says we will try to dominate South America, Africa, and the Middle East. We'll leave Asia to the Japanese and Eastern Europe to the Germans." He reached for one of the roast beef sandwiches they had packed.

"Are there any conservative teachers left in the universities? When I went to school in the sixties, there were at least a few who supported the Vietnam war. What else does your professor say about our foreign policy? You said he was a sociologist, right?"

"Yea, but he's pretty active in political causes on campus and in town. Seems like he's always marching or protesting something. He says we ignore international law whenever we want. Dad, did we pack any brownies?"

"That's the problem with the colleges today; you've got a bunch of hippies and radicals on the faculty left over from the protests against the war who've never worked a day in their lives. They intimidated their teachers and administrators in the sixties with their strikes and sit-ins, got Ph.D.s in the seventies, and got tenure in the eighties. They don't realize the war is over—the times have passed them by. At least your generation seems to have some common sense." He emptied the thermos into his mug and held its warmth in his icy hands. "Anyway, why does he think we want to conquer what he calls the Third World?"

"Hey, I studied this for my final. He says that most American politicians represent the interests of the rich and that the President and the Congress work together to maintain capitalism. Because capitalism demands more and more markets, the United States is driven to dominate other countries. He said it was ridiculous of the President to call the Soviet Union an evil empire when we have a far from angelic empire of our own that already includes most of Latin America. He's always telling us about President Johnson's invasion of the Dominican Republic, Reagan's invasion of some island in the Caribbean that begins with a G, and Bush's invasion of Panama."

"You know, Brad, Thoreau refused to pay his taxes because he opposed our war against Mexico back in the 1840s. I wonder if your Dr. Stokes is willing to go that far in protesting American foreign policy? By the way, it's time for you to file your own income tax return. You can pick up a 1040 form on your next trip to the post office. It's due April 15." Refreshed by food and drink, father and son stepped out into the icy sunshine.

WRITING 1.

If you could pick one person to talk politics with, who would it be? Why? What topics would you like to discuss?

WHAT IS POLITICAL SCIENCE?

The subject of the conversation between Brad Thomas and his father is politics. Unlike physics, with its search for quarks and other mysterious subatomic particles, politics is a subject on which almost everyone has an opinion. Even those Americans, the majority, who do not read the political coverage in their newspapers receive a great quantity of political information and opinion from radio and television news and from current events programming. Opinions, however, no matter how dear they are to us, are not the same as knowledge. If it is true that there is a bewildering array of opinion on political issues, such as the wisdom of the U.S. military operations in the Third World and the immunity of women from the draft registration requirement, is it also true that one of these opinions is true and the others false? In other words, is there a science of politics?

Political science is in fact the oldest of the social sciences. Its founder was the ancient Greek philosopher Socrates, who, although he sought knowledge of all things above and below the earth, was especially attracted to the study of human things. According to Socrates the most important question that a human being can pose is "How ought I to live?" The answer to this question, he taught, is inseparable from the broader inquiry, "How ought we as a community to live?" Socrates, we are told in the writings of his young interlocutors Plato and Xenophon, sought to construct "the best city in speech," the ideal political system, which would serve as a standard by which all existing rulers and regimes could be judged.

Plato's student, Aristotle, described politics as a practical science, like ethics and shipbuilding, as opposed to a theoretical science, like theology and physics. The aim of the practical branches of knowledge is to guide human action, which has as its end something other than knowledge itself—a good life, the prosperity of the community, a cargo ship. The object of the theoretical sciences is not action but knowledge, knowledge of the attributes of God, for example, or of the laws governing the solar system. The study of politics is especially advantageous to founders of countries and to rulers. In a democracy, however, it becomes useful to everyone. Only in a democratic regime are the rulers and the ruled supposed to be the same: "government of the people, by the people, and for the people," in Abraham Lincoln's immortal description. In order for popular self-government to succeed, each citizen must become informed about the workings of federal, state, and local government and must develop informed opinions on a wide variety of controversial public issues, ranging from prohibiting abortion to aiding Zambia.

Democratic citizens have not only more freedom than a dictator's subjects but also more duties. Although we do not go as far as the democracy of ancient Athens, where the citizens met in a single assembly and made the laws directly themselves, and where most political offices were filled by lot from among the citizen body as a whole, the conversation between Mr. Thomas and his son illustrates the range of political responsibilities imposed on U.S. citizens. At eighteen, Brad had to register for possible conscription into the armed forces and, soon after, was expected to register to vote, to go to the polls on election day and cast his ballot, to make himself available to serve as a juror in a civil or criminal trial, and to pay income taxes. In about one-half of the fifty states, voters not only choose their legislators and other political leaders from among competing candidates but also determine policy questions directly through the town meeting or through the popular initiative and referendum.

In contrast to history offerings, most political science courses explore current events. Instructors in American politics courses frequently address issues surrounding campaigns and elections, and the typical fare of those who teach international relations includes U.S. actions affecting other countries, both friend and foe. In political science departments, today's headlines are often the introduction to tomorrow's lecture. Many instructors trained in the science of politics not only inform their students on public issues and help them learn how to enlighten themselves but also show them how to influence political decision making, especially in the American government curriculum.

WRITING 2.

Look at the front page of today's newspaper. Which headlines refer to a political event or issue? Which of these articles interests you most? Why? Does it refer to matters that you would like to know more about? Describe them.

The Subfields of Political Science

In their brief interchange of fact and opinion, Brad and his dad touched upon at least three of the five subfields into which political science is often divided.

American Politics. The Thomases made a number of allusions to American politics, the first subfield, in their discussion of the draft registration law, for instance, and of the failure of Congress to criticize presidents' military ventures. Political scientists within this category tend to specialize in one of the three branches of government or in political parties or interest groups.

Political Theory. Political theory, which traces its roots to the writings of Plato and Aristotle, is less practical and less focused on current events. It is based on the assumption that ideas have consequences; that is, that political events, such as the popular movements in Eastern

Europe in 1989 and 1990 that led to the collapse of one hardline Communist government after another and to democratic reforms and the development of free market economies, are often the product of changes in the theories that people regard as true concerning politics and the human condition. One branch of the theory subfield is the history of political philosophy, in which the teacher and student explore together the classic texts of ancient, medieval, and modern political thought. The careful reading of texts such as Plato's *Republic* or Machiavelli's *The Prince* is not motivated by mere antiquarian interests but by a belief that learning to see the world through the eyes of history's most profound political observers is necessary to acquire a standpoint outside the present from which one can better understand and judge the ideas and prejudices that form the twentieth-century mind. Dr. Stokes, Brad's sociology professor, seems especially interested in the questions posed by Karl Marx and his disciples concerning the imperialistic nature of capitalism.

International Relations.   Brad speculated on a possible division of global influence among the United States, Japan, and Germany. Here he ventured into the domain of the third subfield, international relations. As many as one-half of all political science majors seem primarily interested in the study of the relations among sovereign nation-states. Perhaps this curiosity is due to the high stakes of international politics, in which a dispute between two countries may quickly explode into violence and war or a treaty between the United States and the Soviet Union can result in massive reductions in military spending. International relations issues often lend themselves to dramatic treatment, such as the U.S. response to the taking of American hostages in Iran or the Persian Gulf War. Foreign relations is also a subfield of history.

Comparative Politics.   Part of the allure of the fourth subfield, comparative politics, is identical to that of international relations — the natural curiosity about foreign places. Imagining oneself in Moscow or Tokyo while reading or discussing Soviet or Japanese politics is a pleasant and inexpensive way to travel. Specialists in comparative politics study the political systems of countries other than the United States. They are not so much concerned with the relations between countries as they are in the political systems within a country. Some comparativists focus on what they call political economy, and in fact many economists are concerned with the economies of other countries. There is a subgroup of economists especially interested in the study of economic development in poor countries.

Political Behavior.   Specialists in this area tend to be interested in methodology, that is, in studying how we can obtain real knowledge about political phenomena and move beyond mere opinion or speculation. They tend to be skeptical about the traditional emphasis on distinguishing good regimes from bad regimes and to stress the limitations of nonempirical research. They are likely to concentrate their efforts on the collection of data and to rely on computers, eschewing the "armchair" philosophizing engaged in by scholars in political theory. Behavioralists (not to be confused with behaviorists, who constitute a school within psychology) draw heavily on the scientific method, which has produced undeniably remarkable advances in the physical sciences with its emphasis on experimentation. Behavioralists seek to explain and predict political behavior, not to judge or guide it. Quite a few of these quantitatively oriented political scientists devote themselves to the analysis of voting patterns or to the measurement of public opinion. There is a good deal of overlap here between political science and sociology, which as a discipline is behaviorally oriented and interested in measuring and predicting broad patterns of social behavior. In fact, social methodology courses are often cross-listed in political science and sociology departments.

Career Options

Political science is one of the majors most favored by students in the liberal arts. This popularity is striking, since most college freshmen have not taken a political science course in high school. Another source of wonder is the fact that, unlike many liberal arts majors such as economics or chemistry, political science offers no clear career path to its graduates. The most plausible explanation of student preference for political science is its inherent fascination and the degree to which politics touches our lives. It is thus not surprising that a father and his college-age son choose to discuss politics in a shanty on a frozen pond while they warm themselves with hot coffee and wait for the pickerel and perch to bite.

Political science majors enter a myriad of careers. Most are hired by the same firms that hire other liberal arts majors. Those who do not enter business tend to pursue careers in law, government, journalism, or teaching.

Law. Although many prelaw students major in political science, law schools, unlike medical schools, require no particular undergraduate course of study. Law schools admit students from a variety of backgrounds without specific preference. Law school admissions are based largely on the applicant's undergraduate grade point average and score on the Law School Admissions Test.

Government. The political science major may find a job in nearly any agency or branch of the federal government. There has been little growth, however, in the number of civilian federal employees over the past twenty years. There has been significant increase, however, in the number of state and local government employees, and many political science majors find positions at this level. Popular with some majors is work in the electoral campaign of political candidates — an experience that can result in government employment.

Foreign Service. With the high enrollments in international relations courses, it is not surprising that many political science majors are interested in careers with the foreign service, the diplomatic, consular, commercial, and overseas cultural and information service of the United States. The foreign service assists the President and Secretary of State in planning, conducting, and implementing U.S. foreign policy. Only a small percentage of majors, however, succeed in passing the many hurdles, including a written examination and an oral interview, erected by the State Department.

Journalism. Journalists report on every aspect of human behavior — social, political, and economic. Because much reporting involves political issues and institutions, political science is a logical major for those interested in this career. Writing skills, of course, are critical. In the 1970s investigative reporters such as Bob Woodward became national heroes and contributed to the attractiveness of journalism as a career for college graduates. Like the foreign service, however, journalism has a very tight job market and is highly competitive.

Teaching. Political science, as such, is not usually taught at the secondary level, so majors with teaching ambitions tend to go on to graduate school. A master's degree is necessary for teaching at the junior college level, and a Ph.D. is generally required to obtain a position at a four-year college or university. Again, the job market is tight, and little growth is expected in the size of American institutions of higher education. There is always room, of course, for excellent teachers or scholars who have distinguished themselves in their graduate programs.

THE PUBLIC OPINION POLL

The political science majors who are attracted by the glamor and excitement of political campaigning and who are employed by candidates for local, state, and federal office spend much of their time analyzing and discussing the results of public opinion polls. During the long campaigns characteristic of American politics, the voters themselves are not only polled, usually by telephone, but also bombarded by their morning newspaper and evening news broadcast with the most recent poll data. Scientific sampling of voter preferences has become an indispensable tool in contemporary electoral politics. Periodic polling can alert the candidate that his or her campaign strategy is not working or can indicate weaknesses in the opponent's candidacy that can be fruitfully exploited. These polls are useful because, if done properly, they are accurate.

On Monday, 7 November 1988, for example, the eve of the 1988 presidential election, the Gallup Poll proclaimed that George Bush would defeat Michael Dukakis. The poll showed the Republican candidate leading his Democratic rival in the popular vote by 53 percent to 42 percent with 5 percent undecided. The poll was remarkably prescient, for the actual election results showed Bush with 54 percent and Dukakis with 46 percent. In fact, in twelve of the last thirteen presidential elections, the American people have known who the victor would be before the first voter stepped into a voting booth. The development of scientific public opinion polling in the 1930s made these election forecasts possible.

Today, polls are a feature of daily life in the United States and are used to influence public policy makers as well as voters. Glance through the pages of a daily newspaper or weekly news magazine or watch the network evening news and you are likely to find a report of the results of somebody's poll. While driving to the university today, I heard on the radio news, "This morning, another death row inmate was electrocuted in Florida. Poll reveals that a majority of Americans support capital punishment." On my desk is a newspaper article announcing, "According to latest poll, most Filipinos favor continuation of American military bases in their country." Such barometers of public opinion can play critical roles in the making of political decisions. The first poll may influence one or two more states to prescribe death as a punishment for murder. The second may help persuade the government of the Philippines to allow the Americans to stay in the Clark Air Force and Subic Bay Naval bases. Polls, in fact, have become an essential feature of all democratic regimes and are used both to legitimate and to challenge government policies.

How to Read a Poll

The results of many polls are presented in graphic form and can thus be somewhat daunting to the reader. These tables are actually easy to understand if you know the proper questions to pose. Table 8.1 is typical of those found in political science journals. A political scientist was interested in what American taxpayers think of the way in which the federal government spends their money. According to democratic theory, the spending behavior of the government should reflect the preferences of the people. The researcher selected ten objects of public spending, ranging from programs designed to benefit black Americans to the public schools. He then asked each respondent whether he thought government spending on each of the ten issues was "too little," "about right," or "too much."

TABLE 8.1 Attitudes on Public Spending Issues

	Too Little (%)	About Right (%)	Too Much (%)
Blacks	20.4	58.5	21.0
Food stamps	21.3	46.0	32.6
Defense	27.7	47.2	25.1
Environment	36.5	55.2	8.3
Science	38.3	50.2	11.4
Medicine	49.7	45.4	4.9
Social security	52.1	44.3	3.6
Unemployment	53.8	31.8	14.4
Crime	53.9	41.5	4.6
Public schools	54.4	39.9	5.7

Note: Rows sum to 100 percent. Percentages are responses to the question "Is the federal government spending too little, too much, or about right on [the issue]?" The error margin is + or − 2 percent. Based on a national random telephone survey of 3,496 adult Americans.

WRITING 3.

Interpret the results of the survey shown in Table 8.1. On which issues is there broad public support? On which issues is the public less supportive? Compare, for instance, public attitudes toward spending on crime and defense. Can you infer from these data that Americans place greater value on safe streets than on a secure nation? Does this table help you understand what Americans want from their government?

Understanding the Results

What are the decisions that a survey researcher must make when conceiving of and designing a public opinion poll? If you understand the researcher's options, much of the mystery surrounding the polling process will dissipate, and you will be able to make better use of the published results.

First, what is the population whose opinions are being determined? Is it all registered voters in the United States? Is it all citizens of the Philippines? Is it all college students enrolled in public colleges and universities in Pennsylvania? The population surveyed in Table 8.1 is all adult Americans.

The second question regards how many members of this population were actually interviewed. If the population is small enough, for example, an English composition class of 25 students, it is feasible to ascertain the opinions of every member. Most opinion surveys, however, are confined to a tiny percentage of the whole group. This subpopulation is called a sample. The note with Table 8.1 tells us that 3,496 respondents were interviewed. Most national presidential preference polls employ a smaller sample, usually about 1,200.

Third, how do you know that the opinions or preferences of the small sample accurately represent those of the larger whole? The answer lies in the manner in which the sample was drawn. The most reliable technique for identifying a representative cross-section is random selection. If each voter in the United States had an equal chance of being selected in a presidential poll, for example, then the sample's results for the presidential candidates will faithfully reflect the preferences of the total voting population. The researcher who obtained the findings in Table 8.1 used the technique of random digit dialing, in which every residential telephone number in the United States, regardless of whether it is listed in the telephone book, has an equal chance of being dialed. The randomness of the sample is much more important than its size. This fact was well illustrated by the infamous *Literary Digest* poll of 1936. At the conclusion of the 1936 campaign, the *Literary Digest*, a mass-circulation magazine, published survey results forecasting a landslide victory for the Republican candidate, Alf Landon. Actually, the incumbent Democratic candidate, Franklin Roosevelt, won by a landslide. The magazine sent out more than 10 million ballots. The sample was drawn from automobile registration lists and telephone books. This meant that those who owned neither a telephone nor an automobile were excluded. Moreover, only 25% of the ballots were returned. More devastating was the fact that those who responded favored Landon over Roosevelt and thus did not represent a random sample of all voters. Republicans, although outnumbered, were more intensely committed to their candidate than Democrats and were thus more willing to make the effort to complete and return the survey.

Conventional practice is to settle for an error margin of plus or minus 5 percent. Thus, for the typical presidential poll, the researcher does not claim to be 100 percent certain that, for example, the candidate will receive 55 percent of the votes cast on election day. Rather, the more modest claim is made that that candidate will receive between 50 and 60 percent of the vote. The fourth question, then, asks about the survey's error margin. The reference in the table indicates that the margin of error for each percentage reported is 2%.

Fifth, how were the interviews conducted? Surveys are conducted in person, through the mail, or over the telephone. There are a number of advantages and disadvantages associated with each method. Face-to-face and telephone surveys involve interaction between the interviewer and respondent. Mail surveys are more impersonal but much less costly, especially if the sample is geographically dispersed. Presidential preference polls are nearly always conducted over the telephone because of the need for quick results. The survey of attitudes toward government spending was done by telephone.

The sixth question concerns the purpose of the poll. Why would a researcher want to know how residents of New York City rate its quality of life? Why would a political scientist ask citizens if they would allow an admitted Communist to teach in a college? In the social sciences, public opinion is measured in order to test hunches or beliefs that the researcher has about human behavior. A poll is the social science equivalent of an experiment in the natural sciences. Both experiments and opinion surveys are used to validate or invalidate suppositions about the world. Scientists call these suppositions hypotheses. For instance, a political scientist might hypothesize that richer people tend to be Republicans and that poorer people are often Democrats. A survey that asked respondents to identify their income and party affiliation would have as its purpose the testing of this hypothesis. The researcher's hypothesis can usually be found in the abstract that precedes the findings. Here is the abstract of the article in which Table 8.1 appeared:

> People's attitudes on public spending issues are often depicted as irrational, desiring something for nothing. The data, however, reveal that this proposition may not be true. Most people do want to increase or continue spending on many programs.

The hypothesis, then, tested by the researcher was the common belief that citizens do not support high levels of government spending, even though they may benefit from federal programs. The poll revealed the error of this assumption.

Finally, how many questions did the interviewer pose, and how were the questions worded? At the heart of any poll is the question. Some questionnaires consist of one question, others of several dozen. The note with Table 8.1 indicates that the questionnaire, or interview schedule, consisted of ten questions, one for each category of expenditure.

SUGGESTIONS FOR RESEARCH
Designing and Conducting a Poll

A good way to get a feel for what political scientists do is to design and administer your own questionnaire. Think of how often we attempt to buttress our opinions or arguments by such phrases as "most of my friends agree that . . . ," "most students here favor . . . ," and "people don't care that. . . ." The difficulty with such assertions, of course, is the fact that you rarely have any solid basis for drawing such generalizations. A well-conceived opinion survey provides a firm foundation.

Selecting the Issue

Now that you have been introduced to the public opinion poll, you can design and conduct one yourself. You will need a journal or log book to complete this project.

1. Select a problem or behavior in need of explanation (for example, the conflict between parents and their children, the so-called generation gap, the lack of universal access to health care in the United States).
2. State a hypothesis that you suspect is true and that can be empirically tested (for example, that college students are more liberal than their parents or that Americans have a distaste for socialized medicine).
3. Write in your journal why you think this topic is important and why you are interested in it. Next, identify a hypothesis. How is this supposition related to the general topic of interest?

Designing the Poll

Now you will design the poll.

4. Choose an interview mode—personal interview, telephone survey, or mail questionnaire.
5. Identify a population, such as the students of your university or the students in your English composition class.
6. Choose to survey either the entire population or a sample of it (for example, a random sample of the students in your university or every student in your English composition course). If you choose to survey the opinions of a sample, choose a sample size and a method for drawing a random sample (for example, every twentieth name in the student directory, beginning with the number between one and twenty drawn from a hat).
7. Design the questionnaire. The rule here is parsimony: Avoid unnecessary questions. Every question should contribute to the survey's purpose. Another tip is to arrange the questions in the sequence most likely to elicit complete responses. Some questions require more thought than others, and some are perceived by the respondent as threatening, such as inquiries concerning political affiliation, income, drug use, or sexual behavior. Respondents often fear that interviewers are really salespeople or government agents. The interviewer must overcome reluctance to cooperate. Questionnaires often begin with specific factual questions that are easy to answer and then move on to broader questions of opinion. This arrangement is called the funnel method.

Questions are either closed-ended or open-ended, factual or designed to measure opinions or attitudes. In closed-ended questions, familiar to you as multiple-choice questions on examinations, the respondent must select from answer categories provided by the interviewer. Example:

Q. What is your age?
____ 18–24   ____ 25–34   ____ 35–45   ____ 46–55   ____ 56+

Open-ended questions are not followed by any list of possible answers. Example:

Q. In your opinion, what is the biggest problem facing American society today?

Opinions are expressions of thought or belief; attitudes are the feelings or orientations that underlie opinions. Opposition to capital punishment, for example, is an opinion; political liberalism is an attitude. There are also contingency questions, which the respondent answers only if he or she answered the previous question in a certain way. Example:

Q. Do you play a varsity sport?
____ Yes   ____ No
Q. If you answered yes to the above question, which sport do you play?
____ Football ____ Baseball ____ Hockey ____ Basketball ____ Other

Using the categories of closed-ended and open-ended, classify the following questions taken from a survey of college students.

1. College class? ____ freshman ____ sophomore ____ junior ____ senior ____ grad. student
2. Where do your parents live? city/county _____
   state _____
3. What would you estimate your family's income to be?
   less than $20,000 ____ $20,000 to $50,000 ____ over $50,000 ____
4. Generally speaking, do you usually think of yourself as a Democrat, Republican, or independent?
   Democrat ____   Republican ____   independent ____   other ____
5. If you checked Democrat or Republican, would you call yourself a strong or not-so-strong party supporter?
   strong Democrat ____   strong Republican ____
   not-so-strong Democrat ____   not-so-strong Republican ____
6. Where do you think most students not living with their parents should register and vote?
   at their college address ____   at their parents' address ____
7. If you are registered in your college community, please check any of the following reasons that help explain your choice.
   ____ Voting near college is easier and more convenient than absentee voting or driving to my parents' home.
   ____ I want to have some influence on government policies in my college area.
   ____ I am better informed on politics in my college area than on the affairs of my parents' community.
   ____ I have never lived where my family is now living.

_____ I am more interested in what is going on in my college community than in what is happening where my parents live.
_____ other (please explain)_____

8. If you checked more than one reason in the previous question, rank them by placing a number beside the check mark (1 is most important, 6 is least important).

9. If you are registered where your parents live, please state the reasons for your choice in the space provided:

10. Answer the following question only if your parents live in a different state. My interest in state politics is (check one space):
_____ Greater in parents' state   _____ Greater in college area

What do you think is the purpose of this survey? Which hypothesis is the researcher attempting to test?

8. Draw up a questionnaire or interview schedule. Include both closed-ended and open-ended questions — questions of fact, opinion, and attitude.

Conducting the Poll

9. You may conduct a poll by mail, by telephone, or in person. Most respondents, if they are willing to open their door to a stranger, will answer questions posed by interviewers who come to their home, and experience indicates that only 4 percent of respondents reached by telephone will terminate the interview before it is completed. The response rate for a mail questionnaire, however, is much lower, varying from 20 percent to 50 percent. The low response rate for the _Literary Digest_ poll contributed powerfully to its failure. Critical to persuading recipients to complete a questionnaire is the cover letter. In this letter, the researcher must promise strict confidentiality and must inform the reader of the sponsorship of the survey, its purpose, and the importance of the recipient's cooperation.

Identify the preceding elements in the following cover letter.

Dear Friend:

We are conducting a survey sponsored by the University of Wisconsin-Milwaukee and assisted by the American Civil Liberties Union (ACLU). Our purpose is to learn more about how people like yourself feel about certain aspects of civil liberties and how beliefs are related to behavior. You have been selected at random to participate in this survey — thus, your opinions will represent the opinions of thousands of people much like yourself. We promise you confidentiality. Your name will not be revealed or associated with your response, nor will anyone outside of the project staff here at the University of Wisconsin-Milwaukee be allowed to see your response.

If you choose to conduct your poll by mail, be sure to write a careful cover letter. College students in their cover letters often indicate that they are doing the survey as a requirement for a particular course and that their grade depends on the number of persons who answer the questionnaire. Although some social scientists pay respondents to complete their questionnaires, most researchers appeal to the recipient's altruistic impulses. It is necessary, nevertheless, always to include with the questionnaire a self-addressed, stamped envelope.

10. If you choose to interview the respondents, take notes. Unlike telephone and mail surveys, face-to-face interviews yield information about the respondent's environment and nonverbal messages, which may help explain the respondent's answers. Was the home tidy and clean or dirty and in disarray? Were other people present during the interview, and did they influence the respondent's answers? Was the respondent friendly and open or closed and hostile? Was the respondent distracted by anything in the environment, such as a cooking dinner? How would you describe the respondent's body language? In a personal interview, the researcher can determine the subject's race and sex and approximate age, education, and social class without explicitly asking for this information. Thus, in addition to posing questions from the interview schedule, the interviewer carefully observes the respondent and the environment, making notes and recording this information in an interview journal. The journal is a place for recording and reflecting on the interview situation and often proves invaluable during the data interpretation stage of the research.

Keep your research log with you as you conduct the survey. Note any aspects of the environment or incidents that might have affected the candor of the respondent's answers.

11. If you choose to conduct a telephone survey, prepare a brief introduction similar to the cover letter on page 511 in which you introduce yourself and explain the purpose of your survey. Before posing the first question, tell the respondent approximately how long the interview will take. If you don't get an answer, call back several times, if necessary, at different times of the day. If you leave a message on an answering machine, the respondent is likely either not to return your call or to call back when you are unavailable. Be careful to select the telephone numbers at random.

12. Examine the data collected, and present them in the form of a figure or table accompanied by a narrative. Do the results tend to confirm or deny your hypothesis? What are the broader implications of your findings? What additional research do they inspire?

13. Compose a table presenting your data. Write a description of your study and an analysis of your results.

READINGS

Thomas Jefferson
THE DECLARATION OF INDEPENDENCE

Many Americans regard the Declaration of Independence as the cornerstone of our democracy. Its function in our political system is to provide the theory on which the Constitution, a blueprint for government, rests. The key paragraph in the Declaration tells us the true purpose of government and provides a standard for judging those who wield political power. Some say that a careful reading reveals that the Declaration is not about democracy at all but is actually concerned with freedom.

The Continental Congress meeting in Philadelphia in the summer of 1776 designated a committee of five to compose a declaration of independence. The committee chose Thomas Jefferson to write it. Jefferson was born in Shadwell, Virginia, in 1743 and died in 1826; he was the third president of the United States (1801–1809). Two other committee members, John Adams and Benjamin Franklin, and the full Congress made a few changes in Jefferson's draft, deleting, for example, his uncompromising condemnation of the international slave trade, for which Jefferson blamed the king.

The delegates signed the document on 4 July 1776. Its ringing words have inspired numerous popular revolts and wars of independence, from the French Revolution in 1789 to the struggles for sovereignty waged by many Soviet republics in the 1990s. What are the colonists' major grievances against the king? Who is Jefferson's audience, and what does he want from that audience?

IN CONGRESS, JULY 4, 1776
THE UNANIMOUS DECLARATION OF THE THIRTEEN UNITED STATES OF AMERICA

When in the Course of human events, it becomes necessary for one people to dissolve the political bands which have connected them with another, and to assume among the powers of the earth, the separate and equal station to which the Laws of Nature and of Nature's God entitle them, a decent respect to the opinions of mankind requires that they should declare the causes which impel them to the separation.

We hold these truths to be self-evident, that all men are created equal, that they are endowed by their Creator with certain unalienable Rights, that among these are Life, Liberty and the pursuit of Happiness.

That to secure these rights, Governments are instituted among Men, deriving their just powers from the consent of the governed. That whenever any Form of Government becomes destructive of these ends, it is the Right of the People to alter or to abolish it, and to institute new Government, laying its foundation on such principles and organizing its powers in such form, as to them shall seem most likely to effect their Safety and Happiness. Prudence, indeed, will dictate that Governments long established should not be changed for light and transient causes; and accordingly all experience hath shown that mankind are more disposed to suffer, while evils are sufferable, than to right themselves by abolishing the forms to which they are accustomed. But when a long train of abuses and usurpations, pursuing invariably the same Object, evinces a design to reduce them under absolute Despotism, it is their right, it is their duty, to throw off such Government, and to provide new Guards for their future security. Such has been the patient sufferance of these Colonies; and such is now the necessity which constrains them to alter their former Systems of Government. The history of the present King of Great Britain is a history of repeated injuries and usurpations, all having in direct object the establishment of an absolute Tyranny over these States. To prove this, let Facts be submitted to a candid world.

He has refused his Assent to Laws, the most wholesome and necessary for the public good.

He has forbidden his Government to pass laws of immediate and pressing importance, unless suspended in their operation till his Assent should be obtained; and when so suspended, he has utterly neglected to attend to them.

He has refused to pass other Laws for the accommodation of large districts of people, unless those people would relinquish the right of Representation in the Legislature, a right inestimable to them and formidable to tyrants only.

He has called together legislative bodies at places unusual, uncomfortable, and distant from the depository of their Public Records, for the sole purpose of fatiguing them into compliance with his measures.

He has dissolved Representative Houses repeatedly, for opposing with manly firmness his invasions on the rights of the people.

He has refused for a long time, after such dissolutions, to cause others to be elected; whereby the Legislative Powers, incapable of Annihilation, have returned to the People at large for their exercise; the State remaining in the mean time exposed to all the dangers of invasion from without, and convulsions within.

He has endeavored to prevent the population of these States; for that purpose obstructing the Laws for Naturalization of Foreigners; refusing to pass others to encourage their migration hither, and raising the conditions of new Appropriations of Lands.

He has obstructed the Administration of Justice, by refusing his Assent to Laws for establishing Judiciary Powers.

He has made Judges dependent on his Will alone, for the tenure of their offices, and the amount and payment of their salaries.

He has erected a multitude of New Offices, and sent hither swarms of Officers to harass our people, and eat out their substance.

He has kept among us, in times of peace, Standing Armies without the Consent of our legislatures.

He has affected to render the Military independent of and superior to the Civil Power.

He has combined with others to subject us to a jurisdiction foreign to our constitution, and unacknowledged by our laws; giving his Assent to their Acts of pretended Legislation: For quartering large bodies of armed troops among us: For protecting them, by a mock Trial, from punishment for any Murders which they should commit on the Inhabitants of these States: For cutting off our Trade with all parts of the world: For imposing Taxes on us without our Consent: For depriving us in many cases, of the benefits of Trial by Jury; For transporting us beyond Seas to be tried for pretended offenses; for abolishing the free System of English laws in a neighboring Province, establishing therein an Arbitrary government, and enlarging its Boundaries so as to render it at once an example and fit instrument for introducing the same absolute rule into these Colonies; For taking away our Charters, abolishing our most valuable Laws and altering fundamentally the Forms of our Governments: For suspending our own Legislatures, and declaring themselves invested with power to legislate for us in all cases whatsoever.

He has abdicated Government here, by declaring us out of his Protection and waging War against us.

He has plundered our seas, ravaged our Coasts, burnt our towns, and destroyed the lives of our people.

He is at this time transporting large Armies of foreign Mercenaries to complete the works of death, desolation and tyranny, already begun with circumstances of Cruelty & Perfidy scarcely paralleled in the most barbarous ages, and totally unworthy the Head of a civilized nation.

He has constrained our fellow Citizens taken Captive on the high Seas to bear Arms against their Country, to become the executioners of their friends and Brethren, or to fall themselves by their Hands.

He has excited domestic insurrections amongst us, and has endeavored to bring on the inhabitants of our frontiers, the merciless Indian Savages, whose known rule of warfare, is an undistinguished destruction of all ages, sexes, and conditions.

In every stage of these Oppressions We have Petitioned for Redress in the most humble terms: Our repeated Petitions have been answered only by repeated injury. A Prince, whose character is thus marked by every act which may define a Tyrant, is unfit to be the ruler of a free people.

Nor have We been wanting in attention to our British brethren. We have warned them from time to time of attempts by their legislature to extend an unwarrantable jurisdiction over us. We have reminded them of the circumstances of our emigration and settlement here. We have appealed to their native justice and magnanimity, and we have conjured them by the ties of our common kindred to disavow these usurpations, which would inevitably interrupt our connections and correspondence. They too have been deaf to the voice of justice and consanguinity. We must, therefore, acquiesce in the necessity, which denounces our Separation, and hold them, as we hold the rest of mankind, Enemies in War, in Peace Friends.

We, therefore, the Representatives of the United States of America, in General Congress, Assembled, appealing to the Supreme Judge of the world for the rectitude of our intentions, do, in the Name, and by Authority of the good People of these Colonies, solemnly publish and declare, That these United Colonies are, and of Right ought to be FREE AND INDEPENDENT STATES; that they are absolved from all Allegiance to the British Crown, and that all political connection between them and the State of Great Britain, is and ought to be totally dissolved; and that as Free and Independent States, they have full Power to levy War, conclude Peace, contract Alliances, establish Commerce, and to do all other Acts and Things which Independent States may of right do. And for the support of this Declaration, with a firm reliance on the protection of Divine Providence, we mutually pledge to each other our Lives, our Fortunes, and our sacred Honor.

OPTIONS FOR WRITING

1. Analyze the declaration's indictment of King George III. Is he an illegitimate ruler over the colonists because they did not elect him or because of other reasons? Would the Americans have been justified in rebelling against the crown if the British king had been a benevolent prince? What do you think gives government the right to tell you what you can and cannot do?

2. Describe the meaning of these phrases: "all men are created equal," "right to life," "the pursuit of happiness," and "consent of the governed."

3. Select one of the following relationships, and do some research on both parties.
1. The American colonies and the Kingdom of Great Britain in the 1700s
2. The Confederate States of America and the United States of America in the 1800s
3. A Soviet Republic (such as Latvia, Lithuania, Estonia, the Ukraine, Azerbaijan) and the Soviet Union
4. Quebec and Canada
5. Northern Ireland and the Kingdom of Great Britain
Write a dialogue between a spokesperson for secession and a leader of the country that the smaller group wishes to leave. Include references to public opinion in your dialogue.

Public Opinion and Mass Society

W. H. Auden
THE UNKNOWN CITIZEN

*The next two readings, the work of foreign-born observers of the
United States — a poem, "The Unknown Citizen," by W. H. Auden,
and a chapter, "Of the Principal Source of Belief Among Democratic
Nations," from Alexis de Tocqueville's* Democracy in America —
*raise serious questions about the extent to which democracy threatens
principles which the authors regard as more worthy than majority
rule. As you read, identify those goods which may be imperilled.*

*W. H. Auden (1907–1973) was a poet, critic, and playwright
who was born in York, England. He was quite familiar with American democracy, however, having emigrated to the United States
shortly before the outbreak of World War II and having assumed
U.S. citizenship. He won the Pulitzer Prize for poetry in 1948 for
his work* Age of Anxiety. *Auden considered public opinion a sinister force.*

*Alexis de Tocqueville (1805–1859) was born in Paris, France. A
French lawyer of aristocratic background, he visited the United States
in 1831 as a representative of the French government, traveling from
Boston and New York to Wisconsin and down to New Orleans. During the trip he kept a journal, in which he commented on what he
saw. In 1835 he published the first part of* Democracy in America
*in Belgium, a book that was based on the journal and which im-
mediately skyrocketed him to fame. Tocqueville was the first writer in
modern times to complete a comprehensive investigation of how equality, which he considered to be the essential principle of democracy,
affects every aspect of life within a democratic society.*

*What does Auden think of the power of public opinion in democ-
racy? Which weaknesses in democratic government does Tocqueville
recognize?*

He was found by the Bureau of Statistics to be
One against whom there was no official complaint,
And all the reports on his conduct agree
That, in the modern sense of an old-fashioned word, he was a saint,
For in everything he did he served the Greater Community.
Except for the War till the day he retired
He worked in a factory and never got fired
But satisfied his employers, Fudge Motors Inc.
Yet he wasn't a scab or odd in his views,
For his Union reports that he paid his dues,
(Our report on his Union shows it was sound)

And our Social Psychology workers found
That he was popular with his mates and liked a drink.
The Press are convinced that he bought a paper every day
And that his reactions to advertisements were normal in every way.
Policies taken out in his name prove that he was fully insured,
And his Health-card shows he was once in hospital but left it cured.
Both Producers Research and High-Grade Living declare
He was fully sensible to the advantages of the Installment Plan
And had everything necessary to the Modern Man,
A phonograph, a radio, a car and a frigidaire.
Our researchers into Public Opinion are content
That he held the proper opinions for the time of year;
When there was peace, he was for peace; when there was war, he went.
He was married and added five children to the population,
Which our Eugenist says was the right number for a parent of his
    generation.
And our teachers report that he never interfered with their education.

Was he free? Was he happy? The question is absurd:
Had anything been wrong, we should certainly have heard.

Alexis de Tocqueville
OF THE PRINCIPAL SOURCE OF BELIEF AMONG DEMOCRATIC NATIONS

At different periods dogmatic belief is more or less common. It arises in different ways, and it may change its object and its form; but under no circumstances will dogmatic belief cease to exist, or, in other words, men will never cease to entertain some opinions on trust and without discussion. If everyone undertook to form all his own opinions and to seek for truth by isolated paths struck out by himself alone, it would follow that no considerable number of men would ever unite in any common belief.

But obviously without such common belief no society can prosper; say, rather, no society can exist; for without ideas held in common there is no common action, and without common action there may still be men, but there is no social body. In order that society should exist and, *a fortiori*, that a society should prosper, it is necessary that the minds of all the citizens should be rallied and held together by certain predominant ideas; and this cannot be the case unless each of them sometimes draws his opinions from the common source and consents to accept certain matters of belief already formed.

If I now consider man in his isolated capacity, I find that dogmatic belief is not less indispensable to him in order to live alone than it is to enable him to co-operate with his fellows. If man were forced to demonstrate for himself all the truths of which he makes daily use, his task would never end. He would exhaust his strength in preparatory demonstrations without ever advancing beyond them. As, from the shortness of his life, he has not the time, nor, from the limits of his intelligence, the capacity, to act in this way, he is reduced to take on trust a host of facts and opinions which he has not had either the time or the power to verify for himself, but which men of greater ability have found out, or which the crowd adopts. On this groundwork he raises for himself the structure of his own thoughts: he is not led to proceed in this manner by choice, but is constrained by the inflexible law of his condition. There is no philosopher in the world so great but that he believes a million things on the faith of other people and accepts a great many more truths than he demonstrates.

This is not only necessary but desirable. A man who should undertake to inquire into everything for himself could devote to each thing but little time and attention. His task would keep his mind in perpetual unrest, which would prevent him from penetrating to the depth of any truth or of making his mind adhere firmly to any conviction. His intellect would be at once independent and powerless. He must therefore make his choice from among the various objects of human belief and adopt many opinions without discussion in order to search the better into that smaller number which he sets apart for investigation. It is true that whoever receives an opinion on the word of another does so far enslave his mind, but it is a salutary servitude, which allows him to make a good use of freedom.

A principle of authority must then always occur, under all circumstances, in some part or other of the moral and intellectual world. Its place is variable, but a place it necessarily has. The independence of individual minds may be greater or it may be less; it cannot be unbounded. Thus the question is, not to know whether any intellectual authority exists in an age of democracy, but simply where it resides and by what standard it is to be measured.

I have shown . . . how equality of conditions leads men to entertain a sort of instinctive incredulity of the supernatural and a very lofty and often exaggerated opinion of human understanding. The men who live at a period of social equality are not therefore easily led to place that intellectual authority to which they bow either beyond or above humanity. They commonly seek for the sources of truth in themselves or in those who are like themselves. This would be enough to prove that at such periods no new religion could be established, and that all schemes for such a purpose would be not only impious, but absurd and irrational. It may be foreseen that a democratic people will not easily give credence to divine missions; that they will laugh at modern prophets; and that they will seek to discover the chief arbiter of their belief within, and not beyond, the limits of their kind.

When the ranks of society are unequal, and men unlike one another in condition, there are some individuals wielding the power of superior intelligence, learning, and enlightenment, while the multitude are sunk in ignorance and prejudice. Men living at these aristocratic periods are therefore naturally induced to shape their opinions by the standard of a superior person, or a superior class of persons, while they are averse to recognizing the infallibility of the mass of the people.

The contrary takes place in ages of equality. The nearer the people are drawn to the common level of an equal and similar condition, the less prone does each man become to place implicit faith in a certain man or a certain class of men. But his readiness to believe the multitude increases, and opinion is more than ever mistress of the world. Not only is common opinion the only guide which private judgment retains among a democratic people, but among such a people it possesses a power infinitely beyond what it has elsewhere. At periods of equality men have no faith in one another, by reason of their common resemblance; but this very resemblance gives them almost unbounded confidence in the judgment of the public; for it would seem probable that, as they are all endowed with equal means of judging, the greater truth should go with the greater number.

When the inhabitant of a democratic country compares himself individually with all those about him, he feels with pride that he is the equal of any one of them; but when he comes to survey the totality of his fellows and to place himself in contrast with so huge a body, he is instantly overwhelmed by the sense of his own insignificance and weakness. The same equality that renders him independent of each of his fellow citizens, taken severally, exposes him alone and unprotected to the influence of the greater number. The public, therefore, among a democratic people, has a singular power, which aristocratic nations cannot conceive; for it does not persuade others to its beliefs, but it imposes them and makes them permeate the thinking of everyone by a sort of enormous pressure of the mind of all upon the individual intelligence.

In the United States the majority undertakes to supply a multitude of ready-made opinions for the use of individuals, who are thus relieved from the necessity of forming opinions of their own. Everybody there adopts great numbers of theories, on philosophy, morals, and politics, without inquiry, upon public trust; and if we examine it very closely, it will be perceived that religion itself holds sway there much less as a doctrine of revelation than as a commonly received opinion.

The fact that the political laws of the Americans are such that the majority rules the community with sovereign sway materially increases the power which that majority naturally exercises over the mind. For nothing is more customary in man than to recognize superior wisdom in the person of his oppressor. This political omnipotence of the majority in the United States doubtless augments the influence that public opinion would obtain without it over the minds of each member of the community; but the foundations of that influence do not rest upon it. They must be sought for in the principle of equality itself, not in the more or less popular institutions which men living under that condition may give themselves. The intellectual dominion of the greater number would probably be less absolute among a democratic people governed by a king than in the sphere of a pure democracy, but it will always be extremely absolute; and by whatever political laws men are governed in the ages of equality, it may be foreseen that faith in public opinion will become for them a species of religion, and the majority its ministering prophet.

Thus intellectual authority will be different, but it will not be diminished; and far from thinking that it will disappear, I augur that it may readily acquire too much preponderance and confine the action of private judgment within narrower limits than are suited to either the greatness or the happiness of the human race. In the principle of equality I very clearly discern two tendencies; one leading the mind of every man to untried thoughts, the other prohibiting him from thinking at all. And I perceive how, under the dominion of certain laws, democracy would extinguish that liberty of the mind to which a democratic social condition is favorable; so that, after having broken all the bondage once imposed on it by ranks or by men, the human mind would be closely fettered to the general will of the greatest number.

If the absolute power of a majority were to be substituted by democratic nations for all the different powers that checked or retarded overmuch the energy of individual minds, the evil would only have changed character. Men would not have found the means of independent life; they would simply have discovered (no easy task) a new physiognomy of servitude. There is, and I cannot repeat it too often, there is here matter for profound reflection to those who look on freedom of thought as a holy thing and who hate not only the despot, but despotism. For myself, when I feel the hand of power lie heavy on my brow, I care but little to know who oppresses me; and I am not the more disposed to pass beneath the yoke because it is held out to me by the arms of a million men.

OPTIONS FOR WRITING

1. Rewrite Auden's poem in the form of an expository essay. Make sure that your essay answers these questions: What is Auden's thesis? What evidence does he cite to support his conclusion?

2. Literally, democracy means "rule by the common people," and aristocracy means "rule by the best." Imagine that you come from a society shaped by the aristocratic principle, according to which political power may be exercised only by the most learned and virtuous of the citizens. In your society, books, music, and art are produced always with the aristocratic class in mind. Respect for excellence influences all aspects of your society.

Imagine that you are visiting the United States for the first time and have just arrived in the town where you live. Your purpose is to observe a democratic society. For one week, make daily entries in your journal, describing and commenting on what you see.

3. Analyze what Tocqueville means by the phrase "dogmatic belief." We pride ourselves on living in a free society, in which freedom of speech and press are protected by the Bill of Rights. Are Americans, in your opinion, actually free to say or write whatever they wish? Are there today, as there were in the 1830s, dogmatic beliefs that someone challenges only at great peril to reputation or livelihood? List a few of the current dogmas.

James Madison
THE FEDERALIST NO. 10:
To the People of the State of New York.

The next selection is an essay by James Madison (1751–1836), principal architect of the U.S. Constitution and Bill of Rights. Madison, the fourth President of the United States (1809–1817), was born in Port Conway, Virginia. This piece is the tenth of eighty-five essays written by Madison, Alexander Hamilton, and John Jay and published in the New York newspapers in an effort to persuade the people of New York to support ratification of the constitution proposed by the Philadelphia convention in September 1787. The proponents and opponents of the convention's plan of government called themselves, respectively, Federalists and Anti-Federalists. Thus, the collected essays are known as The Federalist Papers.

In the following essay Madison analyzes the nature, causes, and effects of factions. A faction is any group whose interests are adverse to the interests of other groups or to the common good. A majority faction is a group comprising a majority of the citizens and thus able, in a democracy, to intrude on the rights of the minority. Noting that factions are found in all free societies, Madison searches for a way of controlling rather than suppressing them. What is Madison's solution to the problem of majority faction? Which is better from his point of view, a commercial or agrarian economy?

Among the numerous advantages promised by a well constructed Union, none deserves to be more accurately developed than its tendency to break and control the violence of faction. The friend of popular governments, never finds himself so much alarmed for their character and fate, as when he contemplates their propensity to this dangerous vice. He will not fail therefore to set a due value on any plan which, without violating the principles to which he is attached, provides a proper cure for it. The instability, injustice and confusion introduced into the public councils, have in truth been the mortal diseases under which popular governments have every where perished; as they continue to be the favorite and fruitful topics from which the adversaries to liberty derive their most specious declamations. The valuable improvements made by the American Constitutions on the popular models, both ancient and modern, cannot certainly be too much admired; but it would be an unwarrantable partiality, to contend that they have as effectually obviated the danger on this side as was wished and expected. Complaints are every where heard from our most considerate and virtuous citizens, equally the friends of public and private faith, and of public and personal liberty; that our governments are too unstable; that the public good is disregarded in the conflicts of rival parties; and that measures are too often decided, not according to the rules of justice, and the rights of the minor party; but by the superior force of an interested and over-bearing majority. However anxiously we may wish that these complaints had no foundation, the evidence of known facts will not permit us to deny that they are in some degree true. It will be found indeed, on a candid review of our situation, that some of the distresses under which we labor, have been erroneously charged on the operation of our governments; but it will be found, at the same time, that other causes will not alone account for many of our heaviest misfortunes; and particularly, for that prevailing and increasing distrust of public engagements, and alarm for private rights, which are echoed from one end of the continent to the other. These must be chiefly, if not wholly, effects of the unsteadiness and injustice, with which a factious spirit has tainted our public administrations.

By a faction I understand a number of citizens, whether amounting to a majority or minority of the whole, who are united and actuated by some common impulse of passion, or of interest, adverse to the rights of other citizens, or to the permanent and aggregate interests of the community.

There are two methods of curing the mischiefs of faction: the one, by removing its causes; the other, by controlling its effects.

There are again two methods of removing the causes of faction: the one by destroying the liberty which is essential to its existence; the other, by giving to every citizen the same opinions, the same passions, and the same interests.

It could never be more truly said than of the first remedy, that it is worse than the disease. Liberty is to faction, what air is to fire, an aliment without which it instantly expires. But it could not be a less folly to abolish liberty, which is essential to political life, because it nourishes faction, than it would be to wish the annihilation of air, which is essential to animal life, because it imparts to fire its destructive agency.

The second expedient is as impracticable, as the first would be unwise. As long as the reason of man continues fallible, and he is at liberty to exercise it, different opinions will be formed. As long as the connection subsists between his reason and his self-love, his opinions and his passions will have a reciprocal influence on each other; and the former will be objects to which the latter will attach themselves. The diversity in the faculties of men from which the rights of property originate, is not less an insuperable obstacle to a uniformity of interests. The protection of these faculties is the first object of Government. From the protection of different and unequal faculties of acquiring property, the possession of different degrees and kinds of property immediately results: and from the influence of these on the sentiments and views of the respective proprietors, ensues a division of the society into different interests and parties.

The latent causes of faction are thus sown in the nature of man; and we see them every where brought into different degrees of activity, according to the different circumstances of civil society. A zeal for different opinions concerning religion, concerning Government and many other points, as well of speculation as of practice; an attachment to different leaders ambitiously contending for pre-eminence and power; or to persons of other descriptions whose fortunes have been interesting to the human passions, have in turn divided mankind into parties, inflamed them with mutual animosity, and rendered them much more disposed to vex and oppress each other, than to co-operate for their common good. So strong is this propensity of mankind to fall into mutual animosities, that where no substantial occasion presents itself, the most frivolous and fanciful distinctions have been sufficient to kindle their unfriendly passions, and excite their most violent conflicts. But the most common and durable source of factions, has been the various and unequal distribution of property. Those who hold, and those who are without property, have ever formed distinct interests in society. Those who are creditors, and those who are debtors, fall under a like discrimination. A landed interest, a manufacturing interest, a mercantile interest, a monied interest, with many lesser interests, grow up of necessity in civilized nations, and divide them into different classes, actuated by different sentiments and views. The regulation of these various and interfering interests forms the principal task of modern Legislation, and involves the spirit of party and faction in the necessary and ordinary operations of Government.

No man is allowed to be a judge in his own cause; because his interest would certainly bias his judgment, and, not improbably, corrupt his integrity. With equal, nay with greater reason, a body of men, are unfit to be both judges and parties, at the same time; yet, what are many of the most important acts of legislation, but so many judicial determinations, not indeed concerning the rights of single persons, but concerning the rights of large bodies of citizens, and what are the different classes of legislators, but advocates and parties to the causes which they determine? Is a law proposed concerning private debts? It is a question to which the creditors are parties on one side, and the debtors on the other. Justice ought to hold the balance between them. Yet the parties are and must be themselves the judges; and the most numerous party, or, in other words, the most powerful faction must be expected to prevail. Shall domestic manufactures be encouraged, and in what degree, by restrictions on foreign manufactures? are questions which would be differently decided by the landed and the manufacturing classes; and probably by neither, with a sole regard to justice and the public good. The apportionment of taxes on the various descriptions of property, is an act which seems to require the most exact impartiality; yet, there is perhaps no legislative act in which greater opportunity and temptation are given to a predominant party, to trample on the rules of justice. Every shilling with which they over-burden the inferior number, is a shilling saved to their own pockets.

It is in vain to say, that enlightened statesmen will be able to adjust these clashing interests, and render them all subservient to the public good. Enlightened statesmen will not always be at the helm: Nor, in many cases, can such an adjustment be made at all, without taking into view indirect and remote considerations, which will rarely prevail over the immediate interest which one party may find in disregarding the rights of another, or the good of the whole.

The inference to which we are brought, is, that the *causes* of faction cannot be removed; and that relief is only to be sought in the means of controlling its *effects*.

If a faction consists of less than a majority, relief is supplied by the republican principle, which enables the majority to defeat its sinister views by regular vote: It may clog the administration, it may convulse the society; but it will be unable to execute and mask its violence under the forms of the Constitution. When a majority is included in a faction, the form of popular government on the other hand enables it to sacrifice to its ruling passion or interest, both the public good and the rights of other citizens. To secure the public good, and private rights, against the danger of such a faction, and at the same time to preserve the spirit and the form of popular government, is then the great object to which our enquiries are directed: Let me add that it is the great desideratum, by which alone this form of government can be rescued from the opprobrium under which it has so long labored, and be recommended to the esteem and adoption of mankind.

By what means is this object attainable? Evidently by one of two only. Either the existence of the same passion or interest in a majority at the same time, must be prevented; or the majority, having such co-existent passion or interest, must be rendered, by their number and local situation, unable to concert and carry into effect schemes of oppression. If the impulse and the opportunity be suffered to coincide, we well know that neither moral nor religious motives can be relied on as an adequate control. They are not found to be such on the injustice and violence of individuals, and lose their efficacy in proportion to the number combined together; that is, in proportion as their efficacy becomes needful.

From this view of the subject, it may be concluded, that a pure Democracy, by which I mean, a Society, consisting of a small number of citizens, who assemble and administer the Government in person, can admit of no cure for the mischiefs of faction. A common passion or interest will, in almost every case, be felt by a majority of the whole; a communication and concert results from the form of Government itself; and there is nothing to check the inducements to sacrifice the weaker party, or an obnoxious individual. Hence it is, that such Democracies have ever been spectacles of turbulence and contention; have ever been found incompatible with personal security, or the rights of property; and have in general been as short in their lives, as they have been violent in their deaths. Theoretic politicians, who have patronized this species of Government, have erroneously supposed, that by reducing mankind to a perfect equality in their political rights, they would, at the same time, be perfectly equalized and assimilated in their possessions, their opinions, and their passions.

A republic, by which I mean a government in which the scheme of representation takes place, opens a different prospect, and promises the cure for which we are seeking. Let us examine the points in which it varies from pure democracy, and we shall comprehend both the nature of the cure and the efficacy which it must derive from the union.

The two great points of difference, between a democracy and a republic, are, first, the delegation of the government, in the latter, to a small number of citizens, elected by the rest; secondly, the greater number of citizens, and greater sphere of country, over which the latter may be extended.

The effect of the first difference is, on the one hand, to refine and enlarge the public views, by passing them through the medium of a chosen body of citizens, whose wisdom may best discern the true interest of their country, and whose patriotism and love of justice, will be least likely to sacrifice it to temporary or partial considerations. Under such a regulation, it may well happen, that the public voice, pronounced by the representatives of the people, will be more consonant to the public good, than if pronounced by the people themselves, convened for the purpose. On the other hand the effect may be inverted. Men of factious tempers, of local prejudices, or of sinister designs, may by intrigue, by corruption, or by other means, first obtain the suffrages, and then betray the interest of the people. The question resulting is, whether small or extensive republics are most favorable to the election of proper guardians of the public weal, and it is clearly decided in favor of the latter by two obvious considerations.

In the first place, it is to be remarked that, however small the republic may be, the representatives must be raised to a certain number, in order to guard against the cabals of a few; and that however large it may be, they must be limited to a certain number, in order to guard against the confusion of a multitude. Hence, the number of representatives in the two cases not being in proportion to that of the constituents, and being proportionally greatest in the small republic, it follows, that if the proportion of fit characters be not less in the large than in the small republic, the former will present a greater option, and consequently a greater probability of a fit choice.

In the next place, as each Representative will be chosen by a greater number of citizens in the large than in the small Republic, it will be more difficult for unworthy candidates to practise with success the vicious arts, by which elections are too often carried; and the suffrages of the people being more free, will be more likely to center on men who possess the most attractive merit, and the most diffusive and established characters.

It must be confessed, that in this, as in most other cases, there is a mean, on both sides of which inconveniences will be found to lie. By enlarging too much the number of electors, you render the representative too little acquainted with all their local circumstances and lesser interests; as by reducing it too much, you render him unduly attached to these, and too little fit to comprehend and pursue great and national objects. The Federal Constitution forms a happy combination in this respect; the great and aggregate interests being referred to the national, the local and particular, to the state legislatures.

The other point of difference is, the greater number of citizens and extent of territory which may be brought within the compass of Republican, than of Democratic Government; and it is this circumstance principally which renders factious combinations less to be dreaded in the former, than in the latter. The smaller the society, the fewer probably will be the distinct parties and interests composing it; the fewer the distinct parties and interests, the more frequently will a majority be found of the same party; and the smaller the number of individuals composing a majority, and the smaller the compass within which they are placed, the more easily will they concert and execute their plans of oppression. Extend the sphere, and you take in a greater variety of parties and interests; you make it less probable that a majority of the whole will have a common motive to invade the rights of other citizens; or if such a common motive exists, it will be more difficult for all who feel it to discover their own strength, and to act in unison with each other. Besides other impediments, it may be remarked, that where there is a consciousness of unjust or dishonorable purposes, communication is always checked by distrust, in proportion to the number whose concurrence is necessary.

Hence it clearly appears, that the same advantage, which a Republic has over a Democracy, in controlling the effects of faction, is enjoyed by a large over a small Republic—is enjoyed by the Union over the States composing it. Does this advantage consist in the substitution of Representatives, whose enlightened views and virtuous sentiments render them superior to local prejudices, and to schemes of injustice? It will not be denied, that the Representation of the Union will be most likely to possess these requisite endowments. Does it consist in the greater security afforded by a greater variety of parties, against the event of any one party being able to outnumber and oppress the rest? In an equal degree does the increased variety of parties, comprised within the Union, increase this security? Does it, in fine, consist in the greater obstacles opposed to the concert and accomplishment of the secret wishes of an unjust and interested majority? Here, again, the extent of the Union gives it the most palpable advantage.

The influence of factious leaders may kindle a flame within their particular States, but will be unable to spread a general conflagration through the other States: a religious sect, may degenerate into a political faction in a part of the Confederacy but the variety of sects dispersed over the entire face of it, must secure the national Councils against any danger from that source: a rage for paper money, for an abolition of debts, for an equal division of property, or for any other improper or wicked project, will be less apt to pervade the whole body of the Union, than a particular member of it; in the same proportion as such a malady is more likely to taint a particular county or district, than an entire State.

In the extent and proper structure of the Union, therefore, we behold a Republican remedy for the diseases most incident to Republican Government. And according to the degree of pleasure and pride, we feel in being Republicans, ought to be our zeal in cherishing the spirit, and supporting the character of Federalists.

OPTIONS FOR WRITING

1. Describe Madison's understanding of the chief defects of democracy, "the mortal diseases under which popular governments have every where perished." What do you believe are the strengths and weaknesses of democracy? What other forms of government are there? What are their strong points and weak points?

2. Madison says that there is a connection between the "degrees and kinds of property" citizens possess and their opinions. Do you agree? Give some examples of how the opinions of the rich and poor differ. If poverty were eliminated and we all had the same amount of wealth, would society still be divided into factions?

3. Identify the goals which are more important to Madison than majority rule. Does Madison's solution to the problem of the tyranny of the majority enable the government to ignore public opinion, either temporarily or permanently? In your opinion, does Madison attach insufficient value to public opinion?

Majority Tyranny: American Democracy and the African-American Experience

Frederick Douglass
WHAT TO THE SLAVE IS THE FOURTH OF JULY?
An Address Delivered in Rochester, New York, on 5 July 1852

The next two selections—a speech by Frederick Douglass, a former slave, "What to the Slave Is the Fourth of July?," and an open letter by African-American civil rights leader Martin Luther King, Jr.— raise questions concerning Madison's promise that in the extended, commercial republic of the United States minority rights would be safeguarded. Madison's illustrations of protected minorities are primarily commercial—bankers, merchants, planters, industrialists— and religious. Does his analysis extend to racial minorities? How successful has the Constitution been in safeguarding the interests of African-Americans and other racial minorities and in preventing the majority from treating them unjustly? Does the African-American experience disclose a basic flaw in democracy as a form of government?

Frederick Douglass, whose original name was Frederick Augustus Washington Bailey, was born a slave in Tuckahoe, Maryland, in 1817 and died a free man in 1895. Although slaves were forbidden to learn how to read and write, Douglass nevertheless acquired these skills before his escape to freedom in 1838. He changed his name in order to elude the dreaded slave catchers. Douglass became an abolitionist, working with the Massachusetts Anti-Slavery Society and founding a newspaper dedicated to the destruction of slavery. He was also in much demand as a public speaker in the period of agitation culminating in the Civil War.

Martin Luther King, Jr., was an ordained Baptist minister and the most prominent leader of the civil rights movement in the 1950s and 1960s. Born in Atlanta, Georgia, in 1929 and winner of the Nobel Peace Prize in 1964, he fell to an assassin's bullet in 1968. He fought against laws in the Southern states that required the separation of the races in schools, restaurants, hotels, buses, trains, and other facilities open to the public. King advocated nonviolent resistance to the policy of segregation and was arrested for sitting-in at a luncheon counter reserved for whites. How does King respond to those ministers who had criticized his intentional breaking of the law? What is the difference between revolution and civil disobedience?

Mr. President, Friends and Fellow Citizens: He who could address this audience without a quailing sensation, has stronger nerves than I have. I do not remember ever to have appeared as a speaker before any assembly more shrinkingly, nor with greater distrust of my ability, than I do this day. A feeling has crept over me, quite unfavorable to the exercise of my limited powers of speech. The task before me is one which requires much previous thought and study for its proper performance. I know that apologies of this sort are generally considered flat and unmeaning. I trust, however, that mine will not be so considered. Should I seem at ease, my appearance would much misrepresent me. The little experience I have had in addressing public meetings, in country school houses, avails me nothing on the present occasion.

The papers and placards say, that I am to deliver a 4th [of] July oration. This certainly sounds large, and out of the common way, for me. It is true that I have often had the privilege to speak in this beautiful Hall, and to address many who now honor me with their presence. But neither their familiar faces, nor the perfect gauge I think I have of Corinthian Hall, seems to free me from embarrassment.

The fact is, ladies and gentlemen, the distance between this platform and the slave plantation, from which I escaped, is considerable — and the difficulties to be overcome in getting from the latter to the former, are by no means slight. That I am here to-day is, to me, a matter of astonishment as well as of gratitude. You will not, therefore, be surprised, if in what I have got to say, I evince no elaborate preparation, nor grace my speech with any high sounding exordium. With little experience and with less learning, I have been able to throw my thoughts hastily and imperfectly together; and trusting to your patient and generous indulgence, I will proceed to lay them before you.

This, for the purpose of this celebration, is the 4th of July. It is the birthday of your National Independence, and of your political freedom. This, to you, is what the Passover was to the emancipated people of God. It carries your minds back to the day, and to the act of your great deliverance; and to the signs and to the wonders, associated with that act, and that day. This celebration also marks the beginning of another year of your national life; and reminds you that the Republic of America is now 76 years old. I am glad, fellow-citizens, that your nation is so young. Seventy-six years, though a good old age for a man, is but a mere speck in the life of a nation. Three score and ten is the allotted time for individual men; but nations number their years by thousands. According to this fact, you are, even now, only in the beginning of your national career, still lingering in the period of childhood. I repeat, I am glad this is so. There is hope in the thought, and hope is much needed, under the dark clouds which lower above the horizon. The eye of the reformer is met with angry flashes, portending disastrous times; but his heart may well beat lighter at the thought that America is young, and that she is still in the impressible stage of her existence. May he not hope that high lessons of wisdom, of justice and of truth, will yet give direction to her destiny? Were the nation older, the patriot's heart might be sadder, and the reformer's brow heavier. Its future might be shrouded in gloom, and the hope of its prophets go out in sorrow. There is consolation in the thought that America is young. Great streams are not easily turned from channels, worn deep in the course of ages. They may sometimes rise in quiet and stately majesty, and inundate the land, refreshing and fertilizing the earth with their mysterious properties. They may also rise in wrath and fury, and bear away, on their angry waves, the accumulated wealth of years of toil and hardship. They, however, gradually flow back to the same old channel, and flow on as serenely as ever. But, while the river may not be turned aside, it may dry up, and leave nothing behind but the withered branch, and the unsightly rock, to howl in the abyss-sweeping wind, the sad tale of departed glory. As with rivers so with nations.

Fellow-citizens, I shall not presume to dwell at length on the associations that cluster about this day. The simple story of it is that, 76 years ago, the people of this country were British subjects. The style and title of your "sovereign people" (in which you now glory) was not then born. You were under the British Crown. Your fathers esteemed the English Government as the home government; and England as the fatherland. This home government, you know, although a considerable distance from your home, did, in the exercise of its parental prerogatives, impose upon its colonial children, such restraints, burdens and limitations, as in its mature judgement, it deemed wise, right and proper.

But, your fathers, who had not adopted the fashionable idea of this day, of the infallibility of government, and the absolute character of its acts, presumed to differ from the home government in respect to the wisdom and the justice of some of those burdens and restraints. They went so far in their excitement as to pronounce the measures of government unjust, unreasonable, and oppressive, and altogether such as ought not to be quietly submitted to. I scarcely need say, fellow-citizens, that my opinion of those measures fully accords with that of your fathers. Such a declaration of agreement on my part would not be worth much to anybody. It would, certainly, prove nothing, as to what part I might have taken, had I lived during the great controversy of 1776. To say *now* that America was right, and England wrong, is exceedingly easy. Everybody can say it; the dastard, not less than the noble brave, can flippantly descant on the tyranny of England towards the American Colonies. It is fashionable to do so; but there was a time when to pronounce against England, and in favor of the cause of the colonies, tried men's souls. They who did so were accounted in their day, plotters of mischief, agitators and rebels, dangerous men. To side with the right, against the wrong, with the weak against the strong, and with the oppressed against the oppressor! *here* lies the merit, and the one which, of all others, seems unfashionable in our day. The cause of liberty may be stabbed by the men who glory in the deeds of your fathers. But, to proceed.

Feeling themselves harshly and unjustly treated by the home government, your fathers, like men of honesty, and men of spirit, earnestly sought redress. They petitioned and remonstrated; they did so in a decorous, respectful, and loyal manner. Their conduct was wholly unexceptionable. This, however, did not answer the purpose. They saw themselves treated with sovereign indifference, coldness and scorn. Yet they persevered. They were not the men to look back.

As the sheet anchor takes a firmer hold, when the ship is tossed by the storm, so did the cause of your fathers grow stronger, as it breasted the chilling blasts of kingly displeasure. The greatest and best of British statesmen admitted its justice, and the loftiest eloquence of the British Senate came to its support. But, with that blindness which seems to be the unvarying characteristic of tyrants, since Pharaoh and his hosts were drowned in the Red Sea, the British Government persisted in the exactions complained of.

The madness of this course, we believe, is admitted now, even by England; but we fear the lesson is wholly lost on our present rulers.

Oppression makes a wise man mad. Your fathers were wise men, and if they did not go mad, they became restive under this treatment. They felt themselves the victims of grievous wrongs, wholly incurable in their colonial capacity. With brave men there is always a remedy for oppression. Just here, the idea of a total separation of the colonies from the crown was born! It was a startling idea, much more so, than we, at this distance of time, regard it. The timid and the prudent (as has been intimated) of that day, were, of course, shocked and alarmed by it.

Such people lived then, had lived before, and will, probably, ever have a place on this planet; and their course, in respect to any great change (no matter how great the good to be attained, or the wrong to be redressed by it), may be calculated with as much precision as can be the course of the stars. They hate all changes, but silver, gold and copper change! Of this sort of change they are always strongly in favor.

These people were called tories in the days of your fathers; and the appellation, probably, conveyed the same idea that is meant by a more modern, though a somewhat less euphonious term, which we often find in our papers, applied to some of our old politicians.

Their opposition to the then dangerous thought was earnest and powerful; but, amid all their terror and affrighted vociferations against it, the alarming and revolutionary idea moved on, and the country with it.

On the 2d of July, 1776, the old Continental Congress, to the dismay of the lovers of ease, and the worshippers of property, clothed that dreadful idea with all the authority of national sanction. They did so in the form of a resolution; and as we seldom hit upon resolutions, drawn up in our day, whose transparency is at all equal to this, it may refresh your minds and help my story if I read it.

Resolved, That these united colonies *are*, and of right, ought to be free and Independent States; that they are absolved from all allegiance to the British

Crown; and that all political connection between them and the State of Great Britain *is*, and ought to be, dissolved.

Citizens, your fathers made good that resolution. They succeeded; and today you reap the fruits of their success. The freedom gained is yours; and you, therefore, may properly celebrate this anniversary. The 4th of July is the first great fact in your nation's history — the very ring-bolt in the chain of your yet undeveloped destiny.

Pride and patriotism, not less than gratitude, prompt you to celebrate and to hold it in perpetual remembrance. I have said that the Declaration of Independence is the RING-BOLT to the chain of your nation's destiny; so, indeed, I regard it. The principles contained in that instrument are saving principles. Stand by those principles, be true to them on all occasions, in all places, against all foes, and at whatever cost.

From the round top of your ship of state, dark and threatening clouds may be seen. Heavy billows, like mountains in the distance, disclose to the leeward huge forms of flinty rocks! That *bolt* drawn, that *chain* broken, and all is lost. *Cling to this day — cling to it*, and to its principles, with the grasp of a storm-tossed mariner to a spar at midnight.

The coming into being of a nation, in any circumstances, is an interesting event. But, besides general considerations, there were peculiar circumstances which make the advent of this republic an event of special attractiveness.

The whole scene, as I look back to it, was simple, dignified and sublime.

The population of the country, at the time, stood at the significant number of three millions. The country was poor in the munitions of war. The population was weak and scattered, and the country a wilderness unsubdued. There were then no means of concert and combination, such as exist now. Neither steam nor lightning had then been reduced to order and discipline. From the Potomac to the Delaware was a journey of many days. Under these, and unnumerable other disadvantages, your fathers declared for liberty and independence and triumphed.

Fellow Citizens, I am not wanting in respect for the fathers of this republic. The signers of the Declaration of Independence were brave men. They were great men too — great enough to give fame to a great age. It does not often happen to a nation to raise, at one time, such a number of truly great men. The point from which I am compelled to view them is not, certainly, the most favorable; and yet I cannot contemplate their great deeds with less than admiration. They were statesmen, patriots and heroes, and for the good they did, and the principles they contended for, I will unite with you to honor their memory.

They loved their country better than their own private interests; and, though this is not the highest form of human excellence, all will concede that it is a rare virtue, and that when it is exhibited, it ought to command respect. He who will, intelligently, lay down his life for his country, is a man whom it is not in human nature to despise. Your fathers staked their lives, their fortunes, and their sacred honor, on the cause of their country. In their admiration of liberty, they lost sight of all other interests.

They were peace men; but they preferred revolution to peaceful submission to bondage. They were quiet men; but they did not shrink from agitating against oppression. They showed forbearance; but that they knew its limits. They believed in order; but not in the order of tyranny. With them, nothing was *"settled"* that was not right. With them, justice, liberty and humanity were *"final"*; not slavery and oppression. You may well cherish the memory of such men. They were great in their day and generation. Their solid manhood stands out the more as we contrast it with these degenerate times.

How circumspect, exact and proportionate were all their movements! How unlike the politicians of an hour! Their statesmanship looked beyond the passing moment, and stretched away in strength into the distant future. They seized upon eternal principles, and set a glorious example in their defence. Mark them! . . .

Martin Luther King, Jr.
LETTER FROM BIRMINGHAM JAIL

April 16, 1963

My Dear Fellow Clergymen:

While confined here in the Birmingham city jail, I came across your recent statement calling my present activities "unwise and untimely." Seldom do I pause to answer criticism of my work and ideas. If I sought to answer all the criticisms that cross my desk, my secretaries would have little time for anything other than such correspondence in the course of the day, and I would have no time for constructive work. But since I feel that you are men of genuine good will and that your criticisms are sincerely set forth, I want to try to answer your statement in what I hope will be patient and reasonable terms.

I think I should indicate why I am here in Birmingham, since you have been influenced by the view which argues against "outsiders coming in." I have the honor of serving as president of the Southern Christian Leadership Conference, an organization operating in every southern state, with headquarters in Atlanta, Georgia. We have some eighty-five affiliated organizations across the South, and one of them is the Alabama Christian Movement for Human Rights. Frequently we share staff, educational, and financial resources with our affiliates. Several months ago the affiliate here in Birmingham asked us to be on call to engage in a nonviolent direct-action program if such were deemed necessary. We readily consented, and when the hour came we lived up to our promise. So I, along with several members of my staff, am here because I was invited here. I am here because I have organizational ties here.

But more basically, I am in Birmingham because injustice is here. Just as the prophets of the eighth century B.C. left their villages and carried their "thus saith the Lord" far beyond the boundaries of their home towns, and just as the Apostle Paul left his village of Tarsus and carried the gospel of Jesus Christ to the far corners of the Greco-Roman world, so am I compelled to carry the gospel of freedom beyond my own home town. Like Paul, I must constantly respond to the Macedonian call for aid.

Moreover, I am cognizant of the interrelatedness of all communities and states. I cannot sit idly by in Atlanta and not be concerned about what happens in Birmingham. Injustice anywhere is a threat to justice everywhere. We are caught in an inescapable network of mutuality, tied in a single garment of destiny. Whatever affects one directly, affects all indirectly. Never again can we afford to live with the narrow, provincial, "outside agitator" idea. Anyone who lives inside the United States can never be considered an outsider anywhere within its bounds.

You deplore the demonstrations taking place in Birmingham. But your statement, I am sorry to say, fails to express a similar concern for the conditions that brought about the demonstrations. I am sure that none of you would want to rest content with the superficial kind of social analysis that deals merely with effects and does not grapple with underlying causes. It is unfortunate that demonstrations are taking place in Birmingham, but it is even more unfortunate that the city's white power structure left the Negro community with no alternative.

In any nonviolent campaign there are four basic steps: collection of the facts to determine whether injustices exist; negotiation; self-purification; and direct action. We have gone through all these steps in Birmingham. There can be no gainsaying the fact that racial injustice engulfs this community. Birmingham is probably the most thoroughly segregated city in the United States. Its ugly record of brutality is widely known. Negroes have experienced grossly unjust treatment in the courts. There have been more unsolved bombings of Negro homes and churches in Birmingham than in any other city in the nation. These are the hard brutal facts of the case. On the basis of these conditions, Negro leaders sought to negotiate with the city fathers. But the latter consistently refused to engage in good-faith negotiation.

Then, last September, came the opportunity to talk with leaders of Birmingham's economic community. In the course of the negotiations, certain promises were made by the merchants — for example, to remove the stores' humiliating racial signs. On the basis of these promises, the

Reverend Fred Shuttlesworth and the leaders of the Alabama Christian Movement for Human Rights agreed to a moratorium on all demonstrations. As the weeks and months went by, we realized that we were the victims of a broken promise. A few signs, briefly removed, returned; the others remained.

As in so many past experiences, our hopes had been blasted, and the shadow of deep disappointment settled upon us. We had no alternative except to prepare for direct action, whereby we would present our very bodies as a means of laying our case before the conscience of the local and the national community. Mindful of the difficulties involved, we decided to undertake a process of self-purification. We began a series of workshops on nonviolence, and we repeatedly asked ourselves: "Are you able to accept blows without retaliating?" "Are you able to endure the ordeal of jail?" We decided to schedule our direct-action program for the Easter season, realizing that except for Christmas, this is the main shopping period of the year. Knowing that a strong economic-withdrawal program would be the by-product of direct action, we felt that this would be the best time to bring pressure to bear on the merchants for the needed change.

Then it occurred to us that Birmingham's mayoral election was coming up in March, and we speedily decided to postpone action until after election day. When we discovered that the Commissioner of Public Safety, Eugene "Bull" Connor, had piled up enough votes to be in the run-off, we decided again to postpone action until the day after the run-off so that the demonstrations could not be used to cloud the issues. Like many others, we waited to see Mr. Connor defeated, and to this end we endured postponement after postponement. Having aided in this community need, we felt that our direct-action program could be delayed no longer.

You may well ask, "Why direct action? Why sit-ins, marches, and so forth? Isn't negotiation a better path?" You are quite right in calling for negotiation. Indeed, this is the very purpose of direct action. Nonviolent direct action seeks to create such a crisis and foster such a tension that a community which has constantly refused to negotiate is forced to confront the issue. It seeks so to dramatize the issue that it can no longer be ignored. My citing the creation of tension as part of the work of the nonviolent resister may sound rather shocking. But I must confess that I am not afraid of the word "tension." I have earnestly opposed violent tension, but there is a type of constructive, nonviolent tension which is necessary for growth. Just as Socrates felt that it was necessary to create a tension in the mind so that individuals could rise from the bondage of myths and half truths to the unfettered realm of creative analysis and objective appraisal, so must we see the need for nonviolent gadflies to create the kind of tension in society that will help men rise from the dark depths of prejudice and racism to the majestic heights of understanding and brotherhood.

The purpose of our direct-action program is to create a situation so crisis-packed that it will inevitably open the door to negotiation. I therefore concur with you in your call for negotiation. Too long has our beloved Southland been bogged down in a tragic effort to live in monologue rather than dialogue.

One of the basic points in your statement is that the action that I and my associates have taken in Birmingham is untimely. Some have asked: "Why didn't you give the new city administration time to act?" The only answer that I can give to this query is that the new Birmingham administration must be prodded about as much as the outgoing one, before it will act. We are sadly mistaken if we feel that the election of Albert Boutwell as mayor will bring the millennium to Birmingham. While Mr. Boutwell is a much more gentle person than Mr. Connor, they are both segregationists, dedicated to maintenance of the status quo. I have hoped that Mr. Boutwell will be reasonable enough to see the futility of massive resistance to desegregation. But he will not see this without pressure from devotees of civil rights. My friends, I must say to you that we have not made a single gain in civil rights without determined legal and nonviolent pressure. Lamentably, it is an historical fact that privileged groups seldom give up their privileges voluntarily. Individuals may see the moral light and voluntarily give up their unjust posture; but, as Reinhold Niebuhr has reminded us, groups tend to be more immoral than individuals.

We know through painful experience that freedom is never voluntarily given by the oppressor; it must be demanded by the oppressed. Frankly, I have yet to engage in a direct-action campaign that was "well timed" in the view of those who have not suffered unduly from the disease of segregation. For years now I have heard the word "Wait!" It rings in the ear of every Negro with piercing familiarity. This "Wait" has almost always meant "Never." We must come to see, with one of our distinguished jurists, that "justice too long delayed is justice denied."

We have waited for more than 340 years for our constitutional and God-given rights. The nations of Asia and Africa are moving with jet-like speed toward gaining political independence, but we still creep at horse-and-buggy pace toward gaining a cup of coffee at a lunch counter. Perhaps it is easy for those who have never felt the stinging darts of segregation to say, "Wait." But when you have seen vicious mobs lynch your mothers and fathers at will and drown your sisters and brothers at whim; when you have seen hate-filled policemen curse, kick, and even kill your black brothers and sisters; when you see the vast majority of your twenty million Negro brothers smothering in an airtight cage of poverty in the midst of an affluent society; when you suddenly find your tongue twisted and your speech stammering as you seek to explain to your six-year-old daughter why she can't go to the public amusement park that has just been advertised on television, and see tears welling up in her eyes when she is told that Funtown is closed to colored children, and see ominous clouds of inferiority beginning to form in her little mental sky, and see her beginning to distort her personality by developing an unconscious bitterness toward white people; when you have to concoct an answer for a five-year-old son who is asking, "Daddy, why do white people treat colored people so mean?"; when you take a cross-country drive and find it necessary to sleep night after night in the uncomfortable corners of your automobile because no motel will accept you; when you are humiliated day in and day out by nagging signs reading "white" and "colored"; when your first name becomes "nigger," your middle name becomes "boy" (however old you are) and your last name becomes "John," and your wife and mother are never given the respected title "Mrs."; when you are harried by day and haunted by night by the fact that you are a Negro, living constantly at tiptoe stance, never quite knowing what to expect next, and are plagued with inner fears and outer resentments; when you are forever fighting a degenerating sense of "nobodiness" — then you will understand why we find it difficult to wait. There comes a time when the cup of endurance runs over, and men are no longer willing to be plunged into the abyss of despair. I hope, sirs, you can understand our legitimate and unavoidable impatience.

You express a great deal of anxiety over our willingness to break laws. This is certainly a legitimate concern. Since we so diligently urge people to obey the Supreme Court's decision of 1954 outlawing segregation in the public schools, at first glance it may seem rather paradoxical for us consciously to break laws. One may well ask: "How can you advocate breaking some laws and obeying others?" The answer lies in the fact that there are two types of laws: just and unjust. I would be the first to advocate obeying just laws. One has not only a legal but a moral responsibility to obey just laws. Conversely, one has a moral responsibility to disobey unjust laws. I would agree with St. Augustine that "an unjust law is no law at all."

Now, what is the difference between the two? How does one determine whether a law is just or unjust? A just law is a man-made code that squares with the moral law or the law of God. An unjust law is a code that is out of harmony with the moral law. To put it in the terms of St. Thomas Aquinas: An unjust law is a human law that is not rooted in eternal law and natural law. Any law that uplifts human personality is just. Any law that degrades human personality is unjust. All segregation statutes are unjust because segregation distorts the soul and damages the personality. It gives the segregator a false sense of superiority and the segregated a false sense of inferiority. Segregation, to use the terminology of the Jewish philosopher Martin Buber, substitutes an "I-it" relationship for an "I-thou" relationship and ends up relegating persons to the status of things. Hence segregation is not only politically, economically, and sociologically unsound, it is morally wrong and sinful. Paul Tillich has said that sin is separation. Is not segregation an existential expression of man's tragic separation, his awful estrangement, his terrible sinfulness? Thus it is that I can urge men to obey the 1954 decision of the Supreme Court, for it is morally right; and I can urge them to disobey segregation ordinances, for they are morally wrong.

Let us consider a more concrete example of just and unjust laws. An unjust law is a code that a numerical or power majority group compels a minority group to obey but does not make binding on itself. This is *difference* made legal. By the same token, a just law is a code that a majority compels a minority to follow and that it is willing to follow itself. This is *sameness* made legal.

Let me give another explanation. A law is unjust if it is inflicted on a minority that, as a result of being denied the right to vote, had no part in enacting or devising the law. Who can say that the legislature of Alabama which set up that state's segregation laws was democratically elected? Throughout Alabama all sorts of devious methods are used to prevent Negroes from becoming registered voters, and there are some counties in which, even though Negroes constitute a majority of the population, not a single Negro is registered. Can any law enacted under such circumstances be considered democratically structured?

Sometimes a law is just on its face and unjust in its application. For instance, I have been arrested on a charge of parading without a permit. Now, there is nothing wrong in having an ordinance which requires a permit for a parade. But such an ordinance becomes unjust when it is used to maintain segregation and to deny citizens the First Amendment privilege of peaceful assembly and protest.

I hope you are able to see the distinction I am trying to point out. In no sense do I advocate evading or defying the law, as would the rabid segregationist. That would lead to anarchy. One who breaks an unjust law must do so openly, lovingly, and with a willingness to accept the penalty. I submit that an individual who breaks a law that conscience tells him is unjust, and who willingly accepts the penalty of imprisonment in order to arouse the conscience of the community over its injustice, is in reality expressing the highest respect for law.

Of course, there is nothing new about this kind of civil disobedience. It was evidenced sublimely in the refusal of Shadrach, Meshach, and Abednego to obey the laws of Nebuchadnezzar, on the ground that a higher moral law was at stake. It was practiced superbly by the early Christians, who were willing to face hungry lions and the excruciating pain of chopping blocks rather than submit to certain unjust laws of the Roman Empire. To a degree, academic freedom is a reality today because Socrates practiced civil disobedience. In our own nation, the Boston Tea Party represented a massive act of civil disobedience.

We should never forget that everything Adolf Hitler did in Germany was "legal" and everything the Hungarian freedom fighters did in Hungary was "illegal." It was "illegal" to aid and comfort a Jew in Hitler's Germany. Even so, I am sure that, had I lived in Germany at the time,

I would have aided and comforted my Jewish brothers. If today I lived in a Communist country where certain principles dear to the Christian faith are suppressed, I would openly advocate disobeying that country's antireligious laws.

I must make two honest confessions to you, my Christian and Jewish brothers. First, I must confess that over the past few years I have been gravely disappointed with the white moderate. I have almost reached the regrettable conclusion that the Negro's great stumbling block in his stride toward freedom is not the White Citizen's Counciler or the Ku Klux Klanner, but the white moderate, who is more devoted to "order" than to justice; who prefers a negative peace which is the absence of tension to a positive peace which is the presence of justice; who constantly says, "I agree with you in the goal you seek, but I cannot agree with your methods of direct action"; who paternalistically believes he can set the timetable for another man's freedom; who lives by a mythical concept of time and who constantly advises the Negro to wait for a "more convenient season." Shallow understanding from people of good will is more frustrating than absolute misunderstanding from people of ill will. Lukewarm acceptance is much more bewildering than outright rejection.

I had hoped that the white moderate would understand that law and order exist for the purpose of establishing justice and that when they fail in this purpose they become the dangerously structured dams that block the flow of social progress. I had hoped that the white moderate would understand that the present tension in the South is a necessary phase of the transition from an obnoxious negative peace, in which the Negro passively accepted his unjust plight, to a substantive and positive peace, in which all men will respect the dignity and worth of human personality. Actually, we who engage in nonviolent direct action are not the creators of tension. We merely bring to the surface the hidden tension that is already alive. We bring it out in the open, where it can be seen and dealt with. Like a boil that can never be cured so long as it is covered up but must be opened with all its ugliness to the natural medicines of air and light, injustice must be exposed, with all the tension its exposure creates, to the light of human conscience and the air of national opinion, before it can be cured.

In your statement you assert that our actions, even though peaceful, must be condemned because they precipitate violence. But is this a logical assertion? Isn't this like condemning a robbed man because his possession of money precipitated the evil act of robbery? Isn't this like condemning Socrates because his unswerving commitment to truth and his philosophical inquiries precipitated the act by the misguided populace in which they made him drink hemlock? Isn't this like condemning Jesus because his unique God-consciousness and never-ceasing devotion to God's will precipitated the evil act of crucifixion? We must come to see that, as the federal courts have consistently affirmed, it is

wrong to urge an individual to cease his efforts to gain his basic constitutional rights because the quest may precipitate violence. Society
must protect the robbed and punish the robber.

I had also hoped that the white moderate would reject the myth
concerning time in relation to the struggle for freedom. I have just received a letter from a white brother in Texas. He writes: "All Christians
know that the colored people will receive equal rights eventually, but it
is possible that you are in too great a religious hurry. It has taken Christianity almost two thousand years to accomplish what it has. The teachings of Christ take time to come to earth." Such an attitude stems from
a tragic misconception of time, from the strangely irrational notion that
there is something in the very flow of time that will inevitably cure all
ills. Actually, time itself is neutral; it can be used either destructively or
constructively. More and more I feel that the people of ill will have used
time much more effectively than have the people of good will. We will
have to repent in this generation not merely for the hateful words and
actions of the bad people, but for the appalling silence of the good
people. Human progress never rolls in on wheels of inevitability; it
comes through the tireless efforts of men willing to be co-workers with
God, and without this hard work, time itself becomes an ally of the
forces of social stagnation. We must use time creatively, in the knowledge that the time is always ripe to do right. Now is the time to make
real the promise of democracy and transform our pending national elegy
into a creative psalm of brotherhood. Now is the time to lift our national
policy from the quicksand of racial injustice to the solid rock of human
dignity.

You speak of our activity in Birmingham as extreme. At first I was
rather disappointed that fellow clergymen would see my nonviolent efforts as those of an extremist. I began thinking about the fact that I
stand in the middle of two opposing forces in the Negro community.
One is a force of complacency, made up in part of Negroes who, as a
result of long years of oppression, are so drained of self-respect and a
sense of "somebodiness" that they have adjusted to segregation; and in
part of a few middle-class Negroes who, because of a degree of
academic and economic security and because in some ways they profit
by segregation, have become insensitive to the problems of the masses.
The other force is one of bitterness and hatred, and it comes perilously
close to advocating violence. It is expressed in the various black
nationalist groups that are springing up across the nation, the largest
and best known being Elijah Muhammad's Muslim movement. Nourished
by the Negro's frustration over the continued existence of racial discrimination, this movement is made up of people who have lost faith in
America, who have absolutely repudiated Christianity, and who have
concluded that the white man is an incorrigible "devil."

I have tried to stand between these two forces, saying that we need
emulate neither the "do-nothingism" of the complacent nor the hatred

and despair of the black nationalist. For there is the more excellent way of love and nonviolent protest. I am grateful to God that, through the influence of the Negro church, the way of nonviolence became an integral part of our struggle.

If this philosophy had not emerged, by now many streets of the South would, I am convinced, be flowing with blood. And I am further convinced that if our white brothers dismiss as "rabble-rousers" and "outside agitators" those of us who employ nonviolent direct action, and if they refuse to support our nonviolent efforts, millions of Negroes will, out of frustration and despair, seek solace and security in black nationalist ideologies—a development that would inevitably lead to a frightening racial nightmare.

Oppressed people cannot remain oppressed forever. The yearning for freedom eventually manifests itself, and that is what has happened to the American Negro. Something within has reminded him of his birthright of freedom, and something without has reminded him that it can be gained. Consciously or unconsciously, he has been caught up by the *Zeitgeist*, and with his black brothers of Africa and his brown and yellow brothers of Asia, South America, and the Caribbean, the United States Negro is moving with a sense of great urgency toward the promised land of racial justice. If one recognizes this vital urge that has engulfed the Negro community, one should readily understand why public demonstrations are taking place. The Negro has many pent-up resentments and latent frustrations, and he must release them. So let him march; let him make prayer pilgrimages to the city hall; let him go on freedom rides—and try to understand why he must do so. If his repressed emotions are not released in nonviolent ways, they will seek expression through violence; this is not a threat but a fact of history. So I have not said to my people, "Get rid of your discontent." Rather, I have tried to say that this normal and healthy discontent can be channeled into the creative outlet of nonviolent direct action. And now this approach is being termed extremist.

But though I was initially disappointed at being categorized as an extremist, as I continued to think about the matter I gradually gained a measure of satisfaction from the label. Was not Jesus an extremist for love: "Love your enemies, bless them that curse you, do good to them that hate you, and pray for them which despitefully use you, and persecute you." Was not Amos an extremist for justice: "Let justice roll down like waters and righteousness like an ever-flowing stream." Was not Paul an extremist for the Christian gospel: "I bear in my body the marks of the Lord Jesus." Was not Martin Luther an extremist: "Here I stand; I cannot do otherwise, so help me God." And John Bunyan: "I will stay in jail to the end of my days before I make a butchery of my conscience." And Abraham Lincoln: "This nation cannot survive half slave and half free." And Thomas Jefferson: "We hold these truths to be self-evident, that all men are created equal. . . ." So the question is not whether we will be extremists, but what kind of extremists we will be. Will we be extremists for hate or for love? Will we be extremists for the preservation of injustice or for the extension of justice? In that dramatic scene on Calvary's hill three men were crucified. We must never forget that all three were crucified for the same crime—the crime of extremism. Two were extremists for immorality, and thus fell below their environment. The other, Jesus Christ, was an extremist for love, truth, and goodness, and thereby rose above his environment. Perhaps the South, the nation, and the world are in dire need of creative extremists.

I had hoped that the white moderate would see this need. Perhaps I was too optimistic; perhaps I expected too much. I suppose I should have realized that few members of the oppressor race can understand the deep groans and passionate yearnings of the oppressed race, and still fewer have the vision to see that injustice must be rooted out by strong, persistent, and determined action. I am thankful, however, that some of our white brothers in the South have grasped the meaning of this social revolution and committed themselves to it. They are still all too few in quantity, but they are big in quality. Some—such as Ralph McGill, Lillian Smith, Harry Golden, James McBride Dabbs, Ann Braden, and Sarah Patton Boyle—have written about our struggle in eloquent and prophetic terms. Others have marched with us down nameless streets of the South. They have languished in filthy, roach-infested jails, suffering the abuse and brutality of policemen who view them as "dirty nigger-lovers." Unlike so many of their moderate brothers and sisters, they have recognized the urgency of the moment and sensed the need for powerful "action" antidotes to combat the disease of segregation.

Let me take note of my other major disappointment. I have been so greatly disappointed with the white church and its leadership. Of course, there are some notable exceptions. I am not unmindful of the fact that each of you has taken some significant stands on this issue. I commend you, Reverend Stallings, for your Christian stand on this past Sunday, in welcoming Negroes to your worship service on a nonsegregated basis. I commend the Catholic leaders of this state for integrating Spring Hill College several years ago.

But despite these notable exceptions, I must honestly reiterate that I have been disappointed with the church. I do not say this as one of those negative critics who can always find something wrong with the church. I say this as a minister of the gospel, who loves the church; who was nurtured in its bosom; who has been sustained by its spiritual blessings and who will remain true to it as long as the cord of life shall lengthen.

When I was suddenly catapulted into the leadership of the bus protest in Montgomery, Alabama, a few years ago, I felt we would be supported by the white church. I felt that the white ministers, priests, and rabbis of the South would be among our strongest allies. Instead, some have been outright opponents, refusing to understand the freedom movement and misrepresenting its leaders; all too many others have been more cautious than courageous and have remained silent behind the anesthetizing security of stained-glass windows.

In spite of my shattered dreams, I came to Birmingham with the hope that the white religious leadership of this community would see the justice of our cause and, with deep moral concern, would serve as the channel through which our just grievances could reach the power structure. I had hoped that each of you would understand. But again I have been disappointed. . . .

There was a time when the church was very powerful—in the time when the early Christians rejoiced at being deemed worthy to suffer for what they believed. In those days the church was not merely a thermometer that recorded the ideas and principles of popular opinion; it was a thermostat that transformed the mores of society. Whenever the early Christians entered a town, the people in power became disturbed and immediately sought to convict the Christians for being "disturbers of the peace" and "outside agitators." But the Christians pressed on, in the conviction that they were "a colony of heaven," called to obey God rather than man. Small in number, they were big in commitment. They were too God intoxicated to be "astronomically intimidated." By their effort and example they brought an end to such ancient evils as infanticide and gladiatorial contests.

Things are different now. So often the contemporary church is a weak, ineffectual voice with an uncertain sound. So often it is an archdefender of the status quo. Far from being disturbed by the presence of the church, the power structure of the average community is consoled by the church's silent—and often even vocal—sanction of things as they are.

But the judgment of God is upon the church as never before. If today's church does not recapture the sacrificial spirit of the early church, it will lose its authenticity, forfeit the loyalty of millions, and be dismissed as an irrelevant social club with no meaning for the twentieth century. Every day I meet young people whose disappointment with the church has turned into outright disgust.

Perhaps I have once again been too optimistic. Is organized religion too inextricably bound to the status quo to save our nation and the world? Perhaps I must turn my faith to the inner spiritual church, the church within the church, as the true *ekklesia* and the hope of the world. But again I am thankful to God that some noble souls from the ranks of organized religion have broken loose from the paralyzing chains of conformity and joined us as active partners in the struggle for freedom. They have left their secure congregations and walked the streets of Albany, Georgia, with us. They have gone down the highways of the South on torturous rides for freedom. Yes, they have gone to jail with us. Some have been dismissed from their churches, have lost the support of their bishops and fellow ministers. But they have acted in the faith that right defeated is stronger than evil triumphant. Their witness has been the spiritual salt that has preserved the true meaning of the gospel in these troubled times. They have carved a tunnel of hope through the dark mountain of disappointment.

I hope the church as a whole will meet the challenge of this decisive hour. But even if the church does not come to the aid of justice, I have no despair about the future. I have no fear about the outcome of our struggle in Birmingham, even if our motives are at present misunderstood. We will reach the goal of freedom in Birmingham and all over the nation, because the goal of America is freedom. Abused and scorned though we may be, our destiny is tied up with America's destiny. Before the pilgrims landed at Plymouth, we were here. Before the pen of Jefferson etched the majestic words of the Declaration of Independence across the pages of history, we were here. For more than two centuries our forebears labored in this country without wages; they made cotton king; they built the homes of their masters while suffering gross injustice and shameful humiliation—and yet out of a bottomless vitality they continued to thrive and develop. If the inexpressible cruelties of slavery could not stop us, the opposition we now face will surely fail. We will win our freedom because the sacred heritage of our nation and the eternal will of God are embodied in our echoing demands.

Before closing I feel impelled to mention one other point in your statement that has troubled me profoundly. You warmly commended the Birmingham police force for keeping "order" and "preventing violence." I doubt that you would have so warmly commended the police force if you had seen its dogs sinking their teeth into unarmed, nonviolent Negroes. I doubt that you would so quickly commend the policemen if you were to observe their ugly and inhumane treatment of Negroes here in the city jail; if you were to watch them push and curse old Negro women and young Negro girls; if you were to see them slap and kick old Negro men and young boys; if you were to observe them, as they did on two occasions, refuse to give us food because we wanted to sing our grace together. I cannot join you in your praise of the Birmingham police department.

It is true that the police have exercised a degree of discipline in handling the demonstrators. In this sense they have conducted themselves rather "nonviolently" in public. But for what purpose? To preserve the evil system of segregation. Over the past few years I have consistently preached that nonviolence demands that the means we use must be as pure as the ends we seek. I have tried to make clear that it is wrong to use immoral means to attain moral ends. But now I must affirm that it is just as wrong, or perhaps even more so, to use moral means to preserve immoral ends. Perhaps Mr. Connor and his policemen have been rather nonviolent in public, as was Chief Pritchett in Albany, Georgia, but they have used the moral means of nonviolence to maintain the immoral end of racial injustice. As T. S. Eliot has said,

"The last temptation is the greatest treason: To do the right deed for the wrong reason."

I wish you had commended the Negro sit-inners and demonstrators of Birmingham for their sublime courage, their willingness to suffer, and their amazing discipline in the midst of great provocation. One day the South will recognize its real heroes. They will be the James Merediths, with the noble sense of purpose that enables them to face jeering and hostile mobs, and with the agonizing loneliness that characterizes the life of the pioneer. They will be old, oppressed, battered Negro women, symbolized in a seventy-two-year-old woman in Montgomery, Alabama, who rose up with a sense of dignity and with her people decided not to ride segregated buses, and who responded with ungrammatical profundity to one who inquired about her weariness: "My feets is tired, but my soul is at rest." They will be the young high school and college students, the young ministers of the gospel and a host of their elders, courageously and nonviolently sitting in at lunch counters and willingly going to jail for conscience' sake. One day the South will know that when these disinherited children of God sat down at lunch counters, they were in reality standing up for what is best in the American dream and for the most sacred values in our Judaeo-Christian heritage, thereby bringing our nation back to those great wells of democracy which were dug deep by the founding fathers in their formulation of the Constitution and the Declaration of Independence.

Never before have I written so long a letter. I'm afraid it is much too long to take your precious time. I can assure you that it would have been much shorter if I had been writing from a comfortable desk, but what else can one do when he is alone in a narrow jail cell, other than write long letters, think long thoughts and pray long prayers?

If I have said anything in this letter that overstates the truth and indicates an unreasonable impatience, I beg you to forgive me. If I have said anything that understates the truth and indicates my having a patience that allows me to settle for anything less than brotherhood, I beg God to forgive me.

I hope this letter finds you strong in the faith. I also hope that circumstances will soon make it possible for me to meet each of you, not as an integrationist or a civil rights leader but as a fellow clergyman and a Christian brother. Let us all hope that the dark clouds of racial prejudice will soon pass away and the deep fog of misunderstanding will be lifted from our fear-drenched communities, and in some not too distant tomorrow the radiant stars of love and brotherhood will shine over our great nation with all their scintillating beauty.

Yours in the cause of
Peace and Brotherhood,

Martin Luther King, Jr.

OPTIONS FOR WRITING

1. Write a dialogue between Frederick Douglass and Thomas Jefferson concerning the Fourth of July. On what points do they agree? On which do they disagree?

2. Write a dialogue between Martin Luther King, Jr., and James Madison concerning minority rights under the Constitution. Is Madison critical of King's approach to achieving justice? What does King accuse Madison of failing to take into account?

3. Write an essay on the following topic: "If a law is unjust, does the citizen have an obligation to obey it?" Consider these possible responses to a law you perceive as unfair: (1) I must obey all laws, regardless of my opinion concerning their wisdom, justice, or constitutionality. (2) I can disobey a law only when the government is tyrannical enough to justify revolution and its overthrow. (3) I must obey only those laws which I consider to be just.

Abraham Lincoln
THE GETTYSBURG ADDRESS, 1863

Abraham Lincoln (1809–1865), the sixteenth president of the United States (1861–1865), was born in Hodgenville, Kentucky, and died at the hand of an assassin during his second term in office. He was the first Republican to win the presidency, a political party formed to prevent the extension of slavery to the western territories, and while in the White House led the effort to preserve the union in the face of attempts by eleven southern states to secede and form their own country, the Confederate States of America. In 1863 he emancipated the slaves. At the dedication of a cemetery for the soldiers who died at the battle of Gettysburg in July 1863, one of the decisive battles of the Civil War, Lincoln spoke a few words, intended in part to make possible a reconciliation between North and South after the war. According to Lincoln what is the significance of 1776? What is the purpose of the Civil War?

November 19, 1863

Four score and seven years ago our fathers brought forth on this continent, a new nation, conceived in Liberty, and dedicated to the proposition that all men are created equal.

Now we are engaged in a great civil war, testing whether that nation, or any nation so conceived and so dedicated, can long endure. We are met on a great battle-field of that war. We have come to dedicate a portion of that field, as a final resting place for those who here gave their lives that that nation might live. It is altogether fitting and proper that we should do this.

But, in a larger sense, we can not dedicate—we can not consecrate—we can not hallow—this ground. The brave men, living and dead, who struggled here, have consecrated it, far above our poor power to add or detract. The world will little note, nor long remember what we say here, but it can never forget what they did here. It is for us the living, rather, to be dedicated here to the unfinished work which they who fought here have thus far so nobly advanced. It is rather for us to be here dedicated to the great task remaining before us—that from these honored dead we take increased devotion to that cause for which they gave the last full measure of devotion—that we here highly resolve that these dead shall not have died in vain—that this nation, under God, shall have a new birth of freedom—and that government of the people, by the people, for the people, shall not perish from the earth.

OPTIONS FOR WRITING

1. Describe the subject of Lincoln's speech. What is his tone of voice? What is the purpose of the address, and who is its intended audience? Is he speaking to you? If so, what is he saying to you?

2. Analyze what Lincoln means by "government of the people, by the people, for the people." This statement seems to call for a large role for public opinion in the American political system. Is it consistent with James Madison's beliefs about the place of public opinion?

3. Lincoln's Gettysburg Address is about 250 words long. Write a speech of equal length. Before beginning, identify the subject, purpose, and audience of the speech. Also determine your voice (for example, solemn or humorous, formal or colloquial).

Edward Banfield, Allan Bloom, and Charles Murray
THE PURSUIT OF HAPPINESS:
THEN AND NOW

The following is a conversation among three social scientists who share the unusual honor of having written best-selling books. The subject of the conversation is a phrase from The Declaration of Independence, "the pursuit of happiness." The three interlocutors discuss whether the American people understand the pursuit of happiness in the same way today as they did at the nation's birth.

Edward Banfield (b. 1916) is a professor emeritus of government at Harvard University and author of The Unheavenly City: The Nature and Future of Our Urban Crisis. *Allan Bloom's bestseller is entitled* The Closing of the American Mind: How

Higher Education Has Failed Democracy and Impoverished the Minds of Today's Students. *Bloom (b. 1930) is a professor on the Committee on Social Thought at the University of Chicago. Charles Murray (b. 1943), a fellow at the Manhattan Institute for Policy Research, wrote* Losing Ground: American Social Policy 1950–1980.

Does the pursuit of happiness have a different meaning for most Americans today than it had for Thomas Jefferson? Would you describe these three authors' views as liberal or conservative?

Charles Murray: I concluded my book *Losing Ground* with a thought experiment that goes like this: Let's say you have a two-year-old son or daughter. You know that tomorrow you and your spouse will be run over by a bus, and your child will be orphaned. You are unable to place this child with friends or relatives. Instead, you must choose between two alternatives. One is a pair of poor parents, so poor that your child will sometimes wear hand-me-down—even ragged—clothes, will be teased by schoolmates, and may sometimes go to bed hungry, even though he won't be malnourished. These parents have worked hard all their lives. They will make sure your child goes to school and studies hard, and they will teach your child that integrity, honesty, and self-sufficiency are primary values.

The other choice is parents who are as affectionate to your child as the first couple, but who are incapable of overseeing your child's education. Words like integrity, honesty, and self-sufficiency are meaningless to them. They have plenty of food, shelter, and the rest of the necessities of life.

With which couple will you place your child?

Most people answer—often reluctantly—that they would put their child with the poor couple. If I ask why, they come up with a variety of explanations: "I want my child to become a reflective adult"; "I want my child to grow up valuing things such as self-sufficiency, hard work, and independence." If I were to push far enough, sooner or later the answer would be that they want the child to be able to pursue happiness—long-term, justified satisfaction with life.

Now, I am willing to bet that there is not a nickel's worth of difference among 95 percent of Americans' notions of happiness. Even so, just about everybody is convinced that everybody *else* has an idiosyncratic, hedonistic, ephemeral, or silly view of happiness. They may not have read Aristotle, but they accept an important, nontrivial sense of happiness.

Having said that, we still have a problem. By making the choice for your child, you have in mind a good you are trying to maximize. That good is complex, but nonetheless so important that you are willing to behave in accordance with your understanding of it.

When we think about social policy, shouldn't we try to have the same kind of complex, multidimensional understanding of what we're trying to accomplish?

Government, by setting the rules of the game, enables people to pursue happiness, and that is the entry point for any discussion of the relationship between happiness and social policy. We start with the raw material, the conditions that are required for pursuing happiness. We can all agree that it's difficult to pursue happiness if you're starving. So, material resources are an obvious enabling condition. Safety is another. One of the reasons human beings form communities is to be safe from the tigers beyond the compound. Self-respect is another enabling condition. So is enjoyment or self-fulfillment.

Thinking in these terms changes our approach to social policy. If you think about material resources as an enabling condition for the pursuit of happiness, for example, you are forced to think about poverty in a different way—as something more than an annual income figure alone could pin down. As you start to think about what poverty really is, the operational definition becomes meaningless. I'm not exaggerating. I wrote a book in which the poverty line figured very prominently. I'm not willing to use it anymore, except to say it doesn't mean anything.

Self-respect is as essential to the pursuit of happiness as material resources are. And this is something that statistics like the poverty line can't begin to take into account. If self-respect must consist of the conviction that we can and do measure up, then the implications for social policy are profound.

Folks who deal in policy think about certain topics, but they are oblivious to others. Take the issue of self-fulfillment, or enjoyment. John Rawls addressed this by condensing Aristotle into what he calls the Aristotelian Principle: People enjoy the realization of their capacities. The more complex the capacity or the greater the development of it, the more it can be enjoyed.

A social scientist assembled a variety of people who engaged in various forms of play that they found absorbing and rewarding. He included rock climbers and basketball players and chess players and dancers. In a rigorous social science fashion he analyzed their enjoyment of the activities.

Apparently oblivious to the fact, he came up with a beautiful data statement of the Aristotelian Principle. People enjoy realizing their capacities. They enjoy being pushed to the edge of those capacities. Yet everything we know about how human beings enjoy themselves is at odds with the arguments behind some of the ways we do business as a society.

In the past, policy analysts said that government can provide for material resources because this is one thing government knows how to do. While analysts may have acknowledged the importance of self-respect, enjoyment, and a sense of belonging, they felt free to ignore such notions. People could try to work out these enabling conditions for themselves.

The longer you think about the kinds of issues I've raised, the more obvious it becomes that you can't do business that way. By providing the material resources, you have altered the ways in which other things happen. Such things as self-respect, enjoyment, and "belongingness" are intimately connected to the way in which one provides for one's own material resources.

The findings and the approaches I've been talking about can be used to rationalize either a socialist state or a libertarian one—one in which the government should provide for almost everything or for almost nothing.

We have tried a variety of social experiments that haven't worked very well over the last twenty years. We have to start thinking more imaginatively about what we're trying to accomplish. Thinking about the pursuit of happiness can contribute to that.

Edward Banfield: I intend to limit myself to the question: Has two hundred years of the pursuit of happiness left us more happy or less happy? Almost all of those who have pronounced on this question say it has left us more unhappy. They can be divided into two groups.

First, there are those who say that the pursuit of happiness has turned out to be the pursuit of riches—that our success has corrupted us as individuals and as a society. Second, there are those who say that the pursuit of happiness, or riches, is a treadmill—a foolish waste of time and effort at best. John Adams, in a letter written in retirement to his friend Thomas Jefferson, exemplifies the first view: "Will you tell me how to prevent riches from becoming the effects of temperance and industry? Will you tell me how to prevent riches from producing luxury? And will you tell me how to prevent luxury from producing effeminacy, intoxication, extravagance, vice, and folly?"

Tocqueville was another eminent exponent of this view. Adams and Jefferson were hardly in their graves when Tocqueville began to bewail, in *Democracy in America*, the passions of Americans for physical gratification. In his view it appeared that our main preoccupation was satisfying the body with the conveniences of life. This was not a vicious materialism that we had fallen into, he allowed, but it distracted us from our political duties and enervated the soul, noiselessly unbending its springs of action.

And finally, Aleksandr Solzhenitsyn in his commencement address at Harvard, told us pretty much what Tocqueville had told us—that happiness in America has come to mean wanting things, and the competition for things has dominated our thoughts. Despite our success in getting things, he said, Americans are dissatisfied with themselves and their society. Indeed, he says, they despise it.

This is not the America that I see. Wealth has not prevented America and Americans from being at least as humane and protective of human rights and peace as any society. Indeed, the great calamities that Tocqueville, Solzhenitsyn, and others have spoken of have not eventuated, and what has eventuated has had nothing to do with American wealth. Nazism, Communism, and Muslim fundamentalism were not the results of an excess of material things.

The second criticism—that we are on a treadmill demanding things that we don't really want—is a plausible but much less serious charge. If we're guilty, it's a misdemeanor rather than a felony. Thorstein Veblen, John Kenneth Galbraith—there's one in every generation to tell us that our consumption satisfies our wants rather than our needs. Perhaps it's silly to want a car as a toy rather than as a means of transportation. I am not persuaded of that. I remember the wife of the minister of the church that I was taken to as a child telling my mother that she liked her car because it was the one thing she could control. [Laughter.] It seemed to me the poor woman deserved to have at least one thing that she could control.

On the other hand, if we examine the Founders' understanding of the pursuit of happiness, it is arguable that our pursuit of it has not gotten us very far. Their view was derived from, among others, the philosophy of John Locke.

Jefferson, Adams, and Franklin had read and understood Locke's argument that nature or nature's God created man intending him to be happy. The right to life, liberty, and the pursuit of happiness depended on this.

It being God's intention that all men be happy, the individual has not only to promote his own happiness, but also to take account of the happiness of others. He has an obligation, in Locke's words, to do good. By the light of nature, he writes, we know that we ought to do good to others because it is an obligation of *man*, and we ought to do as much as we can to preserve the rest of mankind, although not at the cost of oneself.

Locke thinks that men should obtain comforts and conveniences by industry. He favors pastimes, but as recreation—that is, interruption of serious work or industry.

Well, how can rationality—the thing that pleasure turns upon—be increased? Children, Locke observed, can be taught to distinguish good from bad, and more important, perhaps, they can be taught self-denial and self-discipline. Indulgent parents are mainly to blame for the mis-education of children, he says, and it will take a tutor of rare qualities to educate a child properly. That certainly amounts to saying that mass education is impossible. Locke would have been amused at the idea that somebody would criticize Harvard and Cornell and Chicago and others for not educating their elite. He would never have expected them to.

PUBLIC OPINION

In Locke's view, public opinion is of crucial importance. Locke says that not one man in 10,000 is indifferent to—or dares act in the face of—public opinion. Although grotesquely, bizarrely wrong in many societies, public opinion offers some hope in a good society. Public opinion, Locke thinks, is a source of second-hand virtue or rationality because the applause of other people's reason will guide one.

So, the question I come to and, alas, end my remarks without answering properly is: What is the case of public opinion today? Locke's view was that men of high reputation ought to be very careful in their use of high reputation so as not to undermine or undercut the substitute for reasonable judgment that most people will have to rely upon.

This is an appropriate place for me to stop because Allan Bloom is a specialist on the subject of how public opinion forms and deforms America and on our potential for happiness today.

Allan Bloom: It's remarkable to come to Washington and find so many people preoccupied with happiness. Happiness is a philosophic issue. Both of our speakers have turned to philosophy for dealing with the comprehensive good. None of the more scientific of the social sciences seems to.

It's an enormous pleasure to talk about philosophic questions with people one respects. And in some sense, that should be the end of my talk, because I would say that's happiness.

Both of the previous speakers seemed to say happiness was the fulfillment of man's nature. When one starts speaking about human nature, what one means is a kind of perfection; something that not everybody can attain but the approximations of which fulfill our humanity. There's a very short list of what the highest human lives are: prophet, saint, legislator, political founder, philosopher, poet. The list has never changed.

The peacock's fan of human nature opens when you study the arguments made for each. When we read about Moses or Jesus, when we see the lives of Socrates or the great rulers — whether it's in Plutarch's *Parallel Lives*, or Thucydides, or Shakespeare's real or imagined kings — we explore the limits of humanity.

One of the greatest public policy uses of a discussion of happiness, or perhaps the only one, is for a statesman to think about what the human possibilities are, and at the same time to see what his nation is. He has before him the task of governing: to encourage the tendencies toward the greatest fulfillments of natural humanity and to discourage the trivial, the wasting of human capacity.

Political regimes always tend to have one dominant principle. Aristocracy's is honor, for example; oligarchy's is money. And each of those has a tendency to distort. A fully educated, thoughtful statesman would, therefore, oppose those tendencies.

Obviously, the great American tendency is equality. Equality always inclines people to say that everybody's achievement is as estimable as every other person's achievement; not to have to envy. And there's a school of public policy now — John Rawls, Ronald Dworkin — that wants to take away envy, not by giving people the virtue of controlling it, but by taking away what's enviable — that is, inequality of talents as well as of money.

Aristotle said that the legislator deals with the comprehensive good. His primary function is to make the citizens good and the doers of noble deeds. The modern legislature, stemming from Locke, tries to provide the *conditions* of happiness or the pursuit of happiness, a much more modest scheme. The question is whether something fundamental has been lost in adopting a more modest scheme.

What we are left with is empty formulas rather than anything substantial or anything to admire. Our only contemporary philosophy is a certain kind of relativism.

At a moment when America most needs to think about both its political unity and the unity of the human beings within it, the only thing the presidents of universities can talk about is diversity: diverse societies, diverse students, and so on. This is perhaps their way of moving away from uncomfortable reflections on what man's perfection might be.

Assaults on classic texts are part of this; because the classic texts encourage discoveries of what is more than mediocre, they give birth to aspirations, and they urge us to develop a capacity for self-contempt.

We would all do well to cut through this ideological assault that attempts to take away all that is uncomfortable; all that would give us aspirations beyond our immediate concept of self.

QUESTIONS

Robert Goldwin: James Madison, in a passage quoted by Charles Murray in his forthcoming book, spoke of "the happiness of the people" as "the object of government." Political leaders would not use such words today. What's the significance of the change in vocabulary? Why has the term "happiness" fallen into disuse?

Banfield: In political matters one has to start from where one is. Only a group like this might be patient enough to hear what somebody thinks Locke thought happiness meant.

But to suppose that the public, or people who form public opinion, can be persuaded to turn back to John Locke, or better yet, to Aristotle, is a pipedream.

Murray: The current hostility toward the concept of happiness is fascinating. It is somehow improper for people who are engaged in the public business to toss around words like that.

One quick answer is that to the extent you use the word happiness as a meaningful concept, you are discarding others—the momentary or the ephemeral pleasures. If you do that and you're engaged in a policy discussion, people can see where you're going to end up.

If you say it's important that people have things besides enough food, shelter, and clothing in their lives, you introduce notions that will be interpreted as saying the state doesn't have an obligation to provide those things, and maybe it shouldn't.

Bloom: There are two tendencies at work. One is the notion that any attempt to say what is good necessarily excludes people who are judged to be not good. Everybody is intimidated by this because ours is supposed to be an inclusive society.

These days the only people we are allowed to call bad are privileged people who don't spend all their time, energies, and money taking care of the disadvantaged. Today, social responsibility consists of making everyone *feel* good.

Parents are generally more sensible. Parents think about what kind of people they want their children to be. And they like to think that their kids are going to *be* good. They have some fairly clear ideas of what good means, and those ideas are very traditional.

I discovered education is a hot issue—not in universities, but among parents. [Laughter.] It's a great force to be tapped. Parents make up a large part of the electorate.

With the Reagan majority, it is assumed that the only thing all parents want their children to do is to be skilled technicians who make money. That parents want children to mint their educations. That has not been my experience. Parents want to convey things to their children that they might lack themselves—aspirations connected with books and learning.

So, discussions about happiness could most easily be part of discussions about education and the concern for the young. How successful that will be, given the fact that the intellectual class is so resolutely know-nothing and is not very accountable now, I don't know. But it's certainly worth trying to tap.

This is a year when we've watched the Senate having no standard other than public opinion. Obviously, statesmen have always given in to their constituencies. But they frequently did it with a tug at their hearts; with a notion that there was something else that could affect them. That has simply disappeared.

HAPPINESS AND INEQUALITY

Goldwin: Allan, did you say that one problem with happiness is that there's something undemocratic about it, that there's inequality in it?

If I understood you correctly, then a real paradox exists, because the assertion that every one of us has an inalienable right to the pursuit of happiness, and that governments exist to secure that right, is in the Declaration of Independence, which is the foundation of our democracy.

If the Declaration of Independence is itself democratic, do you mean that a democratic principle—the pursuit of happiness—is inherently undemocratic because of an implication of inequality?

Bloom: Democracy is problematic, and it shouldn't be a sin to say that. If one chooses democracy, it ought to be on the basis of its advantages and disadvantages.

Again, I would turn to parents. This is something peculiarly American. One of the reasons that socialism has not taken root in this country is because parents don't insist that they themselves attain the heights if their children might. The guarantee to the *pursuit* of happiness is obviously not the guarantee of the *attainment* of happiness. Money, birth, race, and so on do not stand in the way of unequal achievement in our society. That is part of democracy.

Murray: There is something that is odd about the anti-democratic aspect of happiness you were talking about. Among people who are most antagonistic toward applying some of these thoughts to real policy, there is an implicit assumption that only a few can pursue meaningful happiness.

There are a lot of folks out there who say, well, it's okay for you and me who have advantages, and who have gone to college, to think in terms of structuring society so that we have access to these higher goals; but the poor working stiff out there, Joe Six Pack, can't be expected to participate in this. And God forbid that you should expect people in the inner city who are on welfare or who are otherwise disadvantaged to participate.

Bloom: One is always hearing, what about the kid in the inner city, what does Plato have to do with him? There is a beautiful passage from W. E. B. DuBois that says something like "I look at Shakespeare, and he does not wince." And it goes on that way. "I walk and I talk with Plato."

There are problematic aspects to our common culture. The question is whether equality has to be an abstract equality that denies nature, or whether it can take account of natural differences.

One has to keep going back to Aristophanes' beautiful play where everyone is declared equal, and you find the ugly old hags insisting upon the favors of young men. If democracy has to be that, it's not trustworthy.

Murray: One of the most interesting questions is to take someone who is not beautiful or brilliant, who is below average in intelligence—as indeed 50 percent of the population are—and who is below average in industriousness. How can he reach the age of seventy and be satisfied with who he is and what he has done?

The test of a society is that someone can reach the age of seventy and be able to look back and say, I have lived a life that I can be pleased with.

Bloom: The question is whether we should be envious of the peak talents. Of course, everyone wants to have had the level of satisfaction that he can attain. All profit from a society that produces the peaks of human capacity. We should aim for a society in which individuals who are inferior to Shakespeare admire him but recognize that their own humanity is reflected in Shakespeare and is enhanced by it.

It would have been a very poor education indeed that didn't teach us about our own modest talents, and therefore point us higher.

Murray: I am not arguing for a cheapening of the concept of happiness. On the contrary, I am saying that one of the arrogances of our time is that we think that it is something reserved to a relatively small segment of the population, and what we have to do is make sure the rest of society just exists.

To not be too cryptic about this, I would say, for example, that if you are the fellow I was talking about a few minutes ago — the one who doesn't have any special talents, is not going to be famous, is never going to be rich, then if he reaches the age of seventy and can look back and say, I was a good parent to my children, I was a good neighbor, these are important and significant things to have done.

OPTIONS FOR WRITING

1. List the various understandings of happiness that are mentioned in the conversation. What are the implications for government policy of each understanding? Which understanding do you share?

2. According to the participants, is public opinion at present a healthful or noxious influence on America's youth? In your opinion, does public opinion put too high a value on material comforts? If so, what if anything can be done to improve public opinion?

3. Assemble in your imagination three persons of distinct backgrounds whom you admire (for example, a teacher, a rock musician, and a sports star). Imagine that they have met and that the subject of happiness emerges in their discussion. Record their conversation as you think it might occur.

The Baltimore Sun
ELECTION SYSTEM FLAWED, POLL SHOWS

Campaign financing 'is a mess' and 'the system has problems,' many voters say.

In the United States, presidential campaigns are financed by the public by means of a $1 contribution option on income tax returns. The Democratic and Republican presidential candidates during the quadrennial fall campaigns may not accept contributions from other sources. Candidates for seats in the Senate and House of Representatives, however, must raise money from individual, labor union, and corporate donors. In 1990 advocates of public funding of congressional races commissioned a public opinion poll, the results of which are summarized in the following article. Do the poll results support public funding for campaigns by candidates for the Senate and House of Representatives? How would you have answered the questions?

American voters are tired of the way big political contributions influence their congressmen, and a solid majority thinks it would be a good idea for government money to pay for the campaigns instead, according to a poll released today.

The telephone poll, sponsored by People for the American Way, Ralph Nader's Public Citizen, the Advocacy Institute and the ARCA Foundation, found that 18 percent of those surveyed who say they are likely to vote in the 1990 elections think the congressional campaign finance system "is a mess and needs to be fundamentally reformed," while an additional 56 percent agreed "the system has problems and needs to be changed."

Twenty percent said "the system has some problems but is essentially sound," and the remaining 6 percent said they did not know what to think.

The results, said Joan Claybrook, president of Public Citizen, mean "the American public believes Congress no longer represents them." She said voters think the lawmakers instead represent the lobbyists and special interest groups that give them the largest political donations.

While that sort of public dissatisfaction may be a common refrain, Celina Lake, of the survey firm that conducted the poll, said such feelings in the past usually did not apply to a voter's local representative. But in the latest poll, she said, "This new mood has taken on a very personal quality. . . ." One-third say they think their member may be caught up or corrupted by the system."

Though they are dissatisfied, the voters put the issue of campaign finance near the bottom of the list when asked to pick their biggest worries from issues including drugs and crime (38 percent); education (16 percent); the economy (16 percent); taxes (13 percent), and the environment (9 percent).

Those worried most about "corruption and special interest money in politics" (5 percent), ranked barely ahead of "don't know" (2 percent).

Nor did the public seem to know a great deal about the system they dislike. Only 24 percent correctly answered that presidential campaigns are chiefly financed by the federal campaign fund financed by taxpayers' check-off on federal income tax returns.

But the voters did express strong dissatisfaction with some of the specific elements of campaign finance. When asked whether they agreed that political action committees — which collect and distribute donations on behalf of corporations, labor unions and trade associations — should be allowed to contribute to federal election campaigns, 33 percent said yes. Fifty-seven percent said they disagreed. Ten percent did not know.

When asked about possible reforms, 85 percent said they would favor a limit on how much a congressional candidate could spend on a campaign, but the response dropped to 77 percent when asked about a possible limit of "perhaps $500,000."

In the survey, 58 percent said they thought public financing of congressional campaigns was a "good idea" while 33 percent said it was a "bad idea." But the support dropped to 29 percent when respondents were reminded that public money might be spent on "negative campaigns and mudslinging on TV," or for "all campaigns that come along, including the candidates of the Communist Party and the Ku Klux Klan."

The poll sampled 900 registered voters nationwide who said they would probably vote in the 1990 elections. The results had a margin of error of plus or minus 3.3 percentage points.

OPTIONS FOR WRITING

1. Review the summary of the poll results found in the first paragraph of the newspaper article. Does it accurately present those results? Do the findings support Joan Claybrook's conclusions? Joan Claybrook was born in 1937, served as Administrator of the National Highway Traffic Safety Administration under the Carter Administration from 1977 to 1981, wrote *Retreat from Safety: Reagan's Attack on America's Health,* and is the president of Public Citizen. Imagine that you are an opponent of public funding of congressional elections. Write a response to Ms. Claybrook based on the poll data.

2. The poll revealed that the public knows little about the campaign finance system, the subject of the poll. Does public opinion exist concerning issues about which the people have little information? Critics of polling say the poll taker often leads or shapes the respondent's opinion because most people have no clear view on the question posed. Read a local or national newspaper for one week. Identify five controversial issues presently before the President, Congress, or the Supreme Court. How much do you know about each issue, and how much do you think the average citizen knows?

Everett Carll Ladd
ABORTION—THE PARTISAN CONSEQUENCES: Trouble for Both Parties

In 1973 the Supreme Court in Roe v. Wade *found unconstitutional the laws of more than forty states making abortion a criminal offense. The Court found that the right of privacy implied in the Constitution was broad enough to include a woman's decision to terminate her pregnancy. Although permitting some government restrictions during the second and third trimesters, the Court held that a woman's right to abortion was absolute during the first three months of the pregnancy. The decision has provoked numerous efforts to overturn it, including still unsuccessful attempts to persuade Congress to propose a constitutional amendment with that effect and pressure on the Court to reverse its earlier decision.*

Everett Carll Ladd was born in Saco, Maine, in 1937 and wrote, among other books, Transformations of the American Party System: Political Coalitions from the New Deal to the 1970s *and* Where Have All the Voters Gone?: The Fracturing of America's Political Parties. *He is a professor of political science at the University of Connecticut. What effect is the abortion controversy having on the Republican and Democratic parties? Is it hurting one party more than the other?*

What do Americans want their country's policy on abortion to be? And what are the implications for the Democratic and Republican parties of the ever-growing salience of the abortion debate?

The nature of the public's views on abortion is now a hot debate. With the U.S. Supreme Court re-examining in *Webster v. Reproductive Health Services* the policy it set forth sixteen years ago in *Roe v. Wade,* and with feelings running high among both those who want change and those who oppose it, vigorous efforts are being made to promote various interpretations. The very complexity of opinion on the issue gives ample opportunity to those inclinations. People on either side can pick and choose among the various strains in the public's thinking—emphasizing only those parts that agree with their own stands.

In a March national survey by the *Los Angeles Times,* 61 percent said abortion is "morally wrong," and 57 percent said that it is "murder." The same survey, however, found 62 percent opposed to amending the Constitution to prohibit abortion. Accounts that stress one of these elements point in a different direction from those that emphasize the others.

AN OVERVIEW OF PUBLIC SENTIMENT

In fact, although public opinion on abortion is complex, it has been remarkably clear and consistent over the last decade. Substantial majorities of Americans have continued to say a few basic things.

1. *Policy should seek a balance between the mother's claim to choose and the claim accruing to all human life.* Here, as on so many other questions, the public is plainly inclined to the general proposition that individual choice deserves considerable respect. But the public believes that at some point other interests come into play, requiring limits on that choice. The mother should be able to choose to have an abortion—but not for just any reason, and only after taking other important interests into account. The *Los Angeles Times* survey found, for example, 80 percent opposed to abortion "when it is used as a form of birth control." By 53 to 37 percent, the public would require obtaining the consent of the natural father before an abortion is performed, and by 81 to 14 percent they would insist that minors get parental permission.

2. *Neither state nor national government should be permitted to ban all abortions, but government should impose greater restrictions.* By 50 to 34 percent, the *L.A. Times* survey found, the public opposes "wiping out national standards about abortion" and letting each state impose whatever restrictions—including a complete ban—it chooses. And, as noted, a large majority reject a constitutional amendment that would categorically prohibit abortion. People believe that a woman should be able to get a legal abortion when the pregnancy results from rape or from incest, and when there is significant chance the child will be genetically deformed. And in overwhelming numbers, Americans would permit abortions to save the mother's life.

At the same time, large majorities in a poll taken March 27–29 by KRC Communications Research would make abortion illegal in cases where the claim for an abortion rested on the fetus not being of the desired sex (69 percent would make it illegal, 27 percent legal), the father's unwillingness to help raise the child (63 percent illegal, 31 percent legal), the judgment that it was the wrong time in life to have a child (63 to 32 percent), economic exigency (59 to 34 percent), or the belief that the pregnancy would cause excessive emotional strain (53 to 38 percent). Every survey taken in the last fifteen years asking whether abortion should be legal or illegal in various circumstances has found this basic pattern of public response.

3. *Roe v. Wade should not be reversed, but it should be amended.* The *L.A. Times* poll asked its respondents if they favored the court's decision in *Roe* that "permits a woman to get an abortion from a doctor at any time within the first three months of her pregnancy." Forty-six percent said they did, while 35 percent were opposed. The element of constitutionally guaranteed choice stipulated by *Roe* should be retained. It should be noted, however, that this question misstates the *Roe* ruling in one critical regard. The decision bars state-imposed curbs on abortion except to protect the health of the mother at any time in the *first six months of pregnancy.*

But if an important element of choice is to be preserved in the public's view, the full sweep of *Roe* is not. By 57 to 34 percent, respondents to the March 1989 *L.A. Times* survey rejected the proposition that "a pregnant woman should be able to get a legal abortion no matter what the reason"—essentially what *Roe v. Wade* permits. The National Opinion Research Center of the University of Chicago has asked this question annually since 1978, and it has never found the proportion favoring "abortion no matter what the reason" higher than 39 percent. Periodically since 1975, Gallup has asked whether "abortion should be legal under any circumstances, legal under only certain circumstances, or illegal in all circumstances." In no case, including the latest question in a *Newsweek* poll earlier this month—have more than 27 percent endorsed the *Roe* standard of "legal always." Each time at least two-thirds would restrict *Roe.*

The argument goes on in democratic theory over where majority preferences should be followed and where they should be subordinated to minority rights that majorities may not intrude upon. This question will never be resolved in the court of public opinion. On abortion, though, majority opinion is quite clear: *Abortion should not be categorically banned, but it should not be established as an absolute right.*

GROUP DIFFERENCES

Opinions on abortion vary, of course, across different population groups. Women and men hold similar views on most abortion questions, but women are usually found slightly more than men in the anti-abortion camp. Black Americans are slightly more likely than whites to oppose abortion. Regional differences are large, with residents of the Pacific Coast and the Northeast the most supportive of legal abortion and those in the East and West South Central states most opposed.

Two variables stand out in shaping abortion attitudes: (1) *religiosity,* for which frequency of church attendance is perhaps the most reliable survey measure; and (2) *levels of formal education,* where education is important both as a surrogate for overall socioeconomic status and, by itself, in identifying exposure through formal education to contrasting world views. Fifty-nine percent of college graduates in NORC's General Social Surveys (GSS) from 1984 to 1988 think a pregnant woman should be able to get a legal abortion no matter what the reason. Just 24 percent of those whose formal education stopped sometime prior to high school graduation take this stand. Fifty-four percent of those who never attend church favor abortion if the woman wants it "no matter what the reason," the position of only 9 percent who attend church more often than once a week. These two simple measures together explain an extraordinarily high proportion of the differences on abortion questions. Eighty percent of college graduates who rarely if ever attend church back the right to abortion no matter what the reason; just 12 percent with less than a high school education, who regularly attend church, think abortion should be legal in this case.

THE PARTISAN BATTLE

The two parties' stands on abortion could hardly be more dissimilar. In 1984, for example, the Democrats' platform proclaimed that the party "recognizes reproductive freedom as a fundamental human right. We therefore oppose government interference in the reproductive decisions of Americans, especially government interference which denies poor Americans their right to privacy by funding or advocating one or a limited number of reproductive choices only. . . . The Democratic party supports the 1973 Supreme Court decision on abortion rights as the law of the land and opposes any constitutional amendment to restrict or overturn that decision. . . . "

In sharp contrast, the 1984 Republican platform insisted that "the unborn child has a fundamental individual right to life which cannot be infringed. We therefore reaffirm our support for a human life amendment to the Constitution, and we endorse legislation to make clear that the Fourteenth Amendment's protections apply to unborn children. We oppose the use of public revenues for abortion and will eliminate funding for organizations which advocate or support abortions. . . . [W]e reaffirm our support for the appointments of judges . . . who respect traditional family values and the sanctity of innocent human life." The GOP reaffirmed these commitments in its 1988 platform. While the Democrats changed their platform language on abortion substantially in 1988—as part of a drastic shortening of the entire document—they reaffirmed their basic commitment: "We further believe . . . that the fundamental right of reproductive choice should be guaranteed regardless of ability to pay. . . ."

How has its stand on abortion affected each party's electoral fortunes? This question is difficult to answer, of course, because in electoral contests, including that for president, Democrats and Republicans differ on a great variety of issues. Final voter judgments are complex composites. Often no one, including voters themselves, can tell how much any one issue contributed to a vote.

We must be content, then, with a few observations of modest reach. The years since *Roe* have been an era of Republican ascendancy in presidential elections—the arena where policy differences stand out most sharply and are almost certain to have their greatest impact. At the very least, it's hard to make the case that the unequivocal stands against *Roe* in successive party platforms and the positions of Ronald Reagan and George Bush have diminished the GOP's appeal.

Even misstatements of an already strong Republican position against abortion seem not to have hurt. In his first debate with Michael Dukakis, for example, Bush was asked, "If abortions were to become illegal again, do you think that the women who defy the law and have them anyway—as they did before it was okayed by the Supreme Court—and the doctors who performed them, should go to jail?" Bush's answer was "I—I haven't sorted out the penalties, but I do know—I do know that I oppose abortion. . . . As I've seen, abortion is sometimes used as a birth-control device, for heaven's sake—see the millions of these killings—accumulate. . . . And once that illegality is established, then we can come to grips with the penalty side, and of course there's got to be some penalties to enforce the—enforce the law—whatever they may be."

For once Dukakis wasn't slow in responding to a clear opening: "Well, I think what the vice president is saying is that he's prepared to brand a woman a criminal for making this decision. It's as simple as that. I don't think it's enough to come before the American people, who are watching us tonight, and say, 'Well, I haven't sorted it out.' This is a very, very difficult and a fundamental decision. . . . And what he is saying, if I understand him correctly, is that he's prepared to brand a woman a criminal for making this choice." After the debate, campaign chief James Baker and other Bush aides insisted that what the vice president meant to say was something like this: "Of course I don't think the women involved should be sent to prison. I am arguing for a policy of compassion, not retribution." But he didn't say that.

The many polls taken on debate night and in the days immediately following offer no indication that this exchange cut into Bush's support. Some in the political community maintain that the lack of impact was due simply to Baker's adroit damage control. But this seems implausible. It's far more likely that Bush escaped harm because—as the summary of survey findings above indicates—many Americans are dissatisfied with the policy consequences of *Roe v. Wade* and thus accepted, at least in part, Bush's main point that "Yes, my position has evolved, and is continuing to evolve, and it's evolving in favor of life."

INTRAPARTY DIVISIONS

Both parties' leadership encompasses people who have different views on abortion. Some Republican leaders think their party is aligned too outspokenly these days against abortion; some Democrats worry that their party is too supportive of abortion rights. But if there is some concern in both camps, Democrats are giving more public voice to their concerns than are Republicans as the abortion controversy moves front and center in the *Webster* case. On April 6, fifty Democratic members of the House of Representatives signed a letter to their national chairman, Ronald Brown, calling for a shift in party policy. The effort was initiated by John J. LaFalce, a congressman from the Buffalo area.

The fifty Democrats stated that "along with millions of our fellow Democrats, [we] believe the platform plank is bad public policy. We, as good Democrats, simply cannot accept that plank as part of our Democratic heritage and philosophy." The signers went on to argue that the platform commitment to "the fundamental right of reproductive choice" is also bad politics. "A good case can be made," they said, "that the last three presidential elections have turned, at least in part, on the loss of traditional Democrats who have broken with the party over so-called social issues, particularly abortion. . . . The Democratic party is seen more and more as the party of abortion—a sure recipe for losing irretrievably a significant segment of our traditional base of support." The fifty Democrats urged their national chairman "to take appropriate steps to alter the party's course."

Were the situation reversed, and 19 percent of House Republicans were protesting their party's plank against abortion by telling national chairman Lee Atwater to change course by recognizing a "fundamental right of reproductive choice," it would be seen, properly, as a political bombshell. The 19 percent of House Democrats who signed the letter to Ronald Brown were motivated not only by personal beliefs but also by political judgment—that the party was hurting itself politically.

Democratic and Republican leaders are, as groups, far apart on abortion. Rank-and-file members of the two parties, however, for the most part hold strikingly similar views on the issue. The distribution of opinion among all Democratic identifiers differs little from that among Republicans. In NORC-GSS surveys taken from 1984 through 1988, 34 percent of those who identified themselves as strongly committed Democrats said they favored abortion for any reason; 66 percent opposed it. Among strong Republicans the distribution was identical—34 percent in favor, 66 percent opposed. Furthermore, most matched pairs of Democrats and Republicans hold similar views. Seventy-eight percent of Democrats and 76 percent of Republicans with less than a high school education, for example, opposed abortion for any reason. So, too, did 79 percent of Democrats and 82 percent of Republicans among those who attend church regularly (see Table 8.2).

College-educated Democrats and Republicans do differ significantly in their views on abortion. In the NORC surveys, Democratic college graduates maintained, by a margin of nearly two to one, that a woman is entitled to a legal abortion if she wants one for any reason. College-educated Republicans were far more supportive of abortion than other educational groups in the party but still much less so than their Democratic counterparts: they split fifty-fifty on this question.

Evidently, there is a wide range of sentiment on abortion within both camps of partisans. This suggests that both parties are in positions to lose supporters if abortion becomes more of a voting issue following *Webster* and subsequent decisions. The rank-and-file party coalitions thus far have remained remarkably heterogeneous on the issue. Each party is a microcosm of the population, so both can lose if Court decisions on abortion serve to increase public awareness of the parties' positions, which are so sharply opposed.

SMALL DIFFERENCES BETWEEN RANK-AND-FILE PARTISANS

Before exploring further what the partisan fallout might be of giving the contending party positions even greater salience, it might be helpful to introduce a measure of public opinion on abortion that can better cope with what we have seen to be the complexity of the public's judgments. We have created such a measure from three questions included within

TABLE 8.2   Partisan Attitudes and Abortion

Question: Do you think a pregnant woman should, or should not, be able to get a legal abortion no matter what the reason?

	ABORTION STAND			
	Democrats		Republicans	
	Yes	No	Yes	No
National	36%	64%	36%	64%
By partisan intensity:				
Strong	34	66	34	66
Not strong	38	62	38	62
By age:				
18–34 years old	43	57	39	61
35–49 years old	44	56	37	63
50 and over	27	73	33	67
By education:				
Less than H.S. graduate	22	78	24	76
H.S. graduate	37	63	35	66
College graduate	65	35	50	50
By region:				
Northeast	45	55	48	52
Midwest	33	67	30	70
South	29	71	32	68
West	48	52	39	61
By church attendance:				
Low	49	51	55	45
Mid	40	60	42	58
High	22	79	18	82

Source: Surveys by National Opinion Research Center, General Social Surveys, 1984–1988 combined.

Note: Low church attendance = attendance once a year or less, mid = attendance ranging from several times a year up to 2–3 times a month and high = every week (or nearly) and even more frequently.

the March 1989 *Los Angeles Times* survey—items that tap different dimensions of the public's thinking. The first item—the full text of which appears in Table 8.3—asks respondents whether they favor a constitutional amendment categorically banning abortion. A large majority say no. The second question included in our composite measure asks whether "a pregnant woman should, or should not, be able to get a legal abortion no matter what the reason"—the policy that most closely approximates *Roe*. A third question asks whether abortion is morally right or wrong. A large majority think it is morally wrong.

Nearly nine out of ten of these respondents are located in four of the eight positions: 18 percent take the pro-choice position each time; 14 percent say no to a constitutional ban on all abortions and yes to a woman's right to a legal abortion if she wants one for any reason but still indicate that personally they find abortion immoral; 26 percent describe abortion as morally wrong and say that a woman should not be able to choose abortion "no matter what the reason" but reject an absolute constitutional ban; and 30 percent take the anti-abortion position on all three dimensions.

Looking at group responses, we again see that education and religious adherence are enormously powerful predictors. College graduates who rarely or only occasionally attend church, and persons with less than a high school education who attend frequently, occupy opposite poles. Both camps of party identifiers, however, contain large if not exactly comparable proportions of the most religious and the least religious, the most highly educated and the least educated. Overall, Democrats are distributed in roughly the same proportions as Republicans across the four principal response categories that our composite measure defines.

William Schneider argues in the accompanying article that the Republicans have been saved thus far from the consequences of their anti-abortion stand because abortions have gone on even as the party has declared its strong opposition to them. Many Republican voters—especially the upscale and highly educated—have been able to ignore the party's stand because it hasn't seemed terribly consequential. But if *Webster* really cuts back on *Roe*, they would be forced to confront their party's policy. Or, to put the matter a little differently, corresponding to the analysis presented above, less educated, highly religious Republicans could not easily stay in coalition with highly educated, less religious Republicans if court rulings were to make the GOP's stand more salient.

Our analysis shows, however, that by this reckoning the Democrats are at least as vulnerable as the Republicans. Their coalition is still replete with persons who are highly religious and of low formal education; indeed, more of both these groups presently identify themselves as Democrats than as Republicans. Should the abortion issue start to drive dissenting partisans out of their traditional coalitions in far greater proportions than anything we have seen until now, the Democrats are likely to lose more than the GOP. Congressman LaFalce and his forty-nine cosigners obviously agree.

By definition, extremist stands don't find favor. On abortion, two positions are seen by large majorities as extreme: that abortion should be established as an unlimited right, and that it should be categorically banned. Should Republicans come to be seen as the party that would move policy to preclude abortion in all cases, they will surely suffer. But should the Democrats be seen as favoring an unlimited right to abortion, they will suffer. The public wants measured change in the policy set forth by the *Roe* decision.

TABLE 8.3   Index of Abortion Sentiment

Note to readers: This index combines the responses to three questions in the *Los Angeles Times* survey. The questions are:

1. Are you in favor of an amendment to the U.S. Constitution that would prohibit abortions, or are you opposed to that?

2. Do you think a pregnant woman should, or should not be able to get a legal abortion no matter what the reason?

3. Do you believe abortion is morally right or morally wrong?

This index yields eight possible response groups, from those who take the pro-abortion position on all three questions, to those taking an anti-abortion position on all three, with six intermediate combinations. Ninety percent of the responses fit into four of the eight possible categories.

	PRO-ABORTION ON ALL THREE QUESTIONS*	PRO-CHOICE BUT BELIEVE ABORTION IS IMMORAL*	ANTI-ABORTION BUT NO CATEGORIC BAN*	ANTI-ABORTION ON ALL THREE QUESTIONS*
By age:				
18–24 years	21%	14%	25%	30%
25–29	16	16	19	32
30–34	21	19	25	22
35–39	22	13	26	27
40–49	21	12	24	28
50–59	16	15	30	31
60–69	10	11	38	31
70 years and over	18	9	25	38
By sex:				
Male	20	13	29	26
Female	17	14	24	33
By education:				
Less than H.S. grad	14	13	26	36
H.S. grad/ Some college	18	13	27	30
College grad. +	28	16	25	19
By frequency of church attendance:				
Occasionally/rarely	26	17	26	20

Regularly	11	11	28	38
Frequently	6	8	29	44

By church attendance and education:

Occasional/ College grad.	44	21	18	5
Occasional/ H.S. grad.	24	16	29	19
Occasional/ Less than H.S. grad.	21	16	23	30
Regular/ College grad.	19	15	32	24
Regular/ H.S. grad.	11	12	29	38
Frequent/ College grad.	9	10	29	40
Frequent/ Less than H.S. grad.	7	5	35	44
Regular/ Less than H.S. grad.	5	8	21	51
Frequent/ H.S. grad.	5	9	25	46

By party:

Democratic	19	16	27	28
Independent	17	13	29	28
Republican	18	13	25	31

By party and education:

Democrat/ Less than H.S. grad.	11	18	31	30
Republican/ Less than H.S. grad	10	21	25	36
Democrat/ H.S. grad.	21	14	25	30
Republican/ H.S. grad.	18	11	25	31
Democrat/ College grad.	31	18	21	16
Republican/ College grad.	24	13	24	25

By frequency of
church attendance
and party:

Occasional/ Democrat	27	23	21	19
Occasional/ Republican	31	16	25	19
Regular/ Democrat	13	8	27	38
Regular/ Republican	11	12	28	37
Frequent/ Democrat	4	10	36	40
Frequent/ Republican	6	5	26	47

Note: *Column 1 = those taking the pro-abortion position on all three questions. Column 2 = those who say that a pregnant woman should be able to get a legal abortion no matter what the reason and who oppose an amendment banning abortion, but who nonetheless describe abortion as morally wrong. Column 3 = those who describe abortion as morally wrong and who disagree that a woman should be able to get a legal abortion no matter what the reason, but who nonetheless oppose a categoric ban on abortion. Column 4 = those taking the anti-abortion position on all three questions.

Note: Frequent church attendance = more than once a week, regular = once a week to once a month, and occasional/rare = less than once a month.

Source: Survey by the *Los Angeles Times*, March 3–10, 1989.

OPTIONS FOR WRITING

1. Lincoln spoke of "government by the people," yet Professor Ladd indicates that a majority of Americans consider abortion to be morally wrong and the equivalent of murder. Is it possible to square the Supreme Court's policy decision with the principle of majority rule? Does the essay by James Madison help you to understand the paradox of the existence of unpopular laws in a democracy?

2. Write two brief campaign speeches. First, imagine that you are a liberal Democratic candidate for the governorship of your state. How would you interpret the data presented by Professor Ladd in your speech? Now imagine that you are a conservative Republican campaigning for the governor's mansion. How would you change your interpretation of the same data?

3. Select one of the following puzzles and explain it.
   a. The Congress has refused to enact strict gun control laws, even though polls reveal that the people want such controls.
   b. The federal government has a large budget deficit, but the people want a balanced budget.
   c. Courts order children to be bused across neighborhoods in order to achieve racial balance in the schools, even though the people oppose busing.

d. The Equal Rights Amendment to the U.S. Constitution, guaranteeing equal rights for women, was not ratified by the state legislatures, but most people supported it.

4. Is abortion as salient an issue now as it was when Professor Ladd wrote his article in 1989? Which issues dividing the American people dominate the news today? Why do some issues fade from the front pages while others become more important? What role do public opinion pollsters play in this process?

9

THE INSIGHTS
OF SOCIOLOGY

Frederick E. Schmidt

The class of 1988 left behind an unusual gift—a campus communications kiosk. This thirty-two-foot outdoor signboard, covered with advertisements for rides, apartments, and a good time, sets sociologist Schmidt thinking about ways we relate to one another in any social system. Through the kiosk, Schmidt shows us first how we might make assumptions about the message makers and then teaches us how to test those assumptions in the debunking game. The rules of the game are simple, and we can learn a lot about our friends, our professors, and even celebrities as we play.

READINGS

"It's a communications kiosk," the university architect tells me. The elongated rectangle mounted on posts looks like a sign at a train station announcing the local community. Fastened to the kiosk is a torn photograph of Muffey, Amy's missing cat; a single leather glove; a classified ad from *Road and Track* depicting a 1985 MG for sale; and myriads of announcements: a quiltlike display of odd-sized, multicolored slips of paper ranging from a tiny corner of a paper napkin to standard sheets of paper alerting the passer-by to upcoming events and to the selling of plane tickets, trail bikes, computers, cameras, and more. This outdoor kiosk stretches some thirty-two feet, is six feet high, and is mounted against the guardrail of the walkway connecting the bookstore to the library. In one way, it forms the sociological heart of our campus. It provides a tangible source of symbolic exchange extremely useful in seeking to understand human behavior on this campus.

Just what did the graduates of 1988 seek to tell all of us by their gift? Why did the architect design it the way he did? Why a rectangle? The information kiosk, donated to the University by the graduating class of 1988, is a rich source of symbolic interaction. Interaction between and among human beings is the core interest of sociology. Virtually all human interaction is symbolic. For example, words provide critical evidence of symbolic communication. However, they are an imperfect representation of something real. Humans use inferred meanings drawn from words, gestures, posture, and styles of dressing, eating, and working as the basic information upon which to make the decisions affecting our lives.

Who cares? Why bother with these questions, you say? Well, through analysis of the behavior of others we learn about ourselves. These words, just symbols, can get you in trouble. Who says the architect was a "he"? What does the word "he" or "she" symbolize? Words are symbols, an imperfect representation of something real.

The class of 1988 fought to keep this kiosk in a central location. The University administration insisted on a conservative rectangle when the recent alumni really wanted a board in the shape of the school mascot, a catamount. Thus, even the kiosk's shape became a symbol of human communication and some political disagreements. The catamount shape was more than just a big wooden cat; it was the University mascot. The administration worried that putting up a big wooden cat, a symbol, would symbolize something too tacky for the middle of campus. Do you agree? Can you see the administration's point of view?

Sociologists analyze, design, and occasionally even manipulate symbols like these in order to understand and effect change in human behavior and organization. This very chapter you are now reading is one common source of symbolic human exchange sociologists use to affect a reader's thought and subsequent behavior. How do you like that! Are you listening? Do you feel manipulated? Better talk to your instructor.

The kiosk serves as a communication screen between the person who is sending a message (remember that messages are symbols, words, and pictures) and the reader or message receiver. Thus, a basic sociological unit, a dyad, two people — receiver and sender — is formed. A dyad is one kind of social system, an interaction among humans that repeats itself often enough to warrant a label. Behavior in a dyad follows a sometimes predictable pattern. The kingdom for sociology begins with a dyad and then consists of ever larger, familiar social systems to which we all may belong: families, informal groups, clubs, teams, neighborhoods, formal organizations, communities, cities, counties, states, political parties, prisons, military organizations, whole economies, polities (the polity is to political science as the economy is to economics), nations, cultures, and, sometimes in our wildest work, global networks.

This is clearly a vast domain. Our kingdom extends from two people to the United Nations. Sociologists are the imperialists of all the social sciences; we see all the topics studied by the other social sciences — anthropology, psychology, geography, political science, history, and economics — as grist for our mill.

COMPETING PERSPECTIVES

Although there is agreement on the proper extent of the sociological domain, there are also competing perspectives in sociology. Thus, we do not all agree on interpretation. Some sociologists would view the university kiosk as a stage, a blank slate upon which a variety of actors "strut their stuff." These analysts might carefully examine the media and style used to send a message. Did the student writer (who used a napkin corner to advertise a free ride to Boston) mean to suggest a carefree, casual ride? What prompted Amy to tape up Muffey's color snapshot? Were the graduates of 1988 seeking a high-visibility (but relatively low-cost) gift to remind this fall's undergraduates of their recent prowess on campus?

Other sociologists view this kiosk as simple evidence of people trying to exchange goods and services, basic economic activity in a capitalistic system. Is it capitalistic? And is it innocent? Who pays taxes on this informal exchange of goods and services? What about the tiny slip of an index card seeking someone as a house sitter? The announcement that the house in need of a sitter has a full freezer subtly suggests that this is a basic barter economic activity: A free dinner is traded for a weekend of house sitting, and the IRS is none the wiser. Did you ever think that this cute little kiosk would be the scene of illegal activity in an underground economy?

Yet a third sociological perspective might carefully record the value of the goods and services advertised on this board as an indication of the wealth and social class of this particular student body.

A fourth perspective in sociology, that of a family sociologist, might well utilize the forms of interaction symbolized on the board as initial statements in a courting game. Although the card "Call Curt for a good time" is blatantly and somewhat desperately calling for an immediate liaison (has this kid no pride?), the fact that Jan is selling a 1985 BMW suggests that Jan and his or her family might well be worth further investigation as a potential mate capable of supporting an inviting lifestyle. Copy down that number. Similarly, Meggon, who is trying to sell the round-trip British Airlines ticket to Singapore, seems to be a well-traveled woman of some mystery. How did she get that ticket? What plans were interrupted? Is she selling a plane ticket, or is she telling those who read at the kiosk about herself?

These different sociological perspectives are called paradigms. Clearly, sociological paradigms vary greatly. This variation reflects at once the ambiguity—there is no correct perspective—and the excitement of sociological study. Did you see how much fun it can be to let your creative imagination run free as we looked at various sides of the kiosk? Now you play the analyst. Is Jan male or female? Are there clues on that slip of paper advertising the BMW to give you an answer?

COMMONALITIES

Despite these differences in sociological paradigms, most sociologists do agree on some things. What is it that makes sociology a unified discipline? What do sociologists have in common?

Initially, there is consensus on the appropriateness of the general arena in which we operate—all the way from a dyad to global relations. Second, there is a pervasive commitment to apply scientific (or at least systematic) techniques to our investigation of human interaction. Then, there is generally an agreement that some sociologists will be more applied than others. The applied sociologists will work off-campus and be more field oriented, helping communities plan, assisting industry in marketing new products, counseling in schools, running political campaigns, or even designing kiosks. Other sociologists maintain greater interest in theory or in conceptualization and hang out in libraries. Often they may be found in front of college and university classrooms. Regardless of an applied or theoretical orientation, all sociologists agree that human behavior can be understood and that those explanations usually involve group processes rather than simply genetic, biological, or psychological phenomena.

Modern sociologists are not shy about sharing their insights. Just over one hundred years old, sociology is a relatively young discipline, a newcomer to campus. Like many newcomers, sociologists will talk to anyone regarding just about anything, often to the confusion of our audience. Just what do we stand for? What is the correct interpretation of the kiosk? Although we have struggled for respectability (and in fact have made great advances in the application of scientific research techniques for better understanding of social problems), the public is often entertained by our work, challenging us to show that we study more than the trivial aspects of social behavior. We are often accused of reporting what appears to most people to be common sense as highly significant. One example will help you understand this criticism: Sociologists find that as a group of people gets larger, people get alienated. Common sense would dictate, "two is company, three is a crowd." So what? The late Saul Alinsky, an applied sociologist who devoted a lifetime to organizing the poor and oppressed, claimed that "the University of Chicago's Sociology Department [is] an institution that invests $100,000 on a research program to discover the location of brothels that any taxi driver could tell them for nothing."

WRITING 1.

Think through the notion that two is company, three is a crowd. Sociologists note that in a dyad, a two-person relationship, just one path for communication exists. In a triad, a three-person group, communication paths proliferate. Describe a situation in which the common sense approach "two is company, three is a crowd" applies and a situation in which it definitely does not work. As you describe the situations, identify the conditions necessary for this common sense axiom to work. By necessary conditions we mean the way things have to be organized. Is it a school scene, a jail room, or a free-wheeling walk in the woods? What is the time of day? The season? The level of intimacy? For example, different situations—a hockey game as opposed to the back seat of a car—dictate whether the axiom works or not. Under what conditions does the axiom fail? How does basic communication differ in a small group as opposed to a larger one? Can you see that it is not common sense but the social situation that determines whether the axiom works? Describe why this is true.

AN INTRODUCTION TO DEBUNKING

Another activity common to sociologists is playing the debunking game. Alinsky debunked sociological research in his claims that a sociologist is a person who takes public research money only to show how to find a brothel. The fish cartoon in Figure 9.1 (see page 579) debunks truth claims based on power positions. The Doonesbury cartoon in Figure 9.2 (see page 580) debunks male chauvinism. Debunking is basically an intellectual game in which you poke holes in the arguments of others who claim to have learned some useful generalization about human behavior. Following a few of these guidelines will let you play debunking in every classroom, lab, or sociopolitical discussion. Imagine how much fun you can have with these tools when first meeting your new father-in-law. Here, for example, are some common debunking rules:

1. Every social situation has hidden dimensions.
2. Prophecies can become self-fulfilling.
3. Truth claims are tied to one's power position.
4. Behavior is socially determined.
5. Generalizations about behavior depend on context.
6. Generalizations about behavior are related to time.

Rule 1: Every Social Situation Has Hidden Dimensions

An elementary debunking tool deals with obvious and hidden dimensions to almost every social situation. For example, the sociologist Robert K. Merton suggests that an obvious and contributing function of a university is to educate people to be more productive in the society. However, the hidden or unintended purpose of the university is to perpetuate the American class structure by providing an arena where middle-class and upper-class children can meet during prime courtship years. The assumption is that, having met in a summer camp–type atmosphere with minimal chaperoning, couples from the same social class will fall in love and make families. Thus, the main purpose of the University is seen as one perpetuating the class structure of the society.

Formal education (a form of education that takes place in an institution), involves most children in America from ages 5 to 18, approximately 20% of the population. A debunker using the hidden-dimension rule would say that education serves minimally to keep a lot of people off the streets. If one were to add in day care children and workers, college students, teachers, and other school staff, we could probably account for one in four Americans being behind brick walls between 8.00 A.M. and 3:00 P.M. every day, forty weeks a year. Other sociologists who examine institutions note the role played by the family. Often we think of a family as a unit where kids are reared and basic goods consumed. A latent function of the family is to keep parents off the streets as well. If all the moms and dads were to start partying like college students do, society would probably come apart at the seams. The family serves to keep lots of people behind four walls, safe from the cool night air. Note the tremendous baby-sitting function provided by schools and by families.

WRITING 2.

Other applications of this rule regarding the fact that every social situation has hidden dimensions lead us to note that almost every war produces major medical breakthroughs as well as many other technological advances. Does war have a positive side? On the other hand, one latent product of medical advances has been a population explosion created by the simple fact that people live longer. When people live longer, many no longer work, and this elderly, unemployed group creates a strain on the system. Is this a negative side of war? What do you think?

Rule 2: Prophecies Can Become Self-Fulfilling

A second debunking perspective holds that prophecies tend to fulfill themselves. "War is inevitable." "Boys will be boys." A self-fulfilling prophecy is a prophecy which, initially unfounded, becomes true because people believe it. One tragic example of the self-fulfilling prophecy concept occurs when elementary school children are grouped, or "tracked," according to potential performance into fast, medium, and slow streams. Slow-to-develop or disabled children are socially stigmatized by association with the "special" tracks and act out the expectations held by teachers regarding their performance, rarely advancing in the track system. The loss here is not only an individual one, but one to the social system as well. These kids' full contribution to society is never felt.

Other examples of the self-fulfilling prophecy abound. American men are especially vulnerable, entrapped by potentially destructive sex role stereotypes. Seeking a cool, laid-back image, men are often reluctant to engage aggressively in intellectual exchange in the classroom, do not wear seat belts or life jackets, and refuse to fork over a wallet at gun point. Shot dead in a holdup, killed in a car accident, drowned at sea, or staying out of a dynamic exchange of information in a class are all negative behavior outcomes of the self-fulfilling prophecy for college guys.

Rule 3: Truth Claims Are Tied to One's Power Position

A third debunking ground rule comes from an area called the sociology of knowledge. If you examine carefully, you may find that the truth claims of any individual may be directly attributed to that person's social position. Look especially hard at the kind of work the person does in order to understand his or her perspective. Figure 9.1 depicts this principle.

When you employ this guideline to figure out how someone can be so sure of the basic principles governing society, look specifically at the kind of work a person does (or, conversely, doesn't do). Many sociologists are economic determinists, believing that the job one holds ties a person to the economy and to a particular form of economic production. Thus, work dictates how one perceives the world. The kind of job one has is indeed a powerful influence on what one thinks. Rules promoted by people in power often best serve their own specific interests. It can be argued, for example, that mandatory attendance in a college classroom serves no real educational objective; it is simply a way for a professor to use up classroom time taking attendance. Educators have never proved

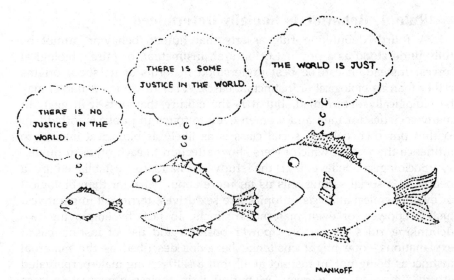

Figure 9.1   The third rule of debunking. (Drawing by Mankoff; © 1981 *The New Yorker Magazine, Inc.*)

that chewing gum in high school affects performance; they simply may not want to pay custodians to scrape it off the bottom of the desks.

Another example of people in authority promoting self-serving ends brings us back to the kiosk. University administrators support the kiosk as a way to facilitate communication in the community. Some sociologists would debunk the promotion of the kiosk on these seemingly reasonable grounds as a deliberate attempt of the University administration to channel, control, and thus "clean up" traditional student graffiti, which—like bubble gum—typically disfigures buildings, sidewalks, and restrooms. Who says one kiosk can communicate as effectively as messages spread all over campus? (See how much fun you can have with these debunking rules? Be careful, however, for they can get you in deep trouble.)

_____

WRITING 3.

Ponder for a moment why operating on the premise that people in power act in their own self-interest may get you in trouble. What does that mean? Give some examples. Explain why these rules may get you in trouble. Consider some other examples of actions based on one's power position: Have you had a class in which the professor uses a book she has written as a text? Do you know why most men suggest that it is a woman's job to change diapers? These and other clues may give you an idea of the way economic power is distributed in societies. See if you can find another good example. Describe it, and then put yourself in the shoes of the powerful person and defend the truth claim.

Rule 4. Behavior Is Socially Determined

A fourth debunking rule asserts that human behavior cannot be fully understood as a product of natural, instinctual, or purely biological forces. Instead, it can be best understood in terms of its social origins rather than its biological or instinctual bases. A sex drive, for example, may be biologically determined, but it is the culture that puts it in gear. In many societies for men and women even to touch in public is forbidden. Within our own culture, social class is as likely as biological instinct to influence the way in which lovers show affection to each other in public.

Sociologists believe that the study of standards established by a people in a social setting tells us far more about behavior than biological or even chemical analysis of topics like sex drives, territorial imperatives, lust for power, or even maternal instincts. In fact, by employing two debunking rules—a person's power position and use of instinct-based explanations—one might challenge behavior described as the maternal instinct as being not an instinct at all, but a self-serving male-perpetuated "truth" imposed on women. Men find it in their self-interest to pass around the story that maternal duties are biologically inseparable from being a woman, a story bound to men's attempts to maintain power and freedom and to avoid some nasty work (as in changing diapers). Gary Trudeau captures the essence of this in a cartoon he drew long before he married Jane Pauley and had two children (Figure 9.2).

Rule 5. Generalizations About Behavior Depend on Context

Another debunking ground rule suggests that generalizations about human behavior be given the context test. A generalization about relationships between friends ("opposites attract," for instance) as a principle about human behavior can be tested in the context of a family, a neighborhood, the community, or several nations. If it is true that friendships form because opposite personality types attract one another, will this principle work in a marriage? In the workplace? Between people of two different racial or religious groups? Between people of different cultures? In

Figure 9.2   The fourth rule of debunking: "A well-established truth." Doonesbury copyright 1975 G. B. Trudeau. Reprinted with permission of Universal Press Syndicate. All rights reserved.

order to make this generalization about behavior, it would have to apply in all these contexts. Such generalizations rarely stand the test of context.

One test of context has to do with looking for common behavior in different places or cultures. Although sociology is a very young discipline and has few generalizations about social behavior that survive the test of context, many behavioral "universals" have been established by anthropologists looking for common patterns in different places. Some pan-cultural phenomena (things that seem to be common in every culture) are universal: All known cultures have some form of family structure, tend toward monogamy (one husband, one wife), are characterized by class distinctions, play sports, use language to communicate, are modest about toilet functions, have bodily adornment, and so on. (Similarly, we have a host of other generalizations that smack of common sense.)

Because our field is so young and we sociologists haven't had time or money to check out all our hunches thoroughly, most generalizations about human behavior are accurate only at specified levels—in dyads, families, communities, *or* nations. Today Dan Rather reports that "the United Kingdom scolded Northern Ireland." This makes absolutely no literal sense. We cannot reduce the behavior of nations to the level of roommates. To do so overlooks vast and important differences in human complexities. It is sociologically incorrect, and you can debunk such statements easily.

However, this same ground rule can be applied to understand better the interaction between levels of analysis. By searching for the ways behavior is influenced by larger (or higher, more general) levels of human organization, we gain a powerful tool in the search for more inclusive information about the ways the social system works.

Consider Figure 9.3, the cartoon by Charles Addams. These poor duffers always thought their shabby lives were really their own fault. Suddenly, a class reunion creates some common consciousness, and they start to wonder about the quality of the school they attended. In our culture, there is a great tendency to reduce complex problems to an individual level. Freshmen with no dates on Friday and Saturday nights often believe that their loneliness is an individual problem, when it is in fact demographic and cultural factors (age and sex grading) that create their problem. For example, on our campus, undergraduate women outnumber the men, two to one. That means, by definition of the situation, that freshman women will have a tough time finding dates on campus. Is that their shortcoming? Social groups that realize the power of the social structure around them to influence their behavior create exciting opportunities for teachers and organizers.

WRITING 4.

Consider the graduates in Figure 9.3. What would you tell these former students? Would you ask them to contribute to the college? How would you remedy the situation? Could you organize them to change their

"I thought it was me, but maybe the school's no damn good."
Figure 9.3   The fifth rule of debunking: "A sociological insight." (Drawing by
Charles Addams; © 1974 *The New Yorker Magazine, Inc.*)

perception? Guess how their experience at school might have influenced
their perception of reality. What kinds of argument might you use to
organize and stimulate these alumni to recognize the power of the institution to affect their individual behavior?

Rule 6: Generalizations About Behavior Are Related To Time

A sixth and final debunking test that may be applied to casual generalizations about human behavior lies in challenging them to stand the
test of history. If the class of '54 had a bad experience at Charles Addams'
university, how did the class of '53 fare? Or the class of 1933? If the

university failed to turn out a successful class in '54, was this a pattern over time or a simple aberration? If a principle works today, did it hold true yesterday? Last year? A decade ago?

Is the communications kiosk a unique form of human communication, or does it have historical roots? Is there a tradition for such forms of communication among human beings? Did cave persons use a communication technique akin to the kiosk when they drew on the back walls of their caves? Does the kiosk represent only a modern form of mural?

Summary of the Rules

You are now well equipped with some of sociology's most powerful tools. First, look for obvious and hidden functions of social organizations. Second, check out the role of self-fulfilling prophecies. Third, identify the power position that influences the generalizer's perspective. Fourth, examine the social control of instinctual behavior. Fifth, be aware of the context in which a generalization is applied, and sixth, apply the test of time to establish laws of human behavior. But be careful: These rules must be used sparingly, or they can paralyze creative work. There is a trap in playing the sociological devil's advocate; one must recognize at the outset that there are simply no generalizations about human behavior and social systems that can withstand the full onslaught of the debunker's repertoire. Too much playing makes one a cynic and in a social system in which optimism prevails, constant debunking can entrap the debunker, label him or her a negative force, and leave the person out in the cold. Some of this country's most brilliant sociologists are so critical that they cannot publish their theories for fear that they will not survive the debunker's challenge.

SOCIOLOGICAL DO-GOODERS: THE BIAS IN THE FIELD

Counteracting the tendency toward cynicism created by knowing how to debunk is a unity apparent among many sociologists who display great enthusiasm and commitment to the study of people and their social systems. The sense of mission is created by the fact that most sociologists share a deep concern for the future of human beings on this earth. People are, after all, the subject matter of our discipline, so we can hardly be faulted for wanting to keep people around.

However, please don't misunderstand sociologists. Keeping people around doesn't necessarily mean that sociologists "like people," or that, as many sociology undergraduates say when asked why they major in sociology, they "like working with people." It is just that sociologists realize that people are the easiest higher forms of intellectual life to talk to on this planet. If we want to survive as a species, we need to understand a bit more about people and about the social systems we build.

The unity, commitment, and sense of mission you may sense among sociologists stem from the fact that many are convinced that time is running out on the human experience. The growing number of people in the global community and the rapid depletion of basic resources create a pressure for some good, accurate findings about our ways of organizing ourselves to eat (the economy), to reproduce (the family or proxy for the family), and to rule (the polity). Therefore, although we struggle to be objective in our work, a personal concern for the preservation of the species leads us to seek a better understanding of social situations, such as social stratification, treatment of the homeless, care for the aged and the dispossessed, minorities, community organization, organizational forms of government, Third World nations, conflict and consensus, the design of organizations, and the impact of institutions. Elements of the sociological imagination were reflected in the preceding discussion of sociology, especially the treatment of debunking ground rules. Despite immensely informative findings about all these topics, sociologists today agree that the most important products of our work so far are the ways we think and approach our work—the sociological imagination.

SUGGESTIONS FOR RESEARCH

Locate a kiosk, bulletin board, or telephone pole in your neighborhood used for exchanging messages.

1. Borrow or copy a message that you find there. Using findings from your field research, describe how people use style (type of paper, size of print, color, weird symbols) rather than content (the actual words in the message) to communicate with one another.

2. Now examine the content of the message. How is it worded? Does the message give you a hint as to the kind of person who wrote the message (age, sex, wealth, year in school)? Is there anything else you can tell abut the author or authors?

3. Imagine that you were going to use the bulletin board to advertise something. How would you write the content? Write it! Now, why did you write it as you did? Analyze your audience: Who were you trying to communicate with? What sociological type of person are you trying to impress with your message—men? Women? Young? Old? Rich? Poor? How do these sociological properties of your intended audience determine the style and content you use to communicate?

4. Once again consider your source of basic information, be it a bulletin board, telephone pole, or kiosk. Identify all the attempts to communicate that represent economic activities, the exchange of goods and services. Can you analyze the information from this source as representing a part of the informal economy? (Read Cheryl Russell's article in the readings.) What are some of the hidden economic dimensions to this area of communication? Are there activities conducted on this board that one might consider illegal? Explain.

READINGS

Joseph Di Bona
BRIDES AND GROOMS WANTED: Looking for a Wife in India—Not for the Faint of Heart

People write for many reasons. Imagine having to write to order a bride! These articles from the Christian Science Monitor *explain one culture's approach to arranging marriages and include letters written to arrange a wedding. Joseph Di Bona is a professor of education at Duke University. He wrote the article on looking for a wife while on sabbatical in India to research student problems. Sheila Tefft is a* Monitor *correspondent. Under what conditions do these traditional forms of marriage work? When do traditional forms of marriage begin to change?*

If you have ever thought of advertising for a husband or a wife, you must consult the Indian matrimonial columns, where experienced hands have been finding mates for as long as anyone remembers.

The bare essentials are easy enough to master. Include your profession, height is important, education a must, earnings are very clearly stated, and of course "community," that catchall category which covers caste, race, religion, region, and anything else you want it to mean. Girls are usually described as fair, meaning light-skinned; "wheatish" is also popular; and homely means accomplished in the domestic arts.

But today many young people are turned off by the perennial search device whereby parents place ads for their children. They say the only ones who are advertised are the losers whose parents have tried everything else—marriage brokers, family connections, the local astrologer, work mates, and anyone else they can find. Their new approach is to advertise directly in slick magazines aimed at a younger crowd.

This qualifies as a daring and exciting development in Indian-arranged marriages, and recently I responded to one such ad. It was placed by Anita K., described as a 40-year-old divorcee. I wrote:

Dear Miss K.,

You will no doubt be surprised to have this belated reply to your matrimonial proposal of some time ago, but the truth is a friend brought it to my attention just yesterday. I am an active 61-year-old divorced professor from the United States working in India temporarily and looking for someone special. I would like to meet you sometime soon in Delhi in order to become better acquainted.

Best Wishes, Joseph.

In about a week, I received this reply.

Dear Mr. Joseph,

Thanks for your letter dated 1 March in response to my matrimonial ad. I was glad to read the particulars given by you and am attracted toward you. I am looking for someone who is mature, understanding, and maybe you are the right man. Incidentally, I have obtained the US visa, and as my plans go I ought to be leaving for America by the end of March 1989. Your plan to visit Delhi at that time would not be of much help if we want to pursue this matter. Although I have one alternative to suggest.

Do you think you can make it to Delhi earlier than that? If yes, that would be lovely, and if not I could visit your place and meet you and we can talk things over. If we happen to check with each other, then I could postpone my departure for America. But now let me give you some information about myself. I have divorced my husband, have one son who is 17 years old and is living with his father who is an army officer. I have no contact with my son since eight years. I am single and lonely. I would like to settle with someone who is considerate, affectionate, and broadminded enough to help me live my life and not rule my life. I am very straightforward. I hate hypocrisy and unfaithfulness. I have had a very bitter experience with my first marriage. In my ad I had given a false name to hide my identity for obvious reasons. My name is Punit, and my height is 5 ft. 7 in, and not 170 cms which was wrongly printed. I have wheatish complexion. I am attractive, smart, and have a cheerful disposition. One of my hobbies is to laugh. Do I sound crazy? I am enclosing a photo, you may kindly send me yours.

Much Love, Punit.

The photo was a knockout postcard-size picture of what looked like a movie queen in her early 20s. What to do next? I decided to consult my neighbor who originally showed me the ad. He has been anxiously searching for a spouse for several years but has not yet found the right girl.

"Shambhu," I asked, "what should I do about Punit?"

"She looks like the right girl for you. She doesn't care about your caste, nationality, or religion, and she seems very smart. I would visit her if I were you, or invite her to come here. Talk to her on the telephone just to hear her voice. I find that's a wonderful way to get to know someone."

I was surprised at how fast things seemed to be moving. I had a much slower time frame in mind, but I was quickly altering my perspective.

"If I invite her to come here," I asked with some hesitancy, "where would she stay, etc.?" The answers were all well-established protocols worked out over eons of experience.

"She will take care of the overnight travel and you pay for the hotel and meals. No, she will not share a room with you. You will get her a room in a nice nearby hotel."

"But, Shambhu, do things always move this quickly?"

He explained his latest effort at wife-hunting. "I just returned from Calcutta where I went to see this girl who happens to be from my same *biradri* (subcaste). I met her family and she is very nice, although she is not very pretty. Not ugly, mind you, but not very pretty. She speaks well, knows English, and I was pleased."

"So you went all the way there, and what happened?"

"We met, we talked, and she said she was ready to make a firm commitment, but I didn't go that far. I have two other girls in Bombay and Bangalore to see first. The one in Bombay is very clever but always talking about her karma and astrology. The one in Bangalore, my brother met and he says she is OK, but physically we are a misfit. I am small and slim. She is a tall, heavy-built Punjabi girl. But he said I should meet her and make my own decision."

"So you want to check out these other girls before you give Calcutta a definite answer."

"That's right, and anyway her father wants to make a site visit to see for himself if all I said checks out. Apparently she had an unfortunate experience recently when a marriage was all sewed up and it turned out the prospective groom was an alcoholic."

"I am getting the hang of this business now. Your advice is to go for it?"

"With a vengeance, my friend," said Shambhu.

"I am now getting my postcard-size photos ready. I have changed my attitude about long-distance phone calls and travel to unheard-of places. I am still not ready to make a commitment after moments of introduction, but I am working on that, too."

"Good," said Shambhu, "that's progress. Remember, this marriage business is not for the faint of heart."

Sheila Tefft
MAIL-ORDER BRIDES GROW WARY

Paramjeet Singh wanted only happiness when she and her husband agreed to their daughter's quick marriage.

Married within 15 days of being introduced to an Indian living in Canada, the Singhs' daughter soon became pregnant. Six months later, after obtaining a visa, she followed her husband to Canada.

Immediately, the marriage began to sour. The husband, whom the Singhs thought was an engineer, worked as a machinist in a factory. His well-to-do family opposed the new wife's efforts to find a job, and after constant harassment, she was ordered out of the family home, along with her two-year-old daughter.

Reticent to end the marriage, the Singhs' daughter is now attempting an uneasy reconciliation with her husband.

"My daughter was so keen to go abroad because we have relatives who are doing well there. At her marriage, I've never seen her so happy," says Mrs. Singh (not her real name). "But now I feel it's not for the best. When I look back, I think we should have waited and investigated more."

In India, a new wariness is tempering the rush for long-distance arranged marriages. For years, many parents here dreamed of marrying their daughter to an established, affluent Indian overseas. Dazzled by prospects for a lifestyle unattainable in India, daughters were sent to the United States, Britain, and other countries. Often, they barely knew their new husbands.

While there are many marital success stories, counselors and social observers say that overseas arranged marriages face tremendous troubles and strains. Indian brides, many of whom have never been away from home, are thrust into a new culture and caught in their husbands' conflicting desires that they adapt to Western ways but also remain traditional.

"Many Indians still look on Americans as greener pastures. They think that if you have two cars, everything is OK," say Anju Chatterjee, co-director of Sanjivini counseling center in New Delhi. "Indians don't realize it's a struggle in America. It's a totally alien culture and very stressful for Indians."

According to American immigration officials, many of the 700,000 Indians in the US are part of a well-educated, accomplished, and affluent community. Indian immigration has jumped from 3,000 in the 1950s, to more than 200,000 in the 1980s.

Yet despite their economic success, many Indians see acute cultural differences between India and the West, and fear the loss of their culture and values. Often they live and socialize in introverted cultural pockets. When it comes to marriage, many seek a spouse from India to preserve their Indian lifestyles.

Some parents living in America send their adolescent daughters back to India to be married. Others return with their teenage children because they fear they will marry foreigners, says Ms. Chatterjee.

That ideal often is clouded by the tensions that arise in making these "green card" marriages work, say counselors and other observers. A "green card" (the color has been changed to pink) gives a foreign national the right to live and work in the US.

The wife must face a long wait for a visa. At the American Embassy in New Delhi, visa applications for about 6,000 Indian spouses are pending. More than 3,000 Indian spouses go to the US every year, waiting an average of two years for their visas.

A New Delhi woman's sister married and followed her husband to

England after a long waiting period for a visa, only to find that he had remarried in the meantime. "The woman is expected to be the good little Indian wife. But if there is trouble, she has no one to turn to for help."

Counselors and sociologists say marital difficulties often are rooted in the Indian man's outdated expectations. Living in the West for a number of years, men may fail to recognize the changes underway in large Indian cities.

"Very often, men tend to think that India is still where it was when they left," say Ms. Chatterjee, the counselor.

Observers in the US say the incidence of divorce among Indian couples is rising. If the couple separates, the woman usually remains abroad because divorced women are not accepted in Indian society. She usually remains isolated from the Indian community in her new home as well.

Despite the strains, many long-distance, arranged marriages work well. But over time, Indian customs are likely to fade overseas. Radha Ramachandran, a New Delhi housewife, has three daughters living in the US, all married in matches supervised and approved by their parents.

"I still believe in this tradition," says Mrs. Ramachandran. "But my grandchildren are growing up in the US. Twenty-five years from now, they will not agree to this arranged marriage."

OPTIONS FOR WRITING

1. Assume that you are visiting India and read about writing for a spouse. Curiosity gets the better of you. Disregarding your natural shyness, you decide to contact an Indian eager to find a spouse whose name has been presented to you by the family. Write a letter of your own paralleling Joseph Di Bona's and describing your interest in finding out more about the prospective mate.

2. Imagine that you have to write for the hand of a fellow American with whom you have fallen in love and with whom you desperately wish to spend the rest of your life. Address the parents of the prospective mate. In your work recall the treatment of the content and style of notes found on the kiosk in the writing assignment earlier in this chapter. What will you say? To whom would it be easier to write? Your lover? The parents?

3. From the letter in the *Monitor*, it is clear that Di Bona tried his hand at the game of mail-order spouse hunting. What are some of the dangers of a person from another culture playing at the serious business of spouse selection? If Di Bona is not an Indian, what ethical questions are raised by his rather tongue-in-cheek approach to wife hunting?

4. What latent functions does a marriage provide? How are some of these unintended aspects of marriage served by a mail-order process? What positive functions could be provided by a mail-order process?

Scholasticus
PROFESSOR PICKERING'S QUICK POETS SOCIETY

> *Some journalists find college courses their beat. In a regular feature entitled "Tenure Track," the* New England Monthly *magazine reports from a variety of New England colleges. In March 1990, "Scholasticus" writes about English 146 at the University of Connecticut. "Scholasticus" is a pseudonym employed by the columnist for this regional magazine. Please realize that the college classroom is traditionally a very closed social occasion. Rarely do colleagues or even guests of the students visit the typical college classroom; consequently, most university classrooms are very isolated places, dominated typically by a single professor. The notion that reporters could cover such an event, in addition to challenging faculty, provides a unique opportunity for analysis of an unusual but very common organizational event.*

Fifteen minutes before class, Professor Samuel Pickering entertains from the second floor of Ratcliffe-Hicks. Rhymes and gospel shouts fill the stairwell. Ghostly incantations lift out over the threshold. Unmentionables resound. Young writers laugh. A visitor must wonder whether the professor will leap through a window or climb atop a desk. Pickering, as it happens, inspired the character John Keating in *Dead Poets Society*, but to think the movie exaggerates his academic style would be an error. The resemblance between John Keating (played by Robin Williams) and Samuel Pickering, Jr., is alarming. The teacher who once led his charges—O Captain! My Captain!—at a prep school in Tennessee twenty years ago no longer stands astride the furniture or lectures from the sill. At the University of Connecticut, particularly at his age, such a step might be a sad mistake. But Professor Pickering, at forty-eight, is not lunatic, nor is he a vulgar man. He makes the same stunning attacks against pomposity, abstraction, rigidity, and pretension. All the film character seems to lack is the real teacher's rich southern drawl and his sly, unsentimental way.

"Now, is there anything you want to bring up about writing?" he asks. "Or the world? Or the meaning of human existence?" The room looks as plain as the inside of a shoe box. A stretch of plywood covers one window. An electrical outlet is missing its plate. From the sparse rows, a young man asks if Pickering could make a living as a writer. Touché, Mr. Pickering.

No, he says. His essays earned only $1,407 two years ago, $2,945 last year, $7,000 during the past eleven months. "I would be starving on the ground," he says "I would be eating at people's toes." The thought makes him shiver. If he had to live on his writing alone, he would probably develop a herniated esophagus, not to mention piles. "And there's no sense wondering about my next book, either," he says. "I know exactly how much money it will make. Fifteen hundred dollars! . . . And we thought we were going to Disney World." He smacks his hands. "Any other questions?"

How was your holiday?

Since Pickering has become semi-famous, the telephone interferes with his family life. Newspapers misquote him. People expect him to be clever or profound when he wants to be dull, left alone to teach, or write little essays about starlings and dandelions and picking up sticks. Some days he would rather leave the world behind for a while and write and write and write.

Any other questions? No?

He passes out blue mimeographed pages, the students' work. "A few po-ems," he says. "A few pomes."

René has written a piece called "Eternal Etude." Not bad, René. "But does anyone have trouble with this . . . étude? This— how should I put it? Comme ci, comme ça . . ."

Pickering dances on his toes, flitting his fingers. "What is the danger of using foreign languages—unless you're Ezra Pound?"

"Don't know what it means?" asks John, a tow-headed young man.

"That's a very good reason, John. If you do not know what the words mean, do not put them in your poem. What other dangers . . . perhaps, perchance, to think, to read, to dream . . . " His voice rises.

"Sounds pompous," René says.

"Haven't you ever known people whenever they talk that spice their language with foreign phrases? I say, 'What in the hell do you mean by that?' Or give it right back to them. Say, 'Mais oui!' Hooo-hooo-hooo-hooo!" The professor titters and the class howls.

"But it's all a facade in some ways, isn't it?" he says, spinning on his heels. "It's the words, after all. It's not the ideas you have. It's the words you use that matter. It's the style. Do you think people will complain that there's no content? Most people who see you have a nice style won't know that it has no content. Come on, give me some words! Twaddle! Twitch! Give me some ugly words—they can't be vulgar."

"Scut!"

"Ratchet!"

"Smut!"

" 'Eternal Etude' is not bad, René. It just seems to be endowed with too much. Maybe it's the word 'eternal.' Of course, I'm addicted to the word 'forever.' Because nothing is forever. Not even love."

A young man snickers.

"Okay," Pickering allows, "love is forever. 'Forever ringing changes upon the bells of time . . .' "

He pauses under the wash of remembered phrases. During some classes it is the lilt of Pope or Milton's meter that stops him. But at this moment he hears Tennyson rippling . . .

> The splendour falls on castle walls
> And snowy summits old in story;
> The long light shakes across the lakes
> And the wild cataract leaps in glory.
> Blow, bugle, blow, set the wild echoes
>   flying,
> Blow, bugle; answer, echoes, dying,
>   dying, dying.

The class sits silently as Pickering peels his hand away from his eyes, having quoted at length. "It doesn't mean doodly-squat," he says. "But it's pretty." And he repeats the lines, slower this time, whispering the last words. Dying, dying. Dying.

"Frightening?" he asks, leaning down, shuffling left to right across the room. He hunkers down to look them in the eyes. "The power of words."

Not everyone bears up in Pickering's class. His scattershot observations confuse the intellect and sometimes strike without warning.

Do not use exclamation points! he cries. I don't like the way they look!

Facilitate? That is an awful word. Facilitators are what they have at universities, aren't they? Sometimes I imagine they're out there lurking with whips.

That sentence, he says, sounds like it comes from the Hardy Boys.

A young woman shyly reads her historical essay about photographing the war in Cambodia. A tall boy murmurs a poem about sharing a cigarette by a beaver dam. Pickering grows impatient, constantly interrupting failed stanzas, forgettable lines.

"Give me pictures, Kimberly Lewis!" he commands the author of the Cambodian war essay. "When we were children and used to look at those picture books of World War II, what photographs did we like the best?"

"The dead soldiers?"

"The bloody sea," says another.

"But as we grew older, we felt guilty about that, didn't we?"

One day last year, Pickering says, he flipped through the newspaper and saw that a friend of his had been killed in the plane crash in Lockerbie, Scotland. "Son of a bitch!" he thought. "My friend was blown up." He got on the phone and started calling people. For the better part of an evening he experienced an extraordinary pleasure conveying bad news.

"Now, I hope you don't misunderstand what I mean," he says, "I was not happy that my friend was killed. I'm not saying that. But after I found out, the news occupied an evening, an otherwise dull evening.

I don't want to admit this, but when you realize something like this about yourself, you come away and you're in the light of truth. And you've got a problem. Isn't it terrible? Now you put that in an essay, and what will people think?"

"You're awful."

"Awful, awful," Pickering echoes. They are quiet for a moment.

Suddenly an excited pulse goes through the room. A boy in the front row has a confession to make. The girl behind him recalls an electrifying phone call from a classmate dishing out word of a friend's death. They have known sinister pleasures.

"The next week after my friend's death," he says, "I picked up *Time* magazine and saw an awful picture of a body hanging off the top of the airplane. You couldn't see a face. And I thought, 'Is that my friend? Could that be . . . I wonder if that's . . . ' No!"

His voice turns to a whisper. "Then I got up and threw the magazine in the garbage can. I didn't want any more of this. This was too much."

It is risky being in a classroom with Professor Pickering. He makes such a striking effort to become familiar. He launches his bombs from behind a veil of high spirits. He admits he has "gone too far . . . on occasion." But that is the romantic way, is it not? he asks. To go a little too far?

Do they still teach children about Bolívar, Magellan, Cortés, Balboa? he wonders. Is Amerigo Vespucci still around? Have you ever looked at the backside of a horse? Has anyone ever climbed up into the seat of a bulldozer? Do you read Alexander Pope? Gretel Ehrlich? How about John MacPhee? Name the most ridiculous parts of human anatomy.

His quizzing continues even as they pack up their belongings to leave.

"Are there any other questions?" he asks, smiling wryly. "Like, why are we here? Is there anything you would like to write? Tell me what interests you. Go! Write! I am waiting."

OPTIONS FOR WRITING

1. Report on a class that you attend. Use a format similar to the one employed by Scholasticus, and develop a pseudonym, if you need to protect yourself in what you have to report.

2. Which debunking rule may help explain why Scholasticus must use a pseudonym? Why?

3. Consider a class that visitors have often attended. How does the activity in that room differ from a more closed class? Recall that you are employing the following debunking rules—hidden dimensions to social situations, truth claims tied to a power position, and generalizations about behavior dependent on context—and explain why each pertains.

David Boaz
YELLOW PERIL REINFECTS AMERICA:
U.S. Hostility Turns to Japan

A surprising amount of solid sociological analysis makes it into the lay press these days. In a Wall Street Journal *piece, David Boaz writes of racism in the contemporary United States.* The New York Times, The Washington Post, *and* The Wall Street Journal *constitute three of the most frequently read newspapers in the United States. Many decision makers read "The Journal" with their coffee each morning, and this paper is thus a most influential one. David Boaz is vice president of the Cato Institute in Washington. The Cato Institute's mission is to "achieve a greater involvement of the intelligent, concerned lay public in questions of policy and the proper role of government." Boaz has recently coedited a Cato Institute book entitled* Beyond the Status Quo.

The House is expected to vote this month on Rep. John Bryant's Foreign Ownership Disclosure Act, which would require foreign investors with a "significant interest" in any business or property to register with the U.S. government.

The growing support for such legislation, which already has passed the House twice, parallels the growth of Japanese companies as significant buyers of American properties alongside traditional investors from Britain, Canada and the Netherlands. Yet discussion of foreign interest always focuses on Japan, which is only the third-largest foreign investor in the U.S., behind Britain and Canada. Could it be that the idea of British and Canadian investors owning American buildings just doesn't frighten Americans because . . . well, because they're white?

It wouldn't be the first time. Racism directed against Asians and Asian-Americans has a long history in this country. In 1882, the Chinese Exclusion Act made the Chinese the first nationality specifically banned from immigrating to this country. It worked. Chinese immigration fell from some 30,000 that year to less than 1,000. Labor leader Samuel Gompers argued, "The superior whites had to exclude the inferior Asiatics, by law, or, if necessary, by force of arms."

From 1854 to 1874, a California law prevented Chinese from testifying in court against white men. The 1879 California constitution denied suffrage to all "natives of China, idiots, and insane persons."

Some harassment was more subtle. For instance, as economist Thomas Sowell points out in "Ethnic America": "License fees in nineteenth-century San Francisco were higher for laundries that did not deliver by horse-and-buggy, and it was made a misdemeanor to carry baskets suspended on a pole across the shoulder—the way the Chinese delivered."

After the turn of the century, the rising sun of Japan became the focus of American hostility. During World War II, the U.S. engaged in a massive propaganda campaign against Japan. As historian John Dower demonstrates in "War Without Mercy: Race and Power in the Pacific War," the enemy in Europe was the madman Hitler, and the enemy in Asia was "the Japs."

The most egregious example of anti-Japanese racism, of course, was Executive Order 9066 by which President Franklin D. Roosevelt ordered more than 110,000 Americans of Japanese ancestry interned in 10 camps. Though there was never a single instance of sabotage or disloyalty by a Japanese-American, the incarceration was upheld by the Supreme Court and endorsed by such opinion-molders as the Los Angeles Times, which editorialized: "A viper is nonetheless a viper wherever the egg is born — so a Japanese-American, born of Japanese parents, grows up to be a Japanese, not an American."

After the war such hostilities seemed to fade. Japan became a staunch American ally and trading partner, and Asian-Americans prospered here. By 1969, Japanese-American and Chinese-American family incomes were, respectively, 128% and 109% of the incomes of white families.

Perhaps they prospered too much. By the 1970s there was a revival of anti-Asian prejudice touched off by several factors, including the influx of Indochinese refugees after the Vietnam War, the academic success of Vietnamese-American students a few years later, and a feeling of U.S. economic decline in the face of the success of the Japanese and Korean economies.

The resurgence of protectionism has often been tinged with racism. In 1980, presidential candidate John Connally warned the Japanese they had "better be prepared to sit on the docks of Yokohama in your little Datsuns and your little Toyotas while you stare at your own little television sets and eat your mandarin oranges, because we've had all we're going to take!" Two years later, Walter Mondale was echoing Connally: "We've been running up the white flag, when we should be running up the American flag! . . . What do we want our kids to do? Sweep up around Japanese computers?" Around the 40th anniversary of the bombing of Hiroshima and Nagasaki, former Sen. Howard Baker pointed out "two facts": "First, we're still at war with Japan. Second, we're losing."

The recent hysteria over foreign investment in the U.S. has an even clearer racist aspect. Los Angeles Times Paul Conrad satirized former President Reagan's "Morning in America" theme by showing the White House surrounded by skyscrapers topped by Japanese flags. A TV ad for presidential candidate Michael Dukakis about the dangers of foreign investment featured a Japanese flag. Martin and Susan Tolchin's book "Buying Into America" contains 15 index references to Japanese investment and a total of one to British, Canadian and Dutch investment.

U.S. liberals frequently accuse conservatives of racism or racial insensitivity. Evidence for such a charge might be found in Sen. Jesse Helms's (R., N.C.) comments during last year's debate over providing compensation to the Japanese-Americans who had been incarcerated in the World War II camps. Mr. Helms suggested such compensation be considered only when the Japanese government compensated the victims of Pearl Harbor — clearly implying Japanese-Americans bore some sort of racial guilt for the misdeeds of the Japanese government.

But there's at least as much anti-Asian prejudice on the left as on the right: Witness Messrs. Mondale, Dukakis, and Conrad. Writing in the *Nation,* Gore Vidal warns we are entering an era in which "the long-feared Asiatic colossus takes its turn as world leader" and calls for a U.S.-Soviet alliance in order to have "an opportunity to survive, economically, in a highly centralized Asiatic world."

Perhaps the most alarming example of the new racism — because of the stature and sobriety of both author and publication — was the late Theodore H. White's 1985 *New York Times Magazine* article, "The Danger from Japan." Mr. White warned that the Japanese were seeking to create another "East Asia Co-prosperity Sphere" — this time by their "martial" trade policies, and that they would do well to "remember the course that ran from Pearl Harbor to the deck of the USS Missouri in Tokyo Bay."

Along with the resurgence of Asian-bashing by pundits and politicians has come an increase in reports of physical Asian-bashing. The Justice Department says incidents of violence against Asians jumped 62% between 1985 and 1986, accounting for 50% of all racial incidents in Los Angeles and 29% in Boston. Much hostility against Asian entrepreneurs has developed in black communities.

In 1982, two unemployed auto workers followed a young Chinese-American man down a Detroit street and beat him to death with a baseball bat — because they thought he was Japanese and thus somehow responsible for their unemployment. A judge at the original sentencing, noting the stress that Japanese imports had caused the men, gave them each three years' probation and a approximate $3,700 fine.

Like anti-Semitism, much of the prejudice against Asian-Americans is based on resentment of the academic and economic success of the group. Rather than admire or emulate the characteristics — hard work, self-discipline, stable families, respect for education — that have made Jews and Asians so successful in America, some Americans convince themselves the alien groups must have somehow "cheated" and deserve to be punished.

This resentment seems to have motivated Patrick Purdy, whose jealousy of the success of Asian immigrants led him to open fire in a Stockton, Calif., schoolyard, killing five Asian-American children. It was elucidated in a series of "Doonesbury" cartoons last year, in which neighbors complained to the parents of an Asian-American student that teaching her "the value of discipline, hard work, and respect for elders" gave her an unfair advantage.

IN SEARCH OF A NEW ENEMY

Besides the costs of protectionism and the ugliness of racism, one more aspect of anti-Asian prejudice is even more ominous. Various Western leaders have taken to declaring the Cold War over. Should events justify that optimistic prediction, there is a possibility Americans will seek a new national adversary. Why? First, because throughout history people have seemed to need an enemy. And second, because at least some American interest groups—possibly including the federal government itself—benefit from the existence of a national enemy. As Thomas Paine wrote in "The Rights of Man," governments do not raise taxes to fight wars, they fight wars to raise taxes.

Who might be America's new enemy? Iran, Libya, South Africa, and Nicaragua might all qualify as devil figures, but none poses a plausible threat to the U.S. It seems entirely likely that those who thrive on fighting enemies will conjure up a new Yellow Peril. Already Japan's eagerness to sell us quality products at good prices is described in military terms: "aggressive" investors, an "invasion" of Toyotas, "an economic Pearl Harbor." Jack Anderson quotes "some strategists" who "fear World War III is an economic war, which we are losing."

Home-grown racism is bad enough. Let's hope it doesn't turn into a race war.

OPTIONS FOR WRITING

1. As one explanation of American anti-Asian prejudice Boaz observes that "throughout history people have seemed to need an enemy." Why is this an example of a self-fulfilling prophecy? Can you identify and discuss other examples of self-fulfilling prophecies?

2. Boaz employs the rules of debunking to challenge American anti-Asian behavior. Select one or two of the debunking rules, and apply them to our anti-Asian behavior patterns to explain, sociologically, why such patterns exist.

Stephen Jay Gould
RACIST ARGUMENTS AND IQ

Whether a relationship exists between race and IQ is a debate that has gone on over the past few decades. This issue reflects at least two of the debunking rules: that of self-fulfilling prophecy and that of the social rather than the biological or genetic origins of behavior. Here the geologist and naturalist Stephen Jay Gould takes a crack at the argument. Gould is a Harvard University geologist and a columnist for Natural History *magazine. The New York Times has called this Antioch University alumnus "an exceptional combination of scientist and science writer." His works hold the interest of both specialists and lay readers and include* Wonderful Life *and* Ever Since Darwin: Reflections in Natural History.

Louis Agassiz, the greatest biologist of mid-nineteenth-century America, argued that God had created blacks and whites as separate species. The defenders of slavery took much comfort from his assertion, for biblical proscriptions of charity and equality did not have to extend across a species boundary. What could an abolitionist say? Science had shone its cold and dispassionate light upon the subject; Christian hope and sentimentality could not refute it.

Similar arguments, carrying the apparent sanction of science, have been continually invoked in attempts to equate egalitarianism with sentimental hope and emotional blindness. People who are unaware of this historical pattern tend to accept each recurrence at face value: that is, they assume that each statement arises from the "data" actually presented, rather than from the social conditions that truly inspire it.

The racist arguments of the nineteenth century were based primarily on craniometry, the measurement of human skulls. Today, these contentions stand totally discredited. What craniometry was to the nineteenth century, intelligence testing has been to the twentieth. The victory of the eugenics movement in the Immigration Restriction Act of 1924 signaled its first unfortunate effect—for the severe restriction upon non-Europeans and upon southern and eastern Europeans gained much support from results of the first extensive and uniform application of intelligence tests in America—the Army Mental Tests of World War I. These tests were engineered and administered by psychologist Robert M. Yerkes, who concluded that "education alone will not place the negro [sic] race on a par with its Caucasian competitors." It is now clear that Yerkes and his colleagues knew no way to separate genetic from environmental components in postulating causes for different performances on the tests.

The latest episode of this recurring drama began in 1969, when Arthur Jensen published an article entitled, "How Much Can We Boost IQ and Scholastic Achievement?" in the *Harvard Educational Review*. Again, the claim went forward that new and uncomfortable information had come to light, and that science had to speak the "truth" even if it refuted some cherished notions of a liberal philosophy. But again, I shall argue, Jensen had no new data; and what he did present was flawed beyond repair by inconsistencies and illogical claims.

Jensen assumes that IQ tests adequately measure something we may call "intelligence." He then attempts to tease apart the genetic and environmental factors causing differences in performance. He does this primarily by relying upon the one natural experiment we possess: identical twins reared apart—for differences in IQ between genetically identical people can only be environmental. The average difference in IQ for identical twins is less than the difference for two unrelated individuals raised in similarly varied environments. From the data on twins, Jensen obtains an estimate of environmental influence. He concludes that IQ has a heritability of about 0.8 (or 80 percent) *within* the population of American and European whites. The average difference between American whites and blacks is 15 IQ points (one standard deviation). He asserts that this difference is too large to attribute to environment, given the high heritability of IQ. Lest anyone think that Jensen writes in the tradition of abstract scholarship, I merely quote the first line of his famous work: "Compensatory education has been tried, and it apparently has failed."

I believe that this argument can be refuted in a "hierarchical" fashion—that is, we can discredit it at one level and then show that it fails at a more inclusive level even if we allow Jensen's argument for the first two levels:

Level I: The equation of IQ with intelligence. Who knows what IQ measures? It is a good predictor of "success" in school, but is such success a result of intelligence, apple polishing, or the assimilation of values that the leaders of society prefer? Some psychologists get around this argument by defining intelligence operationally as the scores attained on "intelligence" tests. A neat trick. But at this point, the technical definition of intelligence has strayed so far from the vernacular that we can no longer define the issue. But let me allow (although I don't believe it), for the sake of argument, that IQ measures some meaningful aspect of intelligence in its vernacular sense.

Level 2: The heritability of IQ. Here again, we encounter a confusion between vernacular and technical meanings of the same word. "Inherited," to a layman, means "fixed," "inexorable," or "unchangeable." To a geneticist, "Inherited" refers to an estimate of similarity between related individuals based on genes held in common. It carries no implications of inevitability or of immutable entities beyond the reach of environmental influence. Eyeglasses correct a variety of inherited problems in vision; insulin can check diabetes.

Jensen insists that IQ is 80 percent heritable. Princeton psychologist Leon J. Kamin has done the dog-work of meticulously checking through details of the twin studies that form the basis of this estimate. He has found an astonishing number of inconsistencies and downright inaccuracies. For example, the late Sir Cyril Burt, who generated the largest body of data on identical twins reared apart, pursued his studies of intelligence for more than forty years. Although he increased his sample sizes in a variety of "improved" versions, some of his correlation coefficients remain unchanged to the third decimal place—a statistically impossible situation. IQ depends in part upon sex and age; and other studies did not standardize properly for them. An improper correction may produce higher values between twins not because they hold genes for intelligence in common, but simply because they share the same sex and age. The data are so flawed that no valid estimate for the heritability of IQ can be drawn at all. But let me assume (although no data support it), for the sake of argument, that the heritability of IQ is as high as 0.8.

Level 3: The confusion of within- and between-group variation. Jensen draws a causal connection between his two major assertions — that the within-group heritability of IQ is 0.8 for American whites, and that the mean difference in IQ between American blacks and whites is 15 points. He assumes that the black "deficit" is largely genetic in origin because IQ is so highly heritable. This is a *non sequitur* of the worst possible kind — for there is no necessary relationship between heritability within a group and differences in mean values of two separate groups.

A simple example will suffice to illustrate this flaw in Jensen's argument. Height has a much higher heritability within groups than anyone has ever claimed for IQ. Suppose that height has a mean value of five feet two inches and a heritability of 0.9 (a realistic value) within a group of nutritionally deprived Indian farmers. High heritability simply means that short farmers will tend to have short offspring, and tall farmers tall offspring. It says nothing whatever against the possibility that proper nutrition could raise the mean height to six feet (taller than average white Americans). It only means that, in this improved status, farmers shorter than average (they may now be five feet ten inches) would still tend to have shorter than average children.

I do not claim that intelligence, however defined, has no genetic basis — I regard it as trivially true, uninteresting, and unimportant that it does. The expression of any trait represents a complex interaction of heredity and environment. Our job is simply to provide the best environmental situation for the realization of valued potential in all individuals. I merely point out that a specific claim purporting to demonstrate a mean genetic deficiency in the intelligence of American blacks rests upon no new facts whatever and can cite no valid data in its support. It is just as likely that blacks have a genetic advantage over whites. And, either way, it doesn't matter a damn. An individual can't be judged by his group mean.

If current biological determinism in the study of human intelligence rests upon no new facts (actually, no facts at all), then why has it become so popular of late? The answer must be social and political. The 1960s were good years for liberalism; a fair amount of money was spent on poverty programs and relatively little happened. Enter new leaders and new priorities. Why didn't the earlier programs work? Two possibilities are open: (1) we didn't spend enough money, we didn't make sufficiently creative efforts, or (and this makes any established leader jittery) we cannot solve these problems without a fundamental social and economic transformation of society; or (2) the programs failed because their recipients are inherently what they are — blaming the victims. Now, which alternative will be chosen by men in power in an age of retrenchment?

I have shown, I hope, that biological determinism is not simply an amusing matter for clever cocktail party comments about the human animal. It is a general notion with important philosophical implications and major political consequences. As John Stuart Mill wrote, in a statement that should be the motto of the opposition: "Of all the vulgar modes of escaping from the consideration of the effect of social and moral influences upon the human mind, the most vulgar is that of attributing the diversities of conduct and character to inherent natural differences."

OPTIONS FOR WRITING

1. Most of the other authors included in this chapter are social scientists or journalists with a decided social science perspective. Describe any differences or similarities you detect in a comparison of Gould's writing style and that of the other authors.

2. Why does a naturalist get into the debate about IQ and race? Identify debunking rules Gould employs in attacking the assumption that race and IQ are associated.

Susan Fraker
WHY WOMEN AREN'T GETTING TO THE TOP

Race, IQ, and the issue of gender affecting behavior concern many Americans. Susan Fraker takes on those who would argue that it is something about being a woman that keeps women from getting jobs. In a clear application of the debunking rule that society determines behavior, Fraker describes the role of men in keeping limits on the number of women CEOs. Fraker is an associate editor at Fortune *Magazine.*

Ten years have passed since U.S. corporations began hiring more than token numbers of women for jobs at the bottom rung of the management ladder. A decade into their careers, how far up have these women climbed? The answer: not as far as their male counterparts. Despite impressive progress at the entry level and in middle management, women are having trouble breaking into senior management. "There is an invisible ceiling for women at that level," says Janet Jones-Parker, executive director of the Association of Executive Search Consultants Inc. "After eight or ten years, they hit a barrier."

The trouble begins at about the $75,000 to $100,000 salary level, and seems to get worse the higher one looks. Only one company on *Fortunes's* list of the 500 largest U.S. industrial corporations has a woman chief executive. That woman, Katharine Graham of the Washington Post Co. (No. 342), readily admits she got the job because her family owns a controlling share of the corporation.

More surprising, given that women have been on the ladder for ten years, is that none currently seems to have a shot at the top rung. Executive recruiters, asked to identify women who might become presidents or chief executives of *Fortune* 500 companies, draw a blank. Even companies that have women in senior management privately concede that these women aren't going to occupy the chairman's office.

Women have only four of the 154 spots this year at the Harvard Business School's Advanced Management Program—a prestigious 13-week conclave to which companies send executives they are grooming for the corridors of power. The numbers aren't much better at comparable programs at Stanford and at Dartmouth's Tuck School. But perhaps the most telling admission of trouble comes from men at the top. "The women aren't making it," confessed the chief executive of a *Fortune* 500 company to a consultant. "Can you help us find out why?"

All explanations are controversial to one faction or another in this highly charged debate. At one extreme, many women—and some men—maintain that women are the victims of blatant sexism. At the other extreme, many men—and a few women—believe women are unsuitable for the highest managerial jobs: they lack the necessary assertiveness, they don't know how to get along in this rarefied world, or they have children and lose interest in—or time for—their careers. Somewhere in between is a surprisingly large group of men and women who see "discrimination" as the major problem, but who often can't define precisely what they mean by the term.

The discrimination they talk about is not the simple-minded sexism of dirty jokes and references to "girls." It is not born of hatred, or indeed of any ill will that the bearer may be conscious of. What they call discrimination consists simply of treating women differently from men. The notion dumbfounds some male managers. You mean to say, they ask, that managerial women don't want to be treated differently from men in any respect, and that by acting otherwise—as I was raised to think only decent and gentlemanly—I'm somehow prejudicing their chances for success? Yes, the women respond.

"Men I talk to would like to see more women in senior management," says Ann Carol Brown, a consultant to several *Fortune* 500 companies. "But they don't recognize the subtle barriers that stand in the way." Brown thinks the biggest hurdle is a matter of comfort, not competence. "At senior management levels, competence is assumed," she says. "What you're looking for is someone who fits, someone who gets along, someone you trust. Now that's subtle stuff. How does a group of men feel that a woman is going to fit? I think it's very hard."

The experience of an executive at a large Northeastern bank illustrates how many managerial women see the problem. Promoted to senior vice president several years ago, she was the first woman named to that position. But she now believes it will be many years before the bank appoints a woman executive vice president. "The men just don't feel comfortable," she says. "They make all sorts of excuses — that I'm not a banker [she worked as a consultant originally], that I don't know the culture. There's a smoke screen four miles thick. I attribute it to being a woman." Similarly, 117 to 300 women executives polled recently by UCLA's Graduate School of Management and Korn/Ferry International, an executive search firm, felt that being a woman was the greatest obstacle to their success.

A common concern among women, particularly in law and investment banking, is that the best assignments go to men. "Some departments — like sales and trading or mergers and acquisitions — are considered more macho, hence more prestigious," says a woman at a New York investment bank. "It's nothing explicit. But if women can't get the assignments that allow them to shine, how can they advance?"

Women also worry that they don't receive the same kind of constructive criticism that men do. While these women probably overestimate the amount of feedback their male colleagues receive, even some men acknowledge widespread male reluctance to criticize a woman. "There are vast numbers of men who can't do it," says Eugene Jennings, professor of business administration at Michigan State University and a consultant to a dozen large companies. A male banking executive agrees: "A male boss will haul a guy aside and just kick ass if the subordinate performs badly in front of a client. But I heard about a woman here who gets nervous and tends to giggle in front of customers. She's unaware of it and her boss hasn't told her. But behind her back he downgrades her for not being smooth with customers."

Sometimes the message that has to be conveyed to a woman manager is much more sensitive. An executive at a large company says he once had to tell a woman that she should either cross her legs or keep her legs together when she sat. The encounter was obviously painful for him. "She listened to me and thanked me and expressed shock at what she was doing," he recalls, with a touch of agony in his voice. "My God, this is something only your mother tells you. I'm a fairly direct person and a great believer in equal opportunity. But it was damn difficult for me to say this to a woman whom I view to be very proper in all other respects."

Research by Anne Harlan, a human resource manager at the Federal Aviation Administration, and Carol Weiss, a managing associate of Charles Hamilton Associates, a Boston consulting firm, suggests that the situation doesn't necessarily improve as the number of women in an organization increases. Their study, conducted at the Wellesley College Center for Research on Women and completed in 1982, challenges the theory advanced by some experts that when a corporation attained a "critical mass" of executive women—defined as somewhere between 30% and 35%—job discrimination would vanish naturally as men and women began to take each other for granted.

Harlan and Weiss observed the effects of different numbers of women in an organization during a three-year study of 100 men and women managers at two Northeastern retailing corporations. While their sample of companies was not large, after their results were published, other companies said they had similar experiences. Harlan and Weiss found that while overt resistance drops quickly after the first few women become managers, it seems to pick up again as the number of women reaches 15%. In one company they studied, only 6% of the managers were women, compared with 19% in the second company. But more women in the second company complained of discrimination, ranging from sexual harassment to inadequate feedback. Could something other than discrimination—very different corporate cultures, say— have accounted for the result? Harlan and Weiss say no, that the two companies were eminently comparable.

Consultants and executives who think discrimination is the problem tend to believe it persists in part because the government has relaxed its commitment to affirmative action, which they define more narrowly than some advocates do. "We're not talking about quotas or preferential treatment," says Margaret Hennig who, along with Anne Jardim, heads the Simmons College Graduate School of Management. "That's stupid management. We just mean the chance to compete equally." Again, a semantic chasm separates women and men. Women like Hennig and Jardim think of affirmative action as a vigorous effort on the part of companies to ensure that women are treated equally and that sexist prejudices aren't permitted to operate. Men think the term means reverse discrimination, giving women preferential treatment.

Legislation such as the Equal Employment Opportunity Act of 1972 prohibits companies from discriminating against women in hiring. The laws worked well—indeed, almost too well. After seven or eight years, says Jennings of Michigan State, the pressure was off and no one pushed hard to see that discrimination was eliminated in selecting people for senior management. Jennings thinks the problem began in the latter days of the Carter Administration, when the economy was lagging and companies worried more about making money than about how their women managers were doing. The Reagan Administration hasn't made equal opportunity a priority either.

What about the belief that women fall behind not because of discrimination, but because they are cautious, unaggressive, and differently motivated than men—or less motivated? Even some female executives believe that women derail their careers by choosing staff jobs over high-risk, high-reward line positions. One woman, formerly with a large consumer goods company and now president of a market research firm, urges women to worry less about sexism and more about whether the jobs they take are the right route to the top. "I spent five years thinking the only reason I didn't become a corporate officer at my former company was because of my sex," she says. "I finally had to come to grips with the fact that I overemphasized being a woman and underemphasized what I did for a living. I was in a staff function — the company didn't live and die by what I did."

Men and women alike tend to believe that because women are raised differently they must manage differently. Research to support this belief is hard to come by, though. The women retail managers studied by Harlan and Weiss, while never quarterbacks or catchers, had no trouble playing on management teams. Nor did they perform less well on standardized tests measuring qualities like assertiveness and leadership. "Women don't manage differently," Harlan says flatly.

In a much larger study specifically addressing management styles, psychologists Jay Hall and Susan Donnell of Teleometrics International Inc., a management training company, reached the same conclusion. They matched nearly 2,000 men and women managers according to age, rank in their organization, kind of organization, and the number of people they supervised. The psychologists ran tests to assess everything from managerial philosophies to the ability to get along with people, even quizzing subordinates on their views of the boss. Donnell and Hall concluded, "Male and female managers do not differ in the way they manage the organization's technical and human resources."

Data on how women's expectations — and therefore, arguably, their performance — may differ from men's are more confusing. Stanford Professor Myra Strober studied 150 men and 26 women who graduated from the Stanford Business School in 1974. When she and a colleague, Francine Gordon, polled the MBAs shortly before graduation, they discovered that the women had much lower expectations for their peak earnings. The top salary the women expected during their careers was only 60% of the men's. Four years later the ratio had fallen to 40%.

Did this mean that women were less ambitious or were willing to take lower salaries to get management jobs? Strober doesn't think so. She says a major reason for the women's lower salary expectations was that they took jobs in industries that traditionally pay less, but which, the women thought, offered opportunities for advancement. Almost 20% of the women in her sample went into government, compared with 3% of the men. On the other hand, no women went into investment banking or real estate development, which each employed about 6% of the men. Strober points out, however, that investment banking and big-time real estate were all but closed to women in the early 1970s. "One way people decide what their aspirations are," she says, "is to look around and see what seems realistic. If you look at a field and see no women advancing, you may modify your goals."

Some of what Mary Anne Devanna found in her examination of MBAs contradicts Strober's conclusions. Devanna, research coordinator of the Columbia Business School's Center for Research in Career Development, matched 45 men and 45 women who graduated from the Columbia Business School from 1969 to 1972. Each paired man and woman had similar backgrounds, credentials, and marital status. The starting salaries of the women were 98% of the men's. Using data collected in 1980, Devanna found a big difference in the salaries men and women ultimately achieved, though. In manufacturing, the highest paying sector, women earned $41,818 after ten years vs. $59,733 for the men. Women in finance had salaries of $42,867 vs. $46,786 for the men. The gap in the service industries was smallest: $36,666 vs. $38,600. She then tested four hypotheses in seeking to explain the salary differences: (1) that women are less successful because they are motivated differently than men, (2) that motherhood causes women to divert attention from their careers, (3) that women seek jobs in low-paying industries, and (4) that women seek types of jobs—in human resources, say—that pay less.

Devanna found no major differences between the sexes in the importance they attached to the psychic or monetary rewards of work. "The women did not expect to earn less than the men," she says. Nor did she find that motherhood led women to abandon their careers. Although several women took maternity leaves, all returned to work full time within six months. Finally, Devanna found no big difference in the MBAs' choice of industry or function, either when they took their first jobs or ten years later.

Devanna concluded that discrimination, not level of motivation or choice of job, accounted for the pay differences. Could the problem simply have been performance—that the women didn't manage as well as men? Devanna claims that while she couldn't take this variable into account specifically, she controlled for all the variables that should have made for a difference in performance—from family background to grades in business school.

In their discussions with male executives, researchers like Devanna hear a recurrent theme—a conviction that women don't take their careers seriously. Even though most female managers were regarded as extremely competent, the men thought they would eventually leave—either to have children or because the tensions of work became too much. Both are legitimate concerns. A woman on the fast track is under intense pressure. Many corporate types believe that she gets much more scrutiny than a man and must work harder to succeed. The pressures increase geometrically if she has small children at home.

Perhaps as a result, thousands of women have careers rather than husbands and children. In the UCLA-Korn/Ferry study of executive women, 52% had never married, were divorced, or were widowed, and 61% had no children. A similar study of male executives done in 1979 found that only 5% of the men had never married or were divorced and even fewer—3%—had no children.

Statistics on how many women bear children and then leave the corporation are incomplete. Catalyst, a nonprofit organization that encourages the participation of women in business, studied 815 two-career families in 1980. It found that 37% of the new mothers in the study returned to work within two months; 68% were back after 4½ months; 87% in eight months. To a company, of course, an eight-month absence is a long time. Moreover, the 10% or so who never come back—most males are convinced the figure is higher—represent a substantial capital investment lost. It would be naive to think that companies don't crank this into their calculation of how much the women who remain are worth.

Motherhood clearly slows the progress of women who decide to take long maternity leaves or who choose to work part time. But even those committed to working full time on their return believe they are sometimes held back—purposely or inadvertently. "Men make too many assumptions that women with children aren't free to take on time-consuming tasks," says Gene Kofke, director of human resources at AT&T. Karen Gonçalves, 34, quit her job as a consultant when she was denied challenging assignments after the birth of her daughter. "I was told clearly that I couldn't expect to move ahead as fast as I had been," she says. Later, when Gonçalves began working at the consulting firm of Arthur D. Little Inc. in Cambridge, Massachusetts, she intentionally avoided discussions of family and children: "I didn't keep a picture of my daughter in the office, and I would travel anywhere, no matter how hard it was for me."

Sometimes pregnancy is more of an issue for the men who witness it than for the women who go through it. Karol Emmerich, 35, now treasurer of Dayton Hudson Corp., was the first high-level woman at the department-store company to become pregnant. "The men didn't really know what to do," she recalls. "They were worried when I wanted to take three months off. But they wanted to encourage me to come back. So they promoted me to treasurer when I was seven months pregnant. Management got a lot of good feedback." Emmerich's experience would please Simmons Dean Anne Jardim, who worries that most organizations aren't doing enough to keep women who want to have children. "It's mind-boggling," she argues. "Either some of the brightest women in this country aren't going to reproduce or the companies are going to write off women in whom they have a tremendous investment."

To the corporation it may seem wasteful to train a woman and then be unable to promote her because she won't move to take the new job. The Catalyst study found that 40% of the men surveyed had moved for their jobs, vs. only 21% of the women. An argument can be made that an immobile executive is worth less to the corporation—and hence may be paid less.

Where women frequently do go is out of the company and into business for themselves. "When the achievements you want aren't forthcoming, it makes going out on your own easier," says a woman who has set up her own consultancy. "I was told I wouldn't make it into senior management at my bank. Maybe I just didn't have it. But the bank never found any woman who did. They were operating under a consent decree and they brought in a lot of women at the vice president level. Every single one of them left." Karen Gonçalves left Arthur D. Little to do part-time teaching and consulting when she was pregnant with her second child. "I didn't think I would get the professional satisfaction I wanted at ADL," she says.

From 1977 to 1980, according to the Small Business Administration, the number of businesses owned by women increased 33% compared with an 11% increase for men — though admittedly the women's increase started from a much smaller base. While it's not clear from the numbers that women are entering the entrepreneurial ranks in greater numbers than they are joining corporations, some experts think so. "It's ironic," says Strober of Stanford. "The problem of the 1970s was bringing women into the corporation. The problem of the 1980s is keeping them there."

A few companies, convinced that women face special problems and that it's in the corporation's interest to help overcome them, are working hard at solutions. At Penn Mutual Life Insurance Co. in Philadelphia, where nearly half the managers are women, executives conducted a series of off-site seminars on gender issues and sex-role stereotypes. Dayton Hudson provides support (moral and financial) for a program whereby women in the company trade information on issues like personal financial planning and child care.

What women need most, the experts say, are loud, clear, continuing statements of support from senior management. Women have come a long way at Merck, says B. Lawrence Branch, the company's director of equal employment affairs, because Chairman John J. Horan insisted that their progress be watched. Merck has a program that identifies 10% of its women and 10% of minorities as "most promising." The company prepares a written agenda of what it will take for them to move to the next level. Progress upward may mean changing jobs or switching functions, so Merck circulates their credentials throughout the company. "We have a timetable and we track these women carefully," says Branch. Since 1979 almost 40% of the net growth in Merck's managerial staff has been women.

Sensitive to charges of reverse discrimination, Branch explains that Merck has for years singled out the best employees to make sure they get opportunities to advance. Women, he notes, were consistently underrepresented in that group. In his view the tracking program simply allows women to get into the competition with fast-track men. Others might not be so charitable. Any company that undertakes to do something on behalf of its managerial women leaves itself open to the charge that it too is discriminating — treating women and men differently.

What everyone may be able to agree on is that opening corporations to competition in the executive ranks is clearly good for performance and profits. But how can a company do this? It can try to find productive part-time work for all employees who want to work part time — even managers. It can structure promotions so that fewer careers are derailed by an absence of a few months or the unwillingness to relocate. It can make sure that the right information, particularly on job openings, reaches everyone. Perhaps most importantly, it can reward its managers for developing talent of all sorts and sexes, penalize them if they don't, and vigilantly supervise the process.

OPTIONS FOR WRITING

1. Refer back to Figure 9.1. How might men in positions of power react to Fraker's question? How might female secretaries respond to the same statements? Would male secretaries differ from female secretaries in their reaction to this piece?

2. Many Americans argue that special organizations which are race, religion, or gender discriminatory should be allowed to exist in a democratic society. Discuss your position on such an issue.

Cheryl Russell
UNDERGROUND ECONOMY

Demographer Cheryl Russell (author of the recently published book 100 Predictions for the Baby Boom: The Next 50 Years) *shows her versatility as she writes on the informal economy for* American Demographics. *Here she includes estimates of the informal economy's impact on American society. Russell's piece shows how the university kiosk might fit into the economic underground.*

The underground economy is alive and well. Almost one-quarter of all American households say they earn money that is not normally reported on income tax returns. Eighteen million households had at least one such way of making some extra dollars, and many families are involved in more than one underground activity, according to a recent survey.

Americans are more than willing to buy goods and services from people selling "on the side" — people who ask to be paid in cash so that the transaction remains undocumented. More than eight of ten American households bought goods and services in this "gray market" in 1981 — spending fully $42 billion. Internal Revenue Service analysts estimate that only $10 billion of this total was reported on income tax returns.

The informal economy, as defined in a study done for the IRS, "includes all activity which is conceptually within the national income accounts definitions but not captured for lack of an adequate auditing trail." It does not include illegal activities such as drug trafficking, prostitution, arson, or illegal gambling. The study, done by the Survey Research Center of the Institute for Social Research at the University of Michigan, cautions that, "the informal economy is not defined by the failure to pay taxes. Some informal vendors file returns to pay taxes, others file returns but do not owe taxes, and still others neither file returns nor pay taxes."

The $42 billion spent in the informal economy is the gross value of sales, not the net income of informal vendors. The Internal Revenue Service estimates that net business income is about 59 percent of gross business receipts, meaning that about $25 billion in unreported income existed in the informal economy in 1981.

In an attempt to estimate the size and nature of the informal market, the Internal Revenue Service contracted with the Institute for Social Research to interview by telephone a representative sample of about 2,000 adults living in households across the U.S. Instead of asking these householders whether they sold items in the informal market, the institute asked instead whether they bought goods or services from informal vendors in the past 12 months, what they bought, and how much they spent.

"It is difficult, if not impossible," the report notes, "to make national measurements of informal economic activity by interviewing vendors. Although the source of their income may be legitimate, they frequently operate at the margin of conformity with requirements for licensing, permit filing, and performance codes. The approach taken in this study was to measure the size of the informal economy by measuring the value of purchases households made from informal vendors."

Interviewers also asked respondents to describe the informal vendors from whom they bought goods and services—what the vendor's regular occupation was, where the vendor sold goods and services, and whether the vendor requested payment in cash. These questions were included in the survey in an effort to weed out any formal economic transactions, and thereby to derive a more accurate estimate of the size of the informal economy.

ROADSIDE STANDS

As with the formal economy, the informal economy revolves around the basics—food and shelter. Over half of the $42 billion spent by consumers in the informal economy was spent on home repair services or food. Though home repair services were the largest dollar category of informal transactions, amounting to $12 billion in 1981, a greater proportion of households bought food from the informal market. Consumers spent $9 billion on food from informal vendors in 1981. Fully 51 million house-holds — 60 percent of all U.S. households — purchased food from road-side stands, farmers' markets, or direct from farmers, according to the survey results.

The informal economy can be nutritious. Fresh fruits and vegetables were the most common food purchase from informal vendors, bought by 50 million households, followed by the purchase of eggs, milk, or cheese, by 11 million households. And it can be tasty. Nearly 10 mil-lion households bought jellies, jams, pickles, honey, cider, cakes, pies, or bread from informal vendors in 1981. Another 7 million households bought meat, poultry, fish, or seafood informally, according to the survey.

But the informal economy is not a major part of food spending. About 11 percent of Americans' total household expenditures go toward food consumed at home. In the formal economy households spend a median of $2,600 per year on food. In the informal economy over one-third of households spent less than $100 for food in 1981, and over half of households spent less than $300.

"In transit" was the way most people reported finding out about informal food vendors. Nearly half of the households that purchased fruits and vegetables, and 42 percent of those that purchased jellies and jams, learned about the vendor while driving by a roadside stand. Word-of-mouth was the most frequent way that purchasers learned of informal vendors selling eggs, milk, and cheese, as well as meat, poul-try, fish, or seafood.

Only 20 percent of households bought home repair services infor-mally. In the formal economy, however, the proportion is not much greater — only 25 percent of households bought formal home repair ser-vices in 1981.

Of those who did buy home repair services from informal vendors only 14 percent spent more than $1,000. In the formal economy 37 per-cent of the households that bought home repair services in 1981 spent over $1,000. The informal market is dominated by smaller construction projects. The research report notes: "An employer who keeps books for employee compensation or who needs to amortize heavy investments in capital equipment is rapidly pushed into formal business style practices."

Carpentry work was the most common type of informal home re-pair, followed by painting and roofing. Together these three activities accounted for 77 percent of underground home repair expenditures.

Other goods and services of importance to the informal economy are child and adult care and domestic services (accounting for 22 percent of the $42 billion spent in the informal market), car and appliance re-pairs (accounting for 9 percent), lawn services (3 percent), cosmetic and sewing services (2 percent), lessons (2 percent), fuel such as coal and wool (2 percent), catering (less than 1 percent), and items purchased at flea markets or from sidewalk vendors (8 percent).

MOONLIGHT SONATA

"For a small investment in a chain saw, and a used but serviceable pick-up truck whose aging springs may be stiffened by an extra leaf installed on a Saturday afternoon, many a young man appears to have gone into the cordwood business. These entrepreneurs may be found on week-ends in an A&P parking lot or slowly plying their wares door-to-door, asking each customer if they have friends who might also want a cord of wood delivered and racked," the report observes.

The sellers in the informal economy range from those who work full-time at it, to the unemployed, the retired, housewives, students, or friends and relatives of the buyer.

About one-quarter of informal vendors were also regularly employed. According to the judgment of the survey respondents, the vendors' informal selling supplemented their regular wages. On the other hand, "a billion dollars of transactions were conducted in the informal economy with vendors who, based on purchaser-supplied information, were full-time-on-the-side vendors," the study notes ironically. "About $4 billion in informal transactions were with friends or relatives."

The biggest consumers in the informal marketplace are the same people who buy the most in the formal marketplace—those with higher educational levels and incomes. "Not only does the probability of being a consumer in the informal economy increase with number of years of education," reports the Survey Research Center, "but the amount spent systematically increases with increasing levels of education." Householders with some college education spent an average of $672 in 1981 in the informal economy, versus less than $300 for people without a high school diploma. This same relationship holds true in the formal economy, because income increases with educational level.

The study examined the ratio of informal expenditures to total expenditures, however, and found little difference by income in the amount spent in the informal economy. White families were more likely to buy from the informal market than were nonwhite families: 85 percent of white families reported buying from the informal market in 1981 versus only 75 percent of nonwhite families. The average white family spent $615 in 1981 in the underground economy, compared to $527 spent by the typical nonwhite family. This difference, the study notes, probably is due to the high incomes of white families.

The amount of money spent in the informal economy increases with age—but only to age 35. Consumption then falls steadily as a householder's age increases. One-third of respondents aged 26 to 35 spent between $100 and $500 in the informal economy in 1981, and 28 percent spent more than $500. Only 12 percent of householders in this age group reported no informal market purchases in 1981. But fully 37 percent of householders aged 65 and older spent nothing in the informal economy in 1981. The rest spent an average of less than $500.

AVON CALLING

Five million householders reported that they could make extra money selling such door-to-door products as those from Avon, Amway, or Tupperware. This was the most frequently mentioned on-the-side activity available to householders. "The activity," the report says, "is on the borderline between the formal and informal economies."

After door-to-door sales, householders were most likely to say they could earn extra money by selling services such as carpentry, painting, plumbing, or masonry. Respondents also reported that they could make money by selling artwork, baby-sitting, grooming dogs, buying and selling cars, playing in bands, or helping people move.

Ten percent of U.S. households reported that they traded or bartered for goods or services. Most people traded their services for someone else's services, such as medical care for legal help or baby-sitting for baby-sitting.

Households most frequently reported lower cost as the biggest advantage of buying goods and services in the informal economy, cited by 57 percent of respondents. Far behind in second place was the better quality of goods and services, mentioned by only 12 percent of respondents.

The major disadvantage in buying from informal vendors was the absence of guarantees and return privileges, mentioned by 45 percent of respondents. And fully 31 percent of respondents cited questionable quality of goods and services as the biggest disadvantage, nearly three times the share of respondents who cited better quality as an advantage.

The recession had an impact on the informal as well as the formal economy. Twenty percent of households reported that they bought less from the informal economy in 1981 than in 1980, one in five because of a decline in their finances. Only 9 percent reported buying more in 1981.

But the prospect for the future is better — 17 percent of households reported that they would purchase more from the informal economy in the next year, while only 14 percent said they would purchase less. Households planned to buy more because of lower costs (cited by 30 percent), greater accessibility to on-the-side vendors, and positive experiences with the informal economy. Of those who intended to buy less, 34 percent said they would need less in the year ahead and 18 percent cited a worsening of their personal finances.

"The reasons for increased activity in the informal economy are related to favorable experience in dealing with informal suppliers — lower prices and quality — while the reasons for decreasing activity have to do with changes in a family's own situation — reduced consumption needs or reduced income. This argues against the informal economy as a second-class market to which one goes in hard times, and supports the hypothesis that the informal vendor is becoming a more important part of the economic system," the report concludes.

OPTIONS FOR WRITING

1. Examine any information kiosk or bulletin board on your campus or community and see if you can find examples of this informal economy that Cheryl Russell describes. Track down and interview participants—both a service or goods provider and a consumer. How is the operation "on the edge" and "in the grey area"?

2. Have you ever participated in the informal economy? How and why do you believe your buying or selling is part of the informal economy?

3. Did you pay taxes on your informal economic activity? (Be aware of the repercussions of a negative answer to this question, and please do not feel obliged to answer.) What do you think of having to pay taxes for having a garage sale, mowing people's lawns, and other activities? Should the government have the right to collect such taxes? What about giving a neighbor some extra fish you catch or trading firewood for babysitting? These are critical economic activities. Should the government figure out a way to put a dollar sign on those exchanges and tax people?

Lawrence Wright
HISTORY MOVES THROUGH ALL OF US ALL THE TIME

The debunker's test of time is reflected in Lawrence Wright's short piece describing his autobiography In the New World: Growing up with America, 1960–1984. *Wright grew up the son of a bank executive in Oklahoma and Texas. He has also written* City Children, Country Summer: A Story of Ghetto Children Among the Amish.

When I was in the third grade, our teacher asked us to fill out an envelope with our "complete address."
NAME: Larry Wright
STREET ADDRESS: 1126 S. 6th St.
CITY: Ponca City
STATE: Oklahoma
COUNTRY: United States of America
CONTINENT: North America
PLANET: Earth
GALAXY: The Milky Way
THE UNIVERSE
So mine read.

I recall, as I filled out each space on the envelope, the sensation of feeling smaller and smaller and smaller. The true measure of my insignificance in the universe had been revealed to me.

Of course it was easy, growing up in Oklahoma and later in Texas, to feel insignificant. The centers of life and power—New York, London, Paris—seemed as far away as the Pleiades. To be in Dallas in '63, at the age of 16, was to sense that one was living offstage, in the wings—that nothing important would ever happen to us. We were nobodies living nowhere.

Later, when there were reports of Dallas schoolchildren laughing at the news of the assassination of President Kennedy, I wondered if I hadn't laughed myself. It was such a relief, such a release of anxiety, such a shocking turn of events. *Something had happened!* Our lives could change after all—they had changed already! At last we had become significant. In the minds of most Americans, we had become the people who murdered John Kennedy.

Twenty years later, I began writing my autobiography, "In the New World," which opens in Dallas in 1960, with the Kennedy-Nixon presidential contest, and ends in the same city in 1984, with Ronald Reagan's triumphant renomination at the Republican National Convention. The book chronicles the rise of what I call the new world—that is, the urban Sunbelt, which was just beginning its explosive growth at the end of the Eisenhower years and would reach its apogee of power and influence in the Reagan era.

It's a personal account of growing up with America—a raw, adolescent country that was just beginning to understand its new place in the world after the great war of my parents' generation. It is, in some respects, an autobiography of the children of the World War II generation—the vast bulge of population known as the Baby Boom. It is told from the perspective of one who was a Dallasite during the Kennedy assassination, a white Southerner during the civil rights movement, a man during the women's movement, and a conscientious objector during the Vietnam war.

It's curious to hear the frequent reaction of my readers that I was fortunate to have grown up "in the middle of everything that was happening." That's not the way it felt at the time. The great joy in writing the autobiography was to discover that history moves through all of us all the time.

It was easy to see this in the case of my father, who was a farm boy in the dust bowl of Kansas until the winds of history lifted him up and carried him off to save civilization in Europe, and then to Japan, and then Korea, and finally deposited the young hero in Dallas, where he became a prosperous banker and one of the builders of the new world.

But history was also with me, and with my generation as we grew to maturity—many of us in the suburbs of this new world our parents had made for us. We were already a phenomenon, the largest and most powerful generation our country had ever produced. We saw the contradictions between what America stood for and what it claimed to be. History was with us as we argued with ourselves and with our parents over what kind of country we wanted to have. History was present at our dining room table as my father and I fought our generational war, blazing away at each other like the Monitor and the Merrimac, about the war, the hippies, the draft, McGovern and Nixon. History was with me as I sat praying about my duty to my country, and deciding, finally, that Vietnam was a war I couldn't fight. Each of these moments was a part of a larger movement that was occurring in families all across America, tearing the generations apart, causing the country to take stock of itself and change directions. This was history being made.

The great danger, I found, in writing such a book is the received memory of "the way it was." It's like a familiar rut in the road. The danger is particularly great for my generation, which looks at itself as a mass. One's memories get swallowed up in a larger generational notion of how we were. The landmarks— the assassinations, the war, the Beatles, Woodstock, etc.—have become such a part of our consciousness that we forget the way we *really* were. So I treated the younger me much as I do subjects I write about for magazines: I interviewed friends, reread newspapers, secured my love letters from my former girlfriend. My parents were especially helpful—for years they've written their own autobiographies in the form of letters to their children. The research wasn't always pleasing, but it was nearly always surprising.

The great lesson, I found, is the danger of conventional wisdom. The record of history is never clear. But as I look back at my opinions in the '60s and '70s—about Kennedy, Nixon, civil rights, the war—I realize how often I was wrong. Yet my thinking then was what almost everyone was thinking. Perhaps I was afraid to think otherwise. So much mischief and unhappiness have been caused in America by rallying around subtle, beguiling, insidious lies. So one message, especially to students, is "do your own thinking."

Reading autobiographies has always been a special pleasure. Now, in writing my life story, it's wonderful to hear people say they could see in it some of *their* life, too.

Perhaps we didn't grow up in the same city or go to the same schools, or come to similar conclusions about who we are or what we want. But these readers see experiences in my life that remind them of their own—moments when they felt as I did: the arguments with my father, for instance, or working up the nerve to propose to the woman I would marry, or deciding it was time to venture into the deep water of parenthood.

Most of us have more in common than we suspect, and this is the great discovery we make in reading about other people's lives. For in doing so we relive our own, and we come to understand something of our own place in the universe.

OPTIONS FOR WRITING

1. How does Wright's article reflect the debunking test of time? Explain, and give some concrete examples of the application of this test.

2. Construct a time line or chronology of your own life, filling in the high-points and key events. What does Wright mean when he says history moves through all of us all the time?

3. Wright claims that history was with him and his father as they fought out the intergenerational battles. What does he mean? Has history been with you as you fought out intergenerational battles? Give an example.

Italo Calvino
SANTA'S CHILDREN

William Weaver translates from the Italian author Italo Calvino a piece called "Santa's Children" from Marcovaldo or the Seasons in the City. *Calvino's hero, Marcovaldo, a blue-collar Italian worker who has a series of misadventures, provides his creator a wonderful character whose Christmastime job as Santa shows the debunking test of context in a wonderfully succinct and colorful short piece. Italo Calvino was born Guilio Einaudi on an island in the Caribbean. His parents, both Italian botanists, soon returned with him to their native Italy. As a youngster, Calvino's curiosity attracted him away from his parents' interests to "another kind of vegetation, that of the human word." His works are simple in form, delightful in style, and immense in meaning. They include* Italian Folktales, If on a Winter's Night A Traveler, *and* The Uses of Literature.

No period of the year is more gentle and good, for the world of industry and commerce, than Christmas and the weeks preceding it. From the streets rises the tremulous sound of the mountaineers' bagpipes; and the big companies, till yesterday coldly concerned with calculating gross product and dividends, open their hearts to human affections and to smiles. The sole thought of Boards of Directors now is to give joy to their fellow-man, sending gifts accompanied by messages of goodwill both to other companies and to private individuals; every firm feels obliged to buy a great stock of products from a second firm to serve as presents to third firms; and those firms, for their part, buy from yet another firm further stocks of presents for the others; the office windows remain aglow till late, specially those of the shipping department, where the personnel work overtime wrapping packages and boxes; beyond the misted panes, on the sidewalks covered by a crust of ice, the pipers advance. Having descended from the dark mysterious mountains, they stand at the downtown intersections, a bit dazzled by the excessive lights, by the excessively rich shop-windows; and heads bowed, they blow into their instruments; at that sound among the businessmen the heavy conflicts of interest are placated and give way to a new rivalry: to see who can present the most conspicuous and original gift in the most attractive way.

At Sbav and Co. that year the Public Relations Office suggested that the Christmas presents for the most important persons should be delivered at home by a man dressed as Santa Claus.

The idea won the unanimous approval of the top executives. A complete Santa Claus outfit was bought: white beard, red cap and tunic edged in white fur, big boots. They had the various delivery men try it on, to see whom it fitted best, but one man was too short and the beard touched the ground; another was too stout and couldn't get into the tunic; another was too young; yet another was too old and it wasn't worth wasting make-up on him.

While the head of the Personnel Office was sending for other possible Santas from the various departments, the assembled executives sought to develop the idea: the Human Relations Office wanted the employees' Christmas packages also to be distributed by Santa Claus, at a collective ceremony; the Sales Office wanted Santa to make a round of the shops as well; the Advertising Office was worried about the prominence of the firm's name, suggesting that perhaps they should tie four balloons to a string with the letters S.B.A.V.

All were caught up in the lively and cordial atmosphere spreading through the festive, productive city; nothing is more beautiful than the sensation of material goods flowing on all sides and, with it, the good will each feels towards the others; for this, this above all, as the skirling sound of the pipes reminds us, is what really counts.

In the shipping department, goods — material and spiritual — passed through Marcovaldo's hands, since it represented merchandise to load and unload. And it was not only through loading and unloading that he shared in the general festivity, but also by thinking that at the end of that labyrinth of hundreds of thousands of packages there waited a package belonging to him alone, prepared by the Human Relations Office; and even more, by figuring how much was due him at the end of the month, counting the Christmas bonus and his overtime hours. With the money, he too would be able to rush to the shops and buy, buy, buy, to give presents, presents, presents, as his most sincere feelings and the general interests of industry and commerce decreed.

The head of the Personnel Office came into the shipping department with a fake beard in his hand. "Hey, you!" he said to Marcovaldo. "See how this beard looks on you. Perfect! You're Santa then. Come upstairs. Get moving. You'll be given a special bonus if you make fifty home deliveries per day."

Got up as Santa Claus, Marcovaldo rode through the city, on the saddle of the motorbike-truck laden with packages wrapped in varicolored paper, tied with pretty ribbons, and decorated with twigs of mistletoe and holly. The white cotton beard tickled him a little but it protected his throat from the cold air.

His first trip was to his own home, because he couldn't resist the temptation of giving his children a surprise. At first, he thought, they won't recognize me. Then I bet they'll laugh!

The children were playing on the stairs. They barely looked up. "Hi, Papà."

Marcovaldo was let down. "Hmph . . . Don't you see how I'm dressed?"

"How are you supposed to be dressed?" Pietruccio said. "Like Santa Claus, right?"

"And you recognized me first thing?"

"Easy! We recognized Signor Sigismondo, too; and he was disguised better than you!"

"And the janitor's brother-in-law!"

"And the father of the twins across the street!"

"And the uncle of Ernestina — the girl with the braids!"

"All dressed like Santa Claus?" Marcovaldo asked, and the disappointment in his voice wasn't due only to the failure of the family surprise, but also because he felt that the company's prestige had somehow been impaired.

"Of course. Just like you," the children answered. "Like Santa Claus. With a fake beard, as usual." And turning their backs on him, the children became absorbed again in their games.

It so happened that the Public Relations Offices of many firms had had the same idea at the same time; and they had recruited a great number of people, jobless for the most part, pensioners, street-vendors, and had dressed them in the red tunic, with the cotton-wool beard. The children, the first few times, had been amused, recognizing acquaintances under that disguise, neighborhood figures, but after a while they were jaded and paid no further attention.

The game they were involved in seemed to absorb them entirely. They had gathered on a landing and were seated in a circle. "May I ask what you're plotting?" Marcovaldo inquired.

"Leave us alone, Papà; we have to fix our presents."

"Presents for who?"

"For a poor child. We have to find a poor child and give him presents."

"Who said so?"

"It's in our school reader."

Marcovaldo was about to say: "You're poor children yourselves!" But during this past week he had become so convinced that he was an inhabitant of the Land of Plenty, where all purchased and enjoyed themselves and exchanged presents, that it seemed bad manners to mention poverty; and he preferred to declare: "Poor children don't exist any more!"

Michelino stood up and asked: "Is that why you don't bring us presents Papà?"

Marcovaldo felt a pang at his heart. "I have to earn some overtime now," he said hastily, "and then I'll bring you some."

"How do you earn it?"

"Delivering presents," Marcovaldo said.

"To us?"

"No, to other people."

"Why not to us? It'd be quicker."

Marcovaldo tried to explain. "Because I'm not the Human Relations Santa Claus, after all; I'm the Public Relations Santa Claus. You understand?"

"No."

"Never mind." But since he wanted somehow to apologize for coming home empty-handed, he thought he might take Michelino with him, on his round of deliveries. "If you're good, you can come and watch your Papà taking presents to people," he said, straddling the seat of the little delivery wagon.

"Let's go. Maybe I'll find a poor child," Michelino said and jumped on, clinging to his father's shoulders.

In the streets of the city Marcovaldo encountered only other red-and-white Santas, absolutely identical with him, who were driving panel-trucks or delivery carts or opening the doors of shops for customers laden with packages or helping carry their purchases to the car. And all these Santas seemed concentrated, busy, as if they were responsible for the operation of the enormous machine of the Holiday Season.

And exactly like them, Marcovaldo ran from one address to another, following his list, dismounted from his seat, sorted the packages in the wagon, selected one, presented it to the person opening the door, pronouncing the words: "Sbav and Company with a Merry Christmas and a Happy New Year," and pocketed the tip.

This tip could be substantial and Marcovaldo might have been considered content, but something was missing. Every time, before ringing at a door, followed by Michelino, he anticipated the wonder of the person who, on opening the door, would see Santa Claus himself standing there before him; he expected some fuss, curiosity, gratitude. And every time he was received like the postman, who brings the newspaper day after day.

He rang at the door of a luxurious house. A governess answered the door. "Oh, another package. Who's this one from?"

"Sbav and Company wish a . . . "

"Well, bring it in," and she led Santa Claus down a corridor filled with tapestries, carpets, and majolica vases. Michelino, all eyes, followed his father.

The governess opened a glass door. They entered a room with a high ceiling, so high that a great fir tree could fit beneath it. It was a Christmas tree lighted by glass bubbles of every color, and from its branches hung presents and sweets of every description. From the ceiling hung heavy crystal chandeliers, and the highest branches of the fir caught some of the glistening drops. Over a large table were arrayed glass, sliver, boxes of candied fruit and cases of bottles. The toys, scattered over a great rug, were as numerous as in a toyshop, mostly complicated electronic devices and model space-ships. On that rug, in an empty corner, there was a little boy about nine years old, lying prone, with a bored, sullen look. He was leafing through an illustrated volume, as if everything around him were no concern of his.

"Gianfranco, look, Gianfranco," the governess said. "You see? Santa Claus has come back with another present?"

"Three hundred twelve," the child sighed, without looking up from his book. "Put it over there."

"It's the three hundred and twelfth present that's arrived," the governess said. "Gianfranco is so clever. He keeps count; he doesn't miss one. Counting is his great passion."

On tiptoe Marcovaldo and Michelino left the house.

"Papà is that little boy a poor child?" Michelino asked.

Marcovaldo was busy rearranging the contents of the truck and didn't answer immediately. But after a moment, he hastened to protest: "Poor? What are you talking about? You know who his father is? He's the president of the Society for the Implementation of Christmas Consumption. Commendatore—"

He broke off, because he didn't see Michelino anywhere. "Michelino! Michelino! Where are you?" He had vanished.

I bet he saw another Santa Claus go by, took him for me, and has gone off after him. . . . Marcovaldo continued his rounds, but he was a bit concerned, and couldn't wait to get home again.

At home, he found Michelino with his brothers, good as gold.

"Say, where did you go?"

"I came home to collect our presents . . . the presents for that poor child. . . ."

"What? Who?"

"The one that was so sad . . . the one in the villa, with the Christmas tree. . . ."

"Him? What kind of a present could you give him?"

"Oh, we fixed them up very nice . . . three presents, all wrapped in silver paper."

The younger boys spoke up: "We all went together to take them to him! You should have seen how happy he was!"

"I'll bet!" Marcovaldo said. "That was just what he needed to make him happy: your presents!"

"Yes, ours! . . . He ran over right away to tear off the paper and see what they were. . . ."

"And what were they?"

"The first was a hammer: that big round hammer, the wooden kind. . . ."

"What did he do then?"

"He was jumping with joy! He grabbed it and began to use it!"

"How?"

"He broke all the toys! And all the glassware! Then he took the second present . . ."

"What was that?"

"A slingshot. You should of seen him. He was so happy! He hit all the glass balls on the Christmas tree. Then he started on the chandeliers . . ."

"That's enough. I don't want to hear any more! And the . . . third present?"

"We didn't have anything left to give, so we took some silver paper and wrapped up a box of kitchen matches. That was the present that made him happiest of all. He said: They never let me touch matches! He began to strike them, and . . ."

"And?"

". . . and he set fire to everything!"

Marcovaldo was tearing his hair. "I'm ruined!"

The next day, turning up at work, he felt the storm brewing. He dressed again as Santa Claus, in great haste, loaded the presents to be delivered onto the truck, already amazed that no one had said anything to him, and then he saw, coming towards him, the three section chiefs: the one from Public Relations, the one from Advertising, and the one from Sales.

"Stop!" they said to him. "Unload everything. At once!"

This is it, Marcovaldo said to himself, and could already picture himself fired.

"Hurry up! We have to change all the packages!" the three section chiefs said. "The Society for the Implementation of Christmas Consumption has launched a campaign to push the Destructive Gift!"

"On the spur of the moment like this," one of the men remarked. "They might have thought of it sooner . . ."

"It was a sudden inspiration the President had," another chief explained. "It seems his little boy was given some ultra-modern gift-articles, Japanese, I believe, and for the first time the child was obviously enjoying himself . . ."

"The important thing," the third added, "is that the Destructive Gift serves to destroy articles of every sort: just what's needed to speed up the pace of consumption and give the market a boost. . . . All in minimum time and within a child's capacities. . . . The President of the Society sees a whole new horizon opening out. He's in seventh heaven, he's so enthusiastic. . . ."

"But this child . . ." Marcovaldo asked, in a faint voice: "did he really destroy much stuff?"

"It's hard to make an estimate, even a hazy one, because the house was burned down. . . ."

Marcovaldo went back to the street, illuminated as if it were night, crowded with Mammas and children and uncles and grannies and packages and balloons and rocking horses and Christmas trees and Santa Clauses and chickens and turkeys and fruit cakes and bottles and bagpipers and chimney-sweeps and chestnut vendors shaking pans of chestnuts over round, glowing, black stoves.

And the city seemed smaller, collected in a luminous vessel, buried in the dark heart of a forest, among the age-old trunks of the chestnut trees and an endless cloak of snow. Somewhere in the darkness the howl of the wolf was heard; the hares had a hole buried in the snow, in the warm red earth under a layer of chestnut burrs.

A jack-hare came out, white, onto the snow, he twitched his ears, ran beneath the moon, but he was white and couldn't be seen, as if he weren't there. Only his little paws left a light print on the snow, like little clover leaves. Nor could the wolf be seen, for he was black and stayed in the black darkness of the forest. Only if he opened his mouth, his teeth were visible, white and sharp.

There was a line where the forest, all black, ended and the snow began, all white. The hare ran on this side, and the wolf on that.

The wolf saw the hare's prints on the snow and followed them, always keeping in the black, so as not to be seen. At the point where the prints ended there should be the hare, and the wolf came out of the black, opened wide his red maw and his sharp teeth, and bit the wind.

The hare was a bit farther on, invisible; he scratched one ear with his paw, and escaped, hopping away.

Is he here? There? Is he a bit farther on?

Only the expanse of snow could be seen, white as this page.

OPTIONS FOR WRITING

1. The latent and manifest functions of social activities were discussed in this treatment of sociology. From the story about Marcovaldo identify and write about the latent or unintended consequences of Christmas in the corporate, capitalist world.

2. In applying the test of context from the debunking rules to the story about Marcovaldo and Santa Claus, Calvino clearly describes Christmas in Italy to generalize about the commercialization of Christmas. From your reading of this story can you discern some differences in the treatment of Christmas between the urban United States and the Italian city Calvino describes? Write about the cultural differences or similarities.

Horace Miner
BODY RITUAL AMONG THE NACIREMA

Whereas Marcovaldo showed us the pancultural universals of basic
human greed, Horace Miner (b. 1912) gives us an inside-outside look
at our own American society. Dr. Horace Miner holds professorships
in both sociology and anthropology at the University of Michigan.
His work in Mali, Nigeria, Algeria, and Uganda serves as the basis
for his The Primitive City of Timbucktoo *and* Oasis and Cas-
bah. *He is the editor of* The City in Modern Africa.

The anthropologist has become so familiar with the diversity of ways in
which different peoples behave in similar situations that he is not apt to
be surprised by even the most exotic customs. In fact, if all of the logically possible combinations of behavior have not been found somewhere
in the world, he is apt to suspect that they must be present in some yet
undescribed tribe. This point has, in fact, been expressed with respect
to clan organization by Murdock (1949:71). In this light, the magical beliefs and practices of the Nacirema present such unusual aspects that it
seems desirable to describe them as an example of the extremes to
which human behavior can go.

Professor Linton first brought the ritual of the Nacirema to the attention of anthropologists twenty years ago (1936:326), but the culture of
this people is still very poorly understood. They are a North American
group living in the territory between the Canadian Cree, the Yaqui and
Tarahumare of Mexico, and the Carib and Arawak of the Antilles. Little
is known of their origin, although tradition states that they came from
the east. According to Nacirema mythology, their nation was originated
by a culture hero, Notgnihsaw, who is otherwise known for two great
feats of strength—the throwing of a piece of wampum across the river
Pa-To-Mac and the chopping down of a cherry tree in which the Spirit
of Truth resided.

Nacirema culture is characterized by a highly developed market
economy which has evolved in a rich natural habitat. While much of the
people's time is devoted to economic pursuits, a large part of these
labors and a considerable portion of the day are spent in ritual activity.
The focus of this activity is the human body, the appearance and health
of which loom as a dominant concern in the ethos of the people. While
such a concern is certainly not unusual, its ceremonial aspects and associated philosophy are unique.

The fundamental belief underlying the whole system appears to be
that the human body is ugly and that its natural tendency is to debility
and disease. Incarcerated in such a body, man's only hope is to avert
these characteristics through the use of the powerful influences of ritual
and ceremony. Every household has one or more shrines devoted to this

purpose. The more powerful individuals in the society have several shrines in their houses and, in fact, the opulence of a house is often referred to in terms of the number of such ritual centers it possesses. Most houses are of wattle and daub construction, but the shrine rooms of the more wealthy are walled with stone. Poorer families imitate the rich by applying pottery plaques to their shrine walls.

While each family has at least one such shrine, the rituals associated with it are not family ceremonies but are private and secret. The rites are normally only discussed with children, and then only during the period when they are being initiated into these mysteries. I was able, however, to establish sufficient rapport with the natives to examine these shrines and to have the rituals described to me.

The focal point of the shrine is a box or chest which is built into the wall. In this chest are kept the many charms and magical potions without which no native believes he could live. These preparations are secured from a variety of specialized practitioners. The most powerful of these are the medicine men, whose assistance must be rewarded with substantial gifts. However, the medicine men do not provide the curative potions for their clients, but decide what the ingredients should be and then write them down in an ancient and secret language. This writing is understood only by the medicine men and by the herbalists who, for another gift, provide the required charm.

The charm is not disposed of after it has served its purpose, but is placed in the charm-box of the household shrine. As these magical materials are specific for certain ills, and the real or imagined maladies of the people are many, the charm-box is usually full to overflowing. The magical packets are so numerous that people forget what their purposes were and fear to use them again. While the natives are very vague on this point, we can only assume that the idea in retaining all the old magical materials is that their presence in the charm-box, before which the body rituals are conducted, will in some way protect the worshipper.

Beneath the charm-box is a small font. Each day every member of the family, in succession, enters the shrine room, bows his head before the charm-box, mingles different sorts of holy water in the font, and proceeds with a brief rite of ablution. The holy waters are secured from the Water Temple of the community, where the priests conduct elaborate ceremonies to make the liquid ritually pure.

In the hierarchy of magical practitioners, and below the medicine men in prestige, are specialists whose designation is best translated "holy-mouth-men." The Nacirema have an almost pathological horror of and fascination with the mouth, the condition of which is believed to have a supernatural influence on all social relationships. Were it not for the rituals of the mouth, they believe that their teeth would fall out, their gums bleed, their jaws shrink, their friends desert them, and their lovers reject them. They also believe that a strong relationship exists between oral and moral characteristics. For example, there is a ritual ablution of the mouth for children which is supposed to improve their moral fiber.

The daily body ritual performed by everyone includes a mouth-rite. Despite the fact that these people are so punctilious about care of the mouth, this rite involves a practice which strikes the uninitiated stranger as revolting. It was reported to me that the ritual consists of inserting a small bundle of hog hairs into the mouth, along with certain magical powders, and then moving the bundle in a highly formalized series of gestures.

In addition to the private mouth-rite, the people seek out a holy-mouth-man once or twice a year. These practitioners have an impressive set of paraphernalia, consisting of a variety of augers, awls, probes, and prods. The use of these objects in the exorcism of the evils of the mouth involves almost unbelievable ritual torture of the client. The holy-mouth-man opens the client's mouth and, using the above mentioned tools, enlarges any holes which decay may have created in the teeth. Magical materials are put into these holes. If there are no naturally occurring holes in the teeth, large sections of one or more teeth are gouged out so that the supernatural substance can be applied. In the client's view, the purpose of these ministrations is to arrest decay and to draw friends. The extremely sacred and traditional character of the rite is evident in the fact that the natives return to the holy-mouth-men year after year, despite the fact that their teeth continue to decay.

It is to be hoped that, when a thorough study of the Nacirema is made, there will be careful inquiry into the personality structures of these people. One has but to watch the gleam in the eye of a holy-mouth-man, as he jabs an awl into an exposed nerve, to suspect that a certain amount of sadism is involved. If this can be established, a very interesting pattern emerges, for most of the population shows definite masochistic tendencies. It was to these that Professor Linton referred in discussing a distinctive part of the daily body ritual which is performed only by men. This part of the rite involves scraping and lacerating the surface of the face with a sharp instrument. Special women's rites are performed only four times during each lunar month, but what they lack in frequency is made up in barbarity. As part of this ceremony, women bake their heads in small ovens for about an hour. The theoretically interesting point is that what seems to be a preponderantly masochistic people have developed sadistic specialists.

The medicine men have an imposing temple, or latipso, in every community of any size. The more elaborate ceremonies required to treat very sick patients can only be performed at this temple. These ceremonies involve not only the thaumaturge but a permanent group of vestal maidens who move sedately about the temple chambers in distinctive costume and headdress.

The latipso ceremonies are so harsh that it is phenomenal that a fair proportion of the really sick natives who enter the temple ever recover.

Small children whose indoctrination is still incomplete have been known to resist attempts to take them to the temple because "that is where you go to die." Despite this fact, sick adults are not only willing but eager to undergo the protracted ritual purification, if they can afford to do so. No matter how ill the supplicant or how grave the emergency, the guardians of many temples will not admit a client if he cannot give a rich gift to the custodian. Even after one has gained admission and survived the ceremonies, the guardians will not permit the neophyte to leave until he makes still another gift.

The supplicant entering the temple is first stripped of all his or her clothes. In every-day life the Nacirema avoids exposure of his body and its natural functions. Bathing and excretory acts are performed only in the secrecy of the household shrine, where they are ritualized as part of the body-rites. Psychological shock results from the fact that body secrecy is suddenly lost upon entry into the latipso. A man, whose own wife has never seen him in an excretory act, suddenly finds himself naked and assisted by a vestal maiden while he performs his natural functions into a sacred vessel. This sort of ceremonial treatment is necessitated by the fact that the excreta are used by a diviner to ascertain the course and nature of the client's sickness. Female clients, on the other hand, find their naked bodies are subjected to the scrutiny, manipulation and prodding of the medicine men.

Few supplicants in the temple are well enough to do anything but lie on their hard beds. The daily ceremonies, like the rites of the holy-mouth-men, involve discomfort and torture. With ritual precision, the vestals awaken their miserable charges each dawn and roll them about on their beds of pain while performing ablutions, in the formal movements of which the maidens are highly trained. At other times they insert magic wands in the supplicant's mouth or force him to eat substances which are supposed to be healing. From time to time the medicine men come to their clients and jab magically treated needles into their flesh. The fact that these temple ceremonies may not cure, and may even kill the neophyte, in no way decreases the people's faith in the medicine men.

There remains one other kind of practitioner, known as a "listener." This witch-doctor has the power to exorcise the devils that lodge in the heads of people who have been bewitched. The Nacirema believe that parents bewitch their own children. Mothers are particularly suspected of putting a curse on children while teaching them the secret body rituals. The counter-magic of the witch-doctor is unusual in its lack of ritual. The patient simply tells the "listener" all his troubles and fears, beginning with the earliest difficulties he can remember. The memory displayed by the Nacirema in these exorcism sessions is truly remarkable. It is not uncommon for the patient to bemoan the rejection he felt upon being weaned as a babe, and a few individuals even see their troubles going back to the traumatic effects of their own birth.

In conclusion, mention must be made of certain practices which have their base in native esthetics but which depend upon the pervasive aversion to the natural body and its functions. There are ritual fasts to make fat people thin and ceremonial feasts to make thin people fat. Still other rites are used to make women's breasts larger if they are small, and smaller if they are large. General dissatisfaction with breast shape is symbolized in the fact that the ideal form is virtually outside the range of human variation. A few women afflicted with almost inhuman hyper-mammary development are so idolized that they make a handsome living by simply going from village to village and permitting the natives to stare at them for a fee.

Reference has already been made to the fact that excretory functions are ritualized, routinized, and relegated to secrecy. Natural reproductive functions are similarly distorted. Intercourse is taboo as a topic and scheduled as an act. Efforts are made to avoid pregnancy by the use of magical materials or by limiting intercourse to certain phases of the moon. Conception is actually very infrequent. When pregnant, women dress so as to hide their condition. Parturition takes place in secret, without friends or relatives to assist, and the majority of women do not nurse their infants.

Our review of the ritual life of the Nacirema has certainly shown them to be magic-ridden people. It is hard to understand how they have managed to exist so long under the burdens which they have imposed upon themselves. But even such exotic customs as these take on real meaning when they are viewed with the insight provided by Malinowski when he wrote (1948:70):

> Looking from far and above, from our high places of safety in the de-veloped civilization, it is easy to see all the crudity and irrelevance of magic. But without its power and guidance early man could not have mastered his practical difficulties as he has done, nor could man have advanced to the higher stages of civilization.

REFERENCES CITED

Linton, Ralph
    1936 The Study of Man. New York, D. Appleton Century Co.
Malinowski, Bronislaw
    1948 Magic, Science, and Religion. Glencoe, The Free Press.
Murdock, George P.
    1949 Social Structure. New York, The Macmillan Co.

OPTIONS FOR WRITING

1. Did you recognize the Nacirema as any people you might know about? Describe your first clue that *Nacirema* is *American* spelled backwards. Explain how that dimension of American culture that you realized was ours fits into a larger picture of who we are as Americans.

2. Many people say that contemporary college life has the ritual and tribal aspects of an isolated, more primitive human group. Describe your average day on campus. How does college life take on a tribal dimension? What activities mirror those of the broader American culture?

10

THE WORLD
OF BIOLOGY

Daniel J. Bean

Biologist Dan Bean accompanies his student Karen as she sets up sampling stations in Stevensville Brook. Karen is surveying communities of aquatic insects that make their homes in the brook. Through her research project we get to see how biologists work. After explaining how scientists formulate a hypothesis, Bean asks us to make an observation of our own about the natural world, turn that observation into a question, and design and run a simple experiment to answer the question.

READINGS

630

When we left the college this morning, Karen and I expected to spend the day hiking in the rain. By midmorning, however, the wind had shifted direction and the sky had cleared, so we left our rain gear along with the car at the last station. For the last thirty minutes we have been hiking a trail up Mount Mansfield. Now, at 2,200 feet, we stop to rest before leaving the trail and heading north through the woods to find the head-waters of Stevensville Brook. It is late spring in Vermont, and the trees and bushes have just begun to open their buds. Mercifully the gnats and blackflies have not yet emerged to perform their rites of passage by drain-ing unwary hikers (those without a good covering of insect repellent) of bodily fluids. Within a month they will be in full flight and at their best in tormenting hikers.

"What if we get lost?" Karen asks. She has a good point. Looking off the trail we can see only a hundred yards into the woods. The buds, while rapidly turning green and beginning to open, provide only a faint hint of color to break up a monotonous landscape of bare-barked trees, unadorned bushes, and partially decayed leaves from last year's foliage. We will have to travel a quarter mile or more to find the stream, and once we leave the trail behind we will have only the slope of the terrain to guide us. Worse, every fallen tree, rotting log, and maple tree looks the same—this is an easy place to lose one's bearings. In a week or so, with foliage out, this section will be a dense mass of hobble bushes and vines grasping at our legs, with a curtain of green leaves obscuring vision within a hundred feet. That's why we will mark a trail to guide our return. As we head for the stream, every so often I tie a piece of blue surveyor's tape to a tree or bush to help us find our way out. In this manner we make our way to that portion of the stream which will be the upper station on the brook. We have now established the last of six stations Karen will need for her study.

The purpose of Karen's study is to determine if the communities of insects, particularly the caddisfly larvae populations (Figure 10.1), differ with respect to altitude.

The highest station, the one we have just established, is located at an elevation of 2,200 feet on the mountain. The lowest is at 650 feet, just

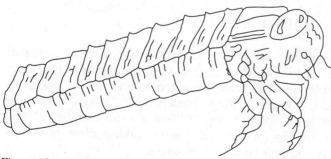

Figure 10.1   Caddisfly larva and case.

before the stream joins Brown's River. The other stations, at 900 feet, 1,400 feet, 1,450 feet, and 1,550 feet, are all at convenient locations where side roads cross the stream or come close to it. Ease of access is important. Karen must check all her stations in a single day to ensure that her samples are not influenced by heavy night rains between two sampling days. Also, water samples and equipment can become quite heavy on a long hike. Only two of Karen's stations, the upper and the lower, require more than a ten-minute hike from the car.

When possible, Karen has selected stream sites that resemble one another in physical structure. They have large rubble or gravel bottoms with depressions deep enough to keep the samplers used to trap the insects under water during periods of low water flow. The exception to this is the upper station—only about two feet across when water is flowing heavily in the spring and after rain storms, barely enough to wet the sand and gravel in the late summer. In other places the stream itself is covered with fallen leaves or with the roots of fallen trees and, in some spots, is only bedrock. During periods of low water the organisms burrow into the sand and gravel bed or withdraw into residual pools, waiting for the next rainstorm to replenish their stream. These conditions are far different from those of the lower stations.

Stream stations one and two are over ten feet wide, with pools of two or more feet of water depth and with flow of considerable velocity. Later in the summer after a thunderstorm, Karen will find her heavy samplers as much as a quarter mile downstream. Station three is located on the main stream at the end of an access road into the national forest. It, too, is wide with deep pools. Stations four and five are at about the same elevation but sample for different purposes. Station four is on the main stream. It is narrower than the lower stations, being supplied by less groundwater. Station five is actually a side stream station. This stream is about the same size as the main stream, and it is important to know what organisms could be swept out of this stream and into Karen's main stream samplers during rainstorms. Now that Karen's stations have been established, the field work on her senior research project can start.

ON BECOMING A BIOLOGIST

Karen's friends frequently ask, "Why do you want to be a biologist? What do you plan to do with your degree after graduation?" Her reply is really quite simple: She has always wanted to answer the questions she asked as a child: "Where do frogs come from?" "Why do the trees change color in the fall?" "What is fog?" "How do fish breathe?" "Why are there so many insects (bugs)?" Of course, asking these questions does not imply that you will become a biologist.

By age five, my son Jon had his own insect collection. He also used to accompany my ecology class on field trips. I would frequently hear my college students ask: "Jon, what is this?" His reply: "Oh, that's a water strider, *Gerris remigis;* see how it walks on the surface." I thought we had another biologist in the family. Now, twenty years later, he is studying to be a history professor.

Jane Goodall, famous for her studies on chimpanzees, answered "curiosity" when asked why she was interested in wildlife. Stephen Jay Gould, a paleontologist at Harvard University, says that he became interested in paleontology when, as a youngster, he saw his first dinosaur at a museum. Karen studies biology not only because she was curious about nature as a child but also because it matches her adult concerns: "because I'm interested in the environment and want to work with an environmental consulting firm." My own interests were aroused by undergraduate courses and fieldwork. In both class and field I became able to think for myself, to ask questions and seek answers through experiments and discussions. My professors and friends played a large role in shaping my decision to become a professional biologist.

It is one thing to want to become a biologist. It is quite another to decide what kind of biologist to become. A biochemist works at the cellular level to determine how genes, membranes, and enzymes function to sustain the living cell or respond to attacks by viruses, chemicals, and bacteria on the organism. Other biologists are interested in the organism itself. A physiologist may study how organs respond to stress, exercise, and chemical agents. The paleontological botanist is interested in the evolution of early plant forms and the environments that shaped those changes. An ecologist may study how acid rain affects lakes, streams, and forests and their organisms, whereas marine biologists do a myriad of types of research on fish, invertebrates, plants, and mammals. These may involve physiology, biochemistry, taxonomy, or evolution.

Regardless of specialization, many biologists work directly to solve a practical problem. This is called applied research, research that looks for the solution to a problem that will have immediate application. Improving crop genetics to increase yield or increase resistance to disease is a form of applied botanical genetics. Testing the effectiveness of a drug for the treatment of a disease is another form.

Other biologists are interested in the ways cells and organs work, usually without regard to solving an immediate problem. This is called basic research. It may be years before the results of a particular study have any practical application. This often confuses the lay person. Why should a scientist conduct research if there is no immediate application or benefit? Very little applied research would reach fruitful completion without the knowledge from years of basic research. Jonas Salk used the information from many basic research studies in developing his polio vaccine. James Watson and Francis Crick were involved in basic research when they solved the riddle of the DNA molecule's structure. The direct application of this knowledge is now used to facilitate studies in genetic engineering.

Whether a biologist is interested in basic or applied research, the study required to reach a level of competence necessary to do meaningful work can be intimidating. During her first three years of college Karen was enrolled in over fourteen science (biology, chemistry, physics) and math courses, as well as her nonscience courses. But now, in her senior year, her study is going to pay off, because she is now conducting her own research.

How do biologists make decisions? How certain are biologists, when they support a view, that their position is the right one? Why do biologists stress the probability of something happening rather than stating that the event will or will not occur?

To the general public it sometimes seems that biologists can't agree, or that they avoid taking a stand. The current debate over global warming is a good example. Issues such as the greenhouse effect are complex and do not lend themselves to easy answers. This highlights the need for everybody to understand the meaning of probability. Indeed, a biologist who has stated that there is the probability of an event happening may also strongly believe that the probability is so low that it will, in all likelihood, never occur. Do you see the paradox in this sentence? Understanding the paradox lies in appreciating how biology is done.

WRITING 1.

Do you or a friend have a plant growing in your dorm room? Is it near the window? Look at it. Does it grow straight up or bend to one side? If it bends, why? How can you test your explanation for the bending? Where would you go to help you understand and explain this phenomenon? Find a plant, make these observations, and experiment with putting it in different places or attitudes. (Turn it around: Does it continue to grow in the original direction? In the opposite direction? Straight up?) Write down your observations, questions, and conclusions. Now go to the library and research the problem to verify your conclusions. Start with a general biology or botany text, and look in the index for plant trophic responses. Then use the references at the end of the chapter on trophic responses to broaden your understanding of the phenomenon. Write a journal entry or short paper explaining what you learned from this experience.

What other common problems have you solved in the past by this "think, try, follow through" technique? Make a list of them. Pick one and write out the steps you followed to reach a solution (or answer), and be prepared to discuss it in class.

ON DOING SCIENCE SCIENTIFICALLY

You've probably heard of the scientific method—a step-by-step approach to solving a problem. An observation leads to a question, the question

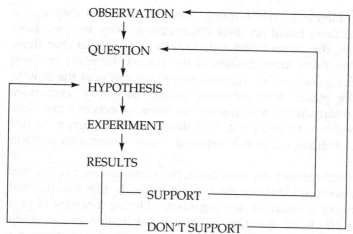

Figure 10.2   Schema for developing and testing hypotheses.

requires an explanation (hypothesis), and the explanation must then be tested by experimentation to determine if it is valid. The results of the experiment will support the hypothesis, not support it, raise new questions, or provide additional observations to restart the cycle (Figure 10.2).

The discovery of penicillin in 1928 by Alexander Fleming offers a famous example of the scientific method. For years microbiologists had attempted to find some chemical means of controlling bacterial growth. Their efforts were frequently frustrated by a fungal growth that contaminated their nutrient plates and made the experiments useless. Fleming encountered the same problem. The chemicals he was testing did not seem to be effective against the bacteria. He did notice, however, that in some of his discarded bacteria plates, colonies of a fungus were growing. Even more interesting, each colony had a ring around it where the bacteria had been killed (observation). Fleming wondered if the fungi could be affecting the bacteria (question) and theorized that the fungus must be responsible for the lack of bacterial growth (hypothesis). In order to test this explanation he needed to devise an experiment. When he deliberately placed a colony of the fungus on his nutrient plates, the bacteria did not grow in the vicinity of the fungus. The demonstration that the fungus *Penicillium* does prevent the growth of bacteria led to other questions: What was the active agent? Could the agent be isolated and purified? How many forms of bacteria were susceptible to the fungal agent? Would the organisms eventually develop resistance? This basic discovery led to the later development of the drug Penicillin for use in controlling bacterial infections such as the pneumonia-causing *Streptococcus pneumoniae*.

It doesn't take an Alexander Fleming, a Jonas Salk, or a Charles Darwin to make observations and ask questions. In our first general biology laboratory at Saint Michael's College each fall we take the students to an open field. We ask teams of students to write a description of the area, observe the distribution of the goldenrod plants, and take measurements of the goldenrods. While doing these assignments they are to keep asking questions based on their observations: Why are the plants clumped? Why are the plants in the center of the clumps taller than those at the edges? Are there more flowers at the tips of the plant or along the stem? Are the galls (swollen regions) more frequent near the ground or higher on the plant? After returning to the laboratory, each team summarizes its information, examines its questions, selects one question, develops a hypothesis to explain it, and designs an experiment to test the hypothesis. Although it is not required, many teams also perform the experiment.

Karen's research project followed much the same process because her course of study required that she do original research. She had decided to do a field project to study stream organisms. During a review of past projects on the effects of elevation on insect distribution in mountain streams, she asked herself if such information was applicable to organisms in similar streams. That is how we came to be standing, literally, on the brink of her stream, ready to find her answer.

WRITING 2.

Each spring, house finches build nests on the sills of the windows in our science building. It is an ideal spot for the nests, between the storm windows and the inner windows. (One of these years we will remember to keep the storm windows down until after the nesting season.) Noticing the nest and the four young birds in it, one of my students, Mike, found a viewing spot where he would not disrupt the feeding behavior of the parent birds. While observing the feeding, Mike realized that the father was an incredible hunter. It took him less than a minute to find and return with food. How did the bird manage it? Curiosity aroused, Mike paid careful attention to the next foraging trip of the male bird as it flew off — all the way to the next window where a veritable delicatessen of dead flies and wasps lay piled on the sill. The solution to Mike's question simply came through more careful observation.

Can you turn an observation into a question, formulate a possible answer to the question (or explanation for the phenomenon observed), and design an experiment to test your explanation? Here are a few suggestions for starters. From which direction do the storms in your area generally come? Why? Is there a relation between wind direction and air temperature? Explain it. Where to the bubbles come from that form on the inside of a glass of cold water? Do bubbles also form on the inside of a glass of warm water?

Make a list of observations. Select one, and ask a question about it. Develop a plausible explanation. Now design an experiment to test your explanation.

In what ways is this assignment similar to Writing 1? How does it differ?

TELLING YOUR STORY

Karen had to build her observation into a research project and eventually report what she saw and measured as well as her results and conclusions. Most of you will not have to go to that length. But learning how to make observations, ask questions, and formulate answers is not only for the scientist.

Gale Lawrence is a New Englander who writes about biology. Although not formally trained in biology, she is the author of books on everyday nature subjects. Her book *The Indoor Naturalist* deals with the topic of nature indoors. In each chapter she writes about common natural phenomena typically found inside of people's houses, such as shower mold or pencil erasers, and brings them into clearer focus for us. Lawrence was not always this attentive to details. In her essay "Fleas" she tells how she came to appreciate life around her by gradually paying more attention to the little details—in this case, where was her cat getting fleas?

> Hussy introduced me to another life form that thrives indoors: her fleas. She had been a stray before I met her and had probably played host to these parasitic, or dependent, insects for as long as she could remember. But after they worked me over the first night she spent indoors with me, I put a flea collar on her and rid her body and our household of her pests.
>
> She didn't have fleas again, or at least she didn't share any of them with me, until we moved to Vermont. This second outbreak taught me how clever fleas can be. We had been in the farmhouse that was to be our new home for only a few days when I noticed Hussy scratching and biting at herself. I was so busy settling in that I ignored her behavior—until I woke up with flea bites once again.

The remainder of the essay not only explains where the new fleas came from but also discusses fleas in general: their life cycles, favorite hosts, feeding habits, and the like.

Biologists find the essay a particularly useful form for speculating about the natural world, especially for discussing a single topic in detail. Stephen Jay Gould uses the essay format for his monthly articles in *Natural History* magazine. His essays address our understanding of the workings of evolution and include such themes as the panda's thumb, hens' teeth, horses' toes, the origin of baseball, and the Cardiff giant. Another biologist (actually a physician researcher), Lewis Thomas, wrote *The Lives of a Cell*, a collection of essays such as "A fear of pheromones" and "Germs, Organelles as Organisms."

Many of my own students prepare essays on topics of interest to them as a way to prepare for oral presentations in class. And many of these student essays found their first life as entries in class or personal journals. Journal entries are in many ways simple essays. Writers use journals to help them focus on one topic before they do detailed research, extensive reading, or careful writing. I use my own journal to keep notes for class, to capture thoughts and ideas for this chapter, to explore possible research ideas, and even just to make lists of things to do. My students include questions from their readings, comments on lecture topics, questions to ask in class, or just plain thoughts on how their education is affecting their lives in general.

The following journal entry was made by an American studies major working as a student volunteer at a federal wildlife refuge in Alaska. The two women in this entry are on a four-day canoe trip to check on the campsites along one of the numerous canoe systems in the refuge.

July 30, 1988

You know life is ok when you sit back and think—"Can't get much better than this"! Another perfect night. It's 9 P.M. and Becky and I are floating on Campers Lake—the sun is real strong and there is a nice breeze—the combination feels great on my face! We have set up camp on a small island—some sign of moose—but no moose now. The loons have come by to check out the trespassers and even let us know just how they felt about our presence. The lake is very quiet—only the leaves echo in the wind.

I wonder about the skitters—they all seem to be swarming but not biting—is this a new batch—not ready yet to suck blood and die—Where are the stragglers from the past scavengers?! I find it too hard to believe they've cooled it for a bit. I wonder—do they come in runs like the salmon?? A huge dragonfly just buzzed by—could he possibly be the answer?? I wonder? The Swanson lakes canoe route is a nice one—smaller—more unique lakes—quite peaceful. Lots of river portages but also lots of lily pads to make the going rough. I wonder why this system has so many lily pads and the Swan lake system doesn't? Could it be that these lakes are not as deep?

Well—a hard day's work done today with a full day ahead of us tomorrow. . . .

Later in the same entry Emma's thoughts turn more biological. As part of her assignments, while in Alaska she is to read *A Sand County Almanac* by Aldo Leopold, an early conservationist.

Natural History! Leopold talks of Nat. Hist. and how right he is. It's so exciting to imagine and wonder about the past and future of the natural things around. I know too little! It's difficult to avoid the desire to want to know names, etc., and see a more rounded picture. I have learned a lot about the history here from the people. The scars (such as the '64 burn) and the natural examples—glaciers, bogs, etc. I need to look behind more of the wonders that amaze me and not simply gloat over their beauty or rarity.

Wow—a noise from above—there it was—a loon gliding in for a landing in front of the canoe—pretty graceful!?! The sound was real neat!

As you can see, journal entries may wander from idea to idea and reveal much of the personal nature of the writer. Note how in the first section Emma's thoughts are on the lake: signs of moose, musings about skitters and the effect of dragonflies on the population size, comments on the canoe route. Then in the section on Leopold we find her wondering what she has learned or still needs to learn. The entry closes with a totally unrelated comment on the landing loon. Emma's journal was outstanding in two respects: her day-to-day experiences were so clear and detailed that I felt I was in Alaska with her, and her attitude about Alaska and Alaskans changed over the summer, which I enjoyed witnessing.

You have just read examples of two different types of observations: those of Gale Lawrence, based on an indoor phenomenon and developed into a finished essay, and those of Emma, written while under the spell of a magical moment in nature. Which do you find more appealing? Which is more informative? Do you see a purpose in each?

It is not necessary to spend time in the field in order to discover questions or topics that interest you. A business major might wonder how social Darwinism relates to big business during the early 1900s. A political science major might raise questions about public health and real-life situations, such as John Snow (1813–1858) did in London in the 1800s, when he convinced the city government that the wells of the city were the source of cholera epidemics.

Years ago a friend of mine was considered a handwriting expert. With a sample of writing, he could describe a variety of personal traits and, usually, the writer's profession. However, he generally missed when he analyzed a biologist's handwriting. He mistakenly assumed that biologists are careful, thoughtful individuals because that's how their published writing appears. Our published articles and books seem to him orderly, with set guidelines, so he concluded that biologists follow set guidelines and are orderly. But he was looking at the finished product rather than the process. Failure and mistakes are common in science, and biologists are not necessarily such organized individuals as he assumed.

You too must always be ready to reexamine your conclusions and premises. Are you really seeing what you are looking at? Is there a better way of examining the data, viewing the situation, or explaining the results?

Now you know a little more about why biologists become biologists, what we do, how we try to accomplish our goals, and what training is required for biology undergraduates. But this is only a short chapter, hardly enough to give you more than a quick introduction. In the section that follows are selected writings of biologists and nonbiologists that will provide more insight into biology. Perhaps they will motivate you to add similar readings to your summer or leisure time reading. And don't ignore your best source for information about biology, the biology major sitting next to you in class or living just down the hall. Ask him or her about the major. Go to one of the biology classes. You might learn something you can use in your own classes.

SUGGESTIONS FOR RESEARCH
Writing Popular Science

The best way to develop your powers of observation is to practice. First, read "Take This Fish and Look at It" by Scudder (in the readings section). Use the following suggestions to develop and write a popular essay on a biological topic in the fashion of Lawrence's essay "Fleas." See also Chad Heise's "Sculpins." Start with an observation (look at a tree or bush or fish in a pet shop's aquarium). What do you see? Write out your observations. Now look again at that scene. What new things did you notice? Write them down. What questions do your observations pose for you? (Why is the tree shaped that way? Are all trees shaped the same way? Why do leaves differ in shape or distribution in different kinds of trees? How does a tree reproduce?) Write out your questions. Now compare your observations and questions with a classmate who has observed the same object or area. Do your two observations and questions match? How do they differ? Why? Now look again for even more detail (remember Scudder's efforts?). Did you touch the object? Smell it? Walk around it (if possible)? If it is appropriate, close your eyes and feel, smell, and listen. Write a description of what each sense contributes to your knowledge.

Now select one of your questions, and develop your essay. List the additional information you need and research for it in the library. Do you think one more visit to the observation site might help?

Samuel H. Scudder
TAKE THIS FISH AND LOOK AT IT

Throughout this chapter I have been stressing the importance of careful observations. This short article is the personal reflection of an outstanding entomologist (studier of insects) of the late nineteenth century. Surprisingly it has nothing to do with insects. Rather, it records his experience as a first-year student at Harvard University, when he petitioned Professor Agassiz to take him on as a student.

As you read this passage, reflect on situations in your own life when you either engaged in a similar quest for knowledge or would have gained from such continuous effort. Do you see what Professor Agassiz was doing? Do you think his technique was fair? How would you respond in a similar situation?

It was more than fifteen years ago that I entered the laboratory of Professor Agassiz, and told him I had enrolled my name in the Scientific School as a student of natural history. He asked me a few questions about my object in coming, my antecedents generally, the mode in which I afterwards proposed to use the knowledge I might acquire, and, finally, whether I wished to study any special branch. To the latter I replied that, while I wished to be well grounded in all departments of zoology, I purposed to devote myself specifically to insects.

"When do you wish to begin?" he asked.

"Now," I replied.

This seemed to please him, and with an energetic "Very well!" he reached from a shelf a huge jar of specimens in yellow alcohol. "Take this fish," he said, "and look at it; we call it a haemulon; by and by I will ask what you have seen."

With that he left me, but in a moment he returned with explicit instructions as to the care of the object entrusted to me.

"No man is fit to be a naturalist," said he, "who does not know how to take care of specimens."

I was to keep the fish before me in a tin tray, and occasionally moisten the surface with alcohol from the jar, always taking care to replace the stopper tightly. Those were not the days of ground-glass stoppers and elegantly shaped exhibition jars; all the old students will recall the huge neckless glass bottles with their leaky, wax-besmeared corks, half eaten by insects, and begrimed with cellar dust. Entomology was a cleaner science than ichthyology, but the example of the Professor, who had unhesitatingly plunged to the bottom of the jar to produce the fish, was infectious; and though this alcohol had a "very ancient and fishlike smell," I really dared not show any aversion within these sacred precincts, and treated the alcohol as though it were pure water. Still I was conscious of a passing feeling of disappointment, for gazing at a fish did not commend itself to an ardent entomologist. My friends at home, too, were annoyed when they discovered that no amount of eau-de-Cologne would drown the perfume which haunted me like a shadow.

In ten minutes I had seen all that could be seen in that fish, and started in search of the Professor—who had, however, left the Museum; and when I returned, after lingering over some of the odd animals stored in the upper apartment, my specimen was dry all over. I dashed the fluid over the fish as if to resuscitate the beast from a fainting fit, and looked with anxiety for a return of the normal sloppy appearance. This little excitement over, nothing was to be done but to return to a steadfast gaze at my mute companion. Half an hour passed—an hour—another hour; the fish began to look loathsome. I turned it over and around; looked it in the face—ghastly; from behind, beneath, above, sideways, at a three-quarters' view—just as ghastly. I was in despair; at an early hour I concluded that lunch was necessary; so, with infinite relief, the fish was carefully replaced in the jar, and for an hour I was free.

On my return, I learned that Professor Agassiz had been at the Museum, but had gone, and would not return for several hours. My fellow-students were too busy to be disturbed by continued conversation. Slowly I drew forth that hideous fish, and with a feeling of desperation again looked at it. I might not use a magnifying-glass; instruments of all kinds were interdicted. My two hands, my two eyes, and the fish: it seemed a most limited field. I pushed my finger down its throat to feel how sharp the teeth were. I began to count the scales in the different rows, until I was convinced that was nonsense. At last a happy thought struck me—I would draw the fish; and now with surprise I began to discover new features in the creature. Just then the Professor returned.

"That is right," said he, "a pencil is one of the best of eyes. I am glad to notice, too, that you keep your specimen wet, and your bottle corked."

With these encouraging words, he added:

"Well, what is it like?"

He listened attentively to my brief rehearsal of the structure of parts whose names were still unknown to me: the fringed gill arches and movable operculum; the pores of the head, fleshy lips and lidless eyes; the lateral line, the spinous fins and forked tail; the compressed and arched body. When I finished, he waited as if expecting more, and then, with an air of disappointment:

"You have not looked very carefully; why," he continued more earnestly, "you haven't even seen one of the most conspicuous features of the animal, which is plainly before your eyes as the fish itself; look again, look again!" and he left me to my misery.

I was piqued; I was mortified. Still more of that wretched fish! But now I set myself to my task with a will, and discovered one new thing after another, until I saw how just the Professor's criticism had been. The afternoon passed quickly; and when, towards its close, the Professor inquired:

"Do you see it yet?"

"No," I replied, "I am certain I do not, but I see how little I saw before."

"That is next best," said he, earnestly, "but I won't hear you now; put away your fish and go home; perhaps you will be ready with a better answer in the morning. I will examine you before you look at the fish."

This was disconcerting. Not only must I think of my fish all night, studying, without the object before me, what this unknown but most visible feature might be; but also, without reviewing my discoveries, I must give an exact account of them the next day. I had a bad memory; so I walked home by Charles River in a distracted state, with my two perplexities.

The cordial greeting from the Professor the next morning was re-assuring; here was a man who seemed to be quite as anxious as I that I should see for myself what he saw.

"Do you perhaps mean," I asked, "that the fish has symmetrical sides with paired organs?"

His thoroughly pleased "Of course! of course!" repaid the wakeful hours of the previous night. After he had discoursed most happily and enthusiastically—as he always did—upon the importance of this point, I ventured to ask what I should do next.

"Oh, look at your fish!" he said, and left me again to my own devices. In a little more than an hour he returned, and heard my new catalogue.

"That is good, that is good!" he repeated; "but that is not all; go on"; and so for three long days he placed that fish before my eyes, forbidding me to look at anything else, or to use any artificial aid. "Look, look, look," was his repeated injunction.

This was the best entomological lesson I ever had—a lesson whose influence has extended to the details of every subsequent study; a legacy the Professor had left to me, as he has left it to so many others, of inestimable value, which we could not buy, with which we cannot part.

A year afterward, some of us were amusing ourselves with chalking outlandish beasts on the Museum blackboard. We drew prancing star-fishes; frogs in mortal combat; hydra-headed worms; stately crawfishes, standing on their tails, bearing aloft umbrellas; and grotesque fishes with gaping mouths and staring eyes. The Professor came in shortly after, and was as amused as any at our experiments. He looked at the fishes.

"Haemulons, every one of them," he said; "Mr. —— drew them."

True; and to this day, if I attempt a fish, I can draw nothing but haemulons.

The fourth day, a second fish of the same group was placed beside the first, and I was bidden to point out the resemblances and differences between the two; another and another followed, until the entire family lay before me, and a whole legion of jars covered the table and surrounding shelves; the odor had become a pleasant perfume; and even now, the sight of an old, six-inch, worm-eaten cork brings fragrant memories.

The whole group of haemulons was thus brought in review; and, whether engaged upon the dissection of the internal organs, the preparation and examination of the bony framework, or the description of the various parts, Agassiz's training in the method of observing facts and their orderly arrangement was ever accompanied by the urgent exhortation not to be content with them.

"Facts are stupid things," he would say, "until brought into connection with some general law."

At the end of eight months, it was almost with reluctance that I left these friends and turned to insects; but what I had gained by this outside experience has been of greater value than years of later investigation in my favorite groups.

OPTIONS FOR WRITING

1. After reading "Take This Fish," read it again. In your journal describe what you discovered the second time that you did not see with the first reading. Now discuss the passage with a classmate. Keep a list of the things your classmate noted that you did not. Write another journal entry recording your final impressions on the value of revisiting the passage. In which of your courses might this approach help you the most?

2. Write a brief essay in the style of the Scudder paper in which you describe a similar learning experience of your own.

Gale Lawrence
FLEAS

The following two essays record the personal experiences of the authors. Gale Lawrence, as you already know from this chapter, is a Vermont naturalist writer. Chad Heise wrote "Sculpins" as a class assignment in an English course at the University of Vermont.

As you read each essay, make careful note of the details given by the authors. Can you visualize the animal? How thoroughly did each writer research and present the information on the animal? Make a list of the kinds of information each author presents about her or his animal.

Hussy introduced me to another life form that thrives indoors: her fleas. She had been a stray before I met her and had probably played host to these parasitic, or dependent, insects for as long as she could remember.

But after they worked me over the first night she spent indoors with me, I put a flea collar on her and rid her body and our household of her pests.

She didn't have fleas again, or at least she didn't share any of them with me, until we moved to Vermont. This second outbreak taught me how clever fleas can be. We had been in the farmhouse that was to be our new home for only a few days when I noticed Hussy scratching and biting at herself. I was so busy settling in that I ignored her behavior — until I woke up with flea bites once again.

I couldn't imagine where she had gotten this new batch of fleas. She hadn't had them when we left our old home, and she had been nowhere except in the car or in our new home since then. The fleas, it turned out, came with the farmhouse. They had been waiting patiently for a new cat or dog to move in because their former host, a large dog belonging to the family who sold the house to me, had moved out on them.

Fleas are accustomed to shifting from one host to another. They are somewhat inconvenienced by the total disappearance of available hosts — as during the month my new house was unoccupied — but they are not necessarily destroyed by such circumstances. Adult fleas can last for several weeks or months without a meal of blood, and because the earlier life stages don't need blood at all, a whole generation can grow up waiting for a new host to move in.

A flea's eggs drop from a cat's or dog's fur and land in the animal's bedding or on the floor. When the eggs hatch a few days or a few weeks later (depending on the temperature), the young, called larvae, feed on particles of organic matter in dust and debris. When the larvae are fully grown, they withdraw into a cocoon to pupate. The duration of the pupal stage, an inactive, nonfeeding period during which the larva *metamorphoses* into an adult, is variable, allowing for a response to conditions such as those encountered by farmhouse fleas.

If a larva enters pupation without a warm-blooded host around to inhabit as an adult, it matures but stays inactive inside its cocoon until it feels the vibrations — the footsteps, perhaps — of a potential host. Only then will it emerge from its inactivity, an adult flea equipped with blood-sucking mouthparts and ready to produce another generation of fleas. My cat inherited the dog's fleas who had, one way or another, managed to survive the month without a host.

Most species of fleas have their favorite hosts — dogs, cats, rodents, or human beings, for instance — but they are also practical enough to settle for what's available in the way of warm blood. Fleas can't live on just any warm-blooded animal, however. They must pick host species that have a way of life compatible with their own. An adult flea likes to feed, drop to the ground for a while, then hop back onto its host — or onto another one — when it's ready to feed again. Because fleas also spend the early stages of their life cycle away from the host's body, they need a host that will still be around when they mature several weeks or months later. The animals that fleas parasitize, therefore, are animals that nest, live in burrows, or sleep in regular spots. Wandering animals like deer don't have fleas. Nor do apes and monkeys. Human beings, with their settled ways, are, in fact, the only primates to have attracted their own species of fleas.

Fleas are well adapted to the parasitic lives they lead. They began to evolve toward their present life-style long ago, when some of the animals around them began to evolve toward warmbloodedness. The insects that became fleas responded to the new circumstances by establishing a place for themselves among newly evolved feathers and fur. But the parasitic habit brought some changes. Fleas lost their wings, for instance, because they no longer needed to fly. They still needed to get from ground to animal or from one animal to another, however, so they developed an alternative method of locomotion — one for which they are justly famous. Fleas can leap 7 or 8 inches (17.5–20 cm) into the air or 12 inches (30 cm) across the floor. A human being would have to high-jump 330 feet (100 m) or broad-jump 990 feet (300 m) to match this performance.

The shape of a flea's body has become tailored to its habitat. It is slender — almost flat — vertically, which enables it to crawl between its host's hairs. The spines on its body slant backward, both to ease its movements forward through the hair, and to catch in the hair when the host animal scratches or bites at it. The flea's outer covering is tough and smooth and therefore difficult for an animal to hold onto with claws or teeth.

It's easy to think of fleas as nothing but small and irritating pests to be gotten rid of as soon as they appear. But if your household pet presents you with them, you might seize the opportunity — as I did the second time around — to examine some of their adaptations with a hand lens before you follow your veterinarian's advice on how best to eliminate them. Fleas are actually impressive little survivors, who manage to live quite well off the warm-blooded animals that evolved around them.

Chad Heise
SCULPINS

During my childhood, I spent much of my time swimming in a small swimming hole that my father had created by damming the brook that bubbled by our house. This swimming hole was large enough for my ten year old frame to explore, and for various species of fish to make their homes. On one particular day, while wearing a diving mask to view some of the fairly large trout I had become familiar with, I spotted a very odd looking creature hovering just above the rocks near the bottom. It was very small — if I hadn't seen its fins moving, I would have thought that it was a small rock. Only about three inches long, the organism had a large head with huge, bugged-out eyes. Just behind its pouting jaws were two fins, spinning like a hummingbird's wings, that allowed the creature to maintain its hovering position. The tail section was long and slender, almost smooth looking, with a small tailfin at the very end. As I approached the beast, almost close enough to touch it, it disappeared, leaving only a cloud of river scum that it had kicked up. It had taken off so fast that I couldn't even begin to see where it had gone. I was intrigued, to say the least.

I described my discovery to my parents, but it was many years later that my father found a picture of the creature in a book, and pointed it out to me. It was called a sculpin, belonging to the *Cottus* genus and Cottidae family of fish. There are about 300 species of Cottidae, 25 of these belonging to the *Cottus* genus. These 25 species of *Cottus* are all freshwater dwellers, but only three of them live in the lakes and streams of Vermont, which is where I met my first one.

I have not, to this day, verified which sculpin my ten year old eyes viewed on that day, but it had to be one of the three species that are common in Vermont. These three species are the mottled sculpin (*Cottus bairdi*), the slimy sculpin (*Cottus cognatus*), and the spoonhead sculpin (*Cottus ricei*). There are only minor distinctive features which allow one to distinguish between these three types of sculpin—they all look relatively the same. One has to observe the pelvic fin rays—fins running along the top or the bottom of the fish—to distinguish the mottled sculpin from the slimy sculpin: the mottled sculpin has four of these fin rays whereas the slimy sculpin has three. The spoonhead sculpin can be identified by its flattened, elongated head, which differs from the other two types of sculpin. . . .

From my encounter with the sculpin and from my research, I have learned that the sculpin is a bottom dweller, making it much different from most other types of fish in Vermont. I remember the sculpin hovering just above the rocks on the bottom, with its huge eyes staring straight ahead. Even in the current, the sculpin didn't move from its spot, due to its circulating frontal, or pectoral fins. What I found to be most interesting, however, was the speed in which the sculpin could move from one hovering position to another. As I would approach it, it would suddenly just disappear. A few minutes later, I would find the sculpin anywhere from two to ten feet away from where it had just been. In my research, I found no explanation for the speed of the sculpin, but apparently this speed is due to the long, slender tail of the fish, which is quite strong.

During the spring, when the water temperature reaches around 50 degrees, the sculpin begins to spawn. The female is either enticed or dragged into a mating den by the male. The mating den is usually the underneath of a rock or overhanging ledge. The female rolls over upside down and deposits her eggs on the ceiling of the den. Sometimes this spawning—deposition and fertilization of eggs—may go on for several hours. The male then chases the female out of the den and may repeat the process with several other females. This is called polygamous spawning.

The sculpin preys mainly on insects and insect larvae that have drifted down to the bottom. Mayflies are the most popular delicacy. On occasion, a larger sculpin might consume a smaller sculpin or a small fish, but usually there is an abundance of insects, so this is uncommon.

Presence of brook trout in a stream usually indicates the presence of sculpin. Brook trout feed on insects, like the sculpin, and have also been known to prey on sculpin. There is evidence that for many years the slimy sculpin has been used as bait for catching brook trout.

The sculpin is a very interesting creature, one which does not look like any other creature that my eyes have ever seen. For me, I only needed to see the sculpin once to be amazed by it. It doesn't look like it belongs in a small freshwater stream; it seems that it would be more at home in the deepest regions of the ocean. It simply looks too odd to belong to the small brook that ran past my home.

The sculpin is an unknown creature to many. Even my grandfather, God rest his soul, had never heard of one, and he had fished (with great success, I might add) the streams of Vermont since the early part of this century. Nonetheless, sculpins do exist, and I find them to be quite interesting creatures. It's been many years since I've seen a sculpin, but I hope to see one again. Unfortunately, the original swimming hole is too small for me now, so I'll have to find a new one.

OPTIONS FOR WRITING

1. Using the factual information from one of these essays, write a story for a young child in which a flea or a sculpin is the central character. Remember the needs and interests of your audience.

2. Both Lawrence and Heise encountered something in their environment that triggered a desire to know more. Find something natural in your world that interests you. Learn all you can about it—from the library, from interviews with experts, and from your own direct observation. Then write an essay on your subject. You might want to tell how you became interested in the topic. If appropriate, include information about the animal's lifestyle and life cycle (birth, life, death).

Lewis Thomas
THE LIVES OF A CELL

Lewis Thomas is a physician, a past president of the Memorial Sloan-Kettering Cancer Center in New York, and a member of the National Academy of Sciences. In addition to being a prolific writer of research papers he is also an excellent writer of books and articles on science and medicine for the lay reader.

The comparison of the earth to a simple cell in Thomas's little book The Lives of a Cell *is not such a strange comparison as it might seem. In the first chapter Thomas makes his case for viewing the earth as a cell.*

Before reading this selection, write a journal entry in which you review what you remember about cells and discuss what you think Thomas might say about the earth as a cell.

We are told that the trouble with Modern Man is that he has been trying to detach himself from nature. He sits in the topmost tiers of polymer, glass, and steel, dangling his pulsing legs, surveying at a distance the writhing life of the planet. In this scenario, Man comes on as a stupendous lethal force, and the earth is pictured as something delicate, like rising bubbles at the surface of a country pond, or flights or fragile birds.

But it is illusion to think that there is anything fragile about the life of the earth; surely this is the toughest membrane imaginable in the universe, opaque to probability, impermeable to death. We are the delicate part, transient and vulnerable as cilia. Nor is it a new thing for man to invent an existence that he imagines to be above the rest of life; this has been his most consistent intellectual exertion down the millennia. As illusion, it has never worked out to his satisfaction in the past, any more than it does today. Man is embedded in nature.

The biologic science of recent years has been making this a more urgent fact of life. The new, hard problem will be to cope with the dawning, intensifying realization of just how interlocked we are. The old, clung-to notions most of us have held about our special lordship are being deeply undermined.

Item. A good case can be made for our nonexistence as entities. We are not made up, as we had always supposed, of successively enriched packets of our own parts. We are shared, rented, occupied. At the interior of our cells, driving them, providing the oxidative energy that sends us out for the improvement of each shining day, are the mitochondria, and in a strict sense they are not ours. They turn out to be little separate creatures, the colonial posterity of migrant prokaryocytes, probably primitive bacteria that swam into ancestral precursors of our eukaryotic cells and stayed there. Ever since, they have maintained themselves and their ways, replicating in their own fashion, privately, with their own DNA and RNA quite different from ours. They are as much symbionts as the rhizobial bacteria in the roots of beans. Without them, we would not move a muscle, drum a finger, think a thought.

Mitochondria are stable and responsible lodgers, and I choose to trust them. But what of the other little animals, similarly established in my cells, sorting and balancing me, clustering me together? My centrioles, basal bodies, and probably a good many other more obscure tiny beings at work inside my cells, each with its own special genome, are as foreign, and as essential, as aphids in anthills. My cells are no longer the pure line entities I was raised with; they are ecosystems more complex than Jamaica Bay.

I like to think that they work in my interest, that each breath they draw for me, but perhaps it is they who walk through the local park in the early morning, sensing my senses, listening to my music, thinking my thoughts.

I am consoled, somewhat, by the thought that the green plants are in the same fix. They could not be plants, or green, without their chloroplasts, which run the photosynthetic enterprise and generate oxygen for the rest of us. As it turns out, chloroplasts are also separate creatures with their own genomes, speaking their own language.

We carry stores of DNA in our nuclei that may have come in, at one time or another, from the fusion of ancestral cells and the linking of ancestral organisms in symbiosis. Our genomes are catalogues of instructions from all kinds of sources in nature, filed for all kinds of contingencies. As for me, I am grateful for differentiation and speciation, but I cannot feel as separate an entity as I did a few years ago, before I was told these things, nor, I should think, can anyone else.

Item. The uniformity of the earth's life, more astonishing than its diversity, is accountable by the high probability that we derived, originally, from some single cell, fertilized in a bolt of lightning as the earth cooled. It is from the progeny of this parent cell that we take our looks; we still share genes around, and the resemblance of the enzymes of grasses to those of whales is a family resemblance.

The viruses, instead of being single-minded agents of disease and death, now begin to look more like mobile genes. Evolution is still an infinitely long and tedious biologic game, with only the winners staying at the table, but the rules are beginning to look more flexible. We live in a dancing matrix of viruses; they dart, rather like bees, from organism to organism, from plant to insect to mammal to me and back again, and into the sea, tugging along pieces of this genome, strings of genes from that, transplanting grafts of DNA, passing heredity as though at a great party. They may be a mechanism for keeping new, mutant kinds of DNA in the widest circulation among us. If this is true, the odd virus disease, on which we must focus so much of our attention in medicine, may be looked on as an accident, something dropped.

Item. I have been trying to think of the earth as a kind of organism, but it is no go. I cannot think of it this way. It is too big, too complex, with too many working parts lacking visible connections. The other night, driving through a hilly, wooded part of southern New England, I wondered about this. If not like an organism, what is it like, what is it *most* like? Then, satisfactorily for that moment, it came to me: it is *most* like a single cell.

OPTIONS FOR WRITING

1. In your journal write a critique of this chapter. Can you see the similarities Thomas is trying to show? What questions can you pose about his

statements? Now go to the library and read the rest of the book (174 pages). Were any of your questions answered in this reading? Do you have additional questions?

John James Audubon
DOWN THE OHIO AND MISSISSIPPI IN SEARCH OF BIRDS, 1820–1821

Journals or diaries are helpful means of recording not only events but feelings and observations. These two journals were written one hundred sixty years and hundreds of miles apart. Each is a record of a river voyage: the first lasting over two months; the latter all of eight hours. Gale Lawrence you know about, but are you familiar with the works of John James Audubon? Audubon spent his life traveling the waterways and roads of this country, sketching and painting birds. His journals describe the harshness of such a life. It is because of Audubon, however, that we know about many of our now extinct birds. Although the original editor modernized some of Audubon's spelling, the sense of the original writing still comes through strongly.

Ohio River, Oct. 12, 1820 I left Cincinnati this afternoon at half past 4 o'clock, on board of Mr. Jacob Aumack's flatboat—bound to New Orleans—the feeling of a husband and a father, were my lot when I kissed my beloved wife & children with an expectation of being absent for seven months—

I took with me Joseph Mason a young man of about 18 years of age[1] of good family and naturally an aimiable youth, he is intended to be a companion, & a friend; and if God will grant us a safe return to our families our wishes will be congenial to our present feelings leaving home with a determined mind to fulfill our object—

Without any money my talents are to be my support and my enthusiasm my guide in my difficulties, the whole of which I am ready to exert to keep, and to surmount.

Nov. 2 We started about 5 and floated down slowly within 2 miles of Henderson when we experienced quite a *gale* and put to on the Indiana shore opposite Henderson—the wind blew so violently that I could only make a very rough drawing of that place—I can scarcely conceive that I stayed there 8 years and passed them comfortably for it undoubtedly is one [of] the poorest spots in the western country according to my present opinion. . . .

So warm tonight that bats are flying near the boats—extremely anxious to be doing something in the drawing way—

[1][Other sources say he was 13.]

Nov. 3 We left our harbour at daybreak and passed Henderson about sunrise, I looked on the mill perhaps for the last time, and with thoughts that made my blood almost cold bid it an eternal farewell —

Nov. 5 The weather fair this morning, the thermometer down at 30 — the sun rose beautiful and reflected through the trees on the placid stream much like a column of lively fire — the frost was heavy on the decks and when the sun shone on it it looked beautiful beyond expression.

Nov. 16 My dear children if ever you read these trifling remarks pay your attention to what follows —

Never be under what is called obligations to men not aware of the value or the meanness of their *conduct*

Never take a passage in any state or vessel without a well understood agreement between you & the owners or clerks & of all things never go for nothing if you wish to save mental troubles & bodily vicissitudes.

Nov. 17 We left early — I took the skiff and went to the mouth of the Ohio, and round the point up the Mississippi —

Eleven years ago on the 2 of January I ascended that stream to St. Genevieve Ferdinand Rozier of *Nantes* my partner in a large keel boat loaded with sundries to a large amount *our* property

The 10th of May 1819 I passed this place in an open skiff bound to New Orleans with two of my slaves —

Now I enter it *poor* in fact *destitute* of all things and relying only on that providential hope the comforter of this wearied mind — in a flat boat a passenger —

The meeting of the two streams reminds me a little of the gentle youth who comes in the world, spotless he presents himself, he is gradually drawn in to thousands of difficulties that make him wish to keep apart, but at last he is overdone mixed, and lost in the vortex. . . .

I saw here two Indians in a canoe they spoke some French, had bear traps, uncommonly clean kept, a few venison hams a gun and looked so independent, free & unconcerned with the world that I gazed on them, admired their spirits, & wished for their condition — here the traveller enters a new world, the current of the stream about 4 miles per hour, puts the steersman on the alert and awakes him to troubles and difficulties unknown on the Ohio, the passenger feels a different atmosphere, a very different prospect. . . .

I bid my farewell to the Ohio at 2 o'clock P.M. and felt a fear gathering involuntarily, every moment draws me from all that is dear to me my beloved wife & children —

Mississippi River, Nov. 19 When we left Cincinnati, we agreed to shave & clean completely every Sunday — and often have been anxious to see the day come for certainly a shirt worn one week, hunting every day and sleeping in buffalo robes at night soon becomes soiled and disagreeable.

Nov. 28 Ever since [I was] a boy I have had an astonishing desire to see much of the world & particularly to acquire a true knowledge of the birds of North America, consequently, I hunted whenever I had an opportunity, and drew every new specimen as I could, or dared *steal time* from my business and having a tolerably large number of drawings that have been generally admired, I concluded that perhaps I could not do better than to travel, and finish my collection or so nearly that it would be a valuable acquisition — my wife hoped it might do well, and I left her once more with an intention of returning in seven or eight months. . . .

We moved from our landing of last night and only crossed the river for the rain lowered the *smoke* so much that it was impossible to see, beyond 20 or 30 yards; played great deal on the flutes, looked at my drawings, read as much as I could and yet found the day very long and heavy for although I am naturally of light spirits and have often tried to keep these good, when off from my home, I have often dull moments of anguish —

Dec. 7 Caught a nice *cat fish* weighing 29 lb. at 3 o'clock this morning — stabbed him . . . but it did not die for one hour — at daybreak the wind stiff ahead, a couple of light showers lulled it, and we put off — Mr. Aumack winged a *white headed eagle,* brought it alive on board, the noble fellow looked at his enemies with a contemptible eye. I tied a string on one of its legs this made him jump overboard. My surprise at seeing it swim well was very great, it used its wings with great effect and would have made the shore distant there about 200 *yards* dragging a pole weighing at least 15 *lbs* — Joseph went after it with a skiff, the eagle defended itself — I am glad to find that its eyes were corresponding with my drawing — this specimen rather less than the one I drew — the female hovered over us and shrieked for some time, exhibiting the *true sorrow* of the *constant mate.* . . .

Our eagle ate of fish freely about one hour after we had him, by fixing a piece on a stick and putting it to its mouth — however while I was friendly Indian toward it it lanced one of its feet and caught hold of my right thumb, made it feel very sore —

Dec. 10 After breakfast we left the post of Arkansas with a wish to see the country above, and so *strong* is my enthusiasm to enlarge the ornithological knowledge of my country that I felt as if I wished myself *rich again* and thereby able to leave my family for a couple of years. . . . We travelled fast — reached the cutoff and landed our skiff. . . . The Indians are still at their canoes, we hailed, and gave them a drachem of whiskey, and as they could not speak either French or English, I *drew* a *deer* with a stroke across its hind parts, and thereby made them know our wants of venison hams —

They brought 2 we gave them 50 *cts* and a couple loads of gun powder to each, brought out smiles, and a cordial shaking of hands — a squaw with them a *handsome woman* waded to us as well as the men and drank freely — whenever I meet *Indians* I feel the greatness of our Creator in all its splendor, for there I see the Man naked from His hand and yet free from acquired sorrow —

Natchez, Dec. 27 I found few men interested towards ornithology except those who had heard or pleased to invent wonderful stories respecting a few species.

. . . having not one cent when I landed here I immediately looked for something to do in the likeness way for our support (unfortunately naturalists are obliged to eat and have some sort of garb) I entered the room of a portrait painter naming himself *Cook* but I assure you he was scarcely fit for a scullion, yet the *gentleman* had some politeness and procured me the drawing of two sketches for $5 each, this was fine sauce to our empty stomachs

. . . the awkwardness I felt when I sat to dinner at the hotel was really justified to me; having not used a fork and scarcely even a plate since I left Louisville, I involuntarily took meat and vegetables with my fingers several times; on board the flatboats we seldom ate together and very often the hungry cooked, this I performed when in need by plucking & cleaning a duck, or a partridge and throwing it on the hot embers; few men have eaten a teal with better appetite than I have dressed in this manner —

Others preferring bacon would cut a slice from the *side* that hung by the chimney and chew that raw with a hard biscuit — Such life is well intended to drill men gradually to hardships to go to sleep with wet muddy clothing on a buffalo skin stretched on a board — to hunt through woods filled with fallen trees, entangled with vines, briars, canes, high rushes and at the same time giving under foot; produces heavy sweats strong appetite, & keeps the imagination free from worldly thoughts, I would advise many *citizens* particularly our Eastern *dandies* to try the experiment — leaving their high-heeled boots, but not their *corsets*, for, this would no doubt be serviceable whenever food giving way, they might wish to depress their stomachs for the occasion —

Dec. 31 I drew this afternoon — and here I have to tell a sad misfortune that took place this morning — having carried under my arm my smallest portfolio and some other articles I laid the whole on the ground and ordered Mr Berthow's servant to take them on board

I unfortunately went off to Natchez again to breakfast the servant forgot my folio on the shore and now I am without, any silver paper, to preserve my drawings, have lost some very valuable drawings, and my beloved wife's likeness — the greater exertions I now must make to try to find it again, but so dull do I feel about it that I am nearly made sick

---

Gale Lawrence
A DAY IN THE URBAN WILDERNESS

Naturalist/author Gale Lawrence and Free Press photographer Irene Ferik recently launched their canoe at daybreak on the

Winooski River. Their goal was to discover what today's "urban wilderness" had to offer. Their findings were recorded diary-style by Lawrence during the eight-mile, eight-hour voyage.

4:30 A.M. — Pitch dark. While we were loading the car I noticed the thin yellowish-orange crescent of the waning moon. It seemed like a good omen.

5:15 A.M. — The morning sky was already light enough to see the faces of other drivers on the road. We stopped at Dunkin Donuts to buy ourselves a treat for later in the morning and saw overlapping shifts at the counter. Two men in formal attire—minus jackets and ties—looked as if they were finishing a night's work (or play), while the others were more obviously starting their day. All of them concentrated on their coffee in relative silence. Even if our car was the only vehicle in the parking lot with a canoe roped on top, I felt briefly a part of the hushed camaraderie among those who are awake this early in the morning.

5:44 A.M. — Sunrise. The sky was overcast, so we hardly noticed it. A pink edging to the clouds the only indication that the sun was now above the eastern horizon. We had intended to be paddling down the Winooski River with the sun rising at our backs, but that was romantic anticipation. We were still shuttling our packs, paddles, cooler, life preservers, thermos jug, and cameras from the car to the canoe at the moment the sun rose.

6 A.M. — The Forest Hills Canoe Access, which is just off West Canal Street in downtown Winooski, is a peaceful place this time of the morning. The crumbling stonework of the abandoned mills creates the sense that we might have slipped backward in history to a time when this section of the Winooski River attracted many of the area's earliest settlers. The falls upriver are the first obstruction Indians and early explorers would have encountered as they paddled up the river from Lake Champlain, so the place where we launched is a likely place for many others to have paused. Directly across the river, in a deep pool at the base of the falls, is a well-known fishing spot called Salmon Hole. Many generations of fishermen have caught pike and trout here.

With the sun a quarter hour above the horizon, we started down the river. Off our bow we saw a flock of gulls on the mud flats. Behind us we heard the sounds of early morning traffic crossing the Winooski Bridge.

6:20 A.M. — We paddled under the railroad bridge that carries infrequent Central Vermont Railway traffic across the river. Just beyond the existing bridge we saw the remains of the original bridge, which was destroyed in the 1927 flood. The twisted girders were humbling. The river we were paddling on was slow and calm—completely non-threatening to novice canoeists after a snowless winter and relatively dry spring and summer—but the river that came roaring through this valley after a rainy fall in 1927 was a powerful and destructive force.

6:35 A.M. — We stopped at the first island below the railroad bridge to enjoy a few minutes of looking back up the river and to eat our donuts as a reward for being under way. A kingfisher rattled at us from the far bank, but the sound of early rush hour traffic was there too to remind us that we were still close to civilization.

7:17 A.M. — As we approached the second island below the bridge, the sound of traffic had faded somewhat. The banks of the river were no longer steep bluffs rising to Burlington on one side and Winooski and Colchester on the other. We were now paddling through the beginnings of the river's broad flood plain. Both banks were low and flat with trees holding onto the soil along the edges. Some were tilted toward the river as if earlier floods had unsettled their roots. Others grew strong and straight with long branches arching over the water. The only sign of human presence along this part of the river was a distant farm building on the Winooski-Colchester side.

7:30 A.M. — I recognized where we were. Many times I have driven to the end of Intervale Road to enjoy the peace and quiet there. I saw the familiar corn fields and recognized the bend in the river that I had looked at often from shore. We paddled around the bend and I had my first look at a part of the river I had never seen from shore. We noticed numerous small birds swooping overhead and discovered that we were passing a colony of bank swallows. The Colchester bank was full of nesting holes, which the birds had dug earlier in the season.

River banks are prime nesting habitat for this species. I have also seen their colonies in sand pits and road cuts, but a river bank seems like a more natural place for them to be. What the bank swallows need is a fresh vertical cut in easily diggable soil, which is exactly what a recently slumped river bank offers them.

While we were watching the bank swallows dart swiftly overhead in pursuit of insects, we saw and heard the first of many airplanes that would fly up the Winooski valley to land at the Burlington Airport that morning.

7:45 A.M. — We spotted a great blue heron wading along the edge of the river in front of us. We paddled toward it as quietly as we could in hopes of getting a picture of this large, long-legged bird as it hunted for fish and frogs near the shore. Then I noticed three more herons flying overhead. We startled the one in the water, and it flew up to join the others. All four eventually landed in a large dead tree down the river a ways. They were so well-camouflaged standing straight and tall among the dead limbs of the tree that when I took my eyes off them, I couldn't find them again.

7:50 A.M. — It began sprinkling. We covered the cameras and concentrated on paddling, hoping to make it to the picnic shelter at the Ethan Allen Farm before we were soaked. Shortly the large green traffic signs at North Avenue and the Beltline came into view way off in the distance. It began to rain harder just as we reached the Canoe Access at the Ethan Allen Farm. We raced for the picnic shelter and sat out the worst of the storm under cover.

9:20 A.M. — Still hazy, chilly, and overcast, but the rain had let up enough that we decided to venture on. We found the river as peaceful as a lake on a windless day. The only sound was the rattling—or was it laughing?—of several kingfishers as we loaded up and started again.

9:25 A.M. — A killdeer feeding on a sandbar let us paddle right by. We had a good look at its handsome brown, white, and black markings, and then it flew off as if to show us its handsome wings, too.

9:45 A.M. — Rush hour for planes. Both military and commercial flights roared overhead one after the other. The only other sounds we could hear were crows cawing in the distance and a truck or farm machine on the Colchester side.

9:55 A.M. — Another shower blew up without warning. We paddled toward shore, where some overhanging willow branches offered shelter, and hoped this one would pass faster than the earlier one had. The rain was gentle and began to fade after about five minutes. The first rain had been somewhat threatening, but this brief shower was refreshing.

10:05 A.M. — Encountered our first human beings on this eight-mile voyage—three men in a Fish and Game motorboat. A few minutes later we saw another man in another Fish and Game boat and told him his friends were about five minutes ahead of him. We thought perhaps they were patrolling for illegal fishermen, but learned later that they were engaged in eel research.

10:20 A.M. — A steep cliff on the Burlington bank let us know we were passing the Ethan Allen Park. Whereas the Ethan Allen Farm is down in the Winooski's floodplain, the Ethan Allen Park occupies higher elevations nearby. The rock outcropping was a surprise after the several miles of low sandy banks we had been paddling through.

10:25 A.M. — More airplanes and a helicopter, but also, from a field on the Colchester side, the soft cooing of a mourning dove.

10:40 A.M. — Turning into a quiet cove at the Old McCrea Farm for an early picnic lunch. The river had been peaceful, but the water in the cove was as still as glass. The overhanging trees were reflected as mirror images in the water, making us feel as if we were paddling across a surface where two worlds met.

10:50 A.M — At the McCrea Farm Canoe Access we encountered a group of children hunting for frogs along the marshy edge of the cove. They were supervised by a teen-age boy who seemed to be a frog expert. The group was enjoying considerable success and held up Mason jars of their catches for us to see.

11:40 A.M. — Left the McCrea Farm for the final leg of our journey.

12:15 P.M. — Encountered a herd of cows on the Colchester bank. One of them was in the water, but climbed ashore as we approached. The day was beginning to heat up now that the morning's rain had passed, but these cows looked quite content among the shade-giving trees with the cool water of the river nearby.

12:38 P.M. — As we approached the Heineberg Bridge, we noticed two young fishermen right under the bridge. We paused to ask them if they were having any luck, and the younger of the two, who was 10-years-old, held up a string of sizeable fish and announced, "Two bass and one northern pike."

12:50 P.M. — Encountered two more fishermen in a large powerboat and asked them the same question. They had caught just one small perch. We told them to head upstream to the bridge and consult with the fishermen there for advice.

1 P.M. — Passed the Sewage Disposal Plant, which we could barely see through the trees.

1:27 P.M. — Reached the Colchester Point Fishing Access near the mouth of the river. Both Fish and Game boats we had encountered earlier were there. They had passed us while we were eating lunch at the Old McCrea Farm. We paused to talk to the Fish and Game staff, who explained their eel research project.

2 P.M. — Left the Fishing Access on the river bank to paddle out the mouth of the Winooski and up the shore of Lake Champlain to an extension of the same Fishing Access on the lake side.

2:15 P.M. — Passed the abutments of the old railroad bridge that used to span the mouth of the Winooski and paddled out into the lake. The water is very shallow here, and shifting sandbars would make navigation close to shore difficult for anything but a canoe.

We felt a sense of victory as we paddled along the sand beach and around the final marshy spit before heading inland. The terns that flew overhead, protesting our invasion of their sandy territory, seemed like a welcoming committee of sorts. We had reached the end of our eight-mile, eight-hour adventure on the Winooski. We had spent most of a late summer day exploring the wildness this ancient river offers as it meanders slowly from the city of Winooski through Burlington and Colchester to empty its waters into Lake Champlain.

OPTIONS FOR WRITING

1. Write a critique of these journals. What is the strength of each journal entry? Does either have a weakness? Is an audience apparent from the style of the writing? Explain.

2. Select a trip or day from your life that you think would make an interesting story, and write about it in journal format. Perhaps your school paper would be interested in printing your remembrance of an Outing Club trip or of a day in the life of a student volunteer. Use Lawrence's technique to describe feelings, surroundings, anticipations.

Stephen Jay Gould
THE CREATION MYTHS OF COOPERSTOWN

Natural History *magazine, published by the American Museum of Natural History in New York City, covers topics from astronomy to zoology. Most of the articles, however, deal with animals. Each month Gould (teacher of biology, geology, and the history of science at Harvard University) writes an essay for the section entitled "This View of Life." These articles explore the history, facts, mysteries, and myths of our attempts to understand evolution.*

In "The Creation Myths of Cooperstown," Gould uses the story of the founding of baseball to illustrate our need to explain beginnings, whether of ourselves or some other object, tradition, or event. Whether an outright hoax such as Piltdown Man or The Cardiff Giant or folk history such as Cooperstown, we seem to thrive on origin myths.

You may either look upon the bright side and say that hope springs eternal or, taking the cynic's part, you may mark P. T. Barnum as an astute psychologist for his proclamation that suckers are born every minute. The end result is the same: you can, Honest Abe notwithstanding, fool most of the people all of the time. How else to explain the long and continuing compendium of hoaxes—from the medieval shroud of Turin to Edwardian Piltdown Man to an ultramodern array of flying saucers and astral powers—eagerly embraced for their consonance with our hopes or their resonance with our fears?

Some hoaxes make a sufficient mark upon history that their products acquire the very status initially claimed by fakery—legitimacy (although as an object of human or folkloric, rather than natural, history. I once held the bones of Piltdown Man and felt that I was handling an important item of Western culture).

The Cardiff Giant, the best American entry for the title of paleontological hoax turned into cultural history, now lies on display in a shed behind a barn at the Farmer's Museum in Cooperstown, New York. This gypsum man, more than ten feet tall, was "discovered" by workmen digging a well on a farm near Cardiff, New York, in October 1869. Eagerly embraced by a gullible public, and ardently displayed by its creators at fifty cents a pop, the Cardiff Giant caused quite a brouhaha around Syracuse, and then nationally, for the few months of its active life between exhumation and exposure.

The Cardiff Giant was the brainchild of George Hull, a cigar manufacturer (and general rogue) from Binghamton, New York. He quarried a large block of gypsum from Fort Dodge, Iowa, and shipped it to Chicago, where two marble cutters fashioned the rough likeness of a naked man. Hull made some crude and minimal attempts to give his statue an aged appearance. He chipped off the carved hair and beard because experts told him that such items would not petrify. He drove darning needles into a wooden block and hammered the statue, hoping to simulate skin pores. Finally, he dumped a gallon of sulfuric acid all over his creation to simulate extended erosion. Hull then shipped his giant in a large box back to Cardiff.

Hull, as an accomplished rogue, sensed that his story could not hold for long and, in that venerable and alliterative motto, got out while the getting was good. He sold a three-quarter interest in the Cardiff Giant to a consortium of highly respected businessmen, including two former mayors of Syracuse. These men raised the statue from its original pit on November 5 and carted it off to Syracuse for display.

The hoax held on for a few more weeks, and Cardiff Giant fever swept the land. Debate raged in newspapers and broadsheets between those who viewed the giant as a petrified fossil and those who regarded it as a statue wrought by an unknown and wondrous prehistoric race. But Hull had left too many tracks—at the gypsum quarries in Fort Dodge, at the carver's studio in Chicago, along the roadways to Cardiff (several people remembered seeing an awfully large box passing on a cart just days before the supposed discovery). By December, Hull was ready to recant, but held his tongue a while longer. Three months later, the two Chicago sculptors came forward, and the Cardiff Giant's brief rendezvous with fame and fortune ended.

The common analogy of the Cardiff Giant with Piltdown Man works only to a point (both were frauds passed off as human fossils) and fails in one crucial respect. Piltdown was cleverly wrought and fooled professionals for forty years, while the Cardiff Giant was preposterous from the start. How could a man turn to solid gypsum, while preserving all his soft anatomy, from cheeks to toes to penis? Geologists and paleontologists never accepted Hull's statue. O. C. Marsh, later to achieve great fame as a discoverer of dinosaurs, echoed a professional consensus in his unambiguous pronouncement: "It is of very recent origin and a decided humbug."

Why, then, was the Cardiff Giant so popular, inspiring a wave of interest and discussion as high as any tide in the affairs of men during its short time in the sun? If the fraud had been well executed, we might attribute this great concern to the dexterity of the hoaxers (just as we grant grudging attention to a few of the most accomplished art fakers for their skills as copyists). But since the Cardiff Giant was so crudely done, we can only attribute its fame to the deep issue, the raw nerve, touched by the subject of its fakery—human origins. Link an absurd concoction to a noble and mysterious subject and you may prevail, at least for a while. My opening reference to P. T. Barnum was not meant sarcastically; he was one of the great practical psychologists of the nineteenth century— and his motto applies with special force to the Cardiff Giant: "No humbug is great without truth at bottom." (Barnum made a copy of the Cardiff

Giant and exhibited it in New York City. His mastery of hype and publicity assured that his model far outdrew the "real" fake when the original went on display at a rival establishment in the same city.)

For some reason (to be explored, but not resolved, in this essay), we are powerfully drawn to the subject of beginnings. We yearn to know about origins, and we readily construct myths when we do not have data (or we suppress data in favor of legend when a truth strikes us as too commonplace). The hankering after an origin myth has always been especially strong for the closest subject of all—the human race. But we extend the same psychic need to our accomplishments and institutions— and we have origin myths and stories for the beginning of hunting, of language, of art, of kindness, of war, of boxing, bowties, and brassieres. Most of us know that the Great Seal of the United States pictures an eagle holding a ribbon reading *e pluribus unum*. Fewer would recognize the motto on the other side (check it out on the back of a dollar bill): *annuit coeptis*—"he smiles on our beginnings."

Cooperstown may house the Cardiff Giant, but the fame of this small village in central New York does not rest upon its celebrated namesake, author James Fenimore, or its lovely Lake Otsego or the Farmer's Museum. Cooperstown is "on the map" by virtue of a different origin myth—one more parochial, but no less powerful, for many Americans, than the tales of human beginnings that gave life to the Cardiff Giant. Cooperstown is the sacred founding place in the official myth about the origin of baseball.

Origin myths, since they are so powerful, can engender enormous practical problems. Abner Doubleday, as we shall soon see, most emphatically did not invent baseball at Cooperstown in 1839 as the official tale proclaims; in fact, no one invented baseball at any moment or in any spot. Nonetheless, this creation myth made Cooperstown the official home of baseball, and the Hall of Fame, with its associated museum and library, set its roots in this small village, inconveniently located near nothing in the way of airports and accommodations. We all revel in bucolic imagery on the field of dreams, but what a hassle when tens of thousands line the roads, restaurants, and port-a-potties during the annual Hall of Fame weekend, when new members are enshrined and two major league teams arrive to play an exhibition game at Abner Doubleday Field, a sweet little 10,000-seater in the middle of town. Put your compass point at Cooperstown, make your radius at Albany—and you'd better reserve a year in advance if you want any accommodation within the enormous resulting circle.

After a lifetime of curiosity, I finally got the opportunity to witness this annual version of forty students in a telephone booth or twenty circus clowns in a Volkswagen. Since Yaz (former Boston star Carl Yastrzemski to the uninitiated) was slated to receive baseball's Nobel in 1989, and his old team was playing in the Hall of Fame game, and since I'm a transplanted Bostonian (although still a New Yorker and not-so-secret Yankee fan at heart), Tom Heitz, chief of the wonderful baseball library at the

Hall of Fame, kindly invited me to join the sardines in this most lovely of all cans.

The silliest and most tendentious of baseball writing tries to wrest profundity from the spectacle of grown men hitting a ball with a stick by suggesting linkages between the sport and deep issues of morality, parenthood, history, lost innocence, gentleness, and so on, seemingly *ad infinitum*. (The effort reeks of silliness because baseball is profound all by itself and needs no excuses; people who don't know this are not fans and are therefore unreachable anyway.) When people ask me how baseball imitates life, I can only respond with what the more genteel newspapers used to call a "barnyard epithet," but now, with growing bravery, usually render as "bullbleep." Nonetheless, baseball is a major item of our culture, and it does have a long and interesting history. Any item or institution with these two properties must generate a set of myths and stories (perhaps even some truths) about its beginnings. And the subject of beginnings is the bread and butter of this column on evolution in the broadest sense. I shall make no woolly analogies between baseball and life; this is an essay on the origins of baseball, with some musings on why beginnings of all sorts hold such fascination for us. (I thank Tom Heitz not only for the invitation to Cooperstown at its yearly acme but also for drawing the contrast between creation and evolution stories of baseball, and for supplying much useful information from his unparalleled storehouse.)

Stories about beginnings come in only two basic modes. An entity either has an explicit point of origin, a specific time and place of creation, or else it evolves and has no definable moment or entry into the world. Baseball provides an interesting example of this contrast because we know the answer and can judge received wisdom by the two chief criteria, often opposed, of external fact and internal hope. Baseball evolved from a plethora of previous stick-and-ball games. It has no true Cooperstown and no Doubleday. Yet we seem to prefer the alternative model of origin by a moment of creation — for then we can have heroes and sacred places. By contrasting the myth of Cooperstown with the fact of evolution, we can learn something about our cultural practices and their frequent disrespect for truth.

The official story about the beginning of baseball is a creation myth, and a review of the reasons and circumstances of its fabrication may give us insight into the cultural appeal of stories in this mode. A. G. Spalding, baseball's first great pitcher during his early career, later founded the sporting goods company that still bears his name and became one of the great commercial moguls of America's gilded age. As publisher of the annual *Spalding's Official Base Ball Guide,* he held maximal power in shaping both public and institutional opinion on all facets of baseball and its history. As the sport grew in popularity, and the pattern of two stable major leagues coalesced early in our century, Spalding and others felt the need for clarification (or merely to codification) of opinion on the hitherto unrecorded origins of an activity that truly merited its common designation as America's "national pastime."

In 1907, Spalding set up a blue ribbon committee to investigate and resolve the origins of baseball. The committee, chaired by A. G. Mills and including several prominent businessmen and two senators who had also served as presidents of the National League, took much testimony but found no smoking gun for a beginning. Then, in July 1907, Spalding himself transmitted to the committee a letter from an Abner Graves, then a mining engineer in Denver, who reported that Abner Doubleday had, in 1839, interrupted a marbles game behind the tailor's shop in Coopers-town, New York, to draw a diagram of a baseball field, explain the rules of the game, and designate the activity by its modern name of "base ball" (then spelled as two words).

Such "evidence" scarcely inspired universal confidence, but the com-mission came up with nothing better—and the Doubleday myth, as we shall soon see, was eminently functional. Therefore, in 1908, the Mills Commission reported its two chief findings: first, "that base ball had its origins in the United States"; and second, "that the first scheme for play-ing it, according to the best evidence available to date, was devised by Abner Doubleday, at Cooperstown, New York, in 1839." This "best evidence" consisted only of "a circumstantial statement by a reputable gentleman"—namely Graves's testimony as reported by Spalding himself.

When cited evidence is so laughably insufficient, one must seek motivations other than concern for truth value. The key to underlying reasons stands in the first conclusion of Mills's committee: hoopla and patriotism (cardboard version) decreed that a national pastime must have an indigenous origin. The idea that baseball had evolved from a wide variety of English stick-and-ball games—although true—did not suit the mythology of a phenomenon that had become so quintessentially American. In fact, Spalding had long been arguing, in an amiable fashion, with Henry Chadwick, another pioneer and entrepreneur of baseball's early years. Chadwick, born in England, had insisted for years that base-ball had developed from the British stick-and-ball game called rounders; Spalding had vociferously advocated a purely American origin, citing the colonial game of "one old cat" as a distant precursor, but holding that baseball itself represented something so new and advanced that a pin-point of origin—a creation myth—must be sought.

Chadwick considered the matter of no particular importance, arguing (with eminent justice) that an English origin did not "detract one iota from the merit of its now being unquestionably a thoroughly American field sport, and a game, too, which is fully adapted to the American character." (I must say that I have grown quite fond of Mr. Chadwick, who certainly understood evolutionary change and its chief principle that historical origin need not match contemporary function.) Chadwick also viewed the committee's whitewash as a victory for his side. He labeled the Mills report as "a masterful piece of special pleading which lets my dear old friend Albert [Spalding] escape a bad defeat. The whole matter was a joke between Albert and myself."

We may accept the psychic need for an indigenous creation myth, but why Abner Doubleday, a man with no recorded tie to the game and who, in the words of Donald Honig, probably "didn't know a baseball from a kumquat"? I had wondered about this for years, but only ran into the answer serendipitously during a visit to Fort Sumter in the harbor of Charleston, South Carolina. There, an exhibit on the first skirmish of the Civil War points out that Abner Doubleday, as captain of the Union artillery, had personally sighted and given orders for firing the first responsive volley following the initial Confederate attack on the fort. Doubleday later commanded divisions at Antietam and Fredericksburg, became at least a minor hero at Gettysburg, and retired as a brevet major general. In fact, A. G. Mills, head of the commission, had served as part of an honor guard when Doubleday's body lay in state in New York City, following his death in 1893.

If you have to have an American hero, could anyone be better than the man who fired the first shot (in defense) of the Civil War? Needless to say, this point was not lost on the members of Mill's committee. Spalding, never one to mince words, wrote to the committee when submitting Graves's dubious testimony: "It certainly appeals to an American pride to have had the great national game of base ball created and named by a Major General in the United States Army." Mills then concluded in his report: "Perhaps in the years to come, in view of the hundreds of thousands of people who are devoted to base ball, and the millions who will be, Abner Doubleday's fame will rest evenly, if not quite as much upon the fact that he was its inventor . . . as upon his brilliant and distinguished career as an officer in the Federal Army."

And so, spurred by a patently false creation myth, the Hall of Fame stands in the most incongruous and inappropriate locale of a charming little town in central New York. Incongruous and inappropriate, but somehow wonderful. Who needs another museum in the cultural maelstroms (and summer doldrums) of New York, Boston, or Washington? Why not a major museum in a beautiful and bucolic setting? And what could be more fitting than the spatial conjunction of two great American origin myths — the Cardiff Giant and the Doubleday Fable? Thus, I too am quite content to treat the myth gently, while honesty requires 'fessing up. The exhibit on Doubleday in the Hall of Fame Museum sets just the right tone in its caption: "In the hearts of those who love baseball, he is remembered as the lad in the pasture where the game was invented. Only cynics would need to know more." Only in the hearts; not in the minds.

Baseball evolved. Since the evidence is so clear (as epitomized below), we must ask why these facts have been so little appreciated for so long, and why a creation myth like the Doubleday story ever gained a foothold. Two major reasons have conspired: first, the positive block of our attraction to creation stories; second, the negative impediment of unfamiliar sources outside the usual purview of historians. English stick-and-ball games of the nineteenth century can be roughly classified into two categories along social lines. The upper and educated classes played cricket, and the history of this sport is copiously documented because the literati write about their own interests, and because the activities of men in power are well recorded (and constitute virtually all of history, in the schoolboy version). But the ordinary pastimes of rural and urban working people can be well nigh invisible in conventional sources of explicit commentary. Working people played a different kind of stick-and-ball game, existing in various forms and designated by many names, including "rounders" in western England, "feeder" in London, and "base ball" in southern England. For a large number of reasons, forming the essential difference between cricket and baseball, cricket matches can last up to several days (a batsman, for example, need not run after he hits the ball and need not expose himself to the possibility of being put out every time he makes contact). The leisure time of working people does not come in such generous gobs, and the lower-class stick-and-ball games could not run more than a few hours.

Several years ago, at the Victoria and Albert Museum in London, I learned an important lesson from an excellent exhibit on the late nineteenth century history of the British music hall. This is my favorite period (Darwin's century, after all), and I consider myself tolerably well informed on cultural trends of the time. I can sing any line from any of the Gilbert and Sullivan operas (a largely middle-class entertainment), and I know the general drift of high cultural interests in literature and music. But here was a whole world of entertainment for millions, a world with its heroes, its stars, its top forty songs, its gaudy theatres — and I knew nothing, absolutely nothing, about it. I felt chagrined, but my ignorance had an explanation beyond personal insensitivity (and the exhibit had been mounted explicitly to counteract the selective invisibility of certain important trends in history). The music hall was the chief entertainment of Victorian working classes, and the history of working people is often invisible in conventional written sources. It must be rescued and reconstituted from different sorts of data; in this case, from posters, playbills, theatre accounts, persistence of some songs in the oral tradition (most were never published as sheet music), recollections of old-timers who knew the person who knew the person. . . .

The early history of baseball — the stick-and-ball game of working people — presents the same problem of conventional invisibility — and the same promise of rescue by exploration of unusual sources. Work continues and intensifies as the history of sport becomes more and more academically respectable, but the broad outlines (and much fascinating detail) are now well established. As the upper classes played a codified and well-documented cricket, working people played a largely unrecorded and much more diversified set of stick-and-ball games ancestral to baseball. Many sources, including primers and boys' manuals, depict games recognizable as precursors to baseball well into the early eighteenth century. Occasional references even spill over into high culture. In *Northanger Abbey,* written at the close of the eighteenth century, Jane Austen remarks: "It was not very wonderful that Catherine . . . should prefer cricket, base ball, riding on horseback, and running about the country, at the age of fourteen, to books." As this quotation illustrates, the name of the game is no more Doubleday's than the form of play.

These ancestral styles of baseball came to America with early settlers and were clearly well established by colonial times. But they were driven ever further underground by Puritan proscriptions of sport for adults. They survived largely as children's games and suffered the double invisibility of location among the poor and the young. But two major reasons brought these games into wider repute and led to a codification of standard forms quite close to modern baseball between the 1820s and the 1850s. First, a set of social reasons, from the decline of Puritanism to increased concern about health and hygiene in crowded cities, made sport an acceptable activity for adults. Second, middle class and professional people began to take up these early forms of baseball, and with this upward social drift came teams, leagues, written rules, uniforms, stadiums, guidebooks: in short, all the paraphernalia of conventional history.

I am not arguing that these early games could be called baseball with a few trivial differences (evolution means substantial change, after all), but only that they stand in a complex lineage, better called a nexus, from which modern baseball emerged, eventually in a codified and canonical form. In those days before instant communication, every region had its own version, just as every set of outdoor steps in New York City generated a different form of stoopball in my youth, without threatening the basic identity of the game. These games, most commonly called town ball, differed from modern baseball in substantial ways. In the Massachusetts Game, a codification of the late 1850s drawn up by ball players in New England towns, four bases and three strikes identify the genus, but many specifics are strange by modern standards. The bases were made of wooden stakes projecting four feet from the ground. The batter (called the striker) stood between first and fourth base. Sides changed after a single out. One hundred runs (called tallies), not higher score after a specified number of innings, spelled victory. The field contained no foul lines, and balls hit in any direction were at play. Most importantly, runners were not tagged out but were retired by "plugging," that is, being hit with a thrown ball while running between bases. Consequently, since baseball has never been a game for masochists, balls were soft—little more than rags stuffed into leather covers—and could not be hit far. (Tom Heitz has put together a team of Cooperstown worthies to re-create town ball for interested parties and prospective opponents. Since few other groups are well schooled in this lost art, Tom's team hasn't been defeated in ages, if ever. "We are the New York Yankees of town ball," he told me. His team is called, quite appropriately in general but especially for this essay, the Cardiff Giants.)

Evolution is continual change, but not insensibly gradual transition; in any continuum, some points are always more interesting than others. The conventional nomination for most salient point in this particular continuum goes to Alexander Joy Cartwright, leader of a New York team that started to play in Lower Manhattan, eventually rented some changing rooms and a field in Hoboken (just a quick ferry ride across the Hudson), and finally drew up a set of rules in 1845, later known as the New York Game. Cartwright's version of town ball is much closer to modern baseball, and many clubs followed his rules — for standardization became ever more vital as the popularity of early baseball grew and opportunity for play between regions increased. In particular, Cartwright introduced two key innovations that shaped the disparate forms of town ball into a semblance of modern baseball. First, he eliminated plugging and introduced tagging in the modern sense; the ball could now be made harder, and hitting for distance became an option. Second, he introduced foul lines, again in the modern sense as his batter stood at a home plate and had to hit the ball within lines defined from home through first and third bases. The game could now become a spectator sport because areas close to the field but out of action could, for the first time, be set aside for onlookers.

The New York Game may be the highlight of a continuum, but it provides no origin myth for baseball. Cartwright's rules were followed in various forms of town ball. His New York Game still included many curiosities by modern standards (twenty-one runs, called aces, won the game, and balls caught on one bounce were outs). Moreover, our modern version is an amalgam of the New York Game plus other town ball traditions, not Cartwright's baby grown up by itself. Several features of the Massachusetts Game entered the modern version in preference to Cartwright's rules. Balls had to be caught on the fly in Boston, and pitchers threw overhand, not underhand as in the New York Game (and in professional baseball until the 1880s).

Scientists often lament that so few people understand Darwin and the principles of biological evolution. But the problem goes deeper. Too few people are comfortable with evolutionary modes of explanation in any form. I do not know why we tend to think so fuzzily in this area, but one reason must reside in our social and psychic attraction to creation myths in preference to evolutionary stories — for creation myths, as noted before, identify heroes and sacred places, while evolutionary stories provide no palpable, particular thing as a symbol for reverence, worship or patriotism. Still, we must remember — and an intellectual's most persistent and nagging responsibility lies in making this simple point over and over again, however noxious and bothersome we render ourselves thereby—that truth and desire, fact and comfort, have no necessary, or even preferred, correlation (so rejoice when they do coincide).

To state the most obvious example in our current political turmoil. Human growth is a continuum, and no creation myth can define an instant for the origin of an individual life. Attempts by antiabortionists to designate the moment of fertility as the beginning of personhood make no sense in scientific terms (and also violate a long history of social definitions that traditionally focused on the quickening, or detected movement, of the fetus in the womb). I will admit—indeed, I emphasized as a key argument of this essay—that not all points on a continuum are equal. Fertilization is a more interesting moment than most, but it no more provides a clean definition of origin than the most interesting moment of baseball's continuum—Cartwright's codification of the New York Game—defines the beginning of our national pastime. Baseball evolved and people grow; both are continua without definable points of origin. Probe too far back and you reach absurdity, for you will see Nolan Ryan on the hill when the first ape hit a bird with a stone; or you will define both masturbation and menstruation as murder—and who will then cast the first stone? Look for something in the middle, and you find nothing but continuity—always a meaningful "before," and always a more modern "after." (Please note that I am not stating an opinion on the vexatious question of abortion—an ethical issue that can only be decided in ethical terms. I only point out that one side has rooted its case in an argument from science that is not only entirely irrelevant to the proper realm of resolution but also happens to be flat-out false in trying to devise a creation myth within a continuum.)

And besides, why do we prefer creation myths to evolutionary stories? I find all the usual reasons hollow. Yes, heroes and shrines are all very well, but is there not grandeur in the sweep of continuity? Shall we revel in a story for all humanity that may include the sacred ball courts of the Aztecs, and perhaps, for all we know, a group of *Homo erectus* hitting rocks or skulls with a stick or a femur? Or shall we halt beside the mythical Abner Doubleday, standing behind the tailor's shop in Cooperstown, and say "behold the man"—thereby violating truth and, perhaps even worse, extinguishing both thought and wonder?

OPTIONS FOR WRITING

1. After reading this article, make a list of other myths with which you are familiar. The myth need not be from biology. For example, Pavlov didn't really use a bell as part of his classical conditioning experiment with dogs. Do we really know who discovered North America? Select a myth, research its origins, and explain how it began and its current status today.

2. Invent a creation myth for a sport of some other institution. Make it as believable as you can.

John Janovy, Jr.
NATURALISTS

Don't be an ornithologist if you can help it. But if you can't
help it, go ahead. . . .

—Frank Chapman

In this opening chapter of his book On Becoming a Biologist, *John
Janovy, Jr., reflects on his upbringing and experiences and on those
of one of his professors, Sutton, as possible influences on their respective career choices.*

*While reading this essay, try to recall incidents from your past
that influenced your choice of a career. If you are still undecided
about a career, what factors influenced your choice of a college or of
a particular course? After reading the chapter, interview one of your
classmates about occasions that influenced his or her choice of career
or college. Did chance play a role in your choice or that of your
classmate?*

It was that idyllic time between Little League and cars with girls. We
lived on the far edge of town. In an afternoon you could set traps,
marvel at the studied placement of possum tracks, and grind the iron
red Oklahoma clay into your very soul. Parents were people who drank
whiskey and played cards. Their friends tried to test my manly inclinations by asking:

"What are you going to be when you grow up, Johnny?"

"A naturalist," I'd reply. They'd smile. Even then I could sense their
thoughts: There's no such thing as a naturalist anymore.

Only my grandfather was sympathetic. He's seen passenger pigeons, known the old west, and watched Indian Territory become the
forty-sixth state. His clothing and demeanor revealed a certain longing.
His house was filled with books of natural history. I remember sitting
for hours staring at a color plate of men spearing a woolly mammoth.
The smell of cigar smoke still takes me back to those days, those books.

"We were born a hundred years too late," he'd say. I never thought
then of the nearly sixty years that separated us. We seemed of the same
generation, at least in our minds.

Since those times humans have placed a biological experiment on
Mars, sent the songs of whales on an odyssey outside the solar system,
passed a city ordinance against gene-splicing experiments, bought stocks
in gene-splicing companies, added words such as "Love Canal" and
"Three Mile Island" to our American lexicon, and put personal computers with prey-predator models in the elementary classroom. The way
things are going, I'd have to say my grandfather was wrong. We were
born a hundred years too soon.

Developments in science since the Second World War have been stunning. There are people alive today who have seen science fiction become reality. The accelerating pace of science and its offspring, technology, has forced us into consideration of questions that in earlier times were the domain of philosophers: Who are we, where are we going, is there an identifiable human nature, is our research immoral? Had I been born a hundred years earlier, my birth would have coincided with another naturalist's epic journey: Charles Darwin would just have finished his voyage on the *Beagle*. In 1837, my parents would never have accepted the idea that a young naturalist's trip could alter our vision of life on Earth. In our time, however, discoveries that assault our senses are familiar events. Yet there remains a shared awareness that confirms the implications of Darwin's world view—namely, that the human species cannot live apart from the planet upon which it evolved. We share a common bond with even the most bizarre beetle of the Peruvian rain forest. A belief in that common bond might, in fact, be the most fundamental characteristic of a biologist.

Scientific, unlike religious, belief is derived from evidence and is subject to modification. Yet belief functions in biology, and in science in general, in much the same way it functions in religion—to direct behavior and maintain values. To truly believe in a common bond with the Peruvian beetle is to hold the insect in high esteem. We respect the bug because of what it represents: life itself. The values that are upheld by a biologist's beliefs are decidedly noncommercial ones. For example, the worth of an organism is found in its contribution to our understanding of life, not necessarily in our ability to convert it into money or prestige.

Humanity as a whole does not seem to share the values of a biologist. This difference is not surprising when you consider the following: Most biologists perceive the human species as only one of the more recent of millions that have occupied the biosphere over the last three and a half billion years, and therefore have enormous interest in the nonhuman components of the natural world.

This view of humanity as a late intruder—perhaps the price of becoming a biologist—is in stark contrast to the values associated with other professions. Attorneys, physicians, businessmen—all are consumed by human activities, conflicts, desires. The collective introspection that marks our species is enforced by these professions. A biologist studies "nature," however, and in doing so inevitably comes to regard humanity as the most effective competitor for the world's resources. The conclusion must be tinged with admiration: No other species' accomplishments approach humanity's accelerating cultural evolution, which in essence represents an escape from the "restrictions" of organic change. But the conclusion must also be tinged with sorrow, for no other species seems to possess the power to destroy overnight what cannot ever, anywhere in the universe, to our knowledge, be replaced. To become a biologist today is to adopt and live with this set of conflicting realizations.

Values are, of course, cultural phenomena. A great body of literature deals with the mechanisms by which such traits are acquired. Briefly summarized, that literature suggests: (1) There are times in early childhood when we are especially receptive to certain environmental influences; (2) early experiences often shape our later behavior; (3) it is not always possible to determine which early experiences translate into which adult behaviors; and (4) once established, certain adult behaviors are exceedingly difficult to change.

Biography seeks to unravel the mystery of life choices and show us by example the effects of experience on our tracks through time. The biographies of biologists always tell of events in which nonhuman organisms are held in high regard. On her deathbed my own mother reflected on her life and talked of times that must have been among her finest. Startlingly young, with an equally young husband off to his first job, she was too broke to go anywhere in a strange land and had a child to entertain. So she did the only thing she could do for free. Every day she put me in a stroller and walked to the Audubon Park Zoo in New Orleans. Who knows what she said to me, if anything? Maybe she just let me look until I was satisfied, then moved on. It would be pure romance to attribute adult career choices to such specific early experiences. But today I cannot pass a zoo without stopping. I stand in front of cages and look until I'm satisfied, then move on. As a senior in college, I encountered a teacher who also took me for a walk, let me look at animals until I was satisfied, then moved on. In May I was to receive a bachelor's degree in mathematics. In March I decided to become a professional biologist.

That teacher was Dr. George M. Sutton, a world-renowned ornithologist who was, at the time, Research Professor of Zoology at the University of Oklahoma. Although I will later address the relationship between teaching and research, as a biologist's life is by definition tangled up in both, for now let it stand that this holder of the highest title a university can bestow, Research Professor, was also a teacher who could direct career choices by example. This message was obvious to all who encountered Sutton. Here was an exceptionally articulate, broadly educated person, as artist who drew upon the poetry of Gerard Manley Hopkins as a teaching device for advanced classes, who was dead-eye with a shotgun, who lived a rich and challenging life, and who was adored by the public. He destroyed any stereotyped image of "biologist." He possessed all the traits, physical and mental, we would like to give our heroes. But overriding them all was his single unshakable belief that, of all the world's resources, none had higher value than birds.

Sutton's own earliest memories included a remarkable incident. His father had taken him walking on a bridge over the Mississippi at Aitkin, Minnesota. A blackbird or grackle landed on the railing. Sutton's father lifted him up, left him standing alone on the railing above the brown and swollen river, and pointed out that the grackle, perched in a similar position, had no fear of falling. George Sutton later claimed the experience was one of two clear and genuine childhood memories in that it had never been mentioned later by his parents. His other genuine memory was of a man who had a collection of bird skins, certainly a unique and impressive phenomenon for Aitkin. One is almost reminded, by these tales, of the metaphorical power of a primitive society's rites of passage. Courage and individuality became symbolized for Sutton, when he was at a very malleable age, by birds. A towering figure at the age of eighty, Sutton continued to express his own courage and individuality through his study of birds.

It's impossible in a book as brief as this to make a complete case for early experience as the crucial factor in life choices. It may also be impossible to account for the effects of a lifelong career as a biologist on the strength of childhood "memories." Especially in the case of prominent, thus in our eyes successful, people, their view of what the public wants to read may influence their choice of words for the introductory paragraphs of autobiographies. Yet, again and again, biologists claim their earliest memories are most often not of humans. Darwin's recollections of the furnishings in his dying mother's room are followed quickly by those of collecting natural items and attempting to identify plants. Charles Darwin described himself at the age of nine as "a naturalist." To support his adult work he had a habit of almost indiscriminate collecting. Writing his biography at the age of seventy, he obviously felt it important to convey this sense of a life spent gathering items from nature.

Biology today, of course, demonstrates how truly monumental is the legacy given to us by naturalist Darwin. Molecular biologists, biochemists, cell physiologists, behaviorists, and ecologists are all able, and sometimes willing, to place their work in an evolutionary context. Geneticists by the very nature of their research are evolutionary biologists without trying to be. While the work of all these scientists may have profound implications for humanity, it is doubtful that much of it is undertaken specifically for that reason. Most of it is done instead to satisfy personal curiosity, or to answer questions that just seem, at the time, to need answers.

Of special interest in this discussion of early life experiences are those of biologists who cannot, as practicing scientists, rightfully be called naturalists. Might even a gene splicer find his or her origins in a childhood fascination with a butterfly? Does a biologist who is captivated by the intricacies of protein synthesis have a certain eye for park squirrels and their acorns? Evidence suggests they do, or at least claim they do. At the age of ten, Thomas Hunt Morgan, father of modern genetics and 1933 Nobel Prize winner, may have been, with his collection of stuffed birds, eggs, insects, and fossils, indistinguishable from the pre-adolescent Darwin. Jacques Monod's father, an avid reader of Darwin, instilled in young Jacques an early interest in biology. And Marshall Nirenberg, 1968 Nobel Laureate who deciphered the genetic code, wrote his M.S. thesis at the University of Florida on the ecology and taxonomy of caddis flies.

Obviously not every potential biologist possesses so clear a set of values as George Sutton, Charles Darwin, and Thomas Hunt Morgan. But the models suggest that values are a legitimate tool, probably in the same category as electron microscopy: that is, they allow you to work in areas, especially areas of thought, you would not have access to otherwise. Like other tools, they may be acquired, although one may possess them and not realize it until confronted with the fact. In retrospect, I had probably always been a biologist, but when I enrolled in George Sutton's class I was trying very hard to be something else. When people later asked why I came back to graduate school, I told them, "Sutton showed me it was all right to be a biologist, after all." What he actually showed me was that the values I held were legitimate ones. The values then asserted themselves and directed my actions.

In the years since that semester with Sutton I've encountered thousands of students, many of them majoring in biology. I could count on one hand the number who were willing or able to discuss values in the same way they could discuss the Krebs cycle. Yet they all must have had some values. I wonder now if we did all those students any favors by structuring a curriculum that emphasized the latest knowledge in biology. They bought textbooks and studied someone else's summary of information that was by then at least five years old; we discussed journal articles to present newer techniques and discoveries. Then, to teach them about why people do things, we sent them to the humanities departments. Did we expect them to integrate the knowledge to arrive at a sense of why people did biology? Yes. But did we try, or do we try today, to assist that integration by straying from the subject of someone else's latest experiments to talk about why that journal article was important to us, or might be important to them, personally? No.

So in one critical area — the *reason* biologists study living organisms our whole lives through — education is left largely to chance, and the responsibility for those lessons falls on student shoulders. The idea that science classes must, from bell to bell, deal only with observations, interpretations, and experimental design is a delusion. Original science cannot ever reveal, except in the most indirect way, why the teacher who presents it so articulately made his or her life choices. Those who ask "Should I become a biologist?" or, "Am I a biologist without knowing it?" thus have the task of ferreting out their role models' values.

OPTIONS FOR WRITING

1. Write an essay explaining how you arrived at your career (school, major) choice. What events were important in helping you make decisions? How firm is your current career goal? What did you learn from Janovy about career choices?

2. Many students enter college with no clear career goals, and four years later, when they're about to graduate, they may still be searching for the right career. Research and write an investigative news article in which you (1) ascertain the percentage of students who enter with unclear career goals, (2) determine the number of graduating seniors who still have no firm career goals, (3) survey the resources available on your campus to help students determine careers, and (4) explain your views on when and how career goals should be made.

David Noonan
DR. DOOLITTLE'S QUESTION

Discover magazine is designed to report current advances in science to the interested general public as well as scientists. In addition to citing brief news items, each issue addresses topics such as AIDS, the fusion energy controversy, the ozone crisis, and Lyme disease in a manner accessible to the general reader.

David Noonan's article from Discover *deals with how science works. "Good science begins with good questions. . . . " The article traces Dr. Doolittle's fascination with blood clotting from his days as a graduate student in 1957 to his current status as a foremost researcher in the field of fibrinogen evolution. His research has led to the discovery of the relationship between fibrinogen molecules in organisms as diverse as humans and the sea cucumber. The experience of Xun Xu, a visiting professor from China, illustrates the way chance can influence the outcome of research. Only because she had to wait a few days for a new project to be set up did Xun Xu perform the extra tests that demonstrated the presence of fibrinogen in the sea cucumber, the lowest form so far found to have this molecule.*

Good science begins with good questions, and more than 30 years ago Russell Doolittle asked himself a great question: Where did blood clotting come from? Of course, he didn't know it was a great question at the time. He was just curious about how something so crucial to the preservation of life had come into existence. So he started climbing up and down the evolutionary tree, analyzing blood from a variety of creatures, searching for an answer. In the process he helped to create the discipline of molecular evolution and to expand our understanding of the principle of natural selection. He developed a number of new research tools, including a data bank that will play a key role in the mapping of the human genome. He shed new light on other, quite diverse problems in biology, such as how normal cells become cancerous and where the AIDS virus may have originated. After three decades of work, more than half his life, about the only thing he hasn't come up with is an answer to his original question.

Doolittle's fascination with blood clotting began in 1957 as a graduate student at Harvard. The young biochemist was working in a lab where the primary subject of study was plasma — the limpid fluid in blood — and the hundreds of proteins found floating in it. "Before that, I'd never paid any attention to plasma proteins," Doolittle says. "Then I found myself in this group where that was all they talked about." His particular task was to study the proteins involved in coagulating human blood. One of nature's most elegant creations, blood clotting in humans and other animals is a complex phenomenon involving the interplay of a dozen different proteins. In the final stages, the protein prothrombin is converted into the enzyme thrombin. Thrombin then converts the protein fibrinogen, which is soluble, into insoluble fibrin, which causes the blood around it to gel. The fibrin thus forms a plug at the site of injury that stops the bleeding. Without the plug we would risk bleeding to death.

In the spring of 1958, after a semester of work with human blood-clotting proteins, Doolittle searched the Harvard bulletin boards for a summer job and found one as a lab assistant at the Marine Biological Laboratory at Woods Hole, Massachusetts. And it was there on Cape Cod that he found his true calling. As he puts it, "That was where I discovered evolution." Working for an ophthalmologist who was studying glaucoma, Doolittle had the unglamorous job of draining eye fluids and blood from different kinds of fish and comparing their chemical composition with that of humans. In the course of his work, he noticed that some fish blood didn't clot as well as human blood. As he pondered this discrepancy, he considered the creatures' different positions on the evolutionary tree, and that was when the big question occurred to him. "My interest in evolution dawned right there," he recalls, "watching the blood drain out of a fish. I asked myself, How in the world did blood clotting ever get started, anyway? And that was, and still is, my main theme: How did this elaborate process ever get put together?"

In pursuit of an answer to that question, Doolittle started examining the blood-clotting protein fibrinogen in a variety of species. His objective was to work his way back in time, back down the evolutionary tree, in order to discover where and when the first blood-clotting system appeared.

With blood clotting, Doolittle, who now calls himself an evolutionary biochemist, had found an ideal model for the study of evolution. As the earliest living organisms evolved from single cells to more complex forms, they developed circulatory systems to supply oxygen and vital nutrients to their multicelled bodies. The larger and more complicated the creatures became, the more elaborate their circulatory systems had to be. Blood clotting, which developed as a way of protecting these systems, was therefore essential to the evolution of life on Earth. Without it, circulatory systems couldn't plug leaks and survive injuries; multi-celled animals, including man, wouldn't be feasible; and only the simplest life-forms, such as algae and bacteria, could exist.

To track the evolution of fibrinogen, Doolittle selected certain species that, taken together, provided him with a portrait of the protein over a period of 450 million years. At one end of the scale he studied human beings, at the other end he studied lampreys, eellike creatures that are among the oldest of the vertebrates. In between the two he looked at a family of even-toed mammals: the artiodactyls, which includes cows, sheep, and pigs. Not surprisingly, comparing the fibrinogen of different species can be a bloody and sometimes strange business.

Doolittle, who has been a professor of biochemistry at the University of California at San Diego since 1964, is a pleasant man, with an easy manner and a ready smile. After all these years, his enthusiasm for his field remains undiminished and contagious; he loves to sit around and indulge in what he calls "the pleasure of thinking about the origin of life." He dresses out of the classic American scientist closet: brown Hush Puppies, brown socks, khaki pants, short-sleeved shirt (with short sleeves that reach to his elbows), and tortoiseshell glasses. The only part of the uniform he eschews is the wrist armor—the gigantic digital watch–calculator—opting instead for a Timex with a black band.

Doolittle looks made for the role of lab-bound scientist. It's hard to picture him on a snowy tundra in Lapland, holding up a beaker to the sliced throat of a freshly killed reindeer in order to catch its blood. But he did take part in such adventures over the years, especially in the early days of his work, when lab methods for isolating proteins were not so sensitive and large amounts of blood were needed.

The Lapland experience took place in 1963, while Doolittle was in Sweden perfecting his skills in analyzing protein structure. That winter, Doolittle and a Swedish colleague journeyed north for the annual reindeer roundup. "We were in a small village there," recalls Doolittle, "and my colleague bought a reindeer for the meat. Since the Laplanders were going to kill it and dress it on the spot, I just stood there with a great big plastic beaker with anticoagulant in it while one of them cut the animal's throat."

A few years later Doolittle found himself in the middle of the Arizona desert with a big game hunter, tracking pronghorn. ("They're called antelope in this country," he explains, "but they're not really antelope. They're pronghorn.") After several long, hot days of hunting, he got what he needed. "Believe me," he says, "that is not the way to collect blood, out there in the desert in the sun."

Like cows, sheep, and pigs, reindeer and pronghorn are artiodactyls, and Doolittle needed their blood to continue his study of that diverse family of mammals. Doolittle also took advantage of his lab's proximity to San Diego's world-famous zoo. For many years he kept a set of bottles on the premises. "If a creature had to be destroyed, the keepers would bleed him into one of my bottles," he recalls. The zoo provided him with blood from such exotic artiodactyls as buffalo, camels, and Persian gazelles.

But it was as a lamprey wrangler that Doolittle made his name. Ugly, slimy, and altogether repulsive, the lamprey is a primitive blood-sucking fish that today exists unchanged from when it first appeared hundreds of millions of years ago. As Doolittle puts it, "Its life-style is 450 million years old." Because of its critical location on the evolutionary tree—it appears just above the notch where vertebrates and inverte-brates diverge—the lamprey has played an important role in Doolittle's work. Since 1959, when he first found signs of fibrinogen in a lamprey, he has drained the blood out of thousands of them to study their clot-ting proteins. "Like salmon, lampreys run up streams in the spring to spawn," Doolittle explains. "So, what you do is, you go up these streams to a place where they get stuck, like a little dam or a fish ladder. Then you wander out into these shallow, dirty New England streams in waders, wearing gloves and carrying a pillowcase. You feel along the bottom until you find one—they use their suckers to latch onto rocks—and then you grab it and thrust it into your pillowcase." On a bulletin board in his office, there's a fading snapshot of Doolittle taken during an early lamprey-collecting trip. He is holding one of the slippery things and grinning for the camera, a man truly in touch with his past.

In a sense the fibrinogen protein found in lampreys is a living fossil, 450 million years old and still chemically active. "It's just so wonderful," says Doolittle, "the way the structure of proteins reflects the whole his-tory of life on Earth."

Proteins are the essential stuff of life. From your toenails to the hair on your head, from your hormones to your blood to your bones, you are, to a large degree, a pile of proteins. There are tens of thousands of proteins in humans and other animals, and they are all made of just 20 different amino acids, repeated many times over and strung together in a particular order, or sequence. Each protein has its own individual se-quence of amino acids, and as a protein evolves, its sequence changes.

What Doolittle did was compare amino acid sequences in the vari-ous types of fibrinogen to determine how much this particular protein had changed over time. For instance, by 1985 he was able to show that the fibrinogen sequences in humans and lampreys were 50 percent iden-tical. In other words, over the course of 450 million years, one half of fibrinogen's amino acid sequence had changed and one half had remained the same.

It is the conserved part of the fibrinogen sequence that is the es-sence of the protein. By way of analogy, think of the essence of a car. A customized hot rod may not look at all like the car that gave rise to it, but if the basic unit, the engine block, is from a Chevrolet, then that's the critical "conserved" part. So if you were looking for Chevrolets at a hot-rod show, where all the cars had been altered somehow, you'd go around checking the engine blocks. Doolittle does the same thing with fibrinogen. He searches the blood of animals for the conserved part of the protein.

Proteins such as fibrinogen evolve because DNA—which codes for proteins—makes mistakes when it replicates itself. "The machine is imperfect," says Doolittle. "Every time a human cell divides, you have to copy four billion chemical bases to make a new double strand of DNA. When that occurs, there are probably a couple of thousand errors every time. We say DNA is delinquent. It is as good as it will probably ever be, but errors are always occurring, making either simple little changes or—many times—grosser ones." In particular, DNA has a tendency to stutter, duplicating a section anywhere from one to hundreds of bases long.

These errors in DNA replication alter the chemical sequences of genes. And altered genes in turn lead to changes in the amino acid sequences of the proteins they make. "The mistakes are made at the genetic level," Doolittle says, "but the rewards and consequences are all judged at the protein level." If the changes are disruptive, they tend to get weeded out. "Much of protein evolution, we believe today, works by what we call natural rejection," he explains. "It throws out all the changes where the errors are terrible." If a change in a sequence is beneficial or benign, on the other hand, it is retained by natural selection. "Duplicate and modify, duplicate and modify. That's the way it works."

The study of evolution from this molecular perspective wasn't possible until the late 1950s. "It had to wait its time," Doolittle explains. "And luckily, I came along at that time." The breakthrough came with the ability of biochemists to sequence a protein for the first time—to work out the exact number and order of its amino acids. By studying these sequences in animals that diverged from a common ancestor, Doolittle was able to determine the degree and rate of change in a protein as it evolved.

Even as he dwells in the molecular world of the protein chemist, buried in the details of amino acid sequences, Doolittle carries in his head an extraordinary panorama of all life over all time. He sees the little picture and the big picture; but for him they are the same picture, and somehow he is able to keep it all in focus. "There are a lot of scientists who live only in the present," Doolittle says. "They want to know how things work, and they don't care where they came from. I think they would be enlightened if they recognized that history could explain a lot.

"Common ancestry is what biology is all about," he says. "A typical bacterium is going to have—at the most—let's say a thousand genes. Half of those genes are ones we have. Then you look at the proteins they code for. And you see the sequences of some of those proteins are also fifty percent identical. So bacteria and humans share a tremendous common ancestry that we can see. We here today are just an instantaneous snapshot over a backdrop of a couple of billion years. You have to keep things in perspective." Key dates in Doolittle's scheme of things include: the first appearance of multicelled organisms 2 billion years ago; the divergence of plant and animal forms a billion years ago; and, most important to Doolittle, the divergence of invertebrates and vertebrates 500 million to 600 million years ago.

By finding fibrinogen in the lamprey, one of the earliest known vertebrates, Doolittle had traced the existence of the protein back 450 million years. But as late as the summer of 1989 he had not detected the protein in an older animal; he could not get past the 450-million-year mark. To continue his march back in time and learn where blood clotting came from, he needed to find fibrinogen in an invertebrate. For a long time, he thought he might find it in lobsters. "Turns out the lobster has a blood-clotting system that has nothing to do with the vertebrate one," he says. "No fibrinogen. An independent concoction. So, false alarm." He and others also looked at sea squirts and horseshoe crabs, among other invertebrates, to no avail.

But even as he was stymied at his primary task, Doolittle succeeded at something else—but it wasn't something he had planned. "Well, chance favors the prepared mind," he says. As Doolittle determined the amino acid sequences of fibrinogen and other proteins over the years, he kept a register, a data base. For the first 20 years, Doolittle simply typed up his sequences and kept them in his files. Then, in 1977, he decided to systematically enter them into a computer. Although it turned out to be a very important decision, it was made for less-than-scientific reasons. "The purpose was to keep my younger son occupied after school," says Doolittle. "He was ten at the time, talented and interested in computers. So I had him come in and enter sequences for me."

Today, with more than 6,000 protein sequences known and that number increasing at the rate of 500 per year, Doolittle depends on a national data bank. But he was a pioneer in creating sequence banks and understanding their usefulness. Right from the start, he programmed his computer to search each new sequence entered against the sequences already on file. "From the very beginning," he says, "the whole point was to get those amino acid sequences so you could line them up and see relationships." Doolittle is just wild about sequence banks both for proteins and genes. "Some people think that they are just repositories of information where people can go and pull out what they are looking for, like numbers from telephone books. But they are much more than that. They are 'connection machines' of a sort. They give new knowledge. Every time you add something into the pot, new knowledge can come out on the basis of the relationships that it finds in there. So they are information generators, not just repositories."

Indeed they are. In 1983 Doolittle entered part of the sequence of a normal growth factor and saw that it closely resembled that of a protein produced by a cancer-causing gene. It was a key piece of evidence that oncogenes are mutated versions of normal genes controlling cell growth. Since then, he has used protein data banks to explore the genealogy of the family of retroviruses that includes both monkey strains and HIV-1 and HIV-2, the human AIDS viruses. His work in this area has led him to quite specific ideas about the origins of the AIDS pandemic. "Current betting," he wrote in the science journal *Nature* in June, "would have to favor two separate horizontal infections of humans during the past twenty to forty years. In one, an individual in West Africa was exposed to a retrovirus from a nonhuman primate, probably a sooty mangabey. In the other, someone in central Africa was infected by another retrovirus, perhaps from an African green monkey, but possibly from an as-yet-unidentified primate."

But the most ambitious role he foresees for sequence data banks will be in the human genome initiative, the planned sequencing of all 100,000 of our genes. "At the beginning, like many scientists, I was aghast that they were going to try to do this," Doolittle admits. "It sounded like a stamp-collecting project that would take funds away from other things." However, after serving on a National Research Council committee in 1987 with James Watson, he changed his mind. Doolittle believes that as human genes are sequenced, fed into data banks, and then searched for against all the gene sequences known from other organisms, tens of thousands of matchups will be made. "We will probably be able to recognize as many as two-thirds of the human genes right off," he says, "and parts of the remaining third." And the same will be true of protein sequences. Doolittle, however, is not so enthusiastic about some other aspects of the project. "The features that I think are positive are completely different from what most other people think are positive. Many people think that somehow there is going to be this great medical benefit that comes from it. I don't see that. In fact I personally think there's going to be a tremendous problem in philosophy and ethics, because you're going to find out the nature of a lot of genetic diseases and you're going to have to ask yourself what you're going to do about them. It's a can of worms, and it could be a terrible thing." One day, for example, it may be possible to fix genetic diseases by replacing a bad gene with a good one. But should gene therapy be applied only to so-called somatic cells, which can't be passed on to the patient's children, in what amounts to a one-shot cure? Or should medicine take the infinitely more drastic step of tinkering with genes in the so-called germ cells, which can be inherited, thus potentially curing a disease once and for all?

Of the two main benefits Doolittle foresees, "one is self-serving and one is not." The one that's not involves education. Doolittle sees the human genome initiative as a great vehicle for revitalizing science teaching in the United States, because he has found that "everybody is interested in the human genome—congressmen, reporters, bus drivers, even teenagers." This natural interest could be exploited, says Doolittle, by making the human genome project the cornerstone of the biology curriculum.

The second big advantage he sees, the self-serving one, concerns evolution. "For an evolutionist," he says, "it's a bonanza." Once every human gene is sequenced, molecular evolutionists will be able to begin tracing them back to their origins to answer the biggest question of them all. "In the long run," he says, "the greatest single scientific advance will come from understanding how we all got here. Evolution is what the human genome initiative is going to come down to."

Of course for Doolittle everything comes down to evolution. When the recombinant DNA technologies came along in the late 1970s, for instance, Doolittle adapted them to his purposes. Since he hadn't been able to find the fibrinogen protein in invertebrates—possibly because these animals make only minute quantities of it—he decided to look for the fibrinogen gene or genes instead. In 1984, using probes that would home in on the DNA coding for the most conserved part of the fibrinogen protein (the engine block), Doolittle went looking for the fibrinogen gene—and didn't find anything. He continued his search through the 1980s. No sign of the gene anywhere.

This past spring, a new associate, Xun Xu, a visiting professor from China, arrived in his lab. Naturally, Doolittle put her to work looking for fibrinogen in an invertebrate, this time in a sea cucumber. Since there wasn't likely to be much, if any, fibrinogen DNA in a sea cucumber, Doolittle decided to use a new, highly sensitive tool in the search. Called polymerase chain reaction, or PCR, it's one of the hottest techniques in genetics. PCR makes it possible to work with very small amounts of a gene by amplifying the tiniest traces of DNA. Doolittle and Xu used the technique in a sort of search-and-amplify mission; if there was even a fragment of the fibrinogen gene in the sea cucumber, PCR would find it and reproduce it over and over again.

So Xu began the search. And it was the same old story. In fact, the assignment looked so unpromising that she came to Doolittle and asked to work on something else. He acquiesced and while her new project was being set up, Xu continued the gene search. It was early July. "And then," Doolittle explains, "she came in one day and said, 'I think I have one.' And I went and looked and there was not a doubt in my mind." The long search was over—they had finally found evidence of a fibrinogen predecessor in an invertebrate.

Doolittle grins as he tells the story. "There are a bunch of people in the world who are going to shrug, but for me this is much more important than anything else." He explains why he never gave up. "I knew it had to be there. We had predicted it was there. It was a matter of knowing how to look." He reflects on the future. "There's a lot more to find out." And he makes a molecular evolution joke. "This was a big step backward." He chuckles as he says it and then changes the subject, anxious not to seem immodest, not wanting to dwell on his success. But the memory of that chuckle lingers, ringing lightly with the unmistakable sound of a certain kind of laugh—the kind of laugh one laughs best.

OPTIONS FOR WRITING

1. Try to recall other examples of good questions leading to good science. Pick one question, and develop it into an essay similar to this one. What do you need to know before writing? What points are you going to make?

2. Consider recent scientific discoveries or theories such as global warming, plate tectonics, the hole in the ozone layer, and the spread of AIDS. Write about the ways one or more of these discoveries has changed your own world or the way you live in it.

James D. Watson
THE DOUBLE HELIX

Between 1950 and 1953 James Watson was a young postdoctoral student at Cambridge University in England. In 1953 he and his professor, Francis Crick, along with physicist Maurice Wilkins, unraveled the mystery of the structure of the DNA molecule. In 1962 the three were honored with the Nobel Prize in Medicine and Physiology. Gunter Stent at the time of his review was a professor in the department of molecular biology at the University of California, Berkeley.

Read the two chapters from Watson's The Double Helix *as though you had to write a book review. Who do you think the audience is? What kind of person do you visualize Watson to be as you read of his "adventures"? What impression do you get of the people of whom Watson writes? Write a journal entry on your reaction to the chapters. Do you want to read the whole book? Did you?*

Now read Stent's review of the book, or, rather, his review of the reviews of the book. What can you learn about Watson from Stent's review? What is your impression of the earlier reviewers? Why do you think their reviews varied so widely? Did you find reading of the reviews helpful to your understanding of the book?

Here I relate my version of how the structure of DNA was discovered. In doing so I have tried to catch the atmosphere of the early postwar years in England, where most of the important events occurred. As I hope this book will show, science seldom proceeds in the straightforward logical manner imagined by outsiders. Instead, its steps forward (and sometimes backward) are often very human events in which personalities and cultural traditions play major roles. To this end I have attempted to re-create my first impressions of the relevant events and personalities rather than present an assessment which takes into account the many facts I have learned since the structure was found. Although the latter approach might be more objective, it would fail to convey the spirit of an adventure characterized both by youthful arrogance and by the belief that the truth, once found, would be simple as well as pretty. Thus many of the comments may seem one-sided and unfair, but this is often the case in the incomplete and hurried way in which human beings frequently decide to like or dislike a new idea or acquaintance. In any event, this account represents the way I saw things then, In 1951–1953: the ideas, the people, and myself.

I am aware that the other participants in this story would tell parts of it in other ways, sometimes because their memory of what happened differs from mine and, perhaps in even more cases, because no two people ever see the same events in exactly the same light. In this sense, no one will ever be able to write a definitive history of how the structure was established. Nonetheless, I feel the story should be told, partly because many of my scientific friends have expressed curiosity about how the double helix was found, and to them, an incomplete version is better than none. But even more important, I believe, there remains general ignorance about how science is "done." That is not to say that all science is done in the manner described here. This is far from the case, for styles of scientific research vary almost as much as human personalities. On the other hand, I do not believe that the way DNA came out constitutes an odd exception to a scientific world complicated by the contradictory pulls of ambition and the sense of fair play.

The thought that I should write this book has been with me almost from the moment the double helix was found. Thus my memory of many of the significant events is much more complete than that of most other episodes in my life. I also have made extensive use of letters written at virtually weekly intervals to my parents. These were especially helpful in exactly dating a number of the incidents. Equally important have been the valuable comments by various friends who kindly read earlier versions and gave in some instances quite detailed accounts of incidents that I had referred to in less complete form. To be sure, there are cases where my recollections differ from theirs, and so this book must be regarded as my view of the matter.

Some of the earlier chapters were written in the homes of Albert Szent-Györgyi, John A. Wheeler, and John Cairns, and I wish to thank them for quiet rooms with tables overlooking the ocean. The later chapters were written with the help of a Guggenheim Fellowship, which allowed me to return briefly to the other Cambridge and the kind hospitality of the Provost and Fellows of King's College.

As far as possible I have included photographs taken at the time the story occurred, and in particular I want to thank Herbert Gutfreund, Peter Pauling, Hugh Huxley, and Gunther Stent for sending me some of their snapshots. For editorial assistance I'm much indebted to Libby Aldrich for the quick, perceptive remarks expected from our best Radcliffe students and to Joyce Lebowitz both for keeping me from completely misusing the English language and for innumerable comments about what a good book must do. Finally, I wish to express thanks for the immense help Thomas J. Wilson has given me from the time he saw the first draft. Without his wise, warm, and sensible advice, the appearance of this book, in what I hope is the right form, might never have occurred.

It was Wilkins who had first excited me about X-ray work on DNA. This happened at Naples when a small scientific meeting was held on the structures of the large molecules found in living cells. Then it was the spring of 1951, before I knew of Francis Crick's existence. Already I was much involved with DNA, since I was in Europe on a postdoctoral fellowship to learn its biochemistry. My interest in DNA had grown out of a desire, first picked up while a senior in college, to learn what the gene was. Later, in graduate school at Indiana University, it was my hope that the gene might be solved without my learning any chemistry. This wish partially arose from laziness since, as an undergraduate at the University of Chicago, I was principally interested in birds and managed to avoid taking any chemistry or physics courses which looked of even medium difficulty. Briefly the Indiana biochemists encouraged me to learn organic chemistry, but after I used a bunsen burner to warm up some benzene, I was relieved from further true chemistry. It was safer to turn out an uneducated Ph.D. than to risk another explosion.

So I was not faced with the prospect of absorbing chemistry until I went to Copenhagen to do my postdoctoral research with the biochemist Herman Kalckar. Journeying abroad initially appeared the perfect solution to the complete lack of chemical facts in my head, a condition at times encouraged by my Ph.D. supervisor, the Italian-trained microbiologist Salvador Luria. He positively abhorred most chemists, especially the competitive variety out of the jungles of New York City. Kalckar, however, was obviously cultivated, and Luria hoped that in his civilized, continental company I would learn the necessary tools to do chemical research, without needing to react against the profit-oriented organic chemists.

Then Luria's experiments largely dealt with the multiplication of bacterial viruses (bacteriophages, or phages for short). For some years the suspicion had existed among the more inspired geneticists that viruses were a form of naked genes. If so, the best way to find out what a gene was and how it duplicated was to study the properties of viruses. Thus, as the simplest viruses were the phages, there had sprung up between 1940 and 1950 a growing number of scientists (the phage group) who studied phages with the hope that they would eventually learn how the genes controlled cellular heredity. Leading this group were Luria and his German-born friend, the theoretical physicist Max

Delbrück, then a professor at Cal Tech. While Delbrück kept hoping that purely genetic tricks could solve the problem, Luria more often wondered whether the real answer would come only after the chemical structure of a virus (gene) had been cracked open. Deep down he knew that it is impossible to describe the behavior of something when you don't know what it is. Thus, knowing he could never bring himself to learn chemistry, Luria felt the wisest course was to send me, his first serious student, to a chemist.

He had no difficulty deciding between a protein chemist and a nucleic-acid chemist. Though only about one half the mass of a bacterial virus was DNA (the other half being protein), Avery's experiment made it smell like the essential genetic material. So working out DNA's chemical structure might be the essential step in learning how genes duplicated. Nonetheless, in contrast to the proteins, the solid chemical facts known about DNA were meager. Only a few chemists worked with it and, except for the fact that nucleic acids were very large molecules built up from smaller building blocks, the nucleotides, there was almost nothing chemical that the geneticist could grasp at. Moreover, the chemists who did work on DNA were almost always organic chemists with no interest in genetics. Kalckar was a bright exception. In the summer of 1945 he had come to the lab at Cold Spring Harbor, New York, to take Delbrück's course on bacterial viruses. Thus both Luria and Delbrück hoped the Copenhagen lab would be the place where the combined techniques of chemistry and genetics might eventually yield real biological dividends.

Their plan, however, was a complete flop. Herman did not stimulate me in the slightest. I found myself just as indifferent to nucleic-acid chemistry in his lab as I had been in the States. This was partly because I could not see how the type of problem on which he was then working (the metabolism of nucleotides) would lead to anything of immediate interest to genetics. There was also the fact that, though Herman was obviously civilized, it was impossible to understand him.

I was able, however, to follow the English of Herman's close friend Ole Maaløe. Ole had just returned from the States (Cal Tech), where he had become very excited about the same phages on which I had worked for my degree. Upon his return he gave up much of his previous research problem and was devoting full time to phage. Then he was the only Dane working with phage and so was quite pleased that I and Gunther Stent, a phage worker from Delbrück's lab, had come to do research with Herman. Soon Gunther and I found ourselves going regularly to visit Ole's lab, located several miles from Herman's, and within several weeks we were both actively doing experiments with Ole.

At first I occasionally felt ill at ease doing conventional phage work with Ole, since my fellowship was explicitly awarded to enable me to learn biochemistry with Herman; in a strictly literal sense I was violating its terms. Moreover, less than three months after my arrival in Copenhagen I was asked to propose plans for the following year. This was no simple matter, for I had no plans. The only safe course was to ask for funds to spend another year with Herman. It would have been risky to say that I could not make myself enjoy biochemistry. Furthermore, I could see no reason why they should not permit me to change my plans after the renewal was granted. I thus wrote to Washington saying that I wished to remain in the stimulating environment of Copenhagen. As expected, my fellowship was then renewed. It made sense to let Kalckar (whom several of the fellowship electors knew personally) train another biochemist.

There was also the question of Herman's feelings. Perhaps he minded the fact that I was only seldom around. True, he appeared very vague about most things and might not yet have really noticed. Fortunately, however, these fears never had time to develop seriously. Through a completely unanticipated event my moral conscience became clear. One day early in December, I cycled over to Herman's lab expecting another charming yet totally incomprehensible conversation. This time, however, I found Herman could be understood. He had something important to let out: his marriage was over, and he hoped to obtain a divorce. This fact was soon no secret—everyone else in the lab was also told. Within a few days it became apparent that Herman's mind was not going to concentrate on science for some time, for perhaps as long as I would remain in Copenhagen. So the fact that he did not have to teach me nucleic-acid biochemistry was obviously a godsend. I could cycle each day over to Ole's lab, knowing it was clearly better to deceive the fellowship electors about where I was working than to force Herman to talk about biochemistry.

At times, moreover, I was quite pleased with my current experiments on bacterial viruses. Within three months Ole and I had finished a set of experiments on the fate of a bacteria-virus particle when it multiplies inside a bacterium to form several hundred new virus particles. There were enough data for a respectable publication and, using ordinary standards, I knew I could stop work for the rest of the year without being judged unproductive. On the other hand, it was equally obvious that I had not done anything which was going to tell us what a gene was or how it reproduced. And unless I became a chemist, I could not see how I would.

I thus welcomed Herman's suggestion that I go that spring to the Zoological Station at Naples, where he had decided to spend the months of April and May. A trip to Naples made great sense. There was no point in doing nothing in Copenhagen, where spring does not exist. On the other hand, the sun of Naples might be conducive to learning something about the biochemistry of the embryonic development of marine animals. It might also be a place where I could quietly read genetics. And when I was tired of it, I might conceivably pick up a biochemistry text. Without any hesitation I wrote to the States requesting permission to accompany Herman to Naples. A cheerful affirmative letter wishing me a pleasant journey came by return post from Washington. Moreover, it enclosed a $200 check for travel expenses. It made me feel slightly dishonest as I set off for the sun.

Maurice Wilkins also had not come to Naples for serious science. The trip from London was an unexpected gift from his boss, Professor J. T. Randall. Originally Randall had been scheduled to come to the meeting on macromolecules and give a paper about the work going on in his new biophysics lab. Finding himself overcommitted, he had decided to send Maurice instead. If no one went, it would look bad for his King's College lab. Lots of scarce Treasury money had to be committed to set up his biophysics show, and suspicions existed that this was money down the drain.

No one was expected to prepare an elaborate talk for Italian meetings like this one. Such gatherings routinely brought together a small number of invited guests who did not understand Italian and a large number of Italians, almost none of whom understood rapidly spoken English, the only language common to the visitors. The high point of each meeting was the day-long excursion to some scenic house or temple. Thus there was seldom chance for anything but banal remarks.

By the time Maurice arrived I was noticeably restless and impatient to return north. Herman had completely misled me. For the first six weeks in Naples I was constantly cold. The official temperature is often much less relevant than the absence of central heating. Neither the Zoological Station nor my decaying room atop a six-story nineteenth-century house had any heat. If I had even the slightest interest in marine animals, I would have done experiments. Moving about doing experiments is much warmer than sitting in the library with one's feet on a table. At times I stood about nervously while Herman went through the motions of a biochemist, and on several days I even understood what he said. It made no difference, however, whether or not I followed the argument. Genes were never at the center, or even at the periphery, of his thoughts.

Most of my time I spent walking the streets or reading journal articles from the early days of genetics. Sometimes I daydreamed about discovering the secret of the gene, but not once did I have the faintest trace of a respectable idea. It was thus difficult to avoid the disquieting thought that I was not accomplishing anything. Knowing that I had not come to Naples for work did not make me feel better.

I retained a slight hope that I might profit from the meeting on the structures of biological macromolecules. Though I knew nothing about the X-ray diffraction techniques that dominated structural analysis, I was optimistic that the spoken arguments would be more comprehensible than the journal articles, which passed over my head. I was specially interested to hear the talk on nucleic acids to be given by Randall. At that time almost nothing was published about the possible three-dimensional configurations of a nucleic-acid molecule. Conceivably this fact affected my casual pursuit of chemistry. For why should I get excited learning boring chemical facts as long as the chemists never provided anything incisive about the nucleic acids?

The odds, however, were against any real revelation then. Much of the talk about the three-dimensional structure of proteins and nucleic acids was hot air. Though this work had been going on for over fifteen years, most if not all of the facts were soft. Ideas put forward with conviction were likely to be the products of wild crystallographers who delighted in being in a field where their ideas could not be easily disproved. Thus, although virtually all biochemists, including Herman, were unable to understand the arguments of the X-ray people, there was little uneasiness. It made no sense to learn complicated mathematical methods in order to follow baloney. As a result, none of my teachers had ever considered the possibility that I might do postdoctoral research with an X-ray crystallographer.

Maurice, however, did not disappoint me. The fact that he was a substitute for Randall made no difference: I had not known about either. His talk was far from vacuous and stood out sharply from the rest, several of which bore no connection to the purpose of the meeting. Fortunately these were in Italian, and so the obvious boredom of the foreign guests did not need to be construed as impoliteness. Several other speakers were continental biologists, at that time guests at the Zoological Station, who only briefly alluded to macromolecular structure. In contrast, Maurice's X-ray diffraction picture of DNA was to the point. It was flicked on the screen near the end of his talk. Maurice's dry English form did not permit enthusiasm as he stated that the picture showed much more detail than previous pictures and could, in fact, be considered as arising from a crystalline substance. And when the structure of DNA was known, we might be in a better position to understand how genes work.

Suddenly I was excited about chemistry. Before Maurice's talk I had worried about the possibility that the gene might be fantastically irregular. Now, however, I knew that genes could crystallize, hence they must have a regular structure that could be solved in a straightforward fashion. Immediately I began to wonder whether it would be possible for me to join Wilkins in working on DNA. After the lecture I tried to seek him out. Perhaps he already knew more than his talk had indicated — often if a scientist is not absolutely sure he is correct, he is hesitant to speak in public. But there was no opportunity to talk to him; Maurice had vanished.

Not until the next day, when all the participants took an excursion to the Greek temples at Paestum, did I get an opportunity to introduce myself. While waiting for the bus I started a conversation and explained how interested I was in DNA. But before I could pump Maurice we had to board, and I joined my sister, Elizabeth, who had just come in from the States. At the temples we all scattered, and before I could corner Maurice again I realized that I might have had a tremendous stroke of good luck. Maurice had noticed that my sister was very pretty, and soon they were eating lunch together. I was immensely pleased. For years I had sullenly watched Elizabeth being pursued by a series of dull nitwits. Suddenly the possibility opened up that her way of life could be changed. No longer did I have to face the certainty that she would end up with a mental defective. Furthermore, if Maurice really liked my sister, it was inevitable that I would become closely associated with his X-ray work on DNA. The fact that Maurice excused himself to go and sit alone did not upset me. He obviously had good manners and assumed that I wished to converse with Elizabeth.

As soon as we reached Naples, however, my daydreams of glory by association ended. Maurice moved off to his hotel with only a casual nod. Neither the beauty of my sister nor my intense interest in the DNA structure had snared him. Our futures did not seem to be in London. Thus I set off to Copenhagen and the prospect of more biochemistry to avoid.

Gunther S. Stent
WHAT THEY ARE SAYING ABOUT HONEST JIM

Who can there be among the readers of *The Quarterly Review of Biology* who does not know by now of James D. Watson's publication of his personal account of the discovery of the structure of DNA? For since it was first serialized in the *Atlantic Monthly* and then brought out in hard covers, a few months ago, *The Double Helix* has furnished one of the major conversational topics in biological circles. The first public intimation that there might be something special about Watson's account was given by newspaper stories last February, which revealed that some months before Harvard University Press had been ordered by its suzerain, the Harvard Corporation, to renounce its earlier agreement to publish this book. These stories are said to have caused Atheneum Press, a commercial publishing house not unaware of the sales appeal of Greater-Boston-banned literature, to increase greatly its initial print order of "The Double Helix," a decision which, in view of the subsequent sales record, seems to have been most wise. And in the meantime there has appeared such a flood of reviews that there can be little point at this late stage in my augmenting that flood by one more pint. The ensemble of reviews of Watson's book is of some interest in its own right, however, and so I have decided to engage in the kind of derivative, second-order scholarship which in British literary circles is often alleged to be typical of American academics, namely, studying not the authors but their critics. As I intend to show here by a brief analysis of six selected reviews of *The Double Helix*, the relativity principle illustrated by the movie "Rashomon" was at work: although all six reviewers are obviously writing about a book by one J. D. Watson, describing the discovery of the structure of DNA and presenting characters named Francis Crick, Maurice Wilkins, Linus Pauling and Rosalind Franklin, one would hardly think that all six reviewers actually read the same book.

Undoubtedly the most important review, in terms of its widespread circulation, was that printed over Philip Morrison's name in *Life Magazine* (March 1, 1968). I find it difficult to believe that someone of the stature of Morrison, a Professor of Physics at M.I.T., actually wrote this shallow piece. More likely, Morrison merely briefed a *Life* rewrite man. (How, for instance, could Morrison have written that passage of his review which says that in Watson's book "there is plenty of clearly put talk about atoms, molecules and hydrogen *bombs*" (italics mine)?) Though the *Life* review points out correctly that this book is an autobiographical account of how Watson "discovered how DNA molecules look" and that "the idea for the double helix had to come somehow, in the way of great new ideas," it has not much else to recommend it in the way of accuracy or depth. Thus *Life* readers, opening their copy of *The Double Helix* expecting to find "the air of a racy novel of one more young man seeking room at the top," would be justified in their belief that they had been had, for Watson certainly does not deliver six dollars worth of "censored movies, smoked salmon, French girls, tailored blazers [which] set the stage on which ambition, deft intrigue and momentary cruelty play their roles." Though Watson is said to have "a sharp eye and an honest tongue," the review evokes a false impression of gentility and niceness, qualities whose absence from *The Double Helix* forms one of its most striking features. Thus, in Copenhagen Watson is said to have "learned chemistry from an 'obviously cultivated' man," whereas Watson actually states that the plan to learn DNA chemistry in Copenhagen was "a complete flop," and that the only time Watson understood what that man was saying had been when he announced that his marriage was over. And Rosalind Franklin is reported to be "rightly and warmly praised for her key x-ray work," whereas one of the chief points of Watson's story is, of course, that Franklin's stubbornness was a major obstacle for Wilkins' working out the structure of DNA; the posthumous praise of Franklin's attainments is relegated to an obviously grafted-on epilogue. The review closes with a reply to the question: "How's Honest Jim?" Apparently blind to the central significance for the whole book of the episode in which Watson is sarcastically greeted in this manner, *Life* inanely lets "our reader answer for him: Fine, just fine."

Ascending the ladder of sophistication to the next rung, we may consider the review in the *Saturday Review* (March 16, 1968) by John Lear, the science editor of that serial. Lear begins his review by saying that "this book is being acclaimed as the Pepys diary of modern science." He then proceeds to prove that this acclaim is unjustified because Watson, unlike Samuel Pepys, was not the Secretary of the British Admiralty and neither participated in the restoration of Charles II nor endured the visitation of London by the plague. Also Watson's writing style, according to Lear, has little distinction. So how can "The Double Helix" resemble Pepys' diary? Good points, those! Lear does not bother to state, however, *who* has actually made the claim he troubles to demolish. Surely not Sir Lawrence Bragg, who, in his foreword to *The Double Helix*, merely suggests that Watson "writes with a Pepys' like frankness." Indeed, it seems precisely Watson's frankness that caused Lear to wonder "what qualities of achievement [Watson's] Nobel award was intended to celebrate." Was it, as "Watson reveals with no apparent regret, his hope that his pretty sister would serve as a romantic decoy in obtaining otherwise inaccessible information essential to his research . . . or his use of "his young friend Peter Pauling to spy on Pauling's brilliant father Linus . . . or "his attempt to bully a proud woman scientist into discussing details of her X-ray studies of DNA"? If it really *was* the intention of the Nobel Committee to celebrate these particular qualities, then it made a serious mistake, for Watson wrote that he merely hoped that Maurice Wilkins" interest in Elizabeth Watson might allow him to join Wilkins' research group; that Peter merely told him that Linus had worked out a structure of DNA and later showed him the by no means secret manuscript describing this structure; and (in the lengthy passage quoted by Lear) that he was merely trying to escape from the laboratory of Rosalind Franklin, who, he feared, was about to strike him. Surely instances of more substantial villainy would have been made known to the Committee.

Lear is worried that *The Double Helix* may have a corrupting effect on the impressionable minds of high school and college students, who, in their idealism, may turn away from becoming scientists once they learn how Watson gained his Nobel prize by knavery. "Fortunately for the future of science, they will acquire a certain amount of perspective from the knowledge that the two men who got the 1962 prize with Watson objected to the text of *The Double Helix* with sufficient vigor to encourage the university press of his home campus — Harvard — to abandon the book's publication." Though Lear's idea of inspiring idealistic youths through preventing the publication of books may not be mainstream *Saturday Review* thought it certainly *is* familiar to John Birch Society adherents. Lear tries to tell the history of genetics, in order to show that Watson's forerunners such as Darwin, Mendel, Miescher and Morgan were all modest fellows who, unlike Watson did not claw their way to public attention. Lear does not have his facts quite straight. He falsely asserts that "it was the great Charles Darwin who first aroused wide interest in inheritance by promulgating the theory of evolution." In fact, such "wide interest" came only at the turn of this century with the rediscovery of Mendel's work, for which rediscovery the study of development rather than evolution paved the way. Equally groundless is

Lear's statement that Darwin did not learn of Mendel's laws of inheritance because Mendel "had as little interest as Darwin did in personal aggrandizement." For Mendel is known to have sent out reprints of his papers to several leading biologists of his day, who simply did not grasp the significance of his work. And contrary to Lear's assertion, it was not the "Darwinian sense of fair play [that] required simultaneous publication with Wallace" but the Darwinian fear of getting scooped. Finally, Lear attributes chemical mutagenesis to Morgan, which was, in fact, discovered by Auerbach and Robson when Morgan was 75 years old. In any case, even if Lear's account *were* accurate, all it would prove is that Watson's predecessors did not write their "Double Helix," no more than did Watson write Pepys' diary. In a final twisting of his blunt knife, Lear suggests that Watson's contribution to the discovery of the DNA structure was not all that great anyway. It was obvious, he intimates, that "there would be in the DNA molecule a spiral stairway with steps in a particular order. The question that remained to be decided was whether the step-plates were within or outside the spiral." This, of course, is a factious distortion of the ideological situation facing Watson and Crick at the outset of their work. At that time the idea that DNA encodes genetic information in the form of a particular nucleotide (or step-plate) order was virtually unknown and it was even less apparent that this order is embodied in a helical, let alone *double* helical, molecule. I wonder what effect Lear's review will have on impressionable minds considering book-reviewing as their life's work. His gall will surely turn off the critical aspirations of any idealistic kid.

We now mount several more rungs on our ladder to reach the next two reviews. The first of these appeared in *The Nation* (March 18, 1968) and was written by J. Bronowski, Senior Fellow in the Salk Institute for Biological Studies and veteran author on matters concerning the social implications of science. Bronowski evidently saw the privately circulated earlier draft of *The Double Helix*, because he notes with some regret that the published version has been "bowdlerized here and there" as a result of objections raised by some of the main protagonists of Watson's story. Nevertheless, Bronowski finds, though some of "the small darts of fun and barbs of malice" are gone, the book has not lost its savor. It still remains "a classical fable about the charmed seventh sons, the antiheroes of folklore who stumble from one comic mishap to the next until inevitably they fall in to the funniest adventure of all: they guess the magic riddle correctly. Though the traditional parts of Rosalind Franklin as the witch and Linus Pauling as the rival suitor have been toned down . . . , they are still unmistakably what they were, mythological postures rather than characters." Bronowski finds that Watson has managed to tell that fairy tale with the quality of innocence and absurdity that children have. "The style is shy and sly, bumbling and irreverent, artless and good-humored and mischievous. . . ." But maybe Watson is not all that artless after all, since Bronowski also recognizes him as playing

Boswell to Crick's Dr. Johnson — "monumentally admired, and (every so often) scored off." (Fortunately, it seems Lear had not gotten wind of the Watson-Boswell analogy).

Bronowski finds that the importance of Watson's book transcends the mere telling of a good story, however, in that "it communicates the spirit of science as no formal account has ever done. . . . It will bring home to the nonscientist how the scientific method really works: that we *invent* a model and then test its consequences, and that it is this conjunction of imagination and realism that constitutes the inductive method." Another important general point brought out by the book is the importance of ruthless criticism for the progress of science: ". . . if you cannot make it and take it without anger, . . . then you are out of place in the world of change that science creates and inhabits."

So far, so good. But in the closing paragraph of his review Bronowski expands his considerations to the general literary scene, and now reveals a view of the relation of contemporary writing to the actual human condition which I find surprising for a man with Bronowski's interests and experience. In that paragraph he seems to abandon his earlier finding that *The Double Helix* is a classical fable in the folkloristic tradition and asserts that "its two happy, bustling, comic anti-heroes are new in literature today, and yet they should be a model for it, because they run head-on against the nostalgia for defeat which haunts the writer's imagery of action now." Bronowski does "not suppose 'The Double Helix' will outsell Truman Capote's 'In Cold Blood' but [thinks that] it is a more characteristic criticism and chronicle of our age, and [that] young men will be fired by it when Perry Smith and Dick Hickock no longer interest even an analyst." How could Bronowski have failed to realize the obvious parallelism between the two books he posits here as antitheses? Quite apart from the strictures of bad taste made by many critics against both Watson and Capote for writing their "true novels," Capote's Smith-Hickock anti-hero pair shares with Watson's self-portrait one essential feature of capital analytical interest: the finding of only transitory existential meaning in action.

The other review which we reach at this level is one in *Science* (March 29, 1968) by Erwin Chargaff, Professor of Biochemistry at Columbia University. Chargaff, as discoverer of the compositional adenine-thymine and guanine-cytosine equivalence in DNA, has an important part in the story told by Watson. To some readers, unfamiliar with Chargaff's speeches and writings over the past dozen years, his review must have seemed surprisingly sarcastic; to other readers, aware of Chargaff's long-standing lack of appreciation of the achievements of Watson and Crick in particular and of the working style of molecular biology in general, the review may have seemed unexpectedly mild. At the very outset Chargaff plays one of his old gambits: stating, *en passant*, that Watson and Crick "popularized" purine-pyrimidine base pairing in DNA. Readers familiar with the Chargaff auto-anthology, "Essays on Nucleic

Acids," will understand that this parlance is to imply that he, Chargaff, and not Watson and Crick, really discovered base-pairing. But if Chargaff *did* discover base-pairing before Watson and Crick, then not only did he not "popularize" it, but he kept it to himself until well after it had become popular.

Chargaff finds that though Watson is not as good a writer of garrulous prose as Sterne, he *has* managed to pull off a "sort of molecular Cholly Knickerbocker" (Lear was only willing to rank Watson with Walter Winchell). Like Lear, Chargaff is bothered by the Pepys' diary analogy but, unlike Lear, he does quote Bragg's foreword. What is significant for Chargaff in this connection is that Pepys, unlike Watson, did not publish his frank observations during his lifetime. Chargaff seems to imply, without actually saying so overtly, that publishing frank impressions of one's contemporaries is rather poor taste, though he does admit that he is not above enjoying some of Watson's revelations about Crick.

. . .

. . . Medawar begins his review by explaining that the significance of the discovery by Watson and Crick went far beyond "merely spelling out the spatial design of a complicated and important molecule. It explained how that molecule could serve genetic purposes. . . . The great thing about their discovery was its completeness, its air of finality. If Watson and Crick had been seen groping toward an answer, if they had published a partly right solution and had been obliged to follow it up with corrections and glosses, some of them made by other people; if the solution had come out piecemeal instead of in a blaze of understanding: then it would still have been a great episode in biological history, but something more in the common run of things: something splendidly well done, but not done in the grand romantic manner." Medawar also points out that in the years following their discovery of the DNA double helix, Watson and Crick showed the way towards the analysis of the genetic code and the understanding of how the genetic material directs the synthesis of proteins. He finds that "it is simply not worth arguing with anyone so obtuse as not to realize that this complex of discoveries is the greatest achievement of science in the twentieth century."

As far as the sense of keen competition conveyed by Watson's story, and the possible shock experienced by lay readers over the revelation that science is not a disinterested search for truth, Medawar is one with Merton in declaring that the notion of indifference to matters of priority is simply humbug. For what accomplishment, he asks, can a scientist call "his" except those things that he has done or thought of first? This does not mean, however, that meanness, secretiveness and sharp practice are not as much despised by scientists as by other decent people in the world of ordinary everyday affairs. Medawar finds, however, that for a person as priority conscious by his own account as Watson, he is not very generous to his predecessors. Why, in particular, did he not give a little more credit to people like Fred Griffith and Oswald Avery, whose work on bacterial transformation had demonstrated that DNA is the genetic material? Medawar's explanation is that this happened not for a lack of generosity but for simply being bored still by matters of scientific history. And why is scientific history boring for most scientists? It is boring because "a scientist's present thoughts and actions are of necessity shaped by what others have done and thought before him; they are a wavefront of a continuous secular process in which The Past does not have a dignified independent existence of its own. Scientific understanding is the integral of a curve of learning; science therefore in some sense comprehends its history within itself."

I can, however, propose an additional explanation for Watson's failure to give what might have seemed proper acknowledgements to the discoverers of the DNA-mediated bacterial transformations, and that is that Avery's discovery of the genetic role of DNA in 1944, like Mendel's discovery of the gene in 1865, was "premature." As mentioned by Watson, DNA did not make its main impact on molecular genetic thought until the extension of Avery's conclusion to bacterial viruses by Hershey and Chase in 1952. It seems to me that the reason for this delay is not, as Lear seems to think, Avery's modesty, but the difficulty of comprehending how the monotonous molecule envisaged by the "tetranucleotide" structure of DNA, the only structural formulation available in the early 1940's, *could* be the carrier of hereditary information. With the abandonment of the "tetranucleotide" concept in the early 1950's and the recognition that DNA molecules could harbor different nucleotide sequences, the way was clear for a simple conception of the genetic code.

Medawar next considers the element of luck in Watson's quick rise to world fame at the age of 25. He does not think that "Watson was lucky except in the trite sense in which we are all lucky or unlucky — that there were several branching points in his career at which he might easily have gone off in a direction other than the one he took." Thus, according to Medawar, Watson *was* lucky to have chosen to enter science rather than literary studies, thereby allowing his "precocity and style of genius" to be clever about something important. Watson was also a highly privileged young man, in that he fell in, before he had yet done anything to deserve it, with an "inner circle of scientists among whom information is passed in a sort of beating of tomtoms, while others await the publication of a formal paper in a learned journal. But because it was unpremeditated we can count it to luck that Watson fell in with Francis Crick, who (whatever Watson may have intended) comes out in this book as the dominant figure, a man of very great intellectual powers."

Considered as literature, Medawar classifies *The Double Helix* as the only entry known to him under the rubric Memoirs, Scientific. "As with all good memoirs, a fair amount of it consists of trivialities and idle chatter. Like all good memoirs, it has not been emasculated by considerations of good taste. Many of the things Watson says about the people in his story will offend them, but his own artless candor excuses him, for he betrays in himself faults graver than those he professes to discern in others. *The Double Helix* is consistent in literary structure. . . . There is no philosophizing or psychologizing to obscure our understanding: Watson displays but does not observe himself. Autobiographies, unlike all other works of literature, are part of their own subject matter. Their lies, if any, are lies *of* their authors but not *about* their authors—who (when discovered in falsehood) merely reveal a truth about themselves, namely, that they are liars."

Medawar believes that Watson's book will become a classic, not only in that it will go on being read, but also in that it presents an object lesson of the nature of the creative process in science. As Watson's story shows, that process involves a rapid alternation of "hypothesis and inference, feedback and modified hypothesis. . . . No layman who reads this book with any kind of understanding will ever think of the scientist as a man who cranks a machine of discovery. No beginner in science will henceforward believe that discovery is bound to come his way if only he practices a certain Method, goes through a well-defined performance of hand and mind."

I hope that Medawar's article will be reprinted in some anthology, so that it too can go on being read as an object lesson of what it takes to write a good review in the borderland between literature and science.

Before closing this review of reviews, I must report that when Watson sent me his manuscript of *The Double Helix* in the fall of 1966 (then still entitled "Honest Jim"), I urged him not to publish it in its original form. I pointed out to him that I considered it to be of rather low literary quality, and that I thought its gossipy style would preclude its being of interest to anyone not personally acquainted with the protagonists of his story. And so, as has almost always been the case for any difference in opinion we have had in the twenty years we have known each other, Watson proved to be right and I wrong.

OPTIONS FOR WRITING

1. Read a book that has been in publication for at least a year, and write a brief review of it. Now find at least three reviews of the book. Prepare a review of the book and reviews in the fashion of Stent's review.

2. Write an essay called "Since *The Double Helix*." Describe the impact of this discovery on biology. What have the principal characters in *The Double Helix* done since the book was written?

3. Write an essay on the Nobel prizes. Why were they established? Who established them? How are the recipients chosen? What is your opinion of their worth?

11

WRITING AND THINKING IN THE PHYSICAL SCIENCES

Tony Magistrale and Michael Strauss

Why does an apple turn brown? What is the relationship between a Tinker Toy–like molecular model and the contents of a glass of water? To answer questions like these, scientists need a different kind of common language, a way of explaining the everyday world of natural phenomena in consistent terms that will allow them to make predictions about what they might observe under particular circumstances. The authors ask us to do several simple experiments and to write up the results.

READINGS

Everyone has heard the story: Sir Isaac Newton, a man who lived in the 1600s, was sitting under an apple tree one lazy summer afternoon when a piece of the tree's fruit fell down and hit him on top of the head. Presumably, Newton cursed, but afterwards did the theory of gravity suddenly occur to him? Hardly. The idea of a force (gravity) pulling such objects as apples to earth was known well before Newton's time. Newton's genius was to hypothesize that this same force could reach to the top of the apple tree, and beyond, out into space itself, to hold the moon in orbit.[1] A connection between the apple and the moon. And the connection could be tested by calculations!

THINKING ABOUT THINGS

How do we reason about the world? What is meant by rational versus irrational thought? How do we define the very concept of reasoning? How does reasoning lead to theories, and how are they developed? The answers help explain what science is. Let's go back to Newton's apple. Take a bite, leaving the remainder of the fruit untouched. Within a short time the bite mark will turn brown. You can observe this, just as you can watch an apple fall from the tree. In the course of an hour, what was once a delicious apple is less so. Following the way of all living things, our apple starts to decompose. If we observe very carefully, we notice that the edges are most susceptible: The brown appears here first. As the exposed apple remains open to the air, the brown areas spread further, until what remains looks nothing like the freshly bitten fruit.

How might we describe what we have seen? How should we choose to think and write about it? Well, that depends on our perspective. To understand and reason about the world, we must first observe it and wonder why things happen the way they do. In all areas of human endeavor, noticing is fundamental and critical because it allows connections to be made. From these connections it is then possible to generate new creative thought. And different people notice different things.

A scientist might be interested in analyzing what causes the brown color when the inside of an apple is exposed to air and how fast it develops under different conditions of temperature and atmospheric environment. A poet, on the other hand, might see the apple's decomposition as a symbol for life itself: The world's youth and beauty must eventually decay. In *The Merchant of Venice* Shakespeare uses an apple as a means for describing the way in which a manipulating individual presents a false front to disguise evil intentions:

> A goodly apple rotten at the heart
> O, what a goodly outside falsehood hath!

---

[1] Jacob Bronowski, "The Nature of Scientific Reasoning" in *Science and Human Values* (New York: Simon and Schuster, Inc., 1956). Bronowski used the example of Newton's apple to illustrate the nature of scientific reasoning.

For many students studying science is an intimidating activity. Some students find the language of the scientist so unlike the way in which they speak that they can find no way to relate it to their lives. Here are some comments written by first-year students in science classes:

> I am glad that [the professor] is trying to tie in chemistry with the real world. That is something that is of great importance to me. I hate to learn trash. Speaking of trash, get rid of lab. I hate lab. Get rid of it (don't try to tell me that it's important either, it isn't).

> I am required to take this course for my major, otherwise I would not be taking it. I find it hard to get into. The material is a little more interesting to me when it relates itself to real things. For example, it is easier to remember a hydrocarbon as being gasoline, but what is a methyl?

> I enjoy learning about tangible objects that have purpose, meaning, and function to a living system. Polysaccharides are so abstract and varying that it gets rather ridiculous and frustrating after a while.

> We have decided through our experience of chemistry that it is boring and its language is foreign and not understandable—it's almost as bad as physics.

The language of science often does seem foreign and too complex for the beginner. This is because it sometimes refers to concepts and ideas that are outside of a student's sensory, social, emotional, or psychological experience. The names of invisible things—such as the polysaccharides and hydrocarbons of chemistry—are numerous and complex; moreover, they do not relate directly to sensory experience. They often refer to observable things in terms of an ultimate submicroscopic structure, which is understandable only in some representative or symbolic form.

For example, take a glass of tap water. What exactly is it? What would happen if we took a microscope, more powerful than any ordinary microscope, and examined a drop of water. What would we see? Perhaps the smallest parts, the atoms and molecules of which things are composed, have properties *unlike* the water in our everyday world (such as color and hardness). The latest scientific theories point to this conclusion. So in order to visualize or conceptualize these atoms and molecules, we invent models or representations of this submicroscopic world. In doing this we must always be careful not to mistake the model for the thing it is supposed to represent.

A number of students, trying to relate everyday substances to the atomic-molecular models presented to them in chemistry class, had real difficulties. One afternoon they were asked to explain the relationship between water or butane gas (substances they experience in the everyday world) and the molecular models of these materials as they were pictured in the chemistry text. These were a few of the responses:

> It's quite hard for me to visualize the structure of
> water when looking at a glass of liquid water. I have no
> clue how little bonds and stuff stick together to make
> such things.

> The structure of butane is the same as the structure of
> the model. That's all I know. It seems like that is
> exactly my problem: trying to relate models and struc-
> tural formulas to real life substances. It's so off the
> wall!

> In, say, a glass of water there are (I think) millions of
> little models. Each molecule of water looks like the
> model (basically) that we can make. Depending upon how
> many molecules are in the glass, that's how many tiny,
> tiny structures there are.

These students had trouble understanding the representative nature of the models of formulas which represent the substances water and butane. One student, however, was able to come to a better comprehension:

> The model is a *representation* [emphasis added] of a mole-
> cule of the substance. It helps us to see the arrangement
> of atoms in a molecule so that we may understand why the
> compound holds certain characteristics, i.e. boiling
> point, reactivity with other compounds, etc.. It also
> helps us to see how the compound exists in space.

Now, let's return to our decomposing apple. The color of an apple that has been cut open changes from white to brown, but an understanding of the nature of the pigment and why it is brown — rather than green or yellow — requires interpretation of the molecular structure of the pigment. What causes brownness, redness, or greenness? To comprehend this fully we need a different kind of common language — a language appropriate for describing a submicroscopic phenomenon. And that's where the complex language of science comes from: It is an attempt to explain the everyday world of natural phenomena in consistent terms and to allow us to make predictions about what we may observe under particular circumstances. These terms often include the symbols and models of a representational world that we use to understand the seeable, touchable world of our senses. The terms have evolved over many years to create a common language among scientists who are making suppositions about the world we touch and see and smell. This evolutionary process has not been linear. Science probes; it does not prove.[2] But a method has grown from the effort, a scientific method of investigation that when carefully and thoroughly applied, can lead to a deeper understanding of the world. But the methodology of science can often be the least exciting part of the discipline, and it is frequently the part that students resent the most. Robert Pirsig comments on methodology in his book *Zen and the Art of Motorcycle Maintenance*:

> The real purpose of the scientific method is to make sure that nature hasn't misled you into thinking you know something you don't actually know. There's not a mechanic or scientist or technician alive who hasn't suffered from that one so much he isn't instinctively on guard. *That's the main reason why so much scientific and mechanical information sounds so dull and so cautious* [emphasis added]. If you go romanticizing scientific information, giving it a flourish here and there, Nature will soon make a complete fool out of you. It does so often enough anyway even when you don't give it opportunities. One must be extremely careful and rigidly logical when dealing with Nature: one logical slip and an entire scientific edifice comes tumbling down.[3]

DOING SCIENCE

Understanding what happens when the inside of an open apple turns from white to brown depends on the perspective of the observer. The observations we make are influenced by a relative understanding of chemistry, biochemistry, physics, sociology, history, subjective interpretations, and influences (whether we were raised, for example, near an apple orchard). Watching an apple brown, a student might question and hypothesize: Where does the brown color come from? And why isn't it some other color? There might be something in the air that causes the brown color. Air is composed mainly of two gases, oxygen and nitrogen. Of these two gases, oxygen is the more reactive. When metallic iron is exposed to the air, it also reacts to give a red-brown compound on the surface of the metal—rust. Rust is a compound of iron and oxygen, and the process of rusting is called oxidation. The reaction of iron with oxygen in the air yields iron oxide, a new compound that is not like iron and not like oxygen. Maybe there's something in the apple that reacts with oxygen in the air and then turns brown. Perhaps something in the apple is oxidizing. That's a good hypothesis.

What is a hypothesis (hypo-thesis)? From the Greek this means "under" thesis, or "not quite a proposition." The dictionary definition says that a hypothesis is a "proposition or set of propositions set up to explain a phenomenon. This can simply be a provisional conjecture to

[2] Gregory Bateson, *Mind and Nature* (New York: E. P. Dutton, 1979), 29.

[3] Robert Pirsig, *Zen and the Art of Motorcycle Maintenance* (New York: William Morrow and Company, 1974), 94.

guide further experiments, or it can be highly probable, based on a large collection of observed facts." The hypothesis results from a lot of thinking about what we observe and what we've previously thought (what Pirsig talks about in his elaboration of inductive and deductive reasoning in the readings section).

WRITING 1.

In a brief and informal fashion, formulate a hypothesis to explain what happens when an Alka-Selzer is dropped into a glass of water, a raw egg is cracked open and dropped into a hot frying pan, or a puddle on your driveway disappears in several hours.

EXPERIMENTS

Consider for a moment: Will a cut-open apple turn brown if we submerge it in water? What if we wrap it in plastic wrap? Will it turn brown more quickly if it is a hot afternoon? Is there a substance we can put on the apple to reverse the browning? To answer these questions, we will be forced to conduct some experiments. If the submerged apple doesn't turn brown, or if plastic wrap preserves the apple's white coloration, then maybe our hypothesis about the existence of oxygen in the air turning apples brown is probable.

When the hypothesis is "proved" by repeated experimentation and observation (that apples brown as a result of a specific chemical reaction between compounds in the apple and oxygen in the air), then it may stand as a theory. Although a theory of apples turning brown really isn't grand enough to compete with major theories, such as the theory of gravity or the quantum theory of light, it is substantiated in the same fashion. But even very grand and well-substantiated theories have one attribute of their hypothesis precursors: They can be abandoned if new, conflicting observations come along. Occasionally a new hypothesis will appear on the scientific scene that is inconsistent with many existing theories and contravenes the accepted order of thought. A new hypothesis can affect the whole structure of scientific thinking. Turmoil and outrage can sweep through the community of scientific scholars, especially if the hypothesis is rapidly embraced by the scientific illiterate.

Examples of once-accepted and then abandoned hypotheses include the need for an ether that purportedly had to exist for light to travel through a vacuum and the Ptolemaic theory that the sun and planets revolved around the earth. The quantum or discontinuous nature of the submicroscopic world, the electromagnetic nature of light, and the structuring of physical reality in terms of space-time are current theories. The ether and Ptolemaic hypotheses have passed into history as failures. The quantum, electromagnetic, and space-time nature of physical reality theories have not—at least not yet, anyway. They are currently viable theories, but they need not remain so. If enough observations contradict these theories, they could go the way of the Ptolemaic solar system and the ether. Science probes, and this probing results in the creation of hypotheses and theories. It never proves them; new information may always cast fresh doubts. This very point is discussed in detail in the readings section by Gregory Bateson, in the essay taken from his book *Mind and Nature*.

Many students of science and some scientists themselves would like to think that their work is a wholly objective, rational, dispassionate search for truth. Scientists often do seek to understand the workings of the world in rational and objective terms, but they do not always agree on what is rational and objective, much less reach a definitive consensus on what is truth. Scientists, like their colleagues in other fields across the university, disagree, maintain passionate convictions, and create work that elicits emotional responses from other scientists and from the public. Nobel laureate Roald Hoffmann breaks from a traditional perception of science as a passionless and narrowly focused field of study to insist on the importance of acknowledging and including in scientific scholarship *personal* reflections, observations, and a communication style that is both literate and relaxed. His purpose is to encourage writers of science to reject the "nice box [of] reductionist understanding" in favor of a more "humanistic" approach that recognizes the coexistence of evolving interpretations of truth. Reveling in the many parallels that he finds between art and science, Hoffmann would have us reconstruct the role of the scientist into that of an artist. The goal of both, he says, should be to render *interpretations* of knowledge rather than dogmatic pronouncements seeking to stifle debate and challenge:

> Scientists would like to think that they acquire truth (morally and ethically valued) and not just knowledge (quite neutral; recall the tree of knowledge of good and evil in Genesis). But I would warn my colleagues that to purvey to the world at large the image of scientists as seekers of truth, rather than reliable knowledge, is dangerous. It makes us out as priests, with the attendant hazards. I suspect much of the exaggerated interest of the public in the rare cases of fraud in science bears some similarity to the prurient interest of the world at large in the moral failings of priests and ministers. I think we gain knowledge, and do that as truthfully as possible.[4]

The way we think and reason about the everyday world is in fact often the way scientists reason about observations in the laboratory. We are constantly hypothesizing about events in our everyday life, and so we are all like scientists.

---

[4] Roald Hoffmann, "Under the Surface of the Chemical Article," *Angewandte Chemie* (International Edition in English) 27 (12): 1596.

WRITING 2.

Slit an apple in half. Wrap one half in plastic wrap, but leave the other half alone. Put the two sections on the desk, and make intermittent observations over the period of an hour. Write down what you see. Cut another apple piece, and place it under water at the bottom of a glass (because apples are less dense than water, you'll need a fork to submerge it). Repeat the same observation and writing process.

WRITING SCIENCE

There are a lot of ways of saying something. An apple's gradual disintegration may appear simple enough, but the language and symbols available for describing the process of disintegration are anything but simple.

A scientific description of apple browning is quite different from an everyday account of the event. The personality of the observers and their individual reactions are removed to some invisible place, and in this void reigns a supposedly objective account that would serve for any observer (although this purported objectivity is never really attainable). There is usually no specific observer in the language of a scientific paper.

The words used in scientific articles often require that the reader have specialized knowledge in a specific field. For example, several scientists writing about apple browning in the *Journal of Food Science* used the following language in their paper: "Enzymatic browning is a function of both the action of PPO and concentration of phenolics in fruits."[5] After reading this statement, the general reader may never wish to eat another apple again. What are phenolics and enzymes, and what are they doing in fruits anyway? Words such as "enzymatic" and "phenolics" require substantial background or interpretation, and the abbreviation "PPO" may even be obscure to a technically competent reader. In the abstract of this paper, the authors have defined the abbreviation as polyphenoloxidase, which doesn't help much if you don't know what enzymes are, or phenols, or oxidation, and so forth.

Scientific writing is often broken up into chunks, each of which is labeled to indicate some aspect of the subject:

1. Abstract
2. Introduction

---

[5] M. Y. Coseteng and C. Y. Lee, "Changes in Apple Polyphenoloxidase and Polyphenol Concentrations in Relation to Degree of Browning," *Journal of Food Science* 52 (4): 985.

3. Materials and methods (with many subgroupings here)
4. Results and discussion
5. References

These subgroupings impart information as concisely and briefly as possible, and the tone of the writing throughout the paper reflects the quest for objectivity:

> Fifty grams of diced apples were weighed into a 250 ml. beaker containing 100 g distilled water. The sample was homogenized in a blender (Waring Commercial Blender, New Hartford, CT) at a Rheostat (The Superior Electric Co., Bristol, CT) setting of 100 for 1 minute. The pH of the sample was measured in duplicate using a digital pH meter (Altex Model 3560 Digital pH meter, Beckman, Irvine, CA).[6]

The idea here is that if you wanted to, you could repeat the procedure and get exactly the same results. If you change anything—for example, suppose your blender came from the Bozo Blender Company of Batavia, New York—then if your results are different, the original authors might point out that you used the wrong blender. If you do everything exactly the same way—and here again is the myth of objectivity—you should get the same results. It is always assumed that the procedure will be independent of the phase of the moon, the mood of the experimenter, the color of the paint on the building in which the experiment is taking place, and a plethora of other seemingly unrelated things. If the results are still different, then other laboratories may try and repeat the whole process to verify the results of the experiment. Agreement among several laboratories using the same general procedure gives credibility to the original observations and to the conclusions that may be drawn from them. The writing must be precise. There is no room for obvious biases or personal interpretations (at least on the surface). You will not find statements like "George thought the second batch of apples turned brown more rapidly, so we decided not to include those in our data sample." On the other hand, convenient exclusions do occur. If one particular piece of data differs markedly from the rest and cannot be reproduced, it is not included in the final version of the paper. It never sees the light of day.

Most scientific papers refer to previous work so that the research being discussed is tied to a framework or history of the subject. A single scientific research study rarely stands alone as a unique and creative contribution that transforms a particular field. Such papers do sometimes appear, but the majority are just part of a larger picture, and the many references that appear throughout a scholarly text glue that particular piece of research in the frame.

Most readers of scientific papers are already acquainted with the subject under discussion. If they are not, and this is often the case for

[6] Coseteng and Lee, "Changes in Apple Polyphenoloxidase"

students beginning work in an area, they must constantly look up the meaning of abbreviations, refer back to previous work, and go to basic textbooks in many fields. This process of beginning is long and arduous. One must become familiar with many new terms and even whole areas of thought before such writing becomes meaningful.

So we must distinguish between writing science and writing about science. They are different activities, often intended for different audiences. A student wanting to write a paper in science (such as chemistry or physics) must ask several questions: What is my objective? What do I want to do? Do I wish to produce a paper that is objective and unemotional or to engage and entertain a nonscientific reader with attention-holding writing? Most scientific papers are not concerned with engaging the reader with lively language; scientific writing is directed to a specific and narrowly defined audience often already interested in the subject. This writing specializes in precise description and an economy of diction. So where does all this leave the student?

Writing an original scientific paper requires real scientific work in progress (or just completed) that is meant to be described to a community of scholars. Often in college or at the university we practice this activity in classrooms and laboratories. Sometimes undergraduates perform actual research that leads to published results. But most of the time students write papers in science classes in an effort to model their writing after the scientific form—introductions, observations, conclusions, and so on. At first this may seem to be a worthless activity. Why bother writing something that is already known and understood? Lab reports are typical examples of such frustration, as expressed by the earlier student comment that referred to laboratory work as "trash." The same experiment may have been performed last year, and the year before that, so it is unlikely that this year's lab report will be considerably different from those which preceded it. So why do it again? Because your professor believes in the importance of helping you understand what it means to model the language, form, and procedures of scientists. And to do this, you often have to start with something as simple as an apple.

WRITING 3.

You have just witnessed an automobile crossing the curb and hitting a tree. Explain this occurrence in scientific language: detached, unemotional, precise, and unambiguous phrasing. Now write another paragraph or two from the subjective position of the person driving the car. Try to capture the essence of this experience.

SUGGESTIONS FOR RESEARCH

1. As a writing exercise with two of your classmates, imagine attending opening day of the World Series. But instead of viewing the

game through your own eyes, assume the perspective of a different person. One classmate will attempt to describe the events as a scientist from MIT. The second will work from the perspective of a Russian who has never seen a baseball game. The third will view the game through the eyes of a ten-year-old child. Here is the assignment: Each of you will write a two-page description of the events that occur from the moment the baseball leaves the hand of the pitcher to the time at which the batter begins to run toward first base. Describe this interval of time in the way that best supports the perspective of the person you are representing.

2.   Select a science department (such as physics, chemistry, or geology) at your school. Make an appointment with someone who works in one of these departments, and interview this person about his or her work. What do you want to ask this person? Why did you pick this particular area of study? Why did the person you are interviewing pick his or her specialization? What types of scientific activities does your subject do in the course of a typical day? Does the person work in a laboratory? If so, what kinds of activities does he or she do there? Describe the interview in an essay.

3.   Ask someone in charge of a research laboratory (at your school, a local hospital, or an industrial lab) for permission to observe the activities of the scientists/technicians working on a given day. Describe the activities you see occurring: The language used, the relationships among individual workers, the amount of repetitious activity, the nature of the clothing, the general physical environment of the laboratory's interior. After you have observed these qualities and characteristics, write a description of what the scientists do in that laboratory and how they behave.

4.   Light a candle. Describe in writing everything you see occurring during the process of the candle's burning. Take special note of the different-colored portions of the flame, the smell, the changes to the candle itself as it burns, the byproducts of its combustion, and the places where the wax gets soft.

READINGS

Robert Pirsig
ZEN AND THE ART OF MOTORCYCLE MAINTENANCE

Robert Pirsig (b. 1928) has established his reputation on one book, Zen and the Art of Motorcycle Maintenance. *This book is an autobiography and a philosophical treatise, offering challenging insights into the nature of scientific reasoning and exploring the nature of rational thought. In the novel, Pirsig tells the story of a cross-country motorcycle trip that he, the narrator, takes with his eleven-year-old son Chris. Pirsig uses this trip to reflect on his relationship with his son and, more importantly, the relationship between science and rationality: "The study of the art of motorcycle maintenance is really a miniature study of the art of rationality itself. Working on a motorcycle, working well, caring, is to become part of a process to achieve an inner peace of mind. The motorcycle is primarily a mental phenomenon." The following excerpt from Chapters 9 and 10 picks up with our cross-country travelers riding a motorcycle through Montana. In it Pirsig summarizes his thoughts about logic and the scientific method in a short Chautauqua, an educational public "lecture."*

Now we follow the Yellowstone Valley right across Montana. It changes from Western sagebrush to Midwestern cornfields and back again, depending on whether it's under irrigation from the river. Sometimes we cross over bluffs that take us out of the irrigated area, but usually we stay close to the river. We pass by a marker saying something about Lewis and Clark. One of them came up this way on a side excursion from the Northwest Passage.

Nice sound. Fits the Chautauqua. We're really on a kind of Northwest Passage too. We pass through more fields and desert and the day wears on.

I want to pursue further now that same ghost that Phaedrus pursued—rationality itself, that dull, complex, classical ghost of underlying form.

This morning I talked about hierarchies of thought—the system. Now I want to talk about methods of finding one's way through these hierarchies—logic.

Two kinds of logic are used, inductive and deductive. Inductive inferences start with observations of the machine and arrive at general conclusions. For example, if the cycle goes over a bump and the engine misfires, and then goes over another bump and the engine misfires, and then goes over a long smooth stretch of road and there is no misfiring, and then goes over a fourth bump and the engine misfires again, one

708

can logically conclude that the misfiring is caused by the bumps. This is induction: reasoning from particular experiences to general truths.

Deductive inferences do the reverse. They start with general knowledge and predict a specific observation. For example, if, from reading the hierarchy of facts about the machine, the mechanic knows the horn of the cycle is powered exclusively by electricity from the battery, then he can logically infer that if the battery is dead the horn will not work. That is deduction.

Solution of problems too complicated for common sense to solve is achieved by long strings of mixed inductive and deductive inferences that weave back and forth between the observed machine and the mental hierarchy of the machine found in the manuals. The correct program for this interweaving is formalized as scientific method.

Actually I've never seen a cycle-maintenance problem complex enough really to require full-scale formal scientific method. Repair problems are not that hard. When I think of formal scientific method an image sometimes comes to mind of an enormous juggernaut, a huge bulldozer—slow, tedious, lumbering, laborious, but invincible. It takes twice as long, five times as long, maybe a dozen times as long as informal mechanic's techniques, but you know in the end you're going to *get* it. There's no fault isolation problem in motorcycle maintenance that can stand up to it. When you've hit a really tough one, tried everything, racked your brain and nothing works, and you know that this time Nature has really decided to be difficult, you say, "Okay, Nature, that's the end of the *nice* guy," and you crank up the formal scientific method.

For this you keep a lab notebook. Everything gets written down, formally, so that you know at all times where you are, where you've been, where you're going and where you want to get. In scientific work and electronics technology this is necessary because otherwise the problems get so complex you get lost in them and confused and forget what you know and what you don't know and have to give up. In cycle maintenance things are not that involved, but when confusion starts it's a good idea to hold it down by making everything formal and exact. Sometimes just the act of writing down the problems straightens out your head as to what they really are.

The logical statements entered into the notebook are broken down into six categories: (1) statement of the problem, (2) hypotheses as to the cause of the problem, (3) experiments designed to test each hypothesis, (4) predicted results of the experiments, (5) observed results of the experiments and (6) conclusions from the results of the experiments. This is not different from the formal arrangement of many college and high-school lab notebooks but the purpose here is no longer just busywork. The purpose now is precise guidance of thoughts that will fail if they are not accurate.

The real purpose of scientific method is to make sure Nature hasn't misled you into thinking you know something you don't actually know.

There's not a mechanic or scientist or technician alive who hasn't suffered from that one so much that he's not instinctively on guard. That's the main reason why so much scientific and mechanical information sounds so dull and so cautious. If you get careless or go romanticizing scientific information, giving it a flourish here and there, Nature will soon make a complete fool out of you. It does it often enough anyway even when you don't give it opportunities. One must be extremely careful and rigidly logical when dealing with Nature: one logical slip and an entire scientific edifice comes tumbling down. One false deduction about the machine and you can get hung up indefinitely.

In Part One of formal scientific method, which is the statement of the problem, the main skill is in stating absolutely no more than you are positive you know. It is much better to enter a statement "Solve Problem: Why doesn't cycle work?" which sounds dumb but is correct, than it is to enter a statement "Solve Problem: What is wrong with the electrical system?" when you don't absolutely *know* the trouble is *in* the electrical system. What you should state is "Solve Problem: What is wrong with cycle?" and *then* state as the first entry of Part Two: "Hypothesis Number One: The trouble is in the electrical system." You think of as many hypotheses as you can, then you design experiments to test them to see which are true and which are false.

This careful approach to the beginning questions keeps you from taking a major wrong turn which might cause you weeks of extra work or can even hang you up completely. Scientific questions often have a surface appearance of dumbness for this reason. They are asked in order to prevent dumb mistakes later on.

Part Three, that part of formal scientific method called experimentation, is sometimes thought of by romantics as all of science itself because that's the only part with much visual surface. They see lots of test tubes and bizarre equipment and people running around making discoveries. They do not see the experiment as part of a larger intellectual process and so they often confuse experiments with demonstrations, which look the same. A man conducting a gee-whiz science show with fifty thousand dollars' worth of Frankenstein equipment is not doing anything scientific if he knows beforehand what the results of his efforts are going to be. A motorcycle mechanic, on the other hand, who honks the horn to see if the battery works is informally conducting a true scientific experiment. He is testing a hypothesis by putting the question to nature. The TV scientist who mutters sadly, "The experiment is a failure; we have failed to achieve what we had hoped for," is suffering mainly from a bad scriptwriter. An experiment is never a failure solely because it fails to achieve predicted results. An experiment is a failure only when it also fails adequately to test the hypothesis in question, when the data it produces don't prove anything one way or another.

Skill at this point consists of using experiments that test only the hypothesis in question, nothing less, nothing more. If the horn honks, and the mechanic concludes that the whole electrical system is working, he is in deep trouble. He has reached an illogical conclusion. The honking horn only tells him that the battery and horn are working. To design an experiment properly he has to think very rigidly in terms of what directly causes what. This you know from the hierarchy. The horn doesn't make the cycle go. Neither does the battery, except in a very indirect way. The point at which the electrical system *directly* causes the engine to fire is at the spark plugs, and if you don't test here, at the output of the electrical system, you will never really know whether the failure is electrical or not.

To test properly the mechanic removes the plug and lays it against the engine so that the base around the plug is electrically grounded, kicks the starter lever and watches the spark-plug gap for a blue spark. If there isn't any he can conclude one of two things: (a) there is an electrical failure or (b) his experiment is sloppy. If he is experienced he will try it a few more times, checking connections, trying every way he can think of to get that plug to fire. Then, if he can't get it to fire, he finally concludes that *a* is correct, there's an electrical failure, and the experiment is over. He has proved that his hypothesis is correct.

In the final category, conclusions, skill comes in stating no more than the experiment has proved. It hasn't proved that when he fixes the electrical system the motorcycle will start. There may be other things wrong. But he does know that the motorcycle isn't going to run until the electrical system is working and he sets up the next formal question: "Solve problem: what is wrong with the electrical system?"

He then sets up hypotheses for these and tests them. By asking the right questions and choosing the right tests and drawing the right conclusions the mechanic works his way down the echelons of the motorcycle hierarchy until he has found the exact specific cause or causes of the engine failure, and then he changes them so that they no longer cause the failure.

An untrained observer will see only physical labor and often get the idea that physical labor is mainly what the mechanic does. Actually the physical labor is the smallest and easiest part of what the mechanic does. By far the greatest part of his work is careful observation and precise thinking. That is why mechanics sometimes seem so taciturn and withdrawn when performing tests. They don't like it when you talk to them because they are concentrating on mental images, hierarchies, and not really looking at you or the physical motorcycle at all. They are using the experiment as part of a program to expand their hierarchy of knowledge of the faulty motorcycle and compare it to the correct hierarchy in their mind. They are looking at underlying form.

A car with a trailer coming our way is passing and having trouble getting back into his lane. I flash my headlight to make sure he sees us. He sees us but he can't get back in. The shoulder is narrow and bumpy.

It'll spill us if we take it. I'm braking, honking, flashing. Christ Almighty, he panics and heads for our shoulder! I hold steady to the edge of the road. Here he COMES! At the last moment he goes back and misses us by inches.

A cardboard carton flaps and rolls on the road ahead of us, and we watch it for a long time before we come to it. Fallen off somebody's truck evidently.

Now the shakes come. If we'd been in a car that would've been a head-on. Or a roll in the ditch.

We pull off into a little town that could be in the middle of Iowa. The corn is growing high all around and the smell of fertilizer is heavy in the air. We retreat from the parked cycles into an enormous, high-ceilinged old place. To go with the beer this time I order every kind of snack they've got, and we have a late lunch on peanuts, popcorn, pretzels, potato chips, dried anchovies, dried smoked fish of some other kind with a lot of fine little bones in it, Slim Jims, Long Johns, pepperoni, Fritos, Beer Nuts, ham-sausage spread, fried pork rind and some sesame crackers with an extra taste I'm unable to identify.

Sylvia says, "I'm still feeling weak."

She somehow thought that cardboard box was our motorcycle rolling over and over again on the highway.

Outside in the valley again the sky is still limited by the bluffs on either side of the river, but they are closer together and closer to us than they were this morning. The valley is narrowing as we move toward the river's source.

We're also at a kind of beginning point in the things I'm discussing at which one can at last start to talk about Phaedrus' break from the mainstream of rational thought in pursuit of the ghost of rationality itself.

There was a passage he had read and repeated to himself so many times it survives intact. It begins:

In the temple of science are many mansions . . . and various indeed are they that dwell therein and the motives that have led them there.

Many take to science out of a joyful sense of superior intellectual power; science is their own special sport to which they look for vivid experience and the satisfaction of ambition; many others are to be found in the temple who have offered the products of their brains on this altar for purely utilitarian purposes. Were an angel of the Lord to come and drive all the people belonging to these two categories out of the temple, it would be noticeably emptier but there would still be some men of both present and past times left inside. . . . If the types we have just expelled were the only types there were, the temple would never have existed any more than one can have a wood consisting of nothing but creepers . . . those who have found favor with the angel . . . are somewhat odd, uncommunicative, solitary fellows, really less like each other than the hosts of the rejected.

What has brought them to the temple . . . no single answer will cover . . . escape from everyday life, with its painful crudity and hopeless dreariness, from the fetters of one's own shifting desires. A finely tempered nature longs to escape from his noisy cramped surroundings into the silence of the high mountains where the eye ranges freely through the still pure air and fondly traces out the restful contours apparently built for eternity.

The passage is from a 1918 speech by a young German scientist named Albert Einstein.

Phaedrus had finished his first year of University science at the age of fifteen. His field was already biochemistry, and he intended to specialize at the interface between the organic and inorganic worlds now known as molecular biology. He didn't think of this as a career for his own personal advancement. He was very young and it was a kind of noble idealistic goal.

The state of mind which enables a man to do work of this kind is akin to that of the religious worshipper or lover. The daily effort comes from no deliberate intention or program, but straight from the heart.

If Phaedrus had entered science for ambitious or utilitarian purposes it might never have occurred to him to ask questions about the nature of a scientific hypothesis as an entity in itself. But he did ask them, and was unsatisfied with the answers.

The formation of hypotheses is the most mysterious of all the categories of scientific method. Where they come from, no one knows. A person is sitting somewhere, minding his own business, and suddenly—flash!—he understands something he didn't understand before. Until it's tested the hypothesis isn't truth. For the tests aren't its source. Its source is somewhere else.

Einstein had said:

Man tries to make for himself in the fashion that suits him best a simplified and intelligible picture of the world. He then tries to some extent to substitute this cosmos of his for the world of experience, and thus to overcome it. . . . He makes this cosmos and its construction the pivot of his emotional life in order to find in this way the peace and serenity which he cannot find in the narrow whirlpool of personal experience. . . . The supreme task . . . is to arrive at those universal elementary laws from which the cosmos can be built up by pure deduction. There is no logical path to these laws; only intuition, resting on sympathetic understanding of experience, can reach them. . . .

Intuition? Sympathy? Strange words for the origin of scientific knowledge.

A lesser scientist then Einstein might have said, "But scientific knowledge comes from *nature*. *Nature* provides the hypotheses." But Einstein understood that nature does not. Nature provides only experimental data.

A lesser mind might then have said, "Well then, *man* provides the hypotheses." But Einstein denied this too. "Nobody," he said, "who has really gone into the matter will deny that in practice the world of phenomena uniquely determines the theoretical system, in spite of the fact that there is no theoretical bridge between phenomena and their theoretical principles."

Phaedrus' break occurred when, as a result of laboratory experience, he became interested in hypotheses as entities in themselves. He had noticed again and again in his lab work that what might seem to be the hardest part of scientific work, thinking up the hypotheses, was invariably the easiest. The act of formally writing everything down precisely and clearly seemed to suggest them. As he was testing hypothesis number one by experimental method a flood of other hypotheses would come to mind, and as he was testing these, some more came to mind, and as he was testing these, still more came to mind until it became painfully evident that as he continued testing hypotheses and eliminating them or confirming them their number did not decrease. It actually *increased* as he went along.

At first he found it amusing. He coined a law intended to have the humor of a Parkinson's law that "The number of rational hypotheses that can explain any given phenomenon is infinite." It pleased him never to run out of hypotheses. Even when his experimental work seemed dead-end in every conceivable way, he knew that if he just sat down and muddled about it long enough, sure enough, another hypothesis would come along. And it always did. It was only months after he had coined the law that he began to have some doubts about the humor or benefits of it.

If true, that law is not a minor flaw in scientific reasoning. The law is completely nihilistic. It is a catastrophic logical disproof of the general validity of all scientific method!

If the purpose of scientific method is to select from among a multitude of hypotheses, and if the number of hypotheses grows faster than experimental method can handle, then it is clear that all hypotheses can never be tested. If all hypotheses cannot be tested, then the results of any experiment are inconclusive and the entire scientific method falls short of its goal of establishing proven knowledge.

About this Einstein had said, "Evolution has shown that at any given moment out of all conceivable constructions a single one has always proved itself absolutely superior to the rest," and let it go at that. But to Phaedrus that was an incredibly weak answer. The phrase "at any given moment" really shook him. Did Einstein really mean to state that truth was a function of time? To state *that* would annihilate the most basic presumption of all science!

But there it was, the whole history of science, a clear story of continuously new and changing explanations of old facts. The time spans of permanence seemed completely random, he could see no order in them. Some scientific truths seemed to last for centuries, others for less than a year. Scientific truth was not dogma, good for eternity, but a temporal quantitative entity that could be studied like anything else.

He studied scientific truths, then became upset even more by the apparent cause of their temporal condition. It looked as though the time spans of scientific truths are an inverse function of the intensity of scientific effort. Thus the scientific truths of the twentieth century seem to have a much shorter life-span than those of the last century because scientific activity is now much greater. If, in the next century, scientific activity increases tenfold, then the life expectancy of any scientific truth can be expected to drop to perhaps one-tenth as long as now. What shortens the life-span of the existing truth is the volume of hypotheses offered to replace it; the more the hypotheses, the shorter the time span of the truth. And what seems to be causing the number of hypotheses to grow in recent decades seems to be nothing other than scientific method itself. The more you look, the more you see. Instead of selecting one truth from a multitude you are *increasing the multitude*. What this means logically is that as you try to move toward unchanging truth through the application of scientific method, you actually do not move toward it at all. You move *away* from it! It is your application of scientific method that is causing it to change!

What Phaedrus observed on a personal level was a phenomenon, profoundly characteristic of the history of science, which has been swept under the carpet for years. The predicted results of scientific enquiry and the actual results of scientific enquiry are diametrically opposed here, and no one seems to pay too much attention to the fact. The purpose of scientific method is to select a single truth from among many hypothetical truths. That, more than anything else, is what science is all about. But historically science has done exactly the opposite. Through multiplication upon multiplication of facts, information, theories and hypotheses, it is science itself that is leading mankind from single absolute truths to multiple, indeterminate, relative ones. The major producer of the social chaos, the inderterminacy of thought and values that rational knowledge is supposed to eliminate, is none other than science itself. And what Phaedrus saw in the isolation of his own laboratory work years ago is now seen everywhere in the technological world today. Scientifically produced antiscience—chaos.

It's possible now to look back a little and see why it's important to talk about this person in relation to everything that's been said before concerning the division between classic and romantic realities and the irreconcilability of the two. Unlike the multitude of romantics who are disturbed about the chaotic changes science and technology force upon the human spirit, Phaedrus, with his scientifically trained classic mind, was able to do more than just wring his hands with dismay, or run away, or condemn the whole situation broadside without offering any solutions.

As I've said, he did in the end offer a number of solutions, but the problem was so deep and so formidable and complex that no one really understood the gravity of what he was resolving, and so failed to understand or misunderstood what he said.

The cause of our current social crises, he would have said, is a genetic defect within the nature of reason itself. And until this genetic defect is cleared, the crises will continue. Our current modes of rationality are not moving society forward into a better world. They are taking it further and further from that better world. Since the Renaissance these modes have worked. As long as the need for food, clothing and shelter is dominant they will continue to work. But now that for huge masses of people these needs no longer overwhelm everything else, the whole structure of reason, handed down to us from ancient times, is no longer adequate. It begins to be seen for what it really is — emotionally hollow, esthetically meaningless and spiritually empty. That, today, is where it is at, and will continue to be at for a long time to come.

I've a vision of an angry continuing social crisis that no one really understands the depth of, let alone has solutions to. I see people like John and Sylvia living lost and alienated from the whole rational structure of civilized life, looking for solutions outside that structure, but finding none that are really satisfactory for long. And then I've a vision of Phaedrus and his lone isolated abstractions in the laboratory — actually concerned with the same crisis but starting from another point, moving in the opposite direction — and what I'm trying to do here is put it all together. It's so big — that's why I seem to wander sometimes.

No one that Phaedrus talked to seemed really concerned about this phenomenon that so baffled him. They seemed to say, "We know scientific method is valid, so why ask about it?"

Phaedrus didn't understand this attitude, didn't know what to do about it, and because he wasn't a student of science for personal or utilitarian reasons, it just stopped him completely. It was as if he were contemplating that serene mountain landscape Einstein had described, and suddenly between the mountains had appeared a fissure, a gap of pure nothing. And slowly, and agonizingly, to explain this gap, he had to admit that the mountains, which had seemed built for eternity, might possibly be something else . . . perhaps just figments of his own imagination. It stopped him.

And so Phaedrus, who at the age of fifteen had finished his freshman year of science, was at the age of seventeen expelled from the University for failing grades. Immaturity and inattention to studies were given as official causes.

There was nothing anyone could have done about it; either to prevent it or correct it. The University couldn't have kept him on without abandoning standards completely.

In a stunned state Phaedrus began a long series of lateral drifts that led him into a far orbit of the mind, but he eventually returned along a route we are now following, to the door of the University itself. Tomorrow I'll try to start on that route.

At Laurel, in sight of the mountains at last, we stop for the night. The evening breeze is cool now. It comes down off the snow. Although the sun must have disappeared behind the mountains an hour ago, there's still good light in the sky from behind the range.

Sylvia and John and Chris and I walk up the long main street in the gathering dusk and feel the presence of the mountains even though we talk about other things. I feel happy to be here, and still a little sad to be here too. Sometimes it's a little better to travel than to arrive.

OPTIONS FOR WRITING

1. Compare the beginning and ending of Pirsig's essay with its main body. How do they differ? What method — style of writing, use of metaphor, and so on — has the author used to draw the reader into the complex issues involved?

2. Pirsig claims, "The real purpose of the scientific method is to make sure nature hasn't misled you into thinking you know something you don't actually know." Write a short summary of the scientific method as Pirsig employs it.

3. Elaborate on the meaning of hypothesis as Pirsig describes it.

Gregory Bateson
EVERY SCHOOL BOY KNOWS

Gregory Bateson (1904–1980) has been described by the New Yorker *as "a distinguished ethnologist, biologist, and anthropologist, and the first man to apply cybernetic and communications theory to such problems as cultural instability, schizophrenia, learning theory, evolution and aesthetics." He is the closest approximation to a Renaissance Man available in the twentieth century. The reading that follows is a small section of a chapter entitled "Every School Boy Knows" from the beginning of Bateson's book* Mind and Nature. *The title is, of course, ironic, for much of what Bateson elaborates on contradicts what many schoolchildren know. In this reading, Bateson shows, in contrast to advertisements of "scientifically proven effective" products, that science never actually proves anything. Science can establish only a high probability for what may be true.*

1. SCIENCE NEVER PROVES ANYTHING

Science sometimes *improves* hypotheses and sometimes *disproves* them. But *proof* would be another matter and perhaps never occurs except in the realms of totally abstract tautology. We can sometimes say that *if* such and such abstract suppositions or postulates are given, *then* such and such must follow absolutely. But the truth about what can be *perceived* or arrived at by induction from perception is something else again.

Let us say that truth would mean a precise correspondence between our description and what we describe or between our total network of abstractions and deductions and some total understanding of the outside world. Truth in this sense is not obtainable. And even if we ignore the barriers of coding, the circumstance that our description will be in words or figures or pictures but that what we describe is going to be in flesh and blood and action—even disregarding that hurdle of translation, we shall never be able to claim final knowledge of anything whatsoever.

A conventional way of arguing this matter is somewhat as follows: Let us say that I offer you a series—perhaps of numbers, perhaps of other indications—and that I provide the presupposition that the series is ordered. For the sake of simplicity, let it be a series of numbers:

$$2, 4, 6, 8, 10, 12$$

Then I ask you, "What is the next number in this series?" You will probably say, "14."

But if you do, I will say, "Oh, no. The next number is 27." In other words, the generalization to which you jumped from the data given in the first instance—that the series was the series of even numbers—was proved to be wrong or only approximate by the next event.

Let us pursue the matter further. Let me continue my statement by creating a series as follows:

$$2, 4, 6, 8, 10, 12, 27, 2, 4, 6, 8, 10, 12, 27, 2, 4, 6, 8, 10, 12, 27 \ldots$$

Now if I ask you to guess the next number, you will probably say, "2." After all, you have been given three repetitions of the sequence from 2 to 27; and if you are a good scientist, you will be influenced by the presupposition called *Occam's razor*, or the *rule of parsimony*: that is, a preference for the simplest assumptions that will fit the facts. On the basis of simplicity, you will make the next prediction. But those facts—what are they? They are not, after all, available to you beyond the end of the (possibly incomplete) sequence that has been given.

You *assume* that you can predict, and indeed I suggest this presupposition to you. But the only basis you have is your (trained) preference for the simpler answer and your trust that my challenge indeed meant that the sequence was incomplete and ordered.

Unfortunately (or perhaps fortunately), it is so that the next fact is never available. All you have is the hope of simplicity, and the next fact may always drive you to the next level of complexity.

Or let us say that for any sequence of numbers I can offer, there will always be a few ways of describing that sequence which will be simple, but there will be an *infinite* number of alternative ways not limited by the criterion of simplicity.

Suppose the numbers are represented by letters:

$$x, w, p, n$$

and so on. Such letters could stand for any numbers whatsoever, even fractions. I have only to repeat the series three or four times in some verbal or visual or other sensory form, even in the forms of pain or kinesthesia, and you will begin to perceive pattern in what I offer you. It will become in your mind—and in mine—a theme, and it will have aesthetic value. To that extent, it will be familiar and understandable.

But the pattern may be changed or broken by addition, by repetition, by anything that will force you to a new perception of it, and these changes can never be predicted with absolute certainty because they have not yet happened.

We do not know enough about how the present will lead into the future. We shall never be able to say, "Ha! My perception, my accounting for that series, will indeed cover its next and future components," or "Next time I meet with these phenomena, I shall be able to predict their total course."

Prediction can never be absolutely valid and therefore science can never *prove* some generalization or even *test* a single descriptive statement and in that way arrive at final truth.

There are other ways of arguing this impossibility. The argument of this book—which again, surely, can only convince you insofar as what I say fits with what you know and which may be collapsed or totally changed in a few years—presupposes that science is a *way of perceiving* and making what we may call "sense" of our percepts. But perception operates only upon difference. All receipt of information is necessarily the receipt of news of *difference*, and all perception of difference is limited by threshold. Differences that are too slight or too slowly presented are not perceivable. They are not food for perception.

It follows that what we, as scientists, can perceive is always limited by threshold. That is, what is subliminal will not be grist for our mill. Knowledge at any given moment will be a function of the thresholds of our available means of perception. The invention of the microscope or the telescope or of means of measuring time to the fraction of a nanosecond or weighing quantities of matter to millionths of a gram—all such improved devices of perception will disclose what was utterly unpredictable from the levels of perception that we could achieve before the discovery.

Not only can we not predict into the next instant of the future, but, more profoundly, we cannot predict into the next dimension of the microscopic, the astronomically distant, or the geologically ancient. As a method of perception—and that is all science can claim to be— science, like all other methods of perception, is limited in its ability to collect the outward and visible signs of whatever may be truth.

Science *probes*; it does not prove.

OPTIONS FOR WRITING

1. Bateson insists that "science, like all other methods of perception, is limited in its ability to collect the outward and visible signs of whatever may be true." What does this phrase mean to you? Can you find an example that illustrates its point?

2. Compare what Bateson means by scientific proof with the advertising phrase heard on television "scientifically proven effective." Why would Bateson believe that such a claim was at least misleading advertising?

3. When tobacco companies say that there is no absolute "proof" that links cigarettes to lung cancer, are they using "proof" in the same manner Bateson refers to it? Why or why not?

Loren Eiseley
THE UNEXPECTED UNIVERSE

Imagine God, as the Poet saith, Ludere in Humanis, to play but a game at Chesse with this world; to sport Himself with making little things great, and great things nothing. Imagine God to be at play with us, but a gamester. . . .

—John Donne

Throughout his career as an anthropologist, Loren Eiseley (1907–1977) attempted to join nature and history as a means for better understanding modern life. He was one of the leading authorities on Darwin, editing a volume of papers for the Darwin society's centennial (1958–1959) celebration commemorating the publication of Darwin's Origin of the Species *in 1859. Interested in art, literature, biology, and history, Eiseley had a career perhaps best summarized in the title of one of his most recent essays, "An Evolutionist Looks at Modern Man." In the following essay, Eiseley writes about his responses to the unexpected and symbolic aspects of the world. It is a very introspective and personal piece.* Time *magazine has written of him: "Eiseley confronts his fellow scientists with the charge that there are more things in heaven and earth than is dreamt of in their philosophy."*

A British essayist of distinction, H. J. Massingham, once remarked perceptively that woods nowadays are haunted not by ghosts, but by a silence and man-made desolation that might well take terrifying material forms. There is nothing like a stalled train in a marsh to promote such reflections—particularly if one has been transported just beyond the environs of a great city and set down in some nether world that seems to partake both of nature before man came and of the residue of what will exist after him. It was night when my train halted, but a kind of flame-wreathed landscape attended by shadowy figures could be glimpsed from the window.

After a time, with a companion, I descended and strolled forward to explore this curious region. It turned out to be a perpetually burning city dump, contributing its miasmas and choking vapors to the murky sky above the city. Amidst the tended flames of this inferno I approached one of the grimy attendants who was forking over the rubbish. In the background, other shadows, official and unofficial, were similarly engaged. For a moment I had the insubstantial feeling that must exist on the borders of hell, where everything, wavering among heat waves, is transported to another dimension. One could imagine ragged and distorted souls grubbed over by scavengers for what might usefully survive.

I stood in silence watching this great burning. Sodden papers were being forked into the flames, and after a while it crossed my mind that this was perhaps the place where last year's lace valentines had gone, along with old Christmas trees, and the beds I had slept on in childhood.

"I suppose you get everything here," I ventured to the grimy attendant.

He nodded indifferently and drew a heavy glove across his face. His eyes were red-rimmed from the fire. Perhaps they were red anyhow.

"Know what?" He swept a hand outward toward the flames.

"No," I confessed.

"Babies," he growled in my ear. "Even dead babies sometimes turn up. From there." He gestured contemptuously toward the city and hoisted an indistinguishable mass upon his fork. I stepped back from the flare of light, but it was only part of an old radio cabinet. Out of it had once come voices and music and laughter, perhaps from the twenties. And where were the voices traveling now? I looked at the dangling fragments of wire. They reminded me of something, but the engine bell sounded before I could remember.

I made a parting gesture. Around me in the gloom dark shapes worked ceaselessly at the dampened fires. My eyes were growing accustomed to their light.

"We get it all," the dump philosopher repeated. "Just give it time to travel, we get it all."

"Be seeing you," I said irrelevantly. "Good luck."

Back in my train seat, I remembered unwillingly the flames and the dangling wire. It had something to do with an air crash years ago and the identification of the dead. Anthropologists get strange assignments. I put the matter out of my mind, as I always do, but I dozed and it came back: the box with the dangling wires. I had once fitted a seared and broken skullcap over a dead man's brains, and I had thought, peering into the scorched and mangled skull vault, it is like a beautiful, irreparably broken machine, like something consciously made to be used, and now where are the voices and the music?

"We get it all," a dark figure said in my dreams. I sighed, and the figure in the murk faded into the clicking of the wheels.

One can think just so much, but the archaeologist is awake to memories of the dead cultures sleeping around us, to our destiny, and to the nature of the universe we profess to inhabit. I would speak of these things not as a wise man, with scientific certitude, but from a place outside, in the role, shall we say, of a city-dump philosopher. Nor is this a strained figure of speech. The archaeologist is the last grubber among things mortal. He puts not men, but civilizations, to bed, and passes upon them final judgments. He finds, if imprinted upon clay, both our grocery bills and the hymns to our gods. Or he uncovers, as I once did in a mountain cavern, the skeleton of a cradled child, supplied, in the pathos of our mortality, with the carefully "killed" tools whose shadowy counterparts were intended to serve a tiny infant through the vicissitudes it would encounter beyond the dark curtain of death. Infinite care had been lavished upon objects that did not equate with the child's ability to use them in this life. Was his spirit expected to grow to manhood, or had this final projection of bereaved parental care thrust into the night, in desperate anxiety, all that an impoverished and simple culture could provide where human affection could not follow?

In a comparable but more abstract way, the modern mind, the scientific mind, concerned as it is with the imponderable mysteries of existence, has sought to equip oncoming generations with certain mental weapons against the terrors of ignorance. Protectively, as in the case of the dead child bundled in a cave, science has proclaimed a universe whose laws are open to discovery and, above all, it has sought, in the words of one of its greatest exponents, Francis Bacon, "not to imagine or suppose, but to *discover* what nature does or may be made to do."

To discover what nature does, however, two primary restrictions are laid upon a finite creature: he must extrapolate his laws from what exists in his or his society's moment of time and, in addition, he is limited by what his senses can tell him of the surrounding world. Later, technology may provide the extension of those senses, as in the case of the microscope and telescope. Nevertheless the same eye or ear with which we are naturally endowed must, in the end, interpret the data derived from such extensions of sight or hearing. Moreover, science since the thirteenth century has clung to the dictum of William of Ockham that hypotheses must not be multiplied excessively; that the world, in essence, is always simple, not complicated, and its secrets accessible to men of astute and sufficiently penetrating intellect. Ironically, in the time of our greatest intellectual and technological triumphs one is forced to say that Ockham's long-honored precepts, however well they have served man, are, from another view, merely a more sophisticated projection of man's desire for order — and for the ability to control, understand, and manipulate his world.

All of these intentions are commendable enough, but perhaps we would approach them more humbly and within a greater frame of reference if we were to recognize what Massingham sensed as lying latent in his wood, or what John Donne implied more than three centuries ago when he wrote:

I am rebegot
of absence, darkness, death:
Things which are not.

Donne had recognized that behind visible nature lurks an invisible and procreant void from whose incomprehensible magnitude we can only recoil. That void has haunted me ever since I handled the shattered calvarium that a few hours before had contained, in microcosmic dimensions, a similar lurking potency.

Some years previously, I had written a little book of essays in which I had narrated how time had become natural in our thinking, and I had gone on to speak likewise of life and man. In the end, however, I had been forced to ask, How Natural is Natural?—a subject that raised the hackles of some of my scientifically inclined colleagues, who confused the achievements of their disciplines with certitude on a cosmic scale. My very question thus implied an ill-concealed heresy. That heresy it is my intent to pursue further. It will involve us, not in the denigration of science, but, rather, in a farther stretch of the imagination as we approach those distant and wooded boundaries of thought where, in the words of the old fairy tale, the fox and the hare say good night to each other. It is here that predictability ceases and the unimaginable begins— or, as a final heretical suspicion, we might ask ourselves whether our own little planetary fragment of the cosmos has all along concealed a mocking refusal to comply totally with human conceptions of order and secure prediction.

The world contains, for all its seeming regularity, a series of surprises resembling those that in childhood terrorized us by erupting on springs from closed boxes. The world of primitive man is not dissimilar. Lightning leaps from clouds, something invisible rumbles in the air, the living body, spilling its mysterious red fluid, lies down in a sleep from which it cannot waken. There are night cries in the forest, talking waters, guiding omens, or portents in the fall of a leaf. No longer, as with the animal, can the world be accepted as given. It has to be perceived and consciously thought about, abstracted, and considered. The moment one does so, one is outside of the natural; objects are each one surrounded with an aura radiating meaning to man alone. To a universe already suspected of being woven together by unseen forces, man brings the organizing power of primitive magic. The manikin that is believed to control the macrocosm by some sympathetic connection is already obscurely present in the poppet thrust full of needles by the witch. Crude and imperfect, magic is still man's first conscious abstraction from nature, his first attempt to link disparate objects by some unseen attraction between them.

2

If we now descend into the early years of modern science, we find the world of the late eighteenth and early nineteenth centuries basking comfortably in the conception of the balanced world machine. Newton had established what appeared to be the reign of universal order in the heavens. The planets—indeed, the whole cosmic engine—were self-regulatory. This passion for order controlled by a divinity too vast to be concerned with petty miracle was slowly extended to earth. James Hutton glimpsed, in the long erosion and renewal of the continents by subterranean uplift, a similar "beautiful machine" so arranged that recourse to the "preternatural," or "destructive accident," such as the Mosaic Deluge, was unnecessary to account for the physical features of the planet.

Time had lengthened, and through those eons, law, not chaos, reigned. The imprint of fossil raindrops similar to those of today had been discovered upon ancient shores. The marks of fossil ripples were also observable in uncovered strata, and buried trees had absorbed the sunlight of far millennia. The remote past was one with the present and, over all, a lawful similarity decreed by a Christian Deity prevailed.

In the animal world, a similar web of organization was believed to exist, save by a few hesitant thinkers. The balanced Newtonian clockwork of the heavens had been transferred to earth and, for a few decades, was destined to prevail in the world of life. Plants and animals would be frozen into their existing shapes; they would compete but not change, for change in this system was basically a denial of law. Hutton's world renewed itself in cycles, just as the oscillations observable in the heavens were similarly self-regulatory.

Time was thus law-abiding. It contained no novelty and was self-correcting. It was, as we have indicated, a manifestation of divine law. That law was a comfort to man. The restive world of life fell under the same dominion as the equally restive particles of earth. Organisms oscillated within severely fixed limits. The smallest animalcule in a hay infusion carried a message for man; the joints of an insect assured him of divine attention. "In every nature and every portion of nature which we can descry," wrote William Paley in a book characteristic of the period, "we find attention bestowed upon even the minutest parts. The hinges in the wing of an earwig . . . are as highly wrought as if the creator had nothing else to finish. We see no signs of diminution of care by multiplicity of objects, or distraction of thought by variety. We have no reason to fear, therefore, our being forgotten, or overlooked, or neglected." Written into these lines in scientific guise is the same humanely protective gesture that long ago had heaped skin blankets, bone needles, and a carved stick for killing rabbits into the burial chamber of a child.

This undeviating balance in which life was locked was called "natural government" by the great anatomist John Hunter. It was, in a sense, like the cyclic but undeviating life of the planet earth itself. That vast elemental creature felt the fall of raindrops on its ragged flanks, was troubled by the drift of autumn leaves or the erosive work of wind throughout eternity. Nevertheless, the accounts of nature were strictly kept. If a continent was depressed at one point, its equivalent arose elsewhere. Whether the item in the scale was the weight of a raindrop or a dislodged boulder on a mountainside, a dynamic balance kept the great beast young and flourishing upon its course.

And as it was with earth, so also with its inhabitants. "There is an equilibrium kept up among the animals by themselves," Hunter went on to contend. They kept their own numbers pruned and in proportion. Expansion was always kept within bounds. The struggle for existence was recognized before Darwin, but only as the indefinite sway of a returning pendulum. Life was selected, but it was selected for but one purpose: vigor and consistency in appearance. The mutative variant was struck down. What had been was; what would be already existed. As in the case of that great animal the earth, of the living flora and fauna it could be said that there was to be found "no vestige of a beginning, — no prospect of an end." An elemental order lay across granite, sea, and shore. Each individual animal peered from age to age out of the same unyielding sockets of bone. Out of no other casements could he stare; the dweller within would see leaf and bird eternally the same. This was the scientific doctrine known as uniformitarianism. It had abolished magic as it had abolished the many changes and shape shiftings of witch doctors and medieval necromancers. At last the world was genuinely sane under a beneficent Deity. Then came Darwin.

3

At first, he was hailed as another Newton who had discovered the laws of life. It was true that what had once been deemed independent creation — the shells in the collector's cabinet, the flowers pressed into memory books — were now, as in the abandoned magic of the ancient past, once more joined by invisible threads of sympathy and netted together by a common ancestry. The world seemed even more understandable, more natural than natural. The fortuitous had become fashionable, and the other face of "natural government" turned out to be creation. Life's pendulum of balance was an illusion.

Behind the staid face of that nature we had worshiped for so long we were unseen shapeshifters. Viewed in the long light of limitless time, we were optical illusions whose very identity was difficult to fix. Still, there was much talk of progress and perfection. Only later did we begin to realize that what Charles Darwin had introduced into nature was not Newtonian predictability but absolute random novelty. Life was bent, in the phrase of Alfred Russel Wallace, upon "indefinite departure." No living thing, not even man, understood upon what journey he had embarked. Time was no longer cyclic or monotonously repetitious. It was historic, novel, and unreturning. Since that momentous discovery, man has, whether or not he realizes or accepts his fate, been moving in a world of contingent forms.

Even in the supposedly stable universe of matter, as it was viewed by nineteenth-century scientists, new problems constantly appear. The discovery by physicists of anitimatter particles having electric charges opposite to those that compose our world and unable to exist in concert with known matter raises the question of whether, after all, our corner of the universe is representative of the entire potentialities that may exist elsewhere. The existence of antimatter is unaccounted for in present theories of the universe, and such peculiarities as the primordial atom and the recently reported flash of the explosion at the birth of the universe, as recorded in the radio spectrum, lead on into unknown paths.

If it were not for the fact the familiarity leads to assumed knowledge, we would have to admit that the earth's atmosphere of oxygen appears to be the product of a biological invention, photosynthesis, another random event that took place in Archeozoic times. That single "invention," for such it was, determined the entire nature of life on this planet, and there is no possibility at present of calling it preordained. Similarly, the stepped-up manipulation of chance, in the shape of both mutation and recombination of genetic factors, which is one result of the sexual mechanism, would have been unprophesiable.

The brain of man, that strange gray iceberg of conscious and unconscious life, was similarly unpredictable until its appearance. A comparatively short lapse of geological time has evolved a humanity that, beginning in considerable physical diversity, has increasingly converged toward a universal biological similarity, marked only by a lingering and insignificant racial differentiation. With the rise of *Homo sapiens* and the final perfection of the human brain as a manipulator of symbolic thought, the spectrum of man's possible social behavior has widened enormously. What is essentially the same brain biologically can continue to exist in the simple ecological balance of the Stone Age or, on the other hand, may produce those enormous inflorescences known as civilization. These growths seemingly operate under their own laws and take distinct and irreversible pathways. In an analogous way, organisms mutate and diverge through adaptive radiation from one or a few original forms.

In the domain of culture, man's augmented ability to manipulate abstract ideas and to draw in this fashion enormous latent stores of energy from the brain has led to an intriguing situation: the range of his *possible* behavior is greater and more contradictory than that which can be contained within the compass of a single society, whether tribal or advanced. Thus, as man's penetration into the metaphysical and abstract has succeeded, so has his capacity to follow, in the same physical body, a series of tangential roads into the future. Likeness in body has, paradoxically, led to diversity in thought. Thought, in turn, involves such vast institutional involutions as the rise of modern science, with its intensified hold upon modern society.

All past civilizations of men have been localized and have had, therefore, the divergent mutative quality to which we have referred. They
have offered choices to men. Ideas have been exchanged, along with
technological innovations, but never on so vast, overwhelming, and sin-
gle-directed a scale as in the present. Increasingly, there is but one way
into the future: the technological way. The frightening aspect of this
situation lies in the constriction of human choices. Western technology
has released irrevocable forces, and the "one world" that has been
talked about so glibly is frequently a distraught conformity produced by
the centripetal forces of Western society. So great is its power over men
that any other solution, any other philosophy, is silenced. Men, unknowingly, and whether for good or ill, appear to be making their last
decisions about human destiny. To pursue the biological analogy, it is
as though, instead of many adaptive organisms, a single gigantic animal
embodied the only organic future of the world.

4

Archaeology is the science of man's evening, not of his midday
triumphs. I have spoken of my visit to a flame-wreathed marsh at night-
fall. All in it had been substance, matter, trailing wires and old
sandwich wrappings, broken toys and iron bedsteads. Yet there was
nothing present that science could not reduce into its elements, nothing
that was not the product of the urban world whose far-off towers had
risen gleaming in the dusk beyond the marsh. There on the city dump
had lain the shabby debris of life: the waxen fragment of an old record
that had stolen a human heart, wilted flowers among smashed beer
cans, the castaway knife of a murderer, along with a broken tablespoon.
It was all a maze of invisible, floating connections, and would be until
the last man perished. These forlorn materials had all been subjected to
the dissolving power of the human mind. They had been wrenched
from deep veins of rock, boiled in great crucibles, and carried miles from
their origins. They had assumed shapes that, though material enough,
had existed first as blueprints in the profound darkness of a living brain.
They had been defined before their existence, named and given shape
in the puff of air that we call a word. That word had been evoked in a
skull box which, with all its contained powers and lurking paradoxes,
has arisen in ways we can only dimly retrace.

Einstein is reputed to have once remarked that he refused to believe
that God plays at dice with the universe. But as we survey the long
backward course of history, it would appear that in the phenomenal
world the open-endedness of time is unexpectedly an essential element
of His creation. Whenever an infant is born, the dice, in the shape of
genes and enzymes and the intangibles of chance environment, are
being rolled again, as when that smoky figure from the fire hissed in my

ear the tragedy of the cast-off infants of the city. Each one of us is a statistical impossibility around which hover a million other lives that were never destined to be born—but who, nevertheless, are being unmanifest, a lurking potential in the dark storehouse of the void.

Today, in spite of that web of law, that network of forces which the past century sought to string to the ends of the universe, a strange unexpectedness lingers about our world. This change in viewpoint, which has frequently escaped our attention, can be illustrated in the remark of Heinrich Hertz, the nineteenth-century experimenter in the electromagnetic field. "The most important problem which our conscious knowledge of nature should enable us to solve," Hertz stated, "is the anticipation of future events, so that we may arrange our present affairs in accordance with such anticipation."

There is an attraction about this philosophy that causes it to linger in the lay mind and, as a short-term prospect, in the minds of many scientists and technologists. It implies a tidiness that is infinitely attractive to man, increasingly a homeless orphan lost in the vast abysses of space and time. Hertz's remark seems to offer surcease from uncertainty, power contained, the universe understood, the future apprehended before its emergence. The previous Elizabethan age, by contrast, had often attached to its legal documents a humble obeisance to life's uncertainties expressed in the phrase "by the mutability of fortune and favor." The men of Shakespeare's century may have known less of science, but they knew only too well unexpected overthrow was implied in the frown of a monarch or a breath of the plague.

The twentieth century, on the other hand, surveys a totally new universe. That our cosmological conceptions bear a relationship to the past is obvious, that some of the power of which Hertz dreamed lies in our hands is all too evident, but never before in human history has the mind soared higher and seen less to cheer its complacency. We have heard much of science as the endless frontier, but we whose immediate ancestors were seekers of gold among great mountains and gloomy forests are easily susceptible to a simplistic conception of the word *frontier* as something conquerable in its totality. We assume that, with enough time and expenditure of energy, the ore will be extracted and the forests computed in board feet of lumber. A tamed wilderness will subject itself to man.

Not so the wilderness beyond the stars or concealed in the infinitesimal world beneath the atom. Wise reflection will lead us to recognize that we have come upon a different and less conquerable region. Forays across its border already suggest that man's dream of mastering all aspects of nature takes no account of his limitations in time and space or of his own senses, augmented though they may be by his technological devices. Even the thought that he can bring to bear upon that frontier is limited in quantity by the number of trained minds that can sustain such an adventure. Ever more expensive grow the tools with which research can be sustained, ever more diverse the social problems which that research, in its technological phase, promotes. To take one single example: who would have dreamed that a tube connecting two lenses of glass would pierce into the swarming depths of our being, force upon us incredible feats of sanitary engineering, master the plague, and create that giant upsurge out of unloosened nature that we call the population explosion?

The Roman Empire is a past event in history, yet by analogy it presents us with a small scale model comparable to the endless frontier of science. A great political and military machine had expanded outward to the limits of the known world. Its lines of communication grew ever more tenuous, taxes rose fantastically, the disaffected and alienated within its borders steadily increased. By the time of the barbarian invasions the vast structure was already dying of inanition. Yet that empire lasted far longer than the world of science has yet endured.

But what of the empire of science? Does not its word leap fast as light, is it not a creator of incalculable wealth, is not space its plaything? Its weapons are monstrous; its eye is capable of peering beyond millions of light-years. There is one dubious answer to this buoyant optimism: science is human; it is of human devising and manufacture. It has not prevented war; it has perfected it. It has not abolished cruelty or corruption; it has enabled these abominations to be practiced on a scale unknown before in human history.

Science is a solver of problems, but it is dealing with the limitless, just as, in a cruder way, were the Romans. Solutions to problems create problems; their solutions, in turn, multiply into additional problems that escape out of scientific hands like noxious insects into the interstices of the social fabric. The rate of growth is geometric, and the vibrations set up can even now be detected in our institutions. This is what the Scottish biologist D'Arcy Thompson called the evolution of contingency. It is no longer represented by the long, slow turn of world time as the geologist has known it. Contingency has escaped into human hands and flickers unseen behind every whirl of our machines, every pronouncement of political policy.

Each one of us before his death looks back upon a childhood whose ways now seem as remote as those of Rome. "Daddy," the small daughter of a friend of mine recently asked, "tell me how it was in olden days." As my kindly friend groped amidst his classical history, he suddenly realized with a slight shock that his daughter wanted nothing more than an account of his own childhood. It was forty years away and it was already "olden days." "There was a time," he said slowly to the enchanted child, "called the year of the Great Depression. In that time there was a very great deal to eat, but men could not buy it. Little girls were scarcer than now. You see," he said painfully, "their fathers could not afford them, and they were not born." He made a half-apologetic gesture to the empty room, as if to a gathering of small reproachful

ghosts. "There was a monster we never understood called Overproduc-
tion. There were," and his voice trailed hopelessly into silence, "so
many dragons in that time you could not believe it. And there was a
very civilized nation where little girls were taken from their parents. . . ." He could not go on. The eyes from Auschwitz, he told me
later, would not permit him.

5

Recently, I passed a cemetery in a particularly bleak countryside. Ad-
joining the multitude of stark upthrust gray stones was an incongruous
row of six transparent telephone booths erected in that spot for reasons
best known to the communications industry. Were they placed there for
the midnight convenience of the dead, or for the midday visitors who
might attempt speech with the silent people beyond the fence? It was
difficult to determine, but I thought the episode suggestive of our dilemma.

An instrument for communication, erected by a powerful unseen
intelligence, was at my command, but I suspect—although I was oddly
averse to trying to find out—that the wires did not run in the proper
direction, and that there was something disconnected or disjointed
about the whole endeavor. It was, I fear, symbolic of an unexpected
aspect of our universe, a universe that, however strung with connecting
threads, is endowed with an open-ended and perverse quality we shall
never completely master. Nature contains that which does not concern
us, and has no intention of taking us into its confidence. It may provide
us with receiving boxes of white bone as cunning in their way as the
wired booths in the cemetery, but, like these, they appear to lack some
essential ingredient of genuine connection. As we consider what appears
to be the chance emergence of photosynthesis, which turns the light of
a far star into green leaves, or the creation of the phenomenon of sex
that causes the cards at the gaming table of life to be shuffled with
increasing frequency and into ever more diverse combinations, it should
be plain that nature contains the roiling unrest of a tornado. It is not the
self-contained stately palace of the eighteenth-century philosophers, a
palace whose doorstep was always in precisely the same position.

From the oscillating universe, beating like a gigantic heart, to the
puzzling existence of antimatter, order, in a human sense, is at least
partially an illusion. Ours, in reality, is the order of a time, and of an
insignificant fraction of the cosmos, seen by the limited senses of a finite
creature. Behind the appearances, as even one group of primitive
philosophers, the Hopi, have grasped, lurks being unmanifest, whose
range and number exceeds the real. This is why the unexpected will
always confront us; this is why the endless frontier is really endless.
This is why the half-formed chaos of the marsh moved me as pro-

foundly as though a new prophetic shape induced by us had risen monstrously from dangling wire and crumpled cardboard.

We are more dangerous than we seem and more potent in our ability to materialize the unexpected that is drawn from our own minds. "Force maketh Nature more violent in the Returne," Francis Bacon had once written. In the end, this is her primary quality. Her creature man partakes of that essence, and it is well that he consider it in contemplation and not always in action. To the unexpected nature of the universe man owes his being. More than any other living creature he contains, unknowingly, the shapes and forms of an uncreated future to be drawn from his own substance. The history of this unhappy century should prove a drastic warning of his powers of dissolution, even when directed upon himself. Waste, uncertain marshes, lie close to reality in our heads. Shapes as yet unevoked had best be left lying amidst those spectral bog lights, lest the drifting smoke of dreams merge imperceptibly, as once it did, with the choking real fumes from the ovens of Belsen and Buchenwald.

"It is very unhappy, but too late to be helped," Emerson had noted in his journal, "the discovery we have made that we exist. That discovery is called the Fall of Man. Ever afterwards we suspect our instruments. We have learned that we do not see directly." Wisdom interfused with compassion should be the consequence of that discovery, for at the same moment one aspect of the unexpected universe will have been genuinely revealed. It lies deep-hidden in the human heart, and not at the peripheries of space. Both the light we seek and the shadows that we fear are projected from within. It is through ourselves that the organic procession pauses, hesitates, or renews its journey. "We have learned to ask terrible questions," exclaimed that same thinker in the dawn of Victorian science. Perhaps it is just for this that the Unseen Player in the void has rolled his equally terrible dice. Out of the self-knowledge gained by putting dreadful questions man achieves his final dignity.

OPTIONS FOR WRITING

1. Eiseley tells us that "the world contains, for all its seeming regularity, a series of surprises resembling those that in childhood terrorized us by erupting on springs from closed boxes." As you look around the world, what do you find puzzling about nature? If you wanted to discover more about this subject, how would you go about investigating it?

2. In the twentieth century, Eiseley asserts, "never before in human history has the mind soared higher and seen less to cheer its complacency." What evidence does Eiseley cite in support of such a sobering conclusion? Do you agree or disagree with his assessment?

3. Eiseley, as well as Owen Barfield in his essay "The Rainbow" that follows, is concerned with human perception and the limits of defining reality.

Create a hypothetical conversation between the two men wherein they discuss the existence of rainbows.

4. If hidden aspects of nature never become part of our human awareness because they are too small to be detected, in what ways do they exist in the world?

Max Born
REFLECTIONS (1965)

Max Born (1882–1970) was a physicist and mathematician who
helped develop the field of quantum mechanics, a creation comparable
to Newtonian physics or Darwin's theory of evolution. Quantum
mechanics shows that on the atomic scale only a statistical interpreta-
tion of events is allowed. In 1954 Born received a Nobel prize for his
work. He went on to write textbooks on atomic physics and optics.
His autobiography, My Life and My Views *(1968), offers abundant*
information about his life and contribution to physics. Born is also
well-known for his concern about the ethical implications of science
and the place of science in the fabric of modern life. He was a gifted
writer and a dedicated teacher with deep insights into the nature of
the physical world, but it was his social conscience that made his
writing so relevant and significant for the general reader. He was an
avid reader of the great philosophers and was thus able to avoid some
of the difficulties that so often confuse naive scientists who try to
write outside their discipline.

I should like to offer a few reflections on the meaning science has for me and for society, and I shall introduce these considerations with the very trivial remark that achievement and success in life depend to a considerable degree on good fortune. I was fortunate in regard to my parents, my wife, my children, my teachers, my pupils, and my collaborators. I was fortunate in surviving two world wars and several revolutions, among them Hitler's, which was most dangerous for a German Jew.

I wish to look at science from two angles, one personal and the other general. Right from the start, as I have already said, I found research great fun, and it has remained enjoyable to this day. This pleasure is a little like that known to anyone who solves crossword puzzles. Yet it is much more than that, perhaps even more than the joy of doing creative work in other professions except art. It consists in the feeling of penetrating the mystery of nature, discovering a secret of creation, and bringing some sense and order into a part of the chaotic world. It is a philosophical satisfaction.

I have tried to read philosophers of all ages and have found many illuminating ideas but no steady progress toward deeper knowledge and understanding. Science, however, gives me the feeling of steady progress: I am convinced that theoretical physics is actual philosophy. It has revolutionized fundamental concepts, e.g., about space and time (relativity), about causality (quantum theory), and about substance and matter (atomistics), and it has taught us new methods of thinking (complementarity) which are applicable far beyond physics. During the last years I have tried to formulate philosophical principles derived from science.

When I was young, very few scientists were needed in industry. The only way they could earn a living was by teaching. I found teaching at a university most enjoyable. To present a scientific subject in an attractive and stimulating manner is an artistic task, similar to that of a novelist or even a dramatic writer. The same holds for writing textbooks. The greater pleasure is in teaching research students. I was lucky to have had a considerable number of men of genius among them. It is marvelous to discover talent and to direct it toward a fertile field of research.

From a personal point of view, therefore, science has given me every satisfaction and pleasure a man can expect from his profession. But during my span of life science has become a matter of public concern and the *l'art pour l'art* standpoint of my youth is now obsolete. Science has become an integral and most important part of our civilization, and scientific work means contributing to its development. Science in our technical age has social, economic, and political functions, and however remote one's own work is from technical application it is a link in the chain of actions and decisions which determine the fate of the human race. I realized this aspect of science in its full impact only after Hiroshima. But then it became overwhelmingly important. It made me ponder over the changes which science has brought about in human affairs during my own time and where they may lead.

In spite of my love of scientific work, the result of my thinking was depressing. This enormous subject cannot be dealt with in a few lines. But a sketch of my life would be incomplete without at least a brief intimation of my view.

It seems to me that the attempt made by nature on this earth to produce a thinking animal may have failed. The reason is not only the considerable and ever increasing probability that a nuclear war may break out and destroy all life on earth. Even if such a catastrophe can be avoided I cannot see any but a dark future for mankind. On account of his brain, man is convinced of his superiority over all other animals; yet whether he, with his state of consciousness, is happier than the dumb animals may be doubted. His history is known for a few thousand years. It is full of exciting events but overall there is a sameness, that is, peace alternating with war, construction with destruction, growth with decline. Always there existed some elementary science developed by philosophers and some primitive technology that was practically independent of science and in the hands of artisans. Both grew very slowly, so slowly that for a long time change was hardly perceptible and without much influence on the human scene. But suddenly, about three hundred years ago, an explosion of mental activity occurred: modern science and technology were born. Since then, they have increased at an ever growing rate, probably faster than exponentially, and are now transforming the human world beyond recognition. But although this is due to the mind, it is not controlled by the mind. It is hardly necessary to give examples of this fact. Medicine has overcome most of the plagues and epidemic diseases and it has doubled the human life span within a single generation: the result is the prospect of catastrophic overpopulation. People are crowded into cities and have lost all contact with nature. Wild animal life is vanishing rapidly. Communication from one place of the globe to the other is almost instantaneous and travel has been speeded up to an incredible extent, with the effect that every little crisis in one corner of the world affects all the rest and makes reasonable politics impossible. The automobile has made the whole countryside accessible to all, but the roads are choked and the places of recreation spoiled. However, this kind of technical miscarriage might be corrected in time by technological and administrative remedies.

The real disease lies deeper. It consists in the breakdown of all ethical principles which have evolved in the course of history and preserved a way of life worth living even through periods of ferocious warfare and wholesale destruction. It is enough to give two examples of the dissolution of traditional ethics by technology: one concerns peace, the other war.

In peace, hard work was the foundation of society. A man was proud of what he had learned to do and of the things he produced with his hands. Skill and application were highly valued. Today there is little left of this. Machines and automation have degraded human work and destroyed its dignity. Today its purpose and reward are money. The money is wanted for buying technical products produced by others for the sake of money.

In war, strength and courage, magnanimity toward the defeated foe, and compassion for the defenseless characterized the ideal soldier. Nothing is left of these. Modern weapons of mass destruction leave no place for ethical restrictions and reduce the soldier to a technical killer.

This devaluation of ethics is due to the length and complication of the path between a human action and its final effect. Most workmen know only their special tiny manipulation in a special section of the production process and hardly ever see the complete product. Naturally they do not feel responsible for this product or for its use. Whether this use is good or bad, harmless or harmful is completely beyond their field of vision. The most horrid result of this separation of action and effect was the annihilation of millions of human beings during the Nazi regime in Germany; the Eichmann type of killers pleaded not guilty because they "did their job" and had nothing to do with its ultimate purpose.

All attempts to adapt our ethical code to our situation in the technological age have failed. The representatives of traditional ethics, the Christian churches, have, as far as I see, found no remedy. The communist states have simply given up the idea of an ethical code valid for every human being and replaced it by the principle that the laws of the state represent the moral code.

An optimist may hope that out of this jungle a new ethics will arise, and arise in time to avoid a nuclear war and general destruction. But against this there is the possibility that no solution of this problem exists because of the very nature of the scientific revolution in human thinking. . . .

The average human being is a naïve realist: i.e., like the animals, he accepts his sense impressions as direct information of reality and he is convinced that all human beings share this information. He is not aware that no way exists of establishing whether one individual's impression (e.g., of a green tree) and that of another (of this tree) is the same and that even the word "same" has no meaning here. Single sense experiences have no objective, i.e., communicable and confirmable, significance. The essence of science is the discovery that relations between two or more sense impressions, particularly statements of equality, can be communicated and checked by different individuals. If the restriction of using only such statements is accepted, one obtains an objective, though colorless and cold, picture of the world. That is the characteristic method of science. It was developed slowly in the so-called classical period of physics (before 1900) and became dominant in modern atomic physics. It has led to an enormous widening of the horizon of knowledge, in the macrocosmos as well as in the microcosmos, and to a stupendous increase of power over the forces of nature. But this gain is paid for by a bitter loss. The scientific attitude is apt to create doubt and skepticism toward traditional, unscientific knowledge and even toward natural, unsophisticated actions on which human society depends.

No one has yet devised a means of keeping society together without traditional ethical principles or of arriving at them by means of the rational methods used in science.

Scientists themselves are an inconspicuous minority; but the impressive successes of technology give them a decisive position in society today. They are aware of a higher objective certainty obtainable by their way of thinking, but they do not see the limitations of it. Their political and ethical judgments are therefore often primitive and dangerous.

The nonscientific mode of thought depends, of course, also on an educated minority, i.e., the lawyers, theologians, historians, philosophers, who by the limitations of their training are unable to understand the most powerful social forces of our time. Thus civilized society is split into two groups, one of which is guided by the traditional humanistic ideas, the other by scientific ones. This situation has recently been discussed by many distinguished thinkers, for example, C. P. Snow. . . . They generally regard it as a weak point of our social institution but believe that it can be remedied by a properly balanced education.

Proposals for an improvement of our educational institutions in this direction are numerous, but so far ineffective. My personal experience is that very many scientists and engineers are fairly well educated people who have some knowledge of literature, history, and other humanistic subjects, who love art and music, who even paint or play an instrument; on the other hand the ignorance and even contempt of science displayed by people with a humanistic education is amazing. Offering myself as an example, I know and enjoy a good deal of German and English literature and poetry, and have even made an attempt to translate a popular German poet into English (Wilhelm Busch). . . . I am also familiar with other European writers: French, Italian, Russian, and others. I love music, and in my younger years played the piano well enough to take part in chamber music or, with a friend, to play simple concertos on two pianos, and occasionally even with an orchestra. I have read and continued to read books on history and our present social, economic, and political situation. I make attempts to influence political opinion by writing articles and giving radio talks. Many of my colleagues share these interests and activities—Einstein was a good violinist; Planck and Sommerfeld were excellent pianists, as are Heisenberg and many others. Concerning philosophy, every modern scientist, particularly every theoretical physicist, is deeply conscious that his work is intricately interwoven with philosophical thinking and that it would be futile without a thorough knowledge of the philosophical literature. This was a leading idea in my own life which I have tried to imbue in my pupils—not of course in order to make them partisans of a traditional school, but to make them able to criticize and to find flaws in the systems and overcome these by new concepts, as Einstein has taught us. Thus I should think that scientists are not cut off from humanistic thinking.

Concerning the other side of the matter, it seems to me rather different. Very many of those I have met whose education has been purely humanistic have no inkling of real scientific thinking. They often know scientific facts, even intricate facts of which I have hardly heard, but they do not know the roots of the scientific method of which I have spoken above; and they seem to be unable to grasp the point of such considerations. It seems to me that skillful, basic scientific thinking is a gift that cannot be taught and is restricted to a small minority.

But in practical affairs, particularly in politics, men are needed who combine human experience and interest in human relations with a knowledge of science and technology. Moreover, they must be men of action and not of contemplation. I have the impression that no method of education can produce people with all the qualities required.

I am haunted by the idea that this break in human civilization, caused by the discovery of the scientific method, may be irreparable. Though I love science I have the feeling that it is so greatly opposed to history and tradition that it cannot be absorbed by our civilization. The political and military horrors and the complete breakdown of ethics which I have witnessed during my lifetime may not be a symptom of an ephemeral social weakness but a necessary consequence of the rise of science—which in itself is among the highest intellectual achievements of man. If this is so, there will be an end to man as a free, responsible being. Should the race not be extinguished by nuclear war, it will degenerate into a species of stupid, dumb creatures under the tyranny of dictators who rule them with the help of machines and electronic computers.

This is no prophecy, only a nightmare. Though I have not taken part in applying scientific knowledge to destructive purposes, like making the A-bomb or the H-bomb, I feel my own responsibility. If my reasoning is correct, the fate of the race is a necessary consequence of the constitution of man, a creature in whom animal instincts and intellectual power are mixed.

However, my reasoning may be quite wrong. I hope so. Someday a man may appear abler and wiser than any in our generation, who can lead the world out of its impasse.

OPTIONS FOR WRITING

1. Born argues, "Science in our technical age has social, economic, and political functions, and however remote one's own work is from technical application it is a link in the chain of actions and decisions which determine the fate of the human race." Choose a contemporary scientific issue that you believe carries deep social, economic, and political implications. What are these implications, and how have they shaped the way in which the public views the science associated with this issue?

2. What is Born's attitude toward technology and modern science? What does he mean by the assertion that they are "so greatly opposed to history and tradition"?

3. The dropping of a nuclear bomb on Hiroshima altered Born's attitude toward science: "Even if such a [worldwide nuclear] catastrophe can be avoided I cannot see but a dark future for mankind." Does this conclusion reflect a fair and balanced perception, or is Born being overly critical of science? How might his pessimism be countered by the positive contributions of science?

C. P. Snow
THE MOMENT (1958)

C. P. Snow (1905–1980) was both a novelist and a scientific researcher. Many of the settings for his fiction are scientific, and he returned often to the theme of the scientist struggling with moral issues in the atomic age. His novel The Affair *(1960) highlighted his interest in portraying men of intellect and their struggle with moral dilemmas. "The Moment" is a chapter from his early novel* The Search, *a story of a young chemist and his advancement in science. In this excerpt the young chemist, Arthur Miles, has just been invited to pursue his research at a famous laboratory. He reluctantly must leave his girlfriend behind.*

It was in that mood, mixed of pleasure at being able to thrust into my work and distress at altering my life with Audrey, that I arrived in Cambridge one cold wet April afternoon.

I was driven by discontent more completely into science than I had been since my first term of research. In the first month I discovered that I had never had such opportunities for work before. Research in Cambridge was on a different scale from anything I had ever seen. There were more great figures than junior lecturers in London. And some of the figures were among the greatest. By now I was used to men who had made their contributions to the structure of modern science; the day when I had been excited at hearing Austin lecture was very far away. But I recaptured some of that old thrill when I saw Rutherford walking underneath the arch of the Cavendish. As I watched him, I remembered the first time I heard his name, when Luard broke out and inspired me with the news of the nuclear atom, when I was in the lowest form at school, twelve years before; it was strange to see a man whose name had become part of my mind.

Before I had been a term in Cambridge, I heard him announce another of the great Cavendish discoveries; the rumour had been running around the laboratories for days, and now I sat in the crowded lecture-room and heard the first authoritative news. In a week it would be told to the Royal Society and published for the world in a month or two: but it made the blood go faster to be told, as though in private, something which had never been heard before and which would alter a great part of our conception of the atom. We were all asking ourselves: how soon are we going to be able to disintegrate atoms as we wish?

I shall not easily forget those Wednesday meetings in the Cavendish. For me they were the essence of all the *personal* excitement in science; they were romantic, if you like, and not on the plane of the highest experience I was soon to know; but week after week I went away through the raw nights with east winds howling from the fens down the old streets, full of a glow that I had seen and heard and been close to the leaders of the greatest movement in the world. The lecture-room, packed from the top gallery to the floor, from the bottom row where professors sat to the ceiling where the degree-students took notes feverishly: the lantern, which, as seemed ironically appropriate in the most famous centre of experimental science, was always giving out: the queer high stretch of excitement that bound us all at times, so that we laughed for relief at every shadow of a joke: the great men. It is all so vivid that even now I can hear the words and feel the same response. There was Rutherford himself; Niels Bohr, the Socrates of atomic science, who talked to us amiably one night in his Danish-English for something like two and a half hours; Dirac, of whom I heard it prophesied very early that he would be another Newton; Kapitza, with a bizarre accent and an unreproducible genius; Eddington, who made some of his Carroll-like jokes; and all the rest, English, Americans, Germans, Russians, who were in atomic physics at the time when the search was hottest.

At those meetings I made some of the friends who were to be important to me later: Constantine and Lüthey I remember meeting on the same night, when W. L. Bragg had given the talk and we three had stayed behind to ask him questions. I had seen Constantine's tawny mane of hair often in the streets, and I heard reports of his eccentric ability. I liked him at sight, but somehow or other I did not see much of him till afterwards. Lüthy was a polite young Bavarian of about my own age, in Cambridge for a couple of terms. He was very useful to me from the start. Looking back, I think I was abler than he, even at the time; I was certainly more original, had more ideas and wider scope; but he had a capacity for detailed scientific criticism and a formal background of physics that I altogether lacked. I suppose he was much the better trained.

Urged on in the atmosphere of science, helped and criticized by Lüthy and some others, and spurred by the success of their researchers, I made great roads into my own work. By Christmas I had done more in eight months than in nearly two years in London. The clue to the structure of the organic group still eluded me; I felt, irritatedly, that the generalisation was almost in my hands, and yet I kept missing it. Lüthy's quick destructive mind wrecked my tentative ideas as soon as I built them up. So, after a few weeks in Cambridge, I left the bigger problem on one side and started on a side-line; and this went so well, and opened up so many speculations worth testing, that I was busy on it for the best part of a year. In that time I published two substantial papers, and had another more ambitious one in hand. I was now getting the name, quite widely, of a very promising young man: in my own subjects there were not many English rivals; I was asked to contribute to all the conferences on crystallography; my personal future was near to being comfortably determined for the next four or five years. My College was one of the few in Cambridge which elect Fellows as the result of an open competition; I was eligible to send in a thesis as soon as I took my doctorate, and my tutor Merton and Macdonald both told me there was no room for doubt.

"I shall be one referee and the other is an admirer of yours," said Macdonald. "They can't get out of taking you." More urbanely, Merton said the same thing: "A good many factors come into Fellowship elections as a rule, you know. But in competitive fellowships ability is peculiarly difficult to ignore except by the rather irregular process of altering the referees' reports. And even with someone more deplorably disreputable than yourself, my dear Miles, a majority would disapprove of such an action."

It was comforting to know that I should be secure for a while. Although I had schooled myself to wait until the end of two years at Cambridge before I thought seriously of position or money, for some time it had not been easy to put these things aside. Myself apart, I was worried by the thought of Audrey. Also, my parents were getting old, and I might have to help keep them. With the future temporarily assured, I turned eagerly once more to the problem which had enticed me for so long.

Now, however, I was in a very different mood to tackle it. I had done enough for place and reputation, and I could afford to gamble on what might be a barren chase. The structure of the organic group was not going to come out easily, I knew; I might very well be wasting a year or more, from the point of view of my career; but my career had been sound enough, and now I was working on something which I could allow to envelop me completely, simply for its own sake, in a way I had not yet known. So strong was this feeling that when I was beginning the work I often kept away from the laboratory for a day, as though my research were a pleasure of which I could, if I pleased, deprive myself. Working on my other problems—my bread-and-butter problems, as it were—I could not waste a day without a twist of uneasiness. Now I was on a piece of work I supremely wanted to do, it was natural to leave it when I was tired, to come back to it when I wished, until I was swept on beyond prudence and ambition and made to think and work and discover until the passion was drained out of me.

There was another reason which gave me far more hope of seeing my way into these molecules at last. I had gained a good deal of experience and technique in research; I had sharpened my mind on Lüthy and the rest, and broadened it on Macdonald's metaphysical schemes; and perhaps more important, I was full of confidence. If I had an idea, it would stand a chance; even if it seemed improbable, it would be looked into; for I had learned by now that more than one of my less likely ideas had worked. This confidence would have been a dangerous state of mind to begin some routine work: I might easily have been careless, simply because my luck had kept coming off. But for work which no one had dared to touch, I had to start with something like an exaggerated belief in myself. I have often thought I was quite unpardonably confident at the time—but perhaps tackling a difficult job was the least objectionable way of showing it.

Almost as soon as I took up the problem again, it struck me in a new light. All my other attempts have been absurd, I thought: if I turn them down and make another guess, then what? The guess didn't seem probable; but none of the others was any good at all. According to my guess, the structure was very different from anything one could have imagined; but that must be true, since the obvious structure didn't fit any of my facts. Soon I was designing structures with little knobs of plasticine for atoms and steel wires to hold them together; I made up the old ones, for comparison's sake, and then I built my new one, which looked very odd, very different from any structure I had ever seen. Yet I was excited—"I think it works," I said, "I think it works."

For I had brought back to mind some calculations of the scattering curves, assuming various models. None of the values had been anything like the truth. I saw at once that the new structure ought to give something much nearer. Hurriedly I calculated: it was a long and tiresome and complicated piece of arithmetic, but I rushed through it, making mistakes through impatience and having to go over it again. I was startled when I got the answer: the new model did not give perfect agreement, but it was far closer than any of the others. So far as I remember, the real value at one point was 1.32, my previous three models gave 1.1, 1.65 and 1.7, and the new one just under 1.4. 'I'm on it, at last,' I thought. 'It's a long shot, but I'm on it at last.'

For a fortnight I sifted all the evidence from the experiments since I first attacked the problem. There were a great many tables of figures, and a pile of X-ray photographs (for in my new instrument in Cambridge I was using a photographic detector); and I had been through most of them so often that I knew them almost by heart. But I went through them again, more carefully than ever, trying to interpret them in the light of the new structure. 'If it's right,' I was thinking, 'then these figures ought to run up to a maximum and then run down quickly.' And they did, though the maximum was less sharp than it should have been. And so on through experiments which represented the work of over a year; they all fitted the structure, with an allowance for a value a shade too big here, a trifle too small there. There were obviously approximations to make, I should have to modify the structure a little, but that it was on the right lines I was certain. I walked to my rooms to lunch one morning, overflowing with pleasure; I wanted to tell someone the news; I waved violently to a man whom I scarcely knew, riding on a bicycle. I thought of sending a wire to Audrey, but decided to go and see her on the following day instead: King's Parade seemed a particularly admirable street, and young men shouting across it were all admirable young men. I had a quick lunch; I wanted to bask in satisfaction, but instead I hurried back to the laboratory so that I could have it all finished with no loose ends left, and then rest for a while. I was feeling the after-taste of effort.

There were four photographs left to inspect. They had been taken earlier in the week and I had looked over them once. Now they had to be definitely measured and entered, and the work was complete. I ran over the first, it was everything I expected. The structure was fitting

even better than in the early experiments. And the second: I lit a cigarette. Then the third: I gazed over the black dots. All was well—and
then, with a thud of the heart that shook me, I saw behind each distinct
black dot another fainter speck. The bottom had fallen out of everything:
I was wrong, utterly wrong. I hunted round for another explanation: the
film might be a false one, it might be a fluke experiment; but the look
of it mocked me: far from being false, it was the only experiment where
I had arrived at precisely the right conditions. Could it be explained any
other way? I stared down at the figures, the sheets of results which I
had forced into my scheme. My cheeks flushing dry, I tried to work this
new photograph into my idea. An improbable assumption, another improbable assumption, a possible experimental error—I went on, fantastically, any sort of criticism forgotten. Still it would not fit. I was wrong,
irrevocably wrong. I should have to begin again.

Then I began to think: If I had not taken this photograph, what
would have happened? Very easily I might not have taken it. I should
have been satisfied with my idea: everyone else would have been. The
evidence is overwhelming, except for this. I should have pulled off a big
thing. I should be made. Sooner or later, of course, someone would do
this experiment, and I should be shown to be wrong: but it would be a
long time ahead, and mine would have been an honourable sort of mistake. On my evidence I should have been right. That is the way everyone would have looked at it.

I suppose, for a moment, I wanted to destroy the photograph. It
was all beyond my conscious mind. And I was swung back, also beyond
my conscious mind, by all the forms of—shall I call it "conscience"—
and perhaps more than that, by the desire which had thrown me into
the search. For I had to get to what I myself thought was the truth.
Honour, comfort and ambition were bound to move me, but I think my
own desire went deepest. Without any posturing to myself, without any
sort of conscious thought, I laughed at the temptation to destroy the
photograph. Rather shakily I laughed. And I wrote in my note-book:

> Mar. 30: Photograph 3 alone has secondary dots, concentric with major dots. This
> removes all possibility of the hypothesis of structure B. The interpretation from Mar.
> 4–30 must accordingly be disregarded.

From that day I understood, as I never had before, the frauds that
creep into science every now and then. Sometimes they must be quite
unconscious: the not-seeing of facts because they are inconvenient, the
delusions of one's own senses. As though in my case I had not seen,
because my unconscious self chose not to see, the secondary ring of
dots. Sometimes, more rarely, the fraud must be nearer to consciousness; that is, the fraud must be realised, even though the man cannot
control it. That was the point of my temptation. It could only be committed by a man in whom the scientific passion was weaker for the time

than the ordinary desires for place or money. Sometimes it would be done, impulsively, by men in whom no faith was strong; and they could forget it cheerfully themselves and go on to do good and honest work. Sometimes it would be done by a man who reproached himself all his life. I think I could pick out most kinds of fraud from among the mistakes I have seen; after that afternoon I could not help being tolerant toward them.

For myself, there was nothing left to do but start again. I looked over the entry in my note-book; the ink was still shining, and yet it seemed to have stood, final, leaving me no hope, for a long time. Because I had nothing better to do, I made a list of the structures I had invented and, in the end, discarded. There were four of them now. Slowly, I devised another. I felt sterile. I distrusted it; and when I tried to test it, to think out its properties, I had to force my mind to work. I sat until six o'clock, working profitlessly; and when I walked out, and all through the night, the question was gnawing at me: 'What is this structure? Shall I ever get it? Where am I going wrong?'

I have never had two sleepless nights together before that week. Fulfillment deferred had hit me; I had to keep from reproaching myself that I had already wasted months over this problem, and now, just as I could consolidate my work, I was on the way to wasting another year. I went to bed late and heard the Cambridge clocks, one after another, chime out the small hours. I would have ideas with the uneasy clarity of night, switch on my light, scribble in my note-book, look at my watch, and try to sleep again; I would rest a little and wake up with a start, hoping that it was morning, to find that I had slept for twenty minutes: until I lay awake in a grey dawn, with all my doubts pressing in on me as I tried with tired eyes to look into the future. 'What is the structure? What line must I take?' And then, as an under-theme, 'Am I going to fail at my first big job? Am I always going to be a competent worker doing little problems?' And another, 'I shall be twenty-six in the winter: I ought to be established. But shall I be getting anywhere?' My ideas, that seemed hopeful when I got out of bed to write them, were ridiculous when I saw them in this cold light.

This went on for three nights, until my work in the daytime was only a pretence. Then there came a lull, when I forgot my worry for a night and slept until mid-day. But, though I woke refreshed, the questions began to whirl round again in my mind. For days it went on, and I could find no way out. I walked twenty miles one day, along the muddy fenroads between the town and Ely, in order to clear my head; but it only made me tired, and I drank myself to sleep. Another night I went to a play, but I was listening not to the actors' words, but to others that formed themselves inside me and were giving me no rest.

While my nerves were still throbbing with work that was getting nowhere, Audrey came up for the week-end. As soon as she met me on the platform, she said:

"You're very worried. And pale. What's gone wrong?"

"Nothing," I said.

"Can't I leave you a fortnight without seeing you look like death?" she said.

We tried to meet each week-end, but she was living at home now, and her father often expected her to entertain his guests.

"I'm quite well," I replied.

We walked towards the gate. She said nothing. I talked on: "But what's the news? I'm rather out of touch. Anything happened in the world? Have you read anything since I saw you?"

I went on until we got into a taxi; then she said:

"Stop that."

I murmured; she took my hand.

"I'm not altogether a fool," she said. "And you've never been able to control your face. And there are lines here—and here—" She traced them, on my forehead and round my mouth—"Why, you're ten years older than when I saw you first."

"It's nearly four years," I said.

"Don't put me off." Her eyes were shining. "What's the matter?"

Although I half-resented it, I was grateful that she was taking me in hand.

"The work's not going too well," I said, and put my arm round her for comfort. "I found there was a hole in my idea."

"A fortnight ago you thought it was almost perfect."

"That was a fortnight ago." I could not help my voice going dulled.

"It's all wrong, now?"

"Quite wrong," I said. "As wrong as anything can be. And I can't see how I can put it right," I added.

She did not try to sympathise in words, but in the way she leaned against my shoulder and glanced up at me I gained more ease than I had had for many days.

"You'll do it, of course," she said at last.

"I'm not so certain," I said. "I might go on for years like this. Just fooling and not seeing any sort of way. It's not easy—"

The line had crept between her eyes.

"I wish I knew this stuff of yours," she burst out. "Then you could talk to me. And it might help a bit."

She was anxious, now. I said:

"Oh, never mind. Let's talk of other things. That'll take me away from it."

But even exchanging private thoughts with Audrey, hearing her say words that had become currency after long use, I still had moments when her voice and mine in reply sounded like noises in the outside world. Disturbing noises which I would get away from if I could. We sat in my rooms and she made me eat lunch and told me of Sheriff's latest affair, and how he had asked her to dinner and introduced his girl—"a little better than Miss Stanton-Browne, but they might be cousins," Audrey said. And she had had a letter from Hunt, who rarely wrote to either of us. He was still at his school, but seemed to be a little less disconsolate. "Why, I don't know," she said. And all the time those names . . . Sheriff . . . Hunt . . . would get mixed in structures that were dancing in my mind. I shook myself free for a while, and I was myself, talking to Audrey. Then she mentioned the Labour Party and my mind leapt to the association Labour Party — MacDonald — Macdonald, my professor — and so to my problem, and I was preoccupied once more.

In the middle of the afternoon Audrey said, suddenly: "It'll be good for you to get out of here for a bit. We'll go somewhere." Rather unwillingly I borrowed a car, and Audrey drove along the London road. I tried to talk, but I was glad when she said something which required no answer. There was a cold wind, but once as we stopped for a moment I caught a smell of spring: it gave me an empty nostalgia, for what I did not know, except some end to this.

We had tea at a village whose name I have forgotten: it must have been Baldock or Stevenage, I think. But I remember the room as sharply as the café where I read my newspaper this morning. It was a stiff, austerely clean little parlour, with hard chairs and round wooden tables; and pale sunshine fell across it on to a grate, where a few lumps of coal lay half burnt. Audrey's hair was the only warm colour in the room. We ate hard little home-made cakes, and Audrey bit at hers firmly, in order to punctuate her views on her women friends.

"What can you do with most of them? What ever are they for? Except have their children and keep their houses, and make their men feel important because they've got a silly woman who believes what they say." She stopped.

"Most of these women haven't the intelligence of a penguin — and they're not as good to look at."

"Really beautiful women are quite as rare," I heard my own voice saying, "as really intelligent ones."

"I don't believe it," she said, "but I'd give anything to meet either after a morning with these — these incubators." She thought a moment.

"I suppose it's inevitable," she added. "I suppose women are meant to be incubators first and foremost. But it's a little strange they should glory in it so."

"Yes," I said, absently.

"I'm ashamed of it when it comes up in myself. And it does come up, you know. Sometimes I'm afraid I'm a real incubator at heart," she laughed. "My dear, when you're all upset like this, and paying no notice to anything I say I ought to get up and go out, if I had a decent independent spirit — but instead I can't help staying to look after you."

I started. My thoughts had stopped going back upon themselves. As I had been watching Audrey's eyes, an idea had flashed through the mist, quite unreasonably, illogically. It had no bearing at all on any of the hopeless attempts I had been making; I had explored every way, I thought, but this was new; and, too agitated to say even to myself that I believed it, I took out some paper and tried to work it out. Audrey was staring with intent eyes. I could not get very far. I wanted my results and tables. But everything I could put down rang true.

"An idea's just come to me," I explained, pretending to be calm. "I don't think there's anything in it. But there might be a little. But anyway I ought to try it out. And I haven't my books. Do you mind if we go back pretty soon?" I fancy I was getting up from the table, for Audrey smiled.

"I'm glad you had some excuse for not listening," she said.

She drove back very fast, not speaking. I made my plans for the work. It couldn't take less than a week, I thought. I sat hunched up, telling myself that it might be all wrong again; but the structure was taking shape, and a part of me was beginning to laugh at my caution. Once I turned and saw Audrey's profile against the fields; but after a moment I was back in the idea.

When I got out at the Cavendish gateway, she stayed in the car. "You'd better be alone," she said.

"And you?"

"I'll sit in Green Street." She stayed there regularly on her week-end visits.

I hesitated. "It's—"

She smiled. "I'll expect you to-night. About ten o'clock," she said.

I saw very little of Audrey that week-end. When I went to her, my mind was active, my body tired, and despite myself it was more comfort than love I asked of her. I remember her smiling, a little wryly, and saying: "When this is over, we'll go away. Right away." I buried my head against her knees, and she stroked my hair. When she left me on the Monday morning, we clung to each other for a long time.

For three weeks I was thrusting the idea into the mass of facts. I could do nothing but calculate, read up new facts, satisfy myself that I had made no mistakes in measuring up the plates: I developed an uncontrollable trick of not being sure whether I had made a particular measurement correctly: repeating it: and then, after a day, the uncertainty returned, and to ease my mind I had to repeat it once more. I could scarcely read a newspaper or write a letter. Whatever I was doing, I was not at rest unless it was taking me towards the problem; and even then it was an unsettled rest, like lying in a fever half-way to sleep.

And yet, for all the obsessions, I was gradually being taken over by a calm which was new to me. I was beginning to feel an exultation, but it was peaceful, as different from wild triumph as it was from the ache in my throbbing nerves. For I was beginning to feel in my heart that I was near the truth. Beyond surmise, beyond doubt, I felt that I was nearly right; even as I lay awake in the dawn, or worked irritably with flushed cheeks, I was approaching a serenity which made the discomforts as trivial as those of someone else's body.

It was after Easter now and Cambridge was almost empty. I was glad; I felt free as I walked the deserted streets. One night, when I left the laboratory, after an evening when the new facts were falling into line and making the structure seem more than ever true, it was good to pass under the Cavendish! Good to be in the midst of the great days of science! Good to be adding to the record of those great days! And good to walk down King's Parade and see the Chapel standing against a dark sky without any stars!

The mingling of strain and certainty, of personal worry and deeper peace, was something I had never known before. Even at the time, I knew I was living in a strange happiness. Or, rather, I knew that when it was over I should covet its memory.

And so for weeks I was alone in the laboratory, taking photographs, gazing under the red lamp at films which still dripped water, carrying them into the light and studying them until I knew every grey speck on them, from the points which were testing my structures down to flaws and scratches on the surface. Then, when my eyes tired, I put down my lens and turned to the sheets of figures that contained the results, the details of the structure and the predictions I was able to make. Often I would say—if this structure is right, then this crystal here will have its oxygen atom 1.2 a.u. from the nearest carbon; and the crystal will break along this axis, and not along that; and it will be harder than the last crystal I measured, but not so hard as the one before, and so on. For days my predictions were not only vaguely right, but right as closely as I could measure.

I still possess those lists of figures, and I have stopped writing to look over them again. It is ten years and more since I first saw them and yet as I read:

PREDICTED	OBSERVED
1.435	1.44
2.603	2.603

and so on for long columns, I am warmed with something of that first glow.

At last it was almost finished. I had done everything I could; and to make an end of it I thought out one prediction whose answer was irrefutable. There was one more substance in the organic group which I could not get in England, which had only been made in Munich; if my general structure was right, the atoms in its lattice could only have one pattern. For any other structure the pattern would be utterly different.

An X-ray photograph of the crystal would give me all I wanted in a single day.

It was tantalizing, not having the stuff to hand. I could write and get some from Munich, but it would take a week, and a week was very long. Yet there seemed nothing else to do. I was beginning to write in my clumsy scientist's German—and then I remembered Lüthy, who had returned to Germany a year ago.

I cabled to him, asking if he would get a crystal and photograph it on his instrument. It would only take him a morning at the most, I thought, and we had become friendly enough for me to make the demand on him. Later in the afternoon I had his answer: "I have obtained crystal will telegraph result to-morrow honoured to assist. Lüthy." I smiled at the "honored to assist," which he could not possibly have left out, and sent off another cable: "Predict symmetry and distances. . . . "

Then I had twenty-four hours of waiting. Moved by some instinct to touch wood, I wanted to retract the last cable as soon as I had sent it. If—if I were wrong, no one else need know. But it had gone. And, nervous as I was, in a way I knew that I was right. Yet I slept very little that night; I could mock, with all the detached part of myself, at the tricks my body was playing, but it went on playing them. I had to leave my breakfast, and drank cup after cup of tea, and kept throwing away cigarettes I had just lighted. I watched myself do these things, but I could not stop them, in just the same way as one can watch one's own body being afraid.

The afternoon passed, and no telegram came. I was persuaded there was scarcely time. I went out for an hour, in order to find it at my rooms when I returned. I went through all the antics and devices of waiting. I grew empty with anxiety as the evening drew on. I sat trying to read; the room was growing dark, but I did not wish to switch on the light, for fear of bringing home the passage of the hours.

At last the bell rang below. I met my landlady on the stairs, bringing in the telegram. I do not know whether she noticed that my hands were shaking as I opened it. It said: "Felicitations on completely accurate prediction which am proud to confirm apologies for delay due to instrumental adjustments. Lüthy." I was numbed for a moment; I could only see Lüthy bowing politely to the postal clerk as he sent off the telegram. I laughed, and I remembered it had a queer sound.

Then I was carried beyond pleasure. I have tried to show something of the high moments that science gave to me; the night my father talked about the stars, Luard's lesson, Austin's opening lecture, the end of my first research. But this was different from any of them, different altogether, different in kind. It was further from myself. My own triumph and delight and success were there, but they seemed insignificant beside this tranquil ecstasy. It was as though I had looked for a truth outside myself, and finding it had become for a moment part of the truth I sought; as though all the world, the atoms and the stars, were wonderfully clear and close to me, and I to them, so that we were part of a lucidity more tremendous than any mystery.

I had never known that such a moment could exist. Some of its quality, perhaps, I had captured in the delight which came when I brought joy to Audrey, being myself content; or in the times among friends, when for some rare moment, maybe twice in my life, I had lost myself in a common purpose; but these moments had, as it were, the tone of the experience without the experience itself.

Since then I never quite regained it. But one effect will stay with me as long as I live; once, when I was young, I used to sneer at the mystics who have described the experience of being at one with God and part of the unity of things. After that afternoon, I did not want to laugh again; for though I should have interpreted the experience differently, I thought I knew what they meant.

OPTIONS FOR WRITING

1. Why is this essay entitled "The Moment," and how does the title relate to the subject of the writing?

2. Snow once wrote another essay about two cultures in which he tried to bridge the gap between the sciences and humanities. Do you see any evidence of this concern in "The Moment"?

3. Throughout "The Moment" we see examples of the writer's personal life, opinions, impressions, and observations. Do these inclusions weaken or deepen the scientific discussion at the heart of the essay?

Roald Hoffmann
UNDER THE SURFACE OF THE CHEMICAL ARTICLE

Roald Hoffmann (b. 1937) won the Nobel prize in chemistry in 1981. The award came for his work in applying molecular orbital theory to chemical reactions. He has received numerous other awards in the past two decades and has been a professor of chemistry at Cornell University since 1965. The reading that follows is part of a larger article (originally a 1988 lecture) that examines in some detail the presuppositions of scientists who are writing for their colleagues. Scientists try, as Hoffmann points out, to express ideas in neutered language devoid of personal motivation and with few references to historical development. And all this is often done with "mind-deadening" similarity, article after article. Hoffmann argues, however, that there is much to be seen under the surface of such writing.

LANGUAGE

Scientists think that what they say is not influenced by the language they use, meaning both the national language (German, French, Chinese) and the words within that language. They think that the words employed, providing they're well-defined, are just representations of an underlying material reality which they, the scientists, have discovered or mathematicized. Because the words are faithful representations of that reality they should be perfectly translatable, into any language.

That position *is* defensible — as soon as the synthesis of the new high-temperature superconductor $YBa_2Cu_3O_{-x}$ was described, it *was* reproduced, in a hundred laboratories around the globe.

But the real situation is more complex. In another sense words are all we have. And the words we have, in any language, are ill-defined, ambiguous. A dictionary is a deeply circular device — just try and see how quickly a chain of definitions closes upon itself. Reasoning and argument, so essential to communication in science, proceed in words. The more contentious the argument, the simpler and more charged the words.

How does a chemist get out of this? Perhaps by realizing what some of our colleagues in linguistics and literary criticism learned over the last century. The word is a sign, a piece of code. It signifies something, to be sure, but what it signifies must be decoded or interpreted by the reader. If two readers have different decoding mechanisms, then they will get different readings, different meanings. The reason that chemistry works around the world, so that BASF can build a plant in Germany or Brazil and expect it to work, is that chemists have in their education been taught the same set of signs.

I think this accounts in part for what *Carl Friedrich von Weizsäcker* noted in a perceptive article on "The Language of Physics": If one examines a physics (read chemistry) research lecture in detail one finds it to be full of imprecise statements, incomplete sentences, halts, etc. The seminar is usually given extemporaneously, without notes, whereas humanists most often read a text verbatim. The language of physics or chemistry lectures is often imprecise. Yet chemists understand those presentations (well, at least some do). The reason is that the science lecturer invokes a code, a shared set of common knowledge. He or she doesn't have to complete a sentence — most everyone knows what is meant halfway through that sentence.

GRAPHICS

The semiotics of chemistry is most apparent in the structures of molecules that grace most every page of a chemical journal, that identify at a glance a paper as chemical. The given, just over a century old, is that the structure of a molecule matters. It's not only what the atomic constituents are. It's also how the component atoms are connected up, how they are arranged in three-dimensional space, and how easily they move from their preferred equilibrium positions. The structure of a molecule, by which I mean the disposition in space of nuclei and electrons, both the static equilibrium structure and its dynamics, determines every physical, chemical, and ultimately biological property of the molecule.

It is crucial for chemists to communicate three-dimensional structural information to each other. The media for that communication are two-dimensional—a sheet of paper, a screen. So one immediately encounters the problem of representation.

Actually that problem is already there. What is a ball-and-stick model of a molecule? Is that reality? Of course not. The model is just one representation of the equilibrium positions of the nuclei, with some further assumptions about bonding. An instructive videotape from the laboratory of F. P. Brooks, Jr. at the University of North Carolina is entitled "What Does a Protein Look Like?" It shows 40 different representations (recalling to my mind the woodcut suite of *Hokusai* entitled "36 Views of Mt. Fuji") of one and the same enzyme, superoxide dismutase—a "ball-and-stick" model, a "space-filling" model, the electrostatic field experienced by a probe charge near the molecule, and so on.

Let me return to the communication problem. Chemists are impelled to communicate three-dimensional information in two dimensions. But they're not *talented* at that. Young people are not selected or select themselves to be chemists on the basis of their artistic ability.

So people are required to do what they're not talented at. That's one definition of life! Chemists cope, by the expedient of inventing a code for communicating three-dimensional structure. *And* they train people in that code. The various elements of that code are known to chemists as Fischer or Newman projections, or as the wedge-dash representation. A molecule of ethane, C_2H_6, is represented in two possible geometries, **1** and **2**. (See Figure 11.1.)

Note another piece of code: carbon is that vertex of the graph which has four lines to it, but it's not labeled C. There are hydrogens at the

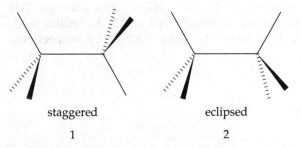

staggered   eclipsed

1   2

Figure 11.1   Geometries of a molecule of ethane (C_2H_6).

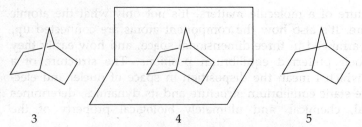

3   4   5

Figure 11.2   A reference set of planes showing three-dimensionality.

ends of the lines. They're also not labeled. The notation is simple: a solid line is in the plane of the paper, a wedge in front, a dashed line in back. Saying that may be enough to make these structures rise from the page for some people, but the neural networks that control representation are effectively etched in, for life, when one handles (in human hands, not in a computer) a ball-and-stick model of the molecule while looking at this picture.

It's fascinating to see the chemical structures floating on the page of every journal and to realize that from such minimal information people can actually *see* molecules in their mind's eye. The clues to three-dimensionality are minimal. The molecules do float, and you're usually discouraged from putting in a reference set of planes to help you see them (3 vs. 4). (See Figure 11.2.)

Some chemists rely so much on the code that they don't draw 3 but 5. What's the difference? One line "crossed" instead of "broken." What a trivial clue to three-dimensional reconstruction, that one part of a molecule is behind another one, is given in 3, absent in 5! The person who draws 5 is making many assumptions about his audience. I bet he or she hardly thinks about that.

The policies of journals, their economic limitations, and the available technology put constraints not only on what is printed but also on how we *think* about molecules. Take norbornane, C_7H_{12}, molecule 3. Until about 1950 no journal in the world was prepared to typeset this structure as 3. Instead you saw it in the journal as 6. (See Figure 11.3.) Now everyone knew since 1874, that carbon was tetrahedral, meaning that the four bonds to it were formed along the four directions radiating out from the center of a tetrahedron to its vertices. You can see this geometry in the two carbon atoms of structures 1 and 2. Molecular models were available or could be relatively easily built. Yet I suspect that

CH_2 ——— CH ——— CH_2
| | |
                CH_2
| | |
CH_2 ——— CH ——— CH_2
6

Figure 11.3   A visual representation of a molecule of norbornane (C_7H_{12})

the image or icon of norbornane that a typical chemist had in his mind around 1925 was **6** and not **3**. He was conditioned by what he saw in a journal or textbook—an image. He was moved to act in synthesizing a derivative of this molecule, for instance, by that unrealistic image.

Maybe it's not that different from the way we approach romance in our lives, equipped with a piecewise reliable set of images from novels and movies.

STYLE

Every manual of scientific writing I've seen exhorts you to use an impersonal, agentless, superrational style. Please give us the facts, gentlemen, and just the facts! Still style rears its head.

My papers are recognizable in a journal just by the proportion of the space given to graphical material, or the way I "line" my orbitals. R. B. Woodward's papers were recognizable in the (constructed) elegance of their scientific storyline, and in the matching elegance, the cadence of his words. I can read a paper by *Jack Dunitz*, by *Rolf Huisgen, Rudolf Hoppe*, or *Bill Doering* and hear their voices in these papers just as surely as I hear the voice of *A. R. Ammons*, a great American poet, or of *Bertolt Brecht*, a German one, when I see their work on a printed page.

It is in the nature of creative human beings to have a style. Why should I write my theory the way *Bill Goddard*, a theorist I admire, does, anymore than you expect *Karlheinz Stockhausen* and *Pierre Boulez* to write piano pieces that sound alike?

DIALECTICAL STRUGGLES

A nice, even-toned, scientific article may hide strong emotional undercurrents, rhetorical maneuvering, and claims of power. One has already been mentioned—the desire to convince, to scream "I'm right, all of you are wrong," clashing with the established rules of civility supposedly governing scholarly behavior. Where this balance is struck depends on the individual.

Another dialogue that is unvoiced is between experiment and theory. There is nothing special about the love-hate relationship between experimentalists and theorists in chemistry. You can substitute "writer" and "critic" and talk about literature, or find the analogous characteristics in economics. The lines of the relationship are easily caricatured—experimentalists think theorists are unrealistic, build castles in the sky. Yet they need the frameworks of understanding that theorists provide. Theorists may distrust experiments, wish that people would do that missing experiment, but where would the theorists be without any contact with reality?

An amusing manifestation of the feelings about this issue is to be found in the occasionally extended quasi-theoretical discussion sections of experimental papers. These sections in part contain a true search for understanding, but in part what goes on in them is an attempt to use the accepted reductionist ideal (with its exaggerated hailing of the more mathematical)—so as to impress one's colleagues. On the other side, I often put more references to experimental work in my theoretical papers than I should, because I'm trying to "buy credibility time" from my experimental audience. If I show experimental chemists that I know of their work, perhaps they'll give me a little time, listen to my wild speculations.

Another struggle, related, is between pure and applied chemistry. It's interesting to reflect that this separation also may have had its roots in Germany in the mid-nineteenth century; it seems to this observer that in the other chemical power of that time, Britain, the distinction was less congealed. Quite typical in a pure chemical paper is a reaching out after some justification in terms of industrial use. But at the same time there is a falling back, an unwillingness to deal with the often unruly, tremendously complicated world of, say, industrial catalysis. And in industrial settings there is a reaching after academic credentials (quite typical, for instance, of the leaders of chemical industry in Germany).

THE ID WILL OUT

I use the subject word in the psychoanalytical sense, referring to the complex of instinctive desires and terrors that inhabit the collective unconscious. On one hand, these irrational impulses, sex and aggression figuring most prominently, are our dark side. On the other hand, they provide the motive force for creative activity.

The irrational seems to be effectively suppressed in the written scientific word. But of course scientists are human, no matter how much they might pretend in their articles that they are not. Their inner illogical forces push out. Where? If you don't allow them in the light of day, on the printed page, then they will creep out or explode in the night, where things are hidden, and no one can see how nasty you are. I refer, of course, to the anonymous refereeing process, and the incredible irrational responses unleashed in it by perfectly good and otherwise rational scientists. You have to let go sometime. . . .

I actually think that what saves the chemical article from dullness is that its language comes under stress. We are trying to communicate things that perhaps cannot be expressed in words but require other signs—structures, equations, graphs. And we are trying hard to eliminate emotion from what we say. Which is impossible. So the words we use occasionally become supercharged with the tension of everything that's *not* being said.

So, many things go on in a scientific article. I will spare you the charts that I've seen hanging in many laboratories, that translate shop-worn phrases into what they really mean. Like "A regime of slow cool-ing over a period of four weeks produced a 90% yield of black crystals of . . . , meaning "I went on vacation and forgot to wash out the flask. When I came back . . . " And so on.

I want to return to the complexity of deciding what is truth in the scientific process. In a recent article, *Harald Weinrich* describes the classic paper of *Watson* and *Crick* on the structure of DNA in *Nature* in 1953. It is succinct, beautifully reasoned, elegant. *David Locke*, in his book, analyzes the rhetorical structure and the use of irony in the same paper. I think most readers were immediately convinced that the Watson and Crick model was the truth, that this was the way it had to be. And so it is (with some minor variation on hydrogen-bonding schemes in un-usual forms of DNA). The Watson and Crick model was and is right. One needs little more.

But then in 1968 *Watson* writes a book, *The Double Helix*, in which he tells the story of how it really happened. Of course, it's a self-cen-tered story, and not kind or fair to *Rosalind Franklin* and others. *Watson's* story is much like one of the four views of an event in *Akira Kurosawa's* masterful film *Rashomon*. It needs other views, which some historians have provided. But there is no question that *Watson's* account is vibrant, full of life. It tells us how he saw the truth, and I think it's a great book.

So (and here I follow *Weinrich*) what *is* the truth: Is it the 1953 paper of *Watson* and *Crick*, or is it the 1968 book by *Watson*? Does the latter diminish the former? It bears reflection.

WHAT IS TO BE DONE?

I have tried to deconstruct, to borrow some language from critical theory, the scientific article, ossified in its present form for over a hundred years. I think I could have done better with a specific text before me, but then I would have run the danger of libel suits or loss of friendship. And it is in the nature of human beings to be unable to criticize, truly, deeply, their own work. So I can't do it to myself. But I'm sure every chemist knows some superb example of what I allude to, especially in the work of one of his less favorite scientists.

The deconstruction is done by me not with malice, but with care. I love this molecular science. I love its richness and the underlying simplicity, but most of all the rich, life-giving variety and connection of all of chemistry. Let me give you an example in Figure 11.4. I see C_2 in a carbon arc and in the tail of Halley's Comet. I see it in acetylene, ethylene, and ethane. I see it in the lovely molecular complexes of *P. Walczanski*, *M. I. Bruce*, and *G. Longoni* and their co-workers, shown in Figure 11.4. I see it in CaC_2 in *W. Jeitschko's* and *A. Simon's* and their co-workers' rare earth carbides. It's staggering!

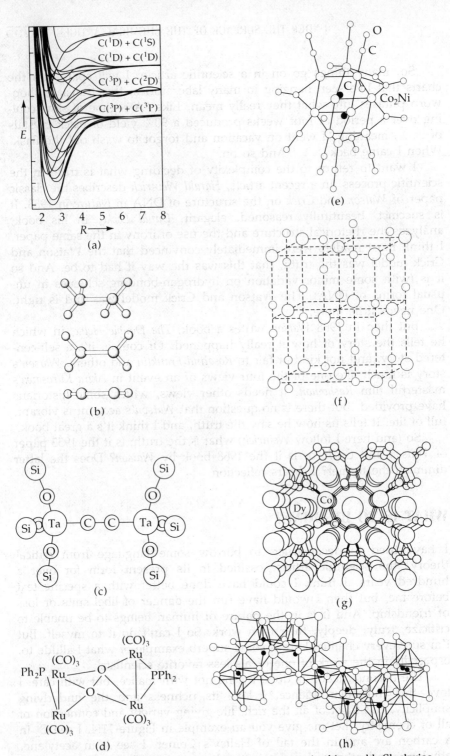

Figure 11.4 Some of the ways in which C_2 finds its way in this world. Clockwise from top left: (a) some calculated potential energy curves for diatomic C_2; (b) ethane, ethylene, acetylene; (c) a dinuclear tantalum complex of C_2; (d) Ru_4C_2 cluster; (e) C_2 inside a Co_3Ni_7 cluster; (f) calcium carbide; (g) $DyCoC_2$; (h) $Gd_{12}C_6I_{17}$.

I know that that richness was created by human beings. So I'm unhappy to see their humanity suppressed in the way they express themselves in print. I also think that there are some real dangers in the present intellectual stance of scientists and in their ritual mode of communication.

Here are the dangers as I perceive them. Acceptance of a facile reductionist philosophy, a vertical mode of understanding appropriated as the *only* mode of understanding, creates a gap between us and our friends in the arts and humanities. They know very well that there isn't only one way of "understanding" or dealing with the death of a parent, or a political election, or a woodcut by *Ernst Ludwig Kirchner*. The world out there is refractory to reduction, and if we insist that it must be reducible, all that we do is to put ourselves into a nice box. The box is the small class of problems that are susceptible to a reductionist understanding.

A second danger, more specific to the scientific article, is that by dehumanizing our mode of communication, by removing emotion, motivation, the occasionally irrational, we may have in fact done much more than chase away the Natural Philosophers. That we've accomplished, to be sure. But 150 years down the line what we have created is a mechanical, ritualized product that 3×10^5 times per year propagates the notion that scientists are dry and insensitive, that they respond only to wriggles in a spectrum. The public at large types us by the nature of our product. How can it do otherwise when we do not make a sufficient effort to explain to the public what it is that we really do in our jargon-barricaded world?

What is to be done? I would argue for a general humanization of the publication process. Let's relax those strictures, editorial or self-imposed, on portraying in words, in a primary scientific paper, motivation, whether personal and scientific, emotion, historicity, even some of the irrational. So what if it takes a little more space? We *can* keep up with the chemical literature, and tell the mass of hack work from what is truly innovative, without much trouble as it is. The humanizing words will not mislead; they may actually encourage us to read more carefully the substance of what is said. I would plead for a valuation and teaching of style, in the written and spoken language of one's own country, as well as in English. I think chemistry has much to gain from reviving the personal, the emotional, the stylistic core of the struggle to discover and create the molecular world.

OPTIONS FOR WRITING

1. Explain how emotions and irrational expressions might surface in a scientific project or article. How might these elements influence scientific writing?

2. In a short paper speculate how the writers of the chemical article included in the readings for this chapter would react to Hoffmann's discussion about the language of scientific writing. Create a dialogue between Hoffmann and these other writers in which each side attempts to justify the need for a certain writing style.

3. Hoffmann argues that too often scientists "suppress their humanity in the way they express themselves in print." Is this true only for scientists, or are writers from other disciplines also capable of doing the same thing? Look through the readings from other disciplines represented in this book, and select some examples that support Hoffmann's critique. How might the authors of these readings justify their writing styles?

T. H. Huxley
THINKING LIKE A SCIENTIST

Thomas Huxley (1825–1895) was a well-known scientist and educator. He was a defender of Darwin's theory of evolution and was concerned with educating England's nonscientific audience about the values of science. He reformed the organization of the English school system. In the following essay, Huxley argues against the popular belief that scientists think differently from everyone else.

The method of scientific investigation is nothing but the expression of the necessary mode of working of the human mind. It is simply the mode at which all phenomena are reasoned about, rendered precise and exact. There is no more difference, but there is just the same kind of difference, between the mental operations of a man of science and those of an ordinary person, as there is between the operations and methods of a baker or of a butcher weighing out his goods in common scales, and the operations of a chemist in performing a difficult and complex analysis by means of his balance and finely-graduated weights. It is not that the action of the scales in the one case, and the balance in the other, differ in the principles of their construction or manner of working; but the beam of one is set on an infinitely finer axis than the other, and of course turns by the addition of a much smaller weight.

You will understand this better, perhaps, if I give you some familiar example. You have all heard it repeated, I dare say, that men of science work by means of induction and deduction, and that by the help of these operations, they, in a sort of sense, wring from Nature certain other things, which are called natural laws, and causes, and that out of these, by some cunning skill of their own, they build up hypotheses and theories. And it is imagined by many, that the operations of the common mind can be by no means compared with these processes, and that they have to be acquired by a sort of special apprenticeship to the craft. To hear all these large words, you would think that the mind of a man of science must be constituted differently from that of his fellow man; but if you will not be frightened by terms, you will discover that you are quite wrong, and that all these terrible apparatus are being used by yourselves every day and every hour of your lives.

There is a well-known incident in one of Molière's plays, where the author makes the hero express unbounded delight on being told that he had been talking prose during the whole of his life. In the same way, I trust, that you will take comfort, and be delighted with yourselves, on the discovery that you have been acting on the principle of inductive and deductive philosophy during the same period. Probably there is not one here who has not in the course of the day had occasion to set in motion a complex train of reasoning, of the very same kind, though differing of course in degree, as that which a scientific man goes through in tracing the causes of natural phenomena.

A very trivial circumstance will serve to exemplify this. Suppose you go into a fruiterer's shop, wanting an apple, — you take up one, and, on biting it, you find it is sour; you look at it, and see that it is hard and green. You take up another one, and that too is hard, green, and sour. The shopman offers you a third; but, before biting it, you examine it, and find that it is hard and green, and you immediately say that you will not have it, as it must be sour, like those that you have already tried.

Nothing can be more simple than that, you think; but if you will take the trouble to analyse and trace out into its logical elements what has been done by the mind, you will be greatly surprised. In the first place, you have performed the operation of induction. You found that, in two experiences, hardness and greenness in apples went together with sourness. It was so in the first case, and it was confirmed by the second. True, it is a very small basis, but still it is enough to make an induction from; you generalise the facts, and you expect to find sourness in apples where you get hardness and greenness. You found upon that a general law, that all hard and green apples are sour; and that, so far as it goes, is a perfect induction. Well, having got your natural law in this way, when you are offered another apple which you find is hard and green, you say, "All hard and green apples are sour; this apple is hard and green, therefore this apple is sour." That train of reasoning is what logicians call a syllogism, and has all its various parts and terms, — its major premiss, its minor premiss, and its conclusion. And, by the help of further reasoning, which, if drawn out, would have to be exhibited in two or three other syllogisms, you arrive at your final determination, "I will not have that apple." So that, you see, you have, in the first place, established a law by induction, and upon that you have founded a deduction, and reasoned out the special conclusion of the particular case. Well now, suppose, having got your law, that at some time afterwards, you are discussing the qualities of apples with a friend: you will say to him, "It is a very curious thing, — but I find that all hard and green apples are sour!" Your friend says to you, "But how do you know that?" You at once reply, "Oh, because I have tried them over and over again, and have always found them to be so." Well, if we were talking science instead of common sense, we should call that an experimental verification. And, if still opposed, you go further, and say, "I have heard from the people in Somersetshire and Devonshire, where a large number of apples are grown, that they have observed the same thing. It is also found to be the case in Normandy, and in North America. In short, I find it to be the universal experience of mankind wherever attention has been directed to the subject." Whereupon, your friend, unless he is a very unreasonable man, agrees with you, and is convinced that you are quite right in the conclusion you have drawn. He believes, although perhaps he does not know he believes it, that the more extensive verifications are,—that the more frequently experiments have been made, and results of the same kind arrived at,—that the more varied the conditions under which the same results are attained, the more certain is the ultimate conclusion, and he disputes the question no further. He sees that the experiment has been tried under all sorts of conditions, as to time, place, and people, with the same result; and he says with you, therefore, that the law you have laid down must be a good one, and he must believe it.

In science we do the same thing;—the philosopher exercises precisely the same faculties, though in a much more delicate manner. In scientific inquiry it becomes a matter of duty to expose a supposed law to every possible kind of verification, and to take care, moreover, that this is done intentionally, and not left to a mere accident, as in the case of the apples. And in science, as in common life, our confidence in a law is in exact proportion to the absence of variation in the result of our experimental verifications. For instance, if you let go your grasp of an article you may have in your hand, it will immediately fall to the ground. That is a very common verification of one of the best established laws of nature—that of gravitation. The method by which men of science establish the existence of that law is exactly the same as that by which we have established the trivial proposition about the sourness of hard and green apples. But we believe it in such an extensive, thorough, and unhesitating manner because the universal experience of mankind verifies it, and we can verify it ourselves at any time; and that is the strongest possible foundation on which any natural law can rest.

So much, then, by way of proof that the method of establishing laws in science is exactly the same as that pursued in common life. Let us now turn to another matter (though really it is but another phase of the same question), and that is, the method by which, from the relations of certain phenomena, we prove that some stand in the position of causes towards the others.

I want to put the case clearly before you, and I will therefore show you what I mean by another familiar example. I will suppose that one of you, on coming down in the morning to the parlour of your house, finds that a tea-pot and some spoons which had been left in the room on the previous evening are gone, — the window is open, and you observe the mark of a dirty hand on the window-frame, and perhaps, in addition to that, you notice the impress of a hob-nailed shoe on the gravel outside. All these phenomena have struck your attention instantly, and before two seconds have passed you say, "Oh, somebody has broken open the window, entered the room, and run off with the spoons and the tea-pot!" That speech is out of your mouth in a moment. And you will probably add, "I know there has; I am quite sure of it!" You mean to say exactly what you know; but in reality you are giving expression to what is, in all essential particulars, an hypothesis. You do not *know* it at all; it is nothing but an hypothesis rapidly framed in your own mind. And it is an hypothesis founded on a long train of inductions and deductions.

What are those inductions and deductions, and how have you got at this hypothesis? You have observed, in the first place, that the window is open; but by a train of reasoning involving many inductions and deductions, you have probably arrived long before at the general law — and a very good one it is — that windows do not open of themselves; and you therefore conclude that something has opened the window. A second general law that you have arrived at in the same way is, that tea-pots and spoons do not go out of a window spontaneously, and you are satisfied that, as they are not now where you left them, they have been removed. In the third place, you look at the marks on the window-sill, and the shoe-marks outside, and you say that in all previous experience the former kind of mark has never been produced by anything else but the hand of a human being; and the same experience shows that no other animal but man at present wears shoes with hob-nails in them such as would produce the marks in the gravel. I do not know, even if we could discover any of those "missing links" that are talked about, that they would help us to any other conclusion! At any rate the law which states our present experience is strong enough for my present purpose. You next reach the conclusion, that as these kinds of marks have not been left by any other animals than men, or are liable to be formed in any other way than by a man's hand and shoe, the marks in question have been formed by a man in that way. You have, further, a general law, founded on observation and experience, and that, too, is, I am sorry to say, a very universal and unimpeachable one, — that some men are thieves; and you assume at once from all these premises — and that is what constitutes your hypothesis — that the man who made the marks outside and on the window-sill, opened the window, got into the room, and stole your tea-pot and spoons. You have now arrived at a *vera causa*; — you have assumed a cause which, it is plain, is competent to produce all the phenomena you have observed. You can explain all these phenomena only by the hypothesis of a thief. But that is a hypothetical conclusion, of the justice of which you have no absolute proof at all; it is only rendered highly probable by a series of inductive and deductive reasonings.

I suppose your first action, assuming that you are a man of ordinary common sense, and that you have established this hypothesis to your own satisfaction, will very likely be to go off for the police, and set them on the track of the burglar, with the view to the recovery of your property. But just as you are starting with this object, some person comes in, and on learning what you are about, says, "My good friend, you are going on a great deal too fast. How do you know that the man who really made the marks took the spoons? It might have been a monkey that took them, and the man may have merely looked in afterwards." You would probably reply, "Well, that is all very well, but you see it is contrary to all experience of the way tea-pots and spoons are abstracted; so that, at any rate, your hypothesis is less probable than mine." While you are talking the thing over in this way, another friend arrives, one of that good kind of people that I was talking of a little while ago. And he might say, "Oh, my dear sir, you are certainly going on a great deal too fast. You are most presumptuous. You admit that all these occurrences took place when you were fast asleep, at a time when you could not possibly have known anything about what was taking place. How do you know that the laws of Nature are not suspended during the night? It may be that there has been some kind of supernatural interference in this case." In point of fact, he declares that your hypothesis is one of which you cannot at all demonstrate the truth, and that you are by no means sure that the laws of Nature are the same when you are asleep as when you are awake.

Well, now, you cannot at the moment answer that kind of reasoning. You feel that your worthy friend has you somewhat at a disadvantage. You will feel perfectly convinced in your own mind, however, that you are quite right, and you say to him, "My good friend, I can only be guided by the natural probabilities of the case, and if you will be kind enough to stand aside and permit me to pass, I will go and fetch the police." Well, we will suppose that your journey is successful, and that by good luck you meet with a policeman; that eventually the burglar is found with your property on his person, and the marks correspond to his hand and to his boots. Probably any jury would consider those facts a very good experimental verification of your hypothesis, touching the cause of the abnormal phenomena observed in your parlour, and would act accordingly.

Now, in this suppositious case, I have taken phenomena of a very common kind, in order that you might see what are the different steps in an ordinary process of reasoning, if you will only take the trouble to analyse it carefully. All the operations I have described, you will see, are involved in the mind of any man of sense in leading him to a conclusion as to the course he should take in order to make good a robbery and punish the offender. I say that you are led, in that case, to your conclusion by exactly the same train of reasoning as that which a man of science pursues when he is endeavouring to discover the origin and laws of the most occult phenomena. The process is, and always must be, the same; and precisely the same mode of reasoning was employed by Newton and Laplace in their endeavours to discover and define the causes of the movements of the heavenly bodies, as you, with your own common sense, would employ to detect a burglar. The only difference is, that the nature of the inquiry being more abstruse, every step has to be most carefully watched, so that there may not be a single crack or flaw in your hypothesis. A flaw or crack in many of the hypotheses of daily life may be of little or no moment as affecting the general correctness of the conclusions at which we may arrive; but, in a scientific inquiry, a fallacy, great or small, is always of importance, and is sure to be in the long run constantly productive of mischievous, if not fatal results.

Do not allow yourselves to be misled by the common notion that an hypothesis is untrustworthy simply because it is an hypothesis. It is often urged, in respect to some scientific conclusion, that, after all, it is only an hypothesis. But what more have we to guide us in nine-tenths of the most important affairs of daily life than hypotheses, and often very ill-based ones? So that in science, where the evidence of an hypothesis is subjected to the most rigid examination, we may rightly pursue the same course. You may have hypotheses and hypotheses. A man may say, if he likes, that the moon is made of green cheese: that is an hypothesis. But another man, who has devoted a great deal of time and attention to the subject, and availed himself of the observations of others, declares that in his opinion it is probably composed of materials very similar to those of which our own earth is made up: and that is also only an hypothesis. But I need not tell you that there is an enormous difference in the value of the two hypotheses. That one which is based on sound scientific knowledge is sure to have a corresponding value; and that which is a mere hasty random guess is likely to have but little value. Every great step in our progress in discovering causes has been made in exactly the same way as that which I have detailed to you. A person observing the occurrence of certain facts and phenomena asks, naturally enough, what process, what kind of operation known to occur in Nature applied to the particular case, will unravel and explain the mystery? Hence you have the scientific hypothesis; and its value will be proportionate to the care and completeness with which its basis had been tested and verified. It is in these matters as in the commonest affairs of practical life: the guess of the fool will be folly, while the guess of the wise man will contain wisdom. In all cases, you see that the value of the result depends on the patience and faithfulness with which the investigator applies to his hypothesis every possible kind of verification.

OPTIONS FOR WRITING

1. How many of the disciplines described in this book require the use of some type of scientific activity? List the disciplines that do, and explain why this is so. Then list those that do not, and justify your selection.

2. Huxley argues that scientists think the same way as the rest of us: "The method of scientific investigation is nothing but the expression of the necessary mode of working of the human mind." Choose any experience that occurred to you today—nothing significant, but ordinary and commonplace. How might Huxley, using the language of inductive and deductive reasoning, interpret this event in the context of his belief that we are all scientists?

3. Compare Huxley's definition of hypothesis to the one offered earlier in this chapter, before the readings. In a short paper discuss which of the two definitions is more definitive.

B. DeCroix, M. J. Strauss, A. DeFusco, and D. C. Palmer
PTERIDINES FROM α-PHENYL-N,N-DI-METHYLACETAMIDINE

Bernard DeCroix and Michael Strauss are chemists at the University De Rouen and the University of Vermont, respectively. Albert De-Fusco and David Palmer were graduate students at the University of Vermont when this article was written. They are now working in the chemical industry. This article is a complex study in organic chemistry, and you do not need to read it for its content. It is more important that you study the form of this piece and consider the manner in which it was constructed. It would be appropriate to read the essay by Roald Hoffmann before looking at this technical piece.

A new synthesis of pteridines from the reaction of chloronitropyrimidines and α-phenyl-substituted amidines is described. It is a useful method for preparing 4-substituted-6-phenyl-7-(N,N-dimethylamino)pteridines. The route complements the synthesis of pteridines from nitrosoaminopyrimidines and arylacetonitriles first described by Timmis and Spickett and developed by Pachter and his colleagues at Smith, Kline, and French Laboratories. The synthesis and reactions of 4-oxygen-substituted 6-phenyl-7-(N,N-dimethylamino)pteridines resulting from reactions of nitrochloropyrimidines and α-phenylamidines are also summarized. The competition between S_NAr displacement and intramolecular cyclization reactions of the pyrimidine precursors is also discussed.

In several previous studies we have reported the use of amidines in preparing benzazocine, indole, benzoquinoline, quinoline, isoquinoline, quinoxaline, and imidazoquinoxaline ring systems. These reactions in-

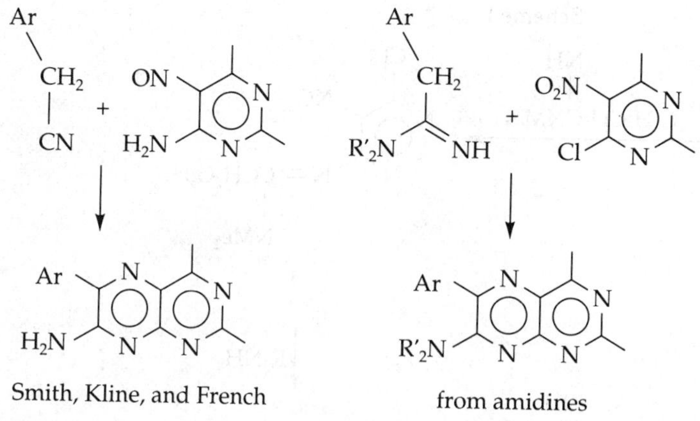

Smith, Kline, and French   from amidines

Figure 11.5

volve nucleophilic annelation of a C–C–N fragment from the amidine on appropriate tri- and dinitro aromatic compounds. The reactions occur in two stages: nucleophilic addition or displacement followed by cyclization on the ring or an adjacent substituent. (See Figure 11.5.)

Although pyrimidines are less reactive toward nucleophiles, we expected that amidine annelation on such substrates in an appropriate fashion could lead to pteridine *N*-oxides and provide a new and useful route to pteridines. Such a synthesis complements the route from nitrosoaminopyrimidines and arylacetonitriles first described by Spickett and Timmis and developed by Pachter and his colleagues at Smith, Kline, and French Laboratories.

One feature of the amidine preparation makes it particularly useful. Since 7-amino functionality in pteridines prepared from nitrosoaminopyrimidines is derived from the nitrile, only primary amino groups will result at C-7 of the product. The amidine route can lead to 4-amino-7-(*N*,*N*-dialkylamino)pteridines. These types of compounds, as well as 4-(*N*-substituted)-7-(*N*,*N* disubstituted)pteridines, are reported here.

The sequence of reactions leading to a series of 4-substituted-6-phenyl-7-(*N*,*N*-dimethylamino)pteridines, **6**, is outlined in Scheme I. (See Figure 11.6.) Reaction of commercially available 4,6-dichloro-5-nitro-pyrimidine, **1** (Aldrich), with ammonia in ethanol yields 4-amino-5-nitro-6-chloropyrimidine, **2**, and a trace of the diamino compound **7**. Compound **2** reacts readily with 2 equiv of α-phenyl-*N*,*N*-dimethylacetamidine to give the substitution product **4a** and 1 equiv of amidine hydrochloride. Compound **2** is not particularly stable, however, and the yield of **4a** is not high (see Experimental Section). Cyclization of **4a** in ethanolic ethoxide gives a good yield of **5a**, however, and upon reduction with dithionite the pteridine **6a** is formed.

The mechanism for the cyclization step is probably similar to that which we have previously proposed for the formation of quinoxaline

Scheme I

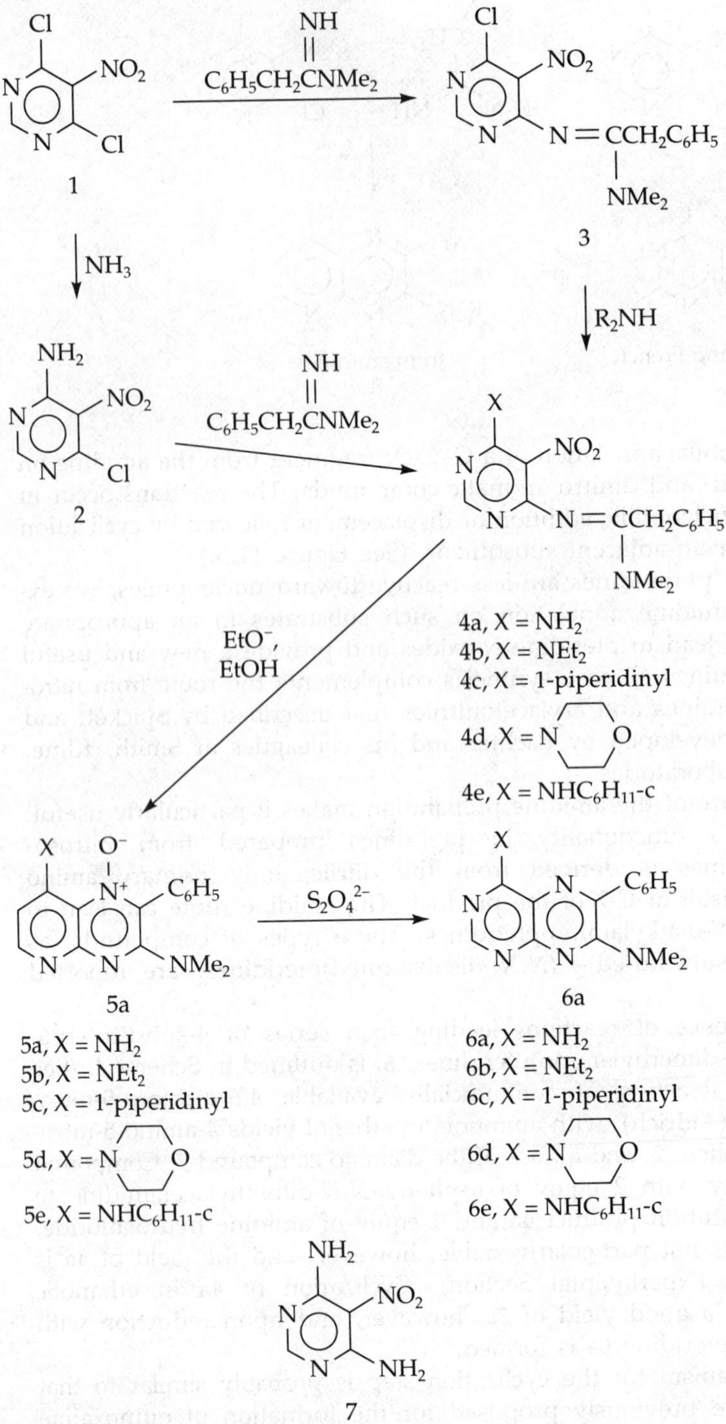
NH
$C_6H_5CH_2CNMe_2$
1
3
NH_3
R_2NH
2
EtO^-, EtOH
$4a, X = NH_2$
$4b, X = NEt_2$
4c, X = 1-piperidinyl
4d, X = N O
$4e, X = NHC_6H_{11}$-c
$S_2O_4^{2-}$
5a
6a
$5a, X = NH_2$
$5b, X = NEt_2$
5c, X = 1-piperidinyl
5d, X = N O
$5e, X = NHC_6H_{11}$-c
$6a, X = NH_2$
$6b, X = NEt_2$
6c, X = 1-piperidinyl
6d, X = N O
$6e, X = NHC_6H_{11}$-c
7

Figure 11.6

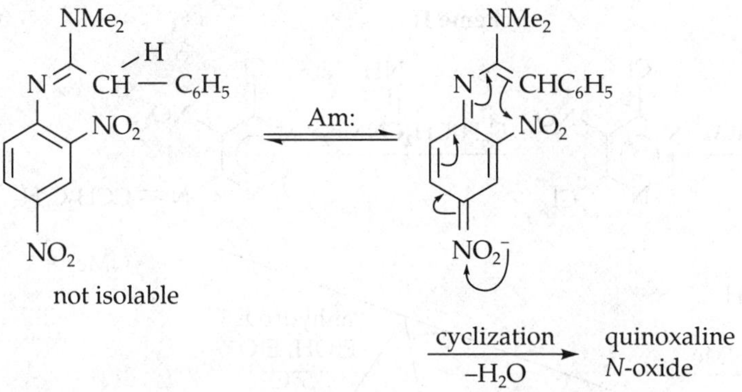

Figure 11.7

N-oxides from reaction of halo dinitro aromatic compounds and amidines. (See Figure 11.7.) Two significant differences are that the initial displacement product **3** is isolable and that strong base is required to cyclize it. Reaction of 1-fluoro-2,4-dinitrobenzene (DNFB) with α-phenyl-*N,N*-dimethylacetamidine gives only the cyclic quinoxaline *N*-oxide product even in the absence of added base. Formation of pteridine *N*-oxides **5a–e** probably occurs as shown in Figure 11.8.

The acidity of the amidine side chain in **4** may in part determine the ease with which cyclization occurs. In an aromatic ring bearing only electron-withdrawing groups (i.e., the product from DNFB and amidine), the amidine methylene is much more acidic. Tautomerization is facile, and rapid cyclization occurs *without added base*. There is another important factor which may contribute to the stability of **4** relative to its dinitrophenyl analogue. The amino group adjacent to the nitro group undergoing attack during cyclization of **4** may reduce the electrophilicity of the nitro group nitrogen sufficiently so that attack occurs only when the nucleophile bears a full negative charge (hence the necessity of added ethoxide).

In order to further clarify the way in which formation of pteridine *N*-oxides occurs, we have qualitatively studied the competition between cyclization of and S$_N$Ar displacement of halogen in **3**. The amines used to displace chloride from **3** in the preparation of **4** (Scheme I) were not

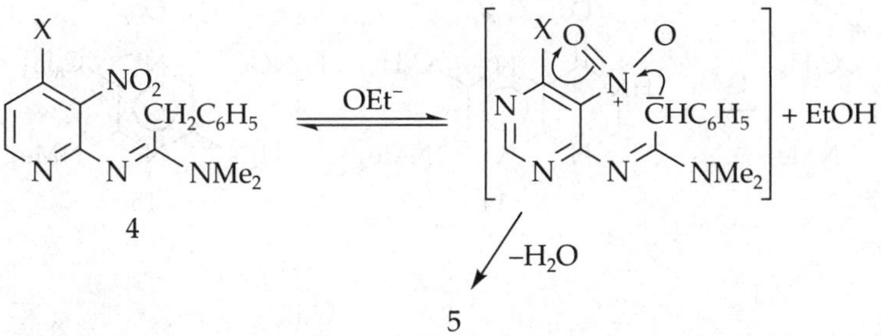

Figure 11.8

Scheme II

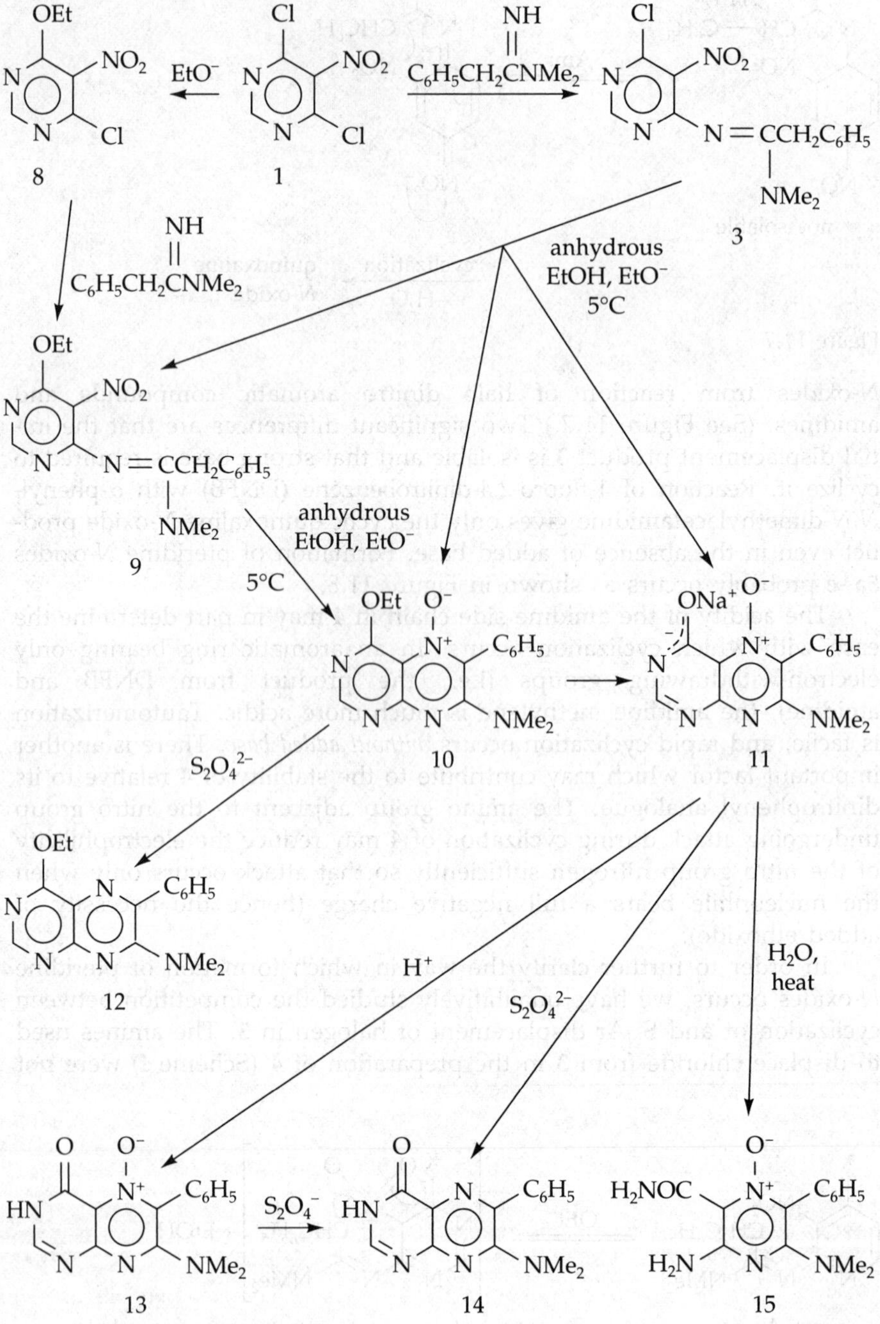

Figure 11.9

sufficiently basic to cause cyclization, and no trace of **5** could be found in the product **4**. On the other hand, treating **3** with ethoxide could result in either displacement of chloride or cyclization or both. The results of such a reaction, as well as further transformations to be described, are summarized in Scheme II. (See Figure 11.9.)

Treatment of **3** with 1 equiv of ethoxide in anhydrous ethanol yields a complex mixture. The composition of this mixture varies depending upon how long the reaction is allowed to stand before workup. After 2 days, the major product is **11**, mixed with sodium chloride which is not easily separated. Acidification of this product yields the pure pteridine *N*-oxide **13** which is easily reduced to pteridine **14** with dithionite. An additional confirmation of structure **11** is the pyrazine *N*-oxide hydrolysis product **15** which results from heating **11** in boiling water for several hours.

Interestingly, if the reaction of **3** with ethoxide is worked up after only 20 min a good yield of a mixture of the substitution product **9**, the substitution–cyclization product **10**, and the cyclized hydrolysis product **11** is obtained. These products could be separated and purified. Compound **9** is converted to **10** by ethoxide at 5 °C (workup after 20 min), and **10** could be easily reduced to the pteridine **12**. Compound **9** was also prepared by reacting **1** with ethoxide to yield **8**. Treatment of **8** with amidine gave a good yield of **9**, identical in all respects with the product resulting from reaction of **3** and ethoxide. Interestingly, reaction of **3** with 2 equiv of ethoxide at 5 °C yields a mixture of **10** and **11** with no contamination by **9**.

It seems clear from the reactions summarized in Scheme II that **9** and **10** are converted to **11** by ethoxide and/or water. Since no cyclized product which contains chlorine, i.e., **16** (see Figure 11.10), can be isolated, it is possible to conclude that S_NAr displacement by ethoxide occurs before cyclization. This is not necessarily true, however, since the chlorine in **16** may be much more susceptible to nucleophilic attack than that in **3** because of the adjacent activating *N*-oxide moiety. Thus, **16**, if formed by a rapid cyclization, could even more rapidly be converted to **10**. A detailed quantitative study of the rate of conversion of **9** to **10** as well as **3** to **9** and **10** would answer this question. Although the reactions were carried out in anhydrous ethanol, hydroxide ion must eventually form from the elimination-aromatization to the *N*-oxides **5**. This

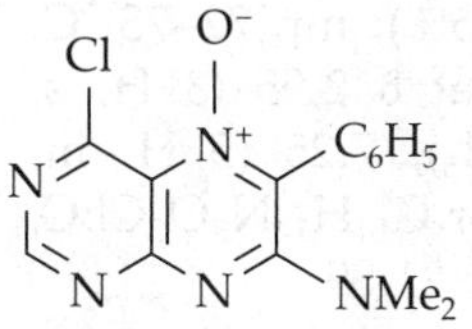

16

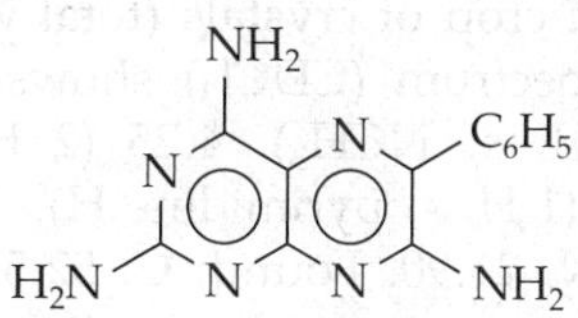

triamterene

Figure 11.10   Figure 11.11

hydroxide is probably the nucleophile responsible for formation of **11**. Another possibility is contamination by small amounts of water, although considerable attention was given to carrying out these reactions under anhydrous conditions.

Compounds similar to **6, 12,** and **14** have substantial diuretic activity, and we expect that the pteridines reported here will also be diuretics. There is still considerable interest in developing potassium-sparing diuretics like triamterene. (See Figure 11.11.) We will report the results of biological testing elsewhere.

EXPERIMENTAL SECTION

All melting points are uncorrected. ^{1}H NMR spectra were run on JEOL C-60 HL and MH-100 spectrometers with Me$_4$Si as an internal reference. Visible and ultraviolet spectra were recorded on a Perkin-Elmer Model 402 UV-visible spectrophotometer. Infrared spectra were recorded on a Perkin-Elmer Model 237 B infrared spectrophotometer. Mass spectra were obtained on a Perkin-Elmer RMU-6D mass spectrometer. Elemental analyses were cross-checked by Galbraith Laboratories, Inc., Knoxville, TN, G. I. Robertson Laboratories, Florham Park, NJ, and Integral Microanalytical Laboratories, Inc., Raleigh, NC, and the analytical laboratories at the University of Rouen.

Compound **1** was obtained from Aldrich Chemical Co., and it was used without further purification. α-Phenyl-*N,N*-dimethylacetamidine was prepared as described previously.

Preparation of 3.   A solution of 3.07 g (0.018 mol) α-phenyl-*N,N*-dimethylacetamidine in 20 mL of dry chloroform was added in small portions to a rapidly stirred solution of 1.83 g (0.0095 mol) of 4,6-dichloro-5-nitropyrimidine in 20 mL of dry chloroform. After 5 days at room temperature, the chloroform was removed with a rotary evaporator, and the resulting oily solid was extracted with four small portions of dry ether (~5 mL each time). This ether was again filtered and evaporated, yielding an oil. About 4 mL of dry ethanol was added to the oil, and the product which rapidly crystallized was filtered off and then washed with dry ethanol. Concentration of the ethanolic filtrate yielded a second crop of crystals (total yield 1.67 g, 55%), mp 72–73 °C. The ^{1}H NMR spectrum (CDCl$_3$) shows absorptions at δ 2.95 (3 H, s, NCH$_3$), 3.10 (3H, s, NCH$_3$), 4.25 (2 H, s, CH$_2$C$_6$H$_5$), 7.25 (5 H, m, C$_6$H$_5$), and 8.45 (1 H, s, pyrimidine H). Anal. Calcd for C$_{14}$H$_{14}$N$_5$O$_2$Cl:C, 52.59; H, 4.41; N, 21.90. Found: C, 52.57; H, 4.42; N, 21.89.

Preparation of 4a.   This compound was prepared from the known 4-amino-5-nitro-6-chloropyrimidine by a procedure similar to that used

TABLE I.   Chemical Shifts (δ) in CDCl₃ and Elemental Analyses of 4b—e

	pyrimidine H	N(CH₃)₂	CH₂C₆H₅	C₆H₅	amine moiety
4b	8.21 s	2.95 s	4.10 s	7.25 s	1.15 (3 H, t), 3.40 (4 H, g)
4c	8.25 s	3.00 s	4.10 s	7.30 s	1.65 (6 H, s), 3.50 (4 H, s)
4d	8.30 s	3.00 s	4.15 s	7.35 s	3.55–3.75 (8 H, m)
4e	8.20 s	3.05 s	4.05 s	7.35 s	1.2–2.1 (10 H, m), 4.2 (1 H, m)

	theoretical, %			found, %		
	C	H	N	C	H	N
4b	60.66	6.78	23.58	60.62	6.73	23.85
4c	61.94	6.56	22.81	61.85	6.64	23.47
4d	58.37	5.98	22.69			
4e	62.81	6.84	21.97	62.17	6.85	22.38

for the preparation of **3** from **1**. The yellow crystalline product was obtained in 25% yield (0.51 g) from 1.25 g of pyrimidine starting material. It was recrystallized from a mixture of benzene and petroleum ether; mp 155–156 °C. The ¹H NMR spectrum (CDCl₃) shows absorption at δ 3.15 (6 H, s, N(CH₃)₂), 4.15 (2 H, s, C*H₂*C₆H₅), 7.35 (2 H, br s, NH₂), 7.50 (5 H, br s, C₆H₅), and 8.40 (1 H, s, pyrimidine H). Anal. Calcd for C₁₄H₁₆N₆O₂: C, 55.99; H, 5.36; N, 27.98. Found: C, 55.79; H, 5.78; N, 26.40. (It should be noted that we have occasionally had some difficulty in obtaining accurate analytical data for nitrogen from some laboratories on compounds where the values exceed 25%.)

In addition to isolating **4a**, an insoluble compound was obtained by filtering the hot solution of **4a** in the recrystallization step. This compound (0.140 g) had a melting point and IR and ¹H NMR spectra identical with those of a sample of 4,6-diamino-5-nitropyrimidine.

Preparation of 4b—e. Compound **3** (0.0015 mol) was dissolved in 10 mL of chloroform and cooled to 0–5 °C in an ice bath. A solution of 0.0031 mol of the amine in 5 mL of chloroform was added very slowly. After 24 h at room temperature, the solvent was removed under vacuum. The remaining yellow solid was washed with ethanol. The crude products were purified by recrystallization from ethanol. All of the compounds **4b–4e** were obtained in 70–80% yield. The melting points are as follows: **4b**, 101–102 °C; **4c**, 133–134 °C; **4d**, 173–175 °C; **4e**, 133–135 °C. The ¹H NMR spectra and elemental analyses are summarized in Table I.

Preparation of 5a–e. A freshly prepared solution of sodium ethoxide in ethanol (3.1 mL, 0.43 M) was added dropwise to a solution of **4a–e** (0.013 mol) in 50 mL of dry ethanol at room temperature. After 5 days, the solvent was removed under vacuum. About 4 mL of dry ethanol was added to the residue, and after the solution was permitted to stand for a few minutes, the yellow crystals which formed were filtered off. These were recrystallized from a benzene-petroleum ether mixture to give yields of **5** ranging from 60 to 80%. The melting points of the products are as follows: **5a**, 221–222 °C; **5b**, 169–170 °C; **5c**, 228–229 °C; **5d**, 237–238 °C; **5e**. 222–223 °C. The ¹H NMR spectra and elemental analyses are summarized in Table II.

Preparation of 6a–e. A mixture of **5** (0.0039 mol) and sodium dithionite (0.013 mol) in 20 mL of 50% aqueous ethanol was heated at ~100 °C for 2 h. The ethanol was then removed on a rotary evaporator, and the yellow crystals which remained in the aqueous mixture were filtered off. Extraction of the aqueous solution with chloroform and evaporation of this solvent gave an additional amount of **6**. The crude product was recrystallized from ethanol-water, providing **6a–e** in approximately 50% yield. The melting points of the products are as fol-

TABLE II.   Chemical Shifts (δ) in CDCl₃ and Elemental Analyses of 5a–e

	pteridine aromatic H	N(CH₃)₂	C₆H₅	amine moiety
5a	8.40 s	2.85 s	7.50 s	6.45 (1 H,br s), 9.30 (1 H, br s)
5b	8.35 s	2.90 s	7.45 s	1.30 (6 H, t), 3.65 (4 H, q)
5c	8.45 s	2.90 s	7.50 s	1.70 (6 H, br s), 3.65 (4 H, br s)
5d	8.45 s	2.90 s	7.45 s	3.80 (8 H, br s)
5e	8.45 s	2.85 s	7.50 s	1.2–2.1 (10 H, m), 4.15 (1 H, m), 10.1 (1 H, br s, NH)

	theoretical, %			found, %		
	C	H	N	C	H	N
5a	59.57	4.99	29.77	58.46	4.84	28.91
5b	63.89	6.55	24.83	63.97	6.85	23.96
5c	65.13	6.32	23.98	65.84	6.38	23.94
5d	61.35	5.72	23.85	62.07	5.84	24.18
5e	65.92	6.63	23.06	65.28	6.84	22.78

TABLE III.   Chemical Shifts (δ) in CDCl$_3$ and Elemental Analyses of 6a–e

	pteridine aromatic H	N(CH$_3$)$_2$	C$_6$H$_5$	amine moiety
6a	8.60 s	3.00 s	7.55 (m, 3 H), 7.80(m, 2 H)	6.55 (br s)
6b	8.55 s	3.00 s	7.40 (m, 3 H), 7.70 (m, 2 H)	1.35 (6 H, t), 4.00 (4 H, q)
6c	8.50 s	2.95 s	7.40 (m, 3 H), 7.70 (m, 2 H)	1.70 (6 H, s), 4.15 (4 H, s)
6d	8.55 s	3.00 s	7.45 (m, 3 H), 7.65 (m, 2 H)	3.85 (4 H, m), 4.35 (4 H, m)
6e	8.60 s	2.95 s	7.50 (m, 3 H), 7.75 (m, 2 H)	1.2–2.2 (10 H, m), 4.20 (1 H, br s), 6.60 (NH, br s)

	theoretical, %			found, %		
	C	H	N	C	H	N
6a	63.15	5.29	31.56	62.90	5.17	31.35
6b	67.06	6.87	26.07			
6c	68.24	6.62	25.13	68.91	6.90	25.40
6d	64.27	5.99	24.98	64.25	6.22	25.54
6e	68.94	6.94	24.12	68.60	6.80	24.41

lows: **6a**, 220–221 °C; **6b**, an oil which could not be recrystallized; **6c**, 157–158 °C; **6d**, 173–174 °C; **6e**, 175–176 °C. The ¹H/NMR spectra and elemental analyses are summarized in Table III.

Preparation of 8.   A freshly prepared solution of sodium ethoxide in ethanol (27.6 mL, 0.43 M) was added dropwise at 0 °C to a stirring solution of 1 (2.50 g, 0.0129 mol) in 20 mL of dry ethanol. After 24 h the sodium chloride was filtered off and the remaining ethanol was removed on a rotary evaporator. The remaining white solid was purified by sublimation to give white crystals, mp 46–47 °C, in ~20% yield. The ¹H NMR spectrum (CDCl$_3$) shows absorption at δ 1.45 (3 H, t, OCH$_2$CH$_3$), 4.65 (2 H, q, OCH$_2$CH$_3$), and 8.75 (1 H, s, pyrimidine H). Anal. Calcd for C$_6$H$_6$N$_3$ClO$_3$: C, 35.22; H, 2.95; N, 20.54. Found: C, 35.24; H, 2.93; N, 20.68.

Preparation of 9.   Compound **9** was prepared from **8** in the same manner as compound **3** was prepared from **1**, except that the reaction mixture was refluxed for 24 h. The yield of product, mp 107–108 °C, was ~60%. The ¹H NMR spectrum shows absorptions at δ 1.35 (3 H, t,

OCH_2CH_3), 3.00 (6 H, br s, $N(CH_3)_2$), 4.20 (2 H, s, $CH_2C_6H_5$), 4.50 (2 H, q, OCH_2CH_3), 7.30 (5 H, s, C_6H_5), and 8.40 (1 H, s, pyrimidine H). Anal. Calcd for $C_{16}H_{19}N_5O_3$: C, 58.35; H, 5.81; N, 21.26. Found: C, 58.08; H, 5.62; N, 20.99.

Preparation of 10, 11, 12, 13, and 14. A solution of sodium ethoxide in ethanol (4.6 mL, 0.43 M) was added dropwise to a solution of **3** (0.32 g, 0.001 mol) in 10 mL of ethanol at 5 °C. The reaction was kept at 5 °C during the addition. After 15 min at this temperature, the solvent was removed under vacuum and the remaining solid was washed with a small portion of dry ethanol. The resulting mixture of **10** and **11** could be separated by extracting the mixture with chloroform which dissolves **10**, leaving **11**. Evaporation of the chloroform provided crude **10** which was recrystallized from distilled water to give 0.135 g (43%) of yellow crystals, mp 195–196 °C. The residue which did not dissolve in chloroform (crude **11** and sodium chloride) was dissolved in water and acidified with 0.5 M HCl to pH 3–4. The acidic solution was extracted four times with small portions of chloroform. The chloroform was then removed under vacuum to yield the crude pteridine *N*-oxide **13** which was recrystallized from ethanol to give 0.045 g (16%) of pure **13**, mp 270–275 °C dec.

The ^{1}H NMR spectrum ($CDCl_3$) of **10** shows absorption at δ 1.50 (3 H, t, OCH_2CH_3), 2.90 (6 H, s, $N(CH_3)_2$), 4.60 (2 H, q, OCH_2CH_3), 7.50 (5 H, s, C_6H_5), and 8.65 (1 H, s, pteridine aromatic H). Anal. Calcd for $C_{16}H_{17}N_5O_2$: C, 61.73; H, 5.50; N, 22.49. Found: C, 61.51; H, 5.51; N, 22.29.

The ^{1}H NMR spectra ($Me_2SO\text{-}d_6$) of **13** shows absorptions at δ 2.70 (6 H, s, $N(CH_3)_2$), 7.45 (5 H, s, C_6H_5), 8.10 (1 H, s, pteridine aromatic H), and 12.10 (1 H, br, s, NH). In $CDCl_3$ these absorptions appear at δ 2.85, 7.45, 8.35, and 12.20, respectively.

When the reaction time exceeds 2 h, **3** yields **11**, contaminated only by a trace of **10**. Compound **10** can also be prepared by reaction of **9** with ethoxide. A solution of sodium ethoxide in ethanol (0.9 mL, 0.43 M) was added dropwise to a solution of **9** (0.115 g, 0.035 mol) in 5 mL of ethanol at 5 °C. After 3 h, the ethanol was removed under vacuum, and the solid residue was washed with ethanol and recrystallized from water to yield 60 mg of **10**. This product is identical in all respects with **10** prepared from **3**. If the reaction is allowed to stand for more than 3 h, increasing amounts of **11** are obtained.

Both **13** and **10** were easily reduced by dithionite to the corresponding pteridines **14** and **12**. These reductions were performed in the same fashion as described for reduction of the derivatives **5a–e**. Crude **12** was recrystallized from a mixture of benzene-petroleum ether to give a 50% yield of pure product, mp 105–106 °C. Crude **14** was recrystallized from water to also yield 50% of pure product, mp 275 °C dec. Compound **14** could also be prepared by treating crude **11**, contaminated by NaCl, with dithionite.

The ^{1}H NMR spectrum (CDCl$_3$ of **12** shows absorptions at δ 1.60 (3 H, t, OCH$_2$CH$_3$), 3.10 (6 H, s, N(CH$_3$)$_2$), 4.85 (2 H, q, OCH$_2$CH$_3$), 7.70 (3 H, m, C$_6$H$_5$), 7.95 (2 H, m, C$_6$H$_5$), and 8.95 (1 H, s, pteridine aromatic proton). Anal. Calcd for C$_{16}$H$_{17}$N$_5$O: C, 65.07; H, 5.79; N, 23.71. Found: C, 65.36; H, 6.03; N, 22.70.

The ^{1}H NMR spectrum (CDCl$_3$) of **14** shows absorptions at δ 3.10 (6 H, s, N(CH$_3$)$_2$), 7.60 (3 H, m, C$_6$H$_5$), 7.90 (2 H, m, C$_6$H$_5$), 8.45 (1 H, s, pteridine aromatic H), 12.90 (1 H, br, NH). Anal. Calcd for C$_{14}$H$_{13}$N$_5$O: C, 62.91; H, 4.90; N, 26.20. Found: C, 62.88; H, 4.70; N, 26.08.

Hydrolysis of 11 to 15. A suspension of compound **11** (0.30 g, 0.001 mol) in water (25 mL) was refluxed for 6 h. The reaction was cooled to room temperature, and the resulting yellow crystals were filtered off. Concentration of the filtrate provided a second crop of crystals for a total yield of 20% (0.055 g) of pure **15**, mp 193–197 °C. Anal. Calcd for C$_{13}$H$_{15}$N$_5$O$_2$: C, 57.12; H, 5.54; N, 25.63. Found: C, 56.76; H, 5.33; N, 24.84. The mass spectrum of this product shows a parent peak at m/e 273 as well as strong absorption at m/e 258, 241, 229, and 213. The ^{1}H NMR spectrum (Me$_2$SO-d$_6$) shows absorptions at δ 2.64 (6 H, s, N(CH$_3$)$_2$), 7.44 (5 H, m, C$_6$H$_5$), 7.88 (2 H, br s, ArNH$_2$), and 9.84 (2 H, br s, CONH$_2$).

Acknowledgment. The authors thank the North Atlantic Treaty Organization for support in the form of a postdoctoral award to B. De-Croix. We also thank the National Institutes of Health for a grant supporting this research (PHS-R01-00450-02). In addition, we acknowledge support from the NIGMS in the form of a Research Career Development Award to M. J. Strauss (PHS-K04-70714-05).

Registry No.— 1, 1, 4316-93-2; **2**, 4316-94-3; **3**, 69352-36-9; **4a**, 69331-05-1; **4b**, 69352-35-8; **4c**, 69331-06-2; **4d**, 69331-07-3; **4e**, 69331-08-4; **5a**, 69331-09-5; **5b**, 69352-34-7; **5c**, 69331-10-8; **5d**, 69331-11-9; **5e**, 69331-12-0; **6a**, 69331-13-1; **6b**, 69331-14-2; **6c**, 69331-15-3; **6d**, 69352-33-6; **6e**, 69331-16-4; **7**, 2164-84-3; **8**, 54851-36-4; **9**, 69331-17-5; **10**, 69331-18-6; **11**, 69331-19-7; **12**, 69331-20-0; **13**, 69331-19-7; **14**, 69331-21-1; **15**, 69331-22-2; α-phenyl-N,N-dimethylacetamidine, 56776-16-0; diethylamine, 109-89-7; piperidine, 110-89-4; morpholine, 110-91-8; cyclohexylamine, 108-91-8.

OPTIONS FOR WRITING

1. What makes this article so difficult to read? Why have the authors included graphics and pictures in this article? And in what ways do the graphic depictions contribute toward understanding the meaning of the article?

2. This article represents the fruits of a collaborative effort of four scientists working and writing together. Such joint effort often occurs in the publication of scientific papers. Why?

3. Consider this article in light of what Hoffmann says about scientific writing. In what ways does this article conform to Hoffmann's thesis on language use, style, and the other elements he associates with scholarship in science? Why do scientists choose to write in such a manner?

Owen Barfield
SAVING THE APPEARANCES: A STUDY IN IDOLATRY

Owen Barfield (b. 1898) was a philosopher and scholar of language and thought, interested in the meaning of words and the evolution of consciousness. He had a lifelong interest in the relationship between science and religion, which is reflected in the books and articles he wrote. In Saving the Appearances: A Study in Idolatry, *he describes the differences between normal human consciousness and the mind of the scientist in understanding worldly phenomena — the appearances. In the first few short chapters that follow, "The Rainbow," "Collective Representation," and "Figuration and Thinking," Barfield examines the nature of perception and its relationship to thinking about what is perceived.*

THE RAINBOW

Look at a rainbow. While it lasts, it is, or appears to be, a great arc of many colours occupying a position out there in space. It touches the horizon between that chimney and that tree; a line drawn from the sun behind you and passing through your head would pierce the centre of the circle of which it is part. And now, before it fades, recollect all you have ever been told about the rainbow and its causes, and ask yourself the question *Is it really there*?

You know, from memory, that if there were a hillside three or four miles nearer than the present horizon, the rainbow would come to earth in front of and not behind it; that, if you walked to the place where the rainbow ends, or seems to end, it would certainly not be "there." In a word, reflection will assure you that the rainbow is the outcome of the sun, the raindrops and your own vision.

When I ask of an intangible appearance or representation, Is it really there? I usually mean, Is it there independently of my vision? Would it still be there, for instance, if I shut my eyes — if I moved towards or away from it. If this is what you also mean by "really there," you will be tempted to add that the raindrops and the sun are really there, but the rainbow is not.

Does it follow that, as soon as anybody sees a rainbow, there "is" one, or, in other words, that there is no difference between an hallucination or a madman's dream of a rainbow (perhaps on a clear day) and an actual rainbow? Certainly not. You were not the only one to see the rainbow. You had a friend with you. (I forbear asking if you both saw "the same" rainbow, because this is a book about history rather than metaphysics, and these introductory chapters are merely intended to clear away certain misconceptions.) Moreover, through the medium of language, you are well aware that thousands of others have seen rainbows in showery weather; but you have never heard of any sane person claiming to have seen one on a sunless or a cloudless day. Therefore, if a man tells you he sees a rainbow on a cloudless day, then, even if you are convinced that he means what he says, and is not simply lying, you will confidently affirm that the rainbow he sees is "not there."

In short, as far as being really there or not is concerned, the practical difference between a dream or hallucination of a rainbow and an actual rainbow is that, although each is a representation or appearance (that is, something which I perceive to be there), the second is a *shared* or collective representation.

Now look at a tree. It is very different from a rainbow. If you approach it, it will still be "there." Moreover, in this case, you can do more than look at it. You can hear the noise its leaves make in the wind. You can perhaps smell it. You can certainly touch it. Your senses combine to assure you that it is composed of what is called solid matter. Accord to the tree the same treatment that you accorded to the rainbow. Recollect all you have been told about matter and its ultimate structure and ask yourself if the tree is "really there." I am far from affirming dogmatically that the atoms, electrons, nuclei, etc., of which wood, and all matter, is said to be composed, are particular and identifiable objects like drops of rain. But if the "particles" (as I will here call them for convenience) *are* there, and are all that is there, then, since the "particles" are no more like the thing I call a tree than the raindrops are like the thing I call a rainbow, it follows, I think, that—just as a rainbow is the outcome of the raindrops and my vision—so, a tree is the outcome of the particles and my vision and my other sense-perceptions. Whatever the particles themselves may be thought to be, the tree, as such, is a representation. And the difference, for me, between a tree and a complete hallucination of a tree is the same as the difference between a rainbow and an hallucination of a rainbow. In other words, a tree which is "really there" is a collective representation. The fact that a dream tree differs in kind from a real tree, and that it is just silly to try and mix them up, is indeed rather literally a matter of "common sense."

This background of particles is of course presumed in the case of raindrops themselves, no less than in that of trees. The relation, *raindrops: rainbow*, is a picture or analogy, not an instance, of the relation, *particles: representation.*

Or again, if anyone likes to press the argument still further and maintain that what is true of the drops must also be true of the particles themselves, and that there is "no such thing as an extra-mental reality," I shall not quarrel with him, but I shall leave him severely alone; because, as I say, this is not a book about metaphysics, and I have no desire to demonstrate that trees or rainbows — or particles — are not "really there" — a proposition which perhaps has not much meaning. This book is not being written because the author desires to put forward a theory of perception, but because it seems to him that certain wide consequences flowing from the hastily expanded sciences of the nineteenth and twentieth centuries, and in particular their physics, have not been sufficiently considered in building up the general twentieth-century picture of the nature of the universe and of the history of the earth and man.

A better term than "particles" would possibly be "the unrepresented," since anything particular which amounts to a representation will always attract further physical analysis. Moreover, the atoms, protons and electrons of modern physics are now perhaps more generally regarded, not as particles, but as notional models or symbols of an unknown supersensible or subsensible base. All I seek to establish in these opening paragraphs is, that, whatever may be thought about the "unrepresented" background of our perceptions, the *familiar* world which we see and know around us — the blue sky with white clouds in it, the noise of a waterfall or a motor-bus, the shapes of flowers and their scent, the gesture and utterance of animals and the faces of our friends — the world too, which (apart from the special inquiry of physics) experts of all kinds methodically investigate — is a system of collective representations. The time comes when one must either accept this as the truth about the world or reject the theories of physics as an elaborate delusion. We cannot have it both ways.

COLLECTIVE REPRESENTATIONS

A representation is something I perceive to be there. By premising that the everyday world is a system of collective representations, it may be thought that we blur the distinction between the fancied and the actual or, following the everyday use of language, between the apparently there and the really there. But this is not so. It only seems to be so because of the very great emphasis which — especially in the last three or four hundred years — the Western Mind has come to lay on the ingredient of spatial depth in the total complex of its perception. I shall return to this later.

As to what is meant by "collective" — any discrepancy between my representations and those of my fellow men raises a presumption of unreality and calls for explanation. If, however, the explanation is satisfactory; if, for instance, it turns out that the discrepancy was due, not to my hallucination, but to their myopia or their dullness, it is likely to be accepted; and then my representation may itself end by becoming collective.

It is, however, not necessary to maintain that collectivity is the *only* test for distinguishing between a representation and a collective representation (though, to creatures for whom insanity is round the corner, it is often likely to be the crucial one).

I am hit violently on the head and, in the same moment, perceive a bright light to be there. Later on I reflect that the light was "not really there." Even if I had lived all my life on a desert island where there was no-one to compare notes with, I might do as much. No doubt I should learn by experience to distinguish the first kind of light from the more practicable light of day or the thunderbolt, and should soon give up hitting myself on the head at sunset when I needed light to go on working by. In both cases I perceive light, but the various criteria of difference between them—duration, for instance, and a sharp physical pain, which the one involves and the other does not, are not difficult to apprehend.

What is required, is not to go on stressing the resemblance between collective representations and private representations, but to remember, when we leave the world of everyday for the discipline of any strict inquiry, that, *if* the particles, or the unrepresented, are in fact all that is *independently* there, then the world we all accept as real is in fact a system of collective representations.

Perception takes place by means of sense-organs, though the ingredient in it of sensation, experienced as such, varies greatly as between the different senses. In touch I suppose we come nearest to sensation without perception; in sight to perception without sensation. But the two most important things to remember about perception are these: *first*, that we must not confuse the percept with its cause. I do not hear undulating molecules of air; the name of what I hear is *sound*. I do not touch a moving system of waves or of atoms and electrons with relatively vast empty spaces between them; the name of what I touch is *matter*. *Second*, I do not perceive any *thing* with my sense-organs alone, but with a great part of my whole human being. Thus, I may say, loosely, that I "hear a thrush singing." But in strict truth all that I ever merely "hear"—all that I ever hear simply by virtue of having ears—is *sound*. when I "hear a thrush singing," I am hearing, not with my ears alone, but with all sorts of other things like mental habits, memory, imagination, feeling and (to the extent at least that the act of attention involves it) will. Of a man who merely heard in the first sense, it could meaningfully be said that "having ears" (i.e. not being deaf) "he heard not."

I do not think either of these two maxims depends on any particular theory of the nature of perception. They are true for any theory of perception I ever heard of—with the possible exception of Bishop Berkeley's. They are true, whether we accept the Aristotelian and medieval conception of form and matter, or the Kantian doctrine of the forms of perception, or the theory of specific sense-energy, or the "primary imagination" of Coleridge, or the phenomenology that underlies Existentialism, or some wholly unphilosophical system of physiology and psychology. On almost any received theory of perception the familiar world — that is, the world which is apprehended, not through instruments and inference, but simply — is for the most part dependent upon the percipient.

FIGURATION AND THINKING

In the conversion of raindrops into a rainbow, or (if you prefer it) the production of a rainbow out of them, the *eye* plays a no less indispensable part than the sunlight — or than the drops themselves. In the same way, for the conversion of the unrepresented into a representation, at least one sentient organism is as much a *sine qua non* as the unrepresented itself; and for the conversion of the unrepresented into representations even remotely resembling our everyday world, at least one nervous system organized about a spinal cord culminating in a brain, is equally indispensable. The rainbow analogy does not imply, nor is it intended to suggest, that the solid globe is as insubstantial as a rainbow. The solid globe is solid. The rainbow is not. Only it is important to know what we mean by solidity. More than that, it is necessary to remember what we meant by solidity in one context, when we go on to use the word or think the thing in another.

It is easy to appreciate that there is no such thing as an unseen rainbow. It is not so easy to grasp that there is no such thing as an unheard noise. Or rather it is easy to grasp, but difficult to keep hold of. And this is still more the case, when we come to the sense of touch. Obvious as it may be to reflection that a system of waves or quanta or discrete particles is no more like solid matter than waves of air are like sound, or raindrops like a rainbow, it is not particularly easy to grasp, and it is almost impossible to keep in mind, that there is no such thing as unfelt solidity.[1] It is much more convenient, when we are listening for example to the geologist, to forget what we learnt about matter from the chemist and the physicist. But it really will not do. We cannot go on for ever having it both ways.

It may be expedient at this point to examine a little further the collective representations and our thinking about them. And it is clearly of little use to begin by asking what they are; since they are everything

---

[1] "The thermometer is below freezing point, the pipe is cracked, and no water comes out of the tap. I know nothing about physics or chemistry; but surely I can say that there is solid ice in the pipe." Certainly you can; and if there was salt in the water, you can say that there is solid, *white* ice in the pipe. I am only pointing out that the solidity you are talking about involves your fancied touch, just as the whiteness involves your fancied glance. Only it is harder to remember.

that is obvious. They are, for instance, the desk I am writing at, the noise of a door being opened downstairs, a Union Jack, an altar in a Church, the smell of coffee, a totem pole, the view from Malvern Hills, and the bit of brain-tissue that is being dissected before a group of students in a hospital laboratory. Some of them we can manipulate, as the lecturer is doing, and as I do when I move the desk. Some of them we cannot. What is important here is that there are, broadly speaking, three different things that we can do with all of them; or, alternatively, they are related to the mind in three different ways.

First, we can simply contemplate or experience them—as when I simply look at the view, or encounter the smell. The whole impression appears then to be given to me in the representation itself. For I am not, or I am not very often, aware of smelling an unidentified smell and then thinking, "That is coffee!" It appears to me, and appears instantly, that I smell coffee—though, in fact, I can no more merely *smell* "coffee" than I can merely *hear* "a thrush singing.". . . It is important to be clear about it. It is plainly the result of an activity of some sort in me, however little I may recollect any such activity.

When a lady complained to Whistler that she did not see the world he painted, he is said to have replied: "No, ma'am, but don't you wish you could?" Both Whistler and the lady were really referring to that activity—which in Whistler's case was intenser than the lady's. Ought it to be called a "mental" activity? Whatever it ought to be called, it really is the percipient's own contribution to the representation. It is all *that* in the representation which is not sensation. For, as the organs of sense are required to convert the unrepresented ("particles") into sensations for us, so *something* is required in us to convert sensations into "things." It is this something that I mean. And it will avoid confusion if I purposely choose an unfamiliar and little-used word and call it, at the risk of infelicity, *figuration*.

Let me repeat it. On the assumption that the world whose existence is independent of our sensation and perception consists solely of "particles," two operations are necessary (and whether they are successive or simultaneous is of no consequence), in order to produce the familiar world we know. First, the sense-organs must be related to the particles in such a way as to give rise to sensations; and secondly, those mere sensations must be combined and constructed by the percipient mind into the recognizable and nameable objects we call "things." It is this world of construction which will here be called *figuration*.

Now whether or no figuration is a mental activity, that is, a kind of thinking, it is clearly not, or it is not *characteristically*, a thinking *about*. The second thing, therefore, that we can do with the representations is to think about them. Here, as before, we remain unconscious of the intimate relation which they in fact have, as representations, with our own organisms and minds. Or rather, more unconscious than before. For now our very attitude is, to treat them as independent of ourselves; to accept their 'outness' as self-evidently given; and to speculate about or to investigate their relations *with each other*. One could perhaps name this process "theorizing" or "theoretical thinking," since it is exactly what is done in most places where science is pursued, whether it be botany, medicine, metallurgy, zoology or any other. But I do not think the term is wide enough. The kind of thing I mean covers other studies as well—a good deal of history, for instance. Nor need it be systematic. There are very few children who do not do a little of it. Moreover, if a common word is chosen, there is the same danger of confusion arising from its occasional use with a less precise intention. Therefore, at the like hazard as before, I propose to call this particular kind of thinking *alpha-thinking*.

Thirdly, we can think about the *nature* of collective representations as such, and therefore about their relation to our own minds. We can think about perceiving and we can think about thinking. We can do, in fact, the kind of thinking which I am trying to do at the moment, and which you will be doing if you think I am right and also if you think I am wrong. This is part of the province of one or two sciences such as physiology and psychology, and of course it is also part of the province of philosophy. It has been called reflection or reflective thinking. But for the same reasons as before, I shall reject the simpler and more elegant term and call it *beta-thinking*.

It should be particularly noted that the distinction here made between alpha-thinking and beta-thinking is not one between two different *kinds* of thinking, such as for instance that which is sometimes made between analytical thinking on the one hand and synthetic or imaginative thinking on the other. It is purely a distinction of subject-matters.

The three operations—*figuration, alpha-thinking* and *beta-thinking*—are clearly distinguishable from one another; but that is not to say that they are divided by impassable barriers at the points where they mutually approach. Indeed the reverse is true. Moreover they may affect each other by reciprocal influence. In the history of the theory of colour, for instance, colour began by being regarded as a primary quality of the coloured object and was later transferred to the status of a "secondary" quality dependent on the beholder. Here we can detect the interaction of alpha-thinking and beta-thinking; and again in the whole influence which experimental science has exerted on philosophy in the last two or three hundred years. This book, on the other hand, will be more concerned with the interaction between figuration and alpha-thinking.

That the former of these affects, and largely determines, the latter hardly needs saying; since the primary product of figuration is the actual subject-matter of most alpha-thinking. That the converse may sometimes also be true, and further, that the borderline between the one and the other is sometimes quite impossible to determine—this is less obvious. Yet a little serious reflection (that is, a little beta-thinking) makes it apparent enough.

Recall for a moment the familiar jingle from *Sylvie and Bruno*, with its persistent refrain of "he thought he saw" followed by "he found it was":

He thought he saw a Banker's Clerk
Descending from the bus
He looked again, and found it was
A hippopotamus.

etc., etc.

This is of course only a very improbable instance of an experience which, in itself, is quite common, especially with those among our representations (and they form the overwhelming majority) which reach us through the sense of sight alone. When we mistake one representation, that is to say one thing, for another, so that there is a transition from an "I thought I saw" to an "I found it was," it is often very difficult indeed to say whether there is first a figuration (based, let us say, on incomplete sensation) and then another and different figuration, producing a different representation; or whether there is one and the same representation, veiled from us at first by some incorrect alpha-thinking, which is subsequently discarded as inapplicable. In the particular case of a puzzled man trying to descry an object spotted far off at sea, it feels more like the latter. Often it feels much more like the former. We have made the mistake before we are aware of having done any thinking at all.

Anyone who wishes to investigate this further should attend carefully to the sort of mistakes we are apt to make on awaking abruptly from deep sleep in a darkened room; especially if it happens to be a strange room. Either way we must conclude that figuration, whether or no it is a kind of thinking, is something which easily and imperceptibly passes over into thinking, and into which thinking easily and imperceptibly passes over. For in both cases there was a representation; otherwise I should not have been deceived. And if the first representation was the result of incorrect thinking, then thinking can do something very much like what figuration does. Alternatively, if it was the result of figuration alone, then the very fact that figuration can "make a mistake" suggests that it has a good deal in common with thinking.

OPTIONS FOR WRITING

1. After reading this essay, do you agree or disagree with Barfield's conclusion that a rainbow would not exist if "eyes" were not there to see it?

2. In your own words, explain what Barfield means by the phrase "collective representation."

3. What is a rainbow, anyway? Although Barfield spends a great deal of time speculating about its existence, he never actually explains precisely what it is—why it looks the way it does, why it takes its peculiar shape and form. Spend some time in the library researching rainbows, and compare what you learn to the information Barfield presents. What material has he left out? Why?

12

THE WORLD
OF BUSINESS

Ronald Savitt

Ronald Savitt takes us on a supermarket tour, pointing out things
we've probably never noticed, asking questions we've never asked.
Why are those jars of expensive salad dressing nestled among the lettuce? Why are certain cereals always on the bottom shelf, others always on the middle one? Using the supermarket as a model, Savitt
explains the place of advertising, personnel management, accounting,
even capitalization in modern U.S. business. Readers are sent to the
store to make their own observations and to analyze advertising materials and personnel practices.

READINGS

SETTING PRICES

Francine Schwadel Ferocious Competition Tests Pricing Skills of a Retail
Manager

The Economist The Value of Friendship

Teri Agins Discount Clothing Stores, Facing Squeeze, Aim to Fashion a
More Rounded Image

MARKETING FAILURES

Christine Donahue How Procter & Gamble Fumbled Citrus Hill

Christine Donahue Citrus Hill: The Brand P&G Wouldn't Let Die

Philip Kotler Don't Mess with Mother Coke

MANAGING RESOURCES

A. L. Minkes What Is Management All About?

Ronald Savitt Zimmerman's: What Do You Do To Make It Happen?

Neil W. Chamberlain The Central Thesis

Did you buy something before you came to class today? If so, you did business. Most of us encounter business everyday. Only on those rare days, when we're hidden away in a forest camp or sailing across the seas, do we not engage in a business transaction or hear about the world of business. Each of us participates as a consumer of goods and services, as an employee or owner, as a government official involved in regulating business, or simply as a citizen. We don't see "business" when we buy that first cup of coffee in the morning, the daily newspaper, or that new sweater that we really cannot do without, but it is there; some of it is easy to see, but not always easy to understand.

Let's examine this familiar but often complex world by taking a walk through a supermarket. I choose this establishment because of its great importance in satisfying the needs of most consumers. Nearly 90% of the nondurable consumer goods—that is, products you use up such as food, soaps, dairy products, and the like—are found in the supermarket. Trying to understand how that vast assortment of goods and services comes into being is an important part of understanding what business is all about.

A JOURNEY THROUGH A SUPERMARKET

For a moment think of yourself as an alien from a distant planet. You need to look at the supermarket not as a familiar place, but as a new one. As we go through it, you need to try to look beyond the obvious.

There are two supermarkets near my house. Both are about the same driving time, but because parking is much easier at Martin's, we'll go there. Martin's lot is larger than the one at the Grand Union, and the store does not look that far from the road. Whether it's true or not I feel like I am closer to the door here. This seems silly, but when you have to push a shopping cart over the winter ice and through the spring slush, it makes a difference. Note that I have parked my car a long way from the store. I do it because I am always concerned about getting my car dented, but today I am doing it so that we can take a good look at the supermarket.

This Tuesday, like all Tuesday mornings, the parking lot is really empty, and we can see its vast size—parking spaces for nearly 500 cars. None will be vacant on Friday evening or Saturday afternoon. Sometimes people will be lined up to get into the lot. The building is big— about 45,000 square feet. That includes the space for display and storage and the preparation areas that we will examine. On our way back to the car we can go around back and look at the loading docks to see where suppliers deliver their goods.

Once inside, we are confronted with twelve check-out counters, three of which are serving people with carts full of groceries. The sign over one check-out says "10 items or less," and there are several people queued up with their purchases in small hand baskets. Customers at the other check-outs have carts crammed with purchases. Grocery carts, which come in a variety of sizes and shapes, help make the supermarket efficient. We should look for the new ones that have a calculator in the handle to keep a running total of the purchases. Store managers believe this cart will bring customers into the store. What do you think?

Before starting, let's look at all of the signs around us. Some direct us to various parts of the store, others promote specific products, and still others note customer service. There is also a pharmacy and a counter for paying bills, buying lottery tickets, and returning empty bottles. Over by the door, there are bins where we can contribute food to the local food bank and boxes where we can recycle plastic bags. If we have time on the way out, we can read the notes on the bulletin board, advertising everything from a request for babysitters to petitions for bike paths. The supermarket is obviously more than a place to buy food. It is an important social institution as well.

Where Goods Are Located

Before we make our rounds inside the supermarket, let us see where things are. This store is so large that it is difficult to see all of the products at once. If we turn to the right, we will be headed toward the produce section. Look at all that lettuce! There are bins of apples, oranges, and lemons; piles of potatoes and onions; and displays of all the things that go into salads, such as tomatoes, radishes, scallions, and mushrooms. These items are for sale, but we need to think about how they all got here. Some of the more exotic items, such as the mangos, came from South America. Lots of the fruit came from California, and there are potatoes from Idaho and Maine. Some of the products have been packaged, including those Shelburne Farm Apples and the organic carrots from California, but there are also bulk apples and carrots. Nestled in the middle of the lettuce—romaine, Boston, and iceberg—are bottles of salad dressing. Is that an accident or was it done on purpose?

Next, along the back wall, we come to the fish counter. What a variety of fish! Salmon, catfish, haddock—even trout swimming in a tank. The fish, shellfish, and shrimp are all nicely laid out on a bed of chipped ice. The display reminds me of a mosaic in a museum in Athens that came from the floor of an ancient fishmonger. Someone has placed a number of recipes all around the fish display. With all the emphasis on avoiding red meat, fish has become more popular, and many people need advice on how to cook it. This area has a carefully designed maritime flavor; the people behind the counter have tall rubber boots and captain hats.

As we move on to the meat counter, we can get a better view of the trout in the tank. I fish, and I just can't think of buying trout here. The meat counter is about 30 feet long, with sections for beef, lamb, and pork. There are also sections for packaged meat products such as sausage and bologna. Here we can also find chicken, game hens, duck. Some of these packages contain whole birds, but others contain all wings, backs, or thighs. A butcher is nowhere to be seen, but if we look carefully we can find a bell. Push it, and out will come a person to provide special help. I really don't know if there is someone in the back cutting meat or whether there are just piles and piles of packaged items. Some stores still have butchers, and you can look through windows to see them.

What was that? We just got a whiff of the bread baking in the in-store bakery. We walked by that too quickly. Let's see what is going on there. The bakery offers free coffee and samples of my favorite cookies—peanut butter oatmeal. Unlike the meat counter, we can see over the bread and cakes to see people preparing items for the ovens—everything from muffins to bagels. I am sure you will agree that it is more pleasant to watch these people work than to watch butchers work. Seeing all of the baking really gives the impression that these goods are fresh. Before we wear out our welcome and eat too many samples, we need to go back through the produce section, past the fish and meat counters, and over to the dairy section.

The sign overhead says "dairy foods," but we can easily see that there is a greater assortment of items than those made from milk. Why is it called dairy? Originally, all of the items did come from milk. We can see skim milk, 2 percent milk, whole milk, butter, and all kinds of cheeses, from cottage to cheddar. But there are other items here as well. Orange juice does not come from cows—certainly not cows in Vermont. What links all of these items? They all need to be stored in coolers. But why not have the bacon here?

Now let's move directly across from produce. Along this wall we find the personal care products, including shaving supplies, shampoo, and toothpaste. This looks more like a drugstore than a place to buy food, with products to take care of the outside of our bodies as well as some for the inside if we eat too much. Two long display racks run from the back of the store to the area just in front of the checkout counters. On both sides of these counters we find a wide variety of items. Let's look at the tooth care section. Here are toothpaste, dental floss, mouthwash, and toothbrushes. Note that there are several brands. My favorite brand, "Tom's of Maine," is right up front at eye level with Crest, Gleam, and Colgate. Martin's even has its own brand of toothpaste, but it is not on the same shelf as Crest. What are the advantages of displaying a product at eye level? How do the various brands get placed where they do?

On the other side of the aisle we can view all of those headache remedies. I rarely buy them, but by the number of brands, sizes, and types, somebody must be getting a lot of headaches. Tylenol, Anacin, and Bayer's Aspirin are all available. Some brands I don't recognize; perhaps I have not seen their ads on TV. Looking at all of these gives me "Excedrin Headache number 1!" Further down the aisle are skin care products, suntan oils, and after-shave lotion.

Let's move to the packaged goods section. Here we can find breakfast cereals, cake mixes, powdered milk, juice in paper cartons, pasta, and crackers and cookies. Take a good look at the various levels of the shelves. What we see most easily is the eye level display. Products displayed there have a better chance of being seen and sold. Many supermarkets charge the producers for the space their products occupy and the location on the shelf. These fees are called slotting fees. Kellogg cereals all seem to be at eye level, but a brand called "Oatios" is way up on the top shelf.

The long aisles that run between the shelves from the back of the store to the front of the store carry most of the rest of the merchandise. Low refrigerator cases are placed along here, in which you find things like frozen orange juice, french fried potatoes, and frozen vegetables; other refrigeration units stand upright and have doors much like your refrigerator at home. Most of the rest of the display units are shelves, though in some stores you will find special display units from which you can scoop out nuts, flour, and dried fruit. There are special display and storage units at the ends of the aisles, and some are even attached to the check-out counters. These are for "impulse items," flashlight batteries, chewing gum, and *TV Guide*: things that shoppers want but forget to put on their shopping lists. We can barely see the clerk behind all of these items. Look at all of the people leafing through magazines as they wait their turn. A lot of unfinished articles go through the check-outs and are finished at home.

We don't have time this morning to inspect each aisle. However, look closely, and note how products that are consumed together are displayed together. For example, potato chips, nuts, and soft drinks are shelved in one place; pasta, sauces, and parmesan cheese in another. Now we want to look beyond the products and begin to understand the business activities that brought all of these items together.

There is more to see, but we cannot see it all on one visit. When you come back, note any changes in the locations of products. There will be changes on a week-to-week basis; special sale items are often given prominent positions. Soft drinks are placed at the ends of the aisles toward the end of the week; new brands of biscuits and crackers are placed near the cheese in special display units. During busy shopping periods, salespeople will be giving samples away. This is a way of promoting the product and learning how customers react to it.

We need to go out around back to see the delivery docks. By this time of day, most of the trucks are on their way back to the major distribution centers. Food products are traditionally delivered late at night or early in the morning. Shipments from local suppliers such as dairies or bakers come in during the day.

WRITING 1.

Go to a nearby supermarket. In your journal make a list of all the items you find at the ends of the aisles and at the check-out counters. Also list all of the breakfast cereals, noting where they are located in the store and how they are displayed on the shelves. Take a good look at the store. Why do the main display aisles run from the back to the front of the store, perpendicular to the check-outs? What kind of merchandise is usually found in the ends of the display units, on the check-out counters? Supermarkets are not exact copies of one another, but there are similarities. What are these similarities, and why do you think they have come about?

BACK TO THE WORLD OF BUSINESS

Instead of going through the supermarket as if we are here to purchase a week's supply of food and household items, let's look at the way the supermarket's activities reflect the world of business. The store's location, the parking lot, and the building itself are obviously part of the public landscape, restricted by laws and regulations governing how the land can be used, how noisy a business can be, and how much traffic is acceptable for the roads. Although we talk about the United States having a free market, that does not mean that firms can do as they please. Other laws monitor how businesses can compete for your dollar, how employees can be treated, and how information and taxes are reported to the government. One of the most important challenges facing a business is determining how to relate to the environment in which it is located. The issues range from preventing major oil spills to choosing the type of packaging material used by supermarkets. Have you seen efforts by supermarkets to be sensitive to the environment?

Keeping Track of It All

Let's look at what is happening at the check-outs. The goods are lifted from the shopping cart to the counter, moved down the conveyer, rung up in the cash register, bagged, and paid for. Underneath this is the collection of data—what items were sold and how much was sold. Accounting keeps track of the business.

Most people think that accounting is "keeping the books." It is actually much broader: Accounting is measuring the sales of items and the development of financial information that allows the supermarket manager to make decisions. For example, there is a continual battle for space in even the largest supermarkets. If the produce manager wants to make space for exotic mushrooms, he or she must know what profits can be made from every square foot of the department. If the average profit per square foot is $4.00 a year, then the decision to increase the space devoted to mushrooms to three square feet will be warranted if profit ends up at $5.50 per square foot per year. However, if the product that is displaced, such as apples, brings people into the store, then cutting apple space can reduce the number of customers and therefore reduce profits. Accounting provides information about the costs of operation, generates data for setting prices and negotiating wages with employees, provides data for the prompt and timely payment of taxes, and develops information about the company for potential investors and present owners.

Where the Money Comes From

By now you have probably wondered about the source of all the merchandise in the supermarket, the way the building got built, and the owner. We need to look beyond the obvious; namely, that the hundreds of tins and packages of food came from manufacturers, that a construction company erected the structure, and that "someone" must own it. What resources were required to make it happen? Funds came from investors including banks, life insurance companies, governments, and individual investors. Each investor evaluates the supermarket's ability to generate profits to pay them a return on their money. They will want to know how well the store is managed and what is done to keep sales up and costs down. Funds can be raised by selling stock in the supermarket. When you buy stock you are really not a lender but an owner, only one among many. Nevertheless, you are providing funds. And as an owner, you hope that your investment will pay dividends; it often happens. Money can also be borrowed from institutions and individuals who give the use of their money in return for interest on a regular basis; they also expect the total lent to be returned at the end of a clearly defined period.

Who Makes It Happen

The physical features of the supermarket are the easiest to see: those colorful fruits and vegetables, cereal boxes, and soup cans, the long aisles stocked with shampoo, and the trout swimming in the tank. But it is the people that really make the business.

Business is all about people. In fact, employees are our supermarket's most important resource. Everyone in this store seems to take a clear interest in trying to help customers; people restocking shelves provide information about the location of various products, and management has telephones on several aisles so that if we are lost we can find out where imported sardines are located (we know that they are not with the fresh fish). Some employees are identifiable by their garments: Produce workers wear waterproof aprons, cashiers wear smocks showing the store's name, and the carry-out people have bright red vests. Would you do that job without a bright red vest?

How employees are recruited, hired, paid, and organized is the focus of human resource management. When we think about businesses we like, those feelings come from the experiences we have with their employees—how friendly they are, how concerned they are with serving our needs, and how helpful they are in solving our problems. Businesses thrive when they provide good customer service, and that comes from the employees.

Supermarket managers believe that shelves should be stocked as soon as they reach a minimum inventory level; employees would rather restock items when the store is closed or during low traffic hours. Who is correct? There is probably *no* single answer, but any solution must consider a number of factors, including the needs for meeting the demands of consumers, the interests of the employees, and the costs of stocking and restocking shelves.

WRITING 2.

Managers are responsible for seeing that company policies are carried out and for ensuring that relevant laws and regulations are followed. Sheila asked Gene, the supermarket's personnel manager, "Why am I receiving a lower wage than Raymond and Arnold? We all stock the shelves and work at the meat counter, and we were hired at the same time." With some concern Gene replied, "You have a different job description. It is a job that pays less than those held by Raymond and Arnold." What argument would Sheila make to get this changed? How might Gene respond? What might happen if Sheila and Gene cannot come to agreement on this matter?

Getting Customers In

Why did all those customers come to this store? The store engaged in marketing: matching consumer needs and wants with products and services. And supermarkets have really been good at that. The average supermarket stocks about 20,000 products, from diet snacks to frozen yogurt. The way that all of these products and services have been assembled, priced, promoted, and displayed is the role of marketing. We have seen that all of this does not come by chance but is driven by management's attempt to meet consumer demands.

We saw customer service cards at the check-outs, which represent one way in which the supermarket managers learn to understand what their customers want. Supermarkets conduct marketing research in other ways. Questionnaires collect information about family size, preferences for specific foods, and satisfaction with the present operation. Several months ago this store changed to environmentally sound cups for the coffee as a result of a survey of its customers. Keeping track of changes in consumer demand and then meeting the demand is crucial for marketing.

Supermarket locations are carefully chosen to be close to customers. The stores are designed to develop a sense of loyalty so that customers think that this is "their store." Stores try to differentiate themselves from their competitors by having the best produce, the freshest bread, the lowest prices, the fastest cashiers, the best baggers, the cleanest stores, and so on.

We are all familiar with the advertising activities of supermarkets. Many of the large ones have a special insert in the newspaper each week, in which we can find special items that arrive from distant places such as mandarin oranges from Japan, items that the store is offering at low price such as coffee, and new products such as television sets. The advertising supplement is a smaller version of the supermarket itself, giving a glimpse of some things we have seen. And, of course it is directed to keep us coming back.

WRITING 3.

Collect the supermarket supplements from your local newspaper; they are often in the Monday edition. Compare the supplements and look at such factors as their size, the way they are printed, whether they use color, and the things they say about each supermarket. Compare the prices of bread, milk, or a brand of cereal from store to store. Can you tell what image each store tried to project from its supplement? Make note of what each store says about itself. Does one stress the quality of its products? Does one try to be the low price leader? How else do they attempt to attract customers?

Marketing is all about competition. As you well know, most communities have several supermarkets, and even small towns usually have more than one store selling food and household products. Competition is the rivalry for your business; supermarkets tell you through their advertising what they offer, at what prices, and why you should shop there. Some prepare fresh orange juice, others have salad bars, and still others have fresh fish sections.

THE BUSINESS TRANSACTION

Of all the things we saw in the supermarket, the most important activity—the sale and purchase between the store and the customer—may not have stuck out. To understand business we really need to look at the transaction. In spite of all your purchases, you may not have thought of business in this way.

Business managers spend time trying to understand how transactions come about and how to make them come about for their firms. We can learn how to sell more by understanding what made the last sale work or by trying to understand why it did not happen. By now you are probably overwhelmed with all those customer service cards that you are given. Well, they are efforts by the business to understand how to be more successful. By taking a close look at the elements that make up a transaction, we can learn more about the world of business. This exercise can make you a better buyer as well as a better seller.

WRITING 4.

Keep a log of all of the purchases that you make for the next three days. Make note of what you buy, where, how much, why, and what happens between you and the seller. Examine your log. Did you compare a variety of brands and stores? Take the most expensive item in your log, and write about the reasons for the purchase. Were there any unpleasant experiences? What went wrong?

Your Last Purchase

Now that you have had a chance to put some words to paper about your last purchase, let's look at what some of my students wrote in class:

> "I missed breakfast and needed something for the day."
> "I walked by the Coke machine and knew I was
>   thirsty."
> "The coffee bun smelled really great; it was a spe-
>   cial for 45 cents."
> "That was the sweater I'd been searching for . . .
>   and it was on sale, real cheap."
> "It was a new brand . . . it sounded great on TV."

One student wanted to buy something to quench her thirst, and although she did get something liquid, it was not what she wanted. To get that far she needed to have the money to make the purchase or have a friend with money to lend; the product had to be produced, shipped, and made available. What she ended up buying, root beer, was not what she wanted. Was she satisfied? How do you think she will behave next time she is thirsty? Other things had to happen to make a transaction take place. Note, too, that not all transactions result in a satisfied customer.

Transactions come about as the result of buyers and sellers performing certain functions. The previous quotes only scratch the surface. We can learn about the elements of a transaction by describing what takes place when we purchase something. Transactions—buying and selling—requiring buyers to have some idea about what consumers want: the sweater, good-tasting coffee, high-speed cars, quiet jazz albums. Sellers must inform buyers as to what is available. Most products are advertised; we learn what is available, where it can be found, and how much it costs.

Risk bearing is also part of a transaction. Our supermarket does marketing research to make certain that it will sell the products that we want. These are market risks that stem from consumers not wanting something. Perishable products, such as milk and eggs, are stocked according to estimates of what can be sold.

Other functions that are part of the transaction include transportation and storage. Getting goods to the store represents transportation, and we certainly saw a great deal of food and health products that require storage.

A single transaction is composed of the following functions: buying, selling, financing, communicating, transporting, storing, risk bearing, and standardizing and grading. We have seen all of these in our trip. The last two were there; for example, we saw large, medium, and small eggs. Standardization is creating acceptable categories; grading is placing each egg in its proper category.

Let me show you what a student wrote about the last time she bought a Coke.

```
I think I have figured it out. . . . The selection of the
Coke in vending machines comes from understanding what
people want. (They) . . . try to get the most popular
brand in front of you--sometimes you won't find what you
want. I guess they hope you will settle for something
. . . but what happens if I walk away? I guess that is
the risk they take. Their research can't reach everybody,
but I guess it is better to know what some folks want
more than just put Coke out there(?) . . .
```

Rebecca then went on to talk about other issues of risk including what happens if the Coke is bad and the security of the vending machine in the dorm basement. "It's been ripped off more than once." Who is responsible for the losses? She got into the issue of standardization and grading: "Now I understand why all soda cans are the same size; they have to fit into vending machines." Well, she is not quite correct. A twelve-ounce tin has become the standard here in the United States, but we are the odd ones out because the rest of the world has gone metric!

Understanding business begins with examining the way we buy and sell goods and services. We don't need to dissect each purchase we make, but it is a valuable way to learn about the world of business.

WRITING 5.

Describe your last purchase—the last transaction you engaged in—in terms of the functions we have defined. You might do this once a week for several weeks until you identify each of the functions as clearly as possible. Each time you write about a purchase and describe what happened you will write more reflectively.

SUGGESTIONS FOR RESEARCH

We learn about the world by making comparisons between the familiar and the unknown and contrasts between seemingly similar things. Go out into your community and visit two business firms offering comparable goods and services, and compare the ways in which they do business. You might consider two automobile dealers, two pizza parlors, two drug stores, or any other businesses that interest you. Be selective in what you compare. Afterward, in an essay, state what you saw, how they differed, and why you chose the firms you did. There is no correct or incorrect approach. Almost every paper will focus on different elements. "When I visited the supermarket," for example, "I looked at such things as (1) access to the store, (2) the product assortment, (3) the store's personality, (4) the people, (5) the lighting, and (6) the ways in which merchandise is displayed."

This would be a good project to do collaboratively, sharing both the research into the businesses and the writing of your results. You might consider writing this report as a feature in the business section of a newspaper, adopting the lively voice used in the front-page essays of the *Wall Street Journal* or the style used for product comparisons in *Consumer Reports*.

READINGS

Setting Prices

Francine Schwadel
FEROCIOUS COMPETITION TESTS THE
PRICING SKILLS OF A RETAIL MANAGER

*Pricing is one of the most difficult decisions managers have to face.
In a capitalist economy, price setting is accomplished in the market
as a result of the actions of sellers and buyers. Sellers have to cover
costs and make profits, and buyers must receive satisfaction from
purchases if the system is going to work. Prices are continuously
changing, and managers are constantly faced with figuring out what
is the "correct" price.*

Two of these readings come from The Wall Street Journal,
*which is the most important business newspaper in the United
States. Published daily, it contains transactions from all of the stock
exchanges in the United States and summaries from those around the
world.* The Wall Street Journal *keeps its readers abreast of major
political and economic events as well as major challenges for business. The other selection here comes from* The Economist, *which is
the prominent business newspaper in Great Britain, although it looks
very much like* Newsweek *or* Time. The Economist *provides a
worldwide view of events in business and includes an important section on American affairs.*

*"Ferocious Competition Tests the Pricing Skills of a Retail Man-
ager" describes the challenges facing Ken Sargent, a Woolworth
manager, during the Christmas season. About 40% of all retail sales
take place between Thanksgiving and Christmas, so having the right
price is important if a retailer is going to be profitable. One way Ken
Sargent establishes his prices is to shop the competition. What other
methods does he use? How else does Woolworth compete with other
stores?*

*Sears, Roebuck, one of America's largest retailers, is attempting
to reposition itself among its competitors by reducing its prices
throughout its operations. According to "The Value of Friendship,"
managers have chosen the "everyday low price" campaign as a means
of creating a new image. Obviously, they hope that the low price
image will be an effective means of increasing sales and improving
the company's performance. How well has this program worked?
Sears's policy has been based on the assumption that consumers are
interested primarily in buying products at the lowest prices. Do you
think that assumption is correct? What other factors do consumers*

796

consider in making choices among products and the stores where they
make the purchases?

    The Woolworth article shows the challenges of making price deci-
sions in a very short run setting, whereas the article on Sears shows
pricing in a long run perspective. What similarities and differences
are there in the two strategies? Do you see any advantages to always
being the low price leader in contrast to having sales during the
year? What might they be?

    Some retail stores have been successful by trying always to be
the low price leaders. According to the third article, "Off-price cloth-
ing chains are finding that low prices alone are no longer enough."
Why has this taken place? What factors do consumers consider in
purchasing clothing items? Can you put these in order of impor-
tance? How important are style, the brand or designer name, and the
store name in the purchase of clothing? Do these factors change when
other products are purchased?

    The following three articles provide different views about the use
of price as a competitive tool. Each seems to provide a correct view,
but all are different. How can you explain that?

Ken Sargent sweeps through the cavernous K mart store here, stopping
to check prices on goods as diverse as Hershey's Kisses, wreath bows
and a plastic exercise device called the Abdominizer.

    He makes a mental record of the gift boxes of potpourri and the
gun-cleaning kits on the main aisles. He doesn't find any Batman videotapes or two-foot-tall Christmas figures that nod their heads and wave
their hands.

    Mr. Sargent's gray suit and maroon tie set him apart from K mart's
sweatsuit and sneakers crowd. In fact, he is no ordinary shopper. He
manages the rival Woolworth store nearby, and his mission today is to
scout out his competitor one last time before the battle to snare this
year's holiday shoppers begins in earnest.

    "I feel pretty good," he says afterwards, jumping into his gray
Honda Accord in the K mart parking lot. "We've done our job as far as
the pricing and presentation for the Christmas season."

    So far as Woolworth Corp. is concerned, he had better be right.
Pricing is paramount in the retail business this season, and discounting
is rampant. It's "an all-out effort to romance the consumer," says retail
consultant Sid Doolittle of Chicago.

    Shoppers have become adept at spotting the promotional hype.
"Consumers today are extraordinarily sophisticated," says Leo Shapiro,
a Chicago market researcher. "They can tell us the average price of an
item they want to buy, a good price, the highest price, and the very
lowest price they think they can find if they really hunt."

    The front-line captains in the pricing fray at the many major chains
are middle-level managers like Mr. Sargent. At Woolworth's Gothic

headquarters building in lower Manhattan, executives do establish national prices, and they recommend displays for their 1,100 variety stores. But they count on store managers to adjust the prices on hundreds of key items, up or down, to keep their stores locally competitive—and profitable. "For us [at headquarters] to lower all the prices to, say, the level of Wal-Mart wouldn't make good sense," says Robert G. Lynn, president and chief executive officer of the company's U.S. Woolworth division.

UP FROM STOCKBOY

Woolworth, like many other retailers, rings up half its yearly profit during the Christmas season. Its profit, then, depends on the pricing intuition of managers like the 44-year-old Mr. Sargent.

The manager, who joined Woolworth straight from high school as a stockboy in upstate New York, has a bigger task than most of his counterparts. He runs a large, two-story operation in a fiercely competitive market where keeping tabs on the enemy is even more imperative than usual. "The stores with the best prices are going to get the customers," he says.

The circulars spilling from the Sunday paper in this Philadelphia suburb show how intense this season's price war has become.

The K mart near Mr. Sargent's store is hyping Moonlight Madness, a three-hour period packed with spur-of-the-moment Blue Light specials. Bradlees, a discount store in the strip mall next to K mart, is shouting about its 25% discounts on Fisher-Price toys. Caldor, another nearby discounter, promotes name-brand watches for as low as $16.99. CVS's drugstore, just down from Mr. Sargent's store in the Oxford Valley Mall here, is ballyhooing its prices on Hershey's Kisses.

K MART AS BELLWETHER

Mr. Sargent worries most about K mart and the local Toys "R" Us store. "I know if I shop K mart," he says, "they've shopped the competition." So he cruises through K mart at least once a week, often on his day off. Several times a year, he also sends an assistant there with a long checklist, which he uses to adjust his prices.

Mr. Sargent has just received from Woolworth headquarters the list of key Christmas items this season. So he dispatches an assistant, JoAnne Oakes, to collect K mart's prices on more than 100 items, including cologne, cameras and candy. Then, he retreats to his drab, windowless office on the lower level of his store to review the list.

He circles 17 K mart prices that undercut his store's. Then he matches them in a column labeled "Your New Price." With a stroke of his red felt-tipped pen, he slashes by 12%, to $21.87, his price on Baseball and Super Mario Land software for the hand-held Nintendo Game Boy video game. He cuts the price on Jean Nate After Bath Splash by 11%, to $12.97. He marks down Old Spice cologne by 8%, to $5.68.

Mr. Sargent has already adjusted his toy prices to make them competitive with Toys "R" Us. He made those changes back in October, when parents, he says, typically start window shopping for gifts.

This time, he drew up his own hit list of 101 items to be surveyed at Toys "R" Us. Using the results as a guide, he reduced prices on more than 50 items, including the Clue board game, popular G.I. Joe figures and a Fisher-Price kiddie sports car.

On most toys, Mr. Sargent decided against matching Toys "R" Us. Instead, he trimmed his prices enough so that when he runs his week-long, 25%-off special sales he will actually undercut his rival's prices. He has planned three of the specials.

The Nintendo Game Boy wasn't on his hit list. Still, Mr. Sargent matched Toys "R" Us's $89.99 price after learning early in November that it was selling Game Boy for $10 less than he was. The report came from a Woolworth sales clerk shopping at Toys "R" Us on her day off. Mr. Sargent then had one of his assistants, posing as a shopper, call to verify the price.

Managers at the nearby K mart and Toys "R" Us stores also routinely monitor their competitors' prices, including Woolworth's. But the managers say they are more concerned about keeping up with other big discount chains and each other than with Mr. Sargent's store. Because Woolworth is smaller and carries a different mix of merchandise, they say, they don't consider it much of a threat.

"They better start!" says Mr. Sargent when told of his rivals' opinion. He adds with a grin: "Maybe that's why I'm selling so many toys."

Over a recent busy weekend, toys were hot items indeed. Mr. Sargent ran a 25%-off sale, trumpeting the news with a big red banner over the toy department and two smaller signs over the mountains of Fisher-Price toy boxes built strategically near the main floor's two entrances to spur impulse purchases.

With the 25% discount, many of Mr. Sargent's toy prices undercut competitors. Monopoly, at $7.41, compared with $8.99 at Toys "R" Us and $9.96 at K mart. Mattel's Li'l Miss Makeup doll cost $17.25, versus $17.99 at Toys "R" Us and $19.97 at K mart. A Little People Farm set from Fisher-Price was $19.49, beating the $21.99 at Toys "R" Us and $24.96 at K mart.

Not all Woolworth's toy prices go so low, however. A 25% discount cut Woolworth's price on a game called Shark Attack to $12.74—still way above the Toys "R" Us price of only $9.99. "You're not going to be right on every single price," Mr. Sargent says.

Even his best deals meet some consumer skepticism. Mr. Sargent tells a young mother, toddler in tow, that a Little People Farm set will cost her only about $19.50 after the 25% discount. The price, she responds, is "too high to begin with. It's only $21.99 at Kiddie City. If they have a sale, it'll be cheaper."

KRYSTLE FOREVER A BOMB?

Mr. Sargent doubts it, but he doesn't argue, and the shopper wanders away.

To make up for the erosion of profits to lower prices, Mr. Sargent redoubles his efforts to keep his store stocked with staples such as needles, threads, pens, pencils, soap dishes and towel bars. They produce higher-than-average profit margins. When weekly deliveries arrive, Mr. Sargent orders his staff to put them on the shelves immediately, bypassing the store's cluttered stock room.

Just before Thanksgiving, Mr. Sargent had moved some high-priced items into prominent locations. A kiosk featuring name-brand watches for as little as $19.95 became a big hit. But, despite his attempt to push Forever Krystle fragrances, sales stunk. After the weekend's rush, he yanked the Forever Krystle line off the top of a glass cologne case and replaced it with Tabu.

"I'm really surprised," he says on the Krystle fiasco. "It's advertised on TV every time you turn around."

STRESS TEST SCORE

Despite this disappointment, Mr. Sargent remains calm. At one point, he dives into a holiday survival kit supplied by the mall and takes a stress test. The Biodot he attaches to his wrist turns lime green, signaling he is "involved," according to the test's color chart. The color is midway between a "very tense" black and a "very relaxed" violet.

"It's tough to be relaxed this time of year," says Mr. Sargent, a smoker who relishes cigarette breaks in his office and in the store's restaurants. "I've got a lot at stake." Store managers like him, whose yearly salaries range between $40,000 and $60,000, can raise their earnings as much as 25% if their stores do well. Mr. Sargent, a family man, has a son in high school and another in college. The family lives in Langhorne.

During and after his sweep through K mart, Mr. Sargent seems confident, even cocky. "They don't have nearly the setup we do," he says of K mart's Nintendo counter. Later, he claims to have the best prices on Hershey's Kisses and red velvet wreath bows. He rejects an assistant's suggestion that he raise his bow price 40 cents to match K mart's. "I'd rather be the leader," he says. "We go through tonnage."

As it turns out, however, Mr. Sargent doesn't *really* have the best prices on bows or Kisses. A closer examination of the items shows that the more expensive bow at K mart is larger, and it later puts out one the same size as Woolworth's for 12 cents less. K mart's package of Kisses is bigger than Woolworth's, making its price per ounce a fraction of a cent less than Woolworth's regular price.

Mr. Sargent doesn't seem perturbed. Over a recent weekend, he was selling Kisses on special at two packages for $3, undercutting K mart's price by two cents an ounce. When the sale ended, he would check out K mart's supplies and pare his price again if his rival still had a lot left. As for the bows, Mr. Sargent vows to match K mart's price.

The price confusion shows how easy it is to make errors in comparison shopping. During her recent trip to K mart, Mrs. Oakes, Woolworth's merchandise coordinator, squints at the fine print on the back of a gift box of Brut deodorant and aftershave lotion to determine whether she has the right item. She can't even find a British Sterling musk set and some of the other colognes she is supposed to check.

There are also distractions. A sales clerk in the camera department asks if she needs help. "No. I was just comparative shopping," she says, looking up from her 26-page list.

K mart is aware of what Mrs. Oakes is doing. She signs in and out at the customer service desk, listing Woolworth as her employer. And she visits the K mart store, list and lead pencil in hand, several times a year.

"You can get stagnant inside your four walls," Mr. Sargent says. "You have to get out and see what's happening."

The Economist
THE VALUE OF FRIENDSHIP

More than a mere store, Sears, Roebuck is an American institution. Eugene Talmadge, a governor of Georgia, used to tell voters: "Your only friends are Jesus Christ, Sears Roebuck and Gene Talmadge." The best man of President-to-be Lyndon Johnson rushed off to a Sears store in San Antonio, Texas, to buy a $2.50 wedding ring for Lady Bird.

But Sears is now an institution in some decay. In a desperate attempt to stop the rot, Sears has thrown away old strengths without finding new ones.

On November 6th Standard & Poor's put $5.4 billion of Sears's debt on its surveillance list for possible downgrading. In an effort to regain the confidence of Wall Street, the company's top managers gave a too-sanguine account of the retail chain's progress to a mass meeting of analysts in New York's Plaza Hotel earlier this month. Only the Polyannas were impressed. Most investors stayed restless.

Sears is engaged in insurance (Allstate), property (Coldwell Banker) and investment banking (Dean Witter) as well as retailing. But its merchandising operation — which includes its famous mail-order catalogue as well as its more than 800 department stores—is closest to the heart of its chief executive, Edward Brennan, who joined Sears in 1956 at the age of 22. "Nothing is more important," says Mr. Brennan. "It is the foundation of our relationship with the American consumer."

Nobody disagrees with Mr. Brennan's three motherhood-and-apple-pie aims for the stumbling stores: to expand market share, to improve operating margins and to increase return on equity. This will require radical structural changes. Sears has lost market share to specialty stores and super-discounters, particularly in hardware and in electronic and electrical goods. Two of the nastiest drops: Sears's share of the paint market is down from a peak of 42% to 18%, and of appliances down from 46% to 32%. The store's durable workaday clothes have acquired a dreary 1950s patina. Sales and profits in recent years have been lucklustre. . . .

In 1988–89 Mr. Brennan and his senior managers have made three big mistakes:

- Introducing a much-touted policy of "everyday low prices." Sears hoped to sell goods more quickly and avoid an incessant round of one-off sales. Explains Mr. Michael Bozic, the boss of the merchandise group: "Too much management, and management time, were being expended on the promotional planning process."

    When Sears slashed prices in March, the strategy looked good, but since then it has backfired. At first customers stormed into the stores: sales of home appliances and electronics were up by about 20% on a year earlier; sales of clothes by 5–10%. But soon people decided to wait until prices went even lower in one of the company's less frequent sales.

    "Everyday low prices" were supposed to convince people that it was pointless to wait for a sale. Since prices were always low, they might as well buy today rather than tomorrow. But in fact Sears has not stopped staging sales and special offers; it is merely staging them less often. Customers, it seems, suspect "everyday low prices" is a con, and the ploy is proving expensive for Sears.

    In the third quarter to September 30, 1989, the sales of the merchandise groups at $6.9 billion were no higher than in the previous year, despite about 5% inflation in the intervening period. Net profit declined to $82.9m from $110.5m in the third quarter of 1988.

- Losing the loyalty of Sears's own staff. A former chief executive of Sears used to boast that the store chain owed its success to "men, merchandise, methods and money—and men come first." The company's salaries and benefits were above average, and Sears employees were generally recognized as better trained and motivated than those of other retailers.

    Sears's poor profit and sales performance made upheaval inevitable. Industry insiders say the store's employees were in a mood to be understanding and recognized thousands of jobs would have to go. They were ready to be tolerant about the chaos caused by virtually every manager acquiring, in Mr. Bozic's words, "a new boss, a new job or a new accountability."

But the management has gone too far in squeezing costs. It has reduced its pensioners' medical benefits, its staff's holiday entitlements, and cut discounts for employees. In many stores employees have turned surly. Unless Sears can regain their confidence, it will lose customers to more obliging rivals. Nordstrom, a Seattle-based chain, is a case in point. The courtesy of its highly-motivated employees has helped Nordstrom increase its sales fivefold (to $2.3 billion) and its net profit sixfold (to $123m) in the 1980s.

- Putting the 1,454-foot Sears Tower, the world's tallest building, up for sale a year ago. Sears hoped that cash-rich Japanese investors would buy it. But no bidders have come forward. Apparently the Japanese don't like to buy too many American national monuments, for fear of provoking a xenophobic backlash. The Sears Tower in Chicago is even more a symbol of America's commercial virility than New York's Rockefeller Centre, snapped up on October 30th by Mitsubishi Estate.

Now Sears cannot afford to withdraw the building from sale, despite Chicago's soft property market. Estimates of its value have dropped from as high as $1.2 billion to $800m–900m. The company is committed to moving its head-office employees to cheaper premises, and it needs the cash. It has started wrestling with a complicated mortgage-equity deal for the 110-storey Tower.

These big mistakes are wounding, not fatal. Despite all the changes, Sears is still trusted by most of its customers. They remain confident that the store will stand behind the goods it sells — and that the goods will never be shoddy. This trust is Sears's bedrock. If it throws away that final asset, it will throw away everything.

Teri Agins

DISCOUNT CLOTHING STORES, FACING SQUEEZE, AIM TO FASHION A MORE ROUNDED IMAGE

Off-price clothing chains are finding that low prices alone are no longer enough.

The discount retailers, starting to feel squeezed by widespread department-store price cutting, are fighting back by stressing factors other than price: they are trying to make their stores easier to shop, showcasing individual items in ads and putting new emphasis on customer service. The chains also are striving to build customer loyalty by offering store credit cards.

"The rules of the game have changed," says Eugene Kosack, chairman of National Brands Outlet, a 45-store menswear chain based in Fair Lawn, N.J. "We can't just win on a price war because when a department store goes on sale, they have a lot more advantages than us." Mr. Kosack says NBO's sales have been flat in the past two years as big retailers such as R.H Macy & Co. emphasized sales and markdowns. NBO, a unit of Dylex Ltd. of Canada, is retraining its salespeople and last month kicked off a $3 million ad campaign that promotes its customer service as its most important attribute.

DIMINISHED ADVANTAGE

Off-price chains, which typically charge 20% to 60% below department stores' regular prices, have gained market share in recent years. According to MRCA Information Services, a Stamford, Conn., market research firm, off-price apparel retailers' market share rose to 7.5% in 1989 from 6.8% in 1987. Apparel sales at department stores, meanwhile, fell to 26.4% in 1989 from 27.3% in 1987 (with the rest of the market split among mail-order houses, mass merchandisers and other outlets).

But widespread discounting by department stores and other regular retailers has given shoppers less reason to buy at discount chains. "The off-pricers have been losing some of their competitive advantage," says Thomas Tashjian, a retail analyst at Seidler Amdec Securities in Los Angeles.

Some off-price companies are feeling the heat. Ross Stores Inc., a 156-store clothing chain based in Newark, Calif., blamed its flat fourth-quarter sales in part on an "unparalleled level of department-store promotions." And last week, the 455-store Dress Barn Inc., Stamford, Conn., said earnings in the fiscal quarter ended Jan. 27 plunged 38%, the biggest drop in the company's 26-year history.

The discounters are being pinched on other fronts as well. Some popular apparel brands such as Harve Benard and Phillips Van Heusen are increasingly bypassing off-price channels. Instead, they are selling most of their excess merchandise through their own networks of factory-outlet stores. At the same time, there's no shortage of off-price operators combing the market for merchandise. "With so many more chains to feed and stock, the best selection of branded goods is harder to come by," says Alan Millstein, a New York retail industry consultant.

In some markets, off-price operators face two unexpected competitors: J.C. Penney & Co. and Sears, Roebuck & Co., both of which are adding more brand-name goods in their stores. With those chains' huge buying power, "most brands would rather sell to a Penney than an off-price operator," says Howard Davidowitz, a New York retail consultant.

Nevertheless, since the 1989 Christmas season, the 153-store Burlington Coat Factory Warehouse Corp. has increased its vendor list of brand-name goods by about 12%, says Monroe Millstein, chairman. He says Burlington Coat Factory's ability to buy huge lots and pay vendors promptly has given it an edge. "Whatever qualms they had about selling to us have been conquered," he says.

Off-price chains are responding to the pressures they face with a variety of strategies. Last Christmas, TJ Maxx, a TJX Cos. off-price chain, shifted away from its long-running slogan "The maximum for minimum at TJ Maxx," to a more direct approach. The new TJ Maxx ads showcase individual items. One ad has a lineup of feet wearing "brand name" athletic shoes, with the discount prices listed.

NBO's new ads, trying to overcome discounters' reputation for spotty service, say the chain's "knowledgeable salespeople" can "help you make easy decisions. We can recommend the best style for you, the best colors for you, or we can just point you in the right direction if you'd rather look on your own."

Some off-price retailers, sensitive to shoppers' criticism that their stores are hard to shop in because they are too crammed with merchandise on racks and in piles, are trying to do a better job at presenting their wares. In 1989, Ross Stores began a remodeling program to group apparel for men and women by segment. This is a radical change from Ross's traditional approach, in which all women's clothes, for example, were hung together on bar racks, separated only by size. "Now, we are segmenting the store by life style and attitude," says a Ross spokeswoman.

For example, the women's department in a remodeled store has a core cosmetics and accessories area, surrounded by separate departments for dresses, sportswear, large sizes, and an "Attitudes for Her" junior's area. Fashions are highlighted by displays on walls, columns and small, free-standing racks. By year end, Ross plans to have one-third of its 161 stores remodeled in this manner.

Some discounters are starting to offer store credit cards, which they say get customers to visit more often, generate bigger purchases and provide an additional marketing opportunity in the form of monthly statements. Filene's Basement, a Boston-based chain, rolled out a store credit card in November, and Burlington Coat Factory plans to add its own card this year.

But with so many stores pushing their bargains, off-price stores may be forced to come up with more marketing innovations to break away from the pack. Peter Brown, a vice president at apparel industry consultants Kurt Salmon Associates, says, "Until the overcapacity in department-store channels is flushed out of the system—which isn't going to be anytime soon—then the off-price retailers are in a very weak position with regard to value."

OPTIONS FOR WRITING

1. In Czechoslovakia, prices for all goods and services have traditionally been set by government agencies. As that country moves toward a market economy, managers of retail enterprises will have to learn how to set prices. Prepare a report on price competition in American retailing.

2. The lowest price paid for an item represents the best value for the purchaser. If this principle held in all cases, stores with the lowest prices would dominate the market, yet we see stores offering the same item, such as a woman's denim skirt, at different prices. Why does this condition occur? Analyze the situation.

3. Besides pricing, retailers use techniques including location, product assortment, advertising, sales promotion, and service to attract customers. Evaluate how these various factors should be used together in order to increase the demand for a local pizza parlor.

Marketing Failures

Christine Donahue
HOW PROCTER & GAMBLE FUMBLED CITRUS HILL

Businesses are stuck in an endless pursuit to discover, develop, and market new products to satisfy their customers. Brands, products, and services come and go like the seasons. Success is difficult to attain. In the last decade product failure has gone from 90 percent to 95 percent. Customers are fickle, competitors are aggressive, and the environment is in constant flux. Managers do not know everything that they should, and often the best-laid plans just don't work out. Although there are general principles for developing new products, they are easier to talk about than to apply. Failures are a source of knowledge, and many companies profit by these experiences. Ford Motor Company failed miserably with the Edsel, yet in less than two years it came back into the market with one of the most popular mass-produced cars ever, the Mustang.

Two of the following readings come from Adweek's Marketing Week. *This is one of numerous business and trade publications that report on events.* Business Week, Forbes, *and* Fortune *are major general business publications that cover a wide variety of topics affecting major corporations.* INC. *reports on the exciting world of entrepreneurship. There are literally hundreds of such publications covering every aspect of business operation, from accounting to human resource management to production to transportation. The other reading comes from Philip Kotler and Gary Armstrong's* Principles of Marketing. *Most business textbooks include small case histories of companies or events affecting business.*

Procter & Gamble is one of the world's leading producers of consumer goods. Among its products are Crest, Folger's Coffee, Ivory Soap, NyQuil, Pampers, and Tide. "How Procter & Gamble Fumbled Citrus Hill" and "Citrus Hill: The Brand P&G Wouldn't Let Die" offer insights into the search and development of new products. After reading these articles, see if you can outline the planning process (that is, product development). Yes, managers make mistakes, but many problems arise because we cannot predict the future. Can you distinguish which of the problems came from being unable to predict the future and which came from management's failure to do its homework?

Coca-Cola apparently violated the rule "if it ain't broke, don't fix it." Or did it, too, make mistakes that might have been avoided? Don't be too hard on the people involved. Remember as you read that you have the advantage of 100% hindsight!

The Procter & Gamble Co. entered the orange-juice business six years ago convinced that its labs could turn out a discernibly better-tasting juice, and that its marketers could turn that taste advantage into gold. That kind of alchemy had worked for P&G many times before and had turned the company into the world's most admired marketer.

Today, P&G has given Citrus Hill's brand management group until the end of the year to turn the brand around. But executives at the company (1987 sales: $17 billion) entertained the idea of selling off the brand and getting out of the $3-billion market before then. Citrus Hill is estimated to have lost at least $200 million since 1982 and it's still not breaking even.

From its birth as a result of misread market research, the story of Citrus Hill is a series of large and small disasters, retold here by a former member of Citrus Hill's brand management group and corroborated by several other members of the group and internal documents. All spoke on the condition that they not be identified. P&G declined to comment.

In the late 1970s, P&G sought to escape flattening growth in its core businesses by finding faster-growing consumer products. Orange juice met a number of criteria, the brand executive recalls. "The orange-juice business was only projected to grow about 10% for the first five years, but that's better than what they were getting in detergent."

As P&G saw it, the category had plenty of room for a third major brand. The leading brands, Coca-Cola Foods' Minute Maid and Beatrice Cos. Inc.'s Tropicana, held only about 30% of the market between them. Small private-label and regional brands accounted for the rest.

Tropicana was charging a premium price for its Tropicana Pure Premium, the only national brand not made from concentrate. If such a quality edge could bolster margins, reasoned P&G, a technique to produce better-tasting orange juice could generate substantial profit. And P&G's engineers said they could do it.

But there was a basic flaw in that reasoning, the marketing executive recalls: "If you look at consumer acceptance of orange juice, the perceived difference between the best and the worst product in the category is narrower than in any other category. P&G needs to compete in categories where they can create a discernable difference and market the heck out of it. Orange juice had less room for improvement than anything."

That didn't stop P&G from taking the first steps in 1981. P&G paid Benn Hill Griffin Jr., a citrus farmer, $19 million for some Florida orange groves and a processing plant. Then P&G sent two brand groups down to Florida. One was to use technology developed by P&G engineers to come up with a new, superior juice, code named C-2431. The second group went to work on making a conventional orange juice, which was called CHC37, or Citrus Hill.

Why a me-too product when a computer model had forecast that another ordinary juice could expect only an 8.1% share—too little to cover costs? "No one cared, because we only wanted to sell it in test market to get some experience in orange juice with it. We were never going to expand it nationally."

That was before Citrus Hill, the conventional blend, scored slightly higher—60% vs. 40%—than Minute Maid and Tropicana in blind taste tests. "All that means is that 10 people out of 100 can tell the difference, but everyone was running around like that was a big deal, saying, 'We have an advantage, every consumer will want it.'"

It took the brand group just nine months, a near record for P&G, to get Citrus Hill into Indiana and Iowa test markets in October 1982. A strong "buy one, get one free" introductory plan convinced 35% of orange-juice drinkers to try Citrus Hill, an extremely strong level.

In fact, too strong. "Somehow they inadvertently shipped in more promotional merchandise than they were supposed to, and that contributed to higher introductory sales." In the first month of testing in Iowa, Citrus Hill's share was 1.2%. In November, the second month, the brand's share climbed to 6.7%.

In December, Citrus Hill's share hit 9%. That's when word reached P&G's Cincinnati headquarters from the other brand group in Florida: The new technology to produce the truly better, P&G-grade orange juice, was a bust. It was too expensive to pay off.

The sudden failure of its original strategy, and the inflated results from Citrus Hill's two test markets, convinced P&G to expand nationally with a brand it only had intended to use as a trial balloon.

"They were excited by the initial results," the former marketer recalls. "They felt it had the potential to be a leading brand. There had been so much bad press about [P&G's] moving too slowly on new products. The decision was, 'It appears we have a winner here, why not expand?' That was three months into test market. We should've waited longer."

Had P&G waited three more months, it would have become clear that Citrus Hill could not sustain a share that had climbed as high as 17.5%. Citrus Hill may have convinced many people to try it, but its repurchase rate was just 50%. By the sixth month, the brand's share was back down to 11.4%.

Still, the rollout went ahead.

"By the time they started having sell-in meetings for the trade, six months into test, it was apparent the brand had leveled out, but P&G had already spent the money, so they went ahead with it."

By that time, Citrus Hill's share had fallen to 8.5%, close to the original computer model's forecast of 8.1%. But that didn't stop P&G from raising projections for Citrus Hill's eventual share of the orange-juice market to between 9.6% and 10%, a point at which Citrus Hill would do better than just break even.

The rollout began in December 1983 on a sour note. "There was an error by the printer, so the color on the labels was all wrong—it was washed out and made the juice look pale and thin."

The label wasn't the only thing that went wrong for P&G. A freeze in Florida during the winter of 1982–83 decimated the harvest of oranges P&G was blending into Citrus Hill. Unable to produce the same blend it had been test-marketing and unwilling to delay the national rollout, P&G began purchasing concentrate on the open market from The Tree-Sweet Cos. and Coca-Cola Foods, the former brand-management team recalls. P&G now was marketing its competition's juice under the Citrus Hill label. Says a member of the team, "The original Citrus Hill product wasn't Citrus Hill."

Those problems were compounded when P&G drafted the sales force for its Folgers coffee brand to sell Citrus Hill as well. "These guys were used to calling on one buyer, and now they were being asked to call on two more buyers, refrigerated and frozen, effectively tripling their workload. Their annual bonuses are tied to volume, but the volume was going to be very small compared to the volume for Folgers, so Citrus Hill just meant a lot more work for no more money."

P&G did try to change that. It gave Folgers salespersons expensive training courses, complete with three-hour audiocassette tapes on orange juice for them to play in their cars. But the coffee sales force still sold Citrus Hill the way they sold coffee. "They were selling a year's worth of orange juice into stores at a time."

That can work for coffee, but unlike coffee, frozen and chilled orange juices do not keep. They deteriorate. According to an internal memo written by P&G management in March 1985, Citrus Hill's frozen product logged six months between the plant and the consumer, compared with 18 days for Minute Maid. Chilled Citrus Hill aged two weeks before sales, compared with Minute Maid's one week. "As a result," says the memo, "there was significant product degradation."

As soon as Citrus Hill achieved national distribution, Minute Maid and Tropicana doubled their ad and promotional spending and mobilized their sales forces. "Minute Maid's sales force slaughtered Citrus Hill on the beaches," says Frank Blod, vice president of marketing for Coca-Cola Foods in 1984 and 1985 and now a partner at New England Consulting Group in Westport, Conn. "They kept the product off the shelves by loading the pipeline with Minute Maid."

Ultimately, Citrus Hill's market share stabilized at 8.5%. All the data indicated that Citrus Hill was perceived by the general public as being every bit as good as Tropicana and Minute Maid. But that wasn't good enough to break people's habits.

Late in 1985, P&G decided it would have to relaunch the brand to salvage its orange-juice business and readied Citrus Hill Select.

Christine Donahue
CITRUS HILL: THE BRAND P&G WOULDN'T LET DIE

TIME, PATIENCE MAY REVIVE JUICE

The sale of Tropicana orange juice to Joseph E. Seagram & Sons Inc. for the dizzying price of $1.2 billion shines an unflattering light on The Procter & Gamble Co.'s Citrus Hill brand, which P&G also has considered selling.

P&G entered the market six years ago with its sights trained on Beatrice Cos.' billion-dollar brand. Since then, almost every shot it fired has missed the mark, and Citrus Hill neither has the volume nor the share to command a price anywhere near Tropicana's. "P&G's stated intention was to become the No. 2 brand in orange juice," says a former member of P&G's brand-management team who worked on the launch of Citrus Hill. That would have placed P&G behind Coca-Cola Food's Minute Maid brand and ahead of Tropicana. P&G would not comment for this article.

P&G's odds for success have looked long since the company's original strategy foundered in 1983. That's when P&G scrapped the technology it was counting on to give it a better-tasting orange juice and launched Citrus Hill, which has the advantage of costing less to produce. Less costly, perhaps, but Citrus Hill also has no discernible advantage over Minute Maid and Tropicana, which controlled the market. Still, P&G ignored research that argued against moving ahead. By 1985,

P&G found itself in the uncomfortable position of marketing ordinary orange juice against two entrenched competitors.

A market research study P&G commissioned showed 43% of orange-juice drinkers had tried Citrus Hill, but a much smaller percentage bought it again, precisely because Citrus Hill offered nothing new. In late 1985, P&G tried to rectify that by relaunching Citrus Hill Select.

The new brand didn't use the advanced technology that P&G's engineers originally had developed — technology that persuaded P&G to get into the orange-juice market in the first place. But while less advanced, the process P&G used for Citrus Hill Select at least promised to make the brand more than just a "me-too" product. Basically, P&G found its own way to inject small amounts of fresh juice into reconstituted juice, giving Citrus Hill Select a slightly better taste than juice made only from concentrate. "It was the best technology available," says the former Citrus Hill marketer.

P&G's in-store sampling program for Citrus Hill Select was its largest ever, and it worked. "Citrus Hill Select was one of the most successful restagings ever by P&G," says the marketer. "It increased market share by 20%, from 8% to 10%."

The company even managed to find at least one solution to the problem of poor trade relations that has plagued the brand from the start. Using DPP analysis, a method of calculating an individual product's contribution to the retailer's bottom line, P&G came up with a fatter, squatter 16-ounce can for its frozen version. The new shape boosted retail profits 30% by occupying less room in the freezer case. Recalls the former Citrus Hill marketer, "The trade got very excited, and it helped shore up spotty distribution of that size."

But for every step forward, P&G took at least one step back. For one, P&G gained virtually no ground on Tropicana and Minute Maid, which had doubled spending on advertising and promotion to defend their combined 30% share of the category.

"As a result of actions by Tropicana and Minute Maid, Citrus Hill's market share came almost exclusively from private-label brands," says Frank Blod, a partner in the Westport, Conn.-based New England Consulting Group who was vice president of marketing for Minute Maid in 1984 and 1985.

Private-label orange juice probably is one of the most profitable private-label businesses for supermarket retailers. There's little branded competition with private-label juice for the price-sensitive segment of the orange-juice market. This allows retailers to keep private-label orange-juice margins higher than in other categories. "It was a very profitable partnership for retailers until Citrus Hill came in and messed it up," says Blod.

And that wasn't the only reason for bad blood between the trade and Citrus Hill. "Before they even launched Citrus Hill, P&G made statements in writing to the grocery trade that they were coming in to shake up the sleepy orange-juice industry, which irritated the trade," says Blod. "It was typical of P&G to be so arrogant to assume that they could go into any market and come to own it over time."

Retailers did take some comfort in the fact that P&G's presence led to a sharply higher level of trade promotion generally. The percentage of orange juice sold to retailers at lower prices went from 39% in 1981, prior to Citrus Hill's introduction, to 47% in 1983 when Citrus Hill was introduced. It kept climbing until more than half of all orange juice was being sold at a discount, according to a recent report by Beverage Marketing, a New York consulting firm.

P&G, the high-cost producer in the category due to its low volume, tried to change that in early 1986. "P&G pulled its trade spending, and that killed them with the trade," recalls Karl Maggard, who spent 20 years at P&G and is now vice president of sales at Tropicana. "Citrus Hill went from a 12% Nielsen share of total orange juice to 3.6% at one point."

In its annual-report for the fiscal year ending in June 1986, P&G reported: "Citrus Hill orange juice increased volume significantly this past year following the expansion late in the previous year of improved Citrus Hill Select." But according Beverage Marketing's report, Citrus Hill dollar sales actually fell by 4.2% in 1986, to $230 million.

The brand group scrambled for other ways to give Citrus Hill its own cachet. It came up with foil-lined cartons to preserve freshness for chilled Citrus Hill. "That was the best thing we did in terms of product," says the former Citrus Hill marketer, and one competitor even copied the move. And in 1986, P&G again tried to apply its technological edge to orange juice, and came out with Citrus Hill Plus Calcium.

According to the Beverage Marketing report, over half of the $15.5 million P&G spent on ads for Citrus Hill in 1986 went to Citrus Hill Plus Calcium. Still Citrus Hill finished up 1987 with 8.5% of the total orange-juice market, higher than the 7.7% it averaged in 1986 but still shy of P&G's break-even point.

Meanwhile both Minute Maid and Tropicana have gained share, although heavy marketing spending has cut deeply into their profits as well. Minute Maid, which dominates the frozen-juice segment of the orange-juice business, now has about 22% of the overall market. Tropicana, whose strength is in chilled juice, now has 18.6% of the overall market, up from 14.5% in 1985.

"The question was always whether the name Citrus Hill and a slightly better product could overcome the fantastic Minute Maid distribution system in frozen juice and the fantastic Tropicana distribution system in chilled juice and their brand names, which had been around forever," says a second former P&G executive who has responsibility for the brand.

In retrospect, the answer is no. Ironically, P&G's original insight, that a discernibly better-tasting juice could prevail even in such a commodity category, has been borne out — by Tropicana. Tropicana Pure Premium, the only major brand not made from concentrate, has a lock on the markets where it's sold. "The total marketing effort was successful, but basically you have to start off with a product the consumer wants," says Bob Weisman, senior vice president of Tropicana.

While Seagram sorts out its Tropicana acquisition, P&G may get some breathing room, and Citrus Hill does have strengths to build on. Scanner data indicates that Citrus Hill is consistently the No. 2 brand behind Tropicana in the Southern California market, for instance, and the brand is also relatively strong in parts of the South. The coffee sales force to which P&G assigned Citrus Hill may be making up for earlier mistakes as they learn how to sell juice.

And Seagram, which is new to supermarkets, will be replacing Beatrice, a seasoned grocery marketer, as one of Citrus Hill's two big competitors. "This will be a real stretch for Seagram," says Tom Pirko, president of Bevmark Inc., a Los Angeles-based beverage consulting firm. "Now is P&G's chance to make a run for it."

Time and P&G's traditional patience in brand-building could be on Citrus Hill's side. "Sometimes a brand that seems mature in terms of growth surprises you," says Pirko.

If nothing else, Citrus Hill will have taught P&G plenty about the food business. Says a former P&G executive who worked on Citrus Hill, "P&G is learning once again that the further you move away from home, the less you can go by the same rules that apply to Tide."

Philip Kotler
DON'T MESS WITH MOTHER COKE

In 1985 the Coca-Cola Company made a spectacular marketing blunder. After 99 successful years, it set aside its long-standing rule — "don't mess with Mother Coke" — and dropped its original formula Coke! In its place came *New* Coke with a sweeter, smoother taste. The company boldly announced the new taste with a flurry of advertising and publicity.

At first, amid the introductory fanfare, New Coke sold well. But sales soon went flat, and the stunned public reacted. Coke began receiving over 1,500 phone calls and many sacks of mail each day from angry consumers. A group called Old Cola Drinkers staged protests, handed out tee-shirts, and threatened a class-action suit unless Coca-Cola brought back the old formula. Most marketing experts predicted that New Coke would be the "Edsel of the Eighties."

After just two months, the Coca-Cola Company brought old Coke back. Called Coke Classic, it sold side-by-side with New Coke on supermarket shelves. The company said that New Coke would remain its "flagship" brand, but consumers had a different idea. By the end of 1985, Classic was outselling New Coke in supermarkets by two to one. By mid-1986, the company's two largest fountain accounts, McDonald's and Kentucky Fried Chicken, had returned to serving Coke Classic in their restaurants.

Quick reaction saved the company from potential disaster. It stepped up efforts for Coke Classic and slotted New Coke into a supporting role. By 1987, Coke Classic was again the company's main brand, and the country's leading soft drink with a 19 percent market share versus Pepsi's 18.5 percent. New Coke became the company's "attack brand"—its Pepsi stopper. With computer-enhanced star Max Headroom leading the charge, company ads boldly compared New Coke's taste with Pepsi's. Still, New Coke managed only a 2 percent market share.

Why was New Coke introduced in the first place? And what went wrong? Many analysts blame the blunder on poor marketing research.

In the early 1980s, though Coke was still the leading soft drink, it was slowly losing market share to Pepsi. For years, Pepsi had successfully mounted the "Pepsi Challenge," a series of televised taste tests showing that consumers preferred the sweeter taste of Pepsi. By early 1985, though Coke led in the overall market, Pepsi led in share of supermarket sales by 2 percent. (That doesn't sound like much, but 2 percent of the huge soft-drink market amounts to $600 million in retail sales.) Coca-Cola had to do something to stop its loss of market share—the solution appeared to be a change in Coke's taste.

Coca-Cola began the largest new product research project in the company's history. It spent over two years and $4 million on research before settling on a new formula. It conducted some 200,000 taste tests—30,000 on the final formula alone. In the blind tests, 60 percent of consumers chose the new Coke over the old, and 52 percent chose it over Pepsi. Research showed that New Coke would be a winner, and the company introduced it with confidence. What happened?

Looking back, Coke's marketing research was too narrowly focused. The research looked only at taste; it did not explore how consumers felt about dropping the old Coke and replacing it with a new version. It took no account of the intangibles—Coke's name, history, packaging, cultural heritage, and image. But to many people, Coke stands beside baseball, hot dogs, and apple pie as an American institution; it represented the very fabric of Americana. Coke's symbolic meaning turned out to be more important to many consumers than its taste. More complete marketing research would have detected these strong emotions.

Coke's managers may also have used poor judgment in interpreting the research and planning strategies around it. For example, they took the finding that 60 percent of consumers preferred New Coke's taste to mean that the new product would win the marketplace—as when a political candidate wins with 60 percent of the vote. But it also meant that 40 percent still wanted the old Coke. By dropping the old Coke, the company trampled the taste buds of its large core of loyal coke drinkers who did not want a change. The company might have been wiser to leave the old Coke alone and introduce New Coke as a brand extension, as was later done successfully with Cherry Coke.

The Coca-Cola Company has one of the largest, best managed, and most advanced marketing research operations in America. Good marketing research has kept the company atop the rough-and-tumble soft-drink market for decades. But marketing research is far from an exact science. Consumers are full of surprises, and figuring them out can be awfully tough.

OPTIONS FOR WRITING

1. Compare the similarities and differences between Procter & Gamble and Coca-Cola in these two failures. Be certain to point out what each company might have done to prevent the circumstances that led to their predicaments. What advice would you offer to the manager of each company? Write a consult's report to one of these companies.

2. One of the challenges of business is to discover general principles that can be used in a number of circumstances. Without using the specific examples—that is, do not mention orange juice—develop general principles. Once you have a list, write a letter to a manufacturer of personal computers about avoiding market failure. Here you should refer specifically to the products.

Managing Resources

A. L. Minkes
WHAT IS MANAGEMENT ALL ABOUT?

Businesses as well as governments, hospitals, nursing homes, universities, and all other types of organizations, get things done through a process called management. It is a complex activity that is defined slightly differently by all who use it. There is simply no best definition, though many have tried to find one. Economists suggest that management is the allocation of scarce resources; as a student you can appreciate that approach in terms of your time and money. Although this is a good starting point, there is more to it.

In "What Is Management All About?" from The Entrepreneurial Manager, *Professor A. L. Minkes offers a comprehensive view of what it is to manage. Minkes, a British scholar, goes beyond a single abstract definition; he describes what a manager confronts on*

*a single day. As you read this piece, look for ways of better manag-
ing your own time. Keep a log of how you use your time for a week.
Do you think you can improve your time management?*

*In "Zimmerman's: What Do You Do to Make It Happen?" you
will find a firsthand glimpse of the challenges facing managers. This
is a case prepared for use in an introductory marketing course. The
materials come from the records of a real firm, though the real company is carefully disguised. The case focuses on one part of the challenges that Suzzane Zimmerman must face if she is going to turn the
business around. As you read through the case, you should identify
external and internal factors that must be dealt with. Appended to
the case are two tables describing some operating results for Zimmerman's. Although you may not be familiar with accounting data,
Table 12.1 provides summary information about what has happened.
Look at that table carefully to see if you can describe in words some
of the things that are happening. For example, can you explain why
sales are going down?*

*As you might expect, the practice of business requires an under-
standing of great volumes of quantitative data. Table 12.2 provides
the results of a survey of Zimmerman's customers. Try to summarize
the results of each of the three sections of the table. Based on the
"Comparison of Zimmermans with Two Favorite Stores," discuss
what Suzzane should do to become more competitive with the other
stores.*

*Professor Neil Chamberlain, who had a distinguished career as
an economist at Yale University, provides a general look at management in "The Central Thesis" from his book* Enterprise and Environment. *He asks you to move from specific examples you have read
and to deal with general principles. His thesis holds that the central
challenge to management is to understand that a firm is an ever-
changing organization in an ever-changing environment. He stresses
the need to know a firm's history and its present and to use these to
develop plans for the future. As you read through his chapter, consider writing a list of factors that have affected business over the past
several years — the energy crisis, new concerns about the environment, and the Gulf War, to mention a few. Consider how each factor
has affected business. Our current concern with pollution is pushing
companies to think about new packaging formats and materials. What
other responses might there be?*

*The future is difficult, if not impossible, to predict. We know
that there will always be forces affecting the ways business must
manage. Some people known as "futurists" have already begun predictions about what events might take place. Some of their analysis is
based on historical trends, but other predictions are guesses. In the
United States we have an aging population: There are more and more
people over the age of 65 who are living longer lives. What effect
will this have on the types of goods and services demanded in the*

next ten or twenty years? Although aging can be predicted from past trends, other forces cannot be so easily defined. We already sense that the demand for a secure and healthy food supply is emerging. What other things might be in our future? How should managers approach the future?

What is management itself? What does it mean, and what are the tasks and qualities which are required of managers?

There are three ways of looking at this topic. The first might be called the conventional way of examining definitions of the kind which many books consider. The second is concerned with the reality of the manager's day, the fragmented life and varied pressures which are the regular experience. The third approach is to analyze management as an idea — what it is that managers are doing when they are engaged in management. This focuses not on the specific functions they perform but on the inherent nature of management activity.

ON DEFINITIONS OF MANAGEMENT

Definitions can serve several purposes. They tell the reader what the subject means, or at least what the author means by it. In this way, they mark out the area of discussion, influence the method of approach to a subject, and simultaneously indicate what is *not* included within it. This can be extremely important; think of the following examples drawn from economics.

In 1932 the late Lord Robbins published his famous book *An Essay on the Nature and Significance of Economic Science,* in which he defined economics as a science which studied the allocation between competing ends of scarce resources which have alternative uses. This definition greatly influenced many economists and the way the subject was studied, because it focused attention on relative scarcity and on prices. That is quite different from studying economics as, say, the history and structure of economic institutions. Jacob Viner said that "economics is what economists do": and Keynes, in his introduction to the *Cambridge Economic Handbook Series* (1922), characterized the theory of economics as a method, "a technique of thinking." This way of looking at the subject inclines economists towards the construction of analytical models rather than the empirical study of behavior in organizations.

Similarly with management: some definitions emphasize the element of co-ordination of resources, others the task of managing people. For some writers, the elements of leadership and direction hold the center of the stage; for others, planning and control are the crucial features.

So what can be picked out as characteristics of management in the profusion of definitions?

1. A first and striking feature of management is that it exists essentially because of the existence of organizations. Of course it is true that individuals are said to manage their affairs, personal, financial, and career: an individual may "manage" his investment portfolio or his estate, and a one-man business, which can hardly be said to be an organization, can be said to require managing. But this is a rather superficial use of the term "management," which means no more than to say that men and women have to look after their business matters and personal concerns. When they are members of organizations, as when they are employed in a firm, their arrangements are part of a network which involves other people, perhaps in very large numbers.

This may seem so obvious as to be hardly worth saying: managers must be very well aware of this. But it is worth emphasizing for a number of reasons. A manager is not a Robinson Crusoe: he does not carry on his activities or make his decisions on his own. Herbert Simon put it in this way, that when an executive makes a decision, he does so with one eye on the matter in hand and one eye on its organizational consequences. Managers know, in other words, that what they do affects other members of the organization and they in turn are affected by the actions of others. Thus management involves a relationship of interdependence, in all kinds of ways. Decisions about production involve requirements for the purchase of materials or components; the transfer of staff from one task to another creates the need to consider the vacancies it causes.

Just as managers are not isolated individuals, so their actions are not isolated incidents, and management requires, therefore, an awareness of a whole set of interrelationships. The study of management is partly the study of managerial action, but it is also the study of how that action is generated and processed in the framework of organization.

2. A second feature is that management is about the genesis and progress of change. In a totally unchanging world, there would be no requirement for management at all. When people say that there is a problem of managing change, they are in a sense understating matters, because management *is about* change. One way of expressing it is to say that in an unchanging world there would only be the administrative task of keeping things going, of administering established routines and procedures. Suppose, for example, that a large retail organization has an established system allowing customers to return articles which they have purchased and which turn out not to be suitable. Marks and Spencer do this: clothing bought in any of their stores can be returned to any other of their stores throughout Britain. The rules which Marks and Spencer apply in this respect are well-known and long-established. A store manager may doubtless exercise discretion in borderline cases, but the procedure appears to be quite standard. This is fundamentally a matter of administration.

Consider another instance: a group of civil servants in a very closely regulated, partly legally-based department (overseas) were discussing with a visiting academic the possibility of running a series of management seminars for the staff. The academic visitor asked some of them what their work consisted of, and they replied "We administer the ordinances." Since they claimed that they had no discretion in interpreting the ordinances and when in doubt "We consult a senior officer," he concluded that they had explicit administrative tasks but they had not shown him that they exercised a managerial function. Once again, this was a matter of administration.

At what point could these examples be translated into a management situation? When a business is considering whether or not to *change* its procedures, or when, as in the case of the civil-servants, the discussion turned to possible *changes* in the organization of their department, management questions were bound to arise. These are quite modest examples of changes, which serve to show, nevertheless, that a transition from administration to management occurs as soon as questions are raised of the type: what procedures should we institute, what new rules are appropriate, what new methods are appropriate? These are management questions: it is only when they have been answered and decisions have been made about them that the task of administering the rules can begin.

Of course, the point has been exaggerated for the sake of exposition: the distinction between management and administration is not always perfectly clear and precise. But the principle is valid.

3. An important approach to definitions of management is that it involves working through other people. The work of managers requires them to organize others: they have to allocate tasks to subordinates and to supervise and control the results. One consequence is that managers are dependent on the skills and performance of other people, and, interestingly enough, this is more significant the higher up the management chain they are. The apex of the pyramid ultimately rests on its base. In a sense, therefore, to be at the top of the organization means both to be in a position of authority and to be in a position of dependence. The balance between authority, and the power conferred by it, and reliance on others will vary from one business to another, depending on their size, managerial style, cultural traditions, and so on. But companies do recognize this factor. For example, John Neville, who was chief executive of Manganese Bronze, spoke of the relationship between the group headquarters and the subsidiaries as one in which the center had to rely on the ability of the senior executives in the subsidiaries. It had to trust them; and the word *trust* was used explicitly by Sir Patrick Meaney, who was chief executive of Thomas Tilling, and Gordon Yardley, managing director of its subsidiary company Newey and Eyre, to describe the relationship between them. In turn, Yardley saw his relationship with his subordinates in the same light: he expressed it by saying that when he planned a visit to a branch of his company, he checked first with the branch manager that it was acceptable. This picture of dependence does not imply absence of authority and power. The

same John Neville made it clear that the subsidiary had to deliver the goods: if not, the company could replace the senior executives with others who would do the job. What this means is that choosing people in whom reliance can be placed, who can be *depended on*, in other words, is a critical task in management. But this dependence which comes from working through other people has two other substantial consequences. One is that management has a waiting aspect; managers spend part of their time waiting for the results of tasks which they have delegated to others. The other, and more important, consequence is that management means taking responsibility for the activities of others. In a marvelous and courageous passage in his history of *The Second World War*, Winston Churchill comments as follows about his horrified discovery that Singapore, far from being a fortress, was acutely vulnerable to land-based attack: "I ought to have known. My advisers ought to have known and I ought to have been told, and I ought to have asked."

Churchill was here emphasizing the doctrine of ultimate responsibility—where the buck stops—and it is a lesson which can be applied at all levels of management where managers are concerned with the work of others who report to them. How this responsibility can be honored and by what means of control, formal and informal, managers can reconcile the burden of responsibility with the delegation of tasks to others (who cannot be supervised every moment of the day) is one of the major management questions in the modern business corporation.

4. Since management is concerned with change, it can be seen to have an entrepreneurial as well as an administrative aspect. There is a good deal of debate about the meaning of the term "entrepreneur," but for the purposes of this chapter entrepreneurship is taken to be concerned with three things:

(a) determination of the mission or basic direction of the enterprise;
(b) choice of strategy for effecting the business purposes;
(c) creation of the corporate structure, i.e. the organizational means for devising and implementing strategy.

Thus Sir Adrian Cadbury in defining the strategic characteristics of Cadbury Schweppes made this series of statements. At one time, before the merger with Schweppes, Cadburys' business could have been defined in terms of its basic raw material, the cocoa bean. Now it could be classified as the supply of snack foods of which it happens that many are covered with chocolate: since, furthermore, the company is essentially a marketing concern, it can be defined in the context of its distribution outlets, e.g. supermarkets.

Similarly, Robin Martin, who, at the head of Tarmac, presided over its development into a major construction company, categorized it within construction and civil engineering, a view which top direction of the company continued to hold. In going on to strategic choice, Martin spoke particularly of diversification, within that context, as a means of fostering growth.

Concern with "mission" and "strategic choice" must lie with managers; with whom else? With which managers and at which levels of the organization are other matters, which belong to later chapters. That they are part of management responsibility is crucial, since from this idea flows a whole set of commitments and tasks, and a picture of what constitutes an effective manager.

The third point mentioned above was the creation of the organization. Professor Ansoff has pointed out that in traditional economic theory the manager was perceived as what he calls "an operator of a fixed arm." By this he meant that the manager was regarded as somebody who took a set of inputs (labor, materials, equipment) and used them in the "best" combinations so as to produce output at minimum cost. In reality, however, a large part of management is concerned with the design and establishment of the structure of the organization. As will be seen later in this book, the formation of strategy is an abstract exercise without the organizational means of making it effective. Textbooks of management rightly concentrate attention on the importance of organization, and this is not a "given": it has to be designed and created. In a very large company with numerous departments and divisions this may seem obvious, but it is interesting that management has to face this task even when the business is of quite modest size. The British industrialist John Crabtree emphasized this point in an unpublished manuscript describing the growth of his firm, which made electrical products, from its inception with "a man and a boy" in 1921 to about 1,000 employees in 1935, when he died. He thought that organizations did not grow "naturally" and that at successive increments of two or three hundred employees, management needed to consider how to reconstruct the ways in which it handled its tasks.

ON THE MANAGER'S WORKING DAY

In a conversation with the author a number of years ago, Professor Bela Gold remarked that at the University of Pittsburgh it had been his custom to take graduate students downtown to observe for themselves how executives actually spent their time. He thought it might disabuse them of the notion that executives sat back in order to brood on long-term strategic developments: it could be that in fact they were struggling to keep the in-tray from overflowing.

The daily life of the manager is filled with specific tasks and current pressures. The managing director of a large British company, when asked how he felt that industrial management differed from academic life, replied that he thought it much more *fragmented*. "I do not find it difficult," he said, "to find a spare hour to devote to one job, but I find it extremely difficult to find two successive hours."

Curzon gives a very apt example of a manager's working day, illustrating an imaginary but realistic factory manager responsible to the company's managing director. His engagement diary records his anticipated arrangements:

0845   Deal with day's correspondence
0915   Meeting with R & D departmental head: discussion on delay in presentation of new design
0930   Meeting with union representative: grievances concerning new shift system
1000   Tour of loading bays: observations of procedures
1030   Meeting with departmental heads: discussion of preliminary estimates for next financial year
1145   Work on preparation of preliminary estimates documents
1230   Working lunch with industrial editor of national newspaper
1345   Further tour loading bays
1415   Further preparation of estimates document
1515   Meeting with . . . overseas marketing manager: discussion on developments in S E Asian markets.

Curzon goes on to comment:

> In the event, the 0930 meeting continues until 1030, and preparation of the estimates document, programmed for 1145, is abandoned in favor of an emergency meeting with factory shop stewards, designed to head off a conflict concerning the allocation of overtime. Throughout [his] day he is involved in the process of communication, e.g. listening, observing, ordering, persuading, writing.

These passages are used by Curzon to stress the manager's role in "the processes of communication," but they also serve to underline four critical aspects of management life. The first, as has already been suggested, is its *fragmentation* and the short time which can be given to individual important topics. The second is the *variety* of matters which come before the manager's attention: new design, union grievance, loading bay procedures, estimates, working lunch with journalist, overseas markets. Thirdly, there is the variety of *people* with whom he is involved: departmental heads, union representative, journalist, company marketing manager. Lastly, there is the problem of *delay and interruption*—the extended 0930 meeting, and the emergency meeting which leads him to defer the preparation of the estimates document, very important job though that must clearly be. And if the experience of being dean of a faculty in a university is any guideline, there are other interruptions: for example, the telephone, the indispensable deadly instrument, and the sheer amount of time it takes to get from one place to another.

It is not surprising, therefore, that writers like Handy should lay stress on the manager's problem of living "in two or more dimensions":

The manager is, above all, responsible for the future. . . .

But this management of the future has to go hand in hand with the responsibility for the present. . . . It is not easy to live in two or more time dimensions at once. It is hard to plan creatively for five years hence with a redundancy interview scheduled for one hour's time. Just as routine drives out non-routine, so the present can easily obliterate the future. By concentrating on the problems of the present the future becomes in its turn a series of present problems or crises, intervention by the manager in a power role becomes legitimate, even essential, there is still less time available for the future, the manager feels indispensable and legitimized by crisis. The cycle has become self-fulfilling. *Unless the manager is able to live successfully in two time dimensions he will make the present more difficult than it need be and will unsuccessfully manage the future.* [Italics added]

This passage has been quoted at length because it forms a whole and poses the well-known problem of reconciling attention to present pressures with the need to attend to future concerns. This is not something which is confined to middle managers. Sir Isaac Wolfson, asked at a University of Birmingham seminar if running so large a business as Great Universal Stores did not give him ulcers, replied—jestingly, it is true—"No: they are for middle managers." But even top managers face the problem of fragmentation and variety of specific problems. It is not difficult to find examples, and those which follow, from the experience of the Midlands Postal Region in Britain, illustrate the point. Senior management could not spend all its time thinking about long-term strategic plans. It had to consider a range of individual topics.

As the mechanization of letter sorting offices advanced, the prospect arose in 1978–9 that, except for early morning mail, the "Stratford-upon-Avon" postmark would disappear, to be replaced by "Coventry" or a generic title. A simple enough matter of efficiency, it might be thought, but in fact a complicated, quite time-consuming affair which engaged attention at senior level. The local MP, district councillors and many local bodies, headed by the Shakespeare Birthplace Trust, lobbied fiercely to retain the Stratford postmark. They argued that it was regarded by overseas tourists, on whom Stratford depends so much for its prosperity, as an important feature for which "Coventry" was no substitute at all. Hence, the simple matter of efficiency turned out to be sufficiently significant to engage attention at the highest Post Office level (with the additional complication that in a public corporation political pressure is more difficult to resist). Or again, a postal business will be seriously affected by the availability and punctuality of the railway service, and any deficiencies may cause short-run crises as well as long-term policy problems. Machinery breakdown or industrial disputes with engineers assume a significance in the context of mechanization which can result in an engagements diary very like the hypothetical one outlined by Curzon.

One more example from the postal business deserves to be cited because it illustrates so well the "localized," specific problems which can occupy the time of managers. The business is labor-intensive, i.e. it has a relatively high input of labour, by contrast with telecommunications. It also involves an important element of what are called unsocial hours, because postal employees who make early morning deliveries of letters have to arrive very early at the sorting offices in preparation for their delivery "walk." Scrupulous though the Post Office may be in explaining this to young recruits to the business, the experience sometimes comes as an unpalatable shock in the dark early hours of winter, and some of them leave within a fairly short time. This creates problems for the business, and hence occupies the attention of managers, both in respect of supply of labor and of the cost of the training which has been invested in personnel and which has to be repeated for the replacement intake.

This chapter has given much attention to specific examples: they are certainly particular, but they are also typical. They are not intended to prove that managers are rushed off their feet all the time, that the pressure is unrelenting, and that time is an inexorable enemy of even a single long-term thought. But they lend practical force to the view expressed in the passage from Handy cited above, and they oblige managers to consider how to secure that life in two dimensions which he regards as essential if they are to perform successfully. That is why companies quite often try to devise means by which their managers can be got away from day-to-day pressures. They may use special "think tank" gatherings away from the office, "brainstorming sessions," seminars, project groups: they may provide for occasions and facilities to encourage informal exchange of ideas.

THE CONCEPT OF MANAGEMENT

So far in this chapter, the implications of some characteristic definitions of management have been considered and some picture of the managerial day has been given. In this penultimate section, the purpose is to analyze the *nature* of management as an idea. In any organization, be it business or otherwise, men and women play many parts; each individual may play more than one part. The finance director of a company will have regard to financial matters and will also contribute to wider policy discussions on the board of directors of the enterprise. A manager may be engaged in some specific function and also be managing a department. The question to be examined now is: what is it that is being done which can properly be called *management*?

Consider an example. Suppose that a young man or woman has graduated from a university with a degree in chemistry and has found a job in the research and development department of a business enterprise. And suppose that he or she is put to work on the chemical properties of the materials which the company utilizes. Clearly such a person cannot be said to be engaged in *management*, since, whatever the formal status in the company, the work is that of a chemist—much as it might be if the same person were working in, say, a university laboratory.

Now suppose that the chemist is promoted to be head of the R & D department. It appears to become immediately obvious that the kind of work—*or significant part of it*—can legitimately be classified as management. Why is this so?

1. In the first place, it is virtually certain that there will no longer be as much time for chemistry and, particularly, for keeping up to date with fresh developments in the subject. Of course this will partly depend on the size of the department: the bigger and more varied its activities, the stronger the argument. (Similar circumstances are experienced by academics who assume significant administrative responsibilities.)

2. The kinds of decision with which the new head of the department is now concerned are quite different. Imagine that the department has been allocated a fixed budget of £x thousand, that it has ten chemically feasible projects in hand, and that to persist with all of them would exceed the budget. The head must accordingly either persuade higher management to increase the budget allocation or pare down the ten projects to, say, the *best* eight. But the criteria for choosing and the language in which the case will be argued will be economical, commercial, market criteria. Interested though the company may be in the inherent intellectual quality of the ideas which are generated in its research laboratories, its budget allocations must be judged against the contribution those ideas will ultimately make to the "bottom line," the profit account of the company.

Or consider again:

3. As head of department, the manager has to think about a variety of staff questions. Colleagues whose projects do not receive what they regard as adequate funding may feel aggrieved. Then there will be matters of recruitment and promotion of staff to consider and questions of how to balance individual talents with organizational harmony. This requires an understanding, once again, of factors other than the chemistry of research products; it requires, rather, the chemistry of organization and human relations, of personnel and social psychology.

This analysis suggests that the transition into management is a movement *from specialist to generalist*. Beginning as a specialist in chemistry, working strictly within that discipline, the chemist has now to be concerned with a range of activities and decisions. This means co-ordinating variables from a variety of disciplines in which it is virtually certain that this particular individual is *not* expert and in which the company does employ experts. Thus, all management can be regarded as *general* management: the phase "specialist management" is a contradiction in terms.

Is this an exaggerated picture of the idea of management? Is it an excessively academic view? Is it not at variance with the earlier sections of this chapter which show the manager as a busy, practical person? Do managers sit back and analyze problems in terms of economics, sociology, and social psychology? Not everybody goes into business with a specialist training in chemistry or accounting or anything else with immediate applicability to a particular aspect of a company's activity. Graduates in English, history, geography, and young men and women who are not graduates at all take jobs in industry and commerce: on the other hand, many entrants have degrees or diplomas in business studies, so that they are quite well-equipped in the relevant disciplines. And even if the analysis is valid, is it not applicable mainly to large and bureaucratic business corporations?

It is true that the story of the chemist is hypothetical and simplified, that it is chosen partly to make a point: but that does not mean that it fails to get at the essence of management. Suppose, for example, that the head of the R & D department is promoted further so that the career progress looks like Figure 12.1

Thus, the further that managers advance, the less can they be seen in a specialist function; and the more departments which fall within their ultimate responsibility, the more evident it becomes that their decisions are generalist and interdisciplinary in character. Although it is perfectly true, therefore, that managers perform specific tasks within spe-

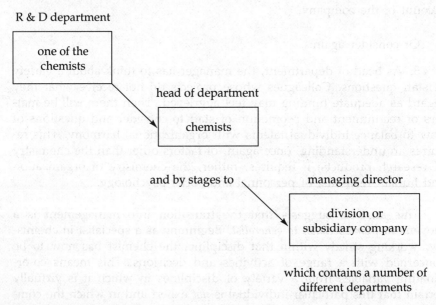

Figure 12.1   Career progress of the head of R & D.

cific functional areas of a company, it is also true that the peculiar characteristic of management as an idea lies in its generalist nature. Sometimes, in fact, this is expressed in the title "general manager" given to managers responsible for an area or division in which they are concerned with a number of departmental functions.

SOME IMPLICATIONS AND CONCLUSIONS

The first implication which may be drawn from the foregoing analysis is by way of being a puzzle or a paradox. On the one hand, there has been a striking increase in the number of "expertises" and experts. Once upon a time, men spoke of the Renaissance man as the ideal, with a wide-ranging culture, and of the generalist, ground perhaps in the classics, as the most appropriate man for top-level administration. But nowadays many subjects which once filled a single textbook have opened up into numbers of separate specialisms: there are accountants and tax accountants, lawyers and company lawyers, systems analysts and computer programmers. How is this compatible with the view that management is general management?

It means, first of all, that the task of management is more complex than in the past, because the number of special fields which are relevant to ultimate decisions is larger and the element of expertise is greater. This means, secondly, that the kind of general training which is suitable for development of managers has also changed, as was already pointed out in 1963 by the Franks Report on *British Business Schools.* This training, whether in formal education or through experience, is more likely to turn on business subjects, but not on any single discipline.

A second implication concerns the problem of promotion in management life. If management is general—so that the head of a police force need not have been a policeman or the head of a postal business a postman—what are the advantages and disadvantages of bringing in managers from outside a company? This question is especially acute in organizations which have a high professional content: hospitals, social work departments, schools, colleges and universities. But they also exist in business. For example, if a company appoints a new sales director, what kind of background is essential or simply desirable? The late Sir Frederick Hooper, who was managing director of Schweppes (a considerable time before its merger with Cadbury), once described how, after looking at a number of candidates who had come up through the sales function, the company eventually chose as director a man from production. He had the qualities of understanding data and handling organization which outweighed his inexperience in the field of sales.

This anecdote is not a universal recommendation, and choices of this kind may raise very difficult problems within an organization. But it illustrates the point about general management and the practical difficulty that can arise in finding suitable general managers in a world where recruits enter on employment in a specific function.

There is a third aspect, which is concerned with what a business enterprise is required to do. In Professor Drucker's view, it exists essentially to supply products to consumers, who have to be willing to pay for them: this is the primary test of its performance and the measure of its success. He particularly, and other writers too, see business management, therefore, as an economic instrument, using economic resources to generate wealth and the power to create wealth. Management derives what Drucker calls its authority from its ability to meet customer demand at the relevant prices, and everything that managers do and all the decisions they make must be assessed against the test of economic performance. This means that the ability to identify where the market lies, to decide who the customer is, and to know how to satisfy wants, are inherent in the management task.

Even in a non-business, non-market situation, decisions have to be made about what are the right things to supply and how they can be most efficiently supplied. But the task of actually managing a complex organization, business or non-business, requires, as Drucker himself appreciates, a variety of skills and activities. The ultimate test may be economic performance but the management tasks cannot be defined solely in terms of economics. If there were a single "bottom line" for every management activity and decision, life would be immeasurably easier for managers: but there is not. Rosemary Stewart, who says that since "Managers' jobs vary so much" she doubted "the truth of the common statement 'a good manager can manage anything,'" adds:

> We quoted Sune Carlson's pioneering study of nine managing directors and subsequent studies, which show that typically the manager's day is a very fragmented one. This makes it harder to organize one's time effectively. Research has shown that *many managers require political skills* as well as the, more commonly emphasized, supervisory skills. [Italics added]

Two further implications may be drawn from the argument of this chapter. One is that a considerable part of the management task is concerned with the *internal environment* of the organization. Managers certainly have to be alert to the external environment, of customers, competitors, technology, government: without that they would be lost. But a great deal of this work centers round internal management: organizational design, committee or board meetings, discussions with other managers about personnel, and generally, in fact, maintaining the health of the organization and ensuring its innovative development.

The other implication is that management is an integrative activity. One of the most forceful expressions of this view is made by Professor Kanter, who distinguishes organizations which are integrative and see problems as wholes from those which work by what she terms "walling off a piece of experience and preventing it from being touched or affected by any new experiences." She emphasizes a point which has been of basic importance in this chapter, that management requires the co-ordination of a variety of specialists, each with an approach to problems which reflects a specific background and training. The strength of an organization resides in its diversity, but, of course, the point is to bring together the diverse views so as to arrive at agreed courses of action. Within an organization, an integrative approach which avoids "walling off" means that ideas can move across internal, departmental frontiers, and that innovative practices can challenge the old and generate change.

Professor Kanter contrasts this approach with what she terms "segmentalism," which "assumes that problems can be solved when they are carved into pieces and the pieces are assigned to specialists who work in isolation." This is another issue: to the extent, however, that it emphasizes the significance of integrating specialisms, it underlines a central point of this chapter.

Ronald Savitt
ZIMMERMAN'S: WHAT DO YOU DO TO MAKE IT HAPPEN?

In April 1988, Suzzane Zimmerman at the age of 33 became the chief executive officer of the department store founded by her grandfather nearly a century ago as a result of her father's death. While she had been brought into the store's operations as a fashion consultant five years ago, she now had full charge of the operations. She had no formal management training but had participated in the store's operations with her father. She had seen the changes in the local retail environment and the recent report of the comptroller clearly suggested that significant changes had to be made in the store if it were to remain in business. She wanted to take charge and bring the store not simply back to where it had been but to make it a major force in the retail market.

Last Monday, Tom Brockhaus presented Suzzane with a summary of the operating results for the last three years; these can be found in Table 12.1. He also chose a few important figures from the larger report. He thought it important for her to know that their inventory turnover was about 15% on the average less than for department stores of their size as reported by the National Retail Merchants Association. Productivity for employees as measured by sales per salesperson, store productivity in general by "dollars per square foot," and selling costs were all out of line with similar size operations—and all worse than the standard

TABLE 12.1 Zimmerman's Selected Operating Data ($)

	1985		1986		1987	
Net Sales	1,137,000	(100.0)*	987,000	(100.0)	974,000	(100.0)
Cost of Goods Sold	637,235	(56.0)	556,789	(56.4)	593,688	(61.0)
Gross Margin	499,765	(44.2)	430,211	(44.0)	380,312	(34.4)
Store Expenses (selected)						
Advertising	29,500	(2.6)	30,100	(3.0)	17,600	(1.8)
Payroll⁺	124,678	(11.0)	127,052	(12.9)	129,708	(13.3)
Total Store Expenses	313,316	(27.6)	304,974	(30.9)	289,571	(29.7)
Contribution to Overhead and Profit	189,411	(16.7)	129,675	(13.1)	94,304	(9.7)

* Figures in "( )" represent percents where Net Sales = 100%.
⁺ Of which sales salaries represented nearly 80% of annual payroll figures.

measures. Tom also pointed out that their cost of goods sold were higher than other stores in their sales class.

Zimmerman's is a full line department store located in a major Northeastern regional market whose trading area included nearly 100,000 people. The market serves three distinct market segments including an urban market, rural agricultural and fishery markets, and a college market which represented about 20% of the population during the school year as well as a significant portion of the store's revenues.

In the trading area, Zimmerman's faced the usual assortment of mass merchants including K mart, Sears, J.C. Penney's as well as a number of specialty stores especially in men's, women's and children's clothing. Currently, Zimmerman's operated from a single downtown location; over its history the store attempted to reflect the needs of each of the three markets. The store had a basement area which offered a number of items for the kitchen including small appliances. It, too, had a variety of products to appeal to each of the markets. As with all regional department stores they provided the traditional wide assortment of customer services including delivery, credit, complaint-handling, bridal, gift wrapping, check cashing, and personal shopping. As with many such department stores it had been the most important retail institution in the community but its position had begun to wane.

Zimmerman's had always tried to serve the market; its motto was: "We succeed by selling goods which are good for all." The store did not aggressively promote itself; indeed it did not have to because it was "the store in town." Promotion was limited to newspaper advertising in the two local newspapers. These ads stressed the wide variety of items which were available and at times looked like inventory lists. The only exception to this pattern were co-operative ads in which they featured specific brands. The sales force was trained to be service oriented though they were compensated on 20% base salary and a 80% commission formula. Price promotion was unheard of except for the traditional mark-downs after the major sales periods such as Christmas. In part the elder Zimmerman argued that because each of the selling floors had a different price line, there was no need to "cut prices unnecessarily." He beleived that customers would go from the "high price to the low price floor" if they wanted a better price.

The trading area until 1976 had been stable with little growth. The residents had traditional New England values; their tastes had not changed over the years and were very conservative. They shopped for value but preferred brand name items. There was limited interest in fashion. In 1976 two major electronic firms built research and development facilities in the area and as a result of associated service industries, the area began to change. Also a major ship repair yard had been opened up. The total employment increased by about 3,000; and the population increased by about 12,000.

Most of the new jobs were filled by people who had previously lived in major metropolitan areas. As Suzzane's father remarked shortly before his death, "The whole country has gone from a sleepy little village dominated by farmers and fisherman to a real city with all of the demands that 'city folk' have." The new residents not only brought additional income but they brought a variety of new tastes and demands. While many shopped at Zimmerman's because it was basically the only "up market" department store, they were not satisfied with it and a number of stores came in to fill the gap. Some data from a very informal customer study are found in Table 12.2.

In the past three years, the number of new specialty stores increased dramatically; included among these are a national toy store, two women's specialty stores, a classy men's clothing store, and several firms in cooking equipment and gourmet foods. A new shopping center is being planned; it will have two major anchors, one of which is thought to be a regional department store from Boston and several more specialty stores. The full list has not been released but there is no doubt that these will increase pressures on Zimmerman's.

Suzzane realizes that if she does not do something quickly, the store will be out of business. She knows that she cannot make it all happen by herself and has sent out tenders to a number of marketing consulting firms. Her letter includes some of the following language: " . . . a complete marketing plan," "an understanding of the information I need to know in order to make decisions," "means of evaluating the plan," and "anything else that is important to make Zimmerman's profitable and an asset to the community." She realizes that the proposals will not include all of the data, but she expects that such a proposal will make assumptions and provide appropriate examples where data are not available.

TABLE 12.2   Zimmerman's Store Survey Selected Responses

1.	When I go to a store in response to an ad, it is more often for a special sale price than for regular merchandise.	Strongly Agree	52.38%
		Agree	20.24%
		Neutral	8.33%
		Disagree	10.71%
		Strongly Disagree	8.33%
2.	I am not as concerned about fashion as I am about modest prices and wearability.	Strongly Agree	10.84%
		Agree	16.87%
		Neutral	24.10%
		Disagree	28.92%
		Strongly Disagree	19.28%
3.	The quality of the clothes I buy is not as important as having the right look.	Strongly Agree	4.71%
		Agree	8.24%
		Neutral	9.41%
		Disagree	32.94%
		Strongly Disagree	44.71%
4.	I don't buy clothes that would make me stand out from everyone else.	Strongly Agree	29.76%
		Agree	15.48%
		Neutral	17.86%
		Disagree	16.67%
		Strongly Disagree	20.42%
5.	I stop wearing clothes only when they wear out, not because they go out of style.	Strongly Agree	11.76%
		Agree	9.41%
		Neutral	24.71%
		Disagree	24.71%
		Strongly Disagree	29.41%

Please rate Zimmerman's on each of the following categories:

1.	Size of selection	Outstanding	3.66%
		Good	69.15%
		Fair	25.61%
		Poor	1.22%
2.	Prices I can afford	Outstanding	8.24%
		Good	78.82%
		Fair	11.67%
		Poor	1.18%
3.	Value for dollars	Outstanding	3.57%
		Good	17.86%
		Fair	64.29%
		Poor	14.29%
4.	Quality of merchandise	Outstanding	3.53%
		Good	12.94%
		Fair	63.53%
		Poor	20.00%

5.	Sales and special offers	Outstanding	3.61%
		Good	13.25%
		Fair	54.22%
		Poor	28.92%
6.	Use of advertising that attracts me to the store	Outstanding	11.25%
		Good	26.25%
		Fair	41.25%
		Poor	21.25%
7.	Range of services offered	Outstanding	15.19%
		Good	58.23%
		Fair	21.52%
		Poor	4.00%
8.	Helpful, knowledgeable staff	Outstanding	5.88%
		Good	15.29%
		Fair	49.41%
		Poor	14.63%
9.	Easy to find what I am looking for in the store	Outstanding	7.14%
		Good	21.43%
		Fair	55.93%
		Poor	15.48%

Comparison of Zimmerman's with Two Favorite Stores

1.	Kitchenware	Zimmerman's	#3
		Elegant Gourmet	#2
		Kitchenwares	#1
2.	Men's clothing	Zimmerman's	#3
		J.C. Penneys	#1
		Parkers	#2
3.	Women's sportswear (medium priced)	Zimmerman's	#2
		J.C. Penney's	#3
		Parkers for Women	#1

Case prepared by Ronald Savitt, School of Business Administration, The University of Vermont, ©1988. The case is intended to be used as the basis of discussion and application of appropriate marketing principles.

Neil W. Chamberlain
THE CENTRAL THESIS

If the theme of this book can be captured in a sentence, it would read something like this: How the business firm uses the discretion available to it to attempt to establish some measure of control over its operations in an environment filled with uncertainty due to change, and to relate itself to a society which is seeking to do the same thing.

In pursuing this theme we shall not be interested in the total population of business firms, most of which are simply extensions of households, conducted by an individual or a "momma and poppa" to provide income to one or a few families—a personal source of livelihood. Our concern is solely with firms which are large enough to require a professional management and staff.

Such a firm is not a single-celled organism, as a proprietorship is likely to be, with all its functions blended in one man's mind. It is composed of a number of specialized parts—shops, departments, divisions, subsidiaries. Firms like General Motors and General Electric have definable specialized subdivisions running into the thousands. Each of these requires not only its own supervision but some higher-level manager who is responsible for coordinating its activities with the activities of other units, to ensure that their respective contributions add up to the product which is wanted. The firm can be looked on as a system— something with explicit overall objectives, its parts meshing together with functional fitness to achieve the result.

The parts, the subsystems, do not, however, contribute their bit to the overall objective of the system with simple machinelike automatism. Constituted as separately definable units, captained by idiosyncratic individuals ranging all the way from the obsessively ambitious to the kind who wants only to get by and be left alone, each unit has its own peculiar set of objectives. These are partly defined by the functional role which the unit plays in the organization—a sales office thinks primarily in terms of its sales quota and not the difficulty of filling orders or the cost of financing them, for example. They are also defined by the personal goals of those who occupy the unit—the sum of such of their aspirations as the firm can help them achieve.

The consequence is that the self-defined objectives of the subunit necessarily diverge from the letter or spirit of the tasks which have been assigned it. The divergence may not be great. It may arise out of an excess enthusiasm for the role it has been given as much as from any deficiency of zeal. Or the individual who is responsible for the subunit may understandably be more concerned with his own welfare than that of the firm.

However great, the divergence is never total. The fact that there *is* a functional role on which performance will be judged guarantees some, and usually a large, congruence of objectives between the overall system and its subsystems. But divergences there will also always be.

At every level of operations, the function of the manager is to coordinate the parts in the level below him, for which he is responsible, in a way that puts the objectives of the larger unit ahead of the partly divergent objectives of the units which compose it. This task involves him in a continuing bargaining relationship with those activities he must try to integrate, as he seeks to induce each person to perform his role in ways which improve the total performance even though they are less satisfying to the purposes of the subunit considered independently. The manager himself is subject to similar bargaining pressures from those in the hierarchy above him, who are doing their best to coordinate his actions with the actions of other related units.

The result is a complex of bargaining relationships rather than a simple chain of command-and-obedience relationships, since pressures and influence run in both directions. Subordinates have their own methods of resisting the demands of superiors and of obtaining a hearing for their own points of view, as anyone who has dealt with a group of workers, organized or unorganized, is aware.

THE FIRM IN THE TIME STREAM

So much is stage setting. At this point the plot begins.

The business firm—this complex of interpersonal relationships—can be viewed as a ship's company embarked on a voyage on an unexplored river with many branches and tributaries, movement along which is a function of time. The network of relationships can, if we wish, be subsumed under the currently popular term, the decision-making process. That process has two primary functions. One is to hold the company together, to prevent its breakup because of either internal conflicts or external difficulties. The other is to move the company, successfully, along its voyage through time. If we view the firm as an organization in a time stream, then the decision-making process is what keeps it afloat, in one piece, and at the same time moving through a changing environment.

Let us concentrate a little further on the time dimension. In the firm's voyage, the *present* is simply a moving front, a transitory position which is the consequence, on the one hand, of its past movements—its history—which have brought it to this present momentary position, and on the other hand, of its future objectives, the point at which it is aiming, toward which it is directing its movement. It is the firm's actual past and its intended future which thus jointly define its actions in the present. In point of time, the present is analytically the least consequential aspect of the firm's operations; it is a moving pinpoint on a constantly extending line.

On the philosophy that we should let bygones be bygones, economists have tended to pay little attention to the effects of the past on the present—this moving front. Even when admitting the past into their consideration, they tend to do so only in the limited sphere of economic history, viewing it with an antiquarian or cultural interest (which of course has its own value) rather than treating it as an ingredient in analysis of the present.

This neglect has probably had less adverse impact on economic reasoning, however, than has the tendency to rule out of theoretical bounds any element of control or purposiveness with respect to the course of economic events. Economic theory is conceived as a body of objective and scientific law, which may be applied for policy purposes. Economic policy is commonly viewed as separate and distinct from economic theory, a different subject matter. If, however — to pursue the analogy of the voyage through time — the system of present relationships is partially determined by the intended, purposive, and controlled movement of the organization through time, then the element of control becomes a necessary *ingredient* of any objective or scientific economic observations. This cause-and-effect relationship is in contrast to the so-called "natural" sciences. We would scarcely presume that some self-willed and consciously selective policy on the part of, say, Mars could affect the relationships among planets already identified, requiring a different set of projections of the paths of heavenly bodies, which in turn would hold only until Saturn, perhaps, chose to modify the paths of the stars in their courses.

A shift of emphasis to the future, with its characteristic of purposive action, does not warrant slighting the firm's present operations. It means only that both present and future impose their independent as well as interdependent interests and requirements.

COUNTERPOINT

If we return for a moment to the notion of the firm as a system, with which we began, we shall recall the need for coordination of the numerous parts in order to achieve the system's objectives. At each level of operation stands a manager whose principal task is to bring those units for which he has supervisory responsibility into a coherent relationship looking to some specified objective. The foreman integrates the specialized activities of the men under him, and the contribution of his shop in turn is coordinated with the contributions of other shops by a general foreman, to whom he is responsible. The production manager is charged with coordinating the flow of materials into the plant, their processing through whatever stages are required, timed with sufficient precision so that no shortage of parts holds back the smooth flow of finished goods. An executive vice-president coordinates the operations of the production manager, the sales manager, and the financial manager. Wherever specialized activities are dependent on other specialized activities, there is need for such coordination.

The objective is the smooth functioning of the firm as though it were a machine. When human idiosyncrasies emerge, the effort is to eliminate or overcome them. This is where the manager's skill of bargaining enters into his task of coordinating. In order to induce the performance which is wanted from some unit, he may have to make concessions. An order—do it this way—is not enough. There are too many methods by which an overbearing boss can be cut down to size—perhaps even eliminated for failure to secure the needed cooperation—for him to have any sense of "final" authority over those who are nominally under his jurisdiction.

But with all the pressures and ploys which enter into the system of relationships, the objective remains to convert the numerous parts into a smoothly functioning whole. As mechanization and computerization play larger roles in corporate processes, the problems which human beings, with their independent aspirations and self-serving goals, introduce into the operations of the firm are reduced. There are fewer people who must be induced. The systematic, machinelike functioning of the firm to accomplish specified objectives comes closer to realization. There is a greater coherence of the parts. An equilibrium in performance is approached—the equilibrium which has been the economist's model of the firm for many years: goods are produced in those quantities which can be marketed at that price which will earn for the firm the largest possible profit under the conditions obtaining. This is the equilibrium of the present point in time.

But at the very time that the efforts of management are bent to this end, the firm continues to move on its time path into the future. The present is a moving front. The surrounding environmental conditions may remain the same for some period, so that there is no need for disturbing the coherent system of relationships which it has been management's purpose to attain. But the environment does change, and sometimes swiftly. The present does not remain the same forever; it does not always continue to display the same features as those which have only recently been experienced. Observations which have been based on an expectation of continuity of conditions no longer hold in the face of a discontinuity. The new terrain or climate may be a hostile one, threatening the very survival of the company. The changing scene may not be conducive to augmenting the welfare of the company—may not be possible to sustain its growth rate.

In order to guard its position and attain expanding objectives, the firm must first be alert to "breaks" in the environmental circumstances under which it operates. It must look for changes which have intruded to make the past a less effective guide to the future, a less certain source of behavioral generalizations.

A sense of history involves not only awareness of how the past instructs. It involves as well sensitivity to the possibility that the past cannot contribute either scientific or probabilistic rules or useful maxims because it differs from the present in respects which are identifiable, explicit, and significant, not just in the commonplace sense that no two events are ever precisely the same.

But change in organizational activity occurs not only as a reaction to a change in historical environment. It comes also because the firm has goals which can only be achieved by changing its course. It throws its hook into the future, as it were, anchoring it in some intended destitution toward which it pulls itself, purposively, modifying its activity and organization as necessary to achieve this end.

This process of adjusting or adapting or reconstituting itself for future objectives involves upsetting the present equilibrium which we have just said it was management's purpose to create. Recognizing that the present is evanescent, and that the firm is being propelled into a future where the equilibrium which it is in the process of achieving will no longer be appropriate, both for historical and purposive reasons, management is faced with the necessity of tearing apart, or at least disturbing, the very system which it finds equally necessary to bring closer to perfection. It must do this in order to keep its organization both viable in the short run and competent to pursue whatever new goals it may set for itself over the longer haul.

This in not some subtle economic paradox which the professional can resolve while the layman fumbles, perplexed, for the answer. It is a genuine dilemma confronting the firm, one which is not subject to resolution but which requires a continuing flow of ad hoc adjustments, compromises, and best judgments. Management cannot wait until the future actually renders the present coherent processes inappropriate and then rebuild a new and more suitable system, since that would be too late. The prime example of the catastrophic consequences of such a policy was provided by the Ford Motor Company in 1928, when for a year it suspended operations while ripping apart its world-famous assembly lines, which had become obsolete, to retool for an environment which it had not bothered to understand or anticipate. At the same time, in its anxiety to build for the future, the firm cannot neglect its present effective functioning, on which its future must be built. The captain of a sinking ship does not spend his time planning his destination; on the other hand, the captain that does not plan his destination may find himself in charge of a sinking ship.

The fact of the matter is that the business firm is constantly subject to two pressures which must be maintained in some sort of balance. There must always be a tendency toward systematic, coherent, efficient organization if the firm's existing goals are to be achieved and if the complex of relationships is to be held together at the present point in time. There must always be a tendency toward a state of equilibrium. At the same time there must also be a tendency toward a breakup of existing relationships and the formation of new ones, because of the intrusion of unavoidable environmental changes and the firm's purposiveness with respect to them. There must be a tendency toward disturbing present relations, toward introducing an element of disequilibrium.

These two tendencies—toward coherence and disturbance, toward equilibrium and disequilibrium—must run together, in a kind of economic counterpoint. Each is necessary to fulfill the intended effect of the other. Without systematic coordination, the firm cannot survive in its present environment. Without taking actions now looking to a changed system of relationships, the organization cannot survive beyond the present.

This economic counterpoint introduces tension into the firm's operations. Although it seeks some balance between the two tendencies or pressures, whatever balance it achieves does not create an atmospheric calm. Storms are always brewing. Conflicts of values and interests arise within the firm between those who see themselves in change, and between those who believe their aspirations will be advanced by one kind of change and others who prefer a different kind. These tensions run all through the organization, through all its subunits, all levels.

THE FIRM IN ITS LARGER ECONOMIC SETTING

Just as the firm explores its environment to discover what opportunities are offered and how it can best exploit them, so does the environment—the social environment—react to the firm in turn. The firm offers society a resource to be exploited for the achievement of the latter's own objectives. To that end it may prod the firm to move along certain lines rather than others, offering inducements. It may close off certain opportunities on which the firm had seized if the exploitation of these seems to disadvantage society rather than reward it. It may impose certain constraints on the ways in which a firm is free to act in the pursuit of objectives.

Thus at any point in time the firm and society have reached a working understanding as to the respects in which each may exploit the other. But that point in time, the present, is one which has its own conflicting tendencies to shake down into an equilibrium, a stable set of relationships, and concomitantly to shake up those relationships as each guides toward a future which it purposefully distinguishes from the present. This interplay between the two entities becomes more explicit and more sophisticated as each develops a greater technical competence in appraising position and course, just as the art of sailing was improved when scientific instrumentation was substituted for celestial navigation.

Certain theoretical and methodological considerations emerge from this approach. One is the temporary quality of generalizations concerning social institutions. Historical discontinuities and purposive conduct operate to prevent the continual cumulation and refinement of a body of scientific knowledge. The observations we make and the behavior we seek to reduce to rule relate to particular periods or epochs, bounded by time and place. We cannot do without generalization—we should wallow helplessly on our voyage if we did—but we ought to be aware of how our behavioral generalizations differ from those relating to nonhuman, nonpurposive, natural phenomena.

Second, and of perhaps greater interest, is the fact that the element of purposiveness introduces the possibility of varieties of behavior free in *some* respects from a tendency to uniformity. The consequence is not to rule out the possibility of generalization, substituting chaotic or anarchic observation, but to suggest that our interest in central tendencies should be accompanied by an interest in a range of behavior, affecting both substance and the durability of behavioral generalizations. It also suggests that the element of planning for control, rather than being viewed as only the application of theory, must be incorporated as an element of theory. Purposiveness is itself a phenomenon which cannot be ruled out of effective generalization.

This analysis is therefore not intended to be antitheoretical, destructive, or negative. Far from such a purpose, it seeks to call attention to facets of economic behavior which deserve more serious attention as we reach for knowledge, however much they may complicate our intellectual efforts.

This is the skeleton outline of the theme which will be elaborated in the succeeding pages. It may be useful to restate here that theme as it was summarized in the first paragraph: How the business firm uses the discretion available to it to attempt to establish some measure of control over its operations in an environment filled with uncertainty due to change, and to relate itself to a society which is seeking to do the same thing.

OPTIONS FOR WRITING

1. Write a letter based on Professor Chamberlain's discussion to Suzzane Zimmerman describing how she should prepare for the future. Try to help her decide what information she should collect and how she should organize it.

2. Minkes provides a means of organizing time effectively. How might Suzzane Zimmerman use this framework to make better use of this scarce resource? Pretend that you are a management consultant, and suggest to her what activities should receive greatest attention. Distinguish between the day-to-day activities and planning for the future.

3. Both Minkes and Chamberlain discuss change. Compare the two approaches. Are they similar or diverse? Which would be easier to explain to a manager?

13

THE PROFESSION OF TEACHING

John H. Clarke

At first they were twenty-six unmotivated tenth graders confronting Hawthorne's *The Scarlet Letter* until one of them claimed that Hester Prynne must be "stupid or something" for wearing the big red letter "A" on her dress. When another student responded, "She's just being spiteful, throwing it back in their faces, you know," the lid blew off the class. As John Clarke tells the rest of the story, we begin to understand that education means making a difference in the lives of people. Clarke asks us to explore our own learning experiences for clues to what makes for effective learning.

READINGS

CHILDREN WITH SPECIAL NEEDS
Torey Hayden   Somebody Else's Kids
Al Young   Chicken Hawk's Dream

MANAGING A CLASS FULL OF DIFFERENCES
Kevin Ryan   Just So They Have Fun
William Glasser, M.D.   The Needs That Drive Us All
Mortimer Adler   The Same Objectives for All
Benjamin Bloom   Innocence in Education
Paulo Freire   The "Banking" Concept of Education

> When the young woman—the mother of this child—stood fully revealed before the crowd, it seemed to be her first impulse to clasp the infant closely to her bosom; not so much by an impulse of motherly affection, as that she might thereby conceal a certain token, which was wrought or fashioned into her dress. . . . On the breast of her gown, in fine red cloth surrounded with an elaborate embroidery and fantastic flourishes of gold thread, appeared the letter "A."
>
> "She hath good skill at her needle, that's certain," remarked one of the female spectators.
>
> Nathaniel Hawthorne, *The Scarlet Letter*, 1850

I'll confess it. The first time I read *The Scarlet Letter*, I fell in love with Hester Prynne. That is the way it happened. I was a sophomore in high school then. For the first few pages, I felt only a distant sort of pity for this woman of the past, branded for adultery with a mysterious sire. The Puritans locked Hester in their jail. They made her fashion an "A" on her breast—adultery. They held her in a dark stone cell to make her talk. For days they interrogated. "Who is the father?" the gray elders asked. She sat in the dark with baby Pearl on her lap and didn't tell them anything. Silence. She kept her silence. That's what first caught my attention. Now I count Hester among my finest teachers, not for her silence, but for what she spoke in action.

When Hester walked through the prison doorway into the bright Massachusetts sunlight, I was startled. She stood tall, taller by a full head than the squat Puritan dignitaries who tormented her. Her black hair shimmered in the sunlight. Her eyes were dark and deep; her forehead, broad. She would walk proudly among the scratchy Puritans and would not compromise her heart. At whatever cost to comfort or reputation, she was fully prepared to live her own life exactly as she imagined it should be led—to wear her sign above her heart for all to see. In black and white Boston, Hester paraded her outrageously luminescent emblem. As she carried baby Pearl from the jail toward her cabin at the forest's edge, my heart followed meekly.

As a high school sophomore, I could not pretend to resemble Hester Prynne. I was much more like her cowering lover, Arthur Dimmesdale, or even her wretched husband, crablike Roger Chillingworth. I was too afraid to look at my own mind, too afraid to stand in front of others. I was pliable. I lacked conviction. I was not one who could endure the shame of prison. I lacked Hester's bravado, her insight. Perhaps I felt her rebellious spirit, but I lacked her courage. When I first imagined Hester's dark figure moving through the Puritan streets of old Boston, I began to ask myself, "Who are you? What do you believe? Would you dare to know yourself and make a vibrant show of it to all you meet?" Of course, when I chose to teach as a profession, I chose to stand in front of others. I also chose to teach *The Scarlet Letter*.

MY KIDS MEET HESTER PRYNNE

I can't remember all their names, all of my students in room 101, but I do remember a few. I remember clearly the day my sophomores joined Hester and me in coloring their sins.

"What does Hester's letter "A" stand for?" I asked limply. The clock stood still. Silence. Twenty minutes to go. The school day would end at 3:00 and we would all be free. "Why does Hester embellish the sign of her sin?"

Big Vic already had his chin on his hand; his eyelids were sagging. Big Vic, class barometer, was dropping fast. No help this time. Margie and Cher had stopped their chatter. No hope there. Even Brenda the Brain, sudden traitor to the cause of truth, had propped up her copy of *The Scarlet Letter* so it would cover up her Algebra I text, in which she was working through the odd-numbered problems. We were doomed. During that last period of the day, late in the football season, twenty-seven sophomores and their teacher were going to die of boredom in the English wing of this high school, in room 101.

"She stupid or something?" Shocked silence. No, the voice was not mine. It wasn't even familiar. I looked up. The question had come from the back row where the angry young man sat. It wasn't Sniper—he was absent. It might have been that hostile kid, Bernie. Yep. Bad Bernie was looking up at me, for the first time all year it seemed. I stared, a little frightened and surely surprised at a reprieve from this unexpected quarter. "She must be stupid, or something," he continued. "Why would she do herself up with a glossy red letter? So people would have something more to laugh at?"

A bubble of interest! I let the silence sit there, boiling Bernie's question. All eyes were open now. Heads were carefully turning, looking toward Bad Bernie at the back of the room. As miracle or looming calamity, Bernie's words had electrified the air. Big Vic had one eye half open and was looking over his shoulder. Pressure was rising. Bernie, of all people, had broken the awful silence with a question. I waited for the tension to build effect. The silence was excruciating. Heat! Margie was the first to break the code of silence.

"She's just being spiteful, throwing it back in their face, you know," Margie began, not to Bad Bernie, but to the air in which we all sweltered. "She's got her kid there and all. And, she's waving it in their face. They threw her in jail, right? They made her have the kid in jail. So she wants them to feel wormy for a while, that's all." As usual, Margie was stirring the soup a bit wildly, but her courage added its medicinal spice. Suddenly, we were all breathing again.

"Why?" I asked to keep it simmering.

"Maybe she was proud of what she did." Aha! Brenda the Brain, one defiant eyebrow arched over her algebra book, was going to cook. As close relative to ancient Hester, Brenda had decided to add a bit for the whole tribe of rebels, past and present. Her algebra book closed itself with a riffle we tried not to hear. "Maybe Hester Pinn, or whatever, was giving them the needle—the whole rotten town, I mean."

The class laughed, unaware how far Brenda's humor reached. One of the bad boys in the back made a needle with his middle finger and started sewing the air. I stared him down forcefully.

"Proud? Right." Bernie continued. "If she's so tough, then why didn't she finger the father?" Crude laughter erupted again from the back row. "I wouldn't give them the satisfaction . . . and I sure wouldn't wear any letter." Bernie stopped, then. Silence filled the room again. I let it sit, not wanting to cool curiosity with early answers.

A rustle of nervous movement. Then silence again. "Bernie wouldn't do it," I said quietly.

"Well, neither would I," Margie broke in. "Not that letter anyway." Rough laughter burst again from the back of the room. The bad boys in the back started inventing letters for Margie and Cher to wear. I walked back there to quiet things down.

"Bernie and Margie wouldn't do it." I repeated, looking back over their hunched shoulders.

"It's crazy."

"It's dumb."

"I ain't doing it."

"We could make our own letters out of colored paper," Brenda offered. "We can gussie them up with those magic markers he keeps in the coffee can." Only one-third of the class dared to vote against her with their eyes.

"I ain't no adulterator," little Dana chirped from her corner.

"You aren't an adulteress," I said quickly to cut off the snickering from the back row.

"None of us are like Hester that way," Brenda said.

"We don't have babies," little Dana commented.

"Yet," grunted a voice from the back.

Coloring Our Sins

"I don't think we have the guts." Reliably abrasive, Brenda had forced the question.

"But we all have something to hide, I bet." She went on. "So lets say we make up our letter, a different one for each of us, the one we are hiding, and we wear it around the town."

"No!" A chorus of refusal. Big Vic was looking wildly around the room.

"So we wear it around the school, then," Brenda compromised. "For just a day or so."

The whole class turned to me. There were huge questions in their looks. What is literature? What is school for? Which questions are good ones? What kind of teacher are you? Why are we here? Is this aging pile of bricks in fact the temple of truth? Will school keep us insulated from life forever? I thought over the "big question" for a long time.

"It is a choice," I said at last. "It's got to be a choice."

But a quiet boy named Darryl was already walking toward the stack of paper on the shelf. He took some scissors and markers from the coffee can. He paused, then carefully selected a sheet of blue paper? "Depressed," I heard him whisper to Dana. And then they had all begun.

How sin boiled over in room 101! How manifold in form and subtle in variation. How rich in texture. The many shades of sin glimmered under the neon sun. Sin revealed its blush and found its shape on scraps of colored paper. We were enraptured, each of us, by the seething liquor of hidden guilt.

The letter "A" was there, of course, once in red to say Angry and once again in blue to say Argues too much. Regal purple bloomed, first to proclaim loneliness and then again as an "S" to say Sad. A red "S" was yelling Screams. Another "L" appeared in pink confessing Lustfulness. A "P" was there for Paranoid and "AL" for Always Late. A fat "F." Like daisies in a summer meadow, three small golden letters "S" nodded to themselves in the sunny window corner.

"Why "S"?" I asked them in a whisper.

"We're all shy!" they sang in cheerful chorus. I scanned the room anxiously, my eyes seeking bodies crushed in this thoughtless rush to the public scaffold. No bodies. All bent eagerly to their craft. Even Bernie the Bad looked absorbed in his work. I couldn't read the dark letter he was making.

"What does your "F" stand for, Cher?" I asked, to turn away those bright eyes. "I call it 'Fraid," said the radiant face, eyes unblinking. "You wanna wear it?"

"You have good skill at your needle, that's for certain." Her smile did not falter.

Then Margie was standing with us too, her awkward body brought erect for the first time in my memory. Before I could inquire, she told me what her letter meant.

"It's "I" for Insecure," she said. I solemnly nodded and suppressed my wonder. And under the remorseless eyes of those two smiling seraphim, I fashioned a letter for that day in pale yellow, without embellishment. A plain yellow "A." Then I looked up into their fearless faces.

"Anxiety," I said. Part of the weight left me immediately. "Leave your letters overnight," I said as the bell rang. "Pick them up in the morning. We'll wear them in the cafeteria. We'll wear them in the hall. In class tomorrow we can each tell our story."

Descending the Scaffold

The next day twenty-six letters filed quietly into room 101 for last period English. Only Bernie was missing. We waited quietly. None of us wanted to start without our leader any more than Hawthorne's Puritans would start a church service without the Reverend Dimmesdale. Long after the bell sounded, he walked slowly through the door—followed by Mr. Greeno, the assistant principal in charge of discipline. We watched. My stomach knotted, then relaxed again. Old Greeno was actually smiling.

"I just came down with Bernie so you wouldn't think he was tardy," Mr. Greeno said, still grinning broadly. He cast his eyes quickly around the room, then snatched them back. "I enjoyed our little chat, hmm," he said to Bernie. Then, to our amazement, he shook Bernie's hand. Even I cringed in discomfort, but Bad Bernie showed no loss of confidence. When Mr. Greeno had left, closing the door behind him, Bernie walked slowly toward his seat at the back wall. The class turned to make a semicircle around the boys in the back of the room.

Bernie had to turn around to show us his letter. Pinned to the back of his black leather jacket there was a black letter "K."

"Kleptomania," he said to us quietly when he was seated. Eyes flashed toward me, then back to Bernie. I don't think I looked surprised. I waited with the others.

"And I guess I'm out of business," Bernie said with a smile.

We sat quietly there. We waited. All the stories would come out but Bernie had to be the first.

"Old Greeno stopped me in the cafeteria," Bernie began. "As usual, he was laying for me. But before he could rag me about whatever it was, he spotted my letter. He asked me what it meant. So I told him."

"Not the truth," his scurrilous friend Bill blurted out.

"Sure. I had spent the day wearing the truth, rather than hiding it. The truth was easy. I just said I was a big "K" for Kleptomaniac and that I made quite a good amount of money moving books and stuff out of the school bookstore and spreading it around the school to whoever might need a book or whatever—at a very reasonable price."

"Very reasonable, but Greeno runs the bookstore!" Margie exclaimed in horror. "Did he run out to call the cops?"

"He just started laughing, that's all. He laughed so hard we had to go down to his office to take a little breather. We split a Coke with the door closed and had ourselves a him-and-me talk."

"Did you tell him everything?" Dana asked.

"I couldn't remember everything," Bernie laughed. "I just told him I was getting tired of stealing, tired of doing crime. The pressure was enormous, you know, just keeping up a business like that. He said he was tired of busting me. We agreed to call it quits. He said he might be able to line me up a job."

"It's O.K., Bernie." Margie said at last. "We can buy our own books from now on."

"Or if we want to lift some stuff, I guess we'll have to lift ourselves," his friend Bill added, to keep the door cracked.

"And that was it?" Margie asked.

"Not quite," Bernie said. Bernie rose to his full stature and walked to the front of the room. From under his jacket, he pulled a large bag of black jelly beans. "They're yours, man," he said, plunking them down on the desk. "Don't worry. I bought these from Greeno—with money. In September, or maybe you didn't realize, I lifted just a few bags from your desk. For a while at the beginning, you used to deal them out to people who were nice—or who came up with some kind of right answer." I nodded, remembering. "So, here they are."

I opened the jelly beans and poured out a few. As the stories unfolded, up to the bell and thereafter, we ate black jelly beans and talked about Hester Prynne.

MAKING A DIFFERENCE IN THE LIVES OF CHILDREN

The purpose of teaching is to make a difference in the lives of young people. Love for learning is essential to good teaching. Love for kids is also a basic requirement. But neither love for the subject nor love for the kids is enough to make a good teacher. We have to learn how to teach by struggling to find answers to questions. Learning to teach well requires an endless cycle of inquiry:

1. How do children grow, naturally, without the help of teachers?
2. How do children learn, beyond the growth that happens naturally?
3. How can teachers intervene to speed and direct the learning process?
4. How can teachers know when they have made a difference?

The questions seem simple, but they can drive a lifetime of inquiry.

How Do Children Grow, Naturally?

In room 101 I looked out over twenty-seven faces. Each face disguised fifteen years of adaptive change to circumstances I could not even imagine. Darryl hardly said a word in class, but he was the first to go for scissors and colored paper. When it came to learning, he was a "doer." When chance gave him something to do, he would do it, then think about what he had done, silently waiting for the next chance to act. The boys in the back were watchers. They had learned early to put some distance between themselves and the demands of authority. I had not grown up in the streets of their neighborhood, where learning was best from a safe distance. Dana spent most of her day talking to her own dream people, talking to the rest of us only when dream and reality came together. How many years had Dana spent working and reworking her dreams? Brenda hid behind her book the way a child hides behind a fence, planning for the right time to leap out and make something happen. Where had Brenda, the learner, learned to hide and wait, then leap out? Children all grow at different rates and in different directions. Their learning has its own unique style. A moment of intense learning for one may be meaningless to another.

At any age we are all learning. Growth may be easiest to see in a baby, whose flailing arms gradually shape ways to use hands for more than parting the air. Older people learn by refining knowledge and polishing skills that are already well established. As in all of nature, the pattern of early growth is the most powerful influence on later growth. All new learning extends from the branches of prior learning. The more we know, the more we can learn.

To make a difference, teachers have to adapt what they do to fit what students have already learned. Each paper letter fashioned in room 101 represented what the students had already learned about themselves. Some were shy. Others were angry. Some were afraid. Starting from that self-knowledge each went on to learn something new, revising old beliefs to accommodate new abilities. Eventually most of them even made room for Hester Prynne in the expanding universe of their minds.

WRITING 1.

Our memories hold in storage a vast number of episodes from early life that struck us at the time as important in some way. Each of these episodes usually marks a moment of learning. Locate a moment in your early school years that is relatively vivid in your memory. Describe the moment in as much detail as you can. Where were you? What did you see? What did you do? What did you feel? Looking back at what you have written, try to explain why this event stuck in your memory. Were you learning something?

How Do Children Learn, Beyond the Growth That Happens Naturally?

The difference between learning in the street and learning in school is the fact that school learning is organized. In the street learning occurs, sometimes propelled by luck, sometimes propelled by mistake. It happens, but none of us can predict how random learning happens or what effects it will produce. Out in the street, a car streaks by, a yellowing piece of paper skitters across the asphalt and pastes itself to the fence, and a toddler, arms outstretched, stumbles along behind the fleeing pigeons. We may learn from any of these events, or we may not. In school learning is arranged so we can see patterns in different kinds of events, not just those occurring outside the window. Our culture has discovered that helping students organize their minds helps them organize, in turn, the world in which they live.

Virtually all the students in room 101, except perhaps Margie and Cher, had learned to hide any part of themselves that implied weakness. Out in the street, they might be attacked wherever they showed vulnerability. Little Dana stood back so the bigger students would not overpower her. Big Vic, despite his size, kept a wary eye to all sides, hoping not to be caught unprepared. The boys in the back, pushed to the wall, kept attackers at bay with an endless barrage of sharp commentary. They had learned to do these things in the street. In school they were protected enough to explore new patterns of behavior; they could earn new choices. What if? What if they organized one day around the idea that weakness should be the main subject of discussion? School should protect risky questioning.

Not all of human experience is organized in patterns. In school, however, the subject areas are all organized that way. History records the flow of events from the past through the present. Mathematics reveals the recurrent patterns embedded in the number system and reflected in experience. English explores the patterns through which meaning emerges from language. Science explains the recurring patterns in the physical universe and in living systems. By understanding the essential patterns that guide life, we gain control over our own lives. Of course, our minds work in patterns, too. By working with organized bodies of information, students can learn to manage better the work of their own minds. Organization is the key to school learning.

WRITING 2.

Imagine that you had been a student in room 101 on the day of Hester's letter. Would you refuse to wear a letter? Would you choose a letter of a lesser sin? Would you wear the letter of your most secret guilt? Write a journal entry describing and explaining your choice.

How Can Teachers Speed and Direct the Learning Process?

Most teachers no longer assume that listening is the best way to learn. When students do things, plan things, watch things, or simply question, learning takes place. Research has shown that teachers have to adapt their art to different needs, using lectures and books for those who need to watch and hear, exercises for those who need to do something, demonstrations for those who like to see it happen, and creative projects for those who dream. By looking for the right moment, a teacher can also help students try out new ways of learning. On the day of the letter, Bernie gave up dreaming in the classroom and used action to try something new. The black "K" gave him a chance to take action in behalf of a new vision. His dreaming probably contained enough discontent with petty crime to support the risk he took. On the day of the letter, the teacher's job was not to talk but to listen and wait; not to direct, but to help; not to lead, but to join in; not to condemn, but to applaud; not to act, but to set the stage for action.

When teaching involves more than just talk, teaching requires a continuous gamble with the lives of young people. What do they know and believe? What do they need to know? What are they willing to try? If all their needs are different, how can we intervene to guide them to a more powerful vision of the way the world works? Which of their many needs gives the teacher the greatest chance for success? Their needs change as they grow and learn. How can we intervene to speed the process of growth? How can we avoid slowing the learning process? Consider Bernie's note sent later in the year—instead of the group project that was due the following Tuesday.

March 29

Dear Techer,
Well, I will not be in scool again today. My grandfather dyed on sunday and the whole family is going back down South to the funral. I don't know when we will be comming back. My group is sposed to do it today. Sory.

Bernie

How many separate problems are embedded in this note? (1) It's late in March, past the middle of the school year. The word "again" suggests that Bernie has been absent quite a bit already. (2) The death of a grandfather can put a strain on any of us. (3) Traveling for an unspecified period makes planning makeup work difficult. (4) Bernie's spelling exhibits a long-standing pattern of errors. (5) Bernie's group depended on him for some part of the presentation. (6) His absence will leave a hole in the gradebook. (7) Bernie is feeling sorry. Bernie is also probably feeling powerless, as fate again intervenes to make his life unmanageable.

WRITING 3.

How should a teacher respond to a letter like Bernie's? Giving no response sends a clear negative message about the teacher's hopes for this student. Any response to any part of the problem has a positive and a negative potential. So, which of Bernie's problems is worth confronting? What informal response will help him move forward? In a short response, write a note to Bernie that will (1) do no harm and (2) do some good.

Teachers often try to focus their written comments on a single issue, hoping for one change at a time. Which problem in Bernie's letter deserves emphasis? How should a teacher respond? If you see what others have written, you will notice that they ranked the problems differently and have offered different kinds of solutions.

How Can Teachers Know When They Have Made a Difference?

Just to return to the classroom day after day, teachers need to know they have made a difference. But sensing that we make a difference is not quite good enough. Parents, principals, and school board members may respect our feelings, but they want evidence. What is evidence? Bernie's bag of black jelly beans is evidence, but few beyond the teacher would understand its meaning. Examination grades are evidence, but they include how much students knew before they took the class, rather than what they learned. Special projects can measure both depth of knowledge and creative problem-solving ability, but good projects can't be sent home in an envelope or sent off with a college application. For ourselves and for all those who depend on teachers for information about people, we need evidence.

To know we have made a difference, we have to be able to identify specific outcomes in the flow of learning and then trace the path of development to those outcomes. We use evidence to identify outcomes; we use evidence to locate the steps along the path. If we are lucky, the path of development may include something we said that a student actually remembers. Most of the time, however, the path of change is marked by steps made by the student, not by the teacher. Homework assignments, studying for tests, reading, conversations with friends, daydreaming, and chance encounters may all provide steps on the path to a learning outcome.

For Bernie the outcome of learning on the day of the letter was the decision to stop ripping off the bookstore. How did Bernie make his way to that outcome? He had just spent an hour with Mr. Greeno, talking about crime and establishing a personal relationship. By chance Mr. Greeno had spotted Bernie in the cafeteria wearing a black letter on his jacket. Bernie had gone to the cafeteria because he had a study hall just before English class. He was wearing a black letter because Darryl had walked over to the scissors can and started cutting a letter. Darryl walked because Brenda had an idea about what they could all do for a challenge. Brenda put down her algebra when Margie started chattering about sex. Way back at the beginning, Bernie had himself asked a question: "She stupid or something?" A question the teacher had asked in the dead silence of room 101 made him uncomfortable. "Why did Hester Prynne wear a scarlet letter?"

What had I done to make a difference? What does any teacher do to make a difference? The question is not as simple as it might appear. Talking, questioning, waiting, and provoking all play a part. Assignments, available materials, and the structure of a school day also contribute. Group dynamics are important, the strange and unreliable chemistry that happens when you mix people in classrooms. How can you plan out a specific change?

WRITING 4.

Looking at your own knowledge, skills, and attitudes, select one attribute that is an outcome of your time in school. What kind of events brought it about? What people helped support the development of that attribute?

Could you plan out a series of events that would teach younger people how to acquire that attribute? What events would you line up? What books? What challenges? Looking at your plan, how confidently can you predict the effects you desire? What other factors might intervene to change the effect?

A PROFESSION AS PROBLEM SOLVING

More than twenty years have passed since Bernie gave me the bag of black jelly beans. I have not seen him since. I have not seen Margie or Cher, Dana, or Big Vic. They all left room 101 to go on and work their own lives. Do I miss them? Surely. They are still my kids. But now I have had thousands of kids, and more keep coming. They bring their bright colors. They bring their chittering laughter. They bring their silence and pain and anger. They all bring their special gifts. We sit in the awful silence struggling to find the right question. I wait. The silence is terrible.

Then, somebody grows strong enough to take a chance. I say "yes." Somebody breaks loose a question. I raise the ante. Somebody else has another way to see it. I probe for evidence and create a path. Some follow; some hold back. Then, a bright flash. "Wait, I have an idea. What if . . . " Who knows how it will happen? Suddenly, we're all moving together, and the goal is clear. Magic.

A professional is a person who has decided to use knowledge to help other people solve the problems they face. Some choose to study law and help people solve legal problems. Others choose medicine to help people solve health problems. Still others choose counseling to help people better manage the progress of their personal lives. Speech therapists, architects, accountants, ministers, urban designers, and engineers all acquire different kinds of knowledge and develop skills in different kinds of problem solving. In choosing a profession, we choose to dedicate our minds and lives to reducing pain in one small corner of the human condition.

READING TO UNDERSTAND PROBLEMS; WRITING TO PROPOSE SOLUTIONS

The reading section includes seven essays or stories that may help you think about different problems in teaching and learning and show you how various solutions may fit these problems. The first three pieces of writing are all narratives, stories about young people as we find them in classrooms and in the streets. Some of the most difficult teaching problems are embedded in these stories: drug use, individual differences in the classroom, and the turmoil that results when too many people occupy one space. The second group of essays, written by experts in education, offer different solutions to the kinds of problems teachers face. Read the stories to understand the problems; read the analyses to evaluate common solutions to these problems. These readings should provoke you to propose your own solution to a teaching or learning problem.

Which of the problems in the stories looks most significant to you? Some students come to school with severe handicaps already in place. Torey Hayden's class includes severely handicapped people. Many individuals drop out of school. Al Young's "Chicken Hawk" represents some of them. Other students become hard to work with as soon as you gather them together in one room. Kevin Ryan describes a first-year teacher in one of those classrooms in "Just So They Have Fun." Which of these problems is most important?

Which solutions should we entertain? William Glasser argues that we can't do anything with all the kids until we reshape schools to respond to the five needs that all of us have. Mortimer Adler has proposed a curriculum that would teach all students the same material in the same classroom. Benjamin Bloom has devised a way to ensure that all students master all the material we present to them—if we give it time and adapt to their differences. Paulo Freire believes that schools need to empower individuals to manage their own lives. Clearly these experts do not agree with each other. Who offers the best solution? What solutions beyond those described should we consider? Your own reading should aim to gather material for your own writing.

SUGGESTIONS FOR RESEARCH

Proposing a Solution

In education, problem solving is often seen as a four-step exercise:

1. Describing the problem in detail. Think of one kind of teaching problem. What actually happens in school or in a community in regard to that problem? Describe your own experience. Locate statistics or expert opinions that also describe the problem.

2. Describe a clear purpose. What purpose follows logically from the problem you have described? If your description is clear and detailed, your purpose in proposing changes should also be clear.

3. Propose specific changes. For the purpose you have described, what specific changes in teaching or school life would you suggest? How would you set up these changes? Who would help? With your changes in place, what would a school day look like to a student?

4. Ascertain the costs for each change. What are the costs of the changes you have proposed, in money, time, school buildings, teacher training, or community life? What would it take to make the change happen?

As you read through the following sections, identify one problem worth solving. Using the library, interviews, and your own experience, try to describe the problem in a way that suggests solutions. Write a proposal in four parts to solve the problem.

READINGS

Children with Special Needs

Torey Hayden
SOMEBODY ELSE'S KIDS

All students do not walk into the classroom ready to learn. As Torey Hayden shows in Somebody Else's Kids, *some children are learning disabled, bringing perceptual problems that may restrict their ability to read, write, or count. Others are emotionally disturbed, with autism being only one of several possible problems. An alarming number of students come to school hungry or suffer abuse in their own homes. Some suffer from their own attempt to compensate for rejection — by getting pregnant or by undercutting their chance to learn in innumerable ways. To succeed with her children, what would Torey Hayden need?*

Al Young is a novelist and short story writer in Chicago, one of the "new" black writers who has focused attention on the plight of kids in the urban ghetto and on the loss our country has incurred through neglect of young people. As you read "Chicken Hawk's Dream," try to find ways to explain the differences among the characters. What has happened to Chicken Hawk that could take him away from Chicago to New York? What could schools do to focus his ambition on things that pay off?

We were piloting a reading series program in the primary grades that year. For me it was not a new program. The school I had previously taught in had also piloted the program. I got to live through the disaster twice.

The program itself was aesthetically outstanding. The publishers had obviously engaged true artistic talent to do the layouts and illustrations. Many of the stories were of literary quality. They were fun stories to read.

Unless, of course, you could not read.

It was a reading series designed for adults, for the adults who bought it, for the adults who had to read it, for the adults who had forgotten what it was like to be six and not know how to read. This series was a response to the community agitators who as forty-year-olds were not fascinated by the controlled vocabulary of a basal reader. They had demanded something more and now they had gotten it. As children's books for adults, those in the series were peerless. In fact, the first time I had encountered the books, I had covertly dragged home every single reader at one time or another because I *wanted* to read them. Of course,

I was twenty-six. We bought the books, the children did not, and in this case we bought the books for ourselves.

For the kids it was all a different matter. Or at least for my kids. I had always taught beginners or failures. For these two groups the reading program was an unmitigated disaster.

The major difficulty was that, in order to appeal to adults from the first pre-primer on, the series had dispensed with the usual small words, short sentences and controlled vocabulary. Even the pictures accompanying the text, though artistic, were rarely illustrative of the story at hand. The first sentence in the very first book intended for nonreading six-year-olds had eight words including one with three syllables. For some of the children this was all right. They managed the first sentence and all the others after it. For the majority of the children, including mine, well . . . in the three years I had used the series, I had memorized the three pre-primers because never in all that time did any of my children advance to another book. Normally, the first three pre-primers were mastered in the first grade, before Christmas.

I was not the only person having problems. In the first year of piloting, word soon got around in the teachers' lounge: None of the first- or second-grade teachers was having much success. Traditionally, publishers of reading series send a chart outlining the approximate place a teacher and her class should be at any given time in the term. We all gauged our reading programs around that chart so that we could have our children properly prepared for the next grade by the end of school. This publisher's chart hung in the lounge that first year, and the five of us, two first-grade teachers, two second-grade teachers, and I with my primary special education class, would moan to see ourselves slip further and further behind where the publisher predicted we should be. No one was going to get through the program on time.

After a few months of struggling we became so incensed over this impossible series that we demanded some sort of explanation from the school district for this insanity. The outcome of the protest had been the arrival from the publishing company of a sales representative to answer our questions. When I brought up the fact that less than half of all the children in the program were functioning where the chart said they should be, I expected I had set myself up to be told my colleagues and I just were not good teachers. But no. The salesman was delighted He smiled and reassured us that we were doing very well indeed. The truth was, he said, only 15 percent of all first graders were *expected* to complete the entire first-grade program during the first grade. The other 85 percent were not.

I was horrified beyond reply. We were using a program that by its very construction set children up to fail. All except the very brightest were destined to be "slow readers." Many, many teachers not hearing this man's words were going to assume that the chart was correct and put their children through an entire year's program under the mistaken belief that all the first-grade material was meant to be done in the first grade, none in the second. That was not too extravagant an assumption, in my opinion. Worst of all, however, was that as the years went on, perfectly ordinary children who were learning and developing at normal rates would fall further and further behind, so that by the fifth or sixth grade they could conceivably be considered remedial readers because they were two or more books behind their grade placement, when in fact they were right where the publisher expected them to be. And of course nothing could ever be said to these children who were reading fourth-grade books in sixth that would convince them that they were anything other than stupid. It was nothing more than statistics to the publishing company. For the kids it was life. That was such a bitterly high price to pay for an aesthetically pleasing book.

Lori was one of the reading series' unwilling victims. Already a handicapped student who undoubtedly would always have trouble with symbolic language, Lori was trapped with an impossible set of books and a teacher who despised both the books and special students.

Edna Thorsen, Lori's teacher, was an older woman with many, many years of experience behind her. Due for retirement the next year, Edna had been in the field since before I was born. In many areas of teaching Edna was superb. Unfortunately, special children was not one of them. She firmly believed that no exceptional or handicapped child should be in a regular classroom, with perhaps the exception of the gifted, and even of that she was unsure. Not only did these children put an unfair burden on the teacher, she maintained, but they disallowed a good education for the rest of the class because of the teacher time they absorbed. Besides, Edna believed, six-year-olds were just too young to be exposed to the rawness of life that the exceptional children represented. There was plenty of time when they were older to learn about blindness and retardation and mental illness.

Edna kept to many of the more traditional methods of teaching. Her class sat in rows, always stood when addressing her, moved in lines and did not speak until spoken to. They also progressed through the reading program exactly according to the chart sent out by the publishing company. If in the second week of November the children were to be, according to the charts, up to Book #2, page 14, all three of Edna's little reading groups were within a few pages one way or the other of Book #2, page 14, the second week in November. She had no concept of the notion that only 15 percent of the children were actually expected to be there and all the rest behind. Her sole responsibility, she said, was to see that all twenty-seven children in her room had gone through the three pre-primers, the primer and the first-grade reader by that last day of school in June and were ready for second grade. That all her children could not read those books had no bearing in Edna's mind on anything. Her job was to present the material and she did. It was theirs to learn it. That some did not was their fault, not hers.

Lori was not doing well. The hoped-for maturation in her brain had not yet occurred. In addition to her inability to pick up written symbols, she continued to display other common behaviors of brain-damaged children such as hyperactivity and a shortened attention span. Although Lori had not been on my original roster of resource students when school convened, she appeared at my door during the first week with Edna close behind. We had here what Edna called a "slowie"; Lori was so dense, Edna told me, you couldn't get letters through her head with a gun.

So for a half hour every afternoon, Lori and I tried to conquer the written alphabet. I had to admit we were not doing stunningly. In the three weeks since we had started, Lori could not even recognize the letters in her first name. She could write L-O-R-I without prompting now; we had accomplished that much. Sort of. It came out in slow, meticulously made letters. Sometimes the O and the R were reversed or something was upside down or occasionally she would start on the right and print the whole works completely backwards. For the most part, though, I could trust her to come close. I had scrapped the pre-reading workbook from the reading series because with two years of kindergarten she had been through it three times and still did not know it. Instead I started with the letters of her name and hoped their relevancy would help.

Her difficulty lay solely with symbolic language: letters, numbers, anything written that represented something, other than a concrete picture. She had long since memorized all the letters of the alphabet orally and she knew their sounds. But she just could not match that knowledge to print.

Teaching her was frustrating. Edna certainly was right on that account. Three weeks and I had already run through all my years of experience in teaching reading. I had tried everything I could think of to teach Lori those letters. I used things I believed in, things I was skeptical about, things I already knew were a lot of nonsense. At that point I wasn't being picky about philosophies. I just wanted her to learn.

We began with just one letter, the L. I made flash cards to drill her, had her cut out sandpaper versions to give her the tactile sensation of the letter, made her trace it half a million times in a pan of salt to feel it, drew the letter on her palm, her arm, her back. Together we made a gigantic L on the floor, taped tiny construction paper L's all over it and then hopped around it, walked over it, crawled on it, all the time yelling L-L-L-L-L-L-L! until the hallway outside the classroom rang with our voices. Then I introduced O and we went through the same gyrations. Three long weeks and still we were only on L and O.

Most of our days went like this:
"Okay, what letter is this?" I hold up a flash card with an O on it.
"M!" Lori shouts gleefully, as if she knows she is correct.
"See the shape? Around and around. Which letter goes around, Lor?" I demonstrate with my finger on the card.

"Oh, I remember now. Q."

"Whoops. Remember we're just working with L and O, Lori. No Q's."

"Oh, yeah." She hits her head with one hand. "Dumb me, I forgot. Let's see now. Hmmmm. Hmmmm. A six? No, no, don't count that; that's wrong. Lemme see now. Uh . . . uh . . . A?"

I lean across the table. "Look at it. See, it's round. Which letter is round like your mouth when you say it? Like this?" I make my mouth O-shaped.

"Seven?"

"Seven is a number. I'm not looking for a number. I'm looking for either an O," and here I make my mouth very obvious, "or an L. Which one makes your mouth look like this?" I push out my lips. "And that's just about the only letter your lips can say when they're like that. What letter is it?"

Lori sticks her lips out like mine and we are leaning so intently toward one another that we look like lovers straining to bridge the width of the table. Her lips form a perfect O and she gargles out LlllllllL."

I go "Ohhhhhhh" in a whisper, my lips still stuck out like a fish's.

"O!" Lori finally shouts. "That's an O!"

"Hey, yeah! There you go, girl. Look at that, you got it." Then I pick up the next card, another O but written in red Magic Marker instead of blue like the last. "What letter is this?"

"Eight?"

So went lesson after lesson after lesson. Lori was not stupid. She had a validated IQ in the nearly superior range. Yet in no way could she make sense of those letters. They just must have looked different to her than to the rest of us. Only her buoyant, irrepressible spirit kept us going. Never once did I see her give up. She would tire or become frustrated but never would she completely resign herself to believing that L and O would not someday come straight.

Al Young
CHICKEN HAWK'S DREAM

Chicken Hawk stayed high pretty much all the time and he was nineteen years old limping down academic corridors trying to make it to twelfth grade.

Unlike his good sidekick Wine, whose big reason for putting up with school was to please his mother, Chicken Hawk just loved the public school system and all the advantages that came with it. He could go on boarding at home, didn't have to work, and could mess over a whole year and not feel he'd lost anything.

He sat behind me in Homeroom Study Hall, sport shirt, creased pants, shiny black pointy-toed stetsons, jacket, processed hair. He'd look around him on lean days and say, "Say, man, why dont you buy this joint off me so I can be straight for lunch, I'd really appreciate it."

One morning he showed up acting funnier than usual. Turns out he was half-smashed and half-drunk because he'd smoked some dope when he got up that morning, then on the way to school he'd met up with Wine, so the two of them did up a fifth of Nature Boy, a brand of sweet wine well known around Detroit. Wine wasnt called Wine for nothing. Between the Thunderbird and Nature Boy he didn't know what to do with himself. He was a jokey kind of lad who drank heavily as a matter of form—his form. "I like to juice on general principle," is the way he put it.

That morning Chicken Hawk eased up to me during a class break. "Man, I had this dream, the grooviest dream I had in a long time, you wanna know how it went?"

By that time I thought I could anticipate anything Chicken Hawk would come up with, but for him to relate a private dream was something else, something new. "What you dream, man?"

"Dreamed I was walkin round New York, you know, walkin round all the places where Bird walked and seen all the shit he seen and all thru this dream I'm playin the background music to my own dream, dig, and it's on alto sax, man, and I'm cookin away somethin terrible and what surprise me is I can do the fingerin and all that jive—I can blow that horn, I know I can blow it in real life, I *know* I can! You know somebody got a horn I can borrow, I'll show everybody what I can do."

"Drew's got an alto and he lives up the street from me. Maybe you could get your chops together on his horn. It dont belong to him tho, it's his brother's and Drew don't hardly touch it, he too busy woodsheddin his drums. I'll ask him if you can come over after school and play some."

"Aw, baby, yeah, nice, that's beautiful, Al, that sure would be beautiful if you could arrange all that. Think maybe Drew'd lemme borrow it for a few days?"

"Well, I don't know about all that, you could ask him."

"Yeah, unh-hunh, know what tune I wanna blow first? Listen to this . . ." and he broke off into whistling something off a very old LP.

Wellsir—Drew said OK, to bring Chicken Hawk on over and we'd see what he could do. "But if you ask me the dude ain't nothin but another pot head with a lotta nerve. On the other hand he might just up and shake all of us up."

Six of us, mostly from the band, went over to Drew's house after school to find out what Chicken Hawk could do with a saxophone. As we went stomping thru the snow, old Wine was passing the bottle— "Just a little taste, fellas, to brace ourselves against the cold, dig it?"

Drew's mother, a gym teacher, took one look at us at the front door and said, "Now I know all you hoodlums is friendsa Drew's but you are not comin up in here trackin mud all over my nice rugs, so go on round the back way and wipe your feet before you go down in the basement, and I mean wipe em good!"

We got down there where Drew had his drums set up and Drew got out his brother's old horn. "Be careful with it, Chicken Hawk, it aint mine and Bruh gon need it when he get back from out the Service."

We all sat around to watch.

Chicken Hawk, tall, cool, took the horn and said, "Uh, show me how you hold this thing, just show me that, show me how you hold it and I'll do the rest."

"Show him how to hold it, Butter."

One of the reed players, a lightskin fellow named Butter, leaned over Chicken Hawk and showed him where to place his fingers on the keys. Chicken Hawk looked at Butter as tho he were insane. "Look here, gimme a little credit for knowin somethin about the thing will you, you aint got to treat me like I'm some little baby."

"Then go ahead and blow it, baby!"

"Damn, I shoulda turned on first, I'd do more better if I was high. Anybody got a joint they can lay on me?"

Everybody started getting mad and restless. Drew said, "Mister Chicken Hawk, sir, please blow somethin on the instrument and shut up!"

"Shit, you dudes dont think I can blow this thing but I mo show you."

"Then kindly show us."

Poor Chicken Hawk, he finally took a deep breath and huffed and puffed but not a sound could he make. "You sure this old raggedy horn work?"

"Dont worry about that, man," Drew told him, "just go head and play somethin. You know—*play?*"

Chicken Hawk slobbered all over the mouthpiece and blew on it and worked the keys until we could all hear them clicking but still no sound. He wiped his lips on his coat sleeve and called his boy Wine over. "Now, Wine, you see me playin on this thing, dont you?"

"Yes, I am quite aware of that, C. H."

"You see me scufflin with it and it still dont make a sound?"

"Yes, I aint heard anything, C. H., my man."

"Then, Wine, would you say—would you say just offhand that it could be that Drew's brother's horn aint no damn good?"

Old Wine looked around the room at each of us and rubbed his hands together and grinned, "Well, uh, now I'd say it's a possibility, but I don't know about that. Would you care for a little taste to loosen you up?"

Chicken Hawk screwed his face up, blew into the instrument and pumped keys until he turned colors but all that came out were some feeble little squeaks and pitiful honks. "Well, gentlemen," he announced, "Ive had it with this axe. It don't work. It's too beat-up to work. It just ain't no more good. I can blow it all right, O yeah—I could play music on it all right but how can you expect me to get into anything on a jive horn?"

Drew took the saxophone and carefully packed it back inside its case. Wine passed Chicken Hawk the Nature Boy and we all started talking about something else. There were no jokes about what had just happened, no See-Now-What-I-Tell-You.

Drew got to showing us new things he'd worked out on drums for a Rock & Roll dance he'd be playing that weekend. He loved to think up new beats. After everyone got absorbed in what Drew was doing, Chicken Hawk and Wine, well-juiced, eased quietly up the back steps.

I saw Chicken Hawk on 12th Street in Detroit. He was out of his mind standing smack on the corner in the wind watching the light turn green, yellow, red, back to green, scratching his chin, and he smiled at me.

"Hey, Chicken Hawk!"

"Hey now, what's goin on?"

"You got it."

"And don't I know it, I'm takin off for New York next week."

"What you gon do in New York?"

"See if I can get me a band together and cut some albums and stuff."

"Well—well, that's great, man, I hope you make it. Keep pushin."

"Gotta go get my instrument out of the pawnshop first, mmmm—you know how it is."

"Yeah, well, all right, take care yourself, man."

OPTIONS FOR WRITING

Torey Hayden

1. What does school look like from the perspective of a disabled person? All of us are disabled somehow. Consider the point of view of a young person with a perceptible disability (different from your own). Can you describe a school day from that perspective? Tell it as a story.

2. Under current law, all young people have a right to education that fits their needs at public expense. Of course, the range of needs is extensive, especially for people with physical or emotional handicaps. Educational research suggests that handicapped students should be "mainstreamed" into regular classes whenever possible. Under what conditions, if any, should teachers separate a child with special needs from other children in regular classrooms? Should behavior make a difference? Morality? Order in the classroom? Intellectual ability? Physical handicap? Can you defend your view? Develop a strong argument for mainstreaming or separating students with a specific handicap.

3. Over the past twenty years, schools have absorbed responsibility for a greater and greater number of social problems, including drug abuse, family

neglect and abuse, civic involvement, and sexuality. Conduct research, through interviews and library sources, that will allow you to distinguish between social issues that the schools should handle and social issues that should be managed in some other way.

Al Young

4. The school years breed both success and failure. Look back over your own school years to find a person your age who failed in some notable way. Write the story of that person in a way that reveals the causes of failure. What solutions are suggested by those causes? How much can a teacher do to effect change?

5. Dreams. All of us need them. They imply a sense of purpose that moves us forward with conviction, energy, and enthusiasm. But dreams can also hurt. When our dreams do not come true, we may sink into despair and stop moving altogether. Write a short personal essay on dreams. Are certain dreams worth pursuing and others self-destructive? Try to base your argument on dreams you have had for your own future or dreams you may have now.

6. How do you fight a drug war? Should the battles take place in church, in the family, in the streets, in hospitals, in school, in the skies over South America? Or is this a battle among forces in the human heart? Select a "drug war" that you believe may be worth fighting. Conduct a library search of sources describing current practice in this kind of drug war. Develop a research paper that describes current practice and makes recommendations.

Managing a Class Full of Differences

Kevin Ryan
JUST SO THEY HAVE FUN

New teachers often begin their work in the classroom believing that goodwill and humor will take them the distance. They are surprised when student energy becomes disruptive and their own energy disappears. As you look at this case study, try to list changes in the teacher's approach that could prevent chaos.

Bill Moore began the school year with confidence. Although he was new to teaching, he felt he understood children. He knew he would be accepted by his fifth grade students. He knew he would be successful.

To Bill, teaching was an art. It could not be learned; it had to be felt. He believed a teacher needed to know certain educational concepts and possess certain technical skills, but the essential prerequisite for teaching success was to like kids. The teacher who liked children would be able to provide meaningful classroom experiences and enable students to enjoy the learning process.

Broad-shouldered and muscular, Bill had the stature of a basketball player. His blond hair, blue eyes and tanned skin accentuated his athletic appearance. When he walked around the room his size was particularly noticeable; he appeared Herculean compared to the small eleven-year-olds seated at their desks.

Bill discovered how enjoyable teaching and children could be during an outdoor education trip in college. He spent four days working with underprivileged boys at a YMCA camp. The experience made him feel needed and gave him a sense of self-worth. Originally a marketing major, Bill became bored with computing figures and understanding theories of consumerism. He felt that teaching was an opportunity to work with real people, not abstract symbols.

Bill began teaching at Flowing Brook Elementary School. It had an enrollment of 500 students and served children in a lower middle-class, suburban community. Most of the students' parents worked in factories; a few held white-collar positions. The homes surrounding the school were small and architecturally simple; all manifested a certain sameness.

The students wore nice but unpretentious clothing. Occasionally a girl would flaunt a new dress; a boy, new tennis shoes; but these occasions were rare.

There were thirty-two students in his classroom, a room intended to hold only twenty-five. The room had a few seasonal decorations attached to the dull blue walls, walls which had not been painted for three years. A melange of colorful leaves dotted the bulletin board and a couple of commercial posters hung above the blackboard.

The textbooks and curriculum guides outlined specifically what each teacher should teach and Bill had them carefully stacked next to his desk. Faculty members at Flowing Brook were not encouraged to deviate from the adopted subject matter sequence. The teacher provided a subject matter-centered curriculum and offered a strong emphasis on the basics.

Bill found it difficult to adjust to a traditional school. He did his student teaching in an open space school and believed that the open concept was the ideal. It enabled the students to enjoy school, their peers, and the teacher. He wanted students to be able to talk when they wished and excuse themselves for a drink or to go to the restroom without asking for the teacher's permission. With a few problems anticipated, the year began.

Alphabetizing was the first major English unit of the year and Bill wanted to make sure that students knew the alphabet well enough to locate words in their dictionaries. "Okay, let's work on those dictionaries for a few minutes." Bill waited impatiently while the students found their dictionaries. His frustration with the students showed on his face; his look was serious and intense. He finally said, "Let's go, hurry up." The students moved slowly around the room until a student in the back of the room reinforced Bill's request and yelled, "Hurry up." The student demand, along with some individualized disciplining by Bill, produced results. The students were reseated, dictionaries in hands.

"Okay, Let's see who can look up the words the fastest." There was a pause and then Bill called out the first word, "Crime!" The students furiously scanned their dictionaries for the correct page.

"I got it," responded one student. Another student repeated the statement, only to be followed by a chorus of "I got it" as other students simultaneously located the correct page.

"Hey!" Bill demanded quiet. "Hey!" His second attempt was louder and more adamant.

The quiet was broken by a frustrated student, "I don't want to play the dictionary game!"

"I don't want to play either," remarked another student.

Bill ignored the comments and gave the next word, "Jigsaw!" Jigsaw was followed by a long list of words: border, smash, motion. . . . Bill moved away from his desk and walked around the room as the students continued to look up words. The room was split almost evenly between those involved and interested, and those bored and indifferent. Bill stopped at one girl's desk to respond to a question. His inattentiveness to the class as a whole seemed to cause the other students to get louder. Bill looked up at the students seated near a corner table, "Hey, hold it down." The noise level decreased as the students at the corner table buried their heads again in their books.

Bill spent a great deal of time during class at his desk. He gave directions, answered questions, and covered lesson material while sitting at the large wooden desk located at the front of the room. Students lined up and waited for his assistance. Class control was difficult because Bill had to help the students standing at his desk, and, at the same time, keep the students at their desks quiet. The difficulty of working with one or two students and keeping the other thirty quiet was particularly noticeable whenever the students worked on independent projects or reports.

One day early in November, for instance, the students were working on sports reports. Bill was helping students at his desk when a loud crash jarred the room. Bill looked up and observed two students, Frank and Dave, standing next to an overturned chair. "Dave, Frank, get back up here. Who told you to go back there?" The students meekly picked up the chair and returned to their seats. Bill looked at the class and said, "All right get out your English books." The students walked around putting some materials away, getting others out. Bill gave them about five minutes for the transition in activities. "Okay, Joan, please read the directions for the assignment on prefixes." The class quieted down. The students discussed the definition of a prefix and gave examples. "For tomorrow I want you to do page 103." The class got louder when Bill stopped talking about the assignment and returned to his desk.

"Don! Amy!" Bill called out the names of two students who were not working on the English assignment. The students started back to work but the rest of the class got louder. Bill stared at the restless students and said, "Mark, you owe me fifty sentences." Mark was leaning back in his chair and staring out the window. There was a pause, the class became a little quieter. "Mike, you owe me fifty sentences." Mike was talking to a neighbor. The class got very quiet. Bill commented, "I guess you folks like to write sentences."

During the first part of the year the lessons in Bill's classes were not dramatic and the planning for instruction minimal. By Christmas the curriculum guides and textbooks were followed almost religiously. The teaching was straightforward. Classes started with a short discussion of a concept and after the discussion Bill gave an assignment. All students did the same work on the same assignments. Bill developed very few individualized lessons; he relied on the packaged materials developed by publishing companies or other teachers.

Bill taught the lowest reading group for the fifth grade, a group he was assigned by his supervisor. There were about twenty students in the group and all read below the grade level. The students spent most of their time working on self-instructional materials and memorizing word lists. Students were encouraged to work on the self-instructional packages but they were seldom given time to look at books in the library.

The reading program Bill used was new and experimental. It emphasized the basic skills and reflected the unwritten philosophy of the district: a teacher should not develop materials for students when packaged materials from a publisher are available. Teachers were expected to use various science and reading programs purchased and adopted by the school district and to implement the programs in the form recommended by the publishers.

The principal told Bill during the first evaluation in October to develop better lesson plans. Initially Bill wrote down only the concept he planned to teach (e.g., alphabetizing or prefixes); he thought up the method and sometimes the assignment when class began. This approach was, in part, a carryover from his student teaching. After talking to the curriculum coordinator, however, Bill developed his plans in more detail. He began including both the concept and methods of instruction. The sequence for teaching concepts and objectives was determined by the various district guides. Bill did not have to determine the "what to teach" just the "how."

Bill wanted to have a reputation as fair and likeable but he felt the school expected him to be tough. Rules were created, therefore, for the students to follow: a raise-your-hand rule, a sit-up-straight rule, a work-hard rule. As long as the students were quiet, the rules were not implemented. When the class was calm, students could respond without raising their hands or carry on conversations with peers. Once it started to get noisy, Bill got tough. The toughness usually manifested itself in a verbal reprimand with Bill calling out a student's name and then delivering a punishment. "Joan, you have fifty sentences to write. Susan, you have the same." Bill's disciplining, particularly at the beginning of the year, was seldom nonverbal and private, it was overt and public.

During late winter the students were working on an assignment when Bill attempted to call the class to order. "Hey! Hey! Hey! What's all the noise? Everyone should be done with their worksheets so turn them in." The class got quieter. "Okay, let's get our books out." Bill walked to the side of the room, waited, and then called on a student to begin reading.

"Nancy, get your own book." Nancy and a friend were sharing a book. Nancy responded, "I want to share with Susie." The class got quieter, Bill looked sternly at Nancy. "Get your own book!" This time it was a command, not a request. Nancy responded pleadingly, "I want to share with Susie." Bill glared at Nancy but did not repeat his command. Nancy moved toward her desk but did not get her book. Bill turned away and called on another student, "Okay, John, would you read next?"

A few minutes later, Bill yelled across the room at John, the student who just finished reading. "John, you know the rule for sitting back in chairs." John looked sheepishly at Bill and bent his head down. "Stand up and pick up your chair." The class was absolutely quiet. John stood up and picked up his chair. He held his chair for the next seven minutes. John held the chair in a variety of positions to keep it from dropping. Bill finally walked over to John, took the chair, unfolded it, and told John to sit down.

The final evaluation by the principal was conducted in March. Bill thought he was doing a good job. The students were enjoying school; they were learning. The principal disagreed. She felt Bill did not have sufficient control; there was too much freedom in his classroom. According to the principal the students needed to be controlled. They must ask for permission to get a drink of water, raise their hands to answer a question, and sit in straight rows while working on assignments. The principal felt Bill was not tough enough. The evaluation was negative. Bill suddenly felt defeated and uncertain.

Other than managerial problems, the principal described very little Bill needed to do to improve. She simply told him to be tougher and plan better. Bill found himself asking questions to which there seemed to be no clear-cut answers: How do I plan better? What is good planning? How do I get tougher? Do I have to make students line up for the restroom? A drink? Do they have to be quiet before leaving the room? Bill began to question his ability to teach. Teaching suddenly seemed difficult.

In accordance with the principal's "get tough" policy, Bill cracked down on misbehaving students. His action created an immediate parental reaction. One parent became angry and protested Bill's inconsistency and questioned his fairness. The parent, Bill, and the principal discussed the problem. Although Bill felt threatened, he stood his ground. More importantly, the principal supported him. The principal's support gave Bill renewed confidence. He knew what the principal wanted and he knew he could do it. He could be tough.

The weather was warm; the room was almost hot. The students were observing a filmstrip. "Hawaii consists of many islands. The islands were created by volcanic action." The students looked at the picture of the islands as one student read the captions. Bill repeated word for word what the student read. The pattern continued until the filmstrip was completed. The students stood up to stretch. "Sit down! Sit down! We have another filmstrip." Bill was firm, the students sat down. Bill started the projector and called on another student to read. "The active volcanoes of Hawaii are Mauna Kea and Mauna Loa." Students struggled with the words, Bill assisted with the pronunciations. He repeated what had been read and discussed it with the class for a few minutes. "John, read next." John tried to read but found the words difficult. Bill took over but like the student he struggled. "The major cities of Hawaii are Honolulu, Kalaupapa, Kahului, Kaitua, and Niulii." The warmth of the room made it difficult for the students to concentrate. Only about one-third of the students looked at the filmstrip; many students played with pencils or fidgeted with books; some had their heads down on their desks.

The filmstrip ended. Bill told the class that there would be a short break. They stood up, started talking and moving around. Bill reacted, "Sit down!" The students looked at Bill but did not settle down. "Before we go to the restroom we all have to sit down." A few students returned to their seats, many remained standing. "4 . . . 3 . . . 2 . . . 1 . . ." When Bill started counting backwards the students ran to their desks. When seated, they put their heads down.

The class was excused for the restroom by tables. "Table 1, you may go . . . Table 4 . . . Table 2 . . ." He excused only those students who were quiet. "Table 6 you are all excused except Mary." The students at Table 6 left, Mary put her head back down. Bill waited, "Okay, Mary, you can go."

Mary looked up somewhat angrily. "What did I do wrong?"

Bill responded immediately, "You were talking. No talking is permitted."

The students returned from the restroom. They straggled in and wandered around while Bill worked at his desk. The principal started talking on the intercom. "Once again, today, someone has set off a firecracker in the restroom. This will not happen again! *All* teachers will accompany *all* students to the restroom and drinking fountains! No students are to be allowed in the hall by themselves! Teachers, this is partly your fault! You have become lax in watching students outside your rooms. Now, let's all do our jobs, and let's put an end to this."

The announcement ended, Bill looked at the class. "Are there any questions concerning what Mrs. Johnson said?"

One student raised his hand, "What would happen if they caught someone with firecrackers?" The students all focused their attention on Bill. A "Yeah, what happens" look appeared on everyone's face.

"Well, if someone is caught he could go to jail, if the judge finds the person guilty."

The students looked frightened. A girl desperately waved her hand and called, "Mr. Moore, Mr. Moore!" Bill gave her permission to talk. "Mr. Moore, what if someone sticks a firecracker in your pocket and you don't know you have it, would you still go to jail?" The students were both frightened and excited as they waited for an answer.

"Well, if you had them and you didn't know it, you probably wouldn't go to jail. The judge would probably set you free."

Bill asked if there were other questions. The class sat quietly. One girl raised her hand, "Mr. Moore, if someone goes to jail is it all right if we visit them?" The students were excited at the possibility. Again the class's attention focused on Bill. He nodded affirmatively. The students responded with excitement; there was clapping and smiling.

"All right, quiet!"

One boy was very excited and called out, "Can we really visit?"

Bill responded quickly, "John, you have talked out of turn. You have one mark." The class got totally quiet. Bill leaned back and put a mark next to John's name.

Bill started the year hoping his students would enjoy school and learn. To a certain extent this was accomplished. Bill viewed enjoyment in interpersonal terms—joking around, solving riddles, and playing games. He often had relaxed conversations with students about sports and current events. The students enjoyed Bill's warmth and often responded physically by touching him affectionately and putting their arms around him, almost like children with a parent. Bill wanted to be liked by the students but he had difficulty knowing how close to be with them. How much joking around should a teacher do? How warm could a teacher be before students would take advantage of the closeness?

One day late in the school year, for example, the students were working on an English assignment. One girl called Bill over to her desk and said she had a riddle: "What has eyes but cannot see?"

Bill stood quietly for a second, a number of students gathered around, smiling and staring at Bill's puzzled face. "I don't know," replied Bill. "What does have eyes and cannot see?"

The girl's smile broadened as she answered, "A potato!" The students who were staring at Bill exploded in laughter and the students around the room looked up to see what had happened.

The class became very loud, Bill's facial expression immediately turned serious, "All right, get out your math books." The commandlike statement caused the class to get quiet. Bill walked to the front of the room, picked up his math book, his face still set in seriousness, and the lesson began.

Knowing how far to go with jokes, how much to plan, how to discipline and how to develop interesting lessons were problems which plagued Bill throughout the year. At the end of the year he had developed some solutions based on what he thought the principal wanted. He was, nevertheless, still struggling to find a teaching style which would permit his open approach to exist in a traditional school. He was still struggling to see himself as a teacher.

OPTIONS FOR WRITING

1. Most of us have encountered at least one teacher in our lives who has truly made a difference—for better or for worse. Write a short personal essay describing the teacher in your own experience who has now proved most influential. What made that teacher influential? Be sure to ground your essay in specific episodes or examples.

2. Teachers have to play many roles in the classroom: (1) *authority figures*, handing out grades and detentions; (2) *experts*, representing knowledge as clearly as possible; (3) *role models*, representing socially acceptable norms; (4) *ego ideals*, supporting student aspiration by conveying an enlarged sense of the possible; (5) *facilitators*, planning events for groups and supporting individual learning; and (6) *persons*, individuals with unique personalities, interests, needs, and desires. Of course, not all people are equally good at filling all of these roles. If you were hiring teachers, which qualities would you seek? What is the order of priority for these roles? How would you recognize a person with the qualities you seek?

3. Should teachers need a license to teach? Conduct library research to answer this question.

William Glasser, M.D.
THE NEEDS THAT DRIVE US ALL

William Glasser is a doctor and a therapist who turned his attention to the schools when he began to believe that schools systematically deprive students of a chance to behave and learn in responsible ways. In walling the students from the world and imposing our authority on them, we prevent them from learning how to understand their own basic needs and how to meet them. To Glasser all of us have the same basic needs. If schools helped us understand how to meet those needs, we would have few disciplinary problems, and students would be actively engaged in satisfying their innate curiosity. They would also tend to graduate with healthy self-esteem and less self-doubt, breaking the neurotic cycle that passes self-limiting habits from one generation to the next.

All living creatures are driven by the basic need to attempt to stay alive and reproduce so that the species will continue. As creatures have evolved from simple to complex, the basic need to survive and reproduce has been augmented by additional basic needs. . . . Humans not only need (1) to survive and reproduce, but also (2) to belong and love, (3) *to gain power*, (4) to be free and (5) to have fun. All five needs are built into our genetic structure as instructions for how we must attempt to live our lives. All are equally important and must be reasonably satisfied if we are to fulfill our biological destiny. I italicize the need for power because, unlike the other four needs that are shared to some extent by many higher animals, the way we continually struggle for power in every aspect of our lives seems uniquely human.

We are also born with no choice but to feel pain when a need is frustrated and pleasure when it is satisfied. The quicker and more severe the frustration, the more pain we feel; the quicker and deeper the satisfaction, the more pleasure we experience. We also feel a continual urge to behave when any need is unsatisfied and we can no more deny this urge than we can deny the color of our eyes. For example, when we are thirsty, we have a great urge to seek water because to satisfy the genetic instruction to survive, we must have sufficient water in our tissues. At birth we may not know what thirst is, but we know that we are unsatisfied. We feel both the pain associated with dehydration and the urge to behave, although at that time we have no idea what to do to satisfy our thirst.

Simple survival instructions like hunger, thirst, and sexual frustration are relatively clear-cut, and we quickly learn what particular discomfort is attached to all the aspects of this need. For example, in the desert, where water is scarce, there is little ambiguity as to what thirst is and what will satisfy it. When we attempt to satisfy the nonsurvival, essentially psychological, needs, such as belonging, fun, freedom and especially power, we run into more difficulty because what will satisfy these needs is much less clearly defined. For example, it is much harder to find a friend than to come in from the cold. The need for power is particularly difficult to satisfy because in many cultures (certainly ours) the mores of the culture condemn those who openly strive for it. Even politicians try to appear humble, emphasizing how much they wish to serve and how little they want to tell us what to do.

But regardless of cultural prejudices, power itself is neither good nor bad. There is nothing bad about wanting a fancy car or a big boat. In fact, if it were not for the need for power, our whole economy would crumble because almost all that is bought and sold, except for bare necessities, is for the sake of power. Except for a few of the classified ads, almost all of the advertisements we are exposed to in any media are for products that will make their purchasers more powerful. No one needs a Porsche to get to work or a designer label on blue jeans.

When someone uses his power to help downtrodden people satisfy any of their needs, especially to get some power, this use of power is humane. But history records few examples of people like Martin Luther King, Jr., who used what power he had for the benefit of the powerless. Instead, history is replete with tyrants who used their power to hurt people, and the reason that so many of us see power as bad is because so many people have been its victims. But even tyrants tend to talk about power as if it is bad: They wish that their enemies would let them be more humble. Their purpose is always to preach the virtues of humility because the more people they can persuade to be humble, the more easily they can both preserve and add to the power that they have.

Power therefore carries a cultural taint which does not seem to extend to the other psychological needs. I know of no culture that denigrates the need to love and belong. Freedom is also cherished by almost all societies, and while fun may not get the recognition it deserves, it seems to be an integral part of both primitive and civilized cultures. That these needs are built into our genetic structure is difficult to prove. It is, however, well known that infants who are given only physical care but no love or attention will become withdrawn, fail to assimilate their food and die of a peculiar starvation called marasmus. This is strong evidence that this need is present and pressing from birth.

Early in our evolution, the psychological needs which have now become separate were probably linked to our need for survival. For example, we are descended from people who learned that they had to nurture each other to survive. Living in groups, cooperating, sharing and caring gave our ancestors so much advantage over those who were less cooperative that our human species gradually became dominant. Certainly the beginning of the separate need to care is seen in many higher animals, and in apes and gorillas it is probably almost as developed as it is in us. Without long-term parental care, no mammalian babies will survive, and anyone reading this is well aware that in humans love between parents and children never seems to run out. Almost all of us are uncomfortable when we are alone for too long, and it is my belief that children whom we call autistic, who seem to have little or no need for others, may be suffering from a defect in this genetic instruction just as surely as a child suffering from a specific genetic defect called Down's syndrome may be retarded and physically handicapped.

While it is easy to understand that people who strive for power may become dominant and have a better chance to survive, most of us have difficulty accepting that this need is written in our genes. As I have mentioned, culturally we have been taught by those in power to be humble and that it is not moral to try to gain too much power. That their teachings have been largely accepted when what they advocate is so obviously self-serving is a tribute to how effective they have been in getting their message across. But also, because we want power so badly, we often support those who are stronger in the hope that they will share a little of what they have with us. And if they are wise, they do. Successful politicians are masters of this approach and the same expertise is not unknown in business, higher education and even religion.

If you look around in any society, you cannot fail to see the all-pervasive effect of this need. Families band together for power, but if they succeed in becoming very powerful, they tend in almost all cases to fight among themselves for the lion's share of what they have. Rather than go over what seems so obvious, just ask yourself one question: Who do you know who is so completely satisfied with his life that he can go a week without complaining that someone has gotten in the way of what he wanted to do? Most of us cannot get through a gripe-free day: To be satisfied with how others have treated us for a week would seem like an eternity.

We are intensely competitive. If we think that we have any chance at all to move beyond bare survival, we are almost all ambitious. We worry about winning, our honor, our pride, our integrity, our desire to be heard, our need to be right, who recognizes us, whether we are achieving enough, rich enough, good-looking, well-dressed, influential—the list is endless. We are easily jealous and "stupid" people call us arrogant when all we are is competent. We worry about status, position and whether we have clout. We are constantly trying to avoid those who would coerce us, manipulate us or use us. That we have often been wronged and seek revenge is much on the minds of many of us. Do people put us down or avoid us when we offer "constructive" criticism of how they live their lives? If what I have written here—and I could go on and on—does not pertain to the way you live your life, then it may be that you are not driven by this need. But then maybe you are not of our species: Among us, even the humble compete for who can be the humblest of all.

You can decide for yourself whether power is used more for good than for evil, but simply as a genetic need it has no morality. Our needs push us for fulfillment; whether in our attempt to satisfy them we do right or wrong is up to each of us to decide. I am spending too much time explaining this need because it is by far, especially for young people, the most difficult to fulfill. As I will explain later, if students do not feel that they have any power in their academic classes, they will not work in school. The same could also be said for teachers. There is no greater work incentive than to be able to see that your effort has a power payoff.

Freedom, another basic need, is often in conflict with power, and even to some extent with belonging. The more power you have, even if you use it for my benefit, the less freedom I have. It seems that there has to be a counterforce to power; unbridled power would be destructive to the survival of the species. Therefore, almost everything said about power could also be reworded into the vocabulary of freedom. For example, we may be inherently competitive but we want the freedom of when and where to compete. We want to win but we want to be free to lose without losing too much. And as much as a child may love her parents, she also wants the freedom to branch out on her own. So you can see that freedom can be in conflict not only with power but also belonging. For example, if you want me around too much, I claim you stifle me, but if you aren't constantly giving me attention, I may claim you don't love me. But this is far from a necessary conflict and most of us are able to figure out compatible ways to satisfy these needs.

Most people, after some thought, have no difficulty accepting that love, power and freedom are as basic as the need to survive. They might, however, question my claim that fun is a basic need. They wonder, do we really need to have fun and what is it, anyway? It's hard to define but we all know that fun is associated with laughter, play and entertainment. It's the part of the job that you don't have to do, but doing it may be the best part of the job. It is never serious, but it is often important: All work and no play makes Jack a dull boy. It can be frivolous, but it doesn't have to be. It is the intangible joy that people experience when they discover how much they share when they didn't expect to get along so well or the unexpected dividend that accompanies a plan that turns out so much better than expected. It can be planned but is much more likely to be spontaneous. It can balance a lot of misery and it is like a catalyst that makes anything we do better and worth doing again and again.

Not only humans have fun, even though we seem to be the only creature who laughs. My observation is that all animals who can make choices as to what to do to fulfill their needs seem at times to have fun. The higher the animal, the more fun: Apes appear to be more fun seeking than dogs or cats. The older the creature, the less it seems interested in fun, but given an opportunity, human beings in the last third of their lives seem as much interested in pursuing fun as young people, especially if they have the time and money to do so. Lower animals, whose behavior is essentially built-in and who do not have much ability to learn, are not involved with fun. If you want a fun pet, you would not choose a turtle.

My guess is that we (and all higher animals who are capable of learning) will survive in direct proportion to how much we can learn. So, driven by the need for fun, we always have a powerful genetic incentive to keep trying to learn as much as we can. Without the relationship between fun and learning we would not learn nearly as much, especially when we are young and have so much to learn. I realize that we also learn for power, love and freedom but to satisfy these often requires long-term dedication. It is the immediate fun of learning that keeps us going day by day, especially when we are young and have so much to learn. Just watch a baby or a puppy at play and you will see that during all the obvious fun and clowning some important learning is going on. In fact, even if all we set out to do is have fun, if we succeed, it is almost impossible not to have learned something new and often important.

When little babies discover something while playing, they squeal for joy because even though they don't realize it, they are having fun. In fact, when any of us are in any situation where we decide that we no longer want to learn, we stop having fun. While old dogs and cats who no longer play could be said to have learned about all they want to know, higher animals like us (and maybe apes and porpoises) never seem to stop pursuing fun, because driven by so many needs, we can never learn enough to satisfy ourselves for any appreciable length of time.

A good comedian is always a good teacher. It is the clear, sharp but unexpected insights of a comic like Bill Cosby that are so filled with learning that we cannot fail to laugh. When highly trained astronauts voyage into space they find that joking and clowning are the best way to keep sharp as they struggle with the unforeseen difficulties that require quick learning. And as you almost always remember, your best teachers were able to make learning so much fun that you may still recall what they taught even though you have very little use for it now. What you remember is the fun, and in doing so, seem not to be able to forget the learning that was a part of it.

Boring is the opposite of fun. It always occurs when we have to spend time without learning: A monotonous task is always boring. If we can find a way to learn while doing something repetitive (for example, listening to the tape of a good book while commuting), this can make a boring ride to and from work fun. In fact, boredom can be defeated by the satisfaction of any basic need (for example, making the task competitive as in a corn-shucking contest or social as Tom Sawyer did when he was painting the fence). A prisoner who is actively planning his escape finds his confinement much less oppressive. Anytime we can introduce power, freedom or belonging into any situation, we find it much more interesting. But as we do, we also find ourselves having fun and cannot help learning along the way. Now we will find ourselves laughing where previously we were yawning. I am sure you have noticed the deadly boredom that pervades any time that you have to spend with someone who "knows it all."

At this point, keeping these needs in mind, ask yourself if the students in your classes sense that they belong, that they are friendly with other students and supportive of you and each other. Do your students realize that there is power in knowledge, and if they do not, have you any program to help them gain this vital belief? For example, do you believe in academic competition, and if you do, do all your students have some chance to win? Or are there just a few high-achieving consistent winners and the rest mostly losers? Do your students have any freedom to choose what to study or any say in how they may prove to you that they are making progress? Are they free to leave class to go to the library or to the gym if their work is done and they are waiting for others to finish? Is there, as in spaceships, some laughter and good-natured clowning in which you are an active participant as they work or discuss assignments? Even if you have not been aware of these needs, have you been concerned that your students find satisfaction in your class?

It is not important now how you answer these questions. What is important is that you keep them in mind as you continue reading this book. While I still have some control theory to explain, the thrust of this book is implied in the previous paragraph: The more students can fulfill their needs in your academic classes, the more they will apply themselves to what is to be learned. How to do this is not easy, but it is also not easy to face class after class in which many students make little effort to learn. In the next two chapters I will attempt to teach you enough applied control theory so that you should be able to see why I suggest the learning-team approach that is the thrust of this book, an approach that should lead you to answer yes to the questions in the previous paragraph.

It is important that you as a teacher understand that the questions asked two paragraphs back apply as much to you as to your students. If you do not find your work satisfying, you will never be able to do it as well as you would like. No class can ever be satisfying unless both teachers and students find it so. Therefore, this book is as much addressed to your satisfaction as to your students'. It will seem to be more about them than you, but this is because anything you can do to help them will help you as well.

OPTIONS FOR WRITING

1. In all likelihood, your school experience helped you satisfy some of your needs but neglected others. Develop a short personal essay that describes the needs most schools meet and the needs they neglect. Make recommendations that would lead schools to meet a larger number of student needs.

2. William Glasser believes that all of us are driven by five needs. He believes that positive learning occurs when we can meet our own needs. After locating those needs in the essay, describe the extent to which schools allow individual students to meet each of these needs. Should schools have this purpose? If schools were set up to let students meet their own needs, what would those schools be like? Would these schools be better or worse than more conventional schools? Write an essay explaining your opinion.

3. Glasser developed "reality therapy" as a way to help disruptive students learn to take control of their own behavior. Conduct library research on reality therapy and draw conclusions on the effectiveness of this approach.

Mortimer Adler
THE SAME OBJECTIVES FOR ALL

Mortimer Adler is a philosopher who noticed that American education had lost track of its purpose—to carry on a common cultural base as

> *a foundation of society. The schools all taught different subjects to students whom they chose to see as increasingly different. To Adler our retreat from a common base of knowledge reflects less a failure of intellect among the students than a failure of conviction and skill among teachers. He proposes common objectives for all students and methods that would allow all students to gain the kind of learning they need to succeed in this culture.*

At the very heart of a multitrack system of public schooling lies an abominable discrimination. The system aims at different goals for different groups of children. One goal, higher than the others, is harder to accomplish. The other goals are lower—and perhaps easier, but, ironically, they are all too frequently not attained.

The one-track system of public schooling that *The Paideia Proposal* advocates has the same objectives for all without exception.

These objectives are not now aimed at in any degree by the lower tracks onto which a large number of our underprivileged children are shunted—an educational dead end. It is a dead end because these tracks do not lead to the result that the public schools of a democratic society should seek, first and foremost, for all its children—preparation to go on learning, either at advanced levels of schooling, or in adult life, or both.

Nor, in the present state of our schools, is that main objective aimed at or attained in any satisfactory measure by the higher track along which a minority of favored children move during their years of basic schooling. That track is higher only in the sense that its aims are more difficult to accomplish. But even it is not now directed to the right objectives.

In the early years, before basic schooling branches out in different directions, it fails badly to teach proficiency in the indispensable skills of learning. Even in these years, when it is still a one-track system, it falls far short of delivering the goods.

To achieve the desired quality of democratic education, a one-track system of public schooling for twelve years must aim directly at three main objectives and make every effort to achieve them to a satisfactory degree.

These three objectives are determined by the vocations or callings common to all children when they grow up as citizens, earning their living and putting their free time to good use.

The first of these objectives has already been mentioned. It relates to that aspect of adult life which we call personal growth or self-improvement—mental, moral, and spiritual. Every child should be able to look forward not only to growing up but also to continued growth in all human dimensions throughout life. All should aspire to make as much of their powers as they can. Basic schooling should prepare them to take advantage of every opportunity for personal development that our society offers.

A second main objective has to do with another side of adult life — the individual's role as an enfranchised citizen of this republic. Citizens are the principal and permanent rulers of our society. Those elected to public office for a term of years are instrumental and transient rulers — in the service of the citizenry and responsible to the electorate.

The reason why universal suffrage in a true democracy calls for universal public schooling is that the former without the latter produces an ignorant electorate and amounts to a travesty of democratic institutions and processes. To avoid this danger, public schooling must be universal in more than its quantitative aspect. It must be universal also in its qualitative aspect. Hence, the second objective of basic schooling — an adequate preparation for discharging the duties and responsibilities of citizenship.

This requires not only the cultivation of the appropriate civic virtues, but also a sufficient understanding of the framework of our government and of its fundamental principles.

The third main objective takes account of the adult's need to earn a living in one or another occupation.

The twelve years of basic schooling must prepare them for this task, *not* by training them for one or another particular job in our industrial economy, but by giving them the basic skills that are common to all work in a society such as ours.

Here then are the three common callings to which all our children are destined: to earn a living in an intelligent and responsible fashion, to function as intelligent and responsible citizens, and to make both of these things serve the purpose of leading intelligent and responsible lives — to enjoy as fully as possible all the goods that make a human life as good as it can be.

To achieve these goals, basic schooling must have for all a quality that can best be defined, *positively*, by saying that it must be general and liberal; and *negatively*, by saying that it must be nonspecialized and nonvocational.

Describing it as nonvocational may appear to be inconsistent with what has been said about its relation to earning a living. However, the schooling proposed is truly vocational in the sense that it aims to prepare children for the three vocations or callings common to all.

It is truly vocational in a further sense. It will prepare the young for earning a living by enabling them to understand the demands and workings of a technologically advanced society, and to become acquainted with its main occupations. It is nonvocational only in the sense that it does not narrowly train them for one or another particular job.

That kind of specialized or particularized job training at the level of basic schooling is in fact the reverse of something practical and effective in a society that is always changing and progressing. Anyone so trained will have to be retrained when he or she comes to his or her job. The techniques and technology will have moved on since the training in school took place.

Why, then, was such false vocationalism ever introduced into our schools? As the school population rapidly increased in the early decades of this century, educators and teachers turned to something that seemed more appropriate to do with that portion of the school population which they incorrectly and unjustly appraised as being uneducable — only trainable. In doing this, they violated the fundamental democratic maxim of equal educational opportunity.

As compared with narrow, specialized training for particular jobs, general schooling is of the greatest practical value. It is good not only because it is calculated to achieve two of the three main objectives at which basic schooling should aim — preparation for citizenship and for personal development and continued growth. It is also good practically because it will provide preparation for earning a living.

Of all the creatures on earth, human beings are the least specialized in anatomical equipment and in instinctive modes of behavior. They are, in consequence, more flexible than other creatures in their ability to adjust to the widest variety of environments and to rapidly changing external circumstances. They are adjustable to every clime and condition on earth and perpetually adjustable to the shock of change.

That is why general, nonspecialized schooling has the quality that most befits human nature. That is why, in terms of practicality and utility, it is better than any other kind of schooling.

But when we recognize that twelve years of general, nonspecialized schooling for all is the best policy — the most practical preparation for work — we should also realize that that is not its sole justification. It is not only the most expedient kind of schooling, but it is also best for the other reasons stated above: because it prepares our children to be good citizens and to lead good human lives.

OPTIONS FOR WRITING

1. Imagine that the school board of the universe will convene next week to decide on the five books that all students in all countries should be required to read and understand before they graduate from secondary school. Write an argument in favor of five specific books.

2. Adler believes that schools could succeed with all children if they narrowed their effort to a few objectives and then taught them well. Develop five or six objectives that should lie at the heart of all schooling. Describe these objectives and your purpose for choosing them. What should all students be able to do when they graduate? What should they all know? What should they all believe? What would schools have to do to guarantee achievement of your objectives to all students?

3. Mortimer Adler's *Paideia Proposal* has inspired the redevelopment of schools across the United States. Conduct library research, and evaluate the success of his proposals in real school settings.

Benjamin Bloom
INNOCENCE IN EDUCATION

Benjamin Bloom started a revolution in education when he began to argue that virtually all students could learn what we want them to learn if we could just be clear about our expectations and set up conditions to support their learning. "Hold high standards for performance," he encouraged. "Let them take as much time as they need to master the material." His "Learning for Mastery" became a central theme in our attempt to reform schools which seemed to be failing an increasing number of students.

After at least 5,000 years of educating the young in the home, in schools, and in the work place, educators frequently complain that almost nothing is really known about the educative process. The complaint becomes a rationalization for the failures of education and an excuse for the quick adoption (and equally rapid rejection) of new educational panaceas. Many educators appear to boast that they are in a state of *innocence* about education.

In striking contrast with professional educators are the host of journalists, reformers, and faddists who are quite certain that they have the true remedy for our educational ills. Most of them get a hearing in the mass media. The more persistent reformers have little difficulty in securing a grant to demonstrate their panacea and in collecting a following of educators who move in their wake for a few years. The libraries and basements of our schools still store the forgotten relics of fads and nostrums which were purchased because they promised to solve our educational problems.

In education, we continue to be seduced by the equivalent of snake-oil remedies, fake cancer cures, perpetual-motion contraptions, and old wives' tales. Myth and reality are not clearly differentiated, and we frequently prefer the former to the latter. It is not difficult to understand why the layman purchases fake cancer cures—he still yearns for a cure even when hope has been denied by a physician. But it would be difficult to explain why a reputable physician would purchase or advocate a fake cure. A parent in despair about the education of his child will seek a remedy no matter how farfetched because he also wants to hope. It is we educators who must look to our own field to ask why we have so much difficulty in distinguishing between myth and reality, or between sound remedies and worthless panaceas.

We have been *innocents* in education because we have not put our own house in order. We need to be much clearer about what we do and do not know so that we don't constantly confuse the two. If I could have one wish for education during the next decade, it would be the systematic ordering of our basic knowledge in such a way that what is known and true can be acted on, while what is superstition, fad, and myth can be recognized as such and used only when there is nothing else to support us in our frustration and despair. In addition, we need to know what new ideas are worth considering and how these ideas can and should be tested.

What do I mean by innocence? A decade ago, most of us were innocents with regard to the smoking of cigarettes. It was a costly habit which some condemned as vile and dirty, while others admired it as manly or sophisticated. No one claimed great virtues for smoking, but it was regarded as little more than a matter of individual taste and habit. Today, the effects of cigarette smoking on the incidence of lung cancer are widely known. We are no longer innocent about smoking cigarettes. We may continue to smoke cigarettes, but we do so with some knowledge of the possible consequences.

A decade ago, a manufacturer of electrical equipment found it expedient to dump the mercury by-products in the nearest body of water. These wastes sank out of sight, and as far as anyone knew that was the end of the matter. Now that researchers have established the links between mercury in the water, mercury in small fish, mercury in larger fish, and mercury deposits in the tissues of people who eat these fish, our manufacturer is no longer an innocent. Ten years ago, he was innocent when he dumped the mercury in the water. Today, if he does it, he does it from malevolence and a disregard for human values.

One could cite many instances in which innocence has been lost during the past few decades. These have been most dramatic with regard to phenomena that are not detectable by the senses (X-rays, carbon monoxide, etc.), that develop over a long time (lead poisoning, water pollution), or that are complex results of many forces in the society (economic cycles, crime, changes in social mores). New knowledge, new methods of detecting and measuring phenomena, and improved communication have made us aware of ways in which we are being influenced by the many forces around us. In some instances we have experienced great frustration because the loss of innocence has not been accompanied by effective ways of preventing or dealing with the problems that have been identified. In other instances, we have quickly learned how to deal responsibly with the new problems.

While I do not think we have equally dramatic instances in education, I believe that we should be less innocent in some aspects of education than we were two decades ago. And, I believe the next decade will establish other areas in which new knowledge and basic principles will force us to alter our educational institutions and educative processes — not so much from taste and whim but because our new awareness requires these changes.

Our innocence in education may, in part, be attributed to our addiction to *correlation and association* in our research. In contrast are those research procedures which seek to establish a *causal chain* that links one set of events to a relatively remote set of results or consequences. As long as we only know the correlation between two variables, we are not likely to be much affected. Our innocence is threatened when evidence accumulates under a wide variety of conditions that the relationships have a causal rather than only an associational basis. And our innocence is really challenged when some of the links between the phenomena are established.

One of the striking things about the loss of innocence is that a single clear presentation of a causal chain is sufficient to change almost everyone who understands and accepts the evidence. Especially for the professionals in a field, innocence may be challenged by a single lecture or publication which presents the links in a causal chain. The professional may persist in his practices, but he can never again do so as an innocent.

What I would like to do in this paper is point up seven areas or processes of education where our innocence is being threatened or challenged. For some of these areas, some of the causal links have already been established. For others, much work is still needed before the causal chain will become clear. I hope some parts of this catalog will be recognized by the readers of this paper and that many will join in the endeavor to do the conceptual and empirical research necessary to establish more complete causal relationships. It is my hope that each reader will prepare his own list of possibilities for reducing our innocence about education.

INDIVIDUAL DIFFERENCES IN LEARNING

Less than a decade ago, most educators accepted the idea that human capacity for school learning differed greatly from one person to another. While we differed in our estimates of the proportion who could learn effectively what the schools had to teach, most of us were certain that only a small percentage (10–15 percent) of students could really learn to some mastery level. Throughout the world, the proportion of students expected to *fail* in school varied from 5 percent to as high as 75 percent. We differed also in the causes we invoked to explain school-learning differences—genetics, motivation, socioeconomic status, language facility, docility, etc. But, we assumed that most of the causes of success or failure in school learning lay outside the school's or the teacher's responsibility. In our innocence, we were content to talk about *equality of opportunity*, by which we thought of each student being given the same learning conditions—it was the students who differed in their use of the opportunity.

More recently, we have come to understand that under appropriate learning conditions, students differ in the *rate* at which they can learn—not in the level to which they can achieve or in their basic capacity to learn. Fundamental research on these ideas is still in process. Studies in which these ideas have been applied to actual school subjects reveal that as many as 90 percent of the students can learn these school subjects up to the same standard that only the top 10 percent of students have been learning under usual conditions. As this research proceeds, special conditions have been discovered under which both the *level* of learning and the *rate* of learning become much the same from student to student. That is, there is growing evidence that much of what we have termed *individual differences in school learning* is the effect of particular school conditions rather than of basic differences in the capabilities of our students.

As we learn more about how individual differences in school learning are maximized or minimized, our responsibility for the learning of our students will become greater and greater. As our understanding of the learning process becomes greater, our loss of innocence will be accompanied by responsibilities and technical complexities which many of us will be loath to take on. Surprisingly, some of the professional and graduate schools have been first to take on these new responsibilities. The teachers at the elementary school level have been slow to learn about these ideas and to accept the responsibilities associated with the loss of innocence.

SCHOOL ACHIEVEMENT AND ITS EFFECT ON PERSONALITY

We have long been aware of the consistency and predictability of measures of school achievement over a number of years. We took this as further evidence of differences in human learning capacity and as validation of our grading and measurement procedures.

While we recognized some of the effects of consistently high or low achievement marks on the student's motivation for further learning and attitude toward the school, we were not aware of or much concerned about the ways in which school achievement influences the student's view of himself or his personality. After all, it was the student who was able or deficient — not the school or the educational process.

During the last two decades (and in part spurred on by the Supreme Court decision on school segregation) many scholars have been trying to determine the relation between school conditions, school achievement, and personality characteristics. Some have been searching for a direct relation between the student's success or failure in school and his view of himself. There is considerable evidence that repeated success in school over a number of years increases the probability of the student's gaining a positive view of himself and high self-esteem. Similarly, there is evidence that repeated failure or low performance in school increases the probability of the student's developing a negative view of himself and a lowered self-esteem. While these relationships between school marks and self-concept are relatively clear, much additional research is needed to establish the causal and interactive links between school achievement and self-view over a number of years.

What is more striking, but less certain, is the evidence that repeated success in school over a number of years (especially at the primary school level) appears to increase the likelihood that an individual can withstand stress and anxiety more effectively than individuals who have a history of repeated failure or low marks in school. To put it bluntly, repeated success in coping with the academic demands of the school appears to confer upon a high proportion of such students a type of immunization against emotional illness. Similarly, repeated failure in coping with the demands of the school appears to be a source of emotional difficulties and mental illness. Thus, while this research is beginning to draw parallels between immunization against physical diseases (e.g., polio, smallpox, etc.) and immunization against emotional diseases, it is also helping us to understand how schools may actually infect children with emotional difficulties. One question that is troubling some workers in this field is why some students who succeed admirably do not develop this immunization, while others who fail repeatedly are able to avoid the emotional difficulties that "should" be their fate.

Associated with some of this research is the remarkable finding that most of the emotional consequences are associated with teacher's marks and judgments rather than with the results of standardized achievement tests. Thus, it is possible to find two schools that do not overlap in their achievement measures, so that the lowest students in the superior school are slightly higher on the standardized achievement measure than the highest students in the inferior school. Under such conditions, the highest students in the inferior school have a more positive view of themselves than the lowest students in the superior school, even though the two groups of students have almost the same level of tested achievement. Indeed, the highest students in the inferior school have almost as positive a view of themselves and their capabilities as the highest students in the superior school. Perhaps the explanation has to do with the fact that most of the evidence of success or failure is in terms of teachers' marks and judgments, which the students receive daily, rather than standardized tests, which are given only once or twice a year with little interpretation to the students or parents. It is the perception of how well one is doing relative to others in the same situation that appears to be a key link between school achievement and personality effects.

Research on the relations between school achievement and mental health is far from complete. I believe that when it is fully established, it will have powerful effects on how we run our schools, mark our students, and even teach them. Especially when we are able to determine how to develop school learning more effectively, will we change from our present innocence about the long-term effects of school achievement (positive or negative) to a more complex view of education and our responsibilities for both the learning of our students and the more basic personality consequences of this learning.

TEACHERS VERSUS TEACHING

The selection and training of teachers have been central problems in education for many centuries. During the past fifty years there has been much research on teacher characteristics and their relation to student learning. This research was intended to improve the selection of students for teacher training and the selection of teachers for particular teaching positions. One could summarize most of this research with the simple statement that the characteristics of teachers have little relation to the learning of their pupils. In spite of the accumulation of a great deal of evidence on this point, in our innocence we still devote much effort to the selection of teachers and the recruitment of teacher-training students on the basis of scholastic aptitude, scholastic achievement, personality characteristics, and interests and attitudes.

More recently, some researchers have taken the position that it is the *teaching*, not the *teacher*, that is the key to the learning of the students. That is, it is not what teachers are *like* but what they *do* in interacting with their students in the classroom that determines what students learn and how they feel about the learning and about themselves. This point of view has led to some of the most fundamental research about the nature of teaching, the role of the teacher in the classroom, and the kinds of learning materials that are useful in promoting particular kinds of learning.

As the role of teaching becomes more central than the characteristics of the teacher, we are likely to become clearer as to the kinds of preservice and in-service teacher training that can improve teaching. Even more important, research on this problem has already broadened our view of teaching from that of a single teacher teaching thirty students to the notion that tutors, aides, and even other students can be helpful in promoting learning. Finally, this view is enlarging our notion of the variety of conditions that can serve in the teaching-learning process. These include new materials and media, new organizations of classrooms, and new relations among teachers and students.

As we shift our attention from the teacher as a person to the variety of ways in which teaching-learning can take place, the nature of the schools—their organization, buildings, and routines—will undergo marked transformations. Innocence in this area has already been challenged, and many of the consequences have already been seen in the schools. While we may no longer be innocent in this area, much research and development must take place before we will understand the many links in the teaching-learning process and the long-term consequences of these new developments for education in the schools and in the larger community.

WHAT CAN BE LEARNED?

When we observe teachers in the process of teaching, we note that there is much emphasis on the learning of information. When we examine teachers' quizzes and final examinations, we also note that most of the questions have to do with the remembering of information presented in the textbook or in the classroom. Schools, teachers, and textbooks are apparently directed toward filling a presumably "empty head" with things to be remembered. Although teachers, curriculum makers, and testers profess more complex objectives for education, the actual emphasis in the classrooms is still largely on the learning of specific information.

During the past two decades the professed objectives of education have changed from knowledge alone to a great variety of cognitive objectives including creativity. The objectives of education increasingly stress interests, attitudes, and values in the affective domain. And human relations, social skills, and new views of man in relation to his society and to himself are frequently expressed in these newer objectives of education.

The links between the learner and the learning process for some of the major cognitive objectives of education, such as application of principles and interpretation of new data, are well known. The links for some of the simpler affective objectives, such as interests and attitudes, are also known. However, there are many complex educational objectives for which we know very little about the kinds of learning processes needed. It is here that the links between the learner and the learning process must still be established.

Thus, while the view of what ought to be learned in the schools has broadened enormously, the teaching-learning processes for many of these new objectives are not fully understood. New research and development are necessary if our understanding of process is to match our new conceptions of educational objectives.

Even more important, classroom teaching in the schools has not caught up with what we already know about the teaching-learning processes necessary for many of the educational objectives which transcend *knowledge* as the primary goal of education. There is a wide gulf between what we want in education and what we do in education. While we want education to accomplish much more than the inculcation of knowledge, we are still partially innocent about how to do it. Even when the experts and gifted teachers know how to do it, this is only rarely transmitted to the majority of the teachers. It is the teachers who are still innocent about the relations between educational objectives and the teaching-learning process.

As we become more fully aware of what it is *possible* for education to do, we are left with major value considerations of what education *ought* to do. Perhaps, it is in this area that educators need to come to terms with themselves and with the rapid changes in students, society, and subjects of the curriculum. Decisions must be made about what is desirable and how to determine it before we shift to the more technical considerations of how to accomplish the new objectives and how to train teachers to support the necessary teaching-learning processes.

MANIFEST AND LATENT CURRICULUM

When we talk about educational objectives, we quickly slip into thoughts about the content of education—the subject matter to be learned—and the behaviors that students should develop with relation to the subject matter. Our schools are thought of in terms of science, mathematics, social studies, foreign languages, literature, and the language arts. We organize curriculum centers and curriculum projects to develop the latest and best views on what should be learned. This, to use the words of the sociologist, is the "manifest" curriculum.

Textbooks are written for the manifest curriculum, syllabi are developed, teachers are trained to teach it, and tests are made to determine how much of this curriculum has been learned. There is no doubt about the importance of this curriculum—it is this to which we devote most of the money, time, and energy available to the schools.

During the past decade, sociologists, anthropologists, and social psychologists have been observing the schools, the ways in which they are organized, and the relations among administrators, teachers, and students. Slowly they have been discovering what may be termed the "latent" curriculum.

Schools teach much about time, order, neatness, promptness, and docility in this latent curriculum. Students learn to value each other and themselves in terms of the answers they give and the products they produce in school. Students learn how to compete with their age mates in school and the consequences of an academic and a social pecking order. The latent curriculum is probably a very effective curriculum for a highly urbanized and technologically oriented society. It develops some of the skills, attitudes, and values relevant to getting and keeping a job, the maintenance of a social status system in the larger society, and many of the attributes necessary for the maintenance of political stability.

Indeed, the latent curriculum is in many respects likely to be more effective than the manifest curriculum. The lessons it teaches are long remembered because it is so pervasive and consistent over the many years in which our students attend school. Its lessons are experienced daily and learned firmly. It is probable that the lessons of the latent curriculum are learned so well because they are spelled out in the behavior of the students and adults in the school and are only rarely verbalized or justified.

Where the manifest and the latent curricula are consistent and support each other, learning is most powerful. It is here that attitudes and values are probably learned most effectively. Where the manifest and the latent curricula are in conflict, one would expect the latent curriculum to become dominant. It is not what we talk about but what we do that becomes important.

Schools can and do have considerable effects on both the cognitive and affective aspects of the manifest curriculum. But to judge the effects of school only in terms of this curriculum is to ignore a great range of other influences resulting from the ways in which we have organized our schools and the processes involved in schooling. We have paid a high price for our innocence in this area because we have ignored the effects of the latent curriculum and because we have permitted so many aspects of this curriculum to develop in response to efficiency and convenience in managing students rather than in response to their educational needs.

Our innocence has been in giving our attention solely to the manifest curriculum while we overlooked the latent one. As we develop skill in recognizing and analyzing the latent curriculum and the relations between the two curricula, the schools will look very different to us. Much research will be necessary before we have a clear picture of the latent curriculum and the ways in which it affects students, teachers, and others in the school. Even more will be required before we will understand how to alter the latent curriculum to make it more consistent with the manifest curriculum, or to make both manifest and latent curricula consistent with objectives of education which relate individual needs and the needs of the society.

ROLE OF TESTING

Of all the technical fields related to education, testing has developed most fully. This field has been most responsive to each new development in statistics and psychometrics. It has made excellent use of computer technology and high-speed scoring and data-processing procedures, and has led the way in defining and evaluating many of the possible objectives of education.

Testing has had a profound influence on decision making in many aspects of education. Tests provide the major evidence on which we select students for scholarships and for places in colleges, graduate schools, and professional schools. We use tests to determine whether our new curricula in science, in preschool education, or in medicine are effective.

In our innocence we have permitted testing to dominate education and to serve as the primary and often the only basis for our most important decisions about students, about teachers, and more recently about curricula and programs. This has had the effect of narrowing our view about what is important and of placing a quantitative emphasis on so many aspects of education. There has been a focus on the concrete, on the measurable, and on the products of education.

Only recently have we begun to ask more searching questions about this rapidly developing technology in education. We have begun to ask how testing and evaluation may serve education rather than dominate it. Some of the more exciting possibilities have emphasized the use of evaluation in the development of learning, teaching, and curricula. Some of the newer emphases have been on the process rather than on the product and on the affective as well as the more complex cognitive objectives of education.

Some workers in the field have been searching for ways in which evaluation can be helpful to teachers in improving the process of teaching. Others have found ways in which evaluation can be used to promote the process of learning. Another group has been searching for ways in which evaluation can be used in the actual formation of a new curriculum to insure that it will be the best possible for the students and teachers who will use it. Others have been using evaluation to set goals that students can attain and have found ways in which evaluation can be used to encourage students and help them develop a sense of accomplishment and a positive self-view.

There is a danger that the loss of innocence about the effects of testing will lead some educators to want to eliminate all testing. Steps already taken in this direction have the effect of eliminating measures of symptoms because we find them disturbing to teachers, students, and parents. The consequences of rash actions of this sort will be to lose many of the benefits evaluation can bring to teaching and learning. Tests can serve education without dominating it. The process of education can be markedly improved as we begin to understand how it can be facilitated by the appropriate use of educational evaluation. Many of the new strategies of teaching-learning are based on the use of formative evaluation at each stage of the process. New efforts to individualize education are dependent on major new efforts in evaluation at the beginning of, during, and at terminal points in the process of learning. It is likely that testing, which hitherto has been largely responsive to mass education, may become our most effective tool in helping the schools to relate education and teaching to the individual.

EDUCATION AS PART OF A LARGER SOCIAL SYSTEM

Education in Western societies is frequently equated with schooling. We support schools to give our children and youth an education. We empower schools to give formal recognition to the amount and type of education an individual has completed by the use of credits, certificates, and academic degrees. Most of our writing and research on education deal only with schools and schooling.

Recently, this equation of education and schooling has been attacked by scholars of education as well as by more radical reformers who insist that much learning can and does take place outside the school. But equally important, research on education and research on various aspects of the society have questioned some of the relations between the school system and other subsystems in the society.

Research into the relation between the schools and the home environment has been one of the more fruitful areas of study stimulated by these questions. Home is a powerful educational environment, especially during the preschool and primary school years. Studies of home environment in the United States, as well as in several other countries, reveal the effect of the home on language development, ability to learn from adults, attitudes toward school learning, and aspirations for further education and the occupational careers and life styles associated with education. It is clear that when the home and the school have congruent learning emphases, the child has little difficulty in his later schooling. But when the home and the school have very divergent approaches to life and learning, the child is likely to be penalized severely by the schools—especially when school attendance is required for ten or more years.

During the past half-decade we have begun to recognize some of the problems raised by disparities between home and school. One approach has been to preempt some of the years preceding regular school by placing children in preschool programs. Other attempts have been made to alter some aspects of the primary school. Still other efforts have been made to alter the home environment. There is no doubt that these attempts to alter the relations between home and school have raised many problems. The resolution of these problems and the appropriate relations between home and school will concern us for many years to come. While our innocence has been threatened by research on the relations between home environments and school, our present knowledge does not provide clear answers to the educational and moral questions raised by our new awareness of these relations.

Schools and peer groups are increasingly in conflict, and the individual appears to learn very different things in these two subsystems of society. Especially during adolescence do we find these two subsystems diverging. The conflicts between the values emphasized by schools and colleges and the values emphasized by various peer groups raise serious questions about the ways in which these two subsystems can be more effectively related. The very obvious differences between these subsystems have already had a marked effect on our innocence in this area. What we desperately need are research and scholarship which will point the way to the resolution of some of the more disturbing conflicts between the schools and adolescent peer groups.

Recent research by economists attempts to understand the relationships between the economic system of a nation and its educational system. It is evident that the relations between education and economics may be very different for societies at different stages of industrialization as well as for societies which have very different political systems. The view that education can be conceived of as an investment in human capital has stimulated educators as well as economists to study the economic effects of different approaches to education. The view of education as both a consumer or cultural good and an investment in human capital alters many of our traditional views about education and its effects. This area of research raises long-term problems about the consequences of this view for support of the schools and support of students in the schools.

There are other subsystems in a nation—religion, mass media, the political system, the status system—which have very complex relations with education. Perhaps the main point is that education is not confined to the school system and that very complex educational and other relations are found between the schools as a subsystem and the other subsystems within a society. While we have tended to think of a system of schooling as relatively insulated from other parts of the society, it is likely that the schools will be under pressure to relate more clearly to the other parts of the social system. Undoubtedly, we will come to regard education during the school-attending period, as well as before and after this period, as most appropriately the concern of many aspects of the society. Increasingly we will try to determine what can best be learned in the schools, what can best be learned elsewhere, and what can be learned only through an effective interrelation of different parts of the social system.

While we know much more about these matters than we did a decade ago, we are still quite innocent in this area. It is in these interactions of the subsystems of a nation in relation to both education and the great social problems that new understanding will most probably develop. One is hard pressed at this time to predict the consequences of this new understanding. But there is little doubt that our innocence will be most severely challenged in this area during the years ahead.

This paper has stressed the need for research which can establish causal links between particular events and relatively remote sets of results and consequences in the field of education. While this way of stating the problem suggests simple linear chains of causal relations, it does not preclude more complex interactive relations among events where *cause* and *effect* are not so easily labeled or permanently fixed. There is no doubt that education involves multiple causes as well as multiple effects and that complex problems in education are likely to be resistant to research based on simple notions of causation and determinism.

Five years ago I undertook to summarize the results of twenty-five years of educational research and concluded with the hope that more *powerful* research strategies might enable us to produce as many crucial substantive pieces of research in the next five years as had been produced in the previous twenty-five years. It is left to others to determine whether this in fact has been accomplished. There is no doubt that the amount of educational scholarship and research has increased greatly and that the quality has improved, especially during the past eight to ten years. Resources have been made available to support educational research as well as the training of able, young scholars in this very demanding field. The partial catalog of advances presented in this paper and cited in the bibliography indicates that these resources have been well used.

These advances in our understanding of education and related phenomena have not always been reflected in our educational practices. I am convinced that little will be done until the meaning and consequences of these new advances are understood by educational scholars, educational leaders, and teachers. I have suggested that these new insights and understandings may be conceived of as the loss of *innocence* about the relations among educational phenomena. This way of posing the problem suggests that the burden of responsibility for appropriate actions and practices rests with the professionals in the field once new ideas are adequately communicated. But long experience in education has left me with the impression that innocence is not easily relinquished and new responsibilities are avoided as long as possible.

OPTIONS FOR WRITING

1. According to writers like Benjamin Bloom, all public school students should be required to master certain basic skills. Currently we make all students go to school until the age of sixteen, then we let them go no matter what they have learned. What would your own high school experience have been like if your classes had included students of all ages who were trying to master one set of basic skills?

2. Scan Bloom's chapter for sentences that reflect his view of the problem in education. Scan again for sentences that point to the solutions he would prefer. Has Bloom noticed all of the problems? Do his solutions appear reasonable? Write a paper explaining the value of his approach or describing the failings of his approach, basing your argument on your own school experience.

Paulo Freire
THE "BANKING" CONCEPT OF EDUCATION

How can schools teach freedom when virtually all school systems aim first to keep students quiet in their seats? How can schools help students manage their own lives when teachers and administrators are the only ones who practice power? How can schools support change when teachers are expected to hand down established knowledge and students are expected to pick it up as it comes? Paolo Freire led a revolution in South American education, and his ideas have begun to modify teaching in other regions, too. Read his selection to identify differences between the schooling you experienced and the schooling he recommends.

A careful analysis of the teacher-student relationship at any level, inside or outside the school, reveals its fundamentally *narrative* character. This relationship involves a narrating Subject (the teacher) and patient, listening objects (the students). The contents, whether values or empirical dimensions of reality, tend in the process of being narrated to become lifeless and petrified. Education is suffering from narration sickness.

The teacher talks about reality as if it were motionless, static, compartmentalized, and predictable. Or else he expounds on a topic completely alien to the existential experience of the students. His task is to "fill" the students with the contents of his narration — contents which are detached from reality, disconnected from the totality that engendered them and could give them significance. Words are emptied of their concreteness and become a hollow, alienated, and alienating verbosity.

The outstanding characteristic of this narrative education, then, is the sonority of the words, not their transforming power. "Four times four is sixteen; the capital of Pará is Belém." The student records, memorizes, and repeats these phrases without perceiving what four times four really means, or realizing the true significance of "capital" in the affirmation "the capital of Pará is Belém," that is, what Belém means for Pará and what Pará means for Brazil.

Narration (with the teacher as narrator) leads the students to memorize mechanically the narrated content. Worse yet, it turns them into "containers," into "receptacles" to be "filled" by the teacher. The more completely he fills the receptacles, the better a teacher he is. The more meekly the receptacles permit themselves to be filled, the better students they are.

Education thus becomes an act of depositing, in which the students are depositories and the teacher is the depositor. Instead of communicating, the teacher issues communiqués and makes deposits which the students patiently receive, memorize, and repeat. This is the "banking" concept of education, in which the scope of the action allowed to the students extends only as far as receiving, filing, and storing the deposits. They do, it is true, have the opportunity to become collectors or cataloguers of the things they store. But in the last analysis, it is men themselves who are filed away through the lack of creativity, transformation, and knowledge in this (at best) misguided system. For apart from inquiry, apart from the praxis, men cannot be truly human. Knowledge emerges only through invention and reinvention, through the restless, impatient, continuing, hopeful inquiry men pursue in the world, with the world, and with each other.

In the banking concept of education, knowledge is a gift bestowed by those who consider themselves knowledgeable upon those whom they consider to know nothing. Projecting an absolute ignorance onto others, a characteristic of the ideology of oppression, negates education and knowledge as processes of inquiry. The teacher presents himself to his students as their necessary opposite; by considering their ignorance absolute, he justifies his own existence. The students, alienated like the slave in the Hegelian dialectic, accept their ignorance as justifying the teacher's existence—but, unlike the slave, they never discover that they educate the teacher.

The *raison d'etre* of libertarian education, on the other hand, lies in its drive towards reconciliation. Education must begin with the solution of the teacher-student contradiction, by reconciling the poles of the contradiction so that both are simultaneously teachers *and* students.

This solution is not (nor can it be) found in the banking concept. On the contrary, banking education maintains and even stimulates the contradiction through the following attitudes and practices, which mirror oppressive society as a whole:

a. the teacher teaches and the students are taught;
b. the teacher knows everything and the students know nothing;
c. the teacher thinks and the students are thought about;
d. the teacher talks and the students listen—meekly;
e. the teacher disciplines and the students are disciplined;
f. the teacher chooses and enforces his choice, and the students comply;
g. the teacher acts and the students have the illusion of acting through the action of the teacher;
h. the teacher chooses the program content, and the students (who were not consulted) adapt to it;
i. the teacher confuses the authority of knowledge with his own professional authority, which he sets in opposition to the freedom of the students;
j. the teacher is the Subject of the learning process, while the pupils are mere objects.

It is not surprising that the banking concept of education regards men as adaptable, manageable beings. The more students work at storing the deposits entrusted to them, the less they develop the critical consciousness which would result from their intervention in the world as transformers of that world. The more completely they accept the passive role imposed upon them, the more they tend simply to adapt to the world as it is and to the fragmented view of reality deposited in them.

The capability of banking education to minimize or annul the students' creative power and to stimulate their credulity serves the interests of the oppressors, who care neither to have the world revealed nor to see it transformed. The oppressors use their "humanitarianism" to preserve a profitable situation. Thus they react almost instinctively against any experiment in education which stimulates the critical faculties and is not content with a partial view of reality but always seeks out the ties which link one point to another and one problem to another.

Indeed, the interests of the oppressors lie in "changing the consciousness of the oppressed, not the situation which oppresses them"; for the more the oppressed can be led to adapt to that situation, the more easily they can be dominated. To achieve this end, the oppressors use the banking concept of education in conjunction with a paternalistic social action apparatus, within which the oppressed receive the euphemistic title of "welfare recipients." They are treated as individual cases, as marginal men who deviate from the general configuration of a "good, organized, and just" society. The oppressed are regarded as the pathology of the healthy society, which must therefore adjust these "incompetent and lazy" folk to its own patterns by changing their mentality. These marginals need to be "integrated," "incorporated" into the healthy society that they have "foresaken."

The truth is, however, that the oppressed are not "marginals," are not men living "outside" society. They have always been "inside" — inside the structure which made them "beings for others." The solution is not to "integrate" them into a structure of oppression, but to transform that structure so that they can become "beings for themselves." Such transformation, of course, would undermine the oppressors' purposes; hence their utilization of the banking concept of education to avoid the threat of student *conscientização*.

The banking approach to adult education, for example, will never propose to students that they critically consider reality. It will deal instead with such vital questions as whether Roger gave green grass to the goat, and insist upon the importance of learning that, on the contrary, Roger gave green grass to the rabbit. The "humanism" of the banking approach masks the effort to turn men into automatons — the very negation of their ontological vocation to be more fully human.

Those who use the banking approach, knowingly or unknowingly (for there are innumerable well-intentioned bank-clerk teachers who do not realize that they are serving only to dehumanize), fail to perceive that the deposits themselves contain contradictions about reality. But, sooner or later, these contradictions may lead formerly passive students to turn against their domestication and the attempt to domesticate reality. They may discover through existential experience that their present way of life is irreconcilable with their vocation to become fully human. They may perceive through their relations with reality that reality is really a *process*, undergoing constant transformation. If men are searchers and their ontological vocation is humanization, sooner or later they may perceive the contradiction in which banking education seeks to maintain them, and then engage themselves in the struggle for their liberation.

But the humanist, revolutionary educator cannot wait for this possibility to materialize. From the outset, his efforts must coincide with those of the students to engage in critical thinking and the quest for mutual humanization. His efforts must be imbued with a profound trust in men and their creative power. To achieve this, he must be a partner of the students in his relations with them.

The banking concept does not admit to such partnership—and necessarily so. To resolve the teacher-student contradiction, to exchange the role of depositor, prescriber, domesticator, for the role of student among students would be to undermine the power of oppression and serve the cause of liberation.

Implicit in the banking concept is the assumption of a dichotomy between man and the world: man is merely *in* the world, not *with* the world or with others; man is spectator, not re-creator. In this view, man is not a conscious being (*corpo consciente*); he is rather the possessor of *a* consciousness: an empty "mind" passively open to the reception of deposits of reality from the world outside. For example, my desk, my books, my coffee cup, all the objects before me—as bits of the world which surrounds me—would be "inside" me, exactly as I am inside my study right now. This view makes no distinction between being accessible to consciousness and entering consciousness. The distinction, however, is essential: the objects which surround me are simply accessible to my consciousness, not located within it. I am aware of them, but they are not inside me.

It follows logically from the banking notion of consciousness that the educator's role is to regulate the way the world "enters into" the students. His task is to organize a process which already occurs spontaneously, to "fill" the students by making deposits of information which he considers to constitute true knowledge. And since men "receive" the world as passive entities, education should make them more passive still, and adapt them to the world. The educated man is the adapted man, because he is better "fit" for the world. Translated into practice, this concept is well suited to the purposes of the oppressors, whose tranquility rests on how well men fit the world the oppressors have created, and how little they question it.

The more completely the majority adapt to the purposes which the dominant majority prescribe for them (thereby depriving them of the right to their own purposes), the more easily the minority can continue to prescribe. The theory and practice of banking education serve this end quite efficiently. Verbalistic lessons, reading requirements, the methods for evaluating "knowledge," the distance between the teacher and the taught, the criteria for promotion: everything in this ready-to-wear approach serves to obviate thinking.

The bank-clerk educator does not realize that there is no true security in his hypertrophied role, that one must seek to live *with* others in solidarity. One cannot impose oneself, nor even merely co-exist with one's students. Solidarity requires true communication, and the concept by which such an educator is guided fears and proscribes communication.

Yet only through communication can human life hold meaning. The teacher's thinking is authenticated only by the authenticity of the students' thinking. The teacher cannot think for his students, nor can he impose his thoughts upon them. Authentic thinking, thinking that is concerned about *reality*, does not take place in ivory tower isolation, but only in communication. If it is true that thought has meaning only when generated by action upon the world, the subordination of students to teachers becomes impossible.

Because banking education begins with a false understanding of men as objects, it cannot promote the development of what Fromm calls "biophily," but instead produces its opposite: "necrophily."

> While life is characterized by growth in a structured, functional manner, the necrophilous person loves all that does not grow, all that is mechanical. The necrophilous person is driven by the desire to transform the organic into the inorganic, to approach life mechanically, as if all living persons were things. . . . Memory, rather than experience; having, rather than being, is what counts. The necrophilous person can relate to an object—a flower or a person—only if he possesses it; hence a threat to his possession is a threat to himself; if he loses possession he loses contact with the world. . . . He loves control, and in the act of controlling he kills life.

Oppression—overwhelming control—is necrophilic; it is nourished by love of death, not life. The banking concept of education, which serves the interests of oppression, is also necrophilic. Based on a mechanistic, static, naturalistic, spatialized view of consciousness, it transforms students into receiving objects. It attempts to control thinking and action, leads men to adjust to the world, and inhibits their creative power.

When their efforts to act responsibly are frustrated, when they find themselves unable to use their faculties, men suffer. "The suffering due to impotence is rooted in the very fact that the human equilibrium has been disturbed." But the inability to act which causes men's anguish also causes them to reject their impotence, by attempting

> . . . to restore [their] capacity to act. But can [they], and how? One way is to submit to and identify with a person or group having power. By this symbolic participation in another person's life, [men have] the illusion of acting, when in reality [they] only submit to and become part of those who act.

Populist manifestations perhaps best exemplify this type of behavior by the oppressed, who, by identifying with charismatic leaders, come to feel that they themselves are active and effective. The rebellion they express as they emerge in the historical process is motivated by that desire to act effectively. The dominant elites consider the remedy to be more domination and repression, carried out in the name of freedom, order, and social peace (that is, the peace of the elites). Thus they can condemn — logically, from their point of view — "the violence of a strike by workers and [can] call upon the state in the same breath to use violence in putting down the strike."

Education as the exercise of domination stimulates the credulity of students, with the ideological intent (often not perceived by educators) of indoctrinating them to adapt to the world of oppression. This accusation is not made in the naïve hope that the dominant elites will thereby simply abandon the practice. Its objective is to call the attention of true humanists to the fact that they cannot use banking educational methods in the pursuit of liberation, for they would only negate that very pursuit. Nor may a revolutionary society inherit these methods from an oppressor society. The revolutionary society which practices banking education is either misguided or mistrustful of men. In either event, it is threatened by the specter of reaction.

Unfortunately, those who espouse the cause of liberation are themselves surrounded and influenced by the climate which generates the banking concept, and often do not perceive its true significance or its dehumanizing power. Paradoxically, then, they utilize this same instrument of alienation in what they consider an effort to liberate. Indeed, some "revolutionaries" brand as "innocents," "dreamers," or even "reactionaries" those who would challenge this educational practice. But one does not liberate men by alienating them. Authentic liberation — the process of humanization — is not another deposit to be made in men. Liberation is a praxis: the action and reflection of men upon their world in order to transform it. Those truly committed to the cause of liberation can accept neither the mechanistic concept of consciousness as an empty vessel to be filled, nor the use of banking methods of domination (propaganda, slogans — deposits) in the name of liberation.

Those truly committed to liberation must reject the banking concept in its entirety, adopting instead a concept of men as conscious beings, and consciousness as consciousness intent upon the world. They must abandon the educational goal of deposit-making and replace it with the posing of problems of men in their relations with the world. "Problem-posing" education, responding to the essence of consciousness — *intentionality* — rejects communiqués and embodies communications. It epitomizes the special characteristic of consciousness: being *conscious of*, not only as intent on objects but as turned in upon itself in a Jasperian "split" — consciousness as consciousness *of* consciousness.

Liberating education consists in acts of cognition, not transferrals of information. It is a learning situation in which the cognizable object (far from being the end of the cognitive act) intermediates the cognitive actors — teacher on the one hand and students on the other. Accordingly, the practice of problem-posing education entails at the outset that the teacher-student contradiction be resolved. Dialogical relations — indispensable to the capacity of cognitive actors to cooperate in perceiving the same cognizable object—are otherwise impossible.

Indeed, problem-posing education, which breaks with the vertical patterns characteristic of banking education, can fulfill its function as the practice of freedom only if it can overcome the above contradiction. Through dialogue, the teacher-of-the-students and the students-of-the-teacher cease to exist and a new term emerges: teacher-students with students-teacher. The teacher is no longer merely the-one-who-teaches, but one who is himself taught in dialogue with the students, who in turn while being taught also teach. They become jointly responsible for a process in which all grow. In this process, arguments based on "authority" are no longer valid; in order to function, authority must be *on the side of* freedom, not *against* it. Here, no one teaches another, nor is anyone self-taught. Men teach each other, mediated by the world, by the cognizable objects which in banking education are "owned" by the teacher.

The banking concept (with its tendency to dichotomize everything) distinguishes two stages in the action of the educator. During the first he cognizes a cognizable object while he prepares his lessons in his study or his laboratory; during the second, he expounds to his students about that object. The students are not called upon to know, but to memorize the contents narrated by the teacher. Nor do the students practice any act of cognition, since the object towards which that act should be directed is the property of the teacher rather than a medium evoking the critical reflection of both teacher and students. Hence in the name of the "preservation of culture and knowledge" we have a system which achieves neither true knowledge nor true culture.

The problem-posing method does not dichotomize the activity of the teacher-student: he is not "cognitive" at one point and "narrative" at another. He is always "cognitive," whether preparing a project or engaging in dialogue with the students. He does not regard cognizable objects as his private property, but as the object of reflection by himself and the students. In this way, the problem-posing educator constantly re-forms his reflections in the reflection of the students. The students—no longer docile listeners—are now critical co-investigators in dialogue with the teacher. The teacher presents the material to the students for their consideration, and re-considers his earlier considerations as the students express their own. The role of the problem-posing educator is to create, together with the students, the conditions under which knowledge at the level of the *doxa* is superseded by true knowledge, at the level of the *logos*.

Whereas banking education anesthetizes and inhibits creative power, problem-posing education involves a constant unveiling of reality. The former attempts to maintain the *submersion* of consciousness; the latter strives for the *emergence* of consciousness and *critical intervention* in reality.

Students, as they are increasingly posed with problems relating to themselves in the world and with the world, will feel increasingly challenged and obliged to respond to that challenge. Because they apprehend the challenge as interrelated to other problems within a total context, not as a theoretical question, the resulting comprehension tends to be increasingly critical and thus constantly less alienated. Their response to the challenge evokes new challenges, followed by new understandings; and gradually the students come to regard themselves as committed.

Education as the practice of freedom—as opposed to education as the practice of domination—denies that man is abstract, isolated, independent, and unattached to the world; it also denies that the world exists as a reality apart from men. Authentic reflection considers neither abstract man nor the world without men, but men in their relations with the world. In these relations consciousness and world are simultaneous: consciousness neither precedes the world nor follows it.

La conscience et le monde sont donnés d'un même coup: extérieur par essence à la conscience, le monde est, par essence relatif à elle.

In one of our culture circles in Chile, the group was discussing . . . the anthropological concept of culture. In the midst of the discussion, a peasant who by banking standards was completely ignorant said: "Now I see that without man there is no world." When the educator responded: "Let's say, for the sake of argument, that all the men on earth were to die, but that the earth itself remained, together with trees, birds, animals, rivers, seas, the stars . . . wouldn't all this be a world?"

"Oh, no," the peasant replied emphatically. "There would be no one to say: 'This is a world.'"

The peasant wished to express the idea that there would be lacking the consciousness of the world which necessarily implies the world of consciousness. I cannot exist without a not-I. In turn, the not-I depends on that existence. The world which brings consciousness into existence becomes the world of that consciousness. Hence, the previously cited affirmation of Sartre: "La conscience et le monde sont donnés d'un même coup."

As men, simultaneously reflecting on themselves and on the world, increase the scope of their perception, they begin to direct their observations towards previously inconspicuous phenomena:

In perception properly so-called, as an explicit awareness [Gewahren], I am turned towards the object, to the paper, for instance. I apprehend it as being this here and now. The apprehension is a singling out, every object having a background in experience. Around and about the paper lie books, pencils, ink-well, and so forth, and these in a certain sense are also "perceived," perceptually there, in the "field of intuition"; but whilst I was turned towards the paper there was no turning in their direction, nor any apprehending of them, not even in a secondary sense. They appeared and yet were not singled out, were not posited on their own account. Every perception of a thing has such a zone of background intuitions or background awareness, if "intuiting" already includes the state of being turned towards, and this also is a "conscious experience," or more briefly a "consciousness of" all indeed that in point of fact lies in the co-perceived objective background.

That which had existed objectively but had not been perceived in its deeper implications (if indeed it was perceived at all) begins to "stand out," assuming the character of a problem and therefore of challenge. Thus, men begin to single out elements from their "background awarenesses" and to reflect upon them. These elements are now objects of men's consideration, and, as such, objects of their action and cognition.

In problem-posing education, men develop their power to perceive critically *the way they exist* in the world *with which* and *in which* they find themselves; they come to see the world not as a static reality, but as a reality in process, in transformation. Although the dialectical relations of men with the world exist independently of how these relations are perceived (or whether or not they are perceived at all), it is also true that the form of action men adopt is to a large extent a function of how they perceive themselves in the world. Hence, the teacher-students and the students-teacher reflect simultaneously on themselves and the world without dichotomizing this reflection from action, and thus establish an authentic form of thought and action.

Once again, the two educational concepts and practices under analysis come into conflict. Banking education (for obvious reasons) attempts, by mythicizing reality, to conceal certain facts which explain the way men exist in the world; problem-posing education sets itself the task of demythologizing. Banking education resists dialogue; problem-posing education regards dialogue as indispensable to the act of cognition which unveils reality. Banking education treats students as objects of assistance; problem-posing education makes them critical thinkers. Banking education inhibits creativity and domesticates (although it cannot completely destroy) the *intentionality* of consciousness by isolating consciousness from the world, thereby denying men their ontological and historical vocation of becoming more fully human. Problem-posing education bases itself on creativity and stimulates true reflection and action upon reality, thereby responding to the vocation of men as beings who are authentic only when engaged in inquiry and creative transformation. In sum: banking theory and practice, as immobilizing and fixating forces, fail to acknowledge men as historical beings; problem-posing theory and practice take man's historicity as their starting point.

Problem-posing education affirms men as beings in the process of *becoming* — as unfinished, uncompleted beings in and with a likewise unfinished reality. Indeed, in contrast to other animals who are unfinished, but not historical, men know themselves to be unfinished; they are aware of their incompletion. In this incompletion and this awareness lie the very roots of education as an exclusively human manifestation. The unfinished character of men and the transformational character of reality necessitate that education be an ongoing activity.

Education is thus constantly remade in the praxis. In order to *be*, it must *become*. Its "duration" (in the Bergsonian meaning of the word) is found in the interplay of the opposites *permanence* and *change*. The banking method emphasizes permanence and becomes reactionary; problem-posing education—which accepts neither a "well-be-haved" present nor a predetermined future—roots itself in the dynamic present and becomes revolutionary.

Problem-posing education is revolutionary futurity. Hence it is prophetic (and, as such, hopeful). Hence, it corresponds to the historical nature of man. Hence, it affirms men as beings who transcend themselves, who move forward and look ahead, for whom immobility represents a fatal threat, for whom looking at the past must only be a means of understanding more clearly what and who they are so that they can more wisely build a future. Hence, it identifies with the movement which engages men as beings aware of their incompletion—an historical movement which has its point of departure, its Subjects and its objective.

The point of departure of the movement lies in men themselves. But since men do not exist apart from the world, apart from reality, the movement must begin with the men-world relationship. Accordingly, the point of departure must always be with men in the "here and now," which constitutes the situation within which they are submerged, from which they emerge, and in which they intervene. Only by starting from this situation—which determines their perception of it—can they begin to move. To do this authentically they must perceive their state not as fated and unalterable, but merely as limiting—and therefore challenging.

Whereas the banking method directly or indirectly reinforces men's fatalistic perception of their situation, the problem-posing method presents this very situation to them as a problem. As the situation becomes the object of their cognition, the naïve or magical perception which produced their fatalism gives way to perception which is able to perceive itself even as it perceives reality, and can thus be critically objective about that reality.

A deepened consciousness of their situation leads men to apprehend that situation as an historical reality susceptible of transformation. Resignation gives way to the drive for transformation and inquiry, over which men feel themselves to be in control. If men, as historical beings necessarily engaged with other men in a movement of inquiry, did not control that movement, it would be (and is) a violation of men's humanity. Any situation in which some men prevent others from engaging in the process of inquiry is one of violence. The means used are not important; to alienate men from their own decision-making is to change them into objects.

This movement of inquiry must be directed towards humanization— man's historical vocation. The pursuit of full humanity, however, cannot be carried out in isolation or individualism, but only in fellowship and solidarity; therefore it cannot unfold in the antagonistic relations between oppressors and oppressed. No one can be authentically human while he prevents others from being so. Attempting *to be more* human, individualistically, leads to *having more*, egotistically: a form of dehumanization. Not that it is not fundamental *to have* in order *to be* human. Precisely because it *is* necessary, some men's *having* must not be allowed to constitute an obstacle to others' *having*, must not consolidate the power of the former to crush the latter.

Problem-posing education, as a humanist and liberating praxis, posits as fundamental that men subjected to domination must fight for their emancipation. To that end, it enables teachers and students to become Subjects of the educational process by overcoming authoritarianism and an alienating intellectualism; it also enables men to overcome their false perception of reality. The world—no longer something to be described with deceptive words—becomes the object of that transforming action by men which results in their humanization.

Problem-posing education does not and cannot serve the interests of the oppressor. No oppressive order could permit the oppressed to begin to question: Why? While only a revolutionary society can carry out this education in systematic terms, the revolutionary leaders need not take full power before they can employ the method. In the revolutionary process, the leaders cannot utilize the banking method as an interim measure, justified on grounds of expediency, with the intention of *later* behaving in a genuinely revolutionary fashion. They must be revolutionary—that is to say, dialogical—from the outset.

OPTIONS FOR WRITING

1. According to Freire, schools should serve the purpose of freeing individuals to manage their own lives. Paradoxically, schools often deprive students of freedom, not only in the short run but over the course of a lifetime. Using your own experience as a guide, write a personal essay that explains whether schools promote freedom or restrict freedom in the short term and in the long term.

2. How much did the banking concept direct your own education? List specific courses and teachers. How much of your own education was a mutually beneficial process of inquiry involving both teachers and students? List teachers and courses for this aspect, too. In a brief essay, describe both kinds of education in your own experience. Then explain which kind brought you the greater value.

14

THE NEW LIBRARY

Mara R. Saule

Research librarian Saule shows us a university library through the eyes of two new students who learn that their preconceptions are out of date. These students discover a world of computer catalogues, government documents, and special collections. Then we look over the shoulder of a psychology professor as she conducts a literature search to see if her idea for a research project is feasible. In the process we learn new ways to do our own library research.

READINGS

William Zinsser A Liberal Education

Richard Saul Wurman The Five Rings

William J. Broad Science Can't Keep Up with Flood of New Journals

Alvin Toffler Information: The Kinetic Image

John Naisbitt From an Industrial Society to an Information Society

Theodore Roszak The Public Library: The Missing Link of the Information Age

"So what's the next stop, Andrew?"

"Hold on. I'll see if I can find the schedule."

Jessica and Andrew sat in front of the student center, scanning their packets of college orientation materials. The two had just met while they were touring the university athletic facilities. Both were first-year students from the southern part of the state and were racquetball "jocks." They hit it off immediately and made plans to play a game of racquetball as soon as the orientation tours were over. First, though, they had to figure out what area of campus they were supposed to look at next.

904

Andrew shaded his eyes from the August sun with his college catalogue. "It looks like the library tour is next, Jess."

Jessica wasn't very excited about seeing the library. She already knew what libraries were like: big old buildings full of musty old books, with stuffy old librarians putting away books and telling people to be quiet. Her high school library was little more than a study hall to her. She really wanted to skip this part of orientation and head back to the gym with Andrew. Jessica was startled when Andrew jumped up, took her hand, and pulled her toward the library.

"You know, I bet we'll be spending a lot of time in the library. We'd better hurry or we'll miss the start of the tour."

THE LIBRARY TOUR

Jessica was a little surprised when they went inside the library. Where were the wooden card catalogue cabinets, like those in her high school library? All she could see were rows and rows of green, glowing computer screens. "Most of the books and magazines owned by the library are listed in the main computer system," the tour guide explained. He continued to talk about the other computers that students could find in the library: "Some computers can be used for word processing, some can help you find newspaper and magazine articles, and still others are hooked into libraries across the country." Jessica wondered how anyone could keep all these computers straight. Still, she thought, computers did make the idea of library research a little more exciting.

Watching Andrew sit down at a computer terminal, Jessica was amazed that he could use the computer so easily.

"Hey, look, Jess. The computer lists some books by someone with my last name, Mercier."

Jessica had a hard time paying attention to Andrew because the library wasn't really very quiet. She heard voices coming from all corners. People moved fast and seemed busy. Groups of students were meeting and talking, their backpacks stuffed full of papers and textbooks. People who looked like professors, wearing corduroy jackets and carrying worn leather satchels, were taking stacks of books to the photocopiers or to the circulation desk. Like the students, they met in pairs or groups and chatted with each other. Other people, probably librarians, were helping students with the computers and pointing them to different service or information desks. Colorful signs announcing a library film festival going on downstairs covered one wall. And Jessica could hear lively music coming from a room marked "Audiovisual Center." A steady flow of people came and left through the clicking turnstiles at the library's entrance. Jessica had the impression that just about everyone on campus was coming through the library's lobby. This place seemed more like a crowded marketplace than a library.

Andrew nudged her side. "Wake up, Jess. We're going this way."

As they walked around the main floor, the tour guide continued to describe the library. He said that it contained over a million volumes of material. Andrew pulled down a book from the shelf and fanned its pages. A million books! Andrew tossed the book to Jessica: "Hey, what do you think could be in all those books?"

The tour guide explained that, in addition to books, the library also housed most of the documents and reports published by the United States government. The library had hundreds of thousands of maps, manuscripts, records, photographs, movies, and even computer programs. "Some of what the library owns is on paper and in books," continued the tour guide, "but a lot of it is on microfilm, and on computer, and even on videodisc." It seemed so impersonal and confusing. Jessica was beginning to worry about how she would ever find information for term papers in this vast, hectic building.

"I wonder how many research papers we'll have to do," Andrew mumbled. Jessica thought maybe he too was feeling a little overwhelmed by all the computers and books and noise. At least she hoped she wasn't the only one who felt lost.

Librarians and other library staff members were eager to help students, the guide continued. Each library department had staff who would explain how to use different information sources and how to find answers to research questions. The guide told his group that the reference desk was the first place to stop for help in finding information. Jessica looked over to the large, imposing wooden reference desk that the guide pointed to. A sign above the desk announced "Information Here," but there was a long line of students waiting for help. Although Jessica should have felt reassured by the number of librarians willing to help, she was still overwhelmed. She decided that she had better learn how to navigate her way through the library soon. The reference librarians looked friendly enough, so Jessica thought she'd come back to the reference desk another time to get better acquainted with the library.

As Jessica and the tour group walked up the library's main staircase to the next floor, she realized that the library certainly wasn't what she had expected it to be: computers instead of catalogs, videodiscs in addition to books, and the rubbery odor of electronic equipment mixing with the smell of books. All in all, Jessica felt a lot more comfortable in the gym than in this place. Andrew wanted to break away from the tour to find all the library study areas and to explore the many floors and hallways of the library: "We'll scope out the best place to meet and study, okay?" Andrew's excitement was beginning to rub off on Jessica; maybe the library wasn't such a bad place after all. They set off to discover on their own what other surprises the library had to offer.

WRITING 1.

Fill out the following library survey, either with a group or on your own. After you have finished the survey, bring your responses to class for group discussion. As a group, write a descriptive story about a college student's typical afternoon in the library.

Library Survey

Recall what you knew and felt about libraries before coming to college.

1. Describe everything you can do in a library (any library).
2. List the different kinds of materials you can find in a library.
3. What kinds of services can you expect in a library?
4. Close your eyes and picture a typical librarian. Describe the person you see.
5. Name everything that you think a librarian does all day.
6. What do you think professors do in a library?

Either on your own or in a group, go to your college library. Explore and observe.

1. List all the different departments or areas in your library (for example, reference, government documents).
2. Describe everything that people (students, faculty, others) are doing in the library.
3. Describe what *you* have done in the library.
4. Name three things (any things) that you were surprised to discover about the library.
5. What do you like about the library?
6. What don't you like about the library?

WRITING 2.

Describe one department or area of your college library. Use your responses to the library survey as a starting point. You might choose from a department such as government documents, maps, reference, periodicals, special collections, rare books, microforms, reserves, audiovisual or from a subject library such as a humanities or science library. Not all libraries will have all these departments. When you write about the library department, be sure to include detailed descriptions of the physical layout and of the materials you found located there. Interview people who work in the department and students or faculty using the area in order to get a better sense of the way people use the department.

WHAT'S A LIBRARY MADE OF?

When you walk through the rows of book stacks in your own college library, it's easy to become overwhelmed, like Jessica, by the sheer number of books and the size of the library. Jessica and Andrew wondered what could be in all those millions of books that the orientation tour guide told them about. If you understand what makes up the books, magazines, and other materials found in a library's stacks, even the biggest library can begin to make sense. It is important to understand why and how books and articles are written, how they are published, and how we can find information that we need from them.

People's Thoughts and Ideas

Earlier chapters of this book described the ways that researchers in different fields structure their thoughts and investigations. The philosopher, biologist, psychologist, sociologist, and political scientist all look at problems in different ways. The biologist examines the natural environment and tries to answer questions about living things. The psychologist studies human behavior and questions why we are the way we are. The political scientist studies the systems we create to govern ourselves. All of these researchers use different tools, different sources of information both inside and outside the library, to solve their problems. As you discovered, they may use surveys, interviews, opinion polls, close observation, statistical analysis, and other methods to test their ideas. Researchers may also use articles written by other researchers as the basis for continuing discussion and analysis.

No matter what field researchers are in, however, they will want to share the methods and results of their research with others. Most often, the vehicle used to share research results is a journal article or book. Some results are also announced at conferences or meetings, but those, too, are usually published later as articles. These journals and books usually wind up in a library where they can be read by other researchers and students. The process of research, writing, and publication is renewed through the library.

The Life of an Idea

Let's look more closely at the way an idea goes from a professor's head to the library and back again. Although researchers will ask different questions and use different research tools, the process of creating, testing, and sharing an idea will be similar no matter what the subject.

Birth of an Idea. Some time during college, you will probably take a psychology course. Let's say your psychology teacher is Dr. Susan Nicholas, a young assistant professor who recently came to your college from the University of California. Dr. Nicholas spends much of her week preparing and giving lectures, grading papers, and holding office hours. Like other professors, she also spends part of her time thinking and asking questions about human behavior and doing research to answer these questions. Dr. Nicholas keeps up with what other psychology professors are doing across the country and internationally by reading books and articles and by attending conferences dealing with the aspect of psychology that interests her most.

Dr. Nicholas's particular interest is child psychology: She wonders why children act and think the way they do. Specifically, she studies how infants develop bonds with their fathers. While observing infants interacting with their fathers, Dr. Nicholas wonders what reactions babies might have to their fathers' prolonged absence. She notices that some babies get agitated when the father leaves their field of sight. Because of all the reading she has done, Dr. Nicholas knows that many researchers have discussed father-infant relations, but she doesn't recall reading anything about infant reactions to separation from the father. She guesses, or hypothesizes, that babies will become irritable and sleepless when the father first leaves. Dr. Nicholas must test her hypothesis on a group of babies so that she can determine whether her predictions about infant behavior are accurate.

Is It a New Idea?   The first step that Dr. Nicholas might take in her investigation is to check whether any other researchers have studied this same subject, because someone may have already made the same, or similar, hypothesis and tested it. Even so, Dr. Nicholas may want to try the study on a new group of infants. Or perhaps someone has made observations about infants and fathers that Dr. Nicholas could use in her own study. Maybe she'll discover someone whom she disagrees with and whose ideas she can test and refute. In order to find out what others have written about infant separation from fathers, Dr. Nicholas goes to the library to look at psychology books and journals.

Although Dr. Nicholas checks the library's catalogue to see if any books have been written on her subject, she knows that books take at least a year to be published after they have been written and that the research in books is therefore not quite new. Chances are that she already knows about research projects that are discussed in books. Furthermore, books cover relatively broad topics, and her interest is very narrow. To find out what new research has been done on her specific subject, Dr. Nicholas needs to look at journal articles.

New ideas are generally published in scholarly journals that, like books, can be found in research libraries. These published journals are not like the personal journals you might keep as a daily record of your own thoughts or observations. Scholarly journals are published several times a year, usually monthly or quarterly, and contain reports and discussions of research. Today there are over 100,000 journals published worldwide covering all areas of research.

Journals may look a lot like magazines to you. They come out regularly and have soft covers. Magazines such as *Time*, *People Magazine*, or *Rolling Stone*, however, have a different audience and focus than journals. Magazines tend to cover popular topics and news items in short articles without bibliographies or footnotes. Magazine articles may serve both to inform and to entertain their readers. Unlike scholarly journals, which are written for focused, research-oriented readers, popular magazines are directed to a broad and diverse audience.

Journal articles describe in detail the methods used to test an idea and the results of that test. They may also discuss ideas, analyze other kinds of written works such as poems or novels, or debate earlier research articles. By reading journal articles, we can follow an author's thinking and research path. Most journal articles also include a list of sources, a bibliography, which tells readers which other books or journal articles the researcher consulted. Dr. Nicholas is excited to get to the library and start looking up her subject to see what research paths psychologists have taken when studying infants and fathers.

Because Dr. Nicholas has been following journals in child psychology, she knows which particular research journals would publish articles about infants and fathers. To find which issue of a journal has a pertinent article, she uses *Psychological Abstracts*, an index that lists all books and journal articles in psychology by subject. It also provides brief summaries, or abstracts, of the articles. Dr. Nicholas's library not only has *Psychological Abstracts* in a printed format but also makes it available on computer for faster searching. Although *Psychological Abstracts* is the major index for psychology, most disciplines have their own indexes and abstracts to help people find articles in other subjects. *Art Index*, *Engineering Index*, *Sociological Abstracts*, and *Biological Abstracts* are only a few of the tools that help students and scholars find what has been written on a topic; most of these, too, can be searched on computer.

In addition to checking journal articles to see what research has been done, Dr. Nicholas talks to other psychologists and keeps her ears open at psychologists' meetings to see if anyone is currently working on a similar problem. She uses all professional networks available to make sure that her idea is original and that she is not duplicating someone else's work. As it turns out, Dr. Nicholas's idea appears to be a new one. She can go ahead and test it.

WRITING 3.

Go to your library and find examples of both a journal and a magazine. Write a short essay in which you compare the format, content, language, and audience of the two. Try to choose a journal and magazine that share a broad subject. For example, you could compare the magazine *Business Week* to the journal *Journal of Finance*. You might compare *Psychology Today* to *American Psychologist* or *Rolling Stone* to *Journal of Music Theory.* Look closely at the overall structure of the publications and at the tone and content of individual articles. How are the journal and magazine different? How are they similar? Who publishes each one? What do you expect their readers to be like? Ask a reference librarian to help you identify magazines and journals that your college library owns.

Planning the Test.   Before Dr. Nicholas can test her idea, she needs to determine what testing methods she will use. For example, she may want to find and interview fathers who have had prolonged separations from their infants. She may want to observe closely infants who have been recently separated from their fathers. She may conduct a written survey of the mothers who were with their babies after the father left.

In this planning stage, Dr. Nicholas might go back to the library to find discussions of different testing methods that have been used with infants so that she knows which methods will work the best. Even though no previous psychological studies have examined how infants react to a father's separation, the methods used in earlier studies involving infants might be applicable to her new study. The library's reference department has exactly the book she needs to give her an overview of testing and evaluation methods for studying infant interactions.

Part of the test-planning process includes making sure that her testing and evaluation methods do not harm the families she is studying and do not infringe on their rights. Dr. Nicholas must therefore present her research plan to a university review board that approves research projects involving human subjects. The review board quickly approves the plan but asks that Dr. Nicholas report to the board periodically to make sure the study stays within its original guidelines.

Testing the Idea.   Now that she has done the background research and the planning, Dr. Nicholas can begin to test her hypothesis. She advertises in the local paper to identify families in which the father has left an infant and asks a few psychology graduate students to help out in the testing process. When she interviews, surveys, and observes parents and infants, she discovers that most babies do get irritable and restless after a father leaves. Some of the babies, however, get more irritable than others, so Dr. Nicholas goes back to the library to look up recent research on differences between infants. She follows the same research process she used earlier, checking *Psychological Abstracts* for articles. It turns out that other researchers have reported that infants from divorced families are more sensitive to changes in their surroundings than infants from nondivorced settings.

As a result of her discoveries in the library, Dr. Nicholas changes her hypothesis to apply only to infants from divorced families. She must now retest her hypothesis on more infants and fathers, focusing on divorced fathers.

The Idea Leaves the Nest. Finally, as a result of her library and laboratory research, Dr. Nicholas believes that her revised hypothesis has been supported. Many of the infants that she studied did become irritable and sleepless when the father first left the family after a divorce. She suspects that the babies reacted this way because of the increased emotional intensity in the household, particularly in the mother, although that hypothesis would need to be tested in a new study. For now Dr. Nicholas is happy that her hypothesis about infants appears to be accurate, at least for the particular group of babies that she studied.

After finding evidence to support her theory, Dr. Nicholas wants to share her results with other researchers who are interested in father-infant interactions. First she writes up her results in a paper that is published in *The Journal of Experimental Child Psychology*. Child psychologists around the world follow this journal to see what new research has been done. Some of them will react to Dr. Nicholas's study and draw new conclusions from it, publishing their reactions in journals; other psychologists will come up with new hypotheses to test as a result of reading Dr. Nicholas's study. Some may repeat the test using different infants to see if Dr. Nicholas's initial results hold up in another test. After reading and hearing reactions to her study, Dr. Nicholas herself may repeat her test to see if she can learn more about father-infant interaction.

In addition to publishing the journal article, Dr. Nicholas also presents her ideas at a conference of psychologists; her discussion is summarized in a book of conference proceedings. Finally, she is asked to write an entire book about infants and fathers based on her recent studies.

Dr. Nicholas also plans to share her research results with students in her Child Psychology 121 course. Not only can the students read about infant behavior in textbooks and journal articles, but they also have the opportunity to learn newly discovered insights about fathers and infants through their teacher, an active researcher.

Back to the Library. The journal article, conference proceedings, and book are all bought by college and university libraries throughout the world. In these research libraries, Dr. Nicholas's ideas and studies are made available to students, researchers, and others interested in human behavior or psychology. *Psychological Abstracts* indexes all of the articles in *The Journal of Experimental Child Psychology*; therefore, when the latest *Psychological Abstracts* comes out, Dr. Nicholas's article will be listed under the subject "infant behavior" so that students and researchers can find it when they are studying infants.

When students are asked to write a psychology term paper, they might find Dr. Nicholas's article or book in the library and use her discoveries to support their own writing. Other psychology professors might use Dr. Nicholas's reports to help them think of new ideas. Local, state, and federal agencies might use her observations to help reform child welfare policies. Finally, divorced parents of infants might find Dr. Nicholas's research helpful in dealing with their own babies. All of these people come to the college library to find answers and generate new ideas.

WRITING 4.

Make an appointment with a professor in a field you might like to study to discuss his or her research process. Ask the professor to explain what his or her research interests are and how he or she goes about testing ideas. How does the library fit into the research? How does the professor share ideas with others? How does his or her research process compare to the one just outlined? It would be helpful to make a list of questions to ask your professor before your meeting. Write a short essay describing your discoveries.

The Stuff of Research

Dr. Nicholas is a psychologist. The raw data, or source materials, for her research are people and accounts of their behavior. The article that Dr. Nicholas wrote for *The Journal of Experimental Child Psychology* as a result of her research can become the source material for other scholars when they publish reactions to her article. As you have seen from the previous chapters, the raw material of research or scholarship in other disciplines can be quite varied: creative texts such as novels and poems for the literary scholar; historical texts such as newspapers and diaries for the historian; living nonhuman things such as streams, trees, and insects for the biologist; a campus kiosk covered with fliers for the sociologist. The texts and other materials that form the basis of investigation and research are called primary sources.

Primary and Secondary Sources. Primary sources are the things that researchers study: statistics, people, rocks, bones, poems, diaries, photographs, historical documents, philosophical texts, paintings, music, scientific papers—anything that provokes questions and is studied for answers and insights. The works that interpret and make conclusions from primary materials are considered secondary sources. Dr. Nicholas's journal articles and conference proceedings and books are secondary sources. In other words, they synthesize and analyze data or the earlier thought or writing of others.

Often secondary sources become primary sources in the chain of research, writing, and publication. Philosophers and scientists use the reports of others' research and thought for their primary materials. A student's history research log or field manual based on the observation of natural phenomena may become a primary source for his or her final research paper.

Libraries contain both primary and secondary materials. The library owns copies of novels as well as journals containing literary criticism written about novels. The library has diaries and letters and the journal articles analyzing them. The library may have photographs or reproductions of paintings along with art historians' articles about the meaning of these works of art. The films, music, statistics, government documents, rare books, and manuscripts found in libraries can all serve as primary sources, depending on the interests and focus of the researcher.

We know, of course, that not all primary sources may be found in libraries. The stuff of research can be found just about anywhere. But secondary sources — the books and journal articles that result from research — can always be found in academic libraries where they are easiest for researchers like Dr. Nicholas, and students like you, to locate. Although no single library will own all journals and books published, many university libraries are linked in an electronic interlibrary network so that they can share materials with one another. Ask the reference librarian if you want to get books or articles from other libraries.

WRITING 5.

Choose a year between 1900 and 1960, and see if you can find a primary source written or created during that year. Remember that a primary source can be a newspaper article, an old magazine article, a photograph — anything! Ask the reference librarian for help finding a primary source. Your source may not even be in the library at all. It could be in your campus art museum or geology building. Now describe as precisely as you can the features of this primary source. What does it look like? Who made it? What is its purpose or function? What is interesting about this source? Does it tell you anything about the time period during which it was created? What questions do you have about the source itself? In addition to writing a brief description of your primary source, list questions you have about the time period or the creator of the source; these questions could form the seed of further research.

Jessica and Andrew Do Research

Jessica and Andrew had settled into college life quite nicely and were enjoying their classes. At least Jessica *was* enjoying them until she realized that her first research paper for Women's History 100 was due in two weeks. When she got together with Andrew for their weekly racquetball game, she found out that he had a History 107 paper due soon, too. Unfortunately, neither Jessica nor Andrew had started working on their papers yet. Andrew figured he could put his paper off for a couple of weeks, but Jessica had no time to lose. It looked as though she couldn't avoid doing research in the library any longer.

Jessica's professor, Dr. Linda Vallejo, told the class that each student should write a fifteen-page research paper on anything that had to do with women's history. At first Jess couldn't think of a topic, so she made a list in her history notebook of questions dealing with women's history that she had always wondered about. Dr. Vallejo asked that students keep a personal history journal, or history research log, in which they could record their steps and reactions in doing research for their papers.

Jessica remembered her grandparents talking about World War II. She wondered what her grandmother and other women did at home while their husbands were away at war. This seemed like a focused topic that interested her and which might have some information available.

Now that she had a topic, Jessica was ready to go to the library to find information.

Asking Reference and Research Questions[1]

Ways to start finding information:

- Think carefully about your project or paper topic. If you can, choose a topic that truly interests you.
- Write out your topic as completely as you can in one or two sentences.
- Write down what you already know about your topic.
- Write down what you still need to find out about your topic.
- List some sources (people, places, books, anything) that you think might help you find the information you need.
- Jot down where you'll go first, second, etc., in your information-seeking journey.

How to ask someone for help in finding information:

- Bring your assignment along to show the librarian and other people you question.
- Describe your topic in a couple of sentences.
- Indicate your time frame for completing the assignment (the due date).
- Identify the purpose for which the information will be used (for example, a speech for English 11).
- Indicate what work you've done so far (for example, searched the catalogue for books or read encyclopedias).
- Estimate the amount of information needed (such as at least six sources on the Civil War or enough material for a twenty-page paper).
- Indicate the level of information sought (such as technical information on electronic circuits or a quick overview of the 1960s).

[1] Adapted from a question sheet by Marsha D. Broadway of Brigham Young University.

- Indicate whether current or historical information is needed.
- Specify the format of materials needed (for example, government documents, newspapers, or videotapes).

Asking the Right Questions. Jessica headed off to the history library to see what she could find about World War II. She soon learned that there was a lot of information about World War II, although she was having trouble finding information about women. When she looked up "women" in the library's computer catalogue, there was a lot of information, but she couldn't find much about World War II and women. She was beginning to get pretty frustrated when the librarian asked if he could help her.

She showed Bill Retski, the history librarian, her assignment and explained to him where she had already looked for information. He told her that she needed to think of different ways to ask her question, to think of synonyms for her topic, so that she could figure out the catalogue and other reference sources. Maybe books about women and war in general would have a chapter about World War II. Jessica should also think of other terms related to war, such as "military." Maybe books on the domestic effects of World War II would have sections about women in them. It was up to her to think about different aspects of her question to determine which index terms might work best.

After talking to the librarian, Jessica realized that research was not a haphazard process. She needed a good strategy for finding the best information for her research paper.

Basic Research Strategy

- *Start a research log or notebook.* Keep track of where you looked for information and how you felt about the information you found.
- *Find a brief overview of your topic.* First check a subject encyclopedia. The reference librarian can help you find specialized encyclopedias (such as an encyclopedia of the Olympics or an encyclopedia of women's history).
- *Break down your topic into key words or subject terms.* Think of synonyms for your topic (for example, for a paper on automobiles, you might also look for books on "motor vehicles," or "cars," or even "transportation"). Use this list when you are searching either printed or computerized indexes.
- *Find books on your topic.* Use the library's computerized or card catalogue, trying different subject terms. Review books by scanning tables of contents or indexes to see if a book covers what you need. Look over bibliographies in the book to find more references.
- *Find journal articles on your topic.* Look up your key words in indexes, abstracts, or subject bibliographies. Ask the librarian to help you identify which indexes would be best. Make use of com-

puterized indexes to make research quicker and more thorough in many subjects. Some indexes provide a special thesaurus, or master list, of subject terms; ask the librarian if a thesaurus is available for any indexes that you will use. Scan journal articles, checking their bibliographies for additional sources.

- *Investigate other sources of information.* Talk to an authority on your topic (perhaps a professor or someone in the local community). Check newspapers. Look at government documents and maps, archives, statistics, pamphlets, special collections, and any other sources you can think of inside or outside of the libraries.
- *Compile a bibliography using a style manual.* The *MLA Handbook* or Turabian's *A Manual for Writers* will help you develop a consistent format.

Finding Background Information.   Jessica wasn't feeling very encouraged. She had been in the history library for an hour and still couldn't find any information. Bill suggested that she try to get an overview of her topic in a subject encyclopedia, like *The Encyclopedia of World War II* or *The Women's Studies Encyclopedia.* Once she had an overview of her topic, she would know better what women did during the war and where to go for more detailed information; many subject encyclopedia articles have bibliographies that lead to more information. Sure enough, *The Women's Studies Encyclopedia* included an article about women and war, which included a long section on World War II. In fact, there was so much information on women and World War II that she decided to narrow her topic even more to women working in factories during World War II. Now Jessica was ready to dig deeper into her subject.

After Jessica left the library, she ran into Andrew in the dorm cafeteria. As he was talking to her about finding information for her history paper, he started to think that maybe he should begin his own history paper soon. It sounded like this college research paper business was going to be more complicated than he thought.

Finding Books.   The next step in Jessica's research strategy was to see which books the library owned about women factory workers during World War II. Jessica's library lists all of the books in a computer catalogue. She discovered by looking at a subject heading book at the reference desk that she could type "women and war" or "women and the military" or "women and work" into the computer as possible subjects. She tried lots of other subjects as well until she got a good list of books.

All of the books she found, however, seemed very broad and were several years old. It was interesting to read what people had written about World War II right after the war happened, but Jessica also wanted to know what researchers were writing now about women and the war. She needed to use more up-to-date journal articles.

Finding Articles. To find journal articles, Jessica needed to use an index listing journal articles by subject. Bill told her that the indexes most appropriate for her topic would be *Sociological Abstracts* or *America: History and Life*; both could be found in the reference department of either the history library or the main library.

By checking the subjects "women," "work," and "war," she found lists of many current articles, including some about factory work. Jessica was surprised to discover that her library had *Sociological Abstracts* in print but also had access to it via computer. Searching by computer made finding articles much quicker and more thorough. Jessica recalled Andrew's ease with the computer during orientation; she would have to tell him about how much fun it was to do research with this computer.

Using Other Sources of Information. Jessica was happy with the books and articles that she had found, but she thought that something was missing from her research. All of the books and articles interpreted information for her. She wanted to find statistics and other primary sources so that she could draw some of her own conclusions. She was pleased to find that the main library's government documents department had many statistical sources that provided all sorts of data to support her observations. She found data on numbers and ages of women, on locations and types of factories, and on length of employment in factories. Jessica even found herself making observations from these data that she hadn't read about in other researchers' writing. She almost felt like she was becoming a researcher herself.

Something else was missing from her research, though. It lacked a personal touch. She called her grandmother to interview her about women's factory work during World War II. Maybe she would talk to Andrew to find out if he knew anything about his grandmothers' activities during the war. Jessica also went to the library's special collections department to see if she could find any diaries written by women during World War II. She found not only diaries but also photographs. Now her research was really beginning to be fun.

Documenting Sources. Jessica couldn't believe how quickly the time passed doing research in the library once she knew exactly what she was looking for. It was less than a week before the paper was due, but Jessica felt confident that she had enough information to write a good paper. Before she began to write, however, she recalled Professor Vallejo's discussion of documenting sources. Dr. Vallejo had made a big point in class about the importance of acknowledging in footnotes and bibliographies where every new idea or every piece of new information came from in order to avoid plagiarizing, or stealing, other people's ideas.

Luckily Jessica had kept track of her sources in her research log, including author names; complete titles of articles, journals, and books;

publisher names and locations; and page numbers cited. This made it easy to put the source information into the *MLA Handbook* format, the format that Dr. Vallejo required. Although figuring out the right way to do bibliographies and notes was a little tricky at first, it became easier once Jessica got the Modern Language Association (MLA) style down. Although Dr. Vallejo asked her students to follow MLA style, Jessica knew that other professors required different citation formats, such as the American Psychological Association (APA) style or the style described in Turabian's *A Manual for Writers*. It would sure make life easier if everyone could agree on one way to do footnotes and bibliographies!

Jessica Gets a "B."   Like the library research itself, writing her paper flowed easily because Jessica was interested in the subject and believed that she had something important to say. Jessica just regretted that she hadn't left time to do a good revision after her first draft. Still, she couldn't wait to show Dr. Vallejo her finished work.

Before handing her paper in, she showed it to Andrew. "Hey, this is pretty good, Jess. You know, this topic could fit my history assignment, too. Do you think I could borrow your paper?" Andrew reacted to Jessica's skeptical look: "Just kidding, of course."

Dr. Vallejo liked her paper, too, and she thought that the paper could get an "A" with some revision. Jessica was rightfully proud of what she had learned and written. She wanted to share her work with her mother and grandmother and to keep up with information about women during World War II.

WRITING 6.

Interview one of your friends who has recently done a research paper. Ask the person what steps he or she took in finding information and in writing the research paper. Try to get your friend to be specific and descriptive. Find out how he or she felt at each step—excited? Bored? Happy? Frustrated? How do his or her research steps compare with Jessica's or with Dr. Nicholas's? Was your friend satisfied with the research and the finished paper? Why or why not? Write a few paragraphs describing your friend's research process.

The Heart of the University

You may have noticed that the processes Jessica and Dr. Nicholas followed to do their research were similar. Even though Jessica was writing a research paper for a class and Dr. Nicholas was writing for publication in scholarly journals, they both used a research strategy that led them to primary and secondary sources inside and outside of the library. Research, whether it is done by you as a student or by your professors, can be exciting, challenging, and frustrating. The beginning of research is an idea that you might get when you are remembering or observing or reading or just thinking. To test and investigate that idea you need to use a wide variety of resources, many of which can be found in libraries.

The library is an important central switching station in the research and discovery process. It is sometimes called the heart of the university because it provides a growing record of the thought and research upon which university teaching and scholarship are based. It is the place where students, professors, and other university scholars go to find out what's been thought and studied before. When students or professors come to the library to read what other researchers have written, they may come up with new ideas to examine, test, and finally write up in more articles and books. And these, too, will probably find their way into the library for still others to look at. The library is one step in an ongoing process of thought, creativity, research, and the acquisition of new knowledge.

READINGS

William Zinsser
A LIBERAL EDUCATION

Writing to Learn by William Zinsser (b. 1922) is really an "I-search" book rather than a research book. The term "I-search," coined by writing theorist Ken Macrorie in Searching Writing, refers to a writing process that explores the writer's own experiences and feelings about a topic before turning to authorities for outside support. During his investigative process, Zinsser discovers as much about himself and his feelings as he does about his subject.

As a writing professor at Yale University, Zinsser had visited an innovative "writing across the curriculum" program at Gustavus Adolphus College in Minnesota. As a result of his visit, Zinsser wanted to make a collection, or anthology, of well-written literature from different academic disciplines (much like A Community of Voices). He wanted to create, he said, "a guided tour of good writing in different crannies of the B.A. curriculum." Instead he wound up writing a memoir about his search for good literature, describing his search process and his feelings about the search and including the results of that search.

"A Liberal Education" seems to fit a different model for doing research than the traditional one presented in this chapter. How would you describe Zinsser's research process?

I didn't know where my search for the literature would end, but I had no trouble deciding where it should begin. My thoughts went back to the period of my life that had been the most broadly educational of all—the decade I spent at Yale. Two jobs that I held there put me in touch with the community of knowledge at its most liberal.

My reason for moving to Yale in 1970 was to teach nonfiction writing. I had never seen Yale before and knew nothing of its traditions except that the bulldog was its mascot and the Whiffenpoofs sang at a place called Mory's, possibly on the tables. I was a fourth-generation New Yorker and had never lived anywhere else. That's also where I had had my career: thirteen years as an editor and a writer with the *New York Herald Tribune* and eleven more as a free-lance writer. Those last eleven years, working alone at home, made me desperate for human contact. Whatever Yale had to offer, I was ready.

Hardly had I unpacked my bags and my children when I got a call from the chairman of the board of the *Yale Alumni Magazine*. A sudden domestic crisis, he said, had left the magazine without an editor. He explained that the magazine had a circulation of more than 100,000 and that it went to all the alumni of Yale College and its nine graduate schools, which included schools of art, architecture, divinity, drama, forestry and environmental studies, law, medicine, music and nursing. Would I like to be the editor?

At first I thought it was an absurd thing for a middle-aged Princeton man to do. But luckily I had a second thought: What quicker way to get to know a great university? Editors are licensed to be curious. Besides, I enjoyed editing more than writing. I liked thinking of story ideas; I liked working with writers and helping them to present their writing at its strongest, and I especially liked the element of surprise: Every day an editor learns something new. I signed up for the job and did it for seven years.

I never stopped to ask, "Who is the typical Yale alumnus? Who am I editing for?" One of my principles is that there is no typical anybody; every reader is different. I edit for myself and I write for myself. I assume that if I consider something interesting or funny, a certain number of other people will too. If they don't, they have two inalienable rights— they can fire the editor and they can stop reading the writer. Meanwhile I draw on two sources of energy that I commend to anyone trying to survive in this vulnerable craft: confidence and ego. If you don't have confidence in what you're doing you might as well not do it.

As editor of Yale's magazine I took the whole university as my domain. I wanted to know what was new in every discipline and what scholars were up to in every cranny of the campus. Yale seemed to have no end, for instance, of collections that were unique: silver and textiles, Babylonian tablets and Tibetan sacred texts, Boswell papers and Franklin papers, manuscripts of Charles Lindbergh and Gertrude Stein. In 1972 I noticed that the Western History Association would be holding its annual meeting in New Haven. Why New Haven? It turned out that one of Yale's professors, Howard R. Lamar, was an eminent Western scholar. I asked him for an article explaining why the Western historians, who had never met east of the Mississippi before, were coming East now.

"In the 1940s Yale filed a claim to much of the history of the trans-Mississippi West," he wrote, "by acquiring the libraries—books, maps, manuscripts, newspapers and paintings—of six great collectors of Western Americana. Put together under one roof, they have made [Yale's] Beinecke Library a rendezvous for students of the West and prompted a course on the history of the West that I have been teaching for twenty-one years." But what most excited Professor Lamar was how "the field of Western history has taken on new dimensions and totally new meanings for the student and the public. The Old West, romantic and heroic, has in two decades become the area that epitomizes the most basic questions facing America today." His article went on to describe how some of the most entrenched American attitudes—toward Indians, toward Mexican-Americans, toward Western heroes, toward the role of pioneer women and families, toward nature and land and water—had changed almost overnight. That was news to me; my clock was still set to John Wayne and Billy the Kid.

Or—to go from land to spirit—here's a piece that originated in the Yale Divinity School. I noticed that the school had on its faculty a Benedictine monk named Aidan Kavanagh, who was a professor of liturgics. Could he explain what a professor of liturgics did? His article met my question head-on in this wonderful paragraph:

No one can teach wisdom, least of all I. But what I can do in my own field of liturgical scholarship is to engage my students in an environment of facts, method and perspective in which wisdom may be learned by us all. In this regard my peculiar field is rich. What we study, ultimately, is not texts but the ways in which people from time out of mind have regularly come together to express those values that they have found to serve them best in their own struggle to survive. I shall never live forever if I cannot make it through tomorrow morning. The strategic end is born in the tactics with which it is pursued. Little things like salt, smells, oil, bread and wine, singing and seed, dancing, laughter and tears, bodies and babies, and even thoughts and words form the tactical fabric of survival with which a liturgical scholar must deal.

On another occasion I arranged for an interview with Bert Waterman, Yale's highly respected wrestling coach. He mentioned that one of his wrestlers, Michael Poliakoff, was a classics major who was writing his senior thesis on combative sport in the ancient world; during his summer vacation he had toured the museums of England, Italy and Greece to look for classical Greek vase paintings that matched the descriptions of sport he had encountered in his classical reading. How could I get so lucky as an editor? I asked Mike Poliakoff about his search. "I chose this topic," he said, "because it's a significant gap in our knowledge of antiquity, though these sports, especially wrestling, permeated every aspect of Greek life." He showed me some photographs he had taken of vases, cups, coins and sculptures, made between 550 B.C. and 430 B.C., which depicted wrestlers and referees in positions that haven't changed since. We made a layout to accompany the interview and he wrote the captions. This was one of them:

A black-figure neck amphora of the Leagros group of Attic pottery, 520–510 B.C. The triumph of civilization over barbarism is represented as Hercules, with utmost skill and grace, defeats the giant Antaeus while the goddess Athena and the god Hermes oversee the contest. Hercules is using a "front chancery," a move popular on the Yale wrestling team today.[1]

Those are just three articles recalled at random from several hundred that popped up in various corners of the university. Most of them were about teaching and learning and research; many were about culture, the arts, libraries and special collections; quite a few were about sports, student attitudes and social change. But all of them delighted me with their unexpectedness and their information. They also taught me a lesson about the integration of knowledge: Separate disciplines are seldom separate. Beyond that, I confirmed what I had always believed about my craft—that there's no subject that can't be made accessible in good English with careful writing and editing.

My education quickened in 1973 when I was appointed master of Branford College, one of Yale's twelve undergraduate residential colleges. Every college has a resident master, who resides over its life as an academic and social community. More than a hundred Fellows are also affiliated with each college—professors, deans, research scientists, librarians and other scholars drawn from every discipline and graduate school. One whom I recall with particular affection was the late Aleksis Rannit, an Estonian poet widely honored in Europe. As a postwar emigré in the United States he had become a librarian and was now curator of the Yale's rich Slavic and East European collections. I once asked him if he would talk at one of the weekly master's teas that I held to expose students to people I admired whom they wouldn't ordinarily meet. I wanted him to talk about his past and to read some of his poems.

I still remember that afternoon for three reasons. One was the broad humanistic canvas of his life in prewar Europe. He seemed to have known every artist and writer who was working on some frontier of creativity. (The painter Georges Braque was a typical frontiersman.) I also remember that when I asked him to conclude the afternoon by reading from a volume of his poems, he stood up. Homage to the poem; the rest had been mere reminiscence. But what I remember most was the beauty of the poetry itself. Estonian is a tonal language with an unusual structure of extended beats, and none of us had ever heard it before. But it needed no translating; if Aleksis announced that the next poem was about a lake in winter, we saw the dead leaves on the ice and felt the chill. We were in the presence of a miracle: the ability of poetry to transcend the language it's written in. The words became music and carried the same kind of emotional weight.

But the Fellow who most nourished me with the inclusiveness of his mind was Willie Ruff, professor of music and of Afro-American studies. A black jazz bassist and French-horn player, Ruff also lived in Branford College and thrived on the ideas that circulated there. One Fellow whose research interested him was Dr. Gilbert H. Glaser, professor of neurology at the Yale School of Medicine and an authority on epilepsy. Ruff had long wanted to know more about rhythm than he knew from the lifelong practice of his art, and he thought Dr. Glaser might lead him to some answers. He proposed that Branford College originate and co-sponsor with the Yale School of Medicine and the Yale School of Music a three-day symposium at which "the best minds in other disciplines would talk about how rhythm is at work in what they do."

I liked the idea, and so did all the people Ruff invited. (Most of them were from Yale.) Some were artists who knew rhythm through the act of creation and could demonstrate it: the jazz drummer Jo Jones, the dancer Geoffrey Holder, the poet John Hollander, some members of a Japanese gamelan orchestra, the harpsichordist and Bach scholar Ralph Kirkpatrick. But the people who gave the seminar its rigor were from disciplines that had nothing to do with performance. The metallurgist Cyril Smith talked about symmetry and dissymmetry in molecular structure. The geologist John Rodgers talked about the strict numerical repetition in the formation of crystals. The zoologist G. Evelyn Hutchinson talked about the rhythmic movement of lake waters; the art historian Malcolm Cormack talked about rhythm in painting, and Dr. Glaser talked about the role of the brain in the physiology and control of rhythm. For three days the rhythmologists turned each other on, and Ruff has used the format ever since to teach an interdisciplinary seminar on rhythm. He keeps finding new rhythmical affinities between seemingly unrelated areas of life and inducing Yale professors — of architecture, of astronomy, of physics — to talk about them.

After I left Yale I kept in touch with Ruff and was rewarded with two of the richest experiences of my life — one in Shanghai, the other in Venice. Not only were they extensions of what I had learned at Yale about the links between widely separated centuries and cultures. They also stretched me as a writer, posing unusually hard problems when I went along on both trips and wrote articles about them that later ran in The New Yorker. One of the underestimated tasks in nonfiction writing is to impose narrative shape on an unwieldy mass of material. That task is so central to this book that I'll briefly describe what Ruff got me into.

The first trip took place in June of 1981. Ruff had spent two years learning Mandarin, his eighth language, in order to introduce jazz to China with the pianist Dwike Mitchell, his long-time partner in the Mitchell-Ruff Duo. The emotional climax of the trip was a concert the two men gave at the Shanghai Conservatory of Music. It began with Ruff explaining in Chinese to three hundred students and professors how jazz originated in the drum languages of West Africa — an oral tradition that was the antithesis of their own tradition — and it ended with Mitchell doing an elegant improvisation on a Chinese piece that one of the students had just performed on the piano. I could hardly believe how many opposite forces were at play in one room. But at the end music was the only force; it had blown every difference away.[2]

Two years later I happened to call Ruff and he mentioned that he was about to go to Venice to play Gregorian chants on his French horn in St. Mark's cathedral at night when nobody else was there. He said it was a dream that went back thirty years to his student days at Yale, when his professor was the composer Paul Hindemith. Hindemith was obsessed by the relationship between music and science — his hero was the astronomer Johannes Kepler — and he was particularly excited by the music that came out of St. Mark's basilica in the 1500s and 1600s, when Venice was the center of the musical world. The church's remarkable acoustics inspired many composers—notably, the Gabrielis, Zarlino and Monteverdi—to create an important new style of polyphonic music.

"Hindemith showed us that that music was a crucial bridge to everything that followed," Ruff said. "It was also the music that spoke most directly to me. I loved the luxurious sound that the Gabrielis achieved in their polychoral compositions, which were played and sung antiphonally from opposite lofts in St. Mark's. Ever since then I've wanted to know what that sound is like."

As for why he wanted to play Gregorian chants, Ruff said it went back to a concert that the singer Paul Robeson once gave at Carnegie Hall. To show that the folk music of many disparate countries has a common source, Robeson sang an East African tribal chant, a thirteenth-century Slovakian plain chant and an American Negro spiritual that were almost identical. Robeson explained that the Abyssinian church and the church of the Sudan were once part of the Eastern church of Byzantium. Thus African music found its way into the Byzantine liturgy, which later filtered out into Europe and colored the Gregorian chants of the early Roman Catholic Church. "So what I'll be playing in St. Mark's," Ruff told me, "is sacred music that has been played in that church since the Middle Ages. And because those chants are also at the core of my spirituals I'm going to play some of them, too."

Such a convergence of ancient streams was something I didn't want to miss, and I asked Ruff if I could meet him in Venice. He said he didn't know if he could get the necessary permission; he needed to play when St. Mark's was empty so that he could test its acoustics and make a tape recording. I said I'd take my chances—betting on Ruff is a no-risk proposition. As it turned out, getting permission was a story in itself—a miniseries of ecclesiastical rebuffs. But finally Ruff persuaded (in Italian) an old monsignor to let him use St. Mark's for two hours after the last mass adjourned at seven-thirty.

Even now I find it hard to believe that those two hours happened to me. In summer, St. Mark's is visited by twenty-five thousand tourists a day. But on that night, except for the sacristan who let us in, Ruff and I were the only people there. The first note that Ruff blew on his French horn told us that Hindemith had been right—the note seemed to seek out every crevice in the five immense domes and to linger long after it should have died away. Ruff opened a book called the *Liber Usualis* and began to play some of the oldest chants in the Catholic liturgy: Glorias and Kyries from various masses, a Sanctus, an Agnus Dei, and the beautiful "Pange Lingua." The sound was extraordinarily pure.

I sat in the nave and watched the daylight ebb out of the church. Suddenly the gold mosaics in the domes were drained of color and the interior was dark. The sacristan came and put a candle next to Ruff's book. Ruff kept playing. He and I were alone with our thoughts—a thousand years had been collapsed into two hours. I was listening to music that had been played in St. Mark's since it opened in 1067.

Outside in the square, a clock struck nine. Ruff closed his *Liber Usualis* and stood under the central dome and played "Were You There When They Crucified My Lord?" The great Negro spiritual sounded as majestic as the Gregorian chants. When Ruff finished, the sacristan came hurrying from wherever he had been. *"Bene! Bene!"* he said, clapping his hands, trying to convey his joy, though his face said it all. That the American spiritual moved him more than the chants of his own Catholic liturgy was the final mystery of the night, although, finally, it was no mystery; all the spirituals that Ruff played, including the pentatonic "Go Down, Moses," were so similar to what he had played earlier that I could hardly tell which was which. Not that I was in any mood to try.[3]

Back in New York, trying to write my article, I felt overwhelmed (as I had with the Shanghai piece) by the richness of the material.[4] The story had no end of connections between different centuries and civilizations, including a visit to Stravinsky's grave. Too much had been thrown at me, and I would need to throw quite a lot at the reader. It's not enough for a nonfiction writer to just write good, clean sentences; he must organize those sentences into a coherent shape, taking the reader on a complicated trip—often with several flashbacks—without losing him or boring him. In this case a reader couldn't begin to accompany Ruff on his rounds—intellectually or emotionally—without knowing something about Hindemith and the acoustics of St. Mark's, about the Gabrielis and the Venetian school, about the Byzantine liturgy and the Gregorian chants and the Negro spirituals with which they share a distant ancestry. But too many facts would kill the reader's enjoyment of the adventure itself, which, beneath all its layers, was just an old-fashioned story of a pilgrim on a quest.

Whenever I embark on a story so overloaded with good material I despair of ever getting to the end—of covering all the ground I know I'll need to cover to tell the story right. In my gloom it helps me to remember two things. One is that writing is linear and sequential. If sentence B logically follows sentence A, and if sentence C logically follows sentence B, I'll eventually get to sentence Z. I also try to remember that the reader should be given only as much information as he needs and not one word more. Anything else is a self-indulgence. Prior knowledge of the subject, incidentally, isn't a requirement; only the ability to arrange information in narrative order. Readers may well have thought I was an expert on the Venetian school of music. In fact I had never heard of the Venetian school of music or the Gabrielis until Ruff told me he was going to Venice, and I didn't learn any other details until I flew there and met him at a café overlooking the Grand Canal. The trip was instant education—sufficient, at least, to enable me to tell my story to other generalists like myself.

After that came the hard part: wrestling my new-found education into a narrative that moved logically from A to Z. The only thing I knew at the beginning was how I wanted the article to end: "The sacristan unbolted the door and gave us a warm Italian goodbye and we stepped out into the crowded streets of Venice." But every preceding sentence was slow labor: the steady accretion of detail and the equally steady removal of whatever I had put in that I realized wasn't doing necessary work or that the reader could figure out for himself. (I had learned by long travail a far from obvious lesson: Readers must be given room to bring their own emotions to a piece so crammed with emotional content; the writer must tenaciously resist explaining why the material is so moving.) Only when the job was over did I enjoy it. I don't like to write, but I take great pleasure in having written—in having finally made an arrangement that has a certain inevitability, like the solution to a mathematical problem. Perhaps in no other line of work is delayed gratification so delayed.

So much for the acoustics of St. Mark's and the carpentry of writing. I've told the story because this is a book about process: the process of transmitting information clearly and simply. Only by repeated applications of process—writing and rewriting and pruning and shaping—can we hammer out a clear and simple product.

Now, as I began to think about my book, I thought of my years at Yale and all the teachers there, like Willie Ruff, who took me into their special worlds. I especially remembered Yale professors who cared about good writing even though their subject wasn't English.

The first ones who came to mind were the historians; they were the writing stars of the faculty. They understood that writing is the mechanism by which a historian passes his knowledge on to the next generation, and they insisted on good writing in their student's papers before they considered whether the paper was good history. I also recalled professors in other disciplines who saw clear writing as the corollary of clear thinking—and therefore as a key to learning.

I made a list of about ten and sent them a letter. I said I was looking for brief examples—around five hundred words—of good writing in their discipline that would be accessible to someone of high school age. Had they written any such passages themselves? (I knew they had.) If not, would they recommend a passage that some other scholar had written? The response was swift and generous. Envelopes containing photocopies of admired passages began to come back in the mail, and the accompanying letters often steered me to writers I hadn't known about or raised points I hadn't thought about. Edmund S. Morgan, for instance, my favorite stylist among the history professors, wrote:

"I find I am hard put to pick a passage of five hundred words, because the passages I like best usually depend on the preparation of the reader in earlier passages that give resonance to things said later. Indeed the quality I call resonance is what hits me hardest in all writing.

And what resounds is not merely things said earlier but common knowledge and experience that everyone can relate to. I'm sending you a few passages from Samuel Eliot Morison (whom I consider the best historical writer, not necessarily the best historian, of this century) and from Perry Miller and George Otto Trevelyan. I'm not sure any of them will be appropriate for you because their principal virtue is their suggestiveness (resonance), not their clarity."

Fair enough: Resonance would have to be factored into the equation. Yet I had no trouble detecting it in the brief passage that Professor Morgan sent me from one of his own books, *The Birth of the Republic,* which he diffidently included along with Morison, Miller and Trevelyan. I wasn't surprised to find that I liked it better than anything else in his package:

> The government of Great Britain had not been designed to cover half the globe, and when Englishmen were not busy extending their possessions still farther, they were apt to regard the problem of turnpikes in Yorkshire as vastly more important than the enforcement of the Navigation Acts in New York. Administration of the colonies was left to the King, who turned it over to his Secretary of State for the Southern Department (whose principal business was England's relations with southern Europe). The Secretary left it pretty much to the Board of Trade and Plantations, a sort of Chamber of Commerce with purely advisory powers. The Board of Trade told the Secretary what to do; he told the royal governors; the governors told the colonists; and the colonists did what they pleased.
>
> This system, or lack of system, had at least one virtue: it did no harm, a fact evidenced by the rolling prosperity of mother country and colonies alike. The British Empire, however inefficient in its management, was very much a going concern, and wise men on both sides of the Atlantic believed that its success was intimately connected with the bumbling way in which it was run. They saw both the prosperity and the inefficiency of the empire as results of the freedom that prevailed in it. Freedom, inefficiency, and prosperity are not infrequently found together, and it is seldom easy to distinguish between the first two. The British Empire was inefficient, but its inhabitants were prosperous, and they were free.[5]

The passage is hard to beat for clarity—and for warmth and humanity and a leavening touch of humor. But surely it also has resonance. If resonance is the product of "common knowledge and experience that everyone can relate to," there's nobody who can't relate to the experience of government-by-bumbling—and no American who can't relate to the balancing act called American democracy, a marvel of inefficiency that has somehow never quite lost us our prosperity or our freedom.

Another professor on my list was Dr. David F. Musto, professor of psychiatry and the history of medicine at the Yale School of Medicine, one of whose special interests is the history of drug addiction in America. In 1972 he brought me an eye-opening piece for the *Yale Alumni Magazine*—at least it opened *my* eyes—which said that "the use of opiates like heroin and morphine in the United States has been so great, compared with other nations, that some American scientists around World War I called heroin or morphine addiction 'the American disease.'" Cocaine use was even more common. "From about 1880 to 1900," Musto wrote, "cocaine was a standard stimulant or tonic, and some of our most popular soda pops had cocaine in them."[6]

To illustrate these startling facts in a layout, Dr. Musto brought me some turn-of-the-century advertisements in which pharmaceutical firms extolled the therapeutic value of their drugs. One, for instance, was for Metcalf's Coca Wine, whose active ingredient was cocaine. Two other ads proudly introduced heroin as a cough suppressant. One was run by Bayer, who later made aspirin in the same laboratory. The second ad, run by Martin H. Smith & Co., Chemists, declared: "The problem of administering heroin in proper doses in such form as will give the therapeutic virtues of this drug full sway, and will suit the palate of the most exacting adult or the most capricious child, has been solved by the pharmaceutical compound known as GLYCO-HEROIN. The results attained with Glyco-Heroin in the alleviation and cure of cough are attested by numerous clinical studies that have appeared in the medical journals within the past few years." The adult dosage was one teaspoonful every two hours, with a half-dosage suggested for children over ten, and five to ten drops for children of three and older.

After that I kept track of David Musto's articles because he seemed to be a vigilante on a dimly lit frontier, where the ignorance of doctors meets the acquiescence of the sick. When I asked him for some examples of his writing, he sent me a recent piece from the *Bulletin of the New York Academy of Medicine*. It began like this:

It is a sad paradox that the healing arts can cause sickness and disease. From witch doctors and early Western medicine, down to the era of William Harvey or Benjamin Rush, the posthumous "Father of American Psychiatry," we deal with a profession which for centuries routinely inflicted grievous bodily harm without qualm and, further, often at the behest of society. Physicians confidently treated battle wounds with boiling oil and infectious diseases with blistering, vomiting and purging.

Many of these treatments lasted into our century, among them calomel, or mercurous chloride, perennially popular with physicians and the public and still prescribed in the period between the two world wars. Phlebotomy or bleeding was considered legitimate almost as long. Even Sir William Osler, the most noted physician in the English-speaking world, recommended phlebotomy for selected cases of pneumonia as late as 1909.

The medical profession has a long record of treating patients with useless or harmful remedies, often in clinical settings of complete mutual confidence. Iatrogenic diseases, complications and injury have been, in fact, common in the history of medicine. We may look upon addiction to certain dispensed drugs as one variation among the occasional effects of drug therapies.[7]

"Iatrogenic" means "caused by medical treatment." It's a medical term with a precise meaning, and Dr. Musto was writing for a medical journal. Still, his use of the term doesn't invalidate his article as an example of clear writing for anybody. "Iatrogenic" is easy enough to look up, as I just did. Not only did I enjoy learning a new word; Webster's definition adds an ironic phrase that makes the rest of Dr. Musto's piece all the more disturbing: "said esp. of imagined symptoms, ailments or disorders induced by a physician's words or actions." Here's how his story continues:

> During the 19th century, with the development of organic chemistry and the manufacturing pharmaceutical industry, the purity of natural substances improved. As the composition of natural substances such as opium and coca leaves was separated into several active ingredients, the potency of drugs increased. Further, modes of application were improved so that these active ingredients, such as morphine, could be more effectively introduced into the body's physiology. Here the most dramatic step forward was the development of the hypodermic syringe. By the second half of the 19th century several addicting forms of opium were available. . . .
>
> Because of the enormous humanitarian value of reducing pain and fear, [opium] became a pawn in the vigorous competition for patients among health deliverers. There were more people offering health care — homeopaths, regular physicians, natural bone-setters, local wise ones and so on — than communities needed. Confusion over medical theories, the abundance of physicians and a growing objection by patients to the severe treatments meted out by regular physicians — they called it "heroic treatment" — made an opiate a very attractive remedy: it was painless, it worked, it relieved pain and worry and it made tolerable a host of aliments whose cause and proper treatment were completely unknown. Small wonder that the importation of crude opium into the United States started to rise early in the century and grew more rapidly than the population. In 1840, when importation statistics commenced, to the mid-1890s, when the per capita consumption began to level off, the amount of crude opium for each person in the United States grew from 12 grains to 52 grains.

The article goes on to document the steady march of iatrogenic addiction in this country, noting that "the most important play of America's greatest playwright," Eugene O'Neill's Long Day's Journey into Night, is "a drama of iatrogenic addiction" and pointing out that the dangers of "physician-induced dependence" have proliferated in our own time with the mass production of tranquilizers and other anxiety-reducing pills. "Great temptations are held out to physicians who are able to relieve symptoms in spite of the dangers inherent in the drugs' multiple and often addictive effects."

Dr. Musto's article was just the kind I had hoped to find for my book, bringing a scholar's knowledge to a complex situation or issue. I wanted to present enough examples from enough fields to suggest that every discipline has an accessible literature waiting to be found by teachers and students. I wanted to eliminate such excuses as "It can't be done" and "There's nothing out there."

History and writing are of course natural allies, whether it's colonial history or medical history; one couldn't live without the other. But what would I get from professors in fields where writing was a more unlikely bedfellow — geology, for instance — or where it had rarely been allowed in bed at all? And what about all those conveniently vague humanities? I remembered that the late Brand Blanshard, professor of philosophy emeritus at Yale, once gave me a small book called *On Philosophical Style*, in which he explained how to write about that most vaporous of subjects. Such courage doesn't come along every day. I got out his book and took hope from this early passage:

> Hard as philosophy is, there have been writers who have actually succeeded in making it intelligible and even exciting, not to the exceptionally gifted alone, but to a wide public. Socrates talked it, and Plato wrote it, in a way that some millions of readers have not been willing to forget. Bergson, without once descending to vulgarity, made it for a time one of the excitements of Paris. The British tradition in philosophy has been exceptionally fertile in writers with the gift of making crooked things straight. So if a philosophical writer cannot be followed, the difficulty of his subject can be pleaded only in mitigation of his offense, not in condonation of it. There are too many expert witnesses on the other side.[8]

So I began to cast my net for expert witnesses. But what I first needed to know more about was how writing was related to learning. How much do we learn about a subject through writing that we wouldn't learn in any other way? To find some of the answers I would have to return to Gustavus Adolphus College and see how that first term of writing across the curriculum had gone.

NOTES

[1] After graduation Michael Poliakoff became a professor of classics.

[2] "Shanghai Blues," by William Zinsser, *The New Yorker*, Sept. 21, 1981. Also in *Willie and Dwike: An American Profile*, by William Zinsser. Harper & Row, 1984.

[3] *Profile*, by William Zinsser. Harper & Row, 1984. What Ruff's tape recorder heard that night in Venice is available on a record. "Willie Ruff Solo French Horn: Gregorian Chant, Plain Chant and Spirituals." Recorded in St. Mark's cathedral. Kepler Records, P.O. Box 1779, New Haven, CT 06507.

[4] "Resonance," *The New Yorker*, April 23, 1984. Also in *Willie and Dwike*.

[5] Edmund S. Morgan, *The Birth of the Republic*. University of Chicago Press, 1956, 1977.

[6] David F. Musto, "As American as Apple Pie," *Yale Alumni Magazine*, January 1972.

[7] David F. Musto, "Iatrogenic Addiction: The Problem, Its Definition and History," *Bulletin of the New York Academy of Medicine*, Second series, Vol. 61, No. 8, October 1985.

[8] Brand Blanshard, *On Philosophical Style*. Greenwood Press, 1969.

OPTIONS FOR WRITING

1. What is the main idea of "A Liberal Education"? Describe in a short essay what Zinsser was searching for in this chapter, and describe what he found.

2. Choose one of the writing samples presented in this reading. In a few pages, discuss why you think it is (or isn't) good writing. What did you (or didn't you) like about the way the passage was written? Use specific examples from the passage to support your views.

Richard Saul Wurman
THE FIVE RINGS

Do you nod your head knowingly when someone mentions a book, an artist, or a news story that you have actually never heard of before? Do you feel depressed because you don't know what all of the buttons are for on your VCR? If you answered "yes" to these questions, then Richard Saul Wurman (b. 1935) would diagnose you as suffering from information anxiety. Wurman's 1989 book Information Anxiety *examines the effects that the proliferation of information has on individuals and society today. Really "more a collage than a book," as one reviewer described it,* Information Anxiety *includes personal anecdotes, diagrams, pictures, quotations, and other information "bites" to frame the pages of its text, generating in the reader a true feeling for information anxiety's scope.*

In "The Five Rings," Wurman outlines five different types of information. As you read through this section, think about how each ring can result in information anxiety. What about the different types of information described makes you a little anxious, or uncomfortable?

We are all surrounded by information that operates at varying degrees of immediacy to our lives. These degrees can be roughly divided into five rings (see Figure 14.1); although what constitutes information on one level for one person may operate on another level for someone else. The rings radiate out from the most personal information that is essential for our physical survival to the most abstract form of information that encompasses our personal myths, cultural development, and sociological perspective.

The first ring is *internal* information — the messages that run our internal systems and enable our bodies to function. Here, information takes the form of cerebral messages. We have perhaps the least control over this level of information, but are the most affected by it.

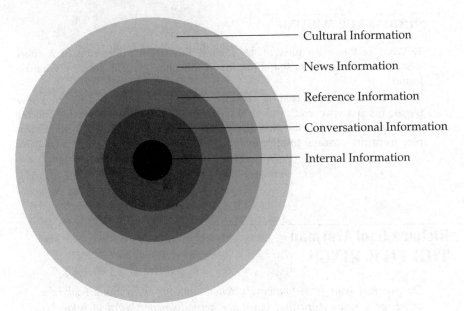

Figure 14.1   The five "information" rings.

The second ring is *conversational* information. It is the formal and informal exchanges and conversations that we have with the people around us, be they friends, relatives, coworkers, strangers in checkout lines, or clients in business meetings. Conversation is a prominent source of information, although we tend to play down or ignore its role, perhaps because of the informality of its nature. Yet this is the source of information over which we have the most control, both as givers and receivers of information.

The third ring is *reference* information. This is where we turn for the information that runs the systems of our world — science and technology — and, more immediately, the reference materials to which we turn in our own lives. Reference information can be anything from a textbook on quantum physics to the telephone book or dictionary.

The fourth ring is *news* information. This encompasses current events — the information that is transmitted via the media about people, places, and events that may not directly affect our lives, but can influence our vision of the world.

The fifth ring is *cultural* information, the least quantifiable form. It encompasses history, philosophy, and the arts, any expression that represents an attempt to understand and come to terms with our civilization. Information garnered from other rings is incorporated here to build the body of information that determines our own attitudes and beliefs, as well as the nature of our society as a whole.

Although there are specific characteristics inherent to the transmission of information at each of these levels, their systems are remarkably similar and often they are fraught with the same problems and pitfalls. Within each is the potential for anxiety. And cumulatively, the grappling with information at each of these levels can weigh us down and induce a state of helplessness. It can paralyze thinking and prevent learning.

Information anxiety can afflict us at any level and is as likely to result from too much as too little information.

There are several general situations likely to induce *information anxiety*: not understanding information; feeling overwhelmed by the amount of information to be understood; not knowing if certain information exists; not knowing where to find information; and, perhaps the most frustrating, knowing exactly where to find the information, but not having the key to access it. You are sitting in front of your computer, which contains all of the spread sheets that will justify the money you are spending to develop a new product, but you can't remember the name of the file. The information remains just out of your grasp.

You are trying to describe yourself as a lover of wine, but you have no idea how to spell the word "oenophile." Now dictionaries are quite useful if you know how to spell, but if you can't remember how the word starts, you're in trouble. This is the nightmare of inaccessibility— trying to find something when you don't know what it is listed under. How do you ask for something if you don't know how to spell it or you don't know what it's called? This is *information anxiety*.

We are surrounded by reference materials, but without the ability to use them, they are just another source of anxiety. I think of them as buddhas, sitting on my shelf with all that information and a knowing smile. It's a challenge for me to get access to them and to make them more accessible to others.

OPTIONS FOR WRITING

1. Choose one ring of information that Wurman defines. Recall a recent experience when you have been confused about internal, conversational, reference, news, or cultural information that you were receiving. Describe the experience, how you felt during the experience, and how it illustrates an instance of your own information anxiety.

2. Can you see a correlation between information anxiety and the composing process, particularly when writing accounts of research or other investigations? Have you ever felt writing anxiety? Write a brief essay in which you define and illustrate writing anxiety, creating your own rings to help classify and define the problem.

3. Reread William Zinsser's essay "A Liberal Education." Describe how and when he feels information anxiety. Use the context of "The Five Rings" to describe the kinds of information Zinsser finds. How does he deal with the information overload he feels?

William J. Broad
SCIENCE CAN'T KEEP UP WITH FLOOD OF NEW JOURNALS

The following New York Times *article describes some of the effects of the explosion in the number of scholarly and scientific journals being written and published each day. The author, William Broad (b. 1951) discusses the dangers of uncontrolled growth in scientific literature. What concerns you about this publishing mania? What implications do you see for your own research projects?*

The number of scientific articles and journals being published around the world has grown so large that it is starting to confuse researchers, overwhelm the quality-control systems of science, encourage fraud and distort the dissemination of important findings.

At least 40,000 scientific journals are now estimated to roll off presses around the world, flooding libraries and laboratories with more than a million new articles each year.

While no one knows exactly how many new journals have appeared in recent years, the literature surge and its associated problems have prompted a series of worried editorials and, somewhat ironically, scientific articles. The American Medical Association is planning an international conference on improving biomedical publications.

"The modern scientist sometimes feels overwhelmed by the size and growth rate of the technical literature," said Michael J. Mahoney, a professor of education at the University of California at Santa Barbara who has written about the journal glut.

Belver C. Griffith, a professor of library and information science at Drexel University of Philadelphia, said: "People had expected the exponential growth to slow down. The rather startling thing is that it seems to keep rising."

Much of the growth is seen as a healthy part of the success and expansion of the scientific enterprise in the 20th century. But experts say at least part of it is symptomatic of fundamental ills, including a publish-or-perish ethic among researchers that is stronger now than ever and encourages shoddy, repetitive, useless or even fraudulent work.

Surveys have shown that the majority of scientific articles go virtually unread. But the world of scientific publishing does not always operate according to the laws of supply and demand. Some scientific journals are little more than vanity publications to which authors pay "page charges" to have their work in print.

Criticizing what is called a "publishing mania," *The New Republic* recently noted that some 2,400 scholarly articles are generated each year in sociology alone. It said useless journals stocked by university libraries were contributing to the skyrocketing cost of college education and proposed that "periodicals go first" in a bout of "book burning."

While other proposed remedies are less radical, they nonetheless are considered important since the smooth functioning of the publication process is crucial to the health of science. At its heart, research is a profoundly social process based on written discourse among scientists in widely separated laboratories.

The article explosion, which began after World War II and has been accelerating ever since, is said to be caused primarily by sharp increases in the ranks of researchers. The National Science Foundation notes that from 1976 to 1986, the number of scientists in the United States more than doubled, rising from 959,500, to 2,186,300.

An added factor is that new technology is lowering age-old barriers to science publication, said Katherine S. Chiang, chairman of the science and technology section of the American Library Association and a librarian at Cornell University. "It's much easier to publish these days," she said. "The new technologies are allowing more information to be generated and controlled. Now there's desktop printing. And some journals are disseminated and read electronically."

Researchers know that having many articles on a bibliography helps them win employment, promotions and Federal grants. But the publish-or-perish imperative gives rise to such practices as undertaking trivial studies because they yield rapid results, and needlessly reporting the same study in installments, magnifying the apparent scientific output. In some cases, authors pad their academic bibliographies by submitting the same paper simultaneously to two or more journals, getting multiple credit for a single piece of work.

"The quality of research has been seriously influenced by the growing pressure to publish voluminously," wrote Dr. Mahoney of the University of California last year in the *Journal of Social Behavior and Personality*.

A final factor is the growth of research "factories," where large teams of researchers churn out paper after paper. Since authorship in these cases is shared, the laboratory chief sometimes has as many as 600 or 700 publications listed on his bibliography.

MORE AND MORE OUTLETS

The upshot of all this is a continuing surge in the number of new journals. Experts estimate that the scientific literature now doubles every 10 to 15 years.

One result of this growth is that almost any submission can get into print, experts say. In the past, many barriers, including panels of scientific "referees" who reviewed manuscripts submitted for publication, left would-be authors out in the cold.

Dr. Drummond Rennie, a senior editor at the *Journal of the American Medical Association*, wrote recently: "There seems to be no study too fragmented, no hypotheses too trivial, no literature citations too biased or too egotistical, no design too warped, no methodology too bungled, no presentation of results too inaccurate, too obscure, and too contradictory, no analysis too self-serving, no argument too circular, no conclusions too trifling or too unjustified, and no grammar and syntax too offensive for a paper to end up in print."

Another result is an inflation in the status of leading journals, experts said. These publications are seen as beacons in stormy seas, often becoming powerful national institutions devoted to screening information and directing its release to both scientists and journalists.

Some experts say top journals can attract too much attention and distort the flow of scientific findings. Marcello Truzzi, a sociologist at Eastern Michigan University, said, "Some of the pre-eminence tends to be artificial."

OVERLOOKING IMPORTANT WORK

Distortion can result when minor journals are neglected. Scientists in every field can cite horror stories of how brilliant papers in obscure journals were long overlooked.

The literature proliferation also leads to confusion about what is new, Dr. Truzzi said. "People discover the same thing over and over when a search of the literature would show it's old stuff," he said.

One of the most worrisome results of the literature growth is the apparent overloading of the quality-control systems of science, including the watchful eyes of co-authors and referee panels that scrutinize submissions to journals. A spate of recent cases of scientific fraud in which gross errors of fact and logic have slipped through the safety nets suggests that the system is seriously taxed.

The most notorious case involved a young heart researcher, John R. Darsee, who in the early 1980's was found to have fabricated much of the data for more than 100 papers he wrote while working at Harvard and Emory universities. Analysis of the case, published last year in *Nature* magazine by Walter W. Stewart and Ned Feder, assessed the vigilance of referees, journal editors and Dr. Darsee's 47 co-authors, 24 of whom were at Emory and 23 at Harvard. It found an "abundance of errors" in the papers, some minor but some "so glaring as to offend common sense."

The *Nature* article said the episode raised serious questions about the adequacy of the review mechanisms intended to insure the accuracy of reports in the nation's top scientific journals.

Many solutions to the problems have been proposed, but only a few acted upon. Journal editors are today struggling to crack down on authors who carve up [a] single study in several parts or who send [the] same paper simultaneously to two or more journals.

QUALITY VS. QUANTITY

Some experts have suggested that the vast numbers of scientific journals be drastically reduced or, at the very least, that their processes be subject to much greater scrutiny.

In this spirit, the American Medical Association plans to sponsor an international congress on peer review in biomedical publication next year. Dr. Rennie said it would "stress responsibility, as it applies to authors and editors and the improvement of quality control."

Dr. Marcia Angell, senior deputy editor of *The New England Journal of Medicine*, has focused on the individual scientists, calling for a ceiling on the number of publications submitted for reviews of promotion of financing.

"At present, it is nearly impossible for those evaluating a researcher who has a long bibliography to become acquainted with all of the work," she wrote in *The Annals of Internal Medicine*. "If the number were limited, the emphasis would shift from quantity of the research to its quality."

Some experts are generally skeptical of reforms. Thomas P. Stosser, editor of the *Journal of Clinical Investigation*, recently wrote, "Despite the complaints and some modest and radical proposals for change, the literature proliferation, like bad weather and taxes, remains something to be endured but apparently impossible to modify."

OPTIONS FOR WRITING

1. Go to your college library, and try to find as many journals as you can that deal with a particular subject. For example, you might try to identify all the journals your library owns that deal with biology, English literature, or women's studies. Ask the reference librarian for help in finding journals. Look through several issues of a few different journals, and make a list of twenty to thirty different individual article titles. Do you notice any pattern in article topics? Write a short essay describing your exploration of scholarly and scientific journals.

2. Interview one of your college professors about journal articles in his or her field. You might ask him or her to read this newspaper article and to describe how it relates to his or her own discipline. Write a short essay reporting on your interview.

3. Why do you think the readers of such a large, popular newspaper as *The New York Times* would be interested in the quantity and quality of scientific publishing? Write a few paragraphs describing your vision of the typical *New York Times* reader and his or her reaction to this article.

Alvin Toffler
INFORMATION: THE KINETIC IMAGE

Both Future Shock *and* Megatrends *deal with political, economic, and social trends that are reshaping American society.* Future Shock, *a best-selling book first published in 1970, is described by its author as "a book about what happens to people when they are overwhelmed by change. It is about the ways in which we adapt — or fail to adapt — to the future." In the chapter "Information: The Kinetic Image," Alvin Toffler (b. 1927) addresses the ideas that great amounts of information bombard us from all media and that that information changes the way we view ourselves and our world. Although some critics argue that* Future Shock *itself bombards us with too much information and images, it was, nonetheless, one of the first books to address the effects of the "information explosion."*

In Megatrends, *published in 1982, John Naisbitt (b. 1922) identifies ten trends that will have great effects on American society. The most important trend, or shift, is the movement from an industrial society to an information society. Also a best-seller,* Megatrends *sold over six million copies and is still used, like* Future Shock, *as a text in college business and sociology courses.*

As you read the following excerpts from Future Shock *and* Megatrends, *think about the different attitudes toward information that the authors present. Is the information explosion a positive or negative development? How does Broad's article from the* New York Times *about scientific publishing fit into Toffler's and Naisbitt's predictions?*

In a society in which instant food, instant education and even instant cities are everyday phenomena, no product is more swiftly fabricated or more ruthlessly destroyed than the instant celebrity. Nations advancing toward super-industrialism sharply step up their output of these "psycho-economic" products. Instant celebrities burst upon the consciousness of millions like an image-bomb — which is exactly what they are.

Within less than one year from the time a Cockney girl-child nicknamed "Twiggy" took her first modelling job, millions of human beings around the globe stored mental images of her in their brain. A dewy-eyed blonde with minimal mammaries and pipestem legs, Twiggy exploded into celebrityhood in 1967. Her winsome face and malnourished figure suddenly appeared on the covers of magazines in Britain, America, France, Italy and other countries. Overnight, Twiggy eyelashes, mannikins, perfumes and clothes began to gush from the fad mills. Critics pontificated about her social significance. Newsmen accorded her the kind of coverage normally reserved for a peace treaty or a papal election.

By now, however, our stored mental images of Twiggy have been largely erased. She has all but vanished from public view. Reality has confirmed her own shrewd estimate that "I may not be around here for another six months." For images, too, have become increasingly transient — and not only the images of models, athletes or entertainers. Not long ago I asked a highly intelligent teenager whether she and her classmates had any heroes. I said, "Do you regard John Glenn, for example, as a hero?" (Glenn being, lest the reader has forgotten, the first American astronaut to orbit in space.) The child's response was revealing. "No," she said, "he's too old."

At first I thought she regarded a man in his forties as being too old to be a hero. Soon I realized this was mistaken. What she meant was that Glenn's exploits had taken place too long ago to be of interest. (John H. Glenn's history-making flight occurred in February, 1962.) Today Glenn has receded from the foreground of public attention. In effect, his image has decayed.

Twiggy, the Beatles, John Glenn, Billie Sol Estes, Bob Dylan, Jack Ruby, Norman Mailer, Eichmann, Jean-Paul Sartre, Georgi Malenkov, Jacqueline Kennedy — thousands of "personalities" parade across the stage of contemporary history. Real people, magnified and projected by the mass media, they are stored as images in the minds of millions of people who have never met them, never spoken to them, never seen them "in person." They take on a reality almost as (and sometimes even more) intense than that of many people with whom we do have "in-person" relationships.

We form relationships with these "vicarious people," just as we do with friends, neighbors and colleagues. And just as the through-put of real, in-person people in our lives is increasing, and the duration of our average relationship with them decreasing, the same is true of our ties with the vicarious people who populate our minds.

Their rate of flow-through is influenced by the real rate of change in the world. Thus, in politics, for example, we find that the British prime ministership has been turning over since 1922 at a rate some 13 percent faster than in the base period 1721–1922. In sports, the heavyweight boxing championship now changes hands twice as fast as it did during our father's youth. Events, moving faster, constantly throw new personalities into the charmed circle of celebrityhood, and old images in the mind decay to make way for the new.

The same might be said for the fictional characters spewed out from the pages of books, from television screens, theaters, movies and magazines. No previous generation in history has had so many fictional characters flung at it. Commenting on the mass media, historian Marshall Fishwick wryly declares: "We may not even get used to Super-

Hero, Captain Nice and Mr. Terrific before they fly off our television screens forever."

These vicarious people, both live and fictional, play a significant role in our lives, providing models for behavior, acting out for us various roles and situations from which we draw conclusions about our own lives. We deduce lessons from their activities, consciously or not. We learn from their triumphs and tribulations. They make it possible for us to "try on" various roles or life styles without suffering the consequences that might attend such experiments in real life. The accelerated flow-through of vicarious people cannot but contribute to the instability of personality patterns among many real people who have difficulty in finding a suitable life style.

These vicarious people, however, are not independent of one another. They perform their roles in a vast, complexly organized "public drama" which is, in the words of sociologist Orrin Klapp, author of a fascinating book called *Symbolic Leaders*, largely a product of the new communications technology. This public drama, in which celebrities upstage and replace celebrities at an accelerating rate, has the effect, according to Klapp, of making leadership "more unstable than it would be otherwise. Contretemps, upsets, follies, contests, scandals, make a feast of entertainment or a spinning political roulette wheel. Fads come and go at a dizzying pace. . . . A country like the United States has an open public drama, in which new faces appear daily, there is always a contest to steal the show, and almost anything can happen and often does." What we are observing, says Klapp, is a "rapid turnover of symbolic leaders."

This can be extended, however, into a far more powerful statement: what is happening is not merely a turnover of real people or even fictional characters, but a more rapid turnover of the images and image-structures in our brains. Our relationships with these images of reality, upon which we base our behavior, are growing, on average, more and more transient. The entire knowledge system in society is undergoing violent upheaval. The very concepts and codes in terms of which we think are turning over at a furious and accelerating pace. We are increasing the rate at which we must form and forget our images of reality.

TWIGGY AND THE K-MESONS

Every person carries within his head a mental model of the world—a subjective representation of external reality. This model consists of tens upon tens of thousands of images. These may be as simple as a mental picture of clouds scudding across the sky. Or they may be abstract inferences about the way things are organized in society. We may think of this mental model as a fantastic internal warehouse, an image emporium in which we store our inner portraits of Twiggy, Charles De Gaulle or

Cassius Clay, along with such sweeping propositions as "Man is basically good" or "God is dead."

Any person's mental model will contain some images that approximate reality closely, along with others that are distorted or inaccurate. But for the person to function, even to survive, the model must bear some overall resemblance to reality. As V. Gordon Childe has written in *Society and Knowledge*, "Every reproduction of the external world, constructed and used as a guide to action by an historical society, must in some degree correspond to that reality. Otherwise the society could not have maintained itself; its members, if acting in accordance with totally untrue propositions, would not have succeeded in making even the simplest tools and in securing therewith food and shelter from the external world."

No man's model of reality is a purely personal product. While some of his images are based on first-hand observation, an increasing proportion of them today are based on messages beamed to us by the mass media and the people around us. Thus the degree of accuracy in his model to some extent reflects the general level of knowledge in society. And as experience and scientific research pump more refined and accurate knowledge into society, new concepts, new ways of thinking, supersede, contradict, and render obsolete older ideas and world views.

If society itself were standing still, there might be little pressure on the individual to update his own supply of images, to bring them in line with the latest knowledge available in the society. So long as the society in which he is embedded is stable or slowly changing, the images on which he bases his behavior can also change slowly. But to function in a fast-changing society, to cope with swift and complex change, the individual must turn over his own stock of images at a rate that in some way correlates with the pace of change. His model must be updated. To the degree that it lags, his responses to change become inappropriate, he becomes increasingly thwarted, ineffective. Thus there is intense pressure on the individual to keep up with the generalized pace.

Today change is so swift and relentless in the techno-societies that yesterday's truths suddenly become today's fictions, and the most highly skilled and intelligent members of society admit difficulty in keeping up with the deluge of new knowledge—even in extremely narrow fields.

"You can't possibly keep in touch with all you want to," complains Dr. Rudolph Stohler, a zoologist at the University of California at Berkeley. "I spend 25 percent to 50 percent of my working time trying to keep up with what's going on," says Dr. I. E. Wallen, chief of oceanography at the Smithsonian Institution in Washington. Dr. Emilio Segre, a Nobel prizewinner in physics, declares: "On K-mesons alone, to wade through all the papers is an impossibility." And another oceanographer, Dr. Arthur Stump, admits: "I don't really know the answer unless we declare a moratorium on publications for ten years."

New knowledge either extends or outmodes the old. In either case it compels those for whom it is relevant to reorganize their store of images. It forces them to relearn today what they thought they knew yesterday. Thus Lord James, vice-chancellor of the University of York, says, "I took my first degree in chemistry at Oxford in 1931." Looking at the questions asked in chemistry exams at Oxford today, he continues, "I realize that not only can I not do them, but that I never *could* have done them, since at least two-thirds of the questions involve knowledge that simply did not exist when I graduated." And Dr. Robert Hilliard, the top educational broadcasting specialist for the Federal Communications Commission, presses the point further: "At the rate at which knowledge is growing, by the time the child born today graduates from college, the amount of knowledge in the world will be four times as great. By the time that same child is fifty years old, it will be thirty-two times as great, and 97 percent of everything known in the world will have been learned since the time he was born."

Granting that definitions of "knowledge" are vague and that such statistics are necessarily hazardous, there still can be no question that the rising tide of new knowledge forces us into ever-narrower specialization and drives us to revise our inner images of reality at ever-faster rates. Nor does this refer merely to abstruse scientific information about physical particles or genetic structure. It applies with equal force to various categories of knowledge that closely affect the everyday life of millions.

THE FREUDIAN WAVE

Much new knowledge is admittedly remote from the immediate interests of the ordinary man in the street. He is not intrigued or impressed by the fact that a noble gas like xenon can form compounds — something that until recently most chemists swore was impossible. While even this knowledge may have an impact on him when it is embodied in new technology, until then, he can afford to ignore it. A good bit of new knowledge, on the other hand, is directly related to his immediate concerns, his job, his politics, his family life, even his sexual behavior.

A poignant example is the dilemma that parents find themselves in today as a consequence of successive radical changes in the image of the child in society and in our theories of childrearing.

At the turn of the century in the United States, for example, the dominant theory reflected the prevailing scientific belief in the primacy of heredity in determining behavior. Mothers who had never heard of Darwin or Spencer raised their babies in ways consistent with the world views of these thinkers. Vulgarized and simplified, passed from person to person, these world views were reflected in the conviction of millions of ordinary people that "bad children are a result of bad stock," that "crime is hereditary," etc.

In the early decades of the century, these attitudes fell back before the advance of environmentalism. The belief that environment shapes personality, and that the early years are the most important, created a new image of the child. The work of Watson and Pavlov began to creep into the public ken. Mothers reflected the new behaviorism, refusing to feed infants on demand, refusing to pick them up when they cried, weaning them early to avoid prolonged dependency.

A study by Martha Wolfenstein has compared the advice offered parents in seven successive editions of *Infant Care*, a handbook issued by the United States Children's Bureau between 1914 and 1951. She found distinct shifts in the preferred methods for dealing with weaning, thumb-sucking, masturbation, bowel and bladder training. It is clear from this study that by the late thirties still another image of the child had gained ascendancy. Freudian concepts swept in like a wave and revolutionized childrearing practices. Suddenly, mothers began to hear about "the rights of infants" and the need for "oral gratification." Permissiveness became the order of the day.

Parenthetically, at the same time that Freudian images of the child were altering the behavior of parents in Dayton, Dubuque and Dallas, the image of the psychoanalyst changed, too. Psychoanalysts became culture heroes. Movies, television scripts, novels and magazine stories represented them as wise and sympathetic souls, wonder-workers capable of remaking damaged personalities. From the appearance of the movie *Spellbound* in 1945, through the late fifties, the analyst was painted in largely positive terms by the mass media.

By the mid-sixties, however, he had already turned into a comical creature. Peter Sellers in *What's New Pussycat?* played a psychoanalyst much crazier than most of his patients, and "psychoanalyst jokes" began to circulate not merely among New York and California sophisticates, but through the population at large, helped along by the same mass media that created the myth of the analyst in the first place.

This sharp reversal in the public image of the psychoanalyst (the public image being no more than the weighted aggregate of private images in the society) reflected changes in research as well. For evidence was piling up that psychoanalytic theory did not live up to the claims made for it, and new knowledge in the behavioral sciences, and particularly in psychopharmacology, made many Freudian therapeutic measures seem quaintly archaic. At the same time, there was a great burst of research in the field of learning theory, and a new swing in childrearing, this time toward a kind of neo-behaviorism, got under way.

At each stage of this development a widely held set of images were attacked by a set of counter-images. Individuals holding one set were assailed by reports, articles, documentaries, and advice from authorities, friends, relatives and even casual acquaintances who accepted conflicting views. The same mother, turning to the same authorities at two different times in the course of raising her child, would receive, in effect, somewhat different advice based on different inferences about reality. While for the people of the past, childrearing patterns remained stable for centuries at a time, for the people of the present and the future, it has, like so many other fields, become an arena in which successive waves of images, many of them generated by scientific research, do battle.

In this way, new knowledge alters old. The mass media instantly and persuasively disseminate new images, and ordinary individuals, seeking help in coping with an ever more complex social environment, attempt to keep up. At the same time, events—as distinct from research as such—also batter our old image structures. Racing swiftly past our attention screen, they wash out old images and generate new ones. After the freedom rides and the riots in black ghettoes only the pathological could hang on to the long-cherished notion that blacks are "happy children" content with their poverty. After the Israeli blitz victory over the Arabs in 1967, how many still cling to the image of the Jew as a cheekturning pacifist or a battlefield coward?

In education, in politics, in economic theory, in medicine, in international affairs, wave after wave of new images penetrate our defenses, shake up our mental models of reality. The result of this image bombardment is the accelerated decay of old images, a faster intellectual through-put, and a new profound sense of the impermanence of knowledge, itself.

A BLIZZARD OF BEST SELLERS

This impermanence is reflected in society in many subtle ways. A single dramatic example is the impact of the knowledge explosion on that classic knowledge-container, the book.

As knowledge has become more plentiful and less permanent, we have witnessed the virtual disappearance of the solid old durable leather binding, replaced at first by cloth and later by paper covers. The book itself, like much of the information it holds, has become more transient.

A decade ago, communications systems designer Sol Cornberg, a radical prophet in the field of library technology, declared that reading would soon cease to be a primary form of information intake. "Reading and writing," he suggested, "will become obsolete skills." (Ironically, Mr. Cornberg's wife is a novelist.)

Whether or not he is correct, one fact is plain: the incredible expansion of knowledge implies that each book (alas, this one included) contains a progressively smaller fraction of all that is known. And the paperback revolution, by making inexpensive editions available everywhere, lessens the scarcity value of the book at precisely the very moment that the increasingly rapid obsolescence of knowledge lessens its long-term informational value. Thus, in the United States a paperback appears simultaneously on more than 100,000 newsstands, only to be swept away by another tidal wave of publications delivered a mere thirty days later. The book thus approaches the transience of the monthly magazine. Indeed, many books are no more than "one-shot" magazines.

At the same time, the public span of interest in a book—even a very popular book—is shrinking. Thus, for example, the life span of best sellers on *The New York Times* list is rapidly declining. There are marked irregularities from year to year, and some books manage to buck the tide. Nevertheless, if we examine the first four years for which full data on the subject is available, 1953–1956, and compare this with a similar period one decade later, 1963–1966, we find that the average best seller in the earlier period remained on the list a full 18.8 weeks. A decade later this had shrunk to 15.7 weeks. Within a ten-year-period, the life expectancy of the average best seller had shrunk by nearly one-sixth.

We can understand such trends only if we grasp the elemental underlying truth. We are witnessing an historic process that will inevitably change man's psyche. For across the board, from cosmetics to cosmology, from Twiggy-type trivia to the triumphant facts of technology, our inner images of reality, responding to the acceleration of change outside ourselves, are becoming shorter-lived, more temporary. We are creating and using up ideas and images at a faster and faster pace. Knowledge, like people, places, things and organizational forms, is becoming disposable.

John Naisbitt
FROM AN INDUSTRIAL SOCIETY TO AN INFORMATION SOCIETY

THE FIVE KEY POINTS

The five most important things to remember about the shift from an industrial to an information society are:

- The information society is an economic reality, not an intellectual abstraction.
- Innovations in communications and computer technology will accelerate the pace of change by collapsing the *information float*.
- New information technologies will at first be applied to old industrial tasks, then, gradually, give birth to new activities, processes, and products.

- In this literacy-intensive society, when we need basic reading and writing skills more than ever before, our education system is turning out an increasingly inferior product.
- The technology of the new information age is not absolute. It will succeed or fail according to the principle of high tech/high touch.

The Information Economy Is Real

If we are to speak of an information economy, we must be able to measure it in concrete terms. How much of the nation's wealth is actually produced in the information sector? How many of us earn a living in information jobs?

Without answers to these questions, most of us will probably choose to pledge continued allegiance to the economic reality we have experienced firsthand, the industrial era, where we produced "real" goods with "real" price tags. We will dismiss the information economy as ephemeral paperwork existing only as an adjunct to goods-producing sectors.

Documenting the information economy is difficult, to be sure. Pinpointing the economics of the creation, production, and distribution of information requires quantifying and codification of highly detailed minutiae.

Fortunately, these questions have been asked and extensively answered in a landmark study by information specialist Dr. Marc Porat. Under the sponsorship of the U.S. Department of Commerce, Porat painstakingly dissected the nation's economy and established criteria for labeling a job or part of a job and its income as part of the information sector or the goods-producing sector, or something other.

"Stating precisely who is an information worker and who is not is a risky proposition," writes Porat. However, his study documents his conclusions extensively enough to convince the information economy's skeptics.

Porat sorted through some 440 occupations in 201 industries, identified the information jobs, and compiled their contribution to the GNP. Questionable jobs were excluded so that the study's conclusions err on the conservative side.

Porat's study is incredibly detailed. He begins with the obvious sorting-out and tallying-up of the economic value of easily identifiable information jobs such as clerks, librarians, systems analysts, calling this first group the *Primary Information Sector*. According to Porat's calculations for the year 1967, 25.1 percent of the U.S. GNP was produced in the Primary Information Sector, that is, the part of the economy that produces, processes, and distributes information goods and services. Included here are computer manufacturing, telecommunications, printing, mass media, advertising, accounting, and education, as well as risk-management industries, including parts of the finance and insurance businesses.

But Porat's study goes on to deal with the more difficult questions that have overwhelmed other researchers. How does one categorize those individuals holding information jobs with manufacturers and other noninformation firms? To answer this question required "tearing firms apart in an accounting sense into information and non-information parts."

Porat creates a new information grouping called the *Secondary Information Sector*. It quantifies the economic contribution of information workers employed in noninformation firms.

These workers produce information goods and services for internal consumption within goods-producing and other companies. In effect their information products are sold on a fictitious account to the goods-producing side of the company. The Secondary Information Sector generated an additional 21.1 percent of the GNP.

Porat's study concludes, then, that the information economy accounted for some 46 percent of the GNP and more than 53 percent of income earned. This was in 1967.

Porat is unwilling to estimate how much the information economy has grown since, except to say it has increased, "by leaps and bounds."

Porat's study leaves little room for doubt. David Birch's more recent finding that only 5 percent of the almost 20 million new jobs created in the 1970s were in manufacturing (almost 90 percent were in information, knowledge, or service jobs) further substantiates the fact that we are now a nation of information workers. For example, while the total labor force grew only 18 percent between 1970 and 1978, the number of administrators and managers grew more than three times that rate—58 percent. Health administrators grew at an astounding 118 percent; public officials were up 76 percent; bankers, 83 percent; systems analysts, 84 percent. In contrast, engineers grew by less than 3 percent.

New York City, once a leading light of industrial America, has lost half the manufacturing jobs it had in 1947. The city lost 40,000 manufacturing jobs in the years between 1977 and 1980 alone. In contrast, New York is experiencing a boom in information jobs. The Regional Planning Association estimates that more than half of New York's gross city product is now generated by people who work in information. In recent years, legal services have replaced apparel as New York City's leading export.

Several states are attempting to replicate the industry-to-information shift that seems to have occurred naturally in New York City. The key strategy is to offer more incentives to high-tech information companies:

- California's Governor Jerry Brown wants the state to offer direct subsidies to high-tech information companies.
- In 1980 North Carolina invested millions in a new microelectronics research center. General Electric Company promptly decided to build a new plant nearby.

- The Minnesota legislature is considering financing the expansion of the University of Minnesota's microelectronics facility in order to attract more high-tech information firms.
- Ohio has established a $5-million fund to make direct loans to high-technology companies.

The cities, states, and companies that plan for the new information age will be in a key position to reap its rewards. And those rewards will be ample.

Today's information companies have emerged as some of the nation's largest. AT&T grossed $58 billion in 1981, far surpassing the GNP of many nations. Other information companies include IBM, ITT, Xerox, RCA, all the banks and insurance companies, the broadcasters, publishers, and computer companies. Almost all of the people in these companies and industries spend their time processing information in one way or another and generating value that is purchased in domestic and global markets.

Collapsing the Information Float

The pace of change will accelerate even more as communications technology collapses the information float. The life channel of the information age is communication. In simple terms, communication requires a sender, a receiver, and a communication channel. The introduction of increasingly sophisticated information technology has revolutionized that simple process. The net effect is a faster flow of information through the information channel, bringing sender and receiver closer together, or collapsing the information float — the amount of time information spends in the communication channel. If I mail a letter to you, it takes three or four days for you to receive it. If I send you a letter electronically, it will take a couple of seconds. That is collapsing the information float. If you respond to my electronic letter within an hour, we have negotiated our business in an hour rather than a week, accelerating life and commerce. Any changes that are occurring will occur much faster because of this foreshortening of the information float.

When President Lincoln was shot, the word was communicated by telegraph to most parts of the United States, but because we had no links to England, it was five days before London heard of the event. When President Reagan was shot, journalist Henry Fairlie, working at his typewriter within a block of the shooting, got word of it by telephone from his editor at the *Spectator* in London, who had seen a rerun of the assassination attempt on television shortly after it occurred.

One way to think about the foreshortening of the information float is to think about when the world changed from trading goods and services to standardized currencies. Just imagine how that speeded up transactions. Now, with the use of electrons to send money around the world at the speed of light, we have almost completely collapsed the money information float. The shift from money to electronics is as basic as when we went from barter to money.

To the benefit of both sender and receiver, the new technology has opened up new information channels with wider range and greater sophistication. It has shortened the distance between sender and receiver and increased the velocity of the information flow. But most importantly, it has collapsed the information float.

With the coming of the information society, we have for the first time an economy based on a key resource that is not only renewable but self-generating.

Now, more than 100 years after the creation of the first data communication devices, we stand at the threshold of a mammoth communication revolution. The combined technologies of the telephone, computer, and television have merged into an integrated information and communication system that transmits data and permits instantaneous interactions between persons and computers. As our transportation network carried the products of industrialization in the past, so too will this emerging communications network carry the new products of the information society. This new integrated communication system will fuel the information society the way energy—electricity, oil, nuclear—kept the industry society humming and the way natural power—wind, water, and brute force—sustained agricultural society.

We have for the first time an economy based on a key resource that is not only renewable, but self-generating. Running out of it is not a problem, but drowning in it is. For example:

- Between 6,000 and 7,000 scientific articles are written each day.
- Scientific and technical information now increases 13 percent per year, which means it doubles every 5.5 years.
- But the rate will soon jump to perhaps 40 percent per year because of new, more powerful information systems and an increasing population of scientists. That means that data will double every twenty months.
- By 1985 the volume of information will be somewhere between four and seven times what it was only a few years earlier.

We are drowning in information but starved for knowledge.

This level of information is clearly impossible to handle by present means. Uncontrolled and unorganized information is no longer a resource in an information society. Instead, it becomes the enemy of the information worker. Scientists who are overwhelmed with technical data complain of information pollution and charge that it takes less time to do an experiment than to find out whether or not it has already been done.

Information technology brings order to the chaos of information pollution and therefore gives value to data that would otherwise be useless. If users—through information utilities—can locate the information they need, they will pay for it. The emphasis of the whole information society shifts, then, from supply to *selection*.

This principle is the driving force behind the new electronic publishers who provide on-line data bases, communication channels for sorting through and selecting. These new businesses are selling a medium, not information as such.

The on-line information selection business has already become a $1.5-billion-a-year enterprise; approximately 80 percent of the business gives users direct access to sources (source data bases), while the other 20 percent (bibliographic data bases) tells the user where to find what is sought. Just listing some of the resources is instructive. For example, available through Lockheed's Dialog system are over 100 separate data bases allowing the user access to such diverse informational sources as the National Agricultural Library, The Foundation Grants Index, The Maritime Research Information Service (MRIS), the Social Science Citation Index (SSCI), and World Aluminum Abstracts (WAA).

Despite all of the excitement generated, very few Americans have computers, but their numbers are increasing at a staggering rate:

- From the beginning of time through 1980 there were only 1 million computers, estimates the president of Commodore International Ltd., a major manufacturer of personal computers. Commodore alone expects to match that figure in 1982.
- Dataquest, Inc., a Cupertino, California, market research firm, estimates that over half a million personal computers were sold in 1980, and that the total will grow *at least* 40 percent annually.
- Apple Computers, a pioneer in the field of personal computers, has sold more than a quarter of a million computers since its beginning in 1977, and currently is selling around 20,000 every month.
- In 1977, only 50 stores catered to computer hobbyists; by 1982 there were 10,000.

Lack of good software is holding back, for now, the widespread use of personal computers in our homes. Better software will eventually sell more hardware (computers), which in turn will attract more software. It will work the way the introduction of high-fidelity equipment worked in this country. When first introduced, there was little software (records), but as hardware sales grew, the market became large enough to attract the development of more software. With more wonderful software available, sales of hi-fi equipment took off. After a critical point the hardware and the software fed on each other, which is what will happen to computers.

The home computer explosion is upon us, soon to be followed by a software implosion to fuel it.

It is projected that by the year 2000, the cost of a home computer system (computer, printer, monitor, modem, and so forth) should only be about twice that of the present telephone-radio-recorder-television system. Before then, computers in homes will approach the necessary critical mass, first in California. Community-wide information services will work this way as well. At some point, some city in the United States will have a sufficient number of home computers (San Diego is a good bet) so that the local newspaper, say, the San Diego *Union*, will give up publishing the hundreds and hundreds of stock listings, on dearer and dearer newspaper stock, and offer self-selected stocks printed out by individual order each afternoon on individual home computers. Such service will sell more computers — which will encourage additional software offerings. Again, it is a shift from supply to selection.

In the future, editors won't tell us what to read: We will tell editors what we choose to read.

Anthony Smith in his 1980 book, *Goodbye Gutenberg*, has usefully pointed out that we are at the beginning of a period that will witness a shift from author to receiver in the "sovereignty over text." For hundreds of years, authors and editors have decided what to put in the packages they create for us — newspapers, magazines, television programs — and we pick among them, deciding what we want to read or watch. Now, with the new technologies, we will create our own packages, experiencing sovereignty over text. It will evolve over a long period of time, but the accumulated impact of people exercising sovereignty over text will undoubtedly have a strong effect on the new society we are shaping.

OPTIONS FOR WRITING

1. Write your own definition of the information explosion. How does this explosion affect different aspects of your life? Is the vast amount of information available to us a positive or a negative development?

2. Naisbitt wrote in *Megatrends* that "we are drowning in information but starved for knowledge." Using the Naisbitt, Toffler, and Broad articles, write a short essay discussing the meaning of Naisbitt's observation. Use examples from all three essays.

3. Both *Megatrends* and *Future Shock* were well-known best-sellers that are still being used as texts in college courses. Using these two excerpts write a short essay discussing why the writing styles and content of the two books appeal to a broad audience. What is interesting or appealing about these works?

4. Toffler's "Information: The Kinetic Image" is full of contemporary allusions. In other words, Toffler often refers to specific people, places, events, and things that were current or popular in the 1960s — but which may be unfamiliar to us in the 1990s. Choose a paragraph from Toffler's piece that has many contemporary allusions, and make a list of the names or terms that you do not understand. Bring this list to your library's reference department, and try to determine the former significance of each item on your list. In a few paragraphs, discuss why an author would want to use contemporary allusions.

Theodore Roszak
THE PUBLIC LIBRARY: THE MISSING LINK
OF THE INFORMATION AGE

The subtitle to Theodore Roszak's The Cult of Information *is "The Folklore of Computers and the True Art of Thinking." The book is about our perception of computers and the product that computers generate: information. Roszak believes that, because of "advertising hype, media fictions, and commercial propaganda," we ascribe to the computer mystical and fantastic powers at the expense of our own creative and analytical thinking. He also proposes some ways that we could use the computer to help us think. In particular, the library and librarians can provide the "missing link" between computers and the public.*

As you read this essay, think about your perceptions of libraries and librarians. How do those perceptions compare to what Roszak is saying?

It is a curious fact that the contemporary discussion of information so rarely touches upon the library. Yet America's city, county, and state libraries represent the best-developed reference and reading service available to the general public. A genuinely idealistic institution, the library has been offering intellectual sustenance to our society since the days of Benjamin Franklin; indeed, as a concept, it grows out of that Age of Reason which invented the democratic politics the Age of Information is now supposed to serve.

Perhaps the library has become the missing link between the computer and the public because, in the minds of computer enthusiasts, it is too closely associated with print-on-paper to seem part of the technology that fascinates them. But the library's commitment to books hardly precludes its use of electronic apparatus; a great deal of the material that has gone into the major data bases was formerly embodied in the reference books that have long been the librarian's major tools. Accordingly, libraries have followed where their reference sources have led; they can and do use computers, where they can find the funding to buy into the technology.

There may be other reasons why computer enthusiasts so often ignore the library. The major commercial thrust behind the cult of information is to sell computers. Library sales count for very little compared to the prospect of putting a privately owned microcomputer into every home. Indeed, if computers were readily available free of charge in the library, that might dissuade some potential customers from buying. There is also the matter of marketing imagery. The personal computer has been dressed up as an affluent, middle-class appliance—like the Cuisinart and the stereo set. Its use in the library associates it with ideas of public budgeting and thrifty purchasing, a sensible investment meant to serve a distinctly lower status populace. In its democratic outreach, the library contacts a clientele that may even include the genuinely poor, whom the data merchants do not regard as any sort of market at all. Significantly, the computer industry has given its product away as free samples in the schools in order to seed its market, but never to the libraries.

There may be one more, rather revealing reason why the library enjoys such low visibility in the Information Age. It is distinctly a female workplace, one of the traditional women's professions. Stereotypically, the library is associated with a certain prim and mannerly feminine subservience that is bound up with the age-old culture of books. In contrast, high tech deals with powerful machines that represent billion dollar investments. High tech is an aggressive masculine operation, a world of high-rolling entrepreneurs, bustling executives, and world-beating decision makers. In the near background, there are the inspired inventors and genius hackers of the technology, more male types. The sexual stereotype overlaps with the class stereotype of the library, lending it an unlikely image for ambitious futuristic brainstorming. The futurologists, for example, who have done so much to popularize the notion of the Information Age, give it no attention whatever.

All this is unfortunate because if computerized information services have any natural place in society, it is in the public library. There, the power and efficiency of the technology can be maximized, along with its democratic access. In preparing this book, I found myself dependent at numerous important points on the reference services of librarians. It is help I have long taken for granted as a teacher and writer, so readily available and convenient to use that one may not even register its value. But this time, because I was involved with a critique of the ethos and economics of information, I found myself giving more attention to the librarians I worked with. On several occasions, they performed data base searches for me that produced a wealth of material I would have been hard-pressed to uncover for myself even on a well-connected personal computer. For one thing, the librarians had access to many more data bases than I could afford to rent. For another, their use of the data bases was far more expert than mine could ever be. They knew the protocols and peculiarities of different data base services; they knew which it paid to try, and they knew the best strategies for tapping them quickly. Some data bases are quite tricky to use; an amateur might wander about in them for many expensive minutes or hours, finding little of value. It takes daily hands-on experience to go hunting for information in just the right way in just the right places. It is a special skill that few home computer users will ever be able to develop to a professional librarian's level of speed and precision.

There was another advantage the librarians enjoyed. By virtue of their training and experience, they knew when *not* to use the computer. As a fully stocked information service, the library includes a multitude of standard reference books which are often the best, quickest, cheapest place to look up a fact. For that matter, librarians know where to look beyond their own resources: special archives, private collections, authorities and experts in the field. Most librarians have built up a file of such less visible sources over the years. One inquiry that was made for me for this book culminated in a phone call to the Office of the Joint Chiefs of Staff in Washington, where the librarian had a contact. I have had searches run which have extended to queries (by letter or phone) to out-of-the-way government agencies, journalists, hobbyists, and enthusiasts. Librarians know what many dedicated hackers overlook: as an information-processing instrument, the computer supplements other sources, it does not replace them.

Here, then, in the libraries of the nation, we have an existing network spread across the society, stationed in almost every neighborhood, and in the charge of experienced people who have always honored a strong ethic of public service. If the equipment for computerized reference facilities were concentrated in local libraries or, better still for reasons of economy, if every local library were linked to a generously funded regional reference center, this would be the fastest and cheapest way for the general public to gain open access to whatever benefits the Information Age may have to offer. Private, profit-making, computer-based information services (of which there are a growing number) are not viable substitutes for what the library can provide as a public reference service, if it is given the chance to show what it can do. Such businesses simply take the service out of the public domain. How painful it is, then, to realize that so much of the money that might have gone out in tax dollars to libraries has been diverted into the purchase of home computers, an approach that finishes by buying the public less information for its dollars. Interestingly, this repeats the economic pattern that has worked to degrade Benjamin Franklin's other great contribution to democratizing information: the post office. There, too, the public utility has been left underfunded, its money diverted toward the more expensive telecommunications and overnight delivery systems of the private sector, all of which operate primarily for the benefit of heavy users in the corporate economy. These examples should remind us that making the democratic most of the Information Age is a matter not only of technology but also of the social organization of that technology. If many libraries cannot provide the first class information services they would wish to offer, it is only for lack of the funds to do so. They cannot buy the equipment, rent the services, and hire the personnel.

It should not be thought, incidentally, that the work reference librarians do for the public needs to be limited to academic and intellectual matters. In the course of the last generation, many public libraries have expanded their information services to include referrals, pamphlets, contacts that cover a wide range of community social needs: legal assistance, tenants' rights, unemployment benefits, job training, immigration, health, welfare, and consumers' problems. The object is to put members of the public in touch with groups and agencies that can help with daily matters of livelihood and survival. This is not the kind of information one finds in most commercial data bases; and while the service may overlap the function of some electronic bulletin boards, the library can make it available to those who cannot afford to own a computer.

One more point. The library is not only there as a socially owned and governed institution, a true people's information service; it is staffed by men and women who maintain a high respect for intellectual values. Because they are also the traditional keepers of the books, the librarians have a healthy sense of the hierarchical relationship between data and ideas, facts and knowledge. They know what one goes to a data base to find and what one goes to a book to find. In their case, the computers might not only generate more information for the public, but information itself is more likely to stay in its properly subordinate place in the culture.

OPTIONS FOR WRITING

1. Roszak contrasts the popular image of libraries and librarians with the image of the computer industry and the people who work in it. Compare your image of libraries and librarians that you presented in the library survey to Roszak's popular image. In a few paragraphs, discuss why you think libraries suffer from such a negative image. Do you agree that it is because librarianship has been viewed as a female profession? Do other traditionally female professions (e.g., nursing, elementary school teaching) have the same image problem?

2. Roszak writes about public libraries, but his observations apply to academic libraries as well. Imagine that you have been asked to write a proposal to enhance the library's image for students on campus. Write a short essay telling the library what to do to make itself more relevant to student life.

CHAPTER AUTHOR BIOGRAPHIES

Daniel Bean is a professor of biology at Saint Michael's College, Colchester, Vermont. He is coauthor of *Writer's Guide: Life Sciences*. His nonbiological activities include conducting workshops on writing to learn and serving as a resource person on the college's peer support teaching resource group.

Arthur W. Biddle is an associate professor of English at the University of Vermont, where he teaches courses in American literature and writing. His current project, *The Thinking Book*, reflects his interest in writing and critical thinking across the curriculum. *Angles of Vision: Reading, Writing and the Study of Literature* is his latest book.

Lynne Bond is a professor of psychology and dean of the graduate college at the University of Vermont. She has published many research articles on aspects of cognitive and social development and has focused on the relationship of writing, discourse, and intellectual development. Her most recent books include *Primary Prevention and Promotion in the Schools, Families in Transition*, and *Writer's Guide: Psychology*.

John H. Clarke is an associate professor of secondary education at the University of Vermont, where he works with teachers and schools designing curricula and developing new ways to teach. To encourage critical thinking across the curriculum, he wrote *Patterns of Thinking* and is working on *The Thinking Book*.

Toby Fulwiler directs the writing program at the University of Vermont, where he also teaches writing and American literature. He is the author of *College Writing* and *Teaching With Writing* and is the editor of *The Journal Book*.

Carl G. Herndl is an assistant professor of English at North Carolina State University, where he teaches writing and British literature. He has published essays about both literature and rhetoric and is currently writing a book about the connections between rhetoric and cultural studies.

Diane Price Herndl is an assistant professor of English at the University of Vermont, where she teaches American literature and feminist studies. Her book *Invalid Women: Figuring Feminine Illness in American Fiction and Culture* is forthcoming from the University of North Carolina Press.

Kenneth M. Holland is a professor of political science and chair of the department at Memphis State. His books include *The Political Role of Law Courts in Modern Democracies*, *Judicial Activism in Comparative Perspective*, and *Writer's Guide: Political Science* (with Arthur W. Biddle). He leads faculty workshops on writing across the curriculum.

Lynda McIntyre is an associate professor of studio art and director of art education at the University of Vermont. She has directed multi-arts and integrated arts programs and has represented the United States on cultural exchanges with China, Australia, and the USSR. She has received fellowships from MacDowell, Yaddo, Ossabaw, and the VCCA in painting, and her paintings are shown in the United States, Europe, and Australia.

Tony Magistrale is an associate professor of English at the University of Vermont. He has published books and articles on American fiction, composition, and writing across the curriculum. He directs the freshman composition program at UVM.

Derk Pereboom is an associate professor of philosophy at the University of Vermont. He has published articles on seventeenth and eighteenth century philosophy, particularly on the thought of the eighteenth-century German philosopher Immanuel Kant.

Karen Wiley Sandler is vice president and dean of academic affairs and associate professor of French at Juniata College. She has taught all levels of language and literature with special interest in using writing in foreign language pedagogy. Coauthor of *Tour de Grammaire: A Study Guide for French*, she has published articles on Renaissance literature, pedagogy, and women's studies.

Mara R. Saule is a library associate professor and directs the library instruction program at the University of Vermont. She also teaches expository writing at the university. Saule is the author of two recent books: *Teaching Technologies in Libraries* and *CD-ROM and Other Optical Information Systems: Implementation Issues for Libraries*.

Ronald Savitt is the John L. Beckley professor of American business at the University of Vermont. He teaches marketing and works with small businesses in new product development. His research interests lie in business history. One of his most recent publications is "Looking Back to See Ahead: Writing the History of American Retailing," in the *Journal of Retailing*, Fall 1989. He is currently working on a history of retailing in the United States.

Frederick E. Schmidt is an associate professor of sociology and directs the Center for Rural Studies at the University of Vermont's College of Agriculture and Life Sciences. He conducts applied research, including recent investigations of community involvement in local economic development, activities in the underground economy, and other issues of rural development in the United States, the USSR, Scotland, and Central America.

Henry Steffens is a professor of history at the University of Vermont. He teaches and publishes in the fields of history of science and European history. Over the past five years he has focused his interests on the uses of writing in teaching. He has conducted writing-across-the-curriculum workshops and summer courses for teachers at all grade levels, emphasizing the uses of both formal and informal writing for teaching content most effectively. *Writer's Guide: History*, written with Mary Jane Dickerson, is one of the results of his interest.

Michael Strauss is currently a professor of chemistry at the University of Vermont. A former ICI fellow and research career development awardee of the NIH, Dr. Strauss has research interests in physical, organic, and heterocyclic chemistry. He has given workshops around the country on pedagogy and on writing across the curriculum.

ACKNOWLEDGMENTS

CHAPTER 1

"Writing:" From William Stafford, "A Way of Writing," which first appeared in *Field* #2 (Spring 1979).

"Freewriting": From Peter Elbow, *Writing Without Teachers* (New York: Oxford University Press, 1973). Copyright © 1973 by Oxford University Press, Inc. Reprinted by permission.

"College Journals": From Toby Fulwiler, *College Writing* (Glenview, IL: Scott Foresman, 1988). Copyright © 1988. Reprinted by permission of Toby Fulwiler.

"Making Meaning Clear": From Donald Murray, "Learning by Teaching," *The Journal of Basic Writing* (Fall/Winter 1981). Reprinted by permission of the Author and Roberta Pryor, Inc. Copyright © 1982 by Donald M. Murray, Boynton/Cook—Heinemann Educational Books.

"Writing as a Mode of Learning": From Jane Emig, "Writing as a Mode of Learning," *College Composition and Communication* (May 1977). Copyright 1977 by the National Council of Teachers of English. Reprinted with permission.

"Starting Support Groups for Writers": From Marge Piercy, *Parti-Colored Blocks for a Quilt* (Ann Arbor, MI: University of Michigan Press, 1982), pp. 154–160. Reprinted by permission of the University of Michigan Press.

CHAPTER 2

"The Death of the Ball Turret Gunner": From Randall Jarrell, *The Complete Poems* (New York: Farrar, Straus & Giroux, Inc., 1945). Copyright © 1945 by Mrs. Randall Jarrell. Renewal copyright © 1972 by Mrs. Randall Jarrell. Reprinted by permission of Farrar, Straus & Giroux, Inc.

"The Altars in the Street": From Denise Levertov, *Poems 1960–1967* (New York: New Directions Publishing Corporation, 1966). Copyright © 1966 by Denise Levertov Goodman. Reprinted by permission of New Directions Publishing Corporation.

"The Eternal City:" From A. R. Ammons, *Collected Poems 1951–1971* (New York: W. W. Norton & Company, Inc., 1972). Reprinted by permission of W. W. Norton & Company, Inc. Copyright © 1972 by A. R. Ammons.

"A & P": From John Updike, *Pigeon Feathers and Other Stories* (New York: Alfred A. Knopf, Inc., 1962). Copyright © 1962 by John Updike. Reprinted by permission of Alfred A. Knopf, Inc. Originally appeared in "The New Yorker."

"A Supermarket in California": From Allen Ginsberg, *Collected Poems 1947–1980* (New York: Harper & Row, Publisher, Inc., 1955). Copyright © 1955 by Allen Ginsberg. Reprinted by permission of Harper & Row, Publishers, Inc.

"Metaphors": From Sylvia Plath, *The Collected Poems of Sylvia Plath*, edited by Ted Hughes (New York: Harper & Row, Publisher, Inc., 1960). Copyright © 1960 by Ted Hughes. Reprinted by permission of Harper & Row, Publishers, Inc.

"One of These Days": From Gabriel Garcia Marquez, *Collected Stories* (New York: Harper & Row, Publisher, Inc., 1984). Copyright © 1984 by Gabriel Garcia Marquez. Reprinted by permission of HarperCollins Publishers.

"Huh": From Wanda Coleman, *Heavy Daughter Blues: Poems & Stories 1968–1986* (Santa Rosa, CA: Black Sparrow Press, 1987). Copyright © 1987 by Wanda Coleman. Reprinted with the permission of Black Sparrow Press.

"Doing Battle with the Wolf" and "Drone": From Wanda Coleman, *African Sleeping Sickness: Stories & Poems* (Santa Rosa, CA: Black Sparrow Press, 1979). Copyright © 1979 by Wanda Coleman. Reprinted with the permission of Black Sparrow Press.

"The Apt Anger of Wanda Coleman": Reprinted by permission of Stacy Gevry.

"Doing Battle with the Wolf: A Critical Introduction to Wanda Coleman's Poetry": From Tony Magistrale, *Black American Literature Forum*, Vol 23 (Fall 1989). Reprinted by permission.

"Introduction: What Is Literature?": From Terry Eagleton, *Literary Theory: An Introduction* (Minneapolis, MN: University of Minnesota Press, 1983). Reprinted by permission of the University of Minnesota Press.

CHAPTER 3

on the Composition of The Memoirs of Hadrian" from Marguerite Yourcenar, *Memoirs of Hadrian* (New York: Farrar, Straus & Giroux, Inc., 1954). Copyright © 1954 by Marguerite Yourcenar. Renewal copyright © 1982 by Marguerite Yourcenar. Reprinted by permission of Farrar, Straus and Giroux, Inc.

"Crewmen Who Dropped A-Bomb Tour Nation Selling Mementos": From Mike Carter, "Crewmen Who Dropped A-Bomb Tour Nation Selling Mementos," in *The Burlington Press* (August 13, 1990). Reprinted by permission of the Associated Press. Copyright © 1990 the Associated Press.

"Why We Can Be Trusted": From Theo Sommer, "Why We Can Be Trusted," in *Newsweek* (July 9, 1990). Copyright © 1990, Newsweek, Inc. All rights reserved. Reprinted by permission.

"Korea's Heartbreaking Hills": From Angus Deming, "Korea's Heartbreaking Hills," in *Newsweek* (June 18, 1991). Copyright © 1991, Newsweek, Inc. All rights reserved. Reprinted by permission.

CHAPTER 4

"Hiroshima Remembered: The U.S. Was Wrong": from Gar Alperovitz, "Hiroshima Remembered: The U.S. Was Wrong," in *The New York Times* (August 4, 1985). Copyright © 1985 by The New York Times Company. Reprinted by permission.

"Hiroshima Remembered: The U.S. Remembered: The U.S. Was Right": From John Connor, "Hiroshima Remembered: The U.S. Was Right," in *The New York Times* (August 4, 1985). Copyright © 1985 by The New York Times Company. Reprinted by permission.

"Supreme Emergency": From Michael Walzer, *Just and Unjust Wars: A Moral Argument with Historical Illustrations* (New York: Basic Books, Inc., 1977). Copyright © 1977 by Basic Books, Inc. Reprinted by permission of Basic Books, Inc., Publishers, New York.

"Existentialism Is a Humanism": From Jean-Paul Sartre, *Existentialism and Human Emotions*, translated by P. Mairet (New York: Philosophical Library, 1947). Reprinted by permission of Allied Books.

"Death": From Thomas Nagel, *Mortal Questions* (New York: Cambridge University Press, 1979). Reprinted by permission of Cambridge University Press.

"Famine, Affluence, and Morality": From Peter Singer, "Famine, Affluence, and Morality," in *Philosophy and Public Affairs* 1, No. 3. Reprinted by permission of Princeton University Press. Copyright © Princeton University Press 1972.

CHAPTER 5

CHAPTER 6

day, 1969). Copyright © 1966, 1982 by Edward T. Hall. Used by permission of Doubleday, a division of Bantam Doubleday Dell Publishing Group, Inc.

"Talking to the Owls and Butterflies": From John Fire/Lame Deer and Richard Erdoes, *Lame Deer: Seeker of Visions* (New York: Simon & Schuster, 1972). Copyright © 1972 by John Fire/Lame Deer and Richard Erdoes. Reprinted by permission of Simon & Schuster, Inc.

"The Handmaid's Tale": From Margaret Atwood, *The Handmaid's Tale* (Boston: Houghton Mifflin Company, 1985). Copyright © 1985 by O. W. Toad, Ltd. Reprinted by permission of Houghton Mifflin Co.

"Bryn Mawr Commencement Address": From Ursula K. Le Guin, *Dancing at the Edge of the World: Thoughts on Words, Women, and Places* (New York: Grove Press, Inc., 1989). Copyright © 1989 by Ursula K. Le Guin. Used by permission of Grove Press, Inc.

"The Blanket Around Her": By Joy Harjo. Used by permission of the author.

"Parts of a Poem": From Wendy Rose, *Lost Copper* (Banning, CA: Malki Museum Press, 1980). Used by permission of Malki Museum Press.

"Two Women Speaking": By Linda Hogan. Used by permission of the author.

"The Medium Is the Metaphor": From Neil Postman, *Amusing Ourselves to Death* (New York: Penguin, 1985). Copyright © 1985 by Neil Postman. Reprinted by permission of the publisher, Viking Penguin, a division of Penguin Books USA Inc.

"Myth": © Muriel Rukeyser, by permission of William L. Rukeyser.

"Social Talk": From Lewis Thomas, *The Lives of a Cell* (New York: Bantam, 1972). Copyright © 1972 by Lewis Thomas. Reprinted by permission of Viking Penguin, a division of Penguin Books USA Inc.

"The Tuscan Zoo": From Lewis Thomas, *The Medusa and the Snail* (New York: Penguin, 1977). Copyright © 1977 by Lewis Thomas. Reprinted by permission of Viking Penguin, a division of Penguin Books USA Inc.

CHAPTER 7

"The Mindset of Health": From Ellen J. Langer, *Mindfulness* (Reading, MA: Addison-Wesley Publishing Company, 1989). © 1989 by Ellen J. Langer. Reprinted with permission of Addison-Wesley Publishing Co., Inc., Reading, Massachusetts.

"The Healing Brain": From Robert Ornstein and David Sobel, *The Healing Brain* (New York: Simon & Schuster, 1987). Copyright © 1987 by the

CHAPTER 8

"The Pursuit of Happiness: Then and Now": From Edward Banfield, Allan Bloom, and Charles Murray, "The Pursuit of Happiness," in *Public Opinion* (May/June 1988). Reprinted with the permission of the American Enterprise Institute for Public Policy Research, Washington, D.C.

"Electoral System Flawed, Poll Shows": From *The Baltimore Sun* (March 4, 1990). Reprinted by permission of The Baltimore Sun. Copyright © 1990.

"Abortion: The Partisan Consequences": From Everett Carll Ladd, "Abortion: The Partisan Consequences," in *Public Opinion* (May/June 1989). Reprinted with the permission of the American Enterprise Institute for Public Policy Research, Washington, D.C.

CHAPTER 9

"Brides and Grooms Wanted": From Joseph Di Bona, "Brides and Grooms Wanted," in *The Christian Science Monitor* (April 19, 1989). Copyright © 1989 by The Christian Science Publishing Society. Reprinted by permission of the author.

"Mail-Order Brides Grow Wary": From Sheila Tefft, "Mail-Order Brides Grow Wary," in *The Christian Science Monitor* (November 2, 1989). Reprinted by permission from *The Christian Science Monitor*. © 1989 The Christian Science Publishing Society. All rights reserved.

"Professor Pickering's Quick Poets Society": From Scholasticus, "Professor Pickering's Quick Poets Society," in *New England Monthly* (March 1990). Reprinted by permission.

"Yellow Peril Reinfects America:" From David Boaz, "Yellow Peril Reinfects America," in *The Wall Street Journal* (April 7, 1989). Reprinted by permission of David Boaz.

"Racist Arguments and IQ": From Steven Jay Gould, *Ever Since Darwin: Reflections in Natural History* (New York: W. W. Norton & Company, 1973). Reprinted by permission of W. W. Norton & Company, Inc. Copyright © 1977 by Stephen Jay Gould. Copyright © 1973, 1974, 1975, 1976, 1977 by The American Museum of Natural History.

"Why Women Aren't Getting to the Top": From Susan Fraker, "Why Women Aren't Getting to the Top," in *Fortune* (April 16, 1984). Copyright © 1984 Time Inc. All rights reserved.

"Underground Economy": From Cheryl Russell, "Underground Economy," in *American Demographics* (October 1983). Reprinted with permission. © American Demographics, October 1983.

"History Moves Through All of Us All the Time": From Lawrence Wright, "History Moves Through All of Us All the Time," in *The Chris-*

tian Science Monitor (April 22, 1988). Reprinted by permission of the author.

"Santa's Children": From Italo Calvino, *Marcovaldo or the Seasons in the City*, translated from the Italian by William Weaver (Orlando, FL: Harcourt Brace Jovanovich, 1963). Copyright © 1963 by Giulio Einaudi editore s.p.a., Torino. English translation copyright © 1983 by Harcourt Brace Jovanovich, Inc., and Martin Secker & Warburg Limited. Reprinted by permission of Harcourt Brace Jovanovich, Inc.

"Body Ritual among the Nacirema": From Horace Miner, "Body Ritual Among the Nacirema," in *American Anthropologist* 58, no. 3 (1956). Reproduced by permission of the American Anthropological Association. Not for further reproduction.

CHAPTER 10

"Fleas": From Gale Lawrence, *The Indoor Naturalist* (Englewood Cliffs, NJ: Prentice-Hall, 1986). © 1986. Used by permission of the publisher, Prentice-Hall Press/A Division of Simon & Schuster, Inc., New York, N.Y. 10023.

"Sculpins": From Chad Heise. © 1988. Used by permission of the author.

"The Lives of a Cell": From Lewis Thomas, *The Lives of a Cell: Notes of a Biology Watcher* (New York: Penguin, 1971). Copyright © 1971 by The New England Journal of Medicine. Reprinted by permission of the publisher, Viking Penguin, a division of Penguin Books USA Inc.

"Down the Ohio and Mississippi in Search of Birds, 1820–1821": From John James Audubon, *The Best Writing of John James Audubon*, edited by Scott Russell Sanders (Bloomington, IN: Indiana University Press, 1986). Reprinted by permission of Indiana University Press.

"A Day in the Urban Wilderness": Reprinted by permission of the author.

"The Creation Myths of Cooperstown": From Stephen Jay Gould, "The Creation Myths of Cooperstown," in *Natural History* (November 1989). Reprinted with permission from *Natural History*, November 1989. Copyright the American Museum of Natural History, 1989.

"Naturalists": From John Janovy, Jr., *On Becoming a Biologist* (New York: Harper & Row, Publisher, 1985). Copyright © 1985 by John Janovy, Jr. Reprinted by permission of Harper & Row, Publishers, Inc.

"Dr. Doolittle's Question": From David Noonan, "Dr. Doolittle's Question," in *Discover* (February 1990). © 1990 Discover Publications.

CHAPTER 11

CHAPTER 12

"Ferocious Competition Tests the Pricing Skills of a Retail Manager": From Francine Schwadel, in *The Wall Street Journal* (December 11, 1989). Reprinted by permission of The Wall Street Journal. © 1989 Dow Jones & Company, Inc. All rights reserved.

"The Value of Friendship": From "The Value of Friendship," in *The Economist* (November 11, 1989). © 1989 The Economist Newspaper Limted. Reprinted with permission.

"Discount Clothing Stores, Facing Squeeze, Aim to Fashion a More Rounded Image": From Teri Agins, "Discount Clothing Stores, Facing Squeeze, Aim to Fashion a More Rounded Image," in *The Wall Street Journal* (March 15, 1990). Reprinted by permission of The Wall Street Journal. © 1990 Dow Jones & Company, Inc. All rights reserved.

"How Procter & Gamble Fumbled Citrus Hill": From Christine Donahue, "How Procter & Gamble Fumbled Citrus Hill," in *Marketing Week* (March 7, 1988). Reprinted with permission.

"Citrus Hill: The Brand P&G Wouldn't Let Die": From Christine Donahue, "Citrus Hill: The Brand P&G Wouldn't Let Die," *Marketing Week* (March 14, 1988). Reprinted with permission.

"Don't Mess with Mother Coke": From Philip Kotler and Gary Armstrong, *Principles of Marketing*, 4th ed. (Englewood Cliffs, NJ: Prentice-Hall, 1989). Copyright 1989. Reprinted by permission of Prentice-Hall, Inc.

"What Is Management All About?": From A. L. Minkes, *The Entrepreneurial Manager: Decisions, Goals, and Business Ideas* (New York: Penguin Books, 1987). Copyright © 1987 A. L. Minkes.

"The Central Thesis": From Neil W. Chamberlain, *Enterprise and Environment* (New York: McGraw-Hill, 1966). Copyright © 1966. Reprinted by permission of the publisher.

CHAPTER 13

"Somebody Else's Kids": From Torey Hayden, *Somebody Else's Kids* (New York: G. P. Putnam's Sons, 1981). Reprinted by permission of The Putnam Publishing Group. Copyright © 1981 by Torey L. Hayden.

"Chicken Hawk's Dream": From Al Young, "Chicken Hawk's Dream," in *Stanford Short Stories 1968* (Stanford, CA: Stanford University Press, 1968). Copyright © 1966 by Al Young. Reprinted by permission of the author.

"Just So They Have Fun": From Kevin Ryan, *Biting the Big Apple* (White Plains, NY: Longman). Reprinted by permission of Longman, Inc., a division of Addison-Wesley.

CHAPTER 14